CW01594523

EDUGORILLA
PUBLICATION

NEET PG

Medical Entrance Exam

Latest Edition
Practice Kit

08 Tests
08 Mock Test

Based On Real Exam Pattern

✓ Thoroughly Revised and Updated

✓ Detailed Analysis of all MCQs

Title	: NEET PG Medical Entrance Exam
Author Name	: Mr. Rohit Manglik
Published By	: EduGorilla Community Pvt. Ltd.
Publishers Address	: 12/651, First Floor Opp. Arvindo Park, Near Jama Masjid, Indira Nagar, Lucknow, Uttar Pradesh-226016, India

Copyright EduGorilla

ISBN : 978-93-90893-72-0

Second Edition

Disclaimer EduGorilla

Compiled and created by EduGorilla Community Pvt. Ltd

Editor's Note

ROHIT MANGLIK
CEO, EduGorilla

Dear Applicants,

People say *"Success comes to those who work hard."* But I've seen people working hard for their exams day in and day out for marginal success. While others succeed in their examinations by putting in just half the work. So are they God Gifted? No! I believe that it's because they work *smart* and not just *hard*. Similarly, for your exams, you should strategize your preparation so as to increase the likelihood of success. Well with EduGorilla get ready to increase your *chances of selection* in your exam by *16x*.

EduGorilla helps you in not only working *hard* but also working in a *smart and strategic* manner. With EduGorilla's preparation package, you get a chance to make your exam preparation easy, and a fun learning path towards selection. Finding the right path to your preparations can be difficult if you don't know in which direction to head. Don't worry, we have you covered! EduGorilla will be your guide to success in your journey. With our Preparation Package, you can prepare strategically and beat the exam in just one attempt.

EduGorilla's Preparation Package includes-

- **Test Series**
- **Books**

Our preparation package is handcrafted as per the latest changes, expert opinions, and students' discretion. Thus, enabling you to get through each stage of the selection process for your exam.

Our Books are designed by the teachers and experts of the respective exam with a combined 150+ years of experience; to provide you with easy, efficient, and effective learning. Our books are smart, in the sense that not only do they give you the answers to the questions but also provide similar questions for practice.

EduGorilla's competent Test Series gives you real-time experience and confidence through which you can clear your offline or online exam in just one attempt. We currently host 83,000+ mock tests for 1,440+ competitive and academic exams.

Thus, EduGorilla misses no chance to assist you in your preparation and covers all stages of the exam, so that you don't have to look anywhere else.

We provide complete preparation packages for defense, banking, teaching, and other National & State-Level exams. Hence, it doesn't matter which exam you aspire to because you will reach your success.

ALL THE BEST !

Let EduGorilla be your Guide to Success.

Rohit Manglik,
Founder and CEO, EduGorilla

Mock Test 01

PART A

Q.1 Which of the following muscular valve controls the flow of digestive juice from the hepatopancreatic duct to the duodenum?

A. Sphincter of Oddi **B.** Semilunar valve
C. Ileocaecal valve **D.** Pyloric sphincter

Q.2 The movement at the following joint permits a person to look towards the right or left:

A. Atlanto-occipital joint
B. Atlanto-axial joint
C. C2-C3 joint
D. C3-C4 joint

Q.3 The intricately and prodigiously looped system of veins and arteries that lie on the surface of the epididymis is known as :

A. Choroid plexus **B.** Tuberal plexus
C. Pampiniform plexus **D.** Pectiniform septum

Q.4 While exposing the kidney from behind, all of the following nerves are liable to injury except:

A. Lateral cutaneous nerve of thigh
B. Ilioinguinal nerve
C. Subcostal nerve
D. Iliohypogastric nerve

Q.5 Which of the following movements will not be affected by the involvement of the L5 Nerve root?

A. Thigh adduction **B.** Knee Flexion
C. Knee Extension **D.** Toe Extension

Q.6 Barr body is found in the following phase of the cell cycle:

A. Interphase **B.** Metaphase
C. G^1 phase **D.** Telophase

Q.7 All of the following physiological processes occur during the growth at the epiphyseal plate except:

A. Proliferation and hypertrophy
B. Calcification and ossification
C. Vasculogenesis and erosion
D. Replacement of red bone marrow with yellow marrow

Q.8 The type of joint between the sacrum and the coccyx is a:

A. Symphysis **B.** Synostosis
C. Synchondrosis **D.** Syndesmosis

Q.9 Single uriniferous tubule does not contain

A. Loop of Henle
B. Collecting duct
C. Distal convoluted tubule
D. Bowman's capsule

Q.10 All of the following are branches of the external carotid artery except:

A. Superior thyroid artery
B. Anterior Ethmoidal artery
C. Occipital artery
D. Posterior auricular artery

Q.11 The maximum amount of urea is present in:

A. Dorsal Aorta **B.** Hepatic Vein
C. Renal Vein **D.** Hepatic Portal Vein

Q.12 Polar bodies are formed during:

A. Spermatogenesis **B.** Organogenesis
C. Oogenesis **D.** Morphogenesis

Q.13 Upper limb weight is transmitted to axial skeleton by all except?

A. Coracoacromial ligament
B. Claviculoclavicular [interclavicular] ligament
C. Costoclavicular ligament
D. Acromioclavicular ligament

Q.14 Which of the following among axillary lymph nodes is a terminal group?

A. Pectoral **B.** Central **C.** Lateral **D.** Apical

Q.15 Which one ofthe following is the correct statement during operation on the submandibular gland?

A. The submandibular gland is seen to wrap around the posterior border of mylohyoid.
B. The facial artery rind vein are divided as they course through the deep part of the gland,
C. The hypoglossal nerve is seen to loop under the submandibular duct
D. Damage to the lingual nerve will cause loss of sensation to the posterior third of the tongue

Q.16 A midline cleft lip is due to the failure of fusion between:

A. Maxillary processes
B. Medial nasal processes
C. Medial and lateral nasal process
D. Medial nasal and maxillary process.

Q.17 Lumbar hemivertebra results due to the abnormal development of:

A. Dorsal sclerotome
B. Intermdiate cell mass
C. Notocord
D. Ventral sclerotome

Q.18 Which of the following organs is not involved in calcium homeostasis?

A. Kidneys **B.** Skin
C. Intestines **D.** Lungs

Q.19 The cell bodies of orexinergic neurons are present in:

A. Locus ceruleus
B. Dorsal raphe
C. Lateral hypothalamic area

D. Hippocampus

Q.20 The hyperkinetic features of Huntington's disease are due to the loss of:
A. Nigrostriatal dopaminergic system
B. Intrastriatal cholinergic system
C. GABA-ergic and cholinergic system
D. Intrastriatal GABA-ergic and cholinergic system

Q.21 On electromyography, all of the following features suggest denervation, except:
A. Unrgulated firing of individual muscle fibres
B. Small short-duration polyphasic action potentials
C. Presence of positive sharp waves
D. Spontaneous firing of motor units

Q.22 Follicular stimulating hormone receptors are present on:
A. Theca cells
B. Granulosa cells
C. Leydig cells
D. Basement membrane of ovarian follicle

Q.23 Which of the following organs secretes zinc in large amount in man?
A. Seminal vesicle B. Prostate
C. Epididymis D. Vas

Q.24 Which of the following favours filtration at the arteriolar end of the capillary bed.
A. Decrease in hydrostatic pressure of capillaries
B. Increase in hydrostatic pressure of capillaries
C. Increase in oncotic pressure of capillaries
D. Decrease in oncotic pressure of interstitium

Q.25 For PCR which of the following is not required:
A. Taq polymerase
B. dNTP
C. Primer
D. Radiolabelled DNA probe

Q.26 In isometric exercise all are increased except :
A. Heart rate
B. Cardiac output
C. Mean arterial pressure
D. Systemic vascular resistance

Q.27 Renin is secreted by -
A. PCT
B. DCT
C. Collecting duct
D. Juxatglomerular apparatus

Q.28 Juxtaglomerular apparatus lies in relation to:
A. Proximal convoluted tubule
B. Ascending loop of Henle
C. Descending loop of Henle
D. Glomerulus

Q.29 Cerebral blood flow is regulated by all except:
A. Blood pressure
B. Arterial PCO2
C. Potassium ions
D. Cerebral metabolic rate

Q.30 Which of the following hormone is not secreted by the kidney:
A. Renin B. Angiotensin I
C. Erythropoietin D. 1, 25 DHCC

Q.31 Toxic effects of high oxygen tension include all of the following except:
A. Pulmonary edema
B. Decreased cerebral blood flow
C. Retinal damage
D. CNS excitation and convulsion

Q.32 Delta waves are seen in:
A. Deep sleep
B. REM sleep
C. Awake state
D. Stage I NREM sleep

Q.33 The processing of short term memory to long term memory is done in:
A. Prefrontal cortex B. Hippocampus
C. Neocortex D. Amygdala

Q.34 Broca's area is concerned with:
A. Word formation B. Comprehension
C. Repetition D. Reading

Q.35 Mitochondrial DNA is:
A. Closed circular B. Nicked circular
C. Linear D. Open circular

Q.36 Which type of RNA has the highest percentage of modified base?
A. mRNA B. tRNA C. rRNA D. snRNA

Q.37 Microsatellite sequence is:
A. Small satellite
B. Extra chromosomal DNA
C. Short sequence (2-5) repeat DNA
D. Looped-DNA

Q.38 The type of enzyme inhibtion in which succinate dehydrogenase reaction is inhibited by malonate is an example of:
A. Noncompetitive B. Uncompetitive
C. Competitive D. Allosteric

Q.39 Which of the following estimates blood creatinine level most accurately.
A. Jaffe method
B. Kinetic jaffe method
C. Technicon method
D. Enzyme assay

Q.40 Chymotrypsinogen is a:
A. Zymogen B. Carboxypeptidase
C. Transaminase D. Elastase

Q.41 Same aminoacid is coded by multiple codons. This property is known as:

A. Degeneracy
B. Frame-shift mutation
C. Transcription
D. Mutation

Q.42 Increased level of lipoprotein(a) predisposes to:

A. Liver cirrhosis
B. Atherosclerosis
C. Nephrotic syndrome
D. Pancreatitis

Q.43 Increased copper excretion in urine is seen in all except:

A. Primary sclerosing cholangitis
B. Wilson's disease
C. Primary biliary cirrhosis
D. Hepatocellular carcinoma

Q.44 End product of purine metabolism in non primate mammals is:

A. Uric acid **B.** Ammonia
C. Urea **D.** Allantoin

Q.45 SYBR Green Dye is used for:

A. HPLC
B. Immunofluorescence
C. PCR
D. ELISA

Q.46 Rapid method of chromosome identilication in intersex is:

A. FISH (Fluorescent in situ hybridization)
B. PCR (Polymerase chain reaction)
C. SSCP (Single stranded conformation polymorphism)
D. Karyotyping

Q.47 Enzyme responsible for complete oxidation of glucose to Carbon dioxide and water is present in:

A. Cytosol
B. Mitochondria
C. Lysosomes
D. Endoplasmic reticulum

Q.48 Dinitrophenol causes:

A. Inhibition of ATP synthase
B. Inhibition of electron transport
C. Uncoupling of oxidation and phosphorylation
D. Accumulation of ATP

Q.49 Within the RBC, hypoxia stimulates glycolysis by which of the following regulating pathways?

A. Hypoxia Stimulates pyruvate dehydrogenase by increased 2,3 DPG
B. Hypoxia inhibits hexokinase
C. Hypoxia stimulates release of all Glycolytic enzymes from Band 3 on RBC membrane
D. Activation of the regulatory enzymes by high PH

Q.50 Study of multiplication of proteins in disease process is called:

A. Proteomics **B.** Genomics
C. Glycomics **D.** Nucleomics

PART B

Q.51 Serum C_3 is persistently low in the following?

A. Post streptococcal glomerulonephritis
B. Membranoproliferative glomerulonephritis
C. Lupus nephritis
D. Glomerulonephritis related to bacterial endocarditis

Q.52 All of the following are associated with low complement levels except:

A. Lupus nephritis
B. Mesangio capillary glomerulonephritis
C. Diarrhea-associated hemolytic uremic syndrome
D. Post—infections glomerulonephritis

Q.53 Males who are sexually under developed with rudimentary testes and prostate glands, sparse pubic and facial hair, long arms and legs and large hands & feet are likely to have the chromosome complement of:

A. 45, XYY **B.** 46, XY **C.** 46, XXY **D.** 46, X

Q.54 Which of the following gene defect is associated with development of medullary carcinoma of thyroid?

A. RET protooncogene **B.** FAP gene
C. Rb gene **D.** BRCA 1 gene

Q.55 To which of the following family of chemical mediators of inflammation, the Lipoxins belong?

A. Kinin system
B. Cytokines
C. Chemokines
D. Arachidonic acid metabolite

Q.56 The membrane protein, clathrin is involved in:

A. Cell motility
B. Receptor-mediated endocytosis
C. Exocytosis
D. Cell shape

Q.57 Differential expression of same gene depending on parent of origin is referred to as:

A. Genomic imprinting **B.** Mosaicism
C. Anticipation **D.** Nonpenetrance

Q.58 Which one of the following is not a feature of liver histology in Non cirrhotic portal fibrosis (NCPF)?

A. Fibrosis in and around the portal tracts
B. Thrombosis of the medium and small portal vein branches
C. Non specific inflammatory cell infiltrates in the portal tracts
D. Bridging fibrosis

Q.59 Characteristic feature in kidney biopsy from a child with hemolytic uremic syndrome is:

A. Thrombotic microangiopathy
B. Proliferative glomerulonephritis
C. Focal segmental glomerulosclerosis
D. Minimal change disease

Q.60 In which of the following conditions bilateral contracted kidneys are characteristically seen?

A. Amyloidosis
B. Diabetes mellitus
C. Rapidly progressive (crescentic) glomerulonephritis
D. Benign nephrosclerosis

Q.61 Atypical pneumonia can be caused by the following microbial agents except?

A. Mycoplasma pneumoniae
B. Legionella pneumophila
C. Human Coronavirus
D. Klebsiella pneumoniae

Q.62 Aschoff' s nodules are seen in:

A. Subacute bacterial endocarditis
B. Libman-Sacks endocarditis
C. Rheumatic carditis
D. Non—bacterial Thrombotic endocarditis

Q.63 Which of the following statements pertaining to leukemia is correct?

A. Blasts of acute myeloid leukemia are typically sudan black negative.
B. Blasts of acute lymphoblastic leukemia are typically myeloperoxidase positive.
C. Low leucocyte alkaline phosphatase score is characteristically seen in blastic phase of chronic myeloid leukemia.
D. Tartrate resistant acid phosphatase positivity is typically seen in hairy cell leukemia.

Q.64 The subtype of Hodgkin's disease, which is histologically distinct from all the other subtypes. is:

A. Lymphocyte predominant
B. Nodular sclerosis
C. Mixed cellularity
D. Lymphocyte depleted

Q.65 The classification proposed by the International Lymphoma Study Group for non Hodgkin's lymphoma is known as:

A. Kiel classification
B. REAL classification
C. WHO classification
D. Rappaport classification

Q.66 In familial Mediterranean fever, the gene encoding the following protein undergoes mutation:

A. Pyrin
B. Perforin
C. Atrial natriuretic factor
D. Immunoglobulin light chain

Q.67 Which type of Amyloidosis is caused by mutation of the transthyretin protein?

A. Familial Mediterranean fever
B. Familial amyloidotic polyneuropathy
C. Dialysis associated amyloidosis
D. Prion protein associated amyloidosis

Q.68 One of the following stains is specific for Amyloid?

A. Periodic Acid schiff (PAS)
B. Alizarin red
C. Congo red
D. Von—Kossa

Q.69 Which one of the following is not used as a tumor marker in testicular tumours?

A. AFP **B.** LDH **C.** HCG **D.** CEA

Q.70 An example of a tumour suppressor gene is:

A. Myc **B.** Fos **C.** Ras **D.** Rb

Q.71 All endothelial cells produce thrombomodulin except those found in:

A. Hepatic circulation
B. Cutaneous circulation
C. Cerebral microcirculation
D. Renal circulation

Q.72 In apoptosis, Apaf^{-1} is activated by release of which of the following substances from the mitochondria?

A. Bcl 2 B. Bax
C. Bcl-XL D. Cytochrome C

Q.73 Fibrinoid necrosis may be observed in all of the following, except:

A. Malignant hypertension
B. Polyarteritis nodosa
C. Diabetic glomerulosclerosis
D. Aschoff's nodule

Q.74 A peripheral smear with increased neutrophils, basophils, eosinophils, and platelets is highly suggestive of:

A. Acute myeloid leukemia
B. Acute lymphoblastic leukemia
C. Chronic myelogenous leukemia
D. Myelodysplastic syndrome

Q.75 Which of the following is characteristically not associated with the development of interstitial lung disease?

A. Organic dusts
B. Inorganic dusts
C. Toxic gaes e.g. chlorine, sulphur dioxide
D. Inhalation of tobacco smoke

Q.76 Inhaled nitric oxide is used:

A. For stabilizing systemic hemodynamics
B. In case of jaundice
C. To prevent CNS complication
D. For reducing pulmonary hypertension

Q.77 A patient of peptic ulcer was prescribed ranitidine and sucralfate in the morning hours. Why is this combination incorrect:

A. Ranitidine combines with sucralfate and prevents its action.
B. Combination of these two drugs produces serious side effects like agranulocytosis.
C. Ranitidine decreases the gastric pH so sucralfate is not able to act.
D. Sucralfate inhibits absorption of ranitidine.

Q.78 All the following statements regarding interactions of levodopa are correct except:

A. In Parkinsonism, phenothiazines reduce its efficacy.
B. It is a prodrug.
C. Pyridoxine reduces effect of levodopa in parkinsonism.
D. Domperidone blocks levodopa induced emesis and its therapeutic potential.

Q.79 Which of the following action is ascribed to delta type of opioid receptors?

A. Supraspinal analgesia
B. Respiratory depression
C. Euphoria
D. Reduced intestinal motility

Q.80 Morphine can be used in all the following conditions except:

A. Head injury **B.** Asthma
C. Hypothyroidism **D.** Diabetes

Q.81 Which of the following statements is not true regarding sulfonamides:

A. Sulfasalazine is absorbed well from GIT.
B. Crystalluria can occur with sulfonamide administration.
C. Sulfonamide administration to Newborn may cause Kernicterus.
D. Sulfonamides are of value in treatment of infections due to Nocardia species.

Q.82 A 60 year old man with rheumatic mitral stenosis with atrial fibrillation is on therapy for a fast ventricular rate. While on treatment, he developed a regular pulse of 64/min. The most likely drug being administered was:

A. Verapamil **B.** Digoxin
C. Carvedilol **D.** Propranolol

Q.83 Which of the following does not bind to GABA receptor chloride channels?

A. Ethanol **B.** Alfaxalone
C. Zolpidem **D.** Buspirone

Q.84 All of the following Anticancer agents cause bone marrow depression except?

A. Chlorambucil **B.** Daunorubicin
C. Doxorubicin **D.** Flutamide

Q.85 All of the following statements about an alpha-glucosidase inhibitor are true except:

A. Reduces intestinal absorption of carbohydrates.
B. Effective in both type I & 2 diabetes.
C. Hypoglycemia is a common & serious side effect.
D. Can be used with other oral Hypoglycemic drugs.

Q.86 Which one of the following statements about biguanides is not true?

A. Don't stimulate insulin Release
B. Decrease hepatic glucose production
C. Renal Dysfunction is not a contraindication for their use
D. Can be combined with sulfonylureas

Q.87 Sympathomimetic drugs are useful in the therapy of all of the following conditions except?

A. Acute decompensated heart failure
B. Hypotension
C. Hypertension
D. Erectile dysfunction

Q.88 In which of the following phases of clinical trial of drug, ethical clearance is not required?

A. Phase I **B.** Phase II **C.** Phase III **D.** Phase IV

Q.89 A highly ionized drug:

A. Is excreted mainly by the kidneys
B. Crosses the placental barrier easily
C. Is well absorbed from the intestine
D. Is highly protein bound

Q.90 A young pregnant woman presents with fulminant hepatic failure. The most likely aetiological agent is:

A. Hepatitis B virus **B.** Hepatitis C virus
C. Hepatitis E virus **D.** Hepatitis A virus

Q.91 Etarcept acts by one of the following mechanisms:

A. By blocking tumor necrosis factor
B. By blocking bradykinin synthesis
C. By inhibiting cyclo-oxygenase-2
D. By blocking lipoxygenase

Q.92 Nevirapine is a:

A. Protease inhibitor
B. Nucleoside reverse transcriptase inhibitor
C. Non-nucleoside reverse transcriptase inhibitor
D. Fusion inhibitor

Q.93 The group of antibiotics which possess additional anti-inflammatory and immunomodulatory activity is:

A. Tetracyclines
B. Polypeptide antibiotics
C. Fluoroquinolones
D. Macrolides

Q.94 One of the following is not penicillinase susceptible:

A. Amoxicillin **B.** Penicillin G
C. Piperacillin **D.** Cloxacillin

Q.95 Inverse agonist of benzodiazepine receptor is:

A. Phenobarbitone **B.** Flumazenil
C. Beta-carboline **D.** Gabapentin

Q.96 A woman with infertility receives an ovary transplant from her sister who is an identical Twin. What type of graft it is?

A. Xenograft **B.** Autograft
C. Allograft **D.** Isograft

Q.97 The capsule of Cryptococcus neoformans in a CSF sample is best seen by:

A. Gram stain
B. India ink preparation
C. Giemsa stain
D. Methenamine-Silver stain

Q.98 Which of the following is not a neuroparasite?

A. Taenia solium **B.** Acanthamoeba

C. Naegleria D. Trichinella spiralis

Q.99 Viruses can be isolated from clinical samples by cultivation in the following except:

A. Tissue culture
B. Embryonated eggs
C. Animals
D. Chemically defined media

Q.100 Which one of the following statements is true regarding Chlamydia pneumoniae:

A. Fifteen serovars have been identified as human pathogens.
B. Mode of transmission is by the airborne bird excreta.
C. The Cytoplasmic inclusions present in the sputum specimen are rich in glycogen.
D. The group specific antigen is responsible for the production of complement fixing antibodies.

Q.101 Chlamydia trachomatis is associated with the following except:

A. Endemic trachoma
B. Inclusion conjunctivitis
C. Lymphogranuloma venereum
D. Community acquired pneumonia

Q.102 The most common pathogens responsible for nosocomial pneumonias in the ICU are:

A. Gram positive organisms
B. Gram negative organisms
C. Mycoplasma
D. Virus infections

Q.103 The following statements are true regarding melioidosis except:

A. It is caused by Burkholderia mallei.
B. The agent is a gram negative aerobic bacteria.
C. Bipolar staining of the aetiological agent is seen with methylene blue stain.
D. The most common form of melioidosis is pulmonary infection.

Q.104 A child was diagnosed to be suffering from diarrhoea due to Campylobacter jejuni. Which of the following will be the correct environmental conditions of incubation of the culture plates of the stool sample:

A. Temperature of 42°C and microaerophilic
B. Temperature of 42°C and 10% carbon dioxide
C. Temperature of 37°C and microaerophilic
D. Temperature of 37°C and 10% carbon dioxide

Q.105 All of the following Vibrio sp. are halophilic, except:

A. V. cholerae **B.** V. parahaemolyticus
C. V. alginolyticus **D.** V. fluvialis

Q.106 A vitreous aspirate from a case of metastatic endophthalmitis on culture yields Gram-positive round to oval cells, 12-14 microns in size. The aspirate on Gram staining shows the presence of pseudohyphae. Which of the following is the most likely aetiological agent?

A. Aspergillus **B.** Rhizopus
C. Candida **D.** Fusarium

Q.107 Which of the following parasitic infestation can lead to malabsorption syndrome?

A. Amoebiasis
B. Ascariasis
C. Hookworm infestation
D. Giardiasis

Q.108 With reference to Bacteroides fragilis the following statements are true, except:

A. B. fragilis is the same frequent anaerobe isolated from clinical samples.
B. B. fragilis is not uniformly sensitive to metronidazole.
C. The lipopolysaccharide formed by B. fragilis is structurally and functionally different from the conventional endotoxin.
D. Shock and disseminated intravascular coagulation are common in Bacreriodes bacteremia.

Q.109 A young male patient presented with urethral discharge. On urine examination pus cells were found but no organisms. Which method would be the best for culture.

A. Mc coy cell line
B. Thayer martin medium
C. L J medium
D. Levinthal medium

Q.110 Which of the following bacteria act by increasing cAMP.

A. Vibrio cholera
B. Staphylococcus aureus
C. E. coli heat stable toxin
D. Salmonella

Q.111 A person working in an abattoir presented with a pustule on his hand which turned into ulcer, which will best help in diagnosis.

A. Trichrome methylene blue
B. Carbel fuschin
C. Acid fast stain
D. Calcoflour white

Q.112 A elderly male presented with fever, chest pain and dry cough. Sputum was cultured on charcoal yeast medium, the organism identified will be -

A. H.influenza
B. Moraxella catarrhalis
C. Legionella
D. Burkholderia cepacia

Q.113 Most common cause of Traveller's diarrhoea:

A. Enterotoxigenic E. coli
B. Enterohemorrhagic E. coli
C. Enteropathogenic E. coli
D. Enreroinvasive E. coli

Q.114 A farmer presents with pustules, which show Gram Positive Cocci on smear. Culture shows Beta hemolysis, and organisms are Catalase negative. To show that the identified organism is group A streptococci, which of the following test should be done?

A. Bacitracin sensitivity
B. Optochin sensitivity
C. Novobiocin sensitivity

D. Bile solubility

Q.115 Components of Innate immunity that are active against viral cells includes:

A. NK cells B. Cytotoxic T cells
C. B cell D. Memory B cell

Q.116 Preservation of brain is not required in:

A. Alkaloid poisoning
B. Organophosphorus poisoning
C. Volatile organic poisoning
D. Heavy metal poisoning

Q.117 Sexual asphyxia is associated with which of the following sexual behaviour.

A. Masochism B. Sadism
C. Fetichism D. Voyeurism

Q.118 Abortion stick used in criminal abortion causes abortion by the mechanism of:

A. Uterine contraction
B. Stimulation of uterine nerves
C. Uterine infection & necrosis
D. Placental separation

Q.119 Hemoperfusion with charcoal is useful in poisoning with:

A. Barbiturate poisoning
B. Methyl alcohol
C. Lithium
D. Ethylene glycol

Q.120 Dialysis is useful in poisoning with all of the following except:

A. Methyl alcohol B. Barbiturates
C. Ethylene glycol D. Copper sulphate

Q.121 Which is not an aryl phosphate.

A. Parathion B. Tik-20
C. Malathion D. Paraoxon

Q.122 Spalding's sign is seen in:

A. Drowning B. Mummification
C. Adipocere D. Maceration

Q.123 Acrodynia is associated with:

A. Mercury B. Phenolic acid
C. Oxalic acid D. Carbolic acid

Q.124 The most fixed part of the intestine is

A. Duodenum B. Jejunum
C. Colon D. Ileum

Q.125 "Nutmeg liver" refers to

A. Amoebic hepatitis
B. Pyogenic abscess
C. Chronic venous congestion
D. Portal cirrhosis

Q.126 The required temperature for sterilization against spores in a Hot-air oven is:

A. 120-140°C for one hour
B. 140-160°C for one hour
C. 160-180°C for one hour
D. 180-200°C for one hour

Q.127 Juvenile Justice (Care and Protection of Children) Act was passed by the Government of India in?

A. 1984 B. 1993 C. 2000 D. 2004

Q.128 True statement about Himalayan Goitre Belt:

A. 2400 Km wide.
B. Largest goitre belt in the world.
C. Extends from Kashmir in the west to Naga hills in the east.
D. All of them.

Q.129 Toxoid is prepared from:

A. Exotoxin B. Endotoxin
C. Both of above D. None of these

Q.130 If prevalence of diabetes is 10%, the probability that three people selected at random from the population will have diabetes is:

A. 0.01 B. 0.03 C. 0.001 D. 0.003

Q.131 If each value of a given group of observations is multiplied by 10 the standard deviation of the resulting observations is:

A. Original std. Deviation x 10
B. Original std. Deviation /10
C. Original std. Deviation – 10
D. Original std. Deviation itself

Q.132 The National Population Policy of India has set the following goals except:

A. To bring down Total Fertility Rate (TFR) to replacement levels by 2015.
B. To reduce the Infant Mortality Rate to 30 per l000 live births.
C. To reduce the Maternal Mortality Rate to 100 per 100000 live births.
D. 100 percent registration of births, deaths, marriages and pregnancies.

Q.133 Sullivan's index indicates

A. Life free of disability
B. Pregnancy rate per HWY
C. Hookworm eggs/gm of stool
D. Standard of living

Q.134 Which one of the following is not included in the elements of Primary Health Care?

A. Immunization services
B. Family planning services
C. Specialized services
D. Health education regarding water and sanitation

Q.135 The events A and B are mutually exclusive, so:

A. Prob (A or B) = Prob (A) + Prob (B)
B. Prob (A and B) = Prob (A) * Prob (B)
C. Prob (A) = Prob (B)
D. Prob (A) + Prob (B) = 1

Q.136 The PEFR of a group of 11 year old girls follow a normal distribution with mean 300 l/min and standard deviation 20 l/min:

A. About 95% of the girls have PEFR between 260 and 340 l/min
B. The girls have healthy lungs
C. About 5% of girls have PEFR below 260 l/min
D. All the PEFR must be less than 340 l/min

Q.137 The standard normal distribution:

A. Is skewed to the left
B. Has mean = 1.0
C. Has standard deviation = 0.0
D. Has variance = 1.0

Q.138 All of the following statements are true about Congenital Rubella except:

A. It is diagnosed when the infant has IgM antibodies at birth.
B. It is diagnosed when IgG antibodies persist from more than 6 months.
C. Most common congenital defects are deafness, cardiac malformations and cataract.
D. Infection after 16 weeks of gestation results in major congenital defects.

Q.139 For the treatment of case a of class III dog bite, all of the following are correct except:

A. Give Immunoglobulins for passive immunity.
B. Give ARV.
C. Immediately stitch wound under antibiotic coverage.
D. Immediately wash wound with soap and water.

Q.140 'Endemic Disease` means that a disease:

A. Occurs clearly in excess of normal expectancy.
B. Is constantly present in a given population group.
C. Exhibits seasonal pattem.
D. Is prevalent among animals.

Q.141 Infant mortality does not include:

A. Early neonatal mortality
B. Perinatal mortality
C. Post neonatal mortality
D. Late neonatal mortality

Q.142 While applying chi-square test to a contingency table of 4 rows and 4 columns, the degrees of freedom would be:

A. 1 **B.** 4 **C.** 9 **D.** 8

Q.143 The highest percentages of polyunsaturated fatty acids are present in:

A. Groundnut oil **B.** Soyabean oil
C. Margarine **D.** Palm oil

Q.144 The following statements are true regarding leptospirosis, except:

A. It is zoonosis
B. Man is the dead end host
C. Man is an accidental host
D. Lice act as reservoirs of infection

Q.145 Which epidemiological study gives the most accurate result.

A. Meta analysis
B. Cross-sectional study
C. Randomized control trial with double blinding
D. Cohort study

Q.146 True about ASHA (accredited social health activist) is:

A. Mental health worker
B. Involved in minimum need program
C. Deployed $\frac{1}{1000}$ population
D. To replace Anganwadi worker in ICDS

Q.147 Causative toxin for endemic ascites is:

A. Pyrrolizidine
B. Beta-oxalyl amino-alanine
C. Ergot
D. Aflatoxin

Q.148 Vision 2020 "The right to sight" includes all except:

A. Trachoma
B. Epidemic conjunctivitis
C. Cataract
D. Onchocerciasis

Q.149 Chlorine demand of water is measured by-

A. Horrock's appratus **B.** Chlorimeter
C. Double pot **D.** Berkfeld filter

Q.150 Comprehensive emergency obstetric care does not include:

A. Manual removal of placenta
B. Hysterectomy
C. Blood transfusion
D. Cesarean section

PART C

Q.151 Immunosuppressant drugs are consumed with:

A. Major viruses **B.** Peritoneal dialysis
C. Kidney transplant **D.** Hemodialysis

Q.152 All of the following conditions are known to cause diabetes insipidus except:

A. Multiple sclerosis **B.** Head injury
C. Histiocytosis **D.** Viral encephalitis

Q.153 40 year old female came to the OPD with complaints of with depressed mood, insomnia, loss of appetite and lack of interest in surroundings for the past 1 year. These symptoms appeared after loss in a business deal 1 year ago. Which is correct regarding the management?

A. Selective Serotonin Reuptake Inhibitors (SSRI's) are the most effective drugs
B. Antidepressants should be given based on the side effect profile
C. No treatment is required as it is due to loss in a business deal
D. Combination therapy with 2 or more antidepressants

Q.154 A 25 year old female presents with 2 year history of repetitive, irresistible thoughts of contamination with dirt associated with repetitive hand washing. She reports these thoughts to be her own and distressing; but is not able to overcome them along with medications. She is most likely to benefit from which of the following therapies?

A. Exposure and response prevention
B. Systematic desensitization
C. Assertiveness training
D. Sensate focusing

Q.155 One of the following usually differentiates hysterical symptoms from hypochondriacal symptoms:

A. Symptoms do not normally reflect understandable physiological or pathological mechanism
B. Physcial symptoms are prominent which are not explained by organic factors
C. Personality traits are significant
D. Symptoms run a chronic course

Q.156 Bright light treatment has been found to be most effective in treatment of:

A. Anorexia nervosa
B. Seasonal affective disorder
C. Schizophrenia
D. Obsessive compulsive disorder

Q.157 Mutism and akinesis in a person, who appears awake and even alert, is best described as:

A. Twilight state **B.** Oneiroid state
C. Stupor **D.** Delirium

Q.158 Intense nihilism, somatization and agitation in old age are the hallmark symptoms of:

A. Involutional melancholia
B. Atypical depression
C. Somatized depression
D. Depressive stupor

Q.159 Loosening of association is an example of:

A. Formal thought disorder
B. Schneiderian first rank symptoms
C. Perseveration
D. Concrete thinking

Q.160 5-HIAA is a metabolite of:

A. Serotonin **B.** Dopamine
C. Epinephrine **D.** Histamine

Q.161 A middle aged person reported to Psychiatric OPD with the complaints of the fear of leaving home, fear of travelling alone and fear of being in a crowd. He develops marked anxiety with palpitations and swelling if he is in these situations. He often avoids public transport to go to his place of work. The most likely diagnosis is:

A. Generalised anxiety disorder
B. Schizophrenia
C. Personality disorder
D. Agoraphobia

Q.162 The following is not an atypical antipsychotic.

A. Thioridazine **B.** Clozapine
C. Olanzapine **D.** Resperidone

Q.163 Most common substance abuse in India is:

A. Tobacco **B.** Cannabis
C. Alcohol **D.** Heroin

Q.164 Naltrexone is used in opioid addiction because:

A. To treat withdrawl symptoms
B. To treat overdose of opioids
C. Prevent relapse
D. Has addiction potential

Q.165 Delusion is a disorder of:

A. Thought **B.** Perception
C. Insight **D.** Cognition

Q.166 Which of the following is responsible for drug induced pulmonary fibrosis?

A. Phenytoin **B.** Bleomycin
C. Actinomycin D **D.** Cisplatin

Q.167 Conditions associated with thymoma are all except?

A. Myasthenia gravis
B. Cushing's syndrome
C. SIADH
D. Hypogammaglobulinemia

Q.168 Bence Jones proteinuria is seen in?

A. Alpha heavy chain disease
B. Gamma heavy chain disease
C. Mu heavy chain disease
D. Epsilon heavy chain disease

Q.169 Which of the following is false regarding delirium tremens?

A. Tremors
B. Ophthalmoplegia
C. Visual hallucinations
D. Clouding of consciousness

Q.170 Coarctation of aorta is most commonly seen with?

A. ASD
B. VSD
C. PDA
D. Bicuspid aortic valve

Q.171 Disseminated intravascular coagulation (DIC) differs from thrombotic thrombocytopenic purpura. In this reference the DIC is most likely characterized by:

A. Significant numbers of schistocytes
B. A brisk reticulocytosis
C. Decreased coagulation factor levels
D. Significant thrombocytopenia

Q.172 The most sensitive test for the diagnosis of myasthenia gravis is:

A. Elevated serum ACh-receptor binding antibodies
B. Repetitive nerve stimulation test
C. Positive edrophonium test
D. Measurement of jitter by single fibre electromyography

Q.173 All of the following are neurologic channelopathies except:

A. Hypokalemic periodic paralysis

B. Episodic ataxia type 1
C. Familial hemiplegic migraine
D. Spinocerebellar ataxia 1

Q.174 EEG is usually abnormal in all of the following, except:
A. Subacute sclerosing panencephalitis
B. Locked — in state
C. Creutzfeldt — Jakob disease
D. Hepatic encephalopathy

Q.175 Which of the following is a cause of reversible dementia?
A. Subacute combined degeneration
B. Picks disease
C. Creutzfeldt — Jakob disease
D. Alzheimers disease

Q.176 Normal CSF glucose level in the normoglycemic adult is:
A. 20-40 mg/dl **B.** 40-70 mg/dl
C. 70-90 mgdl **D.** 90-110 mg/dl

Q.177 Which one of the following is the most common location of hypertensive bleed in the brain?
A. Putamen/external capsule
B. Pons
C. Ventricles
D. Lobar white matter

Q.178 Which of the following features are seen in lower motor lesions?
A. Flaccid paralysis
B. Hyperactive stretch reflex
C. Spasticity
D. Muscular incordination

Q.179 Cluster headache is characterized by all, except:
A. Affects predominantly females
B. Unilateral headache
C. Onset typically in 20-50 years of life
D. Associated with conjunctival congestion

Q.180 Discriminant function is used for determining the prognosis of?
A. Alcoholic hepatitis
B. Cirrhosis
C. Viral hepatitis
D. Fulminant hepatic failure

Q.181 5'-Nucleotidase activity is increased in:
A. Bone diseases
B. Prostate cancer
C. Chronic renal failure
D. Cholestatic disorders

Q.182 Which one of the following conditions commonly predisposes to Colonic carcinoma?
A. Ulcerative colitis **B.** Crohn's disease
C. Diverticular disease **D.** Ischaemic colitis

Q.183 Serum angiotensin converting enzyme may be raised in all of the following, except:
A. Sarcoidosis
B. Silicosis
C. Berylliosis
D. Bronchogenic carcinoma

Q.184 The abnormal preoperative pulmonary function test in a patient with severe kyphoscoliosis includes:
A. Decreased RV and TLC
B. Reduced FEV1/ FVC ratio
C. Reduced FEF 25-75%
D. Increased FRC

Q.185 All of the following are the causes of relative polycythemia except:
A. Dehydration
B. Dengue haemorrhagic fever
C. Gaisbock syndrome
D. High altitude

Q.186 In which of the following conditions Splenectomy is not useful?
A. Herediatary spherocytosis
B. Porphyria
C. Thalassemia
D. Sickle cell disease with large spleen

Q.187 The presence of anti Saccharomyces cerevisae antibody is a surrogate marker of one of the following:
A. Celiac disease **B.** Crohn's disease
C. Ulcerative colitis **D.** Tropical sprue

Q.188 Anticentromere antibodies are most commonly associated with:
A. Diffuse cutaneous systemic sclerosis
B. Mixed connective tissue disease
C. CREST syndrome
D. Polymyositis

Q.189 Smoking is not a risk factor for development of?
A. Small cell carcinoma
B. Respiratory bronchiolitis
C. Emphysema
D. Bronchiolitis obliterans organizing pneumonia

Q.190 Mycotic abscesses are due to:
A. Bacterial infection **B.** Fungal infection
C. Viral infection **D.** Mixed infection

Q.191 Which of the following is least likely to cause infective endocarditis?
A. Staphylococcus albus
B. Streptococcus faecalis
C. Salmonella typhi
D. Pseudomonas aeruginosa

Q.192 All of the following are true for mitral valve prolapse, except:
A. Transmission may be as an autosomal dominant trait
B. Majority of the cases present with features of mitral regurgitation
C. The valve leaflets characteristically show myxomatous degeneration

D. The disease is one of the common cardiovascular manifestations of Marfan's Syndrome

Q.193 All of the following may occur due to hyperkalemia except:

A. Prolonged PR interval
B. Prolonged QRS interval
C. Prolonged QT interval
D. Ventricular asystole

Q.194 All of the following are major complications of massive transfusion, except:

A. Hypokalemia **B.** Hypothermia
C. Hypomagnesemia **D.** Hypocalcemia

Q.195 All of the following statements regarding primary effusion lymphoma are true except:

A. It generally presents in elderly patients
B. There is often an association with HHV 8
C. The proliferating cells are NK cells
D. Patients are commonly HIV positive

Q.196 Laparoscopic procedure patient develops shoulder pain due to:

A. Subphrenic abscess
B. Positional pain during surgery
C. Subdiaphragmatic migration of gas
D. Injury to liver

Q.197 Gangrene not caused by -

A. Frostbite **B.** Burger's disease
C. Varicose veins **D.** Atherosclerosis

Q.198 The defective migration of neural crest cells results in:

A. Congenital megacolon
B. Albinism
C. Adrenogenital hypoplasia
D. Dentinogenesis imperfecta

Q.199 Which one of the following statements is incorrect in regard to stones in the gallbladder?

A. Pigment stones are due to increased excretion of conjugated bilirubin
B. Are considered a risk factor for the development of gallbladder carcinoma
C. 10% of gallstones are radio-opaque
D. A mucocele of the gallbladder is caused by a stone impacted in Hartman's pouch

Q.200 In which of the following conditions acquired (secondary) megacolon is seen?

A. Fissure in-ano
B. Complete absence of parasympathetic ganglion cells
C. Absence of sympathetic ganglion cells
D. Rectal malignancy

Q.201 A patient has carcinoma of right tongue on its lateral border of anterior $\frac{2^{rd}}{3}$, with lymph node of size 4 cm in level 3 on the side of the neck, stage of disease is:

A. N0 **B.** N1 **C.** N2 **D.** N3

Q.202 Tumor marker for primary hepatocellular carcinoma are all except:

A. Alpha feto protein
B. Alpha 2 macroglobulin
C. PIVKA-2
D. Neurotensin

Q.203 Which of the following colonic polyps is not premalignant.

A. Juvenile polyps
B. Hamartomatous polyps associated with Peutz-Jegher's syndrome
C. Villous adenoma
D. Tubular adenomas

Q.204 Severity of acute pancreatitis correlate with levels of all of the following except:

A. Glucose **B.** Amylase
C. Transaminase **D.** Calcium

Q.205 Stone which is resistant to lithotripsy.

A. Calcium oxalate
B. Triple phosphate stone
C. Cystine stone
D. Uric acid stone

Q.206 Which of the following is not a complication of surgery for thoracic outlet syndrome.

A. Pneumothorax
B. Brachial plexus injury
C. Lymphocutaneous fistula
D. Long thoracic nerve injury

Q.207 Colonic diverticulosis is best diagnosed by -

A. Colonoscopy **B.** Nuclear scan
C. Barium enema **D.** CT scan

Q.208 Most common complication after ERCP is:

A. Acute pancreatitis
B. Acute cholangitis
C. Acute cholecystitis
D. Duodenal perforation

Q.209 Which of the following statements related to gastric injury is not true?

A. Mostly related to penetrating trauma
B. Treatment is simple debridement and suturing
C. Blood in stomach is always related to gastric injury
D. Heals well and fast

Q.210 Most common hormone deficiency seen after intracranial radiation therapy?

A. Prolactin **B.** Gonadotropins
C. ACTH **D.** Growth hormone

Q.211 Which of these tumors is least radiosensitive.

A. Ewing's sarcoma **B.** Osteosarcoma
C. Wilm's tumor **D.** Neuroblastoma

Q.212 In which one of the following conditions is sialography contraindicated?

A. Ductal calculus
B. Chronic parotitis
C. Acute parotitis
D. Recurrent sialadenitis

Q.213 Gardner's syndrome is a rare hereditary disorder involving the colon. It is characterized by:
A. Polyposis colon, cancer thyroid, skin tumours
B. Polyposis in jejunum, pituitary adenoma and skin tumours
C. Polyposis colon, osteomas, epidermal inclusion cysts and fibrous tumours in the skin
D. Polyposis of gastrointestinal tract, Cholangiocarcinoma and skin tumours

Q.214 Apart from Escherichia coli. the other most common organism implicated in acute suppurative bacterial peritonitis is:
A. Bacteroides
B. Klebsiella
C. Peptostreptococcus
D. Pseudomonas

Q.215 Referred pain from all of the following conditions may be felt along the inner side of right thigh, except:
A. Inflamed pelvic appendix
B. Inflamed ovaries
C. Stone in pelvic ureter
D. Pelvic abscess

Q.216 Which is not elevated in a child presenting with jaundice, icterus, pruritus & clay coloured stools.
A. Gamma glutanyl transpeptidase
B. Alkaline phosphatase
C. 5'-nucleotidase
D. Glutamate dehydrogenase

Q.217 Barrett's esophagus is diagnosed by:
A. Squamous metaplasia
B. Intestinal metaplasia
C. Squamous dysplasia
D. Intestinal dysplasia

Q.218 This type of thalassemia disease is Cooley anaemia:
A. Alloimmunization
B. Beta-thalassemia
C. Alpha-thalassemia
D. None of these

Q.219 Pigmented villonodular synovitis most commonly affects :
A. Shoulder
B. Ankle
C. Knee
D. Metatarsophalangeal joint

Q.220 Meralgia paresthetica is due to involvement of:
A. Medical cutaneous nerve of thigh
B. Lateral cutaneous nerve of thigh
C. Sural nerve
D. Femoral nerve

Q.221 Rickets in infancy is characterized by the following except :
A. Craniotabes
B. Rachitic rosary
C. Wide open fontanelles
D. Bowlegs

Q.222 Which is not a deep heat therapy?
A. Short wave diathermy
B. Ultrasound therapy
C. Infrared therapy
D. Microwave therapy

Q.223 Bohler's angle is decreased in fracture of:
A. Calcaneum
B. Talus
C. Navicular
D. Cuboid

Q.224 Which of the following statements is true of primary grade IV-V vesicoureteric reflux in young children?
A. Renal scarring usually begins in the mid polar regions
B. Postnatal scarring may occur even in the absence of urinary tract infections
C. Long term outcome is comparable in patients treated with either antibiotic prophylaxis or surgery
D. Oral amoxicillin is the antibiotic of choice for prophylaxis

Q.225 The most common site of Morgagni hernia :
A. Right anterior
B. Right posterior
C. Left anterior
D. Left posterior

Q.226 Prognosis in head injury is best given by:
A. Glasgow coma scale
B. Age of patient
C. Mode of injury
D. CT head

Q.227 Adjuvant chemotherapy is of definite value in:
A. CA colon
B. CA pancreas
C. CA gall bladder
D. CA esophagus

Q.228 A patient has carcinoma of right tongue on its lateral border of anterior 2/3rd, with lymph node of size 4 cm in level 3 on the side of the neck, stage of disease is:
A. N0
B. N1
C. N2
D. N3

Q.229 True about Branchial cyst is:
A. Cysts are more common than sinuses
B. Mostly arises from 2nd branchial system
C. Causes dysphagia and hoarseness
D. Sinus should always be operated

Q.230 Carcinoembryonic antigens (CEA) is increased in all except:
A. Lung cancer
B. Breast cancer
C. Colon cancer
D. Osteogenic sarcoma

Q.231 True about solitary rectal ulcer syndrome is all/except:
A. Increased muscle layer proliferation
B. Crypt distortion
C. Lamina propria infiltration with lymphocyte
D. Subepithelial fibrosis

Q.232 A patient comes with hematemesis and melena. On the upper GI endoscopy, there was no significant lesion. 2 days later the patient rebleeds. The next line of investigation is:
A. Emergency angiography

B. Repeat upper GI endoscopy
C. Enteroscopy
D. Laparotomy

Q.233 All of the following are true about Lymphoma of the thymus except:
A. More common in females
B. Slow growing
C. Clinically confused with undifferentiated tumors
D. May present with respiratory distress and dysphagia

Q.234 Which of the following is not a histological variant of thyroid neoplasm?
A. Follicular
B. Merkel cell
C. Insular
D. Anaplastic

Q.235 All of the following are complications of supracondylar fracture of humerus in children, except:
A. Compartment syndrome
B. Myositis ossificans
C. Malunion
D. Non-Union

Q.236 The lesions associated with recurrent dislocation of shoulder include all, except:
A. Hill-Sach's lesion
B. Bankart`s lesion
C. Capsular laxity
D. Supraspinatus tear

Q.237 The malunion of supracondylar fracture of the humerus most commonly leads to:
A. Flexion deformity
B. Cubitus varus
C. Cubitus valgus
D. Extension deformity

Q.238 Bankarts lesion involves which part of the glenoid labrum:
A. Anterior
B. Superior
C. Anterosuperior
D. Anteroinferior

Q.239 A 7-year-old child presents with a lesion in the upper tibia. X-ray shows the radiolucent area with Codman's triangle and Sunray appearance. Diagnosis is :
A. Ewing's sarcoma
B. Osteosarcoma
C. Osteoid osteoma
D. Chondrosarcoma

Q.240 All of the following mechanisms of action of oral contraceptive pill are true, except:
A. Inhibition of ovulation
B. Prevention of fertilization
C. Interference with implantation of a fertilized ovum
D. Interference with placental function

Q.241 The investigation of choice in a 55-year-old postmenopausal woman who has presented with postmenopausal bleeding is:
A. Pap smear
B. Fractional curettage
C. Transvaginal ultrasound
D. Ca 125 estimation

Q.242 The cysts in Polycystic Ovarian syndrome are formed by:
A. Failure of atretic follicles to undergo apoptosis
B. Oocyte proliferation
C. Multiple corpus lutea
D. Cystic degeneration of ovarian cortex

Q.243 In which of the following heart diseases maternal mortality is found to be highest?
A. Eisenmenger's complex
B. Coarctation of aorta
C. Mitral stenosis
D. Aortic stenosis

Q.244 A female with recurrent abortion and isolated prolonged APTT is most likely associated with:
A. Lupus anticoagulant
B. DIC
C. Von Willebrand disease
D. Hemophilia

Q.245 PAP smear shows Ca in situ-what is the best next logical procedure
A. Conisation
B. Colposcopy & biopsy
C. Hysterectomy
D. HPV viral D.N.A. testing

Q.246 HRT is useful in all except
A. Flushing
B. Osteoporosis
C. Vaginal atrophy
D. Coronary heart disease

Q.247 Most common heart disease which is associated with maximum mortality during pregnancy
A. Eisenmenger syndrome
B. MS
C. AS
D. VSD

Q.248 After the coming head of breach will have difficulty in delivery in all of the following conditions except
A. Hydrocephalus
B. Placenta previa
C. Incomplete dilatation of cervix
D. Extension of head

Q.249 A premature baby of 34 weeks was delivered. The baby had a bullous lesion on the body. X ray shows periostitis. What is the next investigation?
A. VDRL for mother & baby
B. ELISA for HIV
C. PCR for T.B.
D. Hepatitis surface antigen for mother

Q.250 The most common site of ligation in female sterilisation is:
A. Isthmus
B. Ampullary
C. Cornual
D. Fimbrial

Q.251 A lady presents with Jaundice, abdominal distension and pedal edema after delivering a normal baby. Her clinical condition deteriorates with increasing abdominal distension and severe ascites. Her bilirubin is 5 mg/dl, S.alkaline phosphatase was 450 u/L and ALT 345 u/L. There is tender hepatomegaly 6 cm below the costal margin and ascitic fluid show protein less than 2 mg%. Diagnosis is:

A. Acute fatty liver of pregnancy
B. HELLP syndrome
C. Acute fulminant liver failure
D. Budd Chiari syndrome

Q.252 Ovarian tumour which is bilateral:

A. Dysgerminoma
B. Endodermal sinus tumour
C. Immature teratoma
D. Embryonal cell carcinoma

Q.253 During Pregnancy, deficiency of which of the following leads to neural tube defects?

A. Folic acid **B.** Iron
C. Calcium **D.** Zinc

Q.254 Shape of a nulliparous cervix is:

A. Circular **B.** Transverse
C. Longitudinal **D.** Fimbriated

Q.255 Which of the following condition is screened by "Pap Smear"?

A. Ovarian cancer **B.** Endometrial cancer
C. Cervical cancer **D.** Breast Cancer

Q.256 Prolonged second state of Labour may occur due to:

A. Uterine inertia
B. Epidural analgesia
C. Cephalopelvic disproportion
D. All of the above

Q.257 Prerequisites for internal rotation of the head – A/E:

A. Well – flexed head
B. Efficient uterine contraction
C. Favourable shape of the pelvis
D. Tone of the abdominal muscles

Q.258 The first Movements of the baby felt by the mother are known as?

A. Lightening **B.** Engagement
C. Quickening **D.** Ballottement

Q.259 A 13-year old girl came to the casualty with acute lower abdominal pain. She had cyclical pain for the last 6 months. She has not yet attained her menarche. On examination, a tense bulge was seen in the region of the hymen. The most probable diagnosis is?

A. Mayer-Rokitansky-Küster-Hauser syndrome
B. Imperforate hymen
C. Asherman's syndrome
D. Congenital adrenal hyperplasia

Q.260 Which one is the hazard of induction of labor with Pitocin?

A. Elevation in blood pressure
B. Infection
C. Rupture of uterus
D. Early rupture of membrane

Q.261 What is the commonest cause of Postpartum Hemorrhage?

A. Atonicity of uterus **B.** Subinvolution
C. Birth Injury **D.** Puerperal sepsis

Q.262 The absence of which of the following development milestones in a 12-week -old child indicates a grave prognosis(LQ):

A. Babbling (monosyllables)
B. Vocalization
C. Raise the head to 90% in prone posture
D. Hand-to-hand transfer to the object

Q.263 Pincer grasp develops by months:

A. 5-7 **B.** 9-12 **C.** 8-9 **D.** 12-24

Q.264 Which of the following cannot be done by a 3-year-old child

A. Draw a triangle
B. Draw a circle
C. Can arrange 9 cubes
D. Can go up and down

Q.265 A normally developing 10 months old child should be able to do all the following except:

A. Standalone
B. Play peak to boo
C. Pick up a pellet with thumb and index finger
D. Build a tower of 3-4 cubes

Q.266 A child is below the third percentile for height in growth velocity is normal, but chronological age is more the skeletal age. The most likely diagnosis is:

A. Constitutional delay in growth
B. Genetic short stature
C. Primordial dwarfism
D. Hypopituitarism

Q.267 Generally, a person with Down syndrome has an IQ of

A. 20-30 **B.** 40-50
C. 60-70 **D.** None of the above

Q.268 Peak growth velocity in an adolescent girl is seen just after

A. The appearance of pubic & axillary hair
B. Breast enlargement
C. Onset of menstruation
D. Enlargement of external genitalia

Q.269 A female child has recently learned to eat with a spoon without spilling, to dress and undress herself with supervision and to understand that she is a girl. These skills are the first mastered between the ages of-

A. 2 and 3 years **B.** 3 and 4 years
C. 4 and 5 years **D.** 5 and 6 years

Q.270 Which one of the following is the most common cause of congenital hydrocephalus?

A. Craniosynostosis

B. Intra uterine meningitis
C. Aqueductal stenosis
D. Malformations of the great vein of Galen

Q.271 The most common presentation of a child with Wilms tumor is:
A. An asymptomatic abdominal mass
B. Haematuria
C. Hypertension
D. Hemoptysis due to pulmonary secondary

Q.272 The most common laser used in laryngeal surgery is?
A. Argon laser B. Nd YAG laser
C. CO_2 laser D. KTP laser

Q.273 Hyperacusis in Bell's palsy is due to the paralysis of the following muscle:
A. Tensor tympani B. Levator veli palatini
C. Tensor veli palatini D. Stapedius

Q.274 A lady has bilateral hearing loss for 4 years which worsened during pregnancy. Type of impedance audiometry graph will be:
A. Ad B. As C. B D. C

Q.275 Rhinolalia clausa is associated with all of the following except?
A. Allergic rhinitis B. Palatal paralysis
C. Adenoids D. Nasal polyps

Q.276 Structure not seen in bronchoscopy?
A. Vocal cords
B. Trachea
C. First segmental division of bronchi
D. Subcarinal lymph nodes

Q.277 The most common site of a leak in CSF rhinorrhoea is:
A. Sphenoid sinus B. Frontal sinus
C. Cribriform plate D. Tegmen tympani

Q.278 The most common and earliest manifestation of carcinoma of the glottis is:
A. Hoarseness
B. Haemoptysis
C. Cervical lymph nodes
D. Stridor

Q.279 A 5-year-old patient is scheduled for a tonsillectomy. On the day of surgery, he had a running nose, a temperature of 37.5°C, and a dry cough. Which of the following should be the most appropriate decision for surgery?
A. Surgery should be cancelled
B. Can proceed for surgery if chest is clear and there is no history of asthma
C. Should get Xray chest before proceeding for surgery
D. Cancel surgery for 3 weeks and patient to be put on antibiotics

Q.280 Which is the investigation of choice in assessing hearing loss in neonates?
A. Impedance audiometry
B. Brainstem Evoked Response Audiometry (BERA)
C. Free field audiometry
D. Behavioral audiometry

Q.281 Ophthalmoplegic migraine is best characterised as?
A. Recurrent headache with transient palsy of the ophthalmic nerve
B. Headache associated with irreversible palsy of 3rd nerve
C. Recurrent headache with transient palsy of 3, 4 and/or 6th cranial nerves
D. Headache with optic neuritis

Q.282 Which of the following is false regarding intraocular retinoblastoma?
A. 94% cases are sporadic
B. Individuals with sporadic retinoblastoma do not pass their genes to their children
C. Reese Ellsworth classification is used for predicting visual prognosis following radiotherapy
D. Tumour calcification can be detected by an ultrasound scan

Q.283 Bitemporal hemianopia is a characteristic feature of?
A. Glaucoma
B. Optic neuritis
C. Pituitary tumor
D. Retinitis pigmentosa

Q.284 The most common type of scleritis:
A. Non-necrotizing anterior scleritis
B. Necrotizing anterior scleritis
C. Posterior scleritis
D. None of these

Q.285 Arden index is used for interpretation of?
A. Visual evoked response
B. Electrooculogram
C. Electroretinogram
D. Visual field chartin

Q.286 All of the following are involved in endophthalmitis except?
A. Retina B. Vitreous C. Sclera D. Uvea

Q.287 An 18-year-old boy comes to the eye casualty with a history of injury with a tennis ball. On examination, there is no perforation but there is hyphema. The most likely source of the blood is
A. Iris vessels
B. Circulus iridis major
C. Circulus iridis minor
D. Short posterior ciliary vessels

Q.288 In Von Hippel Lindau Syndrome, retinal vascular tumors are often associated with intracranial hemangioblastoma. Which one of the following regions is associated with such vascular abnormalities in this syndrome?
A. Optic radiation B. Optic tract
C. Cerebellum D. Pulvinar

Q.289 The most common cause of vitreous hemorrhage in adults is:
A. Retinal hole B. Trauma

C. Hypertension **D.** Diabetes

Q.290 Which drug can cause macular toxicity when given intravitreally?

A. Gentamicin **B.** Vancomycin
C. Dexamethasone **D.** Ceftazidime

Q.291 Which is the main source of estrogen and progesterone after the 3 months of pregnancy?

A. Hypothalamus **B.** Pituitary gland
C. Placenta **D.** Ovary

Q.292 The following drug is not helpful in the treatment of ectopic pregnancy:

A. Methotrexate **B.** Misoprostol
C. Actinomycin-D **D.** RU 486

Q.293 Which pituitary hormone is to stimulate the secretion of breast milk from the mammary gland?

A. Prolactin **B.** Vasopressin
C. L.H. **D.** H.C.G.

Q.294 In the Manning scoring system of biophysical profile for fetal monitoring, which parameter is not included

A. Fetal tone
B. Fetal gross body movements
C. Oxytocin challenge test
D. Non-stress test

Q.295 The pseudomyxoma peritonei occurs as a complication of the following ovarian tumor:

A. Serous cystadenoma
B. Mucinous cystadenoma
C. Dysgerminoma
D. Gonadoblastoma

Q.296 Which of the following is the least likely physiological change in pregnancy?

A. Increase in intravascular volume
B. Increase in cardiac output
C. Increase in stroke volume
D. Increase in peripheral vascular resistance

Q.297 Hypothyroidism in pregnancy is least likely to be associated with

A. Recurrent abortions **B.** Polyhydramnios
C. PIH **D.** Preterm labour

Q.298 Late hyperglycemia in pregnancy is associated with

A. Macrosomia
B. IUGR
C. Postmaturity
D. Congenital malformation

Q.299 Endolymph is present in?

A. Bony labyrinth **B.** Scala media
C. Scala vestibule **D.** Scala tympani

Q.300 What is the name of the first secretion from the mother's breast following delivery?

A. Sequestrum **B.** Colostrum
C. Lochia **D.** Leucorrhoea

// Smart Answer Sheet //

Correct Percentage of students who answered correctly. Skipped Percentage of students who skipped.

Q.	Ans.	Correct	Skipped	Q.	Ans.	Correct	Skipped	Q.	Ans.	Correct	Skipped	Q.	Ans.	Correct	Skipped	Q.	Ans.	Correct	Skipped	Q.	Ans.	Correct	Skipped
1	A	49.78 %	17.03 %	22	B	20.96 %	31.44 %	43	D	19.21 %	29.7 %	64	A	11.35 %	54.15 %	85	C	6.11 %	62.01 %	106	C	10.92 %	57.2 %
2	B	34.93 %	31.45 %	23	B	23.14 %	20.09 %	44	D	19.21 %	31.01 %	65	B	10.04 %	61.58 %	86	C	12.23 %	55.46 %	107	D	6.11 %	64.2 %
3	C	44.98 %	29.26 %	24	B	27.95 %	32.31 %	45	C	15.28 %	27.08 %	66	A	7.86 %	55.02 %	87	D	6.55 %	57.21 %	108	D	3.93 %	61.57 %
4	A	21.4 %	31.88 %	25	D	17.47 %	27.07 %	46	A	14.85 %	31.44 %	67	B	13.97 %	56.34 %	88	D	8.73 %	62.45 %	109	A	5.24 %	60.7 %
5	A	17.9 %	22.27 %	26	D	32.31 %	31.88 %	47	B	29.69 %	29.7 %	68	C	17.03 %	63.32 %	89	A	9.17 %	61.14 %	110	A	15.28 %	57.21 %
6	A	18.78 %	31.0 %	27	D	53.28 %	22.27 %	48	C	27.95 %	30.57 %	69	D	10.04 %	61.14 %	90	C	12.23 %	64.63 %	111	A	13.97 %	57.65 %
7	D	20.96 %	28.82 %	28	D	26.64 %	31.44 %	49	C	13.54 %	30.13 %	70	D	11.79 %	43.23 %	91	A	5.68 %	62.01 %	112	C	10.04 %	60.7 %
8	A	20.96 %	31.01 %	29	C	29.69 %	27.08 %	50	A	30.57 %	31.88 %	71	C	14.41 %	55.9 %	92	C	13.1 %	55.02 %	113	A	17.47 %	60.7 %
9	B	18.34 %	29.69 %	30	B	30.57 %	31.0 %	51	A	6.55 %	58.08 %	72	D	7.86 %	55.9 %	93	D	7.42 %	62.01 %	114	A	16.16 %	56.33 %
10	B	27.51 %	31.44 %	31	B	21.83 %	31.01 %	52	C	13.54 %	54.58 %	73	C	10.04 %	61.14 %	94	D	11.35 %	57.21 %	115	A	11.35 %	61.58 %
11	B	16.59 %	27.95 %	32	A	25.33 %	27.51 %	53	C	21.4 %	61.13 %	74	C	16.16 %	48.03 %	95	C	4.37 %	63.32 %	116	D	7.42 %	63.76 %
12	C	39.3 %	31.01 %	33	B	33.19 %	22.71 %	54	A	19.65 %	57.21 %	75	D	7.42 %	62.45 %	96	D	19.21 %	57.21 %	117	A	15.28 %	60.7 %
13	A	20.96 %	22.71 %	34	A	31.88 %	31.44 %	55	D	9.17 %	63.76 %	76	D	11.35 %	60.7 %	97	B	15.28 %	62.89 %	118	A	12.23 %	62.88 %
14	D	26.2 %	31.88 %	35	A	33.19 %	27.07 %	56	B	14.41 %	52.4 %	77	D	8.73 %	62.89 %	98	D	11.79 %	57.64 %	119	A	12.66 %	63.32 %
15	A	12.23 %	25.76 %	36	B	23.58 %	30.57 %	57	A	14.41 %	60.26 %	78	D	11.35 %	54.59 %	99	D	13.97 %	62.45 %	120	D	8.73 %	62.01 %
16	B	20.09 %	29.69 %	37	C	33.62 %	29.7 %	58	D	4.37 %	58.51 %	79	A	5.68 %	63.75 %	100	D	4.8 %	62.01 %	121	C	8.73 %	63.32 %
17	D	12.66 %	30.13 %	38	C	26.2 %	31.01 %	59	A	10.92 %	60.7 %	80	A	12.66 %	58.08 %	101	D	18.34 %	61.14 %	122	D	16.16 %	50.22 %
18	D	33.19 %	31.44 %	39	A	16.59 %	31.88 %	60	D	8.3 %	62.44 %	81	A	5.68 %	60.7 %	102	B	14.85 %	55.89 %	123	A	16.59 %	56.34 %
19	C	19.21 %	19.65 %	40	A	24.45 %	31.01 %	61	D	9.17 %	61.14 %	82	B	13.54 %	58.08 %	103	A	4.8 %	55.9 %	124	A	13.1 %	65.5 %
20	D	19.21 %	26.64 %	41	A	26.2 %	23.58 %	62	C	19.21 %	58.08 %	83	D	9.17 %	57.21 %	104	A	5.68 %	62.44 %	125	C	17.03 %	62.01 %
21	B	17.9 %	24.02 %	42	B	31.88 %	31.44 %	63	D	6.11 %	60.7 %	84	D	13.1 %	54.15 %	105	A	6.55 %	61.57 %	126	C	11.79 %	59.39 %

Q.	Ans.	Correct	Skipped	Q.	Ans.	Correct	Skipped	Q.	Ans.	Correct	Skipped	Q.	Ans.	Correct	Skipped	Q.	Ans.	Correct	Skipped	Q.	Ans.	Correct	Skipped
127	C	6.55 %	63.32 %	148	B	11.79 %	61.57 %	169	B	13.1 %	60.26 %	190	B	13.97 %	68.13 %	211	B	7.42 %	68.56 %	232	D	4.8 %	68.56 %
128	D	23.14 %	61.58 %	149	A	24.45 %	57.65 %	170	D	6.99 %	66.37 %	191	C	10.92 %	65.5 %	212	C	8.73 %	68.56 %	233	B	3.49 %	69.44 %
129	A	11.79 %	53.28 %	150	B	15.28 %	57.65 %	171	C	11.35 %	65.94 %	192	B	4.8 %	69.0 %	213	C	9.17 %	65.94 %	234	B	9.17 %	68.12 %
130	C	8.73 %	58.52 %	151	C	17.03 %	64.63 %	172	C	9.61 %	68.56 %	193	C	5.24 %	68.12 %	214	A	4.37 %	68.12 %	235	D	7.86 %	69.43 %
131	A	5.68 %	55.02 %	152	A	2.62 %	68.56 %	173	D	3.93 %	62.88 %	194	A	8.73 %	69.87 %	215	D	6.11 %	69.87 %	236	D	6.11 %	68.56 %
132	A	10.48 %	61.57 %	153	B	8.3 %	69.43 %	174	B	6.11 %	68.56 %	195	C	4.37 %	67.25 %	216	D	3.49 %	68.56 %	237	B	9.17 %	69.87 %
133	A	14.41 %	62.01 %	154	A	6.55 %	70.31 %	175	A	5.68 %	67.25 %	196	C	13.97 %	69.0 %	217	B	6.55 %	69.0 %	238	A	3.49 %	68.56 %
134	C	25.76 %	59.83 %	155	A	3.06 %	62.01 %	176	B	7.86 %	69.0 %	197	C	13.54 %	68.99 %	218	B	11.35 %	69.0 %	239	B	10.92 %	68.56 %
135	A	3.49 %	63.76 %	156	B	8.3 %	68.56 %	177	A	12.66 %	65.07 %	198	A	5.68 %	69.43 %	219	C	6.55 %	69.43 %	240	D	15.72 %	69.43 %
136	A	7.86 %	61.57 %	157	C	6.99 %	67.68 %	178	A	9.61 %	70.3 %	199	D	4.8 %	68.56 %	220	B	13.54 %	69.87 %	241	B	6.55 %	68.56 %
137	D	4.8 %	63.76 %	158	A	5.68 %	68.12 %	179	A	7.42 %	66.82 %	200	D	7.42 %	68.13 %	221	D	8.3 %	62.88 %	242	A	8.73 %	68.13 %
138	D	10.04 %	62.45 %	159	A	8.73 %	68.13 %	180	A	5.24 %	68.56 %	201	C	9.17 %	69.0 %	222	C	5.68 %	66.37 %	243	A	7.86 %	66.81 %
139	C	20.52 %	62.89 %	160	A	11.79 %	68.56 %	181	D	3.49 %	68.56 %	202	B	6.11 %	65.94 %	223	A	8.3 %	70.3 %	244	A	5.24 %	70.31 %
140	B	20.96 %	62.88 %	161	D	9.17 %	66.81 %	182	A	10.92 %	67.68 %	203	A	10.04 %	67.25 %	224	B	5.24 %	69.0 %	245	B	10.48 %	69.0 %
141	B	16.16 %	62.44 %	162	A	10.48 %	67.69 %	183	D	8.73 %	64.2 %	204	B	4.37 %	68.56 %	225	A	4.8 %	66.82 %	246	D	10.92 %	68.56 %
142	C	6.11 %	62.01 %	163	A	16.59 %	65.07 %	184	A	4.37 %	68.99 %	205	C	9.61 %	68.12 %	226	A	15.28 %	68.13 %	247	A	9.17 %	69.0 %
143	B	16.59 %	56.77 %	164	C	7.42 %	68.56 %	185	D	3.93 %	65.07 %	206	C	6.55 %	69.0 %	227	A	6.99 %	69.43 %	248	B	8.73 %	69.0 %
144	D	10.48 %	63.32 %	165	A	12.23 %	64.63 %	186	B	6.99 %	67.25 %	207	C	14.85 %	68.56 %	228	C	7.42 %	69.0 %	249	A	11.35 %	67.69 %
145	A	7.42 %	58.96 %	166	B	8.73 %	67.69 %	187	B	6.11 %	67.69 %	208	A	7.86 %	68.12 %	229	B	13.54 %	65.5 %	250	A	8.73 %	68.13 %
146	C	16.16 %	60.26 %	167	C	6.11 %	69.0 %	188	C	10.92 %	68.56 %	209	C	9.61 %	66.81 %	230	D	9.61 %	69.43 %	251	D	1.75 %	68.56 %
147	A	3.06 %	64.19 %	168	C	4.37 %	68.99 %	189	D	8.73 %	69.87 %	210	D	6.55 %	68.12 %	231	C	8.3 %	65.5 %	252	A	7.86 %	69.43 %

Q.	Ans.	Correct	Skipped	Q.	Ans.	Correct	Skipped	Q.	Ans.	Correct	Skipped	Q.	Ans.	Correct	Skipped	Q.	Ans.	Correct	Skipped	Q.	Ans.	Correct	Skipped
253	A	18.34 %	69.87 %	261	A	18.78 %	65.5 %	269	A	7.86 %	64.63 %	277	C	18.34 %	65.5 %	285	B	8.73 %	65.07 %	293	A	16.59 %	68.56 %
254	A	9.61 %	67.68 %	262	B	5.68 %	68.56 %	270	C	7.42 %	68.13 %	278	A	12.66 %	69.87 %	286	C	11.35 %	69.44 %	294	C	13.1 %	69.0 %
255	C	20.09 %	68.56 %	263	B	10.48 %	63.76 %	271	A	13.1 %	65.5 %	279	D	10.92 %	66.37 %	287	B	7.42 %	64.63 %	295	B	13.1 %	64.19 %
256	D	14.85 %	69.43 %	264	A	4.8 %	69.44 %	272	C	4.8 %	69.87 %	280	B	17.47 %	68.56 %	288	C	3.06 %	69.87 %	296	D	8.73 %	68.56 %
257	D	6.11 %	68.13 %	265	D	10.04 %	67.69 %	273	D	6.11 %	68.56 %	281	C	11.79 %	64.63 %	289	D	4.37 %	68.12 %	297	B	6.55 %	68.56 %
258	C	17.47 %	69.43 %	266	A	10.48 %	68.12 %	274	B	11.35 %	68.56 %	282	B	4.8 %	67.25 %	290	A	4.8 %	68.56 %	298	A	13.97 %	68.13 %
259	B	17.47 %	65.5 %	267	B	10.92 %	64.63 %	275	B	11.35 %	69.0 %	283	C	11.35 %	70.31 %	291	C	16.16 %	66.81 %	299	B	9.17 %	66.81 %
260	C	9.61 %	68.56 %	268	A	9.61 %	68.99 %	276	D	13.1 %	68.56 %	284	A	5.24 %	69.87 %	292	B	8.73 %	69.44 %	300	B	17.47 %	69.87 %

//Hints and Solutions//

1. The sphincter of Oddi refers to the smooth muscle that surrounds the end portion of the common bile duct and pancreatic duct. This muscle relaxes during a meal to allow bile and pancreatic juice to flow into the intestine.

Hence, the correct option is (A).

2. These joints are classified as gliding or plane joints. The primary movement of the atlantoaxial joint complex is rotation. In rotation, the atlas together with the head, rotate around the dens of the axis. This movement allows us to turn our heads to look towards the left or towards the right.

Hence, the correct option is (B).

3. The pampiniform plexus is a loose network of small veins found within the male spermatic cord. The plexus begins in the scrotum with veins arising from the mediastinum testis, an area of connective tissue at the back of the testis.
Hence, the correct option is (C).

4.

Posterior relations of the kidney:

Diaphragm

Medial and lateral arcuate ligaments

Muscles:

- Psoas major
- Quadratus lumborum
- Transversus abdominis

Subcostal vessels

Nerves:

- Subcostal nerve
- Iliohypogastric nerve
- Ilioinguinal nerve

12th rib (11th rib and 12th ribs in the left kidney)

Hence, the correct option is (A).

5. Thigh adduction is performed by adductor muscles (magnus, longus, brevis) with gracilis and pectineus acting as accessory muscles. None of them are supplied by the L5 nerve root.

Hence, the correct option is (A).

6. Barr bodies are dark staining bodies (sex chromatin body) that represent the inactivated X chromosome. They are attached to the nuclear membrane of interphase cells. The number of Barr bodies is one less than the number of X chromosomes (n^{-1}).
Hence, the correct option is (A).

7. Reconversion of bone marrow is a reverse process of natural replacement of red marrow by yellow marrow. This process involves the appearance of areas of normal red marrow in the places where yellow marrow occurs, and is reverse of conversion.
Hence, the correct option is (D).

8. The sacrococcygeal joint is an articulation between the apex of the sacrum and the base of the coccyx (tailbone). This joint is a symphysis, having the two bones lined by hyaline cartilage and connected by an interposed fibrous disc. In some individuals, the joint might be synovial.
Hence, the correct option is (A).

9. Collection ducts are the larger tubes, each receiving the collecting tubules of several nephrons. The collecting duct does not form a part of the uriniferous tubule. The uriniferous tubule is divided into the proximal tubule, the intermediate (thin) tubule, the distal tubule and the collecting duct.

Hence, the correct option is (B).

10. Anterior ethmoidal artery arises from ophthalmic branch of internal carotid artery.The ophthalmic artery most commonly arises as the first major branch of the internal carotid artery, directly after emerging from the carotid sinus. It arises from the C6 segment of the internal carotid artery, usually at the level of the anterior clinoid process of the sphenoid bone.
Hence, the correct option is (B).

11. Urea is synthesised in the liver. So, the maximum amount of urea is present in the hepatic vein and the minimum in the renal vein. The hepatic veins are the veins that drain de-oxygenated blood from the liver into the inferior vena cava. There are usually three upper hepatic veins draining from the left, middle, and right parts of the liver. These are larger than the group of lower hepatic veins that can number from six to twenty.

Hence, the correct option is (B).

12. A polar body is a small haploid cell that is formed at the same time as an egg cell during oogenesis, but generally does not have the ability to be fertilized. When certain diploid cells in animals undergo cytokinesis after meiosis to produce egg cells, they sometimes divide unevenly.
Hence, the correct option is (C).

13. Transmission of upper limb weight occurs through 2 joints – acromioclavicular joint (scapula to clavicle) and sternoclavicular joint (clavicle to sternum). Acromioclavicular ligament and coracoclavicular ligament (more important) are the ligaments stabilizing the acromioclavicular joint. Sternoclavicular joint is stabilized by anterior and posterior sternoclavicular ligaments, costoclavicular ligaments on each side and the midline interclavicular ligament.
Hence, the correct option is (A).

14. It receives lymphatic drainage from all other axillary nodes.The axillary lymph nodes, also known commonly as axillary nodes, are a group of lymph nodes in the axilla and receive lymph from vessels that drain the arm, the walls of the thorax, the breast and the upper walls of the abdomen.
Hence, the correct option is (D).

15. The two parts are continuous with each other, forming a "U" shape around the posterior border of the mylohyoid muscle. The body of the gland is in and inferior to the digastric triangle and also partly under cover of the mandible. The submandibular gland wraps around the edges of the mylohyoid, and is divided into superficial

and deep lobes above and below the muscle.
Hence, the correct option is (A).

16. Lip cleft can occur as a one-sided (unilateral) or two-sided (bilateral) condition. It is due to the failure of fusion of the maxillary prominence and medial nasal processes (formation of the primary palate).
Hence, the correct option is (B).

17. The sclerotome is the ventral derivative of the somite. Somites are segmental units formed in the paraxial mesoderm on either side of the axial structures, the neural tube and the notochord.
Hence, the correct option is (D).

18. Kidneys – Filtration, reabsorption and excretion of calcium. Also involved in activation of Vitamin D.

Skin – Vitamin D syntheisis

Intestines – Absorption of calcium from diet.
Hence, the correct option is (D).

19. The lateral hypothalamus (LH), also called the lateral hypothalamic area (LHA), contains the primary orexinergic nucleus within the hypothalamus that widely projects throughout the nervous system; this system of neurons mediates an array of cognitive and physical processes, such as promoting feeding behavior.
Hence, the correct option is (C).

20. The hyperkinetic aspects of the movement disorder in HD are thought to be due to the degeneration of striatal neurons (potentially through excitotoxic processes triggered by abnormal glutamatergic transmission in the striatum) that belong to the indirect pathway. GABA is considered an inhibitory neurotransmitter because it blocks, or inhibits, certain brain signals and decreases activity in your nervous system. When GABA attaches to a protein in your brain known as a GABA receptor, it produces a calming effect. This can help with feelings of anxiety, stress, and fear.
Hence, the correct option is (D).

21. Myopathies are characterized by the presence of polyphasic, short-duration, low-amplitude MUAPs. Because each small motor unit is able to generate only a reduced amount of force compared with normal, with little muscle contraction, many MUAPs are recruited.
Hence, the correct option is (B).

22. FSH receptors are located on the granulosa cells of the ovary and the Sertoli cells of the testicle, where FSH binding promotes gamete production in the gonads. Follicle-stimulating hormone (FSH) is a glycoprotein gonadotropin secreted by the anterior pituitary in response to gonadotropin-releasing hormone (GnRH) released by the hypothalamus.
Hence, the correct option is (B).

23. It is estimated that 15% of the population uses zinc supplements to exceed the recommended dietary allowance of 11 mg/d for men. A large body of literature supports a protective role for zinc with regard to prostate cancer progression. Zinc has been found to inhibit prostate cancer cell line growth and invasion.
Hence, the correct option is (B).

24. The hydrostatic pressure is 32 mmHg at the arterial end of capillary (Phc,a) and 15 mmHg at the venous end (Phc,b). Because of the gradient of the hydrostatic pressure along the capillary, filtration usually occurs at the arterial end of the capillary and reabsorption at its venous end.
Hence, the correct option is (B).

25. For a PCR reaction, a DNA primer is not needed. The non-availability of DNA primers is the reason why RNA primers should be used in PCR. The DNA Primase enzyme, which is nothing but RNA polymerase much like mRNA, readily synthesises the RNA primers complementary to the cellular DNA.
Hence, the correct option is (D).

26. Isometric exercise produces a characteristic pressor increase in blood pressure which may be important in maintaining perfusion of muscle during sustained contraction. This response is mediated by combined central and peripheral afferent input to medullary cardiovascular centers.
Hence, the correct option is (D).

27. Renin is an enzyme secreted by the juxtaglomerular cells of the kidney. It interacts with aldosterone in a negative-feedback loop. Renin is mainly produced and released into circulation by the so-called juxtaglomerular epithelioid cells, located in the walls of renal afferent arterioles at the entrance of the glomerular capillary network.
Hence, the correct option is (D).

28. The juxtaglomerular apparatus lies adjacent to the glomerulus and regulates kidney function by maintaining the blood flow to the kidney and the filtration rate. This location is critical to its function in regulating renal blood flow and glomerular filtration rate.
Hence, the correct option is (D).

29. Blood brain barrier is not permeable to ions. Hence they cannot influence cerebral blood flow. Small ions and water molecules can cross the blood-brain barrier through ion channels. Other molecules can be actively transported across endothelial cell membranes by carrier-mediated transporters, receptor-mediated transporters, adsorption-mediated transcytosis, or efflux pumps.
Hence, the correct option is (C).

30. Hormones secreted by the kidney are 1,25 dihydroxycholecalciferol, renin and erythropoietin. The human kidney secretes many hormones: erythropoietin (EPO), calcitriol, vitamin D3, as well as the enzyme renin. The kidneys also produce prostaglandins.
Hence, the correct option is (B).

31. Decreased cerebral blood flow is seen with high oxygen tension. But it is a protective effect caused by cerebral vasoconstriction.

Oxygen toxicity can be both acute and chronic.

Acute toxicity develops following exposure to high oxygen tension even for a short duration. It mostly affects the CNS – Bert effect. It is characterised by muscle twitching, convulsions and coma.

Chronic toxicity develops following long term exposure to relatively lower concentration of oxygen. Pulmonary effects are more common – Smith effect. Manifestations are pulmonary edema, atelectasis and congestion of lung passages.

Retrolental fibroplasia (retinopathy of prematurity) is seen following administration of high concentration of oxygen to neonates. It can lead to blindness. It is caused by angiogenesis.
Hence, the correct option is (B).

32.

Delta waves are the slowest recorded brain waves in human beings. They are found most often in infants and young children, and are associated with the deepest levels of relaxation and restorative, healing sleep. Delta is prominently seen in brain injuries, learning problems, inability to think, and severe ADHD.

- frequency – less than 4Hz
- Seen in deep sleep (stage III and IV of NREM), infants, organic brain damage

Hence, the correct option is (A).

33. Hippocampus is responsible for conversion of short term memory into long term memory. Only the explicit / declarative type of long term memory is formed in the hippocampus. Implicit / non declarative form of long term memory is not formed in the hippocampus. Epilepsy patients who have had both their hippocampi removed cannot form new long term memories of the explicit type. But they retain long term memories that were formed before the surgery – thus hippocampus is not the site of storage of long term memory.
Hence, the correct option is (B).

34. Broca's area is involved in the expressive aspects of spoken and written language (production of sentences constrained by the rules of grammar and syntax). In keeping with its role in speech and language, Broca's area is immediately anterior to the motor and premotor representations of the face, tongue and larynx.
Hence, the correct option is (A).

35. Mitochondrial DNA is the small circular chromosome found inside mitochondria. The mitochondria are organelles found in cells that are the sites of energy production. The mitochondria, and thus mitochondrial DNA, are passed from mother to offspring.
Hence, the correct option is (A).

36. In tRNA, the bases (Adenine, Guanine, Uracil and Cytosine) are modified by methylation, reduction, deamination and rearrangement of glycosidic bonds.
Hence, the correct option is (B).

37. Microsatellite sequences are repetitive DNA sequences usually several base pairs in length. Microsatellite sequences are composed of non-coding DNA and are not parts of genes. They are used as genetic markers to follow the inheritance of genes in families. Microsatellites, Simple Sequence Repeats (SSR), Short Tandem Repeats (STR) and Simple Sequence Length Polymorphisms (SSLP) are found in prokaryotes and eukaryotes.
Hence, the correct option is (C).

38. The enzyme succinate dehydrogenase is a classical example of competitive inhibition with succinic acid as its substrate. A substance similar to the substrate takes part and competes with the substrate for the active site and is known as the inhibitor.
Hence, the correct option is (C).

39. Creatinine remains the gold standard for measuring the glomerular filtration rate and kidney functioning. And Jaffe method remains the default method for estimation of creatinine. Creatinine in serum or urine is determined by Jaffe's reaction where creatinine produces quantitatively an orange color with picric acid in alkaline medium. Alkali is consumed to neutralise the acids in both these cases. For urine creatinine measurement, a direct diluted urine sample is used.
Hence, the correct option is (A).

40. Chymotrypsinogen is an inactive precursor (zymogen) of chymotrypsin, a digestive enzyme which breaks proteins down into smaller peptides. Chymotrypsinogen is a single polypeptide chain consisting of 245 amino acid residues.
Hence, the correct option is (A).

41. Of these 64 codons, 61 represent amino acids, and three are stop signals. Although each codon is specific for only one amino acid (or one stop signal), the genetic code is described as degenerate, or redundant, because a single amino acid may be coded for by more than one codon.
Hence, the correct option is (A).

42. According to the low-density-lipoprotein (LDL) receptor hypothesis, development of atherosclerosis is caused by a high concentration of LDL-cholesterol in the blood, and lowering LDL-cholesterol reverses, or at least retards, atherosclerosis, thus preventing cardiovascular disease.
Hence, the correct option is (B).

43. Increased blood and urine copper concentrations and normal or increased ceruloplasmin levels may indicate exposure to excess copper or may be associated with conditions that decrease copper excretion, such as chronic liver disease, or that release copper from tissues, such as acute hepatitis.
Hence, the correct option is (D).

44. Uric acid is the end product of purine metabolism of humans and some higher primates. In other mammals enzyme urate oxidase is capable to further convert uric acid to allantoin.
Hence, the correct option is (D).

45. SYBR Green is a commonly used fluorescent dye that binds double-stranded DNA molecules by intercalating between the DNA bases. It is used in quantitative PCR because the fluorescence can be measured at the end of each amplification cycle to determine, relatively or absolutely, how much DNA has been amplified.
Hence, the correct option is (C).

46. Fluorescence in situ hybridization (FISH) provides researchers with a way to visualize and map the genetic material in an individual's cells, including specific genes or portions of genes. This may be used for understanding a variety of chromosomal abnormalities and other genetic mutations.
Hence, the correct option is (A).

47. During glycolysis, glucose is broken down in ten steps to two molecules of pyruvate, which then enters the mitochondria where it is oxidised through the tricarboxylic acid cycle to carbon dioxide and water.
Hence, the correct option is (B).

48. Dinitrophenol uncouples oxidation and phosphorylation in the respiratory chain. The hydrogen ions re enter the mitochondrial matrix without ATP synthesis. The energy is released as heat.
Hence, the correct option is (C).

49. Hypoxia stimulates RBC glycolysis by promoting release of all glycolytic enzymes from Band 3 on RBC membrane.
Hence, the correct option is (C).

50. Study of multiplication of proteins in disease process is called a Proteomics. Proteomics is the large-scale study of proteins. Proteins are vital parts of living organisms, with many functions. The

proteome is the entire set of proteins that is produced or modified by an organism or system. Proteomics has enabled the identification of ever increasing numbers of protein.
Hence, the correct option is (A).

51. C_3 is increased in all of the above. But in PSGN, the levels return to normal by 6-8 weeks. Low C_3 and C_4 are characteristic of the glomerulonephritis caused by deposition of circulating immune complex. Normal or nearly normal C_3 with very low C_4 is characteristic of type 2 and type 3 cryoglobulinemia.
Hence, the correct option is (A).

52. Diarrhea-associated HUS or Stx-HUS occurs after infection with Shiga toxin-producing Escherichia coli (STEC) or less frequently after a Shigella dysenteriae infection. Enterohemorrhagic E. coli is the most common cause of Stx-HUS in the United States (US).
Hence, the correct option is (C).

53. The clinical picture is that of Klinefelter syndrome. The correct answer should be 47, XXY. But it is not among the options given. Hence we select 46, XXY as the best option.
Hence, the correct option is (C).

54. Other cancer associated genes:

FAP – Familial adenomatous polyposis

Rb – Retinoblastoma

BRCA 1 – Breast cancer
Hence, the correct option is (A).

55. Other arachidonic acid metabolites are leukotrienes and prostaglandins. Arachidonic acid and its metabolites (prostaglandins and leukotrienes) are now considered intracellular messengers. Arachidonic acid is then metabolized by cyclooxygenase (COX) and 5-lipoxygenase, resulting in the synthesis of prostaglandins and leukotrienes, respectively.
Hence, the correct option is (D).

56. A lattice of clathrin coats the cytosolic pits formed during receptor mediated endocytosis. Clathrin is involved in coating membranes that are endocytosed from the plasma membrane and those that move between the trans-Golgi network (TGN) and endosomes. When coating membranes, clathrin does not link to the membrane directly, but does so via adaptor proteins.
Hence, the correct option is (B).

57. In genomic imprinting, there is preferential expression of an allele depending on its parental origin. Genomic imprinting is an epigenetic phenomenon that causes genes to be expressed in a parent-of-origin-specific manner.Genes however, can also be partially imprinted. Partial imprinting happens when alleles from both parents are differently expressed rather than complete expression and complete suppression of one parents allele.
Hence, the correct option is (A).

58. In NCPF, fibrosis is seen only in portal and periportal region. Bridging fibrosis An advanced stage of liver fibrosis seen in the progressive form of chronic liver diseases. The term "bridging" means 'the formation of "bridge" (by the band of mature & thick fibrous tissue) obliterating portal area to central vein', leads to the formation of pseudolobules.
Hence, the correct option is (D).

59. HUS is classified under thrombotic microangiopathies. Thrombotic microangiopathy (TMA) is a pathology that results in thrombosis in capillaries and arterioles, due to an endothelial injury. It may be seen in association with thrombocytopenia, anemia, purpura and kidney failure. The classic TMAs are hemolytic uremic syndrome and thrombotic thrombocytopenic purpura.
Hence, the correct option is (A).

60. In benign nephrosclerosis, the kidneys may be reduced in size due to cortical scarring and shrinking. Benign nephrosclerosis refers to the renal changes most commonly occurring in association with long-standing hypertension. It is termed benign because it rarely progresses to clinically significant chronic kidney disease or kidney failure.
Hence, the correct option is (D).

61. Klebsiella causes 'typical pneumonia'. Even though these infections are called "atypical," they are not uncommon. This illness, caused by Chlamydia pneumoniae, is most common in school-aged children and usually develops into mild pneumonia or bronchitis.
Hence, the correct option is (D).

62. In medicine, Aschoff bodies are nodules found in the hearts of individuals with rheumatic fever. They result from inflammation in the heart muscle and are characteristic of rheumatic heart disease.
Hence, the correct option is (C).

63. Tartrate resistant acid phosphatase (TRAP) is a test performed on blood cells or bone marrow (biopsy) to confirm a diagnosis of hairy cell leukemia. This test can also be done on blood plasma to look for signs of bone breakdown.
Hence, the correct option is (D).

64. The others are part of classical subtype. Lymphocyte predominant HL is an uncommon subtype composed of vague nodules of numerous reactive lymphocytes admixed with large popcorn-shaped RSC. Unlike classic RSC, the non-classic popcorn-shaped RS cells of NLPHL are CD15 and CD30 negative while positive for the B cell marker CD20.
Hence, the correct option is (A).

65. The International Lymphoma Study Group (I.L.S.G.) developed a consensus list of lymphoid neoplasms, which was published in 1994 as the "Revised European-American Classification of Lymphoid Neoplasms" (R.E.A.L.).
Hence, the correct option is (B).

66. Familial Mediterranean fever (FMF) is an inherited autoinflammatory disease characterized by recurrent episodes (attacks) of fever and acute inflammation of the membranes lining the abdomen, joints, and lungs. MEFV (Mediterranean fever) is a human gene that provides instructions for making a protein called pyrin (also known as marenostrin).
Hence, the correct option is (A).

67. Familial transthyretin amyloidosis (FTA) is caused by changes (mutations) in the TTR gene . This gene is responsible for making a protein called transthyretin which transports vitamin A and a hormone called thyroxin to many parts of the body.
Hence, the correct option is (B).

68. Apple green birefringence of amyloid can be observed when stained with congo red and viewed under polarizing microscope. Amyloid can be identified with the hematoxylin & eosin (H&E) stain as waxy, homogenous, eosinophilic material. Most commonly, amyloid can be identified with the Congo red stain as an "apple-green birefringence" when viewed under polarized microscopic

light.
Hence, the correct option is (C).

69. CEA (Carcinoembryonic antigen) is a tumour marker of adenocarcinoma colon, lung, ovary, pancreas and breast. Carcinoembryonic antigen (CEA) is a protein that is present in certain tissues of a developing baby (fetus). By the time a baby is born, it drops to a very low level. In adults, CEA is normally present at very low levels in the blood but may be elevated with certain types of cancer.
Hence, the correct option is (D).

70. Examples of tumor suppressor genes are the $BRCA_1/BRCA_2$ genes, otherwise known as the "breast cancer genes." People who have a mutation in one of these genes have an increased risk of developing breast cancer (among other cancers). The Rb protein is a tumor suppressor, which plays a pivotal role in the negative control of the cell cycle and in tumor progression. It has been shown that Rb protein (pRb) is responsible for a major G^1 checkpoint, blocking S-phase entry and cell growth.
Hence, the correct option is (D).

71. Thrombomodulin is found on endothelium of arteries, veins, capillaries, and lymphatics, and on syncytiotrophoblast of human placenta. Endothelial regulation of the blood coagulation system. Under physiological conditions, the endothelium prevents thrombosis by providing a surface that discourages the attachment of cells and clotting proteins. The endothelium regulates clot formation in part via its activation of the intravascular PARs.
Hence, the correct option is (C).

72. After the death stimuli, Bcl^{-2} and Bcl-xL precluded the release of the $Apaf^{-1}$ cofactor cytochrome c from mitochondria and the formation of larger Apaf-1 complexes, which are steps that presage apoptosis.
Hence, the correct option is (D).

73. Fibrinoid necrosis is not described in diabetic glomerulosclerosis. Diabetes also can cause progressive scarring of glomeruli. This is called glomerulosclerosis. This scarring often produces nodules (lumps) of scar in the glomeruli and thus is called nodular diabetic glomerulosclerosis.
Hence, the correct option is (C).

74. CML is characterised by increase in neutrophils, basophils, eosinophils, and platelets. None of the other conditions mentioned show increase in basophils and eosinophils. Chronic myelogenous leukemia is a disease in which the bone marrow makes too many white blood cells. Chronic myelogenous leukemia (also called CML or chronic granulocytic leukemia) is a slowly progressing blood and bone marrow disease that usually occurs during or after middle age, and rarely occurs in children.
Hence, the correct option is (C).

75. Causes of interstitial lung disease include asbestos, radiation, connective tissue disorders, fumes, aspiration pneumonia and certain genetic conditions. Tobacco smoke is not implicated.
Hence, the correct option is (D).

76. Inhaled nitric oxide (iNO) gas was approved in 1999 by the FDA to treat hypoxic newborns. The use of iNO has proven effective at reducing pulmonary associated stress and is a staple treatment; yet its beneficial ameliorations reach outside the realm of lung disease.
Hence, the correct option is (D).

77. Ranitidine can increase the gastric pH and prevent polymerization (occurs at a pH < 4) of sucralfate.

Sucralfate decreases the absorption of many drugs including ranitidine.
Hence, the correct option is (D).

78. Domperidone blocks the emesis induced by levodopa. It has no affect on the therapeutic potential. Domperidone acts as a peripherally selective antagonist of the dopamine D_2 and D_3 receptors and provides relief from nausea by blocking receptors at the chemoreceptor trigger zone at the floor of the fourth ventricle.
Hence, the correct option is (D).

79. Functions of delta type opioid receptors are:

- supraspinal analgesia
- spinal analgesia
- modulation of hormone and neurotransmitter release

Hence, the correct option is (A).

80.

Morphine is contraindicated in head injury for the following reasons:

- Causes carbon dioxide retention – this in turn increases intracranial tension.
- Therapeutic doses can cause respiratory depression in head injury patients.
- Vomiting, miosis and altered mentation caused by morphine can interfere with assessment of neurological status.

Morphine should be avoided in those with bronchial asthma as it can precipitate an attack of asthma. But it is not contraindicated. Patients with hypothyroidism are more sensitive to the effects of morphine.
Hence, the correct option is (A).

81. Sulfasalazine is poorly absorbed (10-20%) from the GIT. Sulfasalazine is metabolized by intestinal bacteria, resulting in the release of sulfapyridine and 5-aminosalicylate. The drug is useful in the treatment of active ulcerative colitis as well as in preventing relapses of the disease in remission.
Hence, the correct option is (A).

82. Slow ventricular rate in a patient with atrial fibrillation indicates complete heart block – a complication of digoxin therapy. Digoxin is a type of medicine called a cardiac glycoside. It's used to control some heart problems, such as irregular heartbeats (arrhythmias) including atrial fibrillation. It can also help to manage the symptoms of heart failure, usually with other medicines. Digoxin is only available on prescription.
Hence, the correct option is (B).

83. Buspirone does not act on the GABA receptor. Rather, its most salient interaction with neurotransmitter receptors occurs at the 5-HT1A serotonin receptor. This action is supported by studies focused on receptor binding, anatomical localization, biochemistry,

neurophysiology, and animal behavior.
Hence, the correct option is (D).

84. Side effects of flutamide are gynaecomastia, breast tenderness, liver damage, nausea and hot flushes. It has anti androgenic action.
Hence, the correct option is (D).

85. Important side effects of alpha-glucosidase inhibitors – flatulence, diarrhoea, abdominal pain. They arise due to presence of undigested carbohydrates in the colon which get fermented to short chain fatty acids with gas production.
Hence, the correct option is (C).

86. Biguanides are contraindicated in renal disease, hepatic disease and conditions causing tissue anoxia due to increased risk of lactic acidosis. Renal insufficiency is poor function of the kidneys that may be due to a reduction in blood-flow to the kidneys caused by renal artery disease. Normally, the kidneys regulate body fluid and blood pressure, as well as regulate blood chemistry and remove organic waste.
Hence, the correct option is (C).

87. Erection is mediated by parasympathetic nervous system. Penile erection is triggered by sexual stimulation and sexual arousal. Parasympathetic stimulation via the cavernous nerves initiates the process, causing the coiled helicine arteries to uncoil (by expansion of their lumen), relaxing the smooth muscle in the trabeculae.
Hence, the correct option is (D).

88. Phase IV (post marketing surveillance) does not need any ethical clearance. Clinical trials follow a rigorous series from early, small-scale, Phase 1 studies to late-stage, large scale, Phase 3 studies. If a treatment is successful in one phase, it moves on to the next phase.
Hence, the correct option is (D).

89. Highly ionized drugs are lipid insoluble. Hence they are poorly absorbed by the intestine. They cannot cross the placental barrier easily. And since they are not reabsorbed in the renal tubules, they are excreted in urine.
Hence, the correct option is (A).

90. Hepatitis E causes fulminant hepatic failure in 1-2% of cases (20% in pregnancy). Immunologic changes during pregnancy promote the maintenance of the fetus in the maternal environment by suppression of T cell–mediated immunity, rendering pregnant women more susceptible to viral infections like HEV infection.
Hence, the correct option is (C).

91. Etanercept is a biologic tumor necrosis factor (TNF) inhibitor; the drug acts as a soluble TNF receptor and binds TNF-alpha and TNF-beta. [6] TNF is a cytokine that can bind to TNF receptor 1 ($TNFR_1$) or TNF receptor 2 ($TNFR_2$) and is involved in inflammation and the immune response.
Hence, the correct option is (A).

92. Nevirapine falls in the non-nucleoside reverse transcriptase inhibitor (NNRTI) class of antiretrovirals. Both nucleoside and non-nucleoside RTIs inhibit the same target, the reverse transcriptase enzyme, an essential viral enzyme which transcribes viral RNA into DNA.
Hence, the correct option is (C).

93. Tacrolimus (which is a macrolide) has anti-inflammatory and immunomodulatory activity. Tacrolimus (FK506) is a macrolide immunosuppressant produced by the fungus Streptomyces tsukubaensis. The drug is indicated for liver transplant rejection prophylaxis and is under investigation for use in kidney, cardiac, pancreas, small bowel, and bone marrow transplantation.
Hence, the correct option is (D).

94. Cloxacillin is a penicillinase resistant penicillin. Oxacillin, cloxacillin, and dicloxacillin are other semisynthetic penicillinase-resistant penicillins classified together as isoxazolyl penicillins. They have an antimicrobial spectrum similar to that of methicillin and nafcillin and are active against staphylococci and streptococci.
Hence, the correct option is (D).

95. An inverse agonist is an agent that binds to the same receptor as an agonist but induces a pharmacological response opposite to that agonist. β-carbolines such as methyl-6,7-dimethoxy-4-ethyl- β-carboline-3-carboxylate (DMCM) are convulsant and anxiogenic drugs. They bind to the benzodiazepine receptor site but have reverse effects: they are called 'benzodiazepine inverse agonists'.
Hence, the correct option is (C).

96. An Isograft is a graft of tissue between two individuals who are genetically identical (i.e. monozygotic twins). Isograft refers to tissue transplanted between genetically identical twins. An allograft (termed homograft in older texts) is tissue transplanted between unrelated individuals of the same species. A xenograft (termed heterograft in older texts) is tissue transplanted between individuals of different species.
Hence, the correct option is (D).

97. With India ink preparation, the capsule can be seen as a clear halo around the cell. Negative-staining with nigrosin or India ink is a quick and easy method to gain information about the presence or absence of capsules or any other layers around bacteria. An organism with a capsule will show a halo around the cell.
Hence, the correct option is (B).

98. Trichinella spiralis is seen in striated muscles. Trichinella spiralis is an intracellular parasitic nematode of mammalian striated muscles, found worldwide in many carnivorous and omnivorous animals. There is no stage in the life cycle that is external to the host (in the environment), and transmission is solely from ingestion of another infected host.
Hence, the correct option is (D).

99. Viruses cannot grow in acellular media. Viruses cannot be grown on an ordinary culture medium because they are not actually living organisms. Viruses can be cultivated within suitable hosts, such as a living cell. To study bacteriophages for example bacteria are grown in a suitable growth medium, then bacteriophages are added.
Hence, the correct option is (D).

100.

- Chlamydia trachomatis has atleast 15 identified serotypes. But C. pneumoniae has only one serotype.
- Animals have no role in transmission of C. pneumoniae. Transmission is via air borne route.
- Cytoplasmic inclusions lack glycogen.

Hence, the correct option is (D).

101. Chlamydia pneumoniae causes community acquired pneumonia (CAP can be caused by many other organisms too). Community-acquired pneumonia is defined as pneumonia that is acquired outside the hospital. The most commonly identified pathogens are Streptococcus pneumoniae, Haemophilus influenzae,

atypical bacteria (ie, Chlamydia pneumoniae, Mycoplasma pneumoniae, Legionella species), and viruses.
Hence, the correct option is (D).

102. The most commonly identified organisms were Acinobacter species (34.8%), Pseudomonas aeruginosa (23.9%) and Escherichia coli (15.2%). Trivedi et al,[17] reported an incidence of 9.38% of NP and 38% had ventilator associated pneumonia. Commonest isolates were pseudomonas (55%), Acinetobacter (20%), Staph.
Hence, the correct option is (B).

103. Burkholderia mallei causes glanders – a disease of horses, mules and donkeys.Burkholderia pseudomallei causes melioidosis. Glanders is an infectious disease that is caused by the bacterium Burkholderia mallei. While people can get the disease, glanders is primarily a disease affecting horses. It also affects donkeys and mules and can be naturally contracted by other mammals such as goats, dogs, and cats.
Hence, the correct option is (A).

104. Culture conditions for Compylobacter jejuni

- Low oxygen tension (5%)
- Increased carbon dioxide levels (10%)
- Incubation temperature of 42°C

Hence, the correct option is (A).

105. V. cholerae is non halophilic. The genus can be divided into non-halophilic vibrios, including V. cholerae and other species that are able to grow in media without added salt, and halophilic species such as V. parahaemolyticus and V. vulnificus that require salt for growth.
Hence, the correct option is (A).

106. Candida appears as gram positive round to oval cells and pseudohyphae. Candidiasis is a fungal infection caused by a yeast (a type of fungus) called Candida. Some species of Candida can cause infection in people; the most common is Candida albicans. Candida normally lives on the skin and inside the body, in places such as the mouth, throat, gut, and vagina, without causing any problems.
Hence, the correct option is (C).

107. Intestinal parasites are not only important causes of acute diarrheal illnesses, but they also cause chronic diarrhea and malabsorption. Giardiasis, strongyloidosis and capillariasis are definitive causes of malabsorption of many nutrients.
Hence, the correct option is (D).

108. Bacteroides:

- Gram negative anaerobic bacilli
- Most common anaerobic pathogen isolated from clinical specimens
- Virulence factors include capsular polysaccharides and lipopolysaccharide endotoxin
- Lipopolysaccharide endotoxin is much less toxic compared to other gram negative bacteria
- Hence infections do not directly produce signs of sepsis, which is common in other gram negative bacteria
- Some are resistant to metronidazole

Hence, the correct option is (D).

109. Common causes of urethral discharge in a young male are gonococcus and chlamydia. But in this case, no organisms were found in the pus cells. This indicates that the cause is probably not gonococcus. So in order to check for presence of chlamydia, we have to use cell culture methods such as Mc coy cells.
Hence, the correct option is (A).

110. Vibrio cholerae produces a toxin that increases cAMP levels in intestinal crypt cells, producing a sustained activation of the apical membrane CFTR Cl^- channel leading to excessive Cl^- secretion into the ileum and colon.
Hence, the correct option is (A).

111. The trichrome stain is used to differentiate collagen and smooth muscle. Normal liver biopsies demonstrate tricrhome stained collagen in the portal tracts and around the central vein.
Hence, the correct option is (A).

112. The patient presented with history of pneumonia. Charcoal yeast medium is the special medium for legionella culture. Species of the genus Legionella are Gram-negative, non-spore-forming, rod-shaped, aerobic bacteria. They contain branched-chain fatty acids, have a non-fermentative metabolism, and require L-cysteine and iron salts for growth.
Hence, the correct option is (C).

113. Enterotoxigenic E. coli is the most common cause of traveller's diarrhoea. Bacteria are the most common cause of TD. Overall, the most common pathogen identified is enterotoxigenic Escherichia coli, followed by Campylobacter jejuni, Shigella spp., and Salmonella spp. Enteroaggregative and other E. coli pathotypes are also commonly found in cases of TD.
Hence, the correct option is (A).

114. The bacitracin susceptibility test is used to distinguish Group A streptococci, from other streptococci. When grown on blood agar, Group A streptococci are sensitive to (killed by) the antibiotic bacitracin.
Hence, the correct option is (A).

115. Innate immunity is comprised of different components including physical barriers (tight junctions in the skin, epithelial and mucous membrane surfaces, mucus itself); anatomical barriers; epithelial and phagocytic cell enzymes (i.e., lysozyme), phagocytes (i.e., neutrophils, monocytes, macrophages), inflammation.
Hence, the correct option is (A).

116. The heavy metals most commonly associated with poisoning of humans are lead, mercury, arsenic and cadmium. Heavy metal poisoning may occur as a result of industrial exposure, air or water pollution, foods, medicines, improperly coated food containers, or the ingestion of lead-based paints.
Hence, the correct option is (D).

117. Sexual masochism disorder (SMD) is the condition of experiencing recurring and intense sexual arousal in response to enduring moderate or extreme pain, suffering, or humiliation. There is no universally accepted theory explaining the root of sexual masochism. However, some theories attempt to explain the presence of sexual paraphilias in general. One suggests that paraphilias originate because when inappropriate sexual fantasies are forbidden, they become stronger as they are suppressed.
Hence, the correct option is (A).

118. Abortion stick induces abortion by stimulating uterine contraction. Uterine contraction: The tightening and shortening of

the uterine muscles. During labor, contractions accomplish two things: (1) they cause the cervix to thin and dilate (open); and (2) they help the baby to descend into the birth canal.
Hence, the correct option is (A).

119. Charcoal hemoperfusion has been used to treat patients with life-threatening carbamazepine poisoning. Activated charcoal imbedded in the hemoperfusion cartridge competes with plasma proteins for binding of the drug. Barbiturates are sedative-hypnotics, a type of central nervous system (CNS) depressant used to treat insomnia, seizures, and headaches. Barbiturates may also be used in a hospital setting for pre-operative sedation.
Hence, the correct option is (A).

120. Copper sulfate is used as a fungicide, algaecide, root killer, and herbicide in both agriculture and non-agricultural settings. It is also used as an antimicrobial and molluscicide. Uses for individual products containing copper sulfate vary widely. Dialysis is a treatment for kidney failure that rids your body of unwanted toxins, waste products and excess fluids by filtering your blood. When kidneys fail, your body may have difficulty cleaning your blood and keeping your system chemically balanced.
Hence, the correct option is (D).

121. This entity has been manually annotated by the ChEBI Team. ChEBI Ontology. Outgoing. aryl phosphate is a organic phosphate aryl phosphate is a phosphoric ester. Malathion is a man-made organophosphate insecticide that is commonly used to control mosquitoes and a variety of insects that attack fruits, vegetables, landscaping plants, and shrubs. It can also be found in other pesticide products used indoors and on pets to control ticks and insects, such as fleas and ants.
Hence, the correct option is (C).

122. The Spalding sign refers to the overlapping of the fetal skull bones caused by collapse of the fetal brain. It appears usually a week or more after fetal death in utero. When a fetus dies in utero, there are changes in the skin and tissues termed fetal maceration. This process takes place entirely in the womb and stops once the fetus is delivered. The phenomenon of maceration was first described in 1922 as loss of the vernix and then skin peeling.
Hence, the correct option is (D).

123. Acrodynia gets its name from a pink discolouration and pain affecting the hands and feet. It is associated with irritability, photophobia (sensitivity to light) and polyneuritis (inflamed nerves). Now a rare disease, acrodynia (painful extremities) primarily affects young children. The symptoms of irritability, photophobia, pink discoloration of the hands and feet, and polyneuritis can be attributed to chronic exposure to mercury.
Hence, the correct option is (A).

124. The duodenum continues into the jejunum at the duodenojejunal junction or flexure, which lies to the left of L2 vertebra and is fixed to the retroperitoneum by a suspensory ligament of Treitz. Anatomically, the small bowel can be divided into three parts: the duodenum, jejunum, and ileum.

Hence, the correct option is (A).

125. Nutmeg liver refers to the mottled appearance of the liver as a result of hepatic venous congestion. Radiologically, it is most appreciable on port venous phase imaging on cross-sectional imaging. It is named after the cut appearance of the nutmeg seed. Nutmeg liver is the pathological appearance of the liver caused by chronic passive congestion of the liver secondary to right heart failure. The liver appears "speckled" like a grated nutmeg kernel, from the dilated, congested central veins (dark spots) and paler, unaffected surrounding liver tissue.

Hence, the correct option is (C).

126. The commonly-used temperatures and time that hot air ovens need to sterilize materials are 170 degrees Celsius for 30 minutes, 160 degrees Celsius for 60 minutes, and 150 degrees Celsius for 150 minutes.

Hence, the correct option is (C).

127. It was passed by the Government of India in the year 2000. It was amended in 2006. (Juvenile Justice Act was passed in 1986). An Act to consolidate and amend the law relating to juveniles in conflict with law and children in need of care and protection, by providing for proper care, protection and treatment by catering to their development needs, and by adopting a child-friendly approach in the adjudication and disposition of matters in the best interest of children and for their ultimate rehabilitation through various institutions established under this enactment.
Hence, the correct option is (C).

128. It refers to the area of northern India extending 24ookm from Kashmir in the west to Naga hills in the east where goitre is endemic. It is the largest goitre belt in the world. The following states are included in the Himalayan Goitre Belt:

- Jammu and Kashmir
- Himachal Pradesh
- Delhi
- Punjab
- Haryana
- Uttar Pradesh
- Bihar
- West Bengal
- Sikkin
- Arunachal Pradesh
- Assam
- Mizoram
- Nagaland
- Manipur
- Meghalaya
- Tripura

Hence, the correct option is (D).

129. Toxoid vaccines Toxoid vaccine A vaccine made from a toxin (poison) that has been made harmless but that elicits an immune response against the toxin. are based on the toxin produced by certain bacteria (e.g. tetanus or diphtheria). For example, the tetanus toxoid is derived from the tetanospasmin produced by Clostridium tetani.

Hence, the correct option is (A).

130. Prevalence of diabetes = 0.1

Probability that any one person selected from the population will have diabetes = 0.1

Probability that 3 people selected from the population will all have diabetes = 0.1 × 0.1 × 0.1 = 0.001
Hence, the correct option is (C).

131. $s_N = \sqrt{\frac{1}{N}\sum_{i=1}^{N}(x_i - \overline{x})^2}.$

If we substitute $10 \times$ for $\times$ in the above formula, we can find that the SN (standard deviation of N values) will become $10\ SN$. (After squaring and finding square root).
Hence, the correct option is (A).

132. The goal of The National Population Policy of India is to bring down Total Fertility Rate (TFR) to replacement levels by 2010.
Hence, the correct option is (A).

133. Health expectancy calculated by Sullivan's method is the number of remaining years, at a particular age, that an individual can expect to live in a healthy state. It is computed by subtracting the probable duration of bed disability and inability to perform major activities from the life expectancy.

Hence, the correct option is (A).

134. Specifically, Alma-Ata Declaration has outlined eight essential components of PHC [1], including:

(1) Health education on prevailing health problems and the methods of preventing and controlling them.

(2) Nutritional promotion including food supply.

(3) Supply of adequate safe water and sanitation.

(4) Maternal and the principles of primary health care are accessibility, public participation, health promotion, appropriate technology and intersectoral cooperation. Accessibility means that the five types of health care are universally available to all clients regardless of geographic location.

Hence, the correct option is (C).

135. In mutually exclusive events, the probability of at least one of them occurring will be equal to the sum of their individual probabilities.
Hence, the correct option is (A).

136.

- 95.4% of values lie within 2 SD (standard deviation) of the mean.
- Here, SD = 20 l/min.
- Hence 95.4% of values lie within 300-(2*20) and 300=(2*20).
- Which translates into: About 95% of the girls have PEFR between 260 and 340 l/min.

Hence, the correct option is (A).

137. A standard normal deviation is not skewed to any side. It is symmetrical.

Standard deviation = 1.0

Variance = SD^2 = 1.0
Hence, the correct option is (D).

138. Infection in the first trimester has the greatest risk of congenital anomalies. Infection in second trimester can cause deafness. No major congenital defects are seen in infection after 16 weeks of gestation.
Hence, the correct option is (D).

139. Immediate stitching of bite wounds is contraindicated. It increases the trauma and increases the spread of virus into deeper tissues.
Hence, the correct option is (C).

140. An endemic disease is constantly present in a given population group. Epidemic disease occurs clearly in excess of normal expectancy. The dictionary of epidemiology defines an endemic disease as, "the constant presence of a disease or infectious agent within a given geographic area or population group; may also refer to the usual prevalence of a given disease within such an area or group."
Hence, the correct option is (B).

141. Infant mortality includes death within the first year of life. Perinatal mortality includes late foetal deaths (28 weeks of gestation to birth) and early neonatal deaths (birth to 7 days).

Other terms:

Late neonatal mortality – 7 days to 28 days.

Neonatal mortality – birth to 28 days (early neonatal mortality + late neonatal mortality).

Post neonatal mortality – 28 days to 1 year.
Hence, the correct option is (B).

142. Degree of freedom = (no. of rows – 1) × (no. of columns – 1)

=(4-1) × (4-1)

=3 × 3

=9
Hence, the correct option is (C).

143. Foods and oils with higher amounts of polyunsaturated fats include:

- Walnuts.
- Sunflower seeds.
- Flax seeds or flax oil.
- Fish, such as salmon, mackerel, herring, albacore tuna, and trout.
- Corn oil.
- Soybean oil.
- Safflower oil.

Hence, the correct option is (B).

144. Humans constitute the only known reservoir and host of Borrelia recurrentis. After becoming infected by ingesting an infected blood meal, a louse remains infected throughout its lifetime; however, it cannot transmit Borrelia to its progeny. Head lice are not known to transmit any disease and therefore are not considered a health hazard. Head lice infestations can be asymptomatic, particularly with a first infestation or when an infestation is light.
Hence, the correct option is (D).

145. Meta-analysis is a quantitative, formal, epidemiological study design used to systematically assess the results of previous research to derive conclusions about that body of research. Typically, but not necessarily, the study is based on randomized, controlled clinical trials.
Hence, the correct option is (A).

146. An accredited social health activist (ASHA) is a community health worker instituted by the government of India's Ministry of Health and Family Welfare (MoHFW) as a part of the National Rural Health Mission (NRHM). The mission began in 2005; full implementation was targeted for 2012. The general norm will be 'One ASHA per 1000 population'. In tribal, hilly, desert areas the norm could be relaxed to one ASHA per habitation, dependant on workload etc. The States will also need to work out the district and block-wise coverage/phasing for selection of ASHAs.
Hence, the correct option is (C).

147. t is caused by weed seeds of crotalaria(jhunjhunia). Panicum miliare(Gondhli) which gets contaminated with these seeds. Jhunjhunia seeds found to contain pyrrolizidine alkaloids which are hepatotoxins. Epidemiology The overall mortality is 40%.
Hence, the correct option is (A).

148. The Right to Sight (V2020) is a global program that was established in partnership in 1999 by the International Agency for the Prevention of Blindness (IAPB) and the World Health Organization (WHO) with the joint goal to eliminate avoidable blindness by 2020.
Hence, the correct option is (B).

149. Horrock's apparatus is used to measure cholrine demand. Double pot is a method of well water chlorination. Chlorine demand is the difference between the amount of chlorine added to water or wastewater and the amount of residual chlorine remaining after a given contact time. Chlorine demand may change with dosage, time, temperature, pH, and nature and amount of the impurities in the water.
Hence, the correct option is (A).

150. Basic emergency obstetric services.

- Parenteral oxytocics
- Antibiotics and anticonvulsants
- Assisted deliveries
- Manual extraction of the placenta
- Removal of retained products

Comprehensive emergency obstetric services.

- basic services plus
- Caesarean sections
- Blood transfusions

Hence, the correct option is (B).

151. Mmunosuppressant drugs are used to treat autoimmune diseases. With an autoimmune disease, the immune system attacks the body's own tissue. Because immunosuppressant drugs weaken the immune system, they suppress this reaction. This helps reduce the impact of autoimmune disease on the body. Patients must also take immunosuppressive drugs for the rest of their lives to keep the immune system from attacking transplanted organs. But these drugs can make it hard to fight off infections. The drugs may also boost the risk for diabetes, cancer and other conditions.
Hence, the correct option is (C).

152. The cause of multiple sclerosis is unknown. It's considered an autoimmune disease in which the body's immune system attacks its own tissues. In the case of MS , this immune system malfunction destroys the fatty substance that coats and protects nerve fibers in the brain and spinal cord (myelin).
Hence, the correct option is (A).

153. The history is characteristic of depressive disorder. Antidepressant drugs are to be given. But there are no ideal antidepressants. The treatment should be based on the side effect profile of the drugs.
Hence, the correct option is (B).

154. The history is suggestive of Obsessive Compulsive Disorder. The first line of treatment is Exposure and response prevention. Exposure Response Prevention, commonly referred to as ERP , is a therapy that encourages you to face your fears and let obsessive thoughts occur without 'putting them right' or 'neutralising' them with compulsions.
Hence, the correct option is (A).

155. Hysteria (Conversion disroder) is a condition in which a person has blindness, paralysis, or other nervous system (neurologic) symptoms that cannot be explained by medical evaluation.

Hypochondria is a belief that physical symptoms are signs of a serious illness, even when there is no medical evidence to support the presence of an illness.
Hence, the correct option is (A).

156. Seasonal affective disorder refers to episodes of depression that occur every year during autumn or winter. Symptoms improve in spring and summer. Bright light therapy is used to manage circadian rhythm disorders such as delayed sleep phase syndrome (DSPS), a condition which shifts the normal sleeping pattern outside what is considered the social norm.
Hence, the correct option is (B).

157. Akinetic mutism is a medical term describing patients tending neither to move (akinesia) nor speak (mutism). Patients lack most motor functions such as speech, facial expressions, and gestures, but demonstrate apparent alertness. Some common synonyms of stupor are languor, lassitude, lethargy, and torpor.
Hence, the correct option is (C).

158. Involutional melancholia or involutional depression is a traditional name for a psychiatric disorder affecting mainly elderly or late middle-aged people, usually accompanied with paranoia.
Hence, the correct option is (A).

159. In psychiatry, derailment (also loosening of association, asyndesis, asyndetic thinking, knight's move thinking, or entgleisen) is a thought disorder characterized by discourse consisting of a sequence of unrelated or only remotely related ideas.
Hence, the correct option is (A).

160. 5-HIAA is a metabolite of Serotonin. 5-Hydroxy indoleacetic acid (5-HIAA) is the primary metabolite of serotonin. Serotonin is broken down into 5-hydroxy indoleacetic acid within the liver.This test measures the level of 5-HIAA in the urine. It is often done to detect certain tumors in the digestive tract (carcinoid tumors) and to track a person's condition. The urine test may also be used to diagnose a disorder called systemic mastocytosis and some tumors

of the hormone.
Hence, the correct option is (A).

161. Agoraphobia is a fear of being in situations where escape might be difficult or that help wouldn't be available if things go wrong. Many people assume agoraphobia is simply a fear of open spaces, but it's actually a more complex condition. Someone with agoraphobia may be scared of: travelling on public transport.
Hence, the correct option is (D).

162. Atypical Antipsychotics, or Second Generation Antipsychotic Drugs. These new medications were approved for use in the 1990s. Clozapine, asenapine, olanzapine, quetiapine, paliperidone, risperidone, sertindole, ziprasidone, zotepine, and aripiprazole are atypical antipsychotic drugs.
Hence, the correct option is (A).

163.

Most common substance abuse in India – Tobacco (see statistics below)

Most common substance abuse in the world – ?? Probably tobacco (According to WHO statistics, there is an estimated 1.1 billion tobacco users in the world – corresponds to 1/3 of people above 15 years of age)

Most common illicit substance abuse in India – Cannabis (see statistics below)

Most common illicit substance abuse in the world – Cannabis (see statistics below)

National Household Survey of Drug and Alcohol Abuse in India – Estimated users: (2001)

- Tobacco – 162 million
- Alcohol – 62 million
- Cannabis – 9 million
- Opiates – 2.5 lakh

Cannabis is by far the most widely cultivated, trafficked and abused illicit drug. About 147 million people, 2.5% of the world population, consume cannabis (annual prevalence) compared with 0.2% consuming cocaine and 0.2% consuming opiates.

Hence, the correct option is (A).

164. Naltrexone is used to help narcotic dependents who have stopped taking narcotics to stay drug-free. It is also used to help alcoholics stay alcohol-free. The medicine is not a cure for addiction. "The patients reported decreases in anxiety, pain, and sleeping habits from baseline," Dr. Metyas noted. Naltrexone is an opioid receptor antagonist used to treat alcohol and opioid dependence.
Hence, the correct option is (C).

165. Delusional disorder, previously called paranoid disorder, is a type of serious mental illness called a "psychosis" in which a person cannot tell what is real from what is imagined. The main feature of this disorder is the presence of delusions, which are unshakable beliefs in something untrue.
Hence, the correct option is (A).

166. DRUG INDUCED PULMONARY FIBROSIS – BLEOMYCIN

Bleomycin is a glycopeptide antibiotic obtained from Streptomyces verticillus. It is used for the treatment of Hodgkin's lymphoma, squamous cell carcinomas, and testicular cancer. Bleomycin therapy can result in life-threatening interstitial pulmonary fibrosis. This side effect is seen about 10 percent of patients treated with Bleomycin. There is destruction of Type 1 pneumocytes with hyperplasia of type II pneumocytes.

Other drugs causing pulmonary fibrosis include : Methotrexate, Amiodarone, Busulfan, Sulfasalazine, Carmustine.
Hence, the correct option is (B).

167. SIADH (Syndrome of Inappropriate ADH secretion) is not seen associated with thymomas. Syndrome of inappropriate antidiuretic hormone secretion (SIADH) is a condition in which the body makes too much antidiuretic hormone (ADH). This hormone helps the kidneys control the amount of water your body loses through the urine. SIADH causes the body to retain too much water.
Hence, the correct option is (C).

168. Bence Jones proteinuria is seen in Mu heavy chain disease. It occurs due to the excretion of kappa light chains in urine. The presence of Bence-Jones proteins in urine can be a sign of multiple myeloma or another rare condition called Waldenstrom macroglobulinemia. About 50% to 80% of people with multiple myeloma have Bence-Jones proteins in their urine.
Hence, the correct option is (C).

169. Ophthalmoplegia is seen in Wernicke's encephalopathy. The classic triad of symptoms found in Wernicke encephalopathy is: ophthalmoplegia (later expanded to other eye movement disorders, most commonly affecting the lateral rectus muscle. Lateral nystagmus is most commonly seen although lateral rectus palsy, usually bilateral, may be seen).
Hence, the correct option is (B).

170. Bicuspid aortic valve is the most common anomaly associated with coarctation of aorta (seen in 70%). Coarctation of the aorta is generally present at birth (congenital). Although the condition can affect any part of the aorta, the defect is most often located near a blood vessel called the ductus arteriosus.
Hence, the correct option is (D).

171. In DIC, the levels of coagulation factors are decreased. Whereas in TTP, coagulation factor levels are normal. If more than one clotting factor is decreased, it is usually due to an acquired condition. Acquired deficiencies are rare and may be caused by chronic or acute conditions, including: Excess blood clotting that uses up coagulation factor (e.g., disseminated intravascular coagulation) Liver disease (i.e., cirrhosis).
Hence, the correct option is (C).

172. Edrophonium test has 95% sensitivity for detection of systemic myasthenia gravis and 85% sensitivity for that of ocular variety. Edrophonium is a medication used in the diagnosis of myasthenia gravis. It is in the acetylcholinesterase class of drugs. This activity reviews the indications, action, contraindications for edrophonium as a valuable agent in the management of myasthenia gravis.
Hence, the correct option is (C).

173. Spinocerebellar ataxia (SCA) type 1 is not a neurological channelopathy. But SCA type 6 is a neurological channelopathy. Spinocerebellar ataxia type 1 (SCA1) is a condition characterized by progressive problems with movement. People with this condition

initially experience problems with coordination and balance (ataxia).
Hence, the correct option is (D).

174. In locked in state, normal alpha activity is found in EEG. The presence of predominantly posterior and reactive alpha activity in the EEG is observed in normal individuals with preserved conscience. A similar pattern is observed in most patients with locked-in (deefferented) state.
Hence, the correct option is (B).

175. Subacute combined degeneration is caused by vitamin B_{12} deficiency and is potentially reversible. Subacute combined degeneration is progressive degeneration of the spinal cord due to vitamin B_{12} deficiency. Nerve fibers that control movement and sensation are damaged. People have general weakness, tingling and numbness in the hands and feet, and stiff limbs and may become irritable, drowsy, and confused.
Hence, the correct option is (A).

176. A CSF glucose value of 1.7 mmol/L (± 0.31, range 0.9–2.7 mmol/L; normal CSF glucose) and a CSF glucose vs. blood glucose ratio of 0.35 (± 0.07, range 0.19–0.49; normal ratio 0.65 ± 0.01) in the setting of normoglycemia (blood glucose > 3–5 mmol/L) are highly indicative for GLUT1DS.
Hence, the correct option is (B).

177. In fact, hypertension is the most common cause of intracerebral hemorrhages. They can be conveniently divided according to their typical locations which include, in order of frequency: basal ganglia hemorrhage (especially the putamen) thalamic hemorrhage.
Hence, the correct option is (A).

178. Although both upper and motor neuron lesions result in muscle weakness, they are clinically distinct due to various other manifestations. Unlike UMNs, LMN lesions present with muscle atrophy, fasciculations (muscle twitching), decreased reflexes, decreased tone, negative Babinsky sign, and flaccid paralysis.
Hence, the correct option is (A).

179. Males are predominantly affected by cluster headache. Cluster Headache (CH) is a well-characterized primary headache that mostly affects men, although a progressive decrease in the male-to-female ratio has occurred over time.
Hence, the correct option is (A).

180. The modified Maddrey's discriminant function is used to determine prognosis of alcoholic hepatitis. It is calculated as follows:

$$4.6 \times [\text{prothombin time} - \text{control value (seconds)}] + \text{serum bilirubin } (mg/dl)$$

It is useful in predicting short term prognosis especially mortality within 30 days. A value more than 32 implies poor outcome with one month mortality ranging between 35% to 45%.
Hence, the correct option is (A).

181. 5' nucleotidase and Gamma glutamyl transferase are specific for cholestatic disorders. The liver regulates many important metabolic functions. The 5'-nucleotidase activity is increased in obstructive jaundice, parenchymal liver disease, and hepatic metastases.
Hence, the correct option is (D).

182. Risk of colonic carcinoma is more in Ulcerative colitis compared to Chron's disease.In another population-based study, it was found that the risk for CRC among patients with both UC and Crohn's colitis was approximately 2- to 3-fold greater than the general population and that the risk of rectal cancer was increased 2-fold in UC but not in Crohn's colitis.
Hence, the correct option is (A).

183. Some conditions causing increase in serum angiotensin converting enzyme Silicosis.

- Granulomatous hepatitis
- Asbestosis
- Sarcoidosis
- Leprosy
- Lymphoma

Hence, the correct option is (D).

184. Kyphoscoliosis is a restrictive lung disease. There is decrease in residual volume and total lung capacity. FEV1 and FVC are proportionately decreased. Hence the ratio of FEV1 to FVC remains normal or is increased. The forced expiratory flow rate (FEF) is normal. Functional residual capacity (FRC) is decreased.
Hence, the correct option is (A).

185. People living at high altitudes have absolute polycythemia due to increased erythropoietin synthesis. People living in high altitudes can develop polycythemia. In high altitudes, increased red blood cell production occurs in order to compensate for the low ambient oxygen levels and inadequate tissue oxygenation.
Hence, the correct option is (D).

186. Splenectomy has little role in the management of porphyria. Porphyria is a group of liver disorders in which substances called porphyrins build up in the body, negatively affecting the skin or nervous system. The types that affect the nervous system are also known as acute porphyria, as symptoms are rapid in onset and short in duration.
Hence, the correct option is (B).

187. Saccharomyces cerevisae antibody positivity:

- Chron's disease – 60-70%
- Ulcerative colitis – 10-15%

Hence, the correct option is (B).

188. Anticentromere antibodies are seen mostly in those with CREST syndrome (40-80% patients with CREST syndrome are anticentromere antibody positive). CREST syndrome, also known as the limited cutaneous form of systemic sclerosis (lcSSc), is a multisystem connective tissue disorder. The acronym "CREST" refers to the five main features: calcinosis, Raynaud's phenomenon, esophageal dysmotility, sclerodactyly, and telangiectasia.
Hence, the correct option is (C).

189. Smoking is a known risk factor for small cell carcinoma, respiratory bronchiolitis and emphysema. Bronchiolitis obliterans organizing pneumonia (BOOP) is a lung disease that causes inflammation in the small air tubes (bronchioles) and air sacs (alveoli). BOOP typically develops in individuals between 40-60 years old; however the disorder may affect individuals of any age.
Hence, the correct option is (D).

190. An abscess caused by a fungus, e.g., mycetoma. An abscess in lung tissue, caused by anaerobic bacteria such as Staphylococcus

aureus or Nocardia species.
Hence, the correct option is (B).

191. Infective endocarditis is a rare complication of Salmonella typhi infection. Bacterial. Staphylococcus aureus is the leading cause of infective endocarditis in most parts of the world and is responsible for about 31% of cases. Viridans streptococci and Enterococci are the second and third most common organisms responsible for infective endocarditis. Other Streptococci are also a frequent cause.
Hence, the correct option is (C).

192. Features of Mitral valve prolapse:

- Majority of patients are asymptomatic
- Some present with non specific chest pain, dyspnoea, fatigue or palpitation
- Myxomatous degeneration of heart valves is seen (mostly mitral valve)
- Autosomal dominant pattern of inheritance
- Prominent cardiovascular manifestation of Marfans syndrome
- Mitral regurgitation can occur as a complication due to rupture of chordae tendinae or failure of papillary muscles

Hence, the correct option is (B).

193. Hyperkalemia is a higher than normal level of potassium in the blood. Although mild cases may not produce symptoms and may be easy to treat, severe cases of hyperkalemia that are left untreated can lead to fatal cardiac arrhythmias, which are abnormal heart rhythms.
Hence, the correct option is (C).

194. Massive transfusions can cause hyperkalemia due to loss of potassium from the transfused red cells. Massive transfusion (MT) is a lifesaving treatment of hemorrhagic shock, but can be associated with significant complications. The lethal triad of acidosis, hypothermia, and coagulopathy associated with MT is associated with a high mortality rate.
Hence, the correct option is (A).

195. Primary effusion lymphomas are aggressive malignancies that present as serous effusion without any tumour mass. Natural killer (NK) cells rapidly kill infected, damaged, and transformed cells. NK cells also secrete cytokines and chemokines that directly affect abnormal cells and shape subsequent adaptive immunity.
Hence, the correct option is (C).

196. The stretching and/or injury of the peritoneum and diaphragm by pneumoperitoneum results in tearing of blood vessels, traction of nerves (eg, phrenic nerve), and release of inflammatory mediators, which elicit the referred pain to the shoulder. Subdiaphragmatic free gas is one of the ways of detecting presence of free intraperitoneal gas (i.e. pneumoperitoneum). It is the presence of free, extraluminal gas in the anterior subhepatic space.
Hence, the correct option is (C).

197. Other causes of myonecrosis include envenomation by snakes of the genus Bothrops (family Viperidae), ischemic necrosis, caused by vascular blockage (e.g., diabetes type II), tumours that block or hoard blood supply, and disseminated intravascular coagulation or other thromboses.
Hence, the correct option is (C).

198. Conditions caused by defective migration of neural crest cells:

- Congenital megacolon
- Albinism
- Neurocristopathies
- Melanoma
- Oropharyngeal teratoma

Hence, the correct option is (A).

199. Mucocele of gallbladder is caused by stone impaction in the neck of gall bladder or in the cystic duct. The term gallbladder mucocele refers to an overdistended gallbladder filled with mucoid or clear and watery content. Usually noninflammatory, it results from outlet obstruction of the gallbladder and is commonly caused by an impacted stone in the neck of the gallbladder or in the cystic duct.
Hence, the correct option is (D).

200. Absence of ganglion cells result in congenital megacolon. Fissure in ano causes anal sphincter spasm, but does not result in megacolon. Rectal malignancies cause luminal obstruction leading to development of megacolon.
Hence, the correct option is (D).

201. AJCC staging for oral cavity tumours:

- N0 – No clinically palpable lymph nodes
- N1 – Single ipsilateral node less than 3cm
- N2a – Single ipsilateral lymph node 3-6cm
- N2b – Multiple ipsilateral lymph nodes less than 6cm
- N2c – Bilateral / Contralateral lymph nodes less than 6cm
- N3 – Nodes more than 6cm

Hence, the correct option is (C).

202. The first serologic assay for detection and clinical followup of patients with hepatocellular carcinoma was alpha-fetoprotein (AFP) which has been the standard tumor biomarker for HCC for many years. It is a glycoprotein produced by the fetal liver and yolk sac during pregnancy.
Hence, the correct option is (B).

203. Juvenile polyps are not premalignant. This type of polyp is commonly detected in a colon cancer screening. It carries a high risk of becoming cancerous. They can be pedunculated, but they're commonly sessile. Advanced adenomas have the greatest potential for malignant transformation and are defined as adenomas of diameter ≥1 cm, or those of any size with villous histology or high-grade dysplasia.
Hence, the correct option is (A).

204. Amylase levels can be used to diagnose acute pancreatitis. But there is no correlation between amylase levels and severity of acute pancreatitis. Severe acute pancreatitis (SAP) is characterised by the presence of persistent organ failure irrespective of the time of development in relation to disease onset (i.e. early or late phase). Persistence is defined as organ failure lasting for greater than 48 hours.
Hence, the correct option is (B).

205. Cystine stone is resistant to lithotripsy. Cystine and brushite calculi are the most resistant to ESWL, followed by calcium oxalate monohydrate, struvite, calcium oxalate dihydrate, and uric acid stones. Stone composition affects the resistance to fragmentation and the type of fragments produced.
Hence, the correct option is (C).

206. If symptoms persist after physical therapy and injections, surgery may be recommended. Surgery can involve cutting small muscles of the neck (anterior and middle scalene) and removing the cervical or first rib.
Hence, the correct option is (C).

207. Diverticula are easily visualised with barium enema. Traditionally, barium enema imaging has been the primary method of examining patients in whom diverticulitis is suspected. Barium studies superbly depict diverticula, the colonic mucosa and lumen, spasm, and muscle hypertrophy.
Hence, the correct option is (C).

208. Pancreatitis (inflammation of the pancreas) is the most frequent complication, occurring in about 3 to 5 percent of people undergoing ERCP. When it occurs, it is usually mild, causing abdominal pain and nausea, which resolve after a few days in the hospital. Rarely pancreatitis may be more severe.
Hence, the correct option is (A).

209. Stomach acid can damage your esophagus and cause sores and bleeding. If untreated, gastritis can lead to ulcers or worn-away areas of the stomach lining that can bleed in your GI tract.
Hence, the correct option is (C).

210. Growth hormone deficiency was the most prevalent (45%), followed by gonadotropin deficiency (30%), TSH deficiency (25%) and ACTH deficiency (22%).Growth hormone (GH) or somatotropin, also known as human growth hormones (hGH or HGH) in its human form, is a peptide hormone that stimulates growth, cell reproduction, and cell regeneration in humans and other animals. It is thus important in human development.
Hence, the correct option is (D).

211. Epithelial tumors, or cancers in the narrow sense, are considered to have moderate radio- sensitivity. Among these tumors, undifferen- tiated carcinoma and small cell carcinoma have relatively high radiosensitivity, followed by squa- mous cell carcinoma. Tumor cells can be hypoxic and therefore less sensitive to X-rays because most of their effects are mediated by the free radicals produced by ionizing oxygen.
Hence, the correct option is (B).

212. Acute parotitis is a contraindication for saliography. Acute parotitis presents with sudden onset of indurated, warm, erythematous swelling of the pre- and post-auricular areas, with intense local pain and tenderness. Symptoms are often associated with high fevers, chills, and marked systemic toxicity.
Hence, the correct option is (C).

213. Gardner syndrome is a rare, inherited autosomal dominant disorder characterized by multiple colonic polyps; supernumerary teeth; osteomas of the sinuses and skull; and fatty/epithelial cysts or fibrous tumors, or both, in the skin. A characteristic finding is bilateral, multiple, pigmented, ocular fundus lesions, known as congenital hypertrophy of the retinal epithelium. The development of intestinal polyposis and colorectal adenocarcinoma are key features of Gardner syndrome.
Hence, the correct option is (C).

214. Bacteroides is a genus of Gram-negative, obligate anaerobic bacteria. Bacteroides species are non endospore-forming bacilli, and may be either motile or nonmotile, depending on the species. The DNA base composition is 40–48% GC. Unusual in bacterial organisms, Bacteroides membranes contain sphingolipids.
Hence, the correct option is (A).

215. A pelvic abscess is a life-threatening collection of infected fluid in the pouch of Douglas, fallopian tube, ovary, or parametric tissue. Usually, a pelvic abscess occurs as a complication after operative procedures. It starts as pelvic cellulitis or hematoma spreads to parametrial tissue.
Hence, the correct option is (D).

216. The lack of bilirubin in the intestinal tract is responsible for the pale stools typically associated with biliary obstruction. The cause of itching (pruritus) associated with biliary obstruction is not clear. Some believe it may be related to the accumulation of bile acids/bile salts in the skin. Glutamate dehydrogenase (GLDH, GDH) is an enzyme observed in both prokaryotes and eukaryotic mitochondria. The aforementioned reaction also yields ammonia, which in eukaryotes is canonically processed as a substrate in the urea cycle.
Hence, the correct option is (D).

217. At the current time, a diagnosis of Barrett's esophagus can only be made using endoscopy and detecting a change in the lining of the esophagus that can be confirmed by a biopsy of the tissue. The definitive diagnosis of Barrett's esophagus requires biopsy confirmation of the change in the lining of the esophagus.
Hence, the correct option is (B).

218. Thalassemia Major or Cooley's Anemia. This is the most severe form of beta-thalassemia in which the complete lack of beta protein in the hemoglobin causes life-threatening anemia that requires regular blood transfusions and extensive ongoing medical care.

Hence, the correct option is (B).

219. It is a benign condition characterized by exuberant proliferation of synovial tissue. It affects synovial joints, tendon sheaths, and bursae.
Hence, the correct option is (C).

220. Meralgia paresthetica is characterized by pain, tingling, and numbness in the lateral aspect of thigh. There is no motor deficiency. It is due to the involvement of the lateral cutaneous nerve of the thigh.
Hence, the correct option is (B).

221. Bowlegs appear only after the child starts walking – due to the weight-bearing effect. Bowlegs often develop in the child's first year as part of natural growth for no known cause. Some babies are born with bowlegs. This can happen as the baby grows and the space inside their mother's womb gets tighter, causing the leg bones to curve slightly.
Hence, the correct option is (D).

222. Infrared therapy is a type of superficial heat therapy. Heat therapy, also called thermotherapy, is the use of heat in therapy, such as for pain relief and health. It can take the form of a hot cloth, hot water bottle, ultrasound, heating pad, hydrocollator packs,

whirlpool baths, cordless FIR heat therapy wraps, and others.
Hence, the correct option is (C).

223. **Bohler's angle is formed at the junction of :**

A line joining the posterosuperior part of the calcaneal tuberosity and the uppermost point on the posterior articular surface for the talus-line joining the uppermost point on the posterior articular surface for the talus and the anterior process of the calcaneum.

The normal value is 25-40°. It is decreased in fracture of the calcaneum. (Usually occurs in fall from height.)
Hence, the correct option is (A).

224.

- Renal scarring usually begins in the polar regions.
- Long term outcome is better with surgery.
- Co-trimoxazole is the drug of choice for prophylaxis.

Hence, the correct option is (B).

225. The majority of Bochdalek hernias (80–85%) occur on the left side of the diaphragm, a large proportion of the remaining cases occur on the right side.
Hence, the correct option is (A).

226. Prediction of outcome of severe head injury should be based upon early neurologic signs, including the degree of coma as measured by the Glasgow Coma Scale, brain stem reflexes, central nervous system lesion type, presence of increased intracranial pressure, and multimodality evoked responses.
Hence, the correct option is (A).

227. Adjuvant chemotherapy is an additional treatment given after surgery to lower the risk of the cancer returning. Chemotherapy after surgery is not recommended for routine use in patients with stage II colon cancer. Talk with your doctor about the risks and benefits of adjuvant chemotherapy.
Hence, the correct option is (A).

228. AJCC staging for oral cavity tumors:

- N0 – No clinically palpable lymph nodes.
- N1 – Single ipsilateral node less than 3cm.
- N2a – Single ipsilateral lymph node 3-6cm.
- N2b – Multiple ipsilateral lymph nodes less than 6cm.
- N2c – Bilateral / Contralateral lymph nodes less than 6cm.
- N3 – Nodes more than 6cm.

Hence, the correct option is (C).

229. A branchial cyst, also called a branchial cleft cyst, is a cavity that is present at birth on one side of the neck. The cyst may not be recognized until adolescence as it enlarges and becomes oval in shape. A branchial cyst is a cavity that is a congenital remnant from embryologic development. Branchial cleft cysts are congenital epithelial cysts, which arise on the lateral part of the neck from a failure of obliteration of the second branchial cleft in embryonic development. Phylogenetically, the branchial apparatus is related to gill slits.
Hence, the correct option is (B).

230. CEA is increased in adenocarcinoma of the colon, pancreas, breast, ovary, and lungs. A high level of CEA can be a sign of certain types of cancers. These include cancers of the colon and rectum, prostate, ovary, lung, thyroid, or liver. High CEA levels may also be a sign of some noncancerous conditions, such as cirrhosis, noncancerous breast disease, and emphysema.
Hence, the correct option is (D).

231. Histology of solitary rectal ulcer syndrome shows the relative absence of inflammatory cells in the lamina propria. The degree of lymphocytic infiltration in the lamina propria was graded as normal (degree of lymphocytic infiltrate equal to normal mucosa), 1+ (lymphocytic infiltrate denser than the normal background, but lacking follicle information), and 2+ (dense lymphocytic infiltrate with follicle formation).
Hence, the correct option is (C).

232. In case of rebleed, laparotomy should be done. An exploratory laparotomy, also known as a celiotomy or "ex lap," is a type of major surgery that involves opening the abdomen with a large incision in order to visualize the entire abdominal cavity.
Hence, the correct option is (D).

233. Thymic lymphoma is a malignant neoplasm that originates in the thymus and may extend into the mediastinum and surrounding tissues. The most common thymus diseases are myasthenia gravis (MG), pure red cell aplasia (PRCA), and hypogammaglobulinemia, according to the NLM. Myasthenia gravis occurs when the thymus is abnormally large and produces antibodies that block or destroy the muscles' receptor sites.
Hence, the correct option is (B).

234. Merkel cells are found in the top layer of the skin. These cells are very close to the nerve endings that receive the sensation of touch. Merkel cell carcinoma, also called neuroendocrine carcinoma of the skin or trabecular cancer, is a very rare type of skin cancer that forms when Merkel cells grow out of control.
Hence, the correct option is (B).

235. Complications of supracondylar fracture of humerus

- Injury to arteries and nerves
- Volkmann's ischemia
- Myositis ossificans
- Malunion (results in gunstock deformity)
- Volkmann's ischemic contracture

Hence, the correct option is (D).

236. Lesions associated with recurrent dislocation of the shoulder are :

- Hill-Sach's lesion
- Bankart`s lesion
- Erosion of anterior rim of glenoid cavity
- Capsular laxity
- Subcapsularis deficiency
- Glenoid fossa deficiency

Hence, the correct option is (D).

237. Malunion of supracondylar fracture of humerus results in cubitus varus deformity (gunstock deformity). Cubitus varus (varus means a deformity of a limb) is a common deformity in which the extended forearm is deviated towards the midline of the body. Cubitus varus is often referred to as "Gunstock deformity", due to

the crooked nature of the healing.
Hence, the correct option is (B).

238. Bankart lesion is a lesion of the anterior part of the glenoid labrum of the shoulder. This injury is caused by repeated anterior shoulder subluxations. The dislocation of the shoulder joint (anterior) can damage the connective tissue ring around the glenoid labrum.
Hence, the correct option is (A).

239. Osteosarcoma is a type of bone cancer that begins in the cells that form bones. Osteosarcoma is most often found in the long bones more often the legs, but sometimes the arms but it can start in any bone. In very rare instances, it occurs in soft tissue outside the bone.
Hence, the correct option is (B).

240. Prevents ovulation by inhibition of LH surge

Induce atrophic changes in the endometrium, preventing the nidation

Thickening of cervical mucus preventing entry of sperms

Increases tubal motility, so that the fertilized egg reaches the uterine cavity before the endometrium is receptive for implantation.
Hence, the correct option is (D).

241. A woman having post-menopausal bleeding is to be considered as a case of endometrial carcinoma unless otherwise proved. Among the options given, the best method for the diagnosis of endometrial carcinoma is fractional curettage.
Hence, the correct option is (B).

242. In PCOS, the androgen levels are very high. This prevents atresia from developing follicles. These form cysts of size 2-9mm size in the periphery of the ovary in a necklace pattern.
Hence, the correct option is (A).

243. Women with Eisenmenger's complex have up to 50% mortality during pregnancy. Termination of pregnancy is advised. Eisenmenger syndrome is typically due to an unrepaired hole (shunt) between the main blood vessels or chambers of your heart. This shunt is a heart defect you're born with (congenital). Heart defects that can cause Eisenmenger syndrome include Atrioventricular canal defects.
Hence, the correct option is (A).

244. History of recurrent abortions with isolated prolonged APTT is suggestive of antiphospholipid antibody syndrome. The lupus anticoagulant is one of three primary antiphospholipid antibodies that are associated with an increased risk of thrombosis and antiphospholipid antibody syndrome (APS), an autoimmune disorder characterized by excess blood clot formation, organ failures, and pregnancy complications.
Hence, the correct option is (A).

245. A colposcopy is nearly pain-free. You might feel pressure when the speculum goes in. It might also sting or burn a little when they wash your cervix with the vinegar-like solution. If you get a biopsy, you might have some discomfort.
Hence, the correct option is (B).

246. Coronary heart disease (CHD), or coronary artery disease, develops when the coronary arteries become too narrow. The coronary arteries are the blood vessels that supply oxygen and blood to the heart. CHD tends to develop when cholesterol builds up on the artery walls, creating plaques.
Hence, the correct option is (D).

247. Eisenmenger syndrome refers to any untreated congenital cardiac defect with intracardiac communication that leads to pulmonary hypertension, a reversal of flow, and cyanosis. Eisenmenger syndrome is typically due to an unrepaired hole (shunt) between the main blood vessels or chambers of your heart. This shunt is a heart defect you're born with (congenital). Heart defects that can cause Eisenmenger syndrome include: Atrioventricular canal defects.
Hence, the correct option is (A).

248. Placenta previa is when a pregnant woman's placenta blocks the opening to the cervix that allows the baby to be born. It can cause severe bleeding during pregnancy and delivery. The placenta is an organ that grows inside the lining of your uterus during pregnancy.
Hence, the correct option is (B).

249. Congenital syphilis is the disease that occurs when a mother with syphilis passes the infection on to her baby during pregnancy. Up to 40% of babies born to women with untreated syphilis may be stillborn (a baby born dead) or die from the infection as a newborn.
Hence, the correct option is (A).

250. Tubal ligation (commonly known as having one's "tubes tied") is a surgical procedure for female sterilization in which the fallopian tubes are permanently blocked or removed. This prevents the fertilization of eggs by sperm and thus the implantation of a fertilized egg. Tubal ligation is considered a permanent method of sterilization and birth control.
Hence, the correct option is (A).

251. Acute fatty liver of pregnancy is seen after 34 weeks of pregnancy.

HELLP syndrome is a complication of pre-eclampsia. But it usually resolves after delivery.

Acute fulminant liver failure – the symptoms usually subside after delivery

Budd Chiari syndrome – presents within a few weeks after delivery, but it can also occur during pregnancy. Tender hepatomegaly is a hallmark of Budd Chiari syndrome.
Hence, the correct option is (D).

252. Bilateral disease is seen in 10-15 % of cases of dysgerminoma. Our results demonstrated that most bilateral ovarian tumors detected on MR imaging consisted of serous carcinoma, mature teratoma and metastasis. These tumors should thus be considered as representative bilateral ovarian tumors. In 10 to 15% of cases, mature teratomas involve both ovaries simultaneously.
Hence, the correct option is (A).

253. Inadequate levels of folate (vitamin B9) and vitamin B12 during pregnancy have been found to lead to an increased risk of NTDs. The cause is not clear but may be related to genetics, maternal nutrition (including folic acid deficiency) during pregnancy or other factors. Spina bifida is the most common neural tube defect, affecting approximately one out of every 1,000 newborns.

Hence, the correct option is (A).

254. In a nulliparous cervix, the external os is circular. In the case of the multiparous cervix, the os is a transverse slit. The nulliparous

cervix has a smooth, round external os. The parous cervical os is uneven and wide, often described as having a "fish mouth" appearance.
Hence, the correct option is (A).

255. A **Pap smear** is used to **screen** for cervical cancer. The **Pap smear** is usually done in conjunction with a pelvic exam. In women older than age 30, the Pap test may be combined with a test for human papillomavirus (HPV) a common sexually transmitted infection that can cause cervical cancer. It is used to detect abnormal or potentially abnormal cells from the vagina and the cervix, the narrow bottom portion of a woman's uterus. Various bacterial, fungal, and viral infections of the uterus may also be detected using this test.
Hence, the correct option is (C).

256. The second stage may get unduly prolonged because of cephalopelvic disproportion (CPD), abnormal fetal position, and poor expulsive efforts resulting from conduction analgesia, sedation or maternal exhaustion.
Hence, the correct option is (D).

257. The pelvic floor has a gutter shape with a forward and downward slope, encouraging the fetal head to rotate from the left or right occipito-transverse position a total of 90-degrees, to an occipital-anterior (occiput facing forward) position, to lie under the subpubic arch.
Hence, the correct option is (D).

258. You should feel your baby's first movements, called "**quickening**," between weeks 16 and 25 of your pregnancy. If this is your first pregnancy, you may not feel your baby move until closer to 25 weeks. **Quickening** is the term used to describe the fluttery sensation **experienced** by a **mom**-to-be when she first **feels** her baby move. It often happens between about 17 and 20 weeks of pregnancy, but as every pregnancy is unique, it may happen a littler earlier or later.

Hence, the correct option is (C).

259.

- Imperforate hymen prevents the drainage of menstrual blood.
- This results in the accumulation of blood in the vagina leading to hematocolpos.
- This is visualised as the tense bulge.
- In long-standing cases, it can even lead to hematometra.

Hence, the correct option is (B).

260. Risks of **Pitocin** include contractions that are too close together and that don't give the uterus a chance to relax and recover, which can result in fetal distress. Maternal risks of the medication are water intoxication, pulmonary edema and abnormal sodium levels. overstimulation of the uterus. infection. rupture of the uterus. fetal distress.

Hence, the correct option is (C).

261. Uterine atony is the most common cause of postpartum hemorrhage. Primary causes of postpartum hemorrhage include uterine atony, genital tract lacerations, retained placenta, uterine inversion, abnormal placentation, and coagulation disorders. Uterine atony, or lack of effective contraction of the uterus, is the most common cause of postpartum hemorrhage.

Hence, the correct option is (A).

262. Vocalizations are sounds produced by children before they learn to talk. For children with ASD, vocalizations may continue to be used throughout the life span, particularly if the spoken language does not develop. Vocalizations can be divided into two categories: speechlike and nonspeech.
Hence, the correct option is (B).

263. Between 8 and 12 months, she'll develop a pincer grasp, which means she'll be able to pick up smaller objects (like pieces of food) between her thumb and forefinger. The pincer grasp represents the coordination of the brain and muscles that's necessary to help them gain increasing independence. A baby will typically develop this skill between the ages of9 and 10 months, although this can vary.
Hence, the correct option is (B).

264. Most 3-year-olds can count to three and know the names of some of the numbers up to ten. Your child is also starting to recognize numbers from one to nine. He'll be quick to point it out if he receives fewer cookies than his playmate. Three-year-olds learn best through exploring, using all of their senses to understand their world.
Hence, the correct option is (A).

265. From ages 10 to 12 months, your baby is likely to enjoy: Improved motor skills. Most babies this age can sit without help and pull themselves to a standing position. Creeping, crawling and cruising along the furniture will eventually lead to walking.
Hence, the correct option is (D).

266. Constitutional growth delay is the most common cause of delayed puberty. Children with this growth pattern have a fall-off in their linear growth within the first 2 years of life; after this, growth returns to normal, albeit at a lower growth channel than would be expected for parental heights. Skeletal maturation is also delayed, and the onset of puberty is commensurate with bone age rather than chronologic age.
Hence, the correct option is (A).

267. Most individuals with Down syndrome have mild (IQ: 50–69) or moderate (IQ: 35–50) intellectual disability with some cases having severe (IQ: 20–35) difficulties. Those with mosaic Down syndrome typically have IQ scores 10–30 points higher.
Hence, the correct option is (B).

268. In girls, linear growth accelerates shortly after the- larche (appearance of breast tissue) at a mean age of approximately 10 years. Peak height velocity of 8 cm/y is reached 6 to 12 months prior to menarche at approximately 11.5 years of age. Linear growth decelerates after menarche.
Hence, the correct option is (A).

269. Most 3-year-olds can count to three and know the names of some of the numbers up to ten. Your child is also starting to recognize numbers from one to nine. He'll be quick to point it out if he receives fewer cookies than his playmate.

- Jump in place with both feet.
- Climb up and go down a toddler slide.
- Pedal tricycle.

- Walk up and downstairs when one hand is being held by an adult.
- Stand briefly on one foot when one hand is being held by an adult.
- Walk backward.

Hence, the correct option is (A).

270. The most common cause of congenital hydrocephalus is obstruction of the cerebral aqueduct, the long, narrow passageway between the third and fourth ventricle or cavity of the brain. This condition may result from a blockage, infection, hemorrhage, tumor, or arachnoid cyst.
Hence, the correct option is (C).

271. The most common manifestation of Wilms tumor is an asymptomatic abdominal mass; an abdominal mass occurs in 80% of children at presentation. Abdominal pain or hematuria occurs in 25%.

Hence, the correct option is (A).

272. CO_2 does not penetrate into the deep tissue, hence there is decreased risk of scarring. Patients with laryngeal pathology are often treated with CO_2 laser surgery, usually in the operating room under general anesthesia. Although office-based laser surgery using several other laser types has been investigated, prospective studies on office-based CO_2 laser surgery are scarce.

Hence, the correct option is (C).

273. Loudness hyperacusis may occur in Bell's palsy -- here one of the small protective muscles in the ear, the stapedius, is paralyzed when the 7th nerve is damaged. One would think that there would also be hyperacusis when the 5th nerve is damaged, paralyzing the bigger tensor tympani muscle.
Hence, the correct option is (D).

274. The history is suggestive of otosclerosis. Hence the audiometry graph will be of As type. Otosclerosis is a form of conductive hearing loss. In some cases, as the ear loses its ability to transmit sound, people may first notice low-frequency hearing loss, meaning that low-pitched sounds are harder to hear.
Hence, the correct option is (B).

275. Palatal paralysis causes rhinolalia aperta. It usually presents with acute onset nasal regurgitation of fluids, rhinolalia, and palatal asymmetry. Many causes of this disease, such as infections, trauma, tumor, and brainstem lesions, etc. have been reported.
Hence, the correct option is (B).

276. Structures seen in bronchoscopy are: Uvula, Epiglottis, Vocal cords, Larynx, Trachea, Carina, Segmental bronchi, Subsegmental bronchi

Subcarinal lymph nodes cannot be seen as they are located outside the trachea.

Hence, the correct option is (D).

277. The most common site for spontaneous CSF leak is the cribriform plate followed by the ethmoid roof. Primary CSF leaks can also involve the sphenoid sinus, peri sella, or pterygoid recesses. A CSF leak is a condition that occurs when the CSF leaks through a defect in the dura or the skull and out through the nose or ear. A CSF leak results from a hole or tears in the dura, the outermost layer of the meninges. Causes of the hole or tear can include head injury and brain or sinus surgery.
Hence, the correct option is (C).

278. Carcinoma glottis affects the mobility of the vocal cord and produces hoarseness of voice. This helps in early identification of disease. Persistent hoarseness is the usual presenting symptom of glottic carcinoma. Small vocal cord lesions can result in significant hoarseness, and patients with hoarseness often present at early stages. Glottic tumors can also cause hemoptysis and airway compromise if the tumors are large.

Hence, the correct option is (A).

279. Upper respiratory tract infection is a contraindication for tonsillectomy. So the surgery should be cancelled and the patient should be put on antibiotics.

Hence, the correct option is (D).

280. Brainstem-evoked response audiometry (BERA) is a simple, non-invasive, objective test for early identification of hearing impairment in children and neonates. It can be used as a screening test and is useful in newborns, infants, and other difficult-to-test patients.
Hence, the correct option is (B).

281. Ophthalmoplegic Migraine

- It is a rare condition which was previously considered a type of migraine.
- Recent studies suggest that it is likely to be an inflammatory cranial neuropathy.
- The International Headache Classification has reclassified ophthalmoplegic migraine as a type of neuralgia from its earlier classification as a type of migraine.
- It is characterised by transient migraine-like headache associated with paresis of oculomotor, trochlear and/or abducens nerves.
- To arrive at a diagnosis of ophthalmoplegic migraine, other causes should be ruled out by appropriate investigations (like digital subtraction angiography / magnetic resonance angiography of the brain).

Hence, the correct option is (C).

282. One-third of sporadic cases of retinoblastoma are heritable. The remaining sporadic cases do not pass their genes to their children.
Hence, the correct option is (B).

283. Pituitary tumors compress the optic chiasma and cause bitemporal hemianopia. Pituitary adenomas are benign tumors of the pituitary gland and the most common origin of masses near the sella turcica. This condition is a medical emergency called pituitary apoplexy. The patient will present with acute onset headache, ophthalmoplegia, and visual field defects of bitemporal hemianopia.
Hence, the correct option is (C).

284. Necrotizing anterior scleritis is the most severe form and most common form of scleritis with vision-threatening complications and resultant permanent visual loss. In cases of non-necrotizing scleritis, vision is often maintained unless complications such as uveitis occur.

Hence, the correct option is (A).

285. Arden index is used for the interpretation of an electrooculogram. Clinically, the ratio between the light and dark potentials (sometimes also called the Arden index or Arden ratio) is assessed. If that ratio is less than 1.8 it indicates a malfunction of the structures from which the potential originates. The EOG is also used to monitor eye movements.
Hence, the correct option is (B).

286. Endophthalmitis does not involve the scleral coat of the eye. The sclera is involved only in panophthalmitis. Endophthalmitis is the term used to describe severe inflammation of the tissues inside the eye. The inflammation is typically due to infection by bacteria (eg. Staphylococcus species, Streptococcus species, Gram-negative bacteria) or fungi (eg. Candida, Aspergillus).
Hence, the correct option is (C).

287. Circulus arteriosus major, also called "major Circulus arteriosus of iris" CIA or CIAM, is formed by anastomosis of the anterior ciliary arteries with the Long posterior ciliary arteries at the ciliary body. It supplies the iris, ciliary body and choroid.
Hence, the correct option is (B).

288. The cerebellum (which is Latin for "little brain") is a major structure of the hindbrain that is located near the brainstem. This part of the brain is responsible for coordinating voluntary movements. It is also responsible for a number of functions including motor skills such as balance, coordination, and posture.
Hence, the correct option is (C).

289. Proliferative diabetic retinopathy is the most common cause of spontaneous vitreous hemorrhage in adults. In adults, proliferative diabetic retinopathy is the most frequent cause of vitreous hemorrhage, 31.5-54% in the United States, 6% in London, and 19.1% in Sweden. The other causes of vitreous hemorrhage include the following: Retinal tear.
Hence, the correct option is (D).

290. Vancomycin and Ceftazidime can cause macular toxicity when given in high doses. But macular toxicity has been reported with even low dose of gentamycin.

291. The corpus luteum is the exclusive source of 17β-estradiol during the first 5-6 weeks of gestation. After the first trimester, the placenta is the major source of circulating 17β-estradiol (36). The rate of estrogen production and the level of circulating estrogens increase markedly during pregnancy.

Hence, the correct option is (C).

292. Misoprostol can be used for early abortion. But it is not useful in ectopic pregnancy. Do not use this medicine if you are pregnant or planning to become pregnant. This medicine can cause miscarriage, premature birth, or birth defects if taken during pregnancy. You will need to have a negative pregnancy test within 2 weeks before you start using this medicine.

Hence, the correct option is (B).

293. In response to the infant's suckling at the breast, a surge of **prolactin** is released from the pituitary gland. This suckling-induced **prolactin** release is essential for the mammary gland to produce sufficient milk before the next feeding.

Hence, the correct option is (A).

294. Components of Mannings biophysical profile:

1. Non-stress test
2. Fetal breathing movement
3. Fetal muscle tone
4. Fetal gross body movement
5. Amniotic fluid index

Hence, the correct option is (C).

295. Causes of pseudomyxoma peritonei – Mucinous cystadenoma of the ovary, mucocele of the appendix, carcinoma of the large intestine in men.

Hence, the correct option is (B).

296. There is a decrease in peripheral vascular resistance during pregnancy. In the first trimester, there is a substantial decrease in peripheral vascular resistance, which decreases to a nadir during the middle of the second trimester with a subsequent plateau or slight increase for the remainder of the pregnancy. The decrease is ≈35% to 40% of baseline.

Hence, the correct option is (D).

297. Polyhydramnios is a medical condition describing an excess of amniotic fluid in the amniotic sac. It is seen in about 1% of pregnancies. It is typically diagnosed when the amniotic fluid index (AFI) is greater than 24 cm.

Hence, the correct option is (B).

298. Late hyperglycemia is associated with macrosomia. Hyperglycemia during the conception and organogenesis period has increased the risk of congenital anomalies. The term "fetal macrosomia" is used to describe a newborn who's much larger than average. A baby who is diagnosed as having fetal macrosomia weighs more than 8 pounds, 13 ounces (4,000 grams), regardless of his or her gestational age. About 9% of babies worldwide weigh more than 8 pounds, 13 ounces.

Hence, the correct option is (A).

299. Cross-section of cochlea. (Endolymph is located in the cochlear duct - the light green region at the middle of the diagram.) Endolymph is the fluid contained in the membranous labyrinth of the inner ear. Endolymph, found inside the cochlear duct (scala media), has a unique composition not found elsewhere in the body.
Hence, the correct option is (B).

300. Colostrum is the special milk that is secreted in the first 2–3 days after delivery. It is produced in small amounts, about 40–50 ml on the first day (12), but is all that an infant normally needs at this time. If you notice small drops of clear or yellow fluid leaking from your breasts or staining your bra while you're pregnant, that's colostrum. The colostrum phase of breast milk production lasts until the transitional stage begins (between the second and fifth days after birth).

Hence, the correct option is (B).

Mock Test 02

PART A

Q.1 Deficiency of lysyl hydroxylase causes?

A. Alport syndrome
B. Menkes disease
C. Epidermolysis bullosa
D. Osteogenesis imperfecta

Q.2 The enzyme used for the mapping of hypersensitive sites in recombinant DNA research is?

A. DNA ligase
B. DNA polymerase
C. DNase I
D. Polynucleotide kinase

Q.3 Deficiency of argininosuccinate synthase causes?

A. Hyperargininemia
B. Hyperammonemia type II
C. Argininosuccinicaciduria
D. Citrullinemia

Q.4 All are disorders due to peroxisomal abnormalities except?

A. Pfeiffer syndrome
B. Zellweger syndrome
C. Hyperoxaluria type 1
D. Acatalasemia

Q.5 Rothera's test is utilized for detection of?

A. Glucose **B.** Proteins
C. Urea **D.** Ketone bodies

Q.6 Sphingomyelinase deficiency is characteristic of?

A. Fabry disease
B. Krabbe's disease
C. Tay Sachs disease
D. Niemann Pick disease

Q.7 Nonenzymatic glycosylation or glycation creates glycoproteins by:

A. Chemical addition of sugars to polypeptides
B. Extracellular synthesis
C. Attaching 20 amino acids
D. Secretion into the extracellular matrix

Q.8 All are inhibitors of oxidative phosphorylation except?

A. Carboxin **B.** Oligomycin
C. Valinomycin **D.** Atractyloside

Q.9 Proteins targeted for destruction in eukaryotes are covalently linked to :

A. Clathrin **B.** Pepsin
C. Laminin **D.** Ubiquitin

Q.10 Process used in an expression vector to increase yield of recombinant protein synthesis ?

A. Translation initiation
B. Promoter induction
C. Transcription terminators
D. Multiple cloning sites

Q.11 The structural proteins are involved in maintaining the shape of a cell or in the formation of matrices in the body. The shape of these proteins is:

A. Globular **B.** Fibrous
C. Stretch of beads **D.** Planar

Q.12 Which of the following amino acids has to be supplemented in the diet?

A. phenylalanine **B.** cysteine
C. glutamine **D.** asparagine

Q.13 In which of the following conditions the level of creatinine kinase 1 increase?

A. Myocardial ischemia
B. Brain Ischemia
C. Kidney damage
D. Electrical cardioversion

Q.14 Which of the following substances acts to increase the release of Ca2+ from endoplasmic reticulum?

A. Inositol triphosphate
B. Parathyroid hormone
C. 1,25 dihydroxy cholecalciferol
D. Diacylglycerol

Q.15 The transmembrane region of protein is likely to have:

A. A stretch of hydrophilic amino acids
B. A stretch of hydrophobic amino acids
C. A disulphide loop
D. Alternating hydrophilic and hydrophobic amino acids

Q.16 Shine Dalgarno sequence in bacterial mRNA is near:

A. AUG codon **B.** UAA codon
C. UAG codon **D.** UGA codon

Q.17 Claw hand occurs due to paralysis of:

A. Adductor paralysis
B. Flexor digitorum profundus
C. Extensor Digitorium Longus
D. Extensor Digitorum Communis

Q.18 The posterior interosseous nerve is a continuation of:

A. Anterior interosseous nerve
B. Median nerve
C. Radial nerve
D. Ulnar nerve

Q.19 The powerful supinator of the semi – flexed elbow:

A. Brachialis **B.** Brachioradialis
C. Supinator **D.** Biceps brachii

Q.20 Which of the following is an example of hyaline cartilage:

A. epiglottis

B. tip of nose
C. the apex of arytenoid cartilage
D. pinna

Q.21 Single unit smooth muscles are seen in:
A. Iris **B.** Ductus deferens
C. Ureter **D.** Trachea

Q.22 Hairpin bends of end arteries are present in abundance in which part of the long bone?
A. epiphysis **B.** metaphysis
C. diaphysis **D.** all the above

Q.23 The characteristic feature of compact bone:
A. Volkmann canal
B. Haversian system
C. lamellar arrangement
D. trabeculae

Q.24 Deepest layer of scalp is:
A. Connective tissue
B. Aponeurosis (Epicranial Aponeurosis)
C. Loose areolar tissue (Danger area of scalp)
D. None of these

Q.25 Which of the following movements will not be affected by involvement of the L5 Nerve root?
A. Thigh adduction **B.** Knee Flexion
C. Knee Extension **D.** Toe Extension

Q.26 The Couinaud's segmental nomenclature is based on the position of the
A. Hepatic veins and portal vein
B. Hepatic veins and biliary ducts
C. Portal vein and biliary ducts
D. Portal vein and hepatic artery

Q.27 The first costo-chondral joint is a :
A. Fibrous joint **B.** Synovial joint
C. Syndesmosis **D.** Synchondrosis

Q.28 After radical mastectomy there was injury to the long thoracic nerve. The integrity of the nerve can be tested at the bedside by asking the patient to :
A. Shrug the shoulders
B. Raise the arm above the head on the affected side
C. Touch the opposite shoulder
D. Lift a heavy object from the ground

Q.29 An inhaled foreign body is likely to lodge in the right lung due to all of the following features except:
A. Right lung is shorter and wider than left lung
B. Right principal bronchus is more vertical than the left bronchus
C. Tracheal bifurcation directs the foreign body to the right lung
D. Right inferior lobar bronchus is in continuation with the principal bronchus

Q.30 The following statements concerning chorda tympani nerve are true except that it:
A. Carries secretomotor fibers to submandibular gland
B. Joins lingual nerve in infratemporal fossa
C. Is a branch of facial nerve
D. Contains postganglionic parasympathetic fibers

Q.31 The superior oblique muscle is supplied by:
A. 3rd cranial nerve **B.** 4th cranial nerve
C. 5th cranial nerve **D.** 6th cranial nerve

Q.32 Benign Prostatic hypertrophy results in obstruction of the urinary tract. The specific condition is associated with enlargement of the:
A. Entire prostate gland
B. Lateral lobes
C. Median lobe
D. Posterior lobes

Q.33 While doing thoracocentesis, it is advisable to introduce needle along:
A. Upper border of the rib
B. Lower border of the rib
C. In the center of the intercostal space
D. In the anterior part of the intercostal space

Q.34 Cause of death in cyanide poisoning is:
A. Anoxic anoxia **B.** Anemia anoxia
C. Histotoxic anoxia **D.** Stagnant anoxia

Q.35 The volume of air taken into the lungs in normal respiration is known as:
A. Vital capacity
B. Timed vital capacity
C. Tidal volume
D. Inspiratory reserve volume

Q.36 Retinal isomerase catalyses the conversion of?
A. 11-cis retinal to rhodopsin
B. All trans retinal to 11-cis retinal
C. Lumirhodopsin to metarhodopsin
D. Bathorhodopsin to lumirhodopsin

Q.37 Which is a true statement regarding inhibin?
A. Increases the secretion of GnRH.
B. Molecular weight is between 5000 and 10,000.
C. It is secreted by hypothalamus.
D. It is a glycoprotein.

Q.38 Juxtamedullary nephrons:
A. Have smaller sized glomeruli
B. Possess short loops of Henle
C. Have slow rate of filtration
D. Both descending and ascending limbs of loop of Henle contain thin segments.

Q.39 Regarding somatomedin, which is true?
A. Reduced glucose oxidation in fat
B. Increases chondrogenesis
C. Activity is increased in protein deficiency
D. Activity is increased by glucocorticoids

Q.40 Action of calcitonin is?
A. Increases bone resorption

B. Increases calcium and phosphate absorption from GIT
C. Increases renal formation of 1-25 DHCC
D. Increases renal excretion of calcium and phosphate

Q.41 Through which of the following activities does an organism maintain homeostasis by Regulation processes?
A. Sweating and shivering
B. Formation of thick-walled spores to survive unfavorable conditions
C. Changing body temperature with ambient nature
D. Temporarily moving away from stressful habitat

Q.42 The function of axonemal dynein is?
A. Moves particles to the 'minus' end of microtubule.
B. Binds to actin and produce motion by bending their neck region.
C. Responsible for the beating of flagella and cilia.
D. Moves particles towards 'plus' end of microtubule.

Q.43 Which among the following is the primary action of nitric oxide in the GIT?
A. Contraction of gastrointestinal smooth muscle
B. Relaxation of gastrointestinal smooth muscle
C. Vasodilation
D. Vasoconstriction

Q.44 Pulmonary compliance is not decreased in?
A. COPD
B. Decreased surfactant production
C. Pulmonary congestion
D. Pulmonary fibrosis

Q.45 A newly posted junior doctor had difficulty in finding out base deficit/excess for blood in a given patient. An experienced senior resident advised a quick method to determine acid base composition of blood based onPCO2. Which of the following is the likely method he suggested to predict acidbase composition of blood?
A. Red ford nonuogram
B. DuBio's normogram
C. Goldman constant Field equation
D. Siggard Andersen normogram

Q.46 During the cardiac cycle the opening of the aortic valve takes place at the:
A. Beginning of systole
B. End of isovolumetric contraction
C. End of diastole
D. End of diastasis

Q.47 Patients having acute cardiac failure do not show pedal oedema, because :
A. The plasma oncotic pressure is high
B. There is renal compensation
C. There is an increase in cardiac output
D. There is a fall in the systemic capillary hydrostatic pressure

Q.48 During acclimatization to high altitude all of the following take place except:
A. Increase in minute ventilation
B. Increase in the sensitivity of central chemoreceptors
C. Increase in the sensitivity of carotid body to hypoxia
D. Shift in the oxygen dissociation curve to the left

Q.49 Neuronal degeneration is seen in all of the following except:
A. Crush nerve injury
B. Fetal development
C. Senescence
D. Neuropraxia

Q.50 The fibers from the contralateral nasal hemiretina project to the following layers of the lateral geniculate nucleus:
A. Layers 2, 3 & 5
B. Layers 1, 2 & 6
C. Layers 1, 4 & 6
D. Layers 4, 5 & 6

PART C

Q.51 Which of the following is false regarding neoplastic compressive myelopathy?
A. Most neoplasms are subdural in origin
B. Thoracic spine is most commonly involved
C. Tumor does not cross the disk space to involve adjacent vertebral body
D. Prognosis is poor when motor deficits are established for > 48 hours

Q.52 Identify the wrong statement regarding Bell's palsy:
A. It is the most common form of facial paralysis
B. Paralysis is usually preceded by pain behind the ear
C. MRI reveals swelling and enhancement of gasserian ganglion
D. Presence of incomplete paralysis in first week is the most favourable prognostic sign

Q.53 Which nutritional deficiency is associated with hereditary ataxia?
A. Vitamin B12
B. Vitamin B1
C. Vitamin E
D. Vitamin C

Q.54 Kayser Fleischer Ring is seen in what proportion of Wilson's disease patients with neurologic features?
A. 10% B. 50% C. 80% D. 100%

Q.55 Which of the following is not a feature of right heart failure?
A. Jugular venous distension
B. Hepatomegaly
C. Basal crepitations
D. Ascites

Q.56 Riociguat is used in the treatment of:
A. Gouty arthritis
B. Rheumatoid arthritis
C. Chronic thromboembolic pulmonary hypertension
D. Obesity

Q.57 Which of the following is not a component of Syndrome Z?
A. Obstructive sleep apnoea
B. Blood pressure more than 130/85 mm Hg
C. Fasting triglyceride more than 150mg/dl
D. LDL more than 100mg/dl

Q.58 Most common cause of lobar hemorrhage in elderly age group ?

A. Hypertension
B. Vascular malformation
C. Coagulopathy
D. Amyloid angiopathy

Q.59 Which is the most common preceding infection in bone marrow failure syndromes?

A. Parvo B19 **B.** EBV
C. HIV **D.** Hepatitis

Q.60 Which among the following statements is wrong :

A. Light chains are synthesised in slight excess normally in plasma cells
B. Qualitative assessment of M component can be done by electrophoresis
C. M components are detected in chronic myeloid leukaemia
D. In 20% myelomas, only light chains are produced

Q.61 Most specific symptom of temporal arteritis?

A. Visual loss
B. Jaw claudication
C. Temporal headache
D. Polymyalgia rheumatica

Q.62 The artery that is spared in polyarteritis nodosa?

A. Bronchial artery **B.** Renal artery
C. Coronary artery **D.** Pulmonary artery

Q.63 Generalised painless lymphadenopathy is seen in?

A. Rocky mountain spotted fever
B. Scrub typhus
C. Epidemic typhus
D. Q fever

Q.64 Bacillary angiomatosis is caused by?

A. Bartonella bacilliformis
B. Bartonella rochalimae
C. Rickettsia japonica
D. Bartonella henselae

Q.65 Lipoatrophy can occur in patients treated with?

A. Abacavir **B.** Tenofovir
C. Stavudine **D.** Maraviroc

Q.66 Severe muscle weakness is seen in?

A. Cori disease **B.** Andersen disease
C. McArdle disease **D.** Tarui disease

Q.67 Protein losing enteropathy with mucosal erosion is seen in?

A. Lymphoma
B. Coeliac disease
C. Menetrier's disease
D. Systemic lupus erythematosus

Q.68 All are true regarding hepatitis C infection except?

A. Serum transaminase level is a good predictor of the level of liver fibrosis
B. Telaprevir is effective in management
C. 3% risk of vertical transmission
D. Sharing toothbrushes is a risk factor for transmission

Q.69 Sausage digit is seen in?

A. Rheumatoid arthritis
B. Juvenile idiopathic arthritis
C. Enteropathic arthritis
D. Psoriatic arthritis

Q.70 Ehrlichiosis is a common coinfection with?

A. Lyme disease
B. Louse borne relapsing fever
C. Tick borne relapsing fever
D. Leptospirosis

Q.71 Which of the following is seen in Churg-Strauss syndrome?

A. Sinusitis
B. Raynaud's phenomenon
C. Allergic rhinitis
D. Epistaxis

Q.72 All are true regarding Scheuermann's osteochondritis except?

A. Dorsal kyphosis
B. Autosomal recessive inheritance
C. Predominantly affects adolescent boys
D. Irregular ossification of vertebral endplates

Q.73 Which of the following substances produced by osteoclasts is responsible for digestion of minerals during bone resorption?

A. Hydrochloric acid **B.** Acetic acid
C. Cathepsin K **D.** Sclerostin

Q.74 Collagen fibrils in bone are crosslinked with?

A. Osteopontin **B.** Laminin
C. Fibrillin **D.** Pyridinium

Q.75 Most abundant protein of bone is?

A. Laminin **B.** Osteocalcin
C. Type 1 collagen **D.** Type 2 collagen

Q.76 Which of the following increases bone resorption?

A. Osteoprotegerin (OPG)
B. Oestrogen / testosterone
C. Mechanical loading
D. Interleukin 1

Q.77 Which of the following decreases bone resorption?

A. Receptor activator of nuclear factor kappa B ligand (RANKL)
B. Interleukin 1
C. Osteoprotegerin
D. Tumour necrosis factor

Q.78 Sclerostin is produced by?

A. Osteocytes **B.** Osteoblasts
C. Osteoclasts **D.** Chondrocytes

Q.79 Most common form of arthritis is?

A. Rheumatoid arthritis

B. Psoriatic arthritis
C. Seronegative arthritis
D. Osteoarthritis

Q.80 Which of the following has a male female ratio of 1:1?
A. Rheumatoid arthritis
B. Gout
C. Seronegative spondyloarthritis
D. Polymyalgia rheumatica

Q.81 Triad of skin lesions, asymmetric mononeuritis multiplex and eosinophilia are seen in?
A. Cryoglobulinemic vasculitis
B. Polyarteritis nodosa
C. Churg Strauss Syndrome
D. Giant cell arteritis

Q.82 Which of the following genetic mutation has been described in aortic stenosis?
A. KCNH2
B. KCNQ1
C. NOTCH1
D. SCN5A

Q.83 Which of the following is not a feature of complete heart block onthe ECG:
A. Constant RR interval
B. Constant PP interval
C. Constant PR interval
D. PP interval shorter than RR interval

Q.84 Mitral annular area in systole:
A. Decreases by 10%
B. Decreases by 25%
C. Increases by 10%
D. Increases by 25%

Q.85 Dominant right coronary artery means?
A. Right coronary artery supplies major portion of the myocardium
B. Right coronary artery crosses the crux and gives rise to posterior left ventricular branches
C. Right coronary artery supplies major portion of the left ventricle
D. None of the above

Q.86 Sokolow-Lyon electrocardiographic criteria is for the diagnosis of:
A. Left atrial enlargement
B. Left ventricular hypertrophy
C. Right atrial enlargement
D. Right ventricular hypertrophy

Q.87 Prominent upper lobe vessels in X-ray chest in mitral stenosis indicate:
A. Antler sign
B. Pulmonary venous hypertension
C. Cephalization
D. All of the above

Q.88 Which of the following is not an ideal indication for bioprosthetic valve (compared to mechanical prosthetic valve)?
A. Female planning pregnancy
B. Young adult male
C. Elderly female
D. History of endocarditis

Q.89 Most commonly used route for emergency pericardiocentesis in cardiac tamponade is:
A. Left parasternal
B. Right parasternal
C. Apical
D. Subxiphoid

Q.90 Which of the following is not an Acute aortic syndrome?
A. Acute aortic dissection
B. Acute occlusion of aortic bifurcation
C. Intramural hematoma of aorta
D. Perforating ulcer of aorta

Q.91 A 60 year old man presented to the OPD with symptoms suggestive of acute pancreatitis. He consumes high quantities of alcohol regularly. His symptoms started 4 days ago. But he continued to consume alcohol. He was admitted for further evaluation. Presently, he has severe vomiting. He also complains of dizziness when standing. Examination revealed tenderness in the epigastrium and right hypochondrium. A reddish discolouration is noted in the flanks. Which of the following statements regarding the patient is most accurate?
A. The patient should be evaluated for concomitant appendicitis
B. USG is likely to demonstrate pseudocyst of pancreas
C. Contrast CT scan of the abdomen will reveal severe necrotising pancreatitis
D. Pancreatic calcification will be seen in X-ray abdomen

Q.92 A 30 year old woman presented to the OPD with proximal muscle weakness, ptosis and easy fatigability. Which of following is the most sensitive test to arrive at a diagnosis?
A. Single fiber electromyography
B. Muscle biopsy
C. Measurement of creatinine phosphokinase levels
D. Edrophonium test

Q.93 Symmetric, high voltage, triphasic, slow wave EEG pattern is seen in?
A. Uremic encephalopathy
B. Hypoxic ischemic encephalopathy
C. Hypercapnic encephalopathy
D. Hepatic encephalopathy

Q.94 Use of streptokinase is contraindicated in?
A. Pulmonary embolism
B. AV fistula
C. Thrombophlebitis
D. Intracranial tumour

Q.95 Kayser Fleischer ring is characteristic of ?
A. Pterygium
B. Scleritis
C. Hemochromatosis
D. Wilson's disease

Q.96 Androphonia can be corrected by doing:
A. Type I Thyroplasty
B. Type 2 Thyroplasty
C. Type 3 Thyroplasty
D. Type 4 Thyroplasty

Q.97 Use of seigel's speculum during examination of the ear provides all except:
A. Magnification
B. Assessment of movement of the tympanic membrane

C. Removal of foreign body from the ear
D. As applicator for the powdered antibiotic of ear

Q.98 Sensorineural deafness may be feature of all, except:
A. Nail patella syndrome
B. Distal renal tubular acidosis
C. Bartter syndrome
D. Alport syndrome

Q.99 Which of the following conditions causes the maximum hearing loss?
A. Ossicular disruption with intact tympanic membrane
B. Disruption of malleus and incus as well tympanic membrane
C. Partial fixation of the stapes footplate
D. Ottitis media with effusion

Q.100 A 30 year old male is having Attic cholesteatoma of left ear with lateral sinus thrombophlebitis. Which of the following will be the operation of choice?
A. Intact canal wall mastoidectomy
B. Simple mastoidectomy with Tympanoplasty
C. Canal wall down mastoidectomy
D. Mastoidectomy with cavity obliteration

Q.101 Which of the following is not a typical feature of malignant otitis externa?
A. Caused by Pseudomonas aeruginosa
B. Patients are usually old
C. Mitotic figures are high
D. Patient is immune compromised

Q.102 Which of the following is not a typical feature of Ménière's disease?
A. Sensorineural deafness
B. Pulsatile tinnitus
C. Vertigo
D. Fluctuating deafness

Q.103 Which of the following is the most common etiological agent in paranasal sinus mycoses?
A. Aspergillus spp
B. Histoplasma
C. Conidiobolus coronatus
D. Candida albicans

Q.104 Treatment of choice for glue ear is
A. Myringotomy with cold knife
B. Myringotomy with diode laser
C. Myringotomy with ventilation tube insertion
D. Conservative treatment with analgesics & antibiotics

Q.105 Rhinophyma is associated with:
A. Hypertrophy of the sebaceous glands
B. Hypertrophy of sweat glands
C. Hypertrophy of endothelial cells
D. Hypertrophy of epithelial cells

Q.106 Drug of choice in eclampsia:
A. Oral magnesium sulphate
B. Intravenous magnesium sulphate
C. Oral phenytoin sodium
D. Intravenous phenytoin sodium

Q.107 Patients of Rectovaginal fistula should be initially treated with:
A. Colostomy B. Primary repair
C. Colporrhaphy D. Anterior resection

Q.108 Drug of choice for treatment of intrahepatic cholestasis in pregnancy is?
A. Ursodeoxycholic acid
B. Dexamethasone
C. Antihistamines
D. Cholestyramine

Q.109 The most common side effect of IUCD insertion is:
A. Bleeding B. Pain
C. Pelvic infection D. Ectopic pregnancy

Q.110 In a case of Dysgerminoma of ovary one of the following tumor markers is likely to be raised.
A. Serum HCG
B. Serum alphafetoprotein
C. Serum lactate dehydrogenase
D. Serum inhibin

Q.111 The most common pure germ cell tumor of the ovary is:
A. Choriocarcinoma
B. Dysgerminoma
C. Embryonal cell tumor
D. Malignant Teratoma

Q.112 The most common cause of secondary amenorrhoea in India is:
A. Endometrial tuberculosis
B. Premature ovarian failure
C. Polycystic ovarian syndrome
D. Sheehan's syndrome

Q.113 All of the following appear to decrease hot flushes in menopausal women except:
A. Androgens B. Raloxifene
C. Isoflavones D. Tibolone

Q.114 Aspermia is the term used to describe:
A. Absence of semen
B. Absence of sperm in ejaculate
C. Absence of sperm motility
D. Occurrence of abnormal sperm

Q.115 Which one of the following is the ideal contraceptive for a patient with heart disease:
A. IUCD
B. Depo-Provera
C. Diaphragm
D. Oral contraceptive pills

Q.116 Use of one of the following vaccination is absolutely contraindicated in pregnancy:
A. Hepatitis B B. Cholera
C. Rabies D. Yellow fever

Q.117 Which of the following statements is incorrect in relation to pregnant women with epilepsy?

A. The rate of congenital malformation is increased in the offspring of women with epilepsy
B. Seizure frequency increases in approximately 70% of women
C. Breast feeding is safe with most anticonvulsants
D. Folic acid supplementation may reduce the risk of neural tube defect

Q.118 Infants of diabetic mother are likely to have the following cardiac anomaly:

A. Coarctation of aorta
B. Fallot' s tetrology
C. Ebstein's anomaly
D. Transposition of great arteries

Q.119 All are the risk factors associated with macrosomia except:

A. Maternal obesity
B. Prolonged Pregnancy
C. Previous large infant
D. Short Stature

Q.120 All are the causes of intrauterine growth retardation except:

A. Anemia
B. Pregnancy induced hypertension
C. Maternal heart disease
D. Gestational diabetes

Q.121 The smallest diameter of the true pelvis is:

A. Interspinous diameter
B. Diagonal conjugate
C. True conjugate
D. Intertuberous diameter

Q.122 Which one of the following biochemical parameters is the most sensitive to detect open spina bifida?

A. Maternal serum alpha fetoprotein
B. Amniotic fluid alpha fetoprotein
C. Amniotic fluid acetyl cholinesterase
D. Amniotic fluid glucohexaminase

Q.123 The best period of gestation to carry out chorion villous biopsy for prenatal diagnosis is?

A. 8-10 weeks
B. 10-12 weeks
C. 12-14 weeks
D. 14-16 weeks

Q.124 The following complications during pregnancy increase the risk of postpartum hemorrhage (PPH) except:

A. Hypertension
B. Macrosomia
C. Twin pregnancy
D. Hydramnios

Q.125 A primigravida presents to casualty at 32 weeks gestation with acute pain abdomen for 2 hours, vaginal bleeding and decreased fetal movements. She should be managed by:

A. Immediate cesarean section
B. Immediate induction of labor
C. Tocolytic therapy
D. Magnesium sulphate therapy

Q.126 Which of the following tumors is not commonly known to increase in pregnancy?

A. Glioma
B. Pituitary adenoma
C. Meningioma
D. Neurofibroma

Q.127 Which of the following ovarian tumor is most prone to undergo torsion during pregnancy?

A. Serous cystadenoma
B. Mucinous cystadenoma
C. Dermoid cyst
D. Theca lutein cyst

Q.128 All of the following mechanisms might account for a reduced risk of upper genital tract infection in users of progestin releasing IUDs, except:

A. Reduced retrograde menstruation
B. Decreased ovulation
C. Thickened cervical mucus
D. Decidual changes in the endometrium

Q.129 Prenatal diagnosis at 16 weeks of pregnancy can be performed using all of the following, except:

A. Amniotic fluid
B. Maternal blood
C. Chorionic villi
D. Fetal blood

Q.130 Emergency contraception prevents pregnancy by all of the following mechanisms, except:

A. Delaying/inhibiting ovulation
B. Inhibiting fertilization
C. Preventing implantation of the fertilized egg
D. Interrupting an early pregnancy

Q.131 Which of the following statements is incorrect regarding levonorgestrel releasing intrauterine system:

A. There is increased incidence of menorrhagia
B. This system can be used as hormone replacement therapy
C. This method is useful for the treatment of endometerial hyperplasia
D. Irregular uterine bleeding can be problem initially

Q.132 The most common cause of tubal block in India is

A. Gonorrhea infection
B. Chlamydia infection
C. Tuberculosis
D. Bacterial vaginosis

Q.133 Which surgical procedure has the highest incidence of ureteric injury?

A. Vaginal hysterectomy
B. Abdominal hysterectomy
C. Weitheim's hysterectomy
D. Anterior colporrhaphy

Q.134 The risk of Asherman syndrome is the highest if Dilatation and Curettage (D & C) is done for the following condition:

A. Medical termination of pregancy
B. Missed abortion
C. Dysfunctional uterine bleeding

D. Post partum haemorrhage

Q.135 All are true about separation anxiety disorder except:

A. The prevalence is 3.5% to 5.4%
B. Comorbidity is common
C. Prevalence is higher in girls
D. Average age of onset is 4 years

Q.136 All of the following are example of peripheral neuropathies except?

A. Abetalipoproteinemia
B. Charcot-Marie-Tooth disease
C. Werdnig Hoffman disease
D. Dejerine Sottas disease

Q.137 CA-125 is a marker antigen for the diagnosis of:

A. Colon cancer **B.** Breast cancer
C. Brain cancer **D.** Ovarian cancer

Q.138 Least common cause of ambiguous genitalia in females?

A. 21 hydroxylase deficiency
B. 11 hydroxylase deficiency
C. WNT4 gene mutation
D. Foetal placental steroid sulfatase deficiency

Q.139 Earliest sign of pathological gastroesophageal reflux in infants is?

A. Upper GI bleeding
B. Respiratory symptoms
C. Oesophageal stricture
D. Postprandial regurgitation

Q.140 Blalock and Taussig's shunt is done between:

A. Aorta to the pulmonary artery
B. Aorta to pulmonary vein
C. Subclavian artery to pulmonary vein
D. Subclavian vein to an artery

Q.141 Right sided isomerism is found in association with?

A. Asplenia **B.** Single spleen
C. Two spleens **D.** Multiple spleens

Q.142 Most common cause of meningoencephalitis in children is?

A. HSV **B.** Measles
C. Arbobvirus **D.** Enterovirus

Q.143 Which one of the following drugs is used for fetal therapy of congenital adrenal hyperplasia?

A. Hydrocortisone **B.** Prednisolone
C. Fludrocortisone **D.** Dexamethasone

Q.144 The following features are true for tetralogy of Fallot, except:

A. Ventricular septal defect
B. Right ventricular hypertrophy
C. Atrial septal defect
D. Pulmonary stenosis

Q.145 In a child, non functioning kidney is best diagnosed by:

A. Ultrasonography
B. IVU
C. DTPA renogram
D. Creatinine clearance

Q.146 All of the following are anterior dystrophies except?

A. Reis-Buckler's dystrophy
B. Meesmann's dystrophy
C. Schnyder's dystrophy
D. Stocker-Holt's dystrophy

Q.147 False about Argyll Robertson Pupil is?

A. Accommodation reflex normal
B. Direct pupillary reflex absent
C. Indirect pupillary reflex normal
D. Visual acuity normal

Q.148 Enlarged corneal nerves may be seen in all of the following except:

A. Keratoconus
B. Herpes simplex keratitis
C. Leprosy
D. Neurofibromatosis

Q.149 Horner's syndrome is characterized by all of the following except:

A. Miosis **B.** Enopthalmos
C. Ptosis **D.** Cycloplegia

Q.150 Which one of the following statements is incorrect about Optic glioma?

A. Has a peak incidence in first decade
B. Arises from oligodendrocytes
C. Causes meningeal hyperplasia
D. Is associated with type I neurofibromatosis

Q.151 Typically bilateral inferior subluxation of lens is seen in:

A. Marfan's syndrome **B.** Homocystinuria
C. Hyperinsulinemia **D.** Ocular trauma

Q.152 When should a case of Non-Insulin dependent diabetes mellitus (NIDDM) with a history of diabetes for one year have an ophthalmic examination?

A. As early as feasible
B. After 5 years
C. After 10 years
D. Only after visual symptoms develop

Q.153 SAFE strategy is recommended for the control of :

A. Trachoma
B. Glaucoma
C. Diabetic retinopathy
D. Cataract

Q.154 Band shaped keratopathy is caused by:

A. Amyloid
B. Calcium
C. Monopolysaccharide
D. Lipid

Q.155 The laser procedure, most often used for treating iris neovascularization, is:

A. Goniophotocoagulation
B. Laser trabeculoplasty
C. Panretinal photocoagulation (PRP)
D. Laser iridoplasty

Q.156 Commonest site of urethral carcinoma in males is?
A. Prostatic urethra
B. Penile urethra
C. Bulbomembranous urethra
D. Navicular fossa

Q.157 First autologous renal transplantation was performed by?
A. Hardy **B.** Higgins **C.** Studor **D.** Kavosis

Q.158 Lord's plication is used in the treatment of ?
A. Hydrocele
B. Inguinal hernia
C. Testicular malignancy
D. Varicocele

Q.159 Which of the following structures are connected by Grayhack shunt?
A. Corpora cavernosa and saphenous vein
B. Corpora cavernosa and dorsal vein
C. Corpora cavernosa and corpus spongiosum
D. Corpora cavernosa and glans

Q.160 Which of the following conditions is associated with multiple cutaneous sebaceous adenomas?
A. Turcot's syndrome
B. Cowden syndrome
C. Gardner's syndrome
D. Muir Torre syndrome

Q.161 Which of the following renal calculi is seen associated with proteus infection?
A. Calcium Oxalate **B.** Triple Phosphate
C. Xanthine **D.** Uric Acid

Q.162 Which of the following is the most troublesome source of bleeding during a radical retropubic prostatectomy?
A. Dorsal venous complex
B. Inferior vesical pedicle
C. Superior vesical pedicle
D. Seminal vesicular artery

Q.163 Which of the following catheter materials is most suited for long-term use?
A. Latex **B.** Silicone
C. Rubber **D.** Polyurethane

Q.164 A new born presented with bloated abdomen shortly after birth with passing of less meconium. A full thickness biopsy of the rectum was carried out. Which one of the following rectal biopsy findings is most likely to be present?
A. Fibrosis of submucosa
B. Hyalinisation of the muscular coat
C. Thickened Muscularis propria
D. Lack of ganglion cells

Q.165 Abbey Estlander flap is used in the reconstruction of:
A. Buccal mucosa **B.** Lip
C. Tongue **D.** Palate

Q.166 The most common complication seen in hiatus hernia is:
A. Oesophagitis
B. Aspiration pneumonitis
C. Volvulus
D. Esophageal stricture

Q.167 In which one of the following head and neck cancer, perineural invasion is most commonly seen?
A. Adenocarcinoma
B. Adenoid cystic carcinoma
C. Basal Cell Adenoma
D. Squamous cell carcinoma

Q.168 Lumbar sympathectomy is of value in the management of:
A. Intermittent claudication
B. Distal ischaemia affecting the skin of the toes
C. Arteriovenous Fistula
D. Back pain

Q.169 A blood stained discharge from the nipple indicates one of the following:
A. Breast abscess
B. Fibroadenoma
C. Duct Papilloma
D. Fat Necrosis of Breast

Q.170 The most preferred approach for pituitary surgery at the present time is:
A. Transcranial **B.** Transethmoidal
C. Trans-sphenoidal **D.** Transcallosal

Q.171 Which of the following is not a preferred site for planning vascular access for maintenance hemodialysis?
A. Nondominant extremity
B. Upper limb
C. Radiocephalic AV fistula
D. Saphenofemoral fistula

Q.172 Dacron vascular graft is:
A. Nontextile synthetic **B.** Textile synthetic
C. Nontextile biologic **D.** Textile biologic

Q.173 Allen's test is useful in evaluating:
A. Thoracic outlet compression
B. Presence of cervical rib
C. Integrity of palmar arch
D. Digital blood flow

Q.174 The most common cause of acquired arteriovenous fistula is:
A. Bacterial infection **B.** Fungal infection
C. Blunt trauma **D.** Penetrating trauma

Q.175 Which of the following statements is true regarding testicular tumors?
A. Are embryonal cell carcinomas in 95% of cases
B. Bilateral in up to 10% cases

C. Teratomas are more common than seminomas
D. Usually present after 50 years of age

Q.176 The treatment of choice for squamous cell anal cancer is:
A. Abdominoperineal resection
B. Laser fulgaration
C. Chemoradiotherapy
D. Platinum—based chemotherapy

Q.177 Which of the following drugs is not a part of the 'Triple Therapy' immunosuppression for post-renal transplant patients?
A. Cyclosporine **B.** Azathioprine
C. FK 506 **D.** Prednisolone

Q.178 All of the following modalities can be used for in situ ablation of liver secondaries, except?
A. Ultrasonic waves **B.** Cryotherapy
C. Alcohol **D.** Radiofrequency

Q.179 Biliary stricture developing after laparascopic cholecystectomy usually occurs at which part of the common bile duct?
A. Upper
B. Middle
C. Lower
D. All sides with equal frequency

Q.180 Which one of the following statements is incorrect regarding stones in the common bile duct?
A. Can present with Charcot's triad
B. Are suggested by a bile duct diameter >6 mm in ultrasound
C. ERCP, sphincterotomy and balloon clearance is now the standard treatment
D. When removed by exploration of the common bile ducts the T-tube can be removed after 3 days

Q.181 A patient of post cholecystectomy biliary stricture has undergone an ERCP three days ago. Following this she has developed acute cholangitis. The most likely organism is:
A. Escherichia coli
B. Bacillus fragilis
C. Streptococcus viridans
D. Pseudomonas aeruginosa

Q.182 The tumor, which may occur in the residual breast or overlying skin following wide local excision and radiotherapy for mammary carcinoma, is:
A. Leiomyosarcoma
B. Squamous cell carcinoma
C. Basal cell carcinoma
D. Angiosarcoma

Q.183 In which of the following types of breast carcinoma, would you consider biopsy of opposite breast?
A. Adenocarcinoma-poorly differentiated
B. Medullary carcinoma
C. Lobular carcinoma
D. Comedo carcinoma

Q.184 The most important prognostic factor in breast carcinoma is:
A. Histological grade of the tumor
B. Stage of the tumor at the time of diagnosis
C. Status of estrogen and progesterone receptors
D. Over expression of p53 tumour suppressor gene

Q.185 One of the following is not correct in papillary carcinoma of thyroid:
A. Can be reliably diagnosed using fine needle aspiration cytology
B. Always unifocal
C. Typically spreads to the cervical lymph nodes
D. Requires a total thyroidectomy for large tum

Q.186 Which of the following brain tumours is highly vascular in nature?
A. Glioblastoma
B. Meningiomas
C. C P angle epidermoid
D. Pituitary adenomas

Q.187 Early postoperative complication of ileostomy:
A. Obstruction **B.** Prolapse
C. Diarrhoea **D.** Necrosis

Q.188 Most common biochemical abnormality in congenital pyloric stenosis.
A. Hyperkalemic metabolic acidosis
B. Hypokalemic metabolic acidosis
C. Hyperkalemic metabolic alkalosis
D. Hypokalemic metabolic alkalosis

Q.189 Hypotension in acute spinal injury is due to:
A. Loss of sympathetic tone
B. Loss of parasympathetic tone
C. Orthostatic hypotension
D. Vasovagal attack

Q.190 Least risk of CA breast is seen in:
A. BRCA1
B. BRCA2
C. Li-Fraumeni syndrome
D. Ataxia telangiectasia

Q.191 External hemorrhoids below the dentate line are –
A. Painful
B. Ligation is done as management
C. Skin tag is not seen in these cases
D. May turn malignant

Q.192 The technique employed in radiotherapy to counteract the effect of tumour motion due to breathing is known as:
A. Arc technique **B.** Modulation
C. Gating **D.** Shunting

Q.193 Plethoric lung fields are seen in all of the following conditions, except:
A. Atrial septal defect (ASD)
B. TAPVC (Total Anomalous Pulmonary venous connection)
C. Ebsteins' anomaly

D. Ventricular septal defect

Q.194 On MRI the differential diagnosis of spinal cord edema is:

A. Myelodysplasia
B. Myelomalacia
C. Myeloschisis
D. Cord tumors

Q.195 The diagnostic procedure not done in case of pheochromocytoma.

A. CT scan
B. MRI
C. FNAC
D. MIBG scan

Q.196 A young male is brought unconscious to the hospital with external injuries. CT brain showed no midline shift. Basal cistern was compressed with multiple small haemorrhages. What is the likely diagnosis?

A. Cerebral contusion
B. Cerebral laceration
C. Multiple infarcts
D. Diffuse axonal injuries

Q.197 Metabolic abnomiality seen in congenital hypertrophic pyloric stenosis is:

A. Hypochloremic hypokalemic metabolic alkalosis
B. Hyperchloremic hypokalemic metabolic alkalosis
C. Hypochloremic hypokalemic metabolic acidosis
D. Hyperchloremic hypokalemic metabolic acidosis

Q.198 A patient sustained Traumatic injury to major abdominal vessels. It has been planned to explore the Suprarenal Aorta. the Celiac Axis, the Superior Mesentric Artery, and the Left Renal Artery. What maneuver for exposure is recommended:

A. Cranial Visceral Rotation
B. Caudal Visceral Rotation
C. Left Medial Visceral Rotation
D. Right Medical Visceral Rotation

Q.199 The following is a marker of Paget's disease of breast

A. S- 100
B. HMB 45
C. CEA
D. Neuron specific enolase

Q.200 Chronic burrowing ulcer is caused by:

A. Microaerophilic streptococci
B. Peptostreptococcus
C. Streptococcus viridans
D. Streptococcus pyogenes

PART B

Q.201 Which of the following is true regarding nuclear fluorescence in systemic lupus erythematosus?

A. Rim staining pattern indicates antibodies to double stranded DNA
B. Homogenous staining reflects antibodies specific to centromeres
C. Speckled pattern reflects the presence of antibodies to histones
D. Nucleolar pattern reflects antibodies to chromatin

Q.202 Which of the following is true regarding lymphangioleiomyomatosis?

A. Primarily seen in old age
B. Commonly associated with persistent cough
C. Proliferation occurs in perivascular epithelioid cells
D. Disease is rapidly progressive

Q.203 The proto oncogene associated with Burkitt lymphoma is?

A. ABL
B. BRAF
C. HGF
D. MYC

Q.204 All are true regarding desmoid tumours except?

A. Consist of large infiltrative masses that do not metastasize
B. Most frequent in old age
C. Mutations occur in the APC gene
D. Predominantly seen in women

Q.205 All of the following diseases are caused by trinucleotide repeat mutations affecting non-coding regions except?

A. Fragile X syndrome
B. Myotonic dystrophy
C. Spinocerebellar ataxia
D. Friedreich ataxia

Q.206 Rupture of Charcot Bouchard aneurysm usually causes?

A. Extradural haemorrhage
B. Subdural haemorrhage
C. Subarachnoid haemorrhage
D. Intracerebral haemorrhage

Q.207 Anti LKM antibodies are found in?

A. Inflammatory myopathies
B. Behcet's syndrome
C. HCV infection
D. Primary biliary cirrhosis

Q.208 Which of the following is not an anterior mediastinal tumour?

A. Thymoma
B. Lymphoma
C. Neurogenic tumour
D. Teratoma

Q.209 Not an action of bradykinin?

A. Bronchodilation
B. Vasodilatation
C. Pain
D. Increase in vascular permeability

Q.210 Marker for langerhans cell histiocytosis is?

A. CD 5
B. CD 1a
C. CD 22
D. CD 30

Q.211 A person who is heterozygous for sickle cell anemia has increased resistance for?

A. Malaria
B. Filariasis
C. Dengue haemorrhagic fever
D. Thalassemia

Q.212 Caspases are involved in ?

A. Apoptosis
B. Necrosis
C. Neoplasia
D. Inflammation

Q.213 Most common cause of Down's syndrome is?

A. Translocation
B. Mosaicism
C. Paternal nondisjunction
D. Maternal nondisjunction

Q.214 Which stain is used to study fungal morphology in tissue sections?
A. Periodic acid–Schiff
B. Alizarin Red
C. Masson's Trichrome
D. Von Kossa

Q.215 Psammoma body is not seen in ?
A. Papillary carcinoma of thyroid
B. Follicular carcinoma of thyroid
C. Serous cystadenocarcinoma of ovary
D. Meningiom

Q.216 Which among the following is not a neuronal tumour?
A. Ependymoma B. Ganglioglioma
C. Neurocytoma D. Gangliocytoma

Q.217 Necrotizing lymphadenitis is a characteristic feature of?
A. Hodgkin's disease B. Kikuchi disease
C. Kimura disease D. Castleman disease

Q.218 Which among the following is not an autoimmune disease?
A. Myasthenia gravis
B. Systemic lupus erythematosus
C. Grave's disease
D. Sickle cell disease

Q.219 True statement regarding platelet function defects?
A. Normal platelet count with increased bleeding time
B. Decreased platelet count with increased bleeding time
C. Increased platelet count with increased bleeding time
D. Normal platelet count with normal bleeding time

Q.220 HbH is seen in which of the following conditions?
A. Deletion of 3 beta genes
B. Deletion of 3 alpha genes
C. Deletion of 4 beta genes
D. Deletion of 4 alpha genes

Q.221 All are true about Xanthogranulomatous inflammation except?
A. Associated with tuberculosis
B. Foam cells are present
C. Yellow nodules are present
D. Multi-nucleated giant cells are present

Q.222 Which of the following is most characteristic feature of acute inflammation?
A. Vasodilatation and increased vascular permeability
B. Margination of leukocytes
C. Vasoconstriction
D. Vascular stasis

Q.223 Which of the following enzymes are responsible for generating 'oxygen burst' within neutrophils for killing intracellular bacteria?
A. Superoxide dismutase
B. Glutathione peroxidase
C. Oxidase
D. Catalase

Q.224 Which of the following organelles plays a pivotal role in Apoptosis?
A. Mitochondria
B. Endoplasmic Reticulum
C. Nucleus
D. Golgi Apparatus

Q.225 The blood in the vessels normally does not clot because:
A. Vitamin K antagonists are present in plasma
B. Thrombin has a positive feedback on plasminogen
C. Sodium citrate in plasma chelates calcium ions
D. Vascular endothelium is smooth and coated with glycocalyx

Q.226 Which of the following is not a long acting muscarinic antagonist?
A. Glycopyrronium B. Aclidinium
C. Indacaterol D. Umeclidinium

Q.227 Ibrutinib is used for the management of?
A. Chronic Myelogenous Leukemia
B. Acute Lymphoblastic Leukemia
C. Mantle Cell Lymphoma
D. Lymphocyte rich Hodgkin's Lymphoma

Q.228 Patients suffering from multidrug resistant tuberculosis can be treated with all the following drugs except:
A. Tobramycin B. Amikacin
C. Ciprofloxacin D. Clarithromycin

Q.229 All are true regarding leflunomide except?
A. Inhibits proliferation of stimulated lymphocytes
B. Depresses antibody production by B lymphocytes
C. Can be used in children
D. Can cause thrombocytopenia

Q.230 Which of the following drugs have a narrow therapeutic index?
A. Lithium B. Diazepam
C. Penicillin D. Desipramine

Q.231 Which of the following is an integrase inhibitor currently in use for the treatment of HIV infection?
A. Indinavir B. Elvitegravir
C. Saquinavir D. Raltegravir

Q.232 MAO inhibitors are contraindicated in a patient taking?
A. Pethidine B. Buprenorphine
C. Morphine D. Pentazocin

Q.233 Ethosuximide is the drug of choice for treatment of ?
A. Generalized tonic clonic seizures
B. Absence seizures

C. Simple partial seizures
D. Complex partial seizures

Q.234 Which of the following is not an adverse effect of chronic amiodarone therapy?
A. Pulmonary fibrosis
B. Hypothyroidism
C. Hyperthyroidism
D. Systemic lupus erythematosus

Q.235 Alkalinization of urine is done during the administration of which of the following chemotherapeutic drugs?
A. Ara-C (Cytarabine) B. Methotrexate
C. Cisplatin D. Ifosfamide

Q.236 Which of the following is used in the treatment of meningococcal meningitis in patients allergic to penicillin?
A. Ciprofloxacin B. Teicoplanin
C. Meropenem D. Chloramphenicol

Q.237 Not true about Na+ K+ 2Cl- Co-transporter:
A. It is a glycoprotein
B. 12 membrane spanning domains
C. There are distinct isoforms for secretory and absorptive function
D. The secretory form is found exclusively in thick segment of ascending limb of loop of Henle

Q.238 Which of the following has a uricosuric action:
A. Allopurinol B. Losartan
C. Ramipril D. Atenolol

Q.239 All of the following are known adverse effects of thalidomide, except:
A. Diarrhoea
B. Teratogenicity
C. Deep Vein Thrombosis
D. Peripheral Neuropathy

Q.240 Which of the following antihypertensive drugs should not be used in a patient on Lithium in order to prevent Lithium Toxicity?
A. Clonidine
B. Beta blockers
C. Calcium Channel Blockers
D. Diuretics

Q.241 All of the following statements about Aprepitant are true except?
A. Agonist at Neurokinin receptor (NK1)
B. Crosses blood brain barrier
C. Metabolised by CYP3A4 pathway
D. Ameliorates nausea and vomiting of chemotherapy

Q.242 All of the following statement s about 'Erlotinib' are true except?
A. Tyrosine kinase inhibitor
B. Food decreases its absorption
C. Rashes may occur
D. Used in non small cell lung carcinoma

Q.243 A patient who was given primaquine develops dark coloured urine one day after administration of the drug. The likely diagnosis is:
A. Glucose-6-phosphate dehydrogenase deficiency
B. Glucose-6- phosphatase deficiency
C. Galactose-6-phosphate dehydrogenase deficiency
D. Galactose-6-phosphatase deficiency

Q.244 All of the following statements about serotonin syndrome are true, except:
A. It is not an idiosyncratic reaction
B. Can be caused by SSRI
C. Dantrolene is the drug of choice
D. Associated with hyperthermia and hypertension

Q.245 BAL is useful in treating poisoning due to all except?
A. Lead B. Organic mercury
C. Cadmium D. Arsenic

Q.246 Which of the following statements is true regarding ARBO viruses :
A. Yellow fever is endemic in India
B. Dengue virus has only one serotype
C. Kyasanur Forest disease (KFD) is transmitted by ticks
D. Mosquito of culex vishnui complex is the vector of Dengue fever

Q.247 Draughtsman appearance is seen with colonies of:
A. Pneumococcus B. Streptococcus
C. Staphylococcus D. None of the above

Q.248 The most sensitive method for detecting cervical Chlamydia trachomatis infection is:
A. Direct fluorescent antibody test
B. Enzyme immunoassay
C. Polymerase chain reaction
D. Culture on irradiated McConkey cells

Q.249 Epstein Barr (EB) virus has been implicated in the following malignancies except:
A. Hodgkin's disease
B. Non-Hodgkin's lymphoma
C. Nasopharyngeal carcinoma
D. Multiple myeloma

Q.250 A 20 years old male patient presents to the STD clinic with a genital ulcer. The gram stain of the smear from the ulcer shows gram-negative coccobacilli. The most appropriate media for culture would be:
A. Thayer Martin Medium
B. Blood agar with X & V factors
C. Chocolate agar with IsoVitaleX
D. Teilurite blood agar

Q.251 Regarding gas gangrene one of the following is correct:
A. It is due to Clostridium Botulinum infection
B. Clostridial species are gram-negative spore-forming anaerobes
C. The clinical features are due to the release of protein endotoxin
D. Gas is invariably present in the muscle compartments

Q.252 A man, after skinning a dead animal, developed a pustule on his hand. A smear prepared from the lesion showed the presence of Gram-positive bacilli in long chains which were positive for McFadyean's reaction. The most likely aetiological agent is :

A. Clostridium tetani
B. Listeria monocytogenes
C. Bacillus anthracis
D. Actinomyces sp

Q.253 A microbiologist wants to develop a vaccine for the prevention of attachment of diarrhoeagenic E. coli to the specific receptors in the gastrointestinal tract. All of the following fimbrial adhesions would be appropriate vaccine candidates except :

A. CFA-I **B.** P-Pili **C.** CS-2 **D.** K 88

Q.254 Which of the following infestation leads to malabsorption?

A. Giardia lamblia
B. Ascaris lumbricoides
C. Necator americanus
D. Ancylostama duodenale

Q.255 Which one of the following statements is true regarding Chlamydia pneumonia:

A. Fifteen serovars have been identified as human pathogens
B. Mode of transmission is by the airborne bird excreta
C. The Cytoplasmic inclusions present in the sputum specimen are rich in glycogen
D. The group-specific antigen is responsible for the production of complement-fixing antibodies

Q.256 A child was diagnosed to be suffering from diarrhoea due to Campylobacter jejuni. Which of the following will be the correct environmental conditions of incubation of the culture plates of the stool sample:

A. The temperature of 42°C and microaerophilic
B. The temperature of 42°C and 10% carbon dioxide
C. The temperature of 37°C and microaerophilic
D. The temperature of 37°C and 10% carbon dioxide

Q.257 A bacterial disease that has been associated with the 3 "Rs" i.e., rats, ricefields, and rainfall is:

A. Leptospirosis **B.** Plague
C. Melioidosis **D.** Rodent bite fever

Q.258 All can cause pulmonary eosinophilia except-

A. Necator americanus
B. Ankylostoma duodenale
C. Trichinella spiralis
D. Ascaris lumbricoides

Q.259 The following diseases are associated with Epstein-Barr virus infection, except:

A. Infectious mononucleosis
B. Epidermodysplasia verruciformis
C. Nasopharyngeal carcinoma
D. Oral hairy leukoplakia

Q.260 Which one of the following is true

A. Agar has nutrient properties
B. Chocolate medium is a selective medium
C. Addition of selective substances in a solid medium is called enrichment media
D. Nutrient broth is basal medium

Q.261 An elderly male presented with fever, chest pain and dry cough. Sputum was cultured on charcoal yeast medium, the organism identified will be

A. H.influenza
B. Moraxella catarrhalis
C. Legionella
D. Burkholderia cepacia

Q.262 A person working in an abattoir presented with a papule on hand, which turned into an ulcer. Which will best help in diagnosis?

A. Trichrome Methylene Blue
B. Carbol Fuschin
C. Acid Fast Stain
D. Calcofluor White

Q.263 A patient in an ICU is on a central venous line for the past week. He is on ceftazidime and amikacin. After 7 days of antibiotics, he develops a spike of fever and his blood culture is positive for gram-positive cocci in chains, which are catalase-negative. Following this vancomycin was started but the culture remained positive for the same organism even after 10 days of therapy. The most likely organism causing this infection is

A. Staphylococcus aureus A
B. Virdans streptococci
C. Enterococcus faecalis
D. Coagulase-negative staphylococcus

Q.264 A young male patient presented with UTI. On urine examination, pus cells were found but no organisms. Which method would be best used for culture?

A. Mc Coy culture
B. Thayer martin medium
C. LJ Medium
D. Levinthal Medium

Q.265 A child presents with infective skin lesions of the leg. Culture was done which showed gram-positive cocci in chains and hemolytic colonies. Which of the following tests will best identify the organism?

A. Bile solubility
B. Optochin sensitivity
C. Bacitracin sensitivity
D. Catalase positive

Q.266 In India, magistrate inquest is done in the following cases except:

A. Exhumation cases
B. Dowry deaths within 5 years of marriage
C. Murder cases
D. Death of a person in police custody

Q.267 Sparrow's footmarks are characteristic of?

A. Vitriolage
B. Windshield glass injury

C. Lightning strike
D. Stab injury

Q.268 A 34-year old rickshaw puller has been using heroin for the past ten years. One evening his family members found him unconscious. He was brought to the casualty. On examination, he had tachycardia, shallow breathing, constricted pupils. His blood pressure was 100/70 mm of Hg. He had brisk bilateral deep tendon reflexes. The plantar reflexes were flexor on both sides. Which of the following is the best treatment for him?

A. Buprenorphine **B.** Flumazenil
C. Methadone **D.** Naloxone

Q.269 A middle-aged man presents with paraesthesia of hand and feet. Examination reveals the presence of 'Mees' lines in the nails and raindrop pigmentation in the hands; The most likely causative toxin for the above-mentioned symptoms is :

A. Lead **B.** Arsenic **C.** Thallium **D.** Mercury

Q.270 In which of the following conditions, postmortem caloricity is seen?

A. Massive haemorrhage
B. Cyanide poisoning
C. Corrosive poisoning
D. Septicemia

Q.271 Deep blue colour of hypostasis is seen in death due to poisoning by

A. Potassium cyanide **B.** Phosphorus
C. Aniline dyes **D.** Carbon monoxide

Q.272 The cephalic index of the Indian population is between:

A. 70-75 **B.** 75-80 **C.** 80-85 **D.** 85-90

Q.273 Auto-Rikshaw ran over a child's thigh, there is a mark of the tyre tracks, it is an

A. Contact bruise **B.** Patterned bruise
C. Imprint abrasion **D.** Ectopic bruise

Q.274 In methyl alcohol poisoning there is CNS depression, cardiac depression and optic nerve atrophy. These effects are produced due to:

A. Formaldehyde and formic acid
B. Acetaldehyde
C. Pyridine
D. Acetic acid

Q.275 Mercury will affect which part of the renal tubule

A. PCT **B.** DCT
C. CT **D.** Loop of Henle

Q.276 Safe yield of a water supply source is the yield that is adequate for?

A. 80% of the year
B. 90% of the year
C. 95% of the year
D. The whole of the year

Q.277 Minimum depth for the lining of a sanitary well is?

A. 10 feet **B.** 20 feet **C.** 35 feet **D.** 50 feet

Q.278 Quantity of water available per capita considered adequate to meet the needs of all urban domestic purposes?

A. 100-150 L **B.** 150-200 L
C. 200-250 L **D.** 250-300 L

Q.279 Screening test specificity is the ability of a test to correctly identify:

A. False positives **B.** True positives
C. True negatives **D.** False negatives

Q.280 Non-deliberate cultural practice with the anti-mosquito effect is?

A. Use of mosquito repellents
B. Use of bed nets
C. Use of alkaline detergent for washing clothes
D. Use of larvicides

Q.281 A sewage worker with fever and jaundice presented to the emergency department. Lab investigations revealed increased blood urea nitrogen and serum creatinine – indicative of renal failure. Which of the following antibiotics is preferred in this patient?

A. Erythromycin **B.** Doxycycline
C. Penicillin G **D.** Ciprofloxacin

Q.282 Modes of disease transmission by vectors are all except?

A. Regurgitation
B. Biting
C. Ingestion
D. Rubbing of infected excrement

Q.283 JSY is an acronym for?

A. Janani Suraksha Yojana
B. Jeevan Suraksha Yojana
C. Jeevan Shakthi Yojana
D. Jan Suraksha Yojana

Q.284 Movement across socioeconomic levels is known as?

A. Social insurance **B.** Social mobility
C. Social equality **D.** Social upliftment

Q.285 The usefulness of a 'screening test' in a community depends on its :

A. Sensitivity **B.** Specificity
C. Reliability **D.** Predictive value

Q.286 "Five clean practices" under strategies for elimination of neonatal tetanus include all except :

A. Clean surface for delivery
B. Clean hand of the attendant
C. New blade for cutting the cord
D. Clean airway

Q.287 The following statements about breast milk are true except :

A. The maximum milk output is seen at 12 months
B. The coefficient of uptake of iron in breast milk is 70%
C. Calcium absorption of human milk is better than that of cow's milk
D. It provides about 65 kcals per 100 ml

Q.288 A 10-month-old child weighing 8kg has Bitot spots in both eyes. Which of the following is the most appropriate schedule to prescribe vitamin A to this child?

A. 2 lakh units intramuscular (IM) on day 0, 14
B. 1 lakh units IM on day 0, 14
C. 2 lakh units IM on day 0, 1 and 14
D. 1 lakh units IM on day O, 1 and 14

Q.289 All of the following are the mode of transmission of leprosy except?

A. Breast milk
B. Insect bite
C. Transplacental spread
D. Droplet infection

Q.290 According to International Health Regulations, there is no risk of spread of yellow Fever if the Aedes aegypti index remains below:

A. 1% B. 5% C. 8% D. 10%

Q.291 The following statements are true about DPT vaccine except:

A. Aluminium salt has an adjuvant effect
B. Whole killed bacteria of Bordetella pertussis has an adjuvant effect
C. Presence of acellular pertussis component increases its immunogenicity
D. Presence of H. influenzae type B component increases its immunogenicity

Q.292 A study began in 1970 with a group of 5000 adults in Delhi who were asked about their alcohol consumption. The occurrence of cancer was studied in this group between 1990-1995. This is an example of :

A. Cross-sectional study
B. Retrospective cohort study
C. Concurrent cohort study
D. Case-control study

Q.293 Which one of the following is not source of manager's power:

A. Reward B. Coercive
C. Legitimate D. Efferent

Q.294 Under the WHO 'Vision 2020'program. the 'SAFE' strategy is adopted for which of the following diseases?

A. Trachoma
B. Glaucoma
C. Diabetic retinopathy
D. Onchocerciasis

Q.295 Total cholesterol level = a + b (calorie intake) + c (physical activity) + d (body mass index); is an example of:

A. Simple linear regression
B. Simple curvilinear regression
C. Multiple linear regression
D. Multiple logistic regression

Q.296 The PEFR of a group of 11-year-old girls follow a normal distribution with a mean of 300 l/min and standard deviation of 20 l/min:

A. About 95% of the girls have PEFR between 260 and 340 l/min
B. The girls have healthy lungs
C. About 5% of girls have PEFR below 260 l/min
D. All the PEFR must be less than 340 l/min

Q.297 The following tests are used to check the efficiency of pasteurization of milk except:

A. Phosphatase test
B. Standard plate count
C. Coliform count
D. Methylene blue reduction test

Q.298 Which of the following viral infections is transmitted by tick?

A. Japanese encephalitis
B. Dengue fever
C. Kyasanur forest disease (KFD)
D. Yellow fever

Q.299 Which one of the following is a good index of the severity of an acute disease?

A. Cause specific death rate
B. Case fatality rate
C. Standardized mortality ratio
D. Five year survivial

Q.300 Eicosapentaenoic acid is present in

A. Soyabean oil B. Corn oil
C. Safflower oil D. Fish oil

// Smart Answer Sheet //

Correct Percentage of students who answered correctly. **Skipped** Percentage of students who skipped.

Q.	Ans.	Correct	Skipped	Q.	Ans.	Correct	Skipped	Q.	Ans.	Correct	Skipped	Q.	Ans.	Correct	Skipped	Q.	Ans.	Correct	Skipped	Q.	Ans.	Correct	Skipped
1	B	84.63 %	14.06 %	22	B	85.81 %	12.55 %	43	B	22.95 %	76.72 %	64	D	41.29 %	30.89 %	85	B	88.55 %	10.89 %	106	B	47.85 %	43.2 %
2	C	43.63 %	42.56 %	23	B	83.75 %	15.5 %	44	A	88.86 %	10.32 %	65	C	42.77 %	44.79 %	86	B	26.58 %	70.81 %	107	A	52.43 %	35.36 %
3	D	29.32 %	69.39 %	24	D	86.83 %	12.51 %	45	D	81.01 %	13.3 %	66	B	64.62 %	33.51 %	87	D	57.91 %	36.9 %	108	A	42.77 %	43.04 %
4	A	83.89 %	13.97 %	25	A	40.23 %	58.88 %	46	B	69.93 %	30.05 %	67	A	85.81 %	11.65 %	88	B	48.59 %	49.6 %	109	A	19.59 %	76.14 %
5	D	79.01 %	16.34 %	26	A	81.47 %	12.36 %	47	D	44.22 %	41.96 %	68	A	61.24 %	37.1 %	89	D	50.8 %	37.77 %	110	C	62.34 %	35.88 %
6	D	78.85 %	20.26 %	27	D	76.07 %	17.12 %	48	D	10.88 %	87.99 %	69	D	87.58 %	10.26 %	90	B	53.41 %	37.13 %	111	B	54.37 %	40.57 %
7	A	77.43 %	15.5 %	28	B	27.86 %	68.1 %	49	D	67.51 %	30.06 %	70	A	49.55 %	32.95 %	91	C	49.25 %	42.93 %	112	C	45.46 %	30.9 %
8	A	79.42 %	12.29 %	29	A	45.7 %	35.94 %	50	C	82.76 %	12.13 %	71	C	26.18 %	71.02 %	92	A	61.38 %	32.15 %	113	B	65.84 %	32.42 %
9	D	78.82 %	18.13 %	30	D	77.34 %	12.83 %	51	A	55.2 %	36.49 %	72	B	58.9 %	37.21 %	93	D	47.76 %	31.81 %	114	A	56.24 %	33.14 %
10	B	86.93 %	11.62 %	31	B	80.08 %	10.1 %	52	C	24.12 %	69.44 %	73	A	52.81 %	37.47 %	94	D	43.0 %	53.55 %	115	C	79.32 %	18.07 %
11	B	61.0 %	38.05 %	32	C	58.24 %	31.09 %	53	C	47.88 %	51.34 %	74	D	40.26 %	44.42 %	95	D	48.24 %	32.49 %	116	D	56.5 %	38.56 %
12	A	53.82 %	43.59 %	33	A	78.08 %	19.28 %	54	D	59.9 %	36.88 %	75	C	11.03 %	79.48 %	96	D	69.25 %	30.26 %	117	B	66.13 %	32.72 %
13	B	87.68 %	11.38 %	34	C	85.46 %	14.23 %	55	C	88.56 %	11.14 %	76	D	56.84 %	39.91 %	97	C	54.03 %	34.62 %	118	D	62.29 %	31.37 %
14	A	55.21 %	35.88 %	35	C	89.07 %	10.37 %	56	C	52.86 %	35.97 %	77	C	42.17 %	45.36 %	98	A	87.6 %	10.92 %	119	D	26.61 %	68.51 %
15	B	84.62 %	10.11 %	36	B	87.5 %	12.38 %	57	D	47.06 %	43.44 %	78	A	56.02 %	30.16 %	99	A	55.65 %	38.5 %	120	D	61.49 %	37.52 %
16	A	76.18 %	19.84 %	37	D	51.62 %	39.33 %	58	D	50.27 %	32.77 %	79	D	66.26 %	30.64 %	100	C	69.55 %	30.38 %	121	A	48.74 %	43.41 %
17	A	81.0 %	11.34 %	38	D	56.2 %	43.24 %	59	D	25.76 %	73.55 %	80	C	17.72 %	67.48 %	101	C	58.85 %	38.77 %	122	C	49.54 %	38.12 %
18	C	76.39 %	23.6 %	39	B	87.69 %	11.7 %	60	B	48.16 %	43.81 %	81	C	61.56 %	31.86 %	102	B	64.57 %	32.21 %	123	B	86.33 %	11.17 %
19	D	41.55 %	57.17 %	40	D	89.8 %	10.01 %	61	B	44.87 %	43.32 %	82	C	59.68 %	31.23 %	103	A	69.73 %	30.05 %	124	A	18.47 %	78.59 %
20	B	80.61 %	13.17 %	41	A	88.06 %	10.36 %	62	D	79.07 %	12.88 %	83	C	56.71 %	30.02 %	104	C	29.98 %	69.05 %	125	A	41.97 %	32.53 %
21	C	77.62 %	14.92 %	42	C	78.08 %	21.62 %	63	B	15.37 %	81.75 %	84	D	83.0 %	16.27 %	105	A	64.44 %	33.62 %	126	A	42.9 %	57.05 %

Q.	Ans.	Correct	Skipped	Q.	Ans.	Correct	Skipped	Q.	Ans.	Correct	Skipped	Q.	Ans.	Correct	Skipped	Q.	Ans.	Correct	Skipped	Q.	Ans.	Correct	Skipped
127	C	78.2 %	20.86 %	148	B	56.74 %	30.2 %	169	C	57.13 %	37.82 %	190	D	51.99 %	41.17 %	211	A	89.77 %	10.02 %	232	A	81.51 %	15.33 %
128	B	25.74 %	73.44 %	149	D	57.63 %	38.33 %	170	C	62.58 %	34.17 %	191	A	19.47 %	77.42 %	212	A	45.18 %	46.76 %	233	B	63.7 %	31.91 %
129	D	60.52 %	38.85 %	150	C	64.66 %	31.18 %	171	D	21.97 %	67.67 %	192	C	58.74 %	39.35 %	213	D	80.99 %	10.56 %	234	D	87.12 %	12.25 %
130	D	50.34 %	45.69 %	151	B	23.92 %	69.15 %	172	B	48.13 %	49.25 %	193	C	13.35 %	69.4 %	214	A	83.64 %	14.27 %	235	B	15.06 %	82.26 %
131	A	52.57 %	44.26 %	152	A	43.02 %	51.41 %	173	C	17.35 %	68.83 %	194	B	47.9 %	35.11 %	215	B	64.87 %	34.52 %	236	D	88.02 %	11.83 %
132	C	55.35 %	37.55 %	153	A	49.61 %	34.66 %	174	D	87.95 %	11.86 %	195	C	61.23 %	31.52 %	216	A	27.9 %	70.72 %	237	D	87.67 %	11.61 %
133	C	30.01 %	67.68 %	154	B	82.05 %	11.96 %	175	B	67.6 %	30.31 %	196	D	13.21 %	83.9 %	217	B	51.39 %	31.88 %	238	B	83.94 %	13.26 %
134	D	76.75 %	14.8 %	155	C	45.43 %	30.43 %	176	C	44.2 %	34.3 %	197	A	83.89 %	13.79 %	218	D	83.66 %	13.05 %	239	A	81.87 %	13.86 %
135	D	40.11 %	53.11 %	156	C	62.69 %	36.06 %	177	C	43.72 %	36.9 %	198	C	45.43 %	31.21 %	219	A	80.13 %	18.17 %	240	D	79.52 %	14.19 %
136	C	59.18 %	40.47 %	157	A	14.97 %	79.08 %	178	A	58.01 %	41.46 %	199	C	64.64 %	34.06 %	220	B	58.57 %	40.04 %	241	A	24.15 %	71.05 %
137	D	57.21 %	40.42 %	158	A	57.09 %	42.3 %	179	A	21.23 %	74.92 %	200	A	62.21 %	35.55 %	221	A	61.33 %	37.11 %	242	B	16.36 %	73.18 %
138	D	41.49 %	39.23 %	159	A	69.93 %	30.01 %	180	D	55.22 %	34.62 %	201	A	85.77 %	12.15 %	222	A	43.83 %	54.8 %	243	A	86.51 %	11.19 %
139	B	81.8 %	17.34 %	160	D	55.84 %	32.44 %	181	A	47.26 %	47.17 %	202	C	82.44 %	16.14 %	223	C	21.52 %	73.32 %	244	C	18.45 %	78.1 %
140	A	68.29 %	31.4 %	161	B	81.15 %	18.37 %	182	D	19.08 %	69.66 %	203	D	81.17 %	11.64 %	224	A	87.01 %	10.85 %	245	C	81.65 %	18.1 %
141	A	13.82 %	79.17 %	162	A	20.4 %	70.98 %	183	C	57.26 %	37.83 %	204	B	60.66 %	32.88 %	225	D	65.97 %	32.3 %	246	C	88.51 %	11.22 %
142	D	48.2 %	31.0 %	163	B	57.58 %	33.37 %	184	B	56.1 %	36.39 %	205	C	77.13 %	10.37 %	226	C	87.81 %	11.6 %	247	A	77.59 %	22.28 %
143	D	40.85 %	55.62 %	164	D	46.61 %	42.62 %	185	B	61.99 %	35.67 %	206	D	89.65 %	10.17 %	227	C	84.99 %	10.27 %	248	C	86.92 %	12.18 %
144	C	40.01 %	46.33 %	165	B	28.26 %	68.86 %	186	A	44.86 %	32.07 %	207	C	79.53 %	14.63 %	228	A	79.64 %	10.37 %	249	D	15.31 %	67.78 %
145	C	56.07 %	33.02 %	166	A	62.03 %	35.58 %	187	A	69.35 %	30.34 %	208	C	54.49 %	36.01 %	229	C	83.12 %	10.24 %	250	C	87.3 %	10.11 %
146	C	30.65 %	68.38 %	167	B	40.72 %	44.98 %	188	D	46.64 %	32.02 %	209	A	79.64 %	18.81 %	230	A	19.45 %	68.54 %	251	D	11.92 %	74.07 %
147	C	47.25 %	35.68 %	168	B	32.63 %	67.15 %	189	A	84.29 %	12.04 %	210	B	82.52 %	14.52 %	231	D	83.99 %	11.01 %	252	C	65.24 %	33.36 %

Q.	Ans.	Correct	Skipped	Q.	Ans.	Correct	Skipped	Q.	Ans.	Correct	Skipped	Q.	Ans.	Correct	Skipped	Q.	Ans.	Correct	Skipped	Q.	Ans.	Correct	Skipped
253	B	27.17 %	69.51 %	261	C	78.21 %	13.16 %	269	B	83.7 %	14.54 %	277	B	49.17 %	34.2 %	285	A	78.49 %	14.39 %	293	D	54.59 %	41.57 %
254	A	81.09 %	15.25 %	262	A	76.72 %	18.89 %	270	D	63.52 %	30.15 %	278	B	50.76 %	41.18 %	286	D	63.5 %	32.77 %	294	A	40.07 %	46.52 %
255	D	79.27 %	19.34 %	263	C	43.52 %	52.21 %	271	C	67.29 %	32.62 %	279	C	69.9 %	30.03 %	287	A	80.83 %	16.7 %	295	C	62.0 %	35.42 %
256	A	77.93 %	11.78 %	264	A	49.54 %	34.5 %	272	A	66.04 %	31.63 %	280	C	21.04 %	77.15 %	288	D	58.37 %	39.89 %	296	A	57.64 %	39.88 %
257	A	63.97 %	32.64 %	265	C	63.19 %	36.67 %	273	C	85.47 %	12.15 %	281	C	57.01 %	39.95 %	289	C	89.24 %	10.71 %	297	D	86.57 %	10.35 %
258	C	46.48 %	34.05 %	266	C	40.64 %	54.09 %	274	A	79.89 %	17.51 %	282	C	82.87 %	16.38 %	290	A	63.41 %	31.23 %	298	C	41.66 %	51.22 %
259	B	52.89 %	42.55 %	267	B	60.03 %	37.53 %	275	A	77.24 %	18.21 %	283	A	30.12 %	67.65 %	291	D	57.17 %	36.87 %	299	B	89.48 %	10.0 %
260	D	89.84 %	10.06 %	268	D	68.47 %	31.16 %	276	C	66.13 %	31.24 %	284	B	56.22 %	32.03 %	292	C	28.03 %	69.35 %	300	D	63.99 %	35.44 %

//Hints and Solutions//

1.

- Alport syndrome is caused by a mutation in the collagen genes COL4A3 and COL4A6.
- Epidermolysis bullosa dystrophic is due to mutation in the collagen gene COL7A1.
- Osteogenesis imperfecta is caused by mutations in COL1A1 and COL1A2.

Hence the correct option is (B).

2.

- DNA ligase is used for the joining of DNA molecules.
- DNA polymerase I is used for the synthesis of double-stranded cDNA.
- Polynucleotide kinase is used for T-32 end-labeling of DNA or RNA.

Hence, the correct option is (C).

3.

- Argininosuccinicaciduria is caused by metabolic defects in argininosuccinase.
- Hyperammonemia type II is due to a defect in ornithine transcarbamoylase.
- Hyperargininemia is an autosomal recessive disorder characterized by a defect in the gene for arginase.

Hence, the correct option is (D).

4.

- The peroxisome is an organelle involved in the metabolism of many molecules including fatty acids, purines, and amino acids.
- It is bounded by a single membrane and contains more than 50 enzymes.
- Pfeiffer syndrome is due to mutations in the gene encoding fibroblast growth factor receptor 1 (FGR1).
- It is a craniosynostosis syndrome.

Hence, the correct option is (A).

5.

- Ketone bodies - Rothera's test
- Reducing sugars - Benedict's test, Fehling's test
- Proteins - Heller's nitric acid test, Heat, and acetic acid test
- Bile salts - Hay's test
- Bile pigments - Fouchet's test
- Blood - Benzidine test

Hence, the correct option is (D).

6. Sphingomyelinase deficiency is seen in Niemann Pick disease. The enzymes deficient in the other disease are:

- Fabry disease – alpha-galactosidase
- Krabbe's disease – beta-galactosidase
- Tay Sachs disease – Hexosaminidase A

Hence, the correct option is (D).

7. Nonenzymatic glycosylation or glycation creates glycoproteins by the chemical addition of sugars to polypeptides. Since this type of glycosylation is nonenzymatic, the time and the concentration of sugar control glycosylation. Because people with higher circulating levels of glucose have higher levels of nonenzymatic glycosylation, measurement of the glycosylated hemoglobin A1c is a diagnostic test used to monitor blood sugar levels in persons with diabetes.

Hence, the correct option is (A).

8.

- Carboxin inhibits the transfer of ions from FADH2.
- Oligomycin, Valinomycin, and Atractyloside are inhibitors of oxidative phosphorylation.
- Oligomycin inhibits the flow of protons through Fo.
- Valinomycin is an ionophore that inhibits oxidative phosphorylation.
- Atractyloside inhibits translocase.

Hence, the correct option is (A).

9. Ubiquitin targets proteins (newly synthesised abnormal proteins and old proteins) for destruction.

Hence, the correct option is (D).

10. Expression vectors are plasmids / viruses designed to regulate protein expression in a target cell.

They are used to insert a specific gene into the target cell to produce the desired protein.

They contain regulatory sequences which act as enhancer and promoter regions to bring about efficient transcription of the gene.

An inducible promoter regulates the gene expression and can increase the yield of the recombinant protein.

Hence, the correct option is (B).

11. Important structural proteins are collagen, keratin, myosin, etc. They are fibrous proteins.

Collagen is the major insoluble fibrous protein in the extracellular matrix and in connective tissue. In fact, it is the single most abundant protein in the animal kingdom. The various collagens and the structures they form all serve the same purpose, to help tissues withstand stretching.

Hence, the correct option is (B).

12. There are nine essential amino acids, which you must get through your diet: histidine, isoleucine, leucine, lysine, methionine, phenylalanine, threonine, tryptophan and valine. Food proteins lacking one or more of the essential amino acids can maintain life, but cannot support growth. These foods are known as incomplete proteins, or inadequate proteins. Some examples of food containing incomplete proteins are gelatin, corn, and most flours.

Hence, the correct option is (A).

13. Localisation of CPK isoenzymes

CPK 1 (CPK BB) – Brain

CPK 2 (CPK MB) – Myocardium

CPK 3 (CPK MM) – Skeletal muscle

Hence, the correct option is (B).

14. Inositol triphosphate (IP3) and diacylglycerol (DAG) are second messengers for G protein coupled receptors. IP3 stimulates release of calcium from endoplasmic reticulum. DAG activates protein kinase C.

Hence, the correct option is (A).

15. A stretch of hydrophobic amino acids Cell membrane has a lipid core. Hence the transmembrane region of proteins contain hydrophobic amino acids. The ends of transmembrane proteins contain hydrophilic amino acids.

Hence, the correct option is (B).

16. Shine Dalgarno sequence is important in the initiation of translation. It is sequence of bases (5'-UAGGAGG-3') which is located 6-10 bases upstream of the AUG codon in mRNA.

Hence, the correct option is (A).

17. An ulnar claw, also known as claw hand, or spinster's claw is a deformity or an abnormal attitude of the hand that develops due to ulnar nerve damage causing paralysis of the lumbricals. Cervical spondylosis, ulnar nerve palsy, and ulnar nerve entrapment are all conditions that can cause nerve damage leading to claw hand.

Abnormal wear of the cartilage or bone in your spine can cause compression on your nerves, which can also lead to claw hand.

Hence, the correct option is (A).

18. The posterior interosseous nerve, also known as the dorsal interosseous nerve, is the continuation of the deep branch of the radial nerve after it penetrates the supinator muscle. The posterior interosseous nerve is a motor nerve and sequentially innervates supinator, extensor carpi radialis brevis, extensor digitorum communis, extensor digiti minimi, extensor carpi ulnaris, abductor pollicis, extensor pollicis brevis, extensor pollicis longus, and extensor indicis.

Hence, the correct option is (C).

19. Supinator muscle rotates the radius laterally at the proximal radioulnar joint. Note that biceps brachii cannot act as a supinator when the forearm is fully extended, so the most powerful supination occurs when the elbow joint is flexed to 90 degrees.

The biceps brachii is the primary and most powerful supinator of the flexed forearm; the supinator muscle supinates the forearm in the absence of resistance.

Hence, the correct option is (D).

20. Hyaline cartilage locations include around bones of free-moving joints. This is known as articular cartilage. Another example of hyaline cartilage is the tissue found in the walls of the respiratory tract. This includes the bronchi, the nose, the rings of the trachea, and the tips of the ribs.

Hence, the correct option is (B).

21. Single-unit smooth muscle, or visceral smooth muscle is a type of smooth muscle found in the uterus, gastro-intestinal tract, and the bladder. In SUVSM, a single smooth muscle cell in a bundle is innervated by an autonomic nerve fiber. Single-unit muscle has its muscle fibers joined by gap junctions so that the muscle contracts as a single unit.

Hence, the correct option is (C).

22. The ends of diaphysis near the epiphyses are known as metaphyses. Each metaphysis is the zone of active growth of a long bone. The metaphyses are richly supplied with blood through end arteries forming hair pin bends. This is the common site of osteomyelitis in children.

Hence, the correct option is (B).

23. Compact bone consists of closely packed osteons or haversian systems. The osteon consists of a central canal called the osteonic (haversian) canal, which is surrounded by concentric rings (lamellae) of matrix. Between the rings of matrix, the bone cells (osteocytes) are located in spaces called lacunae.

Hence, the correct option is (B).

24. From superficial to deep, the layers of the scalp are (mnemonic: SCALP)

S – Skin

C – Connective tissue (fibrofatty)

A – Aponeurosis (Epicranial Aponeurosis)

L – Loose areolar tissue (Danger area of scalp)

P – Periosteum

Hence, the correct option is (D).

25. Thigh adduction is performed by adductor muscles (magnus, longus, brevis) with gracilis and pectineus acting as accessory muscles. None of them are supplied by L5 nerve root.

Hence, the correct option is (A).

26. Couinaud's segmental nomenclature is based on position of hepatic veins and portal vein. It is the French system.

Hence, the correct option is (A).

27. Costochondral joints are primary cartilaginous joints / synchondrosis / hyaline cartilage joint. The costochondral joints are the joints between each rib and its costal cartilage. They are primary cartilaginous joints. These joints represent the demarcation of the unossified and ossified part of the rib.

Hence, the correct option is (D).

28. Raise the arm above the head on the affected side

Long thoracic nerve (Nerve of Bell) supplies the serratus anterior muscle.

Serratus anterior rotates the inferior angle of scapula laterally during abduction of the arm above the head – hence it is impaired in injury to long thoracic nerve.

Winging of scapula is another classical feature of long thoracic nerve injury.

Hence, the correct option is (B).

29. An foreign body is more likely to get lodged in the right lung as the right bronchus is wider, shorter and more vertical.

Hence, the correct option is (A).

30. Chorda tympani nerve contains preganglionic parasympathetic fibers. It synapses in the submandibular ganglion.

Hence, the correct option is (D).

31. The superior oblique muscle, or obliquus oculi superior, is a fusiform muscle originating in the upper, medial side of the orbit (i.e. from beside the nose) which abducts, depresses and internally rotates the eye. It is the only extraocular muscle innervated by the trochlear nerve (the fourth cranial nerve).

Hence, the correct option is (B).

32. The median lobe of the prostate is prone to the development of BPH. The posterior lobe of the prostate is prone to the development of malignancy. Benign prostatic hyperplasia (BPH) also called prostate gland enlargement is a common condition as men get older. An enlarged prostate gland can cause uncomfortable urinary symptoms, such as blocking the flow of urine out of the bladder.

Hence, the correct option is (C).

33. The intercostal neurovascular bundle lies along the lower boder of the rib. Hence we should introduce the needle along the upper border of rib to prevent damage to the neurovascular bundle.

Hence, the correct option is (A).

34. Cyanide poisoning is a form of histotoxic hypoxia because the cells of an organism are unable to use oxygen, primarily through the inhibition of cytochrome c oxidase enzyme. Cyanide causes intracellular hypoxia by reversibly binding to mitochondrial cytochrome oxidase. Signs and symptoms of cyanide poisoning usually occur less than 1 minute after inhalation and within a few minutes after ingestion.

Hence, the correct option is (C).

35. The reserve volume is the amount of air that remains in the lungs and passageways after a maximal expiration. Vital capacity is the total of the tidal volume, inspiratory reserve volume, and expiratory reserve volume. In a normal healthy adult lung, the vital capacity usually ranges from 3.5 to 5.5 L of air.

Hence, the correct option is (C).

36.

- When light energy is absorbed by rhodopsin, photoactivation of electrons in the retinal portion of rhodopsin leads to the change of cis form of retinal into the all trans form.
- The first stage in the reformation of rhodopsin is to reconvert the alltrans retinal into 11 cis retinal.
- This process is catalysed by the enzyme – retinal isomerase.

Hence, the correct option is (B).

37.

- Inhibin is secreted by the sertoli cells in males and by the granulosa cells in females.
- It inhibits the secretion of Gonadotrophin Releasing Hormone.
- It is a glycoprotein with molecular weight between 10,000 and 30,000.
- It has potent inhibitory feedback effect on the anterior pituitary gland which in turn provides negative feedback mechanism for the control of spermatogenesis.

Hence, the correct option is (D).

38.

- Juxtamedullary nephrons comprise 14-15% of nephrons in the kidney.
- They have large-sized glomeruli which are situated at the junction of the cortex and medulla of the kidney. The rate of filtration is high.
- They have long loops of Henle which penetrate into the medulla.
- Their Henle loops manifest vascular supply in the form of vasa recta.
- Both descending and ascending limbs of the loop of Henle contain thin segments. (In cortical nephrons, descending limb contains a thin segment whereas the ascending limb contains a thick segment.

Hence, the correct option is (D).

39.

- Somatomedin increases glucose oxidation in fat.
- Activity of somatomedin is reduced by protein deficiency and glucocorticoids.
- It has insulin like effect on tissues and causes lipolysis and increased glucose and amino acid transport by muscle.

Hence, the correct option is (B).

40. Parathormone increases bone resorption while calcitonin inhibits it.

Calcitonin reduces calcium and phosphate absorption from GIT and inhibits the renal formation of 1-25 DHCC.

Hence, the correct option is (D).

41. Sweating & Shivering is one of the techniques by the means by which organisms maintain homeostasis through the regulation process.

- Homeostasis is a condition of optimal functioning of steady internal, physical, and chemical conditions maintained by living systems.
- It refers to stability, balance, or equilibrium within a cell or the body and an organism can keep a constant internal environment.
- Homeostasis is an important characteristic of living things which means the adjusting of systems within a cell because keeping a stable internal environment requires constant adjustments as conditions change inside and outside the cell.

Hence, the correct option is (A).

42.

- Axonemal dynein oscillates and is responsible for the beating of flagella and cilia.
- Cytoplasmic dynein moves particles to the 'minus' end of microtubule.
- Kinesin moves particles towards 'plus' end of microtubule.
- Myosin II binds to actin and produce motion by bending their neck region.

Hence, the correct option is (C).

43.

- Nitric oxide (NO) is produced by the action of Nitric Oxide Synthase (NOS) on L-arginine.
- It acts as an inhibitory neurotransmitter in the gastrointestinal system (other inhibitory neurotransmitters are VIP and PACAP).
- It does not have a membrane-bound receptor.
- It diffuses into the target cells and activates guanyl cyclase.
- Activated guanyl cyclase produces cGMP from GTP.
- cGMP in turn mediates smooth muscle relaxation.

Hence, the correct option is (B).

44. Pulmonary compliance is increased in emphysema (a type of chronic obstructive pulmonary disease). In the other 3 conditions (Decreased surfactant production, Pulmonary congestion and Pulmonary fibrosis), the pulmonary compliance is decreased.

Hence, the correct option is (A).

45. Siggard Andersen normogram helps to predict the acid base status of blood. PCO2 is plotted in the Y axis and pH in the X axis.

Hence, the correct option is (D).

46. Atrio-ventricular valves close at the end of diastole.

Semilunar valves open at the end of isovolumetric contraction phase.

Semilunar valves close at the end of systole.

Atrio-ventricular valves open at the end of isovolumetric relaxation phase.

Hence, the correct option is (B).

47. Edema is due to increase in capillary hydrostatic pressure or decrease in plasma oncotic pressure. Acute cardiac failure is usually due to decrease in cardiac output and hypotension. Capillary hydrostatic pressure falls and hence edema is not seen.

Hence, the correct option is (D).

48. During acclimatization, there is shift of oxygen dissociation curve to the right.This improves oxygen release into tissues.

Hence, the correct option is (D).

49. Neuropraxia is characterized by physiological disruption in conduction. Neurapraxia is a relatively mild type of nerve injury, and it's fairly common. It's often the result of trauma to the body, such as a hard blow to the neck, shoulders, or back. It usually feels like a stinging or burning sensation. Depending on which nerve is affected, there is weakness as well.

Hence, the correct option is (D).

50. Fibers from contralateral nasal hemiretina project to layers 1, 4 & 6 of the lateral geniculate body.Fibers from ipsilateral temporal hemiretina project to layers 2, 3 & 5 of the lateral geniculate body.

Hence, the correct option is (C).

51.

- Any malignant tumour can metastasise to spinal columns, particularly tumours of breast, lung, prostate, kidney, lymphoma and myeloma.
- The most common site is the thoracic spinal column.
- Most neoplasms are epidural in origin, resulting from metastases to adjacent vertebral body.
- Unlike infections of the spinal column, the tumours do not cross the disk space.

Hence, the correct option is (A).

52.

- Bell's palsy is the most common form of facial paralysis.
- It has abrupt onset.
- The paralysis is usually preceded by pain behind the ear.
- Maximum weakness occurs by 48 hours.
- MRI may show swelling and uniform enhancement of geniculate ganglion and facial nerve.

Hence, the correct option is (C).

53. There are two types of hereditary ataxia associated with abnormalities of Vitamin E.

- Abetalipoproteinemia – Impairment of formation and secretion of VLDL in liver resulting in deficiency of deliveryof Vitamin E to tissues including central and peripheral nervous system.
- Ataxia with Vitamin E deficiency (AVED) – Impaired binding of Vitamin E to VLDL, resulting in deficiency of Vitamin E inperipheral tissues.

Hence, the correct option is (C).

54.

- Kayser Fleischer Ring is the result of copper deposition in Descemet's membrane around the cornea.
- It appears as a grayish ring at the limbus.
- It is seen in 80% of patients with Wilson's disease presenting with hepatic dysfunction and in 100% of those with neurologic features.
- Hence slit lamp examination is essential for diagnosis of Wilson's disease presenting with neurologic abnormalities.
- Usual neurologic manifestations in Wilson's disease include tremor that has wing beating character in advanced stages, rigidity, dystonia, dysarthria and dysphagia.
- History of psychiatric disturbances like depression and mood swingsare seen in more than half of those with neurologic features.

Hence, the correct option is (D).

55. Basal crepitations are seen in left heart failure. Other findings in right heart failure are right ventricular third heart sound (heard at left sternal edge, better in inspiration), wide splitting of second heart sound (due to prolonged right ventricular ejection and delay in pulmonary component or P2) and peripheral edema.

Hence, the correct option is (C).

56. Riociguat a soluble guanylate cyclase stimulator. It is the only therapy approved by USFDA for inoperable CTEPH (Chronic thromboembolic pulmonary hypertension). Best treatment for operable cases is pulmonary thromboendarterectomy done in expert centres.

Hence, the correct option is (C).

57. Syndrome Z is a combination of obstructive sleep apnoea and metabolic syndrome. Metabolic syndrome is diagnosed if any three of the following conditions are met:1. Fasting plasma glucose level > 100mg/dl2. Blood pressure > 130/85 mm Hg3. Fasting triglyceride level > 150mg/dl4. HDL cholesterol level < 40mg /dl (men) and < 50mg/dl (women) 5. Waist circumference > 102cm (men) and > 88cm (women).

Hence, the correct option is (D).

58.

- Though hypertension is the most common cause of intracerebral hemorrhage, the usual site for it is putamen, thalamus, pons and cerebellum.
- But lobar hemorrhage in elderly is most commonly due to cerebral amyloid angiopathy, where there is amyloid deposition in the walls of cerebral arteries following arteriolar degeneration.

Hence, the correct option is (D).

59.

- Most common infection preceding bone marrow failure syndrome is hepatitis.
- It is usually sero negative (non-A, non- B, non – C).
- It accounts for 5% of etiologies.
- Parvo virus can cause pure red cell aplasia, but it doesn't usually cause generalised bone marrow failure.

Hence, the correct option is (D).

60.

- Qualitative assessment of M component is done by immune electrophoresis.
- Electrophoresis is used for quantitative assessment of M component.
- M component can also be detected in other lymphoid malignancies, CML, Can breast, colon cancer , non neoplastic condition like cirrhosis, sarcoidosis, rheumatoid arthritis, myasthenia gravis.

Hence, the correct option is (B).

61. Giant cell arteritis (temporal arteritis) is a chronic vasculitis of large and medium vessel arteries, usually affecting the cranial branches of arteries arising from aortic arch.

Jaw claudication is an underreported, yet, a very specific symptom of GCA, with a high positive predictive value.

Hence, the correct option is (B).

62.

- Polyarteritis nodosa is a mulisystem, necrotizing vasculitis of small and medium sized muscular arteries.
- It is characterised by the involvement of renal and visceral arteries.
- Pulmonary arteries are not involved in PAN, although rarely bronchial vessels may be involved.

Hence, the correct option is (D).

63.

- Scrub typhus is caused by Rickettsia tsutsugamushi.
- In severe scrub typhus, the patient develops apathy and prostration.
- Erythematous maculopapular rash appears between 5th and 7th dayinvolving trunk, face and limbs.
- The patient also develops generalised painless lymphadenopathy.

Hence, the correct option is (B).

64.

- Bartonellosis is a group of diseases caused by intracellular gram negative bacilli.
- Bacillary angiomatosis is an HIV associated disease caused by Bartonella henselae.
- It can also be caused by Bartonella quintana.

Hence, the correct option is (D).

65.

- The use of thymidine analogue NRTI stavudine is associated with lipoatrophy.
- When lipoatrophy occurs, therapy should be switched to non thymidine NRTI like abacavir or tenofovir.
- This will result in gradual resolution of lipoatrophy.

Hence, the correct option is (C).

66.

- Andersen disease is a type 4 glycogen storage disease.
- It occurs due to deficiency of brancher enzyme.
- It usually presents in infancy with severe muscle weakness.
- Cirrhosis can also occur.

Hence, the correct option is (B).

67.

- Causes of protein losing enteropathy with mucosal erosion are Crohn's disease, ulcerative colitis, radiation damage and lymphoma.
- Coeliac disease, Menetrier's disease and systemic lupus erythematosus can cause protein losing enteropathy without mucosal erosion.

Hence, the correct option is (A).

68.

- Serum transaminase level in hepatitis C is not a good predictor of the level of liver fibrosis
- A liver biopsy is required to assess the degree of liver damage.
- There is 3% risk for acquisition of chronic hepatitis C by vertical transmission.
- Sharing of toothbrushes and razors is another risk factor.

Hence, th correct option is (A).

69.

- Asymmetrical inflammatory oligoarthritis in seen in psoriatic arthritis.
- It occurs mostly in hands and feet.
- Synovitis of the finger or toe along with tenosynovitis, enthesitis and inflammation of the intervening tissue causes sausage digits.

Hence, the correct option is (D).

70.

- Ehrlichiosis is a tick borne bacterial infection.
- It is caused by bacteria such as Anaplasma phagocytophilum and Ehrlichia chaffeensis.
- It is a common coinfection with a lyme disease.

Hence, the correct option is (A).

71.

- Churg-Strauss syndrome is a small vessel vasculitis.
- The acute presentation includes skin lesions, eosinophilia and asymmetric mononeuritis multiplex.
- There can be a prodromal period lasting many years in which the patient can have allergic rhinitis, nasal polyposis and asthma.
- Treatment is by high dose steroids and cyclophosphamide.
- Maintenance therapy is by low dose steroids, azathioprine, methotrexate and mycophenolate mofetil.

Hence, the correct option is (C).

72.

- Scheuermann's osteochondritis has autosomal dominant inheritance.
- It commonly affects adolescent boys.
- It is characterised by irregular ossification of vertebral endplates and dorsal kyphosis.
- Most patients are asymptomatic.
- It can present with backache which is aggravated by exercise.
- Management is by protective postural exercises with avoidance of excessive activity.

Hence, the correct option is (B).

73.

- Mature osteoclasts attach to bone and form a tight sealing zone.
- They secrete hydrochloric acid and proteolytic enzymes like cathepsin K.
- HCl is involved in digestion of bone minerals.
- Cathepsin K is responsible for degradation of collagen.
- Sclerostin (SOST) is a glycoprotein produced by osteocytes which inhibits bone formation.

Hence, the correct option is (A).

74.

- Collagen fibrils in bone are cross-linked with pyridinium.
- It increases bone strength.
- During bone resorption by osteoclasts, these cross-links are released.
- They act as biochemical markers of bone resorption.
- Pyridinium cross-links can be detected in urine.

Hence, the correct option is (D).

75.

- Most abundant protein of bone is type 1 collagen.
- It is a triple helix formed by two $\alpha1$ peptide chains and one $\alpha2$ peptide chain.

Hence, the corerct option is (C).

76.

- Interleukin 1 stimulates bone resorption and inhibits bone formation.
- Osteoprotegerin is glycoprotein which acts as a decoy receptor for receptor activator of nuclear factor kappa B ligand (RANKL).
- It prevents RANKL induced osteoclastic bone resorption. It is produced by osteoblasts.
- Oestrogen, testosterone and mechanical loading inhibit bone resorption and stimulate bone formation.

Hence, the correct option is (D).

77.

- Osteoprotegerin is glycoprotein which acts as a decoy receptor for receptor activator of nuclear factor kappa B ligand (RANKL).
- It prevents RANKL induced conversion of osteoclast precursors to osteoclasts.
- It is produced by osteoblasts.
- All the other factors mentioned increase bone resorption.

Hence, the correct option is (C).

78.

- Sclerostin (SOST) is a glycoprotein produced by osteocytes.
- They also synthesize receptor activator of nuclear factor kappa B ligand (RANKL).
- Both of these are involved in regulating bone formation and resorption.

Hence, the correct option is (A).

79. Osteoarthritis is the most common form of arthritis. It affects up to 80% of individuals older than 75 years.

Hence, the correct option is (D).

80.

- Seronegative spondyloarthritis has a male : female ratio of 1:1.
- Rheumatoid arthritis and Polymyalgia rheumatica are seen more commonly in females.
- Gout is more common in males.

Hence, the correct option is (C).

81. Churg Strauss Syndrome

- Churg Strauss Syndrome is a small vessel vasculitis.
- Biopsy of the affected site reveals small vessel vasculitis with eosinophilic infiltration of vessel wall.

Cryoglobulinemic vasculitis

- Cryoglobulinemic vasculitis presents with rash over lower limbs, arthralgia, Raynaud's phenomenon and neuropathy.

Polyarteritis nodosa.

- Polyarteritis nodosa presents with fever, myalgia, arthralgia, multisystem involvement and palpable purpura.

Giant cell arteritis

- Cardinal symptom of giant cell arteritis is headache localized to the temporal or occipital region.
- Visual disturbances can occur.
- Catastrophic presentation is with blindness in one eye.
- It is commonly associated with polymyalgia rheumatica.

Hence, the correct option is (C).

82. NOTCH1 mutation can cause severe valvular calcification which can be transmitted in an autosomal dominant pattern. KCNH2 and KCNQ1 are potassium channel genes, mutations of which are seen in long QT syndrome. SCN5A is a sodium channel gene which is mutated in long QT 3 and Brugada syndrome.

Hence, the correct option is (C).

83. In complete heart block the atria and ventricle are totally dissociated. Hence PR interval is totally varying. Constant PR interval would mean sequential atrioventricular activation, which is absent in complete heart block.

Hence, the correct option is (C).

84. In systole, when the ventricle contracts, the mitral annulus also contracts, reducing the mitral annular area by about 25%. This is important in preventing mitral regurgitation in systole. When the left ventricle is dilated, with associated annular dilatation, even in the absence of valvular damage, mitral regurgitation can occur. Similarly, when the left ventricular systolic function is poor, the decrease in a mitral annular area with systole is reduced, paving the way for mitral regurgitation.

Hence, the correct option is (D).

85.

- Crux is the junction of the interventricular and atrioventricular grooves posteriorly.
- The dominant artery crosses the crux and supplies the opposite side.
- If right coronary artery is dominant, it crosses the crux and supplies posterior left ventricular branches.
- If left coronary artery is dominant, it crosses the crux and also gives rise to the left posterior descending artery (LPDA).
- In right dominant system, it is the right coronary artery which gives rise to the posterior descending coronary artery (PDA).
- Sometimes the arteries may be codominant.
- It may be noted that regardless of the anatomical dominance of the coronary arteries, it is always the left coronary artery which supplies the major portion of the left ventricular myocardium (and also the total myocardium as right ventricular myocardial mass is quite low compared to that of left ventricle).
- If the right coronary artery is non dominant, lesions in the non dominant artery are ignored from the point of view of coronary revascularization procedures like percutaneous coronary angioplasty.

Hence, the correct option is (B).

86.

- It is used to detect left ventricular hypertrophy (LVH) using an ECG.
- In a case of LVH, the amplitude of the S wave is increased in right oriented leads (like V1) and that of the R wave is increased in left oriented leads (like V5 and V6).
- LVH is said to be present if:

1. S wave in V1 + R wave in lead V5 or V6 > 3.5 mV or
2. R wave in V5 or V6 > 2.6 mV

- It is one of the simplest ECG criteria for the detection of left ventricular hypertrophy.
- As it is solely dependent on ECG voltages, it can produce erroneous results in certain conditions.
- In obese patients, the voltages will be less even in the presence of LVH.
- Similarly, in thin patients, the voltages will be higher even if they don't have LVH.
- Other factors which modify the lead voltages can also influence the calculation.

Hence, the correct option is (B).

87.

- Mitral stenosis is associated with the development of pulmonary hypertension
- When the severity of pulmonary venous hypertension increases, there is a redistribution of pulmonary blood flow towards the upper lobes.
- This is known as cephalization.

- It is also known as 'Antler sign' and 'Upturned moustache sign'.
- A shadow of the left atrium is seen overlying the right atrium – shadow in shadow sign / double atrial shadow.
- Left atrial dilatation leads to straightening of the left heart border and elevation of the left main bronchus.
- The pulmonary arteries are prominent due to pulmonary arterial hypertension
- Kerley B lines may be seen near the costophrenic angles due to thickened interlobular septa
- The right heart border can be shifted to the right indicating right atrial dilatation secondary to pulmonary hypertension and right ventricular hypertrophy.

Hence, the correct option is (D).

88.

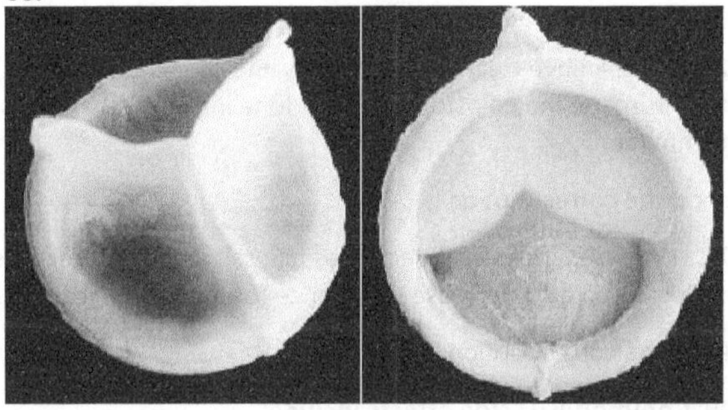

It would be better to implant a mechanical prosthetic valve in an adult male because of the longer projected longevity of the individual and higher chance of degeneration of a bioprosthetic valve due to higher hemodynamic trauma.

Bioprosthetic Heart Valves (Tissue Valves)

- They are heart valves obtained from animals which undergo chemical procedures to make them suitable for implantation in the human heart.
- Porcine valves are the commonly used tissue valves (As the pig heart is the most similar to the human heart).

Advantages:

- Bioprosthetic valves do not require anticoagulant therapy after the valve gets endothelialized (about 3 months).
- In contrast, a mechanical valve requires lifelong anticoagulant therapy.

Disadvantages:

- They have a higher rate of degeneration due to hemodynamic trauma and therefore have a lower projected longevity.

Hence, the correct option is (B).

89.

- Subxiphoid route is used for pericardiocentesis in most cases.
- Earlier apical route was also used for pericardiocentesis.
- But the apical route is seldom used nowadays for fear of injury to coronary arteries (Left anterior descending coronary artery is likely to be injured by the apical route of pericardiocentesis).

Hence, the correct option is (D).

90. Acute aortic syndromes are of 3 types:

1. Aortic dissection
2. Aortic intramural hematoma
3. Penetrating ulcer of the aorta.

- They are an important differential diagnosis of acute coronary syndrome.
- They are characterised by intense tearing pain, the location of which depends on the underlying lesion
- In case of involvement of the ascending aorta, pain is felt in the anterior aspect of thorax and neck
- Pain in the back or the abdomen is seen in involvement of the descending aorta
- Acute aortic syndromes are seen in association with hypertension and collagen vascular disorders like Marfan syndrome

Hence, the correct option is (B).

91. The history and clinical features (Abdominal tenderness, hypotension due to blood loss, Grey Turner's sign) are suggestive of acute pancreatitis with pancreatic necrosis. Hence a contrast CT scan of the abdomen will reveal severe necrotising pancreatitis.

Hence, the correct option is (C).

92.

- The history and clinical features are suggestive of myasthenia gravis.
- Single fiber electromyography is the most sensitive test for the diagnosis of myasthenia gravis.
- Detection of acetylcholine receptor antibodies is the most specific test.
- If single fiber electromyography is not given among the options, the next best choice is edrophonium test.

Hence, the correct option is (A).

93. Symmetric, high voltage, triphasic, slow-wave EEG pattern is characteristic of hepatic encephalopathy.

But it is also seen in other conditions like:

1. Encephalopathy secondary to pulmonary or renal failure
2. Acute hydrocephalus

Hence, the correct option is (D).

94. Absolute contraindications for thrombolysis:

- Previous history of intracranial haemorrhage
- Cerebral vascular lesions (like AV malformations)
- Intracranial malignancy
- Suspected aortic dissection
- Bleeding diathesis

Hence, the correct option is (D).

95. Wilson's disease is characteristic of Wilson's disease. Other conditions in which KF ring is seen are: Chronic active hepatitis, Primary biliary cirrhosis and Intrahepatic cholestatic syndromes.

Hence, the correct option is (D).

96. Androphonia refers to masculinisation of female voice. This can be treated by type 4 thyroplasty. It increases the length and tension of the cord, thereby increasing the pitch of voice.

Hence, the correct option is (D).

97. Uses of Seigel's speculum

- Assess movement of tympanic membrane
- Introduce medicine into the middle ear
- To have a magnified view of ear pathology
- To assess vestibular function by fistula test

Hence, the correct option is (C).

98. Nail-patella syndrome is characterized by abnormalities of the nails, knees, elbows, and pelvis. The features of nail-patella syndrome vary in severity between affected individuals, even among members of the same family. Nail abnormalities are seen in almost all individuals with nail-patella syndrome.

Hence, the correct option is (A).

99. Conductive hearing loss occurs when there is a problem with the way sound is conducted to the inner ear and a structure called the cochlea. The problem may lie in the ear canal, eardrum (tympanic membrane), or the middle ear (ossicles and Eustachian tube). The inner ear remains unaffected in this type of hearing loss.

Hence, the correct option is (A).

100. Attic cholesteatoma is an indication for modified radical mastoidectomy (Canal wall down mastoidectomy). A canal wall down mastoidectomy includes a complete mastoidectomy in addition to removal of the posterior and superior osseous external auditory canal. The tympanic membrane is reconstructed to separate the mucosal lined middle ear space from the mastoid cavity and ear canal.

Hence, the correct option is (C).

101. Malignant otitis externa is an infection, not a malignancy. Hence no mitotic figures are found. Malignant otitis externa is an aggressive infection rather than a malignancy, or cancer. An alternative name for malignant otitis externa is necrotizing external otitis. If it's not treated malignant otitis externa can be life-threatening.

Hence, the correct option is (C).

102. Features of Ménière's disease are:

- Aural fullness
- Fluctuating sensorineural deafness
- Fluctuating tinnitus
- Episodic vertigo

Hence, the correct option is (B).

103. Aspergillus spp. are the commonest etiological agents though the importance of dematiaceous fungi in allergic fungal sinusitis has been stressed.

Hence, the correct option is (A).

104. A myringotomy is a procedure to create a hole in the ear drum to allow fluid that is trapped in the middle ear to drain out. The fluid may be blood, pus and/or water. In many cases, a small tube is inserted into the hole in the ear drum to help maintain drainage.

Hence, the correct option is (C).

105. Rhinophyma is a condition of the external nose caused by hypertrophy of the sebaceous tissue and inflammation of the tissues around the gland over the skin of nose.

Hence, the correct option is (A).

106. Intravenous magnesium sulphate. Intravenous magnesium sulphate is also useful in the treatment of refractory hypokalemia, often associated with hypomagnesemia, and also for the treatment of torsades de pointes.

Hence, the correct option is (B).

107. The definitive treatment is surgery. But to increase the success rate of surgery, the colostomy can be done initially. This decreases inflammation.

Hence, the correct option is (A).

108. Ursodeoxycholic acid decreases bile salt levels and relieves pruritus. It can also decrease the chance for fetal complications.

Hence, the correct option is (A).

109. Common IUD side effects include:

- irregular bleeding for several months.
- lighter or shorter periods or no periods at all.
- symptoms of premenstrual syndrome (PMS), which include headaches, nausea, breast tenderness, and skin blemishes.

Hence, the correct option is (A).

110. Dysgerminomas produce placental alkaline phosphatase and lactate dehydrogenase. Pure dysgerminomas do not produce AFP and HCG.

Hence, the correct option is (C).

111. The most common ovarian germ cell tumor is called dysgerminoma. Signs of ovarian germ cell tumors are swelling of the abdomen or vaginal bleeding after menopause.

Hence, the correct option is (B).

112. Polycystic ovary syndrome (PCOS) is one of the most common causes of secondary amenorrhea. PCOS is the most common cause of ovulatory dysfunction in reproductive-age women.

Hence, the correct option is (C).

113. Raloxifene is an orally administered selective estrogen receptor modulator (SERM). It has estrogenic action on bone and anti-estrogenic actions on the uterus and breast. It is used to prevent osteoporosis postmenopausal women. It is also protective against breast and endometrial cancer. It is not useful in treatment of hot flushes.

Hence, the correct option is (B).

114. Aspermia is the complete lack of semen with ejaculation, which is associated with infertility. Aspermia is the complete lack of semen with ejaculation, due to due to either an inability to transport semen (anejaculation) or to ejaculate in an antegrade direction which is associated with infertility.

Hence, the correct option is (A).

115. Barrier contraceptives are ideal for those with heart disease. Hormonal contraceptives are best avoided.

Hence, the correct option is (C).

116. Theoretically the live attenuated virus in a vaccine could cross the placenta and result in viral infection of the fetus. Owing to this concern, most live attenuated vaccines, including the measles-mumps-rubella (MMR) and varicella vaccines, are contraindicated during pregnancy.

Hence, the correct option is (D).

117. Seizure frequency is increased in approximately 30% of women during pregnancy. Evidence indicates seizure frequency increases during 17-33% of pregnancies. Several possible etiologies have been proposed for this occurrence. Increased renal and hepatic metabolism of AEDs, increased volume of distribution, and changes in serum-binding proteins all impact circulating levels of AEDs.

Hence, the correct option is (B).

118. Most common CVS anomalies in a child born to a diabetic mother: Transposition of great arteries, Ventricular septal defect. The most frequent cardiac anomalies in IDMs include ventricular septal defect, transposition of great arteries and aortic stenosis. Defects involving the great arteries, including truncus arteriosus and double outlet right ventricle, are also more prevalent in IDMs.

Hence, the correct optio is (D).

119. Fetal macrosomia is more likely to be a result of maternal diabetes, obesity or weight gain during pregnancy than other causes. If these risk factors aren't present and fetal macrosomia is suspected, it's possible that your baby might have a rare medical condition that affects fetal growth.

Hence, the correct option is (D).

120. Gestational diabetes is associated with fetal macrosomia. Overt diabetes can cause IUGR. Symmetric or primary IUGR is due to genetic or chromosomal causes, early gestational intrauterine infections (TORCH) and maternal alcohol use. Asymmetric IUGR is more commonly due to extrinsic influences that affect the foetus later in gestation, such as preeclampsia, chronic hypertension, and uterine anomalies.

Hence, the correct option is (D).

121. Interspinous diameter – 10.5cm is the smallest among the options provided. Transverse Diameters Anatomical Transverse Diameter (Bituberous) Obstetric Transverse Diameter (interspinous) Extends between the inner aspects of the ischial tuberosities. Extends between the tips of the ischial spines. It is the smallest diameter of the pelvis 10.5 cm.

Hence, the correct option is (A).

122. Raised specific acetylcholinesterase (AChE) activity in amniotic fluid was consistently found to be associated with fetal intrauterine death and neural tube defects, but in just under half of the samples from pregnancies with spina bifida, the increase was marginal.

Hence, the correct option is (C).

123. Chorionic villus sampling is usually done between weeks 11 and 14 of pregnancy earlier than other prenatal diagnostic tests, such as amniocentesis. You might consider chorionic villus sampling if: You had positive results from a prenatal screening test.

Hence, the correct option is (B).

124. Causes of postpartum haemorrhage:

- Atonicity
- Trauma
- Coagulopathy
- Retained placenta and placental fragments
- Morbidly adherent placenta
- Uterine inversion

Hence, the correct option is (A).

125. Vaginal bleeding at 32 weeks with acute abdominal pain and decreased fetal movements suggests the diagnosis of abruption. Cesarean section should be done immediately to prevent fetal death and development of maternal complications.

Hence, the correct option is (A).

126. Tumours which increase in size during pregnancy:

- Pituitary adenoma
- Neurofibroma
- Meningioma
- Angioma

Hence, the correct option is (A).

127. Dermoid cyst the mot common tumour to undergo torsion during pregnancy. The incidence of ovarian torsion rises 5-fold during pregnancy to approximately 5 per 10,000 pregnancies. Its most common cause in pregnancy is a corpus luteum cyst, which usually regresses spontaneously by the second trimester.

Hence, the correct option is (C).

128. Factors decreasing risk of upper genital tract infection in users of progestin releasing intrauterine contraceptive device:

- Reduced retrograde menstruation – prevents seeding of fallopian tube with bacteria
- Thickened cervical mucus – decreases bacterial penetration
- Decidual changes in the endometrium – making it less susceptible to infection

Hence, the correct option is (B).

129. Fetal blood sampling is done by cordocentesis. It is done in the 18-24 weeks gestational age. Cord blood testing may be used to: Measure blood gases. This helps to see if a baby's blood has a healthy level of oxygen and other substances. Measure bilirubin levels.

Hence, the correct option is (D).

130. Emergency contraception is used to prevent pregnancy. Interruption of an early pregnancy is not contraception – it is termination of pregnancy.

Hence, the correct option is (D).

131. Menorrhagia in older reproductive-age women is typically due to uterine pathology, including fibroids, polyps and adenomyosis. However, other problems, such as uterine cancer, bleeding disorders, medication side effects and liver or kidney disease could be contributing factors.

Hence, the coprrect option is (A).

132. "Tuberculosis (very common in India) is a very common cause of Tubal Blockage." Tubal cannulation may be done immediately after you have a procedure called hysterosalpingography In this, your doctor flushes dye through the catheter to identify and locate a fallopian tube blockage. You may or may not get anesthesia during the procedure. Your doctor might give you a mild sedative to help you relax.

Hence, the correct option is (C).

133. Caesarean section being one of the most performed surgical operations in Nigeria was surprisingly found to be the most common cause of ureteric injury ahead of hysterectomy.

Hence, the correct option is (C).

134. Postpartum bleeding or postpartum hemorrhage (PPH) is often defined as the loss of more than 500 ml or 1,000 ml of blood within the first 24 hours following childbirth. Some have added the requirement that there also be signs or symptoms of low blood volume for the condition to exist.

Hence, the correct option is (D).

135. Separation anxiety disorder is a common childhood anxiety disorder.

It has a prevalence is 3.5% to 5.4%.

It is more common in girls.

The average age of onset is 7.5 years.

Children have unrealistic worries about separation from a major attachment figure.

Comorbidity is common.

Usually present with school refusal and physical complaints related to anxiety.

Hence, the correct option is (D).

136.

- Abetalipoproteinemia is a progressive ataxic neuropathy with retinitis pigmentosa and steatorrhoea.
- Charcot-Marie-Tooth disease is a hereditary motor and sensory neuropathy. It is characterised by weakness of extremities and hammer toe.
- Dejerine Sottas disease is also a hereditary motor and sensory neuropathy. It is associated with distal weakness and ataxia.
- Werdnig Hoffman disease is spinal muscular atrophy type 1. It presents within first 6 months of life. It presents with generalised symmetrical weakness, more in proximal muscle groups with hypotonia.

Hence, the correct option is (C).

137. A CA 125 test measures the amount of the protein CA 125 (cancer antigen 125) in your blood. A CA 125 test may be used to monitor certain cancers during and after treatment. In some cases, a CA 125 test may be used to look for early signs of ovarian cancer in people with a very high risk of the disease.

Hence, the correct option is (D).

138.

- Foetal placental steroid sulfatase deficiency is a rare X-linked condition, and is seen only in males.
- It is not a cause for development of ambiguous genitalia in females.
- The most common cause of ambiguous genitalia in females is Congenital Adrenal Hyperplasia (CAH).
- It is responsible for about 70% of cases.
- 21 hydroxylase deficiency and 11 hydroxylase deficiency are subtypes of CAH.
- Other causes include WNT4 mutation and foetal placental aromatase deficiency.

Hence, the correct option is (D).

139. Gastroesophageal reflux in infants can be of 2 types – Physiological or Pathological.

Physiological reflux

- The infant has regurgitation after feeding, but weight gain is normal.
- There are no respiratory symptoms/features of oesophagitis.

Pathological reflux (gastroesophageal reflux disease)

- Regurgitation is associated with refusal to eat, excessive vomiting, weight loss and failure to thrive.
- The infant has recurrent respiratory features like wheezing, stridor, chronic cough, aspiration, sore throat, hoarseness and recurrent pneumonitis.
- Features of oesophagitis may be present – upper GI bleeding, anemia and Sandifer syndrome (torticollis and dystonia associated with GERD).
- The most frequent complications are failure to thrive and recurrent respiratory symptoms.

Hence, the correct option is (B).

140. Blalock and Taussig's shunt is used in the surgical management of tetralogy of Fallot. It shunts blood from the subclavian artery to the pulmonary artery. That is not given among the list of options. As the subclavian artery is a branch of the aorta, the best answer would be 'aorta to the pulmonary artery.'

Hence, the correct option is (A).

141. Alternate names – Ivemark syndrome/asplenia syndrome.

It is a type of situs anomaly.

Features: asplenia, malrotation of the bowel, transverse liver, gall bladder agenesis, imperforate anus, horseshoe adrenal gland, urethral valves.

The patients are immunocompromised due to the absence of a spleen, most die before 1 year of age.

Hence, the correct option is (A).

142. Enteroviruses are the most common cause of viral meningoencephalitis in children. Non-polio enteroviruses are the most common cause of viral meningitis in the United States, especially from late spring to fall. That is when these viruses spread most often. However, only a small number of people infected with enteroviruses will actually develop meningitis.

Hence, the correct option is (D).

143. In foetuses at risk of virilising congenital adrenal hyperplasia (CAH), prenatal treatment can be offered by administration of dexamethasone (DEX) via the mother, in order to suppress foetal adrenal androgen oversecretion and prevent genital malformations.

Hence, the correct option is (D).

144. Components of Tetralogy of Fallot:

- Pulmonary stenosis
- Overriding aorta
- Ventricular septal defect
- Right ventricular hypertrophy

Hence, the correct option is (C).

145. Isotope renogram is the best modality for renal function estimation. This test provides information on the blood supply, function and flow of urine from the kidneys. A DTPA or MAG3 scan can help your doctor assess individually how each of your kidneys is working and to look for a cause of high blood pressure or other abnormal test result.

Hence, the correct option is (C).

146.

- Anterior (superficial) corneal dystrophy affects epithelium and Bowman's layer.
- Examples include Reis-Buckler's dystrophy, Meesmann's dystrophy and Stocker-Holt's dystrophy.
- Schnyder's dystrophy is a crystalline stromal dystrophy.

Hence, the correct option is (C).

147. Argyll Robertson Pupil

- It is characterised by bilateral constricted pupils.
- Accommodation reflex (near reflex) is normal.
- Pupillary reflex (light reflex) – both direct and indirect – are absent.
- This feature is known as light – near dissociation.
- ARP was first described in neurosyphilis by Douglas Moray Cooper Lamb Argyll Robertson, a Scottish Ophthalmologist.
- It is also seen in other conditions like encephalitis, diabetic neuropathy, multiple sclerosis, stroke etc.

Hence, the correct option is (C).

148. HSV (Herpes Simplex Virus) keratitis is an infection of the cornea—the clear dome that covers the colored part of the eye that is caused by HSV. The infection usually heals without damaging the eye, but more severe infections can lead to scarring of the cornea or blindness.

Hence, the correct option is (B).

149. Components of horner's syndrome –

- Ptosis
- Miosis
- Anhidrosis
- Enophthalmos
- Loss of ciliospinal reflex

Hence, the correct option is (D).

150. Features of optic glioma:

- Cells of origin – astrocytes, oligodendrocytes of optic nerve
- Peak incidence – 2 to 5 years
- Optic glioma is not known to cause meningeal hyperplasia.

Hence, the correct option is (C).

151. Bilateral subluxation of lens:

- Marfan's syndrome – upwards and outwards
- Homocystinuria – downwards and inwards

Hence, the coprrect option is (B).

152. The person may have been diabetic for some time before the diagnosis of NIDDM. Retinopathy may have already occured. Hence, ophthalmological testing should be done as early as possible after diagnosis of NIDDM. If there are no pathologic changes, he should come for review every 6 months / 1 year.

But in case of IDDM (Insulin dependant diabetes mellitus), the patients are diagnosed early in life. There is much less chance of any ophthalmologic disease at the time of diagnosis. Hence ophthalmologic examination is recommended 5 years after the diagnosis of IDDM.

Hence, the correct option is (A).

153. The World Health Organization recommends the SAFE Strategy (Surgery, Antibiotics, Facial cleanliness, and Environmental changes) to control trachoma. 1 Trachoma is an infection that can lead to vision impairment and blindness as well as pain (see our writeup on trachoma).

Hence, the correct option is (A).

154. Band shaped keratopathy occurs due to the accumulation of calcium salts in a band pattern in the anterior corneal layers. The causes of band shaped keratopathy can be broadly divided into six categories: Chronic inflammation: Chronic keratitis, chronic uveitis of any cause and ocular trauma, along with its accompanying chronic Inflammation, are the most common ocular causes of band shaped keratopathy.

Hence, the correct option is (B).

155. Panretinal photocoagulation is the treatment of choice for neovascularization of iris. It stops the angiogenic stimulus from the retina which is responsible for neovascularization.

Hence, the correct option is (C).

156. Commonest site of urethral carcinoma in males is Bulbomembranous urethra. It constitutes about 60% of the cases. Penile urethra is involved in 30% and prostatic urethra is involved in 10%.

Hence, the correct option is (C).

157. First autologous renal transplantation was done by Hardy in the year 1963 and represents a viable option in the management of long or severe upper ureteric strictures.

Hence, the correct option is (A).

158. Lord's plication is a surgical procedure used for the treatment of hydrocele.

The hydrocele fluid is drained and the redundant sac is plicated.

It is used for treatment of small and medium sized hydroceles.

Hence, the correct option is (A).

159. Grayhack shunt connects the corpora cavernosa with the saphenous vein.

It is used for the treatment of ischaemic priapism.

Hence, the correct option is (A).

160. Multiple cutaneous sebaceous adenomas are seen in Muir Torre syndrome. Sebaceous adenoma and sebaceous epithelioma are the most characteristic cutaneous markers of Torre-Muir/Lynch syndrome. They are benign tumours that present as yellow papules or nodules. They can grow on any part of the body but are mostly located on the head, particularly on the face, scalp and eyelids.

Hence, the correct option is (D).

161. High ammonia concentration leads to the formation of triple phosphate stones. This arises when urine is infected with urea splitting organisms like Proteus.

Hence, the correct option is (B).

162. Dorsal venous complex passes over the prostate. It is the most troublesome source of bleeding during a prostatectomy.

Hence, the correct option is (A).

163. Silicone catheters can be used for upto 12 weeks. > 100% silicone – last for 12 weeks and are hypoallergenic. > Latex catheters coated with hydrogel – last 12 weeks but unsuitable in latex allergy patients. > Silicone elastomer – coated on a latex core; tend to be flexible and comfortable and can last 12 weeks; unsuitable in latex allergy patients.

Hence, the correct option is (B).

164. The history is suggestive of congenital aganglionic megacolon (Hirschprung disease). The ganglion cells in the intestinal wall are absent. It occurs due to arrest in migration of neural crest cells.

Hence, the correct option is (D).

165. Abbey Estlander flap (stair step advancement technique) is used in reconstruction of lip since it shows good results with minimum morbidity if performed by experienced hands. The Abbe-Estlander method is useful for the reconstruction of defects affecting 1/3rd to 2/3rd of the lip, including the oral commissure.

Hence, the corerct option is (B).

166. Complications of hiatal hernia may include the following: Intermittent bleeding from associated esophagitis, erosions (Cameron ulcers), or a discrete esophageal ulcer, leading to iron-deficiency anemia. Incarcerated hiatal hernia (rare; observed only with paraesophageal hernia).

Hence, the correct option is (A).

167. Perineural invasion is characteristically seen in adenoid cystic carcinoma. It is the most common malignant tumour of submandibular salivary glands. Adenoid cystic carcinoma (ACC) is a rare form of adenocarcinoma, a type of cancer that begins in glandular tissues . It most commonly arises in the major and minor salivary glands of the head and neck. It can also occur in the breast, uterus, or other locations in the body.

Hence, the correct option is (B).

168. The sympathetic system controls the blood flow to skin (not muscle). Sympathetic tone has a vasoconstrictor effect. Hence lumbar sympathectomy will cause vasodilation and increased blood flow to skin of toes.

Hence, the correct option is (B).

169. Causes of blood stained nipple discharge:

- Intraductal papilloma
- Carcinoma
- Duct ectasia
- Fibrocystic disease

Hence, the correct option is (C).

170. Transsphenoidal literally means "through the sphenoid sinus." It is a surgery performed through the nose and sphenoid sinus to remove pituitary tumors. Transsphenoidal surgery can be performed with an endoscope, microscope, or both. Transnasal transsphenoidal surgery is the surgical approach to remove tumors from the pituitary gland, also known as pituitary adenoma. During the procedure, surgeon approaches the pituitary gland through sphenoid sinus, the air space behind the nose, for removing tumor.

Hence, the correct option is (C).

171. Usual site is forearm of non dominant hand. The femoral vessels are used only if all upper limb vessles have been used. Saphenofemoral arteriovenous fistula is a viable alternative in patients which present no more options for vascular access in upper limbs. It presents good efficacy, low morbidity, complications that may be corrected and good patency rate in long term.

Hence, the correct option is (D).

172. Dacron is a synthetic graft material. It is a type of medical textile. A Dacron graft is made out of a man-made (synthetic) polyester material. It is used to replace natural body tissues. A Dacron graft can be used as a stent to repair an artery, blood vessel, or other hollow structure in your body (such as the tube that carries urine) to hold it open. The graft causes very few reactions.

Hence, the correct option is (B).

173. How to perform allen's test: (To check for patency of radial and ulnar arteries and to confirm integrity of the palmar arterial arch between them):

1. The patient makes a tight fist
2. The examiner compresses the radial and ulnar arteries distally
3. The fist is released and compression of the ulnar artery is released
4. The speed of return of colour to the palm is looked for
5. Steps 1 and 2 are repeated, but release the radial artery compression instead of the ulnar artery
6. Again look for speed of return of colour to the palm

Normally, the colour should return in 5-7seconds. This indicates that the arteries and the palmar arch is patent and functioning well.

Hence, the correct option is (C).

174. The most common etiology for acquired AVFs is penetrating trauma. AVFs also can occur from nontraumatic causes, such as erosion of an aneurysm into a neighboring vein or following surgery for therapeutic purposes (eg, access for hemodialysis).

Hence, the correct option is (D).

175. 15% of familial and 5% of sporadic cases of testicular tumour are bilateral. They are located in the scrotum, behind the penis. They produce testosterone and other male hormones. The testicles also produce and store sperm, the male cells needed for reproduction. nce testicular cancer develops, it can remain within the testicle, or it can spread to lymph nodes in the abdomen or pelvis.

Hence, the correct option is (B).

176. Chemotherapy with radiotherapy (Nigro regimen) is the preferred treatment for anal carcinoma. The present standard of care in terms of treatment is 5-fluorouracil (5-FU) and mitomycin C (MMC) concurrently with radiation, which results in a high level of disease control for small early cancers. Preservation of the anal sphincter is achieved in the majority, although anorectal function is often impaired.

Hence, the correct option is (C).

177. Components of triple therapy immunosuppression for post-renal transplant patients are :

- Cyclosporine
- Azathioprine
- Prednisolone

Hence, the correct option is (C).

178. Ablation of liver secondaries can be done by:

- Cryotherapy
- Radiofrequency ablation
- Microwave ablation
- Injection of chemicals like alcohol and acetic acid

Hence, the correct option is (A).

179. During surgery, the common bile duct may be mistakenly identified as the cystic duct. Hence, surgeon may ligate the common bile duct instead of the cystic duct resulting in the development of a stricture in the upper part.

Hene, the correct option is (A).

180. T tubes are kept in the bile duct for 7-30 days. It allows track to mature and helps prevent bile leak and biliary peritonitis.

Hence, theb correct option is (D).

181. One of the most serious post-ERCP complications is cholangitis leading to subsequent septicemia. Enteric bacteria enter the biliary tree by the hematogenous route or following endoscopic or radiologic manipulation. Improperly disinfected endoscopes and accessories may also introduce infection into the biliary tree.

Hence, the correct option is (A).

182. Angiosarcoma can occur as a late complication following breast conservation surgery. Angiosarcoma is rare cancer that starts in the cells that line blood vessels or lymph vessels. Many times it's a complication of previous radiation treatment to the breast. It can happen 8-10 years after getting radiation treatment to the breast.

Hence, the correct option is (D).

183. Lobular carcinoma has higher incidence of bilaterality compared to other carcinomas. Invasive lobular carcinoma is a type of breast cancer that begins in the milk-producing glands (lobules) of the breast. Invasive cancer means the cancer cells have broken out of the lobule where they began and have the potential to spread to the lymph nodes and other areas of the body.

Hence, the correct option is (C).

184. Involvement of axillary nodes has been the most important prognostic factor for breast cancer. Decisions regarding the use of adjuvant treatment in breast cancer have also largely been based on axillary node involvement.

Hence, the correct option is (B).

185. Papillary carcinoma is usually mulitifocal. Lymphatic spread occurs to cervical lymph nodes (Hematogenous spread occurs in case of follicular carcinoma). Papillary carcinoma (PTC) is the most common form of well-differentiated thyroid cancer, and the most common form of thyroid cancer to result from exposure to radiation. Papillary carcinoma appears as an irregular solid or cystic mass or nodule in a normal thyroid parenchyma.

Hence, the correct option is (B).

186. Glioblastoma multiforme is highly vascular. A hemangioma is a vascular brain tumor that typically develops in the cerebellum, at the back of the brain. A vascular brain tumor is a benign (noncancerous) tumor that's caused by an excess growth of blood vessels in the brain or spinal cord.

Hence, the correct option is (A).

187. Post operative complications that occur with sufficient frequency in ileostomy are : Nipple valve slippage, pouchitis, intestinal obstruction and fistula.

Complications of ileostomy are Obstruction, Vitamin B12 anaemia, Pouchitis, Stoma problems, Valve malfunction and Phantom rectum.

Hence, the ccorrect option is (A).

188. The classic biochemical abnormality in hypertrophic pyloric stenosis is hypochloremic, hypokalemic metabolic alkalosis. Pyloric stenosis can lead to forceful vomiting, dehydration and weight loss. Babies with pyloric stenosis may seem to be hungry all the time. Surgery cures pyloric stenosis.

Hence, the correct option is (D).

189. Possible mechanisms underlying orthostatic hypotension in SCI, such as changes in sympathetic activity, altered baroreflex function, the lack of skeletal muscle pumping activity, cardiovascular deconditioning and altered salt and water balance will be discussed.

Hence, the correct otion is (A).

190. The loss of these brain cells causes some of the movement problems characteristic of ataxia-telangiectasia. Mutations in the ATM gene also prevent cells from responding correctly to DNA damage, which allows breaks in DNA strands to accumulate and can lead to the formation of cancerous tumors.

Hence, the correct option is (D).

191. The dentate line differentiates external and internal hemorrhoids. External hemorrhoids are located below the dentate line and drain via the inferior rectal veins into the pudendal vessels and then into the internal iliac vein. These vessels are covered by anoderm that is comprised of modified squamous epithelium.

Hence, the correct option is (A).

192. Respiratory gating is a technique in radiotherapy in which the radiation is applied during that phase of respiratory cycle in which the tumour is in the best range. This is to prevent unnecessary radiation exposure to normal structures.

Hence, the correct option is (C).

193. Plethoric lung fields are seen in conditions which increase pulmonary blood flow. They are:

- Left to right shunt – ASD, VSD, PDA, Coronary artery fistula into right heart, Aortopulmonary window
- Transposition of great arteries with ASD or VSD
- Truncus arteriosus
- Total anomalous pulmonary venous connection

Hence, the correct option is (C).

194. Myelomalacia occurs when hemorrhaging happens within the spine, or when something halts the flow of blood to the spinal cord – which results in a "softening" of the spinal cord itself.

Hence, the correct option is (B).

195. Traditionally, FNAC has been contraindicated in the diagnosis of pheochromocytoma due to the untoward reactions and its fatality. However, when it is used in the unsuspected cases of EAP which present as abdominal masses, no complication is noted.

Hence, the correct option is (C).

196. Diffuse axonal injuries, It is associated with unconsciousness and CT scan shows multiple petechial haemorrhages.

Hence, the correct option is (D).

197. Hypochloremic alkalosis results from either low chloride intake or excessive chloride wasting. Whereas low chloride intake is very uncommon, excessive chloride wasting often occurs in hospitalized children, usually as a result of diuretic therapy or nasogastric tube suctioning.

Hence, the correct option is (A).

198. Mattox Maneuver, also known as a left medial visceral rotation, is a surgical step to explore and handle Zone 1 and 2 retroperitoneal injuries (aorta, left iliac and pelvic vessels). It starts with incising the parietal peritoneum at the white line of Toldt from the sigmoid colon to the splenic flexure.

Hence, the correct option is (C).

199. CEA(carcinoembryonic antigen) is a type of tumor marker. Tumor markers are substances made by cancer cells or by normal cells in response to cancer in the body. A high level of CEA can be a sign of certain types of cancers. These include cancers of the colon and rectum, prostate, ovary, lung, thyroid, or liver.

Hence, the correct option is (C).

200. Burrowing ulcer / Maleny's ulcer is caused by synergistic infection of microaerophilic non hemolytic streptococci and aerobic hemolytic streptococci. Chronic undermining burrowing ulcer is a cutaneous condition that is a postoperative, progressive bacterial gangrene. It is seen in immunocompromised individuals, mostly after post abdominal surgery and rapidly spreads to involve a large area.

Hence, the correct option is (A).

201. Homogenous staining reflects antibodies specific to chromatin and histones.

Speckled pattern reflects the presence of antibodies to non-DNA nuclear constituents like Sm antigen, SSA and SSB.

Nucleolar pattern reflects antibodies to RNA.

Centromeric pattern is seen in the case of antibodies specific to centromeres.

Hence, the correct option is (A).

202. Proliferation occurs in perivascular epithelioid cells:

- Lymphangioleiomyomatosis is primarily seen in young women of childbearing age.
- The commonest symptom is dyspnoea.
- Proliferation of perivascular epithelioid cells results in distortion of lungs with cystic dilation of terminal air spaces.
- It is a slowly progressing disorder

Hence, the correct option is (C).

203. MYC proto oncogene is associated with Burkitt lymphoma.

ABL is associated with chronic myelogenous leukemia and acute lymphoblastic leukemia.

BRAF is associated with melanoma, leukemia and colon carcinoma.

HGF is associated with hepatocellular carcinoma and thyroid cancer.

Hence, the correct option is (D).

204. Desmoid tumours are commonly seen in the teens to thirties age group.

They are also known as deep fibromatoses.

They usually arise from the musculoaponeurotic structures in the anterior abdominal wall.

Recurrence can occur, but metastasis does not occur.

More common in women.

Hence, the correct option is (B).

205.

- Fragile X syndrome, Myotonic dystrophy and Friedreich ataxia are examples of trinucleotide repeat disorders with expansions affecting non-coding regions.
- Spinocerebellar ataxia, Huntington's disease and Spinobulbar muscular atrophy are trinucleotide repeat disorders with expansions affecting coding regions.

Hence, the correct option is (C).

206. Etiology Of Intracranial Haemorrhage

- Extradural haemorrhage – Torn meningeal artery (especially middle meningeal artery) due to trauma.
- Subdural haemorrhage – Rupture of bridging cortical veins due to trauma.
- Subarachnoid haemorrhage – Rupture of berry aneurysm.
- Intracerebral haemorrhage – Rupture of Charcot Bouchard aneurysm, associated with chronic hypertension.

Hence, the correct option is (D).

207. Anti LKM (Liver Kidney Microsomal) antibodies are of 3 types:

- Anti LKM 1 – Autoimmune hepatitis type II and Chronic hepatitis C
- Anti LKM 2 – Drug-induced hepatitis
- Anti LKM 3 – Chronic Hepatitis D

Antibodies present in the other options:

- Inflammatory myopathies – Anti Jo1 antibody
- Behcet's syndrome – Anti alpha-enolase antibody
- Primary biliary cirrhosis – Anti mitochondrial antibody against E2 subunit of pyruvate dehydrogenase complex

Hence, the correct option is (C).

208. Neurogenic tumours are seen in the posterior mediastinum. Anterior mediastinal masses include Thymomas, teratomas, lymphomas, pheochromocytomas, thyroid and parathyroid lesions.

Hence, the correct option is (C).

209. Bradykinin is a bronchoconstrictor. Bradykinin is a potent endothelium-dependent vasodilator and mild diuretic, which may cause a lowering of the blood pressure. It also causes contraction of non-vascular smooth muscle in the bronchus and gut, increases vascular permeability and is also involved in the mechanism of pain.

Hence, the correct option is (A).

210. Immunohistochemical markers for langerhans cell histiocytosis are :

- CD1a
- HLADR
- CD 68
- S100
- Langerin

Hence, the correct option is (B).

211. Sickle cell trait (heterozygous case of sickle cell anemia) provides protection against malaria. Sickling of RBC's result in the leaking of potassium from the cell. This leads to the death of the malarial parasites within the RBC's.

Hence, the correct option is (A).

212. Caspases are cysteine proteases which play an important role in apoptosis. Caspases are a family of cysteine proteases that serve as primary effectors during apoptosis to proteolytically dismantle most cellular structures, including the cytoskeleton, cell junctions, mitochondria, endoplasmic reticulum, Golgi, and the nucleus.

Hence, the correct option is (A).

213. Maternal nondisjunction in meiosis I is the most common cause of Down's syndrome (95% of total cases). The most common form of Down syndrome is called trisomy 21. This is a condition wherein people have 47 chromosomes in each cell instead of 46. An error in cell division called nondisjunction causes trisomy 21. This error leaves a sperm or egg cell with an extra copy of chromosome 21 before or at conception.

Hence, the correct option is (D).

214. Stains used to demonstrate fungi are Periodic Acid Schiff (PAS) and Methenamine Silver Stain

PAS stains both living and dead fungi, whereas Methenamine Silver stains only living fungi

Massons's Trichrome is used to demonstrate collage, muscle and fibrin

Alizarin Red and Von Kossa are used to demonstrate calcium in tissues

Hence, the correct option is (A).

215. Psammoma bodies are seen in Papillary carcinoma of thyroid, Meningioma, Renal cell carcinoma and in Serous cystadenocarcinoma of ovary.

Hence, the correct option is (B).

216. Ependymoma is a glial tumour

It is derived from ependymal cells of the ventricle

Hence, the correct option is (A).

217. Lymphadenitis can be seen in all of the above mentioned diseases, but necrotizing lymphadenitis is seen only in Kikuchi disease.

Hence, the correct option is (B).

218. Sickle cell disease is a genetic condition which is characterised by mutation in beta globin chain of hemoglobin (glutamic acid is replaced with valine in the 6th position of beta chain).

Hence, the correct option is (D).

219. In platelet function defects, there is normal platelet count with increased bleeding time

The defect lies in platelet function, not number

Hence, the correct option is (A).

220. HbH is formed by 4 beta chains (tetramer of beta chains)

It is seen in alpha thalassemia with deletion of 3 alpha chains

It is precipitated as Heinz bodies within RBC's

Deletion of 4 alpha chains results in formation of Hb Barts (gamma chain tetramer) and is incompatible with life

Hence, the correct option is (B).

221. Xanthogranulomatous inflammation is a condition in which lipid laden macrophages (foam cells) are deposited in various parts of the body

The exact etiopathogenesis is not known

E.coli and proteus are implicated as etiological agents

Mycobacterium tuberculosis is not considered as an etiological agent

Hence, the correct option is (A).

222. Vasodilatation and increased vascular permeability is the most characteristic feature of acute inflammation. Margination of leukocytes and vascular stasis are other prominent features.

Hence, the correct option is (A).

223. NADPH oxidase is responsible for the 'oxygen burst' within neutrophils for killing intracellular bacteria

During the 'oxygen burst', there is an abrupt increase in oxygen consumption and increased synthesis of free radicals

Hence, the correct option is (C).

224. Apoptosis can be initiated by both intracellular and extracellular signals

Mitochondria plays an important role in mediating apoptosis initiated by intracellular signals

Cell surface death receptors play an important role in mediating apoptosis initiated by extracellular signals

Hence, the correct option is (A).

225. Glycocalyx is a general term referring to extracellular polymeric material (glycoprotein) produced by some bacteria, epithelia and other cells. The highly charged glycocalyx of endothelial cells helps prevent platelet adhesion. It also functions to prevent leukocyte adhesion in normal tissues (prevent unwanted inflammation).

Hence, the correct option is (D).

226. Explanation: Indacaterol is a long acting beta 2 agonist used in the treatment of COPD. Glycopyrronium, Aclidinium and Umeclidinium are long acting muscarinic antagonists used in the treatment of COPD.

Hence, the correct option is (C).

227.

- Ibrutinib is an orally administered selective inhibitor of Bruton's tyrosine kinase (BTK).
- It was approved by the US FDA on November 13, 2013 for the treatment of patients with mantle cell lymphoma who have received at least one prior therapy.
- Dose: 560 mg once daily, taken orally.

Hence, the correct option is (B).

228. Second line drugs for treatment of tuberculosis:

- PAS
- Ethionamide
- Kanamycin
- Amikacin
- Capreomycin
- Thiocetazone
- Cycloserine
- Ciprofloxacin
- Ofloxacin
- Rifabutin
- Clarithromycin
- Azithromycin

Hence, the correct option is (A).

229.

- Leflunomide is an immunomodulator.
- It is used in patients with active rheumatoid arthritis.
- It inhibits proliferation of stimulated lymphocytes.
- The active metabolite of leflunomide inhibits dihydroorotate dehydrogenase and pyrimidine synthesis.
- It can depress the antibody production by B cells.
- It should not be used in children and pregnant / lactating women.

Hence, the correct option is (C).

230. Other drugs with narrow therapeutic index:

- Digoxin
- Gentamicin
- Amphotericin B
- Levothyroxine
- Prazosin
- Theophylline
- Quinidine
- Warfarin
- Valproic acid

Hence, the correct option is (A).

231.

- Integrase inhibitors inhibit the enzyme 'integrase' which inserts the viral genome into the host DNA.

- Raltegravir was the first integrase inhibitor approved by the US FDA (in 2007).
- Elvitegravir and Dolutegravir are 2 other integrase inhibitors approved in 2012 and 2013 respectively.
- Raltegravir is the correct answer because at the time of the exam (AIPG 2011), it was the only integrase inhibitor available commercially.

Hence, the correct option is (D).

232. Use of MAO inhibitors in patient taking pethidine / pentazocine can precipitate serotonin syndrome.

Hence, the correct option is (A).

233. Ethosuximide is the drug of choice for treatment of absence seizures. Other drugs used in the management of absence seizures are valproic acid, lamotrigine and clonazepam.

Hence, the correct option is (B).

234. Adverse effects of amiodarone:
-Thyroid function abnormality – hyperthyroidism / hypothyroidism
-Cardiac depression
-Pulmonary alveolitis and fibrosis
-Peripheral neuropathy
-Corneal micro deposits
-Photosensitivity

Hence, the correct option is (D).

235.

- Alkalinization of urine is used in patients receiving high dose methotrexate to promote renal excretion and to avoid nephrotoxicity
- IV Sodium bicarbonate is used to maintain urine pH above 7.0 to avoid precipitation of methotrexate (a weak acid) in the acid pH of renal tubules

Hence, the correct option is (B).

236. Drug of choice – Penicillin G

In case of penicillin resistance, third generation cephalosporins should be used (Ceftriaxone / Cefotaxime)

In case of penicillin / cephalosporin allergy, Chloramphenicol is used

Hence, the correct option is (D).

237. It is a glycoprotein with 12 membrane spanning domains. It is seen in epithelia in various parts of the body and is involved in both absorptive and secretory activities.

There are distinct isoforms for secretory and absorptive function. The absorptive form is found exclusively in thick segment of ascending limb of loop of henle.

Frusemide binds to the Cl- binding site of Na+ K+ 2Cl- Co-transporter and blocks it, thus causing diuresis.

The secretory form is found in the basolateral membrane of most glandular and epithelial cells.

Hence, the correct option is (D).

238. Losartan has a uricosuric action in addition to being an angiotensin receptor blocker. Allopurinol is a xanthine oxidase inhibitor which reduces the synthesis of uric acid.

Hence, the correct option is (B).

239. Constipation is a side effect with thalidomide intake, not diarrhoea.

Other adverse effects of thalidomide:

- Peripheral neuropathy
- Thromboembolism
- Drowsiness
- Teratogenicity
- Fatigue

Hence, the correct option is (A).

240. Diuretics increase sodium loss in urine and increase lithium retention. Hence they should not be used in patients on Lithium.

Hence, the correct option is (D).

241.

- Aprepitant is an NK1 antagonist
- It crosses blood brain barrier and blocks NK1 receptors
- It has an anti emetic action and is used along with chemotherapy regimens
- It is metabolised in liver via CYP3A4 pathway
- It decreases metabolism of drugs metabolised by CYP3A4 pathway (can prolong prothrombin time in patients on warfarin)

Hence, the correct option is (A).

242. Oral bioavailability of erlotinib is 60%

But when taken along with food, it increases to 100%

It should be taken on an empty stomach as there is increased chance of side effects when taken along with food

It is used in treatment of non small cell lung cancer and pancreatic cancer

Important adverse effects are diarrhoea, acneform rash, fatigue and anorexia

Hence, the correct option is (B).

243. Dark colour urine following primaquine administration is due to hemolysis and hemoglobinuria in patients with Glucose-6-phosphate dehydrogenase deficiency.

Hence, the correct option is (A).

244.

- Dantrolene is the drug of choice for malignant hyperthermia
- Serotonin syndrome is a dose related phenomenon and is not idiosyncratic
- It is treated with benzodiazepines, muscle relaxation, endotracheal intubation and mechanical ventilation

- Dantrolene can be used in severe serotonin syndrome with malignant hyperthermia
- Drug of choice in mild / moderate serotonin syndrome – cyproheptadine – an antihistaminic with antiserotonergic action

Hence, the correct option is (C).

245. Complexes formed by combining cadmium / iron with BAL are toxic. Hence BAL (dimercaprol) is contraindicated in treatment of iron / cadmium poisoning.

Hence, the correct option is (C).

246. Yellow fever is not present in India.

Dengue virus has 4 serotypes.

Dengue fever is transmitted by the Aedes mosquito.

Hence, the correct option is (C).

247. The appearance of pneumococcus colonies after prolonged incubation in blood agar – with concentric rings and central combination – also called carrom coin appearance.

Hence, the correct option is (A).

248. Ligase chain reaction and Polymerase chain reaction are the most sensitive methods for the detection of chlamydia.

Hence, the correct option is (C).

249. Epstein Barr (EB) virus-associated conditions:

- Infectious mononucleosis
- Acute transverse myelitis
- Guillain Barre syndrome
- Aplastic anemia
- Chronic fatigue syndrome
- Peripheral neuritis
- T cell lymphoma
- Burkitt's lymphoma
- Hodgkin's disease
- CNS lymphoma
- Lymphoproliferative syndrome
- Gastric carcinoma
- Leiomyosarcoma
- Tonsillar carcinoma
- Nasopharyngeal carcinoma
- Thymoma
- Oral hairy leukoplakia (in adults with HIV)

Hence, the correct option is (D).

250. The clinical picture is suggestive of a soft sore (chancroid) caused by Haemophilus ducreyi. Chocolate agar with IsoVitaleX is used for its culture.

Other culture media:

Thayer Martin Medium – Gonococci

Blood agar with X & V factors – Haemophilus influenzae

Tellurite blood agar – Corynebacterium diphtheria

Hence, the correct option is (C).

251. Clostridia species are the most important agents responsible for gas gangrene. But Clostridium botulinum does not cause gangrene. Clostridia are gram-positive spore-forming anaerobes. Clinical features are due to the release of exotoxin.

Hence, the correct option is (D).

252. The history (animal contact), clinical picture (pustule in the area of contact) and lab findings (gram-positive bacilli in chains with McFadyean reaction positive) are all characteristic of infection by Bacillus anthracis.

Hence, the correct option is (C).

253. P-Pili is involved in the pathogenesis of pyelonephritis. It binds to the P blood group substance on erythrocytes and uroepithelial cells. They have no role in gastrointestinal infection.

Hence, the correct option is (B).

254. Giardiasis can cause fulminant diarrhea and malabsorption. It may even be asymptomatic.

Hence, the correct option is (A).

255. The group-specific antigen is responsible for the production of complement-fixing antibodies.

- Chlamydia trachomatis has at least 15 identified serotypes. But C. pneumonia has only one serotype.
- Animals have no role in the transmission of C. pneumoniae. Transmission is via an airborne route
- Cytoplasmic inclusions lack glycogen

Hence, the correct option is (D).

256. Culture conditions for Campylobacter jejuni

- Low oxygen tension (5%)
- Increased carbon dioxide levels (10%)
- Incubation temperature of 42°C

Hence, the correct option is (A).

257. Rats are important reservoirs. Farmers working in the rice fields are at increased risk of infection. Disease transmission occurs when rainwater contaminated with the urine of rats gets into contact with abraded skin.

Hence, the correct option is (A).

258. Trichinella does not pass through the lungs during its life cycle. The other three pass through the lungs as a part of their life cycle. They cause Löffler's syndrome – in which eosinophils accumulate in the lungs in response to parasitic infection. Strongyloides can also cause Löffler's syndrome.

Hence, the correct option is (C).

259. Epidermodysplasia verruciformis is a rare autosomal recessive disease characterised by increased risk for the development of skin cancer. There is an abnormally high susceptibility to HPV infection of the skin.

Hence, the correct option is (B).

260. Agar has no nutrient properties. Chocolate medium is an enriched media. The addition of selective substances in a liquid medium is called enrichment media.

Hence, the correct option is (D).

261. The patient presented with a history of pneumonia. Charcoal yeast medium is the special medium for legionella culture.

Hence, the correct option is (C).

262. The clinical features are suggestive of cutaneous anthrax. Trichrome methylene blue is used to demonstrate McFadyean's reaction which is characteristic of Bacillus anthracis.

Hence, the correct option is (A).

263. Catalase-negative gram-positive cocci in chains – indicates that they are staphylococci. Enterococci are commonly seen in hospital-acquired infections and they are resistant to cephalosporins and even to vancomycin.

Hence, the correct option is (C).

264. Presence of pus cells without any organisms indicates non gonoccal urethritis. So we need to test for chlamydia. Mc Coy and HeLa cell culture is used for isolation of chlamydia.

Hence, the correct option is (A).

265. The bacitracin susceptibility test is used to distinguish Group A streptococci, from other streptococci. When grown on blood agar, Group A streptococci are sensitive to (killed by) the antibiotic bacitracin.

Hence, the correct option is (C).

266. Cases in which magistrate's inquest is held:

- Dowry death
- Exhumation
- Death in police custody
- Death in a psychiatric hospital
- Death in jail
- Death as a result of police shooting

Hence, the correct option is (C).

267. Sparrow's Foot Marks

- They are bizarre lacerations of the face seen in front seat occupants of a vehicle after a road traffic accident
- The injury is caused by the shattered windshield glass striking the face of the occupant

Hence, the correct option is (B).

268. The clinical features are suggestive of acute heroin intoxication. The drug of choice is naloxone – an opioid antagonist. It reduces the action of heroin. Buprenorphine is a partial opioid agonist. Flumazenil is a benzodiazepine antagonist. Methadone is used in the rehabilitation of opioid addicts.

Hence, the correct option is (D).

269. 'Mees' lines in the nails and raindrop pigmentation of skin are characteristic of arsenic poisoning. Treatment of choice – freshly precipitated hydrated ferric chloride.

Hence, the correct option is (B).

270. Conditions causing postmortem caloricity:

- Disturbance in heat regulation – sunstroke, pontine haemorrhage
- Increased heat production in muscles – tetanus, strychnine poisoning
- Bacterial / viral activity – septicemia / infections
- Intense asphyxia

Hence, the correct option is (D).

271. Colour of post mortem lividity (hypostasis)

- Normal – Bluish pink which later turns into bluish purple
- Carbon monoxide – Bright cherry red
- Cyanide – Pink
- Phosphorous – Dark brown
- Nitrates – Reddish brown
- Chlorates – Chocolate brown
- Hydrogen sulphide – Bluish Green
- Aniline – Deep blue
- Opiates – Black

Hence, the correct option is (C).

272. The cephalic index in different races:

Negroes, Aryans, Aborigines – 70-75

Europeans – 75-80

Mongols, Native Americans, Oriental Asians – 80-85

Hence, the correct option is (A).

273. Imprint abrasions, also known as Impact Abrasions are caused by the stamping of some object against the skin like radiators of cars in vehicular accidents.

Hence, the correct option is (C).

274. Methyl alcohol is converted into formaldehyde by alcohol dehydrogenase. It is in turn converted to formic acid by aldehyde dehydrogenase.

Hence, the correct option is (A).

275. Mercury poisoning (also known as hydrargyria or mercurialism) is a disease caused by exposure to mercury or its compounds.

Hence, the correct option is (A).

276. Water for meeting the requirements of a community can be obtained from various sources like rain, surface water and groundwater.

The safe yield of a source of water is defined as the yield that is adequate for 95% of the year.

Hence, the correct option is (C).

277. The lining of a sanitary well should go down at least 20 feet to ensure that water enters from the bottom and not from the sides of the well.

The lining should extend upwards for about 2-3 feet above the ground.

Hence, the correct option is (B).

278. 2 L is the amount of water required for meeting the physiological requirements of the body every day.

But water is also required for many other activities of daily life such as cooking, washing, bathing, etc.

Taking this into consideration, 150-200 L of water per capita is the amount considered adequate to meet the needs of all urban domestic purposes.

Hence, the correct option is (B).

279. Specificity of a test is the ability to correctly identify True negatives. It is calculated as follows:

$$\text{Specificity} = \frac{\text{Number of true negatives}}{(\text{Number of true negatives} + \text{Number of false positives})}$$

Hence, the correct option is (C).

280. Use of alkaline detergent for washing clothes is a non-deliberate cultural practice with an anti-mosquito effect. Mosquito larva cannot survive in alkaline water.

- Anti larval – Source reduction (elimination of mosquito breeding grounds), use of larvicides (surface films – mineral oils, stomach poisons – Paris Green, contact poisons), biological agents like fungi, nematodes and fish (eg: larvicidal fish – Gambusia affinis)
- Anti adult – Insecticides like DDT (organochlorine), Malathion (organophosphate) and pyrethroids for space sprays and residual sprays. Genetically modified adults have also used screens for homes
- Prevention of mosquito bites – Bed nets, mosquito repellents, insect screens for homes.

Hence, the correct option is (C).

281.

- The history of fever and jaundice in a sewage worker with features of renal failure is suggestive of Weil's disease
- Intravenous penicillin G is the preferred antibiotic for the treatment of Weil's disease
- Erythromycin can be used as an alternative
- In mild cases of leptospirosis, oral therapy with ampicillin/ tetracycline is given
- Doxycycline is used for prophylaxis against leptospirosis

Hence, the correct option is (C).

282. Modes of disease transmission by vectors are:

- Biting
- Regurgitation of ingested material
- Rubbing of infected excrement
- Contamination by body fluids of the vector

Hence, the correct option is (C).

283. Janani Suraksha Yojana is a centrally funded scheme launched in 2005 offering maternity benefits. It aims at lowering maternal mortality and infant mortality by encouraging institutional deliveries.

Hence, the correct option is (A).

284.

- The socioeconomic status of an individual/family can change over time due to the change in their literacy, job and income
- An individual belonging to a low socioeconomic class can move to a higher class by means of better income
- Similarly, an individual in a higher class may move to a lower class due to the loss of his job
- This change in the socioeconomic status of an individual/family over time is known as Social Mobility

Hence, the correct option is (B).

285. A screening test should be sensitive to detect maximum possible cases. Specificity is not as important. After screening, we can apply a confirmatory test with high specificity.

Hence, the correct option is (A).

286. The 5 clean practices are:

1. Clean hands
2. Clean delivery surface
3. Clean cord care
4. Clean blade for cutting cord
5. Clean cord tie and no application on cord stump

Hence, the correct option is (D).

287. The maximum milk output is seen at 5-6 months (730ml/day). At 12 months, it is only 525ml/day.

Hence, the correct option is (A).

288. WHO treatment schedule for active xerophthalmia:

- Medication is given on day 0, 1 and 14
- Same dose on all 3 days
- Oral route preferred
- Age < 1year / any age with weight < 8kg - 50000 IU orally - Age > 1 year – 2 lakh IU orally / 1 lakh IU IM

Hence, the correct option is (D).

289. The following modes are proposed for transmission of leprosy:

- Droplet infection
- Contact spread – direct (skin to skin) and indirect (fomites)
- Others (Breast milk, insect vectors, tattooing)

Hence, the correct option is (C).

290. Aedes aegypti index is the percentage of houses and their premises in a limited well-defined area that show actual breeding of Aedes aegypti larvae. It should be kept below 1%. In addition to this, airports and seaports should be free of Aedes aegypti breeding up to 400m from their perimeters.

Hence, the correct option is (A).

291. Adjuvants increase the immunogenicity of a vaccine so that a lower quantity of antigen is enough to induce a sufficient antibody response. H.influenzae conjugate vaccine (PRP-D) is not useful for immunization against diphtheria. It does not increase the immunogenicity of diphtheria.

Hence, the correct option is (D).

292. In a concurrent study (prospective study), the outcome under study has not yet occurred when the study starts. It requires long-term follow-up. Attrition is a big problem. It is an expensive study.

Hence, the correct option is (C).

293. Types of power:

- Reward power – Ability to give rewards
- Coercive power – Ability to withhold rewards or give punishment
- Legitimate power (position power) – Power bestowed upon a person by his / her position in an organisation
- Expert power – By virtue of one's own knowledge
- Referent power – By virtue of one's personality

Hence, the correct option is (D).

294. SAFE strategy was devised by WHO for the treatment of trachoma. SAFE stands for:

S – Surgery (of the lids for trichiasis)

A – Antibiotics

F – Facial cleanliness

E – Environmental change

Hence, the correct option is (A).

295. Here, the total cholesterol level is depicted as depending upon multiple independent factors. The relationship is linear and not logarithmic. Hence it is multiple linear regression.

Hence, the correct option is (C).

296. 95.4% of values lie within 2 SD (standard deviation) of the mean

Here, SD = 20 l/min

Hence 95.4% of values lie within 300-(2*20) and 300=(2*20)

Which translates into: About 95% of the girls have PEFR between 260 and 340 l/min

Hence, the correct option is (A).

297. Methylene blue reduction test is used to detect the presence of microorganisms in milk. It is done before pasteurization.

Hence, the correct option is (D).

298.

- KFD is transmitted by the bite of hard ticks
- Japanese encephalitis – Culex mosquito
- Dengue fever – Aedes mosquito
- Yellow fever – Aedes mosquito

Hence, the correct option is (C).

299. Case fatality rate = (Deaths due to the particular disease / Total number of cases of the particular disease) × 100

It represents the killing power of the disease.

Hence, the correct option is (B).

300. Eicosapentaenoic acid (EPA) is an omega-3 fatty acid. It's found in the flesh of cold-water fish, including mackerel, herring, tuna, halibut, salmon, cod liver, whale blubber, or seal blubber. It is also found in fish oil supplements, along with docosahexaenoic acid (DHA). Omega-3 fatty acids are part of a healthy diet that helps lower the risk of heart disease.

Hence, the correct option is (D).

Mock Test 03

PART A

Q.1 The cavernous sinus does not communicate with the:

A. Ophthalmic vein
B. Internal jugular vein
C. External jugular vein
D. Pterygoid plexus

Q.2 The artery, which runs along the lower border of posterior belly of digastric is :

A. Lingual
B. Ascending hypophyseal
C. Occipital
D. Palatine

Q.3 Little's area constitutes:

A. Anastomosis between branch of maxillary artery and the branch of facial artery
B. Anastomosis between two branches of facial artery
C. Anastomosis between two branches of maxillary artery
D. None of the above

Q.4 Ophthalmic artery is a branch of:

A. Maxillary artery
B. Sphenopalatine artery
C. ICA
D. ECA

Q.5 All of the following are branches of external carotid artery except:

A. Superior thyroid artery
B. Anterior ethmoidal artery
C. Posterior auricular artery
D. Occipital artery

Q.6 The blood supply of tonsils is:

A. Lingual artery
B. Superior thyroid artery
C. Facial artery
D. Pharyngeal artery

Q.7 Facial artery is the branch of the :

A. Internal carotid artery
B. External carotid artery
C. Superficial temporal
D. Maxilary artery

Q.8 First branch of external carotid artery is:

A. Facial artery
B. Ascending pharyngeal artery
C. Occipital artery
D. Lingual artery

Q.9 Which of the following arteries does not supply the Circle of Willis?

A. Anterior cerebral
B. Middle cerebral
C. Posterior inferior cerebral
D. Posterior communicating

Q.10 The papillae present on margins of the tongue:

A. Fungiform papillae **B.** Filiform papillae
C. Vallate papillae **D.** Foliate papillae

Q.11 Main arterial supply to the tongue is:

A. Lingual artery
B. Facial Artery
C. Ascending palatine artery
D. Ascending pharyngeal artery

Q.12 Ptosis may occur due to damage to:

A. Trochlear nerve
B. Oculomotor
C. Trigeminal nerve
D. Superior oblique muscle

Q.13 Safety muscle of tongue is:

A. Palatoglossus **B.** Styloglossus
C. Genioglossus **D.** Hyoglossus

Q.14 Paralysis of the upper eyelid is due to paralysis of:

A. III **B.** IV **C.** V **D.** VII

Q.15 TMJ is supplied mainly by:

A. Masseteric and auriculotemporal nerve
B. Superficial temporal nerve
C. Facial nerve peripheral branch
D. Posterior auricular nerve

Q.16 The otic ganglion:

A. Is in relation to maxillary nerve
B. Receives preganglionic parasympathetic fibers, through the greater superficial petrosal nerve
C. Sends postganglionic parasympathetic fibers to the auriculotemporal nerve
D. Is related to the tensor tympani

Q.17 The Tongue:

A. Separated from the epiglottis by glossoepiglottic folds
B. Contains 6-10 circumvallate papilla located posterior to sulcus terminals
C. Embryologically derives from 1st branchial arch only
D. Contains foramen caecum which is present on the dorsum of frenulum

Q.18 In jaundice, there is an unconjugated hyperbilirubinemia which is most likely due to :

A. Hepatitis
B. Cirrhosis
C. Obstruction of bile canaliculi
D. Increased breakdown of red cells

Q.19 Which of the following body secretion is maximum?

A. Salivary **B.** Gastric **C.** Sweat **D.** Lacrimal

Q.20 Bile acids are derived from:

A. Bile salts **B.** Bile pigments
C. (A) and (B) **D.** Cholesterol

Q.21 Intrinsic factor which helps in absorption of vitamin B12 is produced by :

A. Parietal cells of stomach
B. Chief cells of stomach
C. Beta cells of pancreas
D. Goblet cells

Q.22 Pharyngeal phase of deglutition :

A. Is a reflex mechanism
B. Vocal cords are closed
C. Is a voluntary mechanism
D. (A) and (B)

Q.23 Nutrients are mainly absorbed in:

A. Small intestine **B.** Large intestine
C. Liver **D.** Stomach

Q.24 All of the following are autocoids except:

A. Histamine **B.** Eicosanoids
C. Serotonin **D.** Insulin

Q.25 Drug receptors for steroids are present in the:

A. Nuclear chromatin **B.** Cell membrane
C. Cytoplasm **D.** Nucleus

Q.26 Which of the following is not a glycoprotein?

A. FSH
B. LH
C. Human chorionic gonadotropin
D. Prolactin

Q.27 Growth hormone is also called as:

A. Somatostatin **B.** Somatomedin
C. Somatocrinin **D.** Somatotropin

Q.28 Function of ADH (Antidiuretic hormone) is:

A. Water reabsorption **B.** Water excretion
C. Na^+ absorption **D.** K^+ secretion

Q.29 Maximum amount of glucose absorption occurs at?

A. PCT **B.** DCT
C. Loop of Henle **D.** None

Q.30 Brush border is seen in?

A. Bowman's capsule
B. Proximal convoluted tubule
C. Distal convoluted tubule
D. Loop of Henle

Q.31 Ammonia in the kidney tubules is excreted in exchange for?

A. $HCO3^-$ **B.** Na^+ **C.** Cl^- **D.** $PO4^{--}$

Q.32 Tidal volume in an adult is:

A. 125 ml **B.** 500 ml **C.** 1500 ml **D.** 2200 ml

Q.33 Surfactant is secreted by:

A. Pneumocyte **B.** Pneumocyte
C. Goblet cells **D.** Pulmonary vessels

Q.34 Smoking causes:

A. Ciliary motility **B.** Cellular hyperplasia
C. Mucous secretion **D.** All of the above

Q.35 Which vitamin is synthesized by intestinal Bacteria?

A. Vitamin B **B.** Vitamin D
C. Vitamin E **D.** Vitamin K

Q.36 Vitamin C is present in largest amount in the body in:

A. Eye **B.** Kidneys
C. Testes **D.** Adrenal Cortex

Q.37 Which of the following is the poorest source of vitamin C?

A. Milk **B.** Guava **C.** Cabbage **D.** Radish

Q.38 The 3 D's, Dermatitis, Diarrhea, Dementia are seen in the deficiency of:

A. Thiamine **B.** Riboflavin
C. Niacin **D.** Pyridoxine

Q.39 Which of the following enzymes require Vitamin C for their activity?

A. Procollagen proline hydroxylase
B. Procollagen amino peptidase
C. Procollagen carboxyl peptidase
D. Lysyl oxidase

Q.40 The following Vitamin is important in non-oxidative decarboxylation, transamination and trans-sulfuration reaction:

A. Riboflavin **B.** Thiamine
C. Pyridoxine **D.** Pantothenic acid

Q.41 Coenzyme A contains which of the following Vitamins?

A. Biotin **B.** Pyridoxine
C. Pantothenic acid **D.** Niacin

Q.42 Vitamin K antagonizes:

A. Corticosteroids
B. Thrombin Formation
C. Bishydroxy Coumarin
D. Production of clotting factors by liver

Q.43 Which of the following is not a polymer of glucose?

A. Glycogen **B.** Cellulose
C. Amylase **D.** Inulin

Q.44 An essential for the conversion of glucose to glycogen in the liver are:

A. UTP **B.** GTP
C. Pyruvate kinase **D.** Guanosine

Q.45 Enzymes concerned with the citric acid cycle are found in the :

A. Nucleus
B. Ribosomes
C. Mitochondria
D. Nonparticulate cytoplasm

Q.46 Cane sugar is:

A. Glucose **B.** Sucrose **C.** Fructose **D.** Maltose

Q.47 Which acid is formed in the citric acid cycle?

A. Oxaloacetic acid **B.** Glutamic acid
C. Nitric acid **D.** Butyric acid

Q.48 Which of the following is an abnormal constituent of urine:

A. Glucose **B.** Creatine
C. Urea **D.** None of the above

Q.49 Which of the following is a non reducing sugar?

A. Glucose **B.** Maltose **C.** Lactose **D.** Sucrose

Q.50 The end product of glycolysis under anaerobic conditions is:

A. Lactic acid **B.** Pyruvic acid
C. Acetoacetic acid **D.** Oxaloacetic acid

PART B

Q.51 The reversible change including the replacement of one type of adult cells with the other type is called:

A. Hyperplasia **B.** Metaplasia
C. Dysplasia **D.** Neoplasia

Q.52 Lack of differentiation of cells is known as:

A. Anaplasia **B.** Metaplasia
C. Dysplasia **D.** Hypertrohpy

Q.53 A simple bacterial test for mutagenic carcinogens is:

A. Ames test **B.** Redox test
C. Bacteriophage **D.** Gene splicing

Q.54 Cellular and flagellar movement is carried out by all of the following except:

A. Intermediate filaments
B. Actin
C. Tubulin
D. Myosin

Q.55 Presence of dermoid cyst in the ovary is an example of:

A. Choristoma **B.** Hamartoma
C. Neoplasia **D.** Teratoma

Q.56 Which of the following is not a feature of malignant neoplasm?

A. Invasion **B.** Encapsulation
C. Metastasis **D.** Anaplasia

Q.57 The most common malignancies found in males are:

A. Lung and oral cavity
B. Brain and parotid
C. Prostate and parotid
D. Brain and prostate

Q.58 Which of the following has best prognosis?

A. Malignant melanoma
B. Squamous cell carcinoma
C. Basal cell carcinoma
D. Osteosarcoma

Q.59 Burkitt's lymphoma is associated with the proliferation of:

A. T cells **B.** B cells
C. Lymph vessels **D.** Lymph nodes

Q.60 The wasting syndrome associated in cancer is called:

A. Achalasia **B.** Cachexia
C. Atelexis **D.** Cacogeusia

Q.61 Onion skin appearance is seen in:

A. Ewing's sarcoma **B.** Osteosarcoma
C. Osteoma **D.** Fibrosarcoma

Q.62 Sunburst appearance and Codman's triangle are seen in:

A. Osteosarcoma **B.** Fibrosarcoma
C. Chondrosarcoma **D.** None of the above

Q.63 Coagulative necrosis is:

A. Characteristic of focal bacterial infections
B. Characteristic of hypoxic death
C. Characterized by loss of tissue architecture
D. None of the above

Q.64 Diabetic gangrene is caused by:

A. Vasospasm **B.** Peripheral neuritis
C. Atherosclerosis **D.** None of the above

Q.65 Liquefactive necrosis is commonly seen in:

A. Brain **B.** Lung **C.** Liver **D.** Spleen

Q.66 Which of the following is correct?

A. Pyknosis - Shrinkage of Nucleus
B. Karyolysis - Dissolution of Nucleus
C. Karyorrhexis - Fragmentation of Nucleus
D. All of the above

Q.67 Stain used for demonstration of amyloid is:

A. Congo Red **B.** Masson's Trichrome
C. Vonkosa **D.** Reticulin

Q.68 The hormone dependent shedding of endometrium is an example of :

A. Necrosis **B.** Autolysis
C. Apoptosis **D.** None of the above

Q.69 Synthesis of DNA occurs in which phase?

A. G1 **B.** G2 **C.** S **D.** M

Q.70 'Physiologic programmed cell death' is termed as:

A. Apoptosis **B.** Lysis
C. Autolysis **D.** Autopsy

Q.71 Anasarca means

A. Abnormal inflammatory process
B. Severe generalized swelling
C. Absence of proliferation of vessels following inflammation
D. Presence of pus

Q.72 Nutmeg liver occurs in:

A. Jaundice
B. Chronic venous congestion
C. Cirrhosis
D. Hepatocellular carcinoma

Q.73 Infarcts are not common in:
A. Both Liver and Lung
B. Liver
C. Kidney
D. Lung

Q.74 Which of the following is true regarding lymphangioleiomyomatosis?
A. Primarily seen in old age
B. Commonly associated with persistent cough
C. Proliferation occurs in perivascular epithelioid cells
D. Disease is rapidly progressive

Q.75 Risk factor for atherosclerosis:
A. Hypertension **B.** Diabetes
C. Smoking **D.** All of them

Q.76 Which of the following is primarily a bactericidal drug?
A. Chloramphenicol **B.** Gentamicin
C. Sulphadiazine **D.** Tetracycline

Q.77 Penicillin is effective against:
A. Neisseria meningitidis
B. Neisseria gonorrhoeae
C. Treponema pallidum
D. All of the above

Q.78 The drug of choice for typhoid is:
A. Tetracycline **B.** Metronidazole
C. Ciprofloxacin **D.** Cefotaxime

Q.79 Desfuroxamide is a drug used for:
A. Kala-azar **B.** Pernicious anemia
C. Pain control **D.** Thalassemia

Q.80 A patient taking which of the following drug should not eat cheese?
A. Tetracycline **B.** Amoxycillin
C. Doxycycline **D.** Triamterene

Q.81 The drug which gives orange-red color to the urine is:
A. Rifampicin **B.** Ethambutol
C. Isoniazid **D.** Streptomycin

Q.82 Bacitracin is a :
A. Oral antibiotic **B.** Topical antibiotic
C. Parenteral antibiotic **D.** All of these

Q.83 Phototoxicity is the side effect of:
A. Penicillin **B.** Demeclocycline
C. Erythromycin **D.** Streptomycin

Q.84 Agent used in oral thrush:
A. Miconazole **B.** Clobetasol
C. Clotrimazole **D.** Amoxycillin

Q.85 Aminoglycosides is :
A. Accumulate in renal failure
B. Inhibit protein synthesis
C. Effective against gram-negative infections
D. All of the above

Q.86 Which of the following is a sign of deep anesthesia?
A. Appearance of tears in eyes
B. Resistance to passive inflation of lungs
C. Fall in blood pressure
D. Patient makes swallowing movements

Q.87 The minimal alveolar concentration (MAC) of halothane is:
A. 75% **B.** 25% **C.** 7.5% **D.** 0.75%

Q.88 Which of the following is used mainly for the induction of general anesthesia?
A. Fentanyl + Droperidol.
B. Ketamine
C. Thiopentone sodium
D. All of the above

Q.89 The general anesthetic having significant cardio depressant activity is:
A. Halothane **B.** Enflurane
C. Ether **D.** Nitrous oxide

Q.90 The immobility produced by general anesthetics in response to painful surgical stimuli is primarily due to their action on:
A. Motor cortex **B.** Basal ganglia
C. Thalamus **D.** Spinal cord

Q.91 The most common side effect of the oral administration of ampicillin is:
A. Anaphylactic shock **B.** Diarrhea
C. Oral candidiasis **D.** Renal failure

Q.92 Which of the following drugs is likely to damage the eighth cranial nerve when administered for a long period of time?
A. Ethambutol **B.** Isoniazid
C. Rifampicin **D.** Streptomycin

Q.93 Mechanism of action of quinolones is:
A. Inhibits DNA gyrase
B. Inhibits bacterial protein synthesis
C. Inhibits bacterial cell wall synthesis
D. Inhibits intake of folic acid

Q.94 Fluconazole is used for the treatment of:
A. Pemphigus **B.** Herpes simplex
C. Candidiasis **D.** Syphilis

Q.95 Ototoxicity and nephrotoxicity is caused by:
A. Antibiotic **B.** Antiemetic
C. Antifungal **D.** Antiviral

Q.96 On a stained slide, Clostridium tetani has the appearance of a:
A. Bunch of grapes **B.** Chain of beads
C. Drum stick **D.** Safety pin

Q.97 In initial stages of typhoid, salmonella can be detected in:
A. Feacus **B.** Urine
C. Blood **D.** All of the above

Q.98 The following are applicable to bacterial genome except:

A. It is composed of DNA
B. It does not contain histones
C. It is circular
D. Its DNA has both introns and extrons

Q.99 Each of the following can cause food poisoning except:
A. Cl. difficile **B.** Staphylococcus
C. Cl. welchii **D.** Cl. botulinum

Q.100 Organ of locomotion in bacteria is:
A. Fimbria **B.** Flagella **C.** Capsule **D.** Cell wall

Q.101 Wasserman test is diagnostic of:
A. Syphilis **B.** Gonorrhea
C. TB **D.** Typhoid

Q.102 In a patient with typhoid, diagnosis after 15 days of onset of fever is best done by:
A. Blood culture **B.** Widal test
C. Stool culture **D.** Urine culture

Q.103 Bacteria with potent exotoxin is:
A. Clostridium tetani **B.** Pseudomonas
C. Shigella **D.** Klebsiella

Q.104 Grape bunch shaped colonies are seen in:
A. Streptococcus **B.** Staphylococcus
C. E.coli **D.** Gonococci

Q.105 Inactivated microorganisms are used in the manufacture of which of the following:
A. Salk vaccine **B.** Tetanus toxoid
C. Sabin's oral vaccine **D.** All of the above

Q.106 The major intestinal pathogens which are non-lactose fermenters are:
A. Salmonella **B.** Klebsiella
C. Escherichia **D.** Paracolons

Q.107 A protoplast is best characterized as a bacterial cell:
A. With a cell wall but free of a capsule
B. Containing a cell wall and a capsule
C. Free of a cell wall and a capsule
D. Uniquely sensitive to penicillin

Q.108 With regards to temperature requirement, most pathogenic bacteria are:
A. Psychrophiles **B.** Mesophiles
C. Cryophiles **D.** Thermophiles

Q.109 Which of the following is anaerobic:
A. E.coli **B.** Bacteroides
C. Pseudomonas **D.** Klebsiella

Q.110 One of the following is a treponemal test for diagnosis of syphilis:
A. FAB **B.** Widal test
C. Wasserman test **D.** Kahn test

Q.111 The vaccine for Japanese Encephalitis is?
A. Live (mutant) vaccine
B. Killed vaccine
C. Live (attenuated) vaccine
D. Live (recombinant) vaccine

Q.112 The mechanism by which most fungi cause disease is:
A. Exotoxin production
B. Lecithinase production
C. Hypersensitivity
D. Coagulase production

Q.113 Germ tubes are formed mainly by:
A. Candida albicans
B. Candida stellatoidea
C. Candida tropicalis
D. Candida pseudotropicalis

Q.114 Fungal infection of human beings is called as:
A. Mucorsis **B.** Mycosis
C. Fungosis **D.** Micromia

Q.115 The culture media for fungus is:
A. Tellurite medium
B. NNN medium
C. Chocolate agar medium
D. Sabourauds medium

Q.116 The brick red color of post mortem lividity is seen in poisoning due to?
A. Carbon monoxide **B.** Hydrogen sulfide
C. Phosphorus **D.** Cyanide

Q.117 Lichtenberg figures are seen in?
A. Heatstroke **B.** Radiation injury
C. Lightning **D.** Electrocution

Q.118 'Paradox gun' is a?
A. Revolver **B.** Shotgun
C. Automatic pistol **D.** Machine gun

Q.119 Danbury tremor is seen in?
A. Mercury poisoning **B.** Iron poisoning
C. Lead poisoning **D.** Arsenic poisoning

Q.120 Kevorkian sign is seen in?
A. Cornea **B.** Retinal vessels
C. Pupil **D.** Vitreous humor

Q.121 Which of the following is true regarding superfecundation?
A. Fertilization of the second ovum in a woman who is already pregnant
B. Occurs in the bipartite uterus
C. Both ova do not always develop to maturity
D. The second fetus is born later as a mature child

Q.122 Scorching results from:
A. The flame emerging from the muzzle
B. Grains of gunpowder being driven into the skin
C. Superficial deposit of smoke on the skin
D. Deposition of lead or other metal in the skin

Q.123 The test to determine blood groups in a bloodstain is:
A. Luminol Spray **B.** Haemin crystal test

C. Kastle-Meyer test D. Lattes crust method

Q.124 Which among the following is a waxy, luminous & translucent poison?

A. Yellow phosphorous
B. Cobra venom
C. Organophosphates
D. Iodine

Q.125 Regarding rugoscopy, all are true except?

A. Palatal rugae are used as a method of identification
B. Palatoprints do not change during growth
C. Primary rugae are less than 3 mm
D. Secondary rugae are 3-5 mm

Q.126 Which theory of social health puts profit ahead of health?

A. Parsonian B. Foucauldian
C. Marxist D. Feminist

Q.127 The purpose is to limit the incidence of disease by controlling causes and risk factors:

A. Primordial prevention
B. Primary prevention
C. Secondary prevention
D. Tertiary prevention

Q.128 The property of a test to identify the proportion of truly ill persons in a population who are identified as ill by a screening test.

A. Sensitivity
B. Specificity
C. Positive predictive value
D. Negative predictive value

Q.129 A study that measures the number of persons with influenza in a calendar year:

A. Cohort study B. Case-control
C. Cross-sectional D. Case report

Q.130 The leading cause of Diarrheal disease is:

A. Enterotoxigenic Escherichia col
B. Salmonella (non-typhoid)
C. Rotavirus
D. Campylobacter jejuni

Q.131 Mammography should be done annually in women of what age?

A. 50 years old and above
B. 60 years old and above
C. 45 years old and above
D. 30 years old and above

Q.132 Samuel Hahnemann is referred to as founding Father of:

A. Ayurveda B. Allopathy
C. Homeopathy D. Yoga

Q.133 Origin of SPM dates back to:

A. 17th Century B. 18th Century
C. 19th Century D. 20th Century

Q.134 Benefits of Socialization of medicine are all except:

A. It eliminates competition among physicians in search of clients
B. It ensures social equity and universal coverage
C. Medical care becomes free for the patients, which is supported by the state
D. Patients can get a good quality of treatment without cost

Q.135 Socialization of medicine means:

A. Study of man as a social being in his total environment
B. Provision of medical services and professional education by the state but operated and regulated by the government
C. Provision of medical services and professional education by the state but operated and regulated by professional groups rather than by the government
D. Study of man as a social being in his whole life

Q.136 Who introduced the concept of social medicine?

A. Rene Sand B. Neumann
C. Jules Guerin D. A Grotjahn

Q.137 Which military surgeon successfully evolved the principle of preventing non-communicable disease with specific diet therapy?

A. Major Walter Reed B. James Lind
C. Major Ronald Ross D. Bruce

Q.138 Who propounded the germ theory of disease?

A. Leeuwenhoek B. Robert Koch
C. Ambroise Pare D. Louis Pasteur

Q.139 Who among the following introduced the concept of the relationship of the environment with human health?

A. Avicenna B. Charaka
C. Hippocrates D. Paracelsus

Q.140 The system of medicine currently not recognized by the Government of India is:

A. Ayurveda/Siddha B. Homeopathy
C. Acupuncture D. Unani

Q.141 The concept of health in Ayurvedic medicine is a state of balance between:

A. Four primary senses of humor
B. Three primary senses of humor
C. Five natural elements
D. None of the above

Q.142 A most common cause of maternal death in India:

A. Severe bleeding B. Unsafe abortion
C. Obstructed labor D. Eclampsia

Q.143 The incidence of tuberculosis in a community is measured by:

A. Sputum smear examination
B. Tuberculin test
C. Mass miniature radiography
D. Mantoux test

Q.144 Kuppuswamy scale for socioeconomic status is used for:

A. Urban population
B. Rural population

C. Urban slum population
D. Any population

Q.145 "Bhopal Gas Tragedy" is an example of:
A. Continuous or repeated exposure epidemic
B. Point source epidemic
C. Slow epidemic
D. Propagated epidemic

Q.146 Tuberculin positive means:
A. Immuno deficient patient
B. Allergic to tuberculin protein
C. The patient is suffering from the disease
D. The patient is infected with mycobacterium

Q.147 Who is known for the discovery of the prevention of scurvy?
A. John Snow B. Louis Pasteur
C. James Lind D. Joseph Lister

Q.148 The most common cancer affecting Indian women is:
A. Cervical cancer B. Breast cancer
C. Ovarian cancer D. Uterine cancer

Q.149 The best parameter to measure air pollution is:
A. SO_2 B. CO_2
C. CO D. All of the above

Q.150 All of the following diseases are transmitted by the Aedes mosquito except:
A. Yellow fever
B. Dengue
C. Chikungunya fever
D. Japanese encephalitis

PART C

Q.151 All of the following are seen in tuberous sclerosis except?
A. Civatte bodies B. Koenen tumors
C. Ash leaf macules D. Shagreen patch

Q.152 An absence of pigment in the skin is called
A. Acanthosis nigricans
B. Albinism
C. Melanism
D. Xanthoderma

Q.153 Pseudo-isomorphic phenomenon is characteristic of?
A. Vitiligo B. Psoriasis
C. DI F D. Plane warts

Q.154 Blaschko's lines represent?
A. Lines of development
B. Dermatomes
C. Lines along blood vessels
D. Lines along lymphatics

Q.155 Most common type of vitiligo is?
A. Segmental vitiligo B. Focal vitiligo
C. Generalized vitiligo D. Mucosal vitiligo

Q.156 Which of the following would be prescribed for acne?
A. Actiq B. Actonel
C. Accu-Check D. Accutane

Q.157 A 36 year old factory worker developed itchy, annular scaly plaques in both groins. Application of a corticosteroid ointment led to temporary relief but the plaques continued to extend at the periphery. The most likely diagnosis is:
A. Erythema annulare centrifugum
B. Granuloma annulare
C. Annular lichen planus
D. Tinea cruris

Q.158 Which of the following is not a cutaneous marker of internal malignancy?
A. Bullous pemphigoid
B. Acanthosis nigricans
C. Dermatomyositis
D. Erythema chronicum migrans

Q.159 An 8-year-old boy from Bihar presents with a 6 months history of an ill-defined, hypopigmented slightly atrophic macule on the face. The most likely diagnosis is:
A. Pityriasis alba
B. Indeterminate leprosy
C. Morphea
D. Calcium deficiency

Q.160 A 6-month-old infant had itchy erythematous papules and exudative lesions on the scalp, face, groins, and axillae for one month. She also had vesicular lesions on the palms. The most likely diagnosis is:
A. Congenital syphilis
B. Seborrheic dermatitis
C. Scabies
D. Psoriasis

Q.161 Airborne contact dermatitis can be diagnosed by:
A. Skin biopsy
B. Patch test
C. Prick test
D. Estimation of serum IgE levels

Q.162 A 3 year old child has eczematous dermatitis on extensor surfaces, His mother has a history of Bronchial asthma Diagnosis should be -
A. Atopic dermatitis
B. Contact dermatitis
C. Seborrhoeic dermatitis
D. Infantile eczematous dermatitis

Q.163 Tuberculids are seen in:
A. Lupus vulgaris
B. Scrofuloderma.
C. Lichen scrofulosorum
D. Erythema nodosum

Q.164 True regarding Pityriasis Rosea is:
A. Self-limiting
B. Chronic relapsing
C. Life-threatening infection

D. Caused by dermatophytes

Q.165 'Chancre redux' is a clinical feature of:

A. Early relapsing syphilis
B. Late syphilis
C. Chancroid
D. Recurrent herpes simplex infection

Q.166 Treatment of alcohol dependence is by all except?

A. Disulfiram B. `Naltrexone
C. Flumazenil D. Acamprosate

Q.167 A 45-year-old farmer has itchy erythematous papular lesions on the face, neck, 'V' area of the chest, dorsum of hands, and forearms for 3 years. The lesions are more severe in summer and improve by 75% in winter. The most appropriate test to diagnose the condition would be:

A. Skin biopsy
B. Estimation of IgE levels in blood
C. Patch test
D. Intradermal prick test

Q.168 Drug used for treatment of nocturnal enuresis is?

A. Trazodone B. Imipramine
C. Chlorpromazine D. Sertraline

Q.169 Most common cause of premature death in schizophrenia is?

A. Drug toxicity
B. Nosocomial infection
C. Homicide
D. Suicide

Q.170 Which is not a cognitive dysfunction?

A. Overgeneralization
B. Thought block
C. Catastrophic thinking
D. Arbitrary inference

Q.171 Which of the following is seen associated with alcoholic paranoia?

A. Drowsiness B. Delusions
C. Hallucinations D. Impulsiveness

Q.172 An 18-year-old student complains of a lack of interest in studies for the last 6 months. He has frequent quarrels with his parents and has frequent headaches. The most appropriate clinical approach would be to:

A. Leave him as a normal adolescent problem
B. Rule out depression
C. Rule out migraine
D. Rule out an oppositional defiant disorder

Q.173 Somatic passivity is seen in?

A. Depression
B. Hypomania
C. Body dysmorphic disorder
D. Paranoid Schizophrenia

Q.174 All are features of autistic disorders except?

A. Stereotypic movements
B. Impairment of social interaction
C. Visual impairment
D. Delay in speech development

Q.175 40 year old female came to the OPD with complaints of depressed mood, insomnia, loss of appetite, and lack of interest in surroundings for the past 1 year. These symptoms appeared after a loss in a business deal 1 year ago. Which is correct regarding the management?

A. Selective Serotonin Reuptake Inhibitors (SSRI's) are the most effective drugs
B. Antidepressants should be given based on the side effect profile
C. No treatment is required as it is due to loss in a business deal
D. Combination therapy with 2 or more antidepressants

Q.176 Delusions in clear consciousness are seen in:

A. Dementia B. Delirium
C. Schizophrenia D. Neurosis

Q.177 Dementia is seen in all except:

A. Schizophrenia B. Head injury
C. Huntington's chorea D. Cannabis

Q.178 Impaired consciousness, visual hallucination, hyperactivity and fragmentary delusions are:

A. Delirium B. Dementia
C. Paranoid psychosis D. Schizophrenia

Q.179 Postural orthostatic tachycardia syndrome is characterised by all except?

A. Women affected more commonly than men
B. Heart rate >120/minute
C. Increase in heart rate >30/minute when standing
D. Usually presents with orthostatic hypotension

Q.180 Who introduced cocaine in psychiatry.

A. Freud B. Jung C. Miller D. Stanley

Q.181 Most common cause of mood congruent delusion is:

A. Schizophrenia B. Mania
C. OCN D. Dementia

Q.182 Which of the following is a mature defense mechanism:

A. Projection B. Reaction formation
C. Anticipation D. Denial

Q.183 Not a proper match:

A. Auditory hallucination - Alcoholism
B. Thought broadcasting-schizophrenia
C. Delusion of infidelity - obsessive-compulsive neurosis
D. Delusion of grandeur - mania

Q.184 Suicidal tendencies are least common with:

A. Alone B. Depression
C. Old age D. Married person

Q.185 Psychoanalysis was introduced by:

A. Freud B. Schielder
C. Dale & Denicker D. Eugen Bluer

Q.186 Thematic perception test is named after:

A. Freud B. Simon paul
C. Douglas D. Wechslers

Q.187 RANKL is produced by all except?

A. Osteocytes
B. Osteoclasts
C. Activated T cells
D. Bone marrow stromal cells

Q.188 The commonest cause of mental retardation is:

A. Alkaptonuria
B. Kluver-Bucy syndrome
C. Korsakoffs syndrome
D. Birth asphyxia

Q.189 Ego's defense mechanism "Undoing" is typically seen in:

A. Depression
B. Schizophrenia
C. Obsessive-compulsive neurosis
D. Hysteria

Q.190 The eight-stage classification of human life is proposed by -

A. Sigmund Freud B. Pavel
C. Strauss D. Erikson

Q.191 The patient presents with altered behavior, delusions & hallucination suggest.

A. Psychotic disorder
B. Confirms schizophrenia
C. Korsakoff s psychosis
D. Obsessive-compulsive neurosis

Q.192 Commonest psychiatric illness in India is:

A. Schizophrenia
B. Endogenous depression
C. Neurotic depression
D. Anxiety neurosis

Q.193 Oedipus complex (given by Sigmund Freud) is seen in:

A. Boys of 1-3 years of age
B. Girls of 1-3 years of age
C. Boys of 3 - 5 years of age
D. Girls of 3-5 years of age

Q.194 Which of the following is a center for recent memory:

A. Parietal cortex
B. Temporal lobe
C. Hippocampus
D. Thalamus and subthalamus

Q.195 Biochemical etiology of Alzheimer's disease relates it to:

A. Acetylcholine B. GABA
C. Serotonin D. Dopamine

Q.196 Which is the most common cause of hypothyroidism?

A. Multinodular goitre
B. Lymphoma of thyroid
C. Hashimoto's thyroiditis
D. Reidel's thyroiditis

Q.197 The most common level of thyroglossal cyst is:

A. Lingual B. Infra-lingual
C. Supra-hyoid D. Infra-hyoid

Q.198 Hashimoto's disease is :

A. A granulomatous thyroiditis
B. An autoimmune thyroiditis
C. Fibrous thyroiditis
D. A viral infection of the thyroid gland

Q.199 A ranula is a:

A. Type of epulis
B. Sublingual thyroid
C. Thyroglossal cyst
D. Cystic swelling in the floor of the mouth

Q.200 Threshold radiation dose for haematological syndrome is?

A. 1 Gy B. 5 Gy C. 20 Gy D. 100 Gy

Q.201 Best investigation for the detection of bone metastases is?

A. X-ray B. CT Scan
C. MRI D. Bone scan

Q.202 Which of the following contrast agents can be used in a patient with renal dysfunction for the prevention of contrast nephropathy?

A. Low osmolar contrast
B. Ionic contrast
C. Fenoldopam
D. Acetylcysteine

Q.203 Egg on side appearance is characteristic of?

A. Tetralogy of Fallot
B. Total anomalous pulmonary venous connection
C. Patent ductus arteriosus
D. Transposition of great arteries

Q.204 Most ionizing radiation among the following is?

A. X rays B. Gamma rays
C. Alpha rays D. Beta rays

Q.205 Which of the following substances are used to coat the walls of a CT scan room for radiation shielding?

A. Tungsten B. Glass C. Lead D. Iron

Q.206 Which one of the following tumors shows calcification on CT Scan:

A. Ependymoma B. Medulloblastoma
C. Meningioma D. CNS Lymphoma

Q.207 Which one of the following is the most preferred route to perform cerebral angiography?

A. Transfemoral route
B. Transaxillary route
C. Direct carotid puncture
D. Transbronchial route

Q.208 Which of the following ultrasound marker is associated with the greatest increased risk for Trisomy 21 in fetus:

A. Echogenic foci in heart

B. Hyperechogenic bowel
C. Choroid plexus cysts
D. Nuchal edema

Q.209 The most sensitive imaging modality for diagnosis of ureteric stones in a patient with acute colic is:
A. X-ray KUB region
B. Ultrasonogram
C. Non-contrast CT scan of the abdomen
D. Contrast-enhanced CT scan of the abdomen

Q.210 The gold standard for the diagnosis of osteoporosis is:
A. Dual-energy X-ray absorptiometry
B. Single energy X-ray absorptiometry
C. Ultrasound
D. Quantitative computed tomography

Q.211 At $t = 0$ there are 6×10^{23} radioactive atoms of a substance, which decay with a disintegration constant equal to $0.01/\text{sec}$. What would be the initial decay rate?
A. 6×10^{23} **B.** 6×10^{22} **C.** 6×10^{21} **D.** 6×10^{20}

Q.212 The technique employed in radiotherapy to counteract the effect of tumor motion due to breathing is known as:
A. Arc technique **B.** Modulation
C. Gating **D.** Shunting

Q.213 Gamma camera in Nuclear Medicine is used for:
A. Organ imaging
B. Measuring the radioactivity
C. Monitoring the surface contamination
D. RIA

Q.214 The MR imaging in multiple sclerosis will show lesions in:
A. White matter **B.** Grey matter
C. Thalamus **D.** Basal ganglia

Q.215 The procedure of choice for the evaluation of an aneurysm is:
A. Ultrasonography
B. Computed tomography
C. Magnetic resonance imaging
D. Arteriography

Q.216 Complications of stellate ganglion block are all except?
A. Mediastinitis **B.** Cardiac arrest
C. Pneumothorax **D.** Mueller's syndrome

Q.217 Anaesthetic implication in Gaisbock's syndrome is?
A. Postoperative respiratory failure
B. Risk of deep vein thrombosis
C. Renal dysfunction
D. Risk of aspiration

Q.218 Thiopental is contraindicated in all of the following except?
A. Porphyria
B. Status asthmaticus
C. Pericardial tamponade
D. Penetrating eye injury

Q.219 Which of the following anaesthetic agents can induce epilepsy?
A. Sevoflurane **B.** Isoflurane
C. Desflurane **D.** Methoxyflurane

Q.220 Contraindications to vasoconstrictors in local anaesthesia?
A. Spinal anaesthesia
B. Epidural anaesthesia
C. Digital nerve block
D. Regional anaesthesia

Q.221 Which of the following is correct regarding colour coding of anaesthetic gases?
A. Oxygen - Black with grey shoulders
B. Nitrous oxide - Blue
C. Cyclopropane - Red
D. Helium - Orange

Q.222 Which of the following agents is not used to provide induced hypotension during surgery?
A. Sodium nitroprusside
B. Hydralazine
C. Mephentermine
D. Esmolol

Q.223 Which of the following agents is used for the treatment of postoperative shivering?
A. Thiopentone **B.** Suxamethonium
C. Atropine **D.** Pethidine

Q.224 Which of the following intravenous induction agents is the most suitable for daycare surgery?
A. Morphine **B.** Ketamine
C. Propofol **D.** Diazepam

Q.225 Which of the following statements is not true about etomidate?
A. It is an intravenous anesthetic
B. It precipitates coronary insufficiency
C. It inhibits cortisol synthesis
D. It causes pain at site of injection

Q.226 In case of reimplantation of an amputated digit, which of the following structures is fixed first?
A. Nerve **B.** Artery **C.** Vein **D.** Bone

Q.227 Agents which decrease bone resorption in osteoporosis are all except?
A. Risedronate **B.** Teriparatide
C. Strontium ranelate **D.** Raloxifene

Q.228

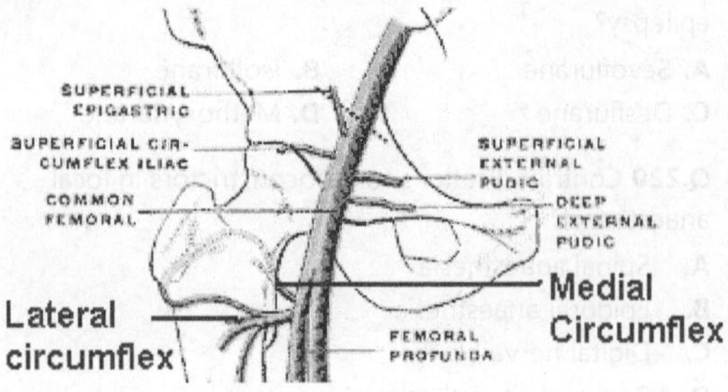

Arteries around the hip joint

Blood supply to head and neck of femur is mainly from?

A. Superficial epigastric artery
B. Medial circumflex femoral artery
C. Lateral circumflex femoral artery
D. Artery of ligamentum teres

Q.229 Which of the following is a characteristic feature of Blount's disease?

A. Genu valgum **B.** Genu varum
C. Coxa vara **D.** Coxa valga

Q.230 Agnes Hunt traction is used for?

A. Flexion deformity of hip
B. Trochanteric fracture
C. Fracture shaft of femur in adults
D. Low backache

Q.231 Triad of Klippel Feil syndrome consists of all except?

A. Low hair line
B. Elevated scapula
C. Short neck
D. Limited neck movements

Q.232 Brown tumor is characteristic of?

A. Hyperparathyroidism
B. Hypoparathyroidism
C. Hyperthyroidism
D. Hypopituitarism

Q.233 Which of the following is tested using the 'Lift off test'?

A. Teres Minor **B.** Subscapularis
C. Supraspinatus **D.** Infraspinatus

Q.234 All are true regarding synovial sarcoma except?

A. More common at extra articular sites
B. Knee and foot are commonly involved
C. Usually seen in individuals less than 50 years of age
D. Originates from the synovial lining

Q.235 Clavicular fracture is treated by?

A. Fixation with plate and screw
B. Open reduction and internal fixation
C. Skeletal traction
D. Figure of eight bandage

Q.236 A joint is innervated by the articular branches of the nerves which supply the muscles which move the joint. This law is known as:

A. Hilton's law **B.** Andry's law
C. Wolff's law **D.** Cushing's law

Q.237 Bone remodeling in response to stress was described by:

A. Harvey Cushing **B.** William Osler
C. Julius Wolff **D.** Nicolas Andry

Q.238 Most common nerve injured in supracondylar fracture humerus?

A. Median
B. Radial
C. Ulnar
D. Anterior interosseous nerve

Q.239 Heberden's Arthropathy affects:

A. Lumbar spine
B. Symmetrically large joints
C. Sacroiliac joints
D. Distal interphalangeal joints

Q.240 Gallow's traction is used for?

A. Fracture shaft of femur
B. Fracture neck of femur
C. Fracture humerus
D. Fracture tibia

Q.241 Duration of second state of labour in a multipara is:

A. 10 minutes **B.** 30 minutes
C. 2 hours **D.** 1 hour

Q.242 Most important conjugate during labour:

A. Anatomical conjugate
B. True conjugate
C. Obstetric conjugate
D. Diagonal conjugate

Q.243 Progression of labour is assessed by:

A. Partograph
B. Cervical dilatation
C. Fetal heart monitoring
D. Status of membranes

Q.244 In android pelvis:

A. Shape is triangular
B. Cavity is convergent
C. Sacral angle less than 90 degrees and inclined forward
D. All of the above

Q.245 All the fetal skull measurements are 9.5 cm except:

A. Bi - parietal
B. Sub mento bregmatic
C. Sub occipito bregmatic
D. Occipitofrontal

Q.246 The best intervention in I stage of labour is:

A. Artificial rupture of membranes with Oxytocin
B. Artificial rupture of membranes with methergine
C. Artificial rupture of membranes with sedation

D. Artificial rupture of membranes only

Q.247 In the partogram devised by WHO, the action line lies ___ hours to the right of the alert line.

A. 2 **B.** 4 **C.** 6 **D.** 8

Q.248 The length of diagonal conjugate is:

A. 5 cm **B.** 13 cm **C.** 13 .5 cm **D.** 10 cm

Q.249 Obstetric conjugate is the distance between:

A. Sacral promontory & inner surface of pubic symphysis
B. Sacral promontory & outer surface of pubic symphysis
C. Sacral promontory & upper edge of pubic symphysis
D. Sacral promontory & lower edge of pubic symphysis

Q.250 A pregnant woman in her third trimester was in a motor vehicle accident presets to the ER. She is stable and no uterine bleeding or contractions. Fetal heart sounds are normal and placenta is intact.

Which of the following is the best next step?

A. Blood type and Rh testing
B. Cesarean section
C. Induction of labor
D. Send her home and follow up the next scheduled visit

Q.251 The highest incidence of Gestational Trophoblastic Disease is in:

A. Australia **B.** Asia
C. North America **D.** Westem Europe

Q.252 The quantity of hormone released by Progestasert per day is?

A. 25 μ g **B.** 45 μg **C.** 65 μg **D.** 85 μg

Q.253 Which of the following is true regarding Organ of Rosenmuller?

A. Forms paraovarian cyst
B. Consist of horizontal tubules in mesovarium
C. Tubules are lined by columnar cells
D. Represents cranial end of the Wolffian body

Q.254 An athletic girl presents with amenorrhea for 3 weeks. Pregnancy test is negative and her vital signs are within normal limits.

Which is the most likely cause of this amenorrhea?

A. Estrogen deficiency
B. Progesterone deficiency
C. Testosterone deficiency
D. Thyroid hormone deficiency

Q.255 All of the following are germ cell tumours except?

A. Mesonephroid tumors
B. Teratoma
C. Dysgerminoma
D. Endodermal sinus tumour

Q.256 Which of the following is not true regarding Large Loop Excision of the Transformation Zone (LLETZ)?

A. Uses low voltage diathermy
B. Applicable only to cervix
C. Loop size greater than 2cm gives a better cone
D. Shorter procedure time compared to laser ablation

Q.257 Solid tumour with cystic areas in between filled with haemorrhagic fluid a accounting for about 20% of all ovarian cancers is?

A. Cystadenocarcinoma
B. Mesonephroid tumors
C. Endometrioid tumour
D. Brenner tumour

Q.258 Moschcowitz repair is done for?

A. Vault prolapse
B. Enterocoele
C. Chronic inversion of uterus
D. Adenomyosis

Q.259 Which is true reqarding Savage syndrome?

A. Receptor defect to gonadotrophic hormones
B. Short stature
C. Ovaries do not contain follicles
D. FSH is normal

Q.260 Which of the following is true regarding RU 486 ?

A. Prevents fertilization
B. Has affinity for estrogen receptors
C. Single dose of 10 mg prevents pregnancy in 90% cases
D. Causes delayed menstruation

Q.261 Absence of corkscrew glands is seen in?

A. Halban's disease
B. Polycystic ovarian disease
C. Irregular ripening
D. Metropathia haemorrhagica

Q.262 All are true regarding medical treatment of endometriosis except?

A. Oral progestins cause decidualization of endometrial tissue
B. Injectable progestagen is used once in 3 months in the management of pain of endometriosis
C. Levonorgestrel releasing intrauterine system reduces dysmenorrhoea in endometriosis
D. Gestrinone is given orally 2.5-5 mg per day to induce endometrial atrophy

Q.263 Which of the following is not a contraindication to pregnancy?

A. Severe pulmonary hypertension
B. Severe obstructive valvular lesions
C. Large secundum atrial septal defect with left to right shunt
D. Marfan syndrome with dilated aorta

Q.264 Gold standard test for measuring B HCG levels in serum is?

A. ELISA
B. Bioassay
C. Radioimmunoassay
D. Latex agglutination test

Q.265 False regarding hormone levels in polycystic ovarian disease?

A. Increased Androgen

B. Increased Prolactin
C. Increased LH
D. Increased LH/FSH ratio

Q.266 Most specific marker for neural tube defects is?

A. Alpha-fetoprotein
B. Unconjugated estriol
C. Acetylcholinesterase
D. Pseudocholinesterase

Q.267 Please identify which of the following are true with regard to pubertal development.

A. Pregnancy is not possible until regular menstruation occurs.
B. Adrenarche is the beginning of breast development.
C. Menarche, or onset of menstruation, is the first manifestation of puberty in the female.
D. Development of a menstrual cycle is dependent upon GnRH pulses increasing in amplitude and frequency.

Q.268 Weight gain in pregnancy depends on all except?

A. Smoking
B. Pre pregnancy weight
C. Ethnicity
D. Maternal age

Q.269 A primigravida in the first trimester of pregnancy was found to be sputumb positive for acid fast bacilli. There is no prior history of tuberculosis. What is the treatment of choice for this patient?

A. Category I DOTS
B. Category II DOTS
C. Category III DOTS
D. Start ATT after delivery

Q.270 Virus responsible for non immune hydrops foetalis is?

A. Cytomegalovirus
B. Herpes simplex virus
C. Hepatitis B virus
D. Parvovirus

Q.271 Plasma retinol value which is considered as marginal in children is?

A. 0.25 to 0.35 μmol L   B. 0.35 to 0.7 μmol L
C. 0.7 to 1.05 μmol L   D. 1.05 to 1.45 μmol L

Q.272 All of the following are features of anorexia nervosa except:

A. Restriction of energy intake relative to requirement
B. Intense fear of gaining weight
C. Symptoms emerge in later adolescence
D. Individual has engaged in recurrent episodes of binging or purging behaviour

Q.273 Which of the following is the fastest growing developmental disorder?

A. Specific learning disorder
B. Intellectual developmental disorder
C. Childhood onset fluency disorder
D. Autism spectrum disorder

Q.274 Which of the following is an X linked disease?

A. Friedreich's ataxia
B. Fabry's disease
C. Osteogenesis imperfecta
D. Cystic fibrosis

Q.275 Differentiating an ASD from a VSD using a chest X-Rays is by detection of?

A. Enlargement of pulmonary artery
B. Enlarged left atrium
C. Dilated aorta
D. Pulmonary plethora

Q.276 A12 year old Boy with hematemesis, melena and mild splenomegaly presented to the paediatrics OPD. Examination revealed absence of jaundice/ascites. Most probable diagnosis is?

A. Extrahepatic Portal Venous Obstruction (EHPVO)
B. Cirrhosis
C. Non Cirrhotic Portal Fibrosis (NCPF)
D. Malaria with disseminated intravascular coagulation

Q.277 Most common malignant orbital tumor in children is?

A. Acute myeloid leukemia
B. Acute lymphoblastic leukemia
C. Rhabdomyosarcoma
D. Cavernous hemangioma

Q.278 An eight year old boy presented to the casualty with high fever, pruritic erythematous rash, joint pain and lymph node enlargement. There is a history of upper respiratory tract infection for which he was on cefaclor 8 days completed of a 10 day course. The most likely diagnosis is?

A. Serum sickness like illness
B. HSP
C. Type III hypersensitivity
D. Kawasaki disease

Q.279 The protective effects of breast milk are known to be associated with:

A. IgM antibodies   B. Lysozyme
C. Mast cells   D. IgA antibodies

Q.280 The appropriate approach to a neonate presenting with vaginal bleeding on day 4 or life is:

A. Administration of vitamin K
B. Investiaation for bleeding disorder
C. No specific therapy
D. Administration of 10ml/kg of fresh frozen plasma over 4 hours

Q.281 The incision used in endomeatal approach to the ear is?

A. Lempert I incision   B. Rosen's incision
C. Lempert II incision   D. Wilde's incision

Q.282 Hitzelberg's sign is:

A. Reduced corneal sensitivity
B. Hypoesthesia of the posterior meatal wall
C. Paraesthesia of face
D. Delayed blink reflex

Q.283 Orbital apex syndrome involves?

A. Olfactory nerve
B. Ophthalmic division of trigeminal nerve
C. Maxillary division of trigeminal nerve
D. Mandibular division of trigeminal nerve

Q.284 All are true regarding mucocele of frontal sinus except?
A. Cystic tender swelling
B. Eggshell crackling can be elicited
C. Displaces the eyeball downward and laterally
D. Treatment is frontoethmoidectpomy

Q.285 Pain in tonsillar fossa and upper neck is characteristic of ?
A. Eagle's syndrome
B. Apert's syndrome
C. Sickler's syndrome
D. Usher's syndrome

Q.286 The following is true for Gradenigo's syndrome?
A. Mastoid tenderness
B. Retro-orbital
C. Hearing loss
D. Sagging of posterosuperior meatal wall

Q.287 Most common site of origin of vestibular schwannoma is?
A. Cochlear nerve
B. Superior vestibular nerve
C. Inferior vestibular nerve
D. Facial nerve

Q.288 Pain pathway from ethmoid sinus is via?
A. Nasociliary nerve
B. Lacrimal nerve
C. Lateral pterygoid nerve
D. Frontal nerve

Q.289 Endolymphatic hydrops is characteristic of:
A. Cholesteatoma
B. Meniere's disease
C. Otosclerosis
D. Gradenigo's syndrome

Q.290 Secondary haemorrhage after tonsillectomy is most commonly seen?
A. 6 hours after surgery
B. 24 hours after surgery
C. 6 days after surgery
D. 14 days after surgery

Q.291 Which of the following is true regarding Mittendorf dot?
A. Glial tissue projecting from optic disc
B. Obliterated vessel running forward into the vitreous
C. Associated with posterior polar cataract
D. Commonest congenital anomaly of hyaloid system

Q.292 All of the following are seen in Favre-Goldman syndrome except?
A. Ectopia lentis
B. Retinoschisis
C. Nyctalopia
D. Pigmentary changes similar to retinitis pigmentosa

Q.293 Stocker's line is seen in?
A. Pinguecula
B. Trachoma
C. Pterygium
D. Concretions

Q.294 Cogan's syndrome is associated with?
A. Keratitis
B. Conjunctivitis
C. Iritis
D. Myopia

Q.295 Gun sign is?
A. Silver wiring of arterioles
B. Deflection of veins at arteriovenous crossing
C. Copper wiring of arterioles
D. Tapering of veins on either side of the crossings

Q.296 Retinoscopy is:
A. Visualization of retina alone
B. Visualization of retina and all other posterior segment contents
C. Objective measurement of the refractive error of the patient
D. Subjective measurement of the refractive error of the patient

Q.297 Bilateral granulomatous panuveitis is seen in?
A. Heerfordt's syndrome
B. Reiter's syndrome
C. Behcet's disease
D. Toxoplasmosis

Q.298 Appendages of the eyes include all except?
A. Lacrimal gland
B. Eyelids
C. Eyebrows
D. Extraocular muscles

Q.299 Diplopia in superior oblique palsy is
A. Vertical diplopia on downward gaze
B. Vertical diplopia on upward gaze
C. Horizontal diplopia on inward gaze
D. Horizontal diplopia on outward gaze

Q.300 Organism most commonly implicated in Late onset endophthalmitis after cataract surgery is?
A. Pseudomonas aeruginosa
B. staphylococcus epidermidis
C. Candida albicans
D. Propionibacterium acnes

// Smart Answer Sheet //

Correct Percentage of students who answered correctly. **Skipped** Percentage of students who skipped.

Q.	Ans.	Correct / Skipped	Q.	Ans.	Correct / Skipped	Q.	Ans.	Correct / Skipped	Q.	Ans.	Correct / Skipped	Q.	Ans.	Correct / Skipped	Q.	Ans.	Correct / Skipped
1	C	89.36 % / 10.34 %	22	D	12.69 % / 78.98 %	43	D	77.51 % / 18.0 %	64	C	41.44 % / 42.22 %	85	D	10.25 % / 82.07 %	106	A	84.21 % / 13.67 %
2	C	58.37 % / 34.57 %	23	A	15.06 % / 80.4 %	44	A	77.34 % / 22.09 %	65	A	45.24 % / 38.94 %	86	C	79.33 % / 10.36 %	107	C	81.88 % / 10.28 %
3	A	19.48 % / 75.0 %	24	D	86.82 % / 11.14 %	45	C	67.7 % / 31.33 %	66	D	53.92 % / 31.39 %	87	D	42.9 % / 34.16 %	108	B	40.52 % / 41.44 %
4	C	42.99 % / 32.19 %	25	C	65.28 % / 31.48 %	46	B	68.15 % / 31.75 %	67	A	59.47 % / 39.91 %	88	C	68.84 % / 30.69 %	109	B	89.97 % / 10.01 %
5	B	45.86 % / 35.48 %	26	D	86.85 % / 11.46 %	47	A	55.52 % / 37.86 %	68	C	78.28 % / 12.23 %	89	A	11.51 % / 86.9 %	110	A	42.88 % / 42.98 %
6	C	80.79 % / 16.12 %	27	D	64.62 % / 32.2 %	48	A	79.78 % / 13.89 %	69	C	49.95 % / 41.34 %	90	D	87.24 % / 10.99 %	111	B	76.11 % / 11.29 %
7	B	32.47 % / 67.26 %	28	A	40.83 % / 35.87 %	49	D	49.07 % / 35.96 %	70	A	42.55 % / 53.66 %	91	B	47.7 % / 43.41 %	112	C	55.85 % / 34.8 %
8	B	51.49 % / 38.64 %	29	A	88.02 % / 10.78 %	50	A	65.35 % / 32.1 %	71	B	85.51 % / 12.98 %	92	D	82.09 % / 13.58 %	113	A	40.79 % / 32.87 %
9	C	82.9 % / 11.16 %	30	B	85.84 % / 11.27 %	51	B	24.74 % / 71.05 %	72	B	76.42 % / 11.93 %	93	A	60.44 % / 37.29 %	114	B	83.78 % / 12.06 %
10	A	85.27 % / 14.03 %	31	B	84.43 % / 13.98 %	52	A	89.14 % / 10.4 %	73	A	85.13 % / 13.42 %	94	C	83.0 % / 15.32 %	115	D	78.96 % / 13.39 %
11	A	77.38 % / 13.83 %	32	B	58.85 % / 37.23 %	53	A	76.31 % / 10.15 %	74	C	86.19 % / 13.37 %	95	A	76.57 % / 21.28 %	116	D	25.15 % / 73.73 %
12	B	42.86 % / 50.35 %	33	B	87.75 % / 10.36 %	54	A	69.25 % / 30.63 %	75	D	86.23 % / 12.51 %	96	C	85.22 % / 13.42 %	117	C	18.67 % / 75.44 %
13	C	80.62 % / 16.36 %	34	D	87.51 % / 10.57 %	55	D	55.19 % / 30.08 %	76	B	47.02 % / 30.78 %	97	C	89.54 % / 10.45 %	118	B	18.72 % / 74.15 %
14	A	80.48 % / 17.04 %	35	D	81.7 % / 13.42 %	56	B	77.06 % / 18.7 %	77	D	84.3 % / 12.94 %	98	D	60.96 % / 35.27 %	119	A	76.66 % / 12.27 %
15	A	87.21 % / 12.06 %	36	D	85.6 % / 11.45 %	57	A	12.34 % / 85.71 %	78	C	84.56 % / 10.83 %	99	A	89.19 % / 10.17 %	120	B	87.42 % / 10.91 %
16	C	55.37 % / 43.11 %	37	A	80.35 % / 13.63 %	58	C	50.93 % / 46.97 %	79	D	85.73 % / 10.39 %	100	B	79.34 % / 13.2 %	121	C	85.98 % / 11.43 %
17	A	82.74 % / 13.32 %	38	C	55.06 % / 34.87 %	59	B	77.17 % / 16.6 %	80	A	89.03 % / 10.72 %	101	A	87.98 % / 11.66 %	122	A	76.51 % / 22.75 %
18	D	88.4 % / 11.19 %	39	A	78.57 % / 21.34 %	60	B	66.21 % / 30.02 %	81	A	78.45 % / 19.59 %	102	B	48.18 % / 48.09 %	123	D	77.49 % / 19.37 %
19	B	82.71 % / 14.04 %	40	C	78.73 % / 20.87 %	61	D	89.5 % / 10.09 %	82	B	81.09 % / 11.33 %	103	A	77.52 % / 15.81 %	124	A	80.19 % / 17.7 %
20	D	84.09 % / 13.74 %	41	C	40.97 % / 41.57 %	62	A	78.48 % / 12.76 %	83	B	67.77 % / 30.39 %	104	B	63.15 % / 33.43 %	125	B	41.12 % / 56.39 %
21	A	78.18 % / 16.01 %	42	C	79.23 % / 17.55 %	63	B	88.49 % / 10.61 %	84	C	77.01 % / 14.38 %	105	A	88.53 % / 10.03 %	126	C	85.37 % / 11.6 %

Q.	Ans.	Correct	Skipped	Q.	Ans.	Correct	Skipped	Q.	Ans.	Correct	Skipped	Q.	Ans.	Correct	Skipped	Q.	Ans.	Correct	Skipped	Q.	Ans.	Correct	Skipped
127	B	83.12 %	13.89 %	148	B	65.72 %	32.27 %	169	D	77.48 %	22.35 %	190	D	22.04 %	73.45 %	211	C	84.56 %	14.2 %	232	A	81.14 %	14.67 %
128	B	86.27 %	13.42 %	149	D	61.16 %	37.33 %	170	B	85.48 %	12.53 %	191	A	80.65 %	18.88 %	212	C	86.44 %	12.4 %	233	B	81.87 %	12.82 %
129	C	78.36 %	15.37 %	150	A	79.14 %	12.05 %	171	B	13.25 %	74.57 %	192	C	82.27 %	16.85 %	213	B	84.35 %	14.32 %	234	D	86.06 %	11.56 %
130	C	79.44 %	10.13 %	151	A	86.03 %	11.53 %	172	B	80.94 %	12.47 %	193	C	86.64 %	13.22 %	214	A	81.56 %	13.18 %	235	D	85.69 %	14.3 %
131	A	82.34 %	13.23 %	152	B	78.48 %	11.22 %	173	D	83.16 %	11.51 %	194	C	86.03 %	13.8 %	215	D	12.74 %	76.08 %	236	A	85.7 %	14.27 %
132	C	87.71 %	12.29 %	153	D	64.09 %	30.48 %	174	C	43.11 %	39.96 %	195	A	87.22 %	10.04 %	216	D	89.05 %	10.27 %	237	C	76.35 %	18.23 %
133	B	13.04 %	84.22 %	154	A	81.66 %	18.2 %	175	B	66.55 %	32.78 %	196	C	84.86 %	11.68 %	217	B	85.31 %	11.01 %	238	D	88.49 %	10.08 %
134	D	61.16 %	38.41 %	155	C	81.17 %	11.43 %	176	C	85.91 %	10.19 %	197	D	83.72 %	11.17 %	218	C	87.91 %	10.79 %	239	D	86.05 %	10.24 %
135	C	87.69 %	11.16 %	156	D	48.11 %	48.89 %	177	D	76.05 %	20.91 %	198	B	87.69 %	10.05 %	219	A	79.97 %	13.21 %	240	A	87.86 %	10.34 %
136	C	85.85 %	13.97 %	157	D	81.0 %	17.19 %	178	A	77.41 %	15.93 %	199	B	88.3 %	11.41 %	220	C	76.8 %	17.09 %	241	B	89.95 %	10.01 %
137	B	84.2 %	12.29 %	158	D	42.67 %	49.68 %	179	D	86.05 %	12.27 %	200	A	65.39 %	32.2 %	221	B	82.64 %	10.25 %	242	C	83.19 %	12.0 %
138	D	85.12 %	12.16 %	159	B	80.59 %	17.97 %	180	A	63.84 %	32.14 %	201	D	85.45 %	12.83 %	222	C	79.21 %	20.33 %	243	A	88.89 %	10.62 %
139	C	79.89 %	14.38 %	160	C	78.92 %	19.36 %	181	B	79.31 %	16.29 %	202	A	84.62 %	11.57 %	223	D	81.99 %	10.81 %	244	D	82.21 %	13.62 %
140	C	89.88 %	10.05 %	161	B	89.18 %	10.23 %	182	A	87.82 %	10.47 %	203	D	88.3 %	11.04 %	224	C	78.76 %	19.35 %	245	D	86.09 %	11.54 %
141	B	81.06 %	16.96 %	162	A	76.28 %	21.83 %	183	C	17.33 %	74.41 %	204	C	63.29 %	35.48 %	225	B	49.08 %	40.61 %	246	A	84.11 %	12.36 %
142	A	76.68 %	15.23 %	163	C	81.18 %	11.45 %	184	D	23.47 %	70.55 %	205	C	83.04 %	10.23 %	226	D	16.29 %	76.52 %	247	B	85.26 %	11.09 %
143	A	83.11 %	14.92 %	164	A	76.43 %	18.47 %	185	A	89.0 %	10.66 %	206	C	77.28 %	16.85 %	227	B	85.25 %	11.61 %	248	C	81.09 %	14.68 %
144	A	76.57 %	12.93 %	165	A	42.49 %	38.82 %	186	D	20.78 %	77.61 %	207	A	60.49 %	37.86 %	228	B	83.75 %	10.95 %	249	A	80.85 %	10.31 %
145	B	77.85 %	21.17 %	166	C	68.73 %	30.73 %	187	B	30.67 %	68.62 %	208	D	86.16 %	11.1 %	229	B	26.33 %	68.65 %	250	A	28.54 %	67.39 %
146	A	89.55 %	10.37 %	167	C	40.85 %	32.1 %	188	D	80.17 %	13.22 %	209	C	60.34 %	30.56 %	230	A	82.31 %	15.99 %	251	B	46.49 %	53.25 %
147	A	84.7 %	14.36 %	168	B	85.23 %	10.34 %	189	C	42.2 %	35.99 %	210	A	89.85 %	10.01 %	231	B	46.81 %	32.17 %	252	C	16.49 %	73.63 %

Q.	Ans.	Correct Skipped	Q.	Ans.	Correct Skipped	Q.	Ans.	Correct Skipped	Q.	Ans.	Correct Skipped	Q.	Ans.	Correct Skipped	Q.	Ans.	Correct Skipped
253	D	63.31 % 35.93 %	261	D	79.49 % 11.79 %	269	A	19.27 % 68.05 %	277	C	31.15 % 67.7 %	285	A	64.73 % 33.82 %	293	C	89.87 % 10.0 %
254	A	80.1 % 19.01 %	262	D	40.89 % 30.81 %	270	D	80.28 % 13.85 %	278	A	67.1 % 32.13 %	286	B	76.58 % 17.52 %	294	A	89.29 % 10.45 %
255	A	83.8 % 15.15 %	263	C	66.32 % 32.01 %	271	C	64.97 % 30.68 %	279	D	40.0 % 37.43 %	287	B	82.58 % 12.09 %	295	D	76.06 % 11.35 %
256	C	79.02 % 19.75 %	264	C	84.31 % 11.96 %	272	C	76.06 % 15.11 %	280	C	84.74 % 11.05 %	288	A	77.38 % 11.66 %	296	C	79.99 % 17.87 %
257	C	32.47 % 67.53 %	265	B	78.71 % 12.22 %	273	D	53.93 % 42.11 %	281	B	89.72 % 10.26 %	289	B	59.6 % 36.35 %	297	A	82.62 % 16.0 %
258	B	60.82 % 30.06 %	266	C	76.42 % 10.9 %	274	B	87.13 % 12.66 %	282	B	47.3 % 42.99 %	290	C	86.37 % 11.55 %	298	D	77.25 % 16.3 %
259	A	89.53 % 10.33 %	267	D	79.98 % 10.44 %	275	B	78.89 % 14.37 %	283	C	85.94 % 11.75 %	291	C	77.68 % 19.46 %	299	A	89.54 % 10.27 %
260	D	86.43 % 11.3 %	268	A	59.14 % 34.29 %	276	A	14.15 % 74.86 %	284	A	78.11 % 13.86 %	292	A	88.76 % 11.0 %	300	D	16.88 % 79.25 %

//Hints and Solutions//

1. Free communication exists between the many rich venous plexuses about the base of the skull. Relatively large channels, the superior and inferior petrosal sinuses unite the sigmoid sinus with the cavernous sinus. The superior ophthalmic vein drains directly into the cavernous sinus through the superior orbital fissure.

The inferior ophthalmic vein may drain posteriorly directly into the cavernous sinus or to the pterygoid plexus. The pterygoid plexus communicates with the cavernous sinus through the foramina ovale, spinosum, and rotundum. Blood also leaves the superior and inferior ophthalmic veins to enter first the anterior facial vein, then goes to a separate channel that connects the internal and external jugular veins.

Hence, the correct option is (C).

2. The occipital artery arises in the neck anterior to the mastoid protuberance from the posterior aspect of the carotid. It branches from the carotid just a little above the facial artery.

The occipital artery passes posteriorly, parallel and deep to the posterior belly of the digastric muscle, and passes in a groove on the temporal bone medial to the mastoid process.

Hence, the correct option is (C).

3. Little's area is situated in the anterior inferior part of nasal septum just above the vestibule. This vascular area is most common site of nose bleed in children and young adults. 4 arteries anastomose here to form a plexus known as the Kiesselbach's plexus. These are: (i) Anterior Ethmoidal artery (Branch of ophthalmic artery) (ii) Septal branch of Sphenopalatine artery (Branch of maxillary artery) (iii) Septal branch of greater palatine artery (Branch of maxillary artery) (iv) Septal branch of superior labial artery (Branch of facial artery).

Hence, the correct option is (A).

4. Ophthalmic artery (OA) is the first intracranial branch of internal carotid artery (ICA). It arises soon after ICA emerges from the cavernous sinus, follows a short intracranial course, transverses the optic canal, and enters the orbit.

Hence, the correct option is (C).

5. The external carotid artery has eight branches: the Superior thyroid, Ascending pharyngeal, Lingual, Facial, Occipital, Posterior auricular, Maxillary, and Superficial temporal arteries.

While the anterior and posterior ethmoidal arteries both arise from the ophthalmic artery, a branch of the internal carotid artery (ICA).

Hence, the correct option is (B).

6. The palatine tonsils are supplied by branches of the external carotid artery: the inferior tonsillar artery via the facial artery, the superior tonsillar artery via the greater palatine branch of the maxillary artery, the posterior tonsillar artery from the ascending pharyngeal arteries and the facial artery, and the anterior tonsillar artery from the dorsal lingual artery.

Hence, the correct option is (C).

7. The blood supply is the facial artery, which is a branch of the external carotid artery. It passes from the medial of the mandible to the lateral side after traveling through the submandibular gland and rounding the lower mandibular inferior border. It becomes tortuous as it anastomoses with the angular artery.

Hence, the correct option is (B).

8. The first branch of the external carotid is the superior thyroid artery. It runs downwards alongside the larynx, to reach the upper pole of the thyroid gland.

Hence, the correct option is (B).

9. The posterior inferior cerebellar artery (or PICA) is an artery that provides blood flow to the cerebellum, a part of the brain located behind the top of the brain stem, which helps with functions related to movement and coordination.

Hence, the correct option is (C).

10. The papillae present on the margins of the tongue is Fungiform papillae. Filiform papillae cover most of the dorsal surface of the anterior 2/3 of the tongue, with fungiform interspaced. Just in front of the sulcus terminalis lies a V-shaped line of circumvallate papillae, and on the posterior aspects of the lateral margins of the tongue lie the foliate papillae.

Hence, the correct option is (A).

11. The main arterial supply to the tongue is the lingual artery. The tongue receives its blood supply primarily from the lingual artery, a branch of the external carotid artery. The lingual veins drain into the internal jugular vein. The floor of the mouth also receives its blood supply from the lingual artery.

Hence, the correct option is (A).

12. Ptosis may occur due to damage to the Oculomotor. Ptosis may be caused by damage to the muscle which raises the eyelid, damage to the superior cervical sympathetic ganglion or damage to the nerve (3rd cranial nerve (oculomotor nerve)) which controls this muscle.

Hence, the correct option is (B).

13. The safe muscle of the tongue is genioglossus. The genioglossus arises from the mandible and protrudes the tongue. It is also known as the tongue's "safety muscle" since it is the only muscle that propels the tongue forward. The hyoglossus, arises from the hyoid bone and retracts and depresses the tongue.

Hence, the correct option is (C).

14. Oculomotor nerve palsy is an eye condition resulting from damage to the third cranial nerve or a branch thereof. The third cranial nerve also controls constriction of the pupil, the position of the upper eyelid, and the ability of the eye to focus. A complete third nerve palsy causes a completely closed eyelid and deviation of the eye outward and downward.

Hence, the correct option is (A).

15. TMJ is supplied mainly by the masseteric and auriculotemporal nerve. The masseteric nerve passes laterally, above the pterygoideus externus, in front of the temporomandibular articulation, and behind the tendon of the temporalis; it crosses the mandibular notch with the masseteric artery, to the deep surface of the masseter, in which it ramifies nearly as far as its anterior border.

Hence, the correct option is (A).

16. The otic ganglion sent postganglionic parasympathetic fibers to the auriculotemporal nerve. The otic ganglion is a small peripheral parasympathetic ganglion residing immediately below the foramen ovale. It is related topographically to the mandibular nerve but is functionally related to the glossopharyngeal nerve.

Hence, the correct option is (C).

17. The Tongue separated from the epiglottis by glossoepiglottic folds. The anterior or lingual surface of the epiglottis is curved forward, and covered on its upper, free part by a mucous membrane which is reflected on to the sides and root of the tongue, forming a median and two lateral glossoepiglottic folds; the lateral folds are partly attached to the wall of the pharynx.

Hence, the correct option is (A).

18. In jaundice, there is an unconjugated hyperbilirubinemia which is most likely due to the increased breakdown of red cells. High unconjugated bilirubin may be due to excess red blood cell breakdown, large bruises, genetic conditions such as Gilbert's syndrome, not eating for a prolonged period of time, newborn jaundice, or thyroid problems.

Hence, the correct option is (D).

19. Gastric secretion is increased with fasting and inhibited by eating. Ghrelin stimulates gastric motility, gastric emptying and gastric acid secretion. Increases in acid secretion are via vagal pathways resulting in increased histamine release. In addition, ghrelin stimulates growth hormone and insulin secretion.

Hence, the correct option is (B).

20. Bile acids are derived from cholesterol. An acid made by the liver that works with bile to break down fats. On a more technical level, bile acids are steroid carboxylic acids derived from cholesterol. The primary bile acids are cholic and chenodeoxycholic acids. They are conjugated with glycine or taurine before they are secreted into the bile.

Hence, the correct option is (D).

21. The intrinsic factor is a protein that helps your intestines absorb vitamin B12. It is made by cells in the stomach lining. The intrinsic factor (IF) is a glycoprotein produced by the parietal cells (oxyntic cells) located at the gastric body and fundus. Intrinsic factor plays a crucial role in the transportation and absorption of the vital micronutrient vitamin B12 (cobalamin, Cbl) by the terminal ileum.

Hence, the correct option is (A).

22. The pharyngeal swallow is started by the oral phase and subsequently is coordinated by the swallowing center on the medulla oblongata and pons. The reflex is initiated by touch receptors in the pharynx as a bolus of food is pushed to the back of the mouth by the tongue, or by stimulation of the palate (palatal reflex). During the pharyngeal phase, the vocal folds close to keep food and liquids from entering the airway. The larynx rises inside the neck and the epiglottis moves to cover it, providing even more airway protection.

Hence, the correct option is (D).

23. The small intestine is the main site of nutrient absorption, and it is in fact the largest of the digestive organs in terms of surface area. The small intestine (small bowel) is about 20 feet long and about an inch in diameter. Its job is to absorb most of the nutrients from what we eat and drink.

Hence, the correct option is (A).

24. Autacoids or "autocoids" are biological factors (molecules) that act as local hormones, have a brief duration, and act near their site of synthesis and on another hand. Insulin helps to regulate blood sugar levels. After you eat, carbohydrates break down into glucose, a sugar that is the body's primary source of energy. Glucose then enters the bloodstream.

Hence, the correct option is (D).

25. Drug receptors for steroids are present in the cytoplasm. Steroid hormone receptors are found in the nucleus, cytosol, and also on the plasma membrane of target cells. They are generally intracellular receptors (typically cytoplasmic or nuclear) and initiate signal transduction for steroid hormones which lead to changes in gene expression over a time period of hours to days.

Hence, the correct option is (C).

26. Prolactin is a glycoprotein secreted by adenohypophysis of the pituitary gland which stimulates the production and secretion of milk. Glycoproteins are proteins that contain oligosaccharide chains (glycans) covalently attached to amino acid side-chains. The carbohydrate is attached to the protein in a cotranslational or posttranslational modification. This process is known as glycosylation. Secreted extracellular proteins are often glycosylated.

Hence, the correct option is (D).

27. Growth hormone (GH), also called somatotropin or human growth hormone, peptide hormone secreted by the anterior lobe of the pituitary gland. It stimulates the growth of essentially all tissues of the body, including bone.

Hence, the correct option is (D).

28. The antidiuretic hormone binds to receptors on cells in the collecting ducts of the kidney and promotes reabsorption of water back into the circulation. These channels transport solute-free water through tubular cells and back into the blood, leading to a decrease in plasma osmolarity and an increased osmolarity of urine.

Hence, the correct option is (A).

29. PCT(Proximal convoluted tubule) is lined by a simple cuboidal brush border epithelium which increases the surface area for reabsorption. Nearly all of the essential nutrients and 70-80 percent of electrolytes and water are reabsorbed by this segment. Glucose is absorbed actively by PCT. It is reabsorbed using a cotransporter with sodium.

Hence, the correct option is (A).

30. A Brush border is seen in the proximal convoluted tubule. The proximal convoluted tubule which is the longest part of the renal tubule has a simple tall cuboidal epithelium, with a brush border (microvilli). The epithelium almost fills the lumen, and the microvilli increase the surface area by 30-40 fold.

Hence, the correct option is (B).

31. Ammonia in the kidney tubules is excreted in exchange for Na^+. The ammonium is transported into the renal lumen in exchange for sodium by a luminal sodium/ammonium exchanger. The ammonium is then "lost" or excreted into the urine with filtered

chloride as its anion. This generates new bicarbonate (via glutamine metabolism) while excreting an acid (ammonium chloride).
Hence, the correct option is (B).

32. Tidal volume (symbol V_T or TV) is the lung volume representing the normal volume of air displaced between normal inhalation and exhalation when extra effort is not applied. In a healthy, young human adult, tidal volume is approximately 500 ml per inspiration or 7 ml/kg of body mass.

Hence, the correct option is (B).

33. Surfactant is secreted by pneumocyte. Surfactant is a macroaggregate molecule secreted by type 2 pneumocytes as the infant approaches term gestation. Surfactant is made up of 90% phospholipid and 10% proteins (surfactant protein [SP] A, B, C, and D). The primary function of surfactant is to reduce surface tension in the lung.

Hence, the correct option is (B).

34. Smoking causes cancer, heart disease, stroke, lung diseases, diabetes, and chronic obstructive pulmonary disease (COPD), which includes emphysema and chronic bronchitis. Smoking also increases the risk for tuberculosis, certain eye diseases, and problems of the immune system, including rheumatoid arthritis.

Hence, the correct option is (D).

35. Vitamin K is synthesized by intestinal Bacteria. Thiamine, folate, biotin, riboflavin, and pantothenic acid are water-soluble vitamins that are plentiful in the diet, but that is also synthesized by gut bacteria. Likewise, it has been estimated that up to half of the daily Vitamin K requirement is provided by gut bacteria.

Hence, the correct option is (D).

36. Vitamin C is present in the largest amount in the body in the adrenal cortex. The total body content of vitamin C ranges from 300 mg (at near scurvy) to about 2 g. High levels of vitamin C (millimolar concentrations) are maintained in cells and tissues and are highest in leukocytes (white blood cells), eyes, adrenal glands, pituitary gland, and brain.

Hence, the correct option is (D).

37. Milk is a poor source of vitamin C. Milk contains high quantities of vitamins A and vitamin B, such as thiamine, nicotinic acid and riboflavin, although it is a low source of vitamin C & vitamin E.

Hence, the correct option is (A).

38. Pellagra is a disease caused by low levels of niacin, also known as vitamin B-3. It's marked by dementia, diarrhea, and dermatitis, also known as "the three Ds". If left untreated, pellagra can be fatal.

Hence, the correct option is (C).

39. Vitamin C deficiency is associated with defective connective tissue, particularly in wound healing. Ascorbate is required for hydroxylation of proline residues in procollagen and hydroxyproline stabilizes the collagen triple helical structure. Consequently, ascorbate stimulates procollagen secretion.

Hence, the correct option is (A).

40. Vitamin is important in non-oxidative decarboxylation, transamination and trans-sulfuration reaction with pyridoxine. Pyridoxine is vitamin B6. Vitamins occur naturally in foods such as meat, poultry, nuts, whole grains, bananas, and avocados. Vitamin B6 is important for many processes in the body.

Hence, the correct option is (C).

41. Pantothenic acid is a component of coenzyme A . Pantothenic acid (as a part of phosphopantetheine) is also present at the active site of acyl carrier protein (ACP), a component of the fatty acid synthesis complex. Both forms are present in foods.

Hence, the correct option is (C).

42. Dicoumarol (bishydroxycoumarin) increases the half-life of tolbutamide in diabetics and in normal patients. Fungal spoilage of coumarin-producing crops results in the fusing of coumarins to form dicoumarol, also known as bis-hydroxycoumarin. Dicoumarol is an anticoagulant that acts as a vitamin K antagonist by inhibiting its bioavailability.

Hence, the correct option is (C).

43. Starch, DNA, and Cellulose are prime examples of natural polymers. When a large number of glucose molecules are held together by a glycosidic bond it turns into a polymer. Inulin is a mixture of linear fructose polymers with different chain length and a glucose molecule at each C2 end. Inulin belongs to the fructan group of polysaccharides and serves as a carbohydrate storage in many plant species.
Hence, the correct option is (D).

44. An essential for converting Glucose to Glycogen in Liver is UTP.

Glycogenesis is the formation of glycogen from glucose. Glycogen is synthesized depending on the demand for glucose and ATP (energy). If both are present in relatively high amounts, then the excess of insulin promotes the glucose conversion into glycogen for storage in liver and muscle cells.

Hence, the correct option is (A).

45. The Krebs cycle enzymes are membrane proteins found within the matrix of the mitochondria except for succinate dehydrogenase which is an integral membrane protein locked to the inner mitochondrial membrane.

Hence, the correct option is (C).

46. Cane sugar (cane juice, cane juice crystals), contains a high concentration of sucrose. Disaccharide – also known as double sugar, is made when two monosaccharides (aka simple sugars) are joined together. Examples include sucrose, lactose, and maltose.

Hence, the correct option is (B).

47. Oxaloacetate is an intermediate of the citric acid cycle, where it reacts with acetyl-CoA to form citrate, catalyzed by citrate synthase. It is also involved in gluconeogenesis, the urea cycle, the glyoxylate cycle, amino acid synthesis, and fatty acid synthesis. Oxaloacetate is also a potent inhibitor of complex II.

Hence, the correct option is (A).

48. Glucose is an abnormal constituent of urine. Abnormal constituents most commonly found in urine are protein (proteinuria) glucose (glycosuria) and acetone (ketonuria), and all may have a significance that must not be ignored.

Hence, the correct option is (A).

49. Sucrose is a non-reducing sugar because the anomeric carbon of both the monosaccharides is involved in glycoside or acetal formation.

Hence, the correct option is (D).

50. Lactic acid formed during anaerobic glycolysis enters the gluconeogenic pathway after oxidation to pyruvate by lactate dehydrogenase. After intense exercise, the lactic acid produces diffuses from the muscle into the blood and is taken up by the liver to be converted into glucose and glycogen.
Hence, the correct option is (A).

51. Metaplasia, the reversible substitution of one type of fully differentiated cell for another type within a given adult tissue, can also be a sequela to cell injury.

Metaplasia occurs when there is abnormal stimulation of tissue growth, generally because of faulty wound healing from a persistent toxic insult or constant mechanical disruption of the injured area.
Hence, the correct option is (B).

52. Anaplasia is a qualitative alteration of differentiation. Anaplastic cells are typically poorly differentiated or undifferentiated and exhibit advanced cellular pleomorphism.

Hence, the correct option is (A).

53. The Ames test is a widely employed method that uses bacteria to test whether a given chemical can cause mutations in the DNA of the test organism. More formally, it is a biological assay to assess the mutagenic potential of chemical compounds.
Hence, the correct option is (A).

54. Intermediate filaments form a cellular scaffolding that help cells to resist external pressure. Perhaps the most important function of intermediate filaments is to provide mechanical support for the plasma membrane where it comes into contact with other cells or with the extracellular matrix. Unlike microfilaments and microtubules, intermediate filaments do not participate in cell motility.

Hence, the correct option is (A).

55. Ovarian dermoid cysts, or teratomas, are made up of a variety of different cell types. They're a type of ovarian germ cell tumor. Usually, these tumors are benign, but occasionally they can be malignant.

Hence, the correct option is (D).

56. Cytologic features of malignant neoplasms include:

- Increased nuclear size (with increased nuclear/cytoplasmic ratio--N/C ratio).
- Variation in nuclear or cell size (pleomorphism).
- Lack of differentiation (anaplasia).
- Increased nuclear DNA content with subsequent dark staining on H and E slides (hyperchromatism).

Thus, Encapsulation is not a feature of malignant neoplasm.

Hence, the correct option is (B).

57. Lung cancer was the most common cancer in men worldwide, contributing 15.5% of the total number of new cases diagnosed in 2018. Lip cancer, the most common form of oral cancer, affects mostly men. Lip cancer is divided into two types: squamous cell and basal cell. The most common type of lip cancer forms in the squamous cells, which are the thin, flat cells that line the lips and mouth.

Hence, the correct option is (A).

58. The prognosis for patients with basal cell carcinoma is excellent, with a 100% survival rate for cases that have not spread to other sites. Nevertheless, if BCC is allowed to progress, it can result in significant morbidity, and cosmetic disfigurement is not uncommon.

Hence, the correct option is (C).

59. Burkitt lymphoma (BL) is a highly malignant B-cell tumor associated with Epstein-Barr Virus (EBV) infection. Although BL can be effectively treated in adults and children, leading to high survival rates, its ability to mask itself from the immune system makes BL an intriguing disease to study.

Hence, the correct option is (B).

60. Cancer cachexia is a wasting syndrome characterized by weight loss, anorexia, asthenia and anemia. The pathogenicity of this syndrome is multifactorial, due to a complex interaction of tumor and host factors. The signs and symptoms of cachexia are considered as the prognostic parameters in cancer patients.

Hence, the correct option is (B).

61. Typically radiographic appearance of Ewing's sarcoma is that of a permeative destruction of bone. It is associated with a soft tissue mass. Lesions can cause a lamination type of periosteal reaction (onion skinning) or vertical speculation.

Hence, the correct option is (A).

62. Osteosarcoma of the distal femur, demonstrating dense tumor bone formation and a sunburst pattern of periosteal reaction. Another pattern seen in rapidly growing processes is called the Codman's triangle. This is a bit of a misnomer, since there really is not a complete triangle.

Hence, the correct option is (A).

63. Coagulative necrosis is characterized by the formation of a gelatinous (gel-like) substance in dead tissues in which the architecture of the tissue is maintained, and can be observed by light microscopy. Coagulation occurs as a result of protein denaturation, causing albumin to transform into a firm and opaque state. This pattern of necrosis is typically seen in hypoxic (low-oxygen) environments, such as infarction. Coagulative necrosis occurs primarily in tissues such as the kidney, heart and adrenal glands. Severe ischemia most commonly causes necrosis of this form.

Hence, the correct option is (B).

64. Dry gangrene may develop slowly. It occurs most commonly in people who have arterial blood vessel disease, such as atherosclerosis, or in people who have diabetes. Wet gangrene. Gangrene is referred to as "wet" if there's a bacterial infection in the affected tissue.

Hence, the correct option is (C).

65. In the brain: Due to excitotoxicity, hypoxic death of cells within the central nervous system can result in liquefactive necrosis. This is a process in which lysosomes turn tissues into pus as a result of lysosomal release of digestive enzymes. Loss of tissue architecture means that the tissue can be liquefied.

Hence, the correct option is (A).

66. (A). Pyknosis involves the shrinkage or condensation of a cell with increased nuclear compactness or density; karyorrhexis refers to subsequent nuclear fragmentation. Pyknosis and karyorrhexis are degenerative changes that are often observed in nonseptic exudates.

(B). Karyolysis (from Greek karyon—kernel, seed, or nucleus), and lysis, "to separate") is the complete dissolution of the chromatin of a dying cell due to the enzymatic degradation by endonucleases. The whole cell will eventually stain uniformly with eosin after karyolysis.

(C). Karyorrhexis (from Greek karyon, "kernel, seed or nucleus", and rhexis, "bursting") is the destructive fragmentation of the nucleus of a dying cell whereby its chromatin is distributed irregularly throughout the cytoplasm.

Hence, the correct option is (D).

67. Staining with Congo Red dye (CR) is one of the major methods used to detect the amyloid structure of protein aggregates. Staining with Congo Red dye (CR) is one of the major methods used to detect the amyloid structure of protein aggregates.

Hence, the correct option is (A).

68. Accumulated evidence suggests that apoptosis helps to maintain cellular homeostasis during the menstrual cycle by eliminating senescent cells from the functional layer of the uterine endometrium during the late secretory and menstrual phase of the cycle.

Hence, the correct option is (C).

69. Fortunately, our cells have defense mechanisms to shield us from these damaging events. In the eukaryotic cell cycle, chromosome duplication occurs during "S phase" (the phase of DNA synthesis) and chromosome segregation occurs during "M phase" (the mitosis phase).

Hence, the correct option is (C).

70. Apoptosis is the process of programmed cell death (PCD) that may occur in multicellular organisms. Biochemical events lead to characteristic cell changes (morphology) and death. These changes include blebbing, cell shrinkage, nuclear fragmentation, chromatin condensation, and chromosomal DNA fragmentation.

Hence, the correct option is (A).

71. Anasarca is general swelling of the whole body that can occur when the tissues of the body retain too much fluid. The condition is also known as extreme generalized edema.

Hence, the correct option is (B).

72. A nutmeg liver appearance is due to a perfusion abnormality of the liver usually as the result of hepatic venous congestion. When hepatic veins are congested, contrast is prevented from diffusing through the liver in a normal manner.

Hence, the correct option is (B).

73. Infarcts are not common in both liver and lungs. Infarction is tissue death (necrosis) due to inadequate blood supply to the affected area. It may be caused by artery blockages, rupture, mechanical compression, or vasoconstriction.

Hence, the correct option is (A).

74.

- Lymphangioleiomyomatosis is primarily seen in young women of childbearing age.
- The commonest symptom is dyspnoea.
- Proliferation of perivascular epithelioid cells results in distortion of lungs with cystic dilation of terminal air spaces.
- It is a slowly progressing disorder.

Hence, the correct option is (C).

75. The exact cause of atherosclerosis isn't known. However, certain traits, conditions, or habits may raise your risk for the disease. These conditions are known as risk factors. The more risk factors you have, the more likely it is that you'll develop atherosclerosis.

Major Risk Factors

- Unhealthy blood cholesterol levels. This includes high LDL cholesterol (sometimes called 'bad" cholesterol) and low HDL cholesterol (sometimes called "good" cholesterol).
- High blood pressure, Blood pressure is considered high if it stays at or above $140/90$ mmHg over time. If you have diabetes or chronic kidney disease high blood pressure is defined as $130/80$ mmHg or higher. (The mmHg is millimeters of mercury - the units used to measure blood pressure,
- Smoking, Smoking can damage and tighten blood vessels, raise cholesterol levels, and raise blood pressure. Smoking also doesn't allow enough oxygen to reach the body's tissues.
- Insulin resistance, This condition occurs if the body can't use its insulin properly, insulin is a hormone that helps move blood sugar into cells where it's used as an energy source. Insulin resistance may lead to diabetes.
- Diabetes, With this disease, the body's blood sugar level is too high because the body doesn't make enough insulin or doesn't use its insulin properly.

Hence, the correct option is (D).

76. Gentamicin is bactericidal and is a broad-spectrum antibiotic (except against streptococci and anaerobic bacteria). Its mechanism of action involves inhibition of bacterial protein synthesis by binding to 30S ribosomes.

Hence, the correct option is (B).

77. (A). Meningococcal infections are usually treated with penicillin, ampicillin, or a combination of penicillin and chloramphenicol. Isolates of Neisseria meningitides with increased levels of resistance to penicillin.

(B). Neisseria gonorrhoeae, the bacterium that causes the sexually transmitted infection gonorrhea, has developed antibiotic resistance to many antibiotics. The bacteria was first identified in 1879. In the 1940s effective treatment with penicillin became available, but by the 1970s resistant strains predominated.

(C). Although penicillin is still effective, clinically significant resistance to macrolides, a second-line alternative to penicillin, has emerged. Macrolide-resistant strains of Treponema pallidum are now prevalent in several developed countries.

Hence, the correct option is (D).

78. Ciprofloxacin (Cipro): Proven to be highly effective for typhoid and paratyphoid fevers. Defervescence occurs in 3-5 d, and convalescent carriage and relapses are rare. Other quinolones (eg, ofloxacin, norfloxacin, pefloxacin) usually are effective. If vomiting or diarrhea is present, should be given IV.

Hence, the correct option is (C).

79. Desfuroxamide is a drug used for thalassemia. Thalassemia is an inherited blood disorder that causes your body to have less hemoglobin than normal. Hemoglobin enables red blood cells to carry oxygen. Thalassemia can cause anemia, leaving you fatigued.

Hence, the correct option is (D).

80. Dairy products such as milk, yogurt, and cheese can interfere with certain medications, including antibiotics such as tetracycline, doxycycline, and ciprofloxacin. Tetracycline is used to treat a wide variety of infections, including acne. It is an antibiotic that works by stopping the growth of bacteria. This antibiotic treats only bacterial infections. It will not work for viral infections (such as common cold, flu).

Hence, the correct option is (A).

81. Rifampicin will cause urine, saliva, sputum, sweat, teeth, and tears to turn a reddish-orange to reddish-brown color. This is to be expected while you are using this medicine. This effect may also cause soft contact lenses to become permanently discolored.

Hence, the correct option is (A).

82. Bacitracin is a topical antibiotic used as first aid to help prevent infection from minor abrasions, wounds, and burns. These drugs are used in similar ways, but they contain different active ingredients.

Hence, the correct option is (B).

83. Phototoxicity is the side effect of Demeclocycline. Adverse effects of Demeclocycline. Less serious side effects may include:

- Sores or swelling in your rectal or genital area;
- Mild nausea, vomiting, diarrhea, loss of appetite;
- White patches or sores inside your mouth or on your lips;
- Swollen tongue, trouble swallowing;
- Vaginal itching or discharge.

Hence, the correct option is (B).

84. Clotrimazole lozenge is only approved for the treatment of fungal infections of the mouth or throat. It may also be used to prevent these infections in patients receiving treatments that may weaken the body's immune system (e.g.chemotherapy). Clotrimazole is known as an azole antifungal agent.

Hence, the correct option is (C).

85. (A). Nephrotoxicity induced by aminoglycosides manifests clinically as non oliguric renal failure, with a slow rise in serum creatinine and a hypoosmolar urinary output developing after several days of treatment.

(B). Aminoglycosides inhibit protein synthesis in bacteria by binding irreversibly to the 30S ribosomal subunit. This inhibits transfer of aminoacyl-tRNA to the peptidyl site, causing premature termination of the peptide chain; it also increases the frequency of misreading of mRNA.

(C). Aminoglycosides are potent bactericidal antibiotics that act by creating fissures in the outer membrane of the bacterial cell. They are particularly active against aerobic, gram-negative bacteria and act synergistically against certain gram-positive organisms.

Hence, the correct option is (D).

86. Anesthetic drugs, which are used to put you to sleep during surgery, can affect your blood pressure. Changes can happen while you're being put to sleep and then when you're coming off of the drugs. In some people, anesthesia causes a significant drop in blood pressure.

Hence, the correct option is (C).

87. The minimum alveolar concentration (MAC) for isoflurane (1.15%) is one-and-one-half times that for halothane (0.75%) and two-thirds that for enflurane (1.7%).

Hence, the correct option is (D).

88. Sodium thiopental is an ultra-short-acting barbiturate and has been used commonly in the induction phase of general anesthesia. Its use has been largely replaced with that of propofol, but may retain some popularity as an induction agent for rapid-sequence induction and intubation, such as in obstetrics.

Hence, the correct option is (C).

89. In general halothane, like most volatile anesthetics, causes a dose-dependent reduction in arterial blood pressure and cardiac output. Unique to halothane is the decreased heart rate as the carotid baroreceptor reflex is blunted. Like most other inhalational agents, halothane causes a decrease in hepatic flow.

Hence, the correct option is (A).

90. Inhaled anesthetic-induced immobility is primarily mediated by an action on the spinal cord, as a consequence of anesthetic action upon motor neuron excitability and upon nociceptive neurons of the spinal cord dorsal horn. Actions on specific receptors have an effect on their synaptic transmission.

Hence, the correct option is (D).

91. The more common side effects of ampicillin oral capsule can include nausea. vomiting, diarrhea. Diarrhea is characterized by loose, watery stools or a frequent need to have a bowel movement. Most often, antibiotic-associated diarrhea is mild and requires no treatment. Diarrhea typically clears up within a few days after you stop taking the antibiotic.

Hence, the correct option is (B).

92. Streptomycin drugs damage the eighth cranial nerve when administered for a long period of time. Streptomycin belongs to a class of drugs known as aminoglycoside antibiotics. It works by killing the organisms that cause the infection. This drug may also be used to treat other serious infections (e.g. Mycobacterium avium complex-MAC, tularemia, endocarditis, plague) along with other medications.

Hence, the correct option is (D).

93. Quinolones inhibit replication of bacterial DNA by blocking the ligase domain of bacterial DNA gyrase (topoisomerase II); some also inhibit topoisomerase IV. These enzymes relax DNA supercoils and enable DNA replication and repair. The effect of quinolones is bactericidal.

Hence, the correct option is (A).

94. Fluconazole is used to treat serious fungal or yeast infections, such as vaginal candidiasis, oropharyngeal candidiasis (thrush, oral thrush), esophageal candidiasis (candida esophagitis), other candida infections (including urinary tract infections, peritonitis [inflammation of the lining of abdomen or stomach], and infections that may occur in different parts of the body), or fungal (cryptococcal) meningitis. This medicine works by killing the fungus or yeast or preventing its growth.

Hence, the correct option is (C).

95. Ototoxicity and nephrotoxicity are caused by the antibiotic. Nephrotoxicity and ototoxicity are clinically significant dose-related adverse effects associated with second-line anti-tubercular injectables drugs (aminoglycosides and capreomycin) used during the intensive phase of treatment of multi-drug resistant tuberculosis (MDR-TB) patients.

Hence, the correct option is (A).

96. Clostridium tetani is a motile, anaerobic, spore-forming bacteria (terminal spores with drum stick appearance). Clostridium tetani is a gram-positive, spore-forming, motile, anaerobic bacillus. Typically measuring 0.3 to 0.5 μm in width and 2 to 2.5 μm in length, the vegetative form often develops long filament-like cells in culture. Motility is produced by peritrichous flagella coating the cell surface.

Hence, the correct option is (C).

97. Classically, the course of untreated typhoid fever is divided into four individual stages, each lasting approximately one week. Diagnosis is made by any blood, bone marrow or stool cultures and with the Widal test (demonstration of salmonella antibodies against antigens O-somatic and H-flagellar).

Hence, the correct option is (C).

98. (A). Most bacteria have a genome that consists of a single DNA molecule (i.e., one chromosome) that is several million base pairs in size and is "circular" (doesn't have ends like chromosomes of eukaryotic organisms).

(B). Escherichia coli is a bacterium, which doesn't have any histones. It is a system that is naïve to histones and hasn't evolved to deal with histone: DNA structures. Instead, histones are being incorporated in the bacterial genome without affecting key processes in the cell, like replication or transcription.

(C). A circular chromosome is a chromosome in bacteria, archaea, mitochondria, and chloroplasts, in the form of a molecule of circular DNA, unlike the linear chromosome of most eukaryotes. Most prokaryotic chromosomes contain a circular DNA molecule – there are no free ends to the DNA.

Hence, the correct option is (D).

99. (A). Clostridium difficile, also known as C. difficile or C. diff, is bacteria that can infect the bowel and cause diarrhea. The infection most commonly affects people who have recently been treated with antibiotics.

(B). Staph food poisoning is a gastrointestinal illness caused by eating foods contaminated with toxins produced by the bacterium Staphylococcus aureus (Staph) bacteria.

(C). Clostridium welchii type A is a common agent of food poisoning when allowed to proliferate to large numbers in cooked foods, usually meat and poultry.

(D). Botulism is a disease caused by the bacterium scientifically known as Clostridium botulinum. Botulism food poisoning occurs when a toxin produced by the bacteria is consumed in improperly preserved foods. The disease is caused by a potent neurotoxin produced by the bacteria.

Hence, the correct option is (A).

100. A flagellum is a locomotory organ in motile bacteria. The filament is its longest portion. Flagella are microscopic hair-like structures involved in the locomotion of a cell. The word "flagellum" means "whip". The flagella have a whip-like appearance that helps to propel a cell through the liquid. Some special flagella are used in few organisms as sensory organs that can sense changes in pH and temperature.

Hence, the correct option is (B).

101. The Wassermann test or Wassermann reaction (WR) is an antibody test for syphilis, named after the bacteriologist August Paul von Wassermann, based on complement fixation. It was the first blood test for syphilis and the first in the nontreponemal test (NTT) category.

Hence, the correct option is (A).

102. In a patient with typhoid, diagnosis after 15 days of onset of fever is best done by Widal test. The Widal test is one method that may be used to help make a presumptive diagnosis of enteric fever, also known as typhoid fever.

The Widal agglutination test, developed by F Widal in 18961 to aid in the diagnosis of typhoid fever, utilizes a suspension of killed Salmonella typhi as antigen, to detect typhoid fever in serum from suspected typhi-infected patients who present with febrile illness.

Hence, the correct option is (B).

103. Bacteria with potent exotoxin is Clostridium tetani. Well-known exotoxins include botulinum toxin produced by Clostridium botulinum; Corynebacterium diphtheriae toxin, produced during life-threatening symptoms of diphtheria; tetanospasmin produced by Clostridium tetani.

Hence, the correct option is (A).

104. Grape bunch-shaped colonies are seen in Staphylococcus. Staphylococci are irregular (grape-like) clusters of cocci (e.g. Staphylococcus aureus). Tetrads are clusters of four cocci arranged within the same plane (e.g. Micrococcus sp.). Sarcina is a genus of bacteria that are found in cuboidal arrangements of eight cocci (e.g. Sarcina ventriculi).

Hence, the correct option is (B).

105. Vaccines against rabies, polio (the Salk vaccine), some forms of influenza, and cholera are made from inactivated microorganisms. Another type of vaccine is a subunit vaccine, which is made from proteins found on the surface of infectious agents. Vaccines for influenza and hepatitis B are of that type.

Hence, the correct option is (A).

106. Lac negative: Organisms unable to ferment lactose will form normal-colored (i.e., un-dyed) colonies. The medium will remain yellow. Examples of non-lactose fermenting bacteria are Salmonella, Proteus species, Yersinia, Pseudomonas aeruginosa and Shigella.

Hence, the correct option is (A).

107. Protoplasts are cells that have had their cell wall removed, usually by digestion with enzymes. Cellulase enzymes digest the cellulose in plant cell walls while pectinase enzymes break down the pectin holding cells together. Once the cell wall has been removed the resulting protoplast is spherical in shape.

Hence, the correct option is (C).

108. Pathogens are usually mesophiles. Mesophiles grow best at moderate temperatures in the range of 20°C to about 45°C. Thermophiles and hyperthermophiles are adapted to life at temperatures above 50°C. Adaptations to cold and hot temperatures require changes in the composition of membrane lipids and proteins.

Hence, the correct option is (B).

109. The most common anaerobe implicated in abdominal infections is Bacteroides fragilis followed by Lactobacillus and Clostridium species. Anaerobes are also a common cause of liver abscesses. The common anaerobes associated are Bacteroides and Fusobacterium species.

Hence, the correct option is (B).

110. The fluorescent treponemal antibody absorption (FTA-ABS) test is a blood test that checks for the presence of antibodies to Treponema pallidum bacteria. These bacteria cause syphilis. Syphilis is a sexually transmitted infection (STI) that's spread through direct contact with syphilitic sores.

Hence, the correct option is (A).

111.

- The vaccine for Japanese Encephalitis is a killed vaccine.
- The virus is grown in mouse brain and is inactivated by formalin.
- Influenza vaccines can be of various types Live (mutant), Live (attenuated), and Live (recombinant) forms.

Hence, the correct option is (B).

112. The mechanism by which most fungi cause disease is hypersensitivity. Hypersensitivity (also called hypersensitivity reaction or intolerance) refers to undesirable reactions produced by the normal immune system, including allergies and autoimmunity.

Hence, the correct option is (C).

113. A germ tube is an outgrowth produced by spores of spore-releasing fungi during germination. It is particularly indicated for colonies of white or cream color on fungal culture, where a positive germ tube test is strongly indicative of Candida albicans.

Hence, the correct option is (A).

114. The fungal infection of human beings is called mycosis. Mycosis is a fungal infection of animals, including humans. Mycoses are common and a variety of environmental and physiological conditions can contribute to the development of fungal diseases. Inhalation of fungal spores or localized colonization of the skin may initiate persistent infections; therefore, mycoses often start in the lungs or on the skin.

Hence, the correct option is (B).

115. The culture media for fungus is the Sabourauds medium. General-purpose media that are commonly used for fungal culture are Sabouraud dextrose, malt extract, and less commonly brain heart infusion medium. To prevent contamination of the medium by bacteria, chloramphenicol is used but prevents the growth of Actinomyces, which others grow well on Sabouraud dextrose agar.

Hence, the correct option is (D).

116. Some poisons impart characteristic colorations which are known as postmortem lividity.

Cyanide - Brick red

Carbon monoxide - Cherry pink

Hydrogen sulfide - Greenish blue

Phosphorus - Brown

Hence, the correct option is (D).

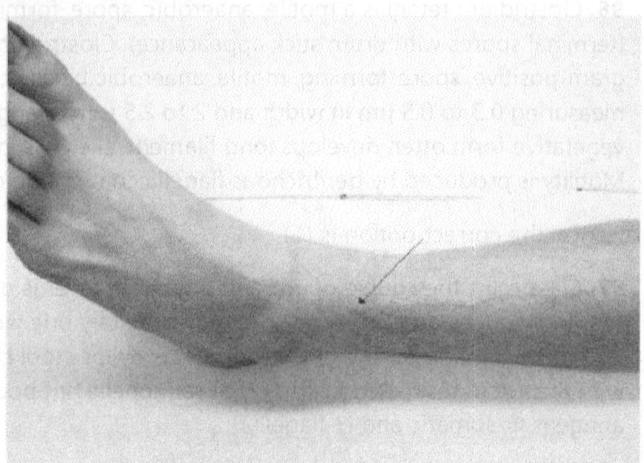

Lichtenberg figures in the leg of a person – notice the red branching pattern

117.

- Lichtenberg figure is an external lesion seen in a lightning strike.
- Superficial, thin, tortuous markings are seen on the skin.
- When the pattern resembles a fern leaf, it is called Lichtenberg figures or filigree burns.

Hence, the correct option is (C).

118. The ball and shotgun, often also known by the marketing name paradox gun, is a shotgun capable of firing both shot and solid projectiles. A Paradox Gun is a shotgun with a partially rifled barrel that enables it to shoot both slugs and shot with reasonable accuracy

Hence, the correct option is (B).

119. Danbury tremor is a classical and consistent manifestation of mercury poisoning. It is a coarse intentional tremor interspersed with jerky movements. It begins in the hand and progresses to lips, tongue, arms, and legs.

Hence, the correct option is (A).

120. Kevorkian sign is a postmortem change that occurs in the retinal vessels. It is characterized by the fragmentation of the blood column in the retinal vessels. It appears within minutes after death and lasts for about 1 hour. It can be visualized by using an ophthalmoscope.

Hence, the correct option is (B).

121.

- Superfecundation is the fertilization of 2 ova discharged from the ovary at the same period by 2 separate acts of coitus committed at short intervals.
- Both ova do not always develop to maturity.
- One fetus may get aborted early or die and get retained until labour.
- Fertilization of a second ovum in a woman who is already pregnant is superfoetation.
- It can occurs in a bipartite uterus.

Hence, the correct option is (C).

122. Scorching results from the flame emerging from the muzzle.

- Peppering – Grains of gunpowder being driven into the skin.
- Smudging – Superficial deposit of smoke on the skin.
- Lead ring / Metal ring around entry wound – Deposition of lead or other metal in the skin.

Hence, the correct option is (A).

123. The common blood groups ABO, MNS, and Rh systems can be determined in a bloodstain by the Lattes crust method. Luminol spray is used to identify bloodstains that are no longer visible due to washing of crime scene. Kastle-Meyer test is used to identify visible bloodstains. Haemin crystal test is a confirmatory test for bloodstains.

Hence, the correct option is (D).

124.

Yellow phosphorous

Yellow phosphorous s a waxy, luminous & translucent poison.

- Yellow phosphorous (white phosphorous) is a waxy & translucent material that becomes luminous in the dark.
- Cobra venom is a transparent yellow viscous liquid.
- Iodine is a bluish-black solid which sublimates into a noxious violet-pink gas.

Hence, the correct option is (A).

125.

- Primary rugae are 5-10mm or more.
- Secondary rugae are 3-5mm.
- Fragmented rugae are less than 3mm.
- Palatal rugae are unique to each person.
- Harrison Allen, in 1889, suggested the use of palatal rugae for identity verification.

Hence, the correct option is (C).

126. Marxists argue that medicine serves a key function in capitalist societies: it blames the victims of diseases, which are caused by the capitalists' pursuit of profit, for their own condition.

Hence, the correct option is (C).

127. Primary prevention: It aims to prevent disease or injury before it ever occurs. This is done by preventing exposures to hazards that cause disease or injury, altering unhealthy or unsafe behaviors that can lead to disease or injury, and increasing resistance to disease or injury should exposure occur.

Hence, the correct option is (B).

128. Specificity is defined as the ability of the test to identify correctly those free of disease in the screened population. This is expressed as the proportion of those without disease correctly identified by a negative screening test result.

Hence, the correct option is (B).

129. A cross-sectional survey was undertaken with the European Union (EU) the Member States and Norway and Iceland to describe seasonal influenza immunization in the 2006-7 season, in particular, to identify country-specific recommendations for risk groups, obtain vaccine uptake information and allow comparison with global recommendations. A standardized questionnaire was completed electronically by each country's project gatekeeper. Of the 29 countries surveyed, 28 recommended seasonal influenza vaccination for older age groups (22 for those aged > 65 years), and in one country vaccines were recommended for all age groups.

Hence, the correct option is (C).

130. Rotavirus is the leading cause of acute diarrhea and causes about 40% of hospitalizations for diarrhea in children under 5. Most diarrheal germs are spread from the stool of one person to the mouth of another. These germs are usually spread through contaminated water, food, or objects.

Hence, the correct option is (C).

131. Women ages 40 to 44 should have the choice to start annual breast cancer screening with mammograms (x-rays of the breast) if they wish to do so. Women age 45 to 54 should get mammograms every year. Women 55 and older should switch to mammograms every 2 years or can continue yearly screening.

Hence, the correct option is (A).

132. The day commemorates the birth anniversary of Dr Christian Friedrich Samuel Hahnemann, a German physician best known for creating the system of alternative medicine called homoeopathy. Dr Samuel Hahnemann, the founder and father of Homoeopathy, was born on April 10, 1755, in Meissen, Saxony, near Dresden.

Hence, the correct option is (C).

133. The origin of SPM dates back to the 18th century. Suspended particulate matter (SPM) refers to fine solid or liquid particles that are suspended in Earth's atmosphere (such as soot, smoke, dust, and pollen). Exposure to SPM (especially very small particles, which can more easily infiltrate the respiratory system) has been strongly linked to negative cardiorespiratory health impacts and even premature death.

Hence, the correct option is (B).

134. Socialization of medicine leads to all:

(A). Free medical care supported by the state.

(B). Eliminates the competition among physicians in search of clients.

(C). Ensures social equity, universal coverage of health services.

Hence, the correct option is (D).

135. Socialized medicine: medical and hospital services for the members of a class or population administered by an organized group (such as a state agency) and paid for from funds obtained usually by assessments, philanthropy, or taxation.

Hence, the correct option is (C).

136. Jules Guerin in 1848 introduced the term 'social medicine'. Although pioneers such as Neumann (1847), Virchow (1848) had propounded that medicine was social science, the idea could not gain ground. Alfred Grotjahn in 1911 related social factors to the etiology of disease and called it 'Social Pathology'. Rene Sand in 1912 founded the Belgian Social Medicine Association.

Hence, the correct option is (C)

137. James Lind (1716-1794), the British naval surgeon, based on his observations on sailors living on stored/preserved rations onboard ships successfully brought down the prevalence of scurvy among them by mandatory issuance of one fresh lime per day to each sailor. British sailors thence became known as 'Limeys'. Major Walter Reed is associated with the discovery of yellow fever transmission with Aedes, Major Ronald Ross with the transmission of malaria by a mosquito, and Bruce with African sleeping sickness transmission by Tse Tse fly.

Hence, the correct option is (B).

138. Louis Pasteur (1822-1895) demonstrated the presence of bacteria in the air, thereby disproving the theory of 'spontaneous generation' of disease. The theory was strengthened subsequently by the discovery of a series of microbes in quick succession, i.e. Anthrax bacillus in 1877, Gonococcus in 1847, Typhoid bacillus, and Pneumococcus in 1880, Tubercle bacillus in 1882, Cholera vibrio in 1883, and so on.

Hence, the correct option is (D).

139. Hippocrates, conventionally considered as the Father of Modern Medicine, introduced the concept of human health is closely related to the environment. He authored a treatise titled, "Airs, Waters, and Places".

Hence, the correct option is (C).

140. Acupuncture and acupressure are well known therapeutic modalities of Chinese origin. As yet these are not recognized as separate entities of disease management in India.

Hence, the correct option is (C).

141. Ayurveda conceptualizes disease as being due to an imbalance between three senses of humor (tridosha) namely Vata (wind), Pitta (bile), and Kapha (phlegm or mucous), whereas the hypothesis in Greek medicine was based on four senses of humor, i.e. blood, phlegm, black bile, and yellow bile.

Hence, the correct option is (B).

142. The major complications that account for nearly two-thirds of all maternal deaths are severe bleeding (mostly bleeding after childbirth), infections (usually after childbirth), high blood pressure during pregnancy (pre-eclampsia and eclampsia), complications from delivery, and unsafe abortions.

Hence, the correct option is (A).

143. Smear microscopy should be performed for all suspected cases of TB, including individuals with cough lasting more than two weeks and cases of suspected extrapulmonary TB. sputum culture is a test to find germs (such as TB bacteria) that can cause an infection. A sample of sputum is added to a substance that promotes the growth of bacteria. If no bacteria grow, the culture is negative.

Hence, the correct option is (A).

144. The modified Kuppuswamy scale is commonly used to measure SES in urban and rural areas. This scale was devised by Kuppuswamy in 1976 and consists of a composite score which includes the education and occupation of the Family Head along with income per month of the family, which yields a score of 3–29.

Hence, the correct option is (A).

145. Point source epidemic:

It is also known as "single exposure epidemic".
In this case, the time of exposure is brief and essentially simultaneous

- All the resultant cases develop the disease within the incubation period of disease at the same time.
- Epidemic curve, in this case, shows a sharp peak and sharp decline.
- Clustering of cases' in a narrow interval of time: All cases develop within one incubation period' of the diseases; examples:- Food poisoning, Measles, Chickenpoxholera, BHOPAL GAS TRAGEDY.

Hence, the correct option is (B).

146. Tuberculosis (TB) is caused by a bacterium called Mycobacterium tuberculosis. The bacteria usually attack the lungs, but TB bacteria can attack any part of the body such as the kidney, spine, and brain. The test is "positive" if there is a bump of a certain size where the fluid was injected. This means you probably have TB germs in your body. Most people with a positive TB skin test have latent TB infection.

Hence, the correct option is (A).

147. John Snow is known for the discovery of the prevention of scurvy. Scurvy can be prevented by a diet that includes vitamin C-rich foods such as amla, bell peppers (sweet peppers), blackcurrants, broccoli, chili peppers, guava, kiwifruit, and parsley.

Hence, the correct option is (A).

148. The most common cancer affecting Indian women is Breast cancer. Breast cancer is cancer that develops from breast tissue. Signs of breast cancer may include a lump in the breast, a change in breast shape, dimpling of the skin, fluid coming from the nipple, a newly-inverted nipple, or a red or scaly patch of skin. In those with a distant spread of the disease, there may be bone pain, swollen lymph nodes, shortness of breath, or yellow skin.

Hence, the correct option is (B).

149. The EPA has identified six pollutants as "criteria" air pollutants because it regulates them by developing human health-based and/or environmentally-based criteria (science-based guidelines) for setting permissible levels. These six pollutants are carbon monoxide, lead, nitrogen oxides, ground-level ozone, particle pollution (often referred to as particulate matter), and sulfur oxides.

Hence, the correct option is (D).

150. Yellow fever is a serious, potentially deadly flu-like disease spread by mosquitoes. It's characterized by a high fever and jaundice. Jaundice is the yellowing of the skin and eyes, which is why this disease is called yellow fever.

Hence, the correct option is (A).

151.

- Civatte bodies are seen in lichen planus, which represent necrotic keratinocytes in dermis.
- Ash leaf macules are the earliest cutaneous markers of tuberous sclerosis.
- Koenen tumors are subungual fibromas.
- Shagreen patches are collagen naevi usually seen on the lower back.

Hence, the correct option is (A).

152. Albinism is a group of inherited disorders that results in little or no production of the pigment melanin, which determines the color of the skin, hair, and eyes. Melanin also plays a role in the development of certain optical nerves, so all forms of albinism cause problems with the development and function of the eyes.

Hence, the correct option is (B).

153. Pseudo-Isomorphic phenomenon

- Isomorphic phenomenon (also known as Koebner phenomenon) is a phenomenon in which new skin lesions appear at the site of injury.
- It is named after Heinrich Köbner, a German dermatologist.
- Isomorphic phenomenon is seen in conditions like psoriasis, vitiligo, and lichen planus.
- Pseudo-isomorphic phenomenon (Pseudo-Koebner phenomenon) is characterized by the appearance of similar skin lesions at the site of injury infective lesions like plane warts and molluscum contagiosum.
- It occurs due to the spread of the infective agent (virus) to the new site.

Hence, the correct option is (D).

154. Blaschko's lines, also called the lines of Blaschko, named after Alfred Blaschko, are lines of normal cell development in the skin. These lines are invisible under normal conditions. They become apparent when some diseases of the skin or mucosa manifest themselves according to these patterns.

Hence, the correct option is (A).

155. Generalized vitiligo is the most common type when macules appear in various places on the body. Generalized vitiligo (also called nonsegmental vitiligo), which is the most common form, involves loss of pigment (depigmentation) in patches of skin all over the body. Depigmentation typically occurs on the face, neck, and scalp, and around body openings such as the mouth and genitals.

Hence, the correct option is (C).

156. Accutane is a form of vitamin A. It reduces the amount of oil released by oil glands in your skin and helps your skin renew itself more quickly. Accutane is used to treat severe nodular acne. It is usually given after other acne medicines or antibiotics have been tried without successful treatment of symptoms. Accutane may also be used for other purposes not listed in this medication guide.

Hence, the correct option is (D).

157. Tinea cruris is characterized by itchy, annular scaly plaques in both groins. There are central clearing and advancement at the periphery. Jock itch (tinea cruris) is a fungal infection that causes a red and itchy rash in warm and moist areas of the body. The rash often affects the groin and inner thighs and may be shaped like a ring.

Hence, the correct option is (D).

158. Erythema chronicum migrans is the rash often seen during the early stage of Lyme disease. It is not associated with internal malignancy. Acanthosis nigricans is associated with gastrointestinal malignancies. Dermatomyositis is strongly associated with a wide range of cancers including ovarian, lung, and gastrointestinal. Bullous pemphigoid is postulated to have a weak association with internal malignancy.

Other cutaneous markers of internal malignancy:

- Acquired ichthyosis
- Extramammary Paget disease
- Palmoplantar keratoderma
- Paraneoplastic pemphigus
- Necrolytic migratory erythema
- Erythema gyratum repens
- Sweet disease

Hence, the correct option is (D).

159. Bihar is a known endemic region for Indeterminate leprosy refers to a very early form of leprosy that consists of a single skin lesion with slightly diminished sensation to touch. It will usually progress to one of the major types of leprosy. leprosy. Indeterminate leprosy refers to a very early form of leprosy that consists of a single skin lesion with a slightly diminished sensation to touch. It will usually progress to one of the major types of leprosy.

Hence, the correct option is (B).

160. Scabies is a skin infestation caused by a mite known as the Sarcoptes scabies. Untreated, these microscopic mites can live on your skin for months. They reproduce on the surface of your skin and then burrow into it and lay eggs. This causes an itchy, red rash to form on the skin.

Hence, the correct option is (C).

161. Airborne contact dermatitis can be diagnosed by a patch test. Patch tests are used in patients with dermatitis, to find out whether their skin condition may be caused or aggravated by a contact allergy. Patch tests are not the same as skin prick tests, which are used to diagnose hay fever allergy (house dust mite, grass pollens and cat dander). Skin prick tests have very limited value for patients with skin rashes.

Hence, the correct option is (B).

162. Atopic dermatitis (eczema) is a condition that makes your skin red and itchy. It's common in children but can occur at any age. Atopic dermatitis is long-lasting (chronic) and tends to flare periodically. It may be accompanied by asthma or hay fever. No cure has been found for atopic dermatitis.

Hence, the correct option is (A).

163. Tuberculids are seen in lichen scrofulosorum. The tuberculids are a heterogeneous group of cutaneous disorders associated with tuberculous infections elsewhere in the body or in other parts of the skin. They include lichen scrofulosorum, papulonecrotic tuberculid, and erythema induratum-nodular vasculitis.

Hence, the correct option is (C).

164. Pityriasis rosea is a common self-limiting rash that usually starts with a herald patch on the trunk and progresses along the Langer lines to a generalized rash over the trunk and limbs. The diagnosis is based on clinical and physical examination findings.

Hence, the correct option is (A).

165. 'Chancre redux' is a clinical feature of early relapsing syphilis. Early latent syphilis is latent syphilis where infection occurred within the past 12 months. Late latent syphilis is latent syphilis where infection occurred more than 12 months ago. Latent syphilis can last for years.

Hence, the correct option is (A).

166. Flumazenil is a benzodiazepine antagonist. It is not used for the treatment of alcohol dependence. Flumazenil (also known as flumazepil, code name Ro 15-1788) is a selective GABAA receptor antagonist administered via injection, otic insertion, or intranasally. Therapeutically, it acts as both an antagonist and antidote to benzodiazepines (particularly in cases of overdose), through competitive inhibition.

Hence, the correct option is (C).

167. The history is suggestive of photodermatitis. Patch test is used for the diagnosis of photodermatitis.

Patch test (photo patch test): Here, 2 patches containing photosensitizing material is applied on 2 different sites on the body. One of them is irradiated with UVA rays. The other is kept as control. The development of eczema is looked for up to 72 hours.

Analysis of results:

- No development of eczema - patient does not have photodermatitis.
- Development of eczema under the patch Irradiated with UVA - Photodermatitis.
- Development of eczema under both patches - Contact dermatitis.

Hence, the correct option is (C).

168. Treatment of nocturnal enuresis

(1). Enuresis alarm systems are the preferred treatment for children with nocturnal enuresis.

- These detect the moisture of urine when there is nocturnal enuresis.
- An alarm is triggered which wakes up the child.
- These systems are of 3 types - wearable alarms, wireless alarms and pad type alarms.
- Alarm systems also have the least relapse rate among the various modalities of treatment.

(2). Motivational therapy

- The child is rewarded for keeping dry at night. But punishment for bedwetting is discouraged.
- There is limited evidence to support the efficacy of this approach.

(3). Drug therapy

- Pharmacological treatment for nocturnal enuresis is reserved for cases that do not respond to treatment with enuresis alarms.
- Desmopressin is the preferred drug. It is given at night to reduce urine production during sleep.
- Tricyclic antidepressants like imipramine can also be used. But use is limited due to side effects.

Hence, the correct option is (B).

169.

- Life expectancy of patients with schizophrenia is decreased by approximately 15 to 25 years.
- Suicide is the most important cause of premature death in patients with schizophrenia.
- There is a 20 fold increased risk of suicide compared to the general population.
- Suicide attempts may occur without warning or expression of intent.
- Cancer is the second most frequent cause of mortality in schizophrenics.
- The rates of metabolic syndrome and cardiovascular disorders are also increased.

Hence, the correct option is (D).

170. Thought block is not cognitive dysfunction. Thought blocking is a thought condition usually caused by a mental health condition such as schizophrenia. During thought blocking, a person stops speaking suddenly and without explanation in the middle of a sentence.

Hence, the correct option is (B).

171. Delusions are seen as associated with alcoholic paranoia.

- Alcoholic paranoia is an alcohol-induced psychotic disorder.
- It is characterized by delusions (mostly of persecution/jealousy/reference).
- Auditory hallucinations may also be seen.

Hence, the correct option is (B).

172. The given features are not something that may be considered a normal adolescent problem. Also, the headache described here cannot be classified under migraine. The oppositional defiant disorder often presents at a younger age. Therefore it is necessary to rule out depression.

Hence, the correct option is (B).

173. Somatic passivity is a Schneiderian first rank of Schizophrenia. Paranoid schizophrenia is characterized by predominantly positive symptoms of schizophrenia, including delusions and hallucinations. These debilitating symptoms blur the line between what is real and what isn't, making it difficult for the person to lead a typical life.

Hence, the correct option is (D).

174. Visual impairment, also known as vision impairment or vision loss, is a decreased ability to see to a degree that causes problems not fixable by usual means, such as glasses. Some also include those who have a decreased ability to see because they do not have access to glasses or contact lenses.

Whereas, Autism spectrum disorder (ASD) is a complex developmental condition that involves persistent challenges in social interaction, speech, and nonverbal communication and restricted/repetitive behaviors. The effects of ASD and the severity of symptoms are different in each person.

Hence, the correct option is (C).

175. The history is characteristic of depressive disorder. Antidepressant drugs are to be given. But there are no ideal antidepressants. The treatment should be based on the side effects profile of the drugs.

Hence, the correct option is (B).

176. Delusions are defined as beliefs that conflict with reality. Delusions are one of the most common symptoms of schizophrenia. These beliefs might include -

Persecutory delusions: When a person believes a person, group, or organization is mistreating or harming them despite contradictory evidence.

Hence, the correct option is (C).

177. Option (D) is correct as, Medical cannabis has been investigated as one of the potential alternative treatments for dementia.

Option (A) is incorrect as, Dementia is commonly found in chronic schizophrenic patients who underestimate their ages by 5 years or more, a symptom known as "age disorientation".

Option (B) is incorrect as, Head injury Dementia: Dementia and traumatic brain injury. Over the past 30 years, research has linked moderate and severe traumatic brain injury to a greater risk of developing Alzheimer's disease or another dementia years after the original head injury.

Option (C) is incorrect as, Huntington's disease is an inherited genetic condition that causes dementia. It causes a slow, progressive decline in a person's movement, memory, thinking, and emotional state.

Hence, the correct option is (D).

178. Impaired consciousness, visual hallucination, hyperactivity and fragmentary delusions are delirium. Delirium is an abrupt change in the brain that causes mental confusion and emotional disruption. It makes it difficult to think, remember, sleep, pay attention, and more. You might experience delirium during alcohol withdrawal, after surgery, or with dementia.

Hence, the correct option is (A).

179.

- Postural orthostatic tachycardia syndrome (POTS) is characterised by symptomatic orthostatic intolerance without orthostatic hypotension that is associated with either heart rate of more than 120/minute or increase of >30/minute when standing that subside on sitting/lying down.
- The symptoms of orthostatic intolerance include lightheadedness, blurred vision, palpitation and nausea.
- Usually affects women more than men.
- This syndrome develops between 15 and 50 years of age.

Hence, the correct option is (D).

180. Freud introduced cocaine in psychiatry. Freud developed a wide-ranging interpretation and critique of religion and culture. Though in overall decline as a diagnostic and clinical practice, psychoanalysis remains influential within psychology, psychiatry, and psychotherapy, and across the humanities. He was particularly interested in the potential social impact of psychiatry.

Hence, the correct option is (A).

181. The DSM-IV criteria for mania require: a distinct period that represents a break from pre-morbid functioning, a duration of at least one week, elevated or irritable mood, at least three to four classical manic signs and symptoms, and the absence of any physical factors. Acute mania can be subdivided into classical pure mania, mania with mood-congruent or mood-incongruent psychosis, mixed state, and rapid-cycling mania.

Hence, the correct option is (B).

182. Projection is a mature defense mechanism that involves taking our own unacceptable qualities or feelings and ascribing them to other people. Projection works by allowing the expression of the desire or impulse, but in a way that the ego cannot recognize, therefore reducing anxiety.

Hence, the correct option is (A).

183. Option (C) is correct, Delusional jealousy is a psychotic disorder and should be treated mainly with antipsychotics, while obsessive jealousy resembles obsessive-compulsive.

Option (A) is incorrect, Alcoholic hallucinosis is a rare complication of chronic alcohol abuse characterized by predominantly auditory hallucinations that occur either during or after a period of heavy alcohol consumption.

Option (B) is incorrect, In psychiatry, thought broadcasting is the belief that others can hear or are aware of an individual's thoughts. Thought broadcasting can be a positive symptom of schizophrenia.

Option (D) is incorrect, Grandiosity is a symptom experienced by people with bipolar disorder (BD) during manic and hypomanic episodes. People experiencing grandiose delusions often describe larger-than-life feelings of superiority and invulnerability.

Hence, the correct option is (C).

184. Suicidal tendencies are least common with married people. Suicidal ideation (or suicidal thoughts) is thinking about, considering, or planning suicide. It is not a diagnosis, but is a symptom of some mental disorders and can also occur in response to adverse events without the presence of a mental disorder.

Hence, the correct option is (D).

185. Psychoanalysis was introduced by Freud. It is a method of treating mental disorders, shaped by psychoanalytic theory, emphasizes unconscious mental processes and is sometimes described as "depth psychology." The psychoanalytic movement originated in the clinical observations and formulations of Austrian psychiatrist Sigmund Freud, who coined the term psychoanalysis.

Hence, the correct option is (A).

186. Thematic perception test is named after Wechslers. The TAT is a widely used projective test for the assessment of children and adults. It is designed to reveal an individual's perception of interpersonal relationships. Thirty-one picture cards serve as stimuli for stories and descriptions about relationships or social situations.

Hence, the correct option is (D).

187.

- RANKL (Receptor Activator of Nuclear factor Kappa B Ligand), also known as Tumor necrosis Factor ligand Super Family member 11 (TNFSF11) is produced by osteocytes, activated T cells and bone marrow stromal cells.
- RANKL acts on the RANK receptor present on osteoclasts and their precursors.
- It promotes maturation of osteoclast precursors into mature osteoclasts.

Hence, the correct option is (B).

188. The commonest cause of mental retardation is birth asphyxia. Asphyxia (as-FIX-ee-uh) means lack of oxygen and blood flow to the brain. Birth asphyxia happens when a baby's brain and other organs do not get enough oxygen and nutrients before, during or right after birth.

Hence the correct option is (D).

189. Ego's defense mechanism "Undoing" is typically seen in obsessive-compulsive neurosis. Obsessive-compulsive disorder (OCD), also called obsessive-compulsive neurosis, type of mental disorder in which an individual experiences obsessions or compulsions or both. Either the obsessive thought or the compulsive act may occur singly, or both may appear in sequence.

Hence, the correct option is (C).

190. The eight-stage classification of human life is proposed by Erikson. Psychologist Erik Erikson developed his eight stages of development to explain how people mature. The stages clarify the developmental challenges faced at various points in life.

Hence, the correct option is (D).

191. Psychotic disorders are severe mental disorders that cause abnormal thinking and perceptions. People with psychoses lose touch with reality. Two of the main symptoms are delusions and hallucinations.

Hence, the correct option is (A).

192. The commonest psychiatric illness in India is neurotic depression. A neurotic depression usually involves a cluster of symptoms that include the following: General distress and heightened negative emotion, especially sadness, irritability, disappointment, futility, or agitation/anxiety. General life dissatisfaction. Low self-esteem and identity problems.

Hence, the correct option is (C).

193. The Oedipus complex is a theory of Sigmund Freud and occurs during the Phallic stage of psychosexual development. It involves a boy, aged between 3 and 6, becoming unconsciously sexually attached to his mother, and hostile towards his father (who he views as a rival).

Hence, the correct option is (C).

194. The cerebellum's job is to process procedural memories; the hippocampus is where new memories are encoded; the amygdala helps determine what memories to store, and it plays a part in determining where the memories are stored based on whether we have a strong or weak emotional response to the event.

Hence, the correct option is (C).

195. The biochemical etiology of Alzheimer's disease relates it to acetylcholine. Acetylcholine is the chief neurotransmitter of the parasympathetic nervous system, the part of the autonomic nervous system (a branch of the peripheral nervous system) that contracts smooth muscles, dilates blood vessels, increases bodily secretions, and slows the heart rate.

Hence, the correct option is (A).

196. Inflammation from Hashimoto's disease, also known as chronic lymphocytic thyroiditis, often leads to an underactive thyroid gland (hypothyroidism). Hashimoto's disease is the most common cause of hypothyroidism. It primarily affects middle-aged women but can also occur in men and women of any age and in children.

Hence, the correct option is (C).

197. The cysts can occur anywhere along the course of the thyroglossal duct from the foramen cecum to the thyroid gland although the infrahyoid location is most common: suprahyoid: 20-25% (less common in adults ~5%) at the level of hyoid bone: ~30% (range 15-50%) infrahyoid: ~45% (range 25-65%).

Hence, the correct option is (D).

198. Hashimoto's disease is autoimmune thyroiditis. Autoimmune thyroiditis is a chronic disease in which the body interprets the thyroid glands and its hormone products T3, T4 and TSH as threats, therefore producing special antibodies that target the thyroid's cells, thereby destroying it.

Hence, the correct option is (B).

199. A ranula is a sublingual thyroid. A ranula is a fluid collection or cyst that forms in the mouth under the tongue. It is filled with saliva (spit) that has leaked out of a damaged salivary gland.

Hence, the correct option is (B).

200. Threshold radiation dose for acute radiation syndromes:

- Haematologic / Haematopoietic syndrome -1 Gy
- Gastrointestinal syndrome -5 Gy
- Central nervous system syndrome -20 Gy.

Hence, the correct option is (A).

201. Best investigation for the detection of bone metastases

- Radioisotope bone scan is the preferred method for the detection of bone metastases.
- It is more sensitive than radiography for the detection of most metastases.
- Technetium-99m is the commonly used radioisotope.
- It accumulates in reactive new bone that is formed in the metastases resulting in a 'hot spot' in the scan.
- The amount of accumulation depends on the level of blood flow.
- In some cases, 'cold spots' are also noted due to the absence of bone formation within the lesion.
- The results from a bone scan are not specific as the tracer can accumulate in other areas with increased bone formation such as sites of fracture healing/infection.
- So a bone scan should be followed by other radiological modalities such as CT scan to confirm the lesion.

Hence, the correct option is (D).

202. Prevention of contrast nephropathy

- Non ionic low osmolar contrast agents are preferred in patients with decreased renal function to prevent contrast nephropathy.
- Ionic contrast media have a higher risk for contrast nephropathy, and hence should be avoided.
- The amount of contrast media used should be limited.
- The patient should be well hydrated before the procedure.
- Supplementary interventions include the use of N-acetylcysteine, fenoldopam, theophylline, prostaglandins, and magnesium.

Hence, the correct option is (A).

203. 'Egg on the side' or 'Egg on string' appearance is characteristic of the transposition of great arteries. Egg-on-a-string sign also referred to as egg on its side refers to the cardio mediastinal silhouette seen in the transposition of the great arteries (TGA). The heart appears globular due to an abnormal convexity of the right atrial border and left atrial enlargement and therefore appears like an egg.

Hence, the correct option is (D).

204. Alpha rays have the highest ionization power, whereas gamma rays have the highest penetration power. Alpha particles, also called alpha rays or alpha radiation, consist of two protons and two neutrons bound together into a particle identical to a helium-4 nucleus. They are generally produced in the process of alpha decay, but may also be produced in other ways.

Hence, the correct option is (C).

205. Lead is used as radiation shielding in CT scans, X-ray machines, etc. Lead is a chemical element with the symbol Pb (from the Latin plumbum) and atomic number 82. It is a heavy metal that is denser than most common materials. Lead is soft and malleable, and also has a relatively low melting point.

Hence, the correct option is (C).

206. A highly calcified tumor (seen on a CT scan) is highly suggestive of a benign tumor. Conversely, there are imaging hints of more aggressive meningiomas other than growth rate, such as involving a lot of swelling in the brain around the tumor. Both meningioma and ependymoma show calcification. But it is more common in meningioma. A meningioma is a tumor that forms on membranes that cover the brain and spinal cord just inside the skull. Specifically, the tumor forms on the three layers of membranes that are called meninges. These tumors are often slow-growing. As many as 90% are benign (not cancerous).

Hence, the correct option is (C).

207. To evaluate the feasibility, efficiency, and safety of the transradial approach (TRA) for cerebral angiography versus the transfemoral approach (TFA) in patients. Transcatheter aortic valve implantation: the transfemoral access route is the default access. Transcatheter aortic valve implantation (TAVI) is a widely accepted alternative to surgical aortic valve replacement (SAVR) among non-operable patients or selected high-risk patients with degenerative, severe aortic stenosis.

Hence, the correct option is (A).

208. All the sonographic markers, any finding of a nuchal fold carried the highest LR for trisomy 21. A short humerus carried the second-highest LR for Down syndrome. A short humerus was identified in 48.7% of fetuses with Down syndrome compared with 2.1% of control fetuses, yielding an LR of 23.5.

Hence, the correct option is (D).

209. The most sensitive imaging modality for the diagnosis of ureteric stones in a patient with acute colic is Non-contrast CT scan of the abdomen. A CT scan uses x-rays and computers to create three-dimensional pictures of your urinary tract (kidneys, ureters, and bladder).

Hence, the correct option is (C).

210. The gold standard for the diagnosis of osteoporosis is Dual-energy X-ray absorptiometry. In the absence of a fragility fracture, BMD assessment by dual-energy x-ray absorptiometry (DXA) is the gold standard to diagnose osteoporosis, according to the classification of the World Health Organization (WHO).

Hence, the correct option is (A).

211. Rate of decay = Disintegration constant × Number of radioactive atoms

$$= 0.01 \times 6 \times 10^{23}$$

$$= 6 \times 10^{21}$$

Hence, the correct option is (C).

212. Respiratory gating is a technique in radiotherapy in which the radiation is applied during that phase of respiratory cycle in which the tumor is in the best range. This is to prevent unnecessary radiation exposure to normal structures.

Hence, the correct option is (C).

213. Gamma camera in Nuclear Medicine is used for measuring radioactivity. Scintigraphy ("scint") is the use of gamma cameras to capture emitted radiation from internal radioisotopes to create two-dimensional images. SPECT (single-photon emission computed tomography) imaging, as used in nuclear cardiac stress testing, is performed using gamma cameras.

Hence, the correct option is (B).

214. Multiple sclerosis is a demyelinating disorder. Hence the lesions will be seen in the white matter (due to loss of myelin). White matter is the tissue through which messages pass between different areas of grey matter within the central nervous system. The white matter is white because of the fatty substance (myelin) that surrounds the nerve fibers (axons).

Hence, the correct option is (A).

215. The procedure of choice for the evaluation of an aneurysm is arteriography. It is an x-ray image of the blood vessels used to evaluate various conditions, such as aneurysm, stenosis (narrowing of the blood vessel), or blockages. A dye (contrast) will be injected through a thin flexible tube placed in an artery. This dye will make the blood vessels visible on the x-ray.

Hence, the correct option is (D).

216. Mueller's syndrome is a sign of successful stellate ganglion block in which there is warmth of the face and injection of the tympanic membrane.
Other signs of successful stellate ganglion block include:

- Horner's syndrome
- Lacrimation
- Flushing of conjunctiva and sclera
- Increase in skin temperature
- Engorged veins of the arm
- Flushing of cheek, face, neck and arm
- Anhidrosis of the face and neck
- Stuffiness of the nostril

Complications of stellate ganglion block include:

- Perforation of oesophagus
- Pneumothorax
- cardiac arrest
- Mediastinitis
- Intercostal neuralgia.

Hence, the correct option is (D).

217.

- Gaisbock's syndrome is polycythemia due to reduction in plasma volume.
- It is usually seen in smokers, obese individuals, and in patients with hypertension.
- Anaesthetic implications include cardiovascular problems and the risk of deep vein thrombosis.
- May require venesection.

Hence, the correct option is (B).

218.

- Thiopental is contraindicated in porphyria, status asthmaticus, pericardial tamponade, and severe shock.
- It causes centrally mediated respiratory depression.
- It can cause laryngeal spasm and bronchoconstriction in asthmatics.
- Thiopental causes depression of myocardial contractility.
- Peripheral vascular resistance falls and it can lead to hypotension, which can be exaggerated if there is hypovolemia.

Hence, the correct option is (C).

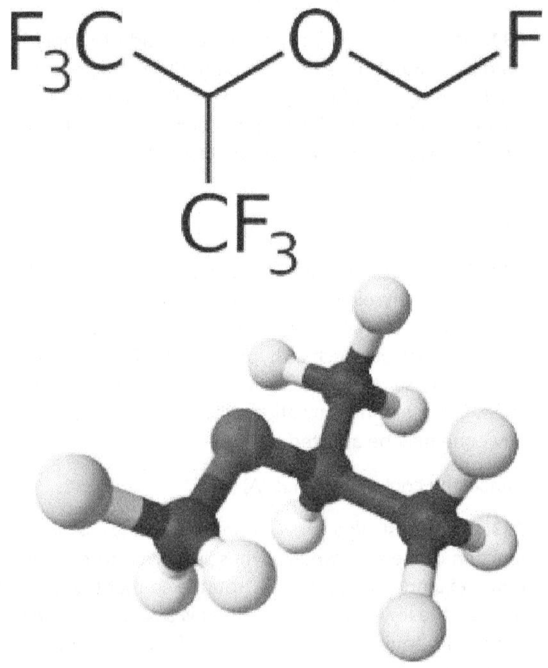

Structure of sevoflurane

219.

- Enflurane and Sevoflurane can induce epilepsy.
- The effect is much more pronounced with Enflurane.
- Tip to remember : Enflurane = Epilepsy (both start with E).
- Enflurane can also increase the intracranial pressure.
- Isoflurane can cause coronary steal syndrome.
- Methoxyflurane is nephrotoxic and can cause high output renal failure.

Hence, the correct option is (A).

220. Contraindications to vasoconstrictors in local anaesthesia

Vasoconstrictors like adrenaline are used with local anaesthetics for decreasing the systemic absorption and to increase the local anaesthetic concentration and duration of nerve block.
But adrenaline should not be used with lignocaine when infiltrating areas of end arterial supply.

- These sites include:
- Fingers
- Toes
- Pinna
- Penis
- Nose

The use of adrenaline in these areas can compromise the blood flow and result in ischaemic injury.

Hence, the correct option is (C).

221. Colour coding of anaesthetic gases

- Oxygen - Black with white shoulders
- Nitrous oxide - Blue
- Cyclopropane - Orange
- Carbon Dioxide - Grey
- Nitrogen - Black
- Helium - Brown
- Air - Grey body with white & black quartered shoulder

Hence, the correct option is (B).

222. Mephentermine acts as an agonist on alpha and beta-adrenergic receptors. This causes increase in cardiac output and blood pressure. Therefore it cannot be used to induce hypotension.

Hence, the correct option is (C).

223. Management of postoperative shivering:

- Drug of choice - Tramadol.
- Alternate drugs - pethidine, pentazocine.
- Supportive treatment - oxygen inhalation (there is increased oxygen consumption during shivering).

Hence, the correct option is (D).

224. Propofol is the induction agent of choice in daycare surgery

- Early induction
- Smooth recovery
- Decreased incidence of post-operative nausea and vomiting.

Hence, the correct option is (C).

225. Disadvantages of etomidate:

- Decrease cortisol synthesis
- Painful injection
- Nausea and vomiting during recovery period
- Produce restlessness and rigidity

Hence, the correct option is (B).

226. Reimplantation of an amputated digit procedure

- Debride the area and clean the wound
- Fixation of bone
- Repair of extensor tendons Repair of flexor tendons
- Arterial repair
- Nerve repair
- Venous repair Closure of the skin wound

Hence, the correct option is (D).

227. Drugs used for treatment of Osteoporosis.

- Drugs that reduce bone resorption (anti-resorptive drugs).
- Selective estrogen receptor modulators - Raloxifene.
- Bisphosphonates - Etidronate, Risedronate, Pamidronate, Alendronate.
- Hormone replacement therapy/estrogen.
- Calcitonin
- Calcium supplements
- Vitamin D

- Denosumab -Monoclonal antibody which inhibits the maturation of osteoclasts by binding to and inhibiting RANKL.

Drugs that increase bone formation.

- Teriparatide

Drugs with both effects (decreases bone resorption and increases bone formation).

- Strontium ranelate

Hence, the correct option is (B).

228. Blood supply to head and neck of femur

- The blood supply to the head and neck of femur comes from:
- Extracapsular arterial ring located at the base of neck of femur
- Artery of ligamentum teres
- Epiphyseal arteries
- Metaphyseal arteries

The extracapsular arterial ring is formed by:

- Posteriorly by branches of medial circumflex femoral artery (major part of blood supply)
- Anteriorly by branches of lateral circumflex femoral artery
- Smaller branches from superior and inferior gluteal artery

Both medial and lateral circumflex femoral arteries are branches of profunda femoris artery.

Artery of ligamentum teres

- It is a branch of obturator artery.
- It contributes a small but variable amount of blood supply.

Hence, the correct option is (B).

229. Blount's disease

- It is named after Walter Putnam Blount.
- It is also known as: Tibia vara, Mau-Nilsonne Syndrome, Blount-Barber syndrome, Erlacher-Blount syndrome, Osteochondrosis deformans tibiae.
- It is a growth disorder of the tibia resulting in progressive bow leg deformity.
- It is also associated with internal tibial torsion and genu recurvatum.
- It is mainly seen in children and adolescents.
- Treatment is by bracing and/or surgery.

Hence, the correct option is (B).

230.

- Agnes Hunt traction is used for correction of mild flexion deformity of hip joint in poliomyelitis.
- Traction used for trochanteric fracture - Russell's traction.
- Traction used for fracture shaft of femur in adults - Perkin's traction.
- Traction used for low backache - Buck's traction.

Hence, the correct option is (A).

231. Elevated scapula can be seen as a part of Klippel Feil syndrome. But it does not constitute the characteristic triad. Sprengel's deformity (also known as high scapula or congenital high scapula) is a rare congenital skeletal abnormality where a person has one shoulder blade that sits higher on the back than the other.

Hence, the correct option is (B).

232. Brown tumor occurs due to the increased osteoclastic activity in hyperparathyroidism. It is a benign mass of reactive tissue. The brown tumor is a bone lesion that arises in settings of excess osteoclast activity, such as hyperparathyroidism. They are a form of osteitis fibrosa cystica. It is not a neoplasm, but rather simply a mass. It most commonly affects the maxilla and mandible, though any bone may be affected.

Hence, the correct option is (A).

233. Lift off test, also know as Gerber's test is used to assess the function of the subscapularis muscle. For performing this test, the arm is extended and internally rotated so that the dorsum of hand rests on the lower back. The patient is asked to lift the hand off the back. This requires internal rotation of the arm brought about by the subscapularis. If the patient is able to perform the maneuver, the subscapularis function is normal and the test is negative.

Hence, the correct option is (B).

234.

- The name synovial sarcoma is a misnomer.
- It does not arise from the synovial lining.
- The name arises from the fact that it histologically resembles synovial tissue.
- Most commonly seen in those between 15 and 35 years of age.
- Males and females are equally affected.
- Most commonly seen in the lower limbs, around knee and foot.
- It is a slow growing tumour with an indolent course (It may be aggressive in later stages).

Hence, the correct option is (D).

235.

- Clavicular fracture heals with good functional results even if there is moderate displacement of the fracture ends.
- Perfect reduction is not essential.
- Treatment consists of a 'Figure of Eight' bandage which is periodically tightened.
- A sling can be used initially to support the upper limb.
- In case of elderly patients with risk of axillary neurovascular compression, only a sling is used instead of the 'figure of eight' bandage.
- Open reduction is done in case of non-union, neurovascular damage, floating shoulder, and wide separation of the fracture ends with interposition of soft tissue.

Hence, the correct option is (D).

236. Hilton's law states that the articular nerves supplying a joint are branches of the nerves that supply the muscles responsible for moving that joint. Hilton's law is described above. Similar observations can be made, to extend the theory; often a nerve will supply both the muscles and skin relating to a particular joint.

Hence, the correct option is (A).

237. Bone remodeling in response to stress was described by German Anatomist/Surgeon Julius Wolff (1836-1902) in the 19th century. Wolff's law states that bone in a healthy person or animal will adapt to the loads it is placed under.

Nicolas Andry (1658-1742), a French doctor coined the term 'Orthopedics'. In his book, he gave the illustration of the crooked tree, which was later used in the symbols of many orthopedic societies around the world.

Hence, the correct option is (C).

238. In order studies, the radial nerve was found to be the one most commonly injured. But recent studies have shown that the median nerve, particularly the anterior interosseous branch is the most commonly damaged in supracondylar fracture of the humerus.

Hence, the correct option is (D).

239. Heberden's nodes seen in distal interphalangeal joints are a characteristic feature of idiopathic osteoarthritis. The DIJ joint (Distal Interphalangeal Joints) is the first knuckle from the top of the finger. It connects the distal phalanx and middle phalanx, which are the two bones at the tip of the finger. Experiencing DIJ (Distal Interphalangeal Joints) joint pain is often a sign of a type of arthritis, such as osteoarthritis or psoriatic arthritis.

Hence, the correct option is (D).

240. Gallow's traction is used in infants and children with femoral fractures.

Indications Gallows Traction:

- Child must weigh less than 12 kg
- Femoral fractures
- Skin must be intact

Hence, the correct option is (A).

241. Second stage

- It is the stage of expulsion of the foetus.
- Begins with full cervical dilatation and ends with the delivery of the foetus.
- Its duration is about 1 hour in primigravida and (1/2) hour in multipara.

Hence, the correct option is (B).

242. The obstetrical conjugate is the distance between the sacral promontory and the inner pubic arch; it should measure 11.5 cm or more. The diagonal conjugate is the distance from the undersurface of the pubic arch to sacral promontory, it is 2 cm longer than the obstetrical conjugate. The transverse diameter of the pelvic inlet measures 13.5 cm.

Hence, the correct option is (C).

243. Progression of labour is assessed by Partograph. Start recording on the partograph when the labour is in active first stage (4 cm or above). Cervical dilatation, the descent of the fetal head and uterine contractions are used in assessing the progress of labour.

Hence, the correct option is (A).

244. The android or male pelvis is more robust, narrower, and taller than the female pelvis. The angle of the male pubic arch and the sacrum are narrower as well. The female pelvis is more delicate, wider and not as high as the male pelvis. The angle of the female pubic arch is wide and round.

Hence, the correct option is (D).

245. All the fetal skull measurements are 9.5 cm except Occipitofrontal. Occipitofrontal is a term relating to the occiput and the frontal direction. Occipitofrontal fasciculus, association fibers in the brain. Occipito-anterior form of cephalic presentation of birth.

Hence, the correct option is (D).

246. The first stage of labor and birth occurs when you begin to feel regular contractions, which cause the cervix to open (dilate) and soften, shorten and thin (effacement). This allows the baby to move into the birth canal. Artificial rupture of membranes (AROM), also known as an amniotomy, is performed by a midwife or obstetrician and was once thought to be an effective means to induce or accelerate labor. Oxytocin injection is used to begin or improve contractions during labor. Oxytocin also is used to reduce bleeding after childbirth. It also may be used along with other medications or procedures to end a pregnancy.

Hence, the correct option is (A).

247. The action line is located 4 hours to the right of the alert line. The partograph was first introduced in 1954 by Friedman graphically depicting the dilatation of the cervix during labour1. Philpott and Castle in 1972 developed Friedman's concept into a tool for monitoring labour by adding the action and alert lines.

Hence, the correct option is (B).

248. The diagonal conjugate is the distance from the undersurface of the pubic arch to the sacral promontory; it is 2 cm longer than the obstetrical conjugate. The transverse diameter of the pelvic inlet measures 13.5 cm.

Hence, the correct option is (C).

249. Pelvic inlet: The obstetrical conjugate is the distance between the sacral promontory and the inner pubic arch; it should measure 11.5 cm or more. The diagonal conjugate is the distance from the undersurface of the pubic arch to sacral promontory; it is 2 cm longer than the obstetrical conjugate. The transverse diameter of the pelvic inlet measures 13.5 cm.

Hence, the correct option is (A).

250. Blood type and Rh testing- RhoGAM should be given in cases of Rh –ve to avoid Rh isoimmunity.

Hence, the correct option is (A).

251. Gestational trophoblastic disease (GTD) is a spectrum of disorders extending from premalignant conditions of hydatidiform mole, which can be further classified into partial (pHM) and complete (CHM) hydatidiform mole, to malignant conditions including invasive mole, choriocarcinoma, and placental site trophoblastic tumor (pSTT). GTD occurs in 1 in 40 000 pregnancies and is commonly seen in Asia.

Hence, the correct option is (B).

252.

- Progestasert is a commonly used IUCD which carries 38 mg of progesterone in silicone oil reservoir.
- It releases 65 μg of hormone per day.
- It acts by forming a thick plug of mucus at the cervical os which prevents penetration by the sperm.

Hence, the correct option is (C).

253.

- Organ of Rosenmuller (epoophoron) represents cranial end of the Wolffian body.
- It consists of vertical tubules in the mesovarium and mesosalpinx.
- The tubule is lined by cubical cells.
- Paroophoron sometimes forms paraovarian cyst.

Hence, the correct option is (D).

254. Estrogen deficiency- Low caloric intake decreases LH and GTRH leading to low estrogen level resulting in infertility, vaginal and breast atrophies.

Hence, the correct option is (A).

255.

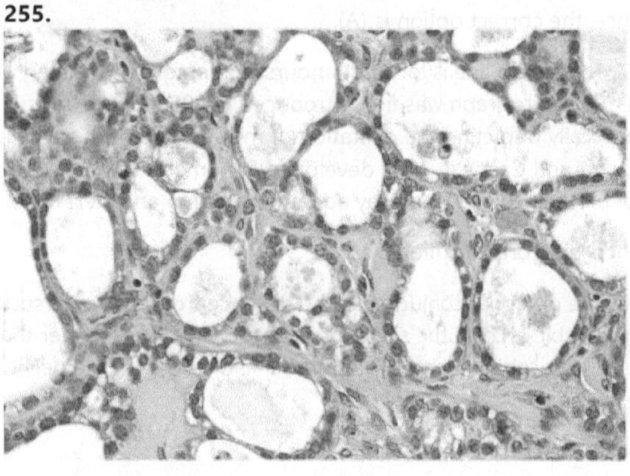

Ovarian clear cell carcinoma.

- Germ cell tumours include Teratoma, Dysgerminoma, Endodermal sinus tumour, Embryonal carcinoma, Polyembryoma, Choriocarcinoma and mixed forms.
- Mesonephroid tumour is an epithelial tumour.
- It is also known as clear cell carcinoma.
- It is an uncommon tumour of ovary.
- It is highly malignant.

Hence, the correct option is (A).

256.

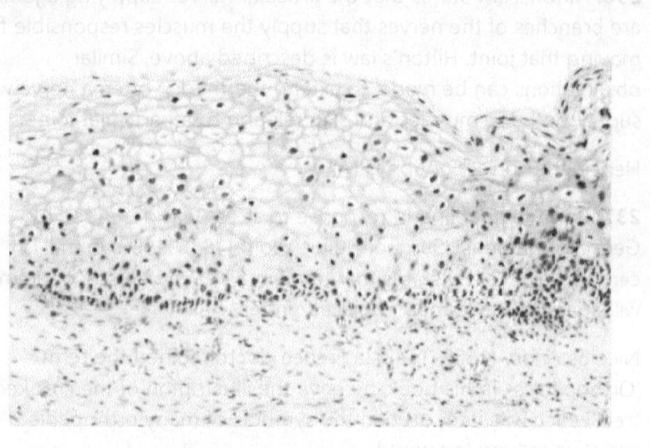

Cervical intraepithelial neoplasia

- Large Loop Excision of the Transformation Zone (LLETZ) uses low voltage diathermy.
- It is used in the treatment of cervical intraepithelial neoplasias.
- It is used only for cervical lesions.
- Loop size lesser than 2cm gives a better cone.
- It is less costly and has shorter procedure time compared to laser ablation.
- But the success rate is similar to laser ablation.

Hence, the correct option is (C).

257.

- Endometrioid tumours account for about 20% of all ovarian cancers.
- They are mostly malignant.
- They are lined by glandular epithelium.
- They are moderate sized solid tumours with cystic areas in between filled with haemorrhagic fluid.
- Ovarian endometriosis coexist in 15% of cases.

Hence, the correct option is (C).

258.

- In Moschcowitz repair, several purse string sutures starting from below are used to obliterate the cul-de-sac of the pouch of Douglas.
- Care should be taken not to include the ureter in the stitch.

Hence, the correct option is (B).

259.

- In Savage syndrome, there is receptor defect to gonadotrophic hormones. The clinical features resemble autoimmune disease.
- Height is normal.
- The ovaries contain follicles.
- FSH is raised.

Hence, the correct option is (A).

260.

- RU 486 (mifepristone) does not prevent fertilization.
- It has affinity for progesterone receptors.
- It blocks the action of progesterone on the endometrium.
- It prevents implantation by causing sloughing and shedding of decidua. Single dose of 10 mg prevents pregnancy in 99.1% cases.

Hence, the correct option is (D).

261.

- The characteristic feature of endometrium in metropathia haemorrhagica is cystic glandular hyperplasia.
- Another important feature is absence of secretory endometrium with absence ofcorkscrew glands.
- Endometrium is usually thick and polypoidal.
- Thin polypi project into the uterine cavity.

Hence, the correct option is (D).

262.

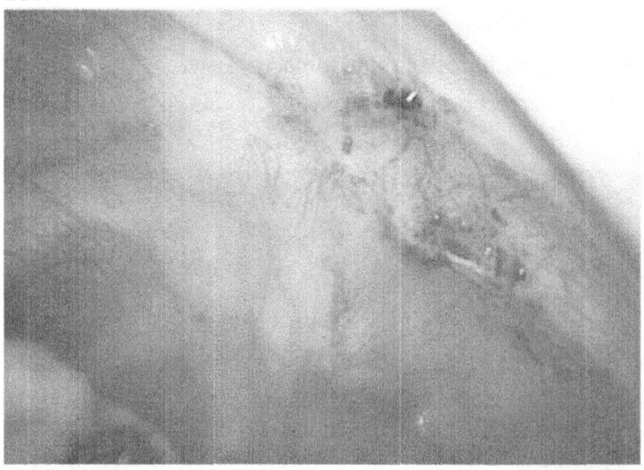

Laparoscopic view of endometriotic lesions in the peritoneum

- Gestrinone has a long half life.
- It is a 19 -nortestosterone derivative.
- It is given orally 2.5 to 5 mg twice weekly for 6 to 9 months.
- It has androgenic, antiprogestagenic, antioestrogenic and antigonadotrophic action.

Hence, the correct option is (D).

263.

- Pregnancy is associated with many haemodynamic changes.
- There is increase in heart rate and cardiac output and decrease in periphera resistance.
- Total blood volume is increased.
- Stenotic lesions and severe cyanotic lesions have a higher complication rate pregnancy.
- Regurgitant lesions and left to right shunts (without pulmonary hypertension) are better tolerated.

Hence, the correct option is (C).

264. Radioimmunoassay is the most sensitive test for measurement of B HCG level serum.

Immunological tests for the diagnosis of pregnancy depend on the detection of in the maternal serum or urine. They are of various types:

- Agglutination inhibition test
- Direct agglutination test
- Enzyme linked immunosorbent assay (ELISA)
- Fluoroimmunoassay (FIA)
- Radioimmunoassay (RIA)
- Immunoradiometric assay (IRMA)

Other uses of B HCG testing:

- Diagnosing ectopic pregnancy
- Monitoring patients who have underwent in vitro fertilization and embryo transfer
- Follow up of patients after treatment of hydatidiform mole and choriocarcinoma

Hence, the correct option is (C).

265. Hormone levels in polycystic ovarian disease.

- Increased Androgen
- Increased Estrogen
- Increased Luteinizing hormone
- Decreased Follicular stimulating hormone
- Increased LH/FSH ratio (>2)
- Increased insulin

Hence, the correct option is (B).

266. Both alpha-fetoprotein and acetylcholinesterase in amniotic fluid are markers for tube defects. But acetylcholinesterase is the most specific marker.

Hence, the correct option is (C).

267. Pregnancy is possible once menarche is achieved. However, early cycles may be irregular and anovulatory. Adrenarche is the onset of growth of pubic hair. Menarche is usually the last manifestation, whereas development of the breast bud is the first (thelarche).

Hence, the correct option is (D).

268. Factors influencing weight gain in pregnancy:

- Maternal age - Increased weight gain in younger women.
- Physical activity - Several studies have demonstrated an inverse relation between weight gain and level of physical activity.
- Prepregnancy weight - Weight gain in pregnancy is generally inversely proportional to BMI (Body Mass Index) in the pre pregnancy period.
- Race/ethnicity - The mean weight gain differs in various ethnic/racial groups.
- Parity - Lower weight gain was noted in multipara Hormonal milieu - Levels of hormones like insulin and leptin can influence weight gain in pregnancy.
- Hormonal milieu - Levels of hormones like insulin and leptin can influence weigh.

- gain in pregnancy.
- Multiple pregnancy - Tend to gain more weight in multiple pregnancy.
- Hyperemesis gravidarum - Lower weight gain in women with hyperemesis.
- gravidarum Anorexia nervosa - Lower weight gain and lower birth weight in anorexic women.
- Substance abuse - Studies have found no significant difference in mean weight gain between smoking and non smoking women. But the birth weight was lower in babies born to women who were smokers.
- Family violence - Greater risk of inadequate weight gain.
- Marital status - Many studies have found that married women were more likely to gain weight than single/divorced women.

Hence, the correct option is (A).

269. Anti tuberculosis treatment in pregnancy.

- Newly smear positive cases of Tuberculosis are treated with Category I DOTS (Directly Observed Treatment Short course) in India.
- The drugs given in category I DOTS - Isoniazid, Rifampicin, Ethambutol and Pyrazinamide are not contraindicated in pregnancy.
- But if the disease is not treated properly, it is harmful for the foetus.
- Streptomycin is not given in pregnant patients as it is teratogenic.

Hence, the correct option is (A).

270. Parvovirus is the commonest infectious etiology for hydrops foetalis. The other viruses implicated include Cytomegalovirus, Hepatitis B virus, Herpes simplex virus, Rubella virus and Adenovirus.

Hence, the correct option is (D).

271.

- The plasma retinol value of 0.7 to 1.05 μmol/L is considered to be marginal.
- Values more than 1.05 μmol/L are considered to be adequate for children.
- Values between 0.35 to 0.7 μmol/L are considered to be deficient.
- If the value is less than 0.35 μmol/L, it is considered to be very deficient.

Hence, the correct option is (C).

272.

- The onset of anorexia nervosa is usually in the early to middle adolescence.
- It is more prevalent in girls.
- They have disturbance in the way in which the body weight or shape is experienced.
- They also cannot recognise the seriousness of the current low body weight. It can be of two types.
- Restricting type - Weight loss occurs through dieting fasting or excessive exercise.
- Binge eating/purging type - In this subtype the person engages in recurrer episodes of binge eating or purging behaviour.
- Bulimia nervosa usually emerges in later adolescence.

Hence, the correct option is (C).

273. Autism spectrum disorder According to the report by Centre for Disease Control, United States of America, the prevalence for autism spectrum disorders has increased from 1 in 110 in 2010 to 1 in 59 in 2018. It is 4 times more prevalent in boys.

Hence, the correct option is (D).

274.

- Fabry's disease is an X linked disease.
- Friedreich's ataxia is an autosomal recessive disease.
- Osteogenesis imperfecta is an autosomal dominant disease.
- Cystic fibrosis is autosomal recessive.

Hence, the correct option is (B).

275.

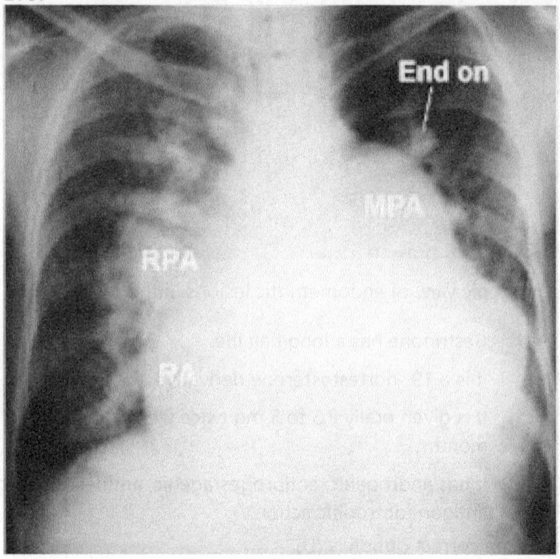

Chest X-ray of a patient with atrial septal defect showing an enlarged right pulmonary artery (RPA), main pulmonary artery (MPA) and right atrium (RA). End-on view of an enlarged pulmonary vessel is also seen.

1. Left atrium is not dilated in a case of atrial septal defect (ASD).
2. It is dilated in patients with ventricular septal defect. (VSD).
3. Pulmonary plethora is present in both ASD and VSD. Pulmonary artery is dilated in both.
4. Size of the aorta is normal in both.

Hence, the correct option is (B).

276.

- Hematemesis, melena and splenomegaly are suggestive of a diagnosis of portal hypertension.
- The first three options can cause portal hypertension.
- But considering the age and sex of the child, Extrahepatic Portal Venous Obstruction (EHPVO) is the most probable diagnosis.
- Non Cirrhotic Portal Fibrosis (NCPF) is usually seen in adult females in the third or fourth decade.
- Cirrhosis is not very common in children, and it is usually accompanied by jaundice/ascites.

Hence, the correct option is (A).

277.

- Most common malignant orbital tumor in children is rhabdomyosarcoma.
- Most common benign orbital tumor in children is dermoid cyst.

Hence, the correct option is (C).

278. Serum sickness like reaction can occur following the use of certain drugs, especially cefaclor in children. It presents with an urticarial/purpuric rash, arthritis, lymphadenopathy and fever. But unlike true serum sickness (a type III hypersensitivity response), it is not caused by circulating immune complexes.

Hence, the correct option is (A).

279. Secretory IgA is the predominant immunoglobulin in breast milk and plays an important role as a specific defence mechanism for the breast-fed baby by providing local immunological protection at mucosal surfaces against bacterial or viral infection or by preventing antigens crossing the epithelial barrier.

Hence, the correct option is (D).

280. Vaginal bleeding can occur in 3rd - 7th day after birth. It occurs due to withdrawal of maternal hormones. It usually subsides in 2-3 days. No specific treatment is required.

Hence, the correct option is (C).

281.

1. Tympanomeatal flap is raised to expose the middle ear in endomeatal approach.
2. Rosen's incision is used in the endomeatal approach for stapedectomy.
3. It is also used for exploratory tympanotomy.

Hence, the correct option is (B).

282.

1. Hitzelberg's sign is seen in acoustic neuroma.
2. It occurs due to the involvement of the 7th cranial nerve.
3. There is early involvement of the sensory fibres which causes hypoesthesia of the posterior meatal wall.
4. Paraesthesia of face and reduced corneal sensitivity occurs due to involvement of the 5th cranial nerve.

Hence, the correct option is (B).

283.

1. Orbital apex syndrome is a complication of paranasal sinus infection.
2. Superior orbital fissure syndrome along with the involvement of maxillary division of trigeminal nerve and optic nerve is known as orbital apex syndrome.
3. In superior orbital fissure syndrome, there is progressive paralysis of abducent, oculomotor and trochlear nerves.

Hence, the correct option is (C).

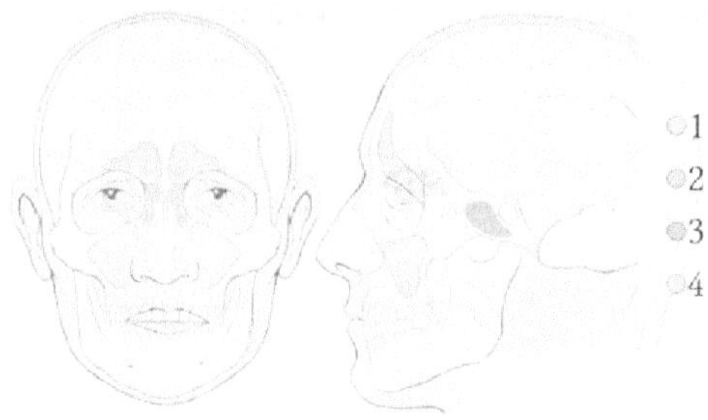

284. Paranasal sinuses - Frontal Sinus (1), Ethmoid Sinus (2), Sphenoid Sinus (3), Maxillary Sinus (4)

1. Mucocele of the frontal sinus is a cystic non tender swelling.
2. It can displace eyeball forward, downward and laterally.
3. The patient presents with headache, diplopia and proptosis.
4. Treatment is frontoethmoidectomy which facilitates free drainage of frontal sinus into the middle meatus.

Hence, the correct option is (A).

285.

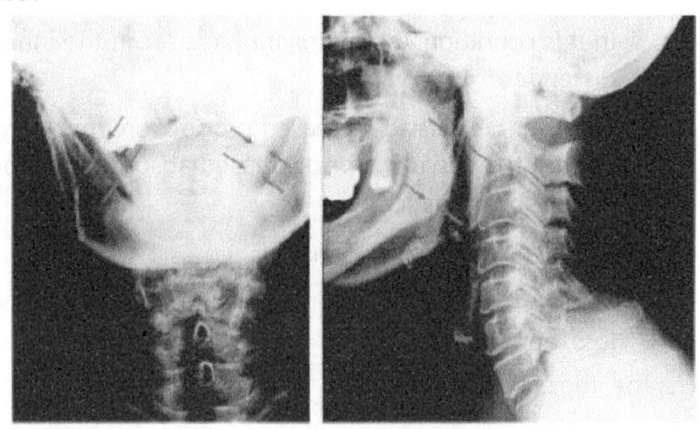

Eagle's syndrome - bilateral ossification of stylohyoid ligaments

1. Eagle's syndrome is characterized by pain in tonsillar fossa and upper neck.
2. Pain radiates of ipsilateral ear.
3. There is aggravation of pain on swallowing.
4. It is caused by calcification of stylohyoid ligament/elongation of stylohyoid process.

Hence, the correct option is (A).

286.

- Gradenigo's syndrome is seen in petrositis.
- It is characterised by lateral rectus palsy, persistent ear discharge and deep-seated ear or retro-orbital pain.
- Mastoid tenderness, hearing loss and sagging of posterosuperior meatal wall are seen acute mastoiditis.

Hence, the correct option is (B).

287. Site of origin of vestibular schwannoma:

- Most common site of origin of vestibular schwannoma is superior vestibular nerve (50-60%).
- It also occurs in the inferior vestibular nerve (40-50%) and cochlear nerve (10%).

Hence, the correct option is (B).

288. 1. Pain sensation from the ethmoid sinus is transmitted by the anterior and posterior ethmoidal branches of the Nasociliary nerve, which in turn is a branch of the trigeminal nerve (ophthalmic division).

2. The other branches of the nasociliary nerve are:

- Long ciliary nerves
- Infratrochlear nerve
- Communicating branch to the ciliary ganglion (long root of the ciliary ganglion).

3. Frontal nerve carries sensations from the forehead, frontal sinus mucosa, and the upper eyelid. it has 2 branches- supraorbital nerve and supratrochlear nerve.

4. Lacrimal nerve innervates the lacrimal gland, conjunctiva, and the lateral upper eyelids.

5. Lateral pterygoid nerve supplies the lateral pterygoid muscle.

Hence, the correct option is (A).

289. Endolymphatic Hydrops:

1. It is another name for Meniere's disease.
2. In this condition, the endolymphatic sac in the inner ear is distended.
3. This is either due to increased production of endolymph by the stria vascularis or decreased absorption through the endolymphatic sac.
4. More commonly seen in males.
5. Clinical features - vertigo, tinnitus, fluctuating hearing loss, aural fullness.

Hence, the correct option is (B).

290. Haemorrhage following tonsillectomy can be of 3 types:

1. Primary haemorrhage (Immediate haemorrhage)

- Occurs during surgery

2. Reactionary haemorrhage (Early haemorrhage)

- Occurs within 24 hours of surgery
- It is due to to the presence of a clot which prevents the compressive action of superior constrictor muscle on the blood vessels.
- It can also occur due to slipping pf a ligature/dislodgement of clot.

3. Secondary haemorrhage (delayed haemorrhage)

- Seen more than 24 hours after surgery.
- Usually seen 5 to 10 days after surgery.
- Occurs due to infection/premature separation of membrane.

Hence, the correct option is (C).

291.

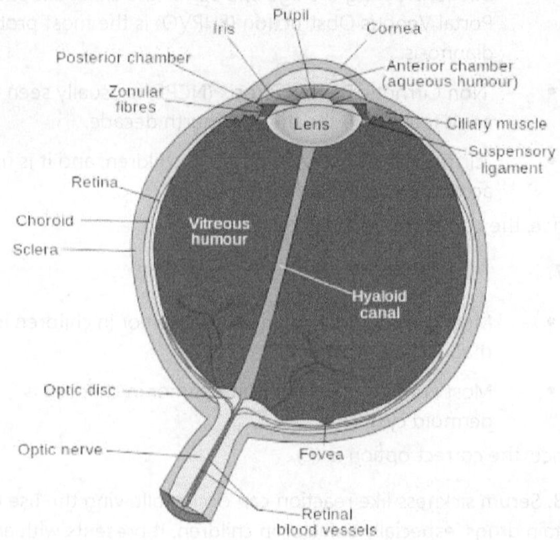

Anatomy of the eye – Hyaloid canal is visible

- Mittendorf dot is a remnant of the anterior end of hyaloid artery.
- It is attached to the posterior lens capsule.
- It is associated with posterior polar cataract.

Hence, the correct option is (C).

292.

- Favre-Goldman syndrome is an autosomal recessive condition.
- It usually presents in childhood with nyctalopia.
- Central and peripheral retinoschisis is present.
- There is marked pigmentary changes similar to retinitis pigmentosa.

Hence, the correct option is (A).

293.

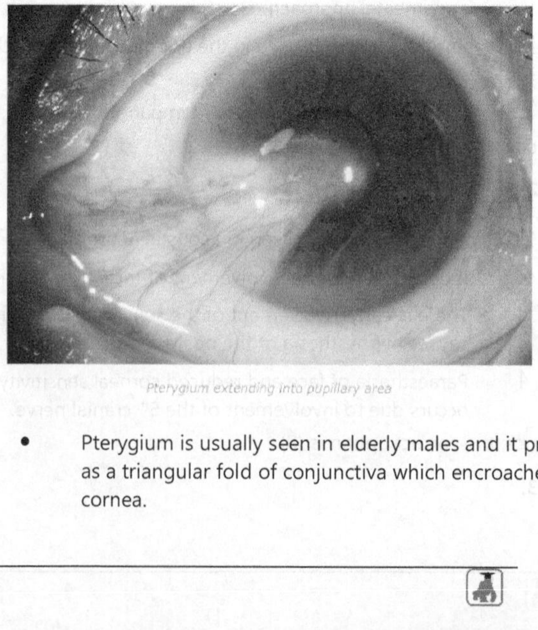

Pterygium extending into pupillary area

- Pterygium is usually seen in elderly males and it presents as a triangular fold of conjunctiva which encroaches the cornea.

- It is usually seen on the nasal side.
- stocker's line is a deposition of iron seen in corneal epithelium anterior to advancing head of pterygium.

Hence, the correct option is (C).

294.

- Cogan' syndrome is seen in middle aged adults.
- The features include intrestitial keratitis, acute tinnitus, vertigo and deafness.
- Treatment is by usage of topical and systemic corticosteroids.
- Early treatment is necessary to prevent permanent deafness and blindness.

Hence, the correct option is (A).

295. Gun sign is seen in grade III hypertensive retinopathy.

The other findings in grade III hypertensive retinopathy include:

- Copper wiring of arterioles
- Banking of veins distal to arteriovenous include
- Right-angle deflection of veins
- Flame shaped haemorrhages
- Cotton wool spots
- Hard exudates.

Hence, the correct option is (D).

296. Retinoscopy (Ret) is a technique to obtain an objective measurement of the refractive error of a patient's eyes. The examiner uses a retinoscope to shine light into the patient's eye and observes the reflection (reflex) off the patient's retina

Hence, the correct option is (C).

297.

- Bilateral granulomatous panuveitis is seen in heerfordt's syndrome(Uveoparotid fever).
- It is also associated with painful enlargement of paratoid glands.
- Cranial nerve palsy, fever, malaise and ski rashes are also seen.

Hence, the correct option is (A).

298. Appendages of the eyes (adnexa of the eye/accessory visual structures) are:

- Eyelids
- Eyebrows
- Conjunctiva
- Lacrimal apparatus

Hence, the correct option is (D).

299. Diplopia in superior oblique palsy:

- In paralysis of the superior oblique muscle (trochlear nerve palsy), maximum diplopia is experienced when the patient looks down.
- This is especially important when the patient tries to climb downstairs and when trying to read a book.
- The patient tries to compensate by tucking the chin towards the chest.

Hence, the correct option is (A).

300. Propionibacterium acnes is a gram-positive, non spore forming bacillus which is most commonly implicated in Late onset endophthalmitis after cataract surgery.

Hence, the correct option is (D).

Mock Test 04

PART A

Q.1 The most widely used method for determining the purity of a protein is?

A. Isoelectric focusing
B. Polyacrylamide gel electrophoresis
C. Ion exchange chromatography
D. High-pressure chromatography

Q.2 The enzyme catalyzing the production of orotidylic acid is?

A. Dihydro orotate
B. Aspartyl transcarbamoylase
C. Dihydro orotate dehydrogenase
D. Orotate phosphoribosyltransferase

Q.3 Deficiency of lysosomal maltase causes?

A. McArdle disease **B.** Andersen disease
C. Cori disease **D.** Pompe disease

Q.4 Which of the following is not a protein misfolding disorder?

A. Tuberculosis
B. Creutzfeldt Jakob disease
C. Alzheimer's disease
D. Cystic fibrosis

Q.5 Which of the following enzymes is responsible for the transfer of amino groups from an amino acid to an alpha-keto acid?

A. Transaminase **B.** Transketolase
C. Deaminase **D.** Lyase

Q.6 Which among the following is a cardioprotective fatty acid?

A. Oleic acid **B.** Omega-3 fatty acid
C. Beta acid **D.** Both A & B

Q.7 Alpha helix and the beta-pleated sheet are examples of:

A. Primary structure
B. Secondary structure
C. Tertiary structure
D. Quaternary structure

Q.8 Cytochrome C of the bacteria has 50% identity of amino acid sequence with that of human. Which of the following is the most conserved parameter in these two proteins?

A. Quarternary structure
B. Tertiary structure
C. Amino acid sequence
D. Loop and turn segments

Q.9 Which of the following elements is known to influence the body's ability to handle oxidative stress?

A. Calcium **B.** Iron
C. Potassium **D.** Selenium

Q.10 A person on a fat-free carbohydrate-rich diet continues to grow obese. Which of the following lipoproteins is likely to be elevated in his blood?

A. Chylomicrons **B.** VLDL
C. LDL **D.** HDL

Q.11 Which of the following is a membrane-bound enzyme that catalyzes the formation of cyclic AMP from ATP?

A. Tyrosine Kinase **B.** Polymerase
C. ATP synthase **D.** Adenylate cyclase

Q.12 Xeroderma pigmentosum is produced as a result of a defect in:

A. DNA polymerase III
B. DNA polymerase I
C. DNA exonuclease
D. DNA ligase

Q.13 Rothera's test is utilized for detection of?

A. Glucose **B.** Proteins
C. Urea **D.** Ketone bodies

Q.14 Site of the urea cycle is?

A. Liver **B.** Kidney **C.** GIT **D.** Lungs

Q.15 The process used in an expression vector to increase the yield of recombinant protein synthesis?

A. Translation initiation
B. Promoter induction
C. Transcription terminators
D. Multiple cloning sites

Q.16 Decreased energy production in thiamine deficiency is due to?

A. It is a cofactor for oxidative reduction
B. It is required for transamination reactions
C. It is a coenzyme for alpha-ketoglutarate dehydrogenase and pyruvate dehydrogenase in the citric acid cycle
D. It is a coenzyme for transketolase in hexose monophosphate shunt

Q.17 Molecules of myoglobin will bind to:

A. 1 molecule of oxygen
B. 16 molecules of oxygen
C. 4 molecules of oxygen
D. 64 molecules of oxygen

Q.18 Which of the following decreases with age?

A. Vital capacity **B.** Systolic BP
C. Pulse pressure **D.** Residual volume

Q.19 Substance not filtered in the pulmonary circulation:

A. Blood clots **B.** Cancer cells
C. Plasma proteins **D.** Gas bubbles

Q.20 Maximum resistance during expiration is due to:

A. Alveolar collapse

B. Expiratory muscle fatigue
C. The dynamic collapse of airways
D. Breaking action of inspiratory muscles

Q.21 Sudden cessation of breathing with maximal expiratory effort is due to:
A. Dynamic airway compression
B. Alveolar collapse
C. Expiratory muscle fatigue
D. Breaking action of inspiratory muscles

Q.22 The maximum amount of carbon dioxide in the human body is transported as:
A. Bicarbonate **B.** Carbide
C. Amylase **D.** None of the above

Q.23 The primary function of the cerebrospinal fluid is to:
A. Protect the brain
B. Provide nutrients to the surrounding tissues
C. Remove waste products
D. All of the above

Q.24 Jellyfish breathe through:
A. Book lungs **B.** Gills
C. Diffusion **D.** None of the above

Q.25 _______ are functional units of food absorption.
A. Red blood cells
B. Small intestine
C. Villi
D. Aggregated lymphoid nodules

Q.26 Night blindness and xerophthalmia are generally conditions associated with the deficiency of which vitamin?
A. Vitamin B **B.** Vitamin K
C. Vitamin B2 **D.** Vitamin A

Q.27 Stomach epithelial cells in the body secrete _______.
A. Hydrochloric acid **B.** Oxytocin
C. Adrenaline **D.** Testosterone

Q.28 Closing volume determines:
A. Transmural pressure
B. Residual volume
C. Small airway resistance
D. Dead space

Q.29 Elbow joint is an example of:
A. hinge joint **B.** gliding joint
C. ball and socket joint **D.** pivot joint

Q.30 A patient is generally advised to specially, consume more meat, lentils, milk, and eggs in the diet only when he suffers from?
A. Scurvy **B.** Kwashiorkor
C. Rickets **D.** Anemia

Q.31 Melatonin is produced by:
A. Thymus **B.** Skin
C. Pituitary **D.** Pineal gland

Q.32 Which part of the human brain is concerned with the regulation of body temperature?
A. Cerebellum **B.** Cerebrum
C. Hypothalamus **D.** Medulla Oblongata

Q.33 The junction between an axon and dendrite is called:
A. Cyton **B.** Synapse
C. Relay **D.** Conduction zone

Q.34 Which of the following muscle is supplied by the anterior division of the mandibular nerve?
A. Medial pterygoid
B. Lateral pterygoid
C. Mylohyoid
D. Anterior belly of digastric

Q.35 All are true regarding axillary artery except?
A. It is a continuation of the subclavian artery.
B. It is crossed by pectoralis minor muscle.
C. It extends from the outer border of the second rib to the lower border of the teres minor.
D. The second part of the axillary artery is posterior to the pectoralis minor muscle.

Q.36 Roof the fourth ventricle is formed by all of the following except?
A. Inferior medullary velum
B. Superior medullary velum
C. Obex
D. Median eminence

Q.37 The branch arising from the main trunk of the mandibular nerve is?
A. Nerve to medial pterygoid
B. Nerve to lateral pterygoid
C. Buccal nerve
D. Auriculotemporal nerve

Q.38 Deep perineal pouch in males does not include?
A. Pudendal nerve
B. Sphincter urethrae
C. Long peroneal nerve
D. Dorsal nerve of the penis

Q.39 Which is true regarding the suprarenal gland?
A. The posterior surface of the left suprarenal is related to the kidney.
B. The posterior surface of the right suprarenal is related to the inferior vena cava.
C. The lateral border of the left suprarenal is related to the left gastric artery.
D. The lateral border of the right suprarenal is related to the right coeliac ganglion.

Q.40 The Pisiform is considered as a sesamoid bone in the tendon of?
A. Flexor digitorum superficialis
B. Flexor digitorum profundus
C. Abductor digiti minimi
D. Flexor carpi ulnaris

Q.41 The largest bursa in the human body is?

A. Subacromial bursa **B.** Prepatellar bursa
C. Infrapatellar bursa **D.** Trochanteric bursa

Q.42 Which is not a part of the hypogastric sheath?
A. Transverse cervical ligament
B. Broad ligament
C. Lateral ligament of the bladder
D. Uterosacral ligament

Q.43 The Chief pronator of the forearm is?
A. Pronator quadratus **B.** Pronator teres
C. Gravity **D.** Flexor carpi radialis

Q.44 Oblique head of adductor pollicis arises from?
A. Trapezium **B.** Trapezoid
C. Capitate **D.** Hamate

Q.45 The Anterior choroidal artery is a branch of?
A. Anterior cerebral artery
B. Posterior cerebral arter
C. Internal carotid artery
D. Anterior communicating artery

Q.46 Which of the following is not a pneumatic bone?
A. Frontal bone **B.** Sphenoid
C. Maxilla **D.** Mandible

Q.47 Muscles supplied by anterior division of mandibular nerve are all except?
A. Medial pterygoid **B.** Lateral pterygoid
C. Temporalis **D.** Masseter

Q.48 Where is the urethral crest located?
A. Membranous urethra
B. Penile urethra
C. Prostatic urethra
D. Bulbar urethra

Q.49 Which is the type of joint seen in the growth plate?
A. Primary cartilaginous
B. Secondary cartilaginous
C. Fibrous joint
D. Plane Joint

Q.50 Which of the following gives rise to the muscular component of the dorsal aorta?
A. Intermediate mesoderm
B. Lateral plate mesoderm
C. Axial mesoderm
D. Paraxial mesoderm

PART B

Q.51 Rose-Waaler test is a?
A. Co-agglutination test
B. Latex agglutination test
C. Slide agglutination test
D. Haemagglutination test

Q.52 Which of the following is an intermediate level disinfectant?
A. Glutaraldehyde
B. Quaternary ammonium compound
C. Hydrogen peroxide
D. Iodophors

Q.53 The best culture medium for primary isolation of H. influenzae is?
A. Chocolate agar **B.** Fildes' agar
C. Levinthal's medium **D.** Nutrient agar

Q.54 Endemic relapsing fever is caused by all except?
A. Borrelia duttonii **B.** Borrelia hermsii
C. Borrelia parkeri **D.** Borrelia recurrentis

Q.55 Which of the following gastroenteritis viruses can spread by air?
A. Sapovirus **B.** Rotavirus
C. Norovirus **D.** Astrovirus

Q.56 Fildes technique is used for the culture of?
A. Clostridium perfringens
B. Clostridium tetani
C. Clostridium botulinum
D. Clostridium difficile

Q.57 Aflatoxin is produced by the fungus?
A. Aspergillus flavus
B. Aspergillus niger
C. Penicillium marneffei
D. Candida albicans

Q.58 All of the following are non-photochromogens except?
A. Mycobacterium ulcerans
B. Mycobacterium xenopi
C. Mycobacterium avium
D. Mycobacterium marinum

Q.59 Which of the following is an enrichment medium?
A. Alkaline peptone water
B. Loeffler serum slope
C. Deoxycholate citrate agar
D. MacConkey's agar

Q.60 Which of the following does not have a polysaccharide capsule related antigen-antibody response?
A. Haemophilus influenzae
B. Neisseria meningitidis
C. Streptococcus pneumonia
D. Bordetella pertussis

Q.61 Erythema chronicum migrans is caused by?
A. Borrelia japonica **B.** Borrelia burgdorferi
C. Borrelia andersonii **D.** Borrelia recurrentis

Q.62 Latent varicella-zoster infection is found in?
A. T cells **B.** B cells
C. Macrophages **D.** Trigeminal ganglion

Q.63 False statement about streptococcus:
A. Cell division occurs along a single axis
B. Part of normal flora in human beings

C. Causes localized infections which do not spread along tissue planes
D. Daughter cells after cell division form a string

Q.64 A patient presented to the OPD with clinical features of pneumonia. Sputum examination of the patient revealed gram-positive cocci with alpha hemolysis on sheep agar. Which test will you do to confirm the diagnosis?

A. Coagulase test
B. Bacitracin sensitivity
C. CAMP test
D. Bile solubility

Q.65 Ehrlich phenomenon is seen in:

A. Mycobacterium TB
B. Proteus
C. Staphylococcus
D. Corynebacterium

Q.66 Metachromatic granules are found in:

A. Diphtheria
B. Mycoplasma
C. Gardenerella vaginalis
D. Chlamydia

Q.67 Albert's staining is done for:

A. Clostridium
B. Corynebacterium
C. Brucella
D. Pneumococcus

Q.68 The incubation period of diphtheria is:

A. 2 - 6 days
B. 2 - 6 hours
C. 2 - 6 weeks
D. 2 - 6 months

Q.69 Brazilian purpuric fever is caused by?

A. Haemophilus haemolyticus
B. Haemophilus aphrophilus
C. Haemophilus aegyptius
D. Haemophilus parainfluenzae

Q.70 Skin test based on neutralization reaction is/are:

A. Casoni test
B. Lepromin test
C. Tuberculin test
D. Tuberculin test

Q.71 Most potent fluoroquinolone against Mycobacterium leprae is?

A. Levofloxacin
B. Ofloxacin
C. Moxifloxacin
D. Ciprofloxacin

Q.72 The antiretroviral drug combination to be avoided is?

A. Zidovudine + Stavudine
B. Zidovudine + Lamivudine
C. Didanosine + Abacavir
D. Didanosine + Zidovudine

Q.73 Basiliximab is:

A. Anti CD3 antibody
B. Anti CD25 antibody
C. IL1 receptor antagonist
D. TNF alpha inhibitor

Q.74 Shortest acting non-benzodiazepine hypnotic is?

A. Zaleplon
B. Zolpidem
C. Zopiclone
D. Eszopiclone

Q.75 Which of the following does not have significant first-pass metabolism?

A. Labetalol
B. Acebutolol
C. Atenolol
D. Metoprolol

Q.76 Which is associated with vaginal carcinoma in female offspring?

A. Diethylstilbestrol
B. Phenytoin
C. ACE inhibitors
D. Indomethacin

Q.77 Which of the following can cause discoloration of teeth in the fetus?

A. Lithium
B. Tetracycline
C. Warfarin
D. Isotretinoin

Q.78 Amylin analogue is?

A. Sitagliptin
B. Liraglutide
C. Nateglinide
D. Pramlintide

Q.79 Intake of which of the following is associated with neural tube defects?

A. Phenytoin
B. Lithium
C. Valproate
D. Phenobarbitone

Q.80 Phocomelia is an adverse effect of?

A. Diethylstilbestrol
B. Thalidomide
C. Valproate
D. Progestins

Q.81 Who is known as the Father of Pharmacology?

A. Oswald Schmiedeberg
B. J Langley
C. Rudolf Buchheim
D. Paul Ehrlich

Q.82 Which of the following is used to decrease the toxicity of amphotericin B?

A. Dose reduction
B. Liposomal delivery systems
C. Supplementing glucose
D. Giving it along with flucytosine

Q.83 Ethosuximide is the drug of choice for treatment?

A. Generalized tonic-clonic seizures
B. Absence seizures
C. Simple partial seizures
D. Complex partial seizures

Q.84 All of the following drugs cross the placenta except?

A. Phenytoin
B. Diazepam
C. Morphine
D. Heparin

Q.85 Which of the following is used for the treatment of chlamydia infection in pregnancy?

A. Tetracycline
B. Erythromycin
C. Azithromycin
D. Doxycycline

Q.86 Simeprevir is used for the treatment of?

A. HIV
B. CMV infection
C. Kaposi sarcoma
D. Chronic Hepatitis C

Q.87 Tyrosine kinase inhibitors are useful in the management of?

A. Acute myeloid leukemia
B. Small cell carcinoma of the lung
C. Gastrointestinal stromal tumors
D. Neurofibromatosis

Q.88 As a side effect the metabolic syndrome is most commonly associated with the following group of medications:
A. Anti-anxiety drugs
B. Anti-depressant drugs
C. Antipsychotic drugs
D. Anticholinergic drugs

Q.89 Mechanism of action of tianeptine in the brain is:
A. Selective serotonin reuptake inhibition
B. Selective serotonin reuptake enhancement
C. Selective dopamine reuptake inhibition
D. Selective norepinephrine reuptake inhibition

Q.90 Prolactin secretion is inhibited by:
A. Dopamine antagonist
B. GABA
C. Neurophysin
D. Bromocriptine

Q.91 Principle organelle involved in the execution of apoptosis is?

[NEET PG, 2014]

A. Nucleus
B. Lysosome
C. Mitochondria
D. Endoplasmic reticulum

Q.92 Some antigen was injected into a rabbit. What antibody will it produce initially?

[NEET PG, 2014]

A. IgG B. IgM C. IgA D. IgD

Q.93 Psammoma bodies are seen in all except?

[NEET PG, 2014]

A. Follicular carcinoma thyroid
B. Papillary carcinoma thyroid
C. Cystadenocarcinoma
D. Meningioma

Q.94 Which complement component is the first common point between involved classical and alternate pathways?
A. C1 B. C2 C. C3 D. C4

Q.95 All are involved in generating free oxygen radical for the killing off bacteria except-
A. Superoxide Dismutase
B. Fenton's reaction
C. NADPH oxidase
D. Glutathione peroxidase

Q.96 Slide fixing in pathology most commonly done by–
A. Formaldehyde B. Alcohol
C. Picric acid D. Glutaraldehyde

Q.97 Various cells respond differently to a second messenger (such as increased cAMP) because they have different?
A. Receptors
B. Enzymatic composition
C. Nuclei
D. Membrane lipids

Q.98 The light brown perinuclear pigment seen on H&F staining of the cardiac muscle fibers in the grossly normal-appearing heart of an 83- year old man at autopsy is due to deposition of?
A. Hemosiderin
B. Lipochrome
C. Cholesterol metabolites
D. Anthracotic pigment

Q.99 The level of alpha-fetoprotein is raised in all of the following except?
A. Cirrhosis of liver
B. Hepatocellular carcinoma
C. Yolk sac tumor
D. Dysgerminoma

Q.100 Brain lipid-binding protein is expressed by which of the following?
A. Mature astrocytes B. Oligodendrocytes
C. Purkinje cells D. Pyramidal neurons

Q.101 A high amylase level in pleural fluid suggests a diagnosis of?
A. Tuberculosis
B. Malignancy
C. Rheumatoid arthritis
D. Pulmonary infarction

Q.102 Which of the following malignant tumors is radioresistant?
A. Ewing's sarcoma B. Retinoblastoma
C. Osteosarcoma D. Neuroblastoma

Q.103 The most important determinant of prognosis in Wilms tumor:
A. Stage of disease
B. Loss of heterozygosity of chromosome 1p
C. Histology
D. Age less than one year at a presentation

Q.104 Hypoglycemia occurs as a paraneoplastic syndrome in:
A. Bronchogenic carcinoma
B. CA pancreas
C. Fibrosarcoma
D. RCC

Q.105 Test for carcinogenicity:
A. Kveim's test B. Ame's test
C. Schilling's test D. Schick test

Q.106 Grading of cancers does not depend on:
A. Degree of differentiation
B. Number of mitoses
C. Architectural features
D. Size of the primary lesion

Q.107 Acid phosphatase is a tumor marker for:

A. Pancreatic carcinoma

B. Prostatic carcinoma

C. Papillary carcinoma of the thyroid

D. Renal cell carcinoma

Q.108 The hallmark change in cell physiology that determines the malignant phenotype:

A. Self-sufficiency in growth signals

B. Sustained angiogenesis

C. Resistance to apoptosis

D. Aerobic glycolysis

Q.109 CA-125 is used is the monitoring and treatment of:

A. Ovarian cancer **B.** Colon cancer

C. Breast cancer **D.** Pancreatic cancer

Q.110 Calcitonin is a marker of:

A. Prostate cancer

B. Medullary carcinoma of the thyroid

C. Pheochromocytoma

D. Pancreatic cancer

Q.111 Molecular profiling of cancer cells is obtained by:

A. Flow cytometry

B. Immunohistochemistry

C. DNA microarray analysis

D. PCR

Q.112 Which is not an antibody associated with retrograde degenerative cerebellar?

A. Anti-Yo **B.** Anti-Hu **C.** Anti-Ri **D.** Anti-Tr

Q.113 An 8-year-old boy completed 8 out of a 10-day course of cefaclor. Now he developed a generalized erythematic rash which is mildly pruritic and lymphadenopathy. Diagnosis is?

A. Kawasaki disease

B. Type 3 hypersensitivity

C. Anaphylaxis

D. Infectious mononucleosis

Q.114 The commonest cause of death in a patient with primary amyloidosis is?

A. Renal failure

B. Cardiac involvement

C. Bleeding diathesis

D. Respiratory failure

Q.115 At the physiological pH, the DNA molecules are?

A. Positively charged **B.** Negatively charged

C. Neutral **D.** Amphipathic

Q.116 Disputed maternity can be solved by using the following tests except?

A. Blood grouping **B.** HLA typing

C. Preciptin test **D.** DNA fingerprinting

Q.117 Contre—coup injuries are seen in :

A. Brain **B.** Diazepam

C. Flumazenil **D.** Ethyl alcohol

Q.118 Paradox gun' is a?

A. Revolver **B.** Shotgun

C. Automatic pistol **D.** Machine gun

Q.119 The combination of alopecia & skin rash, painful peripheral neuropathy, and confusion with lethargy are seen in?

A. Copper poisoning **B.** Nickel poisoning

C. Selenium poisoning **D.** Thallium poisoning

Q.120 Rave drug is?

[NEET PG, 2014]

A. Cannabis **B.** Hashish

C. Ecstasy **D.** Heroin

Q.121 Which among the following is a waxy, luminous & translucent poison?

A. Yellow phosphorus **B.** Cobra venom

C. Organophosphates **D.** Iodine

Q.122 Visualization of gunpowder residue on blood-stained clothes can be facilitated by?

A. Ultraviolet rays **B.** Infrared rays

C. Magnifying lens **D.** Paraffin test

Q.123 Which of the following is used for narco analysis?

A. Atropine **B.** Phenobarbitone

C. Pethidine **D.** Scopolamine

Q.124 A person was brought by police from the railway platform. He is talking irrelevantly. He is having a dry mouth with hot skin, dilated pupils, a staggering gait, and slurred speech. The most probable diagnosis is:

A. Alcohol intoxication

B. Carbamates poisoning

C. Organophosphorus poisoning

D. Dhatura poisoning

Q.125 Hydrogen peroxide is used in all of the following chemical tests for blood except:

A. Benzidine test **B.** Phenolphthalein test

C. Orthotolidine test **D.** Teichmann's test

Q.126 The concept of social medicine was first introduced by:

A. Neuman and Virchow

B. Robert Grotjahrr

C. John Ryle

D. Rene sand

Q.127 The best method for collecting vital statistics in India:

A. Active surveillance

B. Passive surveillance

C. Sentinel surveillance

D. Contact tracing

Q.128 The dose of diphtheria antitoxin is:

A. 1000 to 5000 IU **B.** 10000 to 100000 IU

C. 1000 to 2000 IU **D.** None of them

Q.129 Which of the following is the tertiary level of prevention:

A. Health promotion

B. Specific protection

C. Early diagnosis & treatment

D. Disability limitation

Q.130 Which vaccine is used to prevent death from pneumonia in children?

A. Measles vaccine **B.** Rubella vaccine
C. Chickenpox vaccine **D.** Influenza vaccine

Q.131 In a country, socio-economic progress is best indicated by:

A. Gross net production
B. IMR
C. Annual per capita income of the family
D. Death rate

Q.132 Disease rate is:

A. Risk of susceptibility
B. Usually expressed as a percentage
C. The time period in a calendar year
D. Disease occurrence in a specific time period

Q.133 The concept of levels of prevention aims at:

A. Ascertaining the prognosis of a disease
B. Eradication of a disease
C. Preventing epidemics
D. Intervening in the natural history of a disease

Q.134 The disease which is known as "Father of Public health" is:

A. Smallpox **B.** Rabies
C. Plague **D.** Cholera

Q.135 Quarantine is for:

A. Infective period
B. Shortest incubation period
C. Generation time
D. Longest incubation period

Q.136 In the overhead tank of a hostel, cysts of entameba were found. The best method of disinfection is:

A. Ultraviolet radiation **B.** Boiling
C. Lodination **D.** Chlorination

Q.137 The diagnostic accuracy of a test is determined by:

A. Sensitivity **B.** Specificity
C. Predictive value **D.** None

Q.138 Which is the most economical and best screening?

A. Mosquitos **B.** Direct contact
C. Droplet **D.** Placenta

Q.139 Which of the following is the most powerful chemical disinfectant?

A. Phenol **B.** Lysol
C. Dettol **D.** Pot. permanganate

Q.140 Scientific proof of an etiological factor is given by:

A. Case-control study
B. Cohort study
C. Randomized clinical trial
D. Non-randomized trial

Q.141 Disease imported to a country not otherwise present:

A. Exotic **B.** Enzootic
C. Epizootic **D.** Endemic

Q.142 An odds ratio is derived from:

A. Case-control study
B. Cohort study
C. Randomized clinical trial
D. Non-randomized trial

Q.143 Longitudinal studies are:

A. Are easy to conduct
B. Can detect only one risk factor
C. Can find out the incidence of disease
D. Have increase bias

Q.144 Live attenuated vaccines are:

A. OPV
B. Hepatitis
C. Japanese B encephalitis
D. Chickenpox

Q.145 Vertical transmission is by:

A. Mosquitos **B.** Direct contact
C. Droplet **D.** Placenta

Q.146 Re morbidity indicators except:

A. Period of stay in hospital
B. Doctor: population ratio
C. Attendance of out-patient department
D. Notification rates

Q.147 A vaccine which is given at earliest:

A. BCG **B.** OPV **C.** MMR **D.** DPT

Q.148 Transovarian transmission of infection occurs in:

A. Fleas **B.** Ticks
C. Mosquitos **D.** Sandfly

Q.149 AH is a live vaccine except:

A. 17-D **B.** Rubella **C.** Salk **D.** Measles

Q.150 Descriptive epidemiology studies in relation to:

A. Time **B.** Place **C.** Person **D.** All

PART C

Q.151 A patient presents to the emergency department with abdominal trauma with signs of shock and peritonitis. Airway and breathing were checked. 2 large bore cannulas were inserted to secure IV access. What is the next step in the management of this patient?

A. Immediate exploratory laparotomy with general anesthesia
B. Focused Assessment with Sonography in Trauma (FAST)
C. Laparoscopic visualization of the injury
D. Watch and wait

Q.152 The Abdominal approach is used in?

A. Thiersch operation
B. Delorme's operation
C. Altemier's procedure
D. Ripstein's operation

Q.153 Which of the following is true regarding hereditary pancreatitis?

A. Autosomal recessive disorder
B. Has 80% penetrance
C. Accounts for about 30% of cases of chronic pancreatitis
D. IgG4 concentrations are elevated

Q.154 Stemmer's sign is due to?

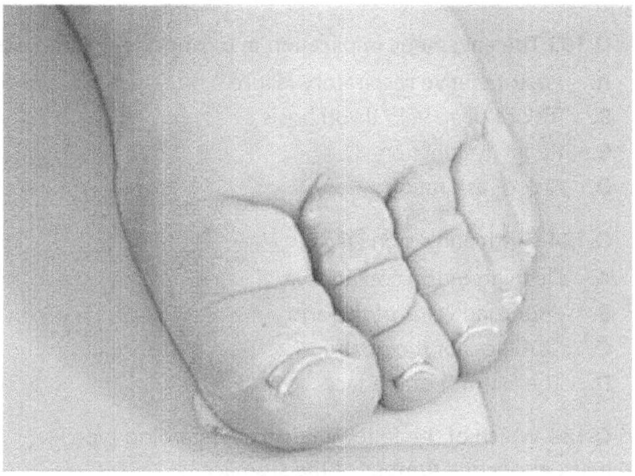

A. Lipodystrophy
B. Retroperitoneal fibrosis
C. Subcutaneous fibrosis
D. Deep vein thrombosis

Q.155 Migratory necrolytic skin rash is seen in?

A. ACTHoma **B.** VIPoma
C. Glucagonoma **D.** Somatostatinoma

Q.156 Delayed obstruction of the urinary tract after TURP is most commonly caused by?

A. Bladder neck stenosis
B. Penoscrotal stricture
C. Bulbar stricture
D. Membranous urethral stricture

Q.157 Which one of the following soft tissue sarcomas frequently metastasizes to lymph nodes?

A. Fibrosarcoma
B. Osteosarcoma
C. Embryonal Rhabdomyosarcoma
D. Alveolar soft part sarcoma

Q.158 Sclerotherapy is ideal for the treatment of:

A. External hemorrhoids
B. Internal hemorrhoids
C. Prolapsed hemorrhoids
D. Strangulated hemorrhoids

Q.159 The earliest manifestation of increased intracranial pressure following head injury is:

A. Ipsilateral pupillary dilatation
B. Contralateral pupillary dilatation
C. Altered mental status
D. Hemiparesis

Q.160 Lymphangiosarcoma was originally described in?

A. Stewart-Treves' syndrome
B. Klippel-Trenaunay's syndrome
C. Milroy's disease
D. Meig's disease

Q.161 Agnes Hunt traction is used for?

A. Flexion deformity of the hip
B. Trochanteric fracture
C. Fracture shaft of femur in adults
D. Low backache

Q.162 The most common type of teratoma of the testis is?

A. Teratoma differentiated
B. Malignant teratoma intermediate
C. Malignant teratoma anaplastic
D. Malignant teratoma trophoblastic

Q.163 Which of the following is tested using the 'Lift off test'?

A. Teres Minor **B.** Subscapularis
C. Supraspinatus **D.** Infraspinatus

Q.164 Which is not true regarding Schatzki's ring?

A. Seen at squamocolumnar junction
B. Associated with reflux disease
C. Circular ring in the proximal oesophagus
D. Respond to dilatation

Q.165 Gallow's traction is used for?

A. Fracture shaft of the femur
B. Fracture neck of the femur
C. Fracture humerus
D. Fracture tibia

Q.166 All are true regarding Caroli's disease except?

A. Intrahepatic stone formation
B. Biliary stasis
C. Commonly presents with ascites
D. Malignant change can occur

Q.167 Heberden's Arthropathy affects:

A. Lumbar spine
B. Symmetrically large joints
C. Sacroiliac joints
D. Distal interphalangeal joints

Q.168 The most common sequelae of tuberculous spondylitis in an adolescent is:

A. Fibrous Ankylosis
B. Bony Ankylosis
C. Pathological dislocation
D. Chronic osteomyelitis

Q.169 All of the following areas are commonly involved sites in pelvic fracture except:

A. Pubic rami **B.** Alae of ileum
C. Acetabulum **D.** Ischial tuberosities

Q.170 A 30-year-old man had a road traffic accident and sustained a fracture of the femur. Two days later he developed sudden breathlessness. The most probable cause can be:

A. Pneumonia
B. Congestive heart failure

C. Bronchial asthma
D. Fat Embolism

Q.171 The Best investigation for the detection of bone metastases is?

A. X-ray **B.** CT Scan
C. MRI **D.** Bone scan

Q.172 In the case of reimplantation of an amputated digit, which of the following structures is fixed first?

A. Nerve **B.** Artery **C.** Vein **D.** Bone

Q.173 In Klippel-Feil syndrome, the patient has all of the following clinical features except:

A. Low hair-line
B. Bilateral Neck webbing
C. Bilateral shortness of sternomastoid muscles
D. Gross limitations of neck movements

Q.174 Most common type of teratoma of the testis is?

A. Teratoma differentiated
B. Malignant teratoma intermediate
C. Malignant teratoma anaplastic
D. Malignant teratoma trophoblastic

Q.175 Which of the following ultrasound marker is associated with the greatest increased risk for Trisomy 21 in the fetus:

A. Echogenic foci in the heart
B. Hyperechogenic bowel
C. Choroid plexus cysts
D. Nuchal edema

Q.176 A joint is innervated by the articular branches of the nerves which supply the muscles which move the joint. This law is known as:

A. Hilton's law **B.** Andry's law
C. Wolff's law **D.** Cushing's law

Q.177 In Radionuclide imaging, the most useful radiopharmaceutical for skeletal imaging is:

A. Gallium 67
B. Technetium sulfur colloid
C. Technetium-99m
D. Technetium—99m linked to Methylene diphosphonate

Q.178 The threshold radiation dose for the hematological syndrome is?

A. 1 Gyw **B.** 5 Gy **C.** 20 Gy **D.** 100 Gy

Q.179 The most accurate investigation for assessing ventricular function is:

A. Multislice CT **B.** Echocardiography
C. Nuclear scan **D.** MRI

Q.180 Which of the following is a characteristic feature of Blount's disease?

A. Genu valgum **B.** Genu varum
C. Coxa vara **D.** Coxa valga

Q.181 The ideal timing of radiotherapy for Wilms tumor after surgery is:

A. Within 10 days
B. Within 2 weeks
C. Within 3 weeks
D. Any time after surgery

Q.182 Which one of the following imaging techniques gives maximum radiation exposure to the patient?

A. Chest X-ray **B.** MRI
C. CT scan **D.** Bone-scan

Q.183 The anesthetic implication in Gaisbock's syndrome is?

A. Postoperative respiratory failure
B. Risk of deep vein thrombosis
C. Renal dysfunction
D. Risk of aspiration

Q.184 Guttmann's sign is?

A. Flushing of the conjunctiva
B. Engorged veins of the arm
C. Stuffiness of the nostril
D. The warmth of the face

Q.185 Which of the following is true regarding type III neuroendocrine tumour of the stomach?

A. Most frequent neuroendocrine tumour of the stomach
B. Serum gastrin is normal
C. High-grade malignant tumour
D. Endoscopic resection is the treatment of choice

Q.186 Which of the following is not a definitive airway?

A. Tracheostomy
B. Orotracheal tube
C. Nasotracheal tube
D. Laryngeal mask airway

Q.187 The mechanism of action of everolimus is?

A. Blocks IL-2 gene transcription
B. Blocks IL-2 receptor signal transduction
C. Blockade of T cells
D. Prevents lymphocyte proliferation

Q.188 A patient presents to the emergency department with abdominal trauma with signs of shock and peritonitis. Airway and breathing were checked. 2 large bore cannulas were inserted to secure IV access. What is the next step in the management of this patient?

A. Immediate exploratory laparotomy with general anaesthesia
B. Focused Assessment with Sonography in Trauma (FAST)
C. Laparoscopic visualization of the injury
D. Watch and wait

Q.189 A most common type of teratoma of the testis is?

A. Teratoma differentiated
B. Malignant teratoma intermediate
C. Malignant teratoma anaplastic
D. Malignant teratoma trophoblastic

Q.190 Which is not true regarding Schatzki's ring?

A. Seen at the squamocolumnar junction
B. Associated with reflux disease
C. Circular ring in the proximal esophagus

D. Respond to dilatation

Q.191 Which of the following is true regarding type III neuroendocrine tumor of the stomach?

A. Most frequent neuroendocrine tumor of the stomach
B. Serum gastrin is normal
C. High-grade malignant tumor
D. Endoscopic resection is the treatment of choice

Q.192 True regarding obstructive azoospermia is?

A. Increased FSH and LH
B. Increased FSH and normal LH
C. Normal FSH and increased LH
D. Normal FSH and LH

Q.193 Areas involved in posterior cerebral artery infarct are all except?

A. Thalamus **B.** Temporal lobe
C. Anterior cortex **D.** Choroid plexus

Q.194 Which of the following is not a component of Total Parenteral Nutrition?

A. Amino acids **B.** Fats
C. Vitamins **D.** Fiber

Q.195 Tumour secreting placental alkaline phosphatase is?

A. Carcinoid tumor
B. Arrhenoblastoma
C. Granulosa cell tumour
D. Dysgerminoma

Q.196 Which of the following is not true regarding the Large Loop Excision of the Transformation Zone (LLETZ)?

A. Uses low voltage diathermy
B. Applicable only to the cervix
C. Loop size greater than 2cm gives a better cone
D. Shorter procedure time compared to laser ablation

Q.197 Solid tumor with cystic areas in between filled with hemorrhagic fluid and accounting for about 20% of all ovarian cancers is?

A. Cystadenocarcinoma
B. Mesonephroid tumors
C. Endometrioid tumor
D. Brenner tumor

Q.198 The characteristics of caput succedaneum – A/E:

A. Crosses midline
B. Crosses the suture line
C. It does not disappear with 2-3 days
D. It is diffuse edematous swelling of the soft tissues of the scalp

Q.199 Which is true regarding Savage syndrome?

A. Receptor defect to gonadotrophic hormones
B. Short stature
C. Ovaries do not contain follicles
D. FSH is normal

Q.200 The absence of corkscrew glands is seen in?

A. Halban's disease
B. Polycystic ovarian disease
C. Irregular ripening
D. Metropathia hemorrhagic

Q.201 Immediate cord ligation is done in:

A. Pre-term babies **B.** Rh incompatibility
C. Both a and b **D.** Anemia

Q.202 True for internal rotation of the head:

A. The Rotation occurs mostly in the cervix
B. In majority of rotation occurs in the pelvic floor
C. The rotation occurs commonly after the crowning of the head
D. Rotation is earlier in primipara than multipara

Q.203 The use of which of the following drugs for the treatment of menorrhagia is not supported by clinical evidence?

A. Tranexamic acid
B. Oral contraceptives
C. Ethamsylate
D. Progesterone only pills

Q.204 The Gold standard test for measuring ß HCG levels in serum is?

A. ELISA
B. Bioassay
C. Radioimmunoassay
D. Latex agglutination test

Q.205 Definition of crowning:

A. Biparietal diameter at the inlet of the pelvis
B. Biparietal diameter at the ischial spine
C. Biparietal diameter at the vulval outlet
D. Biparietal diameter just outside the vulval outlet

Q.206 The Most specific marker for neural tube defects is?

A. Alpha-fetoprotein
B. Unconjugated estriol
C. Acetylcholinesterase
D. Pseudocholinesterase

Q.207 Nodular tags of the hymen in the post-pregnancy period:

A. Carunculae myrtiformes
B. Vestibulae myrtiformes
C. Orficiae myrtiformes
D. Carunculae orificis

Q.208 Engagement of the head occurs when:

A. The greatest horizontal plane – bitemporal is above the pelvic brim
B. The greatest horizontal plane – bitemporal is below the pelvic brim
C. Shortest horizontal plane – biparietal is below the pelvic brim
D. None of the above

Q.209 Which of the following congenital malformations can be diagnosed in the first trimester?

A. Microcephaly **B.** Anencephaly

C. Meningocele **D.** Encephalocele

Q.210 Causes of primary amenorrhoea are all except:

A. Turner syndrome
B. Sheehan's syndrome
C. MRKH syndrome
D. Kallmann syndrome

Q.211 A primigravida in the first trimester of pregnancy was found to be sputum positive for acid-fast bacilli. There is no prior history of tuberculosis. What is the treatment of choice for this patient?

A. Category I DOTS
B. Category II DOTS
C. Category III DOTS
D. Start ATT after delivery

Q.212 The drug of choice for treatment of intrahepatic cholestasis in pregnancy is?

A. Ursodeoxycholic acid
B. Dexamethasone
C. Antihistamines
D. Cholestyramine

Q.213 Is the virus responsible for non-immune hydrops fetal is?

A. Cytomegalovirus
B. Herpes simplex virus
C. Hepatitis B virus
D. Parvovirus

Q.214 Increased nuchal translucency in 13th-week fetal ultrasound characteristic of?

A. Turner syndrome
B. Down's syndrome
C. Hydrocephalus
D. Klinefelter syndrome

Q.215 Which of the following is a Low grade squamous intraepithelial lesion as per the Bethesda system?

A. CIN I
B. CIN II
C. CIN III
D. Squamous metaplasia

Q.216 Which among the following is most commonly associated with carcinoma cervix?

A. HPV 35 **B.** HPV 33 **C.** HPV 18 **D.** HPV 16

Q.217 Estrogen administration in a menopausal woman increases the:

A. Gonadotropin secretion
B. LDL cholesterol
C. Bone mass
D. Muscle mass

Q.218 Which of the following maneuvers is not used for the management of shoulder dystocia?

A. McRoberts maneuver
B. Suprapubic pressure
C. Woods corkscrew maneuver
D. Mauriceau Smellie Veit maneuver

Q.219 Decreased motility of the Fallopian tube is seen associated with?

A. Noonan syndrome
B. PCOD
C. Churg Strauss syndrome
D. Kartagener's syndrome

Q.220 The obstetric conjugate is the distance between:

A. Sacral promontory & inner surface of the pubic symphysis
B. Sacral promontory & outer surface of the pubic symphysis
C. Sacral promontory & upper edge of the pubic symphysis
D. Sacral promontory & lower edge of the pubic symphysis

Q.221 The Sensitivity of uterine musculature:

A. Enhanced by progesterone
B. Enhanced by estrogen
C. Inhibited by estrogen
D. Enhanced by estrogen and inhibited by progesterone

Q.222 Which vitamin deficiency is most commonly seen in a pregnant mother who is on phenytoin therapy for epilepsy?

A. Vitamin B6 **B.** Vitamin B12
C. Vitamin A **D.** Folic acid

Q.223 Which is not included in active management of III state of labor to prevent PPH?

A. Direct oxytocin injection after delivery of shoulder
B. Immediate cutting and cord clamping
C. Prophylactic misoprostol
D. Controlled and sustained cord traction

Q.224 Progression of labor is assessed by:

A. Partograph
B. Cervical dilatation
C. Fetal heart monitoring
D. Status of membranes

Q.225 Most important conjugate during labor:

A. Anatomical conjugate
B. True conjugate
C. Obstetric conjugate
D. Diagonal conjugate

Q.226 The incision used in the endometrial approach to the ear is?

A. Lempert I incision **B.** Rosen's incision
C. Lempert II incision **D.** Wilde's incision

Q.227 Hitzelberger's sign is?

A. Reduced corneal sensitivity
B. Hypoesthesia of the posterior meatal wall
C. Paraesthesia of face
D. Delayed blink reflex

Q.228 Does orbital apex syndrome involve?

A. Olfactory nerve
B. The ophthalmic division of a trigeminal nerve
C. Maxillary division of trigeminal nerve
D. Mandibular division of trigeminal nerve

Q.229 All are true regarding the use of sodium fluoride in otosclerosis except?

A. It inhibits proteolytic enzymes in the cochlea
B. Its use is contraindicated in patients with chronic nephritis
C. It acts by inhibition of osteoblastic activity
D. It is used in patients with positive Schwartz sign

Q.230 Prussak's space is bounded below by?

A. Fibers of a lateral malleolar fold
B. Shrapnell's membrane
C. The short process of malleus
D. Neck of malleus

Q.231 Pain in the tonsillar fossa and upper neck is characteristic of?

A. Eagle's syndrome **B.** Apert's syndrome
C. Sickler's syndrome **D.** Usher's syndrome

Q.232 Ipsilateral immobility of soft palate is seen in?

A. Lermoyez syndrome
B. Ortner's syndrome
C. Costen's syndrome
D. Trotter's syndrome

Q.233 The following is true for Gradenigo's syndrome?

A. Mastoid tenderness
B. Retro-orbital pain
C. Hearing loss
D. Sagging of posterosuperior meatal wall

Q.234 Secondary hemorrhage after tonsillectomy is most commonly seen?

A. 6 hours after surgery
B. 24 hours after surgery
C. 6 days after surgery
D. 14 days after surgery

Q.235 Otoacoustic emissions arise from?

A. Inner hair cells **B.** Outer hair cells
C. Organ of Corti **D.** None of the above

Q.236 A child climbs with alternate steps, builds a tower of 9 cubes, but can tell not his name and cannot say his age and sex, the probable age is:

A. 36 months **B.** 24 months
C. 30 months **D.** 48 months

Q.237 A child's growth variation is normal but bone development is not acc to the chronological age. What is the diagnosis?

A. Genetic
B. Dwarfism
C. Constitutional delay
D. Familial short stature

Q.238 Taste perception of the baby develops at:

A. Birth **B.** 4 month **C.** 6 month **D.** 8 month

Q.239 A 3-month baby will have:

A. Pincer Grasp **B.** Head control
C. Sitting with support **D.** Transfer objects

Q.240 A two-month-old child likely to:

A. Show a positive parachute protective reflex
B. Hold head steady in a seated positive
C. Lift head chest off a flat surface with extended ventral
D. Sustain head level with the body when the placed suspension

Q.241 Adolescent starts at the age of:

A. 7 years **B.** 10 years **C.** 14 years **D.** 17 years

Q.242 Child change rattle from one hand to another at:

A. 1 year **B.** 6 months
C. 3 months **D.** 2 years

Q.243 Short stature, secondary to growth hormone deficiency's associated with:

A. Normal body proportion
B. Low birth weight
C. Normal epiphyseal development
D. Height age equal to skeletal age

Q.244 Order of development of secondary sexual characteristic in male:

A. Testicular development-pubic hair-axillary hair-beard
B. Pubic hair- testicular development -axillary hair -beard
C. Testicular development -beard-pubic hair-axillary hair
D. Axillary hair- beard- pubic hair-testicular development

Q.245 The maximum growth spurt is seen in the girl at, time of:

A. Pubarche **B.** Thelarche
C. Menarche **D.** Adrenarche

Q.246 All of the following are seen in Favre-Goldmann syndrome except?

A. Ectopia lentis
B. Retinoschisis
C. Nyctalopia
D. Pigmentary changes similar to retinitis pigmentosa

Q.247 Axenfeld anomaly is seen in glaucoma associated with?

A. Aniridia
B. Phakomatosis
C. Ectopia lentis
D. Iridocorneal dysgenesis

Q.248 Stocker's line is seen in?

A. Pinguecula **B.** Trachoma
C. Pterygium **D.** Concretions

Q.249 Cogan's syndrome is associated with?

A. Keratitis **B.** Conjunctivitis
C. Iritis **D.** Myopia

Q.250 Which of the following is seen in Lowe's syndrome?

A. Glaucoma **B.** Choroiditis
C. Secondary cataract **D.** Myopia

Q.251 Gunn sign is?

A. Silver wiring of arterioles
B. Deflection of veins at an arteriovenous crossing
C. Copper wiring of arterioles

D. Tapering of veins on either side of the crossings

Q.252 Weiss operation is done for?

A. Cicatricial entropion
B. Senile entropion
C. Senile ectropion
D. Cicatricial ectropion

Q.253 Bilateral granulomatous panuveitis is seen in?

A. Heerfordt's syndrome
B. Reiter's syndrome
C. Behcet's disease
D. Toxoplasmosis

Q.254 Ophthalmoplegic migraine is best characterized as?

A. Recurrent headache with transient palsy of the ophthalmic nerve
B. Headache associated with irreversible palsy of 3rd nerve
C. Recurrent headache with transient palsy of 3, 4, and/or 6th cranial nerves
D. Headache with optic neuritis

Q.255 Which of the following is a topical NSAID for ophthalmic use?

A. Ibuprofen B. Diflunisal
C. Nepafenac D. Oxaprozin

Q.256 A 40-year old woman presents with a 2-year history of erythematous papulopustular lesions on the convexities of the face. There is a background of erythema and telangiectasia. The most likely diagnosis in the patient is:

A. Acne vulgaris
B. Rosacea
C. Systemic lupus erythematosus
D. Polymorphic light eruption

Q.257 Neoplastic dyskeratosis is seen in?

A. Darier's disease
B. Warty dyskeratoma
C. Familial benign pemphigus
D. Actinic keratosis

Q.258 The pseudo-isomorphic phenomenon is characteristic of?

A. Vitiligo B. Psoriasis
C. DLE D. Plane warts

Q.259 Blaschko's lines represent?

A. Lines of development
B. Dermatomes
C. Lines along blood vessels
D. Lines along lymphatics

Q.260 A 27-year-old sexually active male develops a vesiculobullous lesion on the glans soon after taking a paracetamol tablet for fever. The lesion healed with hyperpigmentation. The most likely diagnosis is:

A. Behcet's syndrome B. Herpes genitalis
C. Fixed drug eruption D. Pemphigus Vulgaris

Q.261 An otherwise healthy male presented to the OPD with a curdy white patch on the tongue. The most probable diagnosis is?

A. Candidiasis B. Lichen planus
C. Histoplasmosis D. Aspergillosis

Q.262

The only definite indication for giving systemic corticosteroids in pustular psoriasis is:

A. Psoriatic erythroderma with pregnancy
B. Psoriasis in a patient with alcoholic cirrhosis
C. Moderate arthritis
D. Extensive lesions

Q.263 Anemia with stippling of erythrocytes is seen commonly in which metal toxicity?

A. Lead B. Mercury
C. Manganese D. Arsenic

Q.264 A 45-year-old farmer has itchy erythematous papular lesions on the face, neck, 'V' area of the chest, dorsum of hands, and forearms for 3 years. The lesions are more severe in summer and improve by 75% in winter. The most appropriate test to diagnose the condition would be:

A. Skin biopsy
B. Estimation of IgE levels in the blood
C. Patch test
D. Intradermal prick test

Q.265 A patient had seven irregular hyperpigmented macules on the trunk and multiple small hyperpigmented macules in the axillae and groins since early childhood. There were no other skin lesions. Which is the most likely investigation to support the diagnosis?

A. Slit-lamp examination of the eye
B. Measurement of intraocular tension
C. Examination of fundus
D. Retinal artery angiography

Q.266 Ivermectin is indicated in the treatment of:

A. Syphilis B. Scabies
C. Tuberculosis D. Dermatophytosis

Q.267 Anagen phase of the hair indicates:

A. The phase of activity and growth
B. The phase of transition
C. The phase of resting
D. The phase of degeneration

Q.268 A patient had seven irregular hyperpigmented macules on the trunk and multiple small hyperpigmented macules in the axillae and groins since early childhood. There were no other skin lesions. Which is the most likely investigation to support the diagnosis?

A. Slit lamp examination of eye
B. Measurement of intraocular tension
C. Examination of fundus
D. Retinal artery angiography

Q.269 The drug used for the treatment of nocturnal enuresis is?

A. Trazodone **B.** Imipramine
C. Chlorpromazine **D.** Sertraline

Q.270 False statement regarding Complex Regional Pain Syndrome (CRPS) is?

A. Type 1 CRPS occurs following a nerve injury
B. Type 1 CRPS is also called Reflex Sympathetic Dystrophy
C. It occurs due to adrenergic sensitivity of afferent nociceptors
D. CRPS Type 1 resolves with symptomatic treatment

Q.271 Which of the following is not a feature of pseudohypoparathyroidism?

A. Hyperparathyroidism
B. Hypocalcemia
C. Hypoparathyroidism
D. Hyperphosphatemia

Q.272 Which of the following is a false statement?

A. Acetaminophen does not have anti-inflammatory action
B. NSAIDs with least cardiovascular risk in Naproxen
C. Gastric irritation is more severe with NSAIDs compared to aspirin
D. Non-selective COX-2 inhibitors are contraindicated in postoperative patients

Q.273 Wrong statement about SGLT (sodium-glucose linked transporter):

A. SGLT1 is present in the intestine and kidneys
B. SGLT1 has low capacity and high affinity
C. SGLT2 inhibitors worsen heart failure
D. SGLT2 inhibitors produce weight loss

Q.274 Which of the following is false regarding Multiple Sclerosis (MS)?

A. More common in women and age of onset is between 20-40 years of age
B. Risk factors include vitamin D deficiency and cigarette smoking
C. Pathological hallmark is axonal degeneration
D. HLA DRB1 in MHC class II is associated with 10% of disease risk

Q.275 The following drug is not used for the treatment of type II lepra reaction:

A. Chloroquine **B.** Thalidomide
C. Cyclosporine **D.** Corticosteroids

Q.276 The clinical picture is diagnostic of acne vulgaris. Isotretinoin is used in severe intractable acne. Pterygium of the nail is characteristically seen in:

A. Lichen planus **B.** Psoriasis
C. Tinea unguium **D.** Alopecia areata

Q.277 The main cytokine, involved in erythema nodusum leprosum (ENL) reaction is:

A. Interleukin—2
B. Interferon-gamma
C. Tumor necrosis factor-alpha
D. Macrophage colony-stimulating factor

Q.278 All of the following are true regarding CSF abnormalities in multiple sclerosis except?

A. CSF protein concentration is more than 100 mg/dl
B. CSF IgG index expresses the ratio of IgG to albumin in CSF divided by the same ratio in serum
C. Oligoclonal bands may be absent at onset of multiple sclerosis
D. The number of oligoclonal bands increases with time

Q.279 Max. Joseph's space is a histopathological feature of:

A. Psoriasis Vulgaris **B.** Lichen planus
C. Pityriasis rosea **D.** Parapsoriasis

Q.280 'Chancre redux' is a clinical feature of:

A. Early relapsing syphilis
B. Late syphilis
C. Chancroid
D. Recurrent herpes simplex infection

Q.281 All of the following drugs are effective in the treatment of pityriasis versicolor except:

A. Selenium sulphide **B.** Ketoconazole
C. Griseofulvin **D.** Clotrimazole

Q.282 A 16-year-old boy presented with asymptomatic, multiple, erythematous, annular lesions with a collarette of scales at the periphery of the lesions present on the trunk. The most likely diagnosis is:

A. Pityriasis Versicolor
B. Pityriasis alba
C. Pityriasis rosea
D. Pityriasis rubra pilaris

Q.283 In which of the following conditions Parakeratosis most frequently occurs?

A. Actinic keratoses
B. Seborrheic keratoses
C. Molluscum contagiosum
D. Basal cell carcinoma

Q.284 A 24-year old unmarried woman has multiple nodular, cystic, pustular, and comedonal lesions on the face, upper back, and shoulders for 2 years. The drug of choice for her treatment would be:

A. Acitretin **B.** Isotretinoin
C. Doxycycline **D.** Azithromycin

Q.285 All of the following drugs are effective in the treatment of pityriasis Versicolor except:

A. Selenium sulfide **B.** Ketoconazole
C. Griseofulvin **D.** Clotrimazole

Q.286 Mutation in malignant melanoma-

A. N-myc **B.** CDK2A **C.** RET **D.** None

Q.287 Mycosis fungoides affects:

A. T Cells **B.** B Cells
C. NK Cells **D.** K Cells

Q.288 Civatte bodies are found in:

A. Lichen Planus **B.** Psoriasis
C. Dermatophytosis **D.** Vitiligo

Q.289 Broke's tumor is a tumor of:

A. Superficial dermal vessels
B. Sweat glands
C. Hair follicles
D. Sebaceous glands

Q.290 Reactivation tuberculosis is almost exclusively a disease of the:

A. Lungs **B.** Bones **C.** Joints **D.** Brain

Q.291 Prolonged parasitism in malaria is due to:

A. Antigenic variation
B. Intracellularity of the parasite
C. Immunosuppression
D. Sequestration

Q.292 Which of the following cell types is not a target for the initiation and maintenance of HIV infection?

A. CD4 T cell **B.** Macrophage
C. Dendritic cell **D.** Neutrophil

Q.293 Pautriers abscess is mainly composed of which of the following cells:

A. Eosinophils **B.** Lymphocytes
C. Neutrophils **D.** Macrophages

Q.294 Simplex type of Epidermolysis Bullosa involves mutations in:

A. Keratin 5 **B.** Lamina Lucida
C. Type VII collagen **D.** Dystrophin

Q.295 Selective granular IgA deposit at dermal papillae tips as seen in:

A. Bullous pemphigoid
B. Dermatitis Herpetiformis
C. Lichen planus
D. Pemphigus Vulgaris

Q.296 Linear band of immunofluorescence (due to immunoglobulin deposition) along the dermo-epidermal junction (Ribbon candy pattern) is seen in:

A. Bullous pemphigoid
B. Dermatitis Herpetiformis
C. Pemphigus Vulgaris
D. Lichen planus

Q.297 All are true about basal cell carcinoma except:

A. It is a locally aggressive tumor
B. They are slow-growing and rarely metastasize
C. Associated with mutations that activate Hedgehog pathway signaling
D. A most common site is acral parts

Q.298 Plasmodium falciparum affects all organs except:

A. Lung **B.** Liver **C.** Kidney **D.** Heart

Q.299 Acantholytic cells in Pemphigus are derived from:

A. Stratum granulosum **B.** Stratum basale
C. Langerhans cell **D.** Stratum spinosum

Q.300 The most common cause of premature death in schizophrenia is?

A. Drug toxicity
B. Nosocomial infection
C. Homicide
D. Suicide

// Smart Answer Sheet //

Correct Percentage of students who answered correctly. **Skipped** Percentage of students who skipped.

Q.	Ans.	Correct	Skipped	Q.	Ans.	Correct	Skipped	Q.	Ans.	Correct	Skipped	Q.	Ans.	Correct	Skipped	Q.	Ans.	Correct	Skipped	Q.	Ans.	Correct	Skipped
1	B	48.74 %	47.97 %	22	A	77.84 %	12.1 %	43	A	40.0 %	43.1 %	64	D	83.05 %	13.78 %	85	C	49.59 %	40.37 %	106	D	78.25 %	15.27 %
2	D	28.65 %	70.19 %	23	D	78.97 %	13.58 %	44	C	79.11 %	12.69 %	65	D	41.28 %	54.04 %	86	D	82.86 %	13.82 %	107	B	66.62 %	30.51 %
3	D	61.93 %	33.22 %	24	C	68.67 %	31.01 %	45	C	82.28 %	16.04 %	66	A	81.79 %	10.13 %	87	C	86.95 %	12.32 %	108	D	80.52 %	10.8 %
4	A	88.74 %	11.04 %	25	C	79.84 %	16.88 %	46	D	40.39 %	58.26 %	67	B	77.52 %	13.69 %	88	C	76.4 %	17.15 %	109	A	87.15 %	12.03 %
5	A	50.38 %	48.02 %	26	D	45.44 %	49.19 %	47	A	55.11 %	41.91 %	68	A	88.88 %	10.91 %	89	B	84.97 %	12.38 %	110	B	45.58 %	46.62 %
6	D	62.51 %	35.41 %	27	A	62.18 %	34.0 %	48	C	54.96 %	38.23 %	69	C	21.19 %	78.52 %	90	A	82.31 %	10.38 %	111	C	81.16 %	17.61 %
7	B	60.41 %	35.2 %	28	A	87.13 %	12.17 %	49	A	80.76 %	13.45 %	70	D	83.09 %	11.68 %	91	C	26.43 %	69.9 %	112	B	86.19 %	13.68 %
8	B	58.92 %	33.95 %	29	A	87.51 %	11.56 %	50	B	25.14 %	71.14 %	71	C	44.83 %	30.06 %	92	B	88.72 %	11.12 %	113	B	85.23 %	11.96 %
9	D	76.06 %	14.04 %	30	B	48.65 %	32.55 %	51	D	43.35 %	46.86 %	72	A	79.11 %	10.97 %	93	A	80.69 %	11.14 %	114	B	77.93 %	11.59 %
10	B	79.07 %	20.88 %	31	D	81.51 %	17.33 %	52	D	86.38 %	12.86 %	73	B	69.53 %	30.33 %	94	C	49.85 %	37.37 %	115	B	89.76 %	10.23 %
11	D	77.76 %	11.82 %	32	C	10.86 %	72.83 %	53	B	49.7 %	47.47 %	74	A	77.27 %	14.9 %	95	D	79.01 %	17.45 %	116	C	16.57 %	78.48 %
12	B	56.22 %	38.26 %	33	B	86.36 %	10.63 %	54	D	89.47 %	10.03 %	75	C	77.55 %	13.32 %	96	A	85.88 %	11.36 %	117	A	41.18 %	39.7 %
13	D	49.17 %	43.84 %	34	B	84.0 %	15.28 %	55	C	80.15 %	11.14 %	76	A	23.7 %	70.41 %	97	B	85.58 %	12.21 %	118	B	45.92 %	39.45 %
14	A	82.32 %	11.51 %	35	C	47.9 %	31.35 %	56	B	67.02 %	31.57 %	77	B	85.82 %	14.01 %	98	B	76.43 %	10.18 %	119	D	85.02 %	13.97 %
15	B	77.72 %	12.86 %	36	D	82.41 %	14.6 %	57	A	29.39 %	69.15 %	78	D	79.05 %	13.26 %	99	D	86.22 %	11.72 %	120	C	66.52 %	30.65 %
16	C	84.38 %	14.88 %	37	A	27.59 %	69.24 %	58	D	59.08 %	34.85 %	79	C	82.99 %	16.44 %	100	B	65.91 %	32.29 %	121	A	13.44 %	73.65 %
17	A	86.15 %	10.38 %	38	C	66.6 %	32.72 %	59	C	78.66 %	17.39 %	80	B	81.46 %	11.24 %	101	B	86.77 %	10.43 %	122	B	25.41 %	71.38 %
18	A	87.36 %	11.88 %	39	A	83.78 %	15.17 %	60	D	50.74 %	41.15 %	81	A	87.16 %	11.32 %	102	C	65.43 %	30.82 %	123	D	84.32 %	12.1 %
19	C	80.31 %	19.06 %	40	D	79.79 %	13.05 %	61	B	82.15 %	10.22 %	82	B	12.88 %	69.65 %	103	C	83.28 %	14.94 %	124	D	81.92 %	11.33 %
20	D	27.24 %	71.24 %	41	A	69.68 %	30.15 %	62	D	85.58 %	14.31 %	83	B	55.95 %	39.16 %	104	C	58.03 %	34.99 %	125	D	76.47 %	11.77 %
21	A	57.4 %	39.66 %	42	B	84.73 %	12.53 %	63	C	78.8 %	21.11 %	84	D	84.72 %	13.76 %	105	B	78.56 %	10.14 %	126	A	77.4 %	20.4 %

Q.	Ans.	Correct	Skipped	Q.	Ans.	Correct	Skipped	Q.	Ans.	Correct	Skipped	Q.	Ans.	Correct	Skipped	Q.	Ans.	Correct	Skipped	Q.	Ans.	Correct	Skipped
127	C	85.86 %	12.13 %	148	B	88.34 %	11.19 %	169	D	78.4 %	20.22 %	190	C	47.84 %	37.86 %	211	A	77.09 %	10.95 %	232	D	77.46 %	20.34 %
128	B	19.05 %	72.29 %	149	C	83.11 %	11.28 %	170	D	78.19 %	11.99 %	191	B	76.97 %	13.54 %	212	A	84.61 %	10.87 %	233	B	23.8 %	70.48 %
129	D	84.95 %	13.26 %	150	D	66.89 %	31.01 %	171	D	40.11 %	57.95 %	192	D	48.04 %	37.1 %	213	D	84.94 %	13.44 %	234	C	56.06 %	42.08 %
130	A	81.36 %	13.54 %	151	A	11.11 %	82.76 %	172	D	82.72 %	13.1 %	193	C	45.77 %	40.42 %	214	B	83.88 %	10.21 %	235	B	77.69 %	12.52 %
131	C	83.38 %	11.55 %	152	D	85.6 %	12.1 %	173	C	85.18 %	13.34 %	194	D	87.67 %	11.73 %	215	A	25.78 %	71.7 %	236	C	50.64 %	32.78 %
132	B	64.99 %	32.25 %	153	B	82.21 %	14.0 %	174	B	30.96 %	67.35 %	195	D	52.32 %	39.16 %	216	D	22.99 %	68.16 %	237	C	68.4 %	30.89 %
133	D	14.8 %	79.91 %	154	C	79.88 %	16.29 %	175	D	83.22 %	11.66 %	196	C	28.33 %	71.07 %	217	C	22.69 %	73.73 %	238	A	26.87 %	67.18 %
134	D	83.19 %	12.03 %	155	C	83.25 %	15.67 %	176	A	42.21 %	31.62 %	197	C	41.17 %	32.59 %	218	D	49.75 %	39.85 %	239	B	81.34 %	14.3 %
135	D	20.13 %	73.93 %	156	A	86.88 %	10.25 %	177	D	87.09 %	12.72 %	198	C	23.23 %	67.32 %	219	D	86.92 %	11.23 %	240	D	50.19 %	47.23 %
136	D	52.82 %	44.83 %	157	C	84.85 %	11.81 %	178	A	49.61 %	30.66 %	199	A	81.8 %	14.76 %	220	A	61.23 %	33.1 %	241	B	85.05 %	14.88 %
137	C	21.19 %	72.01 %	158	B	82.69 %	10.7 %	179	B	79.59 %	13.89 %	200	D	76.6 %	16.06 %	221	D	68.25 %	31.05 %	242	B	62.84 %	32.13 %
138	D	78.48 %	12.89 %	159	C	50.69 %	42.15 %	180	B	30.06 %	67.76 %	201	C	15.78 %	74.7 %	222	D	85.72 %	11.23 %	243	A	45.2 %	32.92 %
139	B	67.93 %	30.13 %	160	A	85.53 %	13.97 %	181	A	76.07 %	17.14 %	202	B	76.67 %	16.21 %	223	C	50.71 %	32.27 %	244	A	81.99 %	15.81 %
140	C	64.71 %	31.33 %	161	A	29.21 %	69.59 %	182	C	86.6 %	10.38 %	203	C	85.24 %	11.25 %	224	A	84.11 %	13.01 %	245	C	76.08 %	18.6 %
141	A	86.04 %	12.18 %	162	B	89.28 %	10.08 %	183	B	77.73 %	20.76 %	204	C	65.29 %	32.55 %	225	C	78.8 %	10.52 %	246	A	86.12 %	12.58 %
142	A	87.92 %	11.34 %	163	B	68.94 %	30.13 %	184	C	88.36 %	10.22 %	205	C	68.57 %	31.09 %	226	B	89.57 %	10.04 %	247	D	80.18 %	12.75 %
143	A	15.67 %	78.03 %	164	C	29.08 %	68.76 %	185	B	54.14 %	42.93 %	206	C	67.33 %	31.01 %	227	B	80.64 %	11.98 %	248	C	65.33 %	30.62 %
144	A	88.84 %	10.2 %	165	A	87.0 %	12.12 %	186	D	61.99 %	37.26 %	207	A	64.2 %	30.37 %	228	C	56.59 %	42.14 %	249	A	84.15 %	11.68 %
145	D	82.37 %	12.51 %	166	C	67.62 %	31.79 %	187	B	76.54 %	20.47 %	208	D	49.34 %	48.14 %	229	C	82.62 %	11.57 %	250	A	89.25 %	10.18 %
146	B	15.51 %	73.91 %	167	D	44.46 %	54.04 %	188	A	85.59 %	11.77 %	209	B	79.09 %	10.32 %	230	C	80.09 %	12.43 %	251	D	79.59 %	16.88 %
147	A	79.1 %	11.05 %	168	B	76.41 %	11.85 %	189	B	11.9 %	72.98 %	210	B	61.17 %	35.19 %	231	A	11.87 %	68.93 %	252	B	82.11 %	17.32 %

Q.	Ans.	Correct	Skipped	Q.	Ans.	Correct	Skipped	Q.	Ans.	Correct	Skipped	Q.	Ans.	Correct	Skipped	Q.	Ans.	Correct	Skipped	Q.	Ans.	Correct	Skipped
253	A	18.17 %	77.77 %	261	A	84.06 %	10.92 %	269	B	78.62 %	17.28 %	277	C	83.41 %	11.64 %	285	C	87.71 %	11.63 %	293	B	67.96 %	31.26 %
254	C	78.04 %	20.2 %	262	D	57.8 %	35.84 %	270	A	81.69 %	10.12 %	278	A	82.87 %	10.78 %	286	B	87.22 %	11.09 %	294	A	89.31 %	10.08 %
255	C	15.78 %	73.37 %	263	D	76.68 %	10.93 %	271	C	67.34 %	32.25 %	279	B	83.18 %	15.5 %	287	A	80.31 %	14.67 %	295	B	79.19 %	20.06 %
256	B	82.48 %	15.68 %	264	C	84.27 %	15.21 %	272	C	88.72 %	11.11 %	280	A	82.9 %	16.18 %	288	A	87.92 %	10.66 %	296	A	21.67 %	71.2 %
257	D	78.99 %	11.08 %	265	A	84.17 %	14.9 %	273	C	89.38 %	10.33 %	281	C	83.55 %	15.42 %	289	C	89.17 %	10.04 %	297	D	22.58 %	73.07 %
258	D	47.35 %	45.86 %	266	B	76.64 %	19.36 %	274	C	85.96 %	13.97 %	282	C	79.63 %	13.06 %	290	A	64.62 %	31.5 %	298	A	76.46 %	11.85 %
259	A	45.1 %	44.71 %	267	A	87.15 %	10.38 %	275	C	84.49 %	11.12 %	283	A	59.12 %	40.06 %	291	B	56.21 %	32.26 %	299	D	61.57 %	31.09 %
260	C	53.74 %	41.97 %	268	A	77.77 %	13.36 %	276	A	61.38 %	33.71 %	284	B	81.7 %	17.24 %	292	D	83.77 %	12.95 %	300	D	89.13 %	10.44 %

//Hints and Solutions//

1. Polyacrylamide gel electrophoresis (PAGE) is a technique used almost universally in life science laboratories. The goal of this technique is to separate a mixed sample of proteins to identify and quantify single proteins from the mixture.

Hence, the correct option is (B).

2.

- Orotate phosphoribosyltransferase is the enzyme catalyzing the synthesis of orotidylic acid (Orotidine 5'-monophosphate).
- In the de novo synthesis of pyrimidines, the enzyme aspartyl transcarbamoylase catalyzes the combination of carbamoyl phosphate and aspartate to form carbamoyl aspartate.
- Dihydro orotate catalyzes the production of dihydro orotic acid.
- Dihydro orotate dehydrogenase catalyzes the production of orotic acid from dihydro orotic acid.

Hence, the correct option is (D).

3. Pompe disease belongs to a group of diseases known as the 'lysosomal storage disorders' (LSDs). Pompe disease is a lysosomal storage disorder in which acid alpha-glucosidase (GAA) is deficient or absent. Deficiency of this lysosomal enzyme results in the progressive expansion of glycogen-filled lysosomes in multiple tissues, with cardiac and skeletal muscle being the most severely affected.

Hence, the correct option is (D).

4. Tuberculosis is not a disorder of protein misfolding disorder.

Alzheimer's disease - Abeta deposits in cerebral cortex beta-**amyloid deposits in the cerebral cortex of a patient with Alzheimer's** disease – Immunohistochemistry photomicrograph.

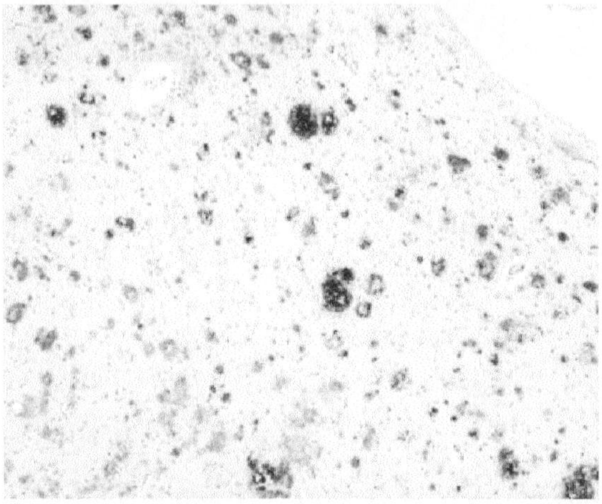

Protein misfolding disorder- Protein misfolding disorders, also known as proteinopathies are conditions in which some proteins become structurally abnormal and impair the function of cells and tissues.

Protein folding is abnormal and they fail to perform normally and may even gain toxic effects.

e.g. Alzheimer's disease (beta-amyloid peptide), Creutzfeldt Jakob disease (prion disease), Cystic fibrosis (CFTR).

Hence, the correct option is (A).

5.

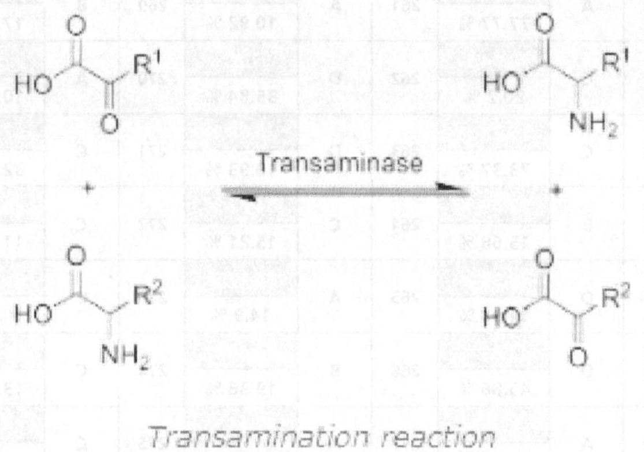

Transamination reaction

transfer of amino groups (Transaminasion)

- Transaminases are responsible for the transfer of an amino group (NH_2) from an amino acid to an alpha-keto acid.
- It results in the formation of new amino acids and alpha-keto acids.
- Transaminases are also known as aminotransferases.
- Pyridoxal phosphate (derived from Vitamin B6) acts as a coenzyme for transamination reactions.
- These reactions are reversible.

Hence, the correct option is (A).

6.

- Palmitic acid and stearic acid are saturated fatty acids – promote atherogenesis.
- Oleic acid is a monounsaturated fatty acid – cardioprotective, reduce LDL.
- Omega-3 fatty acids like linolenic acid and docosahexaenoic acid are cardioprotective.

Hence, the correct option is (D).

7. Alpha helix and the beta-pleated sheet are examples of secondary structure.

- The alpha-helix structure and the beta-pleated sheets contribute to the secondary structures that are held together by hydrogen bonds. The alpha helix has a right-handed spiral conformation. It is a polypeptide chain that is rod-shaped and coiled in a spring-like structure.
- Beta pleated sheets are made of beta strands connected laterally by two or more hydrogen bonds. Each beta-strand is made up of 3 to 10 amino acid residues.

Hence, the correct option is (B).

8. The overall three-dimensional structure of a polypeptide is called its tertiary structure. The tertiary structure is primarily due to interactions between the R groups of the amino acids that make up the protein. Tertiary structure is stabilized by disulfide bonds, ionic interactions, hydrogen bonds, metallic bonds, and hydrophobic interactions. Disulfide bonds are the strongest forces holding the tertiary structure together, as they are covalent bonds.

Hence, the correct option is (B).

9. Selenocysteine is a part of the enzyme glutathione peroxidase which has antioxidant action. Glutathione peroxidase activity is a primary antioxidant defense system that plays a key and fundamental role in the overall defense mechanisms and strategies in biological systems. There are at least eight GPx enzymes in humans, GPx1–GPx8.

Hence, the correct option is (D).

10. A high carbohydrate diet increases lipid synthesis. There is increased synthesis of triglycerides and secretion of VLDL by the liver. VLDL stands for very low-density lipoprotein. Lipoproteins are made up of cholesterol, triglycerides, and proteins. They move cholesterol, triglycerides, and other lipids (fats) to around the body. VLDL is one of the three main types of lipoproteins. VLDL contains the highest amount of triglycerides.

Hence, the correct option is (B).

11. Adenylyl cyclase is the enzyme that synthesizes cyclic adenosine monophosphate or cyclic AMP from adenosine triphosphate (ATP). Cyclic AMP functions as a second messenger to relay extracellular signals to intracellular effectors, particularly protein kinase A. Regulation of intracellular concentrations of cyclic AMP is largely a result in controlling adenylyl cyclase.

Structure and function

- Adenylyl cyclases are integral membrane proteins that consist of two bundles of six transmembrane segments. Two catalytic domains extend as loops into the cytoplasm, as depicted in the figure to the right.
- A soluble (non-membrane bound) form of adenylyl cyclase has recently been characterized in mammalian sperm. This form of the enzyme appears to be activated by bicarbonate ions.
- When adenylyl cyclase is activated, it catalyzes the conversion of ATP to cyclic AMP, which leads to an increase in intracellular levels of cyclic AMP.

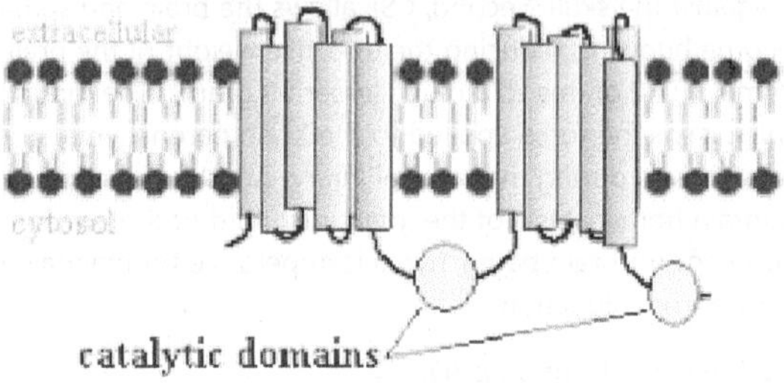

Hence, the correct option is (D).

12. Xeroderma pigmentosum is an autosomal recessive disease with a defect in DNA repair. It is characterized by extreme sensitivity to sunlight. The enzymes affected in this condition are:

1. UV specific endonuclease (most common)
2. DNA polymerase I
3. DNA ligase

Hence, the correct option is (B).

13. Rothera's test is utilized for the detection of ketone bodies.

If Rothera's test is positive before oxidation with H_2O_2 (with a fresh urine sample), then acetone and acetoacetic acid ketone bodies are present. If Rothera's test gives a positive result after oxidation with H_2O_2, then β-hydroxybutyrate is present in urine.

Hence, the correct option is (D).

14. The urea cycle converts excess ammonia into urea in the mitochondria of liver cells. The urea forms then enter the bloodstream, is filtered by the kidneys, and is ultimately excreted in the urine. The urea cycle consists of 4 reactions. The first reaction occurs in the matrix of the mitochondria.

Hence, the correct option is (A).

15. The expression vector and recombinant protein synthesis-

- Expression vectors are plasmids/viruses designed to regulate protein expression in a target cell.
- They are used to insert a specific gene into the target cell to produce the desired protein.
- They contain regulatory sequences that act as enhancer and promoter regions to bring about efficient transcription of the gene.
- An inducible promoter regulates gene expression and can increase the yield of the recombinant protein.

Hence, the correct option is (B).

16.

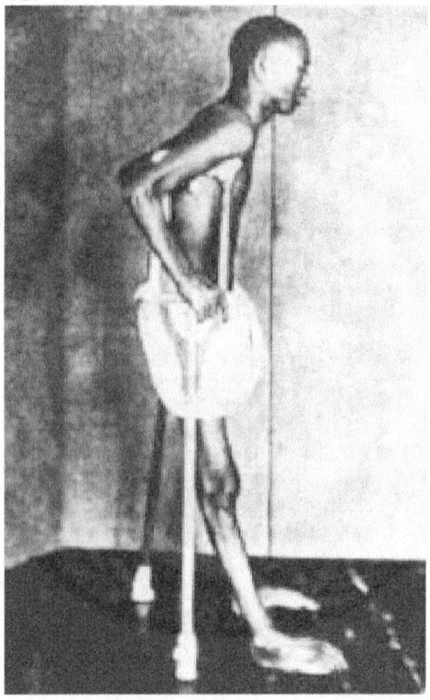

Thiamine–properties, functions, and deficiency disorder-

1. Thiamine (vitamin B1) is a water-soluble vitamin.
2. Thiamine pyrophosphate acts as a coenzyme in the catabolism of carbohydrates and amino acids.
3. It is also required for the biosynthesis of acetylcholine and gamma-aminobutyric acid (GABA).
4. Cereals are the important dietary sources of thiamine.

5. It is present in yeast extract and pork in very high concentrations.
6. It is important for energy production as it is a coenzyme for pyruvate dehydrogenase and alpha-ketoglutarate dehydrogenase in the citric acid cycle (Krebs cycle/Tricarboxylic acid cycle).
7. It is also a coenzyme for transketolase in the pentose phosphate pathway (involved in the production of NADPH).
8. Deficiency of thiamine leads to Beriberi.
9. Alcoholics are prone to develop Wernicke's encephalopathy due to a deficiency of thiamine.
10. The major forms of beriberi are:

- Wet beriberi (cardiovascular disease)
- Dry beriberi (neurological disease)
- Infantile beriberi

Hence, the correct option is (C).

17. Myoglobin is composed of one hundred fifty-three amino acid residues, the majority of which are present in alpha-helices. Myoglobin is a single-chain globular protein with the heme prosthetic group in the center. The Iron located at the center of the heme group interacts with six ligands, the four nitrogen atoms of the porphyrin ring, an imidazole side chain of amino acid residue His-64, and an oxygen molecule. Myoglobin is a cytoplasmic hemoprotein, expressed in cardiac myocytes and oxidative skeletal muscle fibers, which are reversibly bound to an oxygen molecule. Myoglobin mainly functions as an oxygen-storage protein in muscle.

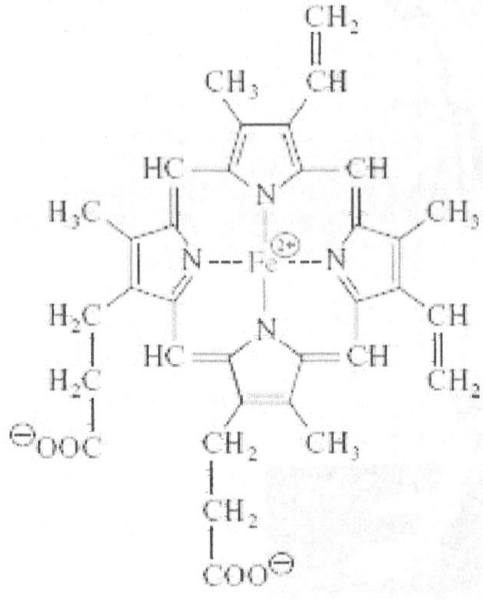

Hence, the correct option is (A).

18. Vital capacity decreases with age.

Vital capacity should be retested by the same method used as when the halo device was in place and also with additional instrumentation that could not previously be used for evaluation. Lung volumes depend on body size, especially height. Total lung capacity (TLC) corrected for age remains unchanged throughout life. Functional residual capacity and residual volume increase with age, resulting in a lower vital capacity.

Hence, the correct option is (A).

19. Pulmonary capillaries also produce substances that break down blood clots. Pulmonary endothelium is a rich source of fibrinolysin activator, which converts plasminogen present in plasma to fibrinolysin, which subsequently breaks down fibrin-to-fibrin degradation products. The lung thus has an efficient fibrinolytic system, which lyses clots in the pulmonary circulation. In addition, the lung is the richest source of heparin (which inhibits coagulation) and thromboplastin (which by converting prothrombin to thrombin, promotes coagulation). So, the lung may play a role in the overall coagulability of blood to promote or delay coagulation and fibrinolysis. Gas bubbles and cancer cells are also filtered in the pulmonary circulation.

Hence, the correct option is (C).

20. Maximum resistance of airway is due to the trachea, but regulation of airway resistance by terminal bronchioles. Expiration in quiet breathing is passive and requires no muscle activity. Compliance of lungs is a measure of stretchability of lungs and hence its total capacity.

Hence, the correct option is (D).

21. Dynamic airway compression occurs when the pressure surrounding the airway exceeds the pressure within the airway lumen. Dynamic compression occurs during inhalation in the external nares, pharynx, and larynx because the pressure within the airways is subatmospheric and the airways are surrounded by atmospheric pressure.

Hence, the correct option is (A).

22. Carbon dioxide can be transported through the blood via three methods. It is dissolved directly in the blood, bound to plasma proteins or hemoglobin, or converted into bicarbonate. The majority of carbon dioxide is transported as part of the bicarbonate system. Carbon dioxide diffuses into red blood cells.

Hence, the correct option is (A).

23. Cerebrospinal fluid (CSF) assists the brain by providing protection, nourishment, and waste removal. CSF provides hydromechanical protection of the neuraxis through two mechanisms. First, CSF acts as a shock absorber, cushioning the brain against the skull. Second, CSF allows the brain and spinal cord to become buoyant, reducing the effective weight of the brain from its normal 1,500 grams to a much lesser 50 grams. The reduction in weight lessens the force applied to the brain parenchyma and cerebral vessels during mechanical injury. Another function of CSF is to maintain homeostasis of the interstitial fluid of the brain. A stable environment for brain parenchyma is imperative for maintaining normal neuronal function.

Hence, the correct option is (D).

24. The thin tissue in jellyfish makes it easier for oxygen to diffuse into their cells. Their bodies consist of an outer layer of tissue, called the epidermis, and an inner layer of tissue called the gastrodermis, which lines their blind guts. The two layers of tissue sandwich an elastic, jellylike substance, called the mesoglea. The mesoglea consists of nonliving material secreted by the living tissues and requires no oxygen itself. This means jellyfish tissue requires very little in the way of diffusion.

Hence, the correct option is (C).

25. The villi and microvilli, with their many folds with finger-like projection, present on the lining of the small intestine, increase the surface area of the intestine for more absorption of the nutrients. The microvilli have protein channels and pumps in their membranes to allow the rapid absorption of food by facilitated diffusion and active transport. Also, the villi contain an epithelial layer, which is only one cell layer thick so that food can pass through easily and be absorbed quickly. This thin layer of cells contains mitochondria to provide the ATP needed for the active transport of certain food molecules. Finally, there is a lacteal branch at the center of the villus, which carries away fats after absorption.

Hence, the correct option is (C).

26. Night blindness, a condition in which a person cannot see in dim light, is generally the earliest clinical manifestation of vitamin A deficiency and is both a sensitive and a specific indicator for low serum retinol levels. Within the eye, vitamin A, in the form of retinal, combines with opsin to produce rhodopsin, the photosensitive visual pigment of rods. Vitamin A deficiency leads to a decline in rhodopsin levels and impaired rod function, manifested as night blindness. In mild cases, night blindness is often only first noticeable following photopic stress from sudden exposure to bright light and results in an increased turnover of rhodopsin.

Hence, the correct option is (D).

27. Four major types of secretory epithelial cells cover the surface of the stomach and extend down into gastric pits and glands: Mucous cells: secrete an alkaline mucus that protects the epithelium against shear stress and acid. Parietal cells: secrete hydrochloric acid. Chief cells: secrete pepsin, a proteolytic enzyme.

Hence, the correct option is (A).

28. To increase or decrease the size (volume) of the chest wall from this resting position requires an alteration of the external or internal pressures acting on it. The contraction of inspiratory muscles expands the chest wall from its resting state and increased its transmural pressure.

Hence, the correct option is (A).

29. The Elbow joint is an example of the hinge joint. The elbow is a hinge joint; it can open and close like a door. The hinge joint allows angular movement in one plane only, increasing or decreasing the angle between the bones e.g. elbow joint, knee joint, etc.

Hence, the correct option is (A).

30. A child may have a diet containing sufficient carbohydrates and fats but still suffers a serious form of malnutrition, This form of malnutrition is known as kwashiorkor. It develops in children whose diets are deficient in protein.

Hence, the correct option is (B).

31. Melatonin is secreted by the pineal gland present between the cerebral hemispheres. Melatonin concentration in blood follows a diurnal cycle, it rises in the evening and drops at noon. Melatonin lightens skin color in certain animals and regulates the working of gonads.

Hence, the correct option is (D).

32. Our internal body temperature is regulated by a part of our brain called the hypothalamus. The hypothalamus checks our current temperature and compares it with the normal temperature of about 37°C. If our temperature is too low, the hypothalamus makes sure that the body generates and maintains heat.

Hence, the correct option is (C).

33. The junction between an axon and dendrite is known as synapses through which nerve impulse is transmitted from one neuron to another. A synapse consists of swelling at the end of nerve fiber called synaptic knob and small synaptic vesicle containing neuro-transmitter-acetylcholine for the transmission of a nerve impulse.

Hence, the correct option is (B).

34. The anterior division of the mandibular nerve supplies lateral pterygoid, masseter, and temporalis. The medial pterygoid is supplied by the nerve to the medial pterygoid which arises from the main trunk of the mandibular nerve.

Hence, the correct option is (B).

35. Axillary artery extends from the outer border of the first rib to the lower border of teres major. Pectoralis minor crosses the axillary artery and divides it into 3 parts. The first part – superior to the muscle. Second part – posterior to the muscle. Third part – inferior to the muscle.

Hence, the correct option is (C).

36. Median eminence is seen on the floor of the fourth ventricle. The roof of the fourth ventricle is formed by Superior medullary velum Inferior medullary velum Superior cerebellar peduncle Tela choroidea of the fourth ventricle Taeniae with the obex.

Hence, the correct option is (D).

37. The mandibular nerve immediately passes between tensor veli palatini, which is medial, and lateral pterygoid, which is lateral, and gives off a meningeal branch (nervus spinosus) and the nerve to medial pterygoid from its medial side. The nerve then divides into a small anterior and large posterior trunk.

Hence, the correct option is (A).

38. The deep perineal pouch is located between the superior and inferior layers of the urogenital diaphragm. The long perineal nerve is located in the superficial perineal pouch. Contents of the deep perineal pouch in males: Muscles – Sphincter urethrae, Deep transverse perineal. Nerves – Dorsal nerve of penis, muscular branch from the perineal nerve. Vessels – deep and dorsal arteries of the penis, the stem of origin of the artery to the bulb of penis, urethral artery.

Hence, the correct option is (C).

39. The posterior surface of the left suprarenal is related to the kidney laterally and left crus of the diaphragm medially. The posterior surface of the right suprarenal is related to the right crus of the diaphragm. The anterior surface of the right suprarenal is related to the inferior vena cavamedially. The lateral border of the left suprarenal is related to the stomach. The medial border of the left suprarenal is related to the left gastric artery. The lateral border of the right suprarenal is related to the liver. The medial border of the right suprarenal is related to the right coeliac ganglion.

Hence, the correct option is (A).

40. Flexor carpi ulnaris is primarily inserted into the pisiform bone. But the muscle action is transmitted through ligaments into the hamate bone (via pisohamate ligament) and the 5th metacarpal bone (via pisometacarpal ligament). Hence, pisiform is considered as a sesamoid bone located in the tendon of flexor carpi ulnaris.

Hence, the correct option is (D).

41. The largest bursa in the body is the subacromial bursa. It is located beneath the coracoacromial arch and the deltoid muscle. The Supraspinatus tendon and the greater tubercle of the humerus are situated underneath the bursa.

Hence, the correct option is (A).

42. The hypogastric sheath is a condensation of the pelvic fascia which transmits vessels and nerves along the lateral pelvic wall towards the pelvic viscera. The broad ligament of the uterus is not a part of the hypogastric sheath. It is a peritoneal fold. Parts of the hypogastric sheath: (1) Anterior lamina – Lateral ligament of the bladder. (2) Middle lamina – Transverse cervical ligament, rectovesical septum in males. (3) Posterior lamina – Presacral fascia, uterosacral ligament.

Hence, the correct option is (B).

43. Muscles involved in pronation of the forearm are: Pronator quadratus Pronator teres The chief pronator is the pronator quadratus. It is assisted by the pronator teres to facilitate rapid movement and when the action is against resistance. Gravity also assists in pronation.

Hence, the correct option is (A).

44. Oblique head of adductor pollicis originates from capitate and the bases of 2nd and 3rd metacarpals. The transverse head originates from the palmar aspect of the third metacarpal. It is inserted into the medial side of the base of the proximal phalanx of the thumb.

Hence, the correct option is (C).

45. The anterior choroidal artery (AChA) is a branch of the intracranial internal carotid, arising distal to the ophthalmic artery but below the circle of Willis. Its size compares with that of cerebral surface artery branches, but its location makes it an uncommon site of occlusion that causes a stroke.

Hence, the correct option is (C).

46. Pneumatic bones are those which enclose an air-filled cavity They are seen in relation to the nasal cavity (paranasal sinuses) and the middle ear The pneumatic bones are Frontal Sphenoid Ethmoid Maxilla Temporal (mastoid air cells).

Hence, the correct option is (D).

47. The anterior division of the mandibular division of the trigeminal nerve has four branches, which are all motor branches except one. The four branches are deep temporal nerves. lateral pterygoid nerves.

Hence, the correct option is (A).

48. In males, the urethral crest is known as the crista urethralis masculine, or the crista phallic, and is a longitudinal fold on the posterior wall of the urethra extending from the uvula of the bladder through the prostatic urethra.

Hence, the correct option is (C).

49. The growth plate is a primary cartilaginous joint. They are also known as synchondrosis / hyaline cartilage joints. The bones are joined by a plate of hyaline cartilage. It does not permit any movement. Other examples: Costochondral joint, I chondro sternal joint, Spheno-occipital joint.

Hence, the correct option is (A).

50. Vascular smooth muscle cells are thought to arise from the splanchnic layer of the paraxial mesoderm. But recent studies have shown that the aortic smooth muscle cells arise from the lateral plate mesoderm.

Hence, the correct option is (B).

51. Rose-Waaler test is a passive haemagglutination test. It is done in rheumatoid arthritis. Autoantibody (RA factor) in the serum acts as an antibody to gamma globulin. RA factor can agglutinate red cells coated with globulins.

Hence, the correct option is (D).

52. Some examples of intermediate disinfectants include water-based phenolics, alcohol-based phenolics, iodophors, sodium hypochlorites, and other chlorine compounds, and alcohol-based quaternary ammonium compounds.

Hence, the correct option is (D).

53. Fildes' agar is made by adding a peptic digest of blood to nutrient agar. It gives copious growth of H. influenzae and it is the best culture medium for the primary isolation of H.

Hence, the correct option is (B).

54. Borrelia recurrentis is a species of Borrelia, a spirochaete bacterium associated with relapsing fever. B. recurrentis is usually transmitted from person to person by the human body louse.

Hence, the correct option is (D).

55. Noroviruses, a group of viruses responsible for over 50 percent of global gastroenteritis cases, can spread by air up to several meters from an infected person according to a new study.

Hence, the correct option is (C).

56. Clostridium tetani is a common soil bacterium and the causative agent of tetanus.

Image result for Fildes technique is used for the culture of?

After incubating anaerobically for 24 hours, if the water of condensation at the bottom of a slope of nutrient agar is inoculated with mixed cell culture, subcultures from the top of the tube will yield a pure growth of tetanus bacillus. This is called the Fildes technique.

Hence, the correct option is (B).

57. Aflatoxins are a family of toxins produced by certain fungi that are found on agricultural crops such as maize (corn), peanuts, cottonseed, and tree nuts. The main fungi that produce aflatoxins are Aspergillus flavus and Aspergillus parasiticus, which are abundant in warm and humid regions of the world.

Hence, the correct option is (A).

58. Mycobacterium marinum (M. marinum) is a slow-growing atypical mycobacterium that is commonly found in bodies of fresh or saltwater in many parts of the world. Skin infections with

Mycobacterium marinum in humans are relatively uncommon and are usually acquired from contact with contents of aquariums or fish.

Hence, the correct option is (D).

59. Enrichment medium is a liquid medium that selectively favors the growth of certain pathogenic bacteria and inhibits commensal bacteria. Loeffler's serum slope is an enriched medium. Deoxycholate citrate agar is a selective medium.

Hence, the correct option is (C).

60. Polysaccharide capsule is an important virulence factor in many organisms like:

- Haemophilus influenzae
- Neisseria meningitidis
- Streptococcus pneumonia
- Klebsiella pneumonia
- Salmonella typhi
- Antibodies against the capsule protect against infection
- The capsule can be used for producing conjugate polysaccharide vaccines (for H. influenzae, N. meningitides, and S. pneumoniae)
- Patients with B cell dysfunction, asplenia (as in sickle cell disease / after splenectomy), and complement defects are highly susceptible to infection with encapsulated organisms

Hence, the correct option is (D).

61. Erythema migrans represents the skin lesion associated with Lyme disease, a tick-borne illness caused by the spirochete Borrelia burgdorferi.

Hence, the correct option is (B).

62. After a primary infection of chickenpox (varicella) (usually in childhood), VZV establishes a latent infection in the trigeminal and dorsal root ganglia.

Hence, the correct option is (D).

63. Causes localized infections that do not spread along tissue planes is a false statement about streptococcus:

Hence, the correct option is (C).

64. The clinical features and microbiological characteristics are suggestive of pneumococcal pneumonia. The diagnosis can be confirmed by Bile solubility and Optochin sensitivity.

Hence, the correct option is (D).

65. Ehrlich-Türk line - the seldom-used term for the thin vertical deposition of material on the posterior surface of the cornea seen in Corynebacterium.

Hence, the correct option is (D).

66. Diphtheria is a serious infection caused by strains of bacteria called Corynebacterium diphtheriae that make toxins (poison).

Metachromatic granules are the cell inclusions mostly found in the prokaryotic cell. It appears red when stained with blue dyes in certain bacteria, yeasts, yeast-like fungi, and protozoa.

Hence, the correct option is (A).

67. Albert's staining technique is a type of special staining technique since it is used to demonstrate a special structure in bacteria. It is chiefly used to demonstrate metachromatic granules found in Corynebacterium diphtheriae.

Hence, the correct option is (B).

68. The incubation period for diphtheria is 2 - 6 days, with a range of 1 - 10 days. The disease can involve almost any mucous membrane.

Hence, the correct option is (A).

69. Brazilian purpuric fever is caused by Haemophilus aegyptius. It is characterized by conjunctivitis which proceeds to fulminant septicemia in infants and children. There is a high fatality. It was first recognized in Brazil in 1984.

Hence, the correct option is (C).

70. The TB skin test is performed by injecting a small amount of fluid (called tuberculin test) into the skin on the lower part of the arm.

Hence, the correct option is (D).

71. Ciprofloxacin has poor activity against Mycobacterium leprae. Ofloxacin, Pefloxacin, Moxifloxacin, and Sparfloxacin have a high level of activity against Mycobacterium leprae. Among them, Moxifloxacin is the most potent.

Hence, the correct option is (C).

72. Unfortunately, some patients are still being prescribed contraindicated antiretroviral regimens that include: 1. stavudine plus zidovudine.

Hence, the correct option is (A).

73. Basiliximab (trade name Simulect) is a chimeric mouse-human monoclonal antibody to the α chain (CD25) of the IL-2 receptor of T cells. It is used to prevent rejection in organ transplantation, especially in kidney transplants.

Hence, the correct option is (B).

74. Zaleplon is the shortest acting non-benzodiazepine hypnotic. It has a selective action on benzodiazepine receptors containing alpha 1 subunit.

Hence, the correct option is (A).

75.

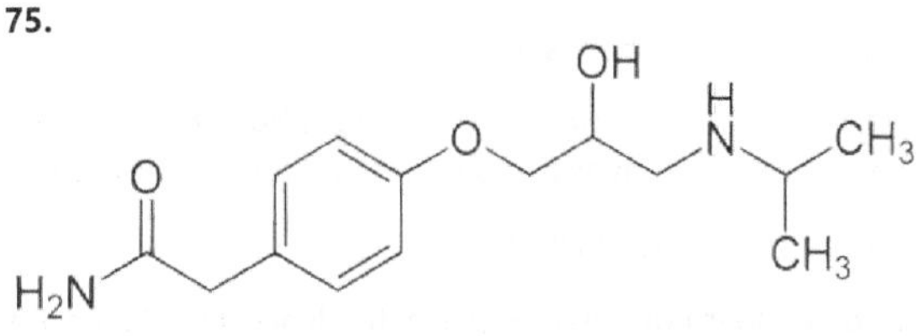

Structure of atenolol

- Atenolol is a selective beta 1 blocker.
- The lipid solubility is low.
- Oral absorption is incomplete.
- First pass metabolism is not significant.

- All other drugs mentioned have significant first-pass metabolism.

Hence, the correct option is (C).

76. Diethylstilbestrol can cause vaginal clear cell adenocarcinoma in girls and young women exposed to it in utero. Phenytoin can cause fetal hydantoin syndrome which is characterized by hypoplasia of the phalanges, cleft lip, cleft palate, and microcephaly. Indomethacin/aspirin can cause premature closure of the ductus arteriosus.

Hence, the correct option is (A).

77. Certain medicines, such as tetracycline, should not be taken by the mother while she is pregnant. These can cause discoloration to the developing teeth of the embryo.

Hence, the correct option is (B).

78. Amylin analogs are used in the treatment of diabetes. They are stable synthetic compounds, which are administered subcutaneously before meals, and work similarly to the physiological amylin.

Pramlintide is only used to treat patients whose blood sugar could not be controlled by insulin or insulin and an oral medication for diabetes.

Hence, the correct option is (D).

79. Valproate is a teratogenic drug that causes spina bifida and other neural tube defects in the fetus when taken by pregnant women. It can also cause heart and limb abnormalities.

Hence, the correct option is (C).

80. Although many factors can cause phocomelia, the prominent roots come from the use of the drug thalidomide and from genetic inheritance.

Hence, the correct option is (B).

81. Oswald Schmiedeberg (1838–1921) is generally recognized as the founder of pharmacology. The son of a Latvian forester, Schmiedeberg obtained his medical doctorate in 1866 with a thesis on the measurement of chloroform in blood.

Hence, the correct option is (A).

82. The right answer is Liposomal delivery systems.

Amphotericin B is an antifungal medication used for serious fungal infections and leishmaniasis.

Hence, the correct option is (B).

83. Ethosuximide is a drug of choice in the absence of seizures and may be effective for myoclonic seizures and tonic or atonic seizures.

Hence, the correct option is (B).

84. Heparin does not cross the placenta. Hence it's safe for use in pregnant patients who need anticoagulation.

Hence, the correct option is (D).

85. Antibiotics to use during pregnancy. Most research has suggested that azithromycin is a safe and effective treatment.

Hence, the correct option is (C).

86. Simeprevir is indicated as a component of combination antiviral treatment for patients with chronic hepatitis C genotype 1 infection.

Hence, the correct option is (D).

87. The right answer is Gastrointestinal stromal tumors.

Tyrosine kinase inhibitors (TKIs) are a type of targeted therapy. TKIs come as pills, taken orally. Targeted therapy identifies and attacks specific types of cancer cells while causing less damage to normal cells.

Hence, the correct option is (C).

88. Hyperglycemia and impaired glucose levels are often seen in patients suffering from diabetes or metabolic syndrome. Atypical antipsychotics can increase the risk of hyperglycemia and impaired glucose levels and subsequently increase the risk of metabolic syndrome.

Hence, the correct option is (C).

89. Tianeptine is an antidepressant agent with a novel neurochemical profile. It increases serotonin (5-hydroxytryptamine; 5-HT) uptake in the brain (in contrast with most antidepressant agents) and reduces stress-induced atrophy of neuronal dendrites.

Hence, the correct option is (B).

90. Dopamine serves as the major prolactin-inhibiting factor or brake on prolactin secretion. Dopamine is secreted into portal blood by hypothalamic neurons, binds to receptors on lactotrophs, and inhibits both the synthesis and secretion of prolactin.

Hence, the correct option is (A).

91. During apoptosis, cytochrome c is released from mitochondria through the actions of the proteins Bax and Bak.

Hence, the correct option is (C).

92. IgM antibodies are produced first and disappear after a few weeks. The first antibodies to be produced in a humoral immune response are always IgM because IgM can be expressed without isotype switching. These early IgM antibodies are produced before B cells have undergone somatic hypermutation and therefore tend to be of low affinity.

Hence, the correct option is (B).

93. Psammoma bodies, which are concentric lamellated calcified structures, are observed most commonly in papillary thyroid carcinoma, Follicular carcinoma (also called Follicular thyroid cancer) is called a "well-differentiated" thyroid cancer like papillary thyroid cancer, but it is typically a bit more malignant (aggressive) than papillary cancer.

Hence, the correct option is (A).

94. The formation of C3 convertases is the point at which the three pathways of complement activation converge, because both the classical pathway and MB-lectin pathway convertases C4b,2b, and the alternative pathway convertase C3b, Bb have the same activity, and they initiate the same subsequent events.

Hence, the correct option is (C).

95. Glutathione peroxidase is a free radical scavenger that converts H_2O_2 to H_2O and O_2. It does not generate free radicals. Superoxide dismutase converts superoxide (O_2–) to H_2O_2.

Hence, the correct option is (D).

96. There are generally three types of fixation processes depending on the initial specimen: Heat fixation: After a smear has dried at room temperature, the slide is gripped by tongs or a clothespin and passed through the flame of a Bunsen burner several times to heat-kill and adhere the organism to the slide.

Hence, the correct option is (A).

97. A large protein enzyme molecule is composed of one or more amino acid chains called polypeptide chains. The amino acid sequence determines the characteristic folding patterns of the protein's structure, which is essential to enzyme specificity.

Hence, the correct option is (B).

98. Lipochrome is a naturally occurring fat-soluble pigment. Lipofuscin, a product of fat breakdown in lysosomes is a type of lipochrome that is associated with the decomposition of cell membranes.

Hence, the correct option is (B).

99. The right answer is Dysgerminoma.

Elevated alpha-fetoprotein refers to a state where alpha-fetoprotein levels are outside of the reference range.

A dysgerminoma is a type of germ cell tumor; it usually is malignant and usually occurs in the ovary.

Hence, the correct option is (D).

100. Oligodendrocytes are a type of large glial cell found in the central nervous system.

Gliomas are the most common primary brain tumors affecting adults.

Hence, the correct option is (B).

101. Elevated levels of pleural fluid amylase are commonly associated with a diagnosis of pancreatitis, pulmonary malignancy, or esophageal rupture, but have been reported in numerous other diseases.

Hence, the correct option is (B).

102. Osteosarcoma tumors are notoriously radioresistant. Radioresistant cancers, including osteosarcoma, typically exhibit considerable potential for relapse and development of metastases following treatment.

Hence, the correct option is (C).

103. The type of Wilms tumour is an important prognostic factor. Tumours with favourable histology have a better prognosis than those with anaplastic (unfavourable) histology.

Hence, the correct option is (C).

104. The right answer is Fibrosarcoma.

Hypoglycemia can oftentimes be the manifestation of a tumor-related paraneoplastic syndrome. Most commonly, the underlying malignancy is an insulinoma or hepatocellular carcinoma.

Hence, the correct option is (C).

105. The Ames test is a widely employed method that uses bacteria to test whether a given chemical can cause mutations in the DNA of the test organism.

Hence, the correct option is (B).

106. Grading is a way of classifying cancer cells. The pathologist gives cancer a grade based on how different they look from normal cells (differentiation), how quickly they are growing and dividing, and how likely they are to spread. Some tumors are described as low grade or high grade.

Hence, the correct option is (D).

107. They also established acid phosphatase as a tumor marker for prostate cancer. From the 1950s through the 1980s, acid phosphatase was widely used to detect, stage, and monitor prostate cancer treatment response, with some success.

Hence, the correct option is (B).

108. Aerobic glycolysis only produces 2 ATP molecules per glucose molecule, which means cancer cells need to uptake more glucose molecules from the microenvironment to meet energy requirements and secrets more lactic acids to the microenvironment for the maintenance of cellular environment homeostasis.

Hence, the correct option is (D).

109. In some cases, a CA 125 test may be used to look for early signs of ovarian cancer in people with a very high risk of the disease.

Hence, the correct option is (A).

110. Calcitonin is a type of tumor marker. Tumor markers are substances made by cancer cells or by normal cells in response to cancer in the body. If too much calcitonin is found in the blood, it may be a sign of a type of thyroid cancer called medullary thyroid cancer (MTC).

Hence, the correct option is (B).

111. Molecular profiling—or "tumor genomic profiling"—is a form of testing that classifies tumors based on this genetic make-up to help diagnose and treat cancer. Using a blood test or biopsy, this testing examines the DNA of cancer cells, looking for genetic mutations that have been acquired by these cells.

Hence, the correct option is (C).

112. The right answer is Anti-Hu.

Not all patients presenting with paraneoplastic cerebellar degeneration and its clinical features have recognizable antineuronal antibodies.

Hence, the correct option is (B).

113. In type III hypersensitivity reaction, an abnormal immune response is mediated by the formation of antigen-antibody aggregates called "immune complexes." They can precipitate in various tissues such as skin, joints, vessels, or glomeruli, and trigger the classical complement pathway.

Hence, the correct option is (B).

114. The commonest cause of death in a patient with primary amyloidosis is Cardiac involvement.

Hence, the correct option is (B).

115. In DNA, the phosphodiester bond is the linkage between the 3' carbon atom of one sugar molecule and the 5' carbon atom of another; importantly these asymmetric bonds mean that each DNA strand has a "direction." Notably, the phosphate groups in the phosphodiester bond are negatively charged at physiological pH.

Hence, the correct option is (B).

116. The Medico-Legal Application of the Serological or Precipitin (Blood) Test. In 1897, Rudolf Kraus introduced the fluid precipitin test. He took bacterial filtrates, which he injected into rabbits. From there, investigators use the precipitin test to determine whether the blood is of animal or human origin.

Hence, the correct option is (C).

117. Contrecoup occurs when a force or blow causes the brain to strike the side of the skull opposite from the point of impact. These injuries often occur in motor vehicle rollover accidents and motorcycle crashes. If not identified, they pose long-term risks for victims.

Hence, the correct option is (A).

118. The ball and shotgun, often also known by the marketing name paradox gun, is a shotgun capable of firing both shot and solid projectiles.

Hence, the correct option is (B).

119.

- The combination of alopecia & skin rash, painful peripheral neuropathy, and confusion with lethargy are known as the 'Thallium triad'.
- It is indicative of chronic thallium poisoning.
- Other symptoms include dystrophy of nails (Mees' lines; also seen in arsenic poisoning), cardiovascular symptoms like hypertension and cardiomyopathy, ophthalmological symptoms like ptosis, ophthalmoplegia, nystagmus, keratitis, lens opacity, and optic atrophy.

Hence, the correct option is (D).

120. MDMA (3,4-methylenedioxy-N-methylamphetamine), widely known as 'Ecstasy' is a psychoactive drug with stimulant and hallucinogenic effects. It produces euphoria. It is consumed by individuals attending clubs and parties.

Hence, the correct option is (C).

121. Yellow phosphorous (white phosphorous) is a waxy & translucent material that becomes luminous in the dark. Cobra venom is a transparent yellow viscous liquid.

Hence, the correct option is (A).

122. Usually, gunpowder residue can be easily seen on clothes.

But in blood-stained/dark colored clothes, it may not be visible to the naked eye or when using a magnifying glass.

In these cases, infrared photography helps in visualizing gunpowder residue/soot.

Hence, the correct option is (B).

123. Drugs used for narcoanalysis are Scopolamine (hyoscine) Sodium thiopental (Sodium Pentothal) Amobarbital (Amytal Sodium).

Hence, the correct option is (D).

124. Typical symptoms of datura poisoning are represented by dry skin and mucosa, flushing, mydriasis, sinus tachycardia, hyperpyrexia, decreased bowel activity, urinary retention, and neurological disorders with ataxia, impaired short-term memory, disorientation, confusion, hallucinations (visual and auditory), psychosis.

Hence, the correct option is (D).

125. Benzidine test, phenolphthalein test, orthotolidine test, and Leucomalachite green test utilize the hydrogen peroxide to detect the presence of blood. Hemoglobin present in the blood is a peroxidase. It oxidizes colorless bases to colored salts in the presence of hydrogen peroxide.

Teichmann's test (haemin crystal test) is done by converting hemoglobin to haemin crystals which are converted to salt in the presence of halogen and form rhombic crystals.

Hence, the correct option is (D).

126. Interests in the relationships between health and social factors began in the 18th century, but the term 'social medicine' was first used in 1848 by a French doctor, Jules Guérin in the year of the February Revolution in France. In the same year, Rudolf Virchow and his colleagues initiated social medicine in Germany.

Hence, the correct option is (A).

127. Vital statistics are accumulated data gathered on live births, deaths, migration, fetal deaths, marriages, and divorces.

Sentinel surveillance is the "monitoring of the rate of occurrence of specific diseases/conditions through a voluntary network of doctors, laboratories and public health departments with a view to assessing the stability or change in health levels of a population".

Hence, the correct option is (C).

128. Diphtheria Antitoxin is prepared by hyperimmunizing horses with diphtheria toxin, blood plasma obtained from the hyperimmunised horses which are rich in antibodies to diphtheria toxin is enzyme refined, purified, and concentrated. The antitoxin has the specific power of neutralizing the toxin secreted by Corynebacterium diphtherea the causative organism of diphtherea. Thus, the dose of diphtheria antitoxin is 10000 to 100000 IU.

Hence, the correct option is (B).

129. The right answer is Disability limitation.

There are 3 levels of disease prevention: Primary Prevention - trying to prevent yourself from getting a disease. Secondary Prevention - trying to detect a disease early and prevent it from getting worse. Tertiary Prevention - trying to improve your quality of life and reduce the symptoms of a disease you already have.

Hence, the correct option is (D).

130. Several effective vaccines are available for the prevention of childhood pneumonia, including two vaccines provided in immunization programs in all countries, Bordetella pertussis and measles vaccines, and two relatively new vaccines, Hib conjugate vaccine (HibCV) and pneumococcal conjugate vaccines (PCVs).

Hence, the correct option is (A).

131. Household monthly income per person is calculated by taking the total gross household monthly income divided by the total number of family members living together.

Hence, the correct option is (C).

132. A prevalence rate is the total number of cases of a disease existing in a population divided by the total population.

Hence, the correct option is (B).

133. It is defined as "all the measures available to reduce or limit impairments and disabilities, and to promote the patients' adjustment to irremediable conditions". Intervention that should be accomplished in the stage of tertiary prevention is disability limitation and rehabilitation.

Hence, the correct option is (D).

134. Cholera is an infectious disease that became a major threat to health during the 1800s.

Hence, the correct option is (D).

135. The right answer is the Longest incubation period.

Quarantine is the separation and restriction of movement or activities of persons who are not ill but who are believed to have been exposed to infection, for the purpose of preventing transmission of diseases. Persons are usually quarantined in their homes, but they may also be quarantined in community-based facilities.

Hence, the correct option is (D).

136. Chlorination can be achieved by using liquefied chlorine gas, sodium hypochlorite solution, or calcium hypochlorite granules and on-site chlorine generators (e.g. WATA). Chlorine is widely applied for the centralized disinfection of drinking water in municipal water supply systems.

Hence, the correct option is (D).

137. The predictive value refers to the likelihood for determining an outbreak or non-outbreak of an infectious disease based on early warning results.

Hence, the correct option is (C).

138. Screening, in medicine, is a strategy used to look for as-yet-unrecognized conditions or risk markers.

The placenta is an organ that develops in your uterus during pregnancy. This structure provides oxygen and nutrients to your growing baby and removes waste products from your baby's blood.

Hence, the correct option is (D).

139. The active ingredient in many Lysol products is benzalkonium chloride, but the active ingredient in the Lysol "Power and Free" line is hydrogen peroxide. Lysol has been used since its invention in the late 19th century as a household and industrial cleaning agent, and previously as a medical disinfectant.

Hence, the correct option is (B).

140. A randomized clinical trial is an experiment. In an RCT, subjects are randomly assigned to one of two or more therapies and then treated in an identical manner for all other potential variables.

Hence, the correct option is (C).

141. Exotic diseases are those which are imported into a country in which they do not otherwise occur, as for example, rabies in the UK.

Hence, the correct option is (A).

142. The right answer is a Case-control study.

The odds of an event happening is defined as the likelihood that an event will occur, expressed as a proportion of the likelihood that the event will not occur. Therefore, if A is the probability of subjects affected and B is the probability of subjects not affected, then odds = A/B.

Hence, the correct option is (A).

143. The right answer is Are easy to conduct.

In a longitudinal study, researchers repeatedly examine the same individuals to detect any changes that might occur over a period of time.

Hence, the correct option is (A).

144. Live attenuated vaccines are produced by modifying a disease-producing ("wild") virus or bacterium in a laboratory. The resulting vaccine organism retains the ability to replicate (grow) and produces immunity, but usually does not cause illness.

Hence, the correct option is (A).

145. Vertical transmission: Passage of a disease-causing agent (pathogen) from mother to baby during the period immediately before and after birth. Transmission might occur across the placenta, in the breast milk, or through direct contact during or after birth. For example, HIV can be a vertically transmitted pathogen.

Hence, the correct option is (D).

146. A morbidity indicator is a value describing the presence of disease in the population, or the degree of risk of an event. The incidence rate, prevalence, and attack rate (AR) are common applications of this concept in epidemiology.

Hence, the correct option is (B).

147. The BCG vaccine was introduced into the UK schedule in 1953. At first, it was offered to children of school leaving age (14 years old) because TB was most common in young adults at this time. Rates of TB in the UK were already falling, and they continued to fall after the vaccine was introduced.

Hence, the correct option is (A).

148. A positive infection status in ticks could occur by the horizontal transmission of rickettsiae from an infected animal host to the tick. The alternative explanation is that the larvae found on the small mammals may be infected with the Rickettsia spp. by transovarial transmission.

Hence, the correct option is (B).

149. Live virus vaccines use the weakened (attenuated) form of the virus. The measles, mumps, and rubella (MMR) vaccine and varicella (chickenpox) vaccine are examples. Killed (inactivated) vaccines are made from a protein or other small pieces taken from a virus or bacteria.

Hence, the correct option is (C).

150. Descriptive epidemiology uses observational studies of the distribution of disease in terms of person, place, and time. The study describes the distribution of a set of variables, without regard to causal or other hypotheses. Personal factors include age, gender, SES, educational level, ethnicity, and occupation.

Hence, the correct option is (D).

151. Maintenance of airway, breathing, and circulation is the first priority. The patient should be intubated in case of airway block. If the breathing is compromised, the patient should be ventilated with a high fraction of inspired oxygen. Large-bore IV cannulas should be inserted and IV fluids should be administered. In case of external bleeding, direct pressure should be applied to control it. Spinal immobilization should be done in cases of suspected spinal cord injury.

Hence, the correct option is (A).

152. Ripstein's operation is the abdominal approach for rectal prolapse. The abdominal approach is recommended in patients with complete rectal prolapse who are otherwise in good health. In Ripstein's operation, the rectosigmoid junction is hitched up to the front of the sacrum using a Teflon sling.

Hence, the correct option is (D).

153. Hereditary pancreatitis is an autosomal dominant disorder. It has 80% penetrance. It is associated with mutations in the cationic trypsinogen gene located on chromosome 7. IgG4 concentrations are elevated in autoimmune pancreatitis.

Hence, the correct option is (B).

154. Stemmer's sign is seen in lymphoedema. The skin on the dorsum of the toes cannot be pinched due to subcutaneous fibrosis. This is called Stemmer's sign. If the examiner cannot pinch the skin of the dorsum of the foot or hand then this positive finding is associated with lymphedema. The purpose of the study was to determine the accuracy of the Stemmer sign to predict lymphedema.

Hence, the correct option is (C).

155. Glucagonoma is a neuroendocrine tumor of the pancreas. It can present with migratory necrolytic skin rash. Other symptoms include glossitis, stomatitis, and angular cheilitis. Diabetes, severe weight loss, and diarrhea can also occur.

Hence, the correct option is (C).

156. The most common cause of delayed obstruction of the urinary tract after Transurethral Resection of the Prostate (TURP) is bladder neck stenosis. Late complications of TURP include: Urethral stricture (3.8%) Bladder neck stenosis (4%) Stress incontinence (2.2%) Sexual dysfunction: retrograde ejaculation (65-70%) and erectile dysfunction (6%). Penoscrotal stricture, Bulbar stricture, Membranous urethral stricture, and Submeatal strictures are subtypes of urethral strictures. Urethral stricture can be treated by the end to end urethroplasty. Bladder neck stenosis can be corrected by endoscopic incision.

Hence, the correct option is (A).

157. Rhabdomyosarcoma is a soft tissue sarcoma that frequently metastasizes to lymph nodes. In stage IV adult soft tissue sarcoma of the retroperitoneum, the tumor is any size, any grade, and may have spread to nearby lymph nodes. Cancer has spread to other parts of the body, such as the lung.

Hence, the correct option is (C).

158. Sclerotherapy is ideal for the treatment of internal hemorrhoids (first degree with bleeding and early second-degree hemorrhoids). Veins and varicose veins can be eliminated with an effective medical procedure called sclerotherapy. The treatment involves injecting a special solution into the vein. The damaged vein is injected with a sclerosing agent.

Hence, the correct option is (B).

159. Early signs and symptoms include changes in mental status, such as disorientation, restlessness, and mental confusion. purposeless movements. increased respiratory effort.

Hence, the correct option is (C).

160. Lymphangiosarcoma was originally described in Stewart-Treves' syndrome(post-mastectomy lymphedema). It affects about 0.5% of patients. Stewart and Treves reported this in a joint paper in 1948. Milroy's disease is familial lymphoedema type 1. Meig's disease is familial lymphoedema type 2.

Hence, the correct option is (A).

161. Agnes Hunt traction is used for the correction of mild flexion deformity of the hip joint in poliomyelitis. Traction used for trochanteric fracture – Russell's traction Traction used for fracture shaft of femur in adults – Perkin's traction Traction used for low backache – Buck's traction

Hence, the correct option is (A).

162. Teratoma arises from totipotent cells in the rete testis. Histologically it is classified into 4 types: Teratoma differentiated Malignant teratoma intermediate Malignant teratoma anaplastic Malignant teratoma trophoblastic The most common type is malignant teratoma intermediate. It contains malignant and incompletely differentiated components.

Hence, the correct option is (B).

163. The liftoff test, also known as Gerber's test is used to assess the function of the subscapularis muscle. For performing this test, the arm is extended and internally rotated so that the dorsum of the hand rests on the lower back. The patient is asked to lift the hand off the back. This requires internal rotation of the arm brought about by the subscapularis. If the patient is able to perform the maneuver, the subscapularis function is normal and the test is negative.

Hence, the correct option is (B).

164. Schatzki's ring is a circular ring seen in the distal oesophagus. It is usually present at the squamocolumnar junction. It is strongly associated with reflux disease. It may be associated with dysphagia and respond to dilatation along with medical anti-reflux therapy.

Hence, the correct option is (C).

165. Gallow's traction is used in infants and children with femoral fractures. Indications Gallows Traction The child must weigh less than 12 kg Femoral fractures Skin must be intact.

Hence, the correct option is (A).

166. Caroli's disease is congenital dilatation of the intrahepatic biliary tree. This disease is complicated by the presence of intrahepatic stone formation. Patients can present with abdominal pain or sepsis. Biliary stasis with stone formation can lead to biliary sepsis. Malignant change in the ductal system can lead to cholangiocarcinoma.

Hence, the correct option is (C).

167. Heberden's nodes seen in distal interphalangeal joints are a characteristic feature of idiopathic osteoarthritis. The most commonly develop on the joints nearest to the fingertips and can cause the fingers to appear crooked. Heberden's nodes only develop in people who have osteoarthritis, or OA, which is a degenerative bone condition. These growths can cause pain, stiffness, and discomfort.

Hence, the correct option is (D).

168. All tuberculous joints except the spine usually heal with fibrous ankylosis. Whereas in the spinal joints, bony ankylosis is seen.

Hence, the correct option is (B).

169. The ischial tuberosity is also the bony point of the bottom that we sit on. An avulsion fracture of the ischial tuberosity is when a small piece of this bone is pulled away from the rest of the pelvis bone. This injury is most commonly seen in adolescent athletes.

Hence, the correct option is (D).

170. The fat globules released from the bone marrow (due to trauma / orthopedic procedures) are deposited in the pulmonary capillary bed. This causes ischemia and inflammation. The symptoms appear 12-72 hours after the trauma. Initial symptoms are tachycardia and tachypnoea. There may be high spiking fever and non-palpable petechiae, especially over the upper body. Neurological symptoms like agitation, delirium, stupor, and coma can occur. (The fat globules may cross the pulmonary circulation via arteriovenous connections).

Hence, the correct option is (D).

171. Radioisotope bone scan is the preferred method for the detection of bone metastases. It is more sensitive than radiography for the detection of most metastases.Technetium-99m is the commonly used radioisotope. It accumulates in the reactive new bone that is formed in the metastases resulting in a 'hot spot' in the scan. The amount of accumulation depends on the level of blood flow. So a bone scan should be followed by other radiological modalities such as a CT scan to confirm the lesion.

Hence, the correct option is (D).

172. REIMPLANTATION OF AN AMPUTATED DIGIT – PROCEDURE:

- Debride the area and clean the wound
- Fixation of bone
- Repair of extensor tendons
- Repair of flexor tendons
- Arterial repair
- Nerve repair
- Venous repair
- Closure of the skin wound

Hence, the correct option is (D).

173. It is a long, bilateral muscle of the neck, which functions to flex the neck both laterally and anteriorly, as well as rotate the head contralaterally to the side of contraction. An acute or chronic condition of neck stiffness with decreased mobility (especially rotation), sometimes followed by aches and pains in the neck and/or pains in body areas distant from the neck (eyes, temples, throat, ears, nose, shoulders), nausea, tinnitus, vertigo, torticollis.

Hence, the correct option is (C).

174.

- Teratoma arises from totipotent cells in the **rete testis**.
- Histologically it is classified into **4 types**:

1. Teratoma differentiated
2. Malignant teratoma intermediate
3. Malignant teratoma anaplastic
4. Malignant teratoma trophoblastic

- The most common type is **malignant teratoma intermediate**.
- It contains malignant and incompletely differentiated components.

Hence, the correct option is (B).

175. They evaluated the significance of the sonographic markers as both isolated and nonisolated findings and calculated the LRs. The most sensitive sonographic markers for trisomy 21 included the nuchal fold, short femur, and an EIF.

Hence, the correct option is (D).

176. Hilton's law states that the articular nerves supplying a joint are branches of the nerves that supply the muscles responsible for moving that joint. The nerve supply to the knee is derived from: branches of the femoral nerve to vastus medialis, and also intermedius and lateralis. from the sciatic by genicular branches of the tibial and common peroneal nerves.

Hence, the correct option is (A).

177. Technetium (Tc-99m) is an isotope commonly used in a number of medical diagnostic imaging scans. Tc99m is used as a radioactive tracer for nuclear medicine; which is a form of medical imaging that assesses how particular parts of our body are working or functioning.

Hence, the correct option is (D).

178. THRESHOLD RADIATION DOSE FOR ACUTE RADIATION SYNDROMES: Haematologic / hematopoietic syndrome – 1 Gy Gastrointestinal syndrome – 5 Gy Central nervous system syndrome – 20 Gy

Hence, the correct option is (A).

179. Echocardiography remains the most frequently performed cardiac imaging investigation and is an invaluable tool for the detailed and accurate evaluation of cardiac structure and function.

Hence, the correct option is (B).

180. It is named after Walter Putnam Blount. It is also known as Tibia vara, Mau-Nilsonne Syndrome, Blount-Barber syndrome, Erlacher-Blount syndrome, Osteochondrosis deformans tibiae. It is a growth disorder of the tibia resulting in progressive bow leg deformity. It is also associated with internal tibial torsion and genu recurvatum. It is mainly seen in children and adolescents. Treatment is by bracing and/or surgery.

Hence, the correct option is (B).

181. Radiotherapy is to be started within 10 days. Delay in starting radiotherapy for Wilm's tumor can result in an increase in relapse rate. Patients with stage IV favorable histology Wilms tumor and lung metastases whose pulmonary lesions do not disappear after 6 weeks of chemotherapy receive whole-lung radiation therapy.

Hence, the correct option is (A).

182. Because CT scans and fluoroscopy use many x-ray scans per procedure, they cause much more radiation exposure than single x-ray scans do. Each CT scan delivers 1 to 10 mSv, depending on the dose of radiation and the part of your body that's getting the test. A low-dose chest CT scan is about 1.5 mSv. The same test at a regular dose is about 7 mSv. The more CT scans you have, the more radiation exposure you get.

Hence, the correct option is (C).

183. Gaisbock's syndrome is polycythemia due to a reduction in plasma volume. It is usually seen in smokers, obese individuals, and patients with hypertension. Anesthetic implications include cardiovascular problems and the risk of deep vein thrombosis. May require venesection.

Hence, the correct option is (B).

184. Guttmann's sign is stuffiness of the nostril which is a sign of successful stellate ganglion block. The other signs of successful stellate ganglion block include Horner's syndrome, engorged veins of the arm, flushing of the conjunctiva and sclera, increase in skin temperature, and anhydrosis of the face and neck.

Hence, the correct option is (C).

185.

- Neuroendocrine tumours of the stomach are rare tumours which comprise about **5%** of all neuroendocrine tumours of the gastrointestinal tract.
- The most frequent neuroendocrine tumour of the stomach is the **type I** tumour.
- **Type III** tumours are **low grade** malignant differentiated tumours.
- **Serum gastrin** is normal.
- The common symptom is **upper gastrointestinal bleeding.**
- Gastrectomy, lymph node resection and resection of liver metastases is the treatment of choice.

Hence, the correct option is (D).

186. Definitive airways prevent aspiration of gastric content, allows for control of ventilation, and permits the delivery of higher concentrations of oxygen. They include endotracheal tubes (nasotracheal/orotracheal), tracheostomy, and cricothyroidotomy.

Hence, the correct option is (D).

187.

- Everolimus is an immunosuppressive agent used in organ transplantation.
- It acts by blocking IL-2 receptor signal transduction.
- It inhibits an intracellular kinase called the mammalian target of rapamycin (mTOR).
- This in turn interferes with intracellular signaling from the IL-2 receptor and arrests T cell division in the G1 phase.

Hence, the correct option is (B).

188. MANAGEMENT OF A CASE OF ABDOMINAL TRAUMA

- Maintenance of airway, breathing, and circulation is the first priority.
- The patient should be intubated in case of airway block.
- If the breathing is compromised, the patient should be ventilated with a high fraction of inspired oxygen.
- Large-bore IV cannulas should be inserted and IV fluids should be administered.
- In case of external bleeding, direct pressure should be applied to control it.
- Spinal immobilization should be done in cases with suspected spinal cord injury.

Indications for laparotomy in blunt trauma abdomen

- Hemodynamically unstable patients with shock.
- Signs of peritonitis.
- Progressive deterioration of the patient's status.
- Identification of hemoperitoneum after Focused Assessment with Sonography in Trauma (FAST) or Diagnostic Peritoneal Lavage (DPL).

Hence, the correct option is (A).

189. Teratoma arises from totipotent cells in the rete testis. Histologically it is classified into 4 types: Teratoma differentiated Malignant teratoma intermediate Malignant teratoma anaplastic Malignant teratoma trophoblastic The most common type is malignant teratoma intermediate. It contains malignant and incompletely differentiated components.

Hence, the correct option is (B).

190. Schatzki's ring is a circular ring seen in the distal esophagus. It is usually present at the squamocolumnar junction. It is strongly associated with reflux disease. It may be associated with dysphagia and respond to dilatation along with medical anti-reflux therapy.

Hence, the correct option is (C).

191. Neuroendocrine tumours of the stomach are rare tumours that comprise about 5% of all neuroendocrine tumours of the gastrointestinal tract. The most frequent neuroendocrine tumour of the stomach is a type I tumour. Type III tumours are low grade malignant differentiated tumours. Serum gastrin is normal. The common symptom is upper gastrointestinal bleeding. Gastrectomy, lymph node resection and resection of liver metastases is the treatment of choice.

Hence, the correct option is (B).

192. In this condition, azoospermia occurs secondary to a bilateral obstruction in the vas deferens or epididymis, Sperm cells are produced, but not ejaculated, The most common cause of obstructive azoospermia is vasectomy, Other causes include congenital absence of vas deferens and obstruction secondary to an infection, The levels of FSH, LH, and testosterone are normal, Testicular volume is usually normal, Treatment is by surgical removal of the obstruction/extraction of sperm from the testis.

Hence, the correct option is (D).

193. Areas involved in posterior cerebral artery infarct Occipital lobe. Inferno-medial temporal lobe. Postero-inferior parietal lobe. Large parts of the thalamus. Midbrain. Posterior part of choroid plexus.

Hence, the correct option is (C).

194. Total parenteral nutrition should provide both energy and other essential nutrients. Carbohydrates, lipids, and amino acids provide energy. The other essential nutrients to be included are minerals, vitamins, and water. Dietary fiber is required only in the case of enteral nutrition. It is not given as a part of parenteral nutrition.

Hence, the correct option is (D).

195. Dysgerminoma corresponds to the seminoma of the testis. It is usually seen in young women or children. It secretes placental alkaline phosphatase.

Hence, the correct option is (D).

196. Large Loop Excision of the Transformation Zone (LLETZ) uses low voltage diathermy. It is used in the treatment of cervical intraepithelial neoplasias. It is used only for cervical lesions. Loop size lesser than 2cm gives a better cone. It is less costly and has a shorter procedure time compared to laser ablation. But the success rate is similar to laser ablation.

Hence, the correct option is (C).

197. Endometrioid tumours account for about 20% of all ovarian cancers. They are mostly malignant. They are lined by glandular epithelium. They are moderate-sized solid tumours with cystic areas in between filled with haemorrhagic fluid. Ovarian endometriosis coexists in 15% of cases.

Hence, the correct option is (C).

198. The main symptom of caput succedaneum is puffiness under the skin of the scalp. The skin is swollen and soft. Pressing on it may result in a dimple in the flesh. The swelling may be on one side or may extend over the midline of the scalp.

Hence, the correct option is (C).

199. Resistant ovary syndrome, previously known as Savage syndrome, is a cause of ovarian failure that can lead to secondary amenorrhea. Resistant ovaries result from a functional disturbance of the gonadotropin receptors in the ovarian follicles. Spontaneous reversal of the receptor resistance may occur.

Hence, the correct option is (A).

200. The characteristic feature of endometrium in neuropathic hemorrhagic is cystic glandular hyperplasia. Another important feature is the absence of secretory endometrium with the absence of corkscrew glands. The endometrium is usually thick and polypoidal. Thin polypi project into the uterine cavity.

Hence, the correct option is (D).

201. Instead, it's clamped and cut between one and three minutes after birth. Currently, most hospitals in the United States practice early (immediate) cord clamping. This means cutting the umbilical cord 10 to 15 seconds after birth or sooner.

Hence, the correct option is (C).

202. As the head descends, the presenting part, usually in the transverse position, is rotated about 45° to anteroposterior (AP) position under the symphysis. Internal rotation brings the AP diameter of the head in line with the AP diameter of the pelvic outlet.

Hence, the correct option is (B).

203. DRUGS USED FOR THE TREATMENT OF MENORRHAGIA Non-hormonal agents Nonsteroidal antiinflammatory drugs They are the first-line treatment in ovulatory menorrhagia Studies have demonstrated a 20-46% reduction in menstrual blood flow Antifibrinolytics Prevent fibrinolysis and breakdown of clots eg: Tranexamic acid, Epsilon aminocaproic acid Ethamsylate.

Hence, the correct option is (C).

204. Radioimmunoassay is the most sensitive test for the measurement of ß HCG levels in serum. Immunological tests for the diagnosis of pregnancy depend on the detection of ß HCG in the maternal serum or urine. They are of various types: Agglutination inhibition test Direct agglutination test Enzyme-linked immunosorbent assay (ELISA) Fluoroimmunoassay (FIA) Radioimmunoassay (RIA) Immunoradiometric assay (IRMA)

Hence, the correct option is (C).

205. This is when you can see the top of your baby's head through the opening of your vagina. This moment happens during the second stage of labor when you push and deliver your newborn. Once your baby crowns, you push out the rest of their body.

Hence, the correct option is (C).

206. Both alpha-fetoprotein and acetylcholinesterase in amniotic fluid are markers for neural tube defects. But acetylcholinesterase is the most specific marker. An AFP test is used to screen for neural tube defects such as spina bifida. An increased level of AFP in the mother's blood has been associated with an increased risk of an open NTD in the baby.

Hence, the correct option is (C).

207. Hymenal tags are outgrowths of extra hymen tissue. These tags usually stick off the edge of the hymen. They're often confused for hymenal polyps, which are stalk-like growths on the hymen. Hymenal tags can also refer to the tissue that remains after the hymen breaks. At pregnancy, the epithelium of hymen becomes very thick and rich in glycogen, which may lead to spontaneous closure.

Hence, the correct option is (A).

208. Engagement of the fetal head is considered to have occurred when the biparietal diameter (BPD), the largest transverse diameter of the fetal head, has traversed the pelvic inlet1, 2. Ultrasound has been applied in the intrapartum assessment of fetal head position6-10.

Hence, the correct option is (D).

209. The congenital anomalies that can be identified in the first trimester are Acrania – A condition in which the flat bones of the cranial vault are partially or completely absent. It is an early stage of anencephaly. Exencephaly – An early stage of anencephaly in which the brain is located outside the skull Anencephaly – Absence of a major part of the brain, skull, and scalp. It is an anomaly that occurs when the rostral end of the neural tube fails to close.

Hence, the correct option is (B).

210. Genetic or inborn conditions are the most common causes of primary amenorrhea. Amenorrhea may result from disorders of the ovaries, pituitary gland, hypothalamus, or uterus. Intensive exercising, extreme weight loss, physical illness, and stress can all result in amenorrhea.

Hence, the correct option is (B).

211. Newly smear-positive cases of Tuberculosis are treated with Category I DOTS (Directly Observed Treatment Short-course) in India. The drugs are given in category I DOTS – Isoniazid, Rifampicin, Ethambutol, and Pyrazinamide are not contraindicated in pregnancy But if the disease is not treated properly, it is harmful to the fetus Streptomycin is not given in pregnant patients as it is teratogenic.

Hence, the correct option is (A).

212. Ursodeoxycholic acid is effective and safe in patients with intrahepatic cholestasis of pregnancy of early-onset, attenuating pruritus and correcting some biochemical abnormalities in the mothers. Ursodeoxycholic acid is a naturally-occurring bile acid that is taken as either a tablet or liquid to try and prevent liver disease in people with cystic fibrosis.

Hence, the correct option is (A).

213. Fetal infection at less than 20 weeks gestational age is associated with an increased risk of fetal death and hydrops; Parvovirus B19 is the most common infectious etiology of non-immune fetal hydrops, with an observed rate of up to 10% for those infected before 20 weeks gestational age.

Hence, the correct option is (D).

214. Increased nuchal translucency (NT) between 11 weeks and 13 weeks plus 6 days is associated with abnormal karyotype, structural malformations, fetal death, and disorders with late postnatal onset, such as Noonan's syndrome. 1-3 Many published studies have suggested that increased NT is associated with poor fetal outcome.

Hence, the correct option is (B).

215. Low-grade squamous intraepithelial lesion (LSIL) is a common abnormal result on a Pap test. It's also known as mild dysplasia. LSIL means that your cervical cells show mild abnormalities. An LSIL, or abnormal Pap result, doesn't mean that you have cancer. The tissue that covers your cervix is made up of squamous cells.

Hence, the correct option is (A).

216. HPV 16 is most commonly associated with carcinoma cervix. It is responsible for 40-70% of all invasive squamous cell cervical cancers. All women are at risk for cervical cancer. It occurs most often in women over age 30. Long-lasting infection with certain types of human papillomavirus (HPV) is the main cause of cervical cancer. HPV is a common virus that is passed from one person to another during sex.

Hence, the correct option is (D).

217. In the early postmenopausal period, hormonal replacement therapy (HRT) produces either stabilization or a slight increase (2-4%) in BMD. In contrast, a significant augmentation of bone mass (especially at the spine) seems to occur in osteopenic women when THR is administered in the late postmenopausal period.

Hence, the correct option is (C).

218. It is a type of obstructed labor in which the anterior shoulder of the fetus fails to deliver after the emergence of the head. Mauriceau Smellie Veit maneuver is used in the management of after coming head in case of breech delivery.

Hence, the correct option is (D).

219. They may even cause hearing loss. The moveable tails, or flagella, of sperm, can also be affected by PCD. This can cause abnormal sperm motility and infertility in men. Women with Kartagener's syndrome can also be infertile, due to impaired cilia motility in the lining of their fallopian tubes.

Hence, the correct option is (D).

220. The obstetrical conjugate is the distance between the sacral promontory and the inner pubic arch; it should measure 11.5 cm or more. The diagonal conjugate is the distance from the undersurface of the pubic arch to the sacral promontory; it is 2 cm longer than the obstetrical conjugate.

Hence, the correct option is (A).

221. When the endometrium is no longer shed, estrogen can cause an overgrowth of cells in the uterus, a condition that can lead to cancer. Progesterone reduces the risk of endometrial (uterine) cancer by making the endometrium thin.

Hence, the correct option is (D).

222. Folic acid absorption is decreased and its excretion is increased in those using phenytoin. Other vitamin deficiencies are seen in phenytoin users: Vitamin D, Vitamin K. Hence pregnant women on phenytoin should take folic acid, cholecalciferol, and phytonadione supplements.

Hence, the correct option is (D).

223. Active management of the third stage of labour involves giving a prophylactic uterotonic, early cord clamping, and controlled cord traction to deliver the placenta. With expectant management, signs of placental separation are awaited and the placenta is delivered spontaneously.

Hence, the correct option is (C).

224. Start recording on the partograph when the labor is the inactive first stage (4 cm or above). Cervical dilatation, the descent of the fetal head, and uterine contractions are used in assessing the progress of labor. Progress in labor is still assessed based on four main signs. These are cervical dilatation/effacement, the station of the presenting part, position of the fetal head, and strength of contractions. Other than the use of a tachograph, these signs have been unchanged since the 17th century.

Hence, the correct option is (A).

225. It is also called the obstetrical conjugate. It is the most important of the pelvic measurements as it is the first boney strait through which the fetus has to pass. It measures about 1.25cm more than the obstetric conjugate and may be felt during a vaginal examination as part of a pelvic assessment.

Hence, the correct option is (C).

226.

1. The tympanometry flap is raised to expose the middle ear in the endometrial approach.
2. Rosen's incision is used in the endometrial approach for stapedectomy.
3. It is also used for exploratory tympanostomy.

Hence, the correct option is (B).

227.

1. Hitzelberger's sign is seen in acoustic neuroma.
2. It occurs due to the involvement of the 7th cranial nerve.
3. There is early involvement of the sensory fibers which causes hypoesthesia of the posterior meatal wall.
4. Paraesthesia of the face and reduced corneal sensitivity occur due to the involvement of the 5th cranial nerve.

Hence, the correct option is (B).

228.

1. Orbital apex syndrome is a complication of paranasal sinus infection.
2. Superior orbital fissure syndrome along with the involvement of maxillary division of the trigeminal nerve and the optic nerve is known as orbital apex syndrome.
3. In superior orbital fissure syndrome, there is progressive paralysis of abducent, oculomotor, and trochlear nerves.

Hence, the correct option is (C).

229. USE OF SODIUM FLUORIDE IN OTOSCLEROSIS
Mechanism of action

- Sodium fluoride promotes osteoblastic activity and inhibits osteoclastic activity
- This helps to decrease the bone remodeling taking place in the osteosclerotic lesions and promotes recalcification
- It also inhibits proteolytic enzymes in the cochlea and helps prevent sensorineural deafness

Indications

- Progressive sensorineural hearing loss
- Radiological evidence of a lesion
- Positive Schwartz sign

Hence, the correct option is (C).

230. Boundaries of Prussak's space: -Superior – Fibers of the lateral malleolar fold -Inferior – Short process of malleus -Lateral – Shrapnell's membrane -Medial – Neck of the malleus.

Hence, the correct option is (C).

231.

1. Eagle's syndrome is characterized by pain in the tonsillar fossa and upper neck.
2. Pain radiates from the ipsilateral ear.
3. There is an aggravation of pain on swallowing.
4. It is caused by calcification of the stylohyoid ligament/elongation of the styloid process.

Hence, the correct option is (A).

232.

1. Trotter's syndrome is seen in nasopharyngeal carcinoma when it spreads laterally and involves the sinus of Morgagni.
2. There is conductive hearing loss, ipsilateral immobility of the soft palate, and neuralgic pain.
3. Ortner's syndrome is characterized by paralysis of recurrent laryngeal nerve and cardiomegaly.
4. Costen's syndrome occurs due to defective bite resulting in temporomandibular joint abnormality.
5. Lermoyez syndrome is a form of Meniere's disease.

Hence, the correct option is (D).

233.

1. Gradenigo's syndrome is seen in petrositis.
2. It is characterized by lateral rectus palsy, persistent ear discharge, and deep-seated ear or retro-orbital pain.
3. Mastoid tenderness, hearing loss, and sagging of the posterosuperior meatal wall are seen in acute mastoiditis.

Hence, the correct option is (B).

234. Haemorrhage following a tonsillectomy can be of 3 types: 1)Primary haemorrhage (Immediate haemorrhage) -Occurs during surgery. 2)Reactionary haemorrhage (Early haemorrhage) -Occurs within 24 hours of surgery. It is due to the presence of a clot that prevents the compressive action of superior constrictor muscle on the blood vessels. It can also occur due to the slipping of a ligature/dislodgement of the clot. 3)Secondary haemorrhage (Delayed haemorrhage) -Seen more than 24 hours after surgery. Usually seen 5 to 10 days after surgery. Occurs due to infection / premature separation of the membrane.

Hence, the correct option is (C).

235. Otoacoustic emissions (OAE) are sounds generated by the action of the outer hair cells that can be recorded in the ear canal that provide a direct measure of cochlear function. Otoacoustic emissions (OAEs) are sounds that arise in the ear canal when (paradoxically) the tympanum receives vibrations transmitted back through the middle ear from the cochlea.

Hence, the correct option is (B).

236. A child climbs with alternate steps, builds a tower of 9 cubes, but can tell not his name and cannot say his age and sex, the probable age is 30 months.

Hence, the correct option is (C).

237. Constitutional growth delay: This condition describes children who are small for their ages but who are growing at a normal rate. They usually have a delayed "bone age," which means that their skeletal maturation is younger than their age in years.

Hence, the correct option is (C).

238. Your baby's sense of taste first starts to develop when she's in the womb (uterus). By the time you're nine weeks pregnant, your unborn baby's mouth and tongue have formed and she has her first tiny tastebuds. While your baby is in the womb, she's surrounded by amniotic fluid.

Hence, the correct option is (A).

239. By 3 months, your baby will have formed a strong attachment to you. They will respond to you with lots of smiles, and might even talk back to you in their own way. The worst of the crying should be nearly over, and you can really enjoy your baby as they grow into their own little person. That all begins to change around 3 months of age when most babies develop enough strength in their neck to keep their head partially upright.

Hence, the correct option is (B).

240. Two-month-old babies can typically see at least 12 inches away, maybe even up to 2 feet or more. You'll know she can see further when you catch your baby smiling when you walk on the other side of the room, or when you see her studying one of her toys on the floor.

Hence, the correct option is (D).

241. Adolescence begins with the onset of physiologically normal puberty and ends when an adult identity and behavior are accepted. This period of development corresponds roughly to the period between the ages of 10 and 19 years, which is consistent with the World Health Organization's definition of adolescence.

Hence, the correct option is (B).

242. Sometime after 6 months, your baby will develop enough hand coordination to be able to manipulate toys more easily and learn how to let go, enabling her to shift toys from hand to hand, examine them from all different angles, and bang different objects together.

Hence, the correct option is (B).

243. Growth hormone deficiency (GHD), also known as dwarfism or pituitary dwarfism, is a condition caused by insufficient amounts of growth hormone in the body. Children with GHD have abnormally short stature with normal body proportions. GHD can be present at birth (congenital) or develop later (acquired).

Hence, the correct option is (A).

244. Male secondary sex characteristics include Growth of body hair, including underarm, abdominal, chest hair, and pubic hair. Growth of facial hair. Enlargement of the larynx (Adam's apple) and deepening of the voice.

Hence, the correct option is (A).

245. Peak growth for girls is typically 6-12 months before the onset of their menstrual cycle (menarche) and then significantly slows down after that. Girls can expect to grow an average of about 2-3 inches after menarche. Boys tend to have their growth spurt about two years later than girls.

Hence, the correct option is (C).

246. Favre-Goldmann syndrome is an autosomal recessive condition. It usually presents in childhood with nyctalopia. Central and peripheral retinoschisis is present. There is marked pigmentary changes similar to retinitis pigmentosa.

Hence, the correct option is (A).

247. Axenfeld anomaly is seen in glaucoma associated with iridocorneal dysgenesis. It is a posterior embryotoxic characterized by prominent Schwalbe's ring.

Hence, the correct option is (D).

248. Pterygium is usually seen in elderly males and it presents as a triangular fold of conjunctiva which encroaches the cornea. It is usually seen on the nasal side. Stocker's line is a deposition of iron seen in the corneal epithelium anterior to the advancing head of the pterygium.

Hence, the correct option is (C).

249. Cogan's syndrome is seen in middle-aged adults. The features include interstitial keratitis, acute tinnitus, vertigo, and deafness. Treatment is by the usage of topical and systemic corticosteroids. Early treatment is necessary to prevent permanent deafness and blindness.

Hence, the correct option is (A).

250. Lowe's syndrome is an ocular-Cerebro-renal syndrome. It is an inborn error of amino acid metabolism. Congenital cataract and glaucoma are the ocular features. Mental retardation, dwarfism, osteomalacia, and muscular hypotonia are the other features seen in this syndrome.

Hence, the correct option is (A).

251. Gunn sign is seen in grade III hypertensive retinopathy. The other findings in grade III hypertensive retinopathy include copper wiring of arterioles. -banking of veins distal to arteriovenous crossings -right-angle deflection of veins -flame-shaped hemorrhages -cotton wool spots hard exudates.

Hence, the correct option is (D).

252. Weiss operation is done for senile entropion. An incision is placed 3mm below the lid margin extending along the whole length of the eyelid. It involved the skin, orbicularis, and the tarsal plate. Mattress sutures are used for correcting the entropion by transposition the tarsus.

Hence, the correct option is (B).

253. Bilateral granulomatous panuveitis is seen in Heerfordt's syndrome (Uveoparotid fever). It is also associated with painful enlargement of parotid glands. Cranial nerve palsy, fever, malaise, and skin rashes are also seen.

Hence, the correct option is (A).

254. It is a rare condition that was previously considered a type of migraine. Recent studies suggest that is it likely to be an inflammatory cranial neuropathy. The International Headache Classification has reclassified ophthalmoplegic migraine as a type of neuralgia from its earlier classification as a type of migraine. It is characterized by transient migraine-like headache associated with paresis of oculomotor, trochlear, and/or abducens nerves. To arrive at a diagnosis of ophthalmoplegic migraine, other causes should be ruled out by appropriate investigations (like digital subtraction angiography / magnetic resonance angiography of the brain).

Hence, the correct option is (C).

255. Nepafenac is a topically administered NSAID sold as 0.1% eye drops. It is used for the treatment of pain and inflammation in patients undergoing cataract surgery. Nepafenac is a prodrug of amfenac that has COX-1 and COX-2 inhibitor activity. Treatment is started 1 day prior to cataract surgery and is continued 2 weeks postoperatively. Side effects include foreign body sensation and decreased visual acuity.

Hence, the correct option is (C).

256. The clinical features are characteristic of rosacea. Rosacea is a commonly encountered chronic inflammatory skin disease in adults with a predilection for highly visible areas of the skin such as the face. It is characterized by flushing, redness, pimples, pustules, and dilated blood vessels.

Hence, the correct option is (B).

257. Dyskeratosis is the premature keratinization of individual keratinocytes. It can be benign or malignant. Benign dyskeratosis is seen in Darier's disease, Warty dyskeratosis, and Familial benign pemphigus. Neoplastic dyskeratosis is seen in Bowen's disease, Squamous cell carcinoma, and Actinic keratosis.

Hence, the correct option is (D).

258. To learn about the pseudo-isomorphic phenomenon, we first need to know what is an isomorphic phenomenon. Isomorphic phenomenon (also known as the Koebner phenomenon) is a phenomenon in which new skin lesions appear at the site of injury. It is named after Heinrich Köbner, a German dermatologist. The isomorphic phenomenon is seen in conditions like psoriasis, vitiligo, and lichen planus. Pseudo-isomorphic phenomenon (Pseudo-Koebner phenomenon) is characterized by the appearance of similar skin lesions at the site of injury infective lesions like plane warts and molluscum contagiosum. It occurs due to the spread of the infective agent (virus) to the new site.

Hence, the correct option is (D).

259. Blaschko's lines are invisible developmental lines of the skin They are thought to represent the pathways of epithelial migration and proliferation in the fetus These were first demonstrated by German dermatologist Alfred Blaschko in 1901. They do not correspond to the path of vessels/nerves/lymphatics Many skin lesions follow Blaschko's lines. eg: Incontinentia pigmenti, Linear lichen planus, Lichen striatus Naevus achromicus.

Hence, the correct option is (A).

260. History and clinical features are characteristic of fixed drug eruption. Fixed drug eruption (FDE) is a distinctive type of cutaneous drug reaction that characteristically recurs in the same locations upon reexposure to the offending drug. The major categories of causative agents of fixed drug eruption include antibiotics, antiepileptics, nonsteroidal anti-inflammatory agents, sildenafil, and phenothiazines, although numerous other agents and certain foods such as cashews and licorice have also been reported as causative agents.

Hence, the correct option is (C).

261. A white curdy patch in the oral cavity in an otherwise healthy individual is characteristic of candidiasis. But immunosuppressive conditions like HIV should be ruled out.

Hence, the correct option is (A).

262. Systemic corticosteroids are not recommended in the treatment of pustular psoriasis. This is because the disease can recur with increased severity once the treatment is stopped. But the best answer is the treatment of extensive lesions. Steroids are very useful as a short term life-saving measure in the severe disease when other drugs have failed.

Hence, the correct option is (D).

263. Arsenic toxicity:

- Mee's lines – not specific, also seen in thallium poisoning.
- Anemia with stippling of erythrocytes.
- Occasionally, pancytopenia and aplastic anemia can develop.

Basophilic stippling is seen in Lead toxicity.

Hence, the correct option is (D).

264. The history is suggestive of photodermatitis. A patch test is used for the diagnosis of photodermatitis. A patch test (photo patch test): Here, 2 patches containing photosensitizing material is applied on 2 different sites on the body. One of them is irradiated with UVA rays. The other is kept in control. Development of eczema is looked for up to 72 hours.

Hence, the correct option is (C).

265. The irregular hyperpigmented macules since early childhood are probably cafe au lait macules. Presence of 6 or more cafe au lait macules is diagnostic of neurofibromatosis type I even when cutaneous neurofibromas are absent. Lisch nodules on the iris can be demonstrated by slit-lamp examination and it helps support the diagnosis.

Hence, the correct option is (A).

266. Ivermectin the only orally effective treatment for scabies. Evidence suggests that oral ivermectin may be a safe and effective treatment for scabies; however, ivermectin is not FDA-approved for this use. Oral ivermectin should be considered for patients who have failed treatment with or who cannot tolerate FDA-approved topical medications for the treatment of scabies.

Hence, the correct option is (B).

267.

In normal hair growth, the hair follicles cycle through distinct phases. 5 Growth, known as anagen, where the hair shaft is actively generated and extends, can last as long as 6 years on the human scalp before entering a period of rest. For example, the anagen phase for eyebrow hairs and pubic hairs is much shorter than the phase for your scalp hairs. During the anagen phase, your hair follicles are pushing out hairs that will continue to grow until they're cut or until they reach the end of their lifespan and fall out.

Hence, the correct option is (A).

268. The irregular hyperpigmented macules since early childhood are probably cafe au lait macules. Presence of 6 or more cafe au lait macules is diagnostic of neurofibromatosis type I even when cutaneous neurofibromas are absent. Lisch nodules on the iris can be demonstrated by slit lamp examination and it helps support the diagnosis.

Hence, the correct option is (A).

269. Enuresis alarm systems are the preferred treatment for children with nocturnal enuresis. Pharmacological treatment for nocturnal enuresis is reserved for cases that do not respond to treatment with enuresis alarms. Desmopressin is the preferred drug. It is given at night to reduce urine production during sleep. Tricyclic antidepressants like imipramine can also be used. But use is limited due to side effects.

Hence, the correct option is (B).

270.

- CRPS Type 1 occurs without obvious nerve injury.
- When the pain and signs of sympathetic dysfunction occur after an identifiable nerve injury, it is termed CRPS Type 2.

Hence, the correct option is (A).

271.

- Pseudohypoparathyroidism (PHP) is a group of inherited disorders characterized by hypocalcemia and hyperphosphatemia.
- Hypocalcemia is due to resistance to parathyroid hormone, which results in hyperplasia of parathyroid glands, and thus causing elevation of PTH levels.

Hence, the correct option is (C).

272.

- Gastric irritation is most severe with aspirin.
- It can cause gastric mucosal erosion and ulceration leading to bleeding and perforation.

Hence, the correct option is (C).

273.

- SGLT2 inhibitors reduce hospitalization for heart failure as demonstrated by multiple cardiovascular outcome trials of various SGLT2 inhibitors.
- They produce glycosuria and weight loss.
- SGLT2 is a high-capacity low-affinity transporter in contrast to SGLT1.
- In kidneys, SGLT2 is present in the proximal part of the tubules while SGLT1 is present more distally.
- The low amount of glucose remaining after transport by the SGLT2 is conserved by SGLT1 located distally as it has a high affinity for glucose compared to SGLT2, produce a virtual absence of glucose in urine.

Hence, the correct option is (C).

274.

- Multiple sclerosis is an autoimmune disease of the central neural system with a relapsing and remitting or progressive course.
- The pathologic hallmark of the disease is demyelination.
- Myelin-specific antibodies are present on degenerating myelin sheaths.
- Surviving oligodendrocytes partially demyelinated surviving axons, which are called shadow plaques.

Hence, the correct option is (C).

275. Drugs used in the treatment of type II lepra reaction are :

- NSAID's
- Thalidomide
- Chloroquine
- Clofazimine
- Corticosteroids
- Parenteral antimony

Hence, the correct option is (C).

276. Dorsal pterygium is most commonly acquired. It arises from conditions involving the proximal nail fold, such as lichen planus, burns, trauma, radiodermatitis, cicatricial pemphigoid, graft-versus-host disease (GVHD), toxic epidermal necrolysis (TEN), pemphigus foliaceous, and Raynaud phenomenon.

Hence, the correct option is (A).

277. Tumour Necrosis Factor-alpha (TNF alpha), is an inflammatory cytokine produced by macrophages/monocytes during acute inflammation and is responsible for a diverse range of signaling events within cells, leading to necrosis or apoptosis. Protein is also important for resistance to infection and cancers.

Hence, the correct option is (C).

278. The following CSF parameters point against a diagnosis of multiple sclerosis:

- Pleocytosis of more than 75 cells/μl.
- Presence of polymorphonuclear lymphocytes.
- The protein concentration of more than 100 mg/dl.

Hence, the correct option is (A).

279. The characteristic feature of Max-Joseph space is formed from the degeneration of basal keratinocytes and anchoring unit disruption. They are regarded as histologic clefts. The colloid bodies ultrastructurally are apoptotic keratinocytes revealing DNA fragmentation in these cells. Lichen planus is an inflammatory skin condition, characterized by an itchy, non-infectious rash on the arms and legs. It consists of small, many-sided, flat-topped, pink, or purple bumps. A significant number of skin specialists believe it might be an autoimmune disease.

Hence, the correct option is (B).

280. A chancre is a painless genital ulcer most commonly formed during the primary stage of syphilis. This infectious lesion forms approximately 21 days after the initial exposure to Treponema pallidum, the gram-negative spirochaete bacterium yielding syphilis.

Hence, the correct option is (A).

281. Griseofulvin is used in the treatment of dermatophyte infections. **Griseofulvin** is a medicine that is **used to treat fungal infections**.

It is mainly **prescribed** for **infections** occurring on the skin or scalp. It is prescribed in particular for an infection called scalp ringworm (also called tinea capitis).

Hence, the correct option is (C).

282. Pityriasis rosea is a viral rash that lasts about 6–12 weeks. It is characterized by a herald patch followed by similar, smaller oval red patches that are located mainly on the chest and back. Its exact cause is unknown. No germ (bacterium, virus, or fungus) has been found in people with the rash. However, certain types of human herpes viruses may be a part of the cause. It is not associated with food, medicines, or stress.

Hence, the correct option is (C).

283. Parakeratosis refers to the incomplete maturation of epidermal keratinocytes, resulting in abnormal retention of nuclei in the stratum corneum. It occurs in many diseases of the skin, particularly in psoriasis. Parakeratosis is a zinc-responsive dermatosis usually observed in 2- to 4-month-old swine. Pigs not allowed access to soil or not supplemented with zinc are more likely to have parakeratosis. The disease is caused by a relative deficiency of zinc.

Hence, the correct option is (A).

284. Isotretinoin capsules are only for severe acne. This is acne with lots of pus-filled spots that may affect the back and chest, as well as the face. Isotretinoin capsules help severe acne by reducing the amount of natural oil made by your skin so blocked pores are less likely.

Hence, the correct option is (B).

285. Griseofulvin is used in the treatment of dermatophyte infections. Oral treatment with agents such as terbinafine, itraconazole, fluconazole, and griseofulvin is used for extensive or refractory cutaneous infections and infections extending into follicles or the dermis (eg, Majocchi's granuloma) or involving nails.

Hence, the correct option is (C).

286. The most common change in melanoma cells is a mutation in the BRAF oncogene, which is found in about half of all melanomas. Other genes that can be affected in melanoma include NRAS, CDKN2A, and NF1. (Usually, only one of these genes is affected.)

Hence, the correct option is (B).

287. Mycosis fungoides is the most common form of a type of blood cancer called cutaneous T-cell lymphoma. Cutaneous T-cell lymphomas occur when certain white blood cells, called T cells, become cancerous; these cancers characteristically affect the skin, causing different types of skin lesions.

Hence, the correct option is (A).

288. Civatte bodies, also known as colloid bodies or hyaline bodies, are regarded as a diagnostic hallmark for lichen planus. Hyperkeratosis, especially hyperorthokeratosis with hypergranulosis, is typical of skin lesions, but not always features of oral lichen planus.

Hence, the correct option is (A).

289. Pilomatricoma, also known as pilomatrixoma, is a type of noncancerous (benign) skin tumor associated with hair follicles. Hair follicles are specialized structures in the skin where hair growth occurs. Pilomatricomas occur most often on the head or neck, although they can also be found on the arms, torso, or legs.

Hence, the correct option is (C).

290. Reactivation TB may occur if the individual's immune system becomes weakened and no longer is able to contain the latent bacteria. The bacteria then become active; they overwhelm the immune process and make the person sick with TB. This also is called TB disease. Tuberculosis (TB) is a disease caused by germs that are spread from person to person through the air. TB usually affects the lungs, but it can also affect other parts of the body, such as the brain, the kidneys, or the spine. A person with TB can die if they do not get treatment.

Hence, the correct option is (A).

291. Malaria parasites are micro-organisms that belong to the genus Plasmodium. There are more than 100 species of Plasmodium, which can infect many animal species such as reptiles, birds, and various mammals. Four species of Plasmodium have long been recognized to infect humans in nature.

Hence, the correct option is (B).

292. The neutrophil chemotaxis recruiter, interleukin-8 (IL-8) has been shown in vitro in may not alter the initial susceptibility of macrophages to HIV infection. Most clinically relevant reservoir, our success could translate to other cell types. HIV primarily targets a type of cell in the immune system called the CD4+ T cell. However, many types of these cells exist, and they are not all equally susceptible to infection by HIV.

Hence, the correct option is (D).

293. Lymphocytes are one of the main types of immune cells. Lymphocytes are divided mainly into B and T cells. B lymphocytes produce antibodies - proteins (gamma globulins) that recognize foreign substances (antigen) and attach themselves to them. B lymphocytes (or B cells) are each programmed to make one specific antibody.

Hence, the correct option is (B).

294. The four major types of epidermolysis bullosa simplex can result from mutations in either the KRT5 or KRT14 gene. These genes provide instructions for making proteins called keratin 5 and keratin 14. Mutations in the COL7A1 gene cause all forms of dystrophic epidermolysis bullosa. This gene provides instructions for making a protein that forms the pieces (subunits) of a larger protein called type VII collagen.

Hence, the correct option is (A).

295. Dermatitis herpetiformis (DH) is a chronic, intensely itchy, blistering skin manifestation of gluten-sensitive enteropathy, commonly known as celiac disease. DH is a rash that affects about 10 percent of people with celiac disease. Sometimes, a direct immunofluorescence test is done, in which the skin around the rash is stained with a dye that will show the presence of IgA antibody deposits.

Hence, the correct option is (B).

296. Bullous pemphigoid (BUL-us PEM-fih-goid) is a rare skin condition that causes large, fluid-filled blisters. They develop on areas of skin that often flex such as the lower abdomen, upper thighs, or armpits. Bullous pemphigoid is most common in older adults. Pemphigoid is caused by a malfunction of the immune system and results in skin rashes and blistering on the legs, arms, and abdomen. Pemphigoid can also cause blistering on the mucous membranes. Mucous membranes produce mucous that helps protect the inside of your body.

Hence, the correct option is (A).

297. Basal cell carcinoma appears as a change in the skin, such as a growth or a sore that won't heal. These changes in the skin (lesions) usually have one of the following characteristics: A pearly white, skin-colored, or pink bump that is translucent, meaning you can see a bit through the surface.

Hence, the correct option is (D).

298. Malaria can damage the kidneys or liver or cause the spleen to rupture. Any of these conditions can be life-threatening. Anemia. Malaria may result in not having enough red blood cells for an adequate supply of oxygen to your body's tissues (anemia). P. falciparum can cause severe malaria because it multiples rapidly in the blood, and can thus cause severe blood loss (anemia).

Hence, the correct option is (A).

299. Acantholysis refers to the loss of attachments between keratinocytes, resulting in the formation of rounded, detached cells within the blister. Pemphigus is characterized by shallow ulcers or fragile blisters that break open quickly. Pemphigoid presents with stronger or "tense" blisters that don't open easily.

Hence, the correct option is (D).

300.

- Life expectancy of patients with schizophrenia is decreased by approximately 15 to 25 years.
- Suicide is the most important cause of premature death in patients with schizophrenia.
- There is a 20 fold increased risk of suicide compared to the general population.
- Suicide attempts may occur without warning or expression of intent.
- Cancer is the second most frequent cause of mortality in schizophrenics.
- The rates of metabolic syndrome and cardiovascular disorders are also increased.

Hence, the correct option is (D).

Mock Test 05

Part A

Q.1 A person is unable to extend his metacarpophalangeal joint. This can result from injury to which nerve -

A. Ulnar nerve injury
B. Radial nerve injury
C. Median nerve injury
D. Posterior Interosseous nerve injury

Q.2 Wrist drop is due to injury of -

A. Ulnar nerve
B. Radial nerve
C. Median nerve
D. Musculocutaneous nerve

Q.3 Which of the following is not supplied by C8 T1 -

A. Abductor pollicis brevis
B. Extensor indices
C. Palmar interossei
D. 3rd & 4th lumbricals

Q.4 Structure passing deep to flexor retinaculum is -

A. Post tibial artery
B. Long saphenous vein
C. Tibialis anterior tendon
D. Peroneus Tertius

Q.5 Which of the following structure is unable in crossing the dorsal surface of the ischial spine

A. Pudendal nerve
B. Nerve to obturator internus
C. Obturator nerve
D. Internal pudendal vessel

Q.6 Inferior most structure of right hilum is -

A. Bronchus
B. Inferior pulmonary vein
C. Pulmonary artery
D. Inferior bronchial vein

Q.7 In a case of chest pain with pericarditis and pericardial effusion, pain is referred by -

A. Phrenic nerve
B. Superficial cardiac plexus
C. Deep cardiac plexus
D. Vagus nerve

Q.8 What does not crossing midline mean?

A. Left gonadal vein
B. Left renal vein
C. Left brachiocephalic vein
D. Hemiazygos vein

Q.9 Ureteric constrictions are at all sites except -

A. Pelviureteric junction
B. Lesser pelvis
C. At ischial spine
D. Urinary bladder wall

Q.10 Which of the following is transmitted through foramen spinosum -

A. Middle meningeal artery
B. Internal carotid artery
C. Facial nerve
D. Mandibular nerve

Q.11 Incudomalleolar joint is an example of:

A. Saddle joint
B. Condylar joint
C. Pivot joint
D. Plane joint

Q.12 All are contents of the interpeduncular fossa except the part-

A. Trochlear nerve
B. Oculomotor nerve
C. Mamillary bodies
D. None of these

Q.13 Cerebellar connection to other parts of the brain is projected through which cell -

A. Golgi cells
B. Basket cells
C. Purkinje cells
D. Oligodendrocytes

Q.14 The cells are belonging to which of the following type of epithelium -

A. Transitional
B. Stratified squamous
C. Stratified cuboidal
D. Stratified columnar

Q.15 Which of the following is not lined by Urothelium

A. Urinary bladder
B. Minor calyx
C. Ureters
D. Membranous urethra

Q.16 The upper 3/4th of vagina develops from -

A. Wolfian duct
B. Mullerian duct
C. Sino vaginal bulb
D. Endoderm

Q.17 The most common cause of delayed umbilical cord separation is

A. Raspberry tumour
B. Leukocyte adhesion deficiency
C. Patent urachus
D. Umbilical granuloma

Q.18 The transition temperature of lipid bilayers of the cell membrane is increased by

A. Cholesterol
B. Saturated fatty acids
C. Hydrocarbons
D. Unsaturated fatty acids

Q.19 Most potent antioxidant -

A. Vitamine E
B. Vitamine A
C. Vitamine K
D. Vitamine C

Q.20 Which of the following does not occur in mitochondria :
A. Citric acid cycle (Kreb's cycle)
B. Glycogenolysis
C. Fatty acid oxidation
D. Electron transport chain

Q.21 Resting membrane potential is mainly due to
A. Na^+ **B.** K^+ **C.** Cl^- **D.** Mg^{++}

Q.22 Almost all transmissible electrically charged particle in excitable tissue is -
A. Na^+ **B.** K^+
C. Cl^- **D.** None of these

Q.23 Which is TRUE regarding nerve conduction
A. All or none phenomenon
B. Conduction independent of amplitude
C. The propagated action potential is generated in dendrites
D. Faster in unmyelinated fibres

Q.24 All are true regarding intrafusal fibres except
A. Nuclear chain fibres are shorter & thinner
B. Nuclear bag fibres are lesser
C. Primary endings excited by bag fibres only
D. Secondary endings excited by chain fibres only

Q.25 True about fatty acid synthesis
A. Occurs in mitochondria
B. Occurs in cytosol
C. Occurs in the endoplasmic reticulum
D. Occurs in ribosomes

Q.26 Where does protein synthesis occur?
A. Smooth ER **B.** Golgi bodies
C. Rough ER **D.** Lysosomes

Q.27 Physiological dead space is?
A. 150 ml **B.** 200 ml **C.** 250 ml **D.** 100 ml

Q.28 Total alveolar ventilation volume (in L/min) is
A. 1.5 **B.** 3.5 **C.** 4.2 **D.** 5

Q.29 The pacemaker potential is due to
A. Fast Na^+ channel
B. Decrease in K^+ permeability
C. Slow Ca^{++} channel
D. Rapid repolarisation

Q.30 Einthoven's law
A. I + III = II **B.** I – III = II
C. I + II + III = 0 **D.** I + III = avL

Q.31 Which of the following structures does not lie in the renal medulla-
A. Juxtaglomerular apparatus
B. Loop of Henle
C. Collecting duct
D. Vasa Recta

Q.32 Proteolytic enzyme Renin is present in?
A. Lungs **B.** Liver **C.** Kidney **D.** Stomach

Q.33 Parietal cell secretes
A. Mucus **B.** Pepsinogens
C. Gastrin **D.** Intrinsic factor

Q.34 The cephalic phase of gastric secretion
A. 20% **B.** 70% **C.** 10% **D.** 100%

Q.35 The mechanism by which pyruvate cytosol is transported to mitochondria is
A. Chloride antiport
B. Proton symport
C. ATP dependent antiport
D. Facilitated uniport

Q.36 Which of the following acts as co-enzymes and not as co-factors
A. Folic acid **B.** Biotin
C. Thiamine **D.** All of these

Q.37 Substrate level phosphorylation is catalysed by which enzyme?
A. Succinate dehydrogenase
B. Alpha-ketoglutarate dehydrogenase
C. Succinate thiokinase
D. Malate dehydrogenase

Q.38 The biosynthesis of the enzyme pyruvate carboxylase is repressed by
A. Insulin **B.** Glucagon
C. Cortisol **D.** Epinephrine

Q.39 Pompe's disease is due to deficiency of which enzyme storage disease
A. Branching enzyme
B. Glucose 6 phosphatase
C. Acid maltase deficiency
D. Muscle phosphorylase

Q.40 1st acetyl group donor in fatty acid synthesis is
A. Malonyl CoA **B.** Palmitate
C. Acetyl CoA **D.** Citrate

Q.41 Acetyl CoA carboxylase is activated by
A. Malonyl CoA **B.** Citrate
C. Palmitoyl CoA **D.** Acetoacetate

Q.42 Which of the following is/are a storage protein
A. Myoglobin **B.** Ovalbumin
C. Ferritin **D.** All of these

Q.43 The main source of energy derived from
A. Fat **B.** Glycogen
C. Lactate **D.** Acetone

Q.44 Thiamine acts as a cofactor in
A. Conversion of pyruvate to acetyl-CoA
B. Transamination reactions
C. Oxidation in the respiratory chain
D. Conversion of pyridoxal to pyridoxal phosphate

Q.45 Consumption of raw egg may lead to the deficiency of
A. Biotin **B.** Riboflavin

C. Thiamine **D.** Avidin

Q.46 True about the coding strand of DNA

a) Acts as a template for mRNA

b) Minus strand

c) Plus strand

d) Matches with RNA transcript that encodes a protein

A. ab **B.** bc **C.** bd **D.** cd

Q.47 All statements are false regarding mature cytoplasmic messenger RNA except-

A. Transcribed from Nuclear DNA

B. Has Thiamine in place of Uracil

C. Sugar is Deoxy Ribose

D. Its molecular weight is more than hn-RNA

Q.48 Which of the following is related to the structure of a codon-

A. Two complementary base pairs

B. Three consecutive nucleotide units

C. An individual ribosome

D. Four individual nucleotides

Q.49 Nobel prize in 2006 was given for the discovery of

A. Lipoxins

B. RNAi

C. DNA

D. β-transcription factor

Q.50 All of these are required for PCR except-

A. Taq polymerase

B. d-NTP

C. Primer

D. Radiolabelled DNA probe

Part B

Q.51 Which of the following is the reason behind delayed prolonged bleeding?

A. Direct injury to endothelial cell

B. Histamine

C. Leukocyte dependent injury

D. IL-I

Q.52 Cardinal signs of Inflammation are all except?

A. Rubor **B.** Tumour **C.** Calor **D.** Cyanosis

Q.53 The first step in the initiation of primary hemostasis for clot formation is?

A. Fibrin deposition **B.** Vasoconstriction

C. Platelet adhesion **D.** Thrombosis

Q.54 Hypoplasia of the gland shown in the Photograph is associated with

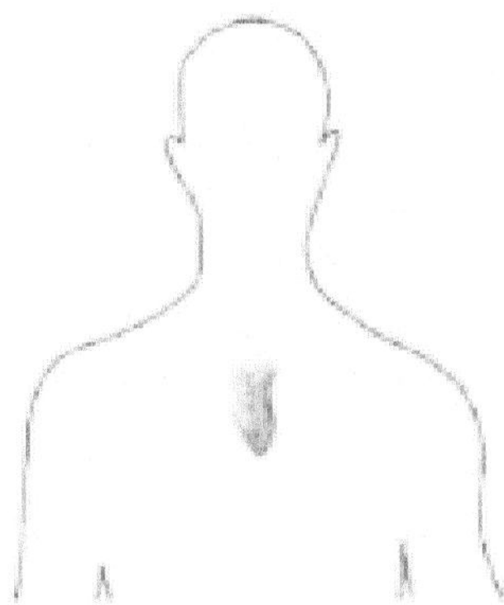

A. Wiskott Aldrich Syndrome

B. IgA deficiency

C. Digeorge syndrome

D. Agammaglobulinemia

Q.55 A 34-year-old, G, P0, presents for genetic counselling at 12 week's gestation. The patient has two sisters and a brother; her father has haemophilia. Her siblings are not affected, but she has a nephew that is:

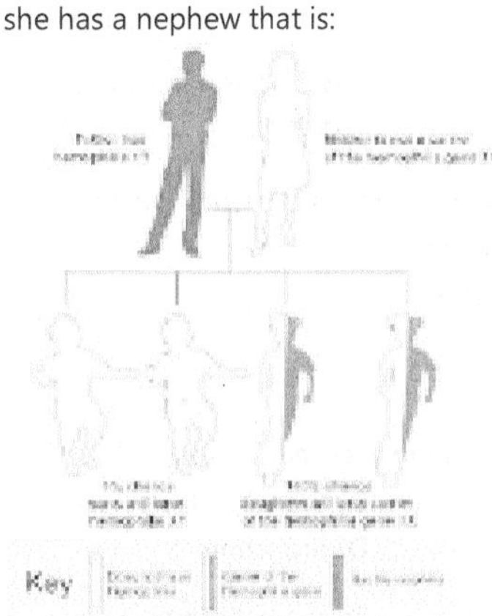

A. Autosomal recessive

B. X-linked inheritance

C. Mitochondrial inheritance

D. Multifactorial inheritance

Q.56 Tumour shown in Photograph is known as

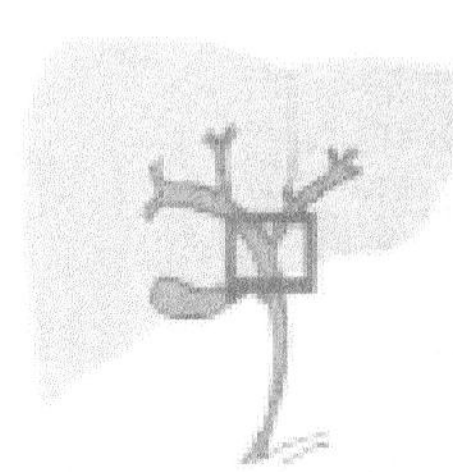

A. Krukenberg tumour

B. Signet ring cell carcinoma

C. Oncocytoma

D. Klatskin tumor

Q.57 Dystrophic calcification is seen in

A. Rickets

B. Atheromatous plaque
C. Hyperparathyroidism
D. Vitamin 'A' intoxication

Q.58 Progenitor hematopoietic stem cells originate in -

A. Bone Marrow **B.** Thymus
C. Lymph node **D.** Spleen

Q.59 Hemophilia manifest clinically as a rise in -

A. PTT **B.** PT **C.** CT **D.** BT

Q.60 Reed Sternberg cells are found in

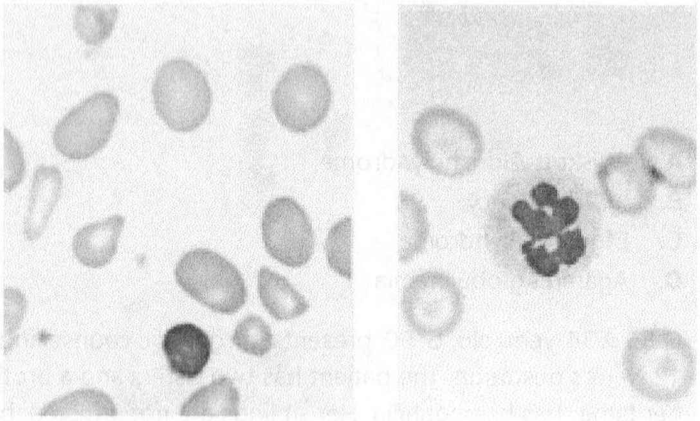

[NEET PG, 2018]

A. Hodgkin's disease **B.** Sickle cell anaemia
C. Thalassemia **D.** CML

Q.61 Best prognostic type of Hodgkin's lymphoma is -

A. Lymphocytic predominant
B. Lymphocytic depletion
C. Mixed cellularity
D. Nodular sclerosis

Q.62 The collapse of the lung is called

A. Emphysema **B.** Bronchiectasis
C. Atelectasis **D.** Bronchitis

Q.63 The protein in glomerular basement membrane responsible for charge-dependent filtration is -

A. Albumin **B.** Collagen type IV
C. Proteoglycan **D.** Fibronectin

Q.64 Mallory Weiss Syndrome is caused due to tear in -

A. The lower esophageal end
B. Crico pharyngeal junction
C. Gastroesophageal junction
D. None of the above

Q.65 Hepatic infarcts are seen in -

A. Pre-eclampsia
B. Chronic venous congestion
C. Shock
D. All of the above

Q.66 Which of the following testicular tumor is not a germ cell neoplasm -

A. Seminoma **B.** Yolk sac tumor
C. Sertoli cell tumor **D.** Teratoma

Q.67 Which of the following joint is characteristically involved in RA. -

A. Spine
B. Sacroiliac joint
C. Metacarpophalangeal joint and proximal interphalangeal joint
D. Wrist joint

Q.68 Neuroglia answerable for phagocytosis is -

A. Fibrous Astrocytes
B. Protoplasmic Astrocytes
C. Oligodendrocytes
D. Microglia

Q.69 Which of the following syndrome is related to Medullary carcinoma of the thyroid.

A. MEN I
B. MEN II
C. Li–Fraumeni syndrome
D. Hashimoto's thyroiditis

Q.70 The highest hurtful potential is in -

A. Epidermal naevus **B.** Junctional naevus
C. Intradermal naevus **D.** None of the above

Q.71 The commonest type of spinal T. B. is -

A. Posterior **B.** Paradiscal
C. Pedicle **D.** Anterior

Q.72 Which of the following is not seen in primary tuberculosis-

A. Cavitation **B.** Caseation
C. Calcification **D.** Giant cell

Q.73 Metastasis in neuroblastoma goes to -

A. Liver **B.** Lung
C. Bone **D.** All of the above

Q.74 Which events in neuroblastoma is associated as 'good' outcome

A. Diploidy
B. N-myc amplification
C. Chromosome 1 p deletion
D. Trk A expression

Q.75 Which of the following conditions is related to Aniridia and Hemihypertrophy -

A. Neuroblastoma
B. Wilm's tumour
C. Non-Hodgkin's lymphoma
D. Germ cell tumour

Q.76 Metabolism of drugs is mostly done by which enzyme

A. Cytochrome C
B. Cytochrome P450
C. Glucuronyl transferase
D. Acetylase

Q.77 100% bioavailability is seen with which route

A. Oral **B.** Intravenous
C. Rectal **D.** Subcutaneous

Q.78 Which of the following is true?

A. As the concentration of the drug increases over the

therapeutic range, only the bound form of the drug increases

B. The bound form is not available for metabolism but is available for excretion

C. Acidic drugs bind to beta globulin and basic drugs bind to albumin

D. Binding sites are non–specific and one drug can displace the other

Q.79 Cholinomimetic drugs can be used for the treatment of all the following conditions EXCEPT:

A. Closed-angle Glaucoma

B. Bradycardia

C. Cobra bite

D. Myasthenia gravis

Q.80 Lid retraction is caused by?

A. Bimatoprost **B.** Latanoprost

C. Brimonidine **D.** Apraclonidine

Q.81 A pupillary dilator is provided by:

A. Postganglionic parasympathetic from Edinger Westphal nucleus

B. Postganglionic sympathetic from cervical sympathetic chain

C. Third cranial nerve

D. Sympathetic fibres of the front-orbital branch of the trigeminal nerve

Q.82 Which of the following drugs can cause hypotension by the release of histamine from mast cells?

A. Aspirin **B.** Procaine

C. Morphine **D.** Sulfadiazine

Q.83 Which of the following drugs can prolong survival in patients with CHF?

A. Furosemide **B.** Amrinone

C. Losartan **D.** Digoxin

Q.84 The site of action of the furosemide is

A. Descending limb of the loop of Henle

B. Thick ascending limb of the loop of Henle

C. Proximal convoluted tubule

D. Distal convoluted tubule

Q.85 Which of the following is not an adverse effect of growth hormone therapy?

A. Carpal tunnel syndrome

B. Hypoglycemia

C. Intracranial hypertension

D. Slipped femoral epiphysis

Q.86 The result of thiopentone on the CNS is rapidly aborted by reason of:

A. Rapid metabolism in the CNS

B. Quick first-pass elimination

C. Redistribution

D. Rapid metabolism in the systemic circulation

Q.87 To prevent exercise-induced bronchial asthma, a drug used is :

A. Sodium cromoglycate

B. Ipratropium bromide

C. Terbutaline

D. Epinephrine

Q.88 Which of the following drugs is not an antiemetic?

A. Ondansetron **B.** Domperidone

C. Metoclopramide **D.** Cinnarizine

Q.89 All of the following drugs are bactericidal except :

A. Isoniazid **B.** Tigecycline

C. Daptomycin **D.** Ciprofloxacin

Q.90 Remifentanil is :

A. Useful for short painful procedures

B. Metabolized by plasma esterases

C. Equipotent as fentanyl

D. All of these

Q.91 All are antithyroid drugs EXCEPT

A. Carbamazepine **B.** Propylthiouracil

C. Methimazole **D.** Carbimazole

Q.92 Bremelanotide is used for :

A. Erectile dysfunction

B. Lower urinary tract symptoms

C. Prostate Cancer

D. Metastatic renal cancer

Q.93 Which among the following does not cause hyperpyrexia? ***[NEET PG, 2014]***

A. MAO Inhibitors **B.** Alcohol

C. Atropine **D.** Amphetamine

Q.94 Which of the following drugs is NOT used in scabies?

A. Benzene hexachloride

B. Permethrin

C. Ciclopirox olamine

D. Crotamiton

Q.95 Prostaglandin analogues have therapeutic utility in the following EXCEPT :

A. Pulmonary hypertension

B. Palliative treatment of patent ductus arteriosus

C. Impotence

D. Inflammatory bowel disease

Q.96 Staining procedure shown in Photograph is used to visualize _______ of the bacterium

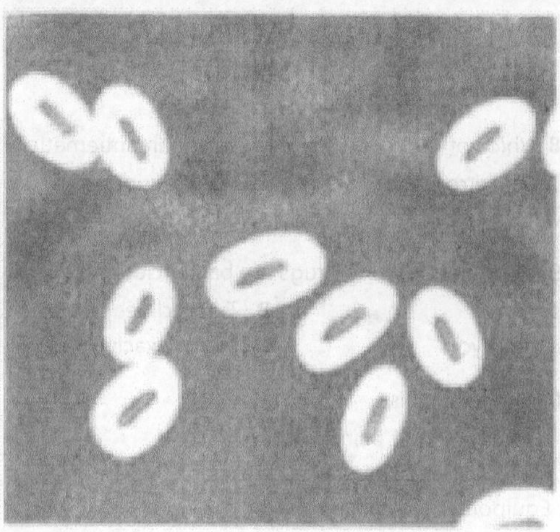

A. Nucleus **B.** Motility
C. Capsule **D.** Ribosomes

Q.97 Mycobacterium tuberculosis was discovered by -
A. Louis Pasteur **B.** Robert Koch
C. Lister **D.** Jenner

Q.98 To see the bacteria, the methods used are -
A. Microscopy
B. Stained preparations
C. Both
D. None of these

Q.99 All are peripheral lymphoid organs except -
A. Lymph nodes
B. Spleen
C. Thymus
D. Mucosa-associated lymphoid tissue

Q.100 B cell maturation takes place in -
A. Thymus **B.** Lymph node
C. Bone marrow **D.** Spleen

Q.101 Innate immunity active against viral cells -
A. NK cells **B.** Cytotoxic T cells
C. B cell **D.** Memory B cell

Q.102 In an inflammatory response, macrophages are usually derived from -
A. Monocytes
B. Reticuloendothelial cells
C. Neutrophils
D. Lymphocytes

Q.103 Which of the following is gram-positive bacillus-
A. Staphylococcus **B.** Streptococcus
C. Listeria **D.** Meningococci

Q.104 "Genital elephantiasis" is caused by all except
A. Lymphogranuloma venereum
B. Chancroid
C. Syphilis
D. Rickettsia

Q.105 Blood culture is positive in which infection of staph. aureus-
A. TSS
B. SSSS
C. Infective endocarditis
D. Impetigo

Q.106 DNA covering material in a virus is called as -
A. Capsomere **B.** Capsid
C. Nucleocapsid **D.** Envelope

Q.107 Both intranuclear and cytoplasmic inclusion is seen in -
A. Poxvirus **B.** Herpesvirus
C. Measles virus **D.** Mumps virus

Q.108 The appearance of cow dry type A inclusion bodies -
A. Granular **B.** Circumscribed
C. In polio **D.** None of these

Q.109 River blindness is caused by:
A. Trichomonas
B. Trichuris
C. Onchocerca volvulus
D. Dracunculus

Q.110 Non-gonococcal urethritis is mostly caused by:
A. Chlamydia and mycoplasma
B. Chlamydia and Streptococcus
C. Chlamydia and treponema
D. Chlamydia and ureaplasama

Q.111 Which of the following acts as an intermediate host of malaria a parasite?
A. Culex **B.** Female anopheles
C. Human **D.** Trombiculid mite

Q.112 The fungi which do not have a sexual phase belong to which of the following groups -
A. Phycomycetes **B.** Fungi Imperfecti
C. Basidiomycetes **D.** Ascomycetes

Q.113 Spherule is a feature of which of the following fungus
A. Blastomyces **B.** Histoplasma
C. Paracoccidioides **D.** Coccidioides

Q.114 Bacteria showing antigenic variation -
A. Yersinia **B.** Bordetella
C. Brucella **D.** Borrelia

Q.115 A most common organism which can contaminate crowded army camps is?
A. Klebsiella
B. E. coli
C. Neisseria meningitidis
D. Staphylococcus

Q.116 Dowry as a punishable offence under IPC act -
A. 304 A **B.** 304 B **C.** 420 **D.** 498

Q.117 Duret Haemorrhage is seen in:
A. Lung **B.** Spleen **C.** Liver **D.** Brain

Q.118 Perjury means giving willful false evidence by a witness while under oath, the witness is liable to be prosecuted for perjury and the imprisonment may extend to 7 years. This falls under which section of IPC?

A. 190 of Indian Penal Code
B. 191 of Indian Penal Code
C. 192 of Indian Penal Code
D. 198 of Indian Penal Code

Q.119 Which of the following offence related to the 509-IPC act-

A. Masturbation in a public place
B. Inquest
C. Dowry death
D. Act intended to insult the modesty of a women

Q.120 Which of the following is related to "Tentative cuts"?

A. Homicide **B.** Accidents
C. Fall from height **D.** Suicide

Q.121 Heat stabilizing in muscles happens overhead temperature (°C) -

A. 30 **B.** 60 **C.** 40 **D.** 50

Q.122 In the case of Hanging neck ligature marks are an example of

A. Bruise **B.** Pressure abrasion
C. Laceration **D.** None of the above

Q.123 Lynching is -

A. Practised in South America
B. Practised by white people on Negros
C. Hanging publically on a tree
D. All of the above

Q.124 In which of the following BAL is not used to treat poisoning due to

A. Organic mercury **B.** Arsenic
C. Lead **D.** Cadmium

Q.125 Eonism is -

A. Desire to identify with the opposite sex
B. Intercourse with a lower animal
C. Female homosexualism
D. Oral sex

Q.126 An Optimal healthy life includes -

A. Moderate physical exercise
B. Sufficient nutrition
C. Mental peace
D. All of the above

Q.127 Missing cases are detected by?

A. Active surveillance
B. Passive surveillance
C. Monitoring
D. Sentinel surveillance

Q.128 All are measurements of mortality except -

A. Crude death rate **B.** Survival rate
C. Incidence **D.** Case fatality rate

Q.129 The Burden of disease is given by -

A. Incidence
B. Crude death rate
C. Cause-specific death rate
D. Proportional mortality rate

Q.130 Any abnormality of anatomical function is-

A. Disease **B.** Impairment
C. Disability **D.** Handicap

Q.131 There is a disease in which overall survival is increased by screening procedure is-

A. Prostate Cancer **B.** Lung Cancer
C. Colon Cancer **D.** Ovarian Cancer

Q.132 In the birth weight of each of the 10 babies born in a hospital in a day is found to be 2.8 kgs, then the standard deviation of this sample will be -

A. 2.8 **B.** 0 **C.** 1 **D.** 0.28

Q.133 A Scatter diagram is drawn to study

A. The trend of a variable over a period of time
B. Frequency of occurrence of events
C. Relationship between two given variables
D. Mean & median values of the given data

Q.134 Measles is infectious during -

A. After 4 days of rash
B. 4 days before and 5 days after the rash
C. Throughout disease
D. Only in the incubation period

Q.135 Which is not a complication of chickenpox -

A. Pancreatitis **B.** Pneumonia
C. Encephalitis **D.** Thrombocytopenia

Q.136 From the following options given below, which one is recognized to do the screening of the school children firstly, under NPCB?

A. Medical officer
B. Ophthalmologic assistant
C. Village health guide
D. School teachers

Q.137 Under the National Programme for Control of Blindness, the goal is to reduce the prevalence of blindness to a level of -

A. 0.1% **B.** 0.3% **C.** 0.5% **D.** 1%

Q.138 Widely practised method of family planning by capable partners in India is -

A. IUCD **B.** OC Pill
C. Sterilization **D.** Nirodh

Q.139 What is the mechanism of action of Glatiramer?

A. Antifungal **B.** Immunomodulator
C. Antiviral **D.** Antibacterial

Q.140 Which of the following statements is not true about breast milk-

A. The maximum milk output is seen at 12 months
B. The coefficient of uptake of iron in breast milk is 70%
C. Calcium absorption of human milk is better than that of

cow's milk

D. It provides about 65 kcals per 100 ml

Q.141 The undersupply in weight for height in a 4 years old child specifies –

A. Acute malnutrition

B. Chronic malnutrition

C. Concomitant acute and chronic

D. Underweight

Q.142 Groundwater has the following advantages except –

A. Likely to be free from pathogenic organisms

B. Usually requires no treatment

C. Supply is likely to be certain even during the dry season

D. Likely to be hard

Q.143 The recommended concentration of iodine in iodised salt at the consumer level is:

A. 20 ppm B. 15 ppm C. 10 ppm D. 5 ppm

Q.144 Additional daily energy requirement during the first six months of a lactating woman is -

A. 350 Kcalories B. 600 Kcalories

C. 550 Kcalories D. 450 Kcalories

Q.145 The incidence of mental illness is the maximum if the causal factors affect a particular period –

A. Perinatal period

B. First five years of life

C. School age

D. Adolescence

Q.146 Average hospital waste produced per bed per day in Government hospital –

A. 1.5-2.0 kg B. 0.5–4 kg

C. 0.5–1 kg D. 0.5–2 kg

Q.147 Following are used in the planning of Health education except –

A. Cover felt needs

B. Using simple words

C. Catchy slogans

D. Ensuring participation

Q.148 Which anti-cancer drug is eliminated by lung:

A. Cyclophosphamide B. 5-FU

C. Enalapril D. Cisplatin

Q.149 Follow–up of cataract operations in the national blindness control program is done by –

A. Active surveillance

B. Passive surveillance

C. Sentinel surveillance

D. Routine check-up

Q.150 The community is described as -

A. A conglomeration people

B. A group of people bound with social norms

C. An association with regulated membership

D. An association patterned the norms of interaction

Part C

Q.151 SIADH- all are features except -

A. Decreased sodium, maintaining the concentrating ability of the urine osmolality (> 100 mOsm)

B. Normal sodium balance maintained indicating excess urinary sodium is due to efficient sodium intake

C. Hypouricemia

D. Low blood pressure due to volume depletion

Q.152 Cardiogenic shock occurs as a result of:

A. Excessive vasodilation and possibly increased capillary permeability.

B. Severe central nervous system trauma that causes a rapid loss in sympathetic stimulation.

C. Reduction in intravascular fluid volume.

D. Myocardial dysfunction.

Q.153 Features of glomerular haematuria -

A. Full of R.B.C. in the high power field

B. Fragmented R.B.C.

C. Dysmorphic R.B.C.

D. Gross haematuria

Q.154 32-year-old AIDS-positive female presented with headaches and nuchal stiffness. On lumbar puncture examination clear CSF was obtained with leucocytes >100/cu.mm. India ink staining was positive. The most probable diagnosis is?

A. Candida Meningitis

B. Cryptococcus meningitis

C. Tubercular Meningitis

D. Cryptosporidium

Q.155 All are present in Fragile X syndrome-

a) FMR

b) Microorchidism

c) Large facies

d) Small ear

A. cd B. ab C. ac D. bd

Q.156 The chance that a health worker gets HIV from an accidental needle prick is -

A. 1% B. 10% C. 95% D. 100%

Q.157 Which is NOT a function of muscles?

A. Cause movement B. Produce heat

C. Absorb nutrients D. Maintain posture

Q.158 Pulsus Bigeminus is seen in therapy with -

A. Beta-blockers

B. ACE inhibitors

C. Digitalis

D. Calcium channel blockers

Q.159 Which of these statements regarding the conduction system of the heart is TRUE

A. The sinoatrial (SA) node of the heart acts as the pacemaker.

B. The SA node is located on the upper wall of the left atrium.

C. The AV node conducts action potentials rapidly through it.

D. Action potentials are carried slowly through the atrioventricular bundle.

Q.160 Which of the following stands for the statement, "Atrioventricular valves open and semilunar valves close during the Ventricular Systole"

A. True
B. False
C. Partially true
D. Partially false

Q.161 Which of these statements correctly applies to intrinsic regulation of the heart?

A. Starling's law of the heart has a major influence on cardiac output.
B. As venous return increases, cardiac output decreases.
C. In response to stretch, cardiac muscle fibers contract with less force.
D. In response to stretch, there is a slight decrease in heart rate.

Q.162 Management of essential hypertension is?

A. No need to treat
B. Diet modification alone
C. Diet modification and drug
D. Invasive surgery

Q.163 In Wilsons disease, copper deposition occurs in -

A. Pons
B. Medulla
C. Cerebellum
D. Basal ganglia

Q.164 The net diffusion of water from one solution of water from one solution through a semipermeable membrane to another solution containing a lower concentration of water is termed-

A. Filtration
B. Diffusion
C. Osmosis
D. Brownian motion

Q.165 CLL is characterized by?

A. Small lymphocytes in peripheral smear
B. Seen commonly in age >50 years persons
C. Hepatosplenomegaly
D. All of the above

Q.166 Desmosomes are helpful in connecting –

A. Keratinocytes
B. Melanocytes
C. Dermis and epidermis
D. Langerhans cells

Q.167 True about stratum lucidum –

a) Sandwiched between S. spinosum and S.granulosum
b) Sandwiched between S. corneum and S.granulosum
c) Contain hair follicle
d) Also known as prickle cell layer
e) Contain degenerated cells

A. ab
B. be
C. ad
D. ce

Q.168 Hypopigmented patches occur in -

A. Becker naevus
B. Freckles
C. Nevus anemicus
D. Nevus Ota

Q.169 An increased incidence of vitiligo is found is –

A. Psoriasis
B. Nutritional deficiency
C. Old age
D. Diabetes mellitus

Q.170 Dennie–Morgan line occurs in –

A. Dermatomyositis
B. SLE
C. Psoriasis vulgaris
D. Atopic dermatitis

Q.171 The most common cause of Airborn Dermatitis in India is –

A. Parthenium
B. Calotropis
C. Dust
D. None of these

Q.172 A most common type of psoriasis –

A. Plaque psoriasis
B. Psoriasis vulgaris
C. Both (A) and (B)
D. Penile psoriasis

Q.173 Auspitz sign is characteristically seen in –

A. Plaque psoriasis
B. Pustular psoriasis
C. Lichen planus
D. Inverse psoriasis

Q.174 A 30-year-old male had severely itchy papula–vesicular lesions on extremities, knees, elbows, and buttocks for one year. tired immunofluorescence staining of the lesions showed IgA deposition at the dermo-epidermal junction. The most probable diagnosis is –

A. Pemphigus vulgaris
B. Bullous pemphigoid
C. Dermatitis herpetiform
D. Nummular eczema

Q.175 A-85 year-old woman with Nikolsky sign–ve, blisters on thigh & trunk, lesions come on & off. What is the cause –

A. Pemphigus vulgaris
B. Pemphigoid
C. Lichen planus
D. Dermatitis herpetiformis

Q.176 Inverted saucer-shaped lesion is found in –

A. Lepromatous leprosy
B. Tuberculoid leprosy
C. Borderline leprosy
D. Indeterminate leprosy

Q.177 About tuberculoid leprosy, false is-

A. Pale-coloured skin
B. CMI is increased
C. A single anaesthetic patch
D. None of these

Q.178 Multiple painful ulcers over glans without in duration is suggestive of –

A. LGV
B. Granuloma inguinale
C. Chancroid
D. 2° syphilis

Q.179 The genital ulcer is seen in A/E –

A. Granuloma inguinale
B. Syphillis

C. LGV
D. Donovanosis

Q.180 Cafe au lait spots seen in?
A. NF
B. Gardner syndrome
C. Cockayne syndrome
D. Down syndrome

Q.181 The Stain used for staining fungal elements –
A. Acid-fast stain B. Mucicarmic
C. Methenamine D. Gram stain

Q.182 Which does not cause Tinea capitis –
A. Epidermophyton
B. Microsporum
C. Trichophyton rubrum
D. Trichophyton violaceum

Q.183 In which of the following, the disturbed orientation is observed
A. Schizophrenia
B. Neurosis
C. Paranoid personality
D. Organic mental disorder

Q.184 Which of the following behavioral problems would suggest an organic brain lesion -
A. Formal thought disorder
B. Auditory hallucinations
C. Visual hallucinations
D. Depression

Q.185 A 16-year-old boy suffering from drug abuse presents with a cross-over of sensory perceptions, such that, sounds can be seen and colors can be heard. Which of the following is that the most likely agent responsible for drug abuse
A. Cocaine B. LSD
C. Marijuana D. PCP

Q.186 Which of the following is not seen in morphine poisoning-
A. Cyanosis
B. Pinpoint pupil
C. Hypertension
D. Respiratory depression

Q.187 Somatic passivity is a feature of-
A. Depressive illness
B. Paranoid Schizophrenia
C. Hypochondriasis
D. Panic disorder

Q.188 Which of the following hallucinations is pathognomonic of schizophrenia -
A. Auditory hallucinations commanding the patient
B. Auditory hallucinations giving running commentry
C. Auditory hallucinations criticizing the patient
D. Auditory hallucinations talking to patient

Q.189 Which of the following conditions is classified under anxiety disorders according to DSM-III
A. Obsessive-compulsive disorder
B. Depression
C. Schizophrenia
D. Bipolar disorder

Q.190 Which of the following is not found in conversion disorder?
A. Jealousy B. Paralysis
C. Anaesthesia D. Abnormal gait

Q.191 Not true about narcolepsy -
A. Sleep sudden
B. Long duration (>3 hrs) of sleep
C. Catapplexy
D. All of the above

Q.192 All are features of autistic disorder except -
A. Mental retardation
B. Absent social smile
C. Onset before 21/2 years
D. Third-person hallucination

Q.193 Electroconvulsive therapy is currently advocated as a line of treatment in the following conditions except -
A. Catatonic schizophrenia
B. Severe depression with psychosis
C. Manic-depressive disorder
D. Obsessive-compulsive disorder

Q.194 Which of the following is a stage of intuitive thought appeared in the jean-Piaget scheme -
A. Sensorimotor
B. Concrete
C. Preoperational stage
D. Formal operations stage

Q.195 Best drug therapy for paranoid schizophrenia in a thinly built 21-years old young male would be-
A. Chlorpromazine B. Risperidone
C. Olanzapine D. Quetiapine

Q.196 March fracture is-
A. Fracture of 4th metatarsal
B. Fracture of 2nd metatarsal
C. Fracture of cuboids
D. Fracture of tibia

Q.197 Callus formation is seen between what duration of fracture healing
A. 0 - 2 weeks B. 2 - 4 weeks
C. 4 - 12 weeks D. 12 -16 weeks

Q.198 Most common muscle damaged in rotator cuff-
A. Supraspinatus B. Infraspinatus
C. Subscapularis D. Teres minor

Q.199 Bankart's lesion is seen at -
A. Post surface of the glenoid labrum
B. Anterior surface of glenoid labrum

C. The Anterior part of the head of the humerus
D. Post part of the head of the humerus

Q.200 If a patient with a suspected fracture of the pelvis has some bleeding from the urethra and is unable to pass urine -
A. He should be encouraged to pass urine after being given antibiotics and analgesics
B. He should be immediately catheterized in the ward
C. A hot water bottle should be given followed by an injection of corbachol
D. He should be prepared for surgery and catheterization attempted in the 0.T

Q.201 Which of the following is the main source to supply blood in the head and neck of the femur?
A. Lateral circumflex femoral Artery
B. Medial circumflex femoral Artery
C. Artery of Ligamentum Teres
D. Popliteal Artery

Q.202 For which fracture, the tube (cylinder) is applied-
A. Shoulder B. Hip C. Pelvis D. Knee

Q.203 All are true regarding whiplash injury except -
A. The Lumbar spine is commonly involved
B. Fractures do not usually cause difficulties
C. A relatively common injury that occurs to a person's neck
D. Hyperextension injury

Q.204 Greenstick fracture is
A. Fracture in adults B. Complete fracture
C. Incomplete fracture D. Fracture spine

Q.205 An 11 years old male having pain in left hip & stumbling on examination constricted abduction & internal rotation, probable diagnosis is -
A. Septic arthritis of the hip
B. Tuberculous arthritis of the hip
C. Congenital dislocation of the hip
D. Perthes disease

Q.206 Reduced digestion of Epiphyseal plate in a growing child occurs in -
A. Rickets B. Osteomalacia
C. Scurvy D. Osteoporosis

Q.207 In Bony ankylosis, there is -
A. Painless, No movement
B. Painful complete movement
C. Painless complete movement
D. Painful incomplete movement

Q.208 The classification system of bone tumours is -
A. Enneking B. Manchester
C. Edmonton D. TNM

Q.209 Type of collagen found in bone is
A. Type 2 B. Type 3 C. Type 4 D. Type 1

Q.210 The contraindication to internal fixation -
A. Physical injury
B. Active infection
C. Intraarticular fracture
D. Fracture dislocation

Q.211 Safety pin index for oxygen cylinder is
A. 3,5 B. 1,5 C. 2,5 D. 1,4

Q.212 Bag and mask ventilation is absolutely contraindicated in –
A. Tracheoesophageal fistula with esophageal atresia and esophagus connected to the trachea
B. Diaphragmatic hernia
C. Meconium aspiration
D. All of the above

Q.213 All of the following are except- advantages of LMA
A. More reliable than a face mask
B. Prevent aspiration
C. Alternative to Endotracheal intubation
D. Does not require a laryngoscope & Visualization

Q.214 A Patient is on regular medications for co-existing medical problems. Which of the following drugs may be stopped safely with minimal risk of adverse effects before an abdominal surgery –
A. Statins
B. Beta Blockers
C. ACE inhibitors/ACE Receptor Blockers
D. Steroids

Q.215 Glycopyrrolate is beer than atropine because –
A. It crosses the blood-brain barrier
B. Not crosses the blood-brain barrier
C. More sedation
D. Antisialague

Q.216 Which of the following is the SAFEST test to be performed in a patient with acutely injured knee joint -
A. Lachmann test
B. Pivot shift test
C. McMurray's test
D. Apley's grinding test

Q.217 A 23-year-old lady with a past of hypersensitivity to neostigmine is displayed for a constituent caesarean part under general anaesthesia. The best muscle intoxicant of choice in this patient should be –
A. Pancuronium B. Atracurium
C. Rocuronium D. Vecuronium

Q.218 Succinylcholine is a muscle relaxant which acts by –
A. Persistent depolarisation
B. Competitive antagonist
C. Mechanism of action uncertain
D. Both (A) and (B)

Q.219 In a young patient who had extensive soft tissue and muscle injury, which of these muscle relaxants used for endotracheal intubation might lead to cardiac arrest –
A. Atracurium B. Suxamethonium
C. Vecuronium D. Pancuronium

Q.220 Commonly used route of administration for general anaesthesia is –

A. Inhalational **B.** Intravenous
C. Intra-arterial **D.** Subcutaneous

Q.221 Thiopentone is used for induction anaesthesia because it is –

A. An ultra-short-acting barbiturate
B. Rapidly redistributed to body fat
C. Rapid redistribution
D. Easy to monitor

Q.222 Among the following anaesthetic drug/inducing agents which should be avoided in a patient with a history of epilepsy-

A. Propofol **B.** Thiopentone
C. Ketamine **D.** Midazolam

Q.223 From which of the following routes absorption of local anaesthetic is maximum?

A. Intercostal **B.** Epidural
C. Bronchial **D.** Caudal

Q.224 Which of the following drugs are believed to be effective in the treatment of postoperative shivering?

A. Ondansetron **B.** Diclofenac Sodium
C. Pethidine **D.** Paracetamol

Q.225 End-tidal CO_2 is increased to the maximum level in –

A. Pulmonary embolism
B. Malignant hyperthermia
C. Extubation
D. Blockage of secretion

Q.226 The concentration of colour in Fetal Doppler is resolved by -

A. Direction flow
B. Velocity of flow
C. Strength of returning echo
D. None of the above

Q.227 True about MRI are all except

A. Not helpful in a breast implant
B. Not good for calcified lesions
C. No radiation exposure
D. Contraindicated in cardiac pacemaker

Q.228 Best investigation for Bronchiectasis is?

A. Chest X-Ray
B. MRI
C. Pulmonary Function Tests
D. HRCT

Q.229 Silhouetting of the left border of the heart (silhouette sign positive) on chest radiograph indicates what pathology

A. Upper lobe **B.** Hilar
C. Lingula **D.** Lower lobe

Q.230 In a Down's syndrome patient posted for surgery, the necessary preoperative investigation to be done is –

A. CT Brain
B. Echocardiography
C. Ultrasound Abdomen
D. X-ray cervical spine

Q.231 A symptomless old patient introduces noise in the carotid artery. Which of the following is the inspection of possibility?

A. Doppler ultrasonography
B. Internal carotid angiography
C. Aortic arch angiography
D. Spiral CT angiography

Q.232 Which of the following is the earliest sign of ulcerative colitis on double-contrast barium enema study -

A. Mucosal granularity
B. Loss of haustrations
C. 'Collar - button' ulcer
D. Lead pipe colon

Q.233 The string of beads appearance on abdominal X-ray is seen in –

A. Small bowel obstruction
B. Large bowel obstruction
C. Carcinoma of stomach
D. Gastric outlet obstruction

Q.234 In Renal cell carcinoma investigation of choice to evaluate inferior vena cava & renal vein for thrombus –

A. IVP **B.** Coloured doppler
C. USG **D.** CT scan

Q.235 The inspection of the solution for viewing of urinary tract tuberculosis (UTTB) is –

A. Plain film X-ray
B. Intravenous urography
C. Ultrasound
D. Computed tomography

Q.236 X-ray features of hypoparathyroidism are the following except –

A. Osteosclerosis
B. Calvarial thickening
C. Subperiosteol resorption
D. Subcutaneous calcification

Q.237 Hair-on end appearance is seen in –

A. Thalassemia
B. Sickle cell anemia
C. Hemochromatosis
D. Megaloblastic anemia

Q.238 Subdural hematoma most commonly results from –

A. Rupture of intracranial aneurysm
B. Injury to cortical bridging veins
C. Rupture of cerebral AVM
D. Haemophilia

Q.239 Phosphorous 32 emits

A. Beta particle **B.** Alpha particle
C. Neutron **D.** X-rays

Q.240 Which of the following is the best technique for differentiating repetition of brain tumour from dispersion therapy-convinced necrosis?

A. MRI
B. Contrast enhanced MRI
C. PET scan
D. CT scan

Q.241 Conjugate of the diagonal is taken as 'a' cm, then obstetric conjugate will be

A. a + 1 cm **B.** a + 2 cm **C.** a - 1 cm **D.** a - 2 cm

Q.242 Time taken for spermatogenesis is (according to tritium-labeled biopsies)

A. 40-50 days **B.** 60-70 days
C. 90-120 days **D.** 70-80 days

Q.243 In which of the following transition meiosis occurs

A. Primary to secondary spermatocyte
B. Second spermatocyte to globular spermatid
C. Germ cells to spermatogonium
D. Spermatogonium to primary spermatocyte

Q.244 Blood transfusion is indicated in the following condition with sickle cell anemia

A. Frequent sickling episodes
B. Twin pregnancy
C. Poor obstetrical outcome
D. All of the above

Q.245 Most delicate test for the observation of iron exhaustion in pregnancy is-

A. Serum iron-binding capacity
B. Serum transferrin
C. Serum iron
D. Serum ferritin

Q.246 Chaser Moir surgery is done is a case of

A. Uterine inversion
B. Vesicovaginal fistula repair
C. Ureterovesical fistula repair
D. Retroverted uterus

Q.247 Post-term labor is seen in:

A. Anencephaly **B.** PID
C. Hydramnios **D.** Multiple pregnancy

Q.248 Best drug for a type of glaucoma shown in the photograph is:

A. Physostigmine **B.** Pilocarpine
C. Latanoprost **D.** Apraclonidine

Q.249 Risk of sear rupture in the classical cesarean section is –

A. 0.9%-12% **B.** 5%-4%
C. 9%- 10% **D.** 4%-9%

Q.250 IUGR is seen in:

A. Rubella **B.** Syphilis
C. CMV **D.** All of the above

Q.251 Best parameter for ultrasound evaluation of IUGR is:

A. Placental membrane
B. Length of femur
C. Abdominal circumference
D. BPD

Q.252 A large baby is born with which complication in pregnancy:

A. Gestational diabetes
B. Gestational hypertension
C. Anaemia
D. None of the above

Q.253 In which of the following, the Oxytocin challenge test for assessing fetal well-being is not contraindicated.

A. Placenta previa **B.** Previous 2 LSCS
C. Breech **D.** Premature labour

Q.254 Sinusoidal heart rate pattern is seen in:

A. Placenta previa
B. Vasa previa
C. Battledore placenta
D. Succenturiate placenta

Q.255 All are an explanation for decreased variability of the fetal heart tracing except-

A. Fetal "sleep state"
B. Prematurity
C. Barbiturate ingestion
D. Fetal stimulation

Q.256 All of the following pelvic structures support the vagina, except:

A. Perineal body
B. Pelvic diaphragm
C. Levator ani muscle
D. Infundibulopelvic ligament

Q.257 True about the timing of LH surge

A. Occur 12 hours before ovulation
B. Occur 12 hours after ovulation
C. Occur 24 hours before ovulation
D. Occur 24 hours after ovulation

Q.258 The cutoff point of serum estrogen level for the diagnosis of ovarian failure:

A. 10 pg/ml **B.** 20 pg/ml **C.** 30 pg/ml **D.** 40 pg/ml

Q.259 False about PCOS:

A. Increased risk of diabetes mellitus
B. Bilateral ovarian cyst
C. Hirsutism
D. High FSH/LH ratio 1:2

Q.260 The vaginal epithelium is derived from:

A. Endoderm of genital ridge
B. Mesoderm of urogenital sinus
C. Endoderm of urogenital sinus
D. Mesoderm of genital ridge

Q.261 A 16-year-old girl with a height of 5 inches presents with primary amenorrhea and rising FSH. The histological finding most consistent with her conditions is?

A. Marfan syndrome
B. Corpus luteal hemorrhage
C. Low oocyte in ovary
D. Pituitary Apoplexy

Q.262 Minimum criteria to diagnose PID include(s):
A. Lower abdominal pain
B. Fever
C. Cervical motion tenderness
D. Leucocytosis

Q.263 Which of the following surgeries of stress incontinence has the long-term success rate is maximum with-
A. Stamey's repair
B. Burch's colposuspension
C. Kelly's stitch
D. Aldridge surgery

Q.264 What are the chances of a normally fertile couple having a baby in one month?
A. 80% B. 25% C. 60% D. 45%

Q.265 Contraceptive vaginal foam tablet "today "contains:
A. Nonoxynol 9 B. Octoxynol 9
C. Menfegol D. None of the above

Q.266 All are the complication of leiomyoma in pregnancy except?
A. Red degeneration B. Obstructed labour
C. PPH D. Placenta previa

Q.267 Best investigation endometriosis is:
A. Laparoscopy B. USG
C. X-ray pelvis D. CT Scan

Q.268 Endometrial hyperplasia is seen in-
A. Endodermal sinus tumor
B. Dysgerminoma
C. PCOD
D. Ca cervix

Q.269 CA 125 is elevated in all except :
A. Tuberculosis
B. Endometriosis
C. Ovarian tumor
D. Polycystic ovarian disease

Q.270 Menstruation is defined as precocious if it starts before the child reaches the age of:
A. 8 years B. 10 years C. 14 years D. 20 years

Q.271 True about head circumference measurement –
A. Measured in supra–orbital ridge
B. Measured hydrocephalus/microcephaly
C. Serial measurement is useful
D. All of these

Q.272 Newborn phase expands up to –
A. 21 days of life B. 30 days of life
C. 28 days of life D. 35 days of life

Q.273 An infant presents with cardiac failure. Examination reveals a weaker femoral pulse when compared to the radial pulse. What is the probable diagnosis?
A. PDA
B. Aorto-iliac vasculitis
C. COA
D. VSD

Q.274 The most common cause of pneumonia in children less than 2 years is?
A. RSV
B. Streptococcus aureus
C. Staphylococcus aureus
D. Klebsiella

Q.275 Congenital hypertrophic pyloric stenosis usually presents –
A. Within 2 days after birth
B. Around 1 week after birth
C. Around 2 weeks after birth
D. Around 2 months after birth

Q.276 Toxic megacolon is seen in –
A. Chronic nonspecific ulcerative colitis
B. Crohn's disease
C. Colonic diverticulosis
D. Hamartomatous polyp

Q.277 % of children with simple febrile seizures developing epilepsy is –
A. 1–2% B. 2–5% C. 5–10% D. 10–20%

Q.278 Which of the following statements is true regarding childhood hurtful is –
A. Wilm's tumour is the commonest
B. AML is the most common malignancy
C. Neuroblastoma arises in the first 4 years
D. None of the above

Q.279 "Haemoglobin E" (HbE) is common in –
A. Punjab B. Kerala
C. Bengal D. Maharashtra

Q.280 Multiple carboxylase deficiency is treated by--
A. Biotin B. Pyridoxine
C. Thiamine D. Folic acid

Q.281 The first branch of the facial nerve is -
A. Greater petrosal nerve
B. Lesser petrosal nerve
C. Chorda-tympani nerve
D. Nerve to the stapedius

Q.282 Lacrimation is affected when facial nerve injury is at -
A. Geniculate ganglion
B. In semicircular canal
C. At sphenopalatine ganglion
D. None of these

Q.283 Dryness of the eye is caused by injury to the facial nerve at-

A. Chorda tympani
B. Cerebellopontine angle
C. Tympanic canal
D. Geniculate ganglion

Q.284 Killian's dehiscence is seen in -
A. Oropharynx **B.** Nasopharynx
C. Cricopharynx **D.** Vocal cords

Q.285 Treatment of Puberphonia is
A. Thyroplasty type III **B.** Thyroplasty type I
C. Thyroplasty type II **D.** Thyroplasty type IV

Q.286 The voice in a patient with Bilateral abductor paralysis of the larynx is
A. Puberphonia
B. Phonasthenia
C. Dysphonia plicae ventricularis
D. Normal or good voice

Q.287 Ranula is -
A. Hypertrophied lymphoid tissue
B. Arises from mucosa of floor of mouth
C. Hard and Hemorrhagic
D. An abscess

Q.288 All are precancerous lesions of oral cavity except -
A. Leukoplakia
B. Erythroplakia
C. Diffuse oral submucous fibrosis
D. Diffuse aphthous ulcers

Q.289 What is the treatment of choice for ethmoidal polyps?
A. Functional Endoscopic sinus surgery with polypectomy
B. Intranasal ethmoidectomy
C. Extra nasal ethmoidectomy
D. Transanal ethmoidectomy

Q.290 Radical mastoidectomy is done for -
A. ASOM
B. CSOM
C. Atticoantral cholesteatoma
D. Acute mastoiditis

Q.291 The axial length of the eyeball at birth is .... % of an adult eye –
A. 100 **B.** 90 **C.** 70 **D.** 40

Q.292 Pinhole can reduce refractive error up to -
A. 3 D **B.** 1 D **C.** 5 D **D.** 10 D

Q.293 A SAFE strategy is for?
A. Bacterial conjunctivitis
B. Viral conjunctivitis
C. Onchocercariasis
D. Trachoma

Q.294 Which of the following organism can penetrate the normal cornea –
a) Gonococcus
b) Pseudomonas
c) Diphtheria
d) Streptococcus
e) Staphylococcus epidermidis
A. a **B.** bc **C.** ad **D.** ac

Q.295 Signs of uveitis –
a) Generalized conjunctival congestion
b) Circumciliary congestion
c) Cells and flare in aqueous
d) Shallow anterior chamber
A. a **B.** c **C.** ac **D.** bc

Q.296 Which of the following statements is correct in regard to aqueous humour-
A. It is secreted at a rate of 2–3 microL/min
B. Secreted by ciliary process
C. Has less protein than plasma
D. All of the above

Q.297 Soft exudates are found in –
A. DM **B.** HTN
C. Toxemia **D.** All of these

Q.298 All are true about optic nerve except -
a) Arises from axons of bipolar neurons
b) 4 cm long
c) Covered by 3 layers continuous with meninges
d) Crossed by the ophthalmic artery
A. ac **B.** ab **C.** ad **D.** bc

Q.299 Bitemporal hemianopia field defect is characteristic of -
A. Glaucoma **B.** Optic neuritis
C. Pituitary tumour **D.** Retinal detachment

Q.300 The function of superior oblique muscle -
A. Intortion **B.** Extortion
C. Lateral rotation **D.** Upward rotation

// Smart Answer Sheet //

Correct Percentage of students who answered correctly. **Skipped** Percentage of students who skipped.

Q.	Ans.	Correct	Skipped	Q.	Ans.	Correct	Skipped	Q.	Ans.	Correct	Skipped	Q.	Ans.	Correct	Skipped	Q.	Ans.	Correct	Skipped	Q.	Ans.	Correct	Skipped
1	D	15.0 %	5.0 %	22	B	2.5 %	55.0 %	43	B	25.0 %	55.0 %	64	D	2.5 %	62.5 %	85	B	10.0 %	62.5 %	106	B	20.0 %	62.5 %
2	B	37.5 %	47.5 %	23	A	32.5 %	55.0 %	44	A	30.0 %	55.0 %	65	D	32.5 %	62.5 %	86	C	12.5 %	65.0 %	107	C	20.0 %	62.5 %
3	B	12.5 %	50.0 %	24	C	12.5 %	57.5 %	45	A	27.5 %	55.0 %	66	C	22.5 %	62.5 %	87	A	25.0 %	62.5 %	108	A	17.5 %	62.5 %
4	A	20.0 %	52.5 %	25	B	27.5 %	55.0 %	46	D	10.0 %	57.5 %	67	C	32.5 %	62.5 %	88	D	35.0 %	62.5 %	109	C	30.0 %	62.5 %
5	C	5.0 %	52.5 %	26	C	30.0 %	55.0 %	47	A	5.0 %	57.5 %	68	D	17.5 %	62.5 %	89	B	12.5 %	62.5 %	110	D	20.0 %	62.5 %
6	B	17.5 %	52.5 %	27	A	35.0 %	55.0 %	48	B	25.0 %	57.5 %	69	B	25.0 %	62.5 %	90	D	27.5 %	62.5 %	111	C	25.0 %	62.5 %
7	A	32.5 %	50.0 %	28	C	17.5 %	57.5 %	49	B	10.0 %	57.5 %	70	B	17.5 %	62.5 %	91	A	32.5 %	62.5 %	112	B	12.5 %	65.0 %
8	A	15.0 %	52.5 %	29	B	5.0 %	55.0 %	50	D	17.5 %	55.0 %	71	B	10.0 %	62.5 %	92	A	12.5 %	62.5 %	113	D	12.5 %	62.5 %
9	C	10.0 %	50.0 %	30	A	22.5 %	57.5 %	51	A	22.5 %	57.5 %	72	A	20.0 %	62.5 %	93	B	12.5 %	62.5 %	114	D	5.0 %	62.5 %
10	A	27.5 %	50.0 %	31	A	30.0 %	55.0 %	52	D	30.0 %	60.0 %	73	D	25.0 %	62.5 %	94	C	27.5 %	62.5 %	115	C	12.5 %	62.5 %
11	A	30.0 %	50.0 %	32	C	30.0 %	55.0 %	53	B	22.5 %	62.5 %	74	D	7.5 %	62.5 %	95	B	7.5 %	62.5 %	116	B	20.0 %	62.5 %
12	D	5.0 %	52.5 %	33	D	30.0 %	55.0 %	54	C	17.5 %	62.5 %	75	B	17.5 %	62.5 %	96	C	25.0 %	62.5 %	117	D	17.5 %	62.5 %
13	C	25.0 %	55.0 %	34	A	20.0 %	55.0 %	55	B	22.5 %	62.5 %	76	B	32.5 %	62.5 %	97	B	32.5 %	62.5 %	118	D	7.5 %	62.5 %
14	A	7.5 %	52.5 %	35	B	10.0 %	55.0 %	56	D	20.0 %	62.5 %	77	B	32.5 %	62.5 %	98	C	32.5 %	62.5 %	119	D	20.0 %	62.5 %
15	D	17.5 %	52.5 %	36	D	30.0 %	55.0 %	57	B	15.0 %	62.5 %	78	D	10.0 %	65.0 %	99	C	22.5 %	62.5 %	120	D	30.0 %	62.5 %
16	B	22.5 %	52.5 %	37	C	10.0 %	57.5 %	58	A	27.5 %	62.5 %	79	B	17.5 %	62.5 %	100	C	22.5 %	62.5 %	121	B	5.0 %	62.5 %
17	B	15.0 %	55.0 %	38	A	17.5 %	57.5 %	59	A	20.0 %	62.5 %	80	D	2.5 %	65.0 %	101	A	32.5 %	62.5 %	122	B	22.5 %	62.5 %
18	B	5.0 %	55.0 %	39	C	22.5 %	55.0 %	60	A	35.0 %	62.5 %	81	B	5.0 %	62.5 %	102	A	20.0 %	62.5 %	123	D	22.5 %	62.5 %
19	A	35.0 %	55.0 %	40	C	20.0 %	55.0 %	61	A	20.0 %	62.5 %	82	C	10.0 %	62.5 %	103	C	32.5 %	62.5 %	124	D	20.0 %	62.5 %
20	B	20.0 %	55.0 %	41	B	7.5 %	55.0 %	62	C	35.0 %	62.5 %	83	C	2.5 %	65.0 %	104	D	17.5 %	62.5 %	125	A	27.5 %	62.5 %
21	B	22.5 %	55.0 %	42	D	27.5 %	55.0 %	63	C	7.5 %	62.5 %	84	B	17.5 %	62.5 %	105	C	15.0 %	62.5 %	126	D	32.5 %	62.5 %

Q.	Ans.	Correct	Skipped	Q.	Ans.	Correct	Skipped	Q.	Ans.	Correct	Skipped	Q.	Ans.	Correct	Skipped	Q.	Ans.	Correct	Skipped	Q.	Ans.	Correct	Skipped
127	D	22.5 %	62.5 %	148	B	25.0 %	62.5 %	169	D	17.5 %	55.0 %	190	A	20.0 %	55.0 %	211	C	25.0 %	55.0 %	232	A	5.0 %	55.0 %
128	C	22.5 %	62.5 %	149	C	7.5 %	62.5 %	170	D	17.5 %	55.0 %	191	B	10.0 %	55.0 %	212	D	37.5 %	55.0 %	233	A	25.0 %	57.5 %
129	D	10.0 %	65.0 %	150	B	32.5 %	65.0 %	171	A	27.5 %	55.0 %	192	D	22.5 %	55.0 %	213	B	7.5 %	55.0 %	234	B	12.5 %	55.0 %
130	B	22.5 %	62.5 %	151	D	7.5 %	52.5 %	172	C	17.5 %	55.0 %	193	D	25.0 %	55.0 %	214	C	17.5 %	57.5 %	235	B	30.0 %	55.0 %
131	C	12.5 %	62.5 %	152	D	20.0 %	52.5 %	173	A	22.5 %	55.0 %	194	C	7.5 %	57.5 %	215	B	15.0 %	55.0 %	236	C	10.0 %	55.0 %
132	B	10.0 %	65.0 %	153	C	7.5 %	55.0 %	174	C	12.5 %	55.0 %	195	C	10.0 %	57.5 %	216	A	25.0 %	55.0 %	237	A	30.0 %	55.0 %
133	C	12.5 %	65.0 %	154	B	37.5 %	55.0 %	175	B	10.0 %	55.0 %	196	B	27.5 %	55.0 %	217	B	25.0 %	55.0 %	238	B	20.0 %	55.0 %
134	B	30.0 %	62.5 %	155	C	12.5 %	55.0 %	176	C	7.5 %	55.0 %	197	C	10.0 %	57.5 %	218	A	10.0 %	55.0 %	239	A	17.5 %	55.0 %
135	A	20.0 %	62.5 %	156	A	32.5 %	55.0 %	177	B	12.5 %	55.0 %	198	A	30.0 %	55.0 %	219	B	25.0 %	55.0 %	240	C	12.5 %	55.0 %
136	D	27.5 %	62.5 %	157	C	22.5 %	55.0 %	178	C	20.0 %	55.0 %	199	B	17.5 %	55.0 %	220	B	25.0 %	55.0 %	241	D	15.0 %	57.5 %
137	C	5.0 %	62.5 %	158	C	15.0 %	55.0 %	179	C	2.5 %	55.0 %	200	D	35.0 %	57.5 %	221	A	22.5 %	55.0 %	242	D	12.5 %	55.0 %
138	D	17.5 %	62.5 %	159	A	32.5 %	55.0 %	180	A	37.5 %	55.0 %	201	B	35.0 %	55.0 %	222	C	20.0 %	55.0 %	243	A	10.0 %	57.5 %
139	B	25.0 %	62.5 %	160	B	12.5 %	57.5 %	181	C	10.0 %	55.0 %	202	D	15.0 %	57.5 %	223	A	12.5 %	55.0 %	244	D	37.5 %	55.0 %
140	A	27.5 %	62.5 %	161	A	22.5 %	57.5 %	182	A	15.0 %	55.0 %	203	A	17.5 %	55.0 %	224	C	27.5 %	55.0 %	245	D	30.0 %	55.0 %
141	A	25.0 %	62.5 %	162	C	30.0 %	55.0 %	183	D	12.5 %	55.0 %	204	C	32.5 %	55.0 %	225	B	15.0 %	55.0 %	246	B	17.5 %	55.0 %
142	D	15.0 %	62.5 %	163	D	30.0 %	55.0 %	184	C	15.0 %	55.0 %	205	D	22.5 %	55.0 %	226	B	10.0 %	55.0 %	247	A	22.5 %	55.0 %
143	B	25.0 %	62.5 %	164	C	25.0 %	55.0 %	185	B	20.0 %	55.0 %	206	A	32.5 %	55.0 %	227	A	15.0 %	55.0 %	248	C	7.5 %	55.0 %
144	B	12.5 %	62.5 %	165	D	37.5 %	55.0 %	186	C	17.5 %	55.0 %	207	A	12.5 %	55.0 %	228	D	32.5 %	55.0 %	249	D	7.5 %	55.0 %
145	B	15.0 %	62.5 %	166	A	15.0 %	55.0 %	187	B	17.5 %	55.0 %	208	A	15.0 %	57.5 %	229	C	5.0 %	57.5 %	250	D	40.0 %	55.0 %
146	B	20.0 %	65.0 %	167	B	15.0 %	55.0 %	188	B	20.0 %	55.0 %	209	D	12.5 %	55.0 %	230	B	27.5 %	55.0 %	251	C	12.5 %	55.0 %
147	C	12.5 %	65.0 %	168	C	15.0 %	55.0 %	189	A	25.0 %	57.5 %	210	B	27.5 %	55.0 %	231	A	17.5 %	55.0 %	252	A	40.0 %	55.0 %

Q.	Ans.	Correct	Skipped	Q.	Ans.	Correct	Skipped	Q.	Ans.	Correct	Skipped	Q.	Ans.	Correct	Skipped	Q.	Ans.	Correct	Skipped	Q.	Ans.	Correct	Skipped
253	C	20.0 %	55.0 %	261	C	10.0 %	55.0 %	269	D	20.0 %	57.5 %	277	A	7.5 %	60.0 %	285	A	15.0 %	62.5 %	293	D	35.0 %	60.0 %
254	B	20.0 %	55.0 %	262	A	20.0 %	55.0 %	270	B	17.5 %	57.5 %	278	C	12.5 %	57.5 %	286	D	5.0 %	60.0 %	294	D	20.0 %	60.0 %
255	D	15.0 %	57.5 %	263	B	25.0 %	55.0 %	271	D	35.0 %	57.5 %	279	C	10.0 %	60.0 %	287	B	30.0 %	60.0 %	295	D	20.0 %	60.0 %
256	D	22.5 %	57.5 %	264	B	5.0 %	60.0 %	272	C	27.5 %	57.5 %	280	A	20.0 %	57.5 %	288	D	25.0 %	60.0 %	296	D	35.0 %	60.0 %
257	C	25.0 %	55.0 %	265	A	25.0 %	57.5 %	273	C	22.5 %	57.5 %	281	A	17.5 %	57.5 %	289	A	25.0 %	60.0 %	297	D	30.0 %	60.0 %
258	B	7.5 %	55.0 %	266	D	25.0 %	57.5 %	274	A	22.5 %	57.5 %	282	A	30.0 %	60.0 %	290	C	22.5 %	60.0 %	298	B	2.5 %	62.5 %
259	D	20.0 %	55.0 %	267	A	25.0 %	57.5 %	275	C	12.5 %	57.5 %	283	D	22.5 %	60.0 %	291	C	10.0 %	62.5 %	299	C	17.5 %	60.0 %
260	C	17.5 %	55.0 %	268	C	12.5 %	57.5 %	276	A	27.5 %	57.5 %	284	C	27.5 %	60.0 %	292	A	12.5 %	62.5 %	300	A	22.5 %	57.5 %

//Hints and Solutions//

1. Option (D) is correct because, in radial nerve head surgery, the most common nerve to get injured is the posterior interosseous nerve. There are thumb and finger drop. Extension of the wrist is spared.

Option (A) is incorrect because the ulnar nerve is what creates the shock-like sensation when you hit the funny bone in your elbow. You may lose sensation and have muscle weakness in your hand if you damage your ulnar nerve. In severe cases, ulnar nerve palsy can cause muscle wasting, or atrophy, that makes the hand look like a claw.

Option (B) is incorrect as injury to the radial nerve may result in radial neuropathy, also called radial nerve palsy. Radial nerve injury may be due to physical trauma, infection, or even exposure to toxins. It often causes numbness and tingling or burning pain.

Option (C) is incorrect as if the median nerve is damaged, the ability to abduct and oppose the thumb may be lost due to paralysis of the thenar muscles.

Hence, the correct option is (D).

2. Option (B) is correct as Radial nerve injury includes.

Clinical features

- Wrist drop, finger drop, thumb drop
- Extension affected of- elbow, wrist, thumb and fingers
- Sensation affected of- posterior surface of arm and forearm and lower lateral half of forearm.

Option (A) is incorrect as symptoms of an ulnar nerve injury include pain, numbness, and loss of muscle strength and coordination in the arm and hand. Symptoms most commonly affect the little finger and the ring finger.

Option (C) is incorrect as signs of a median nerve lesion include weak pronation of the forearm, weak flexion and radial deviation of the wrist, with thenar atrophy and inability to oppose or flex the thumb; - the sensory distribution includes thumb, radial 2 1/2 fingers, and the corresponding portion of the palm.

Option (D) is incorrect as the following features are characteristic of the Musculocutaneous nerve:

The weakness of elbow flexion and forearm supination. Sensory loss over the lateral and volar aspect of the forearm. Weak or absent biceps tendon reflex.

Hence, the correct option is (B).

3. Option (B) is correct as it arises from the distal third of the dorsal part of the body of the ulna and from the interosseous membrane. Like the extensor digiti minimi (i.e. the extensor of the little finger), the tendon of the extensor indicis runs and inserts on the ulnar side of the tendon of the common extensor digitorum.

Option (A) is incorrect as the abductor pollicis brevis is innervated by the recurrent branch of the median nerve (Roots C5- C7 and C8-T1 in the brachial plexus lateral and medial cords respectively).

Option (C) is incorrect as the palmar interossei receive nerve supply from the deep branch of the ulnar nerve. The deep branch of the ulnar nerve arises from nerve roots of C8 and T1 with T1 being the primary innervating segment.

Option (D) is incorrect as the innervation of the lumbrical is dual: the radial first and second lumbrical are supplied by the median nerve (C8, T1) the ulnar third and fourth lumbrical are supplied by the deep branch of the ulnar nerve (C8, T1). This is also not the required answer.

Hence, the correct option is (B).

4. Option (A) is correct as from medial to lateral, structures passing under the flexor retinaculum

- Tibialis posterior
- Flexor digitorum longus
- Posterior tibial vessels
- Tibial nerve
- Flexor hallucis longus

Option (B) is incorrect as the great saphenous vein forms on the dorsum of the foot as the continuation of the medial marginal vein of the foot. It then passes anteriorly to the medial malleolus to ascend at first medial to and then posterior to the medial aspect of the tibia.

Option (C) is incorrect as the tendon passes laterally to the tibialis posterior tendon where it then situated deep to the flexor retinaculum lying in its own synovial sheath along the medial aspect of the sustentaculum tali.

Option (D) is incorrect as it begins at the bifurcation of the common fibular nerve, between the fibula and the proximal part of the fibularis longus. It passes obliquely forward, deep to the extensor digitorum longus, to the front of the interosseous membrane.

Hence, the correct option is (A).

5. Option (C) is correct as Pudendal nerve, internal pudendal vessels, and nerve to obturator internus after leaving the pelvis through the greater sciatic foramen, cross the dorsal aspect of the ischial spine and then re-enter the pelvis through the lesser sciatic foramen.

Option (A) is incorrect because the pudendal nerve originates from the second through the fourth sacral nerves in the sacral plexus. It exits the pelvis through the greater sciatic foramen, crosses over the ischial spine, and then reenters the pelvis through the lesser sciatic foramen.

Option (B) is incorrect as it then crosses the ischial spine, reënters the pelvis through the lesser sciatic foramen, and pierces the pelvic surface of the Obturator internus.

Option (D) is incorrect as the ischial spine provides:

1. attachment to the sacrospinous ligament along its margins and,
2. the origin for the posterior fibres of the levator ani from its pelvic surface.

Its dorsal surface is crossed by the internal pudendal vessels and by the nerve to the obturator intemus.

Hence, the correct option is (C).

6. Option (B) is correct as structures at the hilum- Superior to inferior is as follows:

- Left lung

- Pulmonary artery
- Bronchus
- Inferior pulmonary vein

- Right lung
    - Eparterial bronchus
    - Pulmonary artery
    - Hyparterial bronchus
    - Inferior pulmonary vein

Option (A) is incorrect as the main bronchus is located posterior to the vessels, while the pulmonary artery is superior to the vein.

Option (C) is incorrect because the pulmonary artery is in the middle, and the bronchus and bronchial vessels are located posteriorly.

Option (D) is incorrect as the bronchial veins are small vessels that return blood from the larger bronchi and structures at the roots of the lungs. The right side drains into the azygos vein, while the left side drains into the left superior intercostal vein or the accessory hemiazygos vein.

Hence, the correct option is (B).

7. Option (A) is correct as the parietal pericardium is supplied by the Phrenic nerve. The phrenic nerve originates from the anterior rami of the C3 through C5 nerve roots and consists of motor, sensory, and sympathetic nerve fibers. It provides complete motor innervation to the diaphragm and sensation to the central tendon aspect of the diaphragm.

Option (B) is incorrect as the superficial cardiac plexus is sited on the inferior surface of the arch of the aorta. It is contributed to by both post-ganglionic sympathetic and preganglionic parasympathetic nerves: left inferior cervical cardiac nerve, a branch of the left vagus nerve.

Option (C) is incorrect as it is formed by the cardiac nerves derived from the cervical ganglia of the sympathetic trunk and the cardiac branches of the vagus and recurrent laryngeal nerves except those that supply the superficial cardiac plexus.

Option (D) is incorrect as the vagus nerve supplies sensation to the posterior part of the external auditory canal and external ear.

Hence, the correct option is (A).

8. Option (A) is correct as in the left side, inferior phrenic vein, suprarenal vein, and the gonadal vein drain into the left renal vein, whereas on the right side, they drain into the inferior vena cava directly. So they do not cross the midline on the left side.

Option (B) is incorrect as the left renal vein is longer than the right as it crosses the midline to reach the inferior vena cava (IVC).

Option (C) is incorrect as the left brachiocephalic vein is usually longer than the right because at one point it travels across the body from left to right.

Option (D) is incorrect as it descends to the left of midline, adjacent to the thoracic vertebrae and crosses posteriorly to the aorta at the level of T7-8 to drain into the azygos vein.

Hence, the correct option is (A).

9. Option (C) is correct because, near the ischial spine, the ureter turns downward, anterior ward, and medially just inferior to the uterine vessels, about 2 cm from the cervix (where it may be endangered in hysterectomy).

Option (A) is incorrect as the ureter is constricted at the pelvic ureteric junction.

Option (B) is incorrect as the ureter is constricted at the brim of the lesser pelvis.

Option (D) is incorrect as the ureter is constricted during its oblique passage through the bladder wall.

Hence, the correct option is (C).

10. Option (A) is correct as structures passing through the foramen spinosum are:-

1. Middle meningeal artery
2. Emissary's vein
3. Nervus spinous (a meningeal branch of the mandibular nerve)

Option (B) is incorrect because the internal carotid artery passes through the carotid foramen and the large cavernous sinus and into the medial cranial fossa.

Option (C) is incorrect as at the terminal end of the canal, the facial nerve passes through the stylomastoid foramen, a small aperture around which many muscles and connective tissue structures of the neck make their attachments.

Option (D) is incorrect as it emerges from the mandibular nerve, it passes between the two heads of the lateral pterygoid muscle before heading to its target sites.

Hence, the correct option is (A).

11. Option (A) is correct because saddle joints are said to be biaxial, allowing movement in the sagittal and frontal planes. Examples of saddle joints in the human body include the carpometacarpal joint of the thumb, the sternoclavicular joint of the chest, and the incudomalleolar joint of the middle ear.

Option (B) is incorrect because the radiocarpal joint and the Metacarpophalangeal joint are examples of condyloid joints. The ellipsoid joint is also known as a 'condyloid joint'. An example of an Ellipsoid joint is the wrist; it functions similarly to the ball and socket joint except is unable to rotate 360 degrees; it prohibits axial rotation.

Option (C) is incorrect because a pivot joint is a type of synovial joint that rotates. Two examples of pivot joints in your body are the pivot joint in your neck that allows your head to rotate and the pivot joints between the radius and ulna that rotate your forearm.

Option (D) is incorrect because in a plane joint the mating surfaces of the bones are slightly curved and may be either ovoid or sellar. Only a small amount of gliding movement is found. Examples are the joints between the metacarpal bones of the hand and those between the cuneiform bones of the foot.

Hence, the correct option is (A).

12. Option (D) is correct since we can see that all the options mentioned above are contents of the interpeduncular fossa.

Option (A) is incorrect as the floor of the interpeduncular fossa presents from before backward is optic chiasma, tuber cinereum, tuberal eminences, infundibular stalk, mamillary bodies, and posterior perforated substance, which is pierced by posterior cerebral arteries.

Option (B) is incorrect because the oculomotor and trochlear nerves intervene between superior cerebellar and posterior cerebral arteries in the interpeduncular fossa.

Option (C) is incorrect for the same reason as option (B).

Hence, the correct option is (D).

13. Option (C) is correct as the axons of Purkinje cells are the only output through the cerebellar cortex. However, it should be kept in mind that the output from the cerebellum is through deep nuclei, Purkinje cells axons generally pass to deep nuclei.

Option (A) is incorrect as the Golgi apparatus is responsible for transporting, modifying, and packaging proteins and lipids into vesicles for delivery to targeted destinations.

Option (B) is incorrect as Basket cells are multipolar GABAergic interneurons that function to make inhibitory synapses and control the overall potentials of target cells.

Option (D) is incorrect as Oligodendrocytes are another type of glial cells and these cells are responsible for the myelination of axons in the central nervous system (CNS).

Hence, the correct option is (C).

14. Option (A) is correct as cells of transitional epithelium have an extra reserve of the cell membrane in the form of plate-like areas of cytoplasm containing internalized membranes, which permits the stretching of the epithelium.

Option (B) is incorrect as stratified squamous epithelium is usually protective. The multiple layers are too thick for efficient transport of materials (neither secretory or absorptive). The innermost layer continually produces cells (via mitosis) to replace those lost from the outer surface.

Option (C) is incorrect as it includes absorption, secretion, and excretion. If the cuboidal epithelium is arranged in many layers it forms the stratified cuboidal epithelium. It is found on the inner side of the pancreatic ducts and salivary glands. They mainly help in protection.

Option (D) is incorrect as it is located in the conjunctiva inside the eyelids and areas of tissue transition. It is mostly responsible for the protection and mucous secretion.

Hence, the correct option is (A).

15. Option (D) is correct as Membranous and most of the penile urethra (in males) is lined by pseudostratified or stratified columnar epithelium.

Option (A) is incorrect as the Urinary bladder is lined by the Urothelium.

Option (B) is incorrect as Minor calyx is also lined by Urothelium.

Option (C) is incorrect as Urothelium (transitional epithelium) is found in the renal pelvis, calyces, ureter, urinary bladder, the proximal part of the urethra.

Hence, the correct option is (D).

16. Option (B) is correct as the upper 80% of the vagina is derived from Müllerian epithelium and the lower 20% derived from urogenital sinus epithelium.

Option (A) is incorrect because the Wolffian duct (also known as the mesonephric duct) is one of the paired embryogenic tubules that drain the primitive kidney (mesonephros) to the cloaca. It also gives off a lateral branch forming the ureteric bud. In both the male and the female the Wolffian duct develops into the trigone of the urinary bladder.

Option (C) is incorrect because the sinovaginal bulb is a transitional structure in the development of female genitalia, and is one of a pair of endodermal outgrowths of the urogenital sinus, which later fuse to form the lower part of the vagina. The lower third of the vagina is derived from the urogenital sinus.

Option (D) is incorrect as the endoderm contributes to the epithelia and glands of the gastrointestinal tract, respiratory tract and renal bladder. This layer also contributes to the associated gastrointestinal tract organ development (liver and pancreas).

Hence, the correct option is (B).

17. Option (B) is correct as Leukocyte adhesion deficiency may present with recurrent bacterial infections, defects in neutrophil adhesion, and a delay in umbilical cord sloughing.

Option (A) is incorrect because an umbilical adenoma is a patch of vitellointestinal epithelium left behind when the vitellointestinal duct closed. It may form in a deep sinus in the depths of the umbilicus but commonly protrudes to from it like a raspberry. The mother complains that the baby has a lump at the umbilicus and a mucous discharge.

Option (C) is incorrect because this occurs when the urachus did not seal off and there is a connection between the bladder and the umbilicus. A patent urachus can cause varying amounts of clear urine to leak at the umbilicus.

Option (D) is incorrect as it's a small growth of tissue that forms in the belly button during the first few weeks after the umbilical cord is cut. An umbilical granuloma may not bother your baby. However, it can become infected. This can lead to other symptoms, such as skin irritation around the belly button and a fever.

Hence, the correct option is (B).

18. Option (B) is correct because the temperature at which the crystalline or gel-like state of membrane structures turns into a fluid-like state is known as Transition temperature. Higher the transition temperature, lower the fluidity of the membrane. The transition temperature is increased maximum by the more saturated fatty acids which interact with each other through their long chains strongly and results in lesser fluidity.

Option (A) is incorrect because high levels of cholesterol can increase your risk of heart disease. With high cholesterol, you can develop fatty deposits in your blood vessels

Option (C) is incorrect because Pulmonary toxicity is the result of hydrocarbon aspiration causing direct effects on lung parenchyma. Low-viscosity, highly volatile hydrocarbons, such as kerosene and mineral oils, are easiest to aspirate. These volatile chemicals can displace alveolar oxygen, leading to hypoxia.

Option (D) is incorrect as the greater the degree of unsaturation in fatty acid (i.e., the more double bonds in the fatty acid) the more vulnerable it is to lipid peroxidation (rancidity).

Hence, the correct option is (B).

19. Option (A) is correct because Vitamin E (tocopherol) is the most important antioxidant in the body, acting in the lipid phase of membranes protecting against the effects of free radicals.

Vitamin E is believed to play the most important protective role in the prevention of oxidation of unsaturated fats. In the absence of vitamin E, the quantity of unsaturated fats in the cells becomes diminished, causing abnormal structure and function of such cellular organelles like the mitochondria, the lysosomes, and even the cell membrane.

Option (B) is incorrect because, within the body, vitamin A can be found as retinol, retinal and retinoic acid. The antioxidant activity of vitamin A and carotenoids is conferred by the hydrophobic chain of polyene units that can quench singlet oxygen, neutralize thiyl radicals and combine with and stabilize peroxyl radicals.

Option (C) is incorrect as Vitamin K has antioxidant properties. It protects cellular membranes from damage due to excess free radicals, in a process known as peroxidation. Blood-thinning medication, such as warfarin, can lower the antioxidative potential of vitamin K.

Option (D) is incorrect as Vitamin C is a powerful antioxidant having the ability to donate a hydrogen atom and form a relatively stable ascorbyl-free radical. In addition to neutralizing free radicals with its antioxidant properties, vitamin C also plays a role in controlling infections.

Hence, the correct option is (A).

20. Option (B) is correct because, in the cytosol, glycogen breakdown or glycogenolysis is carried out by two enzymes, glycogen phosphorylase which releases glucose 1-phosphate from the linear chains of glycogen, and glycogen debranching enzyme which untangles the branch points. In the lysosomes, glycogen degradation is catalyzed by α-glucosidase.

Option (A) is incorrect as the citric acid cycle takes place in the matrix of the mitochondria. Through a series of steps, citrate is oxidized, releasing two carbon dioxide molecules for each acetyl group fed into the cycle.

Option (C) is incorrect as fatty acid oxidation is the mitochondrial aerobic process of breaking down a fatty acid into acetyl-CoA units. Fatty acids move in this pathway as CoA derivatives utilizing NAD and FAD.

Option (D) is incorrect because, in eukaryotes, an important electron transport chain is found in the inner mitochondrial membrane where it serves as the site of oxidative phosphorylation through the action of ATP synthase.

Hence, the correct option is (B).

21. Option (B) is correct because resting membrane potential is reached due to the potential difference between ICF and ECF. This is major as a result of the K^+ ion concentration difference in ECF and ICF.

Option (A) is incorrect as sodium is the major cation of the extracellular fluid. It is responsible for one-half of the osmotic pressure gradient that exists between the interior of cells and their surrounding environment.

Option (C) is incorrect as chloride is the predominant extracellular anion. Chloride is a major contributor to the osmotic pressure gradient between the ICF and ECF and plays an important role in maintaining proper hydration. Chloride functions to balance cations in the ECF, maintaining the electrical neutrality of this fluid.

Option (D) is incorrect as Magnesium plays an important intracellular role in decreasing the excitability of smooth muscle, leading to a reduction in smooth muscle tone.

Hence, the correct option is (B).

22. Option (B) is correct as K^+ concentration is higher in ICF. Therefore, the diffusion is highest for K^+ when the cell is at rest.

Option (A) is incorrect as the Na^+ concentration is higher in ECF. Thus, diffusion for Na^+ is least when the cell is at rest.

Option (C) is incorrect as Cl^- concentration higher in ECF. Thus, it also has a higher diffusion but not higher than the diffusion for K^+.

Option (D) is incorrect as diffusion is highest for K+, then Cl- and least for Na+, when the cell is at rest.

Hence, the correct option is (B).

23. Option (A) is correct as the all-or-none law is the principle that the strength by which a nerve or muscle fibre responds to a stimulus is independent of the strength of the stimulus. If that stimulus exceeds the threshold potential, the nerve or muscle fibre will give a complete response; otherwise, there is no response.

Option (B) is incorrect as conduction velocity is highly dependent on rapid signal propagation enabled by myelination.

Option (C) is incorrect as an action potential is generated in axon hillock or its initial segment. Then it propagates at a constant velocity and amplitude through the fibre without any decrement.

Option (D) is incorrect as this propagation is faster in myelinated nerve fibres than the unmyelinated fibres.

Hence, the correct option is (A).

24. Option (C) is correct as contractions of chain fibres can 'drive' the primary sensory ending.

Option (A) is incorrect as nuclear chain fibres are thinner, shorter and more in numbers.

Option (B) is incorrect as nuclear bag fibres are thicker, longer and fewer in numbers.

Option (D) is incorrect as the peripheral part of chain fibres also receives afferent fibres of type Aβ with the second ending (Flower spray). The efferent fibres are Aγ2 static fibres with 'trail ending'.

Hence, the correct option is (C).

25. Option (B) is correct as fatty acids are synthesized in the cytosol, whereas acetyl CoA is formed from pyruvate in mitochondria. Hence, acetyl CoA must be transferred from mitochondria to the cytosol.

Option (A) is incorrect because ATP synthesis occurs in the inner mitochondrial membrane in mitochondria. The enzyme required for the synthesis of ATP is ATP synthase. It is located in the inner mitochondrial membrane. There is the transfer of protons from the matrix to the inner mitochondrial membrane.

Option (C) is incorrect as the ER is the major site at which membrane lipids are synthesized in eukaryotic cells. Because they are extremely hydrophobic, lipids are synthesized in association with already existing cellular membranes rather than in the aqueous environment of the cytosol. Although some lipids are synthesized in association with other membranes, most are synthesized in the ER.

Option (D) is incorrect as ribosomes are the sites in a cell in which protein synthesis takes place. Cells have many ribosomes, and the exact number depends on how active a particular cell is in synthesizing proteins.

Hence, the correct option is (B).

26. Option (C) is correct because protein synthesis is one of the most important biological processes by which individual cells build specific proteins in order to function. Protein synthesis occurs in the rough endoplasmic reticulum, ribosomes and in the nucleus. Note that Rough ER contains ribosomes.

Option (A) is incorrect because the smooth endoplasmic reticulum (smooth ER) is a membranous organelle found in most eukaryotic cells. Its main functions are the synthesis of lipids, steroid hormones, the detoxification of harmful metabolic byproducts and the storage and metabolism of calcium ions within the cell.

Option (B) is incorrect because Glycoprotein synthesis occurs in two organelles in sequences such as the endoplasmic reticulum and the Golgi apparatus.

Option (D) is incorrect because lysosomes are known to contain more than 60 different enzymes, and have more than 50 membrane proteins. Enzymes of the lysosomes are synthesized in the rough endoplasmic reticulum. The enzymes are imported from the Golgi apparatus in small vesicles, which fuse with larger acidic vesicles.

Hence, the correct option is (C).

27. Option (A) is correct as "The normal dead space air in a young adult man is about 150 milliliters.

Option (B) is incorrect as the given data is greater than the defined dead space.

Option (C) is incorrect as the data provided in the option is inappropriate.

Option (D) is incorrect for the same reason as options (B) and (C).

Hence, the correct option is (A).

28. Option (C) is correct as Alveolar ventilation= Respiratory rate × (Tidal volume – Dead space)

Respiratory rate- 12 per minute

Tidal Volume- 500ml

Dead Space- 150 ml

AV= 12× (500-150)= 12 × 350 = 4200ml/min = 4.2L/min

Option (A) is incorrect as total alveolar ventilation volume (in L/min) upon calculating will be 4.2 and not 1.5.

Option (B) is incorrect for the same reason as option (A).

Option (D) is incorrect as we can see in option (C) that total alveolar ventilation volume (in L/min) is estimated as 4.2. So, this option will automatically get wrong.

Hence, the correct option is (C).

29. Option (B) is correct as a direct cause of pacemaker potential.

- Early part- Opening of funny channels producing funny currents due to the increased influx of sodium (major) and potassium (minimal).
- Late part- Opening of T type of calcium channels. The indirect cause of pacemaker potential
- The decrease in the repolarizing potassium efflux.

Option (A) is incorrect as sodium channels mediate fast depolarization and conduct electrical impulses throughout the nerve, muscle and heart.

Option (C) is incorrect as the depolarization causes the voltage-gated Ca^{2+} channels to open allowing the influx of Ca^{2+} that signals the release of neurotransmitters into the synaptic cleft.

Option (D) is incorrect regarding the risk of ventricular fibrillation, it is believed that early repolarization is caused by altered ion channel function (alterations in sodium, potassium and calcium currents have been suggested).

Hence, the correct option is (B).

30. Option (A) is correct as Einthoven's Law states that if electrocardiograms are taken simultaneously with the three limb leads, at any given instant the potential in lead II is equal to the sum of the potentials in leads I and III.

$$\text{Lead I} + \text{Lead III} = \text{Lead II}$$

Option (B) is incorrect as according to the law, the summation of the Lead I and Lead III will be equal to lead II depending on the signs, not the difference of the two will be equal to the rest one.

Option (C) is incorrect as the summation of three is not possible and is contradictory to the equation according to law.

Option (D) is incorrect as in terms of avl it is expressed as:

$$aVL = \frac{(I - III)}{2}$$

Hence, the correct option is (A).

31. Option (A) is correct as the Juxtaglomerular apparatus is the content of the renal cortex and not the part of the renal medulla. So, this is the required answer.

Option (B) is incorrect because a loop of Henle is a thin descending limb, thin ascending limb, medullary part of the thick ascending limb and is a part of the renal medulla. Hence, this is not the required answer.

Option (C) is incorrect as the Medullary part of the collecting duct lies in the renal medulla. Therefore, this is not the required answer.

Option (D) is incorrect as Vasa recta is also the content of the renal medulla. Thus, it is also not the required answer.

Hence, the correct option is (A).

32. Option (C) is correct as

- Renin is a protein enzyme released by the kidneys when the arterial pressure falls too low.
- Renin itself is an enzyme, not a vasoactive substance.
- Renin acts enzymatically on another plasma protein, a globulin called renin substrate (or angiotensinogen), to release a 10-amino acid peptide, angiotensin I.

Option (A) is incorrect because the lungs are involved in immune function through the production and secretion of IgA.

Option (B) is incorrect as the pancreas produces enzymes to help break down proteins, fats and carbohydrates. The gall bladder stores the bile that is produced by the liver.

Option (D) is incorrect as the enzymes that are secreted in the stomach are gastric enzymes. Pepsin is the main gastric enzyme.

Hence, the correct option is (C).

33. Option (D) is correct as an intrinsic factor is a glycoprotein principally secreted by the parietal cells of the stomach. Its secretion is governed by the same biochemical processes that regulate acid secretion and its action is to assist in the absorption of vitamin B_{12}.

Option (A) is incorrect as Mucus is secreted by the stomach epithelial cells, but the mucus is mainly secreted from foveolar cells, found in the necks of the gastric pits. Mucus-secreting cells are the most abundant cell type in the stomach, giving indications of how important mucus is to the functioning stomach.

Option (B) is incorrect as Pepsinogens are synthesized and secreted primarily by the gastric chief cells of the human stomach before being converted into the proteolytic enzyme pepsin, which is crucial for digestive processes in the stomach. Furthermore, pepsin can activate additional pepsinogen autocatalytically.

Option (C) is incorrect as Gastrin is a hormone that is produced by 'G' cells in the lining of the stomach and upper small intestine. During a meal, gastrin stimulates the stomach to release gastric acid. This allows the stomach to break down proteins swallowed as food and absorb certain vitamins.

Hence, the correct option is (D).

34. Option (A) is correct as the Cephalic phase of Gastric acid secretion is 20%.

Option (B) is incorrect as it is the Gastric phase that is 70-80% of the gastric secretion.

Option (C) is incorrect as the given data is inaccurate.

Option (D) is incorrect for the same reason as an option (C).

Hence, the correct option is (A).

35. Option (B) is correct as the Pyruvate is formed from glucose oxidation (glycolysis) in the cytosol. It is transported into the mitochondria along with Er (proton) symport by a monocarboxylate carrier.

Option (A) is incorrect as membrane proteins allow the exchange of chloride ions for bicarbonate ions across the cellular membrane. The action of specific antiporters in this class serve important functions such as allowing the efficient exchange of bicarbonate across red blood cell membranes as they passage through capillaries and the reabsorption of bicarbonate ions by the kidney.

Option (C) is incorrect as an antiporter is an integral protein involved in secondary active transport, which couples the energy of a molecule moving down its concentration gradient to another moving up its concentration gradient. The antiporter simultaneously transports two molecules at the same time in the opposite direction.

Option (D) is incorrect as the uniport proteins are partly responsible for the facilitated diffusion of solutes across cell and organelle membranes.

Hence, the correct option is (B).

36. Option (D) is correct as it covers all the options mentioned above.

Option (A) is incorrect as the vitamin, folic acid, is converted to its coenzyme form, tetrahydrofolic acid, by a pyridine nucleotide-dependent enzyme, dihydrofolate reductase. But, selecting an individual option will not be considered correct.

Option (B) is incorrect as Biotin is a coenzyme for multiple carboxylase enzymes, which are involved in the digestion of carbohydrates, synthesis of fatty acids, and gluconeogenesis. Again, selecting an individual option won't be correct.

Option (C) is incorrect though the active form of thiamine is thiamine pyrophosphate (TPP), which functions as a coenzyme in the metabolism of carbohydrates, lipids, and branched-chain amino acids. Selecting an individual option will not be considered correct.

Hence, the correct option is (D).

37. Option (C) is correct as, in TCA Cycle, Fifth step: Generation of succinate. The reaction involves substrate-level phosphorylation whereby a high-energy phosphate is generated from the energy trapped in the thioester bond of succinyl CoA. The enzyme is succinate thiokinase. The molecule of GDP is phosphorylated to GTP and succinate is formed.

Option (A) is incorrect as the enzyme succinate dehydrogenase catalyzes the removal of two hydrogens from succinate in the sixth reaction of the citric acid cycle. In the reaction, a molecule of FAD, a coenzyme similar to NAD, is reduced to FADH2 as it takes the hydrogens from succinate.

Option (B) is incorrect because Alpha-ketoglutarate dehydrogenase (α-KGDH) is a Krebs cycle enzyme, which catalyses the non-equilibrium reaction converting α-ketoglutarate, coenzyme A and NAD^+ to succinyl-CoA, NADH and CO_2, requiring thiamine pyrophosphate as a cofactor.

Option (D) is incorrect as Malate dehydrogenase (MDH) is an enzyme that reversibly catalyzes the oxidation of malate to oxaloacetate using the reduction of NAD^+ to NADH. This reaction is part of many metabolic pathways, including the citric acid cycle.

Hence, the correct option is (C).

38. Option (A) is correct as Gluconeogenesis is regulated by four key enzymes : (i) Pyruvate carboxylase; (ii) Phosphoenolpyruvate carboxykinase; (iii) Fructose-1, 6-bisphosphatase; and (iv) Glucose-6-phosphatase. The hormone glucagon, epinephrine and glucocorticoids stimulate gluconeogenesis, by inducing these enzymes. Conversely, insulin inhibits gluconeogenesis by repressing their synthesis.

Option (B) is incorrect as Glucagon is a hormone that causes the liver to release glucose into the blood. It is used to quickly increase blood sugar levels in diabetics with low blood sugar (hypoglycemia). This medication may also be used during certain medical tests.

Option (C) is incorrect as cortisol is a steroid hormone that regulates a wide range of processes throughout the body, including metabolism and the immune response. It also has a very important role in helping the body respond to stress.

Option (D) is incorrect as Epinephrine, also called adrenaline, the hormone that is secreted mainly by the medulla of the adrenal glands and that functions primarily to increase cardiac output and to raise glucose levels in the blood.

Hence, the correct option is (A).

39. Option (C) is correct as Pompe's disease (Type H glycogenosis) is due to deficiency of acid maltase (lysosomal α I →4 and α I→6 glucosidase).

Option (A) is incorrect as Glycogen-branching enzyme deficiency (GBED) is an inheritable glycogen storage disease affecting American Quarter Horses and American Paint Horses. It leads to abortion, stillbirths, or early death of affected animals.

Option (B) is incorrect as Glucose-6-phosphatase deficiency (G6P deficiency), or glycogen storage disease type I (GSDI), is a group of inherited metabolic diseases, including types Ia and Ib, characterized by poor tolerance to fasting, growth retardation and hepatomegaly resulting from the accumulation of glycogen and fat in the liver.

Option (D) is incorrect as McArdle disease is a deficiency of muscle phosphorylase. This is an important substance needed to break down glycogen in your muscle cells. The condition causes fatigue and muscle pain during exercise. The disease can lead to dark urine.

Hence, the correct option is (C).

40. Option (C) is correct because Acetyl-CoA acts as a primer to donate 1st 2 carbon atoms (C-15 and C-16) of palmitate. The addition of all the subsequent C2 units is via malonyl-CoA.

Propionyl-CoA acts as a primer (for donating the first 3 carbon atoms) in the synthesis of odd-carbon number fatty acids.

Option (A) is incorrect as Malonyl-CoA is a highly regulated molecule in fatty acid synthesis; as such, it inhibits the rate-limiting step in beta-oxidation of fatty acids.

Option (B) is incorrect as Palmitate is the starting point for other fatty acids that use a set of related reactions to generate the modified chains and head groups of the lipid classes.

Option (D) is incorrect as to obtain cytosolic acetyl-CoA, citrate (produced by the condensation of acetyl CoA with oxaloacetate) is removed from the citric acid cycle and carried across the inner mitochondrial membrane into the cytosol.

Hence, the correct option is (C).

41. Option (B) is correct as Acetyl-CoA carboxylase is an allosteric enzyme, it is activated by citrate and inhibited by long-chain acyl-CoA (palmitoyl CoA).

Option (A) is incorrect as Malonyl-CoA is a three-carbon activated compound, formed by the action of acetyl-CoA carboxylase (ACC) on acetyl-CoA. Although first recognized in lipogenic tissues such as the liver, it is now known to play an important role in the regulation of fatty acid catabolism.

Option (C) is incorrect as the first step is to activate this long-chain fatty acid to produce palmitoyl-CoA by having it react with ATP in the presence of CoA-SH (coenzyme A with functional sulfhydryl group).

Option (D) is incorrect as Acetoacetate is activated by the transfer of CoA from succinyl CoA in a reaction catalyzed by succinyl CoA that is 3-ketoacid CoA transferase.

Hence, the correct option is (B).

42. Option (D) is correct as storage proteins are biological reserves of metal ions and amino acids, used by organisms. Ovalbumin and casein are the storage proteins found in egg white and milk respectively. Ferritin, an iron storage protein, is found in plants and animal tissues.

Option (A) is incorrect although Myoglobin is an oxygen storage protein. It is incorrect as other mentioned proteins are also storage proteins.

Option (B) is incorrect though Ovalbumin is the first protein isolated in pure form and is about half of the total egg albumen protein. The function of ovalbumin is unknown, although it is presumed to be a storage protein. Selecting an individual option when others are also relatable won't be considered correct.

Option (C) is incorrect even Ferritin, an iron storage protein, is found in plants and animal tissues. But, it is incorrect for the same reason as options (A) and (B).

Hence, the correct option is (D).

43. Option (B) is correct as liver glycogen is the first main provider of energy during short-term fasting.

Liver glycogen serves to maintain blood glucose between the meals. Therefore, liver glycogen is the most important reservoir as it comes to play its role in routine condition (between meals). Whereas, adipose tissue fuel is involved only on prolonged fasting and starvation.

Option (A) is incorrect as fat is the body's most concentrated source of energy, providing more than twice as much potential energy as carbohydrate or protein (9 calories per gram versus 4 calories each per gram).

Option (C) is incorrect as lactate is formed from the breakdown of glucose. During this process, the cells make ATP (adenosine triphosphate), which provides energy for most of the chemical reactions in the body. Lactate formation does not use oxygen, so the process is often called anaerobic metabolism.

Option (D) is incorrect as acetone is one of three ketone bodies which are produced in the mammalian liver as an alternative energy source when glucose is not readily available.

Hence, the correct option is (B).

44. Option (A) is correct as TPP acts as a coenzyme for pyruvate dehydrogenase which catalyzes the conversion of pyruvate to acetyl-CoA.

Option (B) is incorrect as it is pyridoxal phosphate that acts as a coenzyme in all transamination reactions and in some oxidation and deamination reactions of amino acids.

Option (C) is incorrect as the cofactors may be inorganic, such as iron-sulfur clusters, or organometallic such as hemes. These cofactors are components of respiratory and photosynthetic electron transport chains as well as metabolic enzymes.

Option (D) is incorrect as Pyridoxal 5'-phosphate (the active form of vitamin B6) is a necessary cofactor for the formation of several important neurotransmitters associated with stress. Within the brain, glutamic acid is converted to GABA via the enzyme glutamate decarboxylase and its cofactor pyridoxal 5'-phosphate.

Hence, the correct option is (A).

45. Option (A) is correct as Biotin deficiency may occur in people who eat an abnormally large amount of uncooked (raw) egg white, which contains avidin, a protein that binds biotin and renders it unavailable for absorption.

Option (B) is incorrect as Riboflavin deficiency usually occurs with other B vitamin deficiencies.

Option (C) is incorrect as risk factors of thiamine deficiency include a diet of mostly white rice, as well as alcoholism, dialysis, chronic diarrhoea, and taking high doses of diuretics.

Option (D) is incorrect as the biotin-avidin complex is simply excreted out of the body. Raw eggs contain avidin, therefore, consuming them can lead to biotin deficiency.

Hence, the correct option is (A).

46. Option (D) is correct as both the statement contained in the option are true about the strand of DNA, that is it is a non-transcribed strand, plus-strand or sense strand. It runs in a '5' → '3' direction.

Coding strand has the same nucleotide sequence and orientation as the transcribed mRNA (except for the replacement of uracil with thymine).

Option (A) is incorrect as the coding strand is also called a non-template strand while the option is saying that it is a template for mRNA. So, this is an incorrect answer.

Option (B) is incorrect as the option contains the choices that are contradictory to each other that is plus strand and minus strand. Hence, this is also not the right answer.

Option (C) is incorrect as the choices in which one is true about the strand of DNA while the other one is not true. So, this option is not correct.

Hence, the correct option is (D).

47. Option (A) is correct as the process of making mRNA from DNA is called transcription, and it occurs in the nucleus. The mRNA directs the synthesis of proteins, which occurs in the cytoplasm.

Option (B) is incorrect as RNA (including mRNA) has Uracil in place of Thiamine while the option is vice-versa. Hence, it is not true about cytoplasmic messenger RNA.

Option (C) is incorrect as the pentose sugar of their nucleotides is 'Ribose' (and not DeoxyRibose). Hence, this is also not true about cytoplasmic messenger RNA.

Option (D) is incorrect as cytoplasmic mature messenger RNA (mRNA) is smaller (less molecular weight) than Heterogeneous Nuclear RNA (hnRNA) and/or Pre-messenger RNA (Pre-mRNA).

Hence, the correct option is (A).

48. Option (B) is correct because a codon is a sequence of 3 nucleotides from 5' → 3' end corresponds to one amino acid.

Option (A) is incorrect as each group of three bases in mRNA constitutes a codon, and each codon specifies a particular amino acid (hence, it is a triplet code).

Option (C) is incorrect as multiple ribosomes can translate a single mRNA molecule at the same time, but all of these ribosomes must begin at the first codon and move along the mRNA strand one codon at a time until reaching the stop codon.

Option (D) is incorrect because the option is contradictory to the correct answer. As three nucleotides are required for a codon that are consecutive in nature, not the four individual nucleotides.

Hence, the correct option is (B).

49. Option (B) is correct as if an investigator introduces into an organism a duplex RNA molecule corresponding in sequence to virtually any mRNA, Dicer nuclease cleaves the duplex into short segments, called small interfering RNAs (siRNAs). These short (21-25 nucleotide long) si RNAs usually form perfect RNA-RNA hybrid with their targets potentially anywhere within the length of mRNA where the complementary sequence exists. Formation of such RNA-RNA duplexes between si RNAs and mRNA results in reduced specific protein production because the si RNA - mRNA complexes are degraded, mostly in specific cytoplasmic organelles termed P-bodies. The process is known as RNA interference (RNAi) for which the Nobel prize was given to Andrew Fire & Craig Mello in 2006.

Option (A) is incorrect as Lipoxins (lipoxygenase interaction products), which are generated by the conjugate activity of both 5- and 15 lipoxygenase, were discovered by Serhan and Samuelsson in 1984 after they incubated 15L-hydroperoxy-5,8,11,13-eicosatetraenoic acid with human leukocytes (Serhan, Hamberg, and Samuelsson, 1984). No Nobel prize was awarded for the discovery of lipoxin.

Option (C) is incorrect as the Nobel Prize in Physiology or Medicine in 1962 was awarded to James Watson, Francis Crick and Maurice Wilkins for their discovery of the molecular structure of DNA, which helped solve one of the most important of all biological riddles.

Option (D) is incorrect as the Nobel Prize in Physiology or Medicine 2012 have been awarded jointly to Sir John B. Gurdon and Shinya Yamanaka "for the discovery that mature cells can be reprogrammed to become pluripotent"

Hence, the correct option is (B).

50. Option (D) is correct as radiolabelled nucleotides are commonly used for the detection of specific nucleic acid sequences. They are typically incorporated enzymatically into DNA and RNA sequences for detection and analysis.

Option (A) is incorrect as the DNA polymerase typically used in PCR is called Taq polymerase, after the heat-tolerant bacterium from which it was isolated (Thermus aquaticus).

Option (B) is incorrect as the function of dNTPs in PCR is to expand the growing DNA strand with the help of Taq DNA polymerase. For performing PCR, we need DNA templet, dNTPs.

Option (C) is incorrect as primers are the strands of DNA (or RNA) that serve as this initial foundation for the DNA replication process, and they are used to demarcate the segment of the DNA template to be amplified. In the PCR process, two primers are matched to the segment of DNA.

Hence, the correct option is (D).

51. Option (A) is correct because direct injury to endothelial cells causes delayed prolonged bleeding because, endothelial cells are central regulators of hemostasis, the balance between the anti- and prothrombotic activities of endothelium determines whether thrombus formation, propagation or dissolution occurs.

Option (B) is incorrect because injured tissue mast cells release histamine, causing the surrounding blood vessels to dilate and increase in permeability. This causes the visible symptoms of a localized allergic reaction, including runny nose, watery eyes, constriction of bronchi, and tissue swelling.

Option (C) is incorrect because leukocytes contain or are capable of producing a number of products that can potentially cause cell injury or modify cell function.

Option (D) is incorrect as the causes of influenza-like illness range from benign self-limited illnesses such as gastroenteritis, rhinoviral disease, and influenza, to severe, sometimes life-threatening, diseases such as meningitis, sepsis, and leukaemia.

Hence, the correct option is (A).

52. <u>Inflammation is characterized by five cardinal signs:</u>

- rubor (redness),
- calor (increased heat)
- a tumour (swelling)
- dolour (pain), and.
- function laesa (loss of function).

Option (D) is correct because Cyanosis is not the Cardinal signs of Inflammation according to the above explanation, hence this will be the correct option.

Option (A) is incorrect as given in the above explanation, Rubor is a Cardinal sign of Inflammation hence this option will not be correct according to the question.

Option (B) is incorrect similarly according to the above explanation Tumour is a Cardinal sign of Inflammation hence this option will not be correct according to the question.

Option (C) is incorrect because according to the above explanation Calor is also a Cardinal sign of Inflammation hence this option will not be correct according to the question.

Hence, the correct option is (D).

53. Option (B) is correct because Vasoconstriction is the narrowing of the blood vessels resulting from contraction of the muscular wall of the vessels, in particular the large arteries and small arterioles. The process is the opposite of vasodilation, the widening of blood vessels.

Option (A) is incorrect because Fibrin deposition, seen as amorphous eosinophilic amyloid-like material, is admixed acute and chronic inflammation and it is associated with alternating denuded and hyperplastic patches of squamous epithelium. The fibrin deposits stain with PAS but do not stain with Congo red.

Option (C) is incorrect because Platelet adhesion is an essential function in response to vascular injury and is generally viewed as the first step during which single platelets bind through specific membrane receptors to cellular and extracellular matrix constituents of the vessel wall and tissues.

Option (D) is incorrect because Thrombosis is the formation of a blood clot, known as a thrombus, within a blood vessel. It prevents blood from flowing normally through the circulatory system.

Hence, the correct option is (B).

54. Option (C) is correct because complete DiGeorge syndrome is characterized by absence or underdevelopment (hypoplasia) of the thymus resulting in very low T cell counts. Infants with complete DiGeorge syndrome have additional symptoms including congenital heart defects and/or hypoparathyroidism. These complications can be significant.

Option (A) is incorrect because Wiskott-Aldrich syndrome is characterized by abnormal immune system function (immune deficiency), eczema (an inflammatory skin disorder characterized by abnormal patches of red, irritated skin), and a reduced ability to form blood clots. This condition primarily affects males.

Option (B) is incorrect because Autoimmune diseases, in which your immune system attacks particular organs or tissues in your own body, can be found with Selective IgA deficiency. Common autoimmune conditions found with IgA deficiency include rheumatoid arthritis and lupus. Some people also have gluten intolerance or inflammatory bowel disease.

Option (D) is incorrect because Agammaglobulinemia is a group of inherited immune deficiencies characterized by a low concentration of antibodies in the blood due to the lack of particular lymphocytes in the blood and lymph. Antibodies are proteins (immunoglobulins, (IgM), (IgG) etc) that are critical and key components of the immune system.

Hence, the correct option is (C).

55. Option (B) is correct as :

- Haemophilia is an X-linked recessive disease. These diseases are more common in men than in women.
- An affected male will not pass the diseases to his sons, but all daughters will be carriers. X-linked recessive diseases are transmitted from carrier women to affected men.

Option (A) is incorrect because Autosomal recessive is one of several ways that a trait, disorder, or disease can be passed down through families. An autosomal recessive disorder means two copies of an abnormal gene must be present in order for the disease or trait to develop.

Option (C) is incorrect because Mitochondrial inheritance is the inheritance of a trait encoded in the mitochondrial genome. Each mitochondrion has a chromosome that is made of DNA (mitochondrial DNA or mtDNA) but is otherwise quite different from the better-known chromosomes in the nucleus. The mitochondrial chromosome is much smaller.

Option (D) is incorrect because Multifactorial inheritance means that "many factors" (multifactorial) are involved in causing a birth defect. The factors are usually both genetic and environmental, where a combination of genes from both parents, in addition to unknown environmental factors, produce the trait or condition.

Hence, the correct option is (B).

56. Option (D) is correct because a Klatskin tumor (or hilar cholangiocarcinoma) is a cholangiocarcinoma (cancer of the biliary tree) occurring at the confluence of the right and left hepatic bile ducts. The disease was named after Gerald Klatskin, who in 1965 described 15 cases and found some characteristics for this type of cholangiocarcinoma.

Option (A) is incorrect because the Krukenberg tumor refers to malignancy in the ovary that metastasized from a primary site, classically the gastrointestinal tract, although it can arise in other tissues such as the breast. Gastric adenocarcinoma, especially at the pylorus, is the most common source.

Option (B) is incorrect because Signet ring cell carcinoma (SRCC) is a rare form of highly malignant adenocarcinoma that produces mucin. It is an epithelial malignancy characterized by the histologic appearance of signet ring cells.

Option (C) is incorrect because an oncocytoma is a tumor made up of oncocytes, epithelial cells characterized by an excessive amount of mitochondria, resulting in an abundant acidophilic, granular cytoplasm. The cells and the tumor that they compose are often benign but sometimes maybe premalignant or malignant.

Hence, the correct option is (D).

57. Option (B) is correct because dystrophic or ectopic mineral deposition occurs in many pathologic conditions, including atherosclerosis. In atherosclerotic plaque, accumulating evidence is consistent with the notion that calcification involves the participation of arterial osteoblasts and osteoclasts.

Option (A) is incorrect because rickets is the inadequate calcification of osteoid into mature bone. Calcification involves the formation of hydroxyapatite crystals.

Option (C) is incorrect because metastatic calcification is the deposition of calcium salts in otherwise normal tissue, because of elevated serum levels of calcium, which can occur because of deranged metabolism as well as increased absorption or decreased excretion of calcium and related minerals, as seen in hyperparathyroidism.

Option (D) is incorrect because vitamin A dietary intake promotes heart valve calcification in vivo. Therefore suggesting that hypervitaminosis A could serve as a new risk factor of CAVD in the human population.

Hence, the correct option is (B).

58. Option (A) is correct as:

- Blood cells first appear during the third week of fetal embryonic development in the yolk sac, but these cells are generated from a primitive stem cell population restricted to the production of myeloid cells.
- Most studies suggest definitive hematopoietic stem cells arise in the mesoderm of the intraembryonic aorta/ gonad/mesonephros region, but evidence also exists for an origin within a small subset of yolk sac-derived cells.
- By the third month of embryogenesis, stem cells derived from the AGM and/or yolk sac migrate to the liver, which is the chief site of blood cell formation until shortly before birth.
- Beginning in the fourth month, stem cells migrate to the bone marrow to commence hematopoiesis at this site.
- By birth, marrow throughout the skeleton is hematopoietically active and virtually the sole source of blood cells.
- Up to the age of puberty, marrow throughout the skeleton remains red and hematopoietically active.
- By age 18 only the vertebrae, ribs, sternum, skull, pelvis, and proximal epiphyseal regions of the humerus and femur retain red marrow, the remaining marrow becoming yellow, fatty, and inactive/

Option (B) is incorrect because the cortex and medulla play different roles in the development of T cells. Cells in the thymus can be divided into thymic stromal cells and cells of hematopoietic origin (derived from bone marrow resident hematopoietic stem cells). Developing T cells are referred to as thymocytes and are of hematopoietic origin.

Option (C) is incorrect because lymph nodes are repositories of B cells, T cells, and other immune system cells, such as dendritic cells and macrophages. They act as filters for foreign particles in the body and are one of the sites where adaptive immune responses are triggered.

Option (D) is incorrect because the spleen is the largest lymphatic organ. It is enclosed by a solid connective tissue capsule composed of dense collagenous connective tissue with a small number of reticular fibres and dispersed smooth muscle cells. The surface of the capsule is covered by a serous membrane with mesothelium.

Hence, the correct option is (A).

59. Option (A) is correct as patients with hemophilia have a deficiency of factor VIII that results in prolonged PTT.

Option (B) is incorrect as prothrombin time (PT) is an assay that tests the extrinsic and common coagulation pathway. So, a Prolonged PT can result from a deficiency of factor V, VII, X, prothrombin or fibrinogen.

Option (C) is incorrect as factor XII deficiency is a rare genetic blood disorder that causes prolonged clotting (coagulation) of blood in a test tube without the presence of prolonged clinical bleeding tendencies. It is caused by a deficiency of the factor XII (Hageman factor), a plasma protein (glycoprotein).

Option (D) is incorrect as bleeding time is not a test for coagulation rathers it tests the ability of the vessels to vasoconstrict and the platelets to form a hemostatic plug.

It is the time taken for a standardized skin puncture to stop bleeding. The normal reference value is between 2-9 minutes.

Hence, the correct option is (A).

60. Option (A) is correct as pathologically, Hodgkin's disease is distinguished from other lymphomas by the presence of Reed Sternberg cells.

Reed Sternberg cells are not absolutely specific for Hodgkin's disease and have also been noticed in cases of infectious mononucleosis and other malignancies including lymphoma, carcinoma and sarcomas.

Option (B) is incorrect because, in sickle cell anaemia, normal red blood cells are rounded and disk-shaped. In sickle cell anaemia, some red blood cells become deformed, so they look like sickles used to cut wheat. These unusually shaped cells give the disease its name.

Option (C) is incorrect as a predominance of hypochromic microcytic cells is found in iron deficiency anaemia, thalassemia, and hereditary sideroblastic anaemia, and in some patients with the anaemia of chronic disorders and with lead intoxication.

Option (D) is incorrect as CML is a clonal bone marrow stem cell disorder in which a proliferation of mature granulocytes (neutrophils, eosinophils and basophils) and their precursors is found.

Hence, the correct option is (A).

61. Option (A) is correct as the prognosis of Hodgkin lymphoma mainly depends on the histological type and staging. Lymphocytic predominant is the best prognostic type of Hodgkin's lymphoma.

Option (B) is incorrect as lymphocytic depletion type is the worst prognosis type of Hodgkin's lymphoma.

Option (C) is incorrect as mixed cellularity is a subtype of classical Hodgkin lymphoma characterized by diagnostic Hodgkin-Reed Sternberg cells in a mixed inflammatory background without sclerosis. Mononuclear Hodgkin cells can be present.

Option (D) is incorrect as nodular sclerosis is a subtype of classical Hodgkin lymphoma characterized by sclerosis, diagnostic Hodgkin and Reed-Sternberg cells and other tumour cells displaying a "lacunar" type morphology. The architectural pattern consists of grouped lacunar cells in lymphoid nodules surrounded by collagen bands.

Hence, the correct option is (A).

62. Option (C) is correct as Atelectasis refers to an incomplete expansion of lungs called Neonatal atelectasis.

The collapse of the previously inflated lung called Acquired atelectasis. This results in areas of relatively airless pulmonary parenchyma.

Option (A) is incorrect as Emphysema is a lung condition that causes shortness of breath. In people with emphysema, the air sacs in the lungs (alveoli) are damaged.

Option (B) is incorrect as Bronchiectasis is a long-term condition where the airways of the lungs become abnormally widened, leading to a build-up of excess mucus that can make the lungs more vulnerable to infection.

Option (D) is incorrect as Bronchitis is an inflammation of the lining of your bronchial tubes, which carry air to and from your lungs. People who have bronchitis often cough up thickened mucus, which can be discolored.

Hence, the correct option is (C).

63. Option (C) is correct as Proteoglycans (PGs) consist of a core protein and linear sugar side chains [glycosaminoglycans (GAGs)] attached to the core protein. The glomerulus is composed of an anastomosing network of capillaries lined by fenestrated endothelium invested by two layers of the epithelium.

The visceral epithelium (podocytes) is incorporated into and becomes an intrinsic part of the capillary wall, separated from endothelial cells by the basement membrane.

The parietal epithelium, situated on Bowman's capsule, lines the urinary space.

Option (A) is incorrect because all anionic molecules (negatively charged) including albumin are repelled by the filtration layer. Serum albumin, often referred to simply as blood albumin, is albumin found in vertebrate blood. Human serum albumin is encoded by the ALB gene.

Option (B) is incorrect as type IV collagen is the main collagen component of the basement membrane. It is network-forming collagen that underlies epithelial and endothelial cells and functions as a barrier between tissue compartments.

Option (D) is incorrect as Fibronectin is a large molecular weight glycoprotein which has been shown to be associated with cell surfaces, extracellular fluids, and connective tissues. Its possible relationship with basement membranes remains controversial. We conclude that fibronectin is probably not part of the basement membranes studied.

Hence, the correct option is (C).

64. Option (D) is correct as the esophagus is the tube that connects your throat to your stomach. Mallory-Weiss syndrome (MWS) is a condition marked by a tear in the mucous membrane, or inner lining, where the esophagus meets the stomach.

Option (A) is incorrect as an esophageal laceration (Mallory-Weiss syndrome) is a tear that does not penetrate the wall of the esophagus. The tear can be caused by forceful vomiting.

Option (B) is incorrect as disorders involving the cricopharyngeal muscles, such as cricopharyngeal dysfunction (CD), include the inability to relax the sphincter (achalasia), delayed relaxation of the cricopharyngeus muscle as the bolus of food moves caudally (asynchrony), and failure to close the sphincter (achalasia).

Option (C) is incorrect as Mallory - Weiss syndrome is characterized by a mucosal tear at the gastroesophageal junction following a bout of forceful retching (or vomiting, coughing or straining).

Hence, the correct option is (D).

65. Option (D) is correct as it is covering all the options mentioned above.

Option (A) is incorrect though in the most severe form of preeclampsia, the presence of HELLP syndrome (defined as hemolysis, elevated liver enzymes and low platelet) with the addition of hepatic compromises, such as hepatic infarction or hematoma, increased the risk of maternal morbidity and mortality. Other options are also relatable so selecting an individual option won't be correct.

Option (B) is incorrect as nutmeg liver refers to the mottled appearance of the liver as a result of hepatic venous congestion. Again selecting an individual option wouldn't be considered as correct.

Option (C) is incorrect as hepatic infarcts are also seen in the condition of shock. But this option is incorrect as well for the same reason as above.

Hence, the correct option is (D).

66. Option (C) is correct as a Sertoli cell tumor, also Sertoli cell tumour (US spelling), is a sex cord-gonadal stromal tumour of Sertoli cells.

Option (A) is incorrect as a seminoma is a germ cell tumor of the testicle or, more rarely, the mediastinum or other extra-gonadal locations.

Option (B) is incorrect as the Yolk sac (Endodermal sinus) tumor (EST) is a member of the germ cell tumor group of cancers.

Option (D) is incorrect as Teratomas are the most common germ cell tumor found in the ovaries.

Hence, the correct option is (C).

67. Option (C) is correct as RA is a chronic multisystem disorder that may affect many tissues and organs but principally attacks the joints, producing a nonsuppurative proliferative and inflammatory synovitis that often progresses to destruction of the articular cartilage and ankylosis of the joint.

Symptoms usually develop in the small joints of the hands, (i.e. metacarpophalangeal & proximal interphalangeal joint), and feet (metatarsophalangeal & interphalangeal) joint.

Option (A) is incorrect as Ankylosing spondylitis (AS) is a type of arthritis in which there is long-term inflammation of the joints of the spine.

Option (B) is incorrect as sacroiliac joints (SIJs) are characteristically involved in SpA leading to joint inflammation of varying degrees, with predominant involvement of its cartilaginous portion.

Option (D) is incorrect as small joints of the hand, wrist, foot, knee, and ankle are characteristically affected by rheumatoid arthritis. A pattern of involvement with the MCP (metacarpophalangeal) joints, PIP (proximal interphalangeal) joints, and the wrist is highly suspicious of rheumatoid arthritis, but not definitive.

Hence, the correct option is (C).

68. Option (D) is correct as Microglial cells are the major phagocytic cells in C.N.S. At the time of injury microglial cells modify to form macrophages called Gitter cells.

Option (A) is incorrect because Fibrous astrocytes are prevalent among myelinated nerve fibres in the white matter of the central nervous system. Organelles seen in the somata of neurons are also seen in astrocytes, but they appear to be much sparser.

Option (B) is incorrect as unlike fibrous astrocytes, protoplasmic astrocytes occur in the grey matter of the central nervous system. They have fewer fibrils within their cytoplasm, and cytoplasmic organelles are sparse so that the somata are shaped by surrounding neurons and fibres.

Option (C) is incorrect as Oligodendrocytes are a type of large glial cell found in the central nervous system. Oligodendrocytes produce the myelin sheath insulating neuronal axons (analogous to Schwann cells in the peripheral nervous system), although some oligodendrocytes (called satellite oligodendrocytes) are not involved in myelination.

Hence, the correct option is (D).

69. Option (B) is correct as Medullary thyroid carcinoma (MTC) is an uncommon neoplasm in children that usually is associated with the multiple endocrine neoplasia (MEN) syndrome types 2A and 2B and with familial medullary thyroid carcinoma (FMTC).

Option (A) is incorrect as Multiple endocrine neoplasia (MEN) type I is a disease in which one or more of the endocrine glands are overactive or forms a tumor. It is passed down through families. The endocrine glands most commonly involved include Pancreas.

Option (C) is incorrect as Li–Fraumeni syndrome is a rare, autosomal dominant, hereditary disorder that predisposes carriers to cancer development. The syndrome is linked to germline mutations of the p53 tumor suppressor gene, which encodes a transcription factor (p53) that normally regulates the cell cycle and prevents genomic mutations.

Option (D) is incorrect as Hashimoto's thyroiditis, also known as chronic lymphocytic thyroiditis and Hashimoto's disease, is an autoimmune disease in which the thyroid gland is gradually destroyed. Early on there may be no symptoms. Over time the thyroid may enlarge, forming a painless goitre.

Hence, the correct option is (B).

70. Option (B) is correct as a malignant melanoma may arise :

- De-novo in apparently normal skin
- In a preexisting pigmented nevus

Malignant change in a benign naevus occurs only in the JUNCTIONAL or compound varieties. Pure dermal naevus is safe.

Option (A) is incorrect as malignant transformation is rare in Epidermal naevus.

Option (C) is incorrect as malignant transformation is rare in Intradermal naevus too.

Option (D) is incorrect as malignant potential is maximum in Junctional naevus that is an option (B). So, this option will automatically get wrong.

Hence, the correct option is (B).

71. Option (B) is correct as the commonest type of spinal T.B. is paradiscal. In this contiguous areas of 2 adjacent vertebrae along with intervening disc are affected. This special pattern of involvement is seen because of the embryology of the vertebra.

The lower half of one vertebra and the upper half of the one below it, along with the intervening disc develop from pair of sclerotomes and have a common blood supply.

Option (A) is incorrect as posterior spinal tuberculosis or tuberculosis of the neural arch is caused by the same type of Mycobacterium tuberculosis which produces classical Pott's spine or anterior spinal tuberculosis

Option (C) is incorrect as pedicle involvement is part of the disease process and usually associated with the relatively severe vertebral body and disc destruction, wide prevertebral abscess, and severe kyphosis. Pedicle involvement can be detected early from MRI and need to be documented as it may influence the treatment strategy.

Option (D) is incorrect as in spinal tuberculosis, characteristically, there is the destruction of the intervertebral disk space and the adjacent vertebral bodies, the collapse of the spinal elements, and anterior wedging leading to the characteristic angulation and gibbous (palpable deformity because of involvement of multiple vertebrae) formation.

Hence, the correct option is (B).

72. Option (A) is correct as cavitation has been detected in 7%-11% of primary lung cancers by plain radiography and in 22% by computed tomography.

Option (B) is incorrect as M. bovis does not produce post-primary tuberculosis in any species. It only produces aggressive primary tuberculosis that can develop small cavities by the erosion of caseating granulomas.

Option (C) is incorrect as foci of calcification in lymph nodes are usually irregularly distributed throughout the node. They result from healed granulomatous infection, usually tuberculosis or histoplasmosis and constitute part of the Ranke complex.

Option (D) is incorrect as tuberculosis is the formation of an organized structure called a granuloma. It consists mainly in the recruitment at the infectious stage of macrophages, highly differentiated cells such as multinucleated giant cells, epithelioid cells and Foamy cells, all these cells being surrounded by a rim of lymphocytes.

Hence, the correct option is (A).

73. Option (D) is correct as it is covering all the options mentioned above. Neuroblastoma is a malignant tumor of the autonomic nervous system.

It has the following peculiarities: -

Most common abdominal cancer of childhood.

Most common cancer of infancy

Most common extracranial solid tumor of childhood (most common solid tumor of childhood is brain tumor).

It is a neuroendocrine tumor, arising from any neural crest element of the sympathetic nervous system.

The primary tumor is localized in the localization of the sympathetic nervous system.

The common sites of neuroblastoma are : -

(i) Adrenal (most common)

(ii) Pelvis

(iii) Cervical area (Neck)

(iv) Posterior mediastinum

(v) Paravertebral retroperitoneum

Metastasis present in 60-70% of children at the time of diagnosis and the most frequent site of metastasis is a skeletal system (bones and bone marrow). Other common sites of metastasis are the liver, lymph nodes and skin. Metastasis to the lung is rare (<3%).

Option (A) is incorrect though the neuroblastoma has spread to the liver, skin. But going for an individual option won't be considered as correct.

Option (B) is incorrect as the children with neuroblastoma usually have metastatic disease at diagnosis; however, the lung metastasis is rarely detected at the initial diagnosis of these children. But it is incorrect for the same reason as an option (A).

Option (C) is incorrect although neuroblastoma often is present at birth, it generally is not detected until the tumor begins to grow and compress the surrounding organs. Cancer cells can metastasize (spread) quickly to other areas of the body, such as lymph nodes, liver, lungs, bones, the central nervous system and bone marrow. It is incorrect for the same reason as well.

Hence, the correct option is (D).

74. Option (D) is correct as the expression of TRKA protein in cancer may confer a more favorable prognosis in certain neoplasms. TRKA expression in neuroblastoma confers a good prognosis via a potential tumor-suppressing role for TRKA and NGF signaling in neuroblastoma cells, resulting in differentiation, growth arrest, and angiogenesis inhibition.

Option (A) is incorrect as tumor cell ploidy is one of the factors; diploid and near-triploid neuroblastomas show poor and excellent clinical outcomes, respectively.

Option (B) is incorrect as N-Myc amplification is a crucial prognostic factor in neuroblastoma, which is associated with almost all features related to poor prognosis and a higher probability of an unfavorable outcome.

Option (C) is incorrect as deletion of a part of the short arm of chromosome 1 is one of the most common chromosomal rearrangements observed in neuroblastoma (NBL) tumors and it is associated with a poor prognosis. No NBL tumour suppressor gene has yet been identified in the region.

Hence, the correct option is (D).

75. Option (B) is correct as Wilm's tumour is associated with three groups of congenital malformations.

The risk of Wilm's tumour is increased in these conditions.

These are -

1. WAGR syndrome - It consists of

- Aniridia
- Mental retardation
- Genital anomalies

The risk of Wilm's tumour is increased by 33% in this syndrome.

2. Denys-Drash syndrome - It consists of

- Gonadal dysgenesis (male pseudohermaphroditism)
- Nephropathy leading to renal failure.
- Majority of patients with this syndrome have renal failure.

3. Beckwith - Wiedemann syndrome - It consists of

- Enlargement of body organs.
- Hemihypertrophy.
- Renal medullary cysts.
- Abnormal large cells in the adrenal cortex.

Option (A) is incorrect as one paraneoplastic syndrome that occurs rarely in people with neuroblastoma causes rapid eye movements and difficulty with coordination. Another rare syndrome causes abdominal swelling and diarrhea.

Option (C) is incorrect as the exact cause of non-Hodgkin lymphoma is unknown. However, there are multiple medical conditions that are associated with an increased risk of developing the disease: Inherited immune deficiencies. Genetic syndromes: Down syndrome, Klinefelter's syndrome (a genetic condition in men caused by an extra X chromosome).

Option (D) is incorrect as androgen insensitivity syndrome is when the body of a person who is genetically male, with 1 X and 1 Y chromosome, is resistant to male hormones called androgens. A person with this syndrome has a higher risk of developing a gonadoblastoma or other germ cell tumours.

Hence, the correct option is (B).

76. Option (B) is correct as biotransformation reactions (metabolism) of drugs can be classified :

A. Non-synthetic (phase I) reactions

Metabolism brings about a change in the drug molecule by:

1. Oxidation
2. Reduction
3. Hydrolysis
4. Cyclization
5. Decyclization

The new metabolite may retain biological activity or it may be an inactive metabolite.

Oxidation is the most important metabolizing reaction.

The most important enzyme for oxidation reaction is cytochrome P450

B. Synthetic (phase II or conjugation) reaction.

Metabolism involves the union of the drug with one of several polar (water-soluble) endogenous molecules that are products of intermediary metabolism, to form a water-soluble conjugate which is readily eliminated by the kidney or, if the molecular weight exceeds 300, in the bile.

Phase II metabolism almost invariably terminates biological activity, i.e. metabolites are usually inactive.

Reactions are:-

1. Acetylation
2. Glucuronide conjugation
3. Glycine conjugation
4. Glutathione conjugation
5. Sulfate conjugation
6. Methylation
7. Nucleotide synthesis

Option (A) is incorrect as cytochrome C is primarily known for its function in the mitochondria as a key participant in the life-supporting function of ATP synthesis. However, when a cell receives an apoptotic stimulus, cytochrome c is released into the cytosol and triggers programmed cell death through apoptosis.

Option (C) is incorrect as glucuronyl transferase is a liver enzyme. It changes bilirubin into a form that can be removed from the body through the bile. It also changes some hormones, medicines, and toxins into non-harmful products.

Option (D) is incorrect as acetyltransferase (or transacetylase) is a type of transferase enzyme that transfers an acetyl group.

Hence, the correct option is (B).

77. Option (B) is correct as the bioavailability of a drug administered intravenously is by definition 100%. Bioavailability is less or equal to 100% for any other route of administration. The term absolute bioavailability is used when the fraction of absorbed drug is related to its i.e. bioavailability.

Option (A) is incorrect as if the oral formulation of a drug has a bioavailability of 50%, one must double the drug dose to achieve the same concentrations in plasma as achieved using the intravenous formulation. Poor oral bioavailability is a major limitation of many drugs administered to horses.

Option (C) is incorrect as drugs administered through the rectal route are absorbed through two different vascular systems, one of which delivers agents to the liver while the second bypasses the liver. As a result, wide variations of bioavailability are seen after rectal administration. References report that 50% of a drug delivered by the rectal route undergoes first-pass metabolism in the liver, but this is a broad approximation, and absorption is often irregular and incomplete.

Option (D) is incorrect as the impact of Subcutaneous Administration of Biotherapeutics on Bioavailability. A drawback of subcutaneous administration of biotherapeutics is the incomplete bioavailability of the injected molecule, which can range widely from 50 to 80% for mAbs and even more for other biotherapeutics.

Hence, the correct option is (B).

78. Option (D) is correct as many drugs can bind to the same binding site in plasma proteins. So displacement by another drug is possible.

Option (A) is incorrect because when drug concentration in plasma increase, both bound form and free form increases. So, it is not true.

Option (B) is incorrect as the bound form is not available for metabolism or excretion. The only free form is available.

Option (C) is incorrect as acidic drugs bind to albumin while basic drugs bind to the α1 acid glycoprotein.

Hence, the correct option is (D).

79. Option (B) is correct as cholinomimetic drugs - Mimics the action of the parasympathetic system (Action of acetylcholine).

It causes Bradycardia. So it cannot be used in bradycardia as it will cause a further decrease in heart rate.

Option (A) is incorrect as cholinergic drugs are useful for the short-term management of angle-closure glaucoma associated with the pupillary block.

Option (C) is incorrect as cholinomimetics could be used for Open-angle glaucoma, Cobra bite.

Option (D) is incorrect as cholinomimetics could also be used for Open-angle glaucoma, Cobra bite and Myasthenia gravis. Myasthenia gravis is a neuromuscular disorder primarily characterized by muscle weakness and muscle fatigue.

Hence, the correct option is (B).

80. Option (D) is correct as the points to remember about Apraclonidine are:

- Sympathomimetic drug
- Indication - Open-angle Glaucoma
- Mechanism of action - Decrease aqueous secretion
- Adverse effect - Upper lid retraction, eye allergy.

Option (A) is incorrect as Bimatoprost ophthalmic may cause a gradual change in the colour of your eyes or eyelids and lashes, usually an increase in brown pigment.

Option (B) is incorrect as Latanoprost is used to treat open-angle glaucoma and ocular hypertension. These conditions are caused by an increase in pressure in your eye. They may cause eye pain or vision changes.

Option (C) is incorrect as Brimonidine is a medication used to treat open-angle glaucoma, ocular hypertension. When applied to the skin it works by causing blood vessels to contract.

Hence, the correct option is (D).

81. Option (B) is correct as Dilator pupillae is supplied by Sympathetic fibres from the cervical sympathetic chain.

Option (A) is incorrect because it is Constrictor pupillae that is supplied by Parasympathetic postganglionic fibres from the Edinger-Westphal nucleus.

Option (C) is incorrect as the oculomotor nerves (third cranial nerves) originate in the midbrain and supply each eye's pupil constrictor, eyelid (levator palpebrae superioris), and muscles that adduct (medial rectus), depress (inferior rectus), and elevate (superior rectus and inferior oblique) the eye.

Option (D) is incorrect as the fibres supply parasympathetic innervation to the lacrimal gland.

Hence, the correct option is (B).

82. Option (C) is correct as basic drugs like morphine, d-TC and amphotericin B etc act as histamine liberators and can cause an acute reaction leading to itching and hypotension.

Option (A) is incorrect as normally, there is a layer that protects the insides of the stomach and intestine from the acid in your stomach. If aspirin is taken at high doses and for a long time, it can slowly damage this layer. This damage can lead to bleeding.

Option (B) is incorrect as the application of procaine leads to the depression of neuronal activity. The depression causes the nervous system to become hypersensitive, producing restlessness and shaking, leading to minor to severe convulsions.

Option (D) is incorrect as side effects reported for sulfadiazine include nausea, loss of appetite, and dizziness.

Hence, the correct option is (C).

83. Option (C) is correct as oral losartan has been found to exert the same beneficial hemodynamic effects as ACE inhibitors in patients with symptomatic heart failure, and in elderly CHF patients, it was found to be associated with lower mortality and better tolerability than others.

Option (A) is incorrect as Furosemide is also used alone or together with other medicines to treat high blood pressure (hypertension). This can damage the blood vessels of the brain, heart, and kidneys, resulting in a stroke, heart failure, or kidney failure.

Option (B) is incorrect as it is a drug that may improve the prognosis in patients with congestive heart failure. Amrinone has been shown to increase the contractions initiated in the heart by high gain calcium-induced calcium release (CICR).

Option (D) is incorrect as in recent trials, digoxin has been shown to reduce morbidity associated with congestive heart failure but to have no demonstrable effect on survival. The goal of digoxin therapy in patients with congestive heart failure is to improve quality of life by reducing symptoms and preventing hospitalizations.

Hence, the correct option is (C).

84. Option (B) is correct as Furosemide is a high efficacy diuretic. They inhibit Na-K-2CL cotransport at the thick ascending limb of the loop of Henle.

Option (A) is incorrect as Furosemide inhibits Na-K-2CL cotransport at the thick ascending limb of the loop of Henle, not the descending limb of the loop of Henle.

Option (C) is incorrect as the proximal tubule is the only site for glucose reabsorption.

Option (D) is incorrect as the distal convoluted tubule (DCT) is a portion of the kidney nephron between the loop of Henle and the collecting tubule.

Hence, the correct option is (B).

85. Option (B) is correct as growth hormone therapy commonly leads to hyperglycemia (not hypoglycemia). Therefore, this is the required answer.

Option (A) is incorrect as the mechanism of carpal tunnel syndrome in acromegaly is that edematous synovial tissues compress the median nerve because oversecretion of growth hormone causes an increase of sodium and water retention in the extracellular fluid. So, this is not the required answer.

Option (C) is incorrect as GHD is often treated with GH therapy. Although the pathogenesis of IH in patients with GHD treated with GH therapy is not fully understood, it is thought that GH increases IGF-1-mediated production of cerebral spinal fluid (CSF) from the choroidal plexus, leading to increased intracranial pressure. So, this is also not the required answer.

Option (D) is incorrect as slipped capital femoral epiphysis (SCFE) is a rare complication of growth hormone (GH) therapy. SCFE developed 2 months after starting GH therapy. Pain over the hip joints or over the knees is an early sign of SCFE.

Hence, the correct option is (B).

86. Option (C) is correct as Thiopentone is a highly lipid-soluble drug. On administration, it quickly reaches the brain and causes anesthesia. But due to high lipid solubility, it again crosses the membranes of the brain and diffuses to other tissues like fat and muscle. As it is not present in the brain, its action is terminated. This is known as re-distribution.

Option (A) is incorrect as the sympathetic nervous system helps regulate both physiologic and metabolic functions. Epinephrine produces metabolic effects--including hyperglycemia, hyperlactatemia, hyperlipemia, increased oxygen consumption, and serum potassium changes.

Option (B) is incorrect as the first pass effect (also known as first-pass metabolism or presystemic metabolism) is a phenomenon of drug metabolism whereby the concentration of a drug, specifically when administered orally, is greatly reduced before it reaches the systemic circulation.

Option (D) is incorrect as the blood flowing through the systemic circulation may also encounter widened passages due to aneurysms.

Hence, the correct option is (C).

87. Option (A) is correct as mast cell stabilizers like cromoglycate and nedocromil are used to prevent exercise-induced asthma. However, corticosteroids are preferred for this indication.

Option (B) is incorrect as Ipratropium is used to control and prevent symptoms (wheezing and shortness of breath) caused by ongoing lung disease (chronic obstructive pulmonary disease-COPD which includes bronchitis and emphysema).

Option (C) is incorrect as Terbutaline is used to prevent and treat wheezing, shortness of breath, and chest tightness caused by asthma, chronic bronchitis, and emphysema.

Option (D) is incorrect as Epinephrine medication is used in emergencies to treat very serious allergic reactions to insect stings/bites, foods, drugs, or other substances.

Hence, the correct option is (A).

88. Option (D) is correct as Cinnarizine is an antihistamine and calcium channel blocker of the diphenylmethylpiperazine group. Therefore, this is not the required answer.

Option (A) is incorrect as Ondansetron (Zofran), a 5-hydroxytryptamine3 receptor agonist, is a potent antiemetic originally used for the treatment of chemotherapy-induced nausea and vomiting. So, this is not the required answer.

Option (B) is incorrect as Domperidone is a specific blocker of dopamine receptors. It speeds gastrointestinal peristalsis, causes prolactin release, and is used as an antiemetic and tool in the study of dopaminergic mechanisms. Hence, it is not the required answer.

Option (C) is incorrect as Metoclopramide is an oral prokinetic and antiemetic agent used in the therapy of gastroesophageal reflux disease, gastroparesis and severe or chemotherapy-induced nausea. Thus, it is also not the required answer.

Hence, the correct option is (D).

89. Option (B) is correct as Tigecycline is a newer drug in the class 'Glycylcyclines.' Its mechanism of action and most properties are similar to tetracyclines. However, it is resistant to the efflux pump (a major mechanism of resistance against tetracyclines).

Option (A) is incorrect as Isoniazid is bactericidal to rapidly dividing mycobacteria but is bacteriostatic if the mycobacteria are slow-growing. It inhibits the cytochrome P450 system and hence acts as a source of free radicals.

Option (C) is incorrect as Daptomycin is a novel antibiotic with rapid in vitro bactericidal activity against gram-positive organisms.

Option (D) is incorrect as for instance, ciprofloxacin, a fluoroquinolone, exhibits a bacteriostatic activity when the replication of DNA is inhibited by inhibiting DNA gyrase and a bactericidal activity caused by bacterial DNA fragmentation. Therefore, this is also not the required answer.

Hence, the correct option is (B).

90. Option (D) is correct as it is covering all the other options mentioned above. Intravenous bolus dosing is not practical because of the short duration of action, rather it is administered by constant i.e. infusion.

Option (A) is incorrect even though due to its short duration of action, it is indicated for short-term painful procedures. Selecting one option when others are also relatable won't be considered correct.

Option (B) is incorrect though remifentanil is the shortest-acting opioid due to its metabolism by plasma esterases. But it is also incorrect as other options are also relatable.

Option (C) is incorrect though the potency is equal to fentanyl and similarly, it can also cause post-operative muscle rigidity. It is incorrect for the same reason as options (A) and (B).

Hence, the correct option is (D).

91. Option (A) is correct as Carbamazepine is used to prevent and control seizures. This medication is known as an anticonvulsant or antiepileptic drug. It is also used to relieve certain types of nerve pain (such as trigeminal neuralgia).

Option (B) is incorrect as Propylthiouracil (PTU) is an oral medication that is used to manage hyperthyroidism which is due to an overactive thyroid gland. It is an anti-thyroid drug that has a mechanism of action that is similar to methimazole (Tapazole).

Option (C) is incorrect as Methimazole (MMI) is an anti-thyroid drug that belongs to drug class thionamides; the FDA-approved uses of which include patients with Graves disease. Patients with toxic multinodular goitre who are poor candidates for surgery or radioactive iodine therapy.

Option (D) is incorrect as Carbimazole is a carbethoxy derivative of methimazole. Its antithyroid action is due to its conversion to methimazole after absorption. Carbimazole is an antithyroid agent that decreases the uptake and concentration of inorganic iodine by the thyroid, it also reduces the formation of di-iodotyrosine and thyroxine.

Hence, the correct option is (A).

92. Option (A) is correct as Bremelanotide functions by activating the melanocortin receptors.

It was shown to be effective in treating sexual dysfunction in both men erectile dysfunction or impotence) and women (sexual arousal disorder).

Option (B) is incorrect as a number of medical treatments for LUTS/BPH exist, such as α-blockers, 5α-reductase inhibitors, anticholinergics, phosphodiesterase type 5 (PDE5) inhibitors, and combination therapies.

Option (C) is incorrect as radiation therapy is a good choice for many men with early-stage prostate cancer. It is also the best treatment for older men or those who have other health problems.

Option (D) is incorrect as Nivolumab (Opdivo) and pembrolizumab (Keytruda) are two of the more common checkpoint inhibitors that can treat metastatic renal cell cancer. Both of these medicines are given through your vein. Nivolumab is given every 2 to 4 weeks. Pembrolizumab is given every 3 weeks.

Hence, the correct option is (A).

93. Option (B) is correct as Ethyl alcohol causes vasodilatation and peripheral circulation increases, resulting in a feeling of warmth, but at the same time, there will be loss of body heat from the skin.

Option (A) is incorrect as MAOI toxicity may present as opisthotonus, muscle rigidity, diaphoresis, hypertension, chest pain, diarrhoea, hallucinations, combativeness, confusion, marked hyperthermia and trismus.

Option (C) is incorrect as in atropine poisoning, Pyrexia (hot as a hare) is a common event and the temperature may be raised by 1 to 6° F.

Option (D) is incorrect because when taken in excess, Amphetamine produces a dry mouth, loss of appetite, irritability, dizziness, loss of sleep, dilated pupils, severe chest pain, restlessness, tachycardia, hypertension, the rise of temperature and death.

Hence, the correct option is (B).

94. Option (C) is correct as this medication is used to treat fungal skin infections such as athlete's foot, jock itch, and ringworm. This medication is also used to treat a skin condition known as pityriasis (tinea versicolor), a fungal infection that causes a lightening or darkening of the skin of the neck, chest, arms, or legs.

Option (A) is incorrect as Lindane, formerly known as gamma benzene hexachloride, is an insecticide and is used to treat scabies and lice infestations. Lindane cream and lotion are usually used to treat only scabies infestation.

Option (B) is incorrect as this medication is used to treat scabies, a condition caused by tiny insects called mites that infest and irritate your skin.

Option (D) is incorrect as Crotamiton works by killing the mites that cause scabies. It also helps relieve itching related to scabies and other skin conditions.

Hence, the correct option is (C).

95. Option (B) is correct as for Palliative treatment of patent ductus arteriosus, indomethacin (drug decreasing PGs) is used.

Option (A) is incorrect though Prostaglandin analogues are useful for pulmonary hypertension.

Option (C) is incorrect as Prostaglandin analogues are also useful for Impotence.

Option (D) is incorrect as Prostaglandin analogues are useful for Inflammatory bowel disease too.

Hence, the correct option is (B).

96. Option (C) is correct as capsule stain is a type of differential stain which uses acidic and basic dyes to stain background & bacterial cells respectively so that the presence of capsule is easily visualized.

Option (A) is incorrect as cell staining is a technique that can be used to better visualize cells and cell components under a microscope. By using different stains, one can preferentially stain certain cell components, such as a nucleus or a cell wall, or the entire cell.

Option (B) is incorrect as the bright field microscope can be used to view motility in a wet mount by reducing the amount of light that passes through the specimen. This is the most common method of observing motility.

Option (D) is incorrect as the first visualization of the shape of the bacterial ribosome and its non-symmetric ribosomal subunits was obtained by the reconstitution of negatively stained electron microscopy (EM) images.

Hence, the correct option is (C).

97. Option (B) is correct as Robert Koch's Discovery of the Tubercle Bacilli. On 24 March 1882, the German doctor Robert Koch communicated to the Berlin Society of Physiology that he had discovered the microorganism responsible for the deadly pulmonary tuberculosis, named Tuberkelvirus in his seminal publication made 2 weeks later.

Option (A) is incorrect as Louis Pasteur discovered that microbes were responsible for souring alcohol and came up with the process of pasteurization, where bacteria is destroyed by heating beverages and then allowing them to cool.

Option (C) is incorrect as Lister successfully introduced carbolic acid (now known as phenol) to sterilise surgical instruments and to clean wounds. Applying Louis Pasteur's advances in microbiology, Lister championed the use of carbolic acid as an antiseptic, so that it became the first widely used antiseptic in surgery.

Option (D) is incorrect as Edward Jenner (1749-1823) Edward Jenner was an English country doctor who introduced the vaccine for smallpox. Previously a keen practitioner of smallpox inoculation, Jenner took the principle a stage further by inducing immunity against this killer disease via exposure to a harmless related disease, cowpox.

Hence, the correct option is (B).

98. Option (C) is correct as it covers both the options given above that are used to see bacteria, i.e.

Bacteria, to be seen they require-

1. Magnification under microscope
2. Staining techniques to produce contrast

Option (A) is incorrect though the Microscopy method is used to see bacteria as individual bacterial cells hard to see because

1. They are too small to be seen by the naked eye.
2. They are almost transparent

But, it is incorrect as the other options are also relatable. So individually it cannot be correct.

Option (B) is incorrect even though a special stain technique is used to examine bacterial spores. Malachite green is used with heat to force the stain into the cells and give them colour. A counterstain, safranin, is then used to give colour to the nonperforming bacteria. At the end of the procedure, spores stain green and other cells stain red. But, it is incorrect for the same reason as of option (A).

Option (D) is incorrect as both the methods that are given in option (A) and (B) are useful to see bacteria. So, this option will automatically get to wrong.

Hence, the correct option is (C).

99. Option (C) is correct as due to their roles in the production of B and T cells, the thymus and bone marrow are considered primary lymphoid organs.

Option (A) is incorrect as Lymph nodes are classified as peripheral lymphoid organs (Vollmerhaus et al., 1981, 1994; Gershwin et al., 1995).

Option (B) is incorrect as Spleen is called peripheral lymphoid organs because of their roles in the production of B and T cells, the thymus and bone marrow are considered primary lymphoid organs.

Option (D) is incorrect as the mucosa-associated lymphoid tissue (MALT) initiates immune responses to specific antigens encountered along all mucosal surfaces. MALT inductive sites are secondary immune tissues where antigen sampling occurs and immune responses are initiated.

Hence, the correct option is (C).

100. Option (C) is correct because the maturation of B- cells takes place in the bone marrow.

Option (A) is incorrect because these are T cells which originate in the bone marrow and mature in the thymus.

Option (B) is incorrect as T-cells mature in the thymus gland or in the lymph nodes. Since the thymus is only 10-15% functional in the adult, the lymph nodes take on greater importance in the maturation process.

Option (D) is incorrect as B cell activation occurs in the secondary lymphoid organs (SLOs), such as the spleen and lymph nodes. After B cells mature in the bone marrow, they migrate through the blood to SLOs, which receive a constant supply of antigen through circulating lymph.

Hence, the correct option is (C).

101. Option (A) is correct as

- NK cells are part of innate immunity
- NK cells are considered to be important in immune surveillance and natural defense against virus-infected and malignant mutant cells.

Option (B) is incorrect as CD8 Cytotoxic Cells Cytotoxic T cells are activated by dendritic cells that express antigen-loaded class I molecules. Dendritic cells ingest intact cells (cross-priming) or free antigens. After processing, antigens are presented in the context of class I or class II molecules.

Option (C) is incorrect as B cells are the part of the adaptive immune system, B cells are responsible for generating antibodies to specific antigens, which they bind via B cell receptors (BCR).

Option (D) is incorrect as B lymphocytes are the cells of the immune system that make antibodies to invading pathogens like viruses. They form memory cells that remember the same pathogen for faster antibody production in future infections.

Hence, the correct option is (A).

102. Option (A) is correct as Mononuclear phagocytes (MP) also known as macrophages or histiocytes are distributed throughout virtual all tissues.

- The macrophage is the dominant cellular player in chronic inflammation.
- MP arise from monoblast in the marrow, and they are released into the circulation as monocytes.
- The monocytes then migrate to tissues and become part of the tissue (fixed) macrophages.

Option (B) is incorrect as the Reticuloendothelial System (RES) consists of cells descending from the monocytes which are able to perform phagocytosis of foreign materials and particles. 90% of the RES is located in the liver.

Option (C) is incorrect as Neutrophils are a type of white blood cell (WBC or granulocyte) that protect us from infections, among other functions. They make up approximately 40 percent to 60 percent of the white blood cells in our bodies,1 and are the first cells to arrive on the scene when we experience a bacterial infection.

Option (D) is incorrect as Lymphocytes are white blood cells that are also one of the body's main types of immune cells. They are made in the bone marrow and found in the blood and lymph tissue. The immune system is a complex network of cells known as immune cells that include lymphocytes.

Hence, the correct option is (A).

103. Option (C) is correct as Listeria is a gram-positive bacillus. Listeria is the only gram-positive bacteria that have endotoxin. (Endotoxin is present only in gram-negative organisms).

Option (A) is incorrect as Staphylococci are also gram-positive aerobic organisms. Staphylococci are Gram-positive cocci not bacilli about 0.5 – 1.0 µm in diameter.

Option (B) is incorrect as Streptococci are Gram-positive, nonmotile, non-spore-forming, catalase-negative cocci (not bacilli) that occur in pairs or chains. Older cultures may lose their Gram-positive character.

Option (D) is incorrect as Meningococci (Neisseria meningitidis) are gram-negative cocci that cause meningitis and meningococcemia.

Hence, the correct option is (C).

104. Option (D) is correct as Rickettsiae and related (rickettsia-like) bacteria (such as Ehrlichia, Anaplasma, and Coxiella burnetii bacteria) are unusual types of bacteria that cause several similar diseases, including the following: Rocky Mountain spotted fever. Epidemic typhus. Ehrlichiosis.

Option (A) is incorrect as Genital elephantiasis can also be caused by bacterial sexually transmitted diseases, specifically lymphogranuloma venereum (LGV) and donovanosis. The bacterium that results in LGV, Chlamydia trachomatis serovar L1-L3, damages the lymphatic system resulting in lymphatic obstruction in the genitals.

Option (B) is incorrect as Chancroid is a genital ulcer disease characterized by painful ulcerous lesions in any of the different regions of the genitalia and regional lymphadenopathy, and is caused by genital infection by the Gram-negative-like, facultatively anaerobic bacterium, Haemophilus ducreyi.

Option (C) is incorrect as Genital elephantiasis means massive enlargement of genitals. In the pre penicillin era, syphilis was the frequent cause of genital elephantiasis. Then was the age of bacterial STI's – donovanosis, LGV; the incidence of which declined with the advent of effective antibiotics.

Hence, the correct option is (D).

105. Option (C) is correct as Blood culture is positive when bacteria present in the blood, i.e. when there is bacteremia.

Infective endocarditis is a complication of staphylococcal aureus bacteremia (SAB). Thus blood culture may be positive.

Option (A) is incorrect as in toxic shock syndrome (TSS) due to staphylococcus aureus, bacteremia is uncommon (in contrast, bacteremia is common in streptococcal TSS).

Option (B) is incorrect as Staphylococcal scalded skin syndrome (SSSS) does not have bacteremia. The symptoms of Staphylococcal scalded skin syndrome (SSSS) include blistering of skin on superficial layers due to the exfoliative toxins released from Staphylococcus aureus.

Option (D) is incorrect as Impetigo also does not have bacteremia. Impetigo is an infection caused by strains of staph or strep bacteria.

Hence, the correct option is (C).

106. Option (B) is correct as the extracellular infectious virus particle is called the virion. The virion consists of a nucleic acid surrounded by a protein coat, the capsid.

Option (A) is incorrect as the capsomere is a subunit of the capsid, an outer covering of protein that protects the genetic material of a virus. Capsomeres self-assemble to form the capsid.

Option (C) is incorrect as the capsid with the enclosed nucleic acid is known as the nucleocapsid.

Option (D) is incorrect as virion may be enveloped or nonenveloped (naked). The envelope is lipoprotein in nature, the lipid is derived from the host cell, while protein is virus-coded.

Enveloped viruses are susceptible to the action of lipid solvents like ether, chloroform and bile salts.

Hence, the correct option is (B).

107. Option (C) is correct as histologic lesions include necrosis of the gastrointestinal epithelium with syncytial cell formation. Intranuclear and intracytoplasmic inclusion bodies characteristic of the measles virus are present in the epithelium, lamina propria, and gut-associated lymphoid tissue.

Option (A) is incorrect as all vertebrate poxviruses have cytoplasmic basophilic (B-type) inclusion bodies, which represent areas of the infected cells that contain large amounts of virus DNA and protein.

Option (B) is incorrect as Intranuclear inclusions, identical to Cowdry type A inclusions seen in other herpesvirus infections, were observed in 46 cases and demonstrated the best correlation with the presence of virions ultrastructurally ($p < 0.0001$).

Option (D) is incorrect as Mumps virus (MuV) infection induces the formation of cytoplasmic inclusion bodies (IBs).

Hence, the correct option is (C).

108. Option (A) is correct as Cowdry type A is of variable size and granular in appearance, e.g. in herpesvirus and yellow fever virus.

Option (B) is incorrect as Cowdry type B is more circumscribed and often multiple, as with adenovirus and poliovirus.

Option (C) is incorrect as we have seen in option (B) that it is Cowdry type B that contains poliovirus.

Option (D) is incorrect as cow dry type A inclusion body has a granular size, i. e. option (A). So, this option will automatically get wrong.

Hence, the correct option is (A).

109. Option (C) is correct as River blindness is caused by Onchocerca volvulus which is transmitted by a black fly.

MNEMONIC:

"BLOOM" B- black fly (Simulium)

L- Leopard rash

O- Onchocerca

R- River blindness

M- Mazzotti test

Option (A) is incorrect as Trichomoniasis is a common sexually transmitted infection caused by a parasite. In women, trichomoniasis can cause a foul-smelling vaginal discharge, genital itching and painful urination. Men who have trichomoniasis typically have no symptoms.

Option (B) is incorrect as Whipworm (Trichuris trichiura) is an intestinal parasite of humans. The larvae and adult worms live in the intestine of humans and can cause intestinal disease. The name is derived from the worm's distinctive whip-like shape.

Option (D) is incorrect as Dracunculiasis, also known as Guinea worm disease (GWD), is an infection caused by the parasite Dracunculus medinensis. A parasite is an organism that feeds off another organism to survive. GWD is spread by drinking water containing Guinea worm larvae.

Hence, the correct option is (C).

110. Option (D) is correct because chlamydia is the most commonly diagnosed cause of non-gonococcal urethritis. The most common bacterial cause of NGU is Chlamydia trachomatis, but it can also be caused by Ureaplasma urealyticum, Haemophilus vaginalis, Mycoplasma genitalium, Mycoplasma hominis, Gardnerella vaginalis, Acinetobacter lwoffi, Ac.

Option (A) is incorrect because chlamydial and genital mycoplasma infections are the most important preventable causes of female infertility and adverse pregnancy outcomes. When they ascend, both of the infections can result in PID—a leading cause of TFI and EP.

Option (B) is incorrect because a streptococcal infection may cause a sore throat. it is also possible to have other throat infections as well as chlamydia. You may also have gonorrhea, another bacterial STI. Just like oral chlamydia.

Option (C) is incorrect because Treponema pallidum is responsible for syphilis. The parasite Chlamydia trachomatis causes a variety of disorders—in women, urethritis, cervicitis, and salpingitis (inflammation of the ureter, cervix, and fallopian tubes, respectively) and, in men, nongonococcal urethritis.

Hence, the correct option is (D).

111. Option (C) is correct as man is the definitive host in most parasitic infections except in Echinococcus granulosus, Plasmodium, Taenia Solium(man is both definitive and intermediate host) Toxoplasma gondii, Sarcocystis lindemanii

In other parasitic infections, man acts as the definitive host, Two intermediate hosts are seen in Lung fluke (paragonimus) Chinese tapeworm (clonorchis) Fish tapeworm (diphyllobothrium latum), Metagonimus Westermann.

Option (A) is incorrect as Culex is a genus of mosquitoes, several species of which serve as vectors of one or more important diseases of birds, humans, and other animals. The diseases they vector include arbovirus infections such as West Nile virus, Japanese encephalitis, or St. Louis encephalitis, but also filariasis and avian malaria.

Option (B) is incorrect as the biting female Anopheles mosquito may carry malaria. Male mosquitoes do not bite so cannot transmit malaria or other diseases. The adult females are generally short-lived, with only a small proportion living long enough (more than 10 days in tropical regions) to transmit malaria.

Option (D) is incorrect as Trombiculosis is a rash caused by trombiculid mites which is often referred to as a chigger bite. Dusting sulfur is used commercially for mite control and can be used to control chiggers in yards.

Hence, the correct option is (C).

112. Option (B) is correct as the fungi imperfection or imperfect fungi, also known as Deuteromycota, the members of this group lack a sexual stage, they are often referred to as imperfect fungi (or formally the Fungi Imperfecti).

Option (A) is incorrect as popularly they are called the algal fungi because they bear a striking resemblance to some of the algae (Vaucheria) in the morphology of the thallus and sex organs.

Option (C) is incorrect as Basidiomycota are filamentous fungi composed of hyphae (except for Basidiomycota-yeast) and reproduce sexually via the formation of specialized club-shaped end cells called basidia that normally bear external meiospores (usually four). These specialized spores are called basidiospores.

Option (D) is incorrect as ascomycetes are 'spore shooters'. They are fungi which produce microscopic spores inside special, elongated cells or sacs, known as 'asci', which give the group its name.

Hence, the correct option is (B).

113. Option (D) is correct as Coccidioides is a dimorphic fungus, it's yeast form is spherule, with a thick doubly refractive wall and filled with endospore. Each endospore gives rise to a spherule.

Option (A) is incorrect as the mould phase of Blastomyces dermatitidis resembles Chrysosporium, Emmonsia, and Scedosporium. However, the latter three are not dimorphic and do not transform into yeast phase at 37°C. Besides, Chrysosporium but not Blastomyces dermatitidis produces arthroconidia.

Option (B) is incorrect as Histoplasma capsulatum produces hyphae-like conidiophores which arise at right angles to the parent hyphae. It has both macro- and microconidia. Macroconidia are tuberculate, thick-walled, round, unicellular, hyaline, large and often have fingerlike projections on the surface.

Option (C) is incorrect as Paracoccidioides brasiliensis is a nonphotosynthetic eukaryote with a rigid cell wall and organelles very similar to those of higher eukaryotes. Being a dimorphic fungus, it has the ability to grow an oval yeast-like form at 37 °C and an elongated mycelial form produced at room temperature.

Hence, the correct option is (D).

114. Option (D) is correct because in the bacterium Borrelia burgdorferi, the cause of Lyme disease, the surface lipoprotein VlsE can undergo recombination which results in antigenic diversity. Bacteria showing antigenic variation are:-

- Neisseria (Meningococci, Gonococci)
- Streptococcus spp
- Mycoplasma
- Borrelia burgdorferi

Option (A) is incorrect as Yersinia doesn't show antigenic variation.

Option (B) is incorrect as Bordetella also does not show antigenic variation.

Option (C) is incorrect for the same reason as an option (A) and (B). Brucella bacteria also do not show antigen variation.

Hence, the correct option is (D).

115. Option (C) is correct as Epidemics of Neisseria meningitides usually occur in closed crowded conditions like jails or army camps.

Option (A) is incorrect as Klebsiella bacteria are normally found in the human intestines (where they do not cause disease). They are also found in human stool (faeces). In healthcare settings, Klebsiella infections commonly occur among sick patients who are receiving treatment for other conditions. Klebsiella species contamination of healthcare workers and the environment.

Option (B) is incorrect as Escherichia coli (abbreviated E. coli) are bacteria found in the intestines of people and animals and in the environment; they can also be found in foods. Most E. coli are harmless and are part of a healthy intestinal tract.

Option (D) is incorrect as Staphylococcus aureus is likely to be a natural contaminant of raw foods of animal origin, although this can be minimised through good hygienic practices.

Hence, the correct option is (C).

116. Option (B) is correct as the Indian criminal laws were comprehensively amended to include dowry as a punishable offence. Section 304B was added to the Indian Penal Code, 1860 ("IPC"), which made dowry death a specific offense punishable with a minimum sentence of imprisonment for 7 years and maximum imprisonment for life.

Option (A) is incorrect as Section 304A in The Indian Penal Code covers death caused by negligence that is whoever causes the death of any person by doing any rash or negligent act not amounting to culpable homicide, shall be punished with imprisonment of either description for a term which may extend to two years, or with fine, or with both.

Option (C) is incorrect as Section 420 of The Indian Penal Court talks about the offence which is committed by the person who cheats another person and thereby induces the deceived to deliver any property. This provision provides punishment for the same.

Option (D) is incorrect as husband or relative of husband of a woman subjecting her to the cruelty that is, however, being the husband or the relative of the husband of a woman, subjects such woman to cruelty shall be punished with imprisonment for a term which may extend to three years and shall also be liable to fine.

Hence, the correct option is (B).

117. Option (D) is correct because duret haemorrhage is a small haemorrhage (or multiple haemorrhages) seen the medulla or pons of patients who are rapidly herniating. The Supratentorial haemorrhage causes the brainstem and mesial temporal lobes to be forced downwards through the tentorial hiatus. As a result of this shift, it is believed that perforating branches from the basilar artery and/or draining veins are damaged with resultant parenchymal haemorrhage. Usually, it is seen in patients with severe herniation for 12-24 hours prior to death.

Option (A) is incorrect because Pulmonary haemorrhage (or pulmonary haemorrhage) is acute bleeding from the lung, from the upper respiratory tract and the trachea, and the alveoli. The onset of pulmonary haemorrhage is characterized by cough productive of blood (hemoptysis) and worsening of oxygenation leading to cyanosis.

Option (B) is incorrect because a splenic hematoma is a localized collection of blood outside of blood vessels and is considered a subset of haemorrhage. Splenic hematomas usually result from abdominal trauma or clotting disorders, or they occur in association with splenic neoplasia, such as hemangiosarcoma or lymphosarcoma.

Option (C) is incorrect because bleeding Varices often due to scarring of the liver or cirrhosis. This increased pressure in the portal vein causes blood to be pushed away from the liver to smaller blood vessels, which are not able to handle the increased amount of blood.

Hence, the correct option is (D).

118. Option (D) is correct as Perjury means giving willful false evidence by a witness while under oath or failure to tell what he knows or believes to be true. The witness is liable to be prosecuted for perjury and the imprisonment may extend up to 7 years (Sec 198, IPC).

Option (A) is incorrect as Sec 190 refers to the threat of refraining a person from applying protection to a public servant.

Option (B) is incorrect as Sec 191 refers to giving false evidence that is Whoever, being legally bound by an oath or by an express provision of law to state the truth or being bound by law to make a declaration upon any subject, makes any statement which is false, and which he either knows or believes to be false or does not believe to be true, is said to give false evidence.

Option (C) is incorrect as Sec 192 refers to fabricating false evidence. Fabricating false evidence: The essence of the offence of fabricating false evidence under Sec. 192 consists in the endeavor to injure another by supplying false data upon which a judicial decision may rest.

Hence, the correct option is (D).

119. Option (D) is correct as Sec 509 IPC deals with the word, gesture, or act intended to insult the modesty of a woman. It includes an act or any nonverbal sound or gesture or any word abusive or nonabusive, which has a sexual connotation to it, made toward a woman to insult or outrage the modesty of a woman.

The punishment for such an offence is 1 year of simple imprisonment or fine or both.

Option (A) is incorrect as masturbation in public would be covered under exhibitionism (a sexual perversion). Exhibitionism is a criminal offence punishable under Sec 294 IPC. Masturbation in front of women would be dealt with under 509 IPC.

Option (B) is incorrect as Inquest-police inquest is Sec 174 CrPC, magistrate inquest Sec 176 CrPC.

Option (C) is incorrect as Dowry's death is Sec 304B IPC.

Hence, the correct option is (D).

120. Option (D) is correct as tentative/trial/hesitation/preliminary wounds: small multiple superficial somewhat parallel and skin-deep cuts usually found on the anterior surface of extremities, chest and abdomen. Unintentional cuts: found on fingers, where a razor blade has been gripped.

Option (A) is incorrect as a homicide requires only a volitional act by another person that results in death, and thus a homicide may result from accidental, reckless, or negligent acts even if there is no intent to cause harm. Even though forensic evidence is collected at virtually every homicide scene, only a few studies have examined its role in investigation and prosecution.

Option (B) is incorrect as a forensic autopsy of a traffic accident fatality needs to both determine the cause of death and identify the mechanism of injury, an analytical task that requires observation of three major traffic accident factors: the body, the vehicles involved, and the scene of the accident.

Option (C) is incorrect as in case of fall from a height, the tissues covering the bony orbital rims are often torn, along with the skin covering the cheekbones and the lower jaw.

Hence, the correct option is (D).

121. "Heat stiffening or heat coagulation is found in bodies exposed to heat i.e. temperatures above 65°C (Reddy)/70°C (Parikh) as is seen in death due to burning, high voltage electrocution (electric shock), or falling into a hot liquid."

Option (B) is correct because from the above explanation it is clear that Heat stiffening in muscles occurs above temperature 60 degrees as given in this option.

Option (A) is incorrect because from the above explanation it is clear that Heat stiffening in muscles occurs above temperature 60 degrees, not 30 degrees as given in this option.

Option (C) is incorrect because from the above explanation it is clear that Heat stiffening in muscles occurs above temperature 60 degrees, not 40 degrees as given in this option.

Option (D) is incorrect because from the above explanation it is clear that Heat stiffening in muscles occurs above temperature 60 degrees, not 50 degrees as given in this option.

Hence, the correct option is (B).

122. Option (B) is correct as the Ligature mark is a type of pressure /imprinted/ contact/patterned abrasion. Patterned abrasions are any impact or pressure abrasions which reproduce the pattern of the object causing it.

Option (A) is incorrect as black and blue marks are often associated with bruises. A bruise, or contusion, appears on the skin due to trauma. Examples of trauma are a cut or a blow to an area of the body. The injury causes tiny blood vessels called capillaries to burst. Blood gets trapped below the skin's surface, which causes a bruise.

Option (C) is incorrect as a laceration is a wound that is produced by the tearing of soft body tissue. This type of wound is often irregular and jagged. A laceration wound is often contaminated with bacteria and debris from whatever object caused the cut.

Option (D) is incorrect as ligature marks are an example of pressure abrasion. So, this option will automatically get wrong.

Hence, the correct option is (B).

123.

Option (D) is correct as it is covering all the other options mentioned above that are true about lynching.

Option (A) is incorrect even though it was practised in a tribal part of India and some southern states of America, for sexual crimes or to take revenge. It is incorrect as other options are also true about lynching, selecting an individual option won't be considered as correct.

Option (B) is incorrect even the name is derived from William Lynch, a white captain in the USA, who used to order hanging of blacks (negroes) on the spot without trial. But it is incorrect for the same reason as of option (A).

Option (C) is incorrect even when it is homicidal hanging in which a suspect, accused or enemy is hanged by a rope from a tree by the mob. It is incorrect for the same reason as of choosing an individual option.

Hence, the correct option is (D).

124. Option (D) is correct as BAL (dimercaprol) is contraindicated in iron and cadmium poisoning. Dimercaprol should not be used in iron, cadmium, selenium, or uranium poisoning because the resulting dimercaprol-metal complexes are more toxic than the metals alone.

Option (A) is incorrect as Mercury poisoning is a type of metal poisoning due to exposure to mercury. It is used in mercury poisoning.

Option (B) is incorrect as Dimercaprol has long been the mainstay of chelation therapy for lead or arsenic poisoning, and it remains an essential drug.

Option (C) is incorrect for the same reason as of option (A) and (C) as BAL is used to treat lead, arsenic and mercury poisoning.

Hence, the correct option is (D).

125. Option (A) is correct as transvestism or Eonism - a transvestite is a person whose whole personality is dominated by the desire to be identified and thought of as a member, of the opposite sex. It is usually found in males who obtain sexual pleasure by wearing a female dress.

Option (B) is incorrect as most people are familiar with the term bestiality, the precise meaning of which has varied in the past but which currently is understood to mean sexual activity between a person and an animal.

Option (C) is incorrect as a lesbian is a homosexual woman. The word lesbian is also used for women in relation to their sexual identity or sexual behaviour, regardless of sexual orientation, or as an adjective to characterize or associate nouns with female homosexuality or same-sex attraction.

Option (D) is incorrect as Oral sex means using your mouth, lips or tongue to stimulate your partner's genitals or anus. But oral sex has official medical names too: oral sex on a woman (the vagina, vulva and clitoris) is called cunnilingus, and oral sex on a man (the penis) is called fellatio.

Hence, the correct option is (A).

126. Option (D) is correct as it is covering all the other options mentioned above, i. e,

Determinants of health

Following determinants of health provide good health, optimal health or positive health.

Genetic configuration → Genetic constitution of an individual can affect health e.g. G-6-PD deficiency.

Level of development → Economic and social development helps to improve health status.

Lifestyle → Moderate physical activity, cessation of smoking and regular exercise prevent the occurrence of CHD. Adequate nutrition, a sound mind (mental peace) and enough sleep also promote health.

Environment → Proper sanitation, adequate safe drinking water and low level of atmospheric pollution promote health.

Health infrastructure → If primary health care facilities are available in the vicinity and such facilities are utilized by the population, the health of individuals and communities is bound to improve.

Option (A) is incorrect even though physical activity or exercise can improve your health and reduce the risk of developing several diseases like type 2 diabetes, cancer and cardiovascular disease. Physical activity and exercise can have immediate and long-term health benefits. Most importantly, regular activity can improve your quality of life. But it is incorrect as other options are also relatable.

Option (B) is incorrect as adequate nutrition is an important aspect of a healthy lifestyle for all individuals, including bank staff. A healthy diet prevents malnutrition and protects from diseases like obesity, heart disease, diabetes, cancer and stroke. It is also incorrect for the same reason as of individual selection of an option.

Option (C) is incorrect as surrounding yourself with those who are stressed or unhappy can increase your levels of stress and unhappiness. Peace of mind is a great way to reduce the stresses of day-to-day life and can help you to become a calmer, more relaxed person overall. This can lead to a happier existence.

Hence, the correct option is (D).

127. Option (D) is correct as the word surveillance is the French word for "watching over" Sentinel surveillance is useful for answering specific epidemiologic questions because sentinel sites may not represent the general population or the general incidence of disease, they may have limited usefulness in analyzing national disease patterns and trends.

Option (A) is incorrect as one way to overcome the limitations of passive surveillance and get a better picture of the disease burden in the community is for health workers to visit health facilities and communities to seek out cases. This is known as active surveillance.

Eradication and elimination programs may require a very active surveillance program aimed at detecting every case.

During outbreak situations, surveillance must be intensified with the introduction of active case finding

Option (B) is incorrect as passive surveillance yields only limited data because many sick people do not visit a health facility and because those cases that do show up may not be correctly classified, recorded, or reported.

Option (C) is incorrect as monitoring is the regular observation and recording of activities taking place in a project or program. Reporting enables the gathered information to be used in making decisions for improving project performance. Monitoring is very important in project planning and implementation.

Hence, the correct option is (D).

128. Option (C) is correct as incidence in epidemiology is a measure of the probability of occurrence of a given medical condition in a population within a specified period of time. Although sometimes loosely expressed simply as the number of new cases during some time period, it is better expressed as a proportion or a rate with a denominator.

Option (A) is incorrect as the crude death rate is defined as "the mortality rate from all causes of death for a population," calculated as the "total number of deaths during a given time interval" divided by the "mid-interval population", per 1,000 or 100,000; for instance, the population of the U.S. was ca.

Option (B) is incorrect as survival rates are derived from life tables or census data, and are used to calculate the number of people that will be alive in the future. Life tables are used to measure mortality, survivorship, and the life expectancy of a population at varying ages.

Option (D) is incorrect as a case fatality rate (CFR, also case fatality risk or case fatality ratio) is the ratio of deaths from a certain disease to the total number of people diagnosed with this disease for a certain period of time. A CFR is conventionally expressed as a percentage and represents a measure of disease severity.

Hence, the correct option is (C).

129. Option (D) is correct as the proportional mortality rate measures the proportion of total death due to a specific cause or proportion of deaths in a particular age group.

It is defined as the "number of deaths due to a particular cause (or in specific age group) per 100 total deaths".

It is the 'simplest measure of estimating the burden of disease' in the community.

It is a useful 'health Status indicator'; indicates the magnitude of preventable mortality.

It is used when population data is not available.

It does not indicate the risk of members of the population contracting or dying from the disease.

Proportional mortality from TB = No. of deaths due to TB in a year / Total no. of deaths in that year × 100

Under 5 proportional mortality rate = No. of deaths under 5 years age / Total no. of deaths during the same period × 100

Option (A) is incorrect as an incidence rate describes how quickly disease occurs in a population. It is based on person-time, so it has some advantages over an incidence proportion. Because person-time is calculated for each subject, it can accommodate persons coming into and leaving the study.

Option (B) is incorrect as the crude death rate is the total number of deaths to residents in a specified geographic area (country, state, county, etc.) divided by the total population for the same geographic area (for a specified time period, usually a calendar year) and multiplied by 100,000.

Option (C) is incorrect as the cause-specific death rate is the number of deaths from a specified cause per 100,000 person-years at risk. The numerator is typically restricted to resident deaths in a specific geographic area (country, state, county, etc.).

Hence, the correct option is (D).

130. Option (B) is correct because impairment is any loss or abnormality of a psychological, physiological or anatomical structure or function.

Option (A) is incorrect because a disease is defined as any abnormal condition of an individual that impairs function.

Option (C) is incorrect because disability (Because of impairment,) is any restriction or inability to perform an activity in a range considered normal for a human being.

Option (D) is incorrect because a handicap is a disadvantage for a given individual, resulting from an impairment/disability, that limits/prevent the fulfillment of a role considered normal (depending on age, sex, social, cultural factors) for that individual.

Hence, the correct option is (B).

131. Option (C) is correct because screening for colorectal cancer (CRC) is employed in an increasing number of countries due to its proven efficacy in reducing CRC incidence and mortality, and an increasing share of CRC cases are diagnosed by screening rather than by symptoms.

Option (A) is incorrect because the FDA initially approved PSA testing in 1986 for monitoring the disease status of prostate cancer patients and, subsequently in 1994, it was endorsed as a screening method for prostate cancer.

Option (B) is incorrect because studies have shown decreased deaths with screening, and overall the benefits of screening outweigh the risks if the correct population is selected. Clinicians must talk about smoking cessation along with screening and patients with positive LDCT must have close follow-ups.

Option (D) is incorrect because advanced ovarian cancer is associated with decreased survival, and increased morbidity with not only the disease itself but also surgery and the effects of chemotherapy. A recent study found that if 75% of ovarian cases can be detected as Stage I or II disease, there would be a 50% reduction in ovarian cancer-related deaths.

Hence, the correct option is (C).

132. Option (B) is correct because standard deviation measures the variation (dispersion) of individual data from the mean. A high standard deviation indicates that the data is dispersed away from the mean. Low standard deviation indicates that the data points tend to be very close to the mean, i.e. data points are clustered close to the mean.

For example, the average height for adult men in the USA is about 70 inches, and the standard deviation is 3 inches. Then -

If dispersion of mean is 1 SD → most men (about 68%) have a height within 3 inches of the mean (67-73) inches.

If dispersion of mean is 2 SD → almost all men (95%) have a height within 6 inches of the mean (64 - 76) inches.

If dispersion is zero SD all men would be exactly 70 inches.

That means the greater the standard deviation greater will be the data spread away from the standard deviation.

Coming back to question

Here all newborn babies have 2.8 kgs of weight.

That means there is no dispersion from the mean.

So, the standard deviation is zero.

Option (A) is incorrect because from the answer we get that the standard deviation will be zero, so there will be no replacement for this answer.

Option (C) is incorrect because from options (A) and (B) we get that standard deviation will be zero and as it is constant, so option (C) will become wrong.

Option (D) is incorrect because from all the three options we get that the answer will be zero that's why it will remain constant and so this option will become an incorrect answer to be selected.

Hence, the correct option is (B).

133. Option (C) is correct because

SCATTER DIAGRAM

- Also known as 'Correlation diagram' or 'Dot diagram'
- Is used to depict 'correlation (relationship) between 2 quantitative variables'
- The vertical axis in the scatter diagram: should be the dependent or the outcome variable
- In a scatter diagram, 2 imaginary lines are drawn along the distribution of dots/scatter

Option (A) is incorrect because line charts, or line graphs, are powerful visual tools that illustrate trends in data over a period of time or a particular correlation. For example, one axis of the graph might represent a variable value, while the other axis often displays a timeline.

Option (B) is incorrect because, in statistics, a histogram is a graphical representation of the distribution of data. It is an estimate of the probability distribution of a continuous variable or can be used to plot the frequency of an event (number of times an event occurs) in an experiment or study.

Option (D) is incorrect because the median provides a helpful measure of the centre of a dataset. By comparing the median to the mean, you can get an idea of the distribution of a dataset. When the mean and the median are the same, the dataset is more or less evenly distributed from the lowest to highest values. The mean is essentially a model of your data set. It is the value that produces the lowest amount of error from all other values in the data set.

Hence, the correct option is (C).

134. Option (B) is correct because there is a list of the period of communicability which is as follows:

Chickenpox: 1 - 2 days before to 4 - 5 days after the appearance of the rash.

Measles: 4 days before to 5 days after the appearance of the rash.

Rubella: 7 days before symptoms to 7 days after the appearance of the rash.

Mumps: 4 - 6 days before symptoms to 7 days thereafter

Influenza: 1 - 2 days before to 1 - 2 days after onset of symptoms

Diphtheria: 14 - 28 days from disease onset.

Pertussis: 7 days after exposure to 3 weeks after the paroxysmal stage.

Poliomyelitis: 7 - 10 days before and after the onset of symptoms.

Hepatitis A: 2 weeks before to 1 week after onset of jaundice.

Hepatitis B: Till disappearance of HBs Ag & appearance of anti-HBs.

Meningococcal: Until absent from nasal and throat discharge.

Tuberculosis: As long as not treated.

Option (A) is incorrect because an infected person is contagious about 2 days before the rash appears. The rash can involve 250 to 500 itchy blisters. Chickenpox continues to be contagious for another 5 to 7 days, or until all of the blisters have become scabs. In most cases, the pox marks heal without scarring.

Option (C) is incorrect because measles is caused by infection with the rubeola virus. The virus lives in the mucus of the nose and throat of an infected child or adult. The disease is contagious for 4 days before the rash appears, and it continues to be contagious for about 4 to 5 days after. so, it isn't infectious throughout the disease.

Option (D) is incorrect because the incubation period for chickenpox is usually 14 to 16 days but can range from 10 to 21 days. A child is infectious 1-2 days before they get the rash until all the blisters have dried up. This usually takes 5 to 7 days. Patients are contagious from 1-2 days before the onset of symptoms. Healthy children are also contagious during the period from 3-5 days before the appearance of the rash to 4 days after the onset of rash.

Hence, the correct option is (B).

135. Option (A) is correct because although generally a benign, self-limited disease, varicella may be associated with serious complications, especially in adults. We present acute pancreatitis- a rare complication, in otherwise healthy patients suffering from chickenpox.

Option (B) is incorrect because varicella pneumonia is the most common and serious complication of chickenpox infection in adults with a reported incidence in healthy adults that is 25-fold greater than in children.

Option (C) is incorrect because cerebellar ataxia, encephalitis and rarely, facial paralysis can be seen as neurological complications of chickenpox. The most serious complication that involves the central nervous system secondary to chickenpox is encephalitis.neurological complications following primary chickenpox infection are extremely rare (0.01–0.03%), although some neurological complications are known.

Option (D) is incorrect because thrombocytopenia is a common haematological complication of chickenpox. Most patients with thrombocytopenia are often asymptomatic or present with only mild cutaneous bleeding. Severe bleeding associated with intracranial haemorrhage or gastrointestinal bleeding is rare.

Hence, the correct option is (A).

136. Option (D) is correct because teachers conducted vision screening of primary school students of their respective schools using the 6/12 Snellen's chart and referred students with a subnormal vision to the optometrist. The Optometrist also validated the screening done by teachers. Optometrist screened the vision of 5% randomly selected children screened by teachers as having normal vision. Descriptive statistics used STATA version 13.0.

Option (A) is incorrect 441 nos. of Medical Officers including In-charge of PHC, Block PHC, and Superintendent of CH have been trained during 2008-09, 2009-2010 & 2010-11 as refresher training. The learner can be a health administrator, a public health specialist, an ophthalmologist or an educationist. Other categories include teachers from medical and nursing schools. This manual is not meant for use by the school teachers.

Option (B) is incorrect because after school teacher's ophthalmologic assistant comes on the list. They prescribed corrective spectacles free for BPL.

Option (C) is incorrect because the primary purpose of the District Health Society is to plan, implement and monitor blindness control activities in the district as per the pattern of assistance approved for the National Programme for Control of Blindness.

Hence, the correct option is (D).

137. Option (C) is correct because the goal of the national program for the control of blindness in India was to reduce blindness in the country to 0.3% by the year 2000. Now the goal for blindness in National Health Policy (NHP) 2002 is to reduce the prevalence of blindness to 0.5% by 2010.

Option (A) is incorrect because as per the Survey in 2001-02, the prevalence of blindness is estimated to be 1.1%.

Option (B) is incorrect because the goal of the national program for the control of blindness in India was to reduce blindness in the country to 0.3% by the year 2000. Now as in 2010 the number has been changed so, 0.3% can't be the correct answer.

Option (D) is incorrect because 1% may come in 2001-2002. As per the Survey in 2001-02, the prevalence of blindness is estimated to be 1.1%.

Hence, the correct option is (C).

138. Option (D) is correct because 21.3% of eligible couples in India have an unmet need for family planning. Various family planning methods help the clients to make informed decisions. Currently, two methods of vasectomy; Conventional and No-Scalpel are practised. under the brand name 'Nirodh'. It is the most widely used method for family planning from others.

Option (A) is incorrect because a rational human resource development plan is in place for the provision of IUCD, mini lap and NSV to empower the facilities (DH, CHC, PHC, SHC) with at least one provider each for each of the services and sub-centers with ANMs trained in IUD insertion.

Option (B) is incorrect as all the spacing methods, viz. IUCDs, Oral Contraceptive Pills(OCPs) and Condoms are available at the public health facilities beginning from the sub-center level.

Option (C) is incorrect because the government has been implementing a Centrally Sponsored Scheme (CSS) since 1981 to compensate the acceptors of sterilization for the loss of wages for the day on which he/she attended the medical facility for undergoing sterilization.

Hence, the correct option is (D).

139. Option (B) is correct as of the mechanism of action:

- Glatiramer acetate is a random polymer composed of four amino acids that are found in myelin basic protein.
- The mechanism of action for glatiramer is unknown, although several have been proposed.
- Administration of glatiramer shifts the population of T cells from pro-inflammatory
- Th1 cells to regulatory Th2 cells that suppress the inflammatory response.
- Given its resemblance to myelin basic protein, glatiramer may also act as a sort of decoy, diverting an autoimmune response against myelin.
- The integrity of the blood-brain barrier is not appreciably affected by glatiramer.
- Glatiramer acetate has been shown in clinical trials to reduce the number and severity of exacerbations

Option (A) is incorrect because the above-mentioned mechanism of action is displayed by amphotericin B, used in the control studies. This antifungal binds to the membrane of the fungal cell membrane (mainly ergosterol) and reorients the sterol molecules, which results in damage to the cytoplasmic membrane.

Option (C) is incorrect because unlike other antimicrobials, antiviral drugs do not deactivate or destroy the microbe (in this case, the virus) but act by inhibiting replication. In this way, they prevent the viral load from increasing to a point where it could cause pathogenesis, allowing the body's innate immune mechanisms to neutralize the virus.

Option (D) is incorrect because the various resistance mechanisms used include:

- Expressions of enzymes capable of altering or degrading antimicrobial agents such as aminoglycosides and beta-lactamases.
- Cell wall alterations, enzymatic drug cleavage or modification, ribosomal mutations, 16S rRNA methylation, and alterations in the β-subunit of RNA polymerase and carbapenemases that provide resistance against different antibiotics.
- The expressions of drug-specific efflux pumps.

Hence, the correct option is (B).

140. Option (A) is correct because, under normal conditions, Indian mothers secrete 450 - 600 ml of milk daily the maximum output of milk is at 5 - 6 months (730 ml/ day) after which the output constantly declines. At 12 months the output is 525 ml/day.

Option (B) is incorrect because iron was supposed to be deficient in breast milk, but recent work has shown that iron contained in human milk has a high level of bioavailability thanks to complex phenomena. The coefficient of uptake of iron in breast milk may be as high as 70% whereas it is only 30 percent for cow's milk and infant formulas.

Option (C) is incorrect because the calcium-phosphorus ratio is high so that uptake of calcium is better than cow's milk'.

Option (D) is incorrect because the energy value of human milk is 64 to 72 kcal per 100 ml.

Hence, the correct option is (A).

141. Option (A) is correct because these indicators are used to measure nutritional imbalance resulting in undernutrition (assessed from underweight, wasting and stunting) and overweight. Child growth is internationally recognized as an important indicator of nutritional status and health in populations. Wasting (deficit in weight for height) → Acute malnutrition.

Option (B) is incorrect because this is a condition that develops when children do not eat the correct balance of nutrients in the first 1,000 days of life (from conception to the age of two), resulting in the irreversible stunting of their cognitive and physical development. Stunting (deficit in height for age) → Chronic malnutrition.

Option (C) is incorrect because in concomitant acute and chronic both, wasting and stunting will come that is, the deficit in weight for height and deficit in height for age.

Option (D) is incorrect because in combined indicator to reflect both acute and chronic malnutrition underweight (low weight for age) comes.

Hence, the correct option is (A).

142. Option (D) is correct because the water gets filtered while percolating through sand & stones.

Option (A) is incorrect because groundwater generally does not get polluted if it is away (at least 20 mtr.) from the sanitary works. The water gets filtered while percolating through sand & stones. Therefore groundwater remains pure and clean.

Option (B) is incorrect since bore well is closed, no risk of getting contaminated. Since it is closed no danger of children or animals falling into it.

Option (C) is incorrect because the temperature of deepwater remains stable. It feels cool in summer and warm in winter. Since the bore is deep, the chances of water remaining available in summer are more.

Hence, the correct option is (D).

143. Option (B) is correct because salt iodization is one of the important measures taken by the National Iodine Deficiency Diseases Control Programme to control iodine deficiency- disorder. The Food Adulteration Act states that iodized salt at the manufacturing level should have no less than 30 ppm and at the consumer level no less than 15 ppm. One of the greatest obstacles to NICCDP is poor iodine stability.

Option (A) is incorrect because it can be assumed that producers' salt containing more than 20 ppm iodine contributes to the elimination of iodine deficiency.

Option (C) is incorrect because as the answer is 15ppm and it cannot be replaced because it is a fixed number, so option C can't be expressed as correct.

Option (D) is incorrect because from the above information we get that 15 ppm will only be the most appropriate answer. So, option D will get automatically wrong for this question.

Hence, the correct option is (B).

144. Option (B) is correct because the energy requirements of women are increased during pregnancy and lactation. - additional 600 kcal daily is needed during the first six months of lactation.

Option (A) is incorrect because the daily diet of a woman should contain an additional 350 calories, 0.5 g of protein during the first trimester and 6.9 g during the second trimester and 22.7 g during the third trimester of pregnancy.

Option (C) is incorrect because during the 1st 6 months the quantity of milk produced by the mother is more and an extra allowance of 550 kcal is made during this period.

Option (D) is incorrect because a woman lactate in 1 to 3 months generates 438 to 521 calories per day.

Hence, the correct option is (B).

145. Option (B) is correct because the first five years of a child's life are fundamentally important. Child development refers to the changes that occur as a child grows and develops in relation to being physically healthy, mentally alert, emotionally sound, socially competent and ready to learn. Recent research confirms that the first five years are particularly important for the development of the child's brain.

Option (A) is incorrect because depression is the most prevalent mental illness in the perinatal period, with around 10 to 14% of mothers affected during pregnancy or after the birth of a baby.

Option (C) is incorrect because at school age not much mental illness has to be seen. They play, study and enjoy their life at that age. They even don't have responsibilities to be taken in their life. so, at this age very less amount of mental illness has to be seen.

Option (D) is incorrect because adolescence is the age at which new things are introduced in life. Few responsibilities and other relations with people are to be made. so, with that mental illness comes at that time but the person would have become so much mature that he/she would cope up with it.

Hence, the correct option is (B).

146. Option (B) is correct because a survey done in Bangalore revealed that the quantity of solid waste generated in hospitals and nursing homes generally varies from ½ to 4 kg per bed per day in Govt. hospitals.

Option (A) is incorrect because the estimated generation of biomedical waste (BMW) in hospital settings is around 1.5-2kg/bed/day, of which the hazardous component is less than 10%.

Option (C) is incorrect because a survey done in Bangalore revealed that the quantity of solid waste generated in hospitals and nursing homes generally varies from ½ to 1 kg per day per bed in nursing homes.

Option (D) is incorrect because a survey done in Bangalore revealed that the quantity of solid waste generated in hospitals and nursing homes generally varies from ½ to 2 kg per day per bed in private hospitals.

Hence, the correct option is (B).

147. Option (C) is correct because slogans are very helpful for attracting people to anything. For any particular topic, slogans become as one of the best techniques as "The public is not interested in health slogans such as "take care of your health" or "be healthy"- "Park".

Option (A) is incorrect because felt needs are needs that the people feel about themselves. If a health program is based on "felt needs" people will gladly participate in the program, and only then it will be a people's program. Very often, there are groups who may have health needs of which they are not aware of. The health educator will have to bring about a recognition of the needs before he proceeds to tackle them.

Option (B) is incorrect because, in India, about 50% of the people are illiterate. So, the health educator must use the simplest possible words.

Option (D) is incorrect because community participation is the key to health education. Health education should aim at encouraging people to work actively with health workers and others in identifying their own health problems and also in developing solutions and plans to work them out.

Hence, the correct option is (C).

148. Option (B) is correct because 5-FU is a metabolite of flucytosine and inhibits the 'thymidine synthetase'. It is a prodrug and requires intracellular conversion into the active and phosphorylated metabolites. It is a short-acting drug with a half-life of 10-15 minutes. It is poorly absorbed by oral route and hence is best given by IV route. It is the drug of choice for colorectal cancer. The most common side effect is gastrointestinal upset. Other side effects include hand foot mouth disease and bone marrow suppression.

Option (A) is incorrect because oral cyclophosphamide is rapidly absorbed and then converted by mixed-function oxidase enzymes (cytochrome P450 system) in the liver to active metabolites. Cyclophosphamide metabolites are primarily excreted in the urine unchanged, and drug dosing should be appropriately adjusted in the setting of renal dysfunction.

Option (C) is incorrect because Enalapril is metabolized in the liver to its active form, enalaprilat. Both enalapril and lisinopril are eliminated by the kidney. The duration of their hypotensive actions averages 24 hours but can last up to 30 hours.

Option (D) is incorrect because a small amount of cisplatin is excreted via the bile and saliva (McEvoy, 1992). After a dose of cisplatin, 15 to 30% of the dose is excreted in the urine in the first 2 to 4 hours (of which 90% is intact cisplatin) 20 to 80% of the dose is recovered in the first 24 hours.

Hence, the correct option is (B).

149. Option (C) is correct because sentinel Surveillance of Blindness is an Initiative of the National Programme for Control of Blindness in India. Sentinel surveillance is an active surveillance system that seeks out data from selected, targeted groups or networks put together for this specific purpose.

Option (A) is incorrect because active surveillance is a way of monitoring localized (early) prostate cancer, rather than treating it straight away. Many men on active surveillance will never need treatment. Active surveillance isn't the same as watchful waiting, which is a different way of monitoring prostate cancer.

Option (B) is incorrect because passive surveillance is the use of local healthcare services to collect data on disease incidence or adverse effects of medicines. It relies on staff and services, who are part of a reporting network, collecting data and generating reports. There is no active search for cases.

Option (D) is incorrect because an annual full body checkup is a routine yearly visit to your doctor to assess your general health. It is an important step in preventing bigger health issues. Your doctor can evaluate your state of well-being and diagnose any potential problems that may be in their beginning stages.

Hence, the correct option is (C).

150. Option (B) is correct because society is a body of individuals of species, generally seen as a community or group, that is outlined by the bounds of functional interdependence, comprising also possible characters or conditions such as cultural identity, social solidarity or eusociality.

Option (A) is incorrect because conglomeration is a fancy word for a bunch of stuff brought together. A huge mob of people could be described as a conglomeration which sounds nicer than a "mob." The "with" should be a reminder that this is a word that brings things or people together.

Option (C) is incorrect because a regulatory association is a corporation without share capital which is composed of its members and which purpose, as established by statute, is to govern and regulate its members in the public interest.

Option (D) is incorrect because patterns of Social Interaction mean the interaction of the people almost every day of our lives. Sociologists have identified five different patterns of social interaction.

- Cooperation
- Competition
- Exchange
- Conflict
- Accommodation

Hence, the correct option is (B).

151. Option (D) is correct because Nausea and vomiting affect approximately one-third of patients with chronic hyponatremia who have a serum sodium concentration of less than 120 mmol/L. Physical examination should include assessment of volume status, as these patients are typically euvolemic. Skin turgor and blood pressure are within the normal range.

Option (A) is incorrect because, in SIADH, serum osmolality is generally lower than urine osmolality. If AVP secretion is shut down completely, urine should have an osmolality of less than 100 mm.

Option (B) is incorrect because it should be noted that aldosterone is unaffected in SIADH and the sodium balance will be usually normal. If isotonic saline is administered, the water will be retained and sodium will be excreted in the urine.

Option (C) is incorrect because Hypouricemia (uric acid < 4 mg/dL) is frequently observed in patients with SIADH during the period of hyponatremia. However, hypouricemia lacks sensitivity and specificity for making the diagnosis of SIADH.

Hence, the correct option is (D).

152. Option (D) is correct because myocardial infarction can lead to cardiogenic shock.

Option (A) is incorrect because it is anaphylactic-shock.

Option (B) is incorrect because it is neurogenic-shock.

Option (C) is incorrect because it is a hypovolemic-shock.

Hence, the correct option is (D).

153. Option (C) is correct because the presence of dysmorphic RBCs with irregular contours and shape in the urine is almost pathognomonic of glomerular haematuria and indicates RBCs egression from the glomerular capillary into the urinary space.

Option (A) is incorrect because hematuria refers to the presence of blood in the urine, as defined as more than 5 to 10 red blood cells per high-power field (RBC/HPF).

Option (B) is incorrect because brown-colored urine, RBC casts, and dysmorphic (small deformed, misshapen, sometimes fragmented) RBCs and proteinuria are suggestive of glomerular hematuria.

Option (D) is incorrect because gross hematuria, or macrohematuria, promotes acute kidney injury (AKI), with subsequent impairment of renal function in a high proportion of patients.

Hence, the correct option is (C).

154. Option (B) is correct because cryptococcal meningitis is a serious infection of the brain and spinal column that can occur in people living with HIV. It is caused by a fungus called Cryptococcus neoformans.

Option (A) is incorrect because candida infections of the central nervous system (CNS) most often involve the meninges. However, intracranial abscesses can occur either as an isolated phenomenon or associated with meningitis. The abscesses are usually small microabscesses, multiple, and associated with disseminated infection in immunocompromised hosts. Candida meningitis can occur as a manifestation of disseminated candidiasis, which most often occurs in premature neonates, in the presence of ventricular drainage devices, and as isolated chronic meningitis. In addition to hematogenous spread, Candida can enter the CNS at the time of craniotomy or through a ventricular shunt.

Option (C) is incorrect because tuberculous meningitis (TBM) is the most common form of central nervous system tuberculosis (TB) and has very high morbidity and mortality. TBM is typically a subacute disease with symptoms that may persist for weeks before diagnosis.

Option (D) is incorrect because cryptosporidium is a genus of apicomplexan parasitic alveolates that can cause a respiratory and gastrointestinal illness (cryptosporidiosis) that primarily involves watery diarrhea (intestinal cryptosporidiosis) with or without a persistent cough.

Hence, the correct option is (B).

155. a) FMR1 (fragile X mental retardation 1) is a human gene that codes for a protein called fragile X mental retardation protein, or FMRP.

b) Macroorchidism is defined as testes twice the normal size for an age without androgenization. Testes will enlarge during treatment with aromatase inhibitors.

c) Aside from intellectual disability, prominent characteristics of the syndrome may include an elongated face, large or protruding ears, flat feet, larger testes (macroorchidism), and low muscle tone.

d) In some cases, however, individuals with a premutation have lower than normal amounts of FMRP. As a result, they may have mild versions of the physical features seen in fragile X syndrome (such as prominent ears) and may experience emotional problems such as anxiety or depression.

Option (C) is correct because of the above explanation.

Option (A) is incorrect because point d is included.

Option (B) is incorrect because at this point b is included.

Option (D) is incorrect because both points are incorrect.

Hence, the correct option is (C).

156. Option (A) is correct because large multi-institutional studies have indicated that the risk of HIV transmission following skin puncture from a needle or sharp object that was contaminated with blood from a person with documented HIV infection is approximately 0.3% and antiretroviral therapy can reduce the risk of infection eightfold.

Option (B) is incorrect because the chance that a health worker gets HIV from an accidental needle prick is not 10%.

Option (C) is incorrect because the option is showing 95% which is not correct.

Option (D) is incorrect because the risk is near about 0.3%.

Hence, the correct option is (A).

157. Option (C) is correct because this is a function of the digestive system. Transport of digested end products from the lumen of the GI tract to the blood or lymph is absorption, and for absorption to happen, the digested foods must first enter the mucosal cells by active or passive transport processes.

Option (A) is incorrect because the main function of the muscular system is movement. Muscles are the only tissue in the body that has the ability to contract and therefore move the other parts of the body.

Option (B) is incorrect because your body will go through the digestion process, breaking down the food you ate into amino acids, and then your bloodstream will carry these nutrients to your muscles to help with muscle growth and repair

Option (D) is incorrect because your skeletal muscles function almost continuously to maintain your posture, making one tiny adjustment after another to keep your body upright. Smooth muscles are involved in many 'housekeeping' functions of the body.

Hence, the correct option is (C).

158. Option (C) is correct because pulsus Bigeminus is recognized as a cause of digitalis toxicity. Pulsus Bigeminus is a disorder of rhythm (irregular rhythm; arrhythmia) most commonly caused by Premature Ventricular Contractions that result in a pulse with an irregular rhythm that alternates in amplitude (pressure) from beat to beat. The most common cause of Pulsus Bigeminus is Digitalis and Pulsus Bigeminus is recognized as a cause of digitalis toxicity.

Option (A) is incorrect because beta-blockers are a class of medications that are predominantly used to manage abnormal heart rhythms, and to protect the heart from a second heart attack after a first heart attack.

Option (B) is incorrect because digitalis, drug obtained from the dried leaves of the common foxglove (Digitalis purpurea) and used in medicine to strengthen contractions of the heart muscle.

Option (D) is incorrect because calcium channel blockers are prescription medications that relax blood vessels and increase the supply of blood and oxygen to the heart while also reducing the heart's workload.

Hence, the correct option is (C).

159. Option (A) is correct because the SA node is the heart's natural pacemaker.

Option (B) is incorrect because the SA node consists of a cluster of cells that are situated in the upper part of the wall of the right atrium (the right upper chamber of the heart).

Option (C) is incorrect because when action potentials reach the AV node, they spread slowly through it.

Option (D) is incorrect because action potentials pass slowly through the atrioventricular node.

Hence, the correct option is (A).

160. Option (B) is correct because the continued ventricular contraction causes the pressure in the ventricle to exceed in the pulmonary trunk and aorta. As a result, the semilunar are forced open and blood is ejected into the pulmonary trunk and aorta.

Option (A) is incorrect because almost immediately the AV valves close (the first heart sound). The pressure in the ventricle continues to increase.

Option (C) is incorrect because, during ventricular systole, contraction of the ventricles causes pressure in the ventricle to increase and the AV valves close.

Option (D) is incorrect because the pressure in the ventricle semilunar is forced open.

Hence, the correct option is (B).

161. Option (A) is correct because the relationship between preload and stroke volume is called Starling's law of the heart.

Option (B) is incorrect because as venous return increased, resulting in an increased preload, cardiac output increases.

Option (C) is incorrect because, in response to increased preload, cardiac muscle fibers contract with greater force.

Option (D) is incorrect because, in response to stretch, there is a slight increase in heart rate.

Hence, the correct option is (A).

162. Option (C) is correct because the mainstay of treatment of essential hypertension is lifestyle, diet modification and drugs.

Option (A) is incorrect because hypertension is a chronic disease. It can be controlled with medication, but it cannot be cured. Therefore, patients need to continue with the treatment and lifestyle modifications as advised by their doctor and attend regular medical follow up, usually for life.

Option (B) is incorrect because in hypertensive patients, in addition to a well-balanced diet, the dietary sodium intake should be limited to 65 to 100 mmol/day. Other recommendations are: following a diet low in saturated fat and cholesterol, and one that emphasizes fruits, vegetables and low-fat dairy products, dietary and soluble fiber, whole grains and protein from the plant sources.

Option (D) is incorrect because the surgical process was not very intrusive.

Hence, the correct option is (C).

163.

Option (D) is correct because the deposition of copper in the basal ganglia results in the clinical manifestations of tremor, dyskinesias, and rigidity. In Wilson's disease, toxic accumulations of copper in the liver cause acute fulminant hepatitis or recurrent hepatitis with hepatic cirrhosis of the course type.

Option (A) is incorrect because the pons (Latin for "bridge") is part of the brainstem, and in humans and other bipeds lies inferior to the midbrain, superior to the medulla oblongata and anterior to the cerebellum. The pons is also called the pons Varolii ("bridge of

Varolius"), after the Italian anatomist and surgeon Costanzo Varolio (1543–75).

Option (B) is incorrect because the medulla oblongata or simply medulla is a long stem-like structure that makes up part of the brainstem. It is anterior and partially inferior to the cerebellum. It is a cone-shaped neuronal mass responsible for autonomic (involuntary) functions ranging from vomiting to sneezing.

Option (C) is incorrect because the cerebellum is the area at the back and bottom of the brain, behind the brainstem. The cerebellum has several functions relating to movement and coordination, including Maintaining balance: The cerebellum has special sensors that detect shifts in balance and movement.

Hence, the correct option is (D).

164. Option (C) is correct because osmosis is defined as the diffusion of water through a semipermeable membrane to a solution with a lower concentration of water.

Option (A) is incorrect because filtration is the process in which fluids are pushed through biologic membranes by unequal processes.

Option (B) is incorrect because diffusion is the process by which molecules move through a substance, seemingly down a concentration gradient, because of the random molecular motion and collision between particles.

Option (D) is incorrect because Brownian motion or pedesis is the random motion of particles suspended in a fluid resulting from their collision with the fast-moving molecules in the fluid.

Hence, the correct option is (C).

165.

- CLL is a disorder of older patients with 90% of cases occurring after the age of 50 years and the median age is 65 yrs.
- Found incidentally Hallmark is absolute lymphocytosis Most are found to have an isolated peripheral blood lymphocytosis during a routine blood test.
- Alternatively, lymphadenopathy, splenomegaly, or both may be detected during a regular physical examination.
- When symptomatic, the most frequent complaint is fatigue or a vague sense of being unwell. Less frequently, enlarged nodes or the development of an infection is the initial complaint, and the most frequent infections are bacterial pneumonia. In contrast to lymphomas, fever and weight loss are uncommon.
- Peripheral Blood The diagnosis is now made with a count of greater than 5 x 10 VI Presence of typical immunophenotypic markers.
- The median lymphocyte count at diagnosis is 30 x IO VL.
- In most patients, the leukemia cells have the morphologic appearance of normal small to medium-sized lymphocytes with clumped chromatin, inconspicuous nucleoli, and a small ring of cytoplasm. Cytoplasmic inclusions occasionally may be observed in CLL cells and may be crystalline, globular, tubular, or rod-shaped Ruptured lymphocytes ("basket" or "smudge" cells) are commonly seen in the blood smear, and the number of these cells increases with the lymphocyte count.
- Stage 0 CLL is characterized by absolute lymphocytosis (high lymphocyte count) without lymphadenopathy (enlarged lymph nodes), hepatosplenomegaly (enlarged liver and spleen), anemia (low red blood cell count), or thrombocytopenia (low platelet count).

Option (D) is correct because it contains all options.

Option (A) is incorrect because it contains only a single point.

Option (B) is incorrect because there are more right options.

Option (C) is incorrect because option A and option B are also right.

Hence, the correct option is (D).

166. Option (A) is correct as desmosomes are the major adhesion complex in the epidermis, anchoring keratin intermediate filaments (IFs) to the cell membrane and bridging adjacent keratinocytes, and allowing cells to withstand trauma.

Option (B) is incorrect as melanocytes remain connected through their dendrites with approximately 30–40 keratinocytes forming the epidermal melanin unit and to the fibroblasts in the underlying dermis.

Option (C) is incorrect because the stratum basale (also called the stratum germinativum) is the deepest epidermal layer and attaches the epidermis to the basal lamina, below which lie the layers of the dermis. The cells in the stratum basale bond to the dermis via intertwining collagen fibers referred to as the basement membrane.

Option (D) is incorrect as Langerhans cells are closely connected with nerve fibers in the epidermis. Thus, Langerhans cells and the nervous system are anatomically and functionally associated.

Hence, the correct option is (A).

167. Option (B) is correct as between the stratum granulosum and corneum in palm and soles, there is an additional layer (addition to 4 layers found elsewhere in the epidermis) called stratum lucidum.

The cells degenerate as they move into stratum lucidum (from deeper layers). As the option has the choices that are true regarding the question, therefore, this is the correct answer.

Option (A) is incorrect as stratum lucidum is sandwiched between the stratum granulosum and corneum in palm and soles, and not between the S. spinosum and S.granulosum. As an option (A) is containing the choices that are contradictory to each other, so this will be incorrect.

Option (C) is incorrect as the prickle cell layer is the other name of the stratum spinosum. And this is not part of stratum lucidum.

Option (D) is incorrect as hair follicles and all other appendages are present in the dermis.

Hence, the correct option is (B).

168. Option (C) is correct as nevus anaemic presents as congenital hypopigmented patches with a well-defined border. They are asymptomatic and typically seen on the upper trunk, although they have also reported on the face and extremities. The distribution of hair, formation of sweat, and skin sensation are unaffected by nevus anaemic.

Option (A) is incorrect because a Becker naevus (nevus in American spelling) is a late-onset epidermal naevus or birthmark occurring mostly in males. It is also known as Becker melanosis. It is due to an overgrowth of the epidermis (upper layers of the skin), pigment cells (melanocytes) and hair follicles.

Option (B) is incorrect because freckles are small brown spots on your skin, often in areas that get sun exposure. In most cases, freckles are harmless. They form as a result of the overproduction of melanin, which is responsible for skin and hair colour (pigmentation). Overall, freckles come from ultraviolet (UV) radiation stimulation.

Option (D) is incorrect because nevus of Ota is a type of dermal melanocytosis (excessive melanocytes in the tissues) that causes the hyperpigmentation of an eye and the surrounding area. It often takes the form of bluish or brownish pigment around the eye, along with this pigment appear on the whites of the eye.

Hence, the correct option is (C).

169.

Option (D) is correct because diabetes mellitus is an autoimmune disease and has been reported in association with vitiligo, and it seems that the incidence of diabetes mellitus is more common in vitiligo patients than in healthy subjects. Vitiligo-associated diabetes mellitus is seen in 1-7% of vitiligo patients in the world.

Option (A) is incorrect because psoriasis is a long-lasting autoimmune disease characterized by patches of abnormal skin. These skin patches are typically red, or purple on some people with darker skin, dry, itchy, and scaly. Psoriasis varies in severity from small, localized patches to complete body coverage.

Option (B) is incorrect because a nutritional deficiency occurs when the body doesn't absorb or get from food the necessary amount of a nutrient. Deficiencies can lead to a variety of health problems. These can include digestion problems, skin disorders, stunted or defective bone growth, and even dementia.

Option (C) is incorrect because vitiligo appears to affect at least 1% to 2% of the population, irrespective of sex, race, or age. In half of all vitiligo cases, onset occurs between the ages of 10 and 30. There are a few reported cases of vitiligo present at birth. Onset in old age also rarely occurs.

Hence, the correct option is (D).

170.

Option (D) is correct because Denny morgan fold is an extra fold of skin beneath lower eyelid which is seen in atopic dermatitis.

Option (A) is incorrect because dermatomyositis is a rare inflammatory disease. Common symptoms of dermatomyositis include a distinctive skin rash, muscle weakness, and inflammatory myopathy, or inflamed muscles. It's one of only three known inflammatory myopathies. Dermatomyositis can affect both adults and children.

Option (B) is incorrect because systemic lupus erythematosus (SLE), also known simply as lupus, is an autoimmune disease in which the body's immune system mistakenly attacks healthy tissue in many parts of the body. Symptoms vary between people and may be mild to severe.

Option (C) is incorrect because of the characteristic plaques on the skin: well-defined plaques of red raised skin that can appear on any area of skin, although the knees, elbows, scalp, and trunk are the most common locations. It is also called plaque psoriasis.

Hence, the correct option is (D).

171. Option (A) is correct as parthenium (congress grass) is the commonest cause of airborne contact dermatitis in India".

Option (B) is incorrect as calotropis is a poisonous plant. The milky latex sap of Calotropis gigantic is a known cause of toxic keratoconjunctivitis and reversible vision loss.

Option (C) is incorrect as pneumoconiosis is a general term given to any lung disease caused by specks of dust that are breathed in and then deposited deep in the lungs causing damage.

Option (D) is incorrect as it is explained in option (A) that parthenium is the most common cause of airborne dermatitis. So, this option will be incorrect.

Hence, the correct option is (A).

172. Option (C) is correct because it is containing both options A and B.

Option (A) is incorrect because option B Psoriasis Vulgaris (also known as chronic stationary psoriasis or plaque-like psoriasis) is also the most common form and affects 85%–90% of people with psoriasis. Plaque psoriasis typically appears as raised areas of inflamed skin covered with silvery-white scaly skin.

Option (B) is incorrect because plaque psoriasis, or psoriasis Vulgaris, is also the most common form of psoriasis. An estimated 80 to 90 percent of people with psoriasis have plaque psoriasis. It's characterized by thick red patches of skin, often with a silver or white scaly layer.

Option (D) is incorrect because psoriasis is an inflammatory skin condition that frequently affects male genitalia. Psoriasis patches on the penis are not as scaly as those on other parts of the body. They may look like well-defined, thin white plaques without scales, or they may have a red ring around them.

Hence, the correct option is (C).

173. Option (A) is correct because auspitz's sign is used as a bed-side test for diagnosis of psoriasis vulgaris/plaque psoriasis (a most common type of psoriasis).

Option (B) is incorrect because pustular psoriasis is a rare and severe form of psoriasis that involves widespread inflammation of the skin and small white or yellow pus-filled blisters or pustules. The pus consists of white blood cells and is not a sign of infection. On light skin, the affected areas will appear red.

Option (C) is incorrect because lichen planus (LIE-Kun PLAY-nus) is a condition that can cause swelling and irritation in the skin, hair, nails and mucous membranes. On the skin, lichen planus usually appears as purplish, itchy, flat bumps that develop over several weeks.

Option (D) is incorrect because inverse psoriasis is a skin condition that causes red and inflamed lesions in the skin folds of the body. It is also known as intertriginous psoriasis. The location and appearance of these lesions set inverse psoriasis apart from other types of psoriasis.

Hence, the correct option is (A).

174. Option (C) is correct as the 30 year male with severely itchy papulovesicular lesions on knees, elbow, buttocks suggests the diagnosis of dermatitis herpetiform. Amongst the vesiculobullous disorders, only dermatitis herpetiform has papulovesicular (papules + vesicles) lesions.

Option (A) is incorrect because pemphigus Vulgaris is a rare, severe autoimmune disease in which blisters of varying sizes break out on the skin and on the lining of the mouth and other mucous membranes. Pemphigus Vulgaris occurs when the immune system mistakenly attacks proteins in the upper layers of the skin.

Option (B) is incorrect because bullous pemphigoid is an autoimmune pruritic skin disease preferentially in elderly people, that may involve the formation of blisters (bullae) in the space between the epidermal and dermal skin layers. The disorder is a type of pemphigoid.

Option (D) is incorrect because nummular eczema, also known as nummular dermatitis or discoid eczema, is a chronic condition that causes coin-shaped spots to develop on the skin. These spots are often itchy and well-defined. They may ooze clear fluid or become dry and crusty.

Hence, the correct option is (C).

175. Option (B) is correct because of in pemphigoid (bullous pemphigoid)

- Age → 85 year
- Blisters on lower body (thigh & trunk)
- Nikolsky's sign negative

Option (A) is incorrect because pemphigus Vulgaris is a rare, severe autoimmune disease in which blisters of varying sizes break out on the skin and on the lining of the mouth and other mucous membranes. Pemphigus Vulgaris occurs when the immune system mistakenly attacks proteins in the upper layers of the skin.

Option (C) is incorrect because lichen planus (LIE-Kun PLAY-nus) is a condition that can cause swelling and irritation in the skin, hair, nails and mucous membranes. On the skin, lichen planus usually appears as purplish, itchy, flat bumps that develop over several weeks.

Option (D) is incorrect because dermatitis herpetiformis (DH) is a chronic autoimmune blistering skin condition, characterized by blisters filled with a watery fluid that is intensely itchy. DH is a cutaneous manifestation of Coeliac disease.

Hence, the correct option is (B).

176. Option (C) is correct because punched out or inverted saucer-shaped lesions are seen in -

- Mid borderline leprosy (BB)
- Borderline lepromatous (BL).

Option (A) is incorrect because lepromatous leprosy is a form of leprosy characterized by pale macules in the skin. It results from the failure of Th1 cell activation which is necessary to eradicate the mycobacteria.

Option (B) is incorrect because tuberculoid leprosy is a milder, less severe form of leprosy. People with this type have only one or a few patches of flat, pale-colored skin (called paucibacillary leprosy). The affected area of the skin may feel numb because of nerve damage underneath. Tuberculoid leprosy is less contagious than other forms.

Option (D) is incorrect because indeterminate leprosy refers to a very early form of leprosy that consists of a single skin lesion with a slightly diminished sensation to touch.

Includes Diseases: Tuberculoid leprosy; Lepromatous leprosy.

Hence, the correct option is (C).

177. Option (B) is correct as, how can cell-mediated immunity (CMI) be increased in leprosy infection. It is decreased in leprosy. So, this is the required answer.

Option (A) is incorrect as people with tuberculoid leprosy have pale-colored skin (called paucibacillary leprosy). The affected area of the skin may feel numb because of nerve damage underneath.

Option (C) is incorrect as people with tuberculoid leprosy type have only one or a few patches of flat.

Option (D) is incorrect as an option (B) was not true about tuberculoid leprosy.

Hence, the correct option is (B).

178. Option (C) is correct because the combination of a painful ulcer with tender adenopathy is suggestive of chancroid; the presence of suppurative adenopathy is almost pathognomonic. Either a clinical presentation of the ulcer(s) not typical of a disease caused by herpes simplex virus (HSV) or a culture-negative for HSV.

Option (A) is incorrect because lymphogranuloma venereum (LGV) is a long-term (chronic) infection of the lymphatic system. It is caused by any of 3 different types (serovars) of the bacteria Chlamydia trachomatis. The bacteria are spread by sexual contact. The infection is not caused by the same bacteria that cause genital chlamydia.

Option (B) is incorrect because granuloma inguinale is a bacterial disease caused by Klebsiella granulomatis (formerly known as Calymmatobacterium granulomatis) characterized by genital ulcers. It is endemic in many less-developed regions.

Option (D) is incorrect because the symptoms of secondary syphilis develop two to eight weeks after a person first becomes infected with primary syphilis. The secondary stage is usually marked by a non-itchy rash. The rash might be confined to one part of your body, or it could spread over several parts. The appearance of the rash varies.

Hence, the correct option is (C).

179. Option (C) is correct because LGV is a subtype of genital ulcer diseases that include other STDs, such as HSV-2, syphilis, and chancroid. This condition is characterized by self-limited genital papules or ulcers followed by painful inguinal and/or femoral lymphadenopathy, which may be the only clinical manifestation at presentation.

Option (A) is incorrect because granuloma inguinale is a bacterial disease caused by Klebsiella granulomatis (formerly known as Calymmatobacterium granulomatis).

Option (B) is incorrect because syphilis is a bacterial infection usually spread by sexual contact. The disease starts as a painless sore — typically on your genitals, rectum or mouth. Syphilis spreads from person to person via skin or mucous membrane contact with these sores.

Option (D) is incorrect because donovanosis is a sexually transmitted genital ulcer disease. The bacterium that causes donovanosis (Klebsiella granulomatis) infects the skin around the genitals, groin or anal area and causes ulcers and destruction of the skin.

Hence, the correct option is (C).

180. Option (A) is correct because having six or more café au lait spots greater than 5 mm in diameter before puberty, or greater than 15 mm in diameter after puberty, is a diagnostic feature of neurofibromatosis type I, but other features are required to diagnose NF-1.

Option (B) is incorrect because Gardner's syndrome, also known as Gardner syndrome or familial colorectal polyposis, is a subtype of familial adenomatous polyposis (FAP). Gardner syndrome is an autosomal dominant form of polyposis characterized by the presence of multiple polyps in the colon together with tumors outside the colon.

Option (C) is incorrect because Cockayne syndrome (CS), also called Neill-Dingwall syndrome, is a rare and fatal autosomal recessive neurodegenerative disorder characterized by growth failure, impaired development of the nervous system, abnormal sensitivity to sunlight (photosensitivity), eye disorders and premature aging.

Option (D) is incorrect because down syndrome is a genetic disorder caused when abnormal cell division results in an extra full or partial copy of chromosome 21. This extra genetic material causes the developmental changes and physical features of Down syndrome.

Hence, the correct option is (A).

181. Option (C) is correct because Grocott methenamine silver stain is preferred for fungi because the periodic acid–Schiff stain tends not to stain two common lung pathogens: Pneumocystis jiroveci and Histoplasma capsulatum.

Option (A) is incorrect because the acid-fast stain is a differential stain used to identify acid-fast organisms such as members of the genus Mycobacterium. Acid-fast organisms are characterized by wax-like, nearly impermeable cell walls; they contain mycolic acid and large amounts of fatty acids, waxes, and complex lipids.

Option (B) is incorrect because mucicarmine stain is a staining procedure used for different purposes. In microbiology the stain aids in the identification of a variety of microorganisms based on whether or not the cell wall-stains intensely red.

Option (D) is incorrect because gram stain or Gram staining, also called Gram's method, is a method of staining used to distinguish and classify bacterial species into two large groups (gram-positive and gram-negative). The name comes from the Danish bacteriologist Hans Christian Gram, who developed the technique.

Hence, the correct option is (C).

182. Option (A) is correct as epidermophyton does not infect hair, it does not cause T. capitis.

Option (B) is incorrect because Microsporum is a genus of fungi that causes tinea capitis, tinea corporis, ringworm, and other dermatophytoses. Microsporum forms both macroconidia and microconidia on short conidiophores.

Option (C) is incorrect because the trichophyton rubrum is a dermatophytic fungus in the phylum Ascomycota. It is an exclusively clonal, anthropophilic saprotroph that colonizes the upper layers of dead skin, and is the most common cause of athlete's foot, fungal infection of the nail, jock itch, and ringworm worldwide.

Option (D) is incorrect because trichophyton violaceum is an anthropophilic, cosmopolitan dermatophyte. It primarily causes tinea capitis and less commonly tinea corporis and tinea unguium.

Hence, the correct option is (A).

183. Option (D) is correct as an orientation to time is labile and quickly disrupted by organic causes. Orientation to place is disturbed later in the disease process.

Option (A) is incorrect as schizophrenia is a serious mental disorder in which people interpret reality abnormally. Schizophrenia may result in some combination of hallucinations, delusions, and extremely disordered thinking and behavior that impairs daily functioning, and can be disabling.

Option (B) is incorrect as Neurosis is a class of functional mental disorders involving chronic distress but neither delusions nor hallucinations. Neurosis may be defined simply as "poor ability to adapt to one's environment, an inability to change one's life patterns, and the inability to develop a richer, more complex, more satisfying personality."

Option (C) is incorrect as the hallmarks of this personality disorder are distrust and suspicion. Individuals who exhibit constitutional paranoia do not normally confide in other people and frequently misread others, redefining innocuous statements and behavior as malevolent.

Hence, the correct option is (D).

184. Option (C) is correct because visual hallucinations are relatively uncommon presentations in medical and psychiatric clinics, where they are generally regarded as a marker of possible underlying "organic" brain disease. Thus, patients with visual hallucinations are often referred for imaging of the brain.

Option (A) is incorrect because a formal thought disorder (FTD) is a disruption of the form or structure of thought. Formal thought disorder also is known as disorganized thinking results in disorganized speech and is recognized as a major feature of schizophrenia and other psychoses.

Option (B) is incorrect because auditory hallucinations are false perceptions of sound. They have been described as the experience of internal words or noises that have no real origin in the outside world and are perceived to be separate from the person's mental processes.

Option (D) is incorrect because depression is classified as a mood disorder. It may be described as feelings of sadness, loss, or anger that interfere with a person's everyday activities.

Hence, the correct option is (C).

185. Option (B) is correct because the characteristic features of acute LSD intoxication are perceptual changes occurring in clear consciousness. These perceptual changes include depersonalization, derealisation, intensification of perceptions, synaesthesias (for example, colors are heard, and sounds are felt), illusions, and hallucinations. In addition, features suggestive of autonomic hyperactivity, such as pupillary dilatation, tachycardia, sweating, tremors, incoordination, palpitations, raised temperature, piloerection, and giddiness can also be present.

Option (A) is incorrect because cocaine, also known as coke, is a strong stimulant most frequently used as a recreational drug. It is commonly snorted, inhaled as smoke, or dissolved and injected into a vein. Mental effects may include loss of contact with reality, an intense feeling of happiness, or agitation.

Option (C) is incorrect because of cannabis, also known as marijuana. Cannabis has mental and physical effects. It causes a high, or stoned, feeling and other effects including a general change in perception, difficulty thinking, impaired short-term memory, altered sense of time, impaired body movement, relaxation, and an increase in appetite.

Option (D) is incorrect because phencyclidine, also known as angel dust among other names, is a drug used for its mind-altering effects. PCP may cause hallucinations, distorted perceptions of sounds, and violent behavior. As a recreational drug, it is typically smoked, but may be taken by mouth, snorted, or injected.

Hence, the correct option is (B).

186. Option (C) is correct because the common factors that can lead to high blood pressure include a diet high in salt, fat, and/or cholesterol. As this doesn't result from morphine poisoning or overdose.

Option (A) is incorrect because manifestations of morphine poisoning include cyanosis.

Option (B) is incorrect because the pinpoint pupil is caused by opiate use. From morphine to heroin and Fentanyl to Percocet and codeine, these medications can cause the pupils to be smaller than 2mm. This is especially true in an overdose situation.

Option (D) is incorrect as an overdose of morphine can cause respiratory depression; as with any medication, there is a therapeutic window above which toxicities occur.

Hence, the correct option is (C).

187. Option (B) is correct because somatic passivity is one of the first-rank symptoms of schizophrenia described by Schneider. Here the patient believes and attributes his bodily function to be under the influence of external force/agency.

Option (A) is incorrect because depression is a mood disorder that causes a persistent feeling of sadness and loss of interest and can interfere with your daily functioning.

Option (C) is incorrect because hypochondriasis or hypochondria is a condition in which a person is excessively and unduly worried about having a serious illness.

Option (D) is incorrect because panic disorder is a type of anxiety disorder. It causes panic attacks, which are sudden feelings of terror when there is no real danger. You may feel as if you are losing control. You may also have physical symptoms, such as. Fast heartbeat.

Hence, the correct option is (B).

188. Option (B) is correct because symptoms for a schizophrenia diagnosis to be made, hallucinations consisting of a running commentary on the person's behavior or thoughts, or two or more voices conversing with one another.

Option (A) is incorrect because command hallucinations are auditory hallucinations that instruct a patient to act in specific ways; these commands can range in seriousness from innocuous to life-threatening.

Option (C) is incorrect because auditory hallucinations are a common and highly distressing positive symptom in patients with schizophrenia. Often, auditory hallucinations present as voices that comment on or criticize the behavior of the patient.

Option (D) is incorrect because auditory hallucinations are one of the most important symptoms for the diagnosis of psychosis, especially schizophrenia. Other types of auditory hallucinations can also occur in schizophrenia, including voices commanding the patient and voices talking directly to him.

Hence, the correct option is (B).

189. Option (A) is correct because Anxiety disorders include: -

1) Panic disorder,

2) Agoraphobia,

3) Specific phobia,

4) Social phobia,

5) Obsessive-compulsive disorder,

6) Post-traumatic stress disorder,

7) Acute stress disorder.

Option (B) is incorrect because depression is a mood disorder that can affect a person's daily life. It may be described as feelings of sadness, loss, or anger. This depressive disorder was added to the DSM-V for children up to 18 years of age who exhibit persistent irritability and frequent episodes of extreme behavioral dyscontrol, which is a pattern of abnormal, episodic, and frequently violent and uncontrollable social behavior without any significant provocation.

Option (C) is incorrect because schizophrenia is characterized by delusions, hallucinations, disorganized speech and behavior, and other symptoms that cause social or occupational dysfunction. DSM-5 raises the symptom threshold, requiring that an individual exhibit at least two of the specified symptoms.

Option (D) is incorrect because bipolar disorders are described by the American Psychiatric Association's Diagnostic and Statistical Manual of Mental Disorders (DSM-5) as a group of brain disorders that cause extreme fluctuation in a person's mood, energy, and ability to function.

Hence, the correct option is (A).

190. Option (A) is correct because jealousy generally refers to the thoughts or feelings of insecurity, fear, and concern over a relative lack of possessions or safety. Jealousy can consist of one or more emotions such as anger, resentment, inadequacy, helplessness or disgust.

Option(B) is incorrect because conversion disorder is a disorder in which a person experiences blindness, paralysis, or other symptoms affecting the nervous system that cannot be explained solely by a physical illness or injury. Symptoms usually begin suddenly after a period of emotional or physical distress or psychological conflict.

Option (C) is incorrect because anaesthesia or anaesthesia (from Greek "without sensation") is a state of controlled, temporary loss of sensation or awareness that is induced for medical purposes. It may include analgesia (relief from or prevention of pain), paralysis (muscle relaxation), amnesia (loss of memory), or unconsciousness.

Option (D) is incorrect as an abnormal gait or a walking abnormality is when a person is unable to walk in the usual way. This may be due to injuries, underlying conditions, or problems with the legs and feet.

Hence, the correct option is (A).

191. Option (B) is correct because in patients with narcolepsy is characterized by a short sleep latency and a sleep-onset REM period in approximately 50% of cases.

Option (A) is incorrect because people with narcolepsy have excessive, uncontrollable daytime sleepiness. They may also suddenly fall asleep at any time, during any type of activity.

Option (C) is incorrect because accessory symptoms in Narcolepsy are cataplexy, hypnagogic hallucination, sleep paralysis.

Option (D) is incorrect because only option B is right in this case.

Hence, the correct option is (B).

192. Option (D) is correct because the third-person hallucination is characteristic of schizophrenia.

Option (A) is incorrect because mental retardation is seen in 50 - 75% of patients with autism.

Option (B) is incorrect because there is the absence of a social smile and eye to eye contact.

Option (C) is incorrect because its onset is before 21/2 years.

Hence, the correct option is (D).

193. Option (D) is correct because electroconvulsive therapy (ECT) is not currently used as a first-line treatment for obsessive-compulsive disorder (OCD). However, several related case reports have demonstrated that ECT seems to be effective for severe OCD, especially when first-line therapies have failed.

Option (A) is incorrect because doctors use electroconvulsive therapy (ECT) to treat severe depression. Sometimes, they also use it to treat other mental illnesses such as schizophrenia. Doctors may also use ECT to ease other symptoms of schizophrenia, such as delusions, hallucinations, or disorganized thinking.

Option (B) is incorrect because major depression is the diagnosis for which ECT is now most frequently recommended in the United States and other western nations, research has continually been conducted on the effectiveness of ECT for the treatment of patients with schizophrenia and mania.

Option (C) is incorrect because electroconvulsive therapy (ECT) is a safe and effective treatment for major depressive disorder, bipolar disorder, catatonia, schizophrenia, and several other conditions. ECT uses an electric current to cause a seizure in the brain and is one of the fastest ways to treat severe symptoms of mental illness.

Hence, the correct option is (D).

194. Option (C) is correct because primitive (intuitive) thinking occurs in the preoperational stage of intellectual development stages by Jean Piaget.

Option (A) is incorrect because the sensorimotor stage is the first of the four stages Piaget uses to define cognitive development. Piaget designated the first two years of an infant life as the sensorimotor stage. During this period, infants are busy discovering relationships between their bodies and the environment.

Option (B) is incorrect because Piaget considered the concrete stage a major turning point in the child's cognitive development because it marks the beginning of logical or operational thought. This means the child can work things out internally in their head (rather than physically try things out in the real world).

Option (D) is incorrect because the formal operational stage begins at approximately age twelve and lasts into adulthood. As adolescents enter this stage, they gain the ability to think in an abstract manner by manipulating ideas in their heads, without any dependence on concrete manipulation.

Hence, the correct option is (C).

195. Option (C) is correct because Olanzapine is a medication that works in the brain to treat schizophrenia. It is also known as a second-generation antipsychotic (SGA) or atypical antipsychotic. Olanzapine rebalances dopamine and serotonin to improve thinking, mood, and behavior and known as the Best drug therapy for paranoid schizophrenia in a thinly built 21-years old young male because it works on many symptoms of schizophrenia.

Option (A) is incorrect because Chlorpromazine, marketed under the trade names Thorazine and Largactil among others, is an antipsychotic medication. It is primarily used to treat psychotic disorders such as schizophrenia but not work on all symptoms of schizophrenia.

Option (B) is incorrect because Risperidone, sold under the brand name Risperdal among others, is an atypical antipsychotic. It is used to treat schizophrenia, bipolar disorder, and irritability associated with autism. It is taken either by mouth or by injection into a muscle. The injectable version is long-acting and lasts for about two weeks but not work on all symptoms of schizophrenia.

Option (D) is incorrect because Quetiapine, sold under the trade name Seroquel among others, is an atypical antipsychotic used for the treatment of schizophrenia, bipolar disorder, and major depressive disorder but not work on all symptoms of schizophrenia.

Hence, the correct option is (C).

196. Option (B) is correct because it is also known as March fractures most commonly occur in the second and third metatarsal bones of the foot. stress fracture of metatarsal bone is the fracture of the distal third of one of the metatarsals occurring because of recurrent stress.

Option (A) is incorrect because fourth metatarsal base fractures are an uncommon foot injury. These fractures can take extended periods of time to heal

Option (C) is incorrect because proximal stress fractures of the second metatarsal are uncommon overuse injuries, exclusively reported in ballet dancers and directly associated with dance-related postures of the foot. Outcomes of conservative treatment are typically unfavorable and often lead to poor union.

Option (D) is incorrect because a tibial shaft fracture occurs along the length of the bone, below the knee and above the ankle. It typically takes a major force to cause this type of broken leg. In many tibia fractures, the smaller bone in the lower leg (fibula) is broken as well.

Hence, the correct option is (B).

197. Option (C) is correct because the stage of callus: This stage lasts for about 4-12 weeks. In this stage, the granulation tissue differentiates further and creates osteoblasts. These cells lay down an intercellular matrix which soon becomes impregnated with calcium salts. This results in the formulation of the callus also called woven bone. The callus is the first sign of union visible on X-rays, usually 3 weeks after the fracture. The formation of this bridge of woven bone imparts good strength to the fracture. Callus formation is slower in adults than in children, and in cortical bones than in cancellous bones. Micromovement induces callus formation.

Option (A) is incorrect because of the disruption of blood flow to the bone, some bone cells around the fracture die. This inflammatory stage ends approximately one week after the fracture.

Option (B) is incorrect because the repairing or reparative phase begins within the first few days after the bone fracture and lasts for about 2 – 3 weeks.

Option (D) is incorrect because Toughening up (6–12 weeks) By 12 weeks after fracture, osteoblasts have transformed the soft callus into a hard callus. The length of the healing period depends on the fracture site.

Hence, the correct option is (C).

198. Option (A) is correct because tears in the tendons of these muscles are called rotator cuff tears. The most commonly affected muscle is the supraspinatus. A combination of susceptible anatomy and a lifetime of wear and tear can cause mechanical abrasion and impingement of the supraspinatus on the acromion bone.

Option (B) is incorrect because the infraspinatus muscle is a thick triangular muscle, which occupies the chief part of the infraspinatus fossa. As one of the four muscles of the rotator cuff, the main function of the infraspinatus is to externally rotate the humerus and stabilize the shoulder joint.

Option (C) is incorrect because the subscapularis is a large triangular muscle which fills the subscapular fossa and inserts into the lesser tubercle of the humerus and the front of the capsule of the shoulder joint.

Option (D) is incorrect because the teres minor is a narrow, intrinsic shoulder muscle that extends from the lateral border of the scapula to the greater tubercle (or tuberosity) of the humerus. It contributes to the "rotator cuff," a capsule of muscles and tendons that collectively stabilize the glenohumeral joint.

Hence, the correct option is (A).

199. Option (B) is correct because a bankart lesion is a lesion of the anterior part of the glenoid labrum of the shoulder. This injury is caused by repeated anterior shoulder subluxations. The dislocation of the shoulder joint (anterior) can damage the connective tissue ring around the glenoid labrum.

Option (A) is incorrect because the labrum remains attached to the periosteum (Figs 6, 9) and undergoes rotation medially to a position along the anterior surface of the scapular neck. The ALPSA lesion can heal in this displaced position, creating a small cleft between the labrum and the glenoid.

Option (C) is incorrect because of anterior and posterior views. The upper or proximal extremity of the humerus consists of the bone's large rounded head joined to the body by a constricted portion called the neck, and two eminences, the greater and lesser tubercles.

Option (D) is incorrect because the lesser tubercle is smaller, anterolaterally placed to the head of the humerus. The lesser tubercle provides insertion to the subscapularis muscle. Both these tubercles are found in the proximal part of the shaft.

Hence, the correct option is (B).

200. Option (D) is correct because it can be diagnosed by surgery.

Option (A) is incorrect as if a patient with a suspected fracture of the pelvis has some bleeding from the urethra and is unable to pass urine he should not be encouraged to pass urine.

Option (B) is incorrect because no attempt should be made to pass a catheter, as this could convert a partial to a complete tear of the urethra.

Option (C) is incorrect as in this case a hot water bottle should be given followed by injection of carbachol is not workable.

Hence, the correct option is (D).

201. Option (B) is correct because the medial circumflex femoral artery along with its retinacular and epiphyseal branches supplies most of the blood supply to the head and neck of femur.

Option (A) is incorrect because the lateral circumflex femoral artery supplies the anterior muscle group of the thigh, as well as the hip and knee joints.

Option (C) is incorrect because the ligamentum teres artery descends from the posterior branch of the obturator artery and attaches at the fovea. This artery is commonly disrupted with dislocations. It is the main blood supply to the femoral head in children.

Option (D) is incorrect because the popliteal artery is the continuation of the femoral artery that begins at the level of the adductor hiatus in the adductor Magnus muscle of the thigh. As it continues down, it runs across the popliteal fossa, posterior to the knee joint.

Hence, the correct option is (B).

202. Option (D) is correct because in some cases, a cast may include the upper and lower arm and the elbow, but leave the wrist and hand free, or the upper and lower leg and the knee, leaving the foot and ankle free. Such a cast may be called a cylinder cast.

Option (A) is incorrect because the goal of treatment is to maintain the function of the shoulder. Most fractures of the body of the scapula are treated without surgery. Ice is used for swelling, and pain medications are used for pain control. The shoulder is immobilized in a shoulder sling for 3-4 weeks until the pain goes away. A shoulder spica cast is used for shoulder fracture.

Option (B) is incorrect because a unilateral hip spica cast is applicable in the hip fracture.

Option (C) is incorrect because bilateral long leg hip spica cast is used in pelvis fracture.

Hence, the correct option is (D).

203. Option (A) is correct because the upper lumbar and lower thoracic spine are the most frequently involved sites. More than one vertebra is typically affected, and the vertebral body is more frequently affected than the posterior arch. Distortion of the spinal column leads to spinal deformities.

Option (B) is incorrect because, in severe cervical spine trauma, these fractures do not usually cause difficulties in diagnosis. However, in whiplash injuries, which are very common and only rarely associated with such fractures, surgical management can be complicated if they are underestimated.

Option (C) is incorrect because whiplash is a relatively common injury that occurs to a person's neck following a sudden acceleration-deceleration force that causes unrestrained, rapid forward and backward movement of the head and neck, most commonly from motor vehicle accidents. The term "whiplash" was first used in 1928.

Option (D) is incorrect because it is the exact injury mechanism that causes whiplash injuries is forceful sudden hyperextension followed by hyperflexion of the cervical vertebrae, mainly spraining the nuchal ligament and the Anterior Longitudinal Ligament respectively.

Hence, the correct option is (A).

204. Option (C) is correct because the greenstick fracture is an incomplete fracture. In which bone is incompletely divided &periosteum remains in continuity.

Option (A) is incorrect because the fracture subtypes can present in children and adults:

- A comminuted fracture is when the bone breaks into several pieces.
- A transverse fracture is when the fracture line is perpendicular to the shaft (long part) of the bone.
- An oblique fracture is when the break is on an angle through the bone.
- A pathologic fracture is caused by a disease that weakens the bone.
- A stress fracture is a hairline crack.

Option (B) is incorrect because complete fractures are fractures where the parts of the bone that have been fractured are completely separated from each other. There is a complete separation of the cortex circumferentially. Complete fractures can be classified as transverse: straight across the bone. oblique: oblique line across the bone.

Option (D) is incorrect because spinal fractures are different than a broken arm or leg, a fracture or dislocation of a vertebra can cause bone fragments to pinch and damage the spinal nerves.

Hence, the correct option is (C).

205. Option (D) is correct because amongst the given options restriction of abduction and internal rotation is seen only in Perthes disease.

Option (A) is incorrect because in septic arthritis:- Restriction of adduction, internal rotation, extension in early stages.

Option (B) is incorrect because in TB hip:-

i) Stage of synovitis:- Restriction of adduction, internal rotation & extension.

ii) Stage of arthritis:- Restriction of abduction, external rotation & extension.

Option (C) is incorrect because in congenital dislocation of the hip:- Restriction of abduction, external rotation.

Hence, the correct option is (D).

206. Option (A) is correct because defective mineralization is seen in both rickets and osteomalacia. However, the question is about defective mineralization in the Epiphyseal plate (growth plate/physics) in a growing child, which is seen in rickets.

Option (B) is incorrect because osteomalacia is a disease of the mature skeleton when physis (epiphyseal plate) has already been fused. There is no physics (epiphyseal plate) in a mature bone.

Option (C) is incorrect because scurvy is a disease resulting from a lack of vitamin C (ascorbic acid). Early symptoms of deficiency include weakness, feeling tired and sore arms and legs. Without treatment, decreased red blood cells, gum disease, changes to hair, and bleeding from the skin may occur.

Option (D) is incorrect because osteoporosis is a bone disease that occurs when the body loses too much bone, makes too little bone, or both. As a result, bones become weak and may break from a fall or, in serious cases, from sneezing or minor bumps. Osteoporosis means "porous bone". Viewed under a microscope, healthy bone looks like a honeycomb.

Hence, the correct option is (A).

207. Ankylosis

Ankylosis is the fusion of bones in a joint leading to stiffness of the joint.

Ankylosis may be : -

1) Fibrous ankylosis: - Two articular surfaces are fused by fibrous tissue.

The features are : -

Some movement of joint is possible (though just a jog of movement).

1. Movements may be painless or painful.
2. The most common cause is tubercular arthritis.

2) Bony ankylosis: - There is a bony union between two articular surfaces. The features are : -

- No movements are possible.
- a Joint is painless
- A most common cause is acute suppurative arthritis (septic arthritis).
- Sometimes, stiffness may also occur due to extra-articular etiology such as in Bum contracture, myositis ossificans, etc. It is called False ankylosis.

From the above explanation,

Option (A) is correct because-

- No movements are possible.
- a Joint is painless

Option (B) is incorrect because pain is not possible.

Option (C) is incorrect because no movement is possible.

Option (D) is incorrect because option A is right.

Hence, the correct option is (A).

208. Option (A) is correct because Enneking's staging of benign & malignant musculoskeletal tumours is based on three criteria:

1. Histological grading,
2. Anatomical size,
3. Presence or absence of regional or distant metastasis.

Option (B) is incorrect as the aim in this study of Manchester diagnostic criteria for NF2* Object was to describe the clinical presentation, differential diagnosis, and risk for neurofibromatosis Type 2 (NF2) in pediatric patients presenting with cerebellopontine angle (CPA) and internal auditory canal (IAC) tumours.

Option (C) is incorrect as the Edmonton Classification System for Cancer Pain (ECS-CP) was developed as a revised version of the Edmonton Staging System (ESS) and was renamed to reflect the intended use for cancer pain classification as a standardized assessment aid to guide clinical management.

Option (D) is incorrect because the TNM Classification of Malignant Tumors is a globally recognized standard for classifying the extent of the spread of cancer. It is a classification system of the anatomical extent of tumour cancers.

Hence, the correct option is (A).

209. Option (D) is correct because over 90% of the collagen in the human body, however, is type I.

The five most common types are:

Type I: skin, tendon, vasculature, organs, bone (the main component of the organic part of the bone)

Type II: cartilage (a main collagenous component of cartilage)

Type III: reticulate (the main component of reticular fibres), commonly found alongside type I

Type IV: forms basal lamina, the epithelium-secreted layer of the basement membrane

Type V: cell surfaces, hair, and placenta.

Option (A) is incorrect because of organs, bone (the main component of the organic part of the bone) Type II: cartilage (a main collagenous component of cartilage).

Option (B) is incorrect because Type III Collagen (Col_3), fibril-forming collagen, is a major extracellular matrix component in a variety of internal organs and skin. It is also expressed at high levels during embryonic skeletal development and is expressed by osteoblasts in mature bone.

Option (C) is incorrect because the main structural protein of the glomerular basement membrane (GBM) is type IV collagen. Type IV collagen is assembled from a family of six distinct chains (reviewed in 14, 15), designated α_1 to α_6.

Hence, the correct option is (D).

210. Option (B) is correct because contraindications to internal fixation include active or suspected infection, compromised soft tissues overlying the fracture, medical or surgical conditions that contraindicate anesthesia (e.g. recent MI) and sever, irreparable neurovascular injury (amputation is better).

Option (A) is incorrect because Type III injuries are more commonly seen in older children where the growth plates have started to close. It is a combination of a horizontal fracture line through the physis and a vertical fracture line which runs from the growth plate through the epiphysis to the articular surface. Displaced injuries may result in a physical bar, leading to growth disturbance and joint incongruity, leading to arthritis.

Option (C) is incorrect because an intraarticular fracture is a bone fracture in which the break crosses into the surface of a joint. This always results in damage to the cartilage. Compared to extraarticular fractures, intraarticular have a higher risk for developing long-term complications, such as posttraumatic osteoarthritis.

Option (D) is incorrect because of fracture-dislocation, a severe injury in which both fracture and dislocation take place simultaneously. Frequently, a loose piece of bone remains jammed between the ends of the dislocated bones and may have to be removed surgically before the dislocation can be reduced.

Hence, the correct option is (B).

211.

Gas	Pin index
Oxygen	2,5
Nitrous oxide	3,5
Cyclopropane	3,6
Air	1,5
Nitrogen	1,4
Entonox (50% O_2+50% N_2O)	Single central (7)
Carbon dioxide (<7.5 %)	2,6
Carbon dioxide (>7.5 %)	1,6

From the above explanation,

Option (C) is correct because 2,5 is the safety pin index for an oxygen cylinder.

Option (A) is incorrect because 3,5 is the safety pin index for Nitrous oxide.

Option (B) is incorrect because 1,5 is the safety pin index for air.

Option (D) is incorrect because 1,4 is the safety pin index for nitrogen.

Hence, the correct option is (C).

212. Bag and mask ventilation is contraindicated when there are increased chances of aspiration like:-

1-Full stomach,

2-Intestinal obstruction,

3-Pregnancy,

4-Hiatus hernia,

5-Diaphragmatic hernia,

6-Tracheoesuphageal fistula,

7-Meconium aspiration syndrome.

From the above explanation,

Option (D) is correct because it is containing all options.

Option (A) is incorrect because other options are also right.

Option (B) is incorrect because it is not containing all the right option.

Option (C) is incorrect because it is not the only correct option.

Hence, the correct option is (D).

213. Option (B) is correct because the disadvantage is it doesn't prevent aspiration of gastric contents.

Option (A) is incorrect because the primary advantage of the LAM over the face mask during general anaesthesia includes the ability to obtain, secure, and maintain a patent airway.

Option (C) is incorrect because the LAM, with its advantages over both the face mask/nasal hood and endotracheal intubation, potentially has a place in oral and maxillofacial surgery by increasing the safety and efficacy of outpatient general anaesthesia in specific situations.

Option (D) is incorrect because the placement of the LMA can be accomplished without muscle relaxants and laryngoscopy. The avoidance of succinylcholine may decrease the incidence of postoperative myalgias. Significant and potentially detrimental hemodynamic changes associated with both laryngoscopy and tracheal intubation are also attenuated and are of shorter duration with the use of the laryngeal mask airway.

Hence, the correct option is (B).

214. Option (C) is correct because Angiotensin-Converting Enzyme Inhibitors and Angiotensin Receptor Blockers should be discontinued 12 to 24 hours before surgery if taken only for hypertension, as they may produce hypotension, which is not responsive to conventional vasopressors.

Option (A) is incorrect as statins should not be stopped abruptly before surgery as their abrupt discontinuation may increase the risk of serious (even life-threatening) complications.

Option (B) is incorrect because if you're taking beta-blockers for high blood pressure, it's important that you continue to take this medication on the day of your surgery and throughout your stay with us. Stopping this medication suddenly can cause a dangerous spike in your blood pressure and heart rate, which might lead to a heart attack.

Option (D) is incorrect because steroid medications, such as Prednisone®, should be continued both during and after surgery. Most likely, your surgeon will give you additional doses at the start of your procedure. This is because long-term steroid therapy suppresses the adrenal gland, which manufactures the steroids your body needs.

Hence, the correct option is (C).

215. Option (B) is correct because Glycopyrrolate is the preferred anticholinergic over atropine and scopolamine because it does not crosse the blood-brain barrier so devoid of central side effects.

Option (A) is incorrect because Glycopyrrolate does not cross the blood-brain barrier nor the placenta. It has a slower diffusion rate relative to other anticholinergic drugs such as atropine and scopolamine.

Option (C) is incorrect because Glycopyrrolate does not produce sedation or emergence delirium.

Option (D) is incorrect because option B is correct.

Hence, the correct option is (B).

216. Option (A) is correct because a positive Lachman test or pivot test is strong evidence of an existing anterior cruciate ligament (ACL) tear, and a negative Lachman test is fairly good evidence against that injury. Although widely used, the anterior drawer is the least helpful manoeuvre for diagnosing an ACL tear.

Option (B) is incorrect because a pivot shift can be used to assess the combined tibiofemoral internal rotation and anterior tibial translation when the ACL is deficient. There are two main components of the pivot shift test that are translation – anterior subluxation of the lateral tibial plateau and rotation – rotation of the tibia relative to the femur.

Option (C) is incorrect because the McMurray test, also known as the McMurray circumduction test is used to evaluate individuals for tears in the meniscus of the knee. A tear in the meniscus may cause a pedunculated tag of the meniscus which may become jammed between the joint surfaces.

Option (D) is incorrect because the Apley's grind test (Apley Compression test) is used to evaluate individuals for problems of the meniscus in the knee. This test is named after Alan Graham Appley (1914 - 1996), a British orthopedic surgeon, who discovered this assessment technique.

Hence, the correct option is (A).

217. Option (B) is correct because this patient has an allergy (hypersensitivity) to neostigmine, So it cannot be used for reversal. Therefore in this condition, non-depolarizing muscle relaxants in which reversal can be avoided should be used:- Atracurium, cisatracurium, mivacurium.

Option (A) is incorrect because Pavulon (pancuronium bromide) Injection is a neuromuscular blocking agent used to provide skeletal muscle relaxation during tracheal intubation and surgery. Pavulon is available in generic form.

Option (C) is incorrect because Rocuronium is used to relax the muscles. It works by blocking the signals between your nerves and your muscles. Rocuronium is given before general anaesthesia in preparing you for surgery. Rocuronium helps to keep your body still during surgery.

Option (D) is incorrect because Vecuronium is used to relax the muscles. It works by blocking the signals between your nerves and your muscles. Vecuronium is given before general anaesthesia in preparing you for surgery. Vecuronium helps to keep your body still during surgery.

Hence, the correct option is (B).

218. Option (A) is correct because Succinylcholine (Anectine) is a synthetic, short-acting depolarizing muscle relaxant. Succinylcholine is used routinely for skeletal muscle relaxation before tracheal intubation.

Option (B) is incorrect because a competitive antagonist binds to the same site as the agonist but does not activate it, thus blocks the agonist's action. A non-competitive antagonist binds to an allosteric (non-agonist) site on the receptor to prevent activation of the receptor.

Option (C) is incorrect because the mechanism of action of Succinylcholine involves what appears to be a "persistent" depolarization of the neuromuscular junction.

Option (D) is incorrect because only option (A) is correct.

Hence, the correct option is (A).

219. Option (B) is correct because Suxamethonium is also commonly used as the sole muscle relaxant during electroconvulsive therapy, favoured for its short duration of action.

Option (A) is incorrect because Atracurium besylate, also known as atracurium besylate, is a medication used in addition to other medications to provide skeletal muscle relaxation during surgery or mechanical ventilation.

Option (C) is incorrect because Vecuronium bromide, sold under the brand name Norcuron among others, is a medication used as part of general anaesthesia to provide skeletal muscle relaxation during surgery or mechanical ventilation.

Option (D) is incorrect because Pancuronium is a typical non-depolarizing curare-mimetic muscle relaxant. It competitively inhibits the nicotinic acetylcholine receptor at the neuromuscular junction by blocking the binding of acetylcholine.

Hence, the correct option is (B).

220. This question is a bit confusing one because of the following two facts:-

"For the induction of anaesthesia, intravenous anaesthetics are used mostly".

"For the maintenance of anaesthesia, inhalational agents are used most commonly".

- But the following statement will clear the doubts.

"Now a day, most of the minor surgical procedures like incision & drainage are done in total intravenous anaesthesia in which intravenous anaesthetics are used for both induction as well as maintenance of anaesthesia".

So,

- For major surgical procedure → i) Induction by intravenous anaesthesia, and ii) Maintenance by inhalational anaesthesia.
- For minor surgical procedure → Induction and maintenance both by intravenous anaesthesia.

Option (B) is correct because "Now a day, most of the minor surgical procedures like incision & drainage are done in total intravenous anaesthesia in which intravenous anaesthetics are used for both induction as well as maintenance of anaesthesia".

Option (A) is incorrect because an inhalational anaesthetic is a chemical compound possessing general anaesthetic properties that can be delivered via inhalation. They are administered through a face mask, laryngeal mask airway or tracheal tube connected to an anaesthetic vaporiser and an anaesthetic delivery system and generally not used.

Option (C) is incorrect because arterial lines are generally not used to administer medication, since many injectable drugs may lead to serious tissue damage and even require amputation of the limb if administered into an artery rather than a vein.

Option (D) is incorrect because local anaesthetics are used to anaesthetize skin, subcutaneous tissue, and peripheral nerves for invasive or surgical procedures. The duration of action of local anaesthetics can range from 30 minutes to 12 hours or more.

Hence, the correct option is (B).

221. Option (A) is correct because sodium thiopental is an ultra-short-acting barbiturate and has been used commonly in the induction phase of general anaesthesia.

Option (B) is incorrect because thiopental is a very fast-acting anaesthetic (20 seconds) and one IV bolus will provide anaesthesia for 5-10 minutes. Redistribution occurs quickly (2-3 minutes) to the lean tissue and then more slowly to body fat.

Option (C) is incorrect because rapid redistribution is responsible for a very short duration of action (rapid recovery), not for induction.

Option (D) is incorrect because option (A) is correct.

Hence, the correct option is (A).

222. Option (C) is correct because ketamine at doses that produce sedative or anaesthetic effects shows anticonvulsant properties.

Option (A) is incorrect because, in individuals with partial epilepsy, propofol sedation alone did not cause seizures. Certain propofol doses within the range of conscious sedation are associated with the cessation of spontaneously occurring interictal spikes.

Option (B) is incorrect because anaesthetists are frequently faced with patients with epilepsy undergoing emergency or elective surgery and patients suffering seizures and status epilepticus in the intensive care unit (ICU). For uncontrolled seizures, treatment with midazolam, thiopental, or propofol is acceptable.

Option (D) is incorrect because Midazolam (Hypnovel) is a short-acting benzodiazepine medication like Diazepam (Valium, Antenex, Duchene) and Clonazepam (Rivotril, Paxam). It is used for emergency treatment/management of prolonged seizures. Sedation during medical procedures.

Hence, the correct option is (C).

223. Option (A) is correct because the peak absorption of local anaesthetic depends on the site of the block. The order of absorption from highest to lowest :Intercostal, intrapleural, intratracheal > caudal / epidural > brachial plexus > distal peripheral > subcutaneous.

Option (B) is incorrect because an epidural is a procedure that injects a local anaesthetic into the space around the spinal nerves in your lower back. This anaesthetic usually blocks the pain from labour contractions and during the birth very effectively. With an epidural, you can usually move and can push your baby out when you need to.

Option (C) is incorrect because when people talk about bronchial asthma, they are really talking about asthma, a chronic inflammatory disease of the airways that causes periodic "attacks" of coughing, wheezing, shortness of breath, and chest tightness. Eosinophils are a type of white blood cell associated with allergic disease.

Option (D) is incorrect as anaesthesia is produced by injection of a local anaesthetic into the caudal canal, the sacral portion of the spinal canal. Caudal anaesthesia is used to provide anaesthesia and analgesia (pain relief) below the umbilicus.

Hence, the correct option is (A).

224. Option (C) is correct because "Unlike other opioid agonists, meperidine (pethidine) frequently terminates shivering regardless of the cause".

Option (A) is incorrect because ondansetron, marketed under the brand name Zofran, is a medication used to prevent nausea and vomiting caused by cancer chemotherapy, radiation therapy, or surgery.

Option (B) is incorrect because diclofenac, sold under the brand name Voltaren among others, is a nonsteroidal anti-inflammatory drug used to treat pain and inflammatory diseases such as gout. It is taken by mouth, used by injection, or applied to the skin.

Option (D) is incorrect because paracetamol, also known as acetaminophen and APAP, is a medication used to treat pain and fever. It is typically used for mild to moderate pain relief.

Hence, the correct option is (C).

225. Option (B) is correct because the unanticipated doubling or tripling of end-tidal CO_2 is the earliest & most sensitive indicator of malignant hyperthermia. The earliest signs seen during anaesthesia are masseter muscle rigidity (MMR), tachycardia, & hypercarbia.

Option (A) is incorrect because a pulmonary embolism is a blood clot that occurs in the lungs. It can damage part of the lung due to restricted blood flow, decrease oxygen levels in the blood, and affect other organs as well. Large or multiple blood clots can be fatal. The blockage can be life-threatening.

Option (C) is incorrect because extubation is the removal of an endotracheal tube (ETT), which is the last step in liberating a patient from the mechanical ventilator. To discuss the actual procedure of extubation, one also needs to understand how to assess readiness for weaning, and management before and after extubation.

Option (D) is incorrect because blocking the secretion of exocrine glands in the head-neck area by the administration of botulinum toxin A.

Hence, the correct option is (B).

226. Using Color Doppler Mode, flow velocities within vessels are colour-coded. The intensity of the colour is a function of velocity. Flow towards and away from the transducer is indicated either as red or blue, respectively. To remember this, use the name of a famous yellow cartoon character as an acronym: BART – Blue Away, Red Towards (with the top of the screen as your reference point).

From the above explanation,

Option (B) is correct because the intensity of colour in Doppler is determined by the velocity of flow.

Option (A) is incorrect because it can not be determined by direction flow.

Option (C) is incorrect because it can not be determined by Strength of returning echo.

Option (D) is incorrect because option (B) is correct.

Hence, the correct option is (B).

227. Option (A) is correct because MRI has evolved to be the most accurate tool in detecting free silicone, its relationship to surrounding structures, and in evaluating implant ruptures. Gel bleed is the normal transudation of microscopic amounts of silicone through an intact breast prosthesis membrane into the surrounding tissues and lymphatics.

Option (B) is incorrect because MRI also cannot detect calcified lesions (calcium deposits in breast tissue that could be a sign of cancer). Finally, MRI can dislodge certain metal devices, such as pacemakers, in some people.

Option (C) is incorrect because radiation is not used, there is no risk of exposure to radiation during an MRI procedure. However, due to the use of the strong magnet, MRI cannot be performed on patients with: Implanted pacemakers. Intracranial aneurysm clips.

Option (D) is incorrect because Magnetic resonance imaging (MRI) is generally contraindicated for patients with a pacemaker (PM) or implantable cardiac defibrillator (ICD), because of the risk of life-threatening interference with the device.

Hence, the correct option is (A).

228. Option (D) is correct because high-resolution computed tomography (HRCT) is the cornerstone in the radiological diagnosis of clinically suspicious cases. HRCT is the most sensitive and specific non-invasive method for diagnosing bronchiectasis.

Option (A) is incorrect because chest x-rays are usually abnormal but are inadequate in the diagnosis or quantification of bronchiectasis. Tram-track opacities are seen in cylindrical bronchiectasis, and air-fluid levels may be seen in cystic bronchiectasis.

Option (B) is incorrect because magnetic resonance imaging is a medical imaging technique used in radiology to form pictures of the anatomy and the physiological processes of the body. MRI scanners use strong magnetic fields, magnetic field gradients, and radio waves to generate images of the organs in the body.

Option (C) is incorrect because pulmonary function tests (PFTs) are noninvasive tests that show how well the lungs are working. The tests measure lung volume, capacity, rates of flow, and gas exchange. This information can help your healthcare provider diagnose and decide the treatment of certain lung disorders.

Hence, the correct option is (D).

229.

The Silhoutte sign	
Shadow of soft tissue structure lost	**Location of lung pathology**
Ascending aorta	Right upper lobe
Aortic arch (**Aortic knuckle**)	Left upper lobe
Upper left heart border	Left upper lobe
Lower right heart border	Right middle lobe
Lower left heart border	**Lingula**
Right hemi-diaphragm	Right lower lobe
Left hemi-diaphragm	Left lower lobe

From the above table,

Option (C) is correct because the left heart border is related to the lingula.

Option (A) is incorrect because ascending aorta and Aortic arch are related to the upper lobe.

Option (B) is incorrect because the left heart border is not related to the hilar.

Option (D) is incorrect because the hemidiaphragm is related to lower lobe.

Hence, the correct option is (C).

230. Option (B) is correct because congenital heart disease (especially endocardial cushion defect) is frequently found in Down's syndrome. Echocardiography is therefore considered necessary preoperative investigation.

Option (A) is incorrect because a CT of the brain is a noninvasive diagnostic imaging procedure that uses special X-ray measurements to produce horizontal or axial, images (often called slices) of the brain.

Option (C) is incorrect because abdominal ultrasonography is a form of medical ultrasonography to visualise abdominal anatomical structures. It uses transmission and reflection of ultrasound waves to visualise internal organs through the abdominal wall.

Option (D) is incorrect because a cervical spine X-ray is a safe and painless test that uses a small amount of radiation to take a picture of the bones in the back of the neck (cervical vertebrae). During the examination, an X-ray machine sends a beam of radiation through the neck, and an image is recorded on a special film or a computer.

Hence, the correct option is (B).

231. Option (A) is correct because bruit over the carotid artery suggests carotid artery stenosis. Duplex scanning (B-mode scan and doppler ultrasonic velocimetry) is the method of choice for assessing the degree of carotid stenosis.

Option (B) is incorrect because carotid angiography is an invasive imaging procedure that involves inserting a catheter into a blood vessel in the arm or leg, and guiding it to the carotid arteries with the aid of a special x-ray machine.

Option (C) is incorrect because an aortic arch-angiogram is an x-ray test that enables us to diagnose a problem (most commonly a narrowing or a blockage) in the arteries supplying your head, neck and arms.

Option (D) is incorrect because spiral CT angiography is a new, minimally invasive technique for vascular imaging that is made possible by combining two recently developed techniques: slip-ring CT scanning and computerized three-dimensional (3D) reconstruction.

Hence, the correct option is (A).

232. Option (A) is correct because the earliest radiological change of UC on barium enema is blurring of the mucosal lining and a fine granularity when the mucosa is seen enface due to edema. Earliest radiological change of Crohn's disease → Aphthous lesions (Bull's eye or Target lesions).

Option (B) is incorrect because the loss of haustra is a sign of chronic ulcerative colitis. Localized a haustral distended colon can be seen on abdominal x-ray during obstruction or volvulus.

Option (C) is incorrect because the collar button-shaped ulcer is a distinctive radiographic manifestation of inflammatory disease of the GI tract.

Option (D) is incorrect because the lead pipe appearance of the colon is the classical barium enema finding in chronic ulcerative colitis, and is also seen with other modalities such as CT or MRI. There is a complete loss of the haustral markings in the diseased segment of the colon, appearing smooth-walled and cylindrical.

Hence, the correct option is (A).

233. Option (A) is correct because

- The string of beads sign is virtually diagnostic of small bowel obstruction.
- The string of beads in radiology

1. Small bowel obstruction
2. Chronic pancreatitis
3. Fibromuscular dysplasia

Option (B) is incorrect because large-bowel obstruction (LBO) is an emergency condition that requires early identification and intervention. It is important to distinguish colonic obstruction from ileus, as well as to distinguish true mechanical obstruction from pseudo-obstruction; treatment differs.

Option (C) is incorrect because stomach cancer, also known as gastric cancer, is cancer that develops from the lining of the stomach. Most cases of stomach cancers are gastric carcinomas, which can be divided into a number of subtypes including gastric adenocarcinomas.

Option (D) is incorrect because gastric outlet obstruction is any disease that mechanically impedes gastric emptying, the normal emptying of the stomach. There is obstruction of the channel of the pylorus and duodenum through which the stomach empties. The cause of the obstruction may be a benign or malignant disease.

Hence, the correct option is (A).

234. Option (B) is correct because Color-coded Doppler sonography (CCDS) was used for the examination of tumour thrombus (n = 7) and benign thrombosis (n = 6) of the inferior vena cava. Therefore, it might be possible to differentiate tumour from nontumor thrombus in the inferior vena cava by using CCDS.

Option (A) is incorrect because an intravenous pyelogram (IVP) is an x-ray examination of the kidneys, ureters and urinary bladder that uses iodinated contrast material injected into veins. An x-ray (radiograph) is a noninvasive medical test that helps physicians diagnose and treat medical conditions.

Option (C) is incorrect because Ultrasonography is a diagnostic medical procedure that uses sound waves to produce images on a screen, which allows medical providers to view internal structures of the body.

Option (D) is incorrect because a CT scan or computed tomography scan makes use of computer-processed combinations of many X-ray measurements taken from different angles to produce cross-sectional images of specific areas of a scanned object, allowing the user to see inside the object without cutting.

Hence, the correct option is (B).

235. Option (B) is correct because all imaging findings may be normal in patients with early genitourinary tuberculosis. Intravenous urography remains the primary modality for the identification of renal, ureteric, and bladder tuberculosis, but findings of urinary tuberculosis are also detectable on ultrasonography, CT scanning, or MRI.

Option (A) is incorrect because plain film x-ray is the most common diagnostic radiological modality used in hospitals today. They were first discovered and used for imaging purposes by Wilhelm Röntgen on 8th November 1895, when he took an image of his wife's hand.

Option (C) is incorrect because an ultrasound scan is a medical test that uses high-frequency sound waves to capture live images from the inside of your body. It's also known as sonography.

Option (D) is incorrect because the term "computed tomography", or CT refers to a computerized x-ray imaging procedure in which a narrow beam of x-rays is aimed at a patient and quickly rotated around the body, producing signals that are processed by the machine's computer to generate cross-sectional images—or "slices"—of the body.

Hence, the correct option is (B).

236. Option (C) is correct because subperiosteal resorption is seen in hyperparathyroidism (not hypoparathyroidism).

Option (A) is incorrect because osteosclerosis is a rare phenomenon in adults with primary hyperparathyroidism since the usual skeletal manifestation is generalized osteopenia.

Option (B) is incorrect because of hypoparathyroidism is generalised osteosclerosis, calvarial thickening, hypoplastic dentition and soft tissue calcifications.

Option (D) is incorrect because hypoparathyroidism manifests predominantly as neuromuscular dysfunction caused by hypocalcemia. Basal ganglia calcification, in particular, is associated with hypoparathyroidism.

Hence, the correct option is (C).

237. Option (A) is correct because the hair-on-end appearance is characteristically and most commonly seen in thalassemia because marrow hyperplasia is more marked in this than other anaemia.

Option (B) is incorrect because sickle cell anaemia is the 2nd most common cause (after thalassemia).

Option (C) is incorrect because hemochromatosis is a disorder where too much iron builds up in your body. Sometimes it's called "iron overload." Normally, your intestines absorb just the right amount of iron from the foods you eat. But in hemochromatosis, your body absorbs too much, and it has no way to get rid of it.

Option (D) is incorrect because megaloblastic anaemia is a condition in which the bone marrow produces unusually large, structurally abnormal, immature red blood cells (megaloblasts). Bone marrow, the soft spongy material found inside certain bones, produces the main blood cells of the body -red cells, white cells, and platelets.

Hence, the correct option is (A).

238. Option (B) is correct because:

Subdural hematoma → Injury to cortical bridging veins

Epidural hematoma → Injury to the middle meningeal artery

Subarachnoid haemorrhage → Rupture of berry (saccular) aneurysm.

Option (A) is incorrect because a ruptured aneurysm releases blood into the subarachnoid space around the brain causing a stroke (left). Different types of aneurysms (right). When an aneurysm bursts, it releases blood into the spaces between the brain and the skull.

Option (C) is incorrect because an AVM rupture occurs because of pressure and damage to the blood vessel. This allows blood to leak (haemorrhage) into the brain or surrounding tissues and reduces blood flow to the brain. Cerebral AVMs are rare.

Option (D) is incorrect because hemophilia is a rare disorder in which your blood doesn't clot normally because it lacks sufficient blood-clotting proteins (clotting factors).

Hence, the correct option is (B).

239. Option (A) is correct because a beta particle also called beta ray or beta radiation is a high-energy, high-speed electron or positron emitted by the radioactive decay of an atomic nucleus during the process of beta decay.

Option (B) is incorrect because an alpha particle is a radioactive particle that is made up of two protons and two neutrons. It is a helium nucleus: that is a helium atom without electrons. Radioactive elements give out alpha particles when they go through a kind of radioactive decay, known as alpha decay.

Option (C) is incorrect because a neutron is a sub-atomic particle with no net electrostatic charge, with a very similar mass to a proton. Neutrons are thought to comprise of one up quark of charge +2/3 and two down quarks of charge -1/3 each, resulting in a net charge of zero. Neutrons are present in almost all atomic nuclei except for Hydrogen.

Option (D) is incorrect because X-rays make up X-radiation, a form of high-energy electromagnetic radiation. Most X-rays have a wavelength ranging from 0.03 to 3 nanometres, corresponding to frequencies in the range 30 petahertz to 30 exahertz and energies in the range 100 eV to 200 keV.

Hence, the correct option is (A).

240. Option (A) is incorrect because magnetic resonance imaging is a medical imaging technique used in radiology to form pictures of the anatomy and the physiological processes of the body. MRI scanners use strong magnetic fields, magnetic field gradients, and radio waves to generate images of the organs in the body.

Option (B) is incorrect because dynamic contrast-enhanced MRI is a method of physiologic imaging, based on fast or ultrafast imaging, with the possibility of following the early enhancement kinetics of a water-soluble contrast agent after intravenous bolus injection.

Option (C) is correct because "MRI or CT scans are often unable to distinguish radiation necrosis from the recurrent tumour, but PET or SPECT scans may demonstrate that glucose metabolism is increased in tumour tissue but decreased in radiation necrosis."

Option (D) is incorrect because a CT scan or computed tomography scan makes use of computer-processed combinations of many X-ray measurements taken from different angles to produce cross-sectional images of specific areas of a scanned object, allowing the user to see inside the object without cutting.

Hence, the correct option is (C).

241. Option (D) is correct because

Obstetrical conjugate

- It is the shortest distance between the sacral promontory and the symphysis pubis
- Normally, this measures 10 cm or more, but it cannot be measured directly by examining fingers
- Thus, for clinical purposes, the obstetrical conjugate is estimated indirectly by subtracting 1.5 to 2 cm from the diagonal conjugate, which is determined by measuring the distance from the lowest margin of the symphysis to the sacral promontory.

Option (A) is incorrect because the diagonal conjugate is the distance from the undersurface of the pubic arch to sacral promontory; it is 2 cm longer than the obstetrical conjugate.

Option (B) is incorrect because the obstetrical conjugate is estimated indirectly by subtracting 1.5 to 2 cm from the diagonal conjugate.

Option (C) is incorrect because it is not the right option.

Hence, the correct option is (D).

242. Option (D) is correct because, for humans, the entire process of spermatogenesis is variously estimated as taking 74 days (according to tritium-labeled biopsies).

Option (A) is incorrect because eros epithelium cycles, spermatogenesis was estimated to take 40.6 days.

Option (B) is incorrect because it is not the right option.

Option (C) is incorrect because, for humans, the entire process of spermatogenesis is variously estimated as taking approximately 120 days (according to DNA clock measurements).

Hence, the correct option is (D).

243. Option (A) is correct because of the transition from mitosis to meiosis. The spermatogonia undergo mitosis to form the primary spermatocytes, which then enter the first meiotic division. They rest for 22 days and then rapidly complete the first meiotic division to form secondary spermatocytes.

Option (B) is incorrect because the spermatid is the haploid male gametic that results from the division of secondary spermatocytes. As a result of meiosis, each spermatid contains only half of the genetic material present in the original primary spermatocyte. Spermatids are connected by cytoplasmic material and have superfluous cytoplasmic material around their nuclei.

Option (C) is incorrect because a spermatogonium (plural: spermatogonia) is an undifferentiated male germ cell. Spermatogonia undergo spermatogenesis to form mature spermatozoa in the seminiferous tubules of the testis.

Option (D) is incorrect because spermatocytes are a type of male gametocyte in animals. They derive from immature germ cells called spermatogonia. They are found in the testis, in a structure known as the seminiferous tubules. There are two types of spermatocytes, primary and secondary spermatocytes. Primary and secondary spermatocytes are formed through the process of spermatocytogenesis.

Hence, the correct option is (A).

244. Indications of Blood transfusion in Sickle Cell Anemia

- Frequent sickling episodes
- Twin pregnancy
- Poor obstetrical outcome
- Severe anemia

Blood transfusion replaces the abnormal cells with normal red cells. The objective of transfusion is to keep the hematocrit value above 25% and the concentration of Hb–Sunder 50%. Prophylactic transfusions during pregnancy remain controversial.

From, the above explanation,

Option (D) is correct because it contains all the right options.

Option (A) is incorrect because twin pregnancy is also right.

Option (B) is incorrect because the poor obstetrical outcome is also right.

Option (C) is incorrect because frequent sickling episodes is also right.

Hence, the correct option is (D).

245. Option (D) is correct because of serum ferritin levels

Indicate iron stores.

Levels < 12mcg/dL indicates iron deficiency anemia.

Levels < 50mcg/dL in early pregnancy suggest depletion of iron stores and that iron supplementation is essential.

However, in cases of chronic inflammation ferritin may be increased.

Option (A) is incorrect because the total iron-binding capacity (TIBC) or sometimes transferring iron-binding capacity is a medical laboratory test that measures the blood's capacity to bind iron with transferrin. It is performed by drawing blood and measuring the maximum amount of iron that it can carry, which indirectly measures transferrin since transferrin is the most dynamic carrier.

Option (B) is incorrect because transferrin is the iron transport protein in serum. In cases of iron deficiency, the degree of transferrin saturation appears to be an extremely sensitive indicator of functional iron depletion. The ferritin levels are depressed when there is a deficiency of storage iron.

Option (C) is incorrect because serum iron is a medical laboratory test that measures the amount of circulating iron that is bound to transferrin (90%) and serum ferritin (10%). Clinicians order this laboratory test when they are concerned about iron deficiency, which can cause anaemia and other problems.

Hence, the correct option is (D).

246. Option (B) is correct because the chaser moir technique is widely used in the repair of the vesicovaginal fistula. Vagina and bladder are separated all around by the flap splitting method and sutured separately in two layers.

Option (A) is incorrect because uterine inversion is when the uterus turns inside out, usually the following childbirth. Symptoms include postpartum bleeding, abdominal pain, a mass in the vagina, and low blood pressure. Rarely inversion may occur not in association with pregnancy.

Option (C) is incorrect because surgeons often will correct the fistula through major gynecological surgery. Newer treatments can include the placement of a stent and are usually successful. In 0.5-2.5% of major pelvic surgeries, a ureterovaginal fistula will form, usually weeks later.

Option (D) is incorrect because a retroverted uterus means the uterus is tipped back so that it aims towards the rectum instead of forward towards the belly. Some women may experience symptoms including painful sex. In most cases, a retroverted uterus won't cause any problems during pregnancy.

Hence, the correct option is (B).

247. Option (A) is correct because post-term labor is seen in anencephaly. The pituitary is absent. It interferes with hormonal control of the onset of labor.

Option (B) is incorrect because pelvic inflammatory disease (PID) is an infection of the female reproductive organs. It usually occurs when sexually transmitted bacteria spread from your vagina to your uterus, fallopian tubes or ovaries. The pelvic inflammatory disease often causes no signs or symptoms.

Option (C) is incorrect because hydramnios is a condition that occurs when too much amniotic fluid builds up during pregnancy. It is also called an amniotic fluid disorder, or polyhydramnios.

Option (D) is incorrect because a pregnancy with more than one fetus is called multiple pregnancies. If more than one egg is released during the menstrual cycle and each is fertilized by a sperm, more than one embryo may implant and grow in your uterus. This type of pregnancy results in fraternal twins (or more).

Hence, the correct option is (A).

248. Option (C) is correct because latanoprost ophthalmic solution is a topical medication used for controlling the progression of glaucoma or ocular hypertension, by reducing intraocular pressure. It is a prostaglandin analog that works by increasing the outflow of aqueous fluid from the eyes. It is also known by the brand name of Xalatan manufactured by Pfizer.

Option (A) is incorrect because physostigmine is used to treat glaucoma as it crosses the blood-brain barrier, it is also used to treat the central nervous system effects of atropine overdose and other anticholinergic drugs overdoses. Physostigmine can reverse both central and peripheral anticholinergic.

Option (B) is incorrect because this medication is used to treat symptoms of dry mouth due to a certain immune disease (Sjogren's syndrome) or from saliva gland damage due to radiation treatments of the head/neck for cancer. Pilocarpine belongs to a class of drugs known as cholinergic agonists.

Option (D) is incorrect because apraclonidine 1% eye drops are used to prevent or reduce increased pressure in the eye during and after certain types of laser eye surgery. Apraclonidine is in a class of medications called alpha-2-adrenergic agonists. It lowers the pressure in the eye by decreasing the amount of fluid produced within the eye.

Hence, the correct option is (C).

249. Risks: The main concern in pregnancies after a non-lower uterine segment scar is the risk of uterine rupture.

- The risk for uterine rupture varies based on the clinical scenario:
- Risk is 4% to 9% for women with a prior classical cesarean who labor, with the overall range in the literature reported as 0.9% to 12%.
- The risk for uterine rupture after myomectomy may be somewhat lower but is difficult to quantitate given small numbers of cases reported in the literature.
- Risks of adverse outcomes do not appear to be elevated for women with multiple prior low-transverse cesarean scars.o The risk for women with a prior uterine rupture is hard to quantify but may be as high as 9-10%.

From the above explanation,

Option (D) is correct because the risk is 4% to 9% for women with a prior classical cesarean.

Option (A) is incorrect because the overall range in the literature reported as 0.9% to 12%.

Option (B) is incorrect because it is not the right answer.

Option (C) is incorrect because the risk for women with a prior uterine rupture is hard to quantify but may be as high as 9-10%.

Hence, the correct option is (D).

250. Option (D) is correct as it is covering all the other options mentioned above, i.e. congenital infections leading to IUGR:

COGDT 10/e, p 289, 290.

Viral: CMV, Rubella, Herpes, Varicella zoster, Influenza, Poliovirus, HIV.

Fernando Arias 3/e, p 110.

Protozoan: Toxoplasma, Malaria, Trypanosoma.

Bacterial: Listeria monocytogenes, Tuberculosis and Syphilis.

Option (A) is incorrect because IUGR is seen in Syphilis. But selecting an individual won't be considered as correct when others are also relatable.

Option (B) is incorrect because IUGR is also seen in CMV. It is incorrect for the same reason as of option (A).

Option (C) is incorrect because IUGR is seen in Rubella. It is incorrect as others are also relatable.

Hence, the correct option is (D).

251. Option (C) is correct because abdominal circumference (AC) is the single most sensitive parameter to detect IUGR. Serial measurements of AC and estimations of fetal weight are more diagnostic to fetal growth restriction.

Option (A) is incorrect because the placental membrane separates maternal blood from fetal blood. The fetal part of the placenta is known as the chorion. The material component of the placenta is known as the decidua basalis.

Option (B) is incorrect because, in human anatomy, the femur is the longest and largest bone. Along with the temporal bone of the skull, it is one of the two strongest bones in the body. The average adult male femur is 48 centimeters (18.9 in) in length and 2.34 cm (0.92 in) in diameter and can support up to 30 times the weight of an adult.

Option (D) is incorrect because Borderline Personality Disorder (BPD) is a condition characterized by difficulties regulating emotion. This means that people who experience BPD feel emotions intensely and for extended periods of time, and it is harder for them to return to a stable baseline after an emotionally triggering event.

Hence, the correct option is (C).

252. Option (A) is correct because gestational diabetes raises your risk of high blood pressure, as well as a preeclampsia-a serious complication of pregnancy that causes high blood pressure and other symptoms that can threaten the lives of both mother and baby. A large baby is born with Gestational diabetes complications in pregnancy.

Option (B) is incorrect because gestational Hypertension also referred to as Pregnancy-Induced Hypertension (PIH) is a condition characterized by high blood pressure during pregnancy. Gestational Hypertension can lead to a serious condition called Preeclampsia, also referred to as Toxemia.

Option (C) is incorrect because anemia during pregnancy increases your risk of premature birth, having a low birth weight baby and postpartum depression. Some studies also show an increased risk of infant death immediately before or after birth.

Option (D) is incorrect because option (A) is correct.

Hence, the correct option is (A).

253. Option (C) is correct because a frank breech (otherwise known as an extended breach) is where the baby's legs are up next to its abdomen, with its knees straight and its feet next to its ears. This is the most common type of breach and this is not related to fetal well so these will be correct options according to the question.

Option (A) is incorrect because the test takes about two hours. The contractions can be uncomfortable. CST is usually safe, but it sometimes triggers early labour. The test is riskier for women who have placenta previa, a higher risk of uterine rupture, or who had a previous C-section.

Option (B) is incorrect because the oxytocin challenge test profile NOT a component of fetal well-being in fetal score Oxytocin challenge test is contraindicated in Placenta previa, Previous 2 LSCS and in premature labour.

Option (D) is incorrect because preterm labour is defined as regular contractions of the uterus resulting in changes in the cervix that start before 37 weeks of pregnancy. Changes in the cervix include effacement (the cervix thins out) and dilation (the cervix opens so that the fetus can enter the birth canal). hence this option will be incorrect according to the question.

Hence, the correct option is (C).

254. Sinusoidal Pattern:

- The stable baseline heart rate of 120 to 160 beats/min with regular oscillations.
- The amplitude of 5 to 15 beats/min (rarely greater).
- Long-term variability frequency of 2 to 5 cycles per minute.
- Fixed or flat short-term variability.
- Oscillation of the sinusoidal waveform above or below a baseline.
- Absence of accelerations.

Causes of Sinusoidal Pattern:

- Serious fetal anemia due to Rh-isoimmunisation/rupture **vasa previa** / fetomaternal hemorrhage/twin to twin transfusion.
- Drugs — Meperidine, morphine, alpha prodine, and butorphanol.
- Amnionitis.
- Fetal distress (+/–).
- Umbilical cord occlusion.

From the above explanation,

Option (B) is correct because the sinusoidal heart rate pattern is seen in vasa previa.

Option (A) is incorrect because, in placenta previa, the placenta is located low in the uterus. The placenta might partially or completely cover the cervix, as shown here. Placenta previa can cause severe bleeding in the mother before or during delivery.

Option (C) is incorrect because placenta battledore (battledore = a beating instrument) is a term describing a placenta where the umbilical cord is attached at the margin. Occurs 7- 9% in singleton pregnancies and 24-33% in twin pregnancies and may affect placental function/fetal growth.

Option (D) is incorrect because the succenturiate placenta is a condition in which one or more accessory lobes develop in the membranes apart from the main placental body to which vessels of fetal origin usually connect them. It is a smaller variant of a bilobed placenta. The vessels are supported only by communicating membranes.

Hence, the correct option is (B).

255.

- Baseline variability on CTG is the oscillation of baseline FHR excluding acceleration and deceleration.
- A variability of 5-25 BPM is a sign of fetal well-being.

Decreased variability is seen in:

- Fetal hypoxia
- Sleep apnoea
- Congenital malformation
- Maternal academia
- Infection
- Drugs are given to mother such as sedatives, magnesium sulfate, antihypertensives

Drugs are given to motor which decreases the baseline variability are:

- Narcotics
- Barbiturates
- Phenothiazines
- Tranquillizers
- General anaesthetics
- Meperidine
- Butorphanol
- MgSO4

According to Williams Increasing gestational age leads to increased baseline variability, so it can be taken prematurity will have decreased variability

Option (D) is correct because from the above explanation it is clear that Fetal stimulation is not an explanation for decreased variability of fetal heart tracing. hence this option will be correct according to the question.

Option (A) is incorrect because from the above explanation it is clear that Fetal "sleep state" is an explanation for decreased variability of the fetal heart tracing

Option (B) is incorrect because from the above explanation it is clear that Prematurity is an explanation for decreased variability of the fetal heart tracing

Option (C) is incorrect because from the above explanation it is clear that Barbiturate ingestion is an explanation for decreased variability of the fetal heart tracing

Hence, the correct option is (D).

256.

- All the options given in the question are somehow related to the vagina, therefore may have a role in supporting the vagina except the infundibulopelvic ligaments.
- The Infundibulopelvic ligament attaches the ovary to tin' lateral pelvic wall arid support the ovary but has no connection to the vagina or uterus, therefore it does not support either structure. So, by exclusion, the answer is an Infundibulopelvic ligament.

Option (D) is correct because from the above explanation it is clear that the Infundibulopelvic ligament supports the vagina. Hence according to the question, this will be the correct option.

Option (A) is incorrect because from the above explanation it is clear that the Perineal body supports the vagina. Hence according to the question, this will not be the correct option.

Option (B) is incorrect because from the above explanation it is clear that Pelvic diaphragm supports the vagina. Hence according to the question, this will not be the correct option.

Option (C) is incorrect because from the above explanation it is clear that Levator ani muscle supports the vagina. Hence according to the question, this will not be the correct option.

Hence, the correct option is (D).

257. LH surge initiates luteinization acting through its receptors about **24-48 hours prior to ovulation.**

Option (C) is correct because from the above explanation it is clear that the timing of LH surge is 24-48 hours prior to ovulation not Occur 24 hours before ovulation as given in this option. Hence, this option will be correct.

Option (A) is incorrect because from the above explanation it is clear that the timing of LH surge is 24-48 hours prior to ovulation not Occur 12 hours before ovulation as given in this option. Hence, this option will not be correct.

Option (B) is incorrect because from the above explanation it is clear that the timing of LH surge is 24-48 hours prior to ovulation not Occur 12 hours after ovulation as given in this option. Hence, this option will not be correct.

Option (D) is incorrect because from the above explanation it is clear that the timing of LH surge is 24-48 hours prior to ovulation not Occur 24 hours after ovulation as given in this option. Hence, this option will not be correct.

Hence, the correct option is (C).

258. Option (B) is correct the diagnosis of menopause is from the classical symptom of hot flush (50%) confirmed by elevated FSH levels to more than 100 mIU/ml and serum estradiol < 20 pg/ml.

Option (A) is incorrect because the cutoff point of serum estrogen level for the diagnosis of ovarian failure is not 10 pg/ml.

Option (C) is incorrect because of the cutoff point of serum estrogen level for the diagnosis of ovarian failure is not 30 pg/ml.

Option (D) is incorrect because it is not the right answer.

Hence, the correct option is (B).

259. Option (D) is correct because, in PCOS the LH:FSH ratio is increased [> 2 : 1].

Option (A) is incorrect because polycystic ovary syndrome is a condition that can affect a woman's ability to produce eggs. PCOS is linked with higher levels of circulating insulin, which is characteristic of type 2 diabetes. A UK study in 2012 showed that the risk of type 2 diabetes for women with PCOS was notably higher.

Option (B) is incorrect because polycystic ovary syndrome (PCOS) affects up to almost 27 percent of women during their childbearing years. It involves cysts in the ovaries, high levels of male hormones, and irregular periods.

Option (C) is incorrect because polycystic ovary syndrome (PCOS), in which the ovaries produce excessive amounts of androgens, is the most common cause of hirsutism and may affect up to 10% of women. Hirsutism is very common and often improves with medical management.

Hence, the correct option is (D).

260. Option (C) is correct as:

- The Vaginal epithelium is derived from the endoderm of the urogenital sinus
- Sinovaginal bulbs fuse to form a vaginal plate which breaks down in the center to form the lumen of the vagina
- Peripheral cells of the vaginal plate form the vaginal epithelium
- The hymen is formed by invagination of the posterior wall of the urogenital sinus

Option (A) is incorrect because the primordial germ cell of the testis develops from the endoderm of the yolk sac and migrates to the genital ridge. Sertoli cells may be derived from coelomic epithelium or the mesenchymal cells of the genital ridge, whereas interstitial cells may develop from myofibroblast-like cells of the mesenchyme.

Option (B) is incorrect because, in males, the UG sinus is divided into three regions: upper, pelvic, and phallic. The upper part gives rise to the urinary bladder and the pelvic part gives rise to the prostatic and membranous parts of the urethra. The female urogenital sinus also gives rise to the urethra and vestibule of the vagina.

Option (D) is incorrect because the paired gonadal primordia arise from the intermediate mesoderm of the mammalian embryo as a genital ridge on either side of the midline in close association with the transitory mesonephric kidney of the embryo.

Hence, the correct option is (C).

261. Option (C) is correct as :

Hypergonadotropic Primary Amenorrhea

Causes

1. Abnormal sex chromosomes: 45,OX, Abnormal X
2. Normal sex chromosomes: 46 XX Pure gonadal dysgenesis, Swyer syndrome, Savage syndrome

Characteristics

Gonadal failure

- These women have streak ovaries with the absence of ovarian follicles.
- No estrogen production.
- Elevated levels of FSH.
- A progesterone challenge test is negative.

Option (A) is incorrect because Marfan syndrome most commonly affects the heart, eyes, blood vessels, and skeleton. People with Marfan syndrome are usually tall and thin with disproportionately long arms, legs, fingers, and toes. The damage caused by Marfan syndrome can be mild or severe. hence this elaboration does not match the 16-year old girl condition hence this will not be the correct option.

Option (B) is incorrect because the basis for corpus luteum hemorrhage (CLH) is an underlying hemostatic failure when the ovum is extruded from the Graafian follicle or an ovarian cyst rupture. There are two categories of women at risk: those who are treated with anticoagulants because of thrombotic disorders, and those with bleeding disorders. so this will not be the correct option.

Option (D) is incorrect because apoplexy means bleeding into an organ or loss of blood flow to an organ. Pituitary apoplexy is commonly caused by bleeding inside a noncancerous (benign) tumor of the pituitary. When pituitary bleeding occurs in a woman during or right after childbirth, it is called Sheehan syndrome. This is a very rare condition.

Hence, the correct option is (C).

262. Option (A) is correct as:

Minimum criteria

- lower abdominal tenderness
- adnexal tenderness
- cervical motion tenderness

Option (B) is incorrect because a temperature greater than 100.4 F in adults or children is considered a fever. Different tests may be done by a doctor, such a blood and imaging tests, to determine the cause of fever and if the cause of the fever needs to be treated.

Option (C) is incorrect because cervical motion tenderness or cervical excitation is a sign found on a gynecological pelvic examination suggestive of pelvic pathology. Classically, it is present in the setting of pelvic inflammatory disease (PID) or ectopic pregnancy and is of some use to help differentiate PID from appendicitis.

Option (D) is incorrect because leukocytosis is white cells (the leukocyte count) above the normal range in the blood. It is frequently a sign of an inflammatory response, most commonly the result of infection, but may also occur following certain parasitic infections or bone tumors as well as leukemia.

Hence, the correct option is (A).

263. Option (B) is correct because the laparoscopic approach results in less postoperative pain, shorter hospitalization and a quicker return to normal activities than the traditional open cut. The colposuspension is generally regarded as the gold standard in treating urinary stress incontinence with a long-term success rate of 85%.

Option (A) is incorrect because all patients were followed-up for a period of 4 to 43 months after surgery. We used Stamey's definition of a cure, which is the absence of urinary incontinence for six months post-operatively.

Option (C) is incorrect because although Marshall-Marchetti-Krantz procedures yielded the most effective repair in the immediate postoperative period, Kelly plications were equally corrective more than three years after surgery (69 and 66%, respectively).

Option (D) is incorrect because cure rates between 84% and 100% have been reported, although there is a high rate of device failure and revision procedures. so it is not constant.

Hence, the correct option is (B).

264.

- Somewhere around 25% of couples will be pregnant at the end of the first month of trying.
- About 50% will have conceived in 6 months. Between 85 and 90% of couples will have conceived at the end of a year.
- Of those that have not conceived, some still will, without any specific help

Option (B) is correct because from the above explanation it is clear that the chances of a normally fertile couple having a baby in one month is 25 % and also given.

Option (A) is incorrect because from the above explanation it is clear that the chances of a normally fertile couple having a baby in one month is 25 %, not 80% as given.

Option (C) is incorrect because from the above explanation it is clear that the chances of a normally fertile couple having a baby in one month is 25 %, not 60% as given.

Option (D) is incorrect because from the above explanation it is clear that the chances of a normally fertile couple having a baby in one month is 25 %, not 45% as given.

Hence, the correct option is (B).

265. "TODAY: It contains 1 gm of NONOX 4 NOL-9"

Option (A) is correct because from the above description it is clear that Contraceptive vaginal foam tablet "today "contains Nonoxynol 9. hence this option will be correct.

Option (B) is incorrect because it is clear from the above description, this option will not be correct.

Option (C) is incorrect because it is clear from the above description, this option will not be correct.

Option (D) is incorrect because it is clear from the above description, this option will not be correct.

Hence, the correct option is (A).

266. Option (D) is correct as:

- Placenta previa risk factors include a previous delivery, age older than 35 and a history of previous surgeries, such as a cesarean section (C-section) or uterine fibroid removal.
- The main symptom is bright red vaginal bleeding without pain during the second half of pregnancy. The condition can also cause severe bleeding before or during delivery.
- Limited physical activity is recommended. A C-section is often required in severe cases.

Option (A) is incorrect because red degeneration is a hemorrhagic infarction of the uterine leiomyoma, which is a well-known complication, especially during pregnancy. As leiomyoma enlarge, they may outgrow their blood supply, resulting in degeneration, thus degeneration occurs primarily in large leiomyomas.

Option (B) is incorrect because obstructed labor, also known as labor dystocia, is when the baby does not exit the pelvis during childbirth due to being physically blocked, despite the uterus contracting normally. Complications for the baby include not getting enough oxygen which may result in death.

Option (C) is incorrect because postpartum bleeding or postpartum hemorrhage (PPH) is often defined as the loss of more than 500 ml or 1,000 ml of blood within the first 24 hours following childbirth. Some have added the requirement that there also be signs or symptoms of low blood volume for the condition to exist.

Hence, the correct option is (D).

267. Option (A) is correct as:

- Laparoscopy is an operation performed in the abdomen or pelvis through small incisions with the aid of a camera.
- The laparoscope aids diagnosis or therapeutic interventions with a few small cuts in the abdomen

Option (B) is incorrect because an ultrasound scan is a medical test that uses high-frequency sound waves to capture live images from the inside of your body. It's also known as sonography.

Option (C) is incorrect because a pelvic X-ray can help find the cause of symptoms such as pain, swelling, or deformity in the pelvic, hip, or upper leg regions, and can detect broken bones after an injury. Also, pelvic X-rays may detect other problems such as cysts, tumors, and later-stage infections of the pelvic bones.

Option (D) is incorrect because CT scans can detect bone and joint problems, like complex bone fractures and tumors. If you have a condition like cancer, heart disease, emphysema, or liver masses, CT scans can spot it or help doctors see any changes. They show internal injuries and bleeding, such as those caused by a car accident.

Hence, the correct option is (A).

268. Option (C) is correct as:

Endometrial hyperplasia especially simple hyperplasia results from circumstances in which it is prolonged increased estrogen production example:

- Follicular cysts of the ovary
- PCOD
- Granulosa and theca cells
- HRT

Option (A) is incorrect because germ cells are the cells in the ovaries and testicles that develop into eggs (ova) in females and sperm in males. An endodermal sinus tumor also called a yolk sac tumor, is a type of germ cell cancer. Endodermal sinus tumors occur most often in children.

Option (B) is incorrect because it usually is malignant and usually occurs in the ovary. Most dysgerminomas are associated with elevated serum lactic dehydrogenase (LDH), which is sometimes used as a tumor marker.

Option (D) is incorrect because cervical cancer is a type of cancer that occurs in the cells of the cervix — the lower part of the uterus that connects to the vagina. Various strains of the human papillomavirus (HPV), a sexually transmitted infection, play a role in causing most cervical cancer.

Hence, the correct option is (C).

269. CA-125

- This is a non-specific tumor marker

- CA-125 is a glycoprotein that is normally not produced by ovarian epithelium but may be produced by both malignant and benign epithelial ovarian tumors.
- Cut off level of CA-125 is < 35 U/mL.

Option (D) is correct because from the above explanation it is clear that CA 125 does not elevate in Polycystic ovarian disease.

Option (A) is incorrect because from the above explanation it is clear that CA 125 is elevated in Tuberculosis.

Option (B) is incorrect because from the above explanation it is clear that CA 125 is elevated in Endometriosis.

Option (C) is incorrect because from the above explanation it is clear that CA 125 is elevated in Ovarian tumors.

Hence, the correct option is (D).

270. Precocious puberty is the appearance of appropriate secondary sexual characters before the age of 8 years and the occurrence of menstruation before 10 years of chronological age. Also, know delayed puberty: is considered delayed when the secondary sexual characters do not appear by the age of 14, and menarche is not established by 16 years of age.

Option (B) is correct because from the above explanation it is clear that Menstruation is defined as precocious if it starts before the child reaches the age of 10 years hence this will be the correct answer according to the question through the explanation.

Option (A) is incorrect because from the above explanation it is clear that Menstruation is defined as precocious if it starts before the child reaches the age of 10 years but in this option, it is given 8 years hence it will not be the correct option.

Option (C) is incorrect because from the above explanation it is clear that Menstruation is defined as precocious if it starts before the child reaches the age of 10 years but in this option, it is given 14 years hence it will not be the correct option.

Option (D) is incorrect because from the above explanation it is clear that Menstruation is defined as precocious if it starts before the child reaches the age of 10 years but in this option, it is given 20 years hence it will not be the correct option.

Hence, the correct option is (B).

271. Option (D) is correct, according to the above explanation it is clear that all other options statements are related to the question and this option includes other options too hence it will be the correct option.

Option (A) is incorrect because head circumference or OFC [occipital frontal circumference] is measured over the most prominent part on the back of the head (occiput) and just above the eyebrows (supraorbital ridges). This can be translated to mean the largest circumference of the head.

Option (B) is incorrect because measure the distance around the back of the child's head with a nonelastic tape measure held above the eyebrows and ears, and plot the measurement on age- and sex-appropriate growth chart. Microcephaly is HC more than 2 SD below the mean.

Option (C) is incorrect because measuring head circumference (HC) is a quick, non-invasive method of determining if infant head size is too large (megacephaly) or too small (microcephaly). When compared with normative growth curves, serial HC measurements are extremely important in monitoring infant health.

Hence, the correct option is (D).

272. Neonate (Newborn)

- From birth to under four weeks of age (< 28 days), the infant is called neonate.
- The neonatal period has been further subdivided into -

1. Early neonatal period → the First week of life (< 7 days)
2. Late neonatal period → 7th to < 28th day

Term neonate (term baby)

- Any neonate born between 37 and < 42 weeks (259 - 293 days) of pregnancy irrespective of the birth weight.

Preterm baby

- Any neonate born before 37 weeks (<259 days) of pregnancy irrespective of the birth weight.

Post-term baby

- Any neonate born at or after 42 weeks (294 days or more) of pregnancy irrespective of the birth weight.

Option (C) is correct because according to the above explanation, the value of this option will be correct.

Option (A) is incorrect because according to the above explanation this option value can not be the answer hence it is incorrect.

Option (B) is incorrect because according to the above explanation this option will not be correct.

Option (D) is incorrect as we came to know that the correct value of this question is defined in an option (C). Hence this option will not be correct.

Hence, the correct option is (C).

273. Option (C) is correct as

- Weak femoral pulse is indicative of the coarctation of the aorta. Normally, the femoral pulse occurs slightly before the radial pulse.
- Weak femoral pulse or femoral pulse felt after the radial pulse is a characteristic feature of COA.
- Coarctation of Aorta (COA) Constrictions of the aorta of varying degrees may occur at any point from the transverse arch to the iliac bifurcation, but 98% occur just below 7 the origin of the left subclavian artery at the origin of the ductus arteriosus (juxtaductal coarctation).
- The anomaly occurs twice as often in males as in females. Coarctation of the aorta may be a feature of Turner syndrome and is associated with a bicuspid aortic valve in more than 70% of patients. Mitral valve abnormalities (a supravalvular mitral ring or parachute mitral valve) and subaortic stenosis are potentially associated lesions. When this group of left-sided obstructive lesions occurs together, they are referred to as the Shone complex. Clinical Manifestations Mostly asymptomatic Some children or adolescents complain about weakness or pain in the legs after exercise.

- Silent hypertension diagnosed on routine physical examination. The disparity in pulsation and blood pressure in the arms and legs.
- The femoral, popliteal, posterior tibial and dorsalis pedis pulses are weak (or absent in up to 40% of patients), in contrast to the bounding pulses of the arms and carotid vessels.
- The radial and femoral pulses should always be palpated simultaneously for the presence of a radial femoral delay. Normally, the femoral pulse occurs slightly before the radial pulse. A radial-femoral delay occurs when blood flow to the descending aorta is dependent on collaterals, in which case the femoral pulse is felt after the radial pulse. In normal persons, systolic blood pressure in the legs obtained by the cuff method is 10-20 mm Hg higher than that in the arms. In the coarctation of the aorta, blood pressure in the legs is lower than that in the arms.

Option (A) is incorrect because patent ductus arteriosus (PDA) is a condition in which the ductus arteriosus does not close. The word "patent" means open. The ductus arteriosus is a blood vessel that allows blood to go around the baby's lungs before birth. hence this option will not be correct.

Option (B) is incorrect because iliac artery disease is caused by the narrowing of the arteries leading to the legs. This narrowing can also be called stenosis. When a leg doesn't receive enough blood flow because of a blockage in an artery, it can cause pain in the lower leg when walking. In severe cases, low blood flow can cause tissue loss.

Option (D) is incorrect because of the ventricular septal defect (VSD): A hole in the septum (the wall) between the lower chambers of the heart (the ventricles). Ventricular Septal Defect is the most common type of heart malformation (congenital heart disease). Hence this option will not be correct.

Hence, the correct option is (C).

274. Option (A) is correct because the respiratory syncytial virus is the most important cause of pneumonia in children less than 2 years of age. At other ages, influenza, parainfluenza, adenovirus are common. bacteria causing pneumonia are klebsiella, S.pneumoniae, E.coli, H.influenza, staphylococci. A typical organism like Mycoplasma and Pneumocystis carinii.

Option (B) is incorrect because of staph infection facts:

Staph infections may cause disease due to direct infection or due to the production of toxins by the bacteria. Boils, impetigo, food poisoning, cellulitis, and toxic shock syndrome are all examples of diseases that can be caused by Staphylococcus.

Option (C) is incorrect because of Staphylococcus aureus Infections

- These bacteria are spread by having direct contact with an infected person, by using a contaminated object, or by inhaling infected droplets dispersed by sneezing or coughing.
- Skin infections are common, but the bacteria can spread through the bloodstream and infect distant organs.

Option (D) is incorrect because to get a klebsiella infection, a person must be exposed to the bacteria. For example, Klebsiella must enter the respiratory (breathing) tract to cause pneumonia, or the blood to cause a bloodstream infection.

Hence, the correct option is (A).

275. The symptoms vomiting usually starts after 3 weeks of age but symptoms may develop as early as1st week of life and as late as 5 months of life. - Nelson

Congenital hypertrophic pyloric stenosis:

- Hypertrophic pyloric stenosis is the commonest surgical disorder of the stomach during infancy.
- Pylorus is thickened and elongated and its lumen is narrowed due to hypertrophy of circular muscle fibers of the pylorus.
- More common in boys.
- More common in infants of blood group 'B' and 'O'.
- Associated congenital defects are → Tracheoesophageal fistula and hypoplasia or agenesis of the inferior labial frenulum.
- May be associated with Turner syndrome, Trisomy 18.
- Symptoms are not present at birth.
- The vomiting usually starts after 3 weeks of age.

Option (C) is correct as above explained this option will be correct.

Option (A) is incorrect because According to the above explanation it will be Around 2 weeks after birth hence this option will not be correct.

Option (B) is incorrect because according to the above explanation this option does not match, hence it will be an incorrect option.

Option (D) is incorrect because in this option the value is 'Around 2 months after birth' hence it will not be the correct option.

Hence, the correct option is (C).

276. Option (A) is correct as of the features of UC :

- Ulcerative colitis involves the rectum and extends proximally.
- In severe cases, the entire colon may be involved Pancolitis.
- It is a disease of continuity, and skip lesions are not found.
- In some patients, distal ileum may also develop mucosal inflammation → backwash ileitis.
- Only mucosa and submucosal layers of the colon are involved, the deep layer is not involved usually.
- Isolated islands of regenerating mucosa bulge upward to create pseudopolyp.
- There is a superficial mucosal ulcer but they are not serpentine as seen in CD.
- Neutrophilic infiltration into crypts leads to the formation of crypt abscess.
- In severe cases of UC, toxic damage to the muscular propria and neural plexus lead to the complete shutdown of neuromuscular function → colon progressively swells to create toxic megacolon.

- There may be epithelial dysplasia with progression to frank carcinoma.

Option (B) is incorrect because colonoscopy is a test that allows a look inside the large intestine (colon). During this test, a physician may see the characteristics of Crohn's disease inside the large intestine. Inflammation in the lining of the colon may look red and swollen and ulcers may look like rows or tracts. so it will be incorrect.

Option (C) is incorrect because diverticula are small pouches in the wall of the digestive tract. They occur when the inner layer of the digestive tract bulges through weak spots in the outer layer. Because this condition typically does not cause symptoms, most people are unaware they have diverticulosis.

Option (D) is incorrect because hamartomatous polyps are tumors, like growths found in organs as a result of faulty development. They are normally made up of a mixture of tissues. Hamartomatous polyps are often found by chance; occurring in syndromes such as Peutz–Jegher syndrome or Juvenile polyposis syndrome.

Hence, the correct option is (A).

277. Option (A) is correct because

- Children with febrile seizures have an increased risk of developing epilepsy.
- Between 2% to 7% of all children with febrile seizures develop epilepsy if followed up to the age of 25 years. The risk depends on the type of febrile seizure:

i) Simple febrile seizures →2% of all children with simple febrile seizures.

ii) Complex febrile seizures → 6-8% of all children with complex febrile seizures.

- Three major risk factors increase the risk of epilepsy: -

1. Complex febrile seizures.
2. Pre-existing neurodevelopmental abnormality.
3. Epilepsy in first degree relatives.

Option (B) is incorrect because according to the above explanation this option will not be correct.

Option (C) is incorrect as we came to know from the above explanation option (A) will be correct hence, this option will not be correct.

Option (D) is incorrect because from the above explanation of option (A) this option can not be true.

Hence, the correct option is (A).

278. Option (C) is correct because of the childhood malignancies

i) The most common tumour in childhood is leukaemias especially acute lymphoblastic leukaemia.

ii) Second most common tumour → Brain tumours

iii) Third most common tumour → Lymphomas

iv) Fourth most common tumour → Neuroblastoma

v) Fifth most common tumours →Wilms tumour

Most of these tumours occur below the age of 5 years.

Option (A) is incorrect because Wilms tumour (also called nephroblastoma) is a type of childhood cancer that starts in the kidneys. It is the most common type of kidney cancer in children. About 9 of 10 kidney cancers in children are Wilms tumours. Cancer starts when cells in the body begin to grow out of control.

Option (B) is incorrect because acute myelogenous leukaemia is caused by damage to the DNA of developing cells in your bone marrow. When this happens, blood cell production goes wrong. The bone marrow produces immature cells that develop into leukemic white blood cells called myeloblasts.

Option (D) is incorrect because option (C) is the correct answer for the question hence this option will not be correct.

Hence, the correct option is (C).

279. "Haemoglobin E (HbE), a common structural haemoglobin variant occurs in very high frequency in countries of south-east Asia and in north-east India, Rabha tribe, one of the scheduled tribes of India, is mainly found in Assam and West Bengal."

Option (C) is correct because from the above explanation it is clear that this will be the correct option.

Option (A) is incorrect because according to the above explanation its answer will be Bengal hence this option will not be correct.

Option (B) is incorrect as we came to know from the above explanation this option will not be the correct answer.

Option (D) is incorrect as we know that the correct answer will be an option (C) hence this option will be incorrect.

Hence, the correct option is (C).

280. Option (A) is correct because of the pathogenesis of multiple carboxylase deficiency:

- Deficiency of either holocarboxylase synthase or biotinidase impairs biotin metabolism.
- Biotin is a cofactor for various carboxylases in the body -
- Impaired metabolism of biotin results in multiple carboxylase deficiency.
- So, for the treatment of multiple carboxylase deficiency, biotin should be given.

Option (B) is incorrect because pyridoxine is used to treat or prevent vitamin B6 deficiency. It is also used to treat a certain type of anaemia (lack of red blood cells). Pyridoxine injection is also used to treat some types of seizures in babies. Pyridoxine taken by mouth (oral) is available without a prescription.

Option (C) is incorrect because thiamine is used to treat or prevent vitamin B1 deficiency. Thiamine injection is used to treat beriberi, a serious condition caused by prolonged lack of vitamin B1. Thiamine taken by mouth (oral) is available without a prescription. Injectable thiamine must be given by a healthcare professional.

Option (D) is incorrect because folic acid helps your body produce and maintain new cells, and also helps prevent changes to DNA that may lead to cancer. As a medication, folic acid is used to treat folic acid deficiency and certain types of anaemia (lack of red blood cells) caused by folic acid deficiency.

Hence, the correct option is (A).

281. Option (A) is correct because it is the first branch and arises from geniculate ganglion(i.e., first genu). It joins the deep petrosal nerve to form vidian nerve(nerve to the pterygoid canal) and carries secretomotor fibers to the lacrimalgland, nasal gland, Palate gland, and pharyngeal gland.

Option (B) is incorrect because it is a branch of the glossopharyngeal nerve (IX) with contributions from the facial (VII) (2-5) and vagus (X) nerves (2) and it originates at the geniculate ganglion, passing forwards through its own canal back into the middle cranial fossa. Here it is between the two layers of the dura mater, passing forwards to exit the skull via foramen ovale to eventually join the otic ganglion.

Option (C) is incorrect because the chorda tympani is a branch of the facial nerve that originates from the taste buds in the front of the tongue, runs through the middle ear, and carries taste messages to the brain.

Option (D) is incorrect because the nerve to stapedius arises from the facial nerve to supply the stapedius muscle. The branch is given off in the facial nerve mastoid segment, as it passes posterior to the pyramidal process. Damage to this branch with resulting paralysis of stapedius leads to hypersensitivity to loud noises (hyperacusis).

Hence, the correct option is (A).

282. Option (A) is correct because first, see the major symptoms of facial nerve palsy : -

1. Loss of lacrimation: - Due to the involvement of greater superficial petrosal nerve.

2. Loss of stapedial reflex: - Due to the involvement of nerve to stapedius.

3. Lack of salivation: - Due to chorda tympani.

4. Loss of taste sensation from Anterior 2/3 of the tongue: - due to chorda tympani.

5. Paralysis of the muscle of facial expression: - Due to terminal (peripheral) branches.

- Now you can make out the site of injury : -
- All the 5 symptoms (i to v) are present → Injury is at or proximal to geniculate ganglion (as all the branches of the facial nerve are involved).
- There is no loss of lacrimation (a greater superficial petrosal nerve is spared) but symptoms (ii) to (v) occur → Injury is distal to the geniculate ganglion but proximal to or at the level of the second genu from where the nerve to stapedius arises.
- Only symptoms (iii) to (v) are present (greater petrosal and nerve to stapedius are spared) → Injury is distal to the second genu but proximal to the origin of chorda tympani, i.e., Injury is between Second genu and mid-portion of the vertical segment.
- Only (Vth) symptom is present → Injury is distal to the origin of chorda tympani, which may be at the level of the stylomastoid foramen.

Option (B) is incorrect because surgical trauma to the lateral semicircular canal (LSC) is a rare complication which does not always result in cochlear damage. ... Histopathological findings (two specimens) were significant for obliterative scarring of the LSC at the site of injury and for the structural integrity of the labyrinth and cochlea. Hence, this option will not be correct.

Option (C) is incorrect because the sphenopalatine ganglion (SPG) is a group of nerve cells that is linked to the trigeminal nerve, the main nerve involved in headache. The SPG, located behind the nose, carries information about sensation, including pain, and also plays a role in autonomic functions, such as tearing and nasal congestion.

Option (D) is incorrect because according to the above explanation there is at least one option is correct as an option (A). Hence, this option will be incorrect.

Hence, the correct option is (A).

283. Option (D) is correct as:

- Dryness in the eye (loss of lacrimation) occurs if the injury is at or proximal to the geniculate ganglion.
- First, see the major symptoms of facial nerve palsy : -
- Loss of lacrimation: - Due to the involvement of greater superficial petrosal nerve.
- Loss of stapedial reflex: - Due to the involvement of nerve to stapedius.
- Lack of salivation: - Due to chorda tympani.
- Loss of taste sensation from Anterior 2/3 of the tongue: - due to chorda tympani.
- Paralysis of the muscle of facial expression: - Due to terminal (peripheral) branches.
- Now you can make out the site of injury : -
- All the 5 symptoms (i to v) are present → Injury is at or proximal to geniculate ganglion (as all the branches of the facial nerve are involved).
- There is no loss of lacrimation (a greater superficial petrosal nerve is spared) but symptoms (ii) to (v) occur → Injury is distal to the geniculate ganglion but proximal to or at the level of the second genu from where the nerve to stapedius arises.
- Only symptoms (iii) to (v) are present (greater petrosal and nerve to stapedius are spared) → Injury is distal to the second genu but proximal to the origin of chorda tympani, i.e., Injury is between Second genu and mid portion of verticle segment.
- Only (Vth) symptom is present → Injury is distal to the origin of chorda tympani, which may be at the level of the stylomastoid foramen.

Option (A) is incorrect because the chorda tympani (CT) nerve carries taste information from the anterior tongue to the brain stem. Injury to the chorda tympani may result in loss or distortion of taste information. The hamster chorda tympani nerve was crushed in the middle ear and the animals were allowed to survive from 2 to 16 weeks. hence this is not related to eye injury hence this will be an incorrect option.

Option (B) is incorrect because the cerebellopontine angle syndrome is a distinct neurological syndrome of deficits that can arise due to the closeness of the cerebellopontine angle to specific cranial nerves. Indications include unilateral hearing loss (85%), speech impediments, disequilibrium, tremors or other loss of motor control.

Option (C) is incorrect because the tympanic nerve contains both sensory and parasympathetic axons: Sensory axons innervate the middle ear including the internal surface of the tympanic membrane. Their cell bodies are found in the superior ganglion of the glossopharyngeal nerve. Hence, this is also not related to the eye injury so it will be incorrect according to the question.

Hence, the correct option is (D).

284. Option (C) is correct as :

- Between these two parts of the inferior constrictor exists a potential gap called Killian's dehiscence.
- It is also called the gateway to tear as perforation can occur at this site during esophagoscopy.
- It is also the site for herniation of pharyngeal mucosa in case of the pharyngeal pouch

Option (A) is incorrect because the oropharynx is the part of the throat just behind the mouth. It starts where the oral cavity stops. It includes the base of the tongue (the back third of the tongue), the soft palate (the back part of the roof of the mouth), the tonsils, and the side and back walls of the throat.

Option (B) is incorrect because the nasopharynx is, by definition, the upper part of the throat behind the nose. The nasopharynx is surrounded by the salpingopharyngeal fold and tubal tonsils, which can become inflamed when infected. It contains adenoid tissue, which fights infection, and the openings to the Eustachian tubes, which lead to the ears.

Option (D) is incorrect because the vocal cords (also called vocal folds) are 2 bands of smooth muscle tissue found in the larynx (voice box). The larynx is set in the neck at the top of the trachea (windpipe). Vocal nodules are noncancerous growths on the vocal cords caused by vocal abuse.

Hence, the correct option is (C).

285. Option (A) is correct as

- Normally, the childhood voice has a higher pitch. When the larynx matures at puberty, vocal cords lengthen and the voice changes to one of lower pitch. This is a feature exclusive to males. Failure of this change leads to the persistence of childhood high-pitched voice and is called puberphonia.
- Type III Thyroplasty- It is used to shorten (relax) the vocal cord. Relaxation of vocal cord lowers the pitch. This procedure is done in mutational falsetto or in those who have undergone gender transformation from female to male.

Option (B) is incorrect because type 1 thyroplasty (medialization thyroplasty) is the most commonly used surgical procedure to correct unilateral vocal cord paralysis (a condition where the vocal cord of one side is paralyzed). Hence, it will not be the correct option.

Option (C) is incorrect because treatment for Adductor Spasmodic Dysphonia by Type 2 Thyroplasty Using Titanium Bridges. The speech disorder in this disease is caused by involuntary and intermittent spasms of the intralaryngeal muscles (Castellon, 2002). There is no curative treatment for this disease.

Option (D) is incorrect because thyroplasty is a procedure performed to change the position of the vocal cord. This is usually performed to improve a patient's voice and ability to cough. Thyroplasty is performed in the operating room with the patient asleep during parts of the surgery. A small cut is made on the neck and the voice box is identified.

Hence, the correct option is (A).

286. Option (D) is correct as:

- The vocal cord vibrates during a speech to produce speech. These vibrations occur due to subglottic airflow when the cord is in adduction (Median & paramedian).
- During normal phonation, the vocal cords are in a median position and during strong whisper, vocal cords are in paramedian position.
- So, for proper voice, the vocal cords should be in median or paramedian position.
- The same occurs in bilateral recurrent laryngeal nerve paralysis, where the vocal cords are in median or paramedian position → Voice is less likely to be impaired.

Now, the question comes to the mind immediately: - Why the voice is affected in unilateral paralysis, in which the cord is in median or paramedian position. The answer is : -

- In unilateral vocal cord paralysis, one cord is paralyzed and vibrates abnormally or does not vibrate at all, therefore it cannot coordinate with the other side (normal) vocal cord. This results in voice problems.

In bilateral paralysis, both vocal cords vibrate abnormally but coordinate with each other, therefore voice is less affected.

Option (A) is incorrect because substantial vocal folds also explain why men tend to have deeper voices than women. During puberty, a surge of sex hormones causes vocal folds to lengthen and build up muscle, more so for boys who experience a spike in testosterone at this time.

Option (B) is incorrect because most commonly, Phonasthenia Is caused by an abnormality with the vocal cords (also known as vocal folds) but there can be other causes from problems with airflow from the lungs or abnormalities with the structures of the throat near the vocal cords.

Option (C) is incorrect because dysphonia plica ventricular is hoarseness due to (a) phonation with the ventricular bands or (b) difficulty in phonation due to the vicarious assumption of the duty of the true vocal cords by the false cords, anatomically known as the ventricular bands.

Hence, the correct option is (D).

287. Option (B) is correct as

- Ranula, also known as mucous retention cyst, is a type of muscle found on the floor of the mouth on one side of the frenulum.
- It arises from the sublingual salivary gland, due to obstruction of its duct and is almost always unilateral.
- It occurs mostly in children and young adults.

Clinical features

- A ranula is usually asymptomatic, and the only complaint is fluctuant swelling with a bluish translucent color.

- Swelling is painless unless it becomes secondarily infected.
- Overlying mucosa is intact and the ranula is not fixed.

Treatment

- Surgical excision of both the gland as well as the lesion. Ranulas are likely to recur if the sublingual gland causing them is not removed with the lesion.

Option (A) is incorrect because it consists of connective tissue formed of reticular fibers, with various types of leukocytes (white blood cells), mostly lymphocytes enmeshed in it, through which the lymph passes. Regions of the lymphoid tissue that are densely packed with lymphocytes are known as lymphoid follicles.

Option (C) is incorrect because the pool of blood in the muscle can form a lump in the area of the damage. Hematomas cause pain, swelling, and tenderness over the area of skin discoloration or deep within the body. A large hematoma may last weeks to months and as it heals it will change color and slowly shrink in size.

Option (D) is incorrect because an abscess is a collection of pus that has built up within the tissue of the body. Signs and symptoms of abscesses include redness, pain, warmth, and swelling. Carbuncles and boils are types of abscess that often involve hair follicles, with carbuncles being larger. They are usually caused by a bacterial infection.

Hence, the correct option is (B).

288. Lesions with an increased risk of malignancy

- Premalignant condition: - Leukoplakia, Erythroplakia, Speckled erythroplakia, chronic hyperplastic, candidiasis.
- Conditions increasing risk: - Oral submucous fibrosis, syphilitic glossitis, sideropenic dysphagia (Paterson Kelly syndrome).
- The risk is doubtful: - Oral lichen planus, DLE, Dyskeratosis congenital.

Option (D) is correct because it is clear from the above explanation Diffuse aphthous ulcers are not the precancerous lesions of the oral cavity.

Option (A) is incorrect as the above explanation it is clear that it is precancerous lesions of the oral cavity.

Option (B) is incorrect as the above explanation it is clear that it is precancerous lesions of the oral cavity.

Option (C) is incorrect as we came to know from the above explanation it is also precancerous lesions of the oral cavity.

Hence, the correct option is (D).

289. Option (A) is correct as :

Surgical treatment of ethmoidal polyps

- Functional endoscopic sinus surgery (FESS): Surgery of choice when available.
- Polypectomy: When there are one or two pedunculated polyps.
- Intranasal ethmoidectomy: Indicated when polyps are multiple and sessile.
- Extra nasal ethmoidectomy: This is indicated when polyps recur after intranasal procedures.
- Transanal ethmoidectomy: Indicated when infection and polypoidal changes are also seen in the maxillary antrum. In this case, the antrum is opened by the Caldwell-Luc approach and the ethmoidal air cells approached through the medial wall of the antrum.

Option (B) is incorrect because intranasal ethmoidectomy is a safe procedure that provides predictable, positive surgical results when accomplished by a knowledgeable rhinology surgeon.

Option (C) is incorrect because ethmoidectomy is the medical name for a procedure that involves removing the partitions between the ethmoid sinuses in order to create larger sinus cavities. This procedure treats sinus infections and sinus obstructions that have been the cause of chronic sinus problems.

Option (D) is incorrect because the first method of treatment is usually proper medication, but sometimes it can be difficult to manage without surgery. Surgery may be performed, the most used being the intranasal (endoscopic) ethmoidectomy. Other types of surgical interventions are external ethmoidectomy and transanal ethmoidectomy.

Hence, the correct option is (A).

290. Option (C) is correct as:

Modified radical mastoidectomy is the surgery of choice for atticoantral cholesteatoma. However, in some situations it is not possible to remove it safely, radical mastoidectomy is indicated.

Indications of radical mastoidectomy

1. When all cholesteatoma cannot be safely removed, e.g. that invading eustachian tube, round window niche, peri labyrinthine or hypotympanic cells.

2. If previous attempts to eradicate chronic inflammatory disease or cholesteatoma have failed.

3. As an approach to petrous apex.

4. Removal of glomus tumour.

5. Carcinoma middle ear. Radical mastoidectomy followed by radiotherapy is an alternative to en bloc removal of the temporal bone in carcinoma middle ear.

Option (A) is incorrect because generally, beta-lactam antibiotics are most successful against gram-positive pathogens for both disruptions of adhesion and postantibiotic effect. Amoxicillin (or erythromycin-sulfisoxazole, in patients who are allergic to penicillin) remains the initial treatment of choice in children with AOM.

Option (B) is incorrect because treatments for CSOM may include topical antibiotics (administered into the ear) with or without steroids, systemic antibiotics (given either by mouth or by injection), topical antiseptics and ear cleaning (aural toileting), all of which can be used on their own or in various combinations.

Option (D) is incorrect because treatment for mastoiditis is with antibiotics. If antibiotics alone do not cure the infection, surgery may be needed to drain the middle ear or to remove part of the infected mastoid bone. The main way to prevent mastoiditis is to prevent ear infections (acute otitis media) or by treating an ear infection right away.

Hence, the correct option is (C).

291. The anteroposterior diameter of the eyeball at birth is about 16.5 mm (70% of the adult size which is attained by 7-8 years).

Option (C) is correct because according to the above explanation this option will be correct.

Option (A) is incorrect as the above explanation it is clear that this option will not be correct because the axial length of the eyeball at birth is 70 %, not 100 %. Hence, this option will not be correct.

Option (B) is incorrect as the above explanation it is clear that this option will not be correct because the axial length of the eyeball at birth is 70 %, not 90 %. Hence, this option will not be correct.

Option (D) is incorrect as the above explanation it is clear that this option will not be correct because the axial length of the eyeball at birth is 70 %, not 40 %. Hence, this option will not be correct.

Hence, the correct option is (C).

292. Option (A) is correct because

- Pin-hole test: It helps in confirming whether the optical correction in the trial frame is correct or not.
- An improvement in visual acuity while looking through a pinhole indicates that optical correction in the trial frame is incorrect.
- A pinhole can reduce refractive error up to 3 D.

Option (B) is incorrect because from the explanation of option (A) it is clear that this option will not be correct.

Option (C) is incorrect as we know that option (A) will be correct according to the question hence this option will not be correct.

Option (D) is incorrect because from the above explanation it is clear that this option will not be correct.

Hence, the correct option is (A).

293. Option (D) is correct as :

A SAFE strategy is used for trachoma

S: Surgery for eyelid

A: Antibiotics

F: Facial hygiene

E: Environmental modifications

Option (A) is incorrect because the two macrolides used in the treatment of bacterial conjunctivitis—erythromycin and azithromycin (AzaSite)—are bacteriostatic agents. Erythromycin is usually recommended only for prophylaxis of neonatal conjunctivitis because the drug has limited activity against S. aureus.

Option (B) is incorrect because most mild cases of viral conjunctivitis clear up on their own within a couple of weeks, without any specific treatment. Cleaning the eyes with water and a clean cloth or sterile pad, applying warm or cool compresses, and using lubricating eye drops, also known as artificial tears, may help to relieve symptoms.

Option (C) is incorrect because the main control strategy for onchocerciasis is currently based on mass treatment with ivermectin. The registration of ivermectin in 1987, and its subsequent donation by Merck & Co., Inc., provided a drug for disease intervention that was applicable in all endemic areas.

Hence, the correct option is (D).

294. The organisms which can penetrate intact corneal epithelium are Neisseria gonorrhea, Haemophilus aegyptius, Corynebacterium diphtheriae, Listeria species and Neisseria meningitides.

Option (D) is correct because from the above explanation it is clear that the statement 'A' and 'C' both organisms can penetrate the normal cornea but this option includes the statements 'A' and 'C'.

Option (A) is incorrect because from the above explanation it is clear that the statement 'A' and 'C' both organisms can penetrate the normal cornea but this option includes only the statement 'A'.

Option (B) is incorrect because from the above explanation it is clear that the statement 'A' and 'C' both organisms can penetrate the normal cornea but this option includes the statements 'B' and 'C'.

Option (C) is incorrect because from the above explanation it is clear that the statement 'A' and 'C' both organisms can penetrate the normal cornea but this option includes the statements 'A' and 'D'.

Hence, the correct option is (D).

295. Signs of acute anterior uveitis

- Circumcorneal (ciliary) congestion.
- Corneal edema, posterior corneal opacities.
- Keratic precipitates (KPs), aqueous flare, aqueous cells, hypopyon, hyphema.
- Muddy iris, Narrow (miotic) pupil, festooned appearance (when dilated with mydriatic), sluggish pupillary reaction, ectropion pupillage, occlusion pupillage.

Option (D) is correct because from the above explanation it is clear that statements 'B' and 'C' are the Signs of uveitis, and this option showing the statement 'B' and 'C'.

Option (A) is incorrect because from the above explanation it is clear that statements 'B' and 'C' are the Signs of uveitis, and this option showing the statement 'a'.

Option (B) is incorrect because from the above explanation it is clear that statements 'B' and 'C' are the Signs of uveitis, and this option showing the statement 'C'.

Option (C) is incorrect because from the above explanation it is clear that statements 'B' and 'C' are the Signs of uveitis, and this option showing the statement 'A' and 'C'.

Hence, the correct option is (D).

296.

- Aqueous is formed by the ciliary body at a rate of 2.3 l/min.
- The most obvious chemical difference between aqueous and plasma is at the level of the protein content of the two fluids. Aqueous has only 1/500 that of plasma protein.
- Aqueous provides nutrition to cornea and lens.

- Normal IOP is 10-21 mm Hg (mean 16+ 2.5 mm Hg).

Option (D) is correct because this option includes every options statement hence this option will be correct according to the question through the above explanation.

Option (A) is incorrect because from the above explanation it is clear that not only 'It is secreted at the rate of 2–3 microL/min' is related to Regarding aqueous humour except this other options are also related to the question fact hence this option will not be correct.

Option (B) is incorrect because from the above explanation it is clear that not only 'Secreted by ciliary process' is related to Regarding aqueous humour except this other options are also related to the question fact hence this option will not be correct.

Option (C) is incorrect because from the above explanation it is clear that not only 'Has less protein than plasma' is related to Regarding aqueous humour except this other options are also related to the question fact hence this option will not be correct.

Hence, the correct option is (D).

297. Causes of soft exudates (cotton wool spots)

- All types of severe hypertension (hypertensive retinopathy) including renal disease, Toxemia of pregnancy.
- Diabetic retinopathy
- Collagen vascular disorders:- SLE, PAN, systemic sclerosis, scleroderma, Wegener's granulomatosis.
- Infections:- AIDS, septic retinitis (including SABE), rarely CMV retinitis in AIDS.
- Microembolization:- IV drug abuse, Post cardiac surgery, Fat embolism or Purtscher retinopathy.
- Other Eale's disease, Adults anemia (Hb < 6.6-8.0 g/d1), Pseudoxanthoma elasticum, Neoplasia (Leukemia, Hodgkin's disease), Sickle cell retinopathy, radiation retinopathy.

Option (D) is correct because this option includes every option statement hence this option will be correct according to the question through the above explanation.

Option (A) is incorrect because from the above explanation it is clear that not only 'DM', is where Soft exudates are found except these other options are also related to the question fact. Hence, this option will not be correct.

Option (B) is incorrect because from the above explanation it is clear that not only 'HTN', is where Soft exudates are found except these other options are also related to the question fact. Hence, this option will not be correct.

Option (C) is incorrect because from the above explanation it is clear that not only 'Toxemia', is where Soft exudates are found except these other options are also related to the question fact. Hence, this option will not be correct.

Hence, the correct option is (D).

298.

- The neurosensory layer of the retina contains three mains neurosensory cells: - Photoreceptors, i.e. rods & cones; bipolar cells (in the inner nuclear layer); and ganglionic cells (in ganglionic cell layer). Axons of ganglionic cells (multipolar cells) form the optic nerve.
- The length of the optic nerve is 47-50 mm.
- Like other parts of CNS, the optic nerve is covered by meningeal sheaths (pia, arachnoid and dura mater) as soon as it leaves the eyeball.
- The intracanalicular part of the optic nerve is crossed by the ophthalmic artery.

Option (B) is correct because according to the above explanation statements 'A' and 'B' are not true about the optic nerve but this option showing statements 'A' and 'B' hence this option will be correct according to the question through the above explanation.

Option (A) is incorrect because according to the above explanation statements 'A' and 'B' are not true about the optic nerve but this option showing statements 'A' and 'C' hence this option will not be correct according to the question through the above explanation.

Option (C) is incorrect because according to the above explanation statements 'A' and 'B' are not true about the optic nerve but this option showing statements 'A' and 'D' hence this option will not be correct according to the question through the above explanation.

Option (D) is incorrect because according to the above explanation statements 'A' and 'B' are not true about the optic nerve but this option showing statements 'B' and 'C' hence this option will not be correct according to the question through the above explanation.

Hence, the correct option is (B).

299. Option (C) is correct as:

- The characteristic visual field defect of the central chiasmatic lesion is bitemporal hemianopia. The pituitary tumor causes central chiasmatic lesions.
- Bitemporal hemianopia results due to central (sagittal) lesion of the optic chiasma, common causes of which are tumors of the pituitary gland (most common), craniopharyngioma, suprasellar meningioma, glioma of the third ventricle, chiasmal arachnoiditis, and third ventricular dilatation.

Option (A) is incorrect as :

Signs of Glaucoma

Loss of peripheral or side vision. This is usually the first sign of vision loss due to glaucoma.

- Seeing halos around lights.
- Vision loss.
- Redness in the eye.
- The eye that looks hazy.
- Nausea or vomiting.
- Pain in the eye and in the head.
- Narrowing of vision (tunnel vision).

Option (B) is incorrect because chronic signs of optic neuritis can include: Persistent visual loss. Most patients with optic neuritis recover functional vision within one year. However, on testing, deficits in color vision, contrast sensitivity, stereo acuity, and light brightness are detectable in most patients at up to two years

Option (D) is incorrect because retinal detachment itself is painless. But warning signs almost always appear before it occurs or has advanced, such as the sudden appearance of many floaters — tiny specks that seem to drift through your field of vision. Flashes of light in one or both eyes (photopsia).

Hence, the correct option is (C).

300. Option (A) is correct as:

- Superior oblique causes intorsion/medial rotation/ internal rotation; abduction and depression.
- There no such movements in the eye called upward rotation or downward rotation. Simply there is elevation and depression.

Option (B) is incorrect because extortion is the wrongful use of actual or threatened force, violence or intimidation to gain money or property from an individual or entity. Extortion generally involves a threat being made to the victim's person or property, or to their family or friends.

Option (C) is incorrect because lateral rotation is a rotating movement away from the midline. This is in the opposite direction of the movements.

Option (D) is incorrect because upward rotation should be incorporated during passive humeral abduction in individuals with hemiplegia post-stroke, especially when the humeral is moved beyond 90° of humeral abduction. Combined movements of scapular and humeral will help maintain the relative movement between the scapula and humerus.

Hence, the correct option is (A).

Mock Test 06

Part A

Q.1 Ape thumb malformation is seen in involvement of -

A. Median nerve **B.** Ulnar nerve
C. Radial nerve **D.** Axillary nerve

Q.2 Froment's sign is characteristically seen in -

A. Ulnar nerve injury
B. Median nerve injury
C. Radial nerve injury
D. Intercostobrachial nerve injury

Q.3 Atrophy of the intrinsic muscles of the hand can be awaited to follow injury of the -

A. Ulnar nerve **B.** Radial nerve
C. Branchial nerve **D.** Axillary nerve

Q.4 In a femoral triangle, the most medial structure seen is

A. Lymphatics **B.** Artery
C. Vein **D.** Nerve

Q.5 Adductor canal lies beneath the -

A. Adductor longus **B.** Adductor magnus
C. Sartorius **D.** Vastus medialis

Q.6 What lies anterior to transverse sinus -

A. Aorta **B.** Pulmonary artery
C. IVC **D.** SVC

Q.7 All the following openings in the right atrium are guarded by valve except -

A. Superior vena cava
B. Inferior vena cava
C. Coronary sinus
D. Atrioventricular opening

Q.8 Sphincter urethra is present in-

A. Prostatic urethra
B. bulbar urethra
C. Membranous urethra
D. Penile urethra

Q.9 The correct relationship of structures at the hilum of a kidney from anterior to posterior is -

A. Renal artery, renal vein, renal pelvis
B. Renal vein, renal artery, renal pelvis
C. Renal pelvis, ranal artery, renal vein
D. None of the above

Q.10 All of the following statements about Sternberg Canal are true, Except -

A. Located anterior and medial to Foramen Rotundum
B. Located posterior and lateral to Foramen Rotundum
C. Caused by incomplete fusion of greater wing of the sphenoid
D. Cause of intrasphenoidal meningocele

Q.11 Suture present between parietal & occipital bones is -

A. Lambdoid suture **B.** Sagittal suture
C. Coronal suture **D.** Metopic suture

Q.12 Falx cerebri contains-

A. Straight sinus
B. Occipital sinus
C. Transverse sinus
D. Anterior intercavernous sinus

Q.13 All the following branches of the Vth nerve supply the dura mater except -

A. Anterior ethmoidal **B.** Posterior ethmoidal
C. Auriculotemporal **D.** Mandibular

Q.14 The Lining epithelium of the vagina is -

A. Pseudostratified columnar epithelium
B. Keratinized stratified squamous epithelium
C. Non keratinized stratified squamous epithelium
D. Ciliated columnar epithelium

Q.15 The Windpipe is lined by -

A. Stratified squamous epithelium
B. Ciliated columnar epithelium
C. Simple columnar epithelium
D. Pseudostratified columnar epithelium

Q.16 The outer layer of the blastocyst forms -

A. Primitive streak **B.** Yolk sac
C. Embryo proper **D.** Trophoblast

Q.17 The development of diaphragm is from?

A. Septum Transversum
B. Pleuropericardial membranes
C. Pleuroperitoneal membranes
D. Both (A) and (C) are true.

Q.18 Enzymatic markers of plasma membrane include all except

A. 5'-nucleotidase
B. Adenylyl cyclase
C. Na^+-K^+-ATPase
D. Galactosyl transferase

Q.19 Among the following, the transmembrane region of the proteins have-

A. A stretch of hydrophilic amino acids
B. A stretch of hydrophobic amino acids
C. A disulphide loop
D. Alternating hydrophilic and hydrophobic amino acids

Q.20 In the cell membrane, the following is true -

A. Lipids are regularly arranged
B. Lipids are symmetrical
C. Protein displaced laterally
D. None

Q.21 Initiation of impulse starts in

A. Axon
B. Axon hillock + initial segment
C. Cell body
D. Dendritic tree

Q.22 Orthodromic conduction is

A. An axon can conduct impulse in one direction only
B. An axon can conduct impulse in both directions
C. The jumping of depolarization from node to node
D. The point at which a runaway spike potential occurs

Q.23 Pseudounipolar cells

A. Sympathetic ganglia
B. Parasympathetic
C. Cranial nerve ganglia
D. Dorsal Root Ganglia

Q.24 Skeletal muscle shrinking ends when

A. Ca^{++} move out of the cytoplasm
B. Ach is absorbed from the Neuromuscular junction
C. Closure and indrawing of receptors
D. Decreased calcium outside reticulum

Q.25 Which one of the following does not increase the force of muscle contraction?

A. Increasing the frequency of activation of motor units
B. Increasing the number of motor units activated
C. Increasing the amplitude of action potentials in the motor neurons
D. Recruiting larger motor units

Q.26 Increase in cytosolic calcium from intracellular storage, during smooth muscle contraction, is/are due to -

A. cAMP **B.** cGMP
C. cCMP **D.** IP3-DAG

Q.27 Pulmonary function changes seen in Emphysema are

A. ↑TLC **B.** ↓RV **C.** ↑FEV_1 **D.** ↑VC

Q.28 The normal intrapleural pressure at the start/beginning of inspiration is ______ cm of H_2O.

A. -8 **B.** -5 **C.** 1.5 **D.** 0

Q.29 Body temperature regulation centre is located at

A. Pituitary **B.** Thalamus
C. Hypothalamus **D.** Basal ganglia

Q.30 The opening of which channel is d/t Plateau phase of ventricular muscle?

A. Na^+ channel
B. K^+ channel
C. Ca–Na channel
D. Closure of Ca^{2+} channel

Q.31 During a complex mitral valve replacement, it is determined that the patient will benefit from brief protective hypothermia. Of the options listed below, which is tend to be the poor substitute for core temperature.

A. Rectum **B.** Bladder
C. Nasopharnyx **D.** None of these

Q.32 Which of the following does not form a filtration barrier in nephrons

A. Podocytes
B. Mesangium
C. Endothelial cell
D. Basement membrane

Q.33 Normal gastric juice contains all except

A. Na^+ **B.** K^+ **C.** Ca^{++} **D.** Mg^{++}

Q.34 The intrinsic element of the citadel is discharged by which of the following cells in gastric glands

A. Chief cells
B. Parietal cells
C. Enterochromaffin cells
D. B cells

Q.35 Transport of ADP in and ATP out of mitochondria is inhibited by

A. Atractyloside **B.** Oligomycin
C. Rotenone **D.** Cyanide

Q.36 Chymotrypsinogen is a form of ________.

A. Zymogen **B.** Carboxypeptidase
C. Transaminase **D.** Clot lysing protein

Q.37 Which of the following is an aldose

A. Ribulose **B.** Ribose
C. Erythrulose **D.** None of these

Q.38 In glycolysis, the first committed step is catalysed by

A. 2, 3 DPG
B. Glucokinase
C. Hexokinase
D. Phosphofructokinase

Q.39 Which of the following metabolites is involved in glycogenolysis, glycolysis and gluconeogenesis?

A. Galactose–1–phosphate
B. Glucose–6–phosphate
C. Uridine diphosphoglucose
D. Fructose–6–phosphate

Q.40 Which organ does not utilise ketone bodies

A. Liver **B.** Brain
C. Skeletal muscles **D.** Cardiac muscles

Q.41 NADPH is required for

A. Gluconeogenesis
B. Glycolysis
C. Fatty acids synthesis
D. Glycogenolysis

Q.42 Which amino acid is scarce in pulses?

A. Lysine **B.** Threonine
C. Methionine **D.** Serine

Q.43 About Denaturation of protein, which is true

A. Biological property persists
B. Primary structure lost
C. Always irreversible

D. Mostly renders protein insoluble.

Q.44 Menkes Kinky hair syndrome is characterized by a congenital deficiency of

A. Serum ceruloplasmin
B. Serum copper
C. Ferochelatase
D. Copper binding ATPase.

Q.45 The pyruvate utilization in tissues is decreased in

A. Pernicious anemia **B.** Scurvy
C. Beriberi **D.** Pellagra

Q.46 Triple bonds are found between which base pairs

A. A–T **B.** C–G **C.** A–G **D.** C–T

Q.47 mRNA is an approving version of

A. tRNA
B. rRNA
C. Ribosomal of DNA
D. A single strand of DNA

Q.48 Ends of chromosomes replicated by

A. Telomerase
B. Centromere
C. Restriction endonuclease
D. Exonuclease

Q.49 Nonsense codons bring about

A. Elongation of the polypeptide chain
B. Pre-translational modification of protein
C. Initiation of protein synthesis
D. Termination of protein synthesis

Q.50 Correct statement about restriction fragment gene -

A. Detected by southern blot
B. Used for identification of the gene for genomic mapping
C. RFLP is a DNA variation sequence
D. All of these

Part B

Q.51 True about Apoptosis include the following except:

A. Inflammation is present
B. DNA breakage
C. Clumping of chromatin
D. Cell shrinkage

Q.52 Complete wound strength is gained by?

A. Never regained **B.** 1 month
C. 6 months **D.** 1 year

Q.53 Virchow triad includes all except:

A. Endothelial injury
B. Abnormal blood flow
C. Hypercoagulability
D. Pulmonary embolism

Q.54 The most important source of the organic compound shown in the photograph is

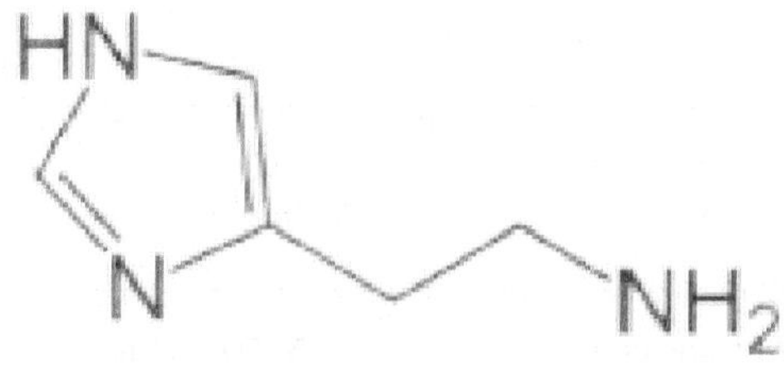

Histamine

A. Eosinophil **B.** Mast cells
C. Neutrophil **D.** Macrophages

Q.55 Which of the following is the most likely inheritance pattern in the pedigree given below-

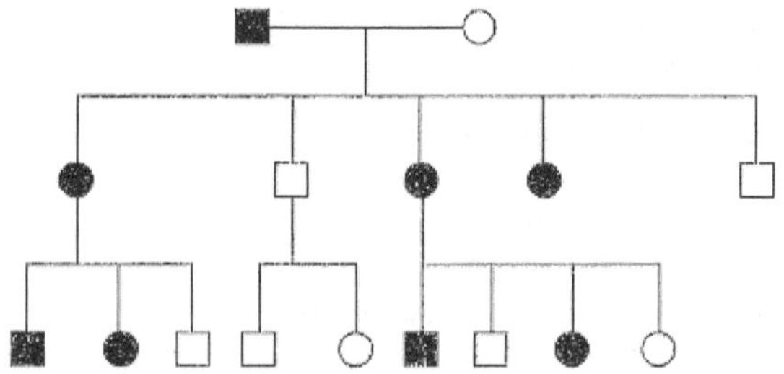

A. Autosomal dominant
B. Mitochondrial
C. Autosomal recessive
D. X-linked dominant

Q.56 Tumour marker for Carcinoma of Organ shown in Photograph is

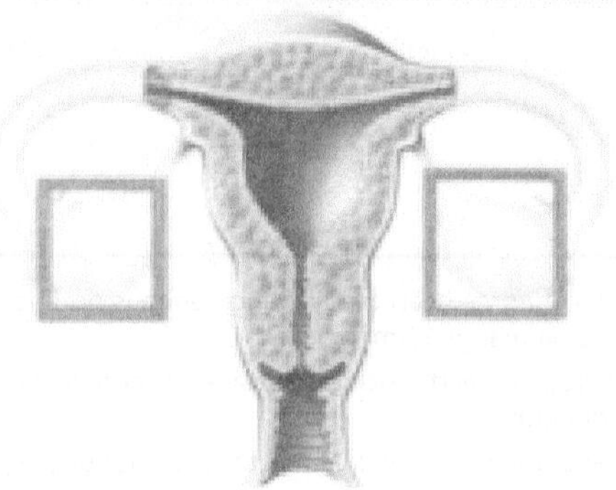

A. PSA **B.** Fibronectin
C. Acid phosphatase **D.** CA 125

Q.57 Solitary hypoechoic lesion of the liver without septate or debris is most likely to be-

A. Hydatid cyst **B.** Caroli's disease
C. Liver abscess **D.** Simple cyst

Q.58 A 22-year-old biker had a road traffic accident with severe injury, after admitting in the hospital his condition suddenly worsens and leads to death, the pathological specimen is provided, what could be likely cause of death?

A. Septic shock

B. Pulmonary thromboembolism
C. Deep vein thrombosis
D. Varicosities of the vein

Q.59 Which of the following is a chemotactic factor:
A. Thromboxanes B. Leukotrienes
C. Prostacyclins D. Prostaglandins

Q.60 Inability to perform the rapid alternating movement is -
A. Past-pointing B. Dysmetria
C. Dysdiadochokinesia D. None

Q.61 Annexin V is associated with:
A. Artherosclerosis B. Inflammation
C. Necrosis D. Apoptosis

Q.62 Which of the following is not component of acinus-
A. Pulmonary lobule
B. Respiratory bronchioles
C. Alveolar ducts
D. Alveolar sac

Q.63 Podocytes are seen in -
A. Bowman's capsule
B. Proximal convoluted tubule
C. Distal convoluted tubule
D. Collecting tubule of the kidney

Q.64 The following image shows:-

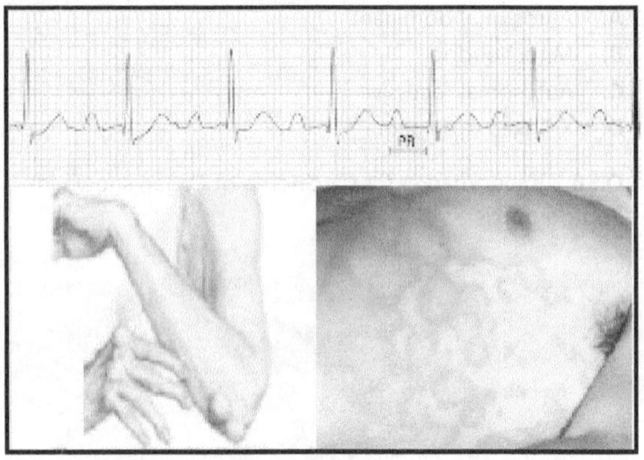

A. Second-degree heart block, Subcutaneous nodule, Erythema marginatum
B. First-degree heart block, Subcutaneous nodule, Erythema marginatum
C. First-degree heart block, Subcutaneous nodule, Erythema nodosum
D. None of these

Q.65 Nutmeg liver is seen in -
A. Right sided heart failure
B. Left sided heart failure
C. Increased pulmonary pressure
D. Decreased pulmonary pressure

Q.66 Carcinoma penis is rarest among -
A. Americans B. Indians
C. Swedes D. Jews

Q.67 Bone resorption markers are all except -
A. Tartrate resistant acid phosphatase
B. Osteocalcin
C. Cross linked-N-telopeptides
D. Urine total free deoxypyridinoline

Q.68 What are gitter cells -
A. Astrocytes
B. Macroglia
C. Modified macrophages in CNS
D. Oligodendrocytes

Q.69 Which of the followings are Anterior pituitary secretes except -
A. Growth hormone B. Prolactin
C. FSH hormone D. Oxytocin

Q.70 Dyskeratosis -
A. Leukoplakia
B. Hyperpigmentation
C. Nail dystrophy
D. Premature keratinisation

Q.71 In a congenital dystrophic variety of epidermolysis bullosa, the mutation is seen in the gene coding for?
A. Laminin 4 B. Collagen type 7
C. Alpha 6 integrin D. Keratin 14

Q.72 In primary T.B. seen -
A. Ghon's focus B. Pleural effusion
C. Miliary mottling D. Fibrosis

Q.73 Which of the following is a reason of Bone affection in scurvy-
A. Bad mineralization of the osteoid tissue
B. Imperfect osteoid matrix formation
C. Defective calcification in osteoid
D. Increased degradation of osteoid tissue

Q.74 Sub-Acute radiation hepatic damage is most marked between-
A. 1-7 days B. 7-21 days
C. 21-40 days D. 40-100 days

Q.75 ESR depends on -
A. Viscosity B. Fibrinogen
C. Rouleaux formation D. All of above

Q.76 Which of the following acid poisoning treated by alkaline diuresis -
A. Morphine B. Amphetamine
C. Phenobarbitone D. Atropine

Q.77 Alkalinization of urine is required for decreasing the poisoning due to:
A. Barbiturates B. Amphetamine
C. Alcohol D. Morphine

Q.78 CYP–450 inducers are:
A. Cimetidine B. Ketoconazole
C. Phenobarbitone D. Theophylline

Q.79 Current ASA standards require that during anaesthesia, systemic blood pressure and heart rate be evaluated at least every

A. 3 minutes **B.** 5 minutes
C. 7 minutes **D.** 10 minutes

Q.80 What is the expected observation in a patient with an expanded pupil not reacting quickly to 1% pilocarpine?

A. Diabetic 3rd nerve palsy
B. Adie's tonic pupil
C. Uncal herniation
D. Pharmacological block

Q.81 Synaptic transmission in the autonomic ganglion is usually:

A. Adrenergic
B. Peptidergic
C. Cholinergic
D. Mediated by substance P

Q.82 Ergometrine is commonly used for :

A. PostPartum Hemorrhage
B. To shorten 2nd stage of labour
C. Dysmenorrhea
D. Toxemia of pregnancy

Q.83 Which of the following drugs is not used for the treatment of congestive heart failure -

A. Nitroglycerin **B.** Spironolactone
C. Nesiritide **D.** Trimetazidine

Q.84 The adverse effect of Losartan are all except:

A. Cough **B.** Hyperkalemia
C. Headache **D.** Angioedema

Q.85 Octreotide is used in all except:

A. Glucagonoma
B. Insulinoma
C. Carcinoid syndrome
D. Glioma

Q.86 Rizatriptan is a drug used for?

A. Prophylaxis of migraine
B. Acute migraine
C. Cluster headache
D. Chronic migraine

Q.87 An anti-emetic drug that also decreases acid secretion due to its action on H_1 receptors is :

A. Promethazine **B.** Domperidone
C. Metoclopramide **D.** Ondansetron

Q.88 An antacid drug that typically causes diarrhoea?

A. Sodium bicarbonate
B. Magnesium hydroxide
C. Calcium bicarbonate
D. Aluminium hydroxide

Q.89 Drug resistance transmitting factor present in bacteria is :

A. Plasmid **B.** Chromosome
C. Introns **D.** Centromere

Q.90 The minimal alveolar concentration of an inhalational anaesthetic is a measure of its :

A. Potency
B. Therapeutic index
C. Diffusibility
D. Oil : water partition coefficient

Q.91 Troglitazone is the drug used in the treatment of:

A. Type 2 diabetes mellitus
B. Petit mal epilepsy
C. Hyperlipidaemia
D. D. Osteoporosis

Q.92 Treatment of choice for SIADH is:

A. Vasopressin **B.** Lithium carbonate
C. Hypertonic Saline **D.** Demeclocycline

Q.93 Which of the following drugs is used for noninfectious uveitis in LUMINATE clinical trial program :

A. Steroid/Infliximab **B.** Cyclosporin
C. Methotrexate **D.** Voclosporin

Q.94 A 17-year-old girl had been taking a drug for the treatment of acne for the last 2 years, which has lead to pigmentation. Which drug could it be?

A. Doxycycline **B.** Minocycline
C. Azithromycin **D.** Chlorpromazine

Q.95 In which of the following Interstitial nephritis is not observed-

A. Diuretics **B.** Beta lactams
C. Allopurinol **D.** Isoniazid

Q.96 The instrument shown in Photograph is sterilized by

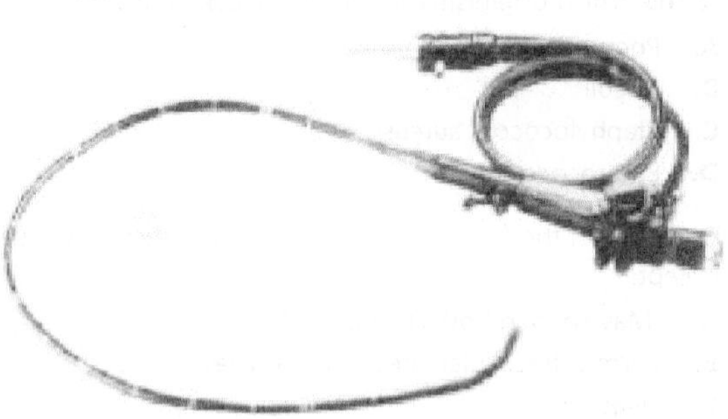

A. Formalin **B.** Autoclaving
C. Boiling **D.** Glutaraldehyde

Q.97 Which of the following statements is not related with Louis Pasteur-

A. Introduction of Complex media
B. Discovery of Rabies vaccine
C. Discovery of M.tuberculosis
D. Disproved spontaneous generation theory

Q.98 Treponema pallidum was innovated by -

A. Robert Koch
B. Twort
C. Schaudinn and Hoffman
D. Ellerman

Q.99 All are autoimmune disease except-
A. Myasthenia gravis
B. Systemic lupus erythematosus
C. Graves' disease
D. Sickle cell disease

Q.100 T cell-subjected to the field is -
A. Cortical follicles of lymph node
B. Medullary cords
C. Mantle layer
D. Paracortical area

Q.101 All of the following are functions of CD4 helper cells, except -
A. Immunogenic memory
B. Produce immunoglobulins
C. Activate macrophages
D. Activate cytotoxic cells

Q.102 All are mononuclear-macrophages except -
A. Histiocytes **B.** Microglia
C. Kupffer cells **D.** B-cells

Q.103 Staph aureus virulence is due to -
A. Pathogenicity correlated with coagulase
B. Endotoxin
C. Hemolysis
D. None of the above

Q.104 In carriers, staphylococci are found in the following sites except -
A. Throat **B.** Nose
C. Skin **D.** None of the above

Q.105 Which organism causes toxic shock syndrome -
A. Pneumococcus
B. E. coli
C. Staphylococcus aureus
D. Enterococcus

Q.106 All of the following are general properties of Viruses except -
A. May contain both DNA and RNA
B. Form extracellular infectious particles
C. Heat labile
D. Not affected by antibiotics

Q.107 Bollinger bodies are spot in -
A. Chickenpox **B.** Cowpox
C. Fowlpox **D.** Smallpox

Q.108 Which is not a DNA virus-
A. Parvovirus **B.** Papovavirus
C. Poxvirus **D.** Rhabdovirus

Q.109 Which of the following is true regarding trematodes-
A. Two host required **B.** Segmented
C. Anus present **D.** Body cavity present

Q.110 Stain with parasite having Charcot-Leyden crystals but no pus cells-
A. Giardia **B.** Taenia
C. E. histolytica **D.** Trichomonas

Q.111 Invasive amoebiasis can be best diagnosed by -
A. ELISA
B. Counter current immunoelectrophoresis
C. Indirect hemagglutination test
D. Complement fixation test

Q.112 Fungi are -
A. Prokaryotes **B.** Eukaryotes
C. Plant **D.** Animals

Q.113 Ascospore is -
A. Asexual spore **B.** Sexual spore
C. Conidia **D.** None of the above

Q.114 Nakayama strain used for which vaccine?
A. Typhoid
B. Chicken pox
C. Japanese encephalitis
D. Yellow fever

Q.115 In which of the following, the Maltese cross is seen on polarizing microscopy-
A. Cryptococcus neoformans
B. Penicillium marneffei
C. Blastomyces
D. Candida albicans

Q.116 Criminal negligence is punishable under Section 304 A for a maximum of -
A. 1 year **B.** 2 years **C.** 3 years **D.** 5 years

Q.117 Which of the following is shared out by CrPC Sec 174-
A. Inquest **B.** Inquiry
C. Murder **D.** Medical negligence

Q.118 Criminal responsibility of a person of Unsound mind in India is incorporated in the Indian Penal Code -
A. Section 302 **B.** Section 84
C. Section 85 **D.** Section 88

Q.119 A subpoena is a somewhat -
A. Decomposed body tissue
B. Designation
C. Document
D. Court tribunal

Q.120 The rate of cooling down of dead bodies in a tropical climate is -
A. 0.2°C/ hours **B.** 0.5°C/ hours
C. 1.0°C/ hours **D.** 1.5°C/ hours

Q.121 Cherry red colour of hypostasis is seen in-
A. CO poisoning **B.** Burns
C. Sulphuric acid **D.** Nitric acid

Q.122 Which of the following is not the part of shotgun -
A. Barrel **B.** Choke bore
C. Bullets **D.** Muzzle

Q.123 Hanging with the feet touching the ground is seen in-

A. Partial hanging **B.** Complete hanging
C. Homicidal hanging **D.** Suicidal hanging

Q.124 All are cardiotoxic except -

A. Aconite **B.** Opium **C.** Oleander **D.** Nicotine

Q.125 Dopamine agonist

A. Clomiphene citrate
B. Bromocriptine mesylate
C. GnRH
D. Dexamethasone

Q.126 Definition of health given by WHO includes which of the following dimension -

A. Social **B.** Economic
C. Mental **D.** All of the above

Q.127 Which of the following is the current trend in Health Care -

A. Qualitative enquiry
B. Community participation
C. Equitable distribution
D. Primary Health Care

Q.128 Sipuleucel-T is used in the treatment of which cancer?

A. Breast **B.** Prostate **C.** Kidney **D.** Pancreas

Q.129 Height in cms, by the cube root of body weight, is term as:

A. Quetelet index **B.** Corpulence index
C. Broca's index **D.** Ponderal index

Q.130 ELISA is executed on people with low generality. What would be the result of executing double screening ELISA tests -

A. Increased sensitivity and positive predictive value
B. Increased sensitivity and negative predictive value
C. Increased specificity and positive predictive value
D. Increased specificity and negative predictive value

Q.131 In a population of 10000 people, the prevalence of a disease is 20%. The sensitivity of a screening test is 95% and specificity is 80%. The positive predictive value of the test will be

A. 45.7% **B.** 54.3% **C.** 15.3% **D.** 98.5%

Q.132 A group of experts discussing and interacting about a particular topic in the presence of an audience is:

A. Symposium **B.** Seminar
C. Panel discussion **D.** Workshop

Q.133 Confidence limit includes -

A. Range & standard deviation
B. Median and standard error
C. Mean and standard error
D. Mode and standard deviation

Q.134 The infectivity of chickenpox continues for -

A. Till the last scab falls off
B. 6 days after onset of rash
C. 3 days after onset of rash
D. Till the fever subsides

Q.135 Not true about varicella infection -

A. Secondary attack rate is 90%
B. Lesions occur on flexor surfaces
C. Only single stage of lesion is present at a time
D. Reactivation occur in 10-30% cases

Q.136 According to WHO, blindness is defined as visual acuity of the better eye, less than

A. 6/60. **B.** 5/60. **C.** 4/60. **D.** 3/60.

Q.137 Which of the following is the least common reason for the heart disease in this country-

A. Rheumatic **B.** Hypertensive
C. Ischaemic **D.** Congenital

Q.138 Following age pyramid denotes

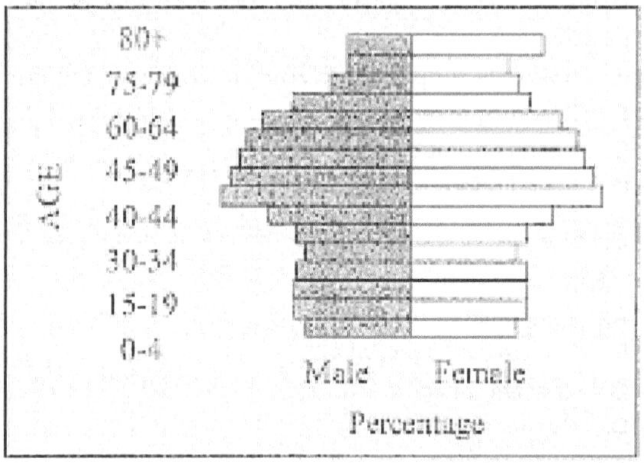

A. Developing country
B. Developed country
C. Underdeveloped country
D. Poor country

Q.139 Demography deals with all except-

A. Mortality **B.** Fertility
C. Morbidity **D.** Marriage

Q.140 Fatty acid characteristically present in breast milk and essential for baby growth –

A. Palmitic acid
B. Arachidonic acid
C. Docosahexaenoic acid
D. Both (B) and (C)

Q.141 MCH care is assessed by –

A. Death rate
B. Birth rate
C. Maternal mortality rate
D. Anemia in mother

Q.142 Daily per capita water consumption for all purposes is –

A. 50-100 litres **B.** 100-150 litres
C. 150–200 litres **D.** 200-250 liters

Q.143 Weight of an Indian reference woman is –

A. 45 kg **B.** 50 kg **C.** 55 kg **D.** 60 kg

Q.144 Energy requirement in late pregnancy –

A. 2500 cal **B.** 1400 cal **C.** 1000 cal **D.** 500 cal

Q.145 Objectives of the National Mental Health programme are all except –

A. Promote community participation
B. Promote the application of mental health knowledge
C. Provides free antipsychotic drugs to all
D. Provide accessibility of mental health care

Q.146 Amount of waste infectious produced in hospitals –

A. 45% **B.** 65% **C.** 80% **D.** 100%

Q.147 Health education –

A. Is health promotion
B. Is health distortion
C. Is delivered through public health agencies only
D. Does not help in prevention of cancer

Q.148 Elements of primary health care include all of the following except –

A. Adequate supply of safe water and basic sanitation
B. Providing essential drugs
C. Health Education
D. Sound referral system

Q.149 Which of the following is not included in Vision 2020 "The right to sight" ____?

A. Trachoma
B. Epidemic conjunctivitis
C. Cataract
D. Onchocerciasis

Q.150 Commonest among diseases with Mendelian inheritance is –

A. Autosomal dominant
B. Autosomal recessive
C. X–linked recessive
D. X–dominant

Part C

Q.151 Notching of ribs occurs in all except?

A. Coarctation of aorta
B. Neurofibromatosis
C. Hypothyroidism
D. Osteogenesis imperfecta

Q.152 Which of the following is measured by Automated Perimeters?

A. Total deviation box plot
B. Pattern deviation plot
C. Grey scale
D. All of the above

Q.153 Urine of a UTI patient has a pH of more than 8, the probable organism is:

A. Ecoli **B.** Proteus
C. Klebsiella **D.** Candida

Q.154 Which drug is used for Mvaesthenia Gravis testing

A. Adrenaline **B.** Phycostigmine
C. Acetylcholine **D.** Edrophonium

Q.155 Which of the following is an example of disorders of sex chromosomes

A. Marfan's syndrome
B. Testicular feminization syndrome
C. Klinefelter's syndrome
D. Down's syndrome

Q.156 False positive ELISA for HIV -

A. Multiple mycloma
B. Lepromatous leprosy
C. SLE
D. All of the above

Q.157 For preservation of alcohol Which chemical is being used ?

A. Potassium acetate **B.** Sodium sulphide
C. Sodium fluoride **D.** Glycerine

Q.158 Carney triad consists of

(A) Gastric carcinoma
(B) Paraganglioma
(C) Pulmonary Chordoma
(D) Carcinoma bronchus
(E) Chondromatosis

A. ABC **B.** CAB **C.** DAB **D.** EBD

Q.159 "Intraepidermal" IgG toppling is spot in:

A. Herpes genitalis **B.** Bullous pemphigoid
C. Pemphigus **D.** SLE

Q.160 This sound is produced during the closure of the semilunar valves-

A. Lubb **B.** Dupp
C. Lubb dupp **D.** Lubb duppshhh

Q.161 What is the prominant feature of ARDS true?

A. Type 2 respiratory failure
B. Lung compliance decreased
C. Increase in diffusion capacity
D. None

Q.162 In ARDS mechanical TV low volume ventilation is

A. 2-3ml/kg **B.** 5-7 ml/kg
C. 5-l0ml/kg **D.** None of these

Q.163 HLA-DR4 is a marker of -

A. Sarcoidosis
B. Rheumatoid arthritis
C. Sero-negative gouty arthritis
D. Psoriasis

Q.164 Which of the following does not cause high anion gap metabolic acidosis -

A. Lactic acidosis
B. Salicylats poisoning
C. Ethylene glycol poisoning
D. Ureterosigmoidostomy

Q.165 The minimum concentration of reduced hemoglobin required for cyanosis is

A. 1gm/dl. **B.** 3 gm/d **C.** 7 gm/d **D.** 5 gm/d

Q.166 Spaghetti and meatball appearance is seen in-

A. Dermatophytes **B.** Pityriasis versicolor
C. Aspergillus **D.** Candida

Q.167 All statements are true regarding skin except –

a. Skin is stratified squamous epithelium
b. Melanocyte & Merkel cells are immigrant cells
c. Keratin filaments are a hallmark of epidermal cells
d. Keratinization process cause hydration of cells
e. Spines of spinous cells are formed from housekeeping organelle

A. de **B.** bc **C.** cd **D.** bd

Q.168 Piebaldism allude to –

A. Androgenetic alopecia
B. Erythema nodosum leprosum
C. Associated with white forelock
D. None of the above

Q.169 Acanthosis nigricans is seen in -

A. Diabetes **B.** GIT cancer
C. Hypothyroidism **D.** All of the above

Q.170 M.C. precipitant of contact dermatitis is –

A. Gold **B.** Nickle **C.** Silver **D.** Iron

Q.171 Determination of Airborne contact dermatitis is possible–

A. Skin biopsy
B. Patch test
C. Prick test
D. Estimation of serum IgE levels

Q.172 Hanging curtain sign is seen in -

A. Pityriasis alba **B.** Pityriasis versicolor
C. Pityriasis rosea **D.** Pitryasis miliaris

Q.173 Typical silvery scales of psoriasis are absent in –

A. Scalp **B.** Knee **C.** Groin **D.** Elbow

Q.174 All are true about erythema multiformis except –

A. Due to Herpes simples
B. Due to sulphonamide
C. Lesion are symmetrical
D. Mucous membrane is usually involved

Q.175 All of the following are bullous lesions except -

A. Pemphigus vulgaris
B. Dermatitis herpetiformis
C. Atopic dermatitis
D. Pemphigoid

Q.176 All are involved in Leprosy except–

A. CNS **B.** Testis **C.** Skin **D.** Cornea

Q.177 Skin smear is negative in which leprosy –

A. Indeterminate **B.** Neuritic
C. Lepromatous **D.** Borderline

Q.178 The highest recurrent cause of frequent genital ulceration in a erotic vital male is –

A. Herpes genitalis **B.** Aphthous ulcer
C. Syphilis **D.** Chancroid

Q.179 Treponema pallidum causes –

A. Condyloma acuminata
B. Condyloma lata
C. Both
D. None

Q.180 Female presents with a history of color change from pallor to cyanosis on exposure to cold in fingers. This condition is mostly associated with?

A. Scleroderma
B. Leukemia
C. Lung infections
D. Hepatosplenomegaly

Q.181 Husband having a suspicion that his wife is having an affair with another man, diagnosis is

A. Delusion **B.** Illusion
C. Hallucination **D.** Delirium

Q.182 A patient gets tingling when his bed light is flashed suddenly. Which type of hallucination is this -

A. Hypnagogic hallucinations
B. Hypnopompic hallucinations
C. Reflex hallucinations
D. Functional hallucinations

Q.183 Features of delirium -

A. Deficit of attention
B. Autonomic instability
C. Altered sleep wake pattern
D. All of the above

Q.184 Fox Fordyce Disease effects:

A. Eccrine Glands **B.** Apocrine glands
C. Pituitary gland **D.** Sebaceous glands

Q.185 The following symptoms may be seen in opium withdrawal -

A. Tremors **B.** Lacrimation
C. Dry nose and mouth **D.** Constipation

Q.186 Which of the following drugs is not used in opioid dependence?

A. Disulfiram **B.** Clonidine
C. Lorazepam **D.** Naltrexone

Q.187 All are features of neurosis except -

A. Symptoms cause subjective distress
B. Contact with reality preserved
C. Personality disturbances
D. Insight is maintained

Q.188 One of the following drug abuse produces a psychosis closely resembling paranoid schizophrenia-

A. Barbiturates **B.** Amphetamines
C. Opioids **D.** Benzodiazepines

Q.189 Anxiety neurosis is manifested by -

A. Difficulty in breathing

B. Complete consciousness
C. Negative thinking
D. All of the above

Q.190 Differentiation of hysterical fits from epileptic fit -
A. Occurs in sleep
B. Injuries to person
C. Incontinence
D. Occurs when people are watching

Q.191 What are the EEG waves recorded for the parietooccipital region with subject awake & eye closed
A. Alpha waves **B.** Beta waves
C. Delta waves **D.** Theta waves

Q.192 Which of the following drugs are used in the treatment of ADHD?
A. Amphetamine **B.** Modafinil
C. Methylphenidate **D.** All

Q.193 ECT is advocated in following except -
A. Chronic schizophrenia
B. Catatonic schizophrenia
C. Severe depression
D. Severe psychoses

Q.194 According to Sigmund Freud, primary process thinking is-
A. Illogical & Bizarre
B. Rational
C. Absent during sleep
D. Logical & unconscious

Q.195 Treatment of depression with suicidal tendencies is?
A. Clozapine **B.** Mitrazapine
C. ECT **D.** Olenzapine

Q.196 Indicators of bone formation include all of the following except -
A. Osteocalcin
B. Alkaline phosphatase
C. Hydroxyproline
D. Type 1 procollegen

Q.197 What diaphysis fracture involve?
A. Skull bones **B.** Long bone
C. Sternum **D.** Ribs

Q.198 Which is true regarding shoulder dislocation -
A. Posterior dislocation is often over-looked
B. Pain is severe in anterior dislocation
C. Radiography may be misleading in posterior dislocation
D. All of the above

Q.199 Avascular necrosis is the commonest in one of the following fracture -
A. Garden 1 and 2 fracture of femoral neck
B. Garden 3 and 4 fracture of femoral neck
C. Sub-trochanteric fracture of femoral neck
D. Baso-trochanteric fracture

Q.200 In the case of a 70-year-old lady with an intracapsular fracture of the neck of femur, the ideal treatment would be -
A. Closed traction
B. Hemiarthropalsty
C. Internal fixation with nail
D. Internal fixation with nail and plate

Q.201 Trochanteric fracture of the femur is best treated by -
A. Dynamic hip screw
B. Inlay plates
C. Plaster in abduction
D. Plaster in abduction and internal rotation

Q.202 Which of the following Treatment of choice be used for old non-united fracture of shaft of the femur -
A. Compression plating
B. Bone grafting
C. Nailing
D. Compression plating with bone grafting

Q.203 The investigation of choice to detect a prolapsed intervertebral disc is?
A. CT Scan **B.** MRI
C. Myelography **D.** Radiograph

Q.204 Hangman's fracture is-
A. Subluxation of C_5 over C_6
B. Fracture dislocation of C_2
C. Fracture dislocation of ankle joint
D. Fracture of odontoid

Q.205 Regarding Perth's disease, which of the following is not correct- -
A. Osteonecrotic osteochondritis
B. Decreased bone age
C. Age of onset has no affect on course
D. Restricted abduction

Q.206 Which of these muscles undergoes wasting first in osteoarthritis knee-
A. Quadriceps only **B.** Hamstrings only
C. Gastronemius **D.** All of the above

Q.207 Chronic persistent neutrophilic discharge is seen in -
A. Chronic osteomyelitis
B. Acute osteomyelitis
C. Septic arthritis
D. None

Q.208 A 10-year child presented with a mid tibial swelling which an x-ray revealed a lytic lesion with sclerotic margins. What is the most likely diagnosis?
A. Eosinophilic granuloma
B. Osteoid osteoma
C. Fibrocortical defect
D. Fibrous dysplasia

Q.209 All are true for Dupuytren's contracture except -
A. Usually 4th finger is involved
B. Bilateral disease is rare
C. Surgical release is useful

D. May be associated with Pyronie disease

Q.210 During the surgical procedure -

A. Tendons should be repaired before nerves
B. Nerves should be repaired before tendons
C. Tendons should not be repaired at the same time
D. None of the above

Q.211 Color of oxygen cylinder is:

A. Black with white color
B. Blue with white color
C. Yellow with white color
D. Grey with grey

Q.212 Bain circuit is Mapleton type circuit –

A. Type A **B.** Type F **C.** Type D **D.** Type E

Q.213 Nasal intubation is contraindicated in –

A. CSF Rhinorrhea
B. Fracture cervical spine
C. Fracture inaudible
D. Short neck

Q.214 All are features of difficult airway except

A. limited mouth opening
B. Micrognathia with macroglossia
C. TMJ ankylosis
D. Increased thyromental distance

Q.215 Malampatti grading is for –

A. Mobility of cervical spine
B. Mobility of atlanto axial joint
C. Assessment of free rotation of neck before intubation
D. Inspection of oral cavity before intubation

Q.216 Pre-anesthetic medication is given to -

A. Reducon of secreon of saliva
B. To prevent undesirable reflexes
C. Reduce anxiety and fear
D. All of the above

Q.217 Shortest acting non depolarizing muscle relaxant –

A. Mivacurium **B.** Vercuronium
C. Atracurium **D.** Succinyl choline

Q.218 The muscle relaxant from the following is responsible for maximum longevity of the action :

A. Atracurium **B.** Vecuronium
C. Rocuronium **D.** Doxacurium

Q.219 Skeletal muscle relaxant of choke in the liver and renal disease is?

A. Atracurium **B.** Mivacurium
C. Gallium **D.** Vecuronium

Q.220 A dentist notices that his 39yr lady patient has scattered, white, 0.2 to 1.5cm, reticulated areas on the buccal mucosa. She says that these lesions have been present for a year. She also has some 0.3cm, pruritic, purple papules on each elbow. A biopsy of a skin lesion shows a band-like infiltrate of lymphocytes at the dermal-epidermal junction along with degeneration of basal keratinocytes. What would you advise the patient?

A. A squamous cell carcinoma is likely to develop.
B. You have systemic lupus erythematosus.
C. You should stop taking all medications.
D. These lesions will probably resolve over time.

Q.221 Use of Thiopentone –

A. Seizure **B.** Truth spell
C. Reduction of ICP **D.** All of the above

Q.222 An intravenous anesthetic agent that is associated with hemodynamic stability, maintenance of CVP with postoperative nausea, vomiting, and myoclonus –

A. Ketamine **B.** Etomidate
C. Propofol **D.** Opioids

Q.223 True about local anesthetic agents-

A. Duration depends on protein binding
B. Potency depends upon lipid solubility
C. LA with low PKa is more active
D. All of the above

Q.224 Sodium bicarbonate, when given with local anesthetics has which of the following effect –

A. Increases speed and quality of anaesthesia
B. Decreases diffusion of the anaesthetic drug
C. Causes rapid elimination of the local anaesthetic
D. Decreases speed and quality of anaesthesia

Q.225 Cause of postoperative hypertension –

A. Pre-operative hypertension
B. Inadequate analgesia
C. Phaeochromocytoma
D. All of the above

Q.226 X - rays are modified -

A. Protons **B.** Electrons
C. Neutrons **D.** Positrons

Q.227 A patient is presented with a metallic foreign body in the eye. Which investigation should not be done:

A. USG **B.** X - ray **C.** CT **D.** MRI

Q.228 Characteristics of BENIGN tumor of the lung in X-ray is

A. Size > 5 cms diameter
B. Cavitation
C. Peripheral location
D. Concentric dense calcification

Q.229 A 55-year-old man who has been on bed rest for the past 10 days, complain of breathlessness and chest pain. The chest X-ray is normal. The next step in the investigation should be –

A. Lung ventilation – perfusion scan
B. Pulmonary arteriography
C. Pulmonary venous wedge angiography
D. Echocardiography

Q.230 All are chest radiographic feature of left atrial enlargement except-

A. Double left heart border
B. Elevated left main bronchus
C. Splaying of carina
D. Enlargement of left atrial appendage

Q.231 Boot shaped heart on chest X-ray is seen in
A. TGA **B.** TAPVC
C. Tetrofogy of fallot **D.** PAPVC

Q.232 Which among the following is false regarding the need for chest radiograph in a patient of the acute abdomen –
A. Supine chest radiograph is the best radiograph for showing presence of a small pnetunoperitoneum
B. A number of chest conditions can present as acute abdominal condition
C. Acute abdominal condition may be complicated by the chest pathology
D. Even when the chest radiograph is normal it acts as a most valuable baseline

Q.233 Which one of the following hepatic lesions can be diagnosed with high accuracy by using nuclear imaging?
A. Hepatocellular carcinoma
B. Hepatic adenoma
C. Focal nodular hyperplacia
D. Cholangiocarcinoma

Q.234 Which of the following agents is used to measure glomerular filtration rate (GFR) –
A. Iodohippurate **B.** Tc99m – DTPA
C. Tc99m – MAG3 **D.** Tc99m – DMSA

Q.235 Arthritis mutilans is seen in:
A. OA
B. Reiters syndrome
C. Psoriatic Arthropathy
D. Rheumatoid arthritis

Q.236 Expansile lytic lesion with fluid-fluid levels within the metaphysis of fibula seen on CT and MRI in an early adolescent female is typical of –
A. Giant cell tumor
B. Aneurysmal bone cyst
C. Hemangioma
D. Fibrous dysplasia

Q.237 Onion - peel appearance is seen in -
A. Ewing's sarcoma **B.** Osteoma
C. Osteosarcoma **D.** Osteoclastoma

Q.238 Which of the following is not an MRI feature of Mesial temporal sclerosis?
A. Atrophy of mammillary body
B. Atrophy of fornix
C. Blurring of Grey white matter junction of ipsilateral temporal lobe
D. Atrophy of hippocampus

Q.239 Investigation of choice for acute subarachnoid hemorrhage –
A. Enhanced MRI **B.** MRI
C. CT-scan **D.** Angiography

Q.240 Cozen's test is for:
A. Golfers elbow **B.** Students elbow
C. Frozen elbow **D.** Tennis elbow

Q.241 Fertilization usually occurs in which part of the fallopian tube
A. Fimbrial end **B.** Ampulla
C. Interstitium **D.** Isthumus

Q.242 The major contribution to the semen from:
A. Testes
B. Seminal vesicles
C. Prostate
D. Bulbourethral and urethral glands

Q.243 Absent fructose content in the seminal fluid suggests
A. Congenital absence of seminal vesicle
B. Partial duct obstruction
C. None
D. Both

Q.244 The diagnostic factor for Choriocarcinoma is:
A. Hypoplastic trophoblasts
B. HCG Level less than 35,000Miu/ml
C. Lung Metastasis
D. None of them

Q.245 Which of the following hematological criteria remains unchanged during pregnancy
A. MCHC **B.** TIBC
C. Blood Volume **D.** S. ferritin

Q.246 The dose of folic acid per day for treating megaloblastic anemia in pregnancy
A. 400 µg **B.** 1 mg **C.** 5 mg **D.** 2 mg

Q.247 Partogram is not used to monitor -
A. Cervical dilatations **B.** Uterine contractions
C. Fetal lung maturity **D.** Descent of head

Q.248 A Patient at 22 weeks gestation is diagnosed as having LUD which occurred at 17 weeks but did not have a miscarriage. This patient is at increased risk for:
A. Septic abortion
B. Recurrent abortion
C. Future infertility
D. Consumptive coagulopathy with hypofibrinogenemia

Q.249 A G2P1 female at 35 weeks experiences uterine contractions. No fetal distress is seen and membranes are not ruptured. Which of the following is to be done?
A. 12 mg betamethasone injection
B. Tocolytic therapy
C. Vaginal swab culture
D. Cervical cerclage

Q.250 Meconium is excreted by a new born till ______ day.
A. 7 **B.** 3 **C.** 6 **D.** 4

Q.251 Fetal cardiac activity is detected with Transvaginal USG as early as?

A. 8 weeks
B. 6 weeks
C. 10 weeks.
D. 12 weeks

Q.252 IUGR is defined when:

A. Birth weight is below the tenth percentile of the average of gestational age
B. Birth weight is below the 20 percentile of the average of gestational age
C. Birth weight is below the 30 percentile of the average of gestational age
D. Weight of baby is less than 1000 gm

Q.253 Increased acidosis and hypoxemia are seen in:

A. Normal Doppler wave form
B. Increased fetal diastolic flow in the middle cerebral artery with absent diastolic flow in the aorta
C. Presence of the 'notch' in the uterine artery
D. Absent umbilical artery

Q.254 Consider the following

1. Reactive NST
2. Absence of deceleration
3. Sinusoidal pattern

Which of the above findings in an antepartum CTG indicate fetal well being :

A. 1 and 2 only
B. 2 and 3 only
C. 1 and 3 only
D. 1, 2 and 3

Q.255 In a female with appendicitis in pregnancy treatment of choice is:

A. Surgery at earliest
B. Abortion with appendectomy
C. Surgery after delivery
D. Continue pregnancy with medical Rx

Q.256 Regarding labia majora, all are correct except:

A. Is homologus to scrotum in males
B. Is supplied by branches of internal and external pudendal arteries
C. Drains into superficial inguinal lymph nodes
D. The broad ligament terminates at its anterior end

Q.257 The ovarian cycle is initiated by:

A. FSH
B. Estrogen
C. LH
D. Progesterone

Q.258 In PCOD which of the following drug is not used for infertility

A. Clomiphene
B. Tamoxifen
C. Spironolactone
D. Testosterone

Q.259 Regarding PCOS and hyperinsulinemia

A. Hyperinsulinemia is observed in about 40% to 80% of women with PCOS
B. Metformin has many other health benefits
C. Metformin causes hypoglycemia in normoglycaemic women
D. Hyperinsulinemia stimulates hepatic synthesis of SHBG

Q.260 About Mayer rokitansky Kuster Hauser syndrome

A. Uterus absent and ovaries present
B. Fallopian tubes are present
C. Typically ovaries are abnormal
D. Secondary sexual characters are not developed.

Q.261 Sensitivity of uterine musculature:

A. Enhanced by progesterone
B. Enhanced by estrogen
C. Inhibited by estrogen
D. Enhanced by estrogen and inhibited by progesterone

Q.262 Gonorrhea — which is not a presenting feature?

A. Hematuria
B. dysuria
C. Discharge
D. Reddened lips of vulva and vagina

Q.263 Postpartum VVF is best repaired after:

A. 6 weeks
B. 8 weeks
C. 3 months
D. 6 months

Q.264 Treatment of genuine stress incontinence:

a. Anterior colporrhaphy
b. Posterior colporrhaphy
c. colposuspension
d. Pelvic floor exercise
e. Sling operation

A. bce
B. bde
C. acde
D. abde

Q.265 Which is not an assisted reproduction technique:

A. GIFT
B. ZIFT
C. IVF and ET
D. Artificial insemination

Q.266 Not a barrier contraceptive:

A. Diaphragm
B. Centochroman
C. Condom
D. Today

Q.267 The most common cause of menorrhagia in the childbearing period:

A. Dysfunctional uterine bleeding
B. Fibroid
C. Pelvic endometriosis
D. Adenomyosis

Q.268 Stage-IIIB endometrial carcinoma true is/are:

a. Vaginal metastasis
b. Lymph node metastasis (paraaortic)
c. Pelvic lymph node involvement
d. Positive peritoneal cytology
e. Rectal invasion

A. c
B. ac
C. ab
D. ad

Q.269 The advantages of cryosurgery over electrocauterization are all except:

A. Less discomfort to the patient.
B. Postoperative bleeding is much less
C. Postoperative vaginal discharge is also much less
D. Cervical stenosis is extremely rare

Q.270 Corpus luteum cyst occurs due to:

A. HCG **B.** Progesterone
C. Estrogen **D.** None of the above

Q.271 A mother comes with her 3-year-old female child with the complaint that child is not eating anything. Her weight is 11 kg (50th percentile) and her height is 88 cm (75th percentile). What should be done next –

A. Vitamin rich tonic to be given
B. Forceful eating
C. Nothing should be done actively and assure the parent
D. Complete investigation for UTI

Q.272 Key features of kangaroo mother care are all the following except?

A. Skin to skin contact between mother and baby
B. Exclusive breast feeding
C. Done for babies with cyanosis
D. Initiated in a facility and continued at home

Q.273 True about fetal circulation –

A. Blood in SVC has more oxygen saturation
B. Pressure in left ventricle is more
C. Brain receives blood with low oxygen saturation
D. Heart receives blood with high oxygen saturation

Q.274 Approx 3-month-old child presents with irregular footer. what is the main reason of it? –

A. Laryngotracheobronchitis
B. Laryngomalacia
C. Respiratory obstruction
D. Foreign body aspiration

Q.275 Which of the following is not the most common renal cystic disease in infants, except ?

A. Polycystic kidney
B. Simple renal cyst
C. Unilateral renal dysplasia
D. Calyceal cyst

Q.276 A child comes with steroid-resistant nephrotic syndrome secondary to FSGS, not responsive to methylprednisolone. What next should be given –

A. Oral cyclophosphamide
B. Oral cyclosporine
C. Oral mycophenolate
D. IV cyclophosphamide

Q.277 Hypsarrhythmia in a child is due to –

A. Grandmal epilepsy **B.** Petitmal epilepsy
C. Myoclonic epilepsy **D.** Reflex epilepsy

Q.278 Common childhood tumors are –

a. Acute lymphoblastic leukemia
b. Chronic lymphoblastic leukemia
c. Chronic myeloid leukemia
d. Brain tumor
e. Wilm's tumor

A. ade **B.** bde **C.** abd **D.** ad

Q.279 The hair on end appearance is seen in X–ray skull in –

a. Thalassemia
b. Hydrocephalus
c. Chronic malaria
d. Sickle cell anemia

A. ad **B.** c **C.** ac **D.** ab

Q.280 Acute malnutrition is manifested by –

A. Weight for age **B.** Weight for height
C. Age for height **D.** Brocas index

Q.281 Adenoids are also called?

A. Nasopharyngeal tonsils
B. Palatine tonsils
C. Faucial tonsils
D. Lingual tonsils

Q.282 Otolith organs are involved with the role of?

A. Oculovestibular reflex
B. Rotary nystagmus
C. Linear acceleration
D. Angular acceleration

Q.283 Hyperacusis is caused by damage to?

A. Stapedius **B.** T. palati
C. T. tympani **D.** All

Q.284 Choana is -

A. Anterior nares **B.** Posterior nares
C. Tonsils **D.** Larynx

Q.285 Osteomeatal complex (OMC) connects-

A. Nasal cavity with maxillary sinus
B. Nasal cavity with sphenoid sinus
C. The two nasal cavities
D. Ethmoidal sinus with ethmoidal bulla

Q.286 Ethmoid bone forms A/E -

A. Superior turbinate **B.** Middle turbinate
C. Inferior turbinate **D.** Uncinate process

Q.287 Lyre sign in seen in-

A. Grave's disease
B. Meniere's disease
C. Lateral sinus thrombosis
D. Carotid body tumour

Q.288 Alternative for SMR -

A. Tympanoplasty
B. Septoplasty
C. Caldwell Luc operation
D. Turboplasty

Q.289 Passavant's ridge is formed by

A. Superior constrictor and palatopharyngeus
B. Inferior constrictor and palatopharyngeus
C. Superior constrictor and palatoglossus
D. Inferior constrictor and palatoglossus

Q.290 In which of the following locations there is a collection of pus in quinsy -

A. Peritonsillar space

B. Parapharyngeal space
C. Retropharyngeal space
D. Within the tonsil

Q.291 Avascular structure of the eye is -
A. Conjuctiva **B.** Cornea
C. Ciliary body **D.** Retina

Q.292 Visual axis is –
A. Center of cornea to retina
B. Object to fovea
C. Center of lens to cornea
D. None

Q.293 Which of the following is seen in chronic contact lens wearer:
A. Inclusion Conjuntivitis
B. Giant papillary Conjunctivitis
C. Vernal keratoconjuntivitis
D. Follicular conjunctivitis

Q.294 Satellite nodules are seen in –
A. Fungal corneal ulcer
B. Tuberculosis
C. Sarcoidosis
D. Viral ulcer

Q.295 Chorioretinitis is caused by –
A. Toxoplasmosis **B.** CMV
C. Oncocerca volvulus **D.** All of the above

Q.296 Treatment of choice for congenital cataract is –
A. Pharmacotherapy
B. Combined cataract surgery and Goniotomy
C. Cataract surgery
D. Pars plana lensectomy with no IOL implant

Q.297 Which of the following is primary glaucoma –
a. Juvenile glaucoma
b. Steroid-induced glaucoma
c. Pigmentary glaucoma
d. Congenital glaucoma
e. Infantile glaucoma
A. ade **B.** bde **C.** abd **D.** ad

Q.298 Cotton wool spots are commonly seen in –
a. AIDS
b. DM
c. Hypertension
d. CMV
A. ab **B.** bc **C.** acd **D.** abc

Q.299 In Holmes-Adie pupil all are true except -
A. There is absent or retarded pupil reactions to light and near
B. Most cases are bilateral
C. Causes reduced or absent accommodation
D. Constricts with 2.5% methacholine

Q.300 III nerve palsy causes all of the following except -
A. Ptosis
B. Mydriasis
C. Medial deviation of eyeball
D. Pupillary reflex lost

// Smart Answer Sheet //

Correct — Percentage of students who answered correctly. Skipped — Percentage of students who skipped.

Q.	Ans.	Correct	Skipped	Q.	Ans.	Correct	Skipped	Q.	Ans.	Correct	Skipped	Q.	Ans.	Correct	Skipped	Q.	Ans.	Correct	Skipped	Q.	Ans.	Correct	Skipped
1	A	35.0 %	3.33 %	22	A	23.33 %	63.34 %	43	D	15.0 %	65.0 %	64	B	15.0 %	61.67 %	85	D	23.33 %	61.67 %	106	A	18.33 %	61.67 %
2	A	16.67 %	58.33 %	23	D	16.67 %	61.66 %	44	D	11.67 %	65.0 %	65	A	31.67 %	63.33 %	86	B	20.0 %	61.67 %	107	C	23.33 %	61.67 %
3	A	30.0 %	60.0 %	24	D	11.67 %	61.66 %	45	C	16.67 %	63.33 %	66	D	25.0 %	63.33 %	87	A	20.0 %	61.67 %	108	D	25.0 %	61.67 %
4	A	25.0 %	58.33 %	25	C	10.0 %	63.33 %	46	B	23.33 %	63.34 %	67	B	10.0 %	63.33 %	88	B	16.67 %	61.66 %	109	A	13.33 %	61.67 %
5	C	16.67 %	58.33 %	26	D	16.67 %	61.66 %	47	D	15.0 %	63.33 %	68	C	26.67 %	61.66 %	89	A	31.67 %	61.66 %	110	C	15.0 %	61.67 %
6	A	18.33 %	58.34 %	27	A	18.33 %	61.67 %	48	A	26.67 %	63.33 %	69	D	30.0 %	61.67 %	90	A	15.0 %	61.67 %	111	A	16.67 %	63.33 %
7	A	18.33 %	58.34 %	28	B	23.33 %	60.0 %	49	D	20.0 %	63.33 %	70	D	18.33 %	61.67 %	91	A	33.33 %	61.67 %	112	B	20.0 %	61.67 %
8	C	11.67 %	60.0 %	29	C	33.33 %	61.67 %	50	D	21.67 %	65.0 %	71	B	16.67 %	63.33 %	92	D	20.0 %	61.67 %	113	B	11.67 %	61.66 %
9	B	16.67 %	61.66 %	30	C	15.0 %	63.33 %	51	A	33.33 %	58.34 %	72	A	35.0 %	61.67 %	93	D	10.0 %	63.33 %	114	C	25.0 %	61.67 %
10	B	8.33 %	63.34 %	31	A	15.0 %	61.67 %	52	A	16.67 %	61.66 %	73	B	13.33 %	63.34 %	94	B	23.33 %	61.67 %	115	A	20.0 %	61.67 %
11	A	25.0 %	63.33 %	32	B	16.67 %	61.66 %	53	D	26.67 %	60.0 %	74	D	11.67 %	65.0 %	95	D	10.0 %	65.0 %	116	B	8.33 %	63.34 %
12	A	20.0 %	60.0 %	33	C	18.33 %	61.67 %	54	B	28.33 %	60.0 %	75	D	33.33 %	61.67 %	96	D	30.0 %	61.67 %	117	A	23.33 %	61.67 %
13	C	15.0 %	61.67 %	34	B	21.67 %	63.33 %	55	D	20.0 %	61.67 %	76	C	21.67 %	61.66 %	97	C	18.33 %	61.67 %	118	B	28.33 %	61.67 %
14	C	30.0 %	60.0 %	35	A	16.67 %	61.66 %	56	D	35.0 %	60.0 %	77	A	23.33 %	61.67 %	98	C	23.33 %	63.34 %	119	C	16.67 %	63.33 %
15	D	18.33 %	63.34 %	36	A	26.67 %	63.33 %	57	D	13.33 %	60.0 %	78	C	11.67 %	61.66 %	99	D	30.0 %	61.67 %	120	B	18.33 %	63.34 %
16	D	21.67 %	63.33 %	37	B	18.33 %	63.34 %	58	B	26.67 %	60.0 %	79	B	16.67 %	63.33 %	100	D	13.33 %	63.34 %	121	A	36.67 %	61.66 %
17	D	30.0 %	61.67 %	38	D	16.67 %	61.66 %	59	B	30.0 %	60.0 %	80	D	11.67 %	63.33 %	101	B	26.67 %	61.66 %	122	C	11.67 %	63.33 %
18	D	11.67 %	61.66 %	39	B	26.67 %	61.66 %	60	C	33.33 %	61.67 %	81	C	18.33 %	63.34 %	102	D	21.67 %	61.66 %	123	A	31.67 %	61.66 %
19	B	10.0 %	63.33 %	40	A	20.0 %	63.33 %	61	D	25.0 %	61.67 %	82	A	31.67 %	61.66 %	103	A	28.33 %	61.67 %	124	B	15.0 %	63.33 %
20	C	11.67 %	63.33 %	41	C	25.0 %	63.33 %	62	A	25.0 %	61.67 %	83	D	13.33 %	63.34 %	104	D	13.33 %	61.67 %	125	B	25.0 %	61.67 %
21	B	30.0 %	61.67 %	42	C	18.33 %	63.34 %	63	A	33.33 %	61.67 %	84	A	18.33 %	61.67 %	105	C	33.33 %	61.67 %	126	D	31.67 %	61.66 %

Q.	Ans.	Correct	Skipped	Q.	Ans.	Correct	Skipped	Q.	Ans.	Correct	Skipped	Q.	Ans.	Correct	Skipped	Q.	Ans.	Correct	Skipped	Q.	Ans.	Correct	Skipped
127	B	21.67 %	63.33 %	148	D	18.33 %	63.34 %	169	D	28.33 %	60.0 %	190	D	30.0 %	60.0 %	211	A	30.0 %	63.33 %	232	A	16.67 %	65.0 %
128	B	16.67 %	61.66 %	149	B	11.67 %	61.66 %	170	B	35.0 %	60.0 %	191	A	20.0 %	61.67 %	212	C	15.0 %	63.33 %	233	C	15.0 %	61.67 %
129	D	16.67 %	61.66 %	150	A	25.0 %	63.33 %	171	B	21.67 %	60.0 %	192	D	28.33 %	60.0 %	213	A	26.67 %	61.66 %	234	B	16.67 %	63.33 %
130	C	8.33 %	65.0 %	151	C	21.67 %	58.33 %	172	C	13.33 %	60.0 %	193	A	15.0 %	60.0 %	214	D	21.67 %	63.33 %	235	C	8.33 %	63.34 %
131	B	6.67 %	66.66 %	152	D	20.0 %	61.67 %	173	C	16.67 %	60.0 %	194	A	13.33 %	61.67 %	215	D	21.67 %	63.33 %	236	B	20.0 %	63.33 %
132	C	25.0 %	61.67 %	153	B	23.33 %	60.0 %	174	D	6.67 %	60.0 %	195	C	25.0 %	60.0 %	216	D	30.0 %	61.67 %	237	A	28.33 %	63.34 %
133	C	8.33 %	65.0 %	154	D	31.67 %	60.0 %	175	C	21.67 %	60.0 %	196	C	10.0 %	60.0 %	217	A	16.67 %	63.33 %	238	C	8.33 %	65.0 %
134	B	20.0 %	61.67 %	155	C	25.0 %	60.0 %	176	A	8.33 %	60.0 %	197	B	31.67 %	61.66 %	218	D	8.33 %	61.67 %	239	C	18.33 %	63.34 %
135	C	16.67 %	61.66 %	156	C	3.33 %	60.0 %	177	B	8.33 %	61.67 %	198	D	21.67 %	60.0 %	219	A	21.67 %	61.66 %	240	D	18.33 %	65.0 %
136	D	23.33 %	63.34 %	157	C	18.33 %	61.67 %	178	A	23.33 %	60.0 %	199	B	13.33 %	63.34 %	220	D	6.67 %	61.66 %	241	B	25.0 %	63.33 %
137	D	23.33 %	61.67 %	158	A	20.0 %	60.0 %	179	B	15.0 %	60.0 %	200	B	20.0 %	63.33 %	221	D	20.0 %	63.33 %	242	B	23.33 %	63.34 %
138	B	21.67 %	61.66 %	159	C	6.67 %	60.0 %	180	A	33.33 %	60.0 %	201	A	21.67 %	63.33 %	222	B	8.33 %	63.34 %	243	D	15.0 %	65.0 %
139	C	11.67 %	63.33 %	160	B	23.33 %	60.0 %	181	A	28.33 %	60.0 %	202	D	25.0 %	63.33 %	223	D	21.67 %	63.33 %	244	D	3.33 %	63.34 %
140	D	20.0 %	61.67 %	161	B	21.67 %	60.0 %	182	C	21.67 %	61.66 %	203	B	28.33 %	61.67 %	224	A	13.33 %	63.34 %	245	A	11.67 %	63.33 %
141	C	26.67 %	61.66 %	162	B	13.33 %	63.34 %	183	D	30.0 %	60.0 %	204	B	25.0 %	61.67 %	225	D	23.33 %	61.67 %	246	B	6.67 %	63.33 %
142	C	15.0 %	65.0 %	163	B	23.33 %	60.0 %	184	B	18.33 %	60.0 %	205	C	21.67 %	61.66 %	226	B	13.33 %	63.34 %	247	C	30.0 %	63.33 %
143	C	23.33 %	61.67 %	164	D	11.67 %	61.66 %	185	B	16.67 %	60.0 %	206	A	15.0 %	63.33 %	227	D	21.67 %	61.66 %	248	D	21.67 %	63.33 %
144	A	28.33 %	61.67 %	165	D	20.0 %	60.0 %	186	A	23.33 %	60.0 %	207	A	23.33 %	61.67 %	228	D	15.0 %	63.33 %	249	C	5.0 %	63.33 %
145	C	20.0 %	65.0 %	166	B	20.0 %	60.0 %	187	C	15.0 %	60.0 %	208	B	18.33 %	61.67 %	229	A	20.0 %	61.67 %	250	B	18.33 %	63.34 %
146	A	20.0 %	65.0 %	167	A	10.0 %	61.67 %	188	B	16.67 %	60.0 %	209	B	11.67 %	61.66 %	230	A	10.0 %	65.0 %	251	B	21.67 %	63.33 %
147	A	35.0 %	63.33 %	168	C	18.33 %	63.34 %	189	D	31.67 %	61.66 %	210	A	20.0 %	61.67 %	231	C	33.33 %	61.67 %	252	A	15.0 %	65.0 %

Q.	Ans.	Correct	Skipped	Q.	Ans.	Correct	Skipped	Q.	Ans.	Correct	Skipped	Q.	Ans.	Correct	Skipped	Q.	Ans.	Correct	Skipped	Q.	Ans.	Correct	Skipped
253	B	16.67 %	65.0 %	261	D	18.33 %	65.0 %	269	C	10.0 %	65.0 %	277	C	16.67 %	66.66 %	285	A	20.0 %	66.67 %	293	B	15.0 %	68.33 %
254	A	21.67 %	63.33 %	262	A	20.0 %	63.33 %	270	A	13.33 %	63.34 %	278	A	21.67 %	66.66 %	286	C	8.33 %	66.67 %	294	A	21.67 %	68.33 %
255	A	20.0 %	63.33 %	263	C	6.67 %	63.33 %	271	C	18.33 %	63.34 %	279	A	25.0 %	66.67 %	287	D	16.67 %	66.66 %	295	D	18.33 %	68.34 %
256	D	20.0 %	63.33 %	264	C	6.67 %	65.0 %	272	C	25.0 %	63.33 %	280	B	23.33 %	66.67 %	288	B	15.0 %	66.67 %	296	C	8.33 %	68.34 %
257	A	15.0 %	63.33 %	265	D	16.67 %	63.33 %	273	D	10.0 %	66.67 %	281	A	30.0 %	66.67 %	289	A	23.33 %	68.34 %	297	A	21.67 %	70.0 %
258	C	10.0 %	63.33 %	266	B	18.33 %	63.34 %	274	B	13.33 %	66.67 %	282	C	8.33 %	66.67 %	290	A	18.33 %	68.34 %	298	D	13.33 %	70.0 %
259	B	13.33 %	65.0 %	267	A	15.0 %	63.33 %	275	C	6.67 %	65.0 %	283	A	23.33 %	66.67 %	291	B	28.33 %	66.67 %	299	B	6.67 %	70.0 %
260	A	20.0 %	65.0 %	268	D	8.33 %	65.0 %	276	B	11.67 %	65.0 %	284	B	23.33 %	66.67 %	292	B	8.33 %	70.0 %	300	C	10.0 %	68.33 %

//Hints and Solutions//

1. Option (A) is correct because in median nerve injury at the wrist, low median nerve injury is what occurs. That means only the thenar muscles are affected. The features shown in this condition include- pen test for abductor pollicis brevis paralysis, opposition and abduction of thumb is lost, ape thumb deformity may be shown and loss of sensation of lateral 2/3rd of palm and lateral three and a half fingers may be seen.

Option (B) is incorrect because an ulnar claw, also known as claw hand, or 'Spinster's Claw' is a deformity or an abnormal attitude of the hand that develops due to ulnar nerve damage causing paralysis of the lumbricals.

Option (C) is incorrect as Radial nerve palsy is a condition that affects the radial nerve and if damage to this nerve occurs, weakness, numbness and an inability to control the muscles served by this nerve may result.

Option (D) is incorrect because Axillary nerve palsy is a neurological condition in which the axillary (also called circumflex) nerve has been damaged by shoulder dislocation. It can cause weak deltoid and sensory loss below the shoulder. Since this is a problem with just one nerve, it is a type of Peripheral neuropathy called mononeuropathy.

Hence, the correct option is (A).

2. Option (A) is correct as Froment's sign is tested for Ulnar nerve injury, by holding a book between the thumb and other fingers. When an ulnar nerve injury is there, adductor pollicis and first palmar interossei are paralysed. This cause the flexor pollicis longus to function while holding the book in a prominent manner of flexion.

Option (B) is incorrect as signs of a median nerve lesion include weak pronation of the forearm, weak flexion and radial deviation of the wrist, with thenar atrophy and inability to oppose or flex the thumb; - the sensory distribution includes thumb, radial 2 and 1/2 fingers, and the corresponding portion of the palm.

Option (C) is incorrect because symptoms of the radial nerve injury may include a sharp or burning pain, as well as unusual sensations in your thumb and fingers. It's common to experience numbness, tingling, and trouble straightening your arm. You may also find that you can't extend or straighten your wrist and fingers.

Option (D) is incorrect because the most common neurologic complication due to axillary dissection is the intercostobrachial nerve syndrome, characterized by fairly constant paresthesias and dull, aching, or burning pain of the upper arm, shoulder, and axilla, and occasionally of the more anterior chest wall.
Hence, the correct option is (A).

3. Option (A) is correct as Ulnar nerve injury causes

- Paralysis of all interossei
- Medial two lumbricals paralysis
- Hypothenar muscles paralysis
- Adductor pollicis paralysis
- Flexor carpi ulnaris paralysis
- Medial two slips of flexor digitorum profundus paralysis
- Ulnar claw hand

Option (B) is incorrect because causes of radial nerve injury include

- fracturing your humerus, a bone in the upper arm.
- sleeping with your upper arm in an awkward position.
- pressure from leaning your arm over the back of a chair.
- using crutches improperly.
- falling on or receiving a blow to your arm.
- long-term constriction of your wrist.

Option (C) is incorrect because most traumatic brachial plexus injuries occur when the arm is forcefully pulled or stretched. Many events can cause the injury, including falls, motor vehicle collisions, knife and gunshot wounds, and most commonly, motorcycle collisions.

Option (D) is incorrect because an axillary nerve injury is characterised by trauma to the axillary nerve: from either a compressive force, a traction injury following anterior dislocation of the shoulder, or a forced abduction movement of the shoulder joint. An axillary nerve injury can cause signs and symptoms of a localized neuropathy.
Hence, the correct option is (A).

4. Option (A) is correct as Lymph nodes of Cloquet/Rosenmuller, Lymphatics, fat, areolar tissue comes under the Medial compartment of the Femoral canal (Femoral sheath).

Option (B) is incorrect because the femoral artery comes under the Lateral compartment of the Femoral canal (Femoral sheath).

Option (C) is incorrect as femoral vein comes under the Intermedius compartment of the Femoral canal (Femoral sheath).

Option (D) is incorrect because the femoral branch of the genitofemoral nerve is also a part of the Lateral compartment of the Femoral canal (Femoral sheath).

Hence, the correct option is (A).

5. Option (C) is correct because, on the medial aspect of the middle third of the thigh, there is an intermuscular cleft known as adductor canal, which lies beneath the Sartorius's muscle. This contains

- Femoral artery
- Femoral vein
- Nerve to vastus medialis
- The posterior division of obturator nerve (Occasional)
- Descending genicular artery
- Saphenous nerve

Option (A) is incorrect as the gracilis origin is located just superficially behind the adductor longus origin. The broad origin of the gracilis is then outlined over the pubic tuberosity with a lateral half of thin tendinous aponeurosis and medial half of thick muscle.

Option (B) is incorrect as the adductor longus muscle lies in front of the adductor Magnus, adductor brevis muscle, the anterior branch of the obturator nerve, and profunda femoris vessels. The pectineus muscle is lateral to it while gracilis lies medially.

Option (D) is incorrect because the Muscles of the Anterior Aspect of the Thigh Four muscles; rectus femoris, vastus lateralis, vastus intermedius and vastus medialis, make up the muscle usually referred to as the quadriceps femoris.

Hence, the correct option is (C).

6. Option (A) is correct as Ascending aorta lies anterior to the transverse sinus.

Option (B) is incorrect as the pulmonary trunk also lies at the anterior of the transverse sinus but it lies behind the aorta.

Option (C) is incorrect as the inferior vena cava (IVC) is the largest vein of the human body. It is located at the posterior abdominal wall on the right side of the aorta.

Option (D) is incorrect because the Superior vena cava, atria lies to the posterior of the transverse sinus.

Hence, the correct option is (A).

7. Option (A) is correct because no valve divides the superior vena cava from the right atrium. Hence, this is the required answer.

Option (B) is incorrect because the Eustachian valve of the Rudimentary semilunar valve is responsible for the opening of the Inferior vena cava to the right atrium. So, this is not the required answer.

Option (C) is incorrect because the Thebesian valve of the Incomplete semicircular valve is responsible for the opening of the Coronary sinus to the right atrium. So, this is not the required answer.

Option (D) is incorrect as the Tricuspid valve is responsible for the opening of AV opening to the Right atrium. So, this is also not the required answer.

Hence, the correct option is (A).

8. Option (C) is correct as the location of the sphincter urethra is at the Membranous part.

Option (A) is incorrect as the nerve supply to the male urethra is derived from the prostatic plexus, which contains a mixture of sympathetic, parasympathetic and visceral afferent fibres.

Option (B) is incorrect as the bulbar urethra lies between the penoscrotal junction and membranous urethra, which includes external urethral sphincter.

Option (D) is incorrect as the penile (spongy) urethra is the longest part of the male urethra.

Hence, the correct option is (C).

9. Option (B) is correct because the order of structures in the hilum of a kidney, from anterior to posterior is :

Renal vein, renal artery, and renal pelvis.

Option (A) is incorrect as renal artery comes at second number in the order. So, this is not the right answer.

Option (C) is incorrect because it also does not represent the correct order of structures in the hilum of a kidney, from anterior to posterior as renal pelvis comes at the last position in the order.

Option (D) is incorrect as the correct order is defined in the option (B). So, this option is not true.

Hence, the correct option is (B).

10. Option (B) is correct because this is not true about Sternberg Canal as we have studied in the above explanation that it is located anterior and medial to Foramen rotundum. Hence, this is the required answer.

Option (A) is incorrect because it lies anterior and medial to foramen rotadum in parasellar region in the middle cranial fossa. So, this is not the required answer.

Option (C) is incorrect because it is caused by incomplete fusion of greater wing of sphenoid with presphenoid at a point where primordial sphenoid portions fuse. So, this is also not the required answer.

Option (D) is incorrect because it is clinically associated with Congenital intrasphenoid meningocele (& encephalocele). Hence, this is also not the required answer.

Hence, the correct option is (B).

11. Option (A) is correct as the joints in the skull are mostly sutures. Suture are fibrous joints which offer no mobility. Lambdoid suture present between the occipital and two parietal bones.

Option (B) is incorrect as Saggital suture is present in the median plane between two parietal bones.

Option (C) is incorrect because Coronal suture is present between the frontal bone and two parietal bones.

Option (D) is incorrect as Metopic suture is present in 3 to 8% of the population; separates 2 halves of the frontal bone.

Hence, the correct option is (A).

12. Option (A) is correct as Falx cerebri contains:

- Superior sagittal sinus
- Inferior sagittal sinus
- Straight sinus

Option (B) is incorrect as Falx Cerebelli that contains Occipital sinus.

Option (C) is incorrect as Tentorium Cerebelli that contains :

- Transverse sinuses
- Superior petrosal sinuses

Option (D) is incorrect as Diaphragma sellae that contains both the Anterior and posterior intercavernous sinus.
Hence, the correct option is (A).

13. Option (C) is correct because the greater auricular nerve (GAN) supplies the main innervation to the anterior portion of the external ear. The auriculotemporal nerve (ATN) also supplies the tragus and helical crus regions while the mastoid branch of the lesser occipital nerve (LON) supplies innervation to most of the posterior surface of the ear. So, this is the required answer.

Option (A) is incorrect as Anterior ethmoidal supplies the anterior cranial fossa. So, this is not the required answer.

Option (B) is incorrect because Posterior ethmoidal is also used in the major supply of anterior cranial fossa. Hence, this is also not the required answer.

Option (D) is incorrect as Nervus meninges medius (a branch of the maxillary nerve), and nervus spinosus (a branch of the mandibular nerve) also used in the supply of the anterior cranial fossa. So, this is also not the required answer.

Hence, the correct option is (C).

14. Option (C) is correct because the vagina is lined by non-keratinized stratified squamous epithelium. The epithelial cells accumulate glycogen as they approach the surface.

Option (A) is incorrect because the respiratory airways are lined by a pseudostratified columnar epithelium with a variety of distinct cell types including ciliated and goblet cells that play crucial roles in mucociliary clearance and host defence.

Option (B) is incorrect as Keratinized cells are specially structured to be waterproof and reduce evaporation from underlying tissues and are therefore an important part of the epidermis or external skin.

Option (D) is incorrect because Ciliated columnar epithelium moves mucus and other substances via cilia and is found in the upper respiratory tract, the fallopian tubes, the uterus, and the central part of the spinal cord. They are the primary target of infection for "common cold viruses" such as coronaviruses, influenza virus and rhinoviruses.

Hence, the correct option is (C).

15. Option (D) is correct because Trachea is lined by Pseudostratified columnar epithelium.

Option (A) is incorrect as the pharynx is lined by non-keratinised squamous stratified epithelium.

Option (B) is incorrect because Respiratory epithelium, or airway epithelium, is a type of ciliated columnar epithelium found lining most of the respiratory tract as respiratory mucosa, where it serves to moisten and protect the airways.

Option (C) is incorrect as the inner lining of the colon and small intestine is a simple columnar epithelium constantly renewed by the proliferation of stem cells residing within pockets, or crypts, along the intestinal wall.

Hence, the correct option is (D).

16. Option (D) is correct as Blastocyst possesses an inner cell mass called embryoblast which subsequently forms the embryo proper, and an outer layer of cells, or trophoblast, which helps to provide nutrition to the embryo.

Option (A) is incorrect because it forms on the dorsal (back) face of the developing embryo, toward the caudal or posterior end.

Option (B) is incorrect because the yolk sac is situated on the front (ventral) part of the embryo; it is lined by extra-embryonic endoderm, outside of which is a layer of extra-embryonic mesenchyme, derived from the epiblast.

Option (C) is incorrect as Embryo proper is the inner cell mass of the blastocyst.

Hence, the correct option is (D).

17. Option (D) is correct as the diaphragm is formed from the following components

Septum transversum

Pleuroperitoneal membranes

As the point covers both the option (A) and (C).

Option (A) is incorrect even though Septum Transversum is used as a component in the development of the diaphragm as in case of option having more true values, going for an option with individual true value will not be considered as the correct answer.

Option (B) is incorrect as the pleuropericardial membranes are fibro-serous walls that separate the pericardial and pleural cavities and anchor the heart inside the mediastinum.

Option (C) is incorrect for the same reason as of option (A) because Pleuroperitoneal membranes are also used in the development of the diaphragm.

Hence, the correct option is (D).

18. Option (D) is correct because Galactosyl transferase is the markers of the Golgi apparatus.

Option (A) is incorrect as 5'-nucleotidase is one of the markers of the plasma membrane. So, this is not the required answer.

Option (B) is incorrect as Adenylyl cyclase is the markers of the plasma membrane. So, this is also not the required answer.

Option (C) is incorrect as Na^+-K^+-ATPase is also one of the markers of the plasma membrane. Hence, this is also not the required answer.

Hence, the correct option is (D).

19. Option (B) is correct as the transmembrane proteins have outer and inner ends which are hydrophilic and a core which is hydrophobic.

So the transmembrane region of the protein is hydrophobic.

Option (A) is incorrect as it is similar to the lipid bilayer, i.e. it has a hydrophobic core.

Option (C) is incorrect because disulfide bonds formed between a pair of oxidized cysteines are important to the structural integrity and proper folding of many proteins.

Option (D) is incorrect because two essential amino acids found in transmembrane, tryptophan and tyrosine, whose side chain contain aromatic structures contribute to the hydrophobicity of helix-bundle membrane protein.

Hence, the correct option is (B).

20. Option (C) is correct because, in the case of membrane proteins, they are able to undergo rotational and lateral movement. However, there is no transverse movement of proteins between the leaflets.

Option (A) is incorrect as lipids are irregularly distributed between the two leaflets. The phospholipids in the plasma membrane are arranged in two layers, called a phospholipid bilayer. Each phospholipid molecule has a head and two tails. The head "loves" water (hydrophilic) and the tails "hate" water (hydrophobic).

Option (B) is incorrect as lipids are irregularly distributed between the two leaflets, thus causing lipid asymmetry, or within the same leaflet, forming a lipid microdomain.

Option (D) is incorrect as option (C) is true about the cell membrane that proteins are displaced laterally in the cell membrane.

Hence, the correct option is (C).

21. Option (B) is correct because axon hillock was the usual site of initiation of action potentials—the trigger zone. It is now thought that the earliest site of action potential initiation is at the initial segment: just between the peak of the axon hillock and the initial (unmyelinated) segment of the axon.

Option (A) is incorrect because axon and initial segment both are the part of the correct answer for this question, so we cannot select only one answer. That's why option A will be incorrect.

Option (C) is incorrect because the soma is the starting point for these protein highways in the cell. The microtubules run down the length of the axon to bring it important supplies, like the neurotransmitters that are used to send signals between neurons.

Option (D) is incorrect because some studies have indicated a role for the dendrites in the process of spike initiation.

Hence, the correct option is (B).

22. Option (A) is correct because an orthodromic impulse runs along an axon in its normal or anterograde direction, away from the soma. In the heart, orthodromic may also refer to an impulse going in the correct direction from the dendrites to axon terminal (from the atria to the ventricles) in contrast to some impulses in re-entry.

Option (B) is incorrect because of unidirectional conduction of an action potential due to transient inactivation of voltage-gated Na^+ channels. At time 0, an action potential (purple) is at the 2-mm position on the axon. The membrane depolarization spreads passively in both directions along the axon.

Option (C) is incorrect because, in myelinated axons, APs appear to "jump" from node to node, in a process called Saltatory conduction, because no depolarization occurs between the nodes.

Option (D) is incorrect because spike potentials are one of the action potentials, which occur in the electrical activity of smooth muscle contraction in animals.

Hence, the correct option is (A).

23. Option (D) is correct because pseudounipolar cells are a type of bipolar cell in which a single process divides into two axons and one goes to the organ (skin or muscle) and other to the spinal cord. This is seen in dorsal root ganglia.

Option (A) is incorrect because low numbers of small neurons [small, intensely fluorescent (SIF) cells] and approximately 5% cholinergic cells are present in the superior cervical sympathetic ganglion (SCG).

Option (B) is incorrect because the parasympathetic nervous system consists of cells with bodies in one of two locations: the brainstem or the sacral spinal cord.

Option (C) is incorrect as among vertebrates there are three major groups of ganglia: Dorsal root ganglia (also known as the spinal ganglia) contain the cell bodies of sensory (afferent) neurons. Cranial nerve ganglia contain the cell bodies of cranial nerve neurons. Autonomic ganglia contain the cell bodies of autonomic nerves.

Hence, the correct option is (D).

24. Option (D) is correct because a protein found in cardiac muscle, called phospholamban (PLB) has been shown to prevent SERCA from working. It does this by binding to the SERCA and decreasing its attraction (affinity) to calcium, therefore preventing calcium uptake into the SR. Failure to remove Ca^{+2} from the cytosol prevents muscle relaxation and therefore means that there is a decrease in muscle contraction too.

Option (A) is incorrect because when calcium is added to or removed from the cytoplasm by transport across the cell membrane or sarcoplasmic reticulum, calcium buffers minimize the effect on changes in cytoplasmic free calcium concentration by binding calcium to or releasing calcium from intracellular proteins.

Option (B) is incorrect because, in the peripheral nervous system, ACh is the neurotransmitter at the neuromuscular junction between the motor nerve and skeletal muscle. In the central nervous system, ACh is found primarily in interneurons, and a few important long-axon cholinergic pathways have also been identified.

Option (C) is incorrect because chest indrawing, as defined by the WHO IMCI guidelines, is the abnormal inward movement of subcostal tissue (ie, the tissue inferior to the costal cartilage of the lower anterior chest wall) during inspiration and in children, chest indrawing often occurs during respiratory diseases with poorly compliant, or "stiff," lungs.

Hence, the correct option is (D).

25. Option (C) is correct because the amplitude of action potential cannot be increased as it follows 'All or none' law. The shape of the action potential is stereotyped; this means that the rise and fall usually have approximately the same amplitude and time course for all action potentials in a given cell. In most neurons, the entire process takes place in about a thousand of a second. Many types of neurons emit action potentials constantly at rates of up to 10–100 per second. However, some types are much quieter and may go for minutes or longer without emitting any action potentials.

Option (A) is incorrect as if more force is needed, then fast oxidative–glycolytic fibres are also stimulated. In order to reach maximum force the help of fast glycolytic fibres is enlisted together with SO and FOG fibres. Maximum force occurs when all motor units of muscle are stimulated and all muscle fibres are contracting.

Option (B) is incorrect as motor unit recruitment refers to the activation of additional motor units to accomplish an increase in contractile strength in a muscle. A motor unit consists of one motor neuron and all of the muscle fibres it stimulates. The activation of one motor neuron will result in a weak but distributed muscle contraction.

Option (D) is incorrect because motor unit recruitment refers to the activation of additional motor units to accomplish an increase in contractile strength in a muscle. The higher the recruitment the stronger the muscle contraction will be.

Hence, the correct option is (C).

26. Option (D) is correct because the release of Ca^{++} from intracellular source, that is sarcoplasmic reticulum, is by IP3-DAG second messenger system, whereas the pumping of Ca^{++} from extracellular space to the cytosol is by Ca^{++} channels. IP3 when bound to its receptors on the sarcoplasmic reticulum, causes the release of calcium into the sarcoplasm.

Option (A) is incorrect because cAMP is a second messenger, used for intracellular signal transduction, such as transferring into cells the effects of hormones like glucagon and adrenaline, which cannot pass through the plasma membrane. It is also involved in the activation of protein kinases. In addition, cAMP binds to and regulates the function of ion channels such as the HCN channels and a few other cyclic nucleotide-binding proteins such as Epac1 and RAPGEF2.

Option (B) is incorrect because cGMP is a common regulator of ion channel conductance, glycogenolysis, and cellular apoptosis. It also relaxes smooth muscle tissues. In blood vessels, relaxation of vascular smooth muscles leads to vasodilation and increased blood flow. cGMP is a secondary messenger in phototransduction in the eye.

Option (C) is incorrect because CCMP is an enhanced data cryptographic encapsulation mechanism designed for data confidentiality and based upon the Counter Mode with CBC-MAC (CCM mode) of the Advanced Encryption Standard (AES) standard. It was created to address the vulnerabilities presented by Wired Equivalent Privacy (WEP), a dated, insecure protocol.

Hence, the correct option is (D).

27. Option (A) is correct as in patients with pulmonary emphysema, lung tissue loss induces a decrease in elastic recoil that is associated with an increase in total lung capacity (TLC), the lung volume at which CT images are obtained after maximal inspiration.

Option (B) is incorrect because restrictive lung diseases are a result of processes that restrict pulmonary expansion. These can be an intrinsic disease such as pulmonary fibrosis and sarcoidosis, or extrinsic processes like kyphosis and morbid obesity. In either case, the result is a restricted expansion, decreased lung volumes, and inadequate ventilation. In the case of RLD, the TLC, FRC, and RV will all be decreased.

Option (C) is incorrect as if reversibility of the Obstructive Defect is present, the physician should determine if the disease is reversible based on the increase in FEV_1 or FVC after bronchodilator treatment.

Option (D) is incorrect because the vital capacity can be used to help differentiate the causes of lung disease. In restrictive lung disease, the vital capacity is decreased. In obstructive lung disease, it is usually normal or only slightly decreased. Vital capacity increases with height and decreases with age.

Hence, the correct option is (A).

28. Option (B) is correct because the intrapleural pressure becomes more negative at the end of inspiration and less negative at expiration. It ranges between -3 and -6 mmHg. At the beginning of inspiration, the pressure is -3.8mmHg (-5 cm of water), and at the end of inspiration (beginning of expiration), it is -6mmHg (-8 cm of water).

Option (A) is incorrect because the normal intrapleural pressure at the end of inspiration is -8cm of H_2O.

Option (C) is incorrect because the overall air resistance will be from 0.5-1.5cm of H_2O.

Option (D) is incorrect as in general, absolute zero pressure is the point where there exists a minimum temperature i.e. zero that can be possible only when the molecular momentum of a system becomes zero. There should not be any motion of particles so there is no collision of particles, kinetic energy nullifies and the temperature becomes zero. But there is no zero pressure seen anywhere.

Hence, the correct option is (B).

29. Option (C) is correct because the temperature of the body is determined by a 'thermostat' located in the hypothalamus. The setpoint of the hypothalamic thermostat is 37 °C but it can be reset.

Option (A) is incorrect because the pituitary gland is called the 'master gland' as the hormones it produces control so many different processes in the body. Through secretion of its hormones, the pituitary gland controls metabolism, growth, sexual maturation, reproduction, blood pressure, and many other vital physical functions and processes.

Option (B) is incorrect because the neuronal information processes necessary for motor control were proposed as a network involving the thalamus as a subcortical motor centre.

Option (D) is incorrect because basal ganglia are strongly interconnected with the cerebral cortex, thalamus, and brainstem, as well as several other brain areas. The basal ganglia are associated with a variety of functions, including control of voluntary motor movements, procedural learning, habit learning, eye movements, cognition, and emotion.

Hence, the correct option is (C).

30. Option (C) is correct because the opening of voltage-gated slow calcium channels results in the plateau phase of the action potential in the myocardium. These slow calcium channels are also called calcium- sodium channels.

Option (A) is incorrect because the action potential begins with the voltage becoming more positive; this is known as depolarization and is mainly due to the opening of sodium channels that allow Na^+ flowing into the cell.

Option (B) is incorrect because the main ions found outside the cell at rest are sodium (Na^+), and chloride (Cl^-), whereas inside the cell it is mainly potassium (K^+). After a delay (known as the absolute refractory period; see below), termination of the action potential then occurs, as potassium channels open, allowing K^+ to leave the cell and causing the membrane potential to return to negative, this is known as repolarization.

Option (D) is incorrect because, in the sinoatrial node, this phase is also due to the closure of the L-type calcium channels, preventing inward flux of Ca^{2+} and the opening of the rapid delayed rectifier potassium channels.

Hence, the correct option is (C).

31. Option (A) is correct because the rectal temperature is said to be the most accurate method for measuring the core temperature.

Option (B) is incorrect because the bladder and pulmonary artery temperatures almost always demonstrated a difference of only 0.1° C to 0.2° C, with bladder temperature being higher.

Option (C) is incorrect because Nasopharnyx can be used as a good substitute for the rectum.

Option (D) is incorrect as we know that rectum is the best answer for the given question. So, option (D) automatically get to be the wrong answer.

Hence, the correct option is (A).

32. Option (B) is correct because the filtration barriers in nephron are:

- Glomerular capillary endothelium
- Basement membrane
- The visceral epithelium of Bowman's capsule with podocytes

Option (A) is incorrect because podocytes are found lining the Bowman's capsules in the nephrons of the kidney. The foot processes known as pedicels that extend from the podocytes wrap themselves around the capillaries of the glomerulus to form the filtration slits.

Option (C) is incorrect because the glomerular filtration barrier has several layers. The first is a glycocalyx made up of proteoglycans and an adsorbed layer of plasma proteins that are located between the endothelial cells and the capillary lumen. Fenestrated endothelial cells form the next layer.

Option (D) is incorrect because the glomerular basement membrane (GBM) is the extracellular matrix component of the selectively permeable glomerular filtration barrier (GFB) that separates the vasculature from the urinary space. The GBM lies between and is initially synthesized by, the glomerular endothelial cells that line the glomerular capillaries and the podocytes (also called visceral epithelial cells) that sit on the opposite side of the GBM within the urinary space.

Hence, the correct option is (B).

33. Option (C) is correct because some non-dairy options include calcium-fortified orange juice, kale, soybeans, some varieties of tofu, canned sardines, and white beans. An 8-ounce glass of fortified orange juice contains about 30% of the recommended Daily Value of calcium, similar to an equal serving of milk.

Option (A) is incorrect because gastric acid, gastric juice, or sometimes known as stomach acid, is a digestive fluid formed in the stomach membrane and is composed of hydrochloric acid, potassium chloride, and sodium chloride.

Option (B) is incorrect because the concentration of potassium in the juices of these patients was uniformly high, averaging 129.95 mgm. percent.

Option (D) is incorrect because mean fasting levels in normal gastric juice were as follows: sodium 47.7 mM, potassium 14.6 mM, calcium 0.8 mM, magnesium 0.36 mM, zinc 13 microM, and copper 1.2 microM: these did not differ significantly in health or disease.

Hence, the correct option is (C).

34. Option (B) is correct as the secretions of the stomach are:

- HCl- Parietal cells/ Oxyntic cells
- The intrinsic factor of Castle- Parietal cells/ Oxyntic cells
- Gastrin- G cells
- Pepsinogen- Chief cells/ Peptic cells
- Somatostatin- D cells
- Histamine- ECL cells

Option (A) is incorrect because chief cells secrete digestive enzymes that cleave the proteins in food into smaller pieces. The main enzyme secreted by chief cells is pepsin. Pepsin is secreted as an inactive enzyme called pepsinogen.

Option (C) is incorrect because enterochromaffin-like (ECL) cells" are a population of cells that are found in the gastric pits of the stomach luminal epithelium and secrete histamine. In response to gastrin released by neighbouring G-cells, secreted histamine from ECL cells acts on parietal cells to stimulate the release of gastric acid.

Option (D) is incorrect because B cells, also known as B lymphocytes, are a type of white blood cell of the small lymphocyte subtype. They function in the humoral immunity component of the adaptive immune system by secreting antibodies.

Hence, the correct option is (B).

35. Option (A) is correct because "Atractyloside inhibits oxidative phosphorylation by inhibiting the transporter of ADP into and ATP out of the mitochondrion".

Option (B) is incorrect because oligomycin is an antibiotic that inhibits ATP synthase by blocking its proton channel (F_0 subunit), which is necessary for oxidative phosphorylation of ADP to ATP (energy production). The inhibition of ATP synthesis would also stop the electron transport chain.

Option (C) is incorrect because rotenone works by interfering with the electron transport chain in mitochondria. It inhibits the transfer of electrons from iron-sulfur centres in complex I to ubiquinone. This interferes with NADH during the creation of usable cellular energy (ATP).

Option (D) is incorrect because the cyanide anion is an inhibitor of the enzyme cytochrome c oxidase (also known as aa3) in the fourth complex of the electron transport chain (found in the membrane of the mitochondria of eukaryotic cells). The binding of cyanide to this enzyme prevents the transport of electrons from cytochrome to oxygen.

Hence, the correct option is (A).

36. Option (A) is correct because chymotrypsinogen is an inactive precursor (zymogen) of chymotrypsin, a digestive enzyme that breaks proteins down into smaller peptides. Chymotrypsinogen is a single polypeptide chain consisting of 245 amino acid residues. A good example of what occurs when some zymogens become active enzymes inside the cells is seen in acute pancreatitis, in which the premature activation of some of the pancreatic enzymes like trypsin, phospholipase A_2 and elastase, produce the autodigestion of pancreatic tissue.

Option (B) is incorrect because carboxypeptidase is an enzyme synthesized in the pancreas and secreted into the small intestine.

Option (C) is incorrect because transaminases or aminotransferases are enzymes that catalyze a transamination reaction between an amino acid and an α-keto acid. They are important in the synthesis of amino acids, which form proteins.

Option (D) is incorrect because in fibrinolysis, a fibrin clot, the product of coagulation, is broken down. Its main enzyme plasmin cuts the fibrin mesh at various places, leading to the production of circulating fragments that are cleared by other proteases or by the kidney and liver.

Hence, the correct option is (A).

37. Option (B) is correct because ribose is an aldopentose (a monosaccharide containing five carbon atoms) that, in its open-chain form, has an aldehyde functional group at one end.

Option (A) is incorrect because ribulose is a ketopentose — a monosaccharide containing five carbon atoms, and including a ketone functional group.

Option (C) is incorrect because D-Erythrulose (also known as erythrulose) is a tetrose carbohydrate with the chemical formula $C_4H_8O_4$. It has one ketone group and so is part of the ketose family. It is used in some self-tanning cosmetics, in general, combined with dihydroxyacetone (DHA).

Option (D) is incorrect as we know that option (B) is the most suited answer for the above question. So, option (D) will automatically get to be the wrong answer.

Hence, the correct option is (B).

38.

Option (D) is correct because phosphofructokinase catalyzes the committed step of glycolysis, meaning that once fructose 1, 6 - bisphosphate is formed it must go for the glycolytic pathway only.

Option (A) is incorrect because 2,3-Diphosphoglycerate (2,3-DPG) is a special intermediate of glycolysis in erythrocytes which is rapidly consumed under conditions of normal oxygen tension. However, when hypoxia is encountered in peripheral tissues, the concentration of 2,3-DPG can accumulate to significant levels within hours.

Option (B) is incorrect because glucokinase (EC 2.7. 1.2) is an enzyme that facilitates phosphorylation of glucose to glucose-6-phosphate. Glucokinase occurs in cells in the liver and pancreas of humans and most other vertebrates.

Option (C) is incorrect because a hexokinase is an enzyme that phosphorylates hexoses (six-carbon sugars), forming hexose phosphate. In most organisms, glucose is the most important substrate of hexokinases, and glucose-6-phosphate is the most important product.

Hence, the correct option is (D).

39. Option (B) is correct because glucose-6-phosphate is the metabolite which:-

Joins glycolysis with glycogenesis and glycogenolysis

Joins glycogenolysis to pentose phosphate pathway (PPP)

Is involved in glycolysis, glycogenesis and gluconeogenesis, glycogenolysis, gluconeogenesis, PPP.

Option (A) is incorrect because glycogen phosphorylase catalyzes the sequential phosphorolysis of glycogen to release glucose 1-phosphate; it is thus the key enzyme in the utilization of muscle and liver reserves of glycogen.

Option (C) is incorrect because uridine diphosphoglucose is an important cofactor of glycosylating enzymes. A simple and high yielding one-pot enzymatic synthesis of UDPG on a gram scale from glucose via hexokinase, phosphoglucomutase and UDPG pyrophosphorylase (UGPase) is described.

Option (D) is incorrect because catalyzes the hydrolysis of fructose 1,6-bisphosphate to fructose 6-phosphate in the presence of divalent cations, acting as a rate-limiting enzyme in gluconeogenesis.

Hence, the correct option is (B).

40. Option (A) is correct because the liver cannot utilize ketone bodies because it lacks enzyme succinyl-CoA-acetoacetate CoA transferase, which is required for the activation of ketone bodies.

Option (B) is incorrect because, in the brain, ketone bodies are also used to make acetyl-CoA into long-chain fatty acids. Ketone bodies are produced by the liver under the circumstances listed above, resultant of intense gluconeogenesis, which is the production of glucose from non-carbohydrate sources (including fatty acids).

Option (C) is incorrect because ketone bodies are oxidized as a fuel source during exercise, are markedly elevated during the post-exercise recovery period, and the ability to utilize ketone bodies is higher in exercise-trained skeletal muscle.

Option (D) is incorrect because ketone bodies can be utilized as a fuel in the heart, brain and muscle, but not the liver.

Hence, the correct option is (A).

41. Option (C) is correct as (Fatty acid synthesis) Cofactor requirements for fatty acid synthesis include NADPH, ATP, Mn^{+2}, biotin (a vitamin B) and HCO^{3-} (as a source of CO_2). NADPH is also required for the reductive synthesis of cholesterol and steroids.

Option (A) is incorrect because Gluconeogenesis (GNG) is a metabolic pathway that results in the generation of glucose from certain non-carbohydrate carbon substrates. From the breakdown of proteins, these substrates include glucogenic amino acids; from the breakdown of lipids, they include glycerol, odd-chain fatty acids; and from other steps, in metabolism, they include pyruvate and lactate.

Option (B) is incorrect because Glycolysis isthe process of breaking down glucose. Glycolysis can take place with or withoutoxygen. Glycolysis produces two molecules of pyruvate, two molecules of ATP, two molecules of NADH, and two moleculesof water.

Option (D) is incorrect because Glycogenolysis is the breakdown of glycogen (n) to glucose-1-phosphate and glycogen (n-1). Glycogen branches are catabolized by the sequential removal of glucose monomers via phosphorolysis, by the enzyme glycogen phosphorylase.

Hence, the correct option is (C).

42. Option (C) is correct as, among plant proteins, pulses are very rich in protein and provide many essential amino acids except methionine. Unlike lysine, which is the limiting amino acid for cereals, the limiting amino acids for pulses were found to be methionine.

Option (A) is incorrect because Lysine is an α-amino acid that is used in the biosynthesis of proteins. lysine are high-protein foods such as eggs, meat, soy, beans and peas, cheese, and certain fish.

Lysine is the limiting amino acid in most cereal grains but is plentiful in most pulses (legumes).

Option (B) is incorrect because Threonine is an amino acid that is used in the biosynthesis of proteins. It contains an α-amino group, a carboxyl group, and a side chain containing a hydroxyl group, making it a polar, uncharged amino acid.

Option (D) is incorrect as serine is a α-amino acid that is used in the biosynthesis of proteins. It contains an α-amino group, a carboxyl group, and a side chain consisting of a hydroxymethyl group, classifying it as a polar amino acid. It can be synthesized in the human body under normal physiological circumstances, making it a nonessential amino acid.

Hence, the correct option is (C).

43. Option (D) is correct because denatured proteins are often insoluble and, therefore, precipitate from solution. Denaturants are also useful in rendering soluble otherwise insoluble forms for proteins and can be used to dissolve aggregates.

Option (A) is incorrect because denaturation does not involve identical changes in protein molecules. A common property of denatured proteins, however, is the loss of biological activity—e.g., the ability to act as enzymes or hormones.

Option (B) is incorrect because the denaturation of proteins involves the disruption and possible destruction of both the secondary and tertiary structures. Since denaturation reactions are not strong enough to break the peptide bonds, the primary structure (sequence of amino acids) remains the same after a denaturation process.

Option (C) is incorrect because denaturation can be irreversible but only in extreme situations not always, like frying an egg.

Hence, the correct option is (D).

44. Option (D) is correct because, Menkes disease ("Kinky" or "steely" hair disease) is a disorder of copper metabolism due to mutations in the gene for a copper-binding P-type ATPase. Defective copper transport across plasma and endoplasmic reticulum membranes result in copper being unavailable for the synthesis of several copper-containing enzymes, including PROTEIN-LYSINE 6-OXIDASE; CERULOPLASMIN; and SUPEROXIDE DISMUTASE.

Option (A) is incorrect because Ceruloplasmin (or caeruloplasmin) is a ferroxidase enzyme that in humans is encoded by the CP gene. Serum ceruloplasmin is a test to check the symptoms of Wilson's disease. Wilson's disease is a rare genetic disorder that causes too much copper to collect in the liver, brain, and other body tissues and organs.

Option (B) is incorrect because, Serum copper is used to measuring the amount of copper in the blood, urine, or liver tissue; to help diagnose and monitor Wilson disease; sometimes to identify copper deficiency or excess.

Option (C) is incorrect because Ferrochelatase is the terminal enzyme of the heme biosynthetic pathway in all cells. It catalyzes the insertion of ferrous iron into protoporphyrin IX, yielding heme. Partially deficient ferrochelatase has been documented in bone marrow, reticulocytes, liver, cultured fibroblasts, and blood or leukocytes from patients with EPP.

Hence, the correct option is (D).

45. Option (C) is correct because the decrease in pyruvate utilization activity results in thiamine deficiency. Thiamine deficiency is a medical condition of low levels of thiamine. A severe and chronic form is known as beriberi.

Option (A) is incorrect because pernicious anaemia is a type of vitamin B_{12} anaemia. The body needs vitamin B_{12} to make red blood cells. Pernicious anaemia is a decrease in red blood cells that occurs when the intestines cannot properly absorb vitamin B_{12}.

Option (B) is incorrect because, scurvy is a disease resulting from a lack of vitamin C. Early symptoms of deficiency include weakness, feeling tired and sore arms and legs.

Option (D) is incorrect because pellagra is a disease caused by a lack of the vitamin niacin (vitamin B_3). Symptoms include inflamed skin, diarrhoea, dementia, and sores in the mouth. Areas of the skin exposed to either sunlight or friction are typically affected first.

Hence, the correct option is (C).

46. Attached to each sugar ring is a nucleotide base, one of the four bases Adenine (A), Guanine (G), Cytosine (C), and Thymine (T).

Option (B) is correct because (C-G pair forms three hydrogen bonds) Guanine pairs with cytosine with 3 hydrogen bonds. This creates a difference in strength between the two sets of Watson and Crick bases.

Option (A) is incorrect because (The A-T pair forms two hydrogen bonds) Adenine pairs with thymine with 2 hydrogen bonds.

Option (C) is incorrect because, in base pairing, adenine always pairs with thymine.

Option (D) is incorrect because, in base pairing, guanine always pairs with cytosine.

Hence, the correct option is (B).

47. Option (D) is correct because mRNA is a complimentary copy of the template strand (non-coding or antisense strand). mRNA strand is similar to the non-template (coding or sense) strand. Thus, both the DNA coding strand and mRNA are complementary to the template strand.

Option (A) is incorrect because transfer ribonucleic acid (tRNA) is a type of RNA molecule that helps decode a messenger RNA (mRNA) sequence into a protein. tRNAs function at specific sites in the ribosome during translation, which is a process that synthesizes a protein from an mRNA molecule.

Option (B) is incorrect because ribosomal ribonucleic acid (rRNA) is a noncoding type of RNA that acts as the primary building block for ribosomes and the assembly line on which protein synthesis occurs in those ribosomes, essential to all living organisms.

Option (C) is incorrect because ribosomal DNA (rDNA) is a DNA sequence that codes for ribosomal RNA. Ribosomes are assemblies of proteins and rRNA molecules that translate mRNA molecules to produce proteins.

Hence, the correct option is (D).

48. Option (A) is correct because Telomerase adds complementary RNA bases to the 3′ end of the DNA strand. Once the 3′ end of the lagging strand template is sufficiently elongated, DNA polymerase adds the complementary nucleotides to the ends of the chromosomes; thus, the ends of the chromosomes are replicated.

Option (B) is incorrect as the centromere is the specialized DNA sequence of a chromosome that links a pair of sister chromatids (a dyad). During mitosis, spindle fibres attach to the centromere via the kinetochore. Centromeres were first thought to be genetic loci that direct the behaviour of chromosomes.

Option (C) is incorrect because a restriction endonuclease is an enzyme that cuts the DNA molecule at, or near to, a specific nucleotide sequence to produce discrete DNA fragments that can be separated by gel electrophoresis.

Option (D) is incorrect because Exonucleases are enzymes that work by cleaving nucleotides one at a time from the end (Exo) of a polynucleotide chain. A hydrolyzing reaction that breaks phosphodiester bonds at either the 3' or the 5' end occurs.

Hence, the correct option is (A).

49. Option (D) is correct because Termination (stop/nonsense) codons signal to terminate the translation. Nonsense mutations show that any one of the three codons is sufficient to terminate protein synthesis within a gene. The UAG, UAA, and UGA triplet sequences are therefore necessary and sufficient to end protein synthesis, whether occurring naturally at the end of a gene or created by mutation within a coding sequence.

Option (A) is incorrect because Elongation of the polypeptide chain involves the addition of amino acids to the carboxyl end of the growing chain. The growing protein exits the ribosome through the polypeptide exit tunnel in the large subunit.

Option (B) is incorrect because Post-translational modification (PTM) refers to the covalent and generally enzymatic modification of proteins following protein biosynthesis. Proteins are synthesized by ribosomes translating mRNA into polypeptide chains, which may then undergo PTM to form the mature protein product.

Option (C) is incorrect because the protein synthetic machinery must select the appropriate starting points for mRNA reading and peptide bond formation. AUG is usually used as the starting codon, and essentially all proteins begin with a methionine. AUG is also the codon for methionine that occurs in the interior of a protein as well.

Hence, the correct option is (D).

50. Option (D) is correct because

- RFLP (Restriction fragment length polymorphism)
- It is a variation in the DNA sequences.
- In this, restriction endo nucleotides are used which cut the DNA into fragments, which all then are detected by southern blotting.
- In can be used for identification of the gene for genetic mapping.

Option (A) is incorrect because it is correct for restriction fragment gene, but individually it is incorrect.

Option (B) is incorrect because it is correct for restriction fragment gene, but individually it is incorrect.

Option (C) is incorrect because it is correct for restriction fragment gene, but individually it is incorrect.

Hence, the correct option is (D).

51. Option (A) is correct because the dead cell and its fragments are rapidly devoured before the contents have leaked out, and therefore cell death by this pathway does not elicit an inflammatory reaction in the host. Thus, no significant inflammation (unlike necrosis). Hence, this is the required answer.

Option (B) is incorrect as radiation causes apoptosis of tumours and surrounding tissue via free radical and dsDNA breakage. Hence, this is not the required answer.

Option (C) is incorrect because it commonly occurs in both apoptotic and necrotic cell death. For apoptosis, the nucleus usually undergoes condensation, chromatin marginalization and fragmentation into a few large and regular chromatin clumps, which are eventually packed into apoptotic bodies.

Option (D) is incorrect as it is characterized by deeply eosinophilic cytoplasm, cell shrinkage, nuclear shrinkage (pyknosis) and basophilia, membrane blebbing, nuclear fragmentation (karyorrhexis), and formation of apoptotic bodies, which are then phagocytosed. So, this is also not the required answer.

Hence, the correct option is (A).

52. Option (A) is correct because "Most wounds do not regain the full tensile strength of unwounded skin after healing is complete".

Option (B) is incorrect as the sutured wound has a tensile strength of 70% of unwounded skin largely because of placement of sutures When sutures are removed, usually at the end of the first week the wound strength is approximately 10% then there is a rapid gain of strength for next 4 weeks i.e. 1 month.

Option (C) is incorrect as it reaches a plateau of wound strength of about 70-80% of unwounded skin by 3rd month and persists at this level for life.

Option (D) is incorrect as we have explained it above that after gaining 70-80% of unwounded skin, it persists at this level for life. So, it will never regain the complete wound strength ever. Hence, this is also not true.

Hence, the correct option is (A).

53. Option (D) is correct as pulmonary embolism is a blockage in one of the pulmonary arteries in your lungs. As this is not related to the Virchow triad, this is the required answer.

Option (A) is incorrect as an endothelial injury is one of the primary influences predispose to thrombus formation. So, this is not the required answer.

Option (B) is incorrect as stasis or turbulence of blood flow or abnormal blood flow is one of the effects of Virchow triad. Hence, this is also not the required answer.

Option (C) is incorrect as Hypercoagulability or blood hypercoagulability - Robbins is also in one of the primary influence of the Virchow triad. Thus, it is not the required answer.

Hence, the correct option is (D).

54. Option (B) is correct as Mast cells are multifunctional bone marrow-derived tissue-dwelling cells that are the major producer of histamine in the body. H1R is expressed in many cells, including mast cells, and are involved in Type 1 hypersensitivity reactions.

Option (A) is incorrect as Eosinophils may modulate immediate hypersensitivity reactions by degrading or inactivating mediators released by mast cells, such as histamine, leukotrienes (which may cause vasoconstriction and bronchoconstriction), lysophospholipids, and heparin.

Option (C) is incorrect as human neutrophils are bona fide histamine-producing cells. Neutrophils store ~0.29 pg/cell and release ~50% of the histamine content in an antigen-dependent manner and on stimulation with other neutrophil agonists.

Option (D) is incorrect as Macrophages (M phi) produce histamine (Hm) when activated by bacterial endotoxin (LPS) through induced histidine decarboxylase (HDC).

Hence, the correct option is (B).

55. Option (D) is correct as it is an X-linked dominant pattern of inheritance.

The features which suggest the X-linked dominant pattern of inheritance are-

- A single abnormal X chromosome is sufficient to express the disease.
- All of the female offspring's of a diseased male XY will receive the abnormal X chromosome and express the disease, whereas none of the male offspring to the diseased father will have the disease (as sons don't receive an X chromosome from their father).
- A diseased mother can transmit the abnormal X chromosome to both daughter and sons equally.Important facts
- If a female is transmitting the disease to all offspring's (both males and females) and a male is not transmitting the disease to any child, it is mitochondrial inheritance.
- If a male is transmitting the disease only to daughters (all daughters) and not to the sons whereas female transmit the disease to half daughters and half of the sons, it is X-linked dominant.
- If only males are affected in a pedigree, it is likely to be an X-linked recessive disease (females act as carriers; only transmit the disease and themselves remain unaffected).
- If there is no sex-predilection and affected individuals transmit the disease to half of the offspring's, it is an autosomal dominant disorder.
- If there is no sex-predilection and affected individuals transmit the disease to one-fourth of the offspring's, it is likely to be an autosomal recessive disorder.

Option (A) is incorrect because Autosomal Dominant is determined if both parents are affected and an offspring is unaffected, the trait must be dominant (parents are both heterozygous). All affected individuals must have at least one affected parent. If both parents are unaffected, all offspring must be unaffected (homozygous recessive).

Option (B) is incorrect because the inheritance of a trait encoded in the mitochondrial genome. Because of the oddities of mitochondria, mitochondrial inheritance does not obey the classic rules of genetics.

Option (C) is incorrect because Autosomal recessive is when any affected founding daughter has 2 unaffected parents the disease must be autosomal recessive. An affected individual must inherit a recessive allele from both parents, so both parents must have an allele.

Hence, the correct option is (D).

56.

Option (D) is correct as CA 125 is elevated in ovarian cancer as well as in some benign conditions. CA 125 is a protein that is a so-called tumour marker or biomarker, which is a substance that is found in greater concentration in tumour cells than in other cells of the body. CA 125 is often measured as a blood test.

Option (A) is incorrect as the PSA test is a blood test used primarily to screen for prostate cancer. The test measures the amount of prostate-specific antigen (PSA) in your blood. PSA is a protein produced by both cancerous and noncancerous tissue in the prostate, a small gland that sits below the bladder in men.

Option (B) is incorrect as the fFN test is a relatively noninvasive tool that can help distinguish between those women who are likely to deliver shortly and those who are not. Fetal fibronectin (fFN) is used to test pregnant women who are between 22 weeks and 35 weeks of pregnancy and are having symptoms of premature labour.

Option (C) is incorrect as this is also known as the serum acid phosphatase test and evaluates the PSA levels in the blood. An acid phosphatase assay kit could be used to measure the level of enzyme in the blood serum.

Hence, the correct option is (D).

57. Option (D) is correct because solitary hypoechoic/anechoic lesion without septae or debris can occur in the early stage of the evolution of the hydatid cyst (Type 1/Simple cyst). However, the diagnosis of hydatid cyst may be considered when focal thickening of the wall is present or when fine hyperechoic spots, due to the hydatid sand, appear in the dependent areas.

Option (A) is incorrect because the parasites form slowly enlarging fluid-filled cysts which may become very large. Cysts occur most commonly in the liver or lungs but may occur in any organ, including the heart, brain, and bones. Cysts often do not cause symptoms unless they become very large or break.

Option (B) is incorrect because the isolated or simple form of Caroli disease is characterized by frequent recurring inflammation of the bile ducts inside the liver. There may also be localized accumulation of pus (abscess), stones that develop inside the bile ducts (intraductal lithiasis), abdominal pain, and/or fever.

Option (C) is incorrect because a liver abscess is a mass filled with pus inside the liver. Common causes are abdominal conditions such as appendicitis or diverticulitis due to hematogenous spread through the portal vein. It can also develop as a complication of a liver injury.

Hence, the correct option is (D).

58. Option (B) is correct because when blood clots form internally following a traumatic injury such as a car accident, they are largely undetected until they start to cause pain and have the potential to cause serious damage and even sudden death. They can form in the legs and cause pulmonary embolism or in the brain and cause intracranial haemorrhage.

Option (A) is incorrect because septic shock is a severe and potentially fatal condition that occurs when sepsis leads to life-threatening low blood pressure. Sepsis develops when the body has an overwhelming response to infection. Knowing how to recognize and prevent septic shock is vital.

Option (C) is incorrect because Deep vein thrombosis (DVT) occurs when a blood clot (thrombus) forms in one or more of the deep veins in your body, usually in your legs. Deep vein thrombosis can cause leg pain or swelling, but also can occur with no symptoms.

Option (D) is incorrect as Varicose veins, also known as varicose or varicosities, occur when your veins become enlarged, dilated, and overfilled with blood. Varicose veins typically appear swollen and raised, and have a bluish-purple or red colour. They are often painful. In most cases, varicose veins appear on the lower legs.

Hence, the correct option is (B).

59. Option (B) is correct because chemotactic factors generated by the interaction of plasma proteins with antigens or pathogens attract neutrophils from the blood to sites of infection. The diffusion of these factors creates a chemical gradient that directs the migration of neutrophils toward the source of the chemotactic factor. One leukotriene, LTB4, is the most potent chemotactic factor in humans.

Option (A) is incorrect because thromboxane A_2 (TXA_2), produced by activated platelets, has prothrombotic properties, stimulating activation of new platelets as well as increasing platelet aggregation. Platelet aggregation is achieved by mediating the expression of the glycoprotein complex GP IIb/IIIa in the cell membrane of platelets.

Option (C) is incorrect because, in healthy vessels, the endothelium expresses constitutive forms of nitric oxide synthase (NOS III) and cyclo-oxygenase (COX-1), which produce the vasoactive hormones NO and prostacyclin, respectively. Both NO and prostacyclin relax blood vessels and inhibit platelet activation.

Option (D) is incorrect because prostaglandins are found in most tissues and organs. They are produced by almost all nucleated cells. They are autocrine and paracrine lipid mediators that act upon platelets, endothelium, uterine, and mast cells. They are synthesized in the cell from the fatty acid arachidonic acid.

Hence, the correct option is (B).

60. Option (C) is correct because dysdiadochokinesia (DDK) is the medical term for an impaired ability to perform rapid, alternating movements (i.e., diadochokinesia). Complete inability is called adiadochokinesia.

Option (A) is incorrect because past-pointing is a physical sign in the disease of the Cerebellum in which, if the eyes are closed, a pointing finger overshoots its intended mark towards the side of the cerebellar damage.

Option (B) is incorrect because dysmetria (English: wrong length) is a lack of coordination of movement typified by the undershoot or overshoot of the intended position with the hand, arm, leg, or eye. It is a type of ataxia. It can also include an inability to judge distance or scale.

Option (D) is incorrect because as from the above we get that option C is correct so, this option automatically get to be as the wrong answer.

Hence, the correct option is (C).

61.

Option (D) is correct because annexin A5 (or annexin V) is a cellular protein in the annexin group. Inflow cytometry, annexin V is commonly used to detect apoptotic cells by its ability to bind to phosphatidylserine, a marker of apoptosis when it is on the outer leaflet of the plasma membrane.

Option (A) is incorrect because atherosclerosis is a disease in which plaque builds up inside your arteries. Arteries are blood vessels that carry oxygen-rich blood to your heart and other parts of your body. Plaque is made up of fat, cholesterol, calcium, and other substances found in the blood. Over time, plaque hardens and narrows your arteries.

Option (B) is incorrect because when inflammation occurs, chemicals from the body's white blood cells are released into the blood or affected tissues to protect your body from foreign substances. This release of chemicals increases the blood flow to the area of injury or infection and may result in redness and warmth.

Option (C) is incorrect because Necrosis is caused by factors external to the cell or tissue, such as infection, toxins, or trauma which result in the unregulated digestion of cell components. In contrast, apoptosis is a naturally occurring programmed and targeted cause of cellular death.

Hence, the correct option is (D).

62. Option (A) is correct because Pulmonary lobule is not a component of the acinus, rather a cluster of 3-5 terminal bronchioles with acinus form pulmonary lobule.

Option (B) is incorrect as Respiratory bronchioles proceed into the alveolar ducts, with immediately branch into alveolar sacs (alveoli).

Option (C) is incorrect as Alveolar ducts are tiny ducts that connect the respiratory bronchioles to alveolar sacs.

Option (D) is incorrect as the alveolar sacs are exactly what they sound like. They are sacs of many alveoli, which are the cells that exchange oxygen and carbon dioxide in the lungs. Since there are many alveolar sacs, this means that there are many alveolar ducts.

Hence, the correct option is (A).

63. Option (A) is correct as Inside the Bowman's capsule, the layers are as follows, from inside to outside -

- A thin layer of fenestrated endothelium
- Glomerular basement membrane
- Visceral epithelium (Podocytes)
- Parietal epithelium

Option (B) is incorrect as Proximal convoluted tubule is the convoluted portion of the vertebrate nephron that lies between Bowman's capsule and the loop of Henle and functions especially in the resorption of sugar, sodium and chloride ions, and water from the glomerular filtrate.

Option (C) is incorrect as the distal convoluted tubule is the nephron segment that lies immediately downstream of the macula densa. Although short in length, the distal convoluted tubule plays a critical role in sodium, potassium, and divalent cation homeostasis.

Option (D) is incorrect as the collecting duct is the last part of a long, twisting tube that collects urine from the nephrons (cellular structures in the kidney that filter blood and form urine) and moves it into the renal pelvis and ureters. Also called renal collecting tubule.

The Bowman's capsule (capsula glomeruli/glomerular capsule) is a cup-like sac at the beginning of tubular component of a nephron.

A glomerulus is enclosed in the sac (Bowman's capsule).

Fluids from blood in the glomerulus are collected in Bowman's capsule (i.e. glomerular filtrate) and further processed along the nephron to form urine.

Outside the Bowman's capsule, there are two poles.

Vascular pole → The side with afferent and efferent arterioles.

Urinary pole → The side with a proximal convoluted tubule.

Hence, the correct option is (A).

64. Option (B) is correct because erythema marginatum is a type of erythema (redness of the skin or mucous membranes) involving pink rings on the torso and inner surfaces of the limbs which come and go for as long as several months. It is found primarily on extensor surfaces. Rheumatic heart disease is a chronic condition that results from years after acute rheumatic fever.

Option (A) is incorrect because second-degree or complete block, or even Stokes-Adams attacks, are signs of RF, and may precede other signs. Here we report a case of RF associated with complete heart block.

Option (C) is incorrect because erythema nodosum is characterized by 1–2-inch (25–51 mm) nodules (rounded lumps) below the skin surface, usually on the shins. These subcutaneous nodules can appear anywhere on the body, but the most common sites are the shins, arms, thighs, and torso. Each nodule typically disappears after around two weeks, though new ones may continue to form for up to six or eight weeks.

Option (D) is incorrect because from the above we analyze that option B is the correct answer. So, option D will get automatically wrong.

Hence, the correct option is (B).

65. Option (A) is correct as the combination of hypoperfusion and retrograde congestion (Chronic passive congestion) acts synergistically to generate centrilobular hemorrhagic necrosis. The liver takes on a variegated mottled appearance reflecting haemorrhage and necrosis in the centrilobular regions, know as nutmeg liver. Chronic passive congestion is seen in RHF.

Option (B) is incorrect as heart failure with reduced ejection fraction (HFrEF), also called systolic failure is a situation when the left ventricle loses its ability to contract normally. The heart can't pump with enough force to push enough blood into circulation.

Option (C) is incorrect because increased pulmonary pressure results in higher pressures within the system, a condition known as pulmonary hypertension.

Option (D) is incorrect as the low pressure is due to the large cross-sectional area of the pulmonary circulation, which results in low resistance.

Hence, the correct option is (A).

66. Option (D) is correct as rates among Jewish men born in Israel are reportedly very close to zero. Hence, this is the required answer.

Option (A) is incorrect as penile cancer is rare in North America and Europe. It's diagnosed in fewer than 1 man in 100,000 each year and accounts for fewer than 1% of cancers in men in the United States. Penile cancer is much more common in some parts of Asia, Africa, and South America.

Option (B) is incorrect as one of the countries with the highest incidence of penile cancer in the world is India, with rates up to 3.32 per 100,000 men in some regions.

Option (C) is incorrect as penile cancer is a rare type of cancer with an age-adjusted incidence in Sweden of 2.1/100,000.

Hence, the correct option is (D).

67. Option (B) is correct as Osteocalcin is a marker of bone formation (not bone resorption). Hence, this is the required answer.

Option (A) is incorrect as Tartrate-resistant acid phosphatase (TRAP) is secreted by osteoclasts and the amount reaching the circulation and a suggested marker of bone resorption. Hence this is not the required answer.

Option (C) is incorrect as Urinary cross-linked N-telopeptide of type I collagen (NTX) is a reliable bone resorption marker in patients with metabolic bone disease.

Option (D) is incorrect as it is excreted unmetabolized in urine and is a specific marker of bone resorption and osteoclastic activity.

Hence, the correct option is (B).

68. Option (C) is correct because Microglial cells are the nervous system counterpart of the monocyte-macrophage system. The unique feature about microglia is that unlike other neuroglial cells it is not developed from neuroectoderm.

- These cells are mesodermal in origin.
- In response to injury, they usually undergo hypertrophy and their cytoplasm becomes filled with debris.
- When the debris-filled in the cytoplasm is usually lipid it is known as Gitter cells, lipophage or foam cell.
- When the debris-filled in the cytoplasm is usually iron the microglia are known as siderophage.

Option (A) is incorrect as Astrocytes are a population of cells with distinctive morphological and functional characteristics that differ within specific areas of the brain.

Option (B) is incorrect as Macroglia are cells that regulate the retinal metabolism and modulate neuron function and blood vessels.

Option (D) is incorrect as Oligodendrocytes produce the myelin sheath insulating neuronal axons (analogous to Schwann cells in the peripheral nervous system), although some oligodendrocytes (called satellite oligodendrocytes) are not involved in myelination.

Hence, the correct option is (C).

69. Option (D) is correct as it is a posterior pituitary that secretes ADH and oxytocin, not the anterior pituitary. Hence, this is the required answer.

Option (A) is incorrect as Anterior pituitary has acidophilic cell named somatotrophs that secrete growth hormone. So, this is not the required answer.

Option (B) is incorrect as there is Lactotrophs named acidophilic cell in the anterior pituitary that secretes prolactin. Therefore, this is also not the required answer.

Option (C) is incorrect as anterior pituitary has Basophilic cell named Gonadotrophs that secretes FSH, LH. Hence, this is also not the required answer.

Hence, the correct option is (D).

70. Option (D) is correct as Dyskeratosis is premature keratinization which occurs in individual cells or group of cells in different strata of the epithelium before they reach the surface. These dyskeratotic cells are large and round with a deep eosinophilic cytoplasm and a hyperchromatic nucleus.

Option (A) is incorrect as Leukoplakia is a condition in which thick, white or greyish patches form usually inside your mouth. Smoking is the most common cause. But other irritants can cause this condition as well. Mild leukoplakia is usually harmless and often goes away on its own.

Option (B) is incorrect as Hyperpigmentation is a common, usually harmless condition in which patches of skin become darker in colour than the normal surrounding skin. This darkening occurs when an excess of melanin, the brown pigment that produces normal skin colour, forms deposits in the skin.

Option (C) is incorrect as Nail dystrophy (distortion and discolouration of normal nail-plate structure), may result from any traumatic or inflammatory process that involves the nail matrix, nail bed, or surrounding tissues.

Hence, the correct option is (D).

71. Option (B) is correct because Dystrophic epidermolysis bullosa is caused by genetic defects (or mutations) within the human COL7A1 gene encoding the protein type VII collagen (collagen VII). DEB-causing mutations can be either autosomal dominant or autosomal recessive.

Option (A) is incorrect because Laminin is vital for the maintenance and survival of tissues. Defective laminins can cause muscles to form improperly, leading to a form of muscular dystrophy, lethal skin blistering disease (junctional epidermolysis bullosa) and defects of the kidney filter (nephrotic syndrome).

Option (C) is incorrect as the ITGA6 protein product is the integrin alpha chain alpha 6. Integrins are integral cell-surface proteins composed of an alpha chain and a beta chain. Specific loss of this integrin chain in the intestinal epithelium, and thus of their hemidesmosomes, induces long-standing colitis and infiltrating adenocarcinomas.

Option (D) is incorrect as Keratin 14 is specifically produced in cells called keratinocytes in the outer layer of the skin (the epidermis). Researchers believe that keratin 14 may also play a role in the formation of sweat glands and the development of patterned ridges on the skin of the hands and feet.

Hence, the correct option is (B).

72. Option (A) is correct because Primary T.B. includes.

- An area of grey-white (size of approx. 1 - 1.50 cm) inflammatory consolidation - called ghon's focus.
- Lymph node.
- Lymphatics and lymphatic channel.

Option (B) is incorrect because the most common causes of pleural effusion are congestive heart failure, pneumonia, malignancies, and pulmonary embolism. Signs and symptoms of pleural effusion include Shortness of breath. Chest pain.

Option (C) is incorrect as Miliary lung mottling is a radiological finding. The most common cause of miliary mottling in a chest radiograph in a developing country is miliary tuberculosis. Tropical pulmonary eosinophilia, varicella pneumonia, pulmonary alveolar lithiasis are other causes which are seen infrequently.

Option (D) is incorrect as Cavity and fibrosis are seen in secondary T.B.

Hence, the correct option is (A).

73. Option (B) is correct because the molecules that are secreted lack tensile strength, are more soluble, and are more vulnerable to enzymatic degradation. Collagen is required for osteoid matrix formation.

Option (A) is incorrect as rickets is defined as the defective mineralization.

Option (C) is incorrect as defective calcification in osteoid is also seen in rickets.

Option (D) is incorrect as an increase in the degradation of osteoid tissue is not responsible for Bone affection in scurvy.

Hence, the correct option is (B).

74. Option (D) is correct as Hepatic radiation damage is not acute, it is subacute and appears within 90 days.

Option (A) is incorrect as Acute radiation damage normally affects rapidly proliferating tissue Epithelium of GIT marked in Latent period 3-5 days.

Option (B) is incorrect as it is Hematopoietic tissue affected by Acute radiation damage marked within the latent period of 2-3 weeks.

Option (C) is incorrect for the same reason as an option (B).

Hence, the correct option is (D).

75. Option (D) is correct as it is covering all the other options mentioned above.

Option (A) is incorrect though When the viscosity is increased, e.g., in polycythemia, ESR is decreased due to jostling. (or pushing one another) effect on the cells as other options also affects ESR. So, going for an individual option will not be considered as correct.

Option (B) is incorrect even Fibrinogen in the blood causes RBCs to stick to each other and thereby fasten the rouleaux formation TESR. But it is incorrect for the same reason as of option (A).

Option (C) is incorrect for the same reason as point (B) as the rouleaux formation affects ESR.

Hence, the correct option is (D).

76. Option (C) is correct as Ionization of acidic drugs is increased in alkaline urine and vice versa. Ionized drugs cannot cross the plasma membrane easily. So is not reabsorbed into the blood from the tubules. Hence, enhanced excretion of the acidic drug through alkaline urine or basic drug through acidic urine.

- In the given choices, only phenobarbitone is acidic.

Option (A) is incorrect as Alkaline diuresis is done to increase excretion of acidic drugs and Morphine is a conjugate base of morphine(1+). It derives from a hydride of a morphinan. So, it is incorrect.

Option (B) is incorrect because Amphetamine is well absorbed in the gut and as it is a weak base hence the more basic the environment the more of the drug is found in a lipid-soluble form and the absorption through lipid-rich cell membranes is highly favoured.

Option (D) is incorrect as typical weak bases include atropine, cocaine, and physostigmine.

Hence, the correct option is (C).

77. Option (A) is correct as ionization of acidic drugs is increased in alkaline urine and vice versa. Ionized drugs cannot cross the plasma membrane easily. So is not reabsorbed into the blood from the tubules. Hence, enhanced excretion of the acidic drug through alkaline urine or basic drug through acidic urine.

- In the given options, the only barbiturate is acidic. Rest all are basic.

Option (B) is incorrect because Amphetamine is well absorbed in the gut and as it is a weak base hence the more basic the environment the more of the drug is found in a lipid-soluble form and the absorption through lipid-rich cell membranes is highly favoured.

Option (C) is incorrect as by the Arrhenius definition of an acid and base, alcohol is neither acidic nor basic when dissolved in water, as it neither produces H^+ nor OH^- in solution. And Alkaline diuresis is done to increase excretion of acidic drugs, and acidic diuresis for basic drugs. So, this is not the required answer.

Option (D) is incorrect as Alkaline diuresis is done to increase excretion of acidic drugs and Morphine is a conjugate base of morphine(1+). It derives from a hydride of a morphinan. So, it is incorrect.

Hence, the correct option is (A).

78. Option (C) is correct as P450 inducers are

- Phenobarbitone
- Rifampicin
- Phenytoin
- Chloral hydrate
- Griseofulvin
- Phenylbutazone
- DDT
- Chronic alcohol ingestion

Option (A) is incorrect as Cimetidine is a potent inhibitor of certain cytochrome P450 (CYP450) enzymes, including CYP1A2, CYP2C9, CYP2C19, CYP2D6, CYP2E1, and CYP3A4. The drug appears to primarily inhibit CYP1A2, CYP2D6, and CYP3A4, of which it is described as a moderate inhibitor.

Option (B) is incorrect as with all azole antifungal agents, ketoconazole works principally by inhibiting the enzyme cytochrome P450 14α-demethylase (CYP51A1). This enzyme participates in the sterol biosynthesis pathway that leads from lanosterol to ergosterol.

Option (D) is incorrect as Enzyme inhibitors reinforce and enzyme inducers reduce the effect of theophylline.

Hence, the correct option is (C).

79. "During the delivery of anaesthesia, the current standard of care is to measure systemic blood pressure and heart rate every 5 minutes at a minimum. The clinical scenario and phase of the operation may mandate more frequent monitoring, which is up to the judgment of the anaesthesia provider."

Option (B) is correct because, during the delivery of anaesthesia, the current standard of care is to measure systemic blood pressure and heart rate every 5 minutes at a minimum.

Option (A) is incorrect because according to the above explanation the heart rate is evaluated at least every 5 minutes, but this option does not match to the explanation hence this will not be correct.

Option (C) is incorrect as we came to know according to the explanation the heart rate be evaluated at least every 5 minutes, but this option does not match to the explanation hence this will not be correct.

Option (D) is incorrect as this option will not be correct according to the above explanation.

Hence, the correct option is (B).

80. Option (D) is correct as Pharmacological block results in receptor blockage and will cause not to respond to pilocarpine 1%. This can be done by Atropine.

Option (A) is incorrect as 3rd Nerve palsy due to diabetes affects the nerve, not the receptor. Palsy causes mydriasis but responds to pilocarpine 1%.

Option (B) is incorrect as Adie's tonic pupil responds to pilocarpine 1% and even diluted solutions at 0.1% due to supersensitivity.

Option (C) is incorrect as Uncal herniation characterized by pupillary dilatation responds to pilocarpine 1%.

Hence, the correct option is (D).

81. Option (C) is correct because an autonomic ganglion is a cluster of nerve cell bodies (a ganglion) in the autonomic nervous system. The two types are sympathetic ganglion and parasympathetic ganglion. Both sympathetic and parasympathetic preganglionic neurons are cholinergic, meaning they release acetylcholine (Ach) at the synapse in the ganglion. Acetylcholine to act on postsynaptic Nicotinic receptors.

Option (A) is incorrect as the function of Adrenergic is enhancing, compared to the inhibiting action of the cholinergic fibres of the parasympathetic system.

Option (B) is incorrect as Peptidergic neurons often coexpress and corelease non-peptide transmitters.

Option (D) is incorrect as the sensory function of substance P is thought to be related to the transmission of pain information into the central nervous system. Substance P coexists with the excitatory neurotransmitter glutamate in primary afferents that respond to painful stimulation.

Hence, the correct option is (C).

82. Option (A) is correct as obstetric indications of ergometrine (Ergonovine):

- To control and prevent Postpartum haemorrhage. It is given at the time of delivery of the anterior shoulder.
- After Caesarean Section/instrumental delivery - to prevent uterine atony.
- To ensure normal involution in multipara.

Option (B) is incorrect as applying fundal pressure by pushing on the mother's abdomen in the direction of the birth canal is often used to assist spontaneous vaginal birth, shorten the length of the second stage and reduce the need for instrumental birth (forceps- or vacuum-assisted) or caesarean section.

Option (C) is incorrect as Nonsteroidal anti-inflammatory drugs (NSAIDs) and combination oral contraceptives (OCs) are the most commonly used therapeutic modalities for the management of primary dysmenorrhea. Treatment of secondary dysmenorrhea involves correction of the underlying organic cause.

Option (D) is incorrect as there are several medicines used to treat high blood pressure (anti-hypertensives) that are considered safe to use in pregnancy. Medicines such as magnesium sulfate can also be given to treat or prevent eclampsia (seizures).

Hence, the correct option is (A).

83. Option (D) is correct as Trimetazidine is a partial fatty acid oxidation inhibitor used for angina pectoris.

Option (A) is incorrect as it happens because something prevents the flow of blood to your heart muscle. Nitroglycerin helps widen the blood vessels so more blood gets to your heart muscle. So, this is not the required answer.

Option (B) is incorrect as Spironolactone, an aldosterone inhibitor is a potassium-sparing diuretic. This medication is used to treat patients with heart failure when systolic dysfunction is present. Spironolactone protects the heart by blocking a certain chemical (aldosterone) in the body that causes salt and fluid build-up. So, this is not the required answer.

Option (C) is incorrect as Nesiritide is a medication used to treat acutely decompensated congestive heart failure with dyspnea at rest or with minimal exertion (such as talking, eating or bathing). Nesiritide is a 32 amino acid recombinant human B-type natriuretic peptide. Hence, this is also not the required answer.

Hence, the correct option is (D).

84. Option (A) is correct because the cough is one of the most frequent side effects associated with angiotensin-converting enzyme inhibitors (ACEIs) but is not thought to be associated with losartan, an angiotensin II receptor antagonist (ARA).

Option (B) is incorrect because the incidence of hyperkalemia associated with the use of the aldosterone receptor antagonists is dose-dependent, with detectable effects even at doses of 25 mg spironolactone per day; the risk of severe hyperkalemia increases with the use of higher dose.

Option (C) is incorrect because 5-HT3 receptor antagonists induce headache with high frequency, in up to 40% of the patients (Veneziano et al. 1995), and headache are the most common adverse effect of the proton pump inhibitors in clinical trials.

Option (D) is incorrect because angioedema accompanies chronic urticaria in 40% of patients, and approximately half have an autoimmune mechanism in which there is IgG antibody directed to the subunit of the IgE receptor (40%) or to IgE itself (5%-10%).

Hence, the correct option is (A).

85. Option (D) is correct because Glioma is a type of tumour that occurs in the brain and spinal cord. Gliomas begin in the gluey supportive cells (glial cells) that surround nerve cells and help them function.

Three types of glial cells can produce tumours. Gliomas are classified according to the type of glial cell involved in the tumour, as well as the tumour's genetic features, which can help predict how the tumour will behave over time and the treatments most likely to work.

Option (A) is incorrect because the only curative therapy for glucagonoma is surgery, and even this is not always successful. Heightened glucagon secretion can be treated with the administration of octreotide, a somatostatin analogue, which inhibits the release of glucagon.

Option (B) is incorrect because Octreotide is an effective treatment of hypoglycemia in more than 50% of patients with insulinoma. Detection of responsive patients was better based on a positive short test with subcutaneous octreotide than on the results of Octreoscan scintigraphy.

Option (C) is incorrect because the drugs most commonly used to treat carcinoid tumours is octreotide (Sandostatin). It can help relieve the flushing and diarrhoea caused by carcinoid syndrome, and slow tumour growth.

Hence, the correct option is (D).

86. Option (B) is correct because "Rizatriptan is taken at the first symptoms of a migraine attack; it is not for everyday use" Stimulation of 5-HT1B/1D receptors can stop an acute migraine attack. Rizatriptan and sumatriptan have comparable potency and selectivity for the 5-HTiD receptors. Use in a migraine: Acute migraine which has failed with NSAIDS Rizatriptan and eletriptan is the most efficacious of the triptans. Triptans are not effective in migraines with aura unless given after the aura is completed and the headache initiated.

Option (A) is incorrect because Prophylactic treatment is not curative, and most patients will still need abortive medications for acute migraine. Before starting prophylactic medications, it is imperative to evaluate if patients are using proper and adequate abortive therapies. Overuse of abortive medications can cause rebound headaches. Depakote and sodium valproate are two anticonvulsant drugs that are used for migraine prophylaxis.

Option (C) is incorrect because Cluster headaches are a series of relatively short but extremely painful headaches every day for weeks or months at a time. You tend to get them at the same time each year, such as the spring or fall. Because of their seasonal nature, people often mistake cluster headaches for symptoms of allergies or business stress. Injectable sumatriptan (Imitrex): Triptans are a class of drugs that can treat migraines. Sumatriptan acts as an agonist for 5-hydroxytryptamine (5-HT) receptors. It can treat migraines, and it can bring rapid relief from cluster headaches. Zolmitriptan (Zomig) is a nasal spray, but it only works for some patients.

Option (D) is incorrect as per the International Headache Society, chronic migraine is defined as headache occurring on 15 or more days per month for more than three months, which, on at least 8 days per month, has the features of migraine headache. Chronic migraine occurs in approximately 1% of the population. causes moderate to severe pain.
Hence, the correct option is (B).

87. Option (A) is incorrect because Promethazine is a first-generation H_1-antihistaminic drug. It is indicated for the treatment of allergic reactions. Because of its anticholinergic action and ability to cross the blood-brain barrier, it can be used as an antiemetic (particularly for prophylaxis of motion sickness) and as an anti-Parkinsonian drug (particularly in drug-induced Parkinsonism).

Acid secretion is reduced mainly by H_2-blocking drugs like ranitidine but even H_1-antihistaminics can also reduce acid secretion at high doses (due to lack of selectivity at such high dose).

Option (B) is incorrect because Domperidone is used to treat symptoms of stomach disorders. It may also be used to prevent nausea and vomiting caused by certain medications. Side effects include headache, dizziness, dry mouth, nervousness, flushing, or irritability may occur the first several days as your body adjusts to the medication.

Option (C) is incorrect because Metoclopramide is used to treat the symptoms of slow stomach emptying (gastroparesis) in patients with diabetes. It works by increasing the movements or contractions of the stomach and intestines. It relieves symptoms such as nausea, vomiting, heartburn, a feeling of fullness after meals, and loss of appetite

Option (D) is incorrect because Ondansetron blocks the actions of chemicals in the body that can trigger nausea and vomiting. Ondansetron is used to prevent nausea and vomiting that may be caused by surgery, cancer chemotherapy, or radiation treatment. Ondansetron may be used for purposes not listed in this medication guide.
Hence, the correct option is (A).

88. Option (B) is correct because extended use or overuse of this medication for constipation may result in dependence on laxatives and ongoing constipation. Overuse may also cause persistent diarrhoea, loss of too much body water (dehydration), and mineral imbalances (e.g., high magnesium).
Side Effects: nausea, vomiting, constipation; increased thirst or urination; muscle weakness, bone pain; confusion, weakness, feeling tired.

Option (A) is incorrect because Sodium bicarbonate, also known as baking soda, is used to relieve heartburn, sour stomach, or acid indigestion by neutralizing excess stomach acid. When used for this purpose, it is said to belong to the group of medicines called antacids. It may be used to treat the symptoms of a stomach or duodenal ulcers.
Side effects: Frequent urge to urinate, headache (continuing), loss of appetite (continuing) mood or mental changes.

Option (C) is incorrect because Calcium bicarbonate medication is used to treat symptoms caused by too much stomach acid such as heartburn, upset stomach, or indigestion. It is an antacid that works by lowering the amount of acid in the stomach. Side effects: loss of appetite, constipation, gas(flatulence), nausea, vomiting, high calcium levels.

Option (D) is incorrect because Aluminium hydroxide is often administered orally for the temporary relief of heartburn or gastroesophageal reflux. It may be used topically, temporarily, to protect and relieve chafed and abraded skin, minor wounds and burns, and skin irritations resulting from friction and rubbing. Patients may also receive it to treat chemo-induced oral mucositis in the form of a mouthwash. Additionally, it is approved for use as an adjuvant in numerous vaccines due to its ability to increase phagocytosis and spur immune responses. It also has approval for use in a wide array of cosmetic products at varying concentrations. Aluminium hydroxide can also serve as a phosphate binder in patients with chronic renal disease. However, its use in this manner is infrequent due to the risk of adverse effects. Commonly, oral aluminium hydroxide is a liquid mixture of both aluminium and magnesium hydroxide.

Hence, the correct option is (B).

89. Option (A) is correct as mechanisms of Acquired Drug Resistance include Plasmid encodes an enzyme that acetylates the drug, thereby inactivating it. Bacteria make an altered 30S ribosomes that do not bind to the drug. Bacteria make altered penicillin-binding proteins, that do not bind to the drug.

Option (B) is incorrect because a chromosome is a deoxyribonucleic acid (DNA) molecule with part or all of the genetic material (genome) of an organism. Most eukaryotic chromosomes include packaging proteins which, aided by chaperone proteins, bind to and condense the DNA molecule to prevent it from becoming an unmanageable tangle.

Option (C) is incorrect because, in some genes, not all of the DNA sequence is used to make protein. Introns are noncoding sections of an RNA transcript, or the DNA encoding it, that are spliced out before the RNA molecule is translated into a protein. The sections of DNA (or RNA) that code for proteins are called exons. Following transcription, new, immature strands of messenger RNA, called pre-mRNA, may contain both introns and exons. The pre-mRNA molecule thus goes through a modification process in the nucleus called splicing during which the noncoding introns are cut out and only the coding exons remain. Splicing produces a mature messenger RNA molecule that is then translated into a protein. Introns are also referred to as intervening sequences.

Option (D) is incorrect because a chromosome is a deoxyribonucleic acid (DNA) molecule with part or all of the genetic material (genome) of an organism. Most eukaryotic chromosomes include packaging proteins which, aided by chaperone proteins, bind to and condense the DNA molecule to prevent it from becoming an unmanageable tangle. This three-dimensional genome structure plays a significant role in transcriptional regulation.
Hence, the correct option is (A).

90. Option (A) is correct as MAC is inversely related to the potency of an inhalational agent. N_2O has a maximum MAC (104%) and is thus the least potent agent. Methoxyflurane is the most potent drug due to the minimum value of MAC.

Option (B) is incorrect as therapeutic Index (TI) A ratio that compares the blood concentration at which a drug becomes toxic and the concentration at which the drug is effective.

Option (C) is incorrect as diffusibility (countable and uncountable, plural diffusibilities) (physics, of a gas or other fluid) A measure of the speed of diffusion. (figuratively, e.g. of a disease) Capacity for spreading.

Option (D) is incorrect as the octanol/water partition coefficient (Kow) is defined as the ratio of a chemical's concentration in the octanol phase to its concentration in the aqueous phase of a two-phase octanol/water system. Values of Kow are thus, unitless.
Hence, the correct option is (A).

91. Option (A) is correct as for the treatment of Type II diabetes mellitus. Troglitazone is used alone or in combination with a sulfonylurea, metformin, or insulin as an adjunct to diet and exercise. Troglitazone is a thiazolidinedione antidiabetic agent that lowers blood glucose by improving target cell response to insulin.

Option (B) is incorrect because Epilepsy is a nervous system disorder that causes seizures. Seizures are temporary changes in brain activity. Doctors categorize and treat different types of epilepsy based on the kind of seizure they cause. Anti-seizure medications can treat absence seizures, for example, ethosuximide (Zarontin), lamotrigine (Lamictal), valproic acid (Depakene, Stavzor).

Option (C) is incorrect because hyperlipidemia is also called high cholesterol. The doctor calls it hyperlipidemia. Either way, it's a common problem. The term covers several disorders that result in extra fats, also known as lipids, in your blood. You can control some of its causes, but not all of them. Hyperlipidemia is treatable. One needs to watch what he eat and also exercise regularly and might need to take a prescription medication, too.

Option (D) is incorrect because Osteoporosis is characterized by low bone mass, microarchitectural disruption, and increased skeletal fragility. Multiple therapeutic regimens have been designed to prevent or treat bone loss in postmenopausal women and older adults. The first step in the prevention or treatment of osteoporosis is ensuring adequate nutrition, particularly maintaining an adequate intake of calcium and vitamin D.
Hence, the correct option is (A).

92. Option (D) is correct because, for patients who cannot adequately restrict free water or have an inadequate response to conservative measures, Demeclocycline (300-600 mg orally twice daily) inhibits the effect of ADH on the distal tubule. The onset of action may require 1 week, and urinary concentrating ability may be permanently impaired, resulting in nephrogenic diabetes insipidus (DI) and even hypernatremia.

Option (A) is incorrect because vasopressin decreases water excretion by the kidneys by increasing water reabsorption in the collecting ducts, hence its other name of antidiuretic hormone. Vasopressin also has a potent constricting effect on arterioles throughout the body.

Option (B) is incorrect because lithium carbonate inhibits thyroid hormone secretion, but unlike iodine, it does not interfere with the accumulation of radioiodine.

Option (C) is incorrect because hypertonic saline-induced inhibition of neutrophil activation and adhesion has been proposed as the main mechanism for its lung-protective properties.

Hence, the correct option is (D).

93. Option (D) is correct because the LUMINATE (Lux Uveitis Multicenter Investigation of a New Approach to Treatment) clinical development program was initiated in 2007 to assess the safety and efficacy of voclosporin for the treatment, maintenance, and control of all forms of noninfectious uveitis.

Option (A) is incorrect because Infliximab and steroids both are effective in the management of moderate to severe steroid-dependent ulcerative colitis. Infliximab is a medication used to treat a number of autoimmune diseases. This includes Crohn's disease, ulcerative colitis, rheumatoid arthritis, ankylosing spondylitis, psoriasis, psoriatic arthritis, and Behçet's disease.

Option (B) is incorrect because Ciclosporin, also spelt cyclosporine and cyclosporin, are an immunosuppressant medication and natural product. It is taken by mouth or by injection into a vein for rheumatoid arthritis, psoriasis, Crohn's disease, nephrotic syndrome, and in organ transplants to prevent rejection.

Option (C) is incorrect because Methotrexate, formerly known as amethopterin, is a chemotherapy agent and immune system suppressant. It is used to treat cancer, autoimmune diseases, ectopic pregnancy, and medical abortions. Types of cancers it is used to include breast cancer, leukaemia, lung cancer, lymphoma, and osteosarcoma.

Hence, the correct option is (D).

94. Option (B) is correct because the patient in question is being treated for acne, the answer should be minocycline. Antibiotics used in acne are erythromycin, clindamycin, tetracycline, and minocycline.

Option (A) is incorrect because Doxycycline is a tetracycline antibiotic that fights bacteria in the body. Doxycycline is used to treat many different bacterial infections, such as acne, urinary tract infections, and others. But Doxycycline does not cause pigmentation on long-term use.

Option (C) is incorrect because Azithromycin is an antibiotic used for the treatment of a number of bacterial infections. This includes middle ear infections, strep throat, pneumonia, traveller's diarrhoea, and certain other intestinal infections, but not use for the treatment of acne.

Option (D) is incorrect because Chlorpromazine, marketed under the trade names Thorazine and Largactil among others, is an antipsychotic medication. It is primarily used to treat psychotic disorders such as schizophrenia. It can cause pigmentation on long-term use but not use in treatment for acne.
Hence, the correct option is (B).

95. Option (D) is correct because Isoniazid, also known as isonicotinylhydrazide (INH), is an antibiotic used for the treatment of tuberculosis. For active tuberculosis, it is often used together with rifampicin, pyrazinamide, and either streptomycin or ethambutol.

Option (A) is incorrect because a diuretic is any substance that promotes diuresis, the increased production of urine. This includes forced diuresis. The side effect of medicines such as thiazide diuretics causes Interstitial nephritis.

Option (B) is incorrect because Drug-induced acute interstitial nephritis (AIN) is a leading cause of acute kidney injury (AKI) in hospitalized patients, and beta-lactam antibiotics are often held responsible. Typically beta-lactam induced AIN is thought to occur between 10 and 21 days of exposure, but limited data is available.

Option (C) is incorrect because Allopurinol is used to treat gout and certain types of kidney stones. It is also used to prevent increased uric acid levels in patients receiving cancer chemotherapy. The side effect of medicines such as allopurinol causes Interstitial nephritis.

Hence, the correct option is (D).

96. Option (D) is correct because Glutaraldehyde, sold under the brand name Cidex and Glutaral among others, is a disinfectant, medication, preservative, and fixative. As a disinfectant, it is used to sterilize surgical instruments and other areas of hospitals. Glutaraldehyde is effective against a range of microorganisms including spores.

Option (A) is incorrect because Formaldehyde sterilization is used where sterilization by steam or high temperature is not possible. Typical equipment suitable for Low-Temperature Steam Formaldehyde processing is Rigid or Flexible Endoscopes. All heat-sensitive instruments for advanced eye surgery like cryo-instruments.

Option (B) is incorrect because an autoclave is used to sterilize surgical equipment, laboratory instruments, pharmaceutical items, and other materials. A very basic autoclave is similar to a pressure cooker; both use the power of steam to kill bacteria, spores, and germs resistant to boiling water and powerful detergents.

Option (C) is incorrect because boiling was the principal method used to kill pathogenic organisms. Boiling is a very simple method of water disinfection. It should be noted that it is designed to kill harmful organisms, and generally does not result in sterile water (free of all microorganisms).

Hence, the correct option is (D).

97. Option (C) is correct because M. tuberculosis, then known as the "tubercle bacillus", was first described on 24 March 1882 by Robert Koch, who subsequently received the Nobel Prize in Physiology or Medicine for this discovery in 1905; the bacterium is also known as "Koch's bacillus".

Option (A) is incorrect because of Complex Media Inc. The complex is an American New York-based media platform for youth culture which was founded as a bi-monthly magazine by fashion designer Marc (Ecko) Milecofsky.

Option (B) is incorrect as virtually all infections with rabies resulted in death until two French scientists, Louis Pasteur and Émile Roux, developed the first rabies vaccination in 1885. Nine-year-old Joseph Meister (1876–1940), who had been mauled by a rabid dog, was the first human to receive this vaccine.

Option (D) is incorrect because Louis Pasteur is credited with conclusively disproving the theory of spontaneous generation with his famous swan-neck flask experiment. He subsequently proposed that "life only comes from life."
Hence, the correct option is (C).

98. Option (C) is correct as, in 1905 Schaudinn and Hoffmann discovered the bacterium that was responsible for syphilis, a spiral-shaped spirochete called Treponema pallidum. The organism was removed from a papula in the vulva of a patient with secondary syphilis.

Option (A) is incorrect because German physician Robert Koch was one of the founders of bacteriology. He discovered the anthrax disease cycle and the bacteria responsible for tuberculosis and cholera. He received the Nobel Prize for Physiology or Medicine in 1905 for his research on tuberculosis.

Option (B) is incorrect because Frederick William Twort FRS (22 October 1877 – 20 March 1950) was an English bacteriologist and was the original discoverer in 1915 of bacteriophages (viruses that infect bacteria). He studied medicine at St Thomas's Hospital, London, was superintendent of the Brown Institute for Animals (a pathology research centre), and was a professor of bacteriology at the University of London.

Option (D) is incorrect because the agents discovered by Ellermann and Bang are now known under the collective term avian leukosis virus or ALV. The virus isolated by Rous bears the name of its discoverer: Rous sarcoma virus. Together, these viruses constitute the avian C-type virus genus, often referred to as avian sarcoma/ leukosis viruses (ASLV).

Hence, the correct option is (C).

99. Option (D) is correct because

- Sickle cell disease is a genetic condition that is characterized by a mutation in the beta-globin chain of haemoglobin (glutamic acid is replaced with valine in the 6th position of beta chain).
- Other given choices like SLE, Graves, and MG are all autoimmune conditions.

Option (A) is incorrect because Myasthenia gravis is a chronic autoimmune neuromuscular disease that causes weakness in the skeletal muscles, which are responsible for breathing and moving parts of the body, including the arms and legs. Myasthenia gravis is an autoimmune disease because the immune system—which normally protects the body from foreign organisms—mistakenly attacks itself.

Option (B) is incorrect because Systemic lupus erythematosus (SLE), also known simply as lupus, is an autoimmune disease in which the body's immune system mistakenly attacks healthy tissue in many parts of the body. Symptoms vary between people and may be mild to severe.

Option (C) is incorrect because Graves' disease is a type of autoimmune problem that causes the thyroid gland to produce too much thyroid hormone, which is called hyperthyroidism. Graves' disease is often the underlying cause of hyperthyroidism.

Hence, the correct option is (D).

100. Option (D) is correct because the paracortex of the lymph node is a T-cell zone. One feature of this region is the high endothelial venule, where circulating lymphocytes leave the bloodstream to enter the node. These postcapillary HEVs can be distinguished by their cuboidal endothelial cells.

Option (A) is incorrect because the cortex of a lymph node is the outer portion of the node, underneath the capsule and the subcapsular sinus. It has an outer part and a deeper part known as the paracortex. The outer cortex consists of groups of mainly in activated B cells called follicles.

Option (B) is incorrect because the Medullary cord is a portion of the medulla of the lymph node which contains lymphatic tissue and project into the medullary sinus. B cells and plasma cells are the main cell types found in the medullary cords.

Option (C) is incorrect because a mantle is a layer inside a planetary body bounded below by a core and above by a crust. Mantles are made of rock or ices and are generally the largest and most massive layer of the planetary body. Mantles are characteristic of planetary bodies that have undergone differentiation by density.

Hence, the correct option is (D).

101. Option (B) is correct because it is not the function of CD4 helper cells. Immunoglobulins, also known as antibodies, are glycoprotein molecules produced by plasma cells (white blood cells). They act as a critical part of the immune response by specifically recognizing and binding to particular antigens, such as bacteria or viruses, and aiding in their destruction.

Option (A) is incorrect because Immunogenic memory is a function of CD4 helper cells. Immunological memory is the ability of the immune system to quickly and specifically recognize an antigen that the body has previously encountered and initiated a corresponding immune response. Memory CD4 help for B cells. Most vaccines act by producing long-lived antibody-producing cells and the same may be true for the long-lived protection that is afforded by natural infections.

Option (C) is incorrect because Activate macrophages are functions of CD4 helper cells. IFN-γ secreted by CD4 T cells can activate macrophages to phagocytose and digest intracellular bacteria and protozoa. In addition, IFN-γ can activate iNOS to produce NOx free radicals to directly kill intracellular bacteria and protozoa.

Option (D) is incorrect because Activate cytotoxic cells are a function of CD4 helper cells. Helper T cells are arguably the most important cells in adaptive immunity, as they are required for almost all adaptive immune responses. They not only help activate B cells to secrete antibodies and macrophages to destroy ingested microbes, but they also help activate cytotoxic T cells to kill infected target cells.
Hence, the correct option is (B).

102. Option (D) is correct because B cells, also known as B lymphocytes, are a type of white blood cell of the small lymphocyte subtype. They function in the humoral immunity component of the adaptive immune system by secreting antibodies.

Option (A) is incorrect because Histiocyte is a type of white blood cell, also called a macrophage, that is created by the bone marrow. They usually stay in place, but when histiocytes are stimulated by infection or inflammation they become active, attacking bacteria and other foreign matter in the body.

Option (B) is incorrect because Microglia are a type of neuroglia (glial cell) located throughout the brain and spinal cord. Microglia account for 10–15% of all cells found within the brain. As the resident macrophage cells, they act as the first and main form of active immune defence in the central nervous system (CNS).

Option (C) is incorrect because Kupffer cells, also known as stellate macrophages and Kupffer–Browicz cells, are specialized macrophages located in the liver, lining the walls of the sinusoids. They form part of the mononuclear phagocyte system.

Hence, the correct option is (D).

103. Option (A) is correct because the most consistent association of virulence is the production of coagulase and to a lesser extent fermentation of mannitol. Coagulase two forms of coagulase exist:- Bound to cell → clumping factor. Excreted from the cell as an enzyme. Clumping factor- It is bound coagulase which is bound to the cell surface. It acts directly on the fibrinogen in plasma and is responsible for the adherence of the organism to fibrinogen which results in clumping. It is detected by the slide coagulase test. Coagulase or free coagulase. It is excreted from the cell as a free enzyme It converts prothrombin to a product that then acts on fibrinogen in the plasma to form a fibrin clot. It is tested by a tube coagulase test.

Option (B) is incorrect because Endotoxin is a type of pyrogen and is a component of the exterior cell wall of Gram-negative bacteria, like E. coli (see image). Endotoxin is a lipopolysaccharide or LPS. LPS consists of the lipid, a portion containing fatty acids and disaccharide phosphates, core polysaccharides and the O-antigen.

Option (C) is incorrect because Hemolysis or hemolysis also known by several other names, is the rupturing of red blood cells (erythrocytes) and the release of their contents (cytoplasm) into surrounding fluid (e.g. blood plasma). Hemolysis may occur in vivo or in vitro (inside or outside the body). One cause of hemolysis is the action of hemolysins, toxins that are produced by certain pathogenic bacteria or fungi. Another cause is intense physical exercise.

Option (D) is incorrect because Staph aureus virulence is due (Pathogenicity correlated with coagulase). As the answer is there in the options, so option (D) is incorrect.
Hence, the correct option is (A).

104. Option (D) is correct because staphylococci are found in all the above options skin, nose and throat. So the answer is an option (D) according to question.

Option (A) is incorrect because, in carriers, staphylococci are found in the throat. Throat swabs are necessary to reliably detect carriers of Staphylococcus aureus (about 38% of persistent carriers in the throat).

Option (B) is incorrect because staph bacteria can lurk in areas deep within the nose. Scientists at the Stanford University School of Medicine have revealed that formerly overlooked sites deep inside the nose may be reservoirs for Staphylococcus aureus, a major bacterial cause of disease.

Option (C) is incorrect because the skin is carriers of staphylococci. They are only able to invade via broken skin or mucous membranes, hence intact skin is an excellent human defence. Once they have invaded they have various ways to avoid host defences.

Hence, the correct option is (D).

105. Option (C) is correct because Staphylococcus aureus causes a range of illnesses, from minor skin infections, such as pimples, impetigo, boils, cellulitis, folliculitis, carbuncles, scalded skin syndrome, and abscesses, to life-threatening diseases such as pneumonia, meningitis, osteomyelitis, endocarditis, toxic shock syndrome, bacteremia, and sepsis. Staphylococcus aureus is a Gram-positive, round-shaped bacterium that is a member of the Firmicutes, and it is a usual member of the microbiota of the body, frequently found in the upper respiratory tract and on the skin.

Option (A) is incorrect because Pneumococci are a type of streptococcus bacteria. The bacteria spread through contact with people who are ill or by healthy people who carry the bacteria in the back of their nose. Pneumococcal infections can be mild or severe. It causes pneumococcal disease. Invasive pneumococcal disease is a life-threatening condition that is fatal in 10 percent of cases.

Option (B) is incorrect because Escherichia coli, also known as E. coli, is a Gram-negative, facultatively anaerobic, rod-shaped, coliform bacterium of the genus Escherichia that is commonly found in the lower intestine of warm-blooded organisms. It produces a powerful toxin that damages the lining of the small intestine, which can cause bloody diarrhoea.

Option (D) is incorrect because Infections commonly caused by enterococci include urinary tract infection (UTIs), endocarditis, bacteremia, catheter-related infections, wound infections, and intra-abdominal and pelvic infections. Many infecting strains originate from the patient's intestinal flora. Enterococcus is a type of bacteria that is typically present in the gut and bowel.
Hence, the correct option is (C).

106. Option (A) is correct because viruses are obligate intracellular parasites. They contain only one type of nucleic acid, either RNA or DNA, never both. Viral genomes consist of DNA or RNA only, never both. DNA and RNA molecules can be double-stranded or single-stranded, linear or circular, segmented (composed of multiple pieces of nucleic acid) or nonsegmented.

Option (B) is incorrect because viruses form extracellular infectious particles, infectious particles present in the supernatant of HCV-infected Huh-7/scr cells efficiently propagate the infection in vitro (54), infectious particles are also physically associated with the infected cells.

Option (C) is incorrect because it is the property of the virus that is very heat labile but stable at low temperatures.

Option (D) is incorrect because viruses insert their genetic material into a human cell's DNA in order to reproduce. Antibiotics cannot kill viruses because bacteria and viruses have different mechanisms and machinery to survive and replicate. The antibiotic has no "target" to attack in a virus.
Hence, the correct option is (A).

107. Option (C) is correct because the cytoplasmic inclusion bodies produced by fowl-pox virus in the chorioallantoic membrane of the egg consist of a mass of virus particles, frequently surrounding an apparently normal component of the cytoplasm. Fowlpox is a disease of chickens and turkeys caused by a DNA virus of the genus Avipoxvirus of the family Poxviridae. Its distribution is worldwide.

Option (A) is incorrect because Chickenpox, also known as varicella, is a highly contagious disease caused by the initial infection with varicella-zoster virus (VZV). The disease results in a characteristic skin rash that forms small, itchy blisters, which eventually scab over. It usually starts on the chest, back, and face.

Option (B) is incorrect because Bollinger bodies are not due to cowpox. Cowpox is a viral skin infection caused by the cowpox or catpox virus. This is a member of the Orthopoxvirus family, which includes the variola virus that causes smallpox. Cowpox is similar to but much milder than the highly contagious and sometimes deadly smallpox disease.

Option (D) is incorrect because Bollinger bodies are not due to smallpox. Smallpox was an infectious disease caused by one of two virus variants, Variola major and Variola minor. The last naturally occurring case was diagnosed in October 1977, and the World Health Organization (WHO) certified the global eradication of the disease in 1980.

Hence, the correct option is (C).

108. Option (D) is correct because Rhabdovirions are enveloped, with bullet-shaped and bacilliform geometries. These virions are about 75 nm wide and 180 nm long. Rhabdoviruses have helical nucleocapsids and their genomes are linear, around 11–15 kb in length. Rhabdoviruses carry their genetic material in the form of negative-sense single-stranded RNA.

Option (A) is incorrect because Parvoviruses are linear, nonsegmented, single-stranded DNA viruses, with an average genome size of 5-6 kilobase pairs (kbp). They are classified as group II viruses in the Baltimore classification of viruses.

Option (B) is incorrect because a papovavirus is any member of the former virus family of Papovaviridae. They are mainly associated with various neoplasms in mammals. Papovaviruses are DNA viruses containing double-stranded DNA, are icosahedral in shape, and do not have a lipoprotein envelope.

Option (C) is incorrect because Poxviruses are brick or oval-shaped viruses with large double-stranded DNA genomes. Poxviruses exist throughout the world and cause disease in humans and many other types of animals. Poxvirus infections typically result in the formation of lesions, skin nodules, or disseminated rash.
Hence, the correct option is (D).

109. Option (A) is correct because it is medically important Fish-Borne Zoonotic Trematodes. They utilize a minimum of two hosts (blood flukes). The final or definitive host for adults and the snail's first intermediate host occurs in the stage cercaria, which is an infective stage.

Option (B) is incorrect because trematodes are leaf-like and unsegmented. Trematodes have heads with suckers but no hooks.

Option (C) is incorrect because trematodes are flattened oval or worm-like animals there is no anus, and waste material must be egested through the mouth.

Option (D) is incorrect because while they have a morphologically and physiologically complex tegument (body covering), trematodes do not have a body cavity. As a result, their organs are bound in parenchyma while the somatic muscle layers in the parenchyma attach to the tegument.
Hence, the correct option is (A).

110. Option (C) is correct because E. histolytica is an intestinal protozoan parasite that causes amebiasis. Humans are the only host for E. histolytica, which is transmitted by faecal-oral contact.

Option (A) is incorrect because Giardia is a microscopic parasite that causes the diarrheal illness known as giardiasis. Giardia (also known as Giardia intestinalis, Giardia lamblia, or Giardia duodenalis) is found on surfaces or in soil, food, or water that has been contaminated with faeces (poop) from infected humans or animals.

Option (B) is incorrect because Taenia is a genus of tapeworms that includes some important parasites of livestock. Members of the genus are responsible for taeniasis and cysticercosis in humans.

Option (D) is incorrect because the trichomonas are rather larger than pus cells and do not stain so that they stand out as clear refractile bodies against a stained background.

Hence, the correct option is (C).

111. Option (A) is correct because serologic ELISA is used to diagnose Invasive amoebiasis. ELISA (enzyme-linked immunosorbent assay) is a plate-based assay technique designed for detecting and quantifying substances such as peptides, proteins, antibodies, and hormones. Other names, such as enzyme immunoassay (EIA), are also used to describe the same technology.

Option (B) is incorrect because counter-current immunoelectrophoresis is a rapid sensitive method for detecting pneumococcal capsular antigens in sputum. Counter Current Immunoelectrophoresis is a modification of immunoelectrophoresis in which antigen and antibody move in opposite directions and form precipitates in the area where they meet in concentrations of optimal proportions.

Option (C) is incorrect because an indirect Hemagglutination test is used for the Diagnosis of Acute Leptospirosis, Antibodies to Cytomegalovirus. An indirect hemagglutination (IHA) test using sonicated extract as the antigen was developed for the detection of antibodies to Clostridium chauvoei. This antigen can be adsorbed onto glutaraldehyde-fixed sheep red blood cells treated with tannic acid and can be destroyed by trypsin and heat treatment.

Option (D) is incorrect because the complement fixation test is an immunological medical test that can be used to detect the presence of either specific antibody or specific antigen in a patient's serum, based on whether complement fixation occurs.
Hence, the correct option is (A).

112. Option (B) is correct because a fungus is a member of a large group of eukaryotic organisms that includes microorganisms such as yeasts and moulds, as well as more familiar mushrooms. The fungi are classified as a kingdom that is separate from plants, animals, and bacteria. Fungi have the following characteristics- Eukaryotic, Possess cell wall, Grows by extending filamentous cells called hyphae, or by budding.

Option (A) is incorrect because Prokaryotes are organisms whose cells do not contain a distinct nucleus, bounded by a nuclear envelope, in contrast to eukaryotic organisms that do have distinct nuclei. Prokaryotes include both the bacteria and the archaea, which appear to be only distantly related to bacteria.

Option (C) is incorrect because fungi are not a plant. The fungi (singular, fungus) once were considered to be plants because they grow out of the soil and have rigid cell walls. Now they are placed independently in their own kingdom of equal rank with the animals and plants and, in fact, are more closely related to animals than to plants.

Option (D) is incorrect because fungi are not an animal. Fungi are living organisms that are distantly related to plants, and more closely related to animals, but rather different from either of those groups.

Hence, the correct option is (B).

113. Option (B) is correct because Ascospores are the sexual propagules of ascomycetes. They are critical for describing most fungi. In ascocarp-forming ascomycetes, ascospores are only found in mature fruiting bodies. Thus, studying spore-bearing ascocarps is essential.

Option (A) is incorrect because asexual spore is the result of asexual reproduction. spore - a small usually single-celled asexual reproductive body produced by many nonflowering plants and fungi and some bacteria and protozoans and that are capable of developing into a new individual without sexual fusion.

Option (C) is incorrect because Conidia are haploid cells genetically identical to their haploid parent. They are produced by conversion of hyphal elements, or are borne on sporogenous cells on or within specialized structures termed conidiophores, and participate in the dispersal of the fungus.

Option (D) is incorrect because Ascospores are sexual spore.
Hence, the correct option is (B).

114. Option (C) is correct because Nakayama strain is a vaccine for Japanese encephalitis. Japanese encephalitis (JE) is an infection of the brain caused by the Japanese encephalitis virus (JEV). While most infections result in little or no symptoms, occasional inflammation of the brain occurs. In these cases, symptoms may include headache, vomiting, fever, confusion and seizures.

Option (A) is incorrect because Vivotif (Typhoid Vaccine Live Oral Ty21a) is a live attenuated vaccine for oral administration only. The vaccine contains the attenuated strain Salmonella typhi Ty21a (1,2). Vivotif is manufactured by the PaxVax Berna GmbH, Switzerland.

Option (B) is incorrect because the chickenpox vaccine is a shot that can protect nearly anyone who receives the vaccine from catching chickenpox. It's also called the varicella vaccine because chickenpox is caused by the varicella-zoster virus. The vaccine is made from live but weakened, or attenuated virus.

Option (D) is incorrect because the 17D vaccine, which is based on a live, attenuated viral strain, is the only commercially available yellow fever vaccine.

Hence, the correct option is (C).

115. Option (A) is correct because Maltese cross pattern under polarized light is seen in:- Babesia, Cryptococcus, Aspergillus nidulans, starch granules, and lipid (cholesterol) droplets. "Fungal ball due to Aspergillus nidulans has a propensity to produce pale staining thick-walled non-viable null cells that show maltese cross birefringence when examined under the polarized light". "On the polarized light, the spores in cryptococcus give maltese cross appearance".

Option (B) is incorrect because Penicillium marneffei infection is an important emerging public health problem, especially among patients infected with human immunodeficiency virus in the areas of endemicity in southeast Asia, India, and China.

Option (C) is incorrect because Blastomyces dermatitis is the causal agent of blastomycosis, an invasive and often serious fungal infection found occasionally in humans and other animals in regions where the fungus is endemic.

Option (D) is incorrect because Candida albicans is an opportunistic pathogenic yeast that is a common member of the human gut flora. It can also survive outside the human body. It is

detected in the gastrointestinal tract and mouth in 40–60% of healthy adults.
Hence, the correct option is (A).

116. Option (B) is correct because criminal negligence is punishable under Section 304 A IPC, for up to 2 years of imprisonment or fine or both.

Option (A) is incorrect because criminal negligence is punishable under Section 304 A for a maximum of 2 years.

Option (C) is incorrect for the reason same as of option (A) (Criminal negligence is punishable under Section 304 A for a maximum of 2 years).

Option (D) is incorrect for the reason same as of option (A) (Criminal negligence is punishable under Section 304 A for a maximum of 2 years).
Hence, the correct option is (B).

117. Option (A) is correct because Sec 174 CrPC deals with police inquest. Section 174 of the Code of Criminal Procedure is a legal provision that deals with the procedure that the police and the magistrate need to follow in cases of suicide and unnatural death.

Option (B) is incorrect because a (domestic) inquiry, in the context of human resource management, is a search for truth, facts are included in Section 75(1) of the Indian Industrial Relation Bill.

Option (C) is incorrect because it is section 303 of the Indian Penal Code that deals with Murder.

Option (D) is incorrect because it is section 304A that deal with Criminal law and medical negligence.
Hence, the correct option is (A).

118. Option (B) is correct because according to section 84 IPC, the act of a person of unsound mind is not an offence.

Option (A) is incorrect because Section 302 IPC is for the punishment of murder.

Option (C) is incorrect because Section 85 IPC i.e. act of a person incapable of judgment by a reason of intoxication (e.g. drunkness) is not an offence if intoxication is caused against his will.

Option (D) is incorrect because Section 88 IPC i.e. Act of a person is not an offence if the act is not intended to cause death/grievous hurt and done by consent in good faith for the person, e.g. Death of patient caused by surgery done by a surgeon.
Hence, the correct option is (B).

119. Option (C) is correct because Summon (subpoena) is a legal document compelling attendance of a witness in a court of law.

Option (A) is incorrect because Decomposition is the process by which organic substances are broken down into simpler organic matter. The gas created by the decomposing body tissue caused the barrel to float and surface.

Option (B) is incorrect because a subpoena is a kind document which is present to the designated presiding officer.

Option (D) is incorrect because Tribunals are specialist judicial bodies which decide disputes in a particular area of law. Most tribunal jurisdictions are part of a structure created by the Courts and Enforcement Act 2007.

Hence, the correct option is (C).

120. Option (B) is correct because the rate of cooling of a dead body in tropical countries (India) is 0.5- 0.7°C/hours.

Option (A) is incorrect because option (B) is correct which is 0.5°C/hours.

Option (C) is incorrect because option (B) is correct which is 0.5°C/hours.

Option (D) is incorrect because, in a temperate climate, it is about 1.5°C/hours.
Hence, the correct option is (B).

121. Option (A) is correct because the cherry red colour of blood is characteristically found in CO poisoning and in about 50% cases in cyanide/HCN poisoning (in 50% cases of cyanide poisoning it is bright red-coloured).

Option (B) is incorrect because a burn is a type of injury to the skin, or other tissues, caused by heat, cold, electricity, chemicals, friction, or radiation. It causes skin Red without blisters.

Option (C) is incorrect because Sulfuric acid also known as vitriol is a mineral acid composed of the elements sulfur, oxygen, and hydrogen, with molecular formula H_2SO_4. causes severe burns with redness, swelling, pain and blurred vision.

Option (D) is incorrect because Nitric acid (HNO_3), also known as aqua fortis and spirit of nitre, is a highly corrosive mineral acid. Nitric acid, red fuming appears as a pale yellow to reddish-brown liquid generating red-brown fumes and having a suffocating odour.
Hence, the correct option is (A).

122. Option (C) is correct because Projectiles of shotgun are lead (or recently steel) shots and pellets (not bullet). Bullets are projectile of the rifled firearm (rifle, pistol, revolver).

Option (A) is incorrect because Barrel is the part of the shotgun.

Option (B) is incorrect because choke bore is the part of the shotgun.

Option (D) is incorrect because the muzzle is the part of the shotgun.

Hence, the correct option is (C).

123. Option (A) is correct because partial hanging is the hanging in which the feet touch the ground or any underlying objects so we consider this as a suicidal case as the weight of the head is enough to cause death.

Option (B) is incorrect because complete hanging: The body is fully suspended and no part of the body touches the ground. Constricting force is the weight of the body.

Option (C) is incorrect because homicidal hanging- in which a person is rendered senseless and then hanged to simulate suicidal death.

Option (D) is incorrect because suicide hanging is the act of intentionally killing oneself via suspension from an anchor-point or ligature point (e.g. an overhead beam or hook) by a ligature or by jumping from a height with a noose around the neck.
Hence, the correct option is (A).

124. Option (B) is correct because Opium is a CNS depressant not cardiotoxic. Opium is dried latex obtained from the seed capsules of the opium poppy Papaver somniferum. Approximately 12 percent of opium is made up of the analgesic alkaloid morphine, which is processed chemically to produce heroin and other synthetic opioids for medicinal use and for the illegal drug trade.

Option (A) is incorrect because Aconitine and its related alkaloids are known cardiotoxins with no therapeutic role in modern western medicine. The rootstocks of Aconitum plants, which contain aconite alkaloids, have been common components of Chinese herbal recipes.

Option (C) is incorrect because Oleander contains cardiotoxic glycosides, such as oleandrin. Cardiac glycosides inhibit Na^{+}/K^{+} ATPase, which leads to increased intracellular Ca^{2+} concentrations and a subsequent positive inotropic effect.

Option (D) is incorrect because Nicotine is Cardiotoxic poisons. Nicotine is a stimulant and potent parasympathomimetic alkaloid that is naturally produced in the nightshade family of plants. It is used for the treatment of tobacco use disorders as a smoking cessation aid and nicotine dependence for the relief of withdrawal symptoms.
Hence, the correct option is (B).

125. Option (B) is correct because bromocriptine, a lysergic acid derivative, acts as a dopamine agonist, to inhibit prolactin release. In most women with elevated serum prolactin levels and amenorrhea–galactorrhea, bromocriptine restores normal menstruation within 6 weeks and causes cessation of galactorrhea by 13 weeks. Bromocriptine therapy also may diminish the size and symptoms of prolactin-secreting pituitary adenomas. Approximately 5% of patients terminate bromocriptine therapy due to nausea, headache, and faintness. These side effects may be minimized by taking the medication with food and by gradually increasing the bromocriptine dose to the appropriate level for the patient.

Option (A) is incorrect because clomiphene citrate acts as an estrogen agonist/antagonist via ER alpha in a coexisting estrogen concentration-dependent way whereas it acts as an estrogen antagonist via ER-beta whether or not estrogen is present.

Option (C) is incorrect because GnRH agonists act as agonists of the GnRH receptor, the biological target of gonadotropin-releasing hormone (GnRH). These drugs can be both peptides and small-molecules.

Option (D) is incorrect because as a glucocorticoid, dexamethasone is an agonist of the glucocorticoid receptor (GR). It will drive the negative feedback system for cortisol secretion in a person with a functional HPA axis.

Hence, the correct option is (B).

126. Option (D) is correct because health definition includes all the above dimension that is Social dimension, Economic dimension, Mental dimension.

Option (A) is incorrect because the social dimension is included in the definition of health which is the quantity and quality of an individual's interpersonal ties and the extent of involvement with the community.

Option (B) is incorrect because the economic dimension is included in the Definition of health. Economic dimension includes health inequalities by gender, ethnicity or socio-economic status (for example by income, education, employment, receipt of benefits at an individual or area level).

Option (C) is incorrect because the mental dimension is included in the Definition of health. A state of balance between oneself and the surrounding world.

Hence, the correct option is (D).

127. Option (B) is correct because Community participation is the current trend in Health Care. Community participation is the process by which individuals and families assume responsibility for their own health and of the community they live in. The community participation approach is a cost-effective way to extend a health care system to the geographical and social periphery of a country.

Option (A) is incorrect because Qualitative research (Qualitative enquiry) encompasses a range of methods that have successfully been used to explore issues of healthcare delivery from patient and provider perspectives. They can help both to illuminate different facets of "quality" and to inform quantitative approaches to researching health care.

Option (C) is incorrect because Equitable distribution means investing more resources in areas where it is needed more. primary care and other services to meet the main health problems in a community must be provided equally to all individuals irrespective of their gender, age, caste, colour, urban/rural location, and social class.

Option (D) is incorrect because Primary Health Care or PHC refers to "essential health care" that is based on scientifically sound and socially acceptable methods and technology. This makes universal health care accessible to all individuals and families in a community.

Hence, the correct option is (B).

128. Option (B) is correct because Sipuleucel-T is the first therapeutic cancer vaccine to demonstrate effectiveness in Phase III clinical trials by prolonging the life of patients who have advanced to the late stage of the disease, metastatic, asymptomatic,hormone-refractory prostate cancer(HRPC).

Option (A) is incorrect because breast cancer occurs when some breast cells begin to grow abnormally. These cells divide more rapidly than healthy cells do and continue to accumulate, forming a lump or mass. It's likely that breast cancer is caused by a complex interaction of your genetic makeup and your environment.

Option (C) is incorrect as having certain genetic conditions, such as von Hippel-Lindau (VHL) disease or inherited papillary renal cell carcinoma. Having a family history of kidney cancer. The risk is especially high in siblings. Being exposed to certain chemicals, such as asbestos, cadmium, benzene, organic solvents, or certain herbicides.

Option (D) is incorrect because cancer of the pancreas is caused when mutated cells grow out of control, forming a tumour. While the exact cause of pancreatic cancer is not known, certain risk factors are strongly linked to the disease, including tobacco smoking and obesity.
Hence, the correct option is (B).

129. Option (D) is correct because height in cms by the cube root of body weight is known as the Ponderal index. Formula: height (cm)/cube root of body weight (kgs).

Option (A) is incorrect because Quetelet's Index, more commonly known as the body mass index (BMI), is a measure of weight relative to height. Originally developed by 19th-century mathematician

Lambert Adolphe Jacques Quetelet, it is a standard measurement that is widely used by health professionals and researchers as an index of body fat. The formula used to calculate this index is the weight (in kilograms) divided by height (in meters squared).

Option (B) is incorrect because the Corpulence Index (CI) or Ponderal Index (PI) is a measure of leanness (corpulence) of a person calculated as a relationship between mass and height. It was first proposed in 1921 as the "Corpulence measure" by Swiss physician Fritz Rohrer and hence is also known as Rohrer's Index.

Option (C) is incorrect because the Broca Index is an estimation of ideal body weight using a height measurement only. The Broca Index was developed by Paul Broca, a French surgeon who lived between 1824 and 1880. The Broca index is only a rough estimate and applies to the range of middle body sizes best. Formula: height in cms -100.

Hence, the correct option is (D).

130. Option (C) is correct because the specificity of ELISA can be increased by carrying out ELISA in a row (series) using different HIV markers. When screening test is used in a series mode: - ↑ Specificity, ↑ PPV, ↓ Sensitivity.

Option (A) is incorrect because Positive predictive value will tell you the odds of you having a disease if you have a positive result. This can be useful in letting you know if you should panic or not. On the other hand, the sensitivity of a test is defined as the proportion of people with the disease who will have a positive result.

Option (B) is incorrect because Negative predictive value where a "true negative" is the event that the test makes a negative prediction, and the subject has a negative result under the gold standard, and a "false negative" is the event that the test makes a negative prediction, and the subject has a positive result under the gold standard.

Option (D) is incorrect because Negative predictive value is the probability that subjects with a negative screening test truly don't have the disease. Increased specificity — when a test does a good job of ruling out people who don't have the disease – usually means that the test has lower sensitivity (more false-negatives).

Hence, the correct option is (C).

131. Option (B) is correct as from the given question,

Sensitivity = 95%

Specificity = 80%

Prevalence = 20%

Thus,

PPV = senstivity × prevalencesenstivity × prevalence + (1-specificity) × (1-prevalence)

Option (A) is incorrect because the question is of the numerical pattern so, there will be only one and fixed answer. so, we get that option (A) is incorrect.

Option (C) is incorrect because as we explained in the above option (A) that the answer in this question is fixed. so, due to this option C is the wrong answer.

Option (D) is incorrect because from the explanation of both of the options A and C we get that the answer is 54.3%. so, option D is the wrong answer.

Hence, the correct option is (B).

132. Option (C) is correct because in panel discussion 4-8 qualified people talk about a topic and discuss a given problem in the presence of an audience.

Option (A) is incorrect because a symposium is a public meeting about a topic in which people give presentations.

Option (B) is incorrect because a seminar is a form of academic instruction, either at an academic institution or offered by a commercial or professional organization.

Option (D) is incorrect because it is a series of meetings usually four or more with emphasis on individual work, within a group with the help of consultants and resource personnel.

Hence, the correct option is (C).

133. Option (C) is correct because, to calculate the confidence limits for a measurement variable, multiply the standard error of the mean times the appropriate t-value. The confidence limit is distributed on either side of the mean and the deviation from the mean is determined by the standard deviation.

Option (A) is incorrect because the standard deviation and range are both measures of the spread of a data set. Each number tells us in its own way how spaced out the data are, as they are both a measure of variation. Although there is not an explicit relationship between the range and standard deviation, there is a rule of thumb that can be useful to relate these two statistics.

Option (B) is incorrect because the term "standard error" is used to refer to the standard deviation of various sample statistics, such as the mean or median. Standard error and standard deviation are measures of variability, while central tendency measures include mean, median, etc.

Option (D) is incorrect as a standard deviation (SD) is the dispersion of a random variable, a measure of the amount by which each value deviates from the mean. The manner of interaction between a ventilator and the person being ventilated, usually defined in terms of what the stimulus is that starts the ventilation.

Hence, the correct option is (C).

134. Option (B) is correct because the period of communicability of patients with varicella is estimated to begin 1–2 days before the onset of rash and ends when all lesions are crusted, typically 4–7 days after onset of rash in immunocompetent people. This period may be longer in immunocompromised people.

Option (A) is incorrect because the blisters release liquid containing the virus, then form crusts or scabs that fall off after 1 to 2 weeks. And as we know that its infectivity will last for 6 days. so it will be the wrong answer.

Option (C) is incorrect because the period of communicability of patients with varicella is estimated to begin 1–2 days before the onset of rash and not after. So, it will be the wrong answer to be selected.

Option (D) is incorrect because the itchy blister rash caused by chickenpox infection appears 10 to 21 days after exposure to the virus and usually lasts about five to 10 days. Other signs and

symptoms, which may appear one to two days before the rash, include Fever.
Hence, the correct option is (B).

135. Option (C) is correct because the characteristic feature of chickenpox is "Pleomorphism", that is, all stages of the rash (papules, vesicles, and crusts) may be seen simultaneously at one time in the same area.

Option (A) is incorrect because Varicella is highly contagious. It is less contagious than measles, but more so than mumps and rubella. Secondary attack rates among susceptible household contacts of persons with varicella are as high as 90% (that is, 9 of 10 susceptible household contacts of persons with varicella will become infected).

Option (B) is incorrect because the symptoms of a skin infection also vary depending on the type. Common symptoms include redness of the skin and a rash. You may also experience other symptoms, such as itching, pain, and tenderness.

Option (D) is incorrect because Varicella incidence ranges from 13 to 16 cases per 1,000 persons per year, with a substantial yearly variation.

Hence, the correct option is (C).

136. Option (D) is correct because WHO has proposed a uniform criterion and defined blindness as "Visual acuity of less than 3/60 or its equivalent". In the absence of appropriate vision charts, the WHO has now added the "inability to count fingers in daylight at a distance of 3 meters" to indicates less than 3/60 or its equivalent.

Option (A) is incorrect as in option (D), it is given that 3/60 is correct so we cannot replace it as it is a fixed number. so, option A will be the wrong answer.

Option (B) is incorrect because as from option (D), we noticed that it is the fixed number. so, it cannot be changed and that's why option (B) will become the wrong answer.

Option (C) is incorrect because from all the other three options we came to know that the answer is in numerical form, so, it cannot be replaced from other options. so, option (C) will become the wrong answer.

Hence, the correct option is (D).

137. Option (D) is correct because considering a birth prevalence of congenital heart disease as 9/1000, the estimated number of children born with congenital heart disease in India is more than 200,000 per year.

Option (A) is incorrect because Rheumatic heart disease, caused by acute rheumatic fever, now bears a lower disease burden in India: It causes 1.1% of total deaths. but it is more than congenital heart disease.

Option (B) is incorrect because Hypertension accounts for an estimated 54 percent of all strokes and 47 percent of all ischemic heart disease events globally.

Option (C) is incorrect because Ischemic heart disease caused 17.8% of deaths and strokes caused 7.1%, according to the study.

Hence, the correct option is (D).

138. Option (B) is correct because, In developed countries, the pyramid generally shows a bulge in the middle and has a narrower base (as in figure given in the question).

Option (A) is incorrect because the pyramid of a developing country (e.g. India) has a broad base and a tapering top as given below:

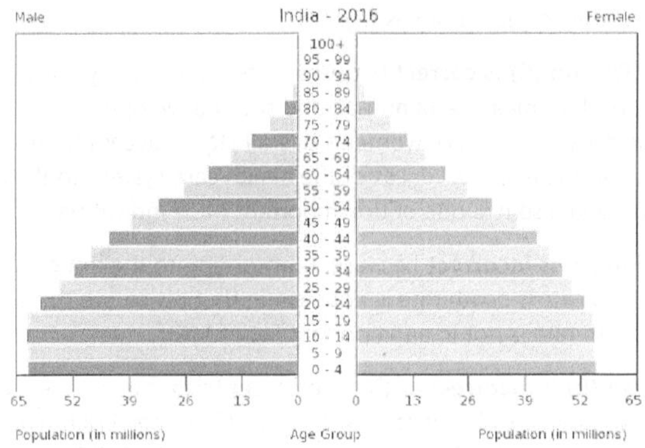

Option (C) is incorrect because underdeveloped also means that it's still a developing country so the graph of it will be almost the same as the developing country.

Option (D) is incorrect because poor countries are those which are still in a developing state. so, the graph for the poor country could come under the graph pattern of a developing country.
Hence, the correct option is (B).

139. Option (C) is correct because morbidity is a term used to describe how often a disease occurs in a specific area or is a term used to describe a focus on death. An example of morbidity is the number of people who have cancer. An example of morbidity is a focus on death.

Option (A) is incorrect because Demography is the scientific study of the human population. It focuses its attention on three readily observable human phenomena:- Change in the population size (growth or decline), The composition of the population, and the distribution of the population. It deals with five "demographic processes", namely fertility, mortality, marriage, migration and social mobility.

Option (B) is incorrect as an explanation in option (A) describes, we have come to the conclusion that it is the part of the five demographic processes.

Option (D) is incorrect because marriage is one of the parts of the five "demographic processes". It means it comes under the demography deals.

Hence, the correct option is (C).

140. Option (D) is correct because as from options (B) and (C) we get that both the options will be correct for the question. So, option D will be the correct answer to be selected.

Option (A) is incorrect because Palmitic acid is the first fatty acid produced during fatty acid synthesis and is the precursor to longer fatty acids. As a consequence, palmitic acid is a major body component of animals.

Option (B) is incorrect because DHA, the 22-carbon, the long-chain fatty acid found in breast milk, plays a key role in the structure and function of neural tissues, most notably those of the retina and brain.

Option (C) is incorrect because Docosahexaenoic acid (DHA) and arachidonic acid (ARA) are long-chain essential fatty acids used as supplements in commercial infant formula. DHA/ARA deficient states are associated with adverse neurological outcomes in animals and humans.

Hence, the correct option is (D).

141. Option (C) is correct because maternal mortality has become an important measure of human and social development. It is particularly revealing of women's overall status, access to health care, and the responsiveness of the health care system to their needs. and also it is one of the important MCH indicators.

Option (A) is incorrect because as according to the important MCH indicators death rate is not seen in that list so, we can say that the death rate is not in an important list of MCH.

Option (B) is incorrect as the adolescent birth rate, defined as the annual number of births to women ages 15–19 per 1,000 women in that age group. This is a progress indicator for the MDG target. and it is not in the MCH indicators.

Option (D) is incorrect because anaemia is one of the important factors associated with a number of maternal and foetal complications. It decreases the woman's reserve to tolerate bleeding either during or after childbirth and makes prone to infections. Anaemia during pregnancy also has been associated with increased risk of intrauterine growth restriction, premature delivery, low birth weight (LBW) and maternal and child mortality.

Hence, the correct option is (C).

142. Option (C) is correct because a daily supply of 150-200 litres per capita is considered as an adequate supply to meet the needs of all urban domestic purposes.

Option (A) is incorrect as according to the World Health Organization (WHO), between 50 and 100 litres of water per person per day is needed to ensure that most basic needs are met and few health concerns arise.

Option (B) is incorrect because according to current estimates, each person consumes approximately 150 litres per day — equating to almost two full bathtubs of water per person per day, or 54,750 litres per person each year. Most of this water is flushed away every day.

Option (D) is incorrect because citizens of Pune consume around 200-250 litres per person, which is almost double the standard usage.
Hence, the correct option is (C).

143. Option (C) is correct because a woman age between 18-29 years should weight around 55kg.

Option (A) is incorrect because a child between the age of 7-13 years should have a weight of 45kg.

Option (B) is incorrect because the average weight for a 13-year-old with height 5.1ft should be around 46kg. Although having 50kg weight is still okay. It depends on your height.

Option (D) is incorrect because a grown adult male may consider 60 kg to be easily manageable to carry. A bodybuilder or professional American Football lineman would yawn if they had to carry 60 kg and maybe could do a hundred reps of 60kg.

Hence, the correct option is (C).

144. Option (A) is correct because a safe energy allowance for the last half of gestation based on indirect calorimetry would be about 1.6 times BEE or 1.5 times REE. This would total about 2500 kcal per day for a pregnant woman with a BEE of 1.1 kcal per minute.

Option (B) is incorrect because, for women who wish to maintain their current weight, the calorie requirement for a resting state is roughly bodyweight times 10. For instance, a 140-pound woman would need roughly 1,400 calories if she slept 24/7 just to support basic biological processes such as breathing and digestion.

Option (C) is incorrect because she should eat 1000 cal at the early age of the pregnancy.

Option (D) is incorrect because the first trimester does not require any extra calories. During the second trimester, an additional 340 calories a day are recommended. For the third trimester, the recommendation is 450 calories more a day than when not pregnant.
Hence, the correct option is (A).

145. Option (C) is correct because antipsychotic medications are used as short or long-term treatment for bipolar disorder to control psychotic symptoms such as hallucinations, delusions, or mania symptoms. These symptoms may occur during acute mania or severe depression. and it doesn't come under the National Mental Health program.

Option (A) is incorrect as to promote community participation in the mental health service development, and to enhance human resource in mental health sub-specialities. As it comes under the National Mental Health program, so it is the objective of that particular program.

Option (B) is incorrect as to encourage the application of mental health knowledge in general healthcare and in social development; it comes under the objectives of the National Mental Health program.

Option (D) is incorrect because to ensure the availability and accessibility of minimum mental healthcare for all in the foreseeable future; is the objective of the National Mental Health program.

Hence, the correct option is (C).

146. Option (A) is correct because the solid wastes generated in hospital and nursing homes generally varies as follows :

1/2 to 4kg/bed/day - Govt. hospital

1/2 to 2kg/bed/day - Private hospital

1/2 to 1kg/bed/day - Nursing home.

Out of all these 45-50% of the wastes are infectious.

Option (B) is incorrect because the higher content of organic food (this is 65% of household waste and 50% in municipal solid waste) is a reflection of cultural values of consuming more cooked food as compared to processed and packaged food.

Option (C) is incorrect because the vast majority of these hospital wastes are just a general sort of waste. According to the World Health Organization, about 80% of the hospital wastes produced by health care activities are general wastes. The remaining 20% of these hospital wastes are considered to be biohazard waste.

Option (D) is incorrect as from the option (A) we analyzed that its less than 50% amount of waste infectious produced so, option (D)

will be the wrong answer.
Hence, the correct option is (A).

147. Option (A) is correct because health education is one strategy for implementing health promotion and disease prevention programs. Health education provides learning experiences on health topics. Health education strategies are tailored to their target population.

Option (B) is incorrect because in psychology, the process of altering or disguising unconscious ideas or impulses so that they become acceptable to the conscious mind.

Option (C) is incorrect because public health professionals work in a variety of settings, there is a special relationship with the governmental public health agencies at the local, state, and federal level. These agencies have a major responsibility for educating and training the current public health workforce and future public health workers who have not received training elsewhere.

Option (D) is incorrect because health education has programs for disease prevention. So, we cannot say that it doesn't provide any help in prevention.
Hence, the correct option is (A).

148. Option (D) is correct because a referral management system is a unique and powerful tool for health providers to keep track of their patient referrals throughout the care continuum. Its main goal is to improve and streamline communication among primary care physicians, specialists, and health providers involved in a patient's care.

Option (A) is incorrect because primary care is the day-to-day healthcare given by a health care provider. Typically this provider acts as the first contact and principal point of continuing care for patients within a healthcare system and coordinates other specialist care that the patient may need. An adequate supply of safe water and basic sanitation is one of the elements of primary health care.

Option (B) is incorrect because primary care is the day-to-day healthcare given by a health care provider. Typically this provider acts as the first contact and principal point of continuing care for patients within a healthcare system and coordinates other specialist care that the patient may need. Provision of essential drugs is one of the essential elements of primary health care.

Option (C) is incorrect as from option (A) and (B) we came to know about the primary health care and also that health education is one of the essential elements of primary health care.

Hence, the correct option is (D).

149. Option (B) is correct because Epidemic keratoconjunctivitis (EKC) is a highly contagious viral conjunctivitis. It is caused by a group of viruses known as adenoviruses that in addition to infections of the ocular surface, are responsible for causing infectious diseases of the gastrointestinal tract and respiratory system illnesses such as the common cold virus, for example. The adenovirus serotypes 8, 19, and 37 are often associated with EKC.

Option (A) is incorrect because VISION2020 aims to eliminate avoidable blindness in the world by 2020 and targets the world's leading causes of avoidable visual impairment: cataract, trachoma, onchocerciasis, childhood blindness (including vitamin A deficiency), and refractive error and low vision.

Option (C) is incorrect because programs emphasize the major causes of blindness: cataract, trachoma, onchocerciasis, childhood blindness, and refractive error. Cataract programs have stressed outreach to underserved areas and the development of additional surgical manpower.

Option (D) is incorrect because long-standing programs have targeted onchocerciasis (OnchocerciasisControl Program and the African Program for Onchocerciasis Control) and trachoma(Global Eradication of Trachoma by 2020), and they have been integrated into the regional implementation plan.
Hence, the correct option is (B).

150. Option (A) is correct because when a person carries an autosomal dominant gene mutation, each offspring carries a 50% chance of inheriting that mutated allele. The most common hereditary cancer syndromes, hereditary breast, and ovarian cancer (HBOC) syndrome and hereditary nonpolyposis colorectal cancer (HNPCC), are autosomal dominant in nature.

Option (B) is incorrect because autosomal recessive is one of several ways that a trait, disorder, or disease can be passed down through families. An autosomal recessive disorder means two copies of an abnormal gene must be present in order for the disease or trait to develop.

Option (C) is incorrect because X-linked recessive inheritance is a mode of inheritance in which a mutation in a gene on the X chromosome causes the phenotype to be always expressed in males (who are necessarily hemizygous for the gene mutation because they have one X and one Y chromosome) and in females who are homozygous for the gene mutation, see zygosity. Females with one copy of the mutated gene are carriers.

Option (D) is incorrect because X-linked dominant inheritance, sometimes referred to as X-linked dominance, is a mode of genetic inheritance by which a dominant gene is carried on the X chromosome.
Hence, the correct option is (A).

151. Option (C) is correct because when the thyroid gland does not produce enough thyroid hormones to meet the needs of the body. The thyroid is underactive. The opposite is hyperthyroidism, where the thyroid produces too much thyroid hormone.

Option (A) is incorrect because It is the result of obstruction of blood flow at the narrowed aortic segment, in conjunction with collateral blood flow through the intercostal arteries. Rib notching occurs along the inferior margin of the third to the eighth ribs; it is caused by the pulsation of dilated intercostal arteries.

Option (B) is incorrect because Non-vascular causes of rib notching include neurofibromatosis, intercostal neuromas and pseudo-rib notching where irregular cortical thickening may occur in the presence of tuberous sclerosis and hyperparathyroidism. Degrees of rib notching on chest radiography may also be of no clinical significance.

Option (D) is incorrect because The hallmark feature of osteogenesis imperfecta is that fragile bones that fracture easily. It affects both bone quality and quantity. kit causes Superior rib notching.

Hence, the correct option is (C).

152. Option (D) is correct because this option is included all other options too so this option will be the correct.

Automated perimetry has made perimetric examination simpler, more accessible and more reproducible, and has, therefore, become a major screening, diagnostic and review modality in patients having any visual Field defect.

- Automated perimetry has many advantages over manual ways of recording the Field.

a. Points in the visual Field are tested randomly so that the subject cannot 'anticipate' where the next stimulus will be presented.

b. The visual Field is tested by a static method which quantifies retinal sensitivity and is more accurate than manual perimetry.

c. Examiner bias is eliminated.

d. There is constant monitoring of Fixation.

e. Abnormal points are re-tested automatically.

f. Built-in, custom-made programs can be selected or further programming is done to perform customized visual Field testing.

Option (A) is incorrect because according to the above explanation it is measured by Automated Perimeters.

Option (B) is incorrect because according to the above explanation it is measured by Automated Perimeters.

Option (C) is incorrect because according to the above explanation it is measured by Automated Perimeters.

Hence, the correct option is (D).

153. Option (B) is correct because a urine pH of 8.5 or 9.0 is indicative of a urea-splitting organism, such as Proteus or Ureaplasma urealyticum; therefore, an asymptomatic patient with a high pH means UTI regardless of the other urine test results.

Option (A) is incorrect because, in the process of collecting the urine, some contamination from skin bacteria is frequent. For that reason, up to 10,000 colonies of bacteria/ml are considered normal. Greater than 100,000 colonies/ml represents urinary tract infection. For counts between 10,000 and 100,000, the culture is indeterminate.

Option (C) is incorrect because Klebsiella UTIs occur when the bacteria enter the urinary tract. It can also happen after using a urinary catheter for a long time. Typically, K. pneumonia causes UTIs in older women.

Option (D) is incorrect because Candiduria is often observed in hospitalized patients. Candiduria is neither a symptom nor a sign, and it is clearly not a disease. The finding of yeast (almost always Candida species) in the urine could mean that the patient has pyelonephritis or cystitis.

Hence, the correct option is (B).

154. Option(D) is correct because the Diagnosis of myasthenia gravis.

1. Myasthenia gravis presents with characteristic clinical features Several special diagnostic Tests for myasthenia Gravis Electrophysiological Testing.
2. Characteristic of myasthenia on electrophysiological testing is a rapid reduction in the amplitude of muscle action potentials evoked during a series of repetitive stimulations of a peripheral nerve at a rate of 3 per second (decrementing response).
3. The traditional and simple method is to stimulate the nerve at 3 Hz and to measure the compound muscle action potential (a decrement of more than 10% when comparing the fifth to the first response is abnormal) Single fiber electromyography.
4. This is more sensitive but technically more difficult than electrophysiological testing. Confirmatory but not specific, often performed in conjunction.
5. This technique demonstrates an inconstancy in the firing of fibers connected to the same motor unit or blocking of successive discharges from single muscle fiber belonging to the same motor unit. Edrophonium and Neostigmine test/Tensilon test.
6. When edrophonium and neostigmine are given intravenously, it produces a transient improvement in strength in patients with myasthenia.

Option(A) is incorrect because this medication is used in emergencies to treat very serious allergic reactions to insect stings/bites, foods, drugs, or other substances. Epinephrine acts quickly to improve breathing, stimulate the heart, raise dropping blood pressure, reverse hives, and reduce swelling of the face, lips, and throat.

Option(B) is incorrect because Physostigmine is a parasympathomimetic, specifically, a reversible cholinesterase inhibitor which effectively increases the concentration of acetylcholine at the sites of cholinergic transmission.

Option(C) is incorrect because they are administered in low doses to reverse the action of muscle relaxants, to treat myasthenia gravis, and to treat symptoms of Alzheimer's disease (rivastigmine, which increases cholinergic activity in the brain).

Hence, the correct option is (D).

155. Option (C) is correct as Klinefelter syndrome is a chromosomal condition that affects male physical and cognitive development. Its signs and symptoms vary among affected individuals.

Affected individuals typically have small testes that do not produce as much testosterone as usual

Option (A) is incorrect because Marfan syndrome (MFS) is a genetic disorder of the connective tissue. The degree to which people are affected varies. People with Marfan tend to be tall and thin, with long arms, legs, fingers, and toes. They also typically have flexible joints and scoliosis.

Option (B) is incorrect because Testicular feminization syndrome now more appropriately called the complete androgen insensitivity syndrome, this is a genetic disorder that makes XY fetuses insensitive (unresponsive) to androgens (male hormones). Instead, they are born looking externally like normal girls.

Option (D) is incorrect because it is a genetic disorder caused by the presence of all or part of the third copy of chromosome 21. It is usually associated with physical growth delays, mild to moderate intellectual disability, and characteristic facial features.

Hence, the correct option is (C).

156. Option (C) is correct because False-positive ELISA is seen in -

1. Antibodies to class II antigens - Recent influenza vaccination.
2. Autoantibodies - Acute viral infections.
3. Hepatic disease - Connective tissue diseases e.g. SLE.
4. ELISA is the standard screening test for HIV infection.
5. It has a sensitivity of > 99.5%, while it is highly sensitive, it is not optimal in regard to specificity. Most commonly used confirmatory test for the diagnosis of HIV infection - a Western Blot test.

Option (A) is incorrect because Multiple myelomas are cancer that forms in a type of white blood cell called a plasma cell. Plasma cells help you fight infections by making antibodies that recognize and attack germs. Multiple myelomas cause cancer cells to accumulate in the bone marrow, where they crowd out healthy blood cells.

Option (B) is incorrect because Lepromatous leprosy is a form of leprosy characterized by pale macules in the skin. It results from the failure of Th1 cell activation which is necessary to eradicate the mycobacteria (Th1 response is required to activate macrophages that engulf and contain the disease).

Option (D) is incorrect because only SLE gives False-positive ELISA for HIV, hence this option will not be correct.

Hence, the correct option is (C).

157. Option (C) is correct because Sodium fluoride is a useful preservative in a suspected case of alcohol poisoning.

It is done with mixing 10 mL of blood with potassium oxalate & sodium fluoride (enzyme inhibitors) for suspected alcohol poisoning.

A preservative (sodium fluoride, 0.5 -2% weight by volume) should be added after collecting a vitreous humor sample for ethanol analysis in postmortem toxicology cases.

Gastric contents can be stored in a saturated salt solution.

Option (A) is incorrect because potassium acetate is used to precipitate dodecyl sulfate (DS) and DS-bound proteins, allowing the removal of proteins from DNA. It is also used as a salt for the ethanol precipitation of DNA. Potassium acetate is used in mixtures applied for tissue preservation, fixation, and mummification.

Option (B) is incorrect because Sodium sulfide is used in the pulp and paper industry, water treatment, textile industry, and various chemical manufacturing processes including the production of rubber chemicals, sulfur dyes, and oil recovery. Along with its hydrate form, sodium sulfide releases hydrogen sulfide (H_2S) when in contact with moist air.

Option (D) is incorrect as it is used as a moisturizer to treat or prevent dry, rough, scaly, itchy skin and minor skin irritations (e.g., diaper rash, skin burns from radiation therapy). Emollients are substances that soften and moisturize the skin and decrease itching and flaking.

Hence, the correct option is (C).

158. Option (A) is correct as:

- Gastric GIST Paraganglioma Pulmonary chondroma.
- "It describes the coexistence of several neoplasms, mainly in young women, including: gastric epithelioid leiomyosarcoma (these are now known to actually be malignant gastrointestinal stromal tumors), pulmonary chondroma, and extra-adrenal paraganglioma".
- Also Know: "Carney complex, also known as LAMB syndrome and NAME syndrome is an autosomal dominant condition comprising myxomas of the heart and skin, hyperpigmentation of the skin (lentiginosis), and endocrine overactivity.
- It is distinct from Carney's triad. Approximately 7% of all cardiac myxomas are associated with Carney complex".

Option (B) is incorrect because according to the explanation of option (A) this option is not correct.

Option (C) is incorrect because according to the explanation of option (A) this option is not correct.

Option (D) is incorrect because according to the explanation of option (A) this option is not correct.
Hence, the correct option is (A).

159. Option (C) is correct because pemphigus causes blistering in the epidermis by virtue of the process of acantholysis. The blisters arise on normal-appearing skin; Immunofluorescence shows deposits of immunoglobulins (usually IgG) and/or C3 in the intercellular spaces around keratinocytes. Antibodies to the intercellular areas of the epidermis are found in the serum. Circulating antibodies to the epidermis are directed against several polypeptide components of the epidermal desmosomes. Their titers somewhat reflect disease activity, and they may contribute to the defective epidermal adhesion. High doses of systemic steroids over prolonged periods usually control the disease.

Option (A) is incorrect because genital herpes is a sexually transmitted disease (STD). This STD causes herpetic sores, which are painful blisters (fluid-filled bumps) that can break open and ooze fluid. About 16 percent of people between the ages of 14 and 49 have this STD.

Option (B) is incorrect because Bullous pemphigoid (BUL-us PEM-fih-goid) is a rare skin condition that causes large, fluid-filled blisters. They develop on areas of skin that often flex — such as the lower abdomen, upper thighs or armpits.

Option (D) is incorrect because SLE is one of a large group of conditions called autoimmune disorders that occur when the immune system attacks the body's own tissues and organs. SLE may first appear as extreme tiredness (fatigue), a vague feeling of discomfort or illness (malaise), fever, loss of appetite, and weight loss.

Hence, the correct option is (C).

160. Option (B) is correct because the second heart sound can be represented by dupp. It occurs at the beginning of ventricular diastole and results from the closure of the semilunar valves.

Option (A) is incorrect because Lubb is the first sound that has a low pitch and produced by the closure of tricuspid and bicuspid valves (collectively called atrioventricular valves) at the beginning of ventricular systole. It is produced by closure of semilunar valves by the end of ventricular systole.

Option (C) is incorrect because the second heart sound can be represented by dupp. It occurs at the beginning of ventricular diastole and results from the closure of the semilunar valves and the first heart sound can be represented by the syllable lubb. It occurs at the beginning of ventricular systole and results from the closure of the AV valves.

Option (D) is incorrect because according to the above explanation this option will not be correct.

Hence, the correct option is (B).

161. Option (B) is correct because decreased lung compliance is a prominent feature of ARDS. Common causes of decreased lung compliance are pulmonary fibrosis, pneumonia, and pulmonary edema. In obstructive lung disease, airway obstruction causes an increase in resistance.

Option (A) is incorrect because Acute Respiratory Distress Syndrome (ARDS) Acute respiratory distress syndrome is a type of respiratory (lung) failure resulting from many different disorders that cause fluid to accumulate in the lungs and oxygen levels in the blood to be too low. but Type 2 respiratory failure is caused by inadequate alveolar ventilation; both oxygen and carbon dioxide are affected.

Option (C) is incorrect because Acute respiratory distress syndrome (ARDS) is a life-threatening condition (PEEP) that may improve oxygen diffusion in affected alveoli, it may result in. diaphragmatic excursion, and increased functional residual capacity.

Option (D) is incorrect because according to above explanation of option (B) this option will not be correct.

Hence, the correct option is (B).

162. Option (B) is correct because in ARDS mechanical TV low volume ventilation is 5-7 ml/kg i.e.,31%.

Option (A) is incorrect because as we know that the correct answer to this question will be 5-7ml/kg. so, automatically 2-3ml/kg will not satisfy the question.

Option (C) is incorrect because from the above option we get that the answer will be 5-7 ml/kg. so, we can say that option (C) will become wrong.

Option (D) is incorrect as we came to know that option B is found to be the correct answer, that's why option (D) will not be the correct answer.

Hence, the correct option is (B).

163. Option (B) is correct because Inherited susceptibility to rheumatoid arthritis (RA) is associated with the DRB1 genes encoding the human leukocyte antigen (HLA)-DR4 and HLA-DR1 molecules. Transgenic mice expressing these major histocompatibility complex (MHC) class II molecules have been developed to generate humanized models for RA.

Option (A) is incorrect because Sarcoidosis is an inflammatory disease that affects multiple organs in the body, but mostly the lungs and lymph glands. In people with sarcoidosis, abnormal masses or nodules (called granulomas) consisting of inflamed tissues form in certain organs of the body. hence it is not related to HLA-DR4.

Option (C) is incorrect because Seronegative rheumatoid arthritis is the diagnosis of rheumatoid arthritis without the presence of certain antibodies in the patient's blood. These indicate that the patient is seropositive and that they possess the antibodies that cause an attack on joints and lead to inflammation. So, it is not related to HLA-DR4.

Option (D) is incorrect because Psoriasis is a long-lasting autoimmune disease characterized by patches of abnormal skin. These skin patches are typically red, or purple on some people with darker skin, dry, itchy, and scaly. Psoriasis varies in severity from small, localized patches to complete body coverage. So, this is also not related to HLA-DR4.

Hence, the correct option is (B).

164. Option (D) is correct because according to the above explanation this is not a reason for the high anion gap. So, this option will be correct according to question.

Causes of High anion gap acidosis

1. Lactic acidosis
2. Toxins
3. Ethylene glycol
4. Methanol
5. Salicylates

Also, there are more causes.

1. Renal failure
2. Ketoacidosis
3. Diabetes
4. Alcohol
5. Starvation

Option (A) is incorrect because according to the above explanation this is the reason for the high anion gap.

Option (B) is incorrect because according to the above explanation this is the reason for the high anion gap.

Option (C) is incorrect because according to above explanation this is reason of high anion gap.

Hence, the correct option is (D).

165. Option (D) is correct As the above explanation, the minimum concentration of reduced hemoglobin is 5 gm/d. So, this option will be correct.

As given

- Cyanosis refers to a bluish color of the skin and mucous membranes resulting from an increased quantity of reduced hemoglobin, or of hemoglobin derivatives, in the small blood vessels of those areas. It is usually most marked in the lips, nail beds, ears, and malar eminences.
- The degree of cyanosis is modified by the color of the cutaneous pigment and the thickness of the skin, as well as by the state of the cutaneous capillaries.
- In some instances, central cyanosis can be detected reliably when the SaO2 has fallen to 85%; in others, particularly in dark-skinned persons, it may not be detected until it has declined to 75%.
- The increase in the quantity of reduced hemoglobin in the mucocutaneous vessels that produce cyanosis may be brought about either by an increase in the quantity of venous blood as a result of dilation of the venules and

venous ends of the capillaries or by a reduction in the Sa in the capillary blood. In sulhaemoglobmemia cyanosis occurs when its level exceeds 0.5gm/dl A methemoglobin level of 15% (i.e.,1.5gm/dl) 3 is associated with visible cyanosis-Nelson.

Option (A) is incorrect As the above explanation the minimum concentration of reduced hemoglobin is 5 gm/d. So, this option will not be correct.

Option (B) is incorrect As the above explanation, the minimum concentration of reduced hemoglobin is 5 gm/d. So, this option will not be correct.

Option (C) is incorrect As the above explanation, the minimum concentration of reduced hemoglobin is 5 gm/d. So, this option will not be correct.

Hence, the correct option is (D).

166. Option (B) is correct because Pityriasis Versicolor is more common in hot, humid climates or in those who sweat heavily, so it may recur each summer. The yeasts can often be seen under the microscope within the lesions and typically have a so-called "spaghetti and meatball appearance" as the round yeasts produce filament.

Option (A) is incorrect because Dermatophyte identification is based on the detection of fungal elements by direct microscopy of clinical specimens combined with culture-based full identification. Phenotypic identification includes macromorphological, micromorphological, and physiological characteristics of the colonies.

Option (C) is incorrect because the fungus is often found growing on dead leaves, stored grain, compost piles, or in other decaying vegetation. It can also be found on marijuana leaves. Although most people are often exposed to aspergillus, infections caused by the fungus rarely occur in people who have a healthy immune system.

Option (D) is incorrect because the common signs of Candida overgrowth are:

- Brain fog, poor memory, ADHD.
- Mood swings, anxiety, depression: 95 percent of serotonin is made in the gut.
- Fatigue and/or fibromyalgia.
- Autoimmune diseases connected to leaky gut (as mentioned above).
- Digestive issues—gas, bloating, constipation.

So, there is no appearance of Spaghetti and meatball so this option will not be correct.

Hence, the correct option is (B).

167. Option (A) is correct because according to the above explanation only this option will be correct because the statements 'd', 'e' are not true regarding skin.

Following events occur during keratinization

1. Increase in cell size
2. Flattening of cells
3. The appearance of new cellular organelles, e.g. lamellar granules in stratum spinosum, keratohyalin granules and odland bodies in stratum granulosum.
4. Metabolism changes from generalized to more focused on the synthesis of molecules (structural proteins and lipids) related to keratinization.
5. Progressive dehydration (not hydration).
6. Progressive shortening and final disappearance of the nucleus.
7. Changes in enzymes with the degradation of cellular organelles and chromatin fragmentation → apoptosis in stratum corneum.
8. Finally, dead cells to break apart and slough away, a process is known as desquamation.

Option (B) is incorrect as this option includes the statements b and c which are related to the skin hence this option will not be correct.

Option (C) is incorrect as this option includes the statements d and c, which are related to the skin hence this option will not be correct.

Option (D) is incorrect as this option includes the statements d and c, which are related to the skin so, this option will not be correct.

Hence, the correct option is (A).

168. Option (C) is correct because Piebaldism is a hypopigmented disorder which is present since birth and is characterized by the congenital white forelock and hypopigmented or depigmented macules on the central part of the forehead, ventral trunk, and upper & lower extremities. Involvement is bilaterally symmetrical.

Option (A) is incorrect because Androgenetic Alopecia is often referred to as 'Male Pattern Hair Loss' or 'Female Pattern Hair Loss'. It is the most common type of hair loss affecting approximately 50% of men over the age of 50 and around 50% of women over the age of 65. Androgenetic Alopecia can also affect younger men and women.

Option (B) is incorrect because Erythema nodosum leprosum (ENL) is an immune-mediated complication of leprosy, characterized by the presence of multiple inflammatory cutaneous nodules and systemic symptoms such as fever, malaise, arthritis, iritis, neuritis, and lymphadenitis.

Option (D) is incorrect because option (C) is correct according to question so this option will not be correct.

Hence, the correct option is (C).

169. Option (D) is correct as all the above explanation this option includes all the options segments hence this option will be correct according to the question.

Option (A) is incorrect because Acanthosis nigricans is a skin condition characterized by areas of dark, velvety discoloration in body folds and creases. The skin changes of acanthosis nigricans (ak-an-THOE-sis NIE-grih-Kuns) typically occur in people who are obese or have diabetes.

Option (B) is incorrect because Malignant acanthosis nigricans is most commonly associated with gastrointestinal adenocarcinomas, as well as genitourinary cancers such as those of the prostate, breast, and ovary. Other cancers, such as those of the lung, stomach, and lymphoma, are occasionally associated with acanthosis nigricans.

Option (C) is incorrect because Acanthosis nigricans, hypothyroidism, and insulin resistance. It is concluded that hypothyroidism may be associated with acanthosis nigricans, that hyperinsulinemia is a regular correlate of the skin disorder, and that treatment of the hypothyroidism does not resolve the hyperinsulinemia or the acanthosis nigricans.

Hence, the correct option is (D).

170. Option (B) is correct because Nickel is the most common sensitizing agent worldwide. Allergic contact dermatitis due to this metal represents great morbidity, as well as cases of systemic allergic contact dermatitis, which can be misdiagnosed as adverse drug reactions, delaying the correct diagnosis and leading to inappropriate treatment. So this option will be correct according to the question.

Option (A) is incorrect because Sometimes ring rash is caused by contact dermatitis. This occurs when your skin comes into contact with an irritant that causes a reaction. Jewelry containing nickel or gold can cause allergic contact dermatitis if a person has an allergy to these metals

Option (C) is incorrect because Contact dermatitis is a common skin reaction, and it is important to determine the causative agent. Silver dermatitis has been infrequently reported in the literature. In the handful of cases that have been reported, five of them were related to occupational exposure to silver compounds.

Option (D) is incorrect because Metal allergy may result in allergic contact dermatitis and also SCD.In the irritant type of contact dermatitis, the most frequent triggers are chemicals such as in soaps, bleach, dyes, and solvents. In allergic contact dermatitis, common allergens include nickel, adhesives, plants, cosmetics, and topical medications. So, it will be incorrect.

Hence, the correct option is (B).

171. Option (B) is correct as of the Diagnosis of Airborne contact dermatitis: The patch test is used to find out causative allergens. Photo patch tests can be useful for excluding light as a factor in the pathogenesis of the lesions. During patch testing, volatile allergens sometimes also cause irritant dermatitis; therefore, high dilutions should be used. So, this option will be correct.

Option (A) is incorrect because this is a test in which A skin biopsy removes cells or skin samples from the surface of your body. The sample taken from a skin biopsy is examined to provide information about your medical condition. A doctor uses a skin biopsy to diagnose or rule out certain skin conditions and diseases.

Option (C) is incorrect because this is a type of test in which A skin prick test, also called a puncture or scratch test, checks for immediate allergic reactions to as many as 40 different substances at once. This test is usually done to identify allergies to pollen, mold, pet dander, dust mites, and foods. In adults, the test is usually done on the forearm.

Option (D) is incorrect because in this Estimation of Ig E may be an important one in treatments for allergy and asthma. In biology, IgE is a class of antibody that plays an important role in allergy and is especially associated with type I hypersensitivity. The serum level of IgE is 0.0003 mg/ml the lowest of all other types of antibodies.

Hence, the correct option is (B).

172. Option (C) is correct because when the skin is stretched across the long axis of a medallion lesion, the scales being finer, lighter and attached at one end tend to fold across the line of stretch, thus hanging curtain sign is seen in pityriasis rosea. So this option will be correct according to the question.

Option (A) is incorrect because Pityriasis alba is a low-grade type of eczema/dermatitis that primarily affects children. No treatment is required for pityriasis alba. The patches usually go away with time. Your doctor may prescribe a moisturizing cream or topical steroid cream such as hydrocortisone to treat the condition.

Option (B) is incorrect as:

- Patches of skin discoloration, usually on the back, chest, neck and upper arms, which may appear lighter or darker than usual.
- Mild itching.
- Scaling.

So, this option will not be correct according to the question.

Option (D) is incorrect because it appears as many white, pink, salmon-colored, tan, or brown patches ranging in size from 1 to 3 cm. The individual lesions can join together to form large patches. Most lesions have a very fine, flaky surface.

Hence, the correct option is (C).

173. Option (C) is correct as Psoriasis is an autoimmune disease that causes plaques, which are itchy, or sore. Some common signs and symptoms include red patches or raised plaques of skin that are covered with silvery scales. these lesions can occur on the genitals or in areas near the genitals, like the upper thighs and groin.

Option (A) is incorrect as Scalp psoriasis appears as red, itchy areas with silvery-white scales. Psoriasis in children often first appears on the scalp. You may notice flakes of dead skin in your hair or on your shoulders, especially after scratching your scalp. The scaly patches, which may bleed when removed, may extend beyond your hairline.

Option (B) is incorrect as areas of plaque may appear anywhere on the body but are most common on the knees and elbows. armpits; groin; under the breasts; behind the knee.

Option (D) is incorrect because psoriasis usually appears as red or pink plaques of raised, thick, scaly skin. However, it can also appear as small flat bumps or large thick plaques. It most commonly affects the skin on the elbows, knees, and scalp, though it can appear anywhere on the body.

Hence, the correct option is (C).

174. Option (D) is correct as Mucous membranes line many tracts and structures of the body, including the mouth, nose, eyelids, trachea (windpipe) and lungs, stomach and intestines, and the ureters, urethra, and urinary bladder. So, according to the question this option will be the correct.

Option (A) is incorrect because Herpes simplex is the primary cause of erythema multiforme, and the virus is present in 70 percent of recurrent erythema multiforme cases. Both types of herpes simplex virus (HSV) can cause the condition, but HSV-1, which also causes cold sores, is responsible for most cases, so, this is related to erythema multiformis so this option is incorrect according to the question.

Option (B) is incorrect as Erythema multiforme usually occurs in adults 20 to 40 years of age,6 although it can be drugs, penicillins, phenothiazines, and sulfonamides. So, according to the question this option will also be incorrect.

Option (C) is incorrect because Erythema multiforme is a skin condition considered to be a hypersensitivity reaction to infections or drugs. It consists of a polymorphous eruption of macules, papules, and characteristic "target" lesions that are symmetrically distributed with a propensity for the distal extremities. So, this option is incorrect according to the question.

Hence, the correct option is (D).

175. Option (C) is correct because Atopic dermatitis (AD), also known as atopic eczema, is a type of inflammation of the skin (dermatitis). It results in itchy, red, swollen, and cracked skin. Clear fluid may come from the affected areas, which often thickens over time. Many people with atopic dermatitis develop hay fever or asthma. So, it will be correct according to the question.

Option (A) is incorrect as Pemphigus Vulgaris (i.e., pemphigus) and bullous pemphigoid (i.e., pemphigoid) are autoimmune disorders in which blistering of the skin is the primary symptom. Pemphigus is unique from pemphigoid in that the blistering can involve the mucous membranes as well as skin. Thus, it is a bullous lesion, so this option will be incorrect according to the question.

Option (B) is incorrect as Dermatitis herpetiformis (DH) is one of the subepidermal autoimmune bullous diseases characterized by skin and intestinal lesions. Skin lesions include polymorphic eruption accompanied by severe pruritus. Intestinal lesions are characterized by atrophy of intestinal villi resulting from an immunological process, so, it is a bullous lesion, so this option will be incorrect according to the question.

Option (D) is incorrect As Bullous pemphigoid (BUL-us PEM-fih-goid) is a rare skin condition that causes large, fluid-filled blisters. They develop on areas of skin that often flex — such as the lower abdomen, upper thighs or armpits. Bullous pemphigoid occurs when your immune system attacks a thin layer of tissue below your outer layer of skin. So, it is a bullous lesion, so this option will be incorrect according to the question.

Hence, the correct option is (C).

176. Option (A) is correct because Lepra bacilli grow better in cooler places, therefore warmer areas of skin and internal organs are spared. Such areas are axilla, groin, scalp, midline back, ovaries, lung and CNS. So, this option will be correct.

Option (B) is incorrect because Testicular affection with leprosy occurs mainly in the lepromatous type. It included age at onset, course, duration of the disease, duration of treatment.

Option (C) is incorrect because a lepromin skin test is performed by injecting a small sample of inactivated M. leprae under your skin. A small lump will form at the injection site, indicating that the correct amount of bacterium has been injected at the correct depth in the skin for the test to be effective. So, this will be incorrect according to the question.

Option (D) is incorrect because, in tuberculoid leprosy, ocular manifestations result from lid closure impairment and reduced corneal sensation, through the involvement of the facial nerve and of the ophthalmic division of trigeminal nerve. So, this will be incorrect according to the question.

Hence, the correct option is (A).

177. Option (B) is correct because

- There should be no confusion at all; skin is not involved in pure neuritic leprosy, therefore skin smear will always (100%) be negative.
- However, you should keep in mind the very important fact that skin smear is also negative in most of the cases of Indeterminate and tuberculoid leprosy. But very rarely skin smear may be positive (as compared to neuritic type where skin smear is negative in 100% of cases).

Option (A) is incorrect because when leprosy is Indeterminate then Skin smear is positive. So, this option will be incorrect.

Option (C) is incorrect because Smear is positive in the multibacillary group (MB), which helps establish a definite diagnosis of leprosy, but sensitivity is low in the paucibacillary group (PB), in which smear is often negative, with a limit of microscopy detection of 104 AARB bacilli per gram of tissue. So, this option will be incorrect according to the question.

Option (D) is incorrect because when leprosy is Borderline then Skin smear is positive. So, this option will be incorrect.

Hence, the correct option is (B).

178. Option (A) is correct As Herpes simplex virus infection and syphilis are the most common causes of genital ulcers in the United States. Noninfectious etiologies, including sexual trauma, psoriasis, Behçet syndrome, and fixed drug eruptions, can also lead to genital ulcers.

Option (B) is incorrect As Possible triggers of aphthous ulcers include Emotional stress. Minor injury to the inside of the mouth, for example from cuts, burns or bites while eating, dental work, hard brushing or ill-fitting dentures.

Option (C) is incorrect As the cause of syphilis is a bacterium called Treponema pallidum. The most common route of transmission is through contact with an infected person's sore during sexual activity. The bacteria enter your body through minor cuts or abrasions in your skin or mucous membranes.

Option (D) is incorrect because Chancroid is a bacterial sexually transmitted disease (STD) caused by infection with Haemophilus ducreyi. It is characterized by painful necrotizing genital ulcers that may be accompanied by inguinal lymphadenopathy. It is a highly contagious but curable disease.

Hence, the correct option is (A).

179. Option (B) is correct As Condylomata lata or condyloma latum is a cutaneous condition characterized by wart-like lesions on the genitals. They are generally symptoms of the secondary phase of syphilis, caused by the spirochete, Treponema pallidum. These lesions hold a high accumulation of spirochetes and are highly infectious. So, this option will be correct.

Option (A) is incorrect because Condyloma acuminata caused by human papillomavirus (HPV). The most common strains of HPV that cause anogenital warts are 6 and 11. HPV is a double-stranded DNA virus primarily spread through sexual contact. There is a chance for Condyloma acuminata to recur after topical treatments.

Option (C) is incorrect because according to the above explanation of both options this option will not be correct.

Option (D) is incorrect because according to the above explanation of option (B), this option will not be correct.

Hence, the correct option is (B).

180. Option (A) is correct History of color change from pallor to cyanosis on cold exposure suggests Raynaud's phenomenon. Raynaud's phenomenon is the most common and earliest manifestation of generalized scleroderma (systemic sclerosis).

Option (B) is incorrect because Leukemia develops when the DNA of developing blood cells, mainly white cells, incurs damage. This causes the blood cells to grow and divide uncontrollably. Healthy blood cells die, and new cells replace them. These develop in the bone marrow. So, according to female, this is not associated with her condition.

Option (C) is incorrect because a lung infection can be caused by a virus, bacteria, and sometimes even a fungus. One of the most common types of lung infections is called pneumonia. A person becomes infected by breathing in the bacteria or virus after a nearby infected person sneezes or coughs. So, according to female, this is not associated with her condition.

Option (D) is incorrect because Hepatosplenomegaly is a disorder where both the liver and spleen swell beyond their normal size, usually due to an infection such as mononucleosis or viral hepatitis. It may also be a sign of another more serious illness such as a lysosomal storage disorder. So, according to female, this is not associated with her condition.

Hence, the correct option is (A).

181. Option (A) is correct because A diagnosis of delusional disorder is made if: The person has one or more delusions that last a month or longer. The person has never been diagnosed with schizophrenia. Hallucinations, if they have them, are related to the themes of their delusions. So, this condition is relating to the situation so it is the correct option.

Option (B) is incorrect As A perception that occurs when a sensory stimulus is present but is incorrectly perceived and misinterpreted, such as hearing the wind as someone crying. Everyone may occasionally experience an illusion. However, illusions are extraordinarily common in people suffering from schizophrenia. So, it is not the correct option according to the given situation in the question. So it will be an incorrect option.

Option (C) is incorrect because It could mean you touch or even smell something that doesn't exist. There are many different causes. It could be a mental illness called schizophrenia, a nervous system problem like Parkinson's disease, epilepsy, or a number of other things. If you or a loved one has hallucinations, thus it is not the correct option according to the given situation in the question. So it will be an incorrect option.

Option (D) is incorrect because the diagnosis of delirium is clinical. No laboratory test can diagnose delirium. The Diagnostic and Statistical Manual of Mental Disorders, Fifth Edition (DSM-5) diagnostic criteria for delirium are as follows: Disturbance in attention (ie, reduced ability to direct, focus, sustain, and shift attention) and awareness. Hence this is also not related to the man situation, so this option will not be the correct option.

Hence, the correct option is (A).

182. Option (C) is correct because it is a form of synaesthesia (a sensory stimulus in one modality resulting in sensory experience in another). A stimulus in one sensory modality produces a hallucination in another sense modality. Thus, this is related to the man's situation so according to the question this option will be the correct.

Option (A) is incorrect because Hypnagogic hallucinations are imagined sensations that seem very real. They occur as a person is falling asleep, and are also referred to as sleep hallucinations. The term hypnopompic describes the period when a person wakes up. Hypnagogic defines the period when a person falls asleep. Thus, this explanation does not relate to the above explanation, so it will be incorrect according to the question.

Option (B) is incorrect As Hypnagogic hallucinations are imagined sensations that seem very real. They occur as a person is falling asleep, and are also referred to as sleep hallucinations. The term hypnopompic describes the period when a person wakes up. thus, this explanation does not relate to the above explanation, so it will be incorrect according to the question.

Option (D) is incorrect As Functional hallucinations are a rare phenomenon, wherein hallucinations are triggered by a stimulus in the same modality and co-occur with it. Although hallucinations in schizophrenia are normally treated using antipsychotics, not all patients respond to them. Thus, this explanation does not relate to the above explanation, so it will be incorrect according to the question.

Hence, the correct option is (C).

183. Clinical features of delirium

- Altered consciousness (clouding of consciousness to coma).
- Cognitive impairment:- Impaired attention, poor concentration,
- disorientation or confusion, altered sensorium, and memory.
- Disturbances (Impairment of immediate and recent memory).
- Perceptual anomalies:- Illusion, Hallucinations.
- Emotional disturbances:- fear & anxiety.
- Language disturbances and psychomotor disturbances (hypoactivity or hyperactivity).
- Disturbance of the sleep-wake cycle.
- Autonomic disturbances:- Tachycardia, sweating, tremors.
- Neurological disturbances:- Tremor, seizure, chloroform movements.

So, according to the above explanation,

Option (D) is correct As all other options statements are the feature of the delirium and this option includes all other options so this will be the correct option.

Option (A) is incorrect As the above explanation this option statement included by the question.

Option (B) is incorrect As the above explanation this option statement included by the question.

Option (C) is incorrect As the above explanation this option statement included by the question.

Hence, the correct option is (D).

184. Option (B) is correct because in Fox-Fordyce disease abnormalities affecting the apocrine sweat glands cause inflammation and enlargement of the glands and the characteristic intense itching. The skin near an affected area may become darkened and dry and multiple, small, raised bumps (papules) may develop.

Option (A) is incorrect because Eccrine glands are uniquely susceptible to a variety of pathologic processes. Alteration in the rate of sweat secretion manifests as hypohidrosis and hyperhidrosis. The obstruction of the eccrine duct leads to miliaria.

Option (C) is incorrect because Non-tumor pituitary diseases like sarcoidosis, histiocytosis, and hemochromatosis can infiltrate the pituitary gland and cause pituitary hormone imbalances. Rarely, infections or autoimmune conditions affect the pituitary gland causing hypophysitis, also characterized by hormonal abnormalities.

Option (D) is incorrect because several medical conditions are related to sebaceous gland pathologies, such as acne, sebaceous hyperplasia, sebaceous adenoma, and sebaceous carcinoma. Acne is a common, complex, chronic disorder of the human pilosebaceous unit that mostly occurs in adolescence and young adulthood.

Hence, the correct option is (B).

185. Option (B) is correct because Opioid withdrawal is accompanied by rhinorrhoea (running nose), lacrimation (excessive tear formation), aching muscles, chills, gooseflesh, and, after 24-48 hours, muscle and abdominal cramps. Drug-seeking behavior is prominent and continues after the physical symptoms have abated.

Option (A) is incorrect because Tremors are involuntary shaking in one or multiple areas of the body and can occur intermittently or be constant. Two of the many possible causes of tremors are acute alcohol withdrawal and excessive alcohol use. Tremors are caused by a problem in the areas of the brain that control the body's muscles.

Option (C) is incorrect because Continuously experiencing dry mouth can be a symptom of alcohol withdrawal. Alcohol withdrawal happens after periods of heavy alcohol use when one tries to quitting alcohol or goes a long enough time without it.

Option (D) is incorrect Constipation is mentioned occasionally as a possible tobacco withdrawal symptom, but no descriptions of tobacco withdrawal syndrome should include constipation.

Hence, the correct option is (B).

186. Option (A) is correct because Disulfiram is used to treat chronic alcoholism. It causes unpleasant effects when even small amounts of alcohol are consumed. These effects include flushing of the face, headache, nausea, vomiting, chest pain, weakness, blurred vision, mental confusion, sweating, choking, breathing difficulty, and anxiety.

Option (B) is incorrect because Clonidine seems best suited for use as a transitional treatment between opiate dependence and induction onto the opiate antagonist naltrexone.

Option (C) is incorrect because Benzodiazepines, such as lorazepam, are often used for short periods of time only. They may produce emotional and/or physical dependence (addiction) even when used as recommended. The use of lorazepam with drugs like opioid medications has led to serious side effects including slowed and difficulty breathing and death.

Option (D) is incorrect because Naltrexone blocks the effects of opioid medication, including pain relief or feelings of well-being that can lead to opioid abuse. An opioid is sometimes called a narcotic. Naltrexone is used as part of a treatment program for drug or alcohol dependence.

Hence, the correct option is (A).

187. Option (C) is correct As Cluster B personality disorders are characterized by dramatic, overly emotional or unpredictable thinking or behavior. They include antisocial personality disorder, borderline personality disorder, histrionic personality disorder, and narcissistic personality disorder.

Option (A) is incorrect because anxiety, sadness or depression, anger, irritability, mental confusion, low sense of self-worth, etc., behavioral symptoms such as phobic avoidance, vigilance, impulsive and compulsive acts, lethargy, etc., cognitive problems such as unpleasant or disturbing thoughts, repetition of thoughts and obsession, habitual.

Option (B) is incorrect because Neurosis, plural neuroses, also called psychoneurosis or plural psychoneuroses, a mental disorder that causes a sense of distress and deficit in functioning. Neuroses are characterized by anxiety, depression, or other feelings of unhappiness or distress that are out of proportion to the circumstances of a person's life.

Option (D) is incorrect because Neurosis and Psychosis are different types of mental disorders. Neurosis refers to a mild mental disorder. While neurosis is a mild mental disorder, psychosis refers to insanity and madness.

Hence, the correct option is (C).

188. Option (B) is correct because DSM-5 lists ten specific personality disorders: Paranoid, schizoid, schizotypal, antisocial, borderline, histrionic, narcissistic, avoidant, dependant and obsessive-compulsive personality disorder.

Option (A) is incorrect As Barbiturates are a class of drugs that were used extensively in the 1960s and 1970s as a treatment for anxiety, insomnia, and seizure disorders. Apart from a few specific indications, they are not commonly prescribed these days.

Option (C) is incorrect because the US Food and Drug Administration (FDA) has approved two opioid agonist medications for the treatment of opioid use disorders: methadone (a Schedule II controlled substance and a full opioid agonist) and buprenorphine (a Schedule III controlled substance and a partial opioid agonist).

Option (D) is incorrect because the benefits and risks of benzodiazepines. Benzodiazepines are a class of psychoactive drugs used to treat a range of conditions, including anxiety and insomnia. They are one of the most widely prescribed medications in the United States, particularly among older patients.

Hence, the correct option is (B).

189. Psychological symptoms of anxiety

- **Cognitive**:- Poor concentration, distractibility, negative automatic thought.
- **Affective**:- Fearfulness, irritability, apprehension, sense of impending doom.
- **Other**:- Derealization, depersonalization, insomnia, normal consciousness.

Option (D) is correct As the above explanation, it is clear that all other options are correct and included in this option so, this option is correct.

Option (A) is incorrect As the above explanation, it is clear that this option statement included in the Anxiety neurosis.

Option (B) is incorrect As the above explanation, it is clear that this option statement included in the Anxiety neurosis.

Option (C) is incorrect As the above explanation, it is clear that this option statement included in the Anxiety neurosis.

Hence, the correct option is (D).

190. Option (D) is correct because

- Hysterical fits (conversion seizure) never occur in sleep (epileptic fit can occur during sleep).
- Injury, tongue biting, and urinary incontinence are rare in conversion seizure (these can occur in epileptic fit).
- Hysterical fits (conversion seizure) usually occur when people are observing (epileptic fit has no relation to people observation).
- Hysterical fits usually occur in a safe place or indoor (epileptic fit can occur anywhere).
- Hysterical fits have normal postictal serum prolactin (serum prolactin may increase in the post-ictal period of epileptic fit).
- There is no or partial amnesia about the episode in conversion seizure (hysterical fits). True convulsion has complete amnesia.

Option (A) is incorrect because occurrence during sleep indicates a true seizure. So, this option is incorrect according to the given question.

Option (B) is incorrect because Mood swings and emotional lability are often caused by damage to the part of the brain that controls emotions and behavior. Often there is no specific event that triggers a sudden emotional response.

Option (C) is incorrect because Incontinence is a lack of control. Sometimes that means you can't help but pee your pants. Another, more pleasant type of incontinence has to do with being undisciplined and addicted to life's pleasures. You probably don't want anything to do with incontinence.

Hence, the correct option is (D).

191. Option (A) is correct because Alpha waves are neural oscillations in the frequency range of 8–12 Hz arising from the synchronous and coherent (in-phase or constructive) electrical activity of thalamic pacemaker cells in humans. They are also called Berger's waves after the founder of EEG.

Option (B) is incorrect because Beta activity refers to a frequency band rather than a distinct (specific) rhythm such as alpha or mu. Beta activity is commonly present in the EEG of healthy people. However, it is often difficult to see because of its low amplitude.

Option (C) is incorrect because Yes, there is an increase because delta and theta waves can occur briefly if a person is emotionally responsive during concentration ration. It is prominent in the EEG wave pattern of an adult who is awake but relaxed with the eyes closed.

Option (D) is incorrect as above explained in option (C) this option is also not correct.

Hence, the correct option is (A).

192. Option (D) is correct because Borderline personality disorder includes a pattern of instability of interpersonal relationships, self-image and marked impulsivity beginning by early adulthood. Recurrent suicidal behavior, self-mutilation, intense anger, difficulty controlling anger and marked mood reactivity are seen.

Option (A) is incorrect because Adjustment disorder is a group of symptoms, such as stress, feeling sad or hopeless, and physical symptoms that can occur after you go through a stressful life event. The symptoms occur because you are having a hard time coping. Your reaction is stronger than expected for the type of event that occurred.

Option (B) is incorrect because Post-traumatic stress disorder (PTSD) is a mental health condition triggered by a terrifying event, causing flashbacks, nightmares and severe anxiety.

Option (C) is incorrect because Paranoid personality disorder (PPD) is one of a group of conditions called eccentric personality disorders. People with PPD suffer from paranoia, an unrelenting mistrust, and suspicion of others, even when there is no reason to be suspicious.

Hence, the correct option is (D).

193. Option (A) is correct because Simple chronic schizophrenia is not an indication for ECT.

Option (B) is incorrect because Doctors may also use ECT to ease other symptoms of schizophrenia, such as delusions, hallucinations, or disorganized thinking. ECT is traditionally used more often to treat depression or bipolar disorder, however, than schizophrenia.

Option (C) is incorrect because Electroconvulsive therapy is one of the best treatments available, says NHS "Severe depression" refers to the pointy end of the depression spectrum, what the Guardian holds dear has been threatened – democracy, civility, truth.

Option (D) is incorrect because electroconvulsive therapy (ECT) to treat severe depression. ECT is traditionally used more often to treat depression or bipolar disorder, however, than schizophrenia. It is thought to be more effective in treating psychosis when mood symptoms are also present.

Hence, the correct option is (A).

194. Option (A) is correct because

- Primary process (related to Id):- Unorganized & non-logical thinking.
- Secondary process (related to Ego):- Reality oriented, goal-directed, logical, rational, concrete and/or abstract conceptual thinking.

Option (B) is incorrect because Rational thinking is the ability to think out of the box, to think critically, to produce "good quality of thoughts" in certain situations to arrive at a rational decision. Rational thinkers are ones who question everything and who are curious about the world.

Option (C) is incorrect As Parasomnias are a category of sleep disorders that involve abnormal movements, behaviors, emotions, perceptions, and dreams that occur while falling asleep, sleeping, between sleep stages, or during arousal from sleep.

Option (D) is incorrect because it is n Freud's psychoanalytic theory of personality, the unconscious mind is a reservoir of feelings, thoughts, urges, and memories that outside of our conscious awareness. Most of the contents of the unconscious are unacceptable or unpleasant, such as feelings of pain, anxiety, or conflict.

Hence, the correct option is (A).

195. Option (C) is correct As ECT is the therapy of choice depression with:

1. Suicidal tendency.
2. Psychomotor retardation.
3. Psychotic and delusional features with the somatic syndrome.
4. Intolerance, contraindication, refractory to drugs.

Option (A) is incorrect because it is an antipsychotic medication that is used to treat severe schizophrenia symptoms in people who have not responded to other medications. It is also used to help reduce the risk of suicidal behavior in people with schizophrenia or similar disorders.

Option (B) is incorrect because Mirtazapine is not a sleeping tablet but it can make you feel sleepy. This can be helpful if you have depression and difficulties getting to sleep. Mirtazapine is also known by the brand name Zispin SolTab.

Option (D) is incorrect because Olanzapine is an antipsychotic medication that affects chemicals in the brain. Olanzapine is used to treat the symptoms of psychotic conditions such as schizophrenia and bipolar disorder (manic depression) in adults and children who are at least 13 years old.

Hence, the correct option is (C).

196. "Markers of bone formation include bone-specific alkaline phosphatase (BAP), osteocalcin (OC) and procollagen peptides. All of these can be measured easily by immunoassay techniques. Of these markers, OC has been extensively studied. However, OC undergoes in vitro degradation, thus, assay results are variable."

Option (C) is correct because Hydroxyproline is a nonessential amino acid derivative formed during post-translational protein modification through hydroxylation of the amino acid proline by the enzyme prolyl hydroxylase which requires vitamin C as a co-factor.

Option (A) is incorrect because According to the above explanation this option is Indicators of bone formation. Which is not correct according to the question part.

Option (B) is incorrect because According to the above explanation this option is Indicators of bone formation. Which is not correct according to the question part.

Option (D) is incorrect According to the above explanation this option is Indicators of bone formation. Which is not correct according to the question part.

Hence, the correct option is (C).

197. Option (B) is correct because "The diaphysis is the main or mid-section (shaft) of a long bone".

1. Long bones are found in the extremities: the arms, legs, hands, and feet (but not the wrists or ankles). As their name indicates, long bones have a long central shaft with knobby end portions.

2. Short bones, which are cube-shaped, are found in confined spaces such as the wrist and ankle.

3. The ribs, shoulder blades, sternum (breastbone), pelvis (hips), and most of the bones of the skull are considered flat bones.

Option (A) is incorrect because Basilar skull fractures include breaks in the posterior skull base or anterior skull base. The former involves the occipital bone, temporal bone, and portions of the sphenoid bone; the latter, superior portions of the sphenoid and ethmoid bones.

Option (C) is incorrect because A sternal fracture is a fracture of the sternum (the breastbone), located in the center of the chest. The injury, which occurs in 5–8% of people who experience significant blunt chest trauma, may occur in vehicle accidents when the still-moving chest strikes a steering wheel or dashboard or is injured by a seatbelt.

Option (D) is incorrect because Rib Fractures, Pneumothorax, and Hemothorax.

Pneumothorax, hemothorax, and diaphragmatic herniation may all occur as a result of these traumatic insults, and myocardial injury is typically fatal. Rib fractures can be single but are often multiple, most often affecting adjacent ribs on one side of the chest.

Hence, the correct option is (B).

198.

- The features of posterior dislocation of the shoulder are not very striking, and for that reason, the injury is often overlooked. An important sign is fixed medial (internal) rotation of the arm, which cannot be rotated outward (externally), even to a neutral position.
- Radiography may be misleading if only the ordinary anteroposterior film is available because the dislocation may not be apparent or at least not obvious on this projection.

Option (D) is correct As according to the above explanation this option true regarding shoulder dislocation because it includes all other options hence it will be correct.

Option (A) is incorrect because according to the above explanation this option true regarding shoulder dislocation.

Option (B) is incorrect because according to the above explanation this option true regarding shoulder dislocation.

Option (C) is incorrect because according to the above explanation this option true regarding shoulder dislocation.

Hence, the correct option is (D).

199. Option (B) is correct because AVN and non-union are almost always seen with displaced fracture (Garden's III & IV) and are less common with undisplaced fractures (Garden's I & II).

Option (A) is incorrect because, in the original description, Garden 1 fractures are characterized as valgus impacted fractures of the subcapital femoral neck involving the lateral cortex and not completely breaching the medial cortex. Garden 2 fractures are subcapital fractures involving both the lateral and medial cortex and have no displacement.

Option (C) is incorrect because Subtrochanteric hip fracture is a break between the lesser trochanter and the area approximately 5 centimeters below the lesser trochanter. The fracture can be classified based on its location: Type II occurs within 2.5 cm below the lesser trochanter and, Type III occurs between 2.5 and 5 cm below the lesser trochanter.

Option (D) is incorrect because Trochanteric fracture involves the proximal femur between the cervical region and the shaft. Subtrochanteric fracture, with a fracture line running from an area within 5 cm distal to the lesser trochanter.

Hence, the correct option is (B).

200. Option (B) is correct because Treatment of choice in patients 70 years or above is arthroplasty; either hemiarthroplasty (if no pre-existing arthritis) or total hip replacement (if pre-existing arthritis is present).

Option (A) is incorrect because Traction means pulling on part of the body. Most often, traction uses devices such as weights and pulleys to put tension on a displaced bone or joint, such as a dislocated shoulder. The tension helps put the joint back in position and keep it still, and this is not related to the ladies' issues, so this option will not be correct.

Option (C) is incorrect because they are held together with special implants, such as plates, screws, nails, and wires. Internal fixation allows shorter hospital stays, enables patients to return to function earlier, and reduces the incidence of nonunion (improper healing) and malunion (healing in improper position) of broken bones.

Option (D) is incorrect because they are held together with special implants, such as plates, screws, nails, and wires. Internal fixation allows shorter hospital stays, enables patients to return to function earlier, and reduces the incidence of nonunion (improper healing) and malunion (healing in improper position) of broken bones.

Hence, the correct option is (B).

201. Option (A) is correct because the Dynamic hip screw (DHS) plate is the implant of choice for fixation. These days proximal femoral nail (PFN) is also commonly used. Dynamic hip screw (DHS) or Sliding Screw Fixation is a type of orthopedic implant designed for fixation of certain types of hip fractures which allows controlled dynamic sliding of the femoral head component along with the construct.

Option (B) is incorrect because An inlay is a design or pattern on an object which is made by putting materials such as wood, gold, or silver into the surface of the object. The Inlay is the technique of putting designs or patterns onto the surfaces of objects.

Option (C) is incorrect because Plaster in abduction occurs when a bone moves away from the midline of the body. Examples of abduction include moving the arms or legs laterally to lift them straight out to the side.

Option (D) is incorrect because Plaster in the abduction and internal rotation is done/used in hip-joint. This probably has no beneficial influence as regards the permanency of the reduction, but it may make a considerable difference to the stability and function if a marginal displacement, or anterior transposition as it is called by some, is the final state of the hip. The so-called "second position" in plaster, with reduced abduction and internal rotation.

Hence, the correct option is (A).

202. Option (D) is correct because Treatment options for femoral shaft non-union are : -

1. Intramedullary interlock nailing with bone grafting (preferred).

2. K-nail with bone grafting.

3. Plating with bone grafting.

And according to the question it is best treated by a compression plate with bone grafting.

Option (A) is incorrect because a dynamic compression plate (DCP) is a metallic plate used in orthopedics for internal fixation of bone, typically after fractures. As the name implies, it is designed to exert dynamic pressure between the bone fragments to be transfixed.

Option (B) is incorrect because Bone grafting is a surgical procedure that uses the transplanted bone to repair and rebuild diseased or damaged bones. A bone graft is a choice for repairing bones almost anywhere in your body. Your surgeon might take bone from your hips, legs, or ribs to perform the graft.

Option (C) is incorrect because Nailing is the act or process of fixing the parts of a broken bone by means of a nail intramedullary nailing. It is used for fixing fragments of bone by use of a nail.

Hence, the correct option is (D).

203. Option (B) is correct because MRI is the investigation of choice for P1D because it shows the following structures clearly Prolapse of disc.

• Compression of cord Any problems with the discs above and below Canal Stenosis.

• Associated features like Ligamentum flavum hypertrophy and facet arthropathy.

Option (A) is incorrect because A computed tomography (CT or CAT) scan allows doctors to see inside your body. It uses a combination of X-rays and a computer to create pictures of your organs, bones, and other tissues. It shows more detail than a regular X-ray.

Option (C) is incorrect because Myelography uses a real-time form of x-ray called fluoroscopy and an injection of contrast material to evaluate the spinal cord, nerve roots and spinal lining (meninges). It is particularly useful for assessing the spine following surgery and for assessing disc abnormalities in patients who cannot undergo MRI.

Option (D) is incorrect because It is used to diagnose or treat patients by recording images of the internal structure of the body to assess the presence or absence of disease, foreign objects, and structural damage or anomaly. During a radiographic procedure, an x-ray beam is passed through the body.

Hence, the correct option is (B).

204. Option (B) is correct because Hangman's fracture is a bilateral fracture of the pars interarticularis of the axis (C_2) with traumatic spondylolisthesis of axis (C_2) over C_3 vertebrae. Thus Hangman's fracture is not simply a fracture, but fracture-dislocation of the axis (C_2).

Option (A) is incorrect because Physiologic anterior subluxation case occurrence at C_5 to C_6 spinal levels. Physiologic anterior subluxation is a phenomenon that is common to the upper pediatric cervical spine and characterized by the normal forward displacement of one cervical vertebra relative to the subjacent one.

Option (C) is incorrect because a dislocated ankle is associated with fractures of the distal ends of the tibia and fibula (called the malleolus) in association with damage to the ligaments that help support the ankle joint. Less commonly, isolated ligament injuries can result in dislocation.

Option (D) is incorrect because A type II odontoid fracture is a break that occurs through a specific part of C_2, the second bone in the neck. Bones of the spine are called vertebrae. The bone involved in the odontoid fracture is the second vertebra, C_2, high up in the neck.

Hence, the correct option is (B).

205. Option (C) is correct because the Age of onset has no effect on the course is not part of Perth's disease.

Option (A) is incorrect because it is a condition where bone dies and stops working or did not respond. Osteochondritis dissecans occurs when a fragment of bone in a joint separates from the rest of the bone because its blood supply is faulty, and there is not enough blood to maintain it.

Option (B) is incorrect because Decreased bone age is a part of Perth's disease. childhood hip disorder initiated by a disruption of blood flow to the head of the femur. Due to the lack of blood flow, the bone dies and causes no increases in bone age.

Option (D) is incorrect because Restricted abduction is a part of Perth's disease. In restricted abduction, the range of motion is reduced, particularly in the abduction and internal rotation, and the patient presents with a limp. Pain is usually mild. Atrophy of thigh muscles may occur from disuse and inequality of leg length.

Hence, the correct option is (C).

206. Option (A) is correct because

- Muscle atrophy particularly involves the quadriceps muscle.
- All periarticular muscles around the knee, the joint may undergo wasting in advanced osteoarthritis knee.
- However muscle atrophy particularly involves the quadriceps which is the earliest muscle to undergo wasting.
- In patients with osteoarthritis knee, quadriceps strengthening exercise form an important management component to protect the articular cartilage from stress.

Option (B) is incorrect because the hamstrings are a groupof muscles and their tendons at the rear of the upper leg. They include thebiceps femoris, semitendinosus, and semimembranosus.
The hamstrings flex the kneejoint and extend the thigh to the backside of the body.

Option (C) is incorrect because The gastrocnemius muscle(plural gastrocnemii) is a superficial two-headed muscle that is in the backpart of the lower leg of humans. It runs from its two heads just above the kneeto the heel, a three joint muscle (knee, ankle and subtalar joints).

Option (D) is incorrect because option (A) is correct which are Quadriceps musclesundergoes wasting first in osteoarthritis knee.

Hence, the correct option is (A).

207. Option (A) is correct because

• The commonest presenting symptom of chronic osteomyelitis is chronic discharging sinus.

• Discharging sinus contains pus (i.e. a mixture of neutrophils and other cells).

Option (B) is incorrect because Acute osteomyelitis is the clinical term for a new infection in the bone. This infection occurs predominantly in children and is often seeded hematogenously. In adults, osteomyelitis is usually a subacute or chronic infection that develops secondary to an open injury to bone and surrounding soft tissue.

Option (C) is incorrect because Septic arthritis, also known as joint infection or infectious arthritis, is the invasion of a joint by an infectious agent resulting in joint inflammation. Symptoms typically include redness, heat, and pain in a single joint associated with a decreased ability to move the joint. The onset is usually rapid.

Option (D) is incorrect because option (A) is correct which is Chronic persistent neutrophilic discharge is seen in chronic osteomyelitis.

Hence, the correct option is (A).

208. Option (B) is correct because:

• An osteoid osteoma is a benign bone tumor that arises from osteoblasts and was originally thought to be a smaller version of an osteoblastoma.

• Osteoid osteomas tend to be less than 1.5 cm in size.

• A tumor can be in any bone in the body but are most common in long bones, such as the femur and tibia.

Option (A) is incorrect because Eosinophilic granuloma function is to detect the presence of disease organisms and communicate that information to other immune system cells. Eosinophilic granuloma most commonly shows up in the skull, legs, ribs, pelvis, and spine.

Option (C) is incorrect because Fibrous cortical defects (FCD) are benign bony lesions and are a type of fibroxanthoma, histologically identical to the larger non-ossifying fibroma (NOF). Fibrous cortical defects typically occur in children (usually 2-15 years), and indeed are one of the most common benign bony lesions, which combined with non-ossifying fibromas are seen in up to 40% of skeletally immature children/adolescents.

Option (D) is incorrect because fibrous dysplasia is a genetic disorder, it's caused by a gene mutation that's not passed from parent to child. There's no cure for the disorder. Treatment, which may include surgery, focuses on relieving pain and repairing or stabilizing bones.

Hence, the correct option is (B).

209. Option (B) is correct because:

• Often both hands are affected (Bilateral disease), one more than the other.

• The earliest sign is a small thickened nodule in the mid-palm opposite the base of the ring finger.

• Gradually this extends distally to involve the ring or little finger.

• There is a rare, curious association with fibrosis of the corpus Cavernosum.

Option (A) is incorrect because Dupuytren disease (DD) is a fibrosing disorder. This condition usually affects the fourth finger (the ring and small fingers).

Option (C) is incorrect because Surgical release is the part of Dupuytren's contracture. If the contracture interferes with hand function, the doctor may recommend surgical treatment. The goal of surgery is to reduce the contracture and improve motion in the affected fingers. The surgical procedures most commonly performed for Dupuytren's contracture.

Option (D) is incorrect because option (D) is true for Dupuytren's contracture. Many men with Peyronie's disease also have Dupuytren's contracture, a connective tissue disorder that causes scar tissue to harden on the palm of the hand. This causes fingers to curve, much like the penis curves in Peyronie's disease.

Hence, the correct option is (B).

210. Option (A) is correct because which is Tendons should be repaired before nerves during the surgical procedure. The sequence of repair (from first to last):

- Bone fixation (first to be done)
- Flexor tendon/muscle repair
- Extensor tendon/muscle repair
- Nerve repair
- Arterial repair
- Venous repair
- Skin grafting or flap if necessary

Option (B) is incorrect because during tendon repair a surgeon will: make one or more small incisions (cuts) in the skin over the damaged tendon. sew the torn ends of the tendon together.

Option (C) is incorrect because Tendons should be repaired. Doctors perform tendon repair surgery to fix a tendon injury. Tendons are tough, stretchy tissues that join muscles to bone.

Option (D) is incorrect because option (A) is correct which is Tendons should be repaired before nerves during the surgical procedure.

Hence, the correct option is (A).

211. Option (A) is correct because the color of the oxygen cylinder is Black with white color.

Option (B) is incorrect because the color of Entonox gas is Blue with white color.

Option (C) is incorrect because the color of the Medical air is Yellow with white color.

Option (D) is incorrect because the color of carbon dioxide is grey with grey color.

Hence, the correct option is (A).

212. Option (C) is correct because Type D is Bain's circuit. Mapleson D or Bain's circuit is best for controlled ventilation. Mapleson B and C are rarely used today. Mapleson D, E, F require higher fresh gas flow to prevent rebreathing. They are next in order of preference list for spontaneous respiration.

Option (A) is incorrect because Type A is the Magill circuit. MAPLETON A - (Magill) CIRCUIT. FGF enters at the end remote from the patient, and there is a Heidbrink one-way pop-off valve at the mask end. Originally C-type systems were common; Magill designed the A circuit to get the bag away from the patient during faciomaxillary surgery.

Option (B) is incorrect because Type F is Jackson - Rees circuit. The Modified Jackson Rees is a popular choice for a non-rebreathing system. The control valve allows you to close the system for hand bagging and then reopen it to a passive condition.

Option (D) is incorrect because Type E is Ayre's T piece. The Mapleson E Ayre's T-piece

• Developed in 1937 by Phillip Ayre (a Newcastle anesthetist)

• used in pediatric patients undergoing cleft palate repair or intracranial surgery.

Hence, the correct option is (C).

213. Option (A) is correct because Nasal intubation is contraindicated in Basal skull fracture, CSF rhinorrhea, coagulopathy, nasal polyp/abscess/foreign body and adenoid.

Option (B) is incorrect because a cervical fracture, commonly called a broken neck, is a catastrophic fracture of any of the seven cervical vertebrae in the neck. Abnormal movement of neck bones or pieces of bone can cause a spinal cord injury resulting in loss of sensation, paralysis, or usually instant death.

Option (C) is incorrect because when an object cracks without necessarily completely breaking to pieces is called Fracture inaudible. This person is difficult or impossible to hear.

Option (D) is incorrect because a Short neck is usually associated with torticollis. Although spasm of the muscles of the nape of the neck is not as prominent as in acute atlantoaxial instability related to trauma, it is remarkable and present. Similarly, neck pain is not as severe as in an acute situation but is frequently associated.

Hence, the correct option is (A).

214. Option (D) is correct because:

• Thyromental distance. Thyromental distance (TMD) measurement is a method commonly used to predict the difficulty of intubation and is measured from the thyroid notch to the tip of the jaw with the head extended.

• If it is less than 7.0 cm with hard scarred tissues, it indicates possible difficult intubation.

Option (A) is incorrect because it is the features of the difficult airway. In difficult airway patients with mandibular fractures often present with very limited mouth opening and are difficult to intubate.

Option (B) is incorrect because it is the features of the difficult airway. micrognathia, macroglossia, hypotonia, and lax joint, airway management can be difficult in a child as well as mental problems due to poor communication. Congenital macroglossia is a condition that consists of an enlarged tongue protruding beyond the alveolar ridge in a resting position.

Option (C) is incorrect because it is the features of the difficult airway. Bird face deformity, receding chin, narrow maxilla, protruding upper incisors with nil or few MMS mouth opening are the features of bilateral TMJ ankylosis.

Hence, the correct option is (D).

215. Option (D) is correct because the Mallampati score is done for:-

• Oral cavity assessment to rule out difficult airway, and

• Sleep apnea evaluation.

Option (A) is incorrect because The cervical spine functions are to provide mobility and stability to the head while connecting it to the relatively immobile thoracic spine. The movement of nodding the head takes place predominantly through flexion and extension at the joint between the atlas and the occipital bone, the atlanto-occipital joint.

Option (B) is incorrect because the atlantoaxial joint is a joint in the upper part of the neck between the first and second cervical vertebrae; the atlas and axis. It is a pivot joint. The atlas and the occipital bone form the atlanto-occipital joint, which allows neck flexion. When you nod your head as if to say "yes," that is neck flexion.

Option (C) is incorrect because Malampatti grading is not for the Assessment of free rotation of neck before intubation.

Hence, the correct option is (D).

216. Option (D) is incorrect as it is covering all the options that are mentioned above.i.e.,

Preanaesthec medication

- Premedication (Preanaesthec medication) refers to the use of drugs before anesthesia to make it more pleasant and safe.

The aims are :

1. Relief of anxiety and apprehension preoperatively and to facilitate smooth induction.

2. Amnesia for preoperative and postoperative events.

3. Supplement analgesic action of anesthetics and potentate them.

4. Decrease secretions and vagal stimulation (undesirable reflex).

5. Anemic effect extending into the postoperative period.

6. Decrease acidity and volume of gastric juice so that it is less damaging if aspirated.

- Drugs used in premedication

1. Sedative - antianxiety → Diazepam/Lorazepam/Midazolam → Lorazepam is used most commonly. → Midazolam is used for daycare surgery.

2. Opioids → Morphine/pethidine

3. Anticholinergics → Atropine/Hyoscine/Glycopyrrolate.

4. Neuroleptics → Haloperidol/chlorpromazine/triflupromazine.

5. H_2 blocker or proton pump inhibitor → Ranitidine/Famotidine, omeprazole/Pantoprazole.

6. Antiemetics → Metoclopramide/Domperidone/Ondansetron.

Option (A) is incorrect as Atropine (0.05 mg/kg i.m.) or glycopyrrolate (0.01 mg/kg i.e., 0.05 mg/kg i.m.) can be administered prior to induction of anesthesia to reduce salivation and protect the heart from vagally mediated bradycardia. Since other options are also considered as Pre-anaesthetic medication, the option is incorrect.

Option (B) is incorrect though the Pre-anaesthetic medication is given in order to prevent undesirable reflexes, but will be considered as incorrect for the same reason as an option (A).

Option (C) is incorrect even in order to reduce anxiety and fear, Pre-anaesthetic medication is given. It is also incorrect as selecting an individual correct option will not be considered as the correct answer.

Hence, the correct option is (D).

217. Option (A) is correct as Mivacurium is the shortest acting nondepolarizing skeletal muscle relaxant.

Option (B) is incorrect as it is a medication used as part of general anesthesia to provide skeletal muscle relaxation during surgery or mechanical ventilation.

Option (C) is incorrect as Atracurium is a medication used in addition to other medications to provide skeletal muscle relaxation during surgery or mechanical ventilation.

Option (D) is incorrect as Suxamethonium (succinylcholine) is the shortest acting skeletal muscle relaxant.

Hence, the correct option is (A).

218. Option (D) is correct as Doxacurium is more potent, but is the least rapid and the longest acting relaxant currently available. When administered in doses of 37 to 80 micrograms/kg, it produces maximum block within 3.5 to 10 min, with a duration of clinical relaxation of 77 to 164 min.

Option (A) is incorrect as Atracurium has an onset of action of approximately 2 minutes when an intubating dose is given. Classified as an intermediate-acting non-depolarizing muscle relaxant with a duration of action of approximately 40 to 45 minutes.

Option (B) is incorrect as Vecuronium is a short-acting nondepolarizing muscle relaxant that is structurally related to pancuronium, with time to onset of action of 1.5 to 2.0 minutes after intravenous bolus infusion, with a duration of effect that lasts only 30 to 40 minutes.

Option (C) is incorrect as Rocuronium is a nondepolarizing neuromuscular blocking agent with a rapid to intermediate onset depending on dose and intermediate duration. Rocuronium, like vecuronium, is longer acting in infants than in children.

Hence, the correct option is (D).

219. Option (A) is correct because atracurium Besylate Injection is a skeletal muscle relaxant used in addition to general anesthesia, to facilitate endotracheal intubation and to provide skeletal muscle relaxation during surgery or mechanical ventilation. Atracurium besylate injection is available in generic form.

Option (B) is incorrect because mivacurium chloride is a short-duration non-depolarizing neuromuscular-blocking drug or skeletal muscle relaxant in the category of non-depolarizing neuromuscular-blocking drugs, used adjunctively in anesthesia to facilitate endotracheal intubation and to provide skeletal muscle relaxation during surgery or mechanical ventilation.

Option (C) is incorrect because a gallium scan uses gallium citrate. It's a drug that has very small amounts of radioactive gallium. A day or two before your scan, your healthcare provider injects the gallium citrate into a vein in your arm. The gallium then travels all over your body. It builds up in any cells that are actively dividing, such as cancer cells. It also binds to cells and proteins involved in inflammation in your body.

Option (D) is incorrect because vecuronium is used to relax the muscles. It works by blocking the signals between your nerves and your muscles. Vecuronium is given before general anesthesia in preparing you for surgery. Vecuronium helps to keep your body still during surgery.

Hence, the correct option is (A).

220. Option (D) is correct because this patient has the classic "pruritic, purple, polygonal papules" of lichen planus, with the distinctive band-like infiltrate of lymphocytes at the dermal-epidermal junction. The lesions of lichen planus are typically self-limited, although the course can run several years. Oral lesions may persist longer. There is no risk for malignancy. Although a lymphocytic infiltrate is present, an infectious or autoimmune cause is not implicated. A drug' eruption should not last this long. Lesions of erythema multiforme are more likely to follow infection drugs, autoimmune diseases, and malignancies.

Option (A) is incorrect because squamous cell carcinoma (SCC) of the skin is caused by DNA damage that leads to abnormal changes (mutations) in the squamous cells in the outermost layer of skin.

Option (B) is incorrect because systemic lupus erythematosus (SLE) is an autoimmune disease. In this disease, the immune system of the body mistakenly attacks healthy tissue. It can affect the skin, joints, kidneys, brain, and other organs.

Option (C) is incorrect because as the term implies, withdrawal reactions occur when a medication is withdrawn or stopped suddenly.

Hence, the correct option is (D).

221. Option (D) is correct as it is covering all the options mentioned above that Thiopental is used for induction in anesthesia, as an anticonvulsant, for cerebroprotection to decrease ICP, for medically induced coma, euthanasia, phobia, truth serum to uncover the truth, to facilitate the recall of painful repressed memories.

Option (A) is incorrect as Coma is induced with anesthetic drugs to achieve complete control of seizure activity. Thiopental sodium and propofol are popularly used for this purpose. Both agents have been found to be effective. But it is incorrect as other options are also correct regarding the question. So, selecting an individual option will be incorrect.

Option (B) is incorrect though Thiopentone is used in truth serum to uncover the truth. But it is also incorrect for the same reason as an option (A).

Option (C) is incorrect as it is also used as a cerebroprotection to decrease ICP. But, it is also incorrect for the same reason as an option (A) and (C).

Hence, the correct option is (D).

222. Option (B) is correct as Etomidate has minimal effect on the cardiovascular system (most cardiostable/hemodynamically stable) and has the highest incidence of nausea & vomiting amongst the inducing agents.

Option (A) is incorrect as the hemodynamic effects of ketamine in the clinical setting are complex and include direct cardiac action and activation of the autonomic nervous system.

Option (C) is incorrect as the hemodynamic effects induced by propofol may, therefore, arise from the reduction of ventricular preload or afterload, depression of myocardial contractility and inhibition of compensatory tachycardia.

Option (D) is incorrect as the physiologic effects of some opioids include hypotension, histamine release, decreased myocardial contractility and effects on cardiac conductivity including the potential to prolong the QT interval.

Hence, the correct option is (B).

223. Option (D) is correct as it is covering all the above-mentioned options. Since combined all the options are true about anesthetic agents, the option is the required answer.

Option (A) is incorrect even when the duration of LAs depends on lipid solubility, protein binding, metabolism, Dose (higher dose produces longer block), vasoconstrictor, and sodium bicarbonate. Selecting an individual option when multiple options are also relatable, will not be considered for evaluation.

Option (B) is incorrect though Potency correlates with lipid solubility. But, it is incorrect for the same reason as an option (A).

Option (C) is incorrect for the same reason as of above-explained options as LA with pKa closer to physiological pH has a more rapid onset of action.

Hence, the correct option is (D).

224. Option (A) is correct because the Addition of sodium bicarbonate increases both onset and duration of action because it raises the pH and more drug is available in Un-ionized form.

Option (B) is incorrect as Indeed, such rate modulates the diffusion speed of anesthetics into lipid membranes; low protonation rates enhance the diffusion for local anesthetics while high ones reduce it. We show also that there is a pH and membrane phase dependence on the local anesthetic diffusion across multiple lipid bilayers.

Option (C) is incorrect as Local anesthetics have a greater affinity for receptors within sodium channels during their activated and inactivated states than when they are in their resting states. Therefore, neural fibers having more rapid firing rates are most susceptible to local anesthetic action.

Option (D) is incorrect as it is explained in option (A) that the addition of sodium bicarbonate leads to an increase in speed and quality of anesthesia. As this option is contradictory from the correct option. So, this option is incorrect.

Hence, the correct option is (A).

225. Option (D) is correct as it is covering all the above-mentioned options. Hence, it is the required answer.

Option (A) is incorrect though Post-operative hypertension is common in patients who already have hypertension (i.e. pre-operative hypertension). As the other given options are also relatable. So, going for an individual option will not be correct.

Option (B) is incorrect as conditions like pheochromocytoma, Cushing syndrome leads to postoperative hypertension. Again this is incorrect due to the same reason as of option (A).

Option (C) is incorrect even when Hypoxia, hypercarbia, and pain due to inadequate analgesia can cause postoperative hypertension. For the same reason as of the above explanations the option is incorrect.

Hence, the correct option is (D).

226. Option (B) is correct as X - rays are the modified electrons from cathode striking the anode both are made up of tungsten which has a high melting point and low vapourization pressure.

Option (A) is incorrect is a proton is a subatomic particle, symbol p or p^+, with a positive electric charge of +1e elementary charge and a mass slightly less than that of a neutron.

Option (C) is incorrect as the neutron is a subatomic particle, symbol n or n^0, with no net electric charge and a mass slightly greater than that of a proton.

Option (D) is incorrect as the positron or antielectron is the antiparticle or the antimatter counterpart of the electron. The positron has an electric charge of +1e, a spin of 1/2, and has the same mass as an electron.

Hence, the correct option is (B).

227. Option (D) is correct as Magnetic resonance imaging (MRI) is contraindicated in cases with a suspected intraocular ferromagnetic foreign body, because the object can easily move in the strong magnetic field, leading to serious and potentially vision-threatening ocular adverse events.

Option (A) is incorrect as bedside handheld sonography can be used to identify the presence of metallic IOFBs with a high positive predictive value. This can be an important adjunct to the physical examination in cases of suspected foreign bodies.

Option (B) is incorrect because conversely, where a metallic IOFB is clinically visible, plain X - ray orbital radiography without subsequent CT orbital imaging may serve to ensure that multiple IOFBs are not present.

Option (C) is incorrect as Eye conditions are common in emergency departments. Intraocular foreign bodies (IOFBs) are a frequent concern. Orbital computed tomography (CT) is traditionally used for evaluation. We sought to evaluate bedside ocular sonography for detecting metallic IOFBs.

Hence, the correct option is (D).

228. Option (D) is correct as Central, concentric, laminar, popcorn or homogeneous (diffuse) calcification is seen in benign lesions.

Option (A) is incorrect as these are made up of "normal" tissues such as cartilage, connective tissue, fat, and muscle but in abnormal amounts. Are usually less than 4 centimeters in diameter.

Option (B) is incorrect as Nodules described as "cavitary," meaning that the interior part of the nodule appears to contain air on X-rays is a characteristic of lung cancer.

Option (C) is incorrect as Peripheral location and infiltrative margin predict invasive features of papillary thyroid microcarcinoma.

Hence, the correct option is (D).

229. Option (A) is correct because this patient has a high clinical likelihood of pulmonary embolism because clinical assessment score is more than 4:-

1. Signs & symptoms of PE (Breathlessness & chest pain) → score 3.0
2. Immobilization (bed rest) > 3 days → score 1.5

So, the total score is 4.5. Therefore, imaging tests should be done. CT contrast is the imaging test of choice.

Option (B) is incorrect as Pulmonary angiography is a test to see how blood flows through the lung. Angiography is an imaging test that uses x-rays and a special dye to see inside the arteries. Arteries are blood vessels that carry blood away from the heart.

Option (C) is incorrect as a new technique of pulmonary vein wedge angiography to delineate pulmonary artery anatomy is described. In retrograde pulmonary vein wedge angiography, the left atrium and pulmonary veins are entered from arterial routes using a specially designed catheter.

Option (D) is incorrect as Echocardiography is a test that uses sound waves to produce live images of your heart. The image is an echocardiogram. This test allows your doctor to monitor how your heart and its valves are functioning. The images can help them spot: blood clots in the heart.

Hence, the correct option is (A).

230. Option (A) is correct as the double left heart border is not the chest radiographic feature of left atrial enlargement. So, this is the required answer.

Option (B) is incorrect because the trachea bifurcates into the right and left main bronchi at the level of the carina, supplying air to the right and left lungs respectively. Since it is also the sign of chest radiographic feature of left atrial enlargement, it is not the required answer.

Option (C) is incorrect as it includes splaying of the carina, with the increase of the tracheal bifurcation angle to over 90 degrees. Thus, it is not the required answer.

Option (D) is incorrect as signs of left atrial enlargement include straightening of left heart border (due to enlargement of the left atrial appendage). So, this is also not the required answer. Hence, the correct option is (A).

231. Option (C) is correct because

Radiological findings of TQF:

i) Boot shaped heart (Coeur en Sabot).

ii) Normal-sized heart (no cardiomegaly).

iii) Pulmonary oligemia.

iv)Right aortic arch (in 25% cases).

Option (A) is incorrect because Egg-on-a-string sign, also referred to as egg on its side, refers to the cardiomediastinal silhouette seen in the transposition of the great arteries (TGA). The heart appears globular due to an abnormal convexity of the right atrial border and left atrial enlargement and therefore appears like an egg.

Option (B) is incorrect because Total anomalous pulmonary venous return (TAPVR) is a congenital (present at birth) heart defect. Due to abnormal development of the fetal heart during the first eight weeks of pregnancy, the vessels that bring oxygen-rich (red) blood back to the heart from the lungs are improperly connected.

Option (D) is incorrect because The syndrome associated with PAPVR is more commonly known as Scimitar syndrome after the curvilinear pattern created on a chest radiograph by the pulmonary veins that drain to the inferior vena cava. This radiographic density often has the shape of a scimitar, a type of curved sword.

Hence, the correct option is (C).

232. For the acute abdomen, chest X-ray is essential because:-

1. For small pneumoperitoneum, a chest x-ray in an upright position (erect) is best.

2. A number of chest conditions may present as an acute abdominal pain (e.g. lower lobe pneumonia, MI).

3. The acute abdominal condition may be complicated by chest pathology, e.g. pleural effusion frequently complicates acute pancreatitis.

4. Even when a chest radiograph is normal it acts as a valuable baseline.

Option (A) is correct As the above explanation it is clear that this statement is false regarding the need for a chest radiograph in a patient of the acute abdomen, hence it will be a correct option according to the question.

Option (B) is incorrect because according to the above-given explanation it is clear that this statement is true regarding the need for a chest radiograph in a patient of the acute abdomen, hence it will be an incorrect option according to the question.

Option (C) is incorrect because according to the above-given explanation it is clear that this statement is true regarding the need for chest radiograph in a patient of the acute abdomen, hence it will be an incorrect option according to the question.

Option (D) is incorrect because according to the above given explanation it is clear that this statement is true regarding the need for a chest radiograph in a patient of the acute abdomen, hence it will be an incorrect option according to the question.

Hence, the correct option is (A).

233. Option (C) is correct because FNH contains both Kupffer cells and hepatocytes, and usually shows increased uptake of both Tc - 99m - SC and Tc - 99m - DISIDA. Therefore, FNH can be diagnosed with high accuracy by using hepatic scintigraphy (nuclear imaging).

Option (A) is incorrect because Tests and procedures used to diagnose hepatocellular carcinoma include, Blood tests to measure liver function. Imaging tests, such as CT and MRI. Liver biopsy, in some cases, to remove a sample of liver tissue for laboratory testing.

Option (B) is incorrect because Hepatic adenoma is usually detected by imaging, typically an ultrasound or CT, as a hyperenhancing liver nodule. Although imaging provides supportive information, a definitive diagnosis of hepatic adenoma requires biopsy of the tissue.

Option (D) is incorrect because Cholangiocarcinoma is suspected based on signs of biliary obstruction, abnormal liver function tests, elevated tumor markers (carbohydrate antigen 19-9 and carcinoembryonic antigen), and ultrasonography showing a bile stricture or a mass, especially in intrahepatic cholangiocarcinoma.

Hence, the correct option is (C).

234. Option (B) is correct because

In dynamic renal scintigraphy:-

- GFR → Tc - 99m - DTPA
- Effective renal plasma flow → Tc-99m - MAG3, I - 123 - OIH.

Option (A) is incorrect because Iodohippurate is indicated in renography to determine renal function, effective renal blood flow, and urinary tract obstruction

Option (C) is incorrect because Radioisotope renography is a form of medical imaging of the kidneys that uses radiolabelling. A renogram, which may also be known as a MAG3 scan, allows a nuclear medicine physician or a radiologist to visualize the kidneys and learn more about how they are functioning.

Option (D) is incorrect because Tc-99m DMSA is a technetium radiopharmaceutical used in renal imaging to evaluate renal structure and morphology, particularly in pediatric imaging for detection of scarring and pyelonephritis.

Hence, the correct option is (B).

235. Option (C) is correct because in the Worst cases of Psoriatic Arthritis both spine and peripheral joints may be involved. Fingers and toes are severely deformed due to erosion and instability of the interphalangeal joints (Arthritis Mutilans). Other features are Sacroiliitis, enthesitis (heel pain) and Spondylitis.

Option (A) is incorrect because OA is the most common form of arthritis, affecting millions of people worldwide. It occurs when the protective cartilage that cushions the ends of your bones wears down over time. Although osteoarthritis can damage any joint, the disorder most commonly affects joints in your hands, knees, hips, and spine.

Option (B) is incorrect because Reiter's syndrome, also known as reactive arthritis, is the classic triad of conjunctivitis, urethritis, and arthritis occurring after infection, particularly those in the urogenital or gastrointestinal tract.

Option (D) is incorrect because Rheumatoid arthritis (RA) is the most common type of autoimmune arthritis. It is caused when the immune system (the body's defense system) is not working properly. RA causes pain and swelling in the wrist and small joints of the hand and feet.

Hence, the correct option is (C).

236. Option (B) is correct because

- Amongst given options, fluid-fluid levels are seen in GCT and ABC.
- The lesion in question is metaphyseal:-

ABC → Metaphyseal

GCT → Epiphyseal

- Age of the patient is early adolescent:-

ABC → Before the age of 20 years

GCT → 20 - 40 years

Option (A) is incorrect because, On bone scintigraphy, most giant cell tumors demonstrate increased uptake on delayed images, especially around the periphery, with a central photogenic region (doughnut sign). Increased blood pool activity is also seen, and can be seen in adjacent bones due to generalized regional hyperemia (contiguous bone activity).

Option (C) is incorrect because MR imaging findings in hemangioma are frequently diagnostic. On T2-weighted images, hemangiomas generally appear as multiple high-signal-intensity lobules that resemble a bunch of grapes. This appearance is due to cavernous or cystic vascular spaces containing stagnant blood.

Option (D) is incorrect because the appearance of fibrous dysplasia is usually smooth and homogenous with endosteal scalloping and cortical thinning The borders are well defined and the cortex is usually intact but thinned due to the expansive nature of the lesion. Other features include the ground-glass matrix.

Hence, the correct option is (B).

237. Option (A) is correct because Onion-peel periosteal reaction is characteristically seen in Ewing's sarcoma.
Note: Onion-peel periosteal reaction may also be seen rarely in osteosarcoma.

Option (B) is incorrect because There are several types of chemical peels ranging in strength from mildly superficial to deeply resurfacing; alpha hydroxy acid peels (AHA), beta hydroxy acid peels (BHA), Jessner peels, retinoic acid peels, trichloroacetic acid peels (TCA), and phenol peels

Option (C) is incorrect because

- Superficial peels, which use mild acids like alpha-hydroxy acid to gently exfoliate.
- Medium peels, which use trichloroacetic or glycolic acid to reach the middle and outer layer of skills.

Option (D) is incorrect because Orange peel-like pitting is a term for skin that looks dimpled or slightly puckered. It may also be called peau d'orange, which is French for "skin of an orange." This type of pitting can happen anywhere on your skin. There are many potential causes of orange peel-like pitting on your skin.

Hence, the correct option is (A).

238. Option (C) is correct because Magnetic resonance imaging-positive temporal lobe atrophy with temporo-polar grey/white matter abnormalities (usually called 'blurring') has been frequently reported in patients with temporal lobe epilepsy associated with hippocampal sclerosis.

Option (A) is incorrect because Associated findings may include atrophy of the ipsilateral mammillary body, fornix, and other parts of the limbic system. Temporal sclerosis and atrophy are demonstrated in the images below. Fluid-attenuated inversion recovery (FLAIR) magnetic resonance images in a 40-year-old patient with complex partial seizures.

Option (B) is incorrect because When severe and long-standing, additional associated findings include 4, atrophy of the ipsilateral fornix and mammillary body. increased signal and or atrophy of the anterior thalamic nucleus. dilatation of temporal horn and temporal lobe atrophy.

Option (D) is incorrect because Associated hippocampal atrophy and gliosis are common. MRI scan commonly displays increased T2 signal and hippocampal atrophy. Mesial temporal sclerosis might occur with other temporal lobe abnormalities (dual pathology). Mesial temporal sclerosis is the most common pathological abnormality in temporal lobe epilepsy.

Hence, the correct option is (C).

239. Option (C) is correct because

Investigation of choice for acute SAH → Non-contrast CT scan

Investigation of choice for chronic SAH → MRI

Option (A) is incorrect because 'Enhancement' refers to a process by which lesions revealed on a breast MRI image increase in contrast at a specific rate over a given short-time-interval, which indicates increased vascularity to the area.

Option (B) is incorrect because Magnetic resonance imaging (MRI) uses a large magnet and radio waves to look at organs and structures inside your body. Health care professionals use MRI scans to diagnose a variety of conditions, from torn ligaments to tumors. MRIs are very useful for examining the brain and spinal cord.

Option (D) is incorrect because Angiography is an imaging test that uses X-rays to view your body's blood vessels. The X-rays provided by an angiography are called angiograms. This test is used to study narrow, blocked, enlarged, or malformed arteries or veins in many parts of your body, including your brain, heart, abdomen, and legs.

Hence, the correct option is (C).

240.

Option (D) is correct because the purpose of Cozen's test (also known as the "resisted wrist extension test" or "resistive tennis elbow test") is to check for lateral epicondylalgia or "tennis elbow".

Option (A) is incorrect because Before diagnosing medial epicondylitis, your doctor may order an X-ray of the inside of your elbow, arm, or wrist to rule out other possible causes of pain, such as a fracture or arthritis.

Option (B) is incorrect because other tests are sometimes needed to rule out other causes of elbow swelling, such as infection (septic arthritis), gout or rheumatoid arthritis. Tests that might be needed include blood tests and an ultrasound scan.

Option (C) is incorrect because the first imaging studies to evaluate a Frozen elbow should be plain radiographs, including anterior-posterior, lateral, and two oblique views. Bony blocks to motion can often be detected using this modality.

Hence, the correct option is (D).

241. Option (B) is correct because fertilization is the process of fusion of spermatozoon with the mature ovum. Almost always fertilization occurs in the ampullary part of the uterine tube. The ferlizable lifespan of the oocyte ranges from 12 - 24 hours whereas that of sperm is 48 - 72 hours.

Option (A) is incorrect because the fimbriae of the uterine tube, also known as fimbriae tube, are small, fingerlike projections at the end of the fallopian tubes, through which eggs move from the ovaries to the uterus. The fimbriae are connected to the ovary.

Option (C) is incorrect because the interstitium is a contiguous fluid-filled space existing between a structural barrier, such as a cell wall or the skin, and internal structures, such as organs, including muscles and the circulatory system.

Option (D) is incorrect because the thyroid gland is located low in the front of the neck, below Adam's apple. The gland is shaped like a butterfly and wraps around the windpipe or trachea. The two wings or lobes on either side of the windpipe are joined together by a bridge, called the isthmus, which crosses over the front of the windpipe.

Hence, the correct option is (B).

242. Option (B) is correct because fluids contributed by the seminal vesicles are approximately 60 percent of the total semen volume; these fluids contain fructose, amino acids, citric acid, phosphorus, potassium, and hormones known as prostaglandins.

Option (A) is incorrect because After emerging from the testes, sperm are stored in the epididymis, in which secretions of potassium, sodium, and glyceryl phosphorylcholine (an energy source for sperm) are contributed to the sperm cells. Sperm mature in the epididymis.

Option (C) is incorrect because The prostate gland is a male reproductive organ whose main function is to secrete prostate fluid, one of the components of semen. The muscles of the prostate gland also help propel this seminal fluid into the urethra during ejaculation

Option (D) is incorrect because the Bulbourethral Glands. The bulbourethral glands (also known as Cowper's glands) are a pair of pea-shaped exocrine glands located posterolateral to the membranous urethra. They contribute to the final volume of semen by producing a lubricating mucus secretion.

Hence, the correct option is (B).

243. Option (D) is correct As the above explanation both are results so this option will be correct according to the question.

The absence of fructose suggests the congenital absence of seminal vesicle or portion of the ductal system or both.

- PESA-percutaneous epididymal sperm aspiration.
- ICSI-intracytoplasmic sperm injection.

Option (A) is incorrect because according to the above explanation, The congenital absence of seminal vesicle is a result of Absent fructose content in the seminal fluid.

Option (B) is incorrect because according to the above explanation, Partial duct obstruction is a result of Absent fructose content in the seminal fluid.

Option (C) is incorrect because according to the above explanation both are results so none option can not be possible.

Hence, the correct option is (D).

244. Option (D) is correct because the Diagnosis of choriocarcinoma is by Histology of a uterine wall showing penetration with marked hyperplastic trophoblastic cells Persistent high HCG levels.

Option (A) is incorrect because Molar pregnancy is an abnormal form of pregnancy in which a non-viable fertilized egg implants in the uterus and will fail to come to term. A molar pregnancy is a gestational trophoblastic disease that grows into a mass in the uterus that has swollen chorionic villi.

Option (B) is incorrect because HCG appears in the blood and urine of pregnant women as early as 10 days after conception. Quantitative HCG measurement helps determine the exact age of the fetus. It can also assist in the diagnosis of abnormal pregnancies, such as ectopic pregnancies, molar pregnancies, and possible miscarriages.

Option (C) is incorrect because Cancer that metastasizes to the lungs is a life-threatening condition that develops when cancer in another area of the body spreads to the lung. Cancer that develops at any primary site can form metastatic tumors. These tumors are capable of spreading to the lungs.

Hence, the correct option is (D).

245. Option (A) is correct because

- MCV increases minimally during pregnancy .
- MCHC remains unchanged.

Option (B) is incorrect because, in pregnancy, increased nutritional demand for iron is reflected in trimester-specific increases in TIBC (1). EDTA complexed the iron in the sample and the added iron for the UIBC test, resulting in a falsely low iron and falsely increased UIBC and TIBC (2, 3).

Option (C) is incorrect because During pregnancy the plasma volume increases by 40-50% and the red blood cell volume increase only by 20–30%. These changes occur mostly in the second trimester and prior to 32 weeks gestation.

Option (D) is incorrect because Ferritin is an acute phase reactant and levels will rise when there is active infection or inflammation. Anemia in pregnancy is defined as hemoglobin (Hb) concentration less than 11 g/dL while low ferritin is defined as SR less than 10 µg/L.

Hence, the correct option is (A).

246. Folic acid deficiency in Pregnancy

- In nonpregnant women, the folic acid requirement is 50 to 100 μg/day.
- During pregnancy, requirements are increased and 400 μg/day is recommended.

The earliest biochemical evidence is low plasma folic acid concentrations.

Normal serum folate levels:

1. Not Pregnant women: 5.4-18ng/ml.
2. 1st trimester: 2.6-15ng/ml.
3. 2nd trimester: 0.8-24ng/ml.
4. 3rd trimester: 1.4-20.7ng/ml.

- Early morphological changes usually include neutrophils that are hypersegmented and newly formed erythrocytes that are macrocytic.
- As the anemia becomes more intense, peripheral nucleated erythrocytes appear, and bone marrow examination discloses megaloblastic erythropoiesis.
- The fetus and placenta extract folate from maternal circulation so effectively that the fetus is not anemic despite severe maternal anemia.

Treatment

- As little as 1mg of folic acid administered orally once daily produces a striking hematological response.
- By 4 to 7 days after beginning folic acid treatment, the reticulocyte count is increased, and leukopenia and thrombocytopenia are corrected.
- American College of Obstetricians and Gynecologists (2013c) have recommended that all women of childbearing age consume at least 400 μg of folic acid daily.

Increased need for Folic acid

- Multifetal pregnancy.
- Hemolytic anemia.
- Crohn disease.
- Alcoholism.
- Inflammatory skin disorders.

Option (B) is correct because in this option the dose of folic acid is 1 mg given which is correct according to the above explanation, hence this option will be correct.

Option (A) is incorrect because in this option the dose of folic acid is 400 μg given which is not correct according to the above explanation, hence this option will not be correct.

Option (C) is incorrect because in this option the dose of folic acid is 5 mg given which is not correct according to the above explanation, hence this option will not be correct.

Option (D) is incorrect because in this option the dose of folic acid is 2 mg given which is not correct according to the above explanation, hence this option will not be correct.

Hence, the correct option is (B).

247. Partograph

- It is a composite graphical record of key data (maternal & fetal) during labor entered against me on a single sheet of paper.
- Components Paentidenficaon Time -recorded at hourly interval Fetal heart rate -
- recorded at every 30 minutes State of membranes & color of liquor -
- to mark T for intact membranes, 'C' for clear & 'M' for meconium-stained liquor **Cervical dilation & descent of the head Uterine contractions Drugs** & fluids Blood pressure -
- every 2 hrs & pulse rate at every 30 minutes Oxytocin Urine analysis Temperature record

Option (C) is correct because Amniocentesis to determine fetal lung maturity is usually done after 32 weeks' gestation because pulmonary maturity is unlikely before this gestational age. The amniotic fluid can be evaluated for a lecithin-to-sphingomyelin (L/S) ratio and the presence or absence of phosphatidylglycerol.

Option (A) is incorrect As the above explanation this is monitored by Partogra, hence this option will not be correct according to the question.

Option (B) is incorrect As the above explanation this is monitored by Partogram, hence this option will not be correct according to the question.

Option (D) is incorrect As the above explanation this is monitored by Partogram, hence this option will not be correct according to the question.

Hence, the correct option is (C).

248. Option (D) is correct As

- When a dead fetus is retained in the uterus for more than 4 weeks (10-20%), there is a possibility of defibrination from silent disseminated intravascular coagulation. i.e, there is a chance for consumption coagulopathy with hypofibrinemia, similar to that seen in intrauterine death of the fetus.
- It is due to the release of thromboplastin from the dead fetus and placenta into the maternal circulation.

Option (A) is incorrect because A septic abortion "is an infection of the placenta and fetus (products of conception) of a pre-viable pregnancy. Infection is centered in the placenta and there is a risk of spreading to the uterus, causing pelvic infection or becoming systemic to cause sepsis and potential damage of distant vital organs." hence this option statement is not correct according to the given situation in the question.

Option (B) is incorrect because Recurrent pregnancy loss (RPL), also referred to as a recurrent miscarriage or habitual abortion, is historically defined as 3 consecutive pregnancy losses prior to 20 weeks from the last menstrual period. hence this option statement is not correct according to the given situation in the question.

Option (C) is incorrect because the use of treatments that can affect the future fertility of men, women, and children and the late effect consequences of infertility and sexual dysfunction can have a lasting impact on a patient's physical and psychological well- being.

Hence, the correct option is (D).

249. Option (C) is correct because

- 12 mg betamethasone injection is indicated in all pregnancies at risk of preterm labor between 28 and 35 weeks to attain lung maturity.
- Since there is no indication of fetal distress it is not given. Tocolytics are used to inhibit contractions and keep the uterus quiescent in case of preterm labor.
- But it is not indicated after 34 weeks. Cervical cerclage is useful in some women with history of preterm labor.
- Thus vaginal swab culture is can be used in this condition as the presence of bacterial vaginosis has been found to be associated with preterm labor and most cases are asymptomatic.

Option (A) is incorrect because betamethasone (bay ta meth a sone) is a corticosteroid. It helps to reduce swelling, redness, itching, and allergic reactions. It is used to treat asthma, allergies, arthritis, Crohn's disease, and ulcerative colitis. It is also used for other conditions, like blood disorders and diseases of the adrenal glands. So, this option will not be correct.

Option (B) is incorrect because Tocolytic medication. Tocolytics are drugs that are used to delay your delivery for a short time (up to 48 hours) if you begin labor too early in your pregnancy. So, this option will not be correct.

Option (D) is incorrect because This is the most common way to do the procedure. Your doctor will use a tool called a speculum to hold your vagina open in order to reach the cervix. She'll then stitch the cervix closed. So, this option will not be correct.

Hence, the correct option is (C).

250.

- The baby may pass meconium in utero or soon after birth, but all healthy newborn babies must evacuate within 24 hours of birth. During the first 2 or 3 days, the baby passes black, tarry (like tar) 'meconium' stools which are followed by greenish (transitional) stools for the next 1 or 2 days.
- The normal breastfed baby usually passes 4-8 semisolid sticky golden yellow stools every day. Some babies may pass stools after each feed due to the 'exaggerated' gastrocolic reflex. The stools are often very small (at times like drippings of the birds) with normal consistency. The babies continue to gain weight.
- Tar means a thick, sticky, brown to black liquid with a pungent odor, obtained by the destructive distillation of wood, coal, peat, shale, etc.

Option (B) is correct as from the above explanation it is clear that Meconium is excreted by a newborn till 3 days so, this option will be correct.

Option (A) is incorrect as from the above explanation it is clear that Meconium is excreted by a newborn till 3 days so, this option will not be correct.

Option (C) is incorrect as from the above explanation it is clear that Meconium is excreted by a newborn till 3 days so, this option will not be correct.

Option (D) is incorrect as from the above explanation it is clear that Meconium is excreted by a newborn till 3 days so, this option will not be correct.

Hence, the correct option is (B).

251. Fetal cardiac activity is detected as early as

With Transvaginal USG	6 weeks of gestational age
With Transabdominal USG	8 weeks of gestational age

Between 5 ½ to 6 ½ weeks, a fetal pole or even a fetal heartbeat may be detected by vaginal ultrasound. The fetal pole is the first visible sign of a developing embryo. This pole structure actually has some curve to it with the embryo's head at one end and what looks like a tail at the other end.

The fetal pole now allows for a crown to rump measurements (CRL) to be taken, so that pregnancy dating can be a bit more accurate. The fetal pole may be seen at a crown-rump length (CRL) of 2-4mm, and the heartbeat may be seen as a regular flutter when the CRL has reached 5mm.

If a vaginal ultrasound is done and no fetal pole or cardiac activity is seen, another ultrasound scan should be done in 3-7 days. Due to the fact that pregnancy dating can be wrong, it would be much too early at this point to make a clear diagnosis of the outcome of the pregnancy.

Option (B) is correct because, at six weeks of pregnancy, an ultrasound can detect a little flutter in the area that will become the future heart of the baby.

Option (A) is incorrect because Fetal cardiac activity is detected with Transvaginal USG as early as 6 weeks.

Option (C) is incorrect because at 10 weeks pregnant has started developing tissue and you can see his arms and legs forming.

Option (D) is incorrect because the detection rate for both valves at 12 weeks was ≥ 90%.

Hence, the correct option is (B).

252. Option (A) is correct because intrauterine growth restriction can result in a baby being small for gestational age (SGA), which is most commonly defined as a weight below the 10th percentile for the gestational age. At the end of pregnancy, it can result in low birth weight.

Option (B) is incorrect because the current WHO criterion for low birth weight is weight less than 2,500 g (5 lb) or below the 10th percentile for gestational age.

Option (C) is incorrect because intrauterine growth retardation (IUGR), which is defined as less than 10 percent of the predicted fetal weight for gestational age.

Option (D) is incorrect because babies weighing less than 1,500 grams (3 pounds, 5 ounces) at birth are considered very low birth weight. Babies who weigh less than 1,000 grams (2 pounds, 3 ounces) are extremely low birth weight.

Hence, the correct option is (A).

253. Option (B) is correct because the Doppler Study of Middle Cerebral Vessels:

- Normally the middle cerebral vessels have high resistance flow and are characterized by little diastolic flow.

- In the case of IUGR, a brain-sparing effect is seen with a reduction in the resistance indices in the middle cerebral vessels (i.e. increased flow) due to the shunting of blood to the brain in IUGR. Whereas in other areas (as aorta in the options) show decreased flow.
- "Increased fetal diastolic flow in the middle cerebral artery with the absent diastolic flow in aorta implies fetal acidemia."

Option (A) is incorrect as Doppler waveforms are traditionally defined as either normal or abnormal. This characteristic waveform is most commonly attributed to arterial flow found distal to high-grade stenosis or occlusion.

Option (C) is incorrect because as far as persistence of diastolic notch in the uterine artery is concerned, it signifies pregnancies destined to develop preeclampsia.

Option (D) is incorrect as Absent end-diastolic flow (AEDF) in an umbilical artery Doppler assessment is a useful feature that indicates underlying fetal vascular stress if detected in mid or late pregnancy.

Hence, the correct option is (B).

254. Reactive NST, i.e. acceleration with fetal movements indicates a healthy fetus.

"Absence of deceleration in the NST is reassuring. Absence of accelerations in the NST may be a sign of fetal compromise."

The sinusoidal pattern is observed with serous fetal anemia, whether from D isoimmunization, ruptured vasa previa, fetomaternal hemorrhage or twin to twin transfusion.

Option (A) is correct According to the above explanation.

Option (B) is incorrect According to the above explanation.

Option (C) is incorrect According to the above explanation.

Option (D) is incorrect According to the above explanation.

Hence, the correct option is (A).

255. Option (A) is correct because the diagnosis of appendicitis during pregnancy is difficult as symptoms of appendicitis viz nausea, vomiting anorexia are normally present in pregnancy. But once the diagnosis is made immediate surgery should be done.

Option (B) is incorrect because pregnancy complications were found to be considerable: 4/12 (33%) who underwent appendectomy for appendicitis during the first trimester aborted spontaneously.

Option (C) is incorrect because perforation increases the risk of morbidity and the risk of preterm delivery and fetal loss. Hence, early surgical intervention is the recommended treatment strategy for appendicitis during pregnancy.

Option (D) is incorrect because if appendicitis is suspected, treatment is prompt surgical exploration. Even though diagnostic errors sometimes lead to the removal of a normal appendix, it is better to operate than to postpone intervention until generalized peritonitis has developed.

Hence, the correct option is (A).

256. Option (D) is correct because it is round ligament and not broad ligament which terminates at its anterior end.

Option (A) is incorrect because the labia majora are homologous to the male scrotum, i.e. they are derived embryologically from the same tissue.

Option (B) is incorrect because the superficial external pudendal artery arises from the medial side of the femoral artery. It supplies the male scrotum and the female labia majora.

Option (C) is incorrect because Labia majora (posterior half) • Drains into → Superficial inguinal → Deep inguinal→ external iliac. Labia minora and prepuce of clitoris • Intercommunicating with the lymphatics of the opposite side in the vestibule and drains into superficial inguinal nodes.

Hence, the correct option is (D).

257. Option (A) is correct because the rise in FSH recruits tertiary-stage ovarian follicles (antral follicles) for entry into the menstrual cycle.

Option (B) is incorrect because estrogen, or estrogen, is the primary female sex hormone. It is responsible for the development and regulation of the female reproductive system and secondary sex characteristics.

Option (C) is incorrect because the Luteinizing hormone is a hormone produced by gonadotropic cells in the anterior pituitary gland. In females, an acute rise of LH triggers ovulation and development of the corpus luteum. In males, where LH had also been called interstitial cell-stimulating hormone, it stimulates Leydig cell production of testosterone.

Option (D) is incorrect because Progesterone is an endogenous steroid and progestogen sex hormone involved in the menstrual cycle, pregnancy, and embryogenesis of humans and other species. It belongs to a group of steroid hormones called the progestogens and is the major progestogen in the body.

Hence, the correct option is (A).

258. Option (C) is correct because Spironolactone is an antiandrogen; used for treating heart failure, liver scarring, or kidney disease.

Option (A) is incorrect because clomiphene citrate is used for induction of ovulation; it can be 50 mg/day increased to 150mg/day; Starting from day 2 to day 6 of the cycle for 5 days.

Option (B) is incorrect because Tamoxifen 10 mg daily for 6 months has been effective in treating male infertility

Option (D) is incorrect because Testosterone 25 -50 mg daily orally improves testicular functions.

Hence, the correct option is (C).

259. In PCOS

- Hyperinsulinemia is seen in 50-70% of cases of PCOS.
- Insulin induces LH to cause thecal hyperplasia and secrete androgens.
- Hyperandrogenism lowers the level of hepatic sex hormone-binding globulin.
- Metformin treats the root causes, rectifies endocrine and metabolic function, improves fertility rate, used as an insulin sensitizer.

- It reduces insulin level, delays glucose absorption, liver production of glucose and improves peripheral resistance.
- Metformin does not cause hypoglycemia in a normoglycemic woman.

From the above explanation, we can say that:

Option (B) is correct because the drug's numerous side benefits associated with the treatment and prevention of diabetes.

Option (A) is incorrect because Hyperinsulinemia is seen in 50-70% of cases of PCOS.

Option (C) is incorrect because Metformin or the glitazones rarely cause hypoglycemia unless taken with insulin stimulators (sulfonylureas or repaglinide) or insulin injections.

Option (D) is incorrect because Hyperandrogenism lowers the level of hepatic sex hormone-binding globulin.

Hence, the correct option is (B).

260. Mayer Rokitansky Kuster Hauser syndrome [MRKH]; Mullerian Agenesis

- Disorder of genital development characterized by the absence of the vagina, an absent or hypoplastic uterus, and normal or hypoplastic fallopian tubes.
- Typically ovaries are normal.
- Secondary sexual characters are well developed [Breast, pubic and axillary hair].
- May be associated with urologic anomalies [unilateral renal agenesis, ectopic or horseshoe kidney and duplication of collecting systems] and Skeletal malformations [Hemivertebrae and scoliosis, Klippel-Feil syndrome which includes the short neck, low hairline, limited range of motion and neurologic symptoms resulting from one or more fused vertebrae].

From the above explanation, we can see that,

Option (A) is correct because disorder of genital development characterized by the absence of the vagina, an absent or hypoplastic uterus, and normal or hypoplastic fallopian tubes.

Option (B) is incorrect because of an absent or hypoplastic uterus and normal or hypoplastic fallopian tubes.

Option (C) is incorrect because typically ovaries are normal.

Option (D) is incorrect because secondary sexual characters are well developed [Breast, pubic and axillary hair].

Hence, the correct option is (A).

261. The uterine muscles are highly sensitive to oxytocin in labour and birth due to upregulation of the sensitivity/concentration of oxytocin receptors by high oestrogen elevations in late pregnancy. Progesterone has been used to inhibit uterine contraction and prevent abortion and preterm labor. The study demonstrates that progesterone inhibits uterine contraction in late pregnancy.

Hence, the correct option is (D).

262. Option (A) is correct because Hematuria is the presence of blood in a person's urine. The two types of hematuria are. gross hematuria-when a person can see the blood in his or her urine. Microscopic hematuria-when a person cannot see the blood in his or her urine, yet it is seen under a microscope.

Option (B) is incorrect because the initial symptoms and signs in women include dysuria, increased vaginal discharge, or vaginal bleeding between periods. Women with gonorrhea are at risk of developing serious complications from the infection, regardless of the presence or severity of symptoms.

Option (C) is incorrect as typical symptoms of gonorrhea include a thick green or yellow discharge from the vagina or penis, pain when peeing and, in women, bleeding between periods. But around 1 in 10 infected men and almost half of infected women do not experience any symptoms.

Option (D) is incorrect because Gonorrhea infections can appear much like common vaginal yeast or bacterial infections. Symptoms include:

- discharge from the vagina (watery, creamy, or slightly green).
- pain or burning sensation while urinating.
- the need to urinate more frequently.
- heavier periods or spotting.

Hence, the correct option is (A).

263. Management of VVF is surgical management:

The timing of surgery -

- Small urinary fistulas sometimes heal spontaneously during the first few weeks.
- However, in a case of established fistula - it is better to wait for about 3 months for all tissue inflammation to subside. If one attempt fails to heal fistula, the second attempt is done after 3 months.
- In fistulas following surgery, the waiting period is 3-6 months.
- In fistulas following radiation: 6 months - 2 years' time can be taken before inflammation subsides.

Techniques of Repair -

Layer technique

- Latzko procedure (for fistulas following hysterectomy)
- Chaser Moir technique.
- Post-operative Management -
- Continuous bladder drainage for 14 days.
- Antibiotic coverage.
- No vaginal examination, P/S, intercourse x 3 months.
- Avoid pregnancy for 2 years.
- In pregnancy after repair of vaginal fistula - elective cesarean is done.

Extra Edge:

This question is an old one so here answer will be 3 months but if this question is repeated now remember the following lines from Williams Gynae. 1st /ed 575-576:

"Timing of repair: Traditional teaching recommends delayed repair of fistulas at 3 - 6 months after injury. However, this old dictum is probably no longer applicable. Most agree that unless there is a severe infection or acute signs of inflammation, waiting is not necessary. Early surgical intervention of uncomplicated fistulas does not affect closure rates, yet appears to reduce social and psychological patient distress (Balivas, 1995). Fistulas identified within the first 24 - 48 hours postoperatively can be safely repaired immediately with success rates of 90 - 100%."

Option (C) is correct as according to the above explanation, VVF is best repaired after 3 months.

Option (A) is incorrect as according to the above explanation, Usually, the repair is performed at 12 weeks duration after the diagnosis.

Option (B) is incorrect as according to the above explanation, the recurrent fistulas were repaired after 3 months.

Option (D) is incorrect as according to the above explanation, delayed repair after 6 months is often followed.

Hence, the correct option is (C).

264.

- Symptoms of pelvic organ prolapse include stress incontinence (inadvertent leakage of urine with physical activity), a vaginal bulge, painful sexual intercourse, back pain, and difficult urination or bowel movements. Colporrhaphy may be performed on the anterior (front) and/or posterior (back) walls of the vagina. An anterior colporrhaphy treats a cystocele or urethrocele, while a posterior colporrhaphy treats a rectocele. Surgery is generally not performed unless the symptoms of the prolapse have begun to interfere with daily life.
- Colporrhaphy is a surgical procedure in humans that repairs a defect in the wall of the vagina. It is the surgical intervention for both cystocele and rectocele. The repair may be to either or both of the anterior or posterior vaginal walls, thus the origin of some of its alternative names
- Burch colposuspension is used to treat stress urinary incontinence (SUI). Stress urinary incontinence is the involuntary leakage of urine during periods of increased intra-abdominal pressure, including exertion such as laughing, coughing, sneezing, coughing, and jumping.
- In stress incontinence, urine leaks when there is a sudden extra pressure ('stress') on the bladder. Urine tends to leak most when you cough, laugh, or exercise (like jump or run). Strengthening the pelvic floor muscles can often cure stress incontinence.
- Sling surgery is the most common surgery doctors use to treat urinary stress incontinence. That's when certain movements or actions, like coughing, sneezing, or lifting, put pressure on your bladder and make you pee a little. The surgeon creates a "sling" out of mesh or human tissue.

Option (C) is correct because of the above explanation.

Option (A) is incorrect because according to the above explanation point b is not valid.

Option (B) is incorrect because point b is not a treatment of genuine stress incontinence.

Option (D) is incorrect because point b is taking place in the option.

Hence, the correct option is (C).

265. Option (D) is correct because Artificial insemination is the deliberate introduction of sperm into a female's cervix or uterine cavity for the purpose of achieving a pregnancy through in vivo fertilization by means other than sexual intercourse.

Option (A) is incorrect because Gamete intrafallopian transfer (GIFT) is a tool of assisted reproductive technology against infertility. Eggs are removed from a woman's ovaries, and placed in one of the Fallopian tubes, along with the man's sperm.

Option (B) is incorrect because Zygote intrafallopian transfer (ZIFT) is an assisted reproductive technology (ART) first used in 1986 to help those who are infertile conceive a child. ZIFT is a hybrid technique derived from a combination of in vitro fertilization (IVF) and gamete intrafallopian transfer (GIFT) procedures.

Option (C) is incorrect because Assisted reproductive technology (ART) is used to treat infertility. It includes fertility treatments that handle both a woman's egg and a man's sperm. It works by removing eggs from a woman's body. The eggs are then mixed with sperm to make embryos. The embryos are then put back in the woman's body. In vitro fertilization (IVF) is the most common and effective type of ART.

Hence, the correct option is (D).

266. Option (B) is correct as Centochroman caused an inhibition in the incorporation of all the three precursors. The implication of these changes in the light of estrogenicity, an agonist.

Option (A) is incorrect because the diaphragm is a barrier method of birth control. It is moderately effective, with a one-year failure rate of around 12% with typical use. It is placed over the cervix with spermicide before sex and left in place for at least six hours after sex. Fitting by a healthcare provider is generally required.

Option (C) is incorrect as a condom is a sheath-shaped barrier device used during sexual intercourse to reduce the probability of pregnancy or a sexually transmitted infection. There are both male and female condoms.

Option (D) is incorrect as today, Vaginal Contraceptive Sponge birth control product is a soft, disposable polyurethane foam sponge containing 1000 mg of nonoxynol 9, which kills sperm on contact. It is inserted into the vagina and while in place provides protection against pregnancy for 24 hours.

Hence, the correct option is (B).

267. Option (A) is correct because abnormal uterine bleeding (formerly, dysfunctional uterine bleeding [DUB]) is irregular uterine bleeding that occurs in the absence of recognizable pelvic pathology, general medical disease, or pregnancy. It reflects a disruption in the normal cyclic pattern of ovulatory hormonal stimulation to the endometrial lining. About 10-15% of women experiences episodes of DUB in the reproductive years of their life. It is common during extremes of reproductive life following pregnancy, during lactation.

Option (B) is incorrect because Fibroids are abnormal growths that develop in or on a woman's uterus. Sometimes these tumors become quite large and cause severe abdominal pain and heavy periods. In other cases, they cause no signs or symptoms at all. The growths are typically benign, or noncancerous. The cause of fibroids is unknown.

Option (C) is incorrect because Endometriosis occurs when bits of the tissue that lines the uterus (endometrium) grow on other pelvic organs, such as the ovaries or fallopian tubes. Outside the uterus, endometrial tissue thickens and bleeds, just as the normal endometrium does during the menstrual cycle.

Option (D) is incorrect because Adenomyosis is a condition in which the inner lining of the uterus (the endometrium) breaks through the muscle wall of the uterus (the myometrium). Adenomyosis can cause menstrual cramps, lower abdominal pressure, and bloating before menstrual periods and can result in heavy periods.

Hence, the correct option is (A).

268.

- Vaginal metastasis means stage IIIB.
- Lymph node involvement is seen from stage MC onwards.
- Bowel involvement /rectal involvement means stage IVA.
- Lung metastasis means stage IVB.
- Serosa involvement/positive peritoneal cytology means stage IIIA. The question is about stage IIIB, so everything involved before it is also included.

Option (D) is correct because, In Stage-IIIB, cancer has spread to the vagina. After surgery, stage IIIB may be treated with chemo and/or radiation.

Option (A) is incorrect because the tumor has spread to the vagina or next to the uterus. Stage $IIIC_1$ cancer has spread to the regional pelvic lymph nodes.

Option (B) is incorrect because it consists of point c which is not right.

Option (C) is incorrect because Metastases to the para-aortic lymph nodes are associated with poor prognosis. Factors associated with para-aortic lymph node dissemination include advanced stage, high histological grade, deep myometrial invasion, cervical involvement, lymphovascular space involvement, and the presence of pelvic lymph node metastases.

Hence, the correct option is (D).

269. Cryosurgery offers advantages over other methods of cancer treatment. It is less invasive than surgery, involving only a small incision or insertion of the cryoprobe through the skin. Consequently, pain, bleeding, and other complications of surgery are minimized. Cryosurgery is less expensive than other treatments and requires shorter recovery time and a shorter hospital stay, or no hospital stay at all. Sometimes cryosurgery can be done using only local anesthesia.

Option (C) is correct because after cryosurgery there will be profuse vaginal discharge for about 2–3 weeks.

Option (A) is incorrect because it is Less discomfort to the patient.

Option (B) is incorrect because in this Postoperative bleeding is much less.

Option (D) is incorrect because in it Cervical stenosis is extremely rare.

Hence, the correct option is (C).

270. Option (A) is correct because the corpus luteum is supported and maintained by the pregnancy hormone human chorionic gonadotrophin or HCG. The corpus luteum begins to decrease in size at around 10 weeks of pregnancy.

Option (B) is incorrect because Progesterone is an endogenous steroid and progestogen sex hormone involved in the menstrual cycle, pregnancy, and embryogenesis of humans and other species. It belongs to a group of steroid hormones called the progestogens and is the major progestogen in the body.

Option (C) is incorrect because Estrogen, or estrogen, is the primary female sex hormone. It is responsible for the development and regulation of the female reproductive system and secondary sex characteristics. There are three major endogenous estrogens in females that have estrogenic hormonal activity: estrone, estradiol, and estriol.

Option (D) is incorrect because it does not contain HCG.

Hence, the correct option is (A).

271. Option (C) is correct because "Allowable normal range of variation in observation, is conventionally taken between 3'd and 97th percentile curves" -Ghai

• This female child has weight (50th percentile) and height (75th percentile) in a normal range of variation (3rd-97th percentile).

• So, nothing should be done actively and the parent should be assured that the weight and height of the child are within a normal range.

Option (A) is incorrect because Vitamin-rich tonic will not help. A vitamin is an organic molecule that is an essential micronutrient that an organism needs in small quantities for the proper functioning of its metabolism.

Option (B) is incorrect because Forceful eating will not help. Forcing children to eat food they don't enjoy could spark tension at mealtimes and damage the parent-child relationship. What's more, making children eat unwanted foods didn't even affect their weight and whether they developed picking eating habits.

Option (D) is incorrect because Complete investigation for UTI will not help. As urinary tract infection (UTI) is an infection in any part of your urinary system — your kidneys, ureters, bladder, and urethra. Most infections involve the lower urinary tract — the bladder and the urethra. The UTI will not affect eating.

Hence, the correct option is (C).

272. Option (C) is correct because except option (C) all other are the key features of kangaroo mother care.

Option (A) is incorrect because it is the key feature of kangaroo mother care. Kangaroo care is a technique practiced on newborns, usually preterm, infants wherein the infant is held, skin-to-skin, with an adult.

Option (B) is incorrect because Exclusive breastfeeding is the key feature of kangaroo mother care. The baby on KMC is breastfed exclusively. Kangaroo mother care promotes early initiation of breastfeeding as compared to other animals. The parent's stable body temperature helps to regulate the neonate's temperature more smoothly than an incubator and allows for readily accessible breastfeeding.

Option (D) is incorrect as initiated in a facility and continued at home are the key features of kangaroo mother care. Cardiopulmonary monitoring, oximetry, supplemental oxygen or nasal (continuous positive airway pressure) ventilation, intravenous infusion, and monitor leads do not prevent kangaroo care. Babies who are in kangaroo care tend to be less prone to apnea and bradycardia and have stabilization of oxygen needs.

Hence, the correct option is (C).

273. Option (D) is correct because

• Blood in IVC has more saturation than blood in SVC as IVC carries the oxygenated blood of the umbilical vein.

• The left ventricular blood has more oxygen saturation that right ventricular blood because it carries the blood of IVC, while blood in the right ventricle is a mixture of blood from IVC and SVC.

• So, the brain and coronary circulation receive blood with higher saturation (through ascending aorta) than the lower half of the body.

• The left ventricular output is approximately half of right ventricular output because the volume of blood reaching in the left atrium is considerably lower than the volume of blood reaching in the right atrium. In fact, the right atrium is the major source of blood to the left atrium.

• Aorta and pulmonary trunk are connected by ductus arteriosis, and the pulmonary trunk has pressure slightly higher or equal to that of aorta → So, blood flows from pulmonary trunk to aorta.

• The pressure in right and left ventricles are equal.

Option (A) is incorrect because Blood oxygen saturation (SO_2) in the superior vena cava (SVC) is approximately 2% to 5% higher than that in the pulmonary artery. This SVC-pulmonary artery gradient in SO_2 varies considerably among individuals, or even within the same person when it is measured at different times

Option (B) is incorrect because the left ventricle is thicker and more muscular than the right ventricle because it pumps blood at a higher pressure.

Option (C) is incorrect because Brain hypoxia is a form of hypoxia or oxygen deficiency affecting the brain. It occurs when the brain does not receive enough oxygen even though blood is still flowing.

Hence, the correct option is (D).

274. Option (B) is correct because

• Laryngomalacia is the most common congenital laryngeal anomaly.

• It is the most common cause of stridor in infants and children.

• Symptoms appear in the first 2 weeks of life and increase in severity for up to 6 months.

• The typical presentation is inspiratory stridor which is exacerbated by any exertion (crying, agitation, feeding), supine position, and viral infection of URT.

• Stridor is due to the partial collapse of a flaccid supraglottic airway during inspiration.

Option (A) is incorrect because Croup, also known as laryngotracheobronchitis, is a type of respiratory infection that is usually caused by a virus. The infection leads to swelling inside the trachea, which interferes with normal breathing and produces the classic symptoms of "barking" cough, stridor, and a hoarse voice.

Option (C) is incorrect because Respiratory obstruction means partial or complete blockage of the breathing passages to the lungs. Causes include the presence of foreign matter, allergic reactions, infections, anatomical abnormalities, and trauma. Associated respiratory distress may be sudden, with only a cough for a warning.

Option (D) is incorrect because Foreign body aspiration occurs when a foreign body enters the airways and causes choking. Objects can enter the esophagus through the mouth, or enter the trachea through the mouth or nose.

Hence, the correct option is (B).

275. Option (C) is correct because the multicystic dysplastic kidney is the commonest form of congenital cystic renal dysplasia and is due to complete ureteric obstruction in fetal life. The condition is usually unilateral; the bilateral disease is lethal.

Multicystic dysplastic kidney

• The multicystic dysplastic kidney is a congenital condition in which the entire kidney is dysplastic with a preponderance of cysts.

• The kidney is replaced by multiple cysts of varying sizes that do not communicate and no identifiable parenchyma is present.

• Contralateral vesicoureteral reflux is present in 15% of cases.

• Contralateral hydronephrosis is present in 5 - 10% cases.

• It is the most common cause of an abdominal mass in a neonate. - Nelson

Option (A) is incorrect because Polycystic kidney disease (PKD) is an inherited disorder in which clusters of cysts develop primarily within your kidneys, causing your kidneys to enlarge and lose function over time. Cysts are noncancerous round sacs containing fluid.

Option (B) is incorrect because Simple kidney cysts are fluid-filled sacs or cysts, that can form in one or both of your kidneys. Simple kidney cysts are usually harmless. Simple kidney cysts don't enlarge the kidneys, replace their normal structure, or cause reduced kidney function like cysts do in people with polycystic kidney disease (PKD).

Option (D) is incorrect because a calyceal diverticulum is a cystic cavity within the kidney that is lined by transitional epithelium and communicates with a calyx or less commonly with the renal pelvis through a narrow isthmus.

Hence, the correct option is (C).

276. Option (B) is correct because the treatment options for the steroid-resistant nephrotic syndrome are:

1. Calcineurin inhibitors (cyclosporine, Tacrolinzus)

2. IV or oral cyclophosphamide

3. Levamisole

4. Mycophenolate

• Pulse corticosteroid

• All the above immunosuppressants are used along with corticosteroids (Prednisolone or methylprednisolone).

• Cyclosporine and cyclophosphamide are most commonly used.

• Despite these options, there is a lack of consensus on first-line appropriate therapy for steroid-resistant nephrotic syndrome.

• According to Indian Journal of pediatric (vol. 46, Jan 17, 2009) the efficacy of these drugs are (in decreasing order): Tacrolimus + Prednisolone > cyclosporine + Prednisolone > IV cyclophosphamide + Prednisolone > Pulse Corticosteroids (IV dexamethasone + oral cyclophosphamide + Prednisolone) > oral cyclophosphamide + Prednisolone.

• So, amongst the given options, the best answer is cyclosporine.

Option (A) is incorrect because Cyclophosphamide is used to treat various types of cancer. It is a chemotherapy drug that works by slowing or stopping cell growth. Cyclophosphamide also works by decreasing your immune system's response to various diseases.

Option (C) is incorrect because Mycophenolate is used in combination with other medications to keep your body from attacking and rejecting your transplanted organ (such as kidney, liver, heart). It belongs to a class of medications called immunosuppressants.

Option (D) is incorrect because it is a chemotherapy drug that works by slowing or stopping cell growth. Cyclophosphamide also works by decreasing your immune system's response to various diseases. It is used to treat a certain type of kidney disease in children after other treatments have not worked.

Hence, the correct option is (B).

277. Option (C) is correct because myoclonic epilepsy (JME) is a type of epilepsy that starts in childhood or the teen years. Myoclonic epilepsy may be Infantile spasm or Infantile myoclonus or West syndrome.

Juvenile myoclonic epilepsy

• Infantile spasm (Infantile myoclonus or West syndrome)

• The onset is usually between 3-8 months of life

It is characterized by a triad of -

i) Salaam spells (sudden dropping of the head & flexion of arms)

ii) Mental retardation

iii) The hypsarrhythmic pattern of EEG (diffuse high voltage slow spike and chaotic activity)

• The spasm occurs in clusters usually on waking.

• The prognosis for normal mental development is poor.

Treatment of infantile myoclonus

• ACTH and corticosteroids are given for 2-12 weeks, depending upon response.

• Vigabatrin is the DOC Now.

Option (A) is incorrect because Grand mal epilepsy usually begins in the pre-school child, or occasionally at puberty. It manifests with a warning (aura), followed by loss of consciousness, tonic and clonic convulsions, and finally a variably prolonged recovery. The aura may consist of a mood change, irritability, brief hallucination or headache, or even the sensation of a strong smell (e.g. burning rubber).

Option (B) is incorrect because Petit mal (absence) epilepsy is one of the most enigmatic of neurological disorders, and there is no widely accepted theory of its etiology. This review covers some of the current issues concerned with the disorder, including treatment and prognosis, neurochemical research, behavioral and psychophysiological effects of wave-spiked discharges, and EEG studies of seizure control.

Option (D) is incorrect because Reflex epilepsy is a condition in which seizures can be provoked habitually by an external stimulus or, less commonly, internal mental processes.

Hence, the correct option is (C).

278. Option (A) is correct because

- Acute lymphoblastic leukemia is the most childhood tumor.
- The brain tumor is the most common childhood tumor.
- Wilm's tumor is the most common childhood tumor.

Here Brain tumor, Wilm's tumor, and Acute lymphoblastic leukemia all are childhood tumors.

Option (B) is incorrect because

- Chronic lymphocytic leukemia (CLL) is the most common leukemia in adults.
- The brain tumor is the most common childhood tumor.
- Wilm's tumor is the most common childhood tumor.

Here Brain tumor, Wilm's tumor is childhood tumor but Chronic lymphocytic leukemia (CLL) is not.

Option (C) is incorrect because

- Acute lymphoblastic leukemia is the most common childhood tumor.
- Chronic lymphocytic leukemia (CLL) is the most common leukemia in adults
- The brain tumor is the most common childhood tumor.

Here Brain tumor, Acute lymphoblastic leukemia is childhood tumor but Chronic lymphocytic leukemia (CLL) is not.

Option (D) is incorrect because

- Acute lymphoblastic leukemia is the most common childhood tumor.
- The brain tumor is the most common childhood tumor.

Here Acute lymphoblastic leukemia, the Brain tumor is a childhood tumor but this option does not contain all tumors so this answer is incorrect.

Hence, the correct option is (A).

279. Option (A) is correct because causes of "Hair on end appearance" is Thalassemia. Bone Changes in Thalassemia.

- Bones become thin and pathological fracture may occur.
- The massive expansion of the marrow of fade and skull produces characteristics .facies.
- Severe maxillary hyperplasia and malocclusion.
- Prominent widening of diploic spaces with "hair on end appearance" caused by vertical trabeculae.
- Crew-cut appearance → striking expansion of hematopoietically active marrow that erodes existing cortical bone and induces new bone formation giving rise to crew-cut appearance.

Causes of "Hair on end appearance" → Sickle cell anemia, hereditary spherocytosis, G-6-PD deficiency

Option (B) is incorrect because Chronic malaria is not a Causes of "Hair on end appearance". Chronic malaria is usually defined as a long-term malarial infection in semi-immune subjects, usually without fever or other acute symptoms. The untreated infection may evolve to hyper-reactive malarial splenomegaly (HMS), a life-threatening complication.

Option (C) is incorrect because causes of "Hair on end appearance" is Thalassemia. Thalassemia is a blood disorder passed down through families (inherited) in which the body makes an abnormal form or inadequate amount of hemoglobin.

But, Chronic malaria is not a Causes of "Hair on end appearance".

Option (D) is incorrect because causes of "Hair on end appearance" is Thalassemia. Thalassemia is a blood disorder passed down through families (inherited) in which the body makes an abnormal form or inadequate amount of hemoglobin. But, Hydrocephalus is not a Causes of "Hair on end appearance". Hydrocephalus is a condition in which an accumulation of cerebrospinal fluid (CSF) occurs within the brain. This typically causes increased pressure inside the skull.

Hence, the correct option is (A).

280. Option (B) is correct because

Weight for height:

- This compares a child's height with the expected weight of a healthy child of the same height.
- A combination of these measurements has been suggested sometimes to distinguish 'type' of malnutrition.
- For example, water low proposed that weight/height allows one to distinguish between children who have suffered malnutrition in the past in front of those who are currently experiencing malnutrition.
- In chronic malnutrition, the child is stunted i.e. his weight for age and height for age are low. Therefore, weight for height cannot diagnose chronic malnutrition as chronic malnutrition affects both weight gain (weight for age) and linear growth (height for age) → Weight deficit is proportionate to the deficit in height.
- In acute malnutrition however his height for age is appropriate but he is wasted (low weight for height and age).
- Thus weight and height measurements together are useful to understand the dynamics of malnutrition, distinguishing between current malnutrition and long-term or chronic malnutrition.
- Wasting (deficit in weight for height) usually signifies acute onset malnutrition.
- Stunting (deficit in height for age) usually signifies a chronic course of malnutrition.
- Wasting and stunting → Acute on chronic malnutrition.
- Underweight (low weight for age) → Combined indicator to reflect both acute and chronic malnutrition.

Option (A) is incorrect because Acute malnutrition is not manifested by Weight for age. The percentage of children who have low weight for age (underweight) can reflect 'wasting' (i.e. low weight for height), indicating acute weight loss, 'stunting', or both. Thus, 'underweight' is a composite indicator and may, therefore, be difficult to interpret. It is defined by = Underweight: weight for age < –2 standard deviations (SD) of the WHO Child Growth Standards median.

Option (C) is incorrect because Acute malnutrition is not manifested by Age for height. The percentage of children with a low height for age (stunting) reflects the cumulative effects of undernutrition and infections since and even before birth. Stunting: height for age < –2 SD of the WHO Child Growth Standards median.

Option (D) is incorrect because the Broca Index (BI) is an estimation of ideal body weight using a height measurement only. The Broca Index was developed by Paul Broca, a French surgeon. The Broca index is only a rough estimate and applies to the range of middle body sizes best.

Hence, the correct option is (B).

281. Option (A) is correct because:

- Adenoids, also known as nasopharyngeal tonsils, are a subepithelial collection of lymphoid tissue at the junction of the roof and posterior wall of the nasopharynx,
- Adenoids act as a barrier to infection.
- Adenoids are subjected to physiological enlargement.
- They are present at birth, enlarge up to 6 years of age and then atrophy and completely disappear by 20 years of age.
- Upper respiratory' tract infections (Rhinitis, sinusitis, tonsillitis) and allergies can cause adenoid hypertrophy.

Option (B) is incorrect because the tonsils (palatine tonsils) are a pair of soft tissue masses located at the rear of the throat (pharynx). Each tonsil is composed of tissue similar to lymph nodes, covered by pink mucosa (like on the adjacent mouth lining). Running through the mucosa of each tonsil are pits, called crypts.

Option (C) is incorrect because Palatine tonsils, commonly called the tonsils and occasionally called the faucial tonsils, are tonsils located on the left and right sides at the back of the throat, which can often be seen as flesh-colored, pinkish lumps.

Option (D) is incorrect because the lingual tonsils are a collection of lymphatic tissue located in the lamina propria of the root of the tongue. This lymphatic tissue consists of the lymphatic nodules rich in cells of the immune system (immunocytes).

Hence, the correct option is (A).

282. Option (C) is correct because:

• Otolith organs: Utricle and saccule are the otolith organs. Their Sensory epithelium is called maculae.

• They are concerned with linear acceleration-deceleration. They sense the position of the head with respect to gravity. Otoliths: They are crystals of calcium carbonate located on the otolithic membrane present in the maculae. Also called otoconia.

Option (A) is incorrect because the oculocephalic reflex and the cold caloric (oculovestibular) reflex are used to test brainstem function in profoundly comatose patients. An intact reflex basically confirms that the brainstem is intact.

Option (B) is incorrect because Torsional (rotary) nystagmus refers to a rotary movement of the globe about its anteroposterior axis. Torsional nystagmus is accentuated on the lateral gaze.

Option (D) is incorrect because Angular acceleration is the time rate of change of angular velocity. In three dimensions, it is a pseudovector. In SI units, it is measured in radians per second squared and is usually denoted by the Greek letter alpha.

Hence, the correct option is (C).

283. Option (A) is correct because

• There is some speculation that the efferent portion of the auditory nerve is selectively damaged while the hair cells that allow us to hear pure tones in an audiometric evaluation remain intact.

• Some have said it involves direct malfunction of the facial nerve; as a result, the stapedius muscle is unable to dampen sound.

Option (B) is incorrect because the tensor veli palatini muscle (tensor palati or tensor muscle of the velum platinum) is a broad, thin, ribbon-like muscle in the head that tenses the soft palate. The tensor veli palatini is found anterior-lateral to the levator veli palatini muscle. Impairment of the tensor veli palatini muscle leads to dysfunction of Eustachian tube opening, impaired middle ear ventilation, and most likely otitis media with effusion.

Option (C) is incorrect because the tensor tympani is a muscle within the ear, located in the bony canal above the osseous portion of the auditory tube. Its role is to damp loud sounds, such as those produced from chewing, shouting, or thunder.

Option (D) is incorrect because option (A) is correct that is hyperacusis is caused by damage of Stapedius.

Hence, the correct option is (A).

284. Option (B) is correct because

• The internal nose is divided into right and left nasal cavities by the nasal septum.

• Each nasal cavity communicates with the exterior through nares or nostrils and with nasopharynx through a posterior nasal aperture or posterior nares or choana.

Option (A) is incorrect because the anterior nares are the external (or "proper") portion of the nostrils (nose). The anterior nares open into the nasal cavity and allow the inhalation and exhalation of air. Each is an oval opening that measures about 1.5 cm anteroposteriorly and about 1 cm in diameter.

Option (C) is incorrect because the tonsils (palatine tonsils) are a pair of soft tissue masses located at the rear of the throat (pharynx). Each tonsil is composed of tissue similar to lymph nodes, covered by pink mucosa (like on the adjacent mouth lining). Running through the mucosa of each tonsil are pits, called crypts.

Option (D) is incorrect because the larynx commonly called the voice box, is an organ in the top of the neck involved in breathing, producing sound and protecting the trachea against food aspiration. The larynx houses the vocal folds and manipulates pitch and volume, which is essential for phonation.

Hence, the correct option is (B).

285. Option (A) is correct because

The stomatal complex is a narrow anatomical region consisting of:-

1. Multiple bony structures (middle turbinate, uncinate process, Bulla ethmoidal).

2. Air spaces (frontal recess, ethmoidal infundibulum, middle meatus)

3. Ostia of anterior ethmoidal, maxillary and frontal sinuses , therefore, connects these sinuses to the nasal cavity.

Option (B) is incorrect because of Sphenoid sinus. Sinuses are air-filled sacs (empty spaces) on either side of the nasal cavity that filter and clean the air breathed through the nose and lighten the bones of the skull. The sphenoid sinuses are located in the sphenoid bone near the optic nerve and the pituitary gland on the side of the skull.

Option (C) is incorrect because the superior meatus connects the nasal cavity with the posterior ethmoid air cells, the middle meatus connects the nasal cavity with the anterior and middle ethmoid air cells and the frontal sinus, and the inferior meatus connects the nasal cavity with the nasolacrimal duct.

Option (D) is incorrect because the ethmoid bulla is usually evaluated on coronal images. These air cells are part of the anterior ethmoid sinuses and make up the superior border of the hiatus semilunaris and maxillary infundibulum and laterally bounded by the lamina papyracea.

Hence, the correct option is (A).

286. Option (C) is correct because "The inferior turbinate is a separate bone, while rest of the turbinates are a part of ethmoidal bone". The inferior turbinate is the largest turbinate and is responsible for the majority of airflow direction, humidification, heating, and filtering of air inhaled through the nose.

The ethmoid bone is one of the 8 bones of the cranium. It is situated at the roof of the nasal cavity and between the two orbital cavities. It contributes to the medial wall of the orbit and forms part of the anterior cranial fossa, where it separates the nasal cavity (inferiorly) from the cranial cavity (superiorly).

Option (A) is incorrect because The superior turbinate is continuous with the middle turbinate and the skull base. At endoscopy, it is found between the middle turbinate and the nasal septum. Its projection forms the medial limits of the superior meatus, into which the posterior ethmoid sinuses drain.

Option (B) is incorrect because The middle turbinate is that part of the lateral mass of the ethmoid bone which projects from the external wall of the nasal cavity, continuous anteriorly with the lateral mass and separated from its posterior portion by a space known as the inferior ethmoidal fissure.

Option (D) is incorrect because the uncinate process is a small part of the pancreas. The uncinate process is the formed prolongation of the angle of junction of the lower and left lateral borders in the head of the pancreas. The word "uncinate" comes from the Latin "uncinatus", meaning "hooked".

Hence, the correct option is (C).

287. Lyre sign is an angiographic finding seen in carotid body tumour of the neck. There is splaying apart of internal and external carotid arteries on angiogram. Carotid body tumors are located at the carotid bifurcation with characteristic splaying of the ICA and ECA, described as the lyre sign. In all modalities, the dense vascularity of these tumors is manifested as prominent contrast enhancement.
Hence, the correct option is (D).

288. Option (B) is correct because

Septoplasty

• Septoplasty is a conservative approach to septal surgery; as much of the septal framework as possible is retained.

• Muco-perichondrial/periosteal flap is generally raised only on one side.

• This operation has almost replaced the SMR operation.

• It can be done in adults as well as in children (in contrast to SMR, which is done only after 17 years).

Option (A) is incorrect because the Office-based myringoplasty alternative is tympanoplasty. Tympanoplasty also called eardrum repair, refers to surgery performed to reconstruct a perforated tympanic membrane (eardrum) or the small bones of the middle ear. Eardrum perforation may result from chronic infection or, less commonly, from trauma to the eardrum.

Option (C) is incorrect because Bone fenestration is a current alternative to the Caldwell-Luc method. Caldwell-Luc surgery, Caldwell-Luc operation, also known as Caldwell-Luc antrostomy, and Radical antrostomy, is an operation to remove irreversibly damaged mucosa of the maxillary sinus. It is done when maxillary sinusitis is not cured by medication or other non-invasive techniques.

Option (D) is incorrect because Radiofrequency surgery has become an increasingly popular alternative to classic turbinate surgery. Tuboplasty refers to a number of surgical operations that attempt to restore patency and functioning of the Fallopian tube(s) so that a pregnancy could be achieved.

Hence, the correct option is (B).

289. Option (A) is correct because It is a mucosal ridge raised by fibers of palatopharyngeus. It encircles the posterior and lateral walls of the nasopharyngeal isthmus. Soft palate, during its contraction, makes firm contact with this ridge to cut off nasopharynx from the oropharynx during the deglutition or speech.

Option (B) is incorrect because The inferior one was joined by the stylopharyngeus and descended along the palatopharyngeal arch to be inserted into the thyroid cartilage and the epiglottis. It is suggested that the superior constrictor and the lateral fibers cooperate as sphincters and the medial fibers and the stylopharyngeus as elevators.

Option (C) is incorrect because The palatoglossus, palatopharyngeus, and stylopharyngeus muscles are intertwined with the superior pharyngeal constrictor muscles. Deep to the parapharyngeal space is the carotid sheath and its contents. The lateral pharyngeal walls and posterior pharyngeal wall function to constrict the diameter of the oropharynx.

Option (D) is incorrect because the outer circular layer of the pharyngeal muscle consists of the superior, middle, and inferior pharyngeal constrictor muscles. The inner longitudinal layer consists of the palatopharyngeus, salpingopharyngeus, and stylopharyngeus muscles.

Hence, the correct option is (A).

290. Option (A) is correct because

• Quinsy consists of suppuration outside the capsule in the area around the capsule.

• There is a collection of pus between the capsule of tonsil and the superior constrictor muscle, i.e. in the peritonsillar area.

Option (B) is incorrect because the parapharyngeal space (also termed the lateral pharyngeal space), is a potential space in the head and the neck. It has clinical importance in otolaryngology due to parapharyngeal space tumors and parapharyngeal abscess developing in this area.

Option (C) is incorrect because the retropharyngeal space is a potential space of the head and neck, bounded by the buccopharyngeal fascia anteriorly and the alar fascia posteriorly. It contains the retropharyngeal lymph nodes.

Option (D) is incorrect because within the tonsil there is no collection of pus in quinsy. The tonsils (palatine tonsils) are a pair of soft tissue masses located at the rear of the throat (pharynx). Each tonsil is composed of tissue similar to lymph nodes, covered by pink mucosa (like on the adjacent mouth lining).

Hence, the correct option is (A).

291. Option (B) is correct because Lens and cornea are avascular structures of the eye, that's why fluorescein angiography can't be used to identify lesions.

Option (A) is incorrect because the conjunctiva is a tissue that lines the inside of the eyelids and covers the sclera (the white of the eye). It is composed of nonkeratinized, stratified squamous epithelium with goblet cells, and stratified columnar epithelium.

Option (C) is incorrect because The ciliary body is a part of the eye that includes the ciliary muscle, which controls the shape of the lens, and the ciliary epithelium, which produces the aqueous humor. The aqueous humor is produced in the non-pigmented portion of the ciliary body.

Option (D) is incorrect because The retina is a thin layer of tissue that lines the back of the eye on the inside. It is located near the optic nerve. The purpose of the retina is to receive light that the lens has focused, convert the light into neural signals, and send these signals on to the brain for visual recognition.

Hence, the correct option is (B).

292. Option (B) is correct because a simple definition of the visual axis is: " A straight line that passes through both the center of the pupil and the center of the fovea".

Option (A) is incorrect because the visual axis does not lie on the line passing through the Center of the cornea to the retina.

Option (C) is incorrect because it is defined as Optical axis, the straight line passing through the geometrical centre of a lens and joining the two centres of curvature of its surfaces.

Option (D) is incorrect because as we know that the best answer for the given question is Object to the fovea. so, option D automatically gets wrong as from all the other three options, one is correct.

Hence, the correct option is (B).

293. Option (B) is correct because Giant papillary conjunctivitis (GPC) is a type of allergic conjunctivitis. In GPC, a foreign body causes prolonged mechanical irritation, which results in a reaction in the eye. Most commonly, contact lenses are the foreign body causing the irritation.

Option (A) is incorrect because

Inclusion Conjunctivitis

- Caused by Chlamydia trachomatis D-K within 5-14 days of birth. Clinical features include mucoid/ mucopurulent discharge, redness in the conjunctiva, swollen lids and pain in eyeballs.

Option (C) is incorrect because Vernal keratoconjunctivitis (VKC) is an allergic eye disease that especially affects young boys. The most common symptoms are itching, photophobia, burning, and tearing. The typical, characteristic signs and symptoms of this disease render the diagnosis of VKC fairly straightforward, even for the general ophthalmologist.

Option (D) is incorrect because
Follicular conjunctivitis

- It is characterized by redness in the conjunctiva, the formation of follicles and discharge from the eyes. It is of following types:
- Epidemic keratoconjunctivitis: adenovirus 8,19; can cause "acute pseudomembranous conjunctivitis" in severe infection.
- Pharyngo-conjunctival fever: caused by adenovirus.
- Herpetic conjunctivitis: caused by HSV_1 (more commonly) and HSV_2 (less commonly).

Hence, the correct option is (B).

294. Option (A) is correct because "The so-called"satellite phenomenon", a ring of punctate opacities around a denser central ulcer, is an important diagnostic feature of fungal corneal ulcer".

Option (B) is incorrect because Tuberculosis (TB) is a disease caused by bacteria called Mycobacterium tuberculosis. The bacteria usually attack the lungs, but they can also damage other parts of the body. TB spreads through the air when a person with TB of the lungs or throat coughs, sneezes, or talks.

Option (C) is incorrect because Sarcoidosis is an inflammatory disease that affects multiple organs in the body, but mostly the lungs and lymph glands. In people with sarcoidosis, abnormal masses or nodules (called granulomas) consisting of inflamed tissues form in certain organs of the body.

Option (D) is incorrect because Herpetic stomatitis is a viral infection of the mouth that causes sores and ulcers. These mouth ulcers are not the same as canker sores, which are not caused by a virus.

Hence, the correct option is (A).

295. Infectious causes of posterior uveitis (chorioretinitis)

- Virus:- CMV, HSV, Herpes zoster, rubella, rubeola (measles)
- Bacteria:- TB, Brucellosis, syphilis, Lyme's disease, Hematogenously spread gram-positive & gram-negative bacteria.
- Fungi Candida, Histoplasma, Blastomycosis, Cryptococcus, Aspergillus.
- Parasite:- Toxoplasma, Toxocara, Cysticercus, Onchocerca.

From the above explanation,

Option (D) is correct because as we know that all the other options are given above are correct. so, we have to choose option (D) as the most appropriate answer.

Option (A) is incorrect because Chorioretinitis is caused by CMV too.

Option (B) is incorrect because Chorioretinitis is caused by Onchocerca too.

Option (C) is incorrect because it is caused by Toxoplasma too.

Hence, the correct option is (D).

296. Option (C) is correct because Treatment of choice for congenital cataract is Cataract surgery with IOL implant and primary posterior capsulotomy.

Option (A) is incorrect because Pharmacotherapy is therapy using pharmaceutical drugs, as distinguished from therapy using surgery (surgical therapy), radiation (radiation therapy), movement (physical therapy), or other modes.

Option (B) is incorrect because Patients undergoing cataract surgery who also have controlled mild to moderate glaucoma are ideal for an ophthalmologist's first cases. Goniotomy, such as that performed with the Kahook Dual Blade (KDB; New World Medical), is a minimally invasive surgical option for glaucoma.

Option (D) is incorrect because Pars plana vitrectomy and lensectomy (PPV-PPL) is an alternative to phacoemulsification and intraocular lens placement in some cases of uveitic cataract.

Hence, the correct option is (C).

297. Primary glaucomas are :

i) Congenital/developmental:- True congenital glaucoma, infantile glaucoma, juvenile glaucoma.

ii) Adult:- Primary open-angle glaucoma, primary angle-closure glaucoma, primary mixed mechanism glaucoma.

Pigmentary glaucoma and steroid-induced glaucoma are secondary glaucomas.

From the above explanation,

Option (A) is correct because all are the Primary glaucomas.

Option (B) is incorrect because Steroid-induced glaucoma is not Primary glaucoma.

Option (C) is incorrect because only Juvenile glaucoma and Infantile glaucoma are primary glaucomas.

Option (D) is incorrect because Infantile glaucoma is also Primary glaucoma.

Hence, the correct option is (A).

298. Causes of soft exudates (cotton wool spots)

- All types of severe hypertension (hypertensive retinopathy) including renal disease, Toxemia of pregnancy.
- Diabetic retinopathy
- Collagen vascular disorders:- SLE, PAN, systemic sclerosis, scleroderma, Wegener granulomatosis.
- Infections:- AIDS, septic retinitis (including SABE), rarely CMV retinitis in AIDS.
- Microembolization:- IV drug abuse, Post cardiac surgery, Fat embolism or Purtscher retinopathy.
- Other Eale's disease, Adults anemia (Hb < 6.6-8.0 g/d1), Pseudoxanthoma elasticum, Neoplasia (Leukemia, Hodgkin's disease), Sickle cell retinopathy, radiation retinopathy.

Option (D) is correct because all points are included.

Option (A) is incorrect because Hypertension is not included.

Option (B) is incorrect because AIDS is not included.

Option (C) is incorrect because Cotton wool spots are not seen in CMV.

Hence, the correct option is (D).

299.

- Adie's tonic pupil (Holmes - Adie pupil) is a unilateral condition (80% of cases). Initially, the pupil does not react to light or accommodation. Subsequently, the pupil does not react to light but reacts slowly and tonically to a near stimulus.
- As there is a defect in post-ganglionic sympathetic innervation to the eye, i.e., there is a deficiency of parasympathetic system, the pupil will react when even a minimum concentration of parasympathomimetic drugs (e.g. pilocarpine, methacholine is given).

Option (B) is correct because Adie's tonic pupil (Holmes - Adie pupil) is a unilateral condition (80% of cases).

Option (A) is incorrect because of in Holmes-Adie pupil there are absent or retarded pupil reactions to light and near.

Option (C) is incorrect because in Holmes-Adie pupil causes reduced or absent accommodation.

Option (D) is incorrect because in Holmes-Adie pupil constricts with 2.5% methacholine.

Hence, the correct option is (B).

300. Option (C) is correct because a complete third nerve palsy causes a completely closed eyelid and deviation of the eye outward and downward. The eye cannot move inward or up, and the pupil is typically enlarged and does not react normally to light.

Option (A) is incorrect because With unilateral third cranial nerve palsy (ie, oculomotor nerve palsy), the involved eye usually is deviated "down and out" (ie, infraducted and abducted), and there may be partial or complete ptosis.

Option (B) is incorrect because the eye will be displaced downward, because the superior oblique (innervated by the fourth cranial or trochlear nerve), is unantagonized by the paralyzed superior rectus, inferior rectus, and inferior oblique. The affected individual will also have ptosis, or drooping of the eyelid, and mydriasis.

Option (D) is incorrect because Oculomotor nerve palsy is an eye condition resulting from damage to the third cranial nerve or a branch thereof.

Hence, the correct option is (C).

Mock Test 07

Part A

Q.1 Tyrosine kinase receptors

A. Have constitutively active tyrosine kinase domains
B. Phosphorylate and activate ras directly
C. Mediate cellular processes involved in growth and differentiation
D. Are not phosphorylated upon activation

Q.2 Physiological anemia of pregnancy is due to

A. Decrease in plasma iron binding capacity
B. Hypoactivity of bone marrow
C. Disproportionate increase in plasma volume
D. Deficiency of vitamin B_{12}

Q.3 Strawberry tongue can be seen in all except:

A. Kawasaki disease
B. Scarlet fever
C. Brucellosis
D. Toxic shock syndrome

Q.4 Clinical findings of which of the following typically includes a rash-like erythema, which spreads throughout the skin of the breast?

A. Inflammatory carcinoma
B. Medullary tumor
C. Colloid tumor
D. Paget's disease

Q.5 The radiographic appearance of the vertebra shown in the image is most common in ?

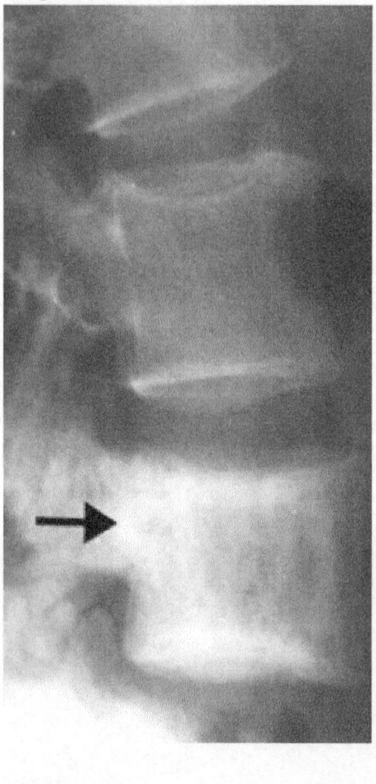

A. Eosininophilic Granuloma
B. Sickle cell anemia
C. Vertebral hemangioma
D. Paget's disease

Q.6 Which of the following isotopes is commonly used in teletherapy?

A. Pd-103 **B.** Co-60 **C.** Tc-99 **D.** Ir-19

Q.7 In patient with back pain, CT spine reveals the following appearance of the vertebra. What is the diagnosis and the sign shown on CT?

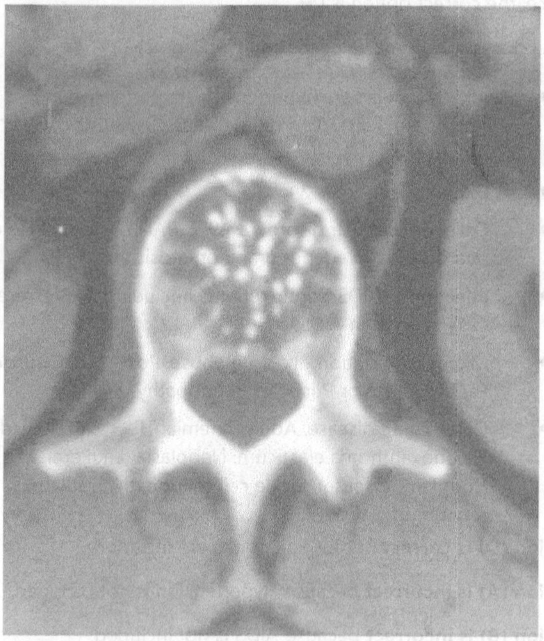

A. Hemangioma, corduroy appearance
B. Hemangioma, polka dot appearance
C. Osteoporosis, H-shape vertebrae
D. Osteoporosis, Polka dot appearance

Q.8 Divorce can be given if there is:

A. Impotence
B. Sterility
C. Premature ejaculation
D. None of the above

Q.9 A 35-year-old woman has been in a women's shelter for past 15 years. She spends most of her day rocking, muttering softly to herself, or looking at her reflection in a small mirror. She needs help with dressing and showering and she often giggles and laughs for no apparent reason. What is the appropriate diagnosis ?

A. Psychotic depression
B. Schizophrenia, paranoid type
C. Shared psychotic disorder
D. Schizophrenia, disorganized type

Q.10 Benzodiazepines those are useful as anticonvulsants have the following properties for increased efficacy

A. Long half-life, and slow entry into the brain
B. Short half-life, and slow entry into the brain
C. Long half-life, and rapid entry into the brain
D. Short half-life, and rapid entry into the brain

Q.11 Treatment of rectal prolapse in childhood is:

A. Lahaut's operation
B. Incision of prolapsed mucosa
C. Thiersch operation
D. Ripstein operation

Q.12 Which of the following changes is a frequent consequence of chronic rheumatic fever ?

A. Anitschkow cells in the endocardium
B. Aschoff bodies in the myocardium
C. Fibrin deposits in the pericardium
D. Stenosis of the mitral valve

Q.13 A patient complaining of having lost his wealth, status as well as his strength and internal body organs has

A. Capgrass Syndrome
B. Fregoli Syndrome
C. Cotard syndrome
D. De Clerambault's Syndrome

Q.14 Mode of action of fluoxetine is:

A. Inhibition of serotonin uptake
B. Inhibition of dopamine uptake
C. Facilitation of adrenergic impulse
D. Facilitation of cholinergic response

Q.15 All of the following are true about Warthin tumor except

A. It is a malignant salivary gland tumor
B. It arises almost always in the parotid gland
C. About 10% are bilateral
D. It has cystic spaces and dense lymphoid stroma

Q.16 Which of the following are characteristic of the secretory phase of the menstrual cycle ?

A. It precedes ovulation
B. It coincides with the development of ovarian follicles
C. It depends on progesterone secretion by the corpus luteum
D. It coincides with rapid drop in estrogen levels

Q.17 True statement about Infraglottic carcinoma larynx:

A. Commonly spreads to mediastinal nodes
B. Second most common carcinoma
C. Most common carcinoma
D. Spreads to submetal nodes

Q.18 Laboratory studies show an elevated serum B-type natriuretic peptide in a 70-year old man with poorly controlled diabetes mellitus, exertional chest pain, bilateral pulmonary rales and pitting edema of legs. Chest radiograph shows prominent right and left heart borders. Which of the following pathologic findings is most likely present in this man?

A. Critical coronary stenosis
B. Left atrial mural thrombus
C. Mitral and tricuspid valve thickening
D. Pericardial fibrinohemorrhagic exudate

Q.19 Under development of which of the following embryonic structures may be related to abnormally thin wall in the smooth part of right atrium in an infant?

A. Pulmonary trunk
B. Conus cordis
C. Sinus venosus
D. Truncus arteriosus

Q.20 The highest concentration of chyle is found in the lymphatics that drain which of the following organs?

A. Small intestine
B. Heart
C. Long bones
D. Spleen

Q.21 The probability of a test detecting a truly positive person from the population of diseased is the:

A. Sensitivity of the test
B. Specificity of the test
C. Positive predictive value of the test
D. Likelihood ratio

Q.22 Criteria for fetal growth are all EXCEPT

A. Height of the uterus
B. Maternal weight gain
C. Ultras onographic measurement of biparietal diameter
D. Ultrasonographic measurement of fetal abdominal circumference

Q.23 Which one of the following statements regarding megalocornea is false?

A. This condition is defined as a clear normal-appearing cornea with a diameter measuring greater than 13 mm
B. This condition is often associated with anterior megalophthalmos, an autosomal dominant disorder
C. The simple form of megalocornea is usually seen as a bilateral condition
D. Tearing and IOP are important factors in the workup

Q.24 Vitreous complications are least seen in surgery in

A. Mature cataract
B. Posterior polar cataracts
C. Nuclear sclerosis grade 2
D. Nuclear sclerosis grade 4

Q.25 An apathetic male child (Image) is having peripheral edema, a "moon" face, and an enlarged, fatty liver. Which of the following basic defects cause this change in the liver?

A. Decreased protein intake leads to decreased lipoproteins
B. Decreased caloric intake leads to hypoalbuminemia
C. Decreased fluid intake leads to hypernatremia
D. Decreased fat absorption leads to hypovitaminosis

Q.26 All are true regarding AFP Surveillance except:

A. WHO recommends it for age less than 15 years
B. Two stool samples are collected per case
C. Non polio AFP rate should be greater than 1 per 100,000 among less than 15 years old
D. Adequate stool specimens should be taken from 100 % AFP

Q.27 The most common premalignant condition of oral carcinoma is:

A. Leukoplakia B. Erythroplakia
C. Lichen planus D. Fibrosis

Q.28 Causes of metabolic alkalosis in a child include all of the following except : -

A. Recurrent vomiting
B. Mineralocorticoid deficiency
C. Bartter's syndrome
D. Thiazide diuretic therapy

Q.29 After receiving a drug to treat UTI (apparently due to Serratia marcescens) for 2 weeks, a 68 year old woman develops headache, nausea/vomiting, vertigo, tinnitus, and progressive loss of hearing. The drug used was most likely a member of which of the following antibiotic classes?

A. Macrolides B. Tetracyclines
C. Cephalosporins D. Aminoglycosides

Q.30 Verrucous carcinoma of the buccal mucosa is identified with which of the following characteristics ?

A. It is faster growing than the epidermoid form
B. It is not associated with tobacco chewing
C. It has a predilection for the gingivobuccal gutter
D. It rarely extends to the mandible

Q.31 Control of urea cycle involves the enzyme:

A. Carbamoyl phosphate synthetase
B. Ornithine transcarbamoylase
C. Argininosuccinase
D. Arginase

Q.32 Fetal sac can be seen using vaginal sonography from the last menstrual period between :

A. 25 - 30 days B. 33 - 35 days
C. 36 - 40 days D. 41 - 45 days

Q.33 Uncomplicated Alcohol withdrawal for patients should be treated with?

A. Diazepam B. Chlordiazepoxide
C. Codeine D. Disulfiram

Q.34 A 25 year old woman complains of nonpuritic and painless red splotchy rash on her chest during intercourse. It usually resolves within a few minutes to a few hours after intercourse. Which of the following is the most likely cause of the rash?

A. Allergic reaction to her partner's pheromones
B. Decreased systolic blood pressure during the plateau phase
C. Increased estrogen during the excitement phase
D. Vasocongestion during the excitement phase

Q.35 A healthy 42 year old woman is found to have a calcium level of 12 mg/dl. She feels well and her physical examination is normal. Further investigation reveals a parathormone (PTH) level of 750 pg/ml (230-630 pg/ml). Which of the following findings is also associated with this disorder ?

A. Osteoblastic lesion of bone
B. Lytic bone lesion
C. Polycythemia
D. Orthostatic hypotension

Q.36 Tzank smear was made from the scrapping of the lesion of a patient having painful tiny vesicular ulcers on lips. Identify the pathogen ?

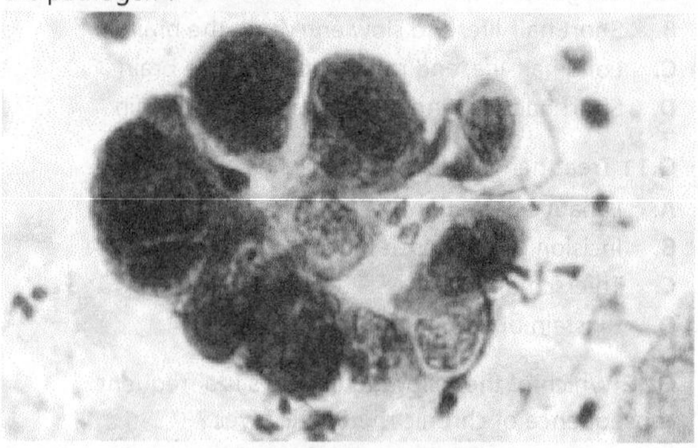

A. HPV B. Parvovirus
C. Herpes simplex D. Varicella zoster

Q.37 Tachyphylaxis is produced by all of the following drugs except :

A. Tyramine B. Ephedrine
C. Amphetamine D. Epinephrine

Q.38 Which of the following symptoms in a newborn infant would prompt a pediatrician to test for cystic fibrosis?

A. Pneumonia
B. Intrauterine growth retardation
C. Meconium ileus
D. Hypochloremic alkalosis

Q.39 An elderly man with end-stage renal disease from hypertensive nephrosclerosis that had been treated by hemodialysis for 14 years presented with a productive cough and fever, from which he recovered. On the basis of following findings (Images) diagnosis of brown tumour was made. Which of the following conditions it may be associated with ?

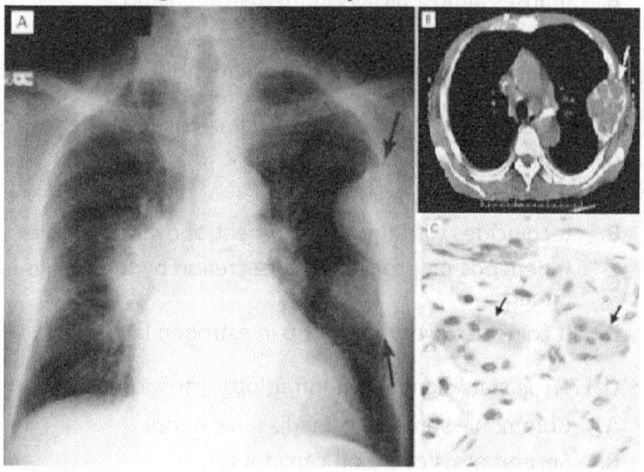

A. Hyperthyroidism
B. Hypothyroidism
C. Hyperparathyroidism
D. Hypoparathyroidism

Q.40 Which of the following laboratory tests would most likely confirm the diagnosis of Prader-Willi syndrome (PWS)?

A. Routine chromosome testing
B. Fluorescence in situ hybridization (FISH) study for subtelomeric rearrangements
C. FISH testing of the 15q11.2-q13 region

D. Lactic acid level

Q.41 Salkowski test is performed for the identification of:

A. Glycerol **B.** Cholesterol
C. Fatty acids **D.** Vitamin D

Q.42 The artery to the ductus deferens is a branch of

A. Inferior epigastric artery
B. Superior Epigastric Artery
C. Superior Vesical Artery
D. Cremasteric Artery

Q.43 Jejunal biopsy in coeliac disease shows

A. Leaf-shaped villi
B. Flattening of the crypts
C. Appearances resembling severe tropical sprue
D. Fissures penetrating into the submucosa

Q.44 Which of the following is not a significant risk factor for the development of heterotopic ossification:

A. Hypertrophic osteoarthritis
B. Ankylosing spondylitis
C. Posttraumatic arthritis
D. Previous osteonecrosis

Q.45 Naproxen is a weak acid with a pKa of 5.2. What percentage of the drug is most likely water soluble in a patient's plasma?

A. 50% **B.** 76%
C. 99% **D.** More than 99%

Q.46 A fracture of the femur occurs through the diaphysis of the femur involves which of the following?

A. Acetabulum
B. Midshaft
C. Medial condyle
D. Anterior cruciate ligament

Q.47 A 55 yrs. male presents with dysphagia, retrosternal discomfort and weight loss. Studies reveal achalasia. Which of the following is most likely recommended primary treatment?

A. Graded pneumatic dilation
B. Calcium channel blockers and nitrates
C. Intrasphincteric injection of botulinum toxin
D. laparoscopic Heller myotomy and partial fundoplication

Q.48 A 50-year-old woman with history of hypertension reported having difficulty reading, what clinical presentation would be expected in this patient?

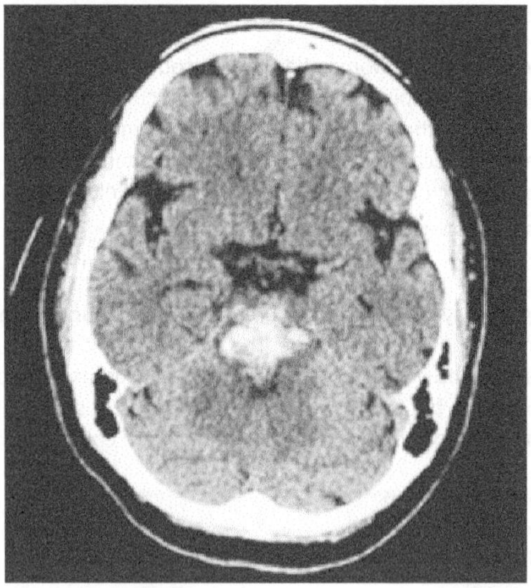

A. Asymmetrical mydriasis
B. Ataxic hemiparesis
C. Hypothermia
D. Quadriplegia

Q.49 Which type of sample can be used to isolate poliovirus earliest?

A. blood **B.** Stool **C.** throat **D.** CSF

Q.50 Consider the following statements regarding mammography -

I - Exposure to low voltage, high amperage x rays.
II - Sensitivity to this test decreases with age.
III - 5 % of breast cancers are missed by population based mammographic screening programmes

A. I, II and III are true **B.** I and II are true
C. II and III are true **D.** I and III are true

Part B

Q.51 Triple therapy for post renal transplant patients include all except

A. Azathioprine **B.** FK 506
C. Prednisolone **D.** Cyclosporine

Q.52 Clinical features of nasopharyngeal angiofibroma are all except:

A. Adolescent male
B. Epistaxis and nasal obstruction is the cardinal symptom
C. Radiotherapy is the Rx of choice
D. Arises from posterior nasal cavity

Q.53 Which of the following is the most likely cause Budd-Chiari syndrome?

A. Obstruction of the intrahepatic sinusoids
B. Thrombosis of the hepatic artery
C. Thrombosis of the hepatic vein
D. Thrombosis of the portal vein

Q.54 Treatment of cord prolapse is based on all of the following factors except :

A. Fetal viability **B.** Fetal maturity

C. Fetal weight **D.** Cervical dilatation

Q.55 A 35-year-old woman has had episodes of light-headedness, irritability, palpitation and difficulty concentrating at her work for the past year. Her haemoglobin is 14.2 g/dL. An abdominal CT scan shows a 1 cm mass in the tail of the pancreas. Which of the following is the most likely diagnosis?

A. Cystadenoma **B.** Insulinoma
C. Pseudocyst **D.** Pheochromocytoma

Q.56 A 55-day-old infant born prematurely is brought with swelling as shown in the image. The swelling is not tender, firm, hot, or red, and it does not transilluminate. It seems to resolve with pressure, but returns when the infant cries or strains. Which of the following is the most appropriate course of action at this point?

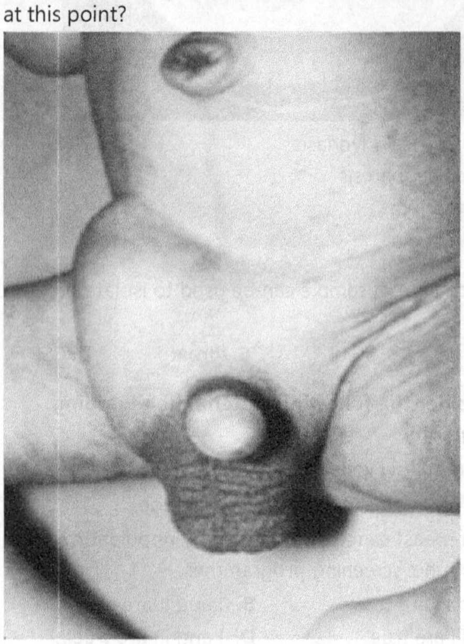

A. Obtain a surgical consultation
B. Perform a needle aspiration
C. Order a barium enema
D. Observe the patient and reassure the patient and family

Q.57 The typical movement of mitral valve calcification is :
A. Upwards and downwards
B. Counter clock wise
C. Side to side
D. Circular

Q.58 Mouse-nibbled appearance of vocal cord is seen in:
A. TB **B.** Syphillis
C. Cancer **D.** Papilloma

Q.59 All of the following are present in the given ECG EXCEPT:

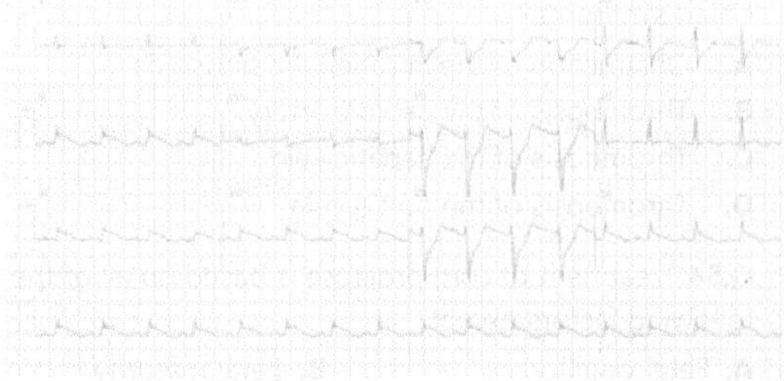

A. Ventricular tachycardia
B. Inferior myocardial ischemia
C. Posterior myocardial ischemia
D. Sinus tachycardia

Q.60 All are true regarding measles vaccine except:
A. Freeze dried live attenuated vaccine
B. Single intramascular dose of 0.5 ml
C. Is occasionally associated with TSS
D. Contraindicated in pregnancy

Q.61 In a pregnant woman, Deep Vein Thrombosis (DVT) is
A. More common in left leg as compare to right leg
B. More common in right leg as compare to left leg
C. Equally common in both the legs
D. An uncommon phenomenon

Q.62 All of the following may be associated with thymoma except
A. Myasthenia gravis
B. Paraneoplastic
C. Hypergammaglobulinemia
D. Pure red cell aplasia

Q.63 A patient having infertility is found to have bilateral cornual block on investigations. Best treatment that can be offered to her would be :
A. In vitro fertilization
B. Tuboplasty
C. Hydrotubation
D. Laparoscopy & hysteroscopy

Q.64 ECG recording of the patient shown below is due to?

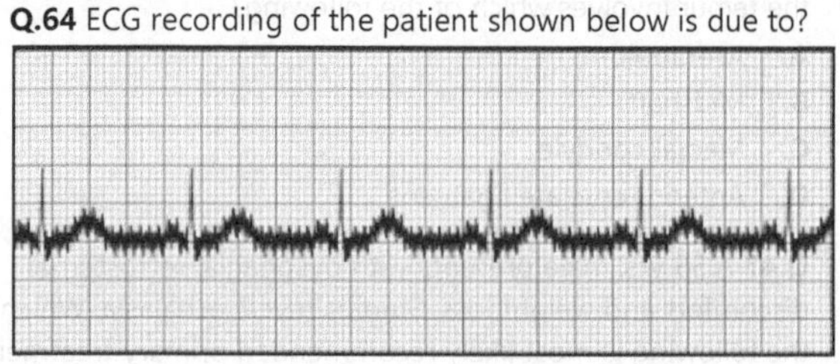

A. Sweating leading to poor electrode contact
B. Electrical interference
C. Restless patient
D. Cable failure

Q.65 A 48-year-old man presents with a three-month history of heartburn after meals which has not been settling with antacids and PPIs. The most appropriate investigation for diagnosing hiatus hernia is:
A. Ultrasound
B. Chest x-ray
C. Upper GI endoscopy
D. Barium meal

Q.66 Apoplexy is:
A. Learning disability
B. Insanity leading to commitment of a crime
C. Sudden onset of bleeding in the brain
D. Injury to the brain due to trauma

Q.67 Hardy Weinberg law states that

A. Relative frequencies of gene allele tends to remain constant from generation to generation
B. Human population and human gene pool is never static
C. Human gene pool changes occur mainly by mutation
D. Harmful genes are eliminated from the gene pool

Q.68 Which of the following structures would most likely be affected by the abscess located between the perineal membrane and the inferior fascia of the pelvic diaphragm within the deep perineal space?
A. Bulbourethral glands
B. Perineal body
C. Superficial transverse perineal muscles
D. Ischiocavernosus muscles

Q.69 The lipoprotein associated with activation of LCAT is
A. HDL **B.** LDL **C.** VLDL **D.** IDL

Q.70 Identify the organism given below?

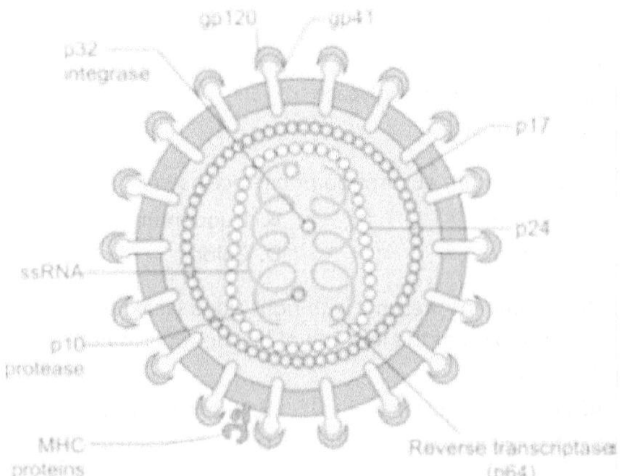

A. Rabies virus **B.** Ebola virus
C. H1N1 virus **D.** HIV virus

Q.71 A 25 year male is presented with pain in abdomen. On USG, mixed echogenicity was found at left renal hilum and a multifocal necrotic mass is detected. Probable diagnosis is ?
A. Metastatic germ cell tumour
B. Transitional cell carcinoma
C. Lymphoma
D. Metastatic malignant melanoma

Q.72 India belongs to which demographic trends:
A. High stationary **B.** Low stationary
C. Early expanding **D.** Late expanding

Q.73 Which of the following cytopathologic findings in pap smear is suggestive of HPV infection?
A. Donovan bodies **B.** Koilocytes
C. Clear cells **D.** Paget cells

Q.74 Risk factors for acalculous cholecystitis include:
A. Extensive burns **B.** Sepsis
C. Multiple trauma **D.** All of the above

Q.75 Cradle of civilization is:
A. Mesopotamia **B.** Haddapa
C. Mohenjodaro **D.** Sindhu ghati

Q.76 In which of the following conditions the serum alkaline phosphatase activities are likely to be reduced?
A. Osteomalacia **B.** Paget's disease
C. Hypophosphatasia **D.** All of the above

Q.77 A 35-year-old female complains of recurrent urticarial lesions she has had for the last 6 months, which occasionally leave a residual discoloration. She also has had arthralgias. The sedimentation rate now is 85 mm/h. The procedure most likely to yield the correct diagnosis in this case would be?
A. A battery of wheal-and-flare allergy skin tests
B. Measurement of total serum IgE concentration
C. Measurement of C1 esterase inhibitor activity
D. Skin biopsy

Q.78 Which of the following medications may most likely increase the uric acid levels in a patient?
A. Acetazolamide
B. Amiloride
C. Spironolactone
D. Hydrochlorothiazide

Q.79 Antihypertensive of choice in Marfans syndrome is:
A. Beta Blockers
B. Ace Inhibitors
C. Prazosin
D. Angiotensin receptor blockers

Q.80 Which of the following statements regarding stress ulceration is true ?
A. It is true ulceration, extending into and through the muscularis mucosa
B. It classically involves the antrum
C. Increased secretion of gastric acid has been shown to play a causative role
D. It frequently involves multiple sites

Q.81 Period of amenorrhea followed by massive bleeding is seen in premenopausal women with:
A. Irregular ripening
B. Irregular shedding
C. Metropathia hemorrhagica
D. All of the above

Q.82 A 2-year-old boy, is brought with multiple bony abnormalities, as shown in the image. A decrease in which of the following is characteristic of this condition?

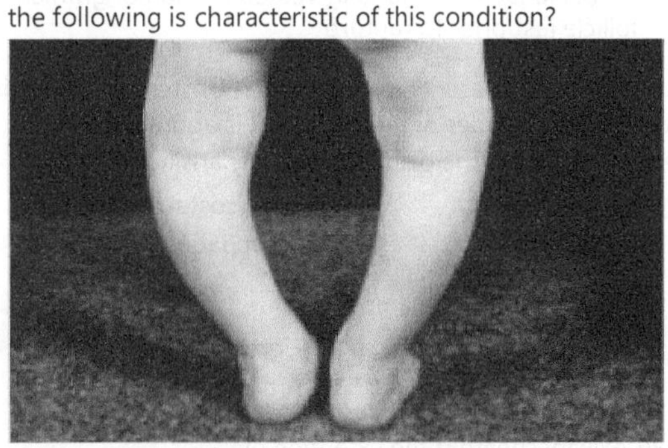

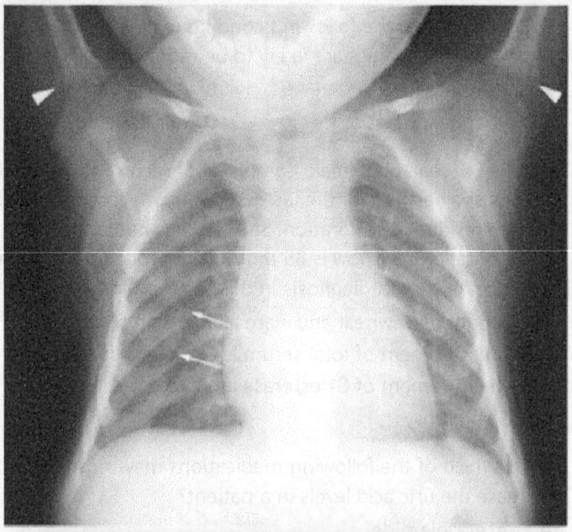

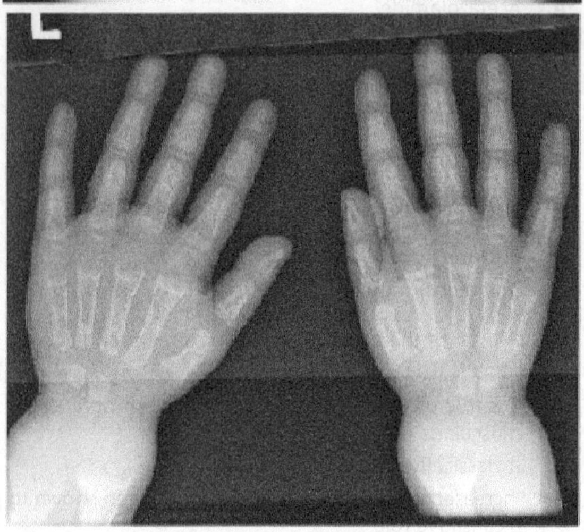

A. Bony osteoblastic activity
B. Calcification of osteoid
C. Serum alkaline phosphatase activity
D. Synthesis of osteoid

Q.83 Characteristics of Mittelschmerz are all except :

A. Pain is usually situated in the hypogastrium
B. It appears in mid menstrual period
C. Pain is usually located on both the ovarian sides irrespective of which ovary is ovulating
D. Probable factors include increased tension of graffian follicle just prior to rupture

Q.84 A woman presents with burning retrosternal chest pain, radiating to the sides of the chest that is aggravated by bending forward. The pain is most likely arising from

A. Heart
B. Intercostal nerves
C. Pancreas
D. Esophagus

Q.85 The epiglottis is example of

A. Elastic cartilage
B. Fibrocartilage
C. Hyaline cartilage
D. Articular

Q.86 Axillary sheath is the extention of

A. Prevertebral fascia
B. Pretacheal fascia
C. Carotid sheath
D. Bucco pharyngeal fascia

Q.87 The following are risk factors for puerperal infection, EXCEPT:

A. Prolonged rupture of the membranes
B. Prolonged pregnancy
C. Prolonged second stage
D. Caesarean section

Q.88 Which of the following is major fuel for brain after several weeks of starvation?

A. Beta hydroxyl butyrate
B. Glucose
C. Glycerol
D. Fatty acids

Q.89 Which of the following is Arachidonate 5-lipoxygenase inhibitor?

A. Zileuton
B. Montelukast
C. Sodium chromoglycate
D. Terbutaline

Q.90 Maximum absorption of bile occurs in :

A. Jejunum
B. Duodenum
C. Ileum
D. Colon

Q.91 A patient presents with right sided weakness of arm and leg. Drooping of the left side of his mouth also noted. Where is the lesion?

A. Left motor cortex
B. Right motor cortex
C. Left brainstem
D. Right brainstem

Q.92 Which of the following grows the colonies on Mac Conkey agar as shown in the image?

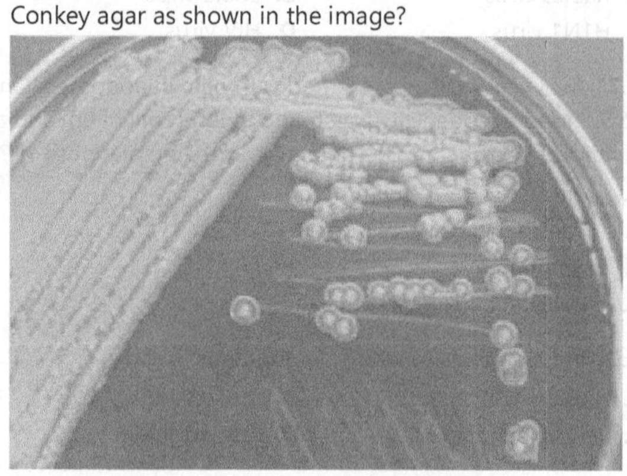

A. Shigella
B. Salmonella
C. Proteus
D. Klebsiella

Q.93 Commonest cause of female pseudohermaphroditism is:

A. Virilizing ovarian tumor
B. Ovarian dysgenesis
C. Exogenous androgen
D. Congenital adrenal hyperplasia

Q.94 The following are the complications of the HIV infection except

A. Cardiac tamponade
B. Pericardial effusion

C. Thromboembolism **D.** Cardiomyopathy

Q.95 Iceberg phenomenon is a part of disease, which presents clinically, screening tests are used for:

A. To detect tip of iceberg
B. To detect clinical cases
C. To detect submerged part [clinical cases]
D. To detect submerged part [sub clinical cases]

Q.96 Which of the following is TRUE regarding the image provided?

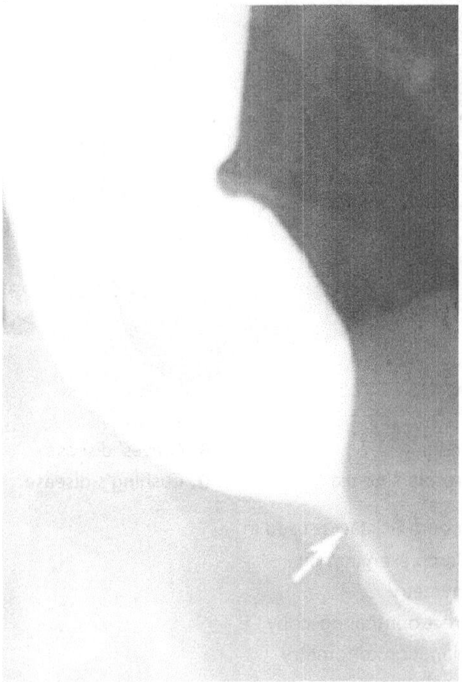

A. Increased tone of lower esophageal sphincter
B. Associated with vitamin A deficiency
C. Not a premalignant condition
D. It's a normal phenomenon

Q.97 Beta adrenergic antagonist are useful antihypertensive agent in all except -

A. Young patients with high renin levels
B. Patients with associated conditions like migraine
C. Patients receiving vasodilators to counteract tachycardia
D. Patients on oral hypoglycemic agents

Q.98 Which of this does not handle the free radicals in lens?

A. Vitamin A **B.** Vitamin C
C. Vitamin E **D.** Catalase

Q.99 Patients with Huntington disease may benefit from treatment with drugs that antagonize

A. GABA **B.** Acetylcholine
C. Dopamine **D.** Serotonin

Q.100 Production of the type of cell shown in Figure is increased by

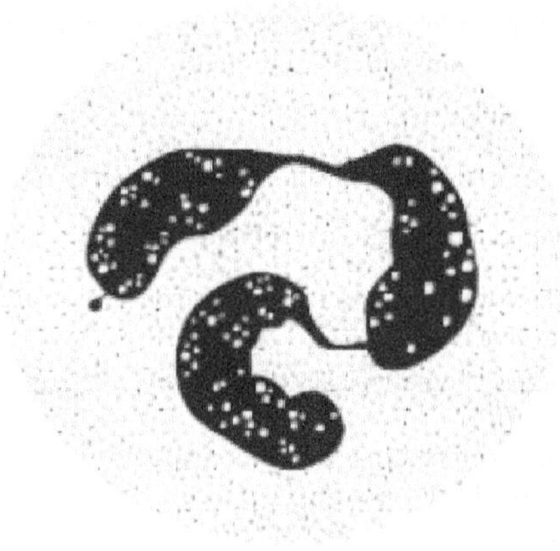

A. Interleukin-2 (IL-2)
B. Granulocyte colony-stimulating factor (G-CSF)
C. Erythropoietin
D. Interleukin-4 (IL-4)

Q.101 A 52-year-old woman presented with indigestion and heartburn occurring shortly after meals. Physical examination revealed mild epigastric tenderness. A radiolabeled-urea breath test is positive. What is the most probable etiologic agent?

A. Campylobacter jejuni
B. Clostridium difficile
C. Helicobacter pylori
D. Shigella dysenteriae

Q.102 During removal of a neurogenic tumor in the posterior mediastinum, the structure indicated by arrow in the given diagram was damaged. What type of nerve fibers were affected by this iatrogenic injury?

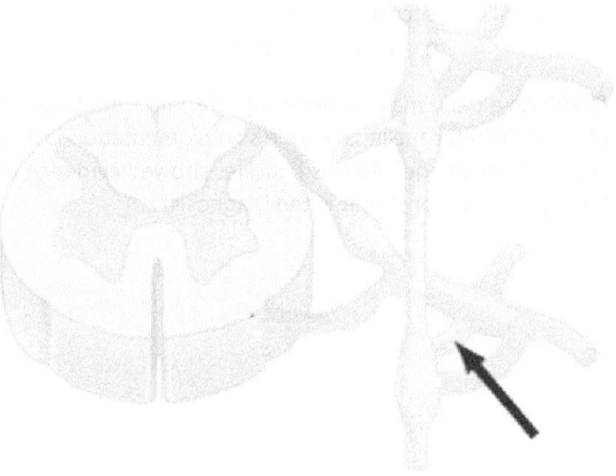

A. Presynaptic sympathetic axons
B. Presynaptic parasympathetic axons
C. Postsynaptic sympathetic axons
D. Postsynaptic parasympathetic axons

Q.103 Stimulation of which of the following might be expected to produce itching?

A. Dorsal root C fibers
B. B fibers in peripheral nerves
C. Dorsal columns of the spinal cord
D. Touch receptors

Q.104 Which of the following medications is most useful for the treatment of premenstrual syndrome?

A. Progesterone
B. Anxiolytics
C. Vitamins
D. Selective serotonin reuptake inhibitors (SSRIs)

Q.105 Which of the following statements concerning acute rheumatic fever is true?

A. Sydenham's chorea typically occurs early in the course of the disease
B. Erythema marginatum is a common finding, occurring in more than 50% of cases
C. Secondary prophylaxis should be initiated in order to decrease recurrent episodes of rheumatic fever
D. Group A streptococci can usually be recovered in the upper respiratory tract of patients with rheumatic fever

Q.106 Which of the following is most characteristic of Huntington disease?

A. Degeneration of upper and lower motor neurons
B. Dopamine depletion and depigmentation of the substantia nigra
C. Increased number of trinucleotide repeats in a gene on chromosome 4
D. Neurofibrillary tangles and amyloid plaques in the cerebral cortex

Q.107 Decrease in heart rate in response to rise in blood pressure is explained by -

A. Baroreflex **B.** Chemoreflex
C. Bainbridge reflex **D.** Hering-Bruer reflex

Q.108 The reliability of visual field testing becomes suspect when pupil diameter decreases below:

A. 4 mm **B.** 3 mm **C.** 2 mm **D.** 1 mm

Q.109 An elderly man presents with chronic fatigability, central obesity, diabetes mellitus. Purple skin pigmentation is noted as shown in the image. Also his knuckles showed evidence of hyperpigmentation. What is the Diagnosis?

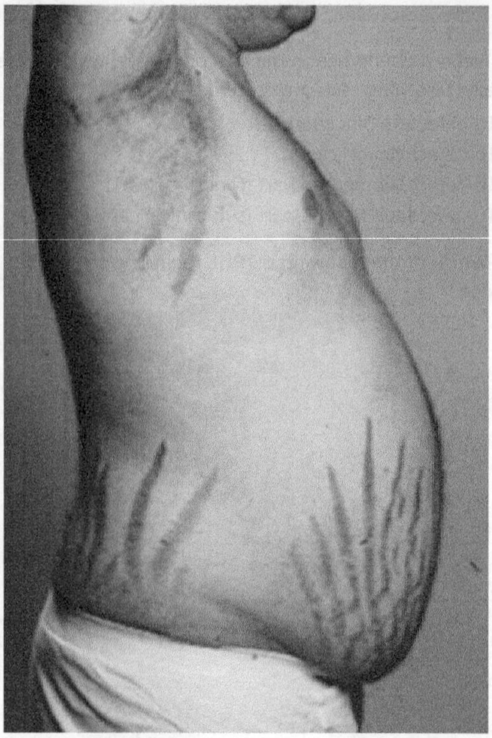

A. Acromegaly **B.** Graves' disease
C. Hyperprolactinemia **D.** Cushing's disease

Q.110 Imbert-Fick law is used in

A. Slit lamp examination
B. Pachymetry
C. Indirect ophthalmoscopy
D. Applanation tonometry

Q.111 The key function of component indicated by arrow in the given diagram of thin filament of skeletal muscle includes

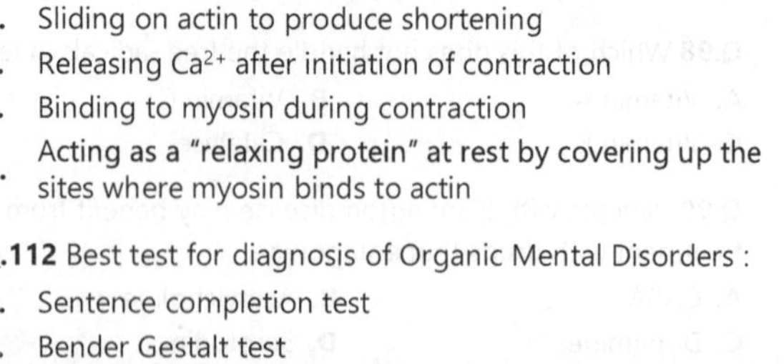

A. Sliding on actin to produce shortening
B. Releasing Ca^{2+} after initiation of contraction
C. Binding to myosin during contraction
D. Acting as a "relaxing protein" at rest by covering up the sites where myosin binds to actin

Q.112 Best test for diagnosis of Organic Mental Disorders :

A. Sentence completion test
B. Bender Gestalt test
C. Rorshach test
D. Thematic Appreciation test

Q.113 Which bacteria act by mechanism of cAMP activation?

A. V. cholerae **B.** B. Cereus
C. B. fragils **D.** Cl. Difficile

Q.114 Which of the following is used to treat digitalis induced ventricular arrhythmia:

A. Phenytoin **B.** Propranolol
C. Quinidine **D.** Diltiazem

Q.115 Which one of the following compound acts as strong inducer but do not act as substrate of β-galactosidase in Escherichia coli :

A. Allolactose
B. Isopropylthiogalactoside (IPTG)
C. Lactose
D. Glucose

Q.116 Shine Dalgarno sequence in prokaryotes is related to

A. Replication **B.** Translation
C. Translocation **D.** Transcription

Q.117 Which of the following diuretic is most likely to cause diabetes mellitus?

A. Acetazolamide **B.** Amiloride
C. Chlorothiazide **D.** Spironolactone

Q.118 What kind of chest radiograph findings might be seen with cyanoacrylate/lipiodol pulmonary embolization ?

A. Prominent pulmonary vasculature that seem to be outlined with a hyperdense coating (vascular cast sign).
B. A very deep costophrenic angle on one side of the chest (deep sulcus sign).
C. A white line at the apex of a lung.
D. More prominent pulmonary vessels in the upper lung zones than in the lower lung zones (cephalization).

Q.119 Aripiprazole an atypical antipsychotic drug, useful in treatment of schizophrenia, is a

A. D2 receptor antagonist
B. D2 receptor partial agonist
C. D2 receptor agonist
D. D2 receptor inverse agonist

Q.120 Rebound phenomenon in the cerebellar lesion occurs because of

A. Exaggerated inverse stretch reflex
B. Loss of cerebellar component of the stretch reflex
C. Loss of the reciprocal inhibition
D. None of the above

Q.121 AFP is a marker of

A. Seminoma
B. Hepatoblastoma
C. Sertoli-Leydig cell tumor
D. Choriocarcinoma

Q.122 An obese and playful 18 month old toddler presents with pallor. He drinks around 2 liters of milk per day. Which laboratory test would most likely reveal the diagnosis?

A. Chest x-ray
B. Examination of stool for ova and parasites
C. Complete blood count
D. Serum haptoglobin

Q.123 Which of the following histologic features would most likely be present in the biopsy specimen of medullary carcinoma of the thyroid?

A. Tumor cells embedded in an amyloid-laden stroma
B. Psammoma bodies
C. Tumor cells with "Orphan Annie" nuclei
D. Infiltrates of lymphocytes with germinal center formation

Q.124 A 74-year-old woman complains of vomiting and intermittent colicky abdominal pain. X rays reveal fluid levels and air in the biliary tree. What is the likely cause?

A. Abdominal adhesions
B. Gallstone ileus
C. Carcinoma of the right colon
D. Abdominal lymphosarcoma

Q.125 Such a presentation is most commonly seen in:

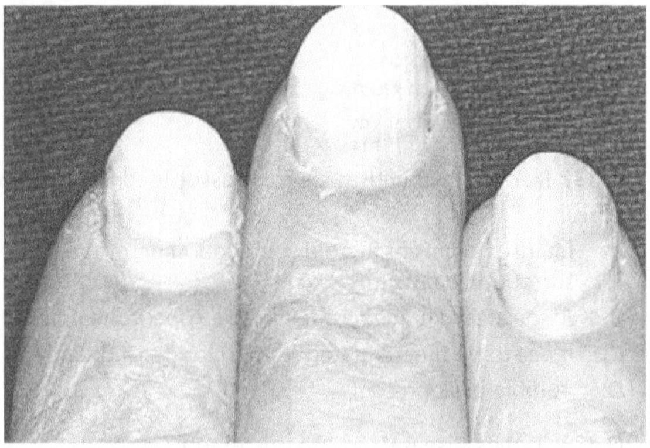

A. Lichen planus **B.** Psoriasis
C. Pemphigus valgaris **D.** Arsenic poisoning

Q.126 Which of the following actions most likely mediates the positive inotropic action of dobutamine?

A. Inhibition of phosphodiesterase
B. Protein kinase-mediated increase in cytoplasmic Ca^{2+} availability
C. Inhibition of the Ca^{2+}/Na^{+} exchanger in cardiac cell membrane
D. Activation of phospholipase A2

Q.127 The risk factors for stroke in a patient with atrial fibrillation include all except :

A. Mitral stenosis
B. Age more than 75 years
C. Spontaneous echo contrast
D. Right ventricular dysfunction

Q.128 A 65-year-old man presents with a tender lump over his right popliteal fossa and severe pain in his leg for 2 days. The lump, which was there a couple of years, has become extremely tender over the last couple of days, the leg has become cold and he is unable to walk. Which of the following is most likely diagnosis?

A. Abdominal aortic aneurysm
B. Internal carotid artery (ICA) stenosis
C. Popliteal artery aneurysm
D. Abdominal compartment syndrome

Q.129 Which one of the following is false regarding Isosorbide mononitrate

A. It does not undergo significant first pass metabolism

B. It has excellent bioavailablity after oral administration

C. It is short acting with half-life of 1-3 min

D. It is one of the active metabolites of Isosorbide dinitrate

Q.130 What is the most common cause of a unilateral neck mass in patients older than 40 years?

A. Reactive lymphadenopathy

B. Hodkin's disease

C. Squamous cell carcinoma

D. Salivary gland infection

Q.131 An elderly patient receiving a blood transfusion develops tachypnea, lumbar pain, tachycardia, and nausea. Which of the following is the most likely explanation?

A. Acute leukemia

B. Fluid overload

C. Hemolysis

D. Pulmonary embolism

Q.132 Riedel's thyroiditis is clinically associated with all, except :

A. Intense fibrosis of thyroid with induration of the surrounding structure occurs

B. Associates with mediastinal and retroperitoneal fibrosis

C. It has to be differentiated from thyroid malignancy

D. Audible bruit present

Q.133 "Lymes Disease"- all are true except

A. Borellia bourgdorferi replicates locally and invades locally

B. Infection progress inspite of good humoral immunity

C. Polymorphonuclear lymphocytosis in CSF suggest meningeal involvement

D. Ig A intrathecally confirms meningitis

Q.134 Most common cause of delayed puberty is :

A. Kallman's syndrome

B. Gonadal dysgenesis

C. Hypothalamic tumor

D. Constitutional

Q.135 Double vision while walking downstairs is seen with lesion of

A. Abducens nerve

B. Occulomotor nerve

C. Trochlear nerve

D. Medial longitudinal Fasciculus

Q.136 Postterm pregnancy is associated with all the following except

A. Transient tachypnea of the newborn

B. Oligohydramnios

C. Meconium aspiration

D. Intrauterine fetal demise

Q.137 A reduction in carotid sinus pressure would cause a decrease in which of the following?

A. Heart rate

B. Myocardial contractility

C. Total peripheral resistance

D. Venous Compliance

Q.138 A woman is found to have a unilateral invasive carcinoma of vulva that is 2 cm in diameter but not associated with evidence of lymph node spread. Initial management should consists of

A. Chemotherapy

B. Radiation therapy

C. Radical vulvectomy

D. Radical vulvectomy and bilateral inguinal lymphadenectomy

Q.139 Shift of medial temporal lobe medially towards tentorial hiatus is referred to as :

A. Sub falcine herniation

B. Uncal herniation

C. Tentorial herniation

D. None of the above

Q.140 Lanugo hair starts forming in which month of intrauterine life?

A. 3 **B.** 4 **C.** 5 **D.** 6

Q.141 Which one of the following test is used to detect malingering?

A. Stenger's test **B.** Bunge's test

C. Weber's test **D.** Rinne's test

Q.142 Which of the following is not a branch of Artery 'A' shown in the Figure?

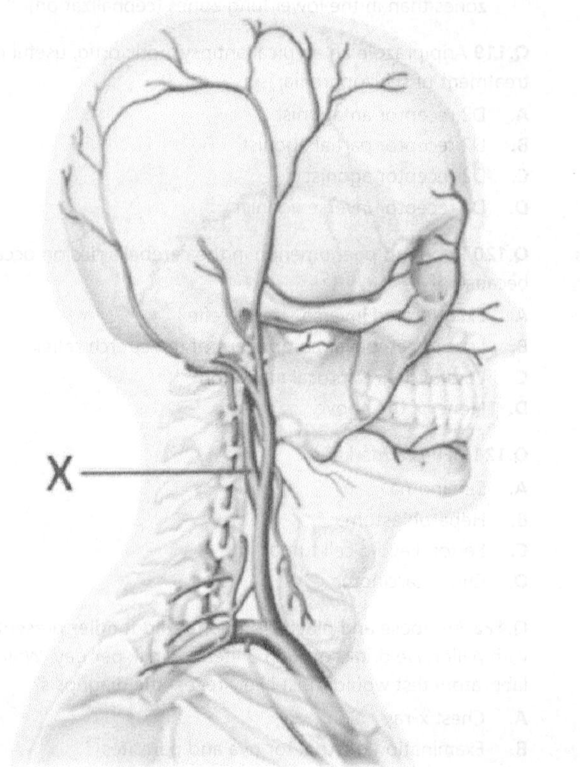

A. Posterior Communicating

B. Posterior Choroidal

C. Anterior Cerebral

D. Anterior Choroidal

Q.143 A 67-year-old man recently diagnosed with benign prostatic hyperplasia was scheduled for surgery. Which of the following drug classes would be absolutely contraindicated in this patient?

A. Alpha-1 blockers
B. Antimuscarinics
C. Beta blockers
D. Alpha-2 agonists

Q.144 Utero-placental blood flow at term in pregnancy is

A. 50 - 75 ml/min
B. 150 - 200 ml/min
C. 350 - 400 ml/min
D. 500 - 700 ml/min

Q.145 A 68-year-old man with a history of a previous myocardial infarction presents complaining of a painful lesion noted on his foot. He has been experiencing pain in his lower legs with ambulation over the last year. The most likely diagnosis is?

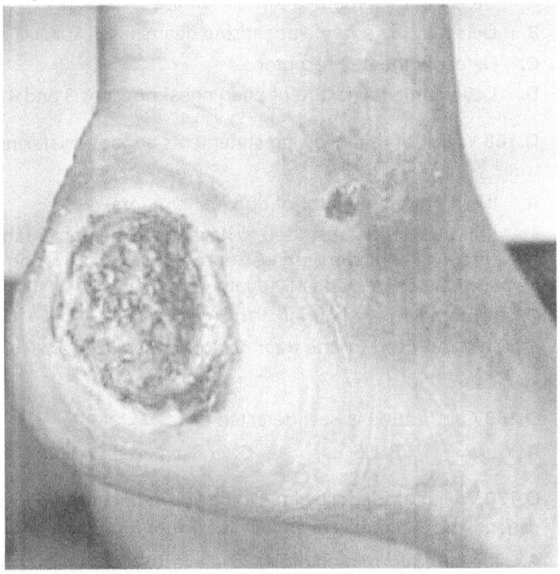

A. Venous stasis ulcer
B. Arterial ulcer
C. Basal cell carcinoma
D. Livedo reticularis

Q.146 During the delivery, it is necessary to do an episiotomy. The tear extends through sphincter of the rectum, but the rectal mucosa is intact. How would you classify this type of episiotomy ?

A. First- degree
B. Second-degree
C. Third-degree
D. Fourth-degree

Q.147 Auricular branch of vagus passes through

A. Mental foramen
B. Pterygoid canal
C. Zygomatic foramen
D. Mastoid canaliculi

Q.148 A patient presents with acute respiratory distress, stridor and inability to speak. Likely diagnosis is:

A. Asthma
B. Aspiration pneumonia
C. Foreign body aspiration
D. Pleural effusion

Q.149 Acrodermatitis enteropathica is:

A. Inherited disorder of excessive excretion of zinc from body
B. Inherited disorder of impaired uptake of zinc from body
C. Inherited disorder of excessive excretion of copper from body
D. Inherited disorder of impaired uptake of copper from body

Q.150 Which is known as Fifth disease:

A. Erythema infectiosum
B. Rubeolla infantum
C. Dukes disease
D. Measles

Part C

Q.151 Rising sun sign is seen in:

A. Glomus jugulare tumour
B. Low jugular bulb
C. Otosclerosis
D. Acoustic neuroma

Q.152 In a patient, serologic test results show HBsAg & anti-HBc as positive and IgM anti-HBc & anti-HBs as negative. What is the correct interpretation?

A. Acutely infected
B. Chronically infected
C. Susceptible
D. Interpretation unclear

Q.153 What is the mechanism of action of Botulinum toxin?

A. It blocks release of acetylcholine.
B. It inhibits glycine and GABA.
C. It is a lecithinase.
D. It is a superantigen.

Q.154 Which of the following malignancies is associated with the skin condition shown here?

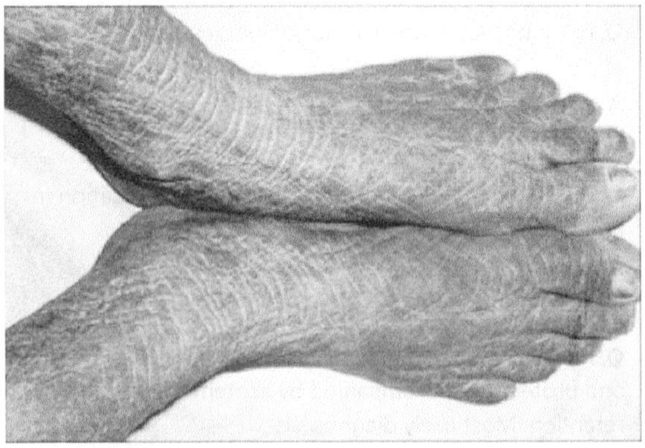

A. Diabetes
B. Gastric carcinoma
C. Malignant melanoma
D. Addison's disease

Q.155 The most common predisposing factor for placenta accrete among the following is

A. Tubal surgery
B. Recent curettage
C. Previous cesarean section
D. Placenta previa

Q.156 Which of the following roentgenographic findings is most commonly seen in infants with bronchiolitis caused by RSV?

A. Hyperinflation **B.** Hilar adenopathy
C. Multilobar infiltrate **D.** Pleural effusion

Q.157 Absent urobilinogen in urine with icterus indicates

A. Liver failure
B. Peri-hepatic obstruction
C. Hemolysis
D. Hepatitis

Q.158 Penetrating injury to NECK is defined as

A. More than 2 cm deep injury
B. Injury to any internal neck organ
C. Violation of platysma
D. Sharp instrument

Q.159 On T1-weighted and T2-weighted MRI, what are the signal characteristics of subacute hemorrhage?

A. Hypointense on T1-weighted and hypointense on T2-weighted images
B. Hyperintense on T1-weighted and hypointense on T2-weighted images
C. Hyperintense on T1-weighted and hyperintense on T2-weighted images
D. Hypointense on T1-weighted and hyperintense on T2-weighted images

Q.160 A 5 year old child presents with coarse facial features, hepatosplenomegaly & progressive loss of developmental milestones. Most likely cause is

A. Mucopolysacharidosis
B. Aminoaciduria
C. Urea cycle deficiency
D. Urea cycle enzyme deficiency

Q.161 Intracytoplasmic inclusion bodies are pathognomonic of

A. Measles **B.** Adenovirus
C. Poliovirus **D.** Rabies

Q.162 Serum marker indicating active viral replication in hepatitis-B is :

A. HBsAg **B.** HBeAg
C. HBcAg **D.** Anti-HBs

Q.163 A 25-year-old man develops abrupt onset of hematuria and proteinuria, accompanied by azotemia and salt and water retention. Most likely diagnosis is

A. Nephrotic syndrome
B. Diabetic nephropathy
C. Nephrolithiasis
D. Acute glomerulonephritis

Q.164 Which of the following is the peritoneal ligament containing splenic vessels at the hilum of the spleen?

A. Hepatoduodenal ligament
B. Coronary ligament
C. Lienorenal ligament
D. Gastrolienal ligament

Q.165 A 44-year-old woman presents with a 3-cm breast mass of 4-month duration. On examination, mammography shows microcalcification and features are suggestive of malignancy. The diagnosis is confirmed by?

A. Needle biopsy
B. Open biopsy from the edge
C. Lymph node biopsy
D. Thermography

Q.166 Which of the following agents has good analgesic and sedative properties but does not cause skeletal muscle relaxation?

A. Enflurane **B.** Nitrous oxide
C. Thiopental **D.** Halothane

Q.167 Which of the following is the most likely cause of chronic granulomatous disease in a 7-year-old boy?

A. Defect in the enzyme NADPH oxidase
B. Defect in the enzyme adenosine deaminase (ADA)
C. Defect in the IL-2 receptor
D. Developmental failure of pharyngeal pouches 3 and 4

Q.168 Which of the following statements about venlafaxine is true?

A. It is a potent inhibitor of dopamine reuptake
B. It has been demonstrated to have the same percentage of response and completeness of response as fluoxetine in severely depressed individuals
C. It can be tapered during 1 to 2 weeks
D. It is approved for the treatment of generalized anxiety disorder

Q.169 Calcification is best detected by :

A. X - ray **B.** USG **C.** CT Scan **D.** MRI

Q.170 Which of the following would you expect to find in a patient whose diet has been low in calcium for 2 months?

A. Increased formation of 24, 25-dihydroxycholecalciferol
B. Decreased amounts of calcium-binding protein in intestinal epithelial cells
C. Increased parathyroid hormone secretion
D. A high plasma calcitonin concentration

Q.171 An 8-month-old female presents with failure to thrive, constipation, fevers, and polydipsia. On evaluation, you find hypokalemia and hyperchloremic metabolic acidosis and suspect Fanconi syndrome. Which of the following would be the most likely inherited cause ?

A. Cystinosis
B. Cystic fibrosis
C. Glycogen storage disease
D. Tyrosinemia

Q.172 True regarding Marshall-Marchetti-Krantz procedure (MMK) for stress incontinence is

A. Urinary retention is very common after an MMK procedure and often requires long-term self-catheterization.
B. Patient has a 5% risk of enterocele formation.
C. The MMK procedure is highly effective, with greater than 90% long-term cure rate.
D. Osteitis pubis occurs in approximately 10% of patients after an MMK, but is easily treated with oral antibiotics.

Q.173 Gamma hemolytic gram positive cocci in chains grown in an ICU patient should be tested for sensitivity to

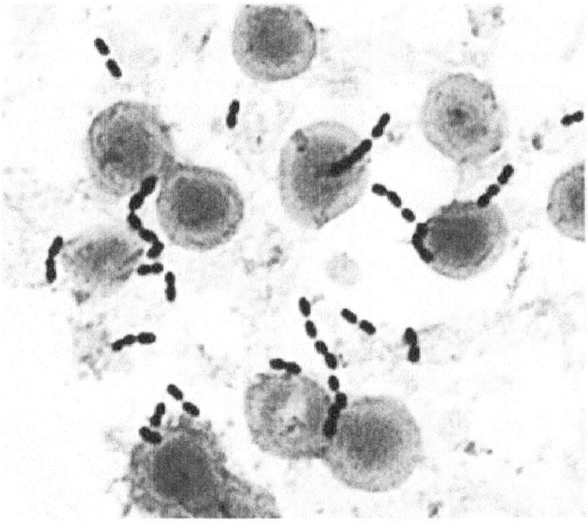

A. Cefepime **B.** Vancomycin
C. Tigycycline **D.** Imepenem

Q.174 A 4-year-old boy has a history of wheezing with colds, but presently suffering from persistent cough and is being given an albuterol MDI with some relief. He has symptoms at least one night out of the week and almost every day. What is the most appropriate medication regimen for this patient?

A. Over-the-counter cough medication
B. Albuterol twice daily
C. Inhaled corticosteroid twice daily plus albuterol as needed
D. Daily systemic corticosteroids

Q.175 All of the following are diagnostic features of neuroleptic malignant syndrome (NMS) EXCEPT:

A. Diaphoresis **B.** Tachypnea
C. Mutism **D.** Tachycardia

Q.176 Action which halts the progress of a disease at its incipient stage and prevents complications:

A. Primary prevention
B. Primordial prevention
C. Secondary prevention
D. Tertiary prevention

Q.177 Consent is required for:

A. Mass immunization
B. Medico-legal autopsy
C. Pathological autopsy
D. Treatment of unconscious patient

Q.178 All the following clostridia are predominantly saccharolytic except:

A. Clostridia septicum
B. Clostridia perfringens
C. Clostridia sporogenes
D. Clostridia acetobutylicum

Q.179 Which of the following is true for SIADH:

A. Hyponatremia with increased plasma osmolality
B. Hypernatremia with decreased plasma osmolality
C. Hyponatremia with decreased plasma osmolality
D. Hypernatremia with increased plasma osmolality

Q.180 Confirmatory diagnosis of rabies on postmortem:

A. Negri bodies in saliva
B. Negri bodies in corneal scrapings
C. Anti-rabies antibodies in blood
D. Negri bodies in brain

Q.181 Out of the following important events, which does not take place at the level of sixth cervical vertebra?

A. At this level lies the junction of larynx and trachea
B. The cricoid cartilage is located here
C. The common carotid artery bifurcates into external and internal carotid arteries
D. The junction of pharynx and esophagus lies at this level

Q.182 Which of the following is true regarding the diagnosis of Tourette disorder?

A. Motor and vocal tics must occur concurrently
B. Onset must be before the age of 21
C. Tics must be present every day consecutively for at least 1 year
D. Multiple motor tics must occur

Q.183 After being severely reprimanded by his employer, a man goes home and is extremely nasty to his wife. What is his behavior an example of?

A. Displacement **B.** Dissociation
C. Rationalization **D.** Conversion

Q.184 The weight of an adult eyeball is

A. 10 gms **B.** 15 gms **C.** 5 gms **D.** 7 gms

Q.185 The eggs seen in the image are of

A. Culex **B.** Aedes
C. Anopheles **D.** Mansonia

Q.186 Xanthogranulomatous pyelonephritis shows the following features except :

A. Accumulation of fatty macrophages
B. Yellow nodules in kidney
C. Association with tuberculosis
D. Presence of plasma cells

Q.187 A 33-year-old man with coeliac disease presents with a blistering rash over the elbows and scalp. The most appropriate treatment is:

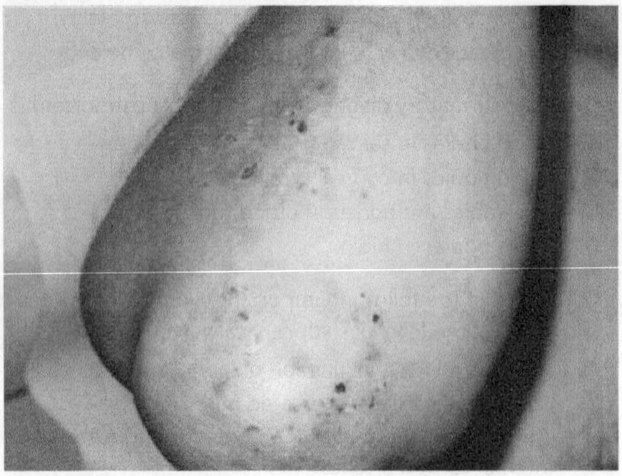

A. Oral prednisolone **B.** Dapsone
C. NSAIDs **D.** Aciclovir

Q.188 Raghu, a 5 year old child, came with scalds of approximately 10% TBSA. He is a known case of juvenile diabetes and has associated inhalation injury. Which of these is not a risk factor for susciptibility to systemic infections -

A. Age (age of children greater than adults)
B. Total burn surface area-TBSA
C. Premorbid diabetes mellitus
D. Inhalation injury

Q.189 Corneal scrapings were taken from a 67 yr old farmer presenting with a corneal ulcer of the right eye. A piece of vegetable matter was embedded in the cornea and scrapings were done. Gram stain (500x magnification) showed numerous narrow angled septate hyphae (figure). Which of the following is the likely etiologic agent?

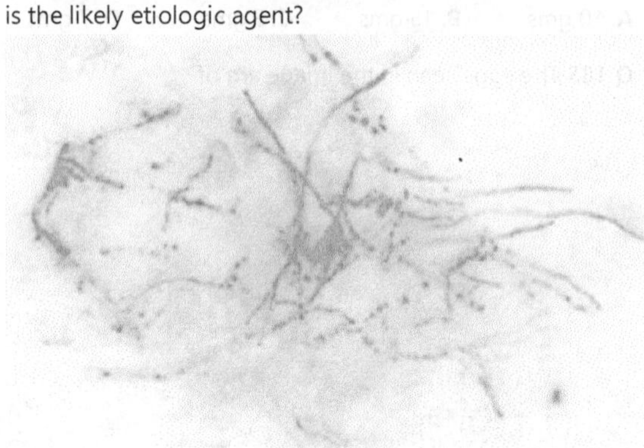

A. Candida **B.** Aspergillus
C. Mucor **D.** Histoplasma

Q.190 A 60-year-old woman experiences mild intermittent right hip pain after falling down a flight of stairs. A radiograph shows calcified, medium-sized arterial branches in the pelvis but no fractures. This radiographic finding most likely represents

A. An incidental observation
B. Benign essential hypertension
C. Long-standing diabetes mellitus
D. Unsuspected hyperparathyroidism

Q.191 Clostridia are implicated in the following except:

A. Botulism
B. Necrotising enterocolitis
C. Bacillary dysentery
D. Pseudomembranous colitis

Q.192 A 47-year-old woman develops headache and double vision. One of her midline sagittal MRIs is shown in figure. On examination, she may have all of the following except:

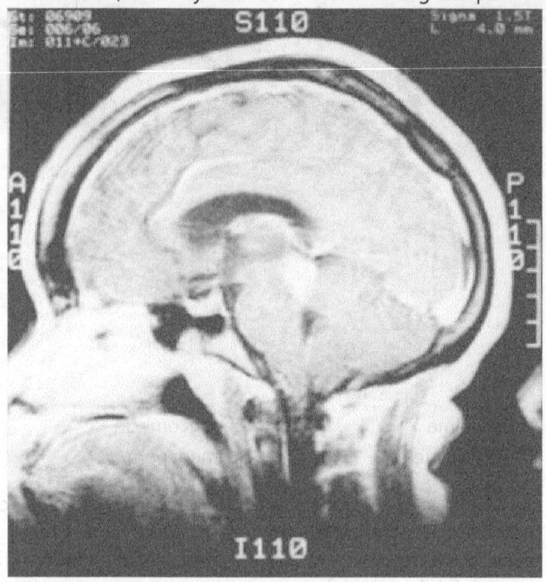

A. Sixth nerve palsy
B. Skew deviation
C. Lid retraction
D. Pupils that react well to a near stimulus but not to light

Q.193 What is the definition of premature ovarian failure?

A. Cessation of menstrual cycles occurring prior to 35 years
B. The start of irregular menstrual cycles at age 38
C. Cessation of menstrual periods prior to age 40
D. The start of irregular menstrual cycles at age 42

Q.194 Regarding investigations in hypospadias all are true except -

A. Urethroscopy and cystoscopy are of value to detect whether internal male sexual organs are developed normally or not
B. Buccal smear and karyotyping to establish genetic sex in penoscrotal and perineal hypospadias
C. Excretory urography to detect additional congenital abnormalities of kidney and ureter
D. Buccal smear and karyotyping to establish genetic sex in glanular hypospadias

Q.195 An 11 year old boy presents with mass in the abdomen and ascites. On imaging the para-aortic lymph nodes are enlarged. On biopsy starry sky appearance (figure) is seen. What is the underlying abnormality?

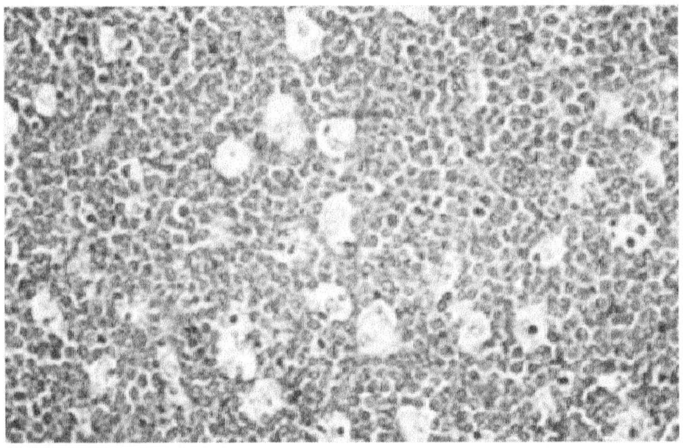

A. P53 gene mutation
B. RB gene mutation
C. Translocation involving BCR-ABL genes
D. Translocation involving MYC-gene

Q.196 The type of mutation shown in the image is known as

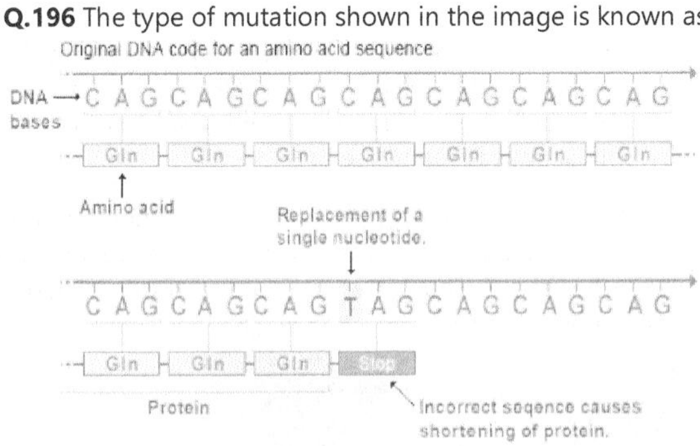

A. Nonsense mutation
B. Missense mutation
C. Frameshift mutation
D. Insertion

Q.197 On the basis of following findings, what is the diagnosis in a 2-year-old with seizures and left hemiparesis?

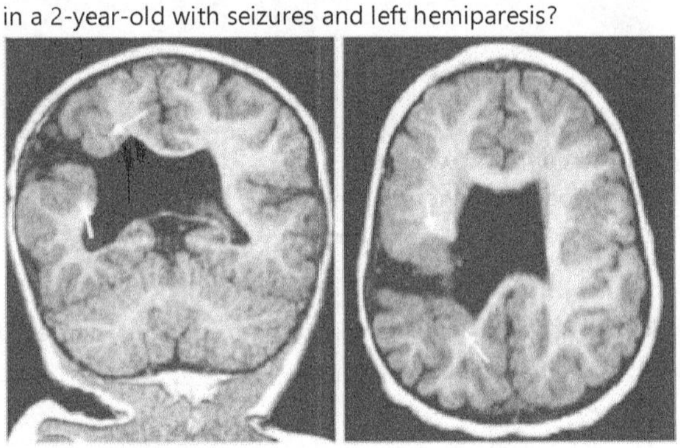

A. Subdural haemorrhage
B. Arnold-Chiari malformation
C. Schizencephaly
D. Lissencephaly

Q.198 False regarding von-Willebrand disease:
A. Normal prothrombin time
B. Normal bleeding time
C. Normal platelet count
D. Normal or slightly increased Partial thromboplastin time

Q.199 Following a right pneumonectomy, the postoperative recovery of a patient is complicated by bronchopleural fistula, which presents with pyrexia, expectoration of large amounts of purulent sputum and a high fluid level on chest radiograph. In addition to positioning the patient to lie on the operated side, what procedure is urgently required?
A. Bronchoscopy
B. Chest drain insertion
C. CT scan of the chest
D. Pulmonary function tests

Q.200 Which of the following is an early sign of prolonged grief?
A. Clinging behavior
B. Self-blame regarding the death
C. Brief hallucinations
D. Anxiety when reminded of loss

Q.201 Untrue about CVP monitoring -
A. Seldinger technique is utilized for cannulation
B. Tip of catheter should be in right atrium
C. Normal is 3 - 10 cm H_2O
D. During catheterization, direction of needle should be towards ipsilateral nipple.

Q.202 The test shown in the image is done for

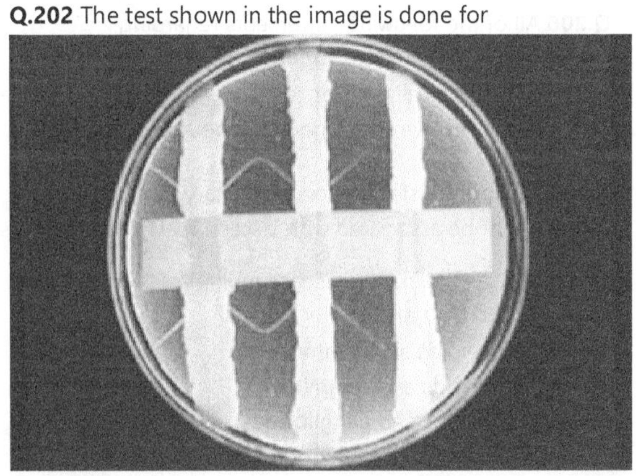

A. Cholera
B. Diptheria
C. Influenza
D. Brucellosis

Q.203 The smear of a patient's peripheral blood is shown in the image. Which of the following substances is most likely to be deficient in this individual?

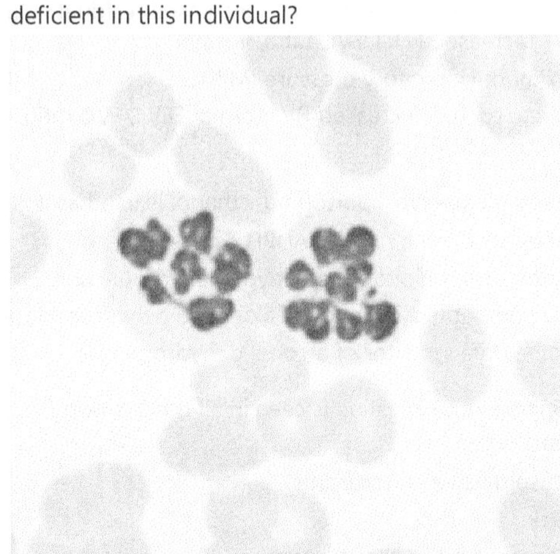

A. Ascorbic acid
B. Folic acid

C. Retinoic acid
D. Vanillylmandelic acid

Q.204 In comparing the secondary structure of proteins, which of the following descriptions applies to both the α-helix and the β-pleated sheet?

A. All peptide bond components participate in hydrogen bonding.
B. N-terminals of chains are together and parallel.
C. The structure is composed of two or more segments of polypeptide chain.
D. N- and C-terminal ends of chains alternate in an antiparallel manner.

Q.205 A patient presenting for evaluation of deafness is found to also have an elevated plasma renin, although his blood pressure is 118/75 mm Hg. Mutation of which of the following single gene would be likely to explain these findings?

A. The gene for barttin
B. The gene for Na+ channel
C. The gene for renin
D. The gene for tyrosine hydroxylase

Q.206 All of the following statements regarding keratoacanthoma are true, except:

A. It is histologically similar to a squamous cell carcinoma.
B. It might resolve spontaneously about subsequent 6 months.
C. It is a form of slowly growing solitary tumour.
D. It might be associated with visceral malignant tumours.

Q.207 The demyelinating disease multiple sclerosis is characterized by a loss of which lipids?

A. Phospholipids and ceramide
B. Sphingolipids and ceramide
C. Sphingolipids and gangliosides
D. Phospholipids and sphingolipids

Q.208 Which of the following pulmonary function tests may correspond to Idiopathic pulmonary fibrosis

A. Increased total lung capacity (TLC), decreased vital capacity (VC), decreased FEV1/FVC ratio
B. Decreased TLC, decreased VC, decreased residual volume (RV), increased FEV1/FVC ratio, normal
C. maximum inspiratory pressure (MIP)
D. Decreased TLC, increased RV, normal FEV1/FVC ratio, decreased MIP

Q.209 In ethylene glycol poisoning, ethanol is used as it is

A. Competitive inhibitor of NADPH oxidase
B. Competitive inhibitor of aldehyde dehydrogenase
C. Non-competitive inhibitor of aldehyde dehydrogenase
D. Competitive inhibitor of alcohol dehydrogenase

Q.210 Gangrene of intestine is seen in all the following conditions, except :

A. Tricuspid valve endocarditis
B. Shock
C. Mesenteric artery thrombosis
D. Volvulus

Q.211 Which of the following is the induction agent of choice in renal patients:

A. Vecuronium
B. Atracurium
C. Pancuronium
D. Rapacuronium

Q.212 Enzyme responsible for respiratory burst reaction is -

A. Peroxidase
B. Hydroxylase
C. NADPH - Oxidase
D. Dehydragenase

Q.213 Disease eradicated from world:

A. Small pox
B. Guineworm
C. Polio
D. Diphtheria

Q.214 Which of the following statements regarding cardiac imaging is correct?

A. Sestamibi imaging can be readily used to identify hibernating myocardium
B. Thallium cannot be readily used to identify hibernating myocardium
C. Dipyridamole stress testing is safe in patients with chronic obstructive pulmonary disease (COPD)
D. The effects of dipyridamole can be reversed with intravenous theophylline

Q.215 An elderly woman presented with a 3-month history of non-healing ulceration on the dorsal hand (image) that had not responded to antibiotics. Her past medical history includes rheumatoid arthritis. What is the diagnosis?

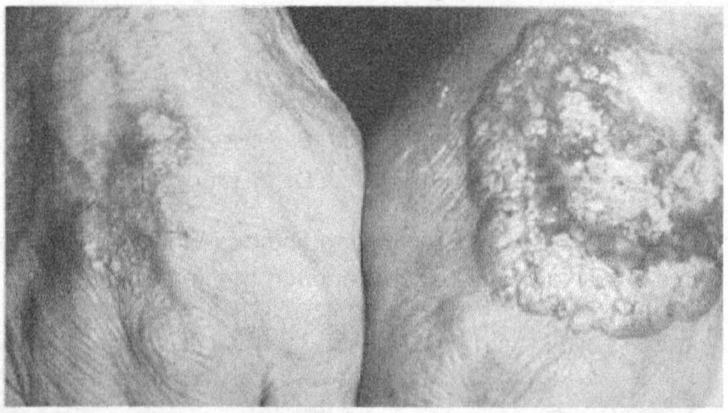

A. Rheumatoid vasculitis
B. Pyoderma gangrenosum
C. Squamous cell carcinoma
D. Keratoacanthoma

Q.216 Bacterial antibiotic resistance is frequently conveyed by

A. A temperate bacteriophage
B. An R-factor plasmid
C. A replicon
D. A lytic bacteriophage

Q.217 A 25-year-old homeless man presents to your office with reports of decreased vision and pain in his right eye for the past 2 days. Examination reveals marked conjunctival injection, a 2-mm hypopyon, and dense vitreous opacities on B-scan ultrasound. You suspect endogenous endophthalmitis, and on further questioning, the patient admits to IV drug abuse. Given the patient's history, which one of the following organisms is the least likely to be involved in this patient's endophthalmitis?

A. C. albicans
B. Staphylococcus species
C. Bacillus cereus

D. Haemophilus influenzae

Q.218 ECG findings of Ostium Secundum atrial septal defect includes all EXCEPT :

A. Left axis deviation
B. rSR' pattern
C. Right ventricle hypertrophy
D. Right atrial hypertrophy

Q.219 Which of the following investigational research procedures can distinguish most clearly whether an isolated 1-cm pedunculated polyp in the sigmoid colon represents hyperplasia of the colonic mucosa or a tubular adenoma?

A. Flow cytometry to quantitate cells in the S phase
B. Histochemical staining for mucin
C. Immunohistochemical staining for keratin
D. Molecular marker of clonality

Q.220 In an outbreak of cholera in a village of 2000 population 20 cases have occurred and 5 have died. Case fatality rate is:

A. 1% B. 0.25% C. 5% D. 25%

Q.221 In sleep apnea syndrome, select the most likely sleep disturbance -

A. Most common cause of excessive daytime sleepiness in the elderly
B. Increased arousals during the night
C. Breakdown of normal temporal organization of sleep-wake cycling
D. Increased slow-wave sleep

Q.222 Montenegro test is done in:

A. Tetanus B. Trachoma
C. Kala azar D. AIDS

Q.223 A 35 year old woman develops hirsutism, deepening of voice and clitorimegaly. A pelvic examination reveals a left ovarian mass. Assuming appropriate diagnostic and staging tests are performed, given this clinical presentation, if the patient requires chemotherapy she should be treated in a fashion analogous to the management of

A. Epithelial ovarian cancer
B. Lymphoma
C. Soft tissue sarcoma
D. Testicular cancer

Q.224 90 percent sensitivity indicates :

A. 90 percent diseased people will give true positive results
B. Detection of positivity cases not in disease
C. It identify correctly those who have not in disease
D. None of the above

Q.225 A 75-year-old man was admitted to the hospital for hip replacement. Which of the following antibiotics would be an appropriate prophylactic agent to be given before surgery?

A. Metronidazole B. Tetracycline
C. Aztreonam D. Cefazolin

Q.226 False statement regarding conduct money

A. It is paid in civil cases
B. It is not paid in criminal cases
C. It is paid in both civil & criminal cases
D. None of the above

Q.227 Leishmania recidivans is seen in infection with:

A. L donovani B. L tropica
C. L braziliensis D. L mexicana

Q.228 Herniation of brain tissue with its dural covering into the nasal cavity is called as:

A. Glioma
B. Neurofibroma
C. Encephalocele
D. Olfactory neuroblastoma

Q.229 In a patient of colon cancer, recurrent perirectal masses compress the pelvic splanchnic nerves. This could affect the organs supplied by which of the following arteries?

A. Right colic artery B. Left colic artery
C. Renal arteries D. Lumbar arteries

Q.230 Conjugated hyperbilirubinemia is seen in

A. Criggler Najjar Syndrome-I
B. Criggler Najjar Syndrome-II
C. Gilbert syndrome
D. Dubin Johnson syndrome

Q.231 A 13-year-old boy is brought to the hospital by his mother after experiencing fever, malaise, and anorexia followed by tender swelling of his parotid glands. Which of the following is the most likely complication to occur in this patient?

A. Myocarditis
B. Orchitis
C. Oophoritis
D. Guillain-Barré syndrome

Q.232 A large retained stone impacted in the distal common bile duct is noted when T-tube cholangiography is performed after choledochostomy. The best management of the stone is :

A. Dissolution with sodium cholate
B. Dissolution with heparin
C. Catheter extraction via the tract of the T-tube
D. Transduodenal papillotomy with endoscopic stone extraction

Q.233 The drug of choice for hypoplastic left heart syndrome is

A. Digoxin B. Prostaglandin E1
C. Milrinone D. Nicardipine

Q.234 The following are imaging features of Renal lymphangiectasia :

A. Renal sinus and perinephric complex cysts seen
B. Kidneys show accentuation of cortico-medullary differentiation
C. Kidneys are usually small
D. Cysts are fluid density on CT scan

Q.235 A 19 year old patient develops intussusception. He was operated and a segment of intestine showing multiple polyps was resected. On the basis of following pathological images, what is the likely diagnosis?

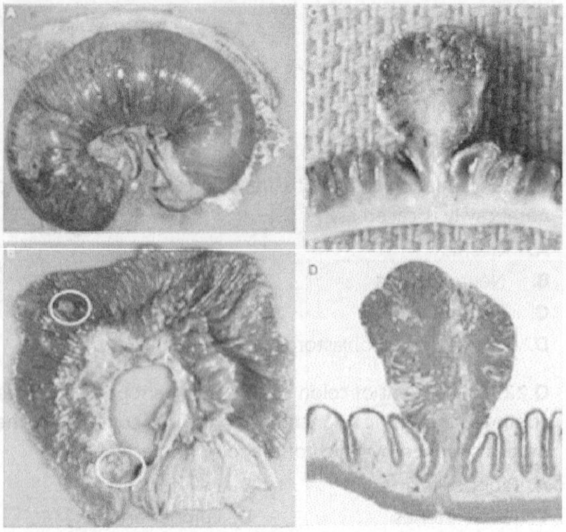

A. Adenocarcinoma
B. Tubulovilluus polyps
C. Hamartomatous polyps
D. Inflammatory polyps

Q.236 A 33-year-old woman, otherwise perfectly well, presents with recurrent episodes of hemoptysis, cough and infection. Her physical examination and lab tests are entirely normal. Which of the following is the most appropriate initial diagnostic test?

A. Gallium scan
B. CT scan of chest
C. Bronchoscopy
D. Pulmonary function tests

Q.237 During intubation of newborn to insert endotracheal tube the blade of laryngoscope is :

A. Curved blade with uncuffed tube
B. Straight blade with Cuffed tube
C. Straight blade with Uncuffed tube
D. Curved blade with cuffed tube

Q.238 Therapeutic gamma irradiation is given to a 50-year-old woman for treatment of a breast carcinoma. The treatments occur over 6 weeks. The neoplasm diminishes in size during this time. Which of the following mechanisms of cellular injury is most likely to account for the efficacy of this radiation therapy?

A. Hyperthermia
B. NK cell lysis
C. Free radical formation
D. Vascular thrombosis

Q.239 Pentameric antibody with a J chain is?

A. IgA **B.** IgG **C.** IgM **D.** IgE

Q.240 Main early complication of TIPSS is :-

A. Perforation of liver capsule
B. Hepatic encephalopathy
C. Shunt stenosis
D. None of the above

Q.241 Vidian neurectomy is done in:

A. Vasomotor rhinitis **B.** Rhinintis sicca
C. Allergic sinusitis **D.** Epistaxis

Q.242 Which of the following conditions is considered an AIDS defining illness?

A. Antibodies to HIV
B. Kaposi sarcoma
C. Oral candidiasis (thrush)
D. Herpes zoster (shingles)

Q.243 Which of the following is the most common presentation of hemophilia A ?

A. Pressure neuropathy **B.** Melera
C. Hematuria **D.** Hemarthrosis

Q.244 True regarding stratified sampling is

A. It is used for hidden population
B. In this method population under study is first divided into homogeneous groups
C. It is used when units of population are natural groups or clusters
D. In this method sampling procedure is carried out in several stages

Q.245 True about Cryoprecipitate?

A. Is prepared by thawing fresh frozen plasma
B. Is rich in fibrinogen
C. May reverse the platelet defect in uremic patients
D. All of the above

Q.246 Which of the following tests is most sensitive for the diagnosis of a pituitary adenoma?

A. Serum prolactin measurement
B. Visual field examination
C. CT scan with contrast injection
D. MRI with gadolinium injection

Q.247 R. Rickettsii causes:

A. Indian tick typhus
B. Rocky mountain spotted fever
C. Rickettsial pox
D. Trench fever

Q.248 Penicillinase resistant pencillin are all except

A. Dicloxacillin **B.** Oxacillin
C. Nafcillin **D.** Ampicillin

Q.249 Which of the following morphologic features is most likely to be present in the liver of a 50-year-old man with a history of chronic alcoholism, but has stopped drinking alcohol 10 years ago and has 35% hematocrit?

A. Concentric "onion-skin" bile duct fibrosis
B. Massive hepatocellular necrosis
C. Periportal PAS-positive globule deposition
D. Portal fibrosis with regenerative nodules

Q.250 A 56 year old woman present with hypertension, anxiety and depression was found to have an adrenal mass when being screened for an abdominal aortic aneurysm. Her 9 am cortisol was 565 nmo/L, 24-hour urine cortisol was normal and 24-hour urine catecholamines were elevated. Most Likely diagnosis is

A. Carcinoid syndrome
B. Conn's syndrome

C. Phaeochromocytoma
D. Metastatic liver disease

Q.251 Heart with the characteristic shape shown in the radiograph is found in?

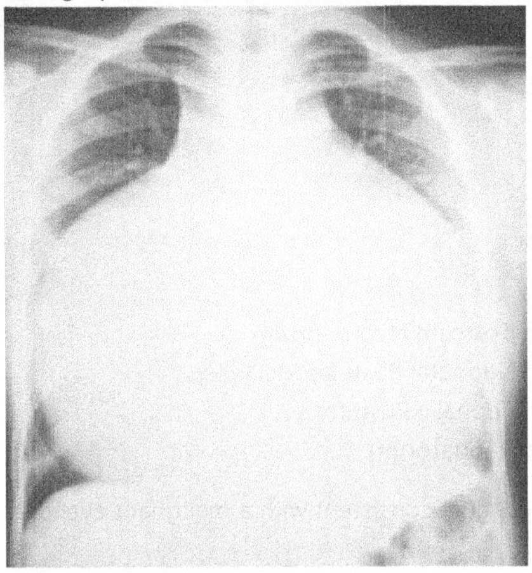

A. Ebstein anomaly **B.** Truncus arteriosus
C. TOF **D.** D-TGA

Q.252 Severity of the disease best assessed by:
A. Disease-specific mortality rate
B. Crude death rate
C. Age-specific mortality rate
D. Case fatality rate

Q.253 The method of female sterilization shown in the figure is known as

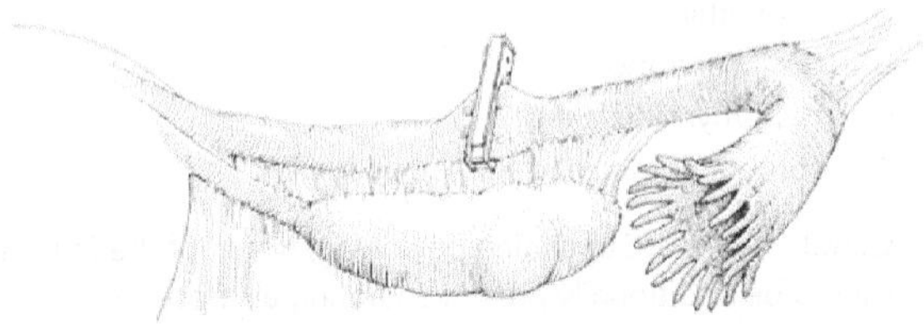

A. Hulka Method **B.** Pomeroy Technique
C. Parkland Method **D.** Adiana procedure

Q.254 Osteomalacia can be prevented by the administration of calcium and :
A. Vitamin A **B.** Vitamin B
C. Vitamin C **D.** Vitamin D

Q.255 Pandemics are caused by:
A. Hepatitis B **B.** Influenza - A
C. Influenza - B **D.** Influenza - C

Q.256 What is the preferred method to diagnose the infection with Chlamydia trachomatis?
A. Nucleic acid amplification
B. Cell culture
C. Cytology (Pap smear)
D. Serology

Q.257 The following sign is least likely to present with which of the following

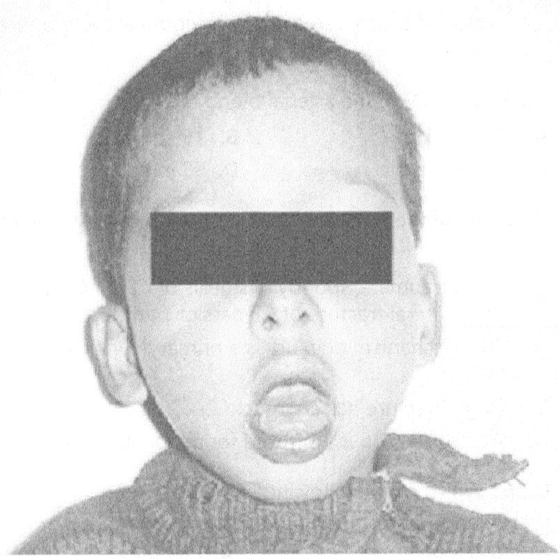

A. Severe anemia with PDA
B. Congenital heart disease
C. Bronchospasm
D. Empysema

Q.258 The commonest site for rheumatoid nodules is :
A. Olecranon process
B. Tendo - Achilles
C. Proximal interphalangeal joints
D. Distal interphalangeal joints

Q.259 What is FALSE about the instrument shown in the image?

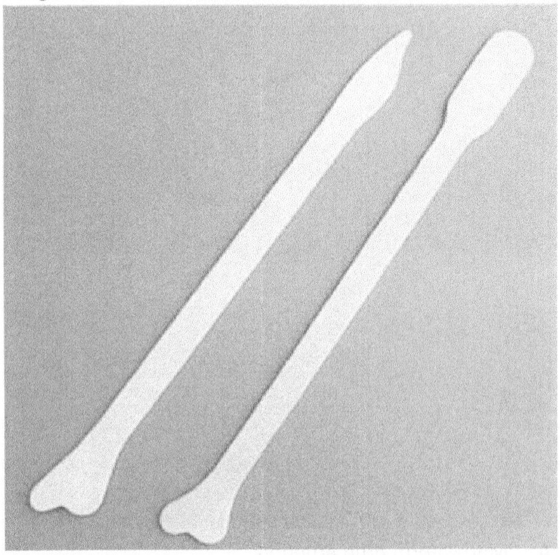

A. Ayre spatula
B. Wooden spatula
C. Long end inserted into cervical canal
D. Primary prevention for cervical cancer

Q.260 Which of the following are incorrectly paired?
A. Lesion of the parietal lobe of the representational hemisphere: unilateral inattention and neglect
B. Lesions of mamillary bodies: loss of recent memory
C. Lesion of the angular gyrus in the categorical hemisphere: nonfluent aphasia

D. Lesion of Broca's area in the categorical hemisphere: slow speech

Q.261 The PO_2 of the arterial blood is

A. 104 mm Hg B. 159 mm Hg
C. 40 mm Hg D. 95 mm Hg

Q.262 All of the following are true for hangman's fracture except?

A. It is a traumatic spondylolisthesis of C2 on C3 as a result of the bilateral fracture of C2 pars or pedicles.
B. The mechanism of injury is a primary hyperflexion of the neck.
C. Type I fracture has an intact C2/C3 disc.
D. A C2/C3 fusion is indicated for a type III fracture.

Q.263 Which of the following is the least likely first clinical presentation of respiratory distress syndrome?

A. Tachypnea B. Cyanosis
C. Wheezing D. Pallor

Q.264 A 36-year-old man receives amoxicillin for presumed bacterial sinusitis. One week later he presents with a diffuse itchy rash. His mucus membranes are normal. Which of the following is the most likely diagnosis?

A. Morbilliform drug eruption
B. Stevens-Johnson syndrome
C. Toxic shock syndrome
D. Urticaria

Q.265 A 12-year-old boy has multiple skin lesions that are diagnosed as von Recklinghausen's syndrome (NF-1). What is TRUE of this condition?

A. It does not show other malignant lesions.
B. It is autosomal recessive.
C. It is associated with optic nerve gliomas.
D. It is characterized by atrioventricular (AV) malformation.

Q.266 The given skin condition (image) present at birth in an infant is most likely

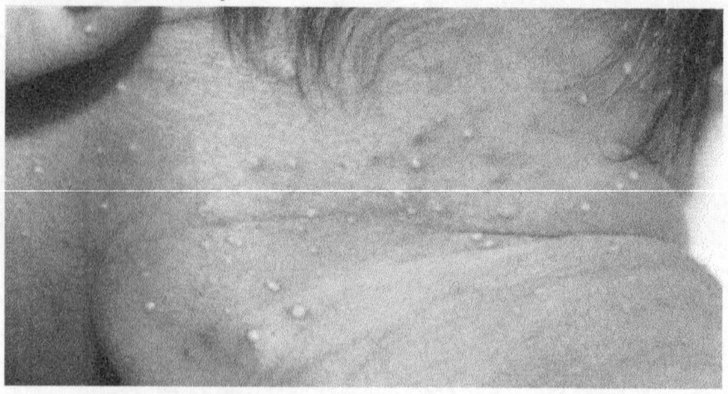

A. Erythema Toxicum Neonatorum
B. Transient Neonatal Pustular Melanosis
C. Neonatal Cephalic Pustulosis
D. Sclerema Neonatorum

Q.267 Features most consistent with a malignant eyelid lesion include:

A. Tenderness, erythema, alteration in pigment pattern
B. Disruption of tarsal architecture, raised pearly margins, pruritus
C. Lash loss, central ulceration, rapid growth
D. Ipsilateral lymph node metastasis, hyperkeratosis, dark pigmentation

Q.268 A 9-year-old girl presents for evaluation of regular vaginal bleeding. History reveals thelarche at age 7 and adrenarche at age 8. Which of the following is the most common cause of this condition in girls?

A. Idiopathic
B. Gonadal tumors
C. Hypothyroidism
D. Tumors of the central nervous system

Q.269 In case of Strychnine poisoning, which of the following should be additionally preserved during autopsy?

A. CSF B. Lung
C. Spinal cord D. Vitreous humor

Q.270 Chicken pox is infective

A. 2 days before and 2 days after rash appearance
B. 2 days before and 5 days after rash appearance
C. 4 days before and 4 days after rash appearance
D. 4 days before and 5 days after rash appearance

Q.271 Cocks peculiar tumor is:

A. Papilloma
B. Infected sebaceous cyst
C. Cylindroma
D. Squamous cell Ca

Q.272 Adverse effects of diphenhydramine can include all of the following except:

A. Dry mouth B. Blurred vision
C. Bradycardia D. Sedation

Q.273 You find a discrete, whitish polyp that extends through the tympanic membrane in a child with a history of recurrent otitis media. This most likely represents which of the following?

A. A cholesteatoma
B. Tympanosclerosis
C. Acute otitis media with perforation and drainage
D. Dislocation of the malleus from its insertion in the tympanic membrane

Q.274 The venom produced by the snake shown in the image is used to make which of the following drugs

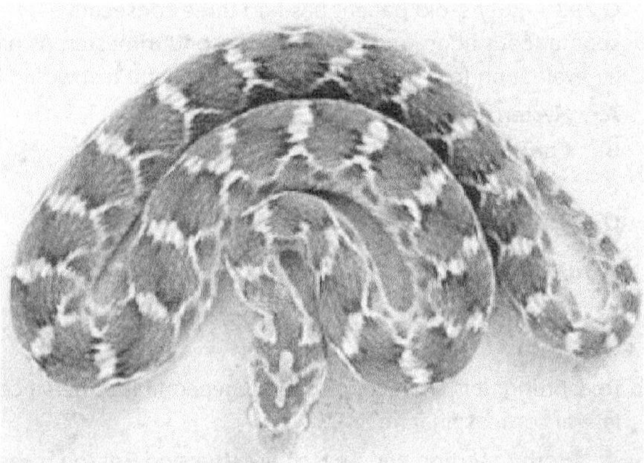

A. Analgesics **B.** Anticoagulant drugs
C. Antimicrobial drugs **D.** Anti-cancer drugs

Q.275 In relation to pregnant women with epilepsy, which of the following statements is incorrect?

A. The rate of congenital malformation is increased in the offspring of women with epilepsy
B. Seizure frequency increases in approximately 70% of women
C. Breastfeeding is safe with most anticonvulsants
D. Folic acid supplementation may reduce the risk of neural tube defect

Q.276 In the physical test illustrated below, the patient is asked to touch his buttocks with his heel while working against resistance. Which muscle group is being tested?

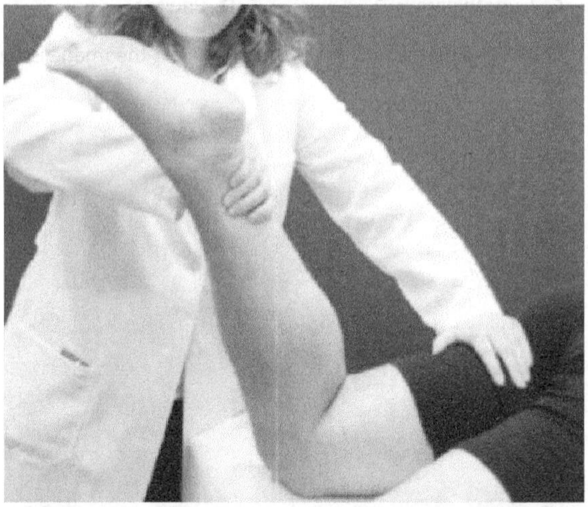

A. Quadriceps femoris **B.** Hamstrings
C. Adductors **D.** Triceps surae

Q.277 An 11-year-old child develops glomerulonephritis a week after he was treated for a sore throat. The causal agent is identified by serotyping of the

A. Capsule
B. M proteins
C. Outer membrane proteins
D. Pili

Q.278 Which of the following is an epimeric pair?

A. Glucose and fructose
B. Glucose and galactose
C. Galactose and mannose
D. Lactose and maltose

Q.279 Which of the following nerve palsy is responsible for the deformity as shown in the image?

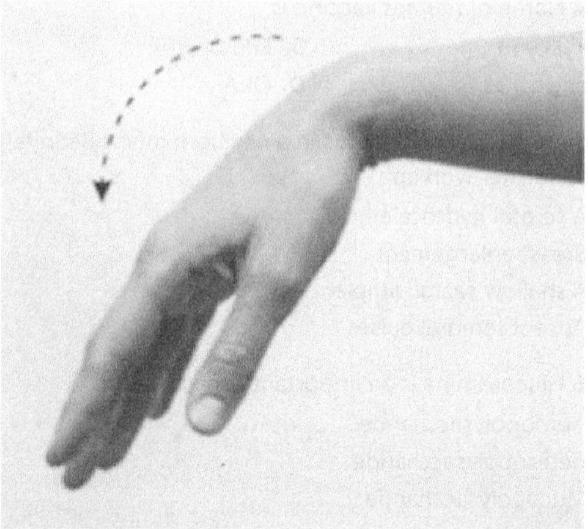

A. Ulnar nerve
B. Radial nerve
C. Musculocutaneous nerve
D. Median nerve

Q.280 A 6-month-old child has an iris lesion and recurrent anterior chamber bleeding. A biopsy of this mass was performed. A high-magnification image of the histology is shown in the figure. Which statement is correct?

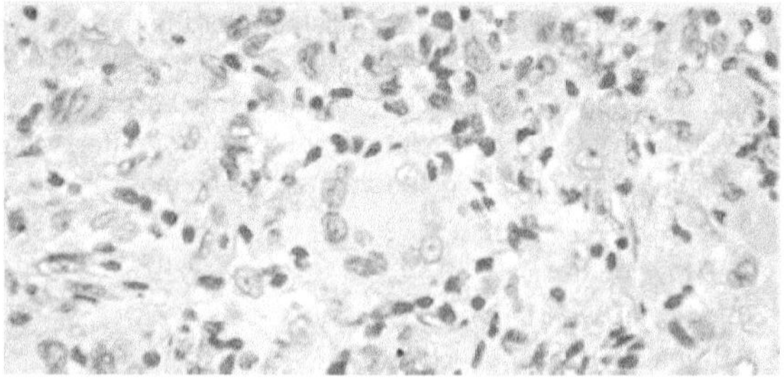

A. The lesion shows pleomorphic cells with a multinucleated tumor cell.
B. This is a benign cutaneous disorder rarely involving the eye.
C. Immunohistochemical stains for macrophages (histiocytes) are negative.
D. Most ocular lesions occur after 1 year of age in this disease entity.

Q.281 What is the mechanism of action of amiodarone?

A. It is a β-receptor antagonist
B. It decreases refractoriness
C. It interferes with outward potassium current
D. It has a relatively short half-life

Q.282 The following is true about prevalence and incidence:

A. Both are rates
B. Prevalence is a rate but incidence is not
C. Incidence is a rate but prevalence is not
D. Both are not rates

Q.283 In the treatment of hydatid cyst PAIR is contraindicated in -
A. Lung cyst
B. Size more than 5 cm
C. Not amenable to treatment with albendazole
D. Multiple cysts

Q.284 Name of mumps vaccine is:
A. Jeryl Lynn B. Edmonston
C. Danish 1331 D. OKA

Q.285 The following findings in a newborn infant definitely require further workup :
A. A scrotal hydrocele
B. Breast enlargement
C. A shallow sacral dimple
D. Absent femoral pulses

Q.286 Glucosamine is an important constituent of
A. Homopolysaccharide
B. Heteropolysaccharide
C. Mucopolysaccharide
D. Dextran

Q.287 True regarding Tolazoline are all except
A. It is a competitive α-adrenergic receptor antagonist
B. It is more potent than phentolamine
C. It is a direct peripheral vasodilator
D. It can be used in the treatment of persistent pulmonary hypertension in newborns

Q.288 A 51-year-old man with increasing abdominal discomfort and abdominal enlargement for the past two years is found to have massive (estimated 3000 gm size) splenomegaly. Laboratory data include Hgb 9 g/dL, WBC count 5,000/microliter, and platelet count 50,000/microliter. Which of the following underlying conditions does he most likely to have?
A. Myelofibrosis
B. Portal hypertension
C. Infectious mononucleosis
D. Hemochromatosis

Q.289 Human leukocyte antigen B27 is associated with all except
A. Anterior uveitis
B. Systemic lupus erythematosus
C. Ankylosing spondylitis
D. Reactive arthritis

Q.290 Phase-4 depolarization of SA nodal cells is caused by which of the following -
A. An increase in the flow of sodium into the cell
B. A decrease in the flow of potassium out of the cell
C. An increase in activity of Na/Ca exchanger
D. A decrease in flow of chloride out of the cell

Q.291 Oral contraceptive of choice in a patient of epilepsy is:
A. Ultra low dose B. Low dose
C. Standard dose D. Sequential

Q.292 Drug not metabolized by liver is :
A. Penicillin G B. Phenytoin
C. Erythromycin D. Rifampicin

Q.293 A 26-yrs-old patient has had three consecutive spontaneous abortions early in the second trimester. As part of an evaluation for this problem, the least useful test would be:
A. Hysterosalpinogram
B. Chromosomal analysis of the couple
C. Endometrial biopsy in the luteal phase
D. Postcoital test

Q.294 Regarding Werdnig Hoffman syndrome
Assertion: The spinal muscular atrophies lead to muscle weakness
Reasoning: It is characterized by degeneration of nerve cells in lateral corticospinal tract
A. Both Assertion and Reason are true, and Reason is the correct explanation for Assertion
B. Both Assertion and Reason are true but Reason is not the correct explanation for Assertion
C. Assertion is true but Reason is false
D. Reason is true but Assertion is false

Q.295 Modified acid-fast stain is used for the diagnosis of
A. Entamoeba histolytica
B. Toxoplasma gondii
C. Cryptosporidium parvum
D. Leishmania donovani

Q.296 Neuroendocrine pathways of the stress response consist of the following except:
A. Spinal cord B. Thyroid
C. Hypothalamus D. Pituitary

Q.297 The epithelium tissue type shown in the image is found in

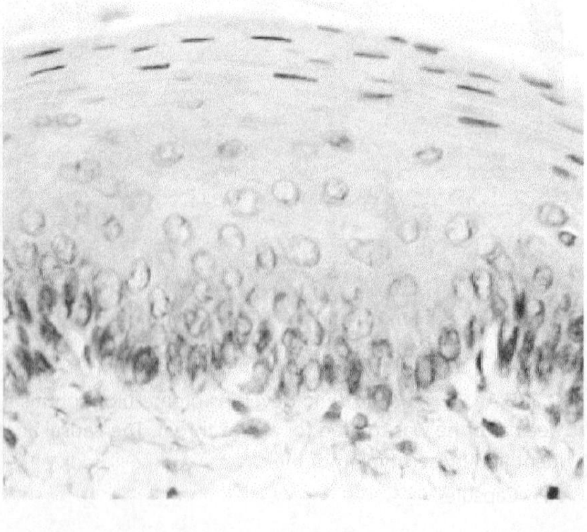

A. Mammary glands
B. Lining of small intestine
C. Inner lining of esophagus
D. Unicellular exocrine gland

Q.298 X-ray of a 47 year old patient presenting with pain and palpable mass in the femur is shown. The solitary tumor is seen with endosteal scalloping and presence of punctate calcification. The most likely diagnosis is

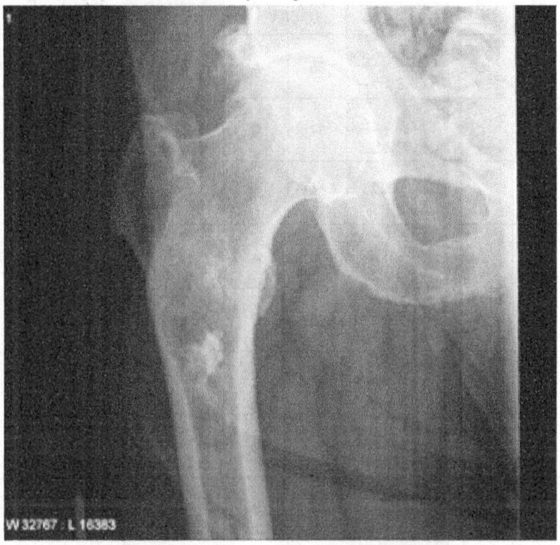

A. Osteosarcoma **B.** Chondrosarcoma
C. Osteopetrosis **D.** Fibrous dysplasia

Q.299 In Benign positional vertigo, semicircular canal involved is:

A. Anterior **B.** Lateral **C.** Posterior **D.** Superior

Q.300 A 25-year-old man complains of 2 weeks of small volume loose, bloody stool. He has urgency to move his bowels. He occasionally has crampy abdominal pain. Barium enema finding is shown below. What is your diagnosis?

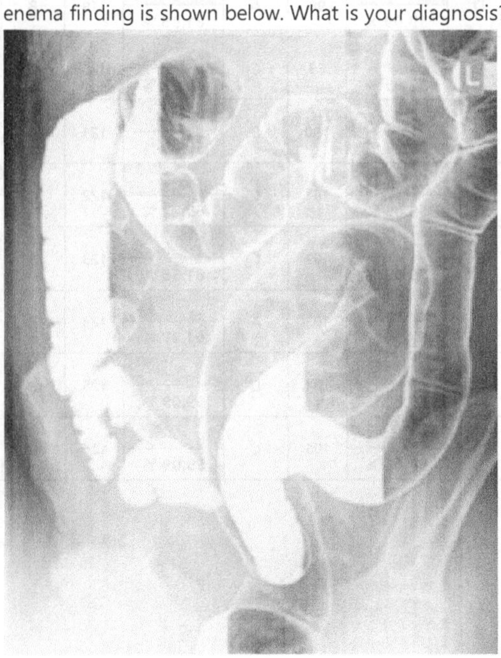

A. Diverticulosis
B. Crohn's disease
C. Ulcerative colitis
D. Irritable Bowel Syndrome

// Smart Answer Sheet //

Correct — Percentage of students who answered correctly. Skipped — Percentage of students who skipped.

Q.	Ans.	Correct	Skipped	Q.	Ans.	Correct	Skipped	Q.	Ans.	Correct	Skipped	Q.	Ans.	Correct	Skipped	Q.	Ans.	Correct	Skipped	Q.	Ans.	Correct	Skipped
1	C	13.64 %	19.31 %	22	B	22.73 %	47.72 %	43	C	20.45 %	51.14 %	64	B	17.05 %	57.95 %	85	A	26.14 %	60.22 %	106	C	15.91 %	61.36 %
2	C	37.5 %	46.59 %	23	B	5.68 %	54.55 %	44	D	12.5 %	52.27 %	65	D	14.77 %	60.23 %	86	A	21.59 %	57.96 %	107	A	12.5 %	59.09 %
3	C	27.27 %	51.14 %	24	C	14.77 %	47.73 %	45	D	11.36 %	54.55 %	66	C	10.23 %	60.22 %	87	B	13.64 %	59.09 %	108	B	13.64 %	62.5 %
4	A	21.59 %	48.86 %	25	A	20.45 %	52.28 %	46	B	26.14 %	48.86 %	67	A	13.64 %	60.22 %	88	A	23.86 %	59.09 %	109	D	32.95 %	59.1 %
5	D	26.14 %	50.0 %	26	D	17.05 %	55.68 %	47	D	29.55 %	52.27 %	68	A	9.09 %	61.36 %	89	A	13.64 %	61.36 %	110	D	12.5 %	62.5 %
6	B	22.73 %	54.54 %	27	A	40.91 %	51.14 %	48	D	13.64 %	53.41 %	69	A	20.45 %	60.23 %	90	C	19.32 %	60.23 %	111	D	13.64 %	59.09 %
7	B	35.23 %	51.13 %	28	B	19.32 %	47.73 %	49	B	36.36 %	51.14 %	70	D	34.09 %	54.55 %	91	C	10.23 %	60.22 %	112	B	11.36 %	61.37 %
8	A	36.36 %	51.14 %	29	D	36.36 %	52.28 %	50	D	21.59 %	53.41 %	71	A	13.64 %	59.09 %	92	D	14.77 %	57.96 %	113	A	29.55 %	60.22 %
9	D	22.73 %	51.13 %	30	C	25.0 %	51.14 %	51	B	23.86 %	59.09 %	72	D	27.27 %	57.96 %	93	D	26.14 %	59.09 %	114	A	7.95 %	60.23 %
10	C	25.0 %	53.41 %	31	A	27.27 %	51.14 %	52	C	23.86 %	56.82 %	73	B	14.77 %	59.09 %	94	C	21.59 %	57.96 %	115	B	17.05 %	60.22 %
11	C	23.86 %	51.14 %	32	B	22.73 %	50.0 %	53	C	11.36 %	60.23 %	74	D	31.82 %	55.68 %	95	D	26.14 %	59.09 %	116	B	14.77 %	62.5 %
12	D	22.73 %	50.0 %	33	B	25.0 %	50.0 %	54	C	20.45 %	57.96 %	75	A	20.45 %	59.1 %	96	A	30.68 %	57.96 %	117	C	12.5 %	60.23 %
13	C	14.77 %	51.14 %	34	D	32.95 %	47.73 %	55	B	23.86 %	59.09 %	76	C	10.23 %	59.09 %	97	D	12.5 %	60.23 %	118	A	11.36 %	62.5 %
14	A	42.05 %	47.72 %	35	B	18.18 %	53.41 %	56	A	28.41 %	59.09 %	77	D	11.36 %	59.09 %	98	A	13.64 %	61.36 %	119	B	14.77 %	62.5 %
15	A	22.73 %	51.13 %	36	C	34.09 %	50.0 %	57	C	12.5 %	60.23 %	78	D	22.73 %	57.95 %	99	C	5.68 %	60.23 %	120	B	10.23 %	62.5 %
16	C	32.95 %	50.0 %	37	D	13.64 %	51.13 %	58	A	21.59 %	59.09 %	79	A	5.68 %	60.23 %	100	B	19.32 %	59.09 %	121	B	23.86 %	57.96 %
17	A	31.82 %	50.0 %	38	C	28.41 %	52.27 %	59	A	10.23 %	61.36 %	80	D	6.82 %	59.09 %	101	C	35.23 %	60.22 %	122	C	11.36 %	56.82 %
18	A	10.23 %	52.27 %	39	C	34.09 %	51.14 %	60	B	14.77 %	59.09 %	81	C	15.91 %	59.09 %	102	C	6.82 %	61.36 %	123	A	17.05 %	57.95 %
19	C	19.32 %	48.86 %	40	C	20.45 %	54.55 %	61	A	25.0 %	60.23 %	82	B	20.45 %	57.96 %	103	A	14.77 %	61.37 %	124	B	28.41 %	59.09 %
20	A	45.45 %	38.64 %	41	B	26.14 %	55.68 %	62	C	12.5 %	59.09 %	83	C	17.05 %	59.09 %	104	D	19.32 %	59.09 %	125	B	15.91 %	60.23 %
21	A	21.59 %	48.86 %	42	C	11.36 %	51.14 %	63	A	22.73 %	60.22 %	84	D	14.77 %	55.68 %	105	C	10.23 %	59.09 %	126	B	12.5 %	61.36 %

Q.	Ans.	Correct	Skipped	Q.	Ans.	Correct	Skipped	Q.	Ans.	Correct	Skipped	Q.	Ans.	Correct	Skipped	Q.	Ans.	Correct	Skipped	Q.	Ans.	Correct	Skipped
127	D	7.95 %	61.37 %	148	C	28.41 %	60.23 %	169	C	27.27 %	60.23 %	190	A	10.23 %	63.63 %	211	B	21.59 %	64.77 %	232	D	17.05 %	59.09 %
128	C	28.41 %	60.23 %	149	B	19.32 %	61.36 %	170	C	17.05 %	60.22 %	191	C	13.64 %	61.36 %	212	C	23.86 %	62.5 %	233	B	13.64 %	63.63 %
129	C	5.68 %	61.37 %	150	A	23.86 %	59.09 %	171	A	5.68 %	59.09 %	192	A	13.64 %	62.5 %	213	A	35.23 %	61.36 %	234	D	5.68 %	63.64 %
130	C	10.23 %	59.09 %	151	A	25.0 %	59.09 %	172	B	3.41 %	62.5 %	193	C	20.45 %	61.37 %	214	D	4.55 %	63.63 %	235	C	18.18 %	62.5 %
131	C	18.18 %	57.96 %	152	B	26.14 %	59.09 %	173	B	21.59 %	61.36 %	194	D	11.36 %	63.64 %	215	B	17.05 %	63.63 %	236	B	18.18 %	61.37 %
132	D	19.32 %	57.95 %	153	A	18.18 %	61.37 %	174	C	27.27 %	60.23 %	195	D	15.91 %	61.36 %	216	B	19.32 %	61.36 %	237	C	15.91 %	62.5 %
133	C	5.68 %	63.64 %	154	B	15.91 %	62.5 %	175	C	22.73 %	62.5 %	196	A	14.77 %	59.09 %	217	D	6.82 %	61.36 %	238	C	13.64 %	61.36 %
134	D	28.41 %	59.09 %	155	D	14.77 %	63.64 %	176	C	15.91 %	61.36 %	197	C	11.36 %	61.37 %	218	A	9.09 %	63.64 %	239	C	21.59 %	63.64 %
135	C	10.23 %	60.22 %	156	A	14.77 %	61.37 %	177	C	19.32 %	61.36 %	198	B	11.36 %	61.37 %	219	D	2.27 %	64.78 %	240	A	9.09 %	61.36 %
136	A	18.18 %	59.09 %	157	B	23.86 %	61.37 %	178	C	9.09 %	63.64 %	199	B	25.0 %	63.64 %	220	D	26.14 %	61.36 %	241	A	27.27 %	62.5 %
137	D	5.68 %	60.23 %	158	C	9.09 %	62.5 %	179	C	13.64 %	61.36 %	200	A	5.68 %	61.37 %	221	A	18.18 %	62.5 %	242	B	25.0 %	62.5 %
138	D	18.18 %	60.23 %	159	B	9.09 %	64.77 %	180	D	30.68 %	59.09 %	201	B	9.09 %	62.5 %	222	C	21.59 %	61.36 %	243	D	22.73 %	61.36 %
139	B	19.32 %	59.09 %	160	A	27.27 %	61.37 %	181	C	14.77 %	61.37 %	202	B	27.27 %	59.09 %	223	D	14.77 %	61.37 %	244	B	10.23 %	62.5 %
140	B	12.5 %	60.23 %	161	D	14.77 %	61.37 %	182	D	6.82 %	62.5 %	203	B	27.27 %	61.37 %	224	A	27.27 %	61.37 %	245	D	25.0 %	61.36 %
141	A	23.86 %	61.37 %	162	B	18.18 %	59.09 %	183	A	21.59 %	59.09 %	204	A	5.68 %	64.77 %	225	D	18.18 %	62.5 %	246	D	19.32 %	60.23 %
142	B	14.77 %	61.37 %	163	D	18.18 %	61.37 %	184	D	17.05 %	60.22 %	205	A	12.5 %	61.36 %	226	C	21.59 %	63.64 %	247	B	28.41 %	62.5 %
143	B	7.95 %	60.23 %	164	C	19.32 %	59.09 %	185	A	15.91 %	63.64 %	206	C	6.82 %	62.5 %	227	A	12.5 %	63.64 %	248	D	21.59 %	61.36 %
144	D	18.18 %	57.96 %	165	A	22.73 %	61.36 %	186	C	17.05 %	61.36 %	207	D	11.36 %	63.64 %	228	C	23.86 %	61.37 %	249	D	15.91 %	61.36 %
145	B	18.18 %	59.09 %	166	B	17.05 %	61.36 %	187	B	20.45 %	60.23 %	208	B	19.32 %	62.5 %	229	B	13.64 %	62.5 %	250	C	28.41 %	60.23 %
146	C	28.41 %	59.09 %	167	A	19.32 %	63.63 %	188	B	10.23 %	62.5 %	209	D	10.23 %	60.22 %	230	D	25.0 %	59.09 %	251	A	15.91 %	61.36 %
147	D	7.95 %	61.37 %	168	D	9.09 %	62.5 %	189	B	22.73 %	62.5 %	210	A	20.45 %	60.23 %	231	B	25.0 %	59.09 %	252	D	23.86 %	61.37 %

Q.	Ans.	Correct	Skipped	Q.	Ans.	Correct	Skipped	Q.	Ans.	Correct	Skipped	Q.	Ans.	Correct	Skipped	Q.	Ans.	Correct	Skipped	Q.	Ans.	Correct	Skipped
253	A	11.36 %	62.5 %	261	D	18.18 %	61.37 %	269	C	18.18 %	62.5 %	277	B	22.73 %	61.36 %	285	D	22.73 %	61.36 %	293	D	14.77 %	61.37 %
254	D	35.23 %	61.36 %	262	B	10.23 %	62.5 %	270	B	22.73 %	59.09 %	278	B	18.18 %	60.23 %	286	C	23.86 %	61.37 %	294	C	10.23 %	63.63 %
255	B	25.0 %	62.5 %	263	C	10.23 %	61.36 %	271	B	27.27 %	60.23 %	279	B	27.27 %	62.5 %	287	B	5.68 %	63.64 %	295	C	21.59 %	62.5 %
256	A	14.77 %	62.5 %	264	A	27.27 %	60.23 %	272	C	18.18 %	61.37 %	280	B	3.41 %	61.36 %	288	A	15.91 %	60.23 %	296	B	11.36 %	59.09 %
257	A	15.91 %	61.36 %	265	C	15.91 %	61.36 %	273	A	17.05 %	61.36 %	281	C	14.77 %	61.37 %	289	B	19.32 %	62.5 %	297	C	9.09 %	62.5 %
258	A	13.64 %	60.22 %	266	B	18.18 %	62.5 %	274	B	30.68 %	61.37 %	282	C	19.32 %	61.36 %	290	A	6.82 %	62.5 %	298	B	19.32 %	60.23 %
259	D	11.36 %	61.37 %	267	C	11.36 %	62.5 %	275	B	10.23 %	63.63 %	283	A	10.23 %	61.36 %	291	C	14.77 %	61.37 %	299	C	15.91 %	61.36 %
260	C	6.82 %	62.5 %	268	A	25.0 %	59.09 %	276	B	27.27 %	61.37 %	284	A	20.45 %	62.5 %	292	A	15.91 %	59.09 %	300	C	19.32 %	61.36 %

//Hints and Solutions//

1. The activation of tyrosine kinase receptors often results in a cellular response that is involved in growth or differentiation. Tyrosine kinase receptors do not have constitutively active receptors; if this were true, there could be no regulation of signaling.

The activation of ras occurs indirectly by the activation of adapter molecules (Grb2 and SOS) that associate with phosphorylated tyrosine residues in the cytoplasmic tail of the receptor. The activation of tyrosine kinase receptors usually involves multimerization into dimers or trimers.
Hence, the correct option is (C).

2. Physiological anemia of pregnancy is due to Disproportionate increase in plasma volume. The increase in the plasma is not matched by an equivalent increase in red cell mass, therefore maternal haematocrit usually decreases resulting in physiological anemia of pregnancy.
Hence, the correct option is (C).

3. Strawberry tongue (or raspberry tongue) is a distinctive enanthem of the dorsum of the tongue characterized by the prominence of inflamed and hypertrophic fungiform papillae together with hyperemia. While it is a diagnostic feature of disorders such as Kawasaki disease and scarlet fever, it can also be seen in various other conditions when it serves as a useful diagnostic indicator.

The topographic alteration leading to strawberry appearance of the tongue is possibly the desquamation of the keratinized epithelium of the filiform papillae. This gives a red denuded appearance to the surface that is interspersed with persistent, inflamed and hypertrophic fungiform papillae (seeds of strawberry). In certain conditions such as scarlet fever, the prominent papillae are initially covered by a white coating giving a "white strawberry" appearance to the tongue. This coating desquamates in a few days giving rise to the typical "red strawberry" tongue.

Most disorders exhibiting strawberry tongue are bacterial toxin-mediated disorders. The bacterial toxins act as superantigens and provoke a nonspecific polyclonal immune cell activation and massive release of inflammatory mediators. Consequently, most of these are multisystem disorders. However, certain other conditions are also associated with this unique morphological alteration.
Hence, the correct option is (C).

4. Inflammatory breast cancer is a very aggressive form of breast cancer characterized by intradermal lymphatic spread of tumor. This type of breast cancer is called "inflammatory" because the breast often looks swollen and red, or inflamed.

Symptoms of inflammatory breast cancer include swelling (edema) and redness (erythema) that affect part of third or more of the breast. The skin of the breast may also appear pink, reddish purple, or bruised. In addition, the skin may have ridges or appear pitted, like the skin of an orange (called peau d'orange). These symptoms are caused by the buildup of fluid (lymph) in the skin of the breast. This fluid buildup occurs because cancer cells have blocked lymph vessels in the skin, preventing the normal flow of lymph through the tissue. Sometimes the breast may contain a solid tumor that can be felt during a physical exam, but more often a tumor cannot be felt.

Additional features of inflammatory breast cancer include the following:

- Compared with other types of breast cancer, inflammatory breast cancer tends to be diagnosed at younger ages.
- Inflammatory breast cancer is more common and diagnosed at younger ages in African American women than in white women.
- Inflammatory breast tumors are frequently hormone receptor negative, which means they cannot be treated with hormone therapies, such as tamoxifen, that interfere with the growth of cancer cells fueled by estrogen.

Inflammatory breast cancer is more common in obese women than in women of normal weight.
Hence, the correct option is (A).

5. The image demonstrates picture frame vertebra sign.

Paget disease of the bone is a common, chronic bone disorder characterised by excessive abnormal bone remodelling. It frequently affects the pelvis, spine, skull and proximal long bones and has characteristic radiographic features.

The majority (approximately three-quarters) of patients are asymptomatic at the time of diagnosis. Presenting symptoms include:

- Localised pain and tenderness
- Increased focal temperature due to hyperaemia (due to hypervascularity)
- Increased bone size: historically changing hat size was a giveaway
- Bowing deformities
- Kyphosis of the spine
- Decreased the range of motion

Polyostotic disease is more prevalent than the monostotic type 1. The most frequent sites of involvement are:

- Spine
- Pelvis (often asymmetric)
- Skull
- Proximal long bones

Radiographic features

Plain radiograph

The early phase features osteolytic (lucent) region which is later followed by coarsened trabeculae and bony enlargement. Sclerotic changes occur much later in the disease process.

Skull

Osteoporosis circumscripta: large, well-defined lytic lesion

Cotton wool appearance: mixed lytic and sclerotic lesions of the skull

Diploic widening: both inner and outer calvarial tables are involved, with the former usually more extensively affected

Tam o'Shanter sign: frontal bone enlargement, with the appearance of the skull falling over the facial bones, like a Tam o' Shanter hat

Spine

Picture frame sign: Paget disease of the spine frequently manifests with cortical thickening and sclerosis encasing the vertebral margins, which gives rise to this appearance on radiographs in mixed phase disease

Squaring of vertebrae: on lateral radiographs, flattening of the normal concavity of the anterior margin of the vertebral body also adds to the rectangular appearance

Vertical trabecular thickening in Paget disease is coarser than the more delicate pattern seen in intraosseous hemangiomas with which it may be confused

Pelvis

Cortical thickening and sclerosis of the iliopectineal and ischiopubic lines

Acetabular protrusio

Enlargement of the pubic rami and ischium

These findings are often asymmetric, and for some reason, are more commonly seen on the right side.

Long bones

Blade of grass or candle flame sign: begins as a subchondral area of lucency with advancing tip of V-shaped osteolysis, extending towards the diaphysis

In rare cases, the disease is isolated to the diaphysis, most commonly in the tibia, rather than subchondral bone, which can cause diagnostic confusion

Lateral curvature (bowing) of the femur

Anterior curvature of the tibia

Signs

Paget disease related signs include:

Tam o' Shanter sign

Blade of grass sign

Osteoporosis circumscripta

Jigsaw pattern bone or mosaic pattern bone

Picture frame vertebra

Cotton wool appearance of bone

Banana fracture

Looser zones

Ivory vertebra sign

MRI

The overall signal characteristics are variable, likely reflecting the natural course of the disease process in different phases.

Several major patterns of involvement have been described

Dominant signal intensity in pagetic bone similar to that of fat; most common pattern: probably corresponds to the early mixed active phase

Relatively low T1 and high T2 signal alteration (also referred as a "speckled" appearance); second most common pattern: probably corresponds to granulation tissue, hypervascularity, and oedema seen in active disease

Low signal intensity on both T1 and T2 images: suggesting the presence of compact bone or fibrous tissue; least common pattern: seen in late blastic inactive phase

Fatty marrow signal is usually preserved in all sequences unless there is a complication.
Hence, the correct option is (D).

6. When a beam of electromagnetic wave or particulate radiation is directed to the tumor site from a distance (100 Cm) it is called teletherapy or external beamradiotherapy.

Radioisotopes which are commonly used for therapeutic purpose are: Radium 226, Cesium-137, gold-198, iodine-125, Cobalt-60, indium-192. Cobalt-60, is the most preferred agent for teletherapy.
Hence, the correct option is (B).

7. Image: Computed tomogram of a vertebral hemangioma. In cross section, bony trabeculae produce a polka-dot appearance.

The polka-dot sign is the result of the replacement of the normal cancellous bone by thickened vertical trabeculae surrounded by fat marrow or vascular lacunae in vertebral intraosseous haemangiomas 2. It is the axial equivalent of the corduroy sign seen on sagittal and coronal images. On CT the dots are white on black fatty background, whereas or MR they are black dots on white background (on non-fat-suppressed T1 or T2-weighted images).
Hence, the correct option is (B).

8. Sec. 11, 12 and 13 of the Hindu Marriage Act, 1955 deals with grounds for void and voidable marriages, and grounds for divorce respectively.

i. Grounds for void and voidable marriage

a. Void marriage, i.e. null from the time of inception

-Bigamy (another marriage without dissolution of earlier marriage)

-Prohibited degree of relationship (related by blood) unless custom permits such marriage

-Sapinda relationship (relationship extending to 3rd generation in the line of ascent through mother and 5th generation through father).

b. Voidable marriage, i.e. it remains valid until annulled by the court

-Impotence

-Unsoundness of mind of either party at the time of marriage

-Consent of either party was obtained by force, fraud or misconception of facts

-Pregnancy of the female by some other person and the husband was ignorant of the fact at the time of marriage.

ii. Grounds for divorce

-Adultery: Voluntary sexual intercourse with any person other than his/her spouse.

-Cruelty: Willful and unjustifiable conduct so as to cause danger to life, limb, or health of another (including mental health).

-Desertion: Abandonment of one spouse without reasonable cause and without consent or against the wish of other.

-Apostasy: Change of religion.

-Unsoundness of mind.

-Virulent leprosy and sexually transmitted diseases including AIDS.

-Renouncing the world.

-Additional grounds for woman: Husband convicted of rape, sodomy or bestiality.
Hence, the correct option is (A).

9. Depending on the predominance of particular symptoms, four subtypes of schizophrenia are recognized: paranoid, disorganized, catatonic, and residual. The essential characteristics of the disorganized type are disorganized speech and behaviour, flat or inappropriate affect, great functional impairment, and inability to perform basic activities such as showering or preparing meals. Grimacing, silly and odd behaviour and mannerisms are common. Hallucinations and delusions, if present, are fragmented and not organized in a coherent theme. This subtype is associated with poor premorbid functions, early insidious onset, and a progressive course without remissions.
Hence, the correct option is (D).

10. Benzodiazepines that are useful as anticonvulsants have a long half-life, and rapid entry into the brain. It is required for efficacy in treatment of status epilepticus.

A short elimination half-life is desirable for benzodiazepines that are useful as hypnotics, although this carries the drawback of increased abuse liability and severity of withdrawal after drug discontinuation.

Benzodiazepines that are useful as antianxiety agents, in contrast, should have a long half-life despite the drawback of the risk of neuropsychological deficits caused by drug accumulation.
Hence, the correct option is (C).

11. Rectal prolapse in children may be seen after an attack of diarrhea, or from loss of weight and consequent loss of fat in the ischiorectalfossa. It may also be associated with fibrocystic disease.

Its treatment include digital repositioning by parents. If digital repositioning fails after 6 weeks trial, injection of 5% phenol in almond oil is administered to pruceaseptic inflammation, so that mucosa become adhered.

Surgery is reserved for non-responders:

a. Thiersch operation: For prolapse in meninomyelocele and sacral agenesis.

b. Lockhart rectopexy:Simplest and safest in childhood complete prolapse.
Hence, the correct option is (C).

12. Rheumatic fever (RF) produces both acute and chronic manifestations. Chronic RE mainly produces damage to cardiac valves.

The mitral valve is most commonly involved, followed by the aortic valve. The stenotic valve has the appearance of a 'fish mouth' or buttonhole.

Hence, the correct option is (D).

13. Cotard delusion is a rare mental illness in which the affected person holds the delusional belief that they are already dead, do not exist, are putrefying, or have lost their blood or internal organs.

The delusion of negation is the central symptom in Cotard's syndrome. The patient afflicted with this mental illness usually denies their own existence, the existence of a certain body part, or the existence of a portion of their body. Cotard's syndrome exists in three stages: (i) Germination stage—the symptoms of psychotic depression and of hypochondria appear; (ii) Blooming stage—the full development of the syndrome and the delusions of negation; and (iii) Chronic stage—continued, severe delusions along with chronic psychiatric depression.
Hence, the correct option is (C).

14. Fluoxetine, like other antidepressants in this class, is classified as a selective serotonin reuptake inhibitor (SSRI). Its mechanism of action appears to be via selective inhibition of serotonin reuptake and downregulation of 5-HT_1 receptors. SSRIs are more selective for inhibiting serotonin reuptake than the tricyclic antidepressant (TCA) drugs. Fluoxetine is metabolized to norfluoxetine, which is an active metabolite.
Hence, the correct option is (A).

15. The gland most likely affected is the parotid gland. Though much less likely to occur than pleomorphic adenoma, Warthin's tumor is the second most common benign parotid tumor.

Warthin's tumor primarily affects older individuals (age 60-70 years). The tumor is slow growing, painless, and usually appears in the tail of the parotid gland near the angle of the mandible. In 5-14% of cases, Warthin's tumor is bilateral, but the two masses usually are at different times. Warthin's tumor is highly unlikely to become malignant.

The appearance of this tumor under the microscope is unique. There are cystic spaces surrounded by two uniform rows of cells with centrally placed pyknotic nuclei. The cystic spaces have epithelium referred to as papillary infoldings that protrude into them. Additionally, the epithelium has lymphoid stroma with germinal center formation.
Hence, the correct option is (A).

16. The secretory phase of the menstrual cycle depends on progesterone secretion and follows the proliferative (follicular) phase. The menstrual phase occurs after the secretory phase. During the follicular phase (approximately days 4 to 16), estrogen produced by the ovaries drives cell proliferation in the base of endometrial glands and the uterine stroma. The proliferative phase culminates with ovulation. The secretory phase (approximately days 16 to 25) is characterized by high progesterone levels from the corpus luteum, a tortuous appearance of the uterine glands, and apocrine secretion by the gland cells. During this phase, maximum endometrial thickness occurs. The menstrual phase (approximately days 26 to 30) is characterized by decreased glandular secretion and eventual glandular degeneration because of decreased production of both progesterone and estrogen by the theca lutein cells. Contraction of coiled arteries and arterioles leads to ischemia and necrosis of the stratum functionale.
Hence, the correct option is (C).

17. Subglottic cancer is the rarest of laryngeal cancer.

• Earliest presentation is a globus or foreign body sensation in throat followed by stridor or laryngeal obstruction.

• Hoarseness is a late feature and occurs due to involvement of glottis or recurrent laryngeal nerve.

• Lymphatic spread occurs to prelaryngeal, pretracheal, paratracheal and lower jugular nodes (i.e. mediastinal nodes.)
Hence, the correct option is (A).

18. The history of diabetes mellitus and the chest pain put ischemic heart disease at the top of the differential diagnosis list for this man, who has findings with both right and left ventricular failure and enlargement, suggesting ischemic cardiomyopathy. An elevated serum B-type natriuretic peptide (which is measured instead of atrial natriuretic peptide) is consistent with heart failure. Occlusive coronary atherosclerosis may lead to multiple infarctions, or may silently cause progressive myofiber loss, but the end stage is ischemic cardiomyopathy.

Atrial mural thrombus formation can occur with aortic valve dysfunction and with dysrhythmias.

Although rheumatic valvulitis with thickening may involve both the left and right sides of the heart, this is unusual, and it is not associated with coronary artery disease.

Pericardial fluid collection may constrict heart motion, without an enlarged heart, and hemopericardium may acutely occur with ventricular rupture.
Hence, the correct option is (A).

19. The right horn of the embryonic sinus venosus gives rise to the smooth part of the right atrium (the sinus venarum). In addition, it forms the roots of the superior and inferior vena cavae. Most of the left sinus horn is obliterated during development. Its major remnant forms the coronary sinus.

The pulmonary trunk and the ascending aorta are formed via the internal spiral septation of the truncus arteriosus. Thus, the pulmonary trunk is a derivative of an embryonic component rather than a source of other structures.

The conus cordis is a derivative of the bulbus cordis. The conus cordis undergoes a complex spiral septation in close coordination with the septation of the ventricle and the truncus arteriosus. Ultimately, the conus cordis forms the right and left ventricular outfl ow channels.

The truncus arteriosus is the cranial third of the bulbus cordis. It undergoes a spiral septation and forms the proximal parts of the pulmonary trunk and the aorta.
Hence, the correct option is (C).

20. Lymphatic capillaries (lacteals) collect the lipids and lipid-soluble vitamins absorbed by the gut and send that chyle through larger lymphatic vessels to the thoracic duct. Thus, the greatest concentration of chyle is found in the intestinal lymphatics (e.g., those draining the small intestine) following meals.

The heart does not produce chyle. Its lymphatic drainage is via standard lymph capillaries to larger lymphatic vessels.

Long bones have medullary cavities containing bone marrow and fat. However, these bones do not have a lymphatic drainage and do not produce chyle.

The spleen does not produce chyle. Its lymphatic drainage is via standard lymph capillaries to larger lymphatic vessels.
Hence, the correct option is (A).

21. • Sensitivity of a screening test detects: true positives among all diseased.

• Specificity of a screening test detects: true negatives among all healthy.

• PPV detects: true positives among all those who are positive on a screening test.

• NPV detects: true negatives among all those who are negative on a screening test.
Hence, the correct option is (A).

22. Maternal weight gain is not a sensitive criteria for fetal growth because contribution of fetal weight to maternal weight gain during pregnancy is less significant than that of water retention and fat accumulation during pregnancy. The total weight gain during the course of a singleton pregnancy is 11kg., out of which fetus contributes only about 3kg.
Hence, the correct option is (B).

23. Megalocornea is an inherited eye disorder in which the corneal diameter is bilaterally enlarged (greater than 13 mm) without an increase in intraocular pressure. It may also be referred to as 'anterior megalophthalmos,' since the entire anterior segment is larger than normal. Features of megalocornea in addition to a deep anterior chamber include astigmatic refractive errors, atrophy of the iris stroma, miosis secondary to decreased function of the dilator muscle, iridodonesis, and tremulousness, subluxation, or dislocation of the lens. Whereas most affected individuals exhibit normal ocular function, complications include cataract development and glaucoma following lenticular dislocation or subluxation. X-linked recessive disorder is the most common pattern, accounting for the male preponderance of the disorder.

Megalocornea sometimes occurs as part of the Marfan syndrome. By 2 years of age, the cornea is approximately adult size. Simple megalocornea is defined as both corneas measuring greater than 13 mm in children older than 2 years, and greater than 12 mm in infants. Congenital glaucoma is associated with epiphora, and increased IOP and must be ruled out of the differential diagnosis.
Hence, the correct option is (B).

24. The posterior capsule is weak in mature, posterior polar cataracts and grade 4 cataracts. Hence occurrence of vitreous complications such as vitreous prolapse in anterior chamber, vitreous loss through wound, nucleus drop in vitreous cavity, following post capsule rupture are greater.

Reference: Risk factors for vitreous complications in resident-performed phacoemulsification surgery, journal of cataract and refractive surgery, nov 2011.
Hence, the correct option is (C).

25. Protein-energy malnutrition (PEM) leads to a spectrum of symptoms from kwashiorkor at one end to marasmus at the other. Marasmus, caused by a lack of caloric intake (i.e., starvation), leads to generalized wasting, stunted growth, atrophy of muscles, and loss of subcutaneous fat. There is no edema or hepatic enlargement. These children are alert, not apathetic, and are ravenous.

In contrast, children with kwashiorkor, which is characterized by a lack of protein despite adequate caloric intake, have peripheral edema, a "moon" face, and an enlarged, fatty liver. The peripheral edema is caused by decreased albumin and sodium retention, while the fatty liver is caused by decreased synthesis of the lipoproteins necessary for the normal mobilization of lipids from liver cells. **Additionally, these children have "flaky paint" areas of skin and abnormal pigmented streaks in their hair ("flag sign").**

In children with marasmus, the skin is inelastic due to loss of subcutaneous fat. In either severe kwashiorkor or marasmus, thymic atrophy may result in the reduction in number and function of circulating T cells. B cell function (i.e., immunoglobulin production) is also depressed, so that these children are highly vulnerable to infections.
Hence, the correct option is (A).

26. Nationwide AFP (acute flaccid paralysis) surveillance is the gold standard for detecting cases of poliomyelitis. The four steps of surveillance are:

Finding and reporting children with acute flaccid paralysis (AFP)

Transporting stool samples for analysis

Isolating and identifying poliovirus in the laboratory

Mapping the virus to determine the origin of the virus strain.

Sensitivity of surveillance: At least one case of non-polio AFP should be detected annually per 100,000 population aged less than 15 years. In endemic regions, to ensure even higher sensitivity, this rate should be two per 100,000.

Completeness of case investigation: All AFP cases should have a full clinical and virological investigation with at least 80% of AFP cases **having 'adequate' stool specimens collected. 'Adequate' stool** specimens are two stool specimens of sufficient quantity for laboratory analysis, collected at least 24 hours apart, within 14 days after the onset of paralysis, and arriving in the laboratory by reverse cold chain and with proper documentation.

Completeness of follow-up: At least 80% of AFP cases should have a follow-up examination for residual paralysis at 60 days after the onset of paralysis.
Hence, the correct option is (D).

27. Oral Premalignant Disorders

The effect on oral mucosa from tobacco smoking range from premalignant conditions to squamous cell carcinoma.

The most common premalignant condition is oral leukoplakia. It is defined as a whitish plaque on the oral mucosa that cannot be characterized by any other disease process. Most common site is buccal mucosa and oral commissures.

Smoking increases the risk of leukoplakia by about six times. If patient stops smoking for 1 year, it will disappear in 60 % of cases.

Features suggestive malignant change in leukoplakia are induration, speckled or nodular appearance.

Chances of malignant changes in leukoplakia increases with increases in age of lesion and age of patient.

All lesions must be biopsied and sent for histology as it has 2-8% risk of malignancy.

Several studies have shown the propensity of leukoplakia to transform into dysplasia, and malignancy and the frequency of transformation range from about 15 to 30%. Erythroplakia and submucosal fibrosis are other less common premalignant conditions; however, they are commonly associated with chewing smokeless tobacco over long periods of time. Out of all the premalignant conditions, progression to malignancy is highest in erythroplakia.
Hence, the correct option is (A).

28. The distal convoluted tubules and cortical collecting ducts of the kidney are the major sites of action of the mineralocorticoids where they induce reabsorption of sodium and secretion of potassium. In the medullary collecting duct, they act in a permissive fashion to allow vasopressin to increase osmotic water flux. Thus, patients with mineralocorticoid deficiency may develop weight loss, hypotension, hyponatremia, and hyperkalemia, whereas patients with mineralocorticoid excess may develop hypertension, hypokalemia, and metabolic alkalosis.
Hence, the correct option is (B).

29. Aminoglycosides cause dose-dependent ototoxicity that involves both cochlear and vestibular function. Nausea, vomiting, and vertigo indicate impairment of vestibular function, and tinnitus and decreased hearing capacity point out that cochlear function is affected.

Macrolides can rarely cause ototoxicity, but they are not active against Serratia marcescens.

Tetracyclines (minocycline) can cause vestibular disturbances, but they are not active against S. marcescens.

Cephalosporins and sulfonamides do not cause ototoxicity.
Hence, the correct option is (D).

30. Verrucous carcinoma is a less aggressive form of locally invasive buccal cancer than the usual epidermoid form. Its frequency is increased in people who chew tobacco. The tumor usually grows very slowly, occurs chiefly in the gingivobuccal gutter, and has a tendency to invade bone. It is identified by its characteristic exophytic, white, shaggy appearance. Wide excision is the best initial treatment for this neoplasm. Even though the tumor may regress in response to radiation, it tends to recur in a more malignant form with metastases. Cervical metastases usually are not present when the lesion is first diagnosed; it is only for the most highly malignant grades of verrucous carcinoma that radical neck dissection and block excision of the cheek are indicated.
Hence, the correct option is (C).

31. Carbamoyl phosphate synthetase I (CPS I) is located in the inner membrane of mitochondria in the liver and, to a lesser extent, in the kidneys and small intestine. It supplies carbamoyl phosphate for the urea cycle. CPS I is specific for ammonia as nitrogen donor and requires N-acetylglutamate as activator.

Hence,the answer is option (A).

32. Fetal sac can be seen using vaginal sonography from the last menstrual period between 33-35 days. This was associated with a chorionic gonadotropin level of about 1000mIU/ml.
Hence, the correct option is (B).

33. THE ALCOHOL WITHDRAWAL SYNDROME

Once the brain has been repeatedly exposed to high doses of alcohol, which is a CNS depressant; any sudden decrease in intake can produce withdrawal symptoms, many of which are the opposite of those produced by intoxication and are consist of cerebral excitation.

Features include tremor of the hands (shakes or jitters); agitation and anxiety; autonomic nervous system overactivity including an increase in pulse, respiratory rate, and body temperature; insomnia, possibly accompanied by bad dreams; and gastrointestinal upset.

These withdrawal symptoms generally begin within 5 to 10 h of decreasing ethanol intake, peak in intensity on day 2 or 3, and improve by day 4 or 5.

Anxiety, insomnia, and mild levels of autonomic dysfunction may persist to some degree for =6 months as a protracted abstinence syndrome, which may contribute to the tendency to return to drinking.

At some point in their lives, between 2 and 5% of alcoholics experience withdrawal seizures, often within 48 h of stopping drinking.

These rare events usually involve a single generalized seizure, and electroencephalographic abnormalities generally return to normal within several days.

Chlordiazepoxide is drug of choice for alcohol withdrawal and it is chosen over diazepam because of longer half life.
Hence, the correct option is (B).

34. The response of women to sexual stimulation is generalized and affects many different organ systems. During the excitement or seduction phase, vasocongestion leads to breast engorgement and the development of a rash on the breasts, chest, and epigastric area, which is called the sex flush. Heart rate and blood pressure also increase during this phase. Vasocongestion also occurs in the clitoris, labia, and vagina, and a transudative lubricant develops in the vagina.

The plateau phase is marked by greater vasocongestion throughout the body and retraction of the clitoris. Changes in hormones such as estrogen are not part of the sexual response.
Hence, the correct option is (D).

35. In hyperparathyroidism bony lesions are lytic and cause pain. The cortical surfaces are thinned and much of the bone is demineralized. The fibrotic bulging lesions within bone are termed brown tumors. Fluid filled cysts can also occur (osteitis fibrosa cystica). Anaemia is common, and the QT interval can be shortened if the calcium is high enough. Hypertension is common. Most patients with hyperparathyroidism have a simple adenoma that functions autonomously so that hormone is secreted with high calcium. In about 10-15% of cases; hyperplasia of all the parathyroid glands is the cause. Differentiation from adenoma is important to determine the correct surgical approach but it is unfortunately, very difficult.
Hence, the correct option is (B).

36. Tzanck smears are used in the diagnosis of herpes infections. The preparation detects multinucleated giant cells. Painful tiny vesicular ulcers on lips, Tzank from the scrapping of the lesion shows multinucleated giant cells. A sample obtained from unroofed vesicles that have appeared within 24 hours provides the best specimen for diagnosis.
Hence, the correct option is (C).

37. Indirect sympathomimetics e.g. ephedrine, amphetamines, tyramine etc show tachyphylaxis. It is defined as rapid development of tolerance when the drug is given repeatedly in short duration. It may be due to depletion of stored neurotransmitter in the vesicle. Epinephrine is directly acting drug.
Hence, the correct option is (D).

38. The newborn with cystic fibrosis generally is asymptomatic. The most common manifestation, meconium ileus, occurs in 15%-20% of CF patients. The ileum is completely obstructed with meconium, which results in intestinal obstruction. The meconium plug syndrome is also seen with an increased frequency in infants with cystic fibrosis, but it is less specific than meconium ileus. Sweat chloride testing in suspected cases of cystic fibrosis has always been troublesome in the newborn period but DNA testing is now available and is 90%-95% sensitive.
Hence, the correct option is (C).

39. Hyperparathyroidism results in disorders of bone and mineral metabolism. Diffuse and focal lesions may arise in multiple bones. The skeletal effects include massive bone resorption, bone fractures, and bone pain, as well as diffuse osteopenia, or circumscribed lytic lesions. On occasion, a patient with undiagnosed hyperparathyroidism presents with a lytic lesion that may be mistaken for a tumor. These lesions are termed "Brown Tumors" due to the presence of old hemorrhage in the lesion. Primary hyperparathyroidism is caused by a parathyroid adenoma, hyperplasia or carcinoma and occurs during the third to fifth decade of life.

Secondary hyperparathyroidism is often the result of chronic renal failure. Several factors contribute to hyperparathyroidism of renal failure including increased phosphorus retention causing decreased calcium, bone resistance to PTH, malabsorbtion of calcium in the gut, and inhibition of 1,25(OH)2D production by increased phosphorous.
Hence, the correct option is (C).

40. Infants with PWS are often hypotonic and may have difficulty gaining weight because of slow feeding. Their neurocognitive development is slow and most children ultimately do not achieve normal intelligence. Obesity due to uncontrolled hunger is frequent. These children are often growth hormone deficient and have hypogonadism. The FISH test of the 15q11.2-q13 region will detect most children with PWS. However, a specific methylation DNA test does exist that will detect those children who inherit the condition as a result of parental disomy, and should be obtained in those children who fit the clinical phenotype for PWS but have normal FISH evaluations. Routine chromosomal testing will be normal in PWS and although it is not "wrong" to order this test as part of the evaluation of a syndromic developmentally delayed child, it is not the best answer. Deletions and rearrangements in the subtelomeric regions of the chromosomes are associated with syndromic mental retardation but again, is not a test that will detect PWS. Mutations in the MECP2 gene are the cause of Rett syndrome. Elevated lactic acid levels are indicative of many different disorders and are not helpful or specific in detecting PWS.
Hence, the correct option is (C).

41. Several reactions given by cholesterol are useful for its qualitative identification and quantitative estimation. These include **Salkowski's test, Liebermann-Burchard reaction and Zak's test.**

Salkowski test: When a chloroform solution of the sterol is treated with an equal volume of conc. H_2SO_4 develops a red to purple colour. The heavier acid, which forms a layer below assumes a yellowish colour with a green fluorescence, whereas the upper chloroform layer becomes bluish red first, and gradually turns

violet-red.
Hence, the correct option is (B).

42. 1. Superior vesical artery supplies many branches to the vesical fundus; from one the artery to the ductus deferens occasionally starts and accompanies the ductus to the testis, anastomosing with the testicular artery. Others supply the ureter. The beginning of the superior vesical artery is the proximal, patent section of the fetal umbilical artery.

2. Often arising with the middle rectal, inferior vesical artery supplies the vesical fundus, prostate, seminal vesicles and lower ureter. Prostatic branches communicate across the midline. The inferior vesical may sometimes provide the artery to the ductus deferens.
Hence, the correct option is (C).

43. Coeliac disease is caused by a reaction to gluten, which are various proteins found in wheat and in other grains such as barley, and rye.Upon exposure to gluten, an abnormal immune response may lead to the production of several different autoantibodies that can affect a number of different organs. In the small-bowel this causes an inflammatory reaction and may produce shortening of the villi lining the small intestine (villous atrophy).The villi are shortened and the crypts lengthened with increased lymphocytic infiltrate.Tropical sprue may also cause subtotal villous atrophy.

Fissures are not found and epithelial cells are normal.
Hence, the correct option is (C).

44. Heterotopic ossification is seen more in men than in women. It is also more common in patients with hypertrophic osteoarthritis, posttraumatic arthritis, ankylosing spondylitis, longer operative times, and especially previous heterotopic bone formation. Anterior and lateral approaches have a higher incidence.
Hence, the correct option is (D).

45. An acidic drug is mainly water soluble when its pKa is lower than the pH of the medium. The amount of water solubility is proportional to the difference between pH and pKa, according to the table given.

Because the pH of plasma is about 7.4, the drug will be greater than 99% water soluble in the patient's plasma.

Difference between pH and pKa	>2.0	2.0	1.0	0.5	0.0
Percentage	>99	99	90	76	50

Hence, the correct option is (D).

46. The physis is the growing cartilaginous portion of the bone. The diaphysis is toward the center and the epiphysis toward the ends of the bone.

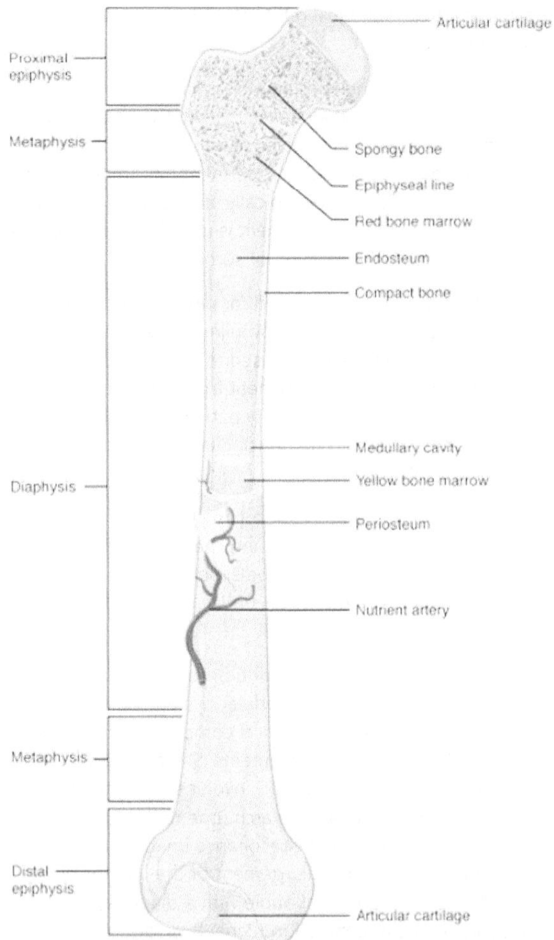

Hence, the correct option is (B).

47. Achalasia is a primary esophageal motility disorder characterized by the absence of esophageal peristalsis and impaired relaxation of the lower esophageal sphincter in response to swallowing. The LES is hypertensive in about 50% of patients. These abnormalities cause a functional obstruction at the gastroesophageal junction.

Initial therapy should be either graded pneumatic dilation (PD) or laparoscopic surgical myotomy with a partial fundoplication in patients fit to undergo surgery. Because of excellent results, a short hospital stay, and a fast recovery time, the primary treatment is considered by many to be a laparoscopic Heller myotomy and partial fundoplication. This treatment provides a fine balance in relieving symptoms of dysphagia by performing the myotomy and in preventing gastroesophageal reflux by adding a partial wrap. The operation relieves symptoms in 85-95% of patients, and the incidence of postoperative reflux is about 20%. Peroral endoscopic myotomy (POEM) has been introduced relatively recently as a novel approach to achalasia.

Pneumatic dilatation is the recommended treatment in those sporadic cases in which surgery is not appropriate. A balloon is inflated at the level of the gastroesophageal junction to blindly rupture the muscle fibers while leaving the mucosa intact. The success rate is 70-80%, and the perforation rate is approximately 5%. If a perforation occurs, emergency surgery is needed to close the perforation and to perform a myotomy. The incidence of pathologic gastroesophageal reflux after the procedure is approximately 30%.

Endoscopic treatment includes an intrasphincteric injection of botulinum toxin to block the release of acetylcholine at the level of the LES, thereby restoring the balance between excitatory and inhibitory neurotransmitters. This treatment has limited value. Only 30% of patients treated endoscopically still have relief of dysphagia 1 year after treatment. This treatment is used in elderly patients who are poor candidates for dilatation or surgery.

Pharmacologic therapy can be used for patients not undergoing PD or myotomy and who have failed botulinum toxin therapy. Calcium channel blockers and nitrates are used to decrease LES pressure. Approximately 10% of patients benefit from this treatment. This treatment is used primarily in elderly patients who have contraindications to either pneumatic dilatation or surgery.
Hence, the correct option is (D).

48. The most common presentation of a pontine hemorrhage is quadriplegia. Small, reactive pupils are characteristic of pontine hemorrhages. Hemiparesis would be expected if the hemorrhage were asymmetrical. Hypothermia is unusual. Upward gaze palsy occurs with midbrain involvement.

She reported having difficulty reading because of oscillopsia. The physical examination revealed pendular nystagmus (two cycles per second) with a predominantly vertical component and some horizontal and torsional eye movements. She also had palatomyoclonus, seen as rhythmic, involuntary contractions of the soft palate and pharyngopalatine arch (one to two cycles per second). T2-weighted magnetic resonance imaging of the brain showed hyperintensity and enlargement of the inferior olivary nuclei, findings that were compatible with a diagnosis of hypertrophic olivary degeneration (Panel B, arrowheads). The condition, which may be caused by trauma, infection, demyelination, neoplasm, or vascular injury in the components of the dentatorubroolivary pathway, results in olivary hypertrophy rather than atrophy. Myoclonic contractions of the soft palate and nystagmus represent the effects of transsynaptic degeneration of the inferior olivary nuclei. After treatment with trihexyphenidyl, there was some improvement in the patient's visual symptoms.

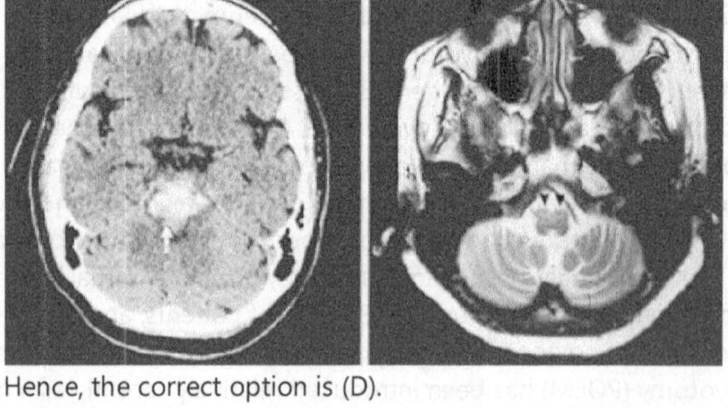

Hence, the correct option is (D).

49. In the early stages, polio may be difficult to differentiate from other forms of acute flaccid paralysis, such as Guillain-Barre Syndrome, transverse myelitis, or traumatic neuritis. All children with acute flaccid paralysis (AFP) should be reported and tested for wild poliovirus within 48 hours of onset, even if doctors are confident on clinical grounds that the child does not have polio. To test for polio, faecal specimens are analyzed for the presence of poliovirus. Because shedding of the virus is variable, two specimens - taken 24-48 hours apart are required. Speed is essential, since the highest concentrations of poliovirus in the stools of infected individuals are found during the first two weeks after onset of paralysis.
Hence, the correct option is (B).

50. Sensitivity to mammography increases with age as breasts become less dense.
Hence, the correct option is (D).

51. Immunosuppression has customarily constituted triple therapy with: (1) a calcineurin inhibitor (cyclosporin); (2) an antiproliferative agent (azathioprine); and (3) a corticosteroid (such as Prednisolone. However, a small number of treatment centres use a policy of initial monotherapy with a calcineurin inhibitor, adding in other agents if necessary.

Tacrolimus is also known as FK506, is an immunosuppressive drug used mainly after allogeneic organ transplant to lower the risk of organ rejection.
Hence, the correct option is (B).

52. <u>Nasopharyngeal Angiofibroma</u>

- Most commonly seen in adolescent males (i.e. option a is correct)
- Most common age of presentation = second decade of life
- Arises from posterior nasal cavity close to sphenopalatine foramen (option d is correct)
- Epistaxis and nasal obstruction are the most common presentation, (correct)
- Recurrent severe epistaxis accompanied by progressive nasal obstruction are the classical symptoms of juvenile angiofibromas at the time of presentation." - Scoff-Brown 7th/ed Vol2p 2438
- TOC is surgical excision (i.e. option c is incorrect)

Hence, the correct option is (C).

53. Budd-Chiari syndrome is caused by occlusion of the hepatic veins that drain the liver. It presents with the classical triad of abdominal pain, ascites, and liver enlargement. The formation of a blood clot within the hepatic veins can lead to Budd-Chiari syndrome.

Abnormalities of the hepatic blood flow occur in various disease states and result in characteristic symptoms. Because of their dual blood supply, arterial occlusion of either the hepatic artery or the portal vein rarely results in liver infarcts. However, thrombosis of branches of the hepatic artery may result in a pale (anemic) infarct, or possibly a hemorrhagic infarct due to blood flow from the portal vein. In contrast, occlusion of the portal vein, which may be caused by cirrhosis or malignancy, may result in a wedge-shaped

red area called an infarct of Zahn. This is a misnomer, however, because it is not really an infarction but instead is the result of focal sinusoidal congestion.

Hepatic vein thrombosis (Budd-Chiari syndrome) is associated with polycythemia vera, pregnancy, and oral contraceptives. Clinically, Budd-Chiari syndrome is characterized by the sudden onset of severe right upper quadrant abdominal pain, ascites, tender hepatomegaly, and hematemesis.
Hence, the correct option is (C).

54. Cord prolapse is an obstetric emergency. After cord prolapse when the cord gets exposed to external environment the whole cord goes into spasm, leading to severe decelerations in fetal heart rate and fetal distress. If the fetus is alive and mature enough for survival, immediate delivery should be alone.

Risk factors for cord prolapse include:

a) Long cord

b) Polyhydramnios

c) Abnormal lie (transverse, beach, and oblique)

d) Multiple pregnancies

e) Floating (unengaged) head
Hence, the correct option is (C).

55. An insulinoma is a neuroendocrine tumor, deriving mainly from pancreatic islet cells, that secretes insulin. Some insulinomas also secrete other hormones, such as gastrin, 5-hydroxyindolic acid, adrenocorticotropic hormone (ACTH), glucagon, human chorionic gonadotropin, and somatostatin. The tumor may secrete insulin in short bursts, causing wide fluctuations in blood levels.

Insulinomas are the most common cause of hypoglycemia resulting from endogenous hyperinsulinism and are characterized clinically by the Whipple triad:

• Presence of symptoms of hypoglycemia (about 85% of patients)

• Documented low blood sugar at the time of symptoms

• Reversal of symptoms by glucose administration

Cystadenomas may produce a mass lesion, but do not have an endocrine function.

Pseudocysts occur as a complication of pancreatitis, which produces abdominal pain. Pseudocysts are a focus of necrotizing inflammation and have irregular borders.

Pheochromocytomas can produce headaches with hypertension from catecholamine release. Most arise in the adrenal medulla. The pancreas is not a site for extra-adrenal pheochromocytoma.
Hence, the correct option is (B).

56. A congenital indirect inguinal hernia is the result of a patent processus vaginalis. This is in contrast to the less common acquired direct inguinal hernia, caused by weakness in the musculature of the inguinal canal. Inguinal hernias are commonly seen in premature infants (16%-25%). Incarceration is common; elective repair is often considered prior to hospital discharge. The diagnosis is so common that diagnostic tests are performed infrequently.
Hence, the correct option is (A).

57. The aortic valve is oriented near the horizontal plane and usually overlies the spine, while the mitral valve is more vertically positioned and lies to the left of the spine.

However, because the valves have a common insertion, it may be difficult to distinguish calcification of one valve from the other in the frontal view. This can be resolved with fluoroscopy in the same projection, because the motion of the aortic valve during the cardiac cycle is near to the vertical while the mitral valve moves more from side to side.
Hence, the correct option is (C).

58. **Tuberculosis:**

Infiltration is especially evident when the arytenoid regions are involved, two pale pyriform swellings showing in these situations; and when the epiglottis is simliarly affected a very characteristics appearance results. Ulceration is frequently seen, especially on the vocal cords. One cord alone may be involved; it looks red, raw, and irregular or serrated in outline. When ulcers occur on the infiltrated regions they present a mouse- nibbled appearance and are usually superficial (Plate XII). Papillomatous vegetations may be noted springing from the interarytenoid region, and are characteristic. When small they are seldom a cause of aphonia; at other times they form tuberculomas of such a size as almost to occlude the glottis, and cause aphonia and considerable dyspnoea. Occasionally an infiltration-paresis of both thyro-arytenoid muscles is evidenced by the spindle-shaped appearance of the glottis on phonation; or one cord-say the right-may appear fixed in the cadaveric position owing to paralysis of the recurrent nerve caused by pressure of thickened pleura or glands. The appearance of one arytenoid and cord fixed in an atypical position is more suggestive of an involvement of the crico-arytenoid articulation.

• Tuberculosis of larynx is always secondary to pulmonary TB.

• Tubercle bacilli reach the larynx by bronchogenic or haematogenous routes.

• Mostly affects males in middle age group.

• Affects posterior part of (Posterior Commissure) larynx more than anterior part.

Clinical Features

• Weakness of voice (earliest symptom), odynophagia, dysphagia.

• Pain radiates to the ears.

• Laryngeal examination shows:

- Vocal cord: Mouse nibbled ulceration

- Arytenoids: show ulceration.

- Interarytenoid region is swollen giving a mammillated appearance"

- Epiglottis shows: Pseudoedema and is called as 'turban epiglottis'.

- Surrounding mucosa is pale
Hence, the correct option is (A).

59. The patient is most likely suffering an acute inferolateral myocardial infarction (MI).

The ST elevations are noted in the inferior leads (II, III, aVF) and in V6 (lateral precordial lead). Also, the striking ST depressions in the anterior precordial leads (V1-V4) are indicative of posterior ischemia.

Here, the presence of ST depressions in an anterior lead represents the mirror of ST elevations in a posterior location. One can visualize the ECG pattern in the anterior leads upside down to see the reciprocal nature of the ST depressions. Although on initial glance, the QRS pattern appears wide in the anterior leads suggesting ventricular tachycardia, on further examination, there are P waves present that are associated with each QRS (seen most clearly in leads II and V1); thus, the rhythm is sinus tachycardia. The wide appearance of the QRS is due to the striking ST deviation.
Hence, the correct option is (A).

60. Measles vaccination

Measles is best prevented by active immunization.

(1) VACCINE: Only live attenuated vaccines are recommended for use; they are both safe and effective, and may be used interchangeably within immunization programmes. Person to person transmission of measles vaccine strains has never been documented. The vaccine is presented as a freeze-dried product. Before use, the lyophilized vaccine is reconstituted with sterile diluent. Each dose of 0.5 ml contains more than1000 viral infective units of the vaccine strain; this is also true when it is presented as an MCV combination. Measles vaccine may also contain sorbitol and hydrolysed gelatin as stabilizers, as well as a small amount of neomycin, but it does not contain thiomersal. In general, it is recommended that freeze-dried vaccine be stored in a refrigerated condition. The diluent must not be frozen but should be cooled before reconstitution. Reconstituted measles vaccine loses about 50 per cent of its potency after 1 hour at 20°C; it loses almost all potency after 1 hour at 37°C. The vaccine is also sensitive to sunlight, hence it is kept in coloured glass vials.

After reconstitution, the vaccine must be stored in the dark at 2-8°C and used within 4 hours.

(2) AGE: The principal problem of measles immunization is timing; immunization before the age of 9 months runs the risk of the vaccine being rendered ineffective by the natural antibodies acquired through the mother. Immunization later than 9 months means that a significant proportion of children will contract measles in the interval between wearing off natural protection, and the introduction of the vaccine. The most effective compromise is immunization as close to the age of 9 months as possible. The WHO Expanded Programme on Immunization recommends immunization at 9 months age. This recommendation has been adopted in India. The age can be lowered to 6 months if there is measles outbreak in the community. For infants immunized between 6 months and 9 months of age, a second dose should be administered as soon as possible after the child reaches the age of 9 months provided that at least 4 weeks have elapsed since the last dose.

In countries where the incidence of measles has declined, the age of immunization is being raised to 12 months in order to avoid the blocking effect of persistent transplacental^ acquired antibody.

(3) ADMINISTRATION: The reconstituted vaccine is generally injected subcutaneously, but it is also effective when administered intramuscularly.

(4) IMMUNE RESPONSES: Measles vaccine induces both humoral and cellular immune responses comparable to those following natural infection, although antibody titres are usually lower. Also, lower average concentrations of maternal antibodies are found in infants born to vaccinated mothers when compared with naturally infected mothers.

Following vaccination, transient measles-specific immunoglobulin (Ig) M antibodies appear in the blood and IgA antibodies appear in mucosal secretions; IgG antibodies persist in the blood for years. Vaccination also induces measles virus-specific CD4+ and CD8+ T lymphocytes.

(5) REACTIONS: When injected into the body, the attenuated virus multiplies and induces a mild "measles" illness (fever and rash) 5 to 10 days after immunization, but in reduced frequency and severity. This may occur in 15 to 20 per cent of vaccinees. The fever may last for 1 - 2 days and the rash for 1 - 3 days. There is no cause for alarm. The vaccines now given rarely cause severe reaction. There is no spread of the virus from the vaccines to contacts.

(6) IMMUNITY: The vaccine has convincingly demonstrated to provide immunity to even severely malnourished children. Immunity develops 11 to 12 days after vaccination and appears to be of long duration, probably for life. One dose of the vaccine given at 11-12 months of age appears to give 99 per cent protection. Infants vaccinated at the age of 9 months show seroconversion of about 90 per cent.

(7) CONTACTS Susceptible contacts over the age of 9-12 months may be protected against measles with measles vaccine, provided that this is given within 3 days of exposure. This is because, the incubation period of measles induced by the vaccine is about 7 days, compared with 10 days for the naturally acquired measles.

(8) CONTRAINDICATIONS: Mild concurrent infections are not considered a contraindication to vaccination, but it should be avoided if the patient has a high fever or other signs of serious disease. Measles vaccine alone, or in combination with other vaccines, should also be avoided by pregnant women. Being in the early stages of HIV infection is not a contraindication to measles vaccination.

People with a history of an anaphylactic reaction to neomycin, gelatin or other components of the vaccine should not be vaccinated. Furthermore, measles vaccine is contraindicated in persons who are severely immunocompromised due to congenital disease, severe HIV infection, advanced leukaemia or lymphoma, serious malignant disease, treatment with high-dose steroids, alkylating agents or antimetabolites, or who receive immuno-suppressive therapeutic radiation.

(9) ADVERSE EFFECTS OF VACCINE: Toxic shock syndrome (TSS) occurs when measles vaccine is contaminated or the same vial is used for more than one session on the same day or next day. The vaccine should not be used after 4 hours of opening the vial. TSS is totally preventable and reflects poor quality of immunization services. The symptoms of TSS are typical. Severe watery diarrhoea, vomiting and high fever are reported within few hours of measles vaccination. There are usually a cluster of cases as all infants vaccinated from contaminated vial will be affected. This may cause death within 48 hours. Case fatality rates are high.

MEASLES AND HIV: Given the severe course of measles in patients with advanced HIV infection, measles vaccination should be routinely administered to potentially susceptible, asymptomatic HIV-positive children and adults.

Vaccination may be considered for those with symptomatic HIV infection if they are not severely immunosuppressed according to conventional definitions. In areas where there is a high incidence of both measles and HIV infection, first dose of measles vaccine may be offered as early as age 6 months. Two additional doses of measles vaccine should be administered to these children according to the national immunization schedule.

Second dose of measles vaccine may be added to the routine immunization schedule in countries that have achieved more than 80% coverage of the first dose of the vaccine at the national level for 3 consecutive years, as determined by the most accurate means available (for example, a well conducted population-based survey or WHO/UNICEF estimates). In general, countries that do not meet this criterion should prioritize improving MCV1 coverage and conducting high-quality follow-up SIAs, rather than adding the second dose to their routine schedule.

COMBINED VACCINE Measles vaccine can be combined with other live attenuated vaccines such as mumps, and rubella vaccines (MMR vaccine), measles, mumps, rubella and varicella (MMRV), and measles and rubella (MR), and such combinations are also highly effective.
Hence, the correct option is (B).

61. Pregnancy increases the risk of deep vein thrombosis (blood clots) and pulmonary embolism. While deep vein thrombosis does not directly endanger the developing fetus, pulmonary embolism can affect fetal health.

Deep vein thrombosis describes the formation of blood clots in blood vessels. Most cases of deep vein thrombosis occur when blood clots form in the large veins of the legs and pelvis.

Pregnant women are more susceptible to deep vein thrombosis than non-pregnant women. Pregnancy causes hormonal changes that increase blood coagulability, a measure of how easily blood clots. In addition, the expanding uterus puts pressure on blood vessels, restricting blood flow from the legs and pelvis back to the heart. Slower blood flow increases the risk of deep vein thrombosis.

DVTs usually develop first in the calf veins, and when they extend, **they "grow" in the direction of venous flow, towards the knees.** When DVTs do not grow, they can be cleared naturally and dissolved into the blood. There is a strong tendency for DVT to develop in the left leg (about 70 to 90% of the time) possibly because of exacerbation of the compressive effects on the left iliac vein due to its being crossed by the right iliac artery.
Hence, the correct option is (A).

62. Thymoma is an uncommon tumor originating from the epithelial cells of the thymus, best known for its association with the neuromuscular disorder myasthenia gravis. It is found in 20% of patients with myasthenia gravis.

Additional associated autoimmune conditions include pure red cell aplasia and Good syndrome (thymoma with combined immunodeficiency and hypogammaglobulinemia).

Paraneoplastic pemphigus is an autoimmune disorder initiated by an underlying neoplasm. Tumor antigens are hypothesized to evoke both a humoral and a cellular immune response that leads to blistering in mucosa and other epithelia.Associated neoplasms include thymoma.

Other reported disease associations of thymoma are with acute pericarditis, agranulocytosis, alopecia areata, ulcerative colitis, **Cushing's disease, hemolytic anemia, limbic encephalopathy,** myocarditis, nephrotic syndrome, panhypopituitarism, pernicious anemia, polymyositis, rheumatoid arthritis, sarcoidosis, scleroderma, sensorimotor radiculopathy, stiff person syndrome, systemic lupus erythematosus and thyroiditis.
Hence, the correct option is (C).

63. Invitro Fertilization is offered to those women who have irreparable / failed tubal damage.

1. Depending on site of block, Tuboplasty is performed with successful pregnancy rate of 27% for fimbrial & 50% for isthmic.

2. Thus, Transvaginal tubal catheterization or hysteroscopy and Tuboplasty have less success rate than IVF, hence IVF would be the best treatment option for her.

3. Proximal tubal occlusions may be approached employing several different therapeutic approaches.

4. In vitro fertilization techniques and microsurgical oviduct reconstruction with reimplantation techniques are two established modalities.

5. Transcervical fallopian tube recanalization techniques now offer a third therapeutic alternative.
Hence, the correct option is (A).

64. The ECG machine is designed to pick up electrical activity within the heart but it will pick up electrical activity from nearby machinery, such as:

- Pumps
- TV
- Drills
- Machinery

You need to repeat the ECG but do as much as you can to correct any modifiable problems.
Hence, the correct option is (B).

65. All the above investigations have been shown to be useful in the diagnosis of a hiatus hernia. However, upper GI barium meals/swallows have been shown to be the most definitive modality in diagnosing hiatus hernias.

Chest x-rays may be normal, but in some cases may show an air fluid level above the level of the left hemi-diaphragm. Upper GI endoscopy is commonly used to assess symptoms of dyspepsia and has not been shown to be as sensitive as barium studies in the detection of hiatus hernias. Positive results obtained with ultrasound scanning may lead to inconsistent and false-positive/negative results due to the operator associated variability regarding technical experience.
Hence, the correct option is (D).

66. Apoplexy: Subarachnoid hemorrhage from rupture of berry aneurysm or cerebral hemorrhage by rupture of cerebral vessels from sudden on-rush of blood to the brain due to excitement or sudden fall from height into cold water.
Hence, the correct option is (C).

67. The Hardy-Weinberg principle (also known as the Hardy-Weinberg equilibrium, model, theorem, or law) states that allele and genotype frequencies in a population will remain constant from generation to generation in the absence of other evolutionary influences. These influences include non-random mating, mutation, selection, genetic drift, gene flow and meiotic drive. Because one or more of these influences are typically present in real populations, the Hardy-Weinberg principle describes an ideal condition against which the effects of these influences can be analyzed.
Hence, the correct option is (A).

68. Bulbourethral (Cowper) glands secrete nonviscous material into the urethra before and during ejaculation to mix with sperm, seminal vesicle fluid, and prostatic fluid to form semen. The bulbourethral glands are found deep to the perineal membrane within the deep perineal compartment, so they are the most likely structures to be affected by the described abscess within the deep perineal compartment.

The perineal body is located at the central point of the perineum where the perineal muscles converge. This unique structure serves as an anchoring point for the perineum and contains collagen and elastic fibers as well as skeletal and smooth muscles. Due to its location between the anal and urogenital triangles of the perineum, it is generally not considered part of the superficial or deep perineal compartments. Therefore, it would not be the most likely structure on this list affected by the described abscess.

The superficial transverse perineal muscles attach to the ischial tuberosities and help to support and stabilize the superficial perineal region. The muscles are, however, located in the superficial perineal space, which is inferior to the perineal membrane, so they would most likely not be affected by this abscess in the deep perineal space.

The ischiocavernosus muscles are paired muscles covering the crura of the penis and the associated erectile tissue, the corpora cavernosa. These muscles force blood within the crura into the distal parts of the corpora cavernosa and compress venous outfl ow via the deep dorsal vein of the penis. Both of these actions increase the turgidity of the penis during erection. However, these muscles are also located in the superfi cial perineal space, which is inferior to the perineal membrane.
Hence, the correct option is (A).

69. HDL scavenges the body cholesterol and blood vessel wall cholesterol by "reverse cholesterol transport". With the help of apo-A, it strips off the cellular cholesterol from peripheral cells and smooth muscle cells of arteries and apo-A, activates the enzyme "LCAT", which helps in esterification of cholesterol. The cholesterol ester formed at the surface, being hydrophobic, moves into the interior and makes the "discoid" HDL to spherical. The mature HDL (good cholesterol) moves to Liver where cholesterol is catabolised.
Hence, the correct option is (A).

70. Worldwide the number of people infected with both HIV and tuberculosis is rising. The HIV virus damages the body's natural defences - the immune system - and accelerates the speed at which tuberculosis progresses from a harmless infection to life-threatening condition. The estimated 10 per cent activation of dormant tuberculosis infection over the life span of an infected person, is increased to 10 per cent activation in one year, if HIV infection is superimposed.

Tuberculosis is already the opportunistic infection that most frequently kills HIV-positive people.

Even in HIV positive cases, tuberculosis can be cured if diagnosed in time and treated properly. Good TB control programme (DOTS) is the best thing that can be done to cure and extend the lives of HIV positive individuals. With correct TB treatment, the HIV positive person having tuberculosis can gain, on an average two additional years of life.
Hence, the correct option is (D).

71. In a young male solitary lymph node enlargement near the renal hilum, having central necrosis is most likely a metastasis from germ cell tumor. Unless proved otherwise.

a. A painless testicular mass is pathognomonic for a testicular malignancy.

b. Ultrasound of the testis is indicated whenever a testicular malignancy is considered and for persistent or painful testicular swelling.

c. If a testicular mass is detected, a radical inguinal orchiectomy should be performed.

d. Back pain from retroperitoneal metastases is common and must be distinguished from musculoskeletal pain. Dyspnea from pulmonary metastases occurs infrequently

e. The staging evaluation for GCT includes a determination of serum levels of fetoprotein (AFP), hCG, and lactate dehydrogenase (LDH). After orchiectomy, a chest radiograph and a CT scan of the abdomen and pelvis should be performed.

f. A chest CT scan is required if pulmonary nodules or mediastinal or hilar disease is suspected.

g. Stage I disease is limited to the testis, epididymis, or spermatic cord.

h. Stage II disease is limited to retroperitoneal (regional) lymph nodes.

i. Stage III disease is disease outside the retroperitoneum, involving supradiaphragmatic nodal sites or viscera.

j. The lymph nodes that are involved first by a right testicular tumor are the interaortocaval lymph nodes just below the renal vessels. For a left testicular tumor, the first involved lymph nodes are lateral to the aorta (para-aortic) and below the left renal vessels.

i. In both cases, further nodal spread is inferior, contralateral, and, less commonly, above the renal hilum. Lymphatic involvement can extend cephalad to the retrocrural, posterior mediastinal, and supraclavicular lymph nodes.

ii. Treatment is determined by tumor histology (seminoma versus nonseminoma) and clinical stage
Hence, the correct option is (A).

72. Demographic characteristics provide an overview of its population size, composition, territorial distribution, changes therein and the components of changes such as nativity, mortality and social mobility. Demographic indicators have been divided into two parts - population statistics and vital statistics.

Population statistics include indicators that measure the population size, sex ratio, density and dependency ratio.

Vital statistics include indicators such as birth rate, death rate, natural growth rate, life expectancy at birth, mortality and fertility rates.

These indicators help in identifying areas that need policy and programmed interventions, setting near and far-term goals and deciding priorities, besides understanding them in an integrated structure.

With a population of 1,364 million in the year 2014, India is the second most populous country in the world, next only to China, whereas seventh in land area. With only 2.4 per cent of the world's land area, India is supporting about 17.5 per cent of the world's population. India's population has been steadily increasing since 1921. The year 1921 is called the "big divide" because the absolute number of people added to the population during each decade has been on the increase since 1921.

India's population is currently increasing at the rate of 16 million each year.

India's population numbered 238 million in 1901, doubled in 60 years to 439 million (1961); doubled again, this time in only 30 years to reach 846 million by 1991. It crossed 1 billion mark on 11 May 2000, and is projected to reach 1.53 billion by the year 2050. This will then make India the most populous country in the world, surpassing China. India belongs to late expanding trend.

THIRD STAGE (Late expanding)

The death rate declines still further, and the birth rate tends to fall. The population continues to grow because births exceed deaths. India has entered this phase. In a number of developing countries (e.g., China, Singapore) birth rates have declined rapidly.
Hence, the correct option is (D).

73. Koilocytes are indicative of HPV-infected epithelial cells. Viral infection causes intracytoplasmic vacuolation that is apparent in cytopathologic and histopathologic preparations.

Donovan bodies represent macrophages stuffed with numerous C.(Donovania) granulomatis organisms. Clear cells are characteristic of clear cell adenocarcinoma of the vagina. Paget cells are characteristic large cells surrounded by a clear, halo-like area that occur in Paget disease of the vulva and Paget disease of the breast.
Hence, the correct option is (B).

74. Acalculous cholecystitis is related to conditions associated with biliary stasis, and include the following:

- Critical illness
- Major surgery or severe trauma/burns
- Sepsis
- Long-term total parenteral nutrition (TPN)
- Prolonged fasting

Other causes of acalculous cholecystitis include the following:

- Cardiac events, including myocardial infarction
- Sickle cell disease
- Salmonella infections
- Diabetes mellitus

Patients with AIDS who have cytomegalovirus, cryptosporidiosis, or microsporidiosis
Hence, the correct option is (D).

75. Contemporary with ancient Egyptian civilization, there existed another civilization in the land which lies between the Euphrates and Tigris rivers, Mesopotamia (now part of Iraq), often called the "Cradle of Civilization", as long as 6,000 years ago.

In ancient Mesopotamia, the basic concepts of medicine were religious, and taught and practised by herb doctors, knife doctors and spell doctors - a classification that roughly parallels our own internists, surgeons and psychiatrists.

Mesopotamia was the cradle of magic and necromancy. Medical students were busy in classifying "demons", the causes of diseases. Geomancy, the interpretation of dreams, and hepatoscopic divination (the liver was considered the seat of life) are characteristic of their medical lore.

Sumerians, Babylonians and Assyrians were the authors of a medical astrology which flourished in the whole of Eurasia. Prescriptions were written on tablets, in cuneiform writing. The oldest medical prescription comes to us from Mesopotamia, dating back to 2100 B.C.
Hence, the correct option is (A).

76. ALP is a most valuable index of osteoblastic activity.

• Increases in serum ALP activity seen in rickets, osteomalacia, hyperparathyroidism and particularly in Paget's disease.

• In primary and secondary malignancies of bone, the level depends on the severity and degree of new bone formation. When the lesion is purely destructive as myelomatosis, the value is normal.

• In hypophosphatasia, where there is defective calcification, low tissue and serum ALP activity is observed.

Total serum AP activity is markedly reduced in hypophosphatasia. Thus, the diagnosis can be suggested in individuals in whom serum AP activity is clearly and consistently subnormal. In general, the more severe the disease, the lower the serum AP activity level appropriate for age. However, AP activity is only a helpful diagnostic indicator as other conditions may also show this finding: early pregnancy, drug administration, hypothyroidism, anemia, celiac disease etc. It must be also noticed that serum AP dramatically varies with age and sex.
Hence, the correct option is (C).

77. Urticaria and angioedema are common disorders, affecting approximately 20% of the population. In acute urticarial angioedema, attacks of swelling are of less than 6 weeks' duration; chronic urticarial angioedema is by definition more long-standing. Urticaria usually is pruritic and affects the trunk and proximal extremities. Angioedema is generally less pruritic and affects the hands, feet, genitalia, and face. This female has chronic urticaria, which probably is due to a cutaneous necrotizing vasculitis. The clues to the diagnosis are the arthralgias, the presence of residual skin discoloration, and the elevated sedimentation rate, which would be uncharacteristic of other urticarial diseases. The diagnosis can be confirmed by skin biopsy. Chronic urticaria rarely has an allergic cause; hence, allergy skin tests and measurement of total IgE levels are not helpful. Measurement of C1 esterase inhibitor activity is useful in diagnosing hereditary angioedema, a disease that is not associated with urticaria. Patch tests are used to diagnose contact dermatitis.
Hence, the correct option is (D).

78. Hydrochlorothiazide is a thiazide diuretic, often used to treat high blood pressure and swelling due to fluid build up. Other uses include diabetes insipidus, renal tubular acidosis, and to decrease the risk of kidney stones in those with high calcium level in the urine. For high blood pressure it is often recommended as a first line treatment

Hydrochlorothiazide can precipitate a gouty attack in predisposed individuals. This is because these agents increase serum uric acid as a result of competition for the organic acid carrier. Loop diuretics can have this effect too.

Acetazolamide is a carbonic anhydrase inhibitor; this agent does not have a significant impact on the levels of uric acid. Amiloride and spironolactone are potassium-sparing diuretics, and they do not have a significant impact on the levels of uric acid either.
Hence, the correct option is (D).

79. Propranolol or other beta-adrenergic blocking agents are effectively used to lower blood pressure and thereby delay or prevent aortic dilatation. Surgical correction of the aorta, aortic valve, and mitral valve has been successful in many patients, but tissues are frequently friable. Patients should be advised of the risks of severe physical and emotional stress and of pregnancy.
Hence, the correct option is (A).

80. Stress ulceration refers to acute gastric or duodenal erosive lesions that occur following shock, sepsis, major surgery, trauma, or burns. These lesions tend to be superficial and can involve multiple sites. McClelland and associates showed that patients subjected to trauma and subsequent hemorrhagic shock do not have increased gastric secretion, but rather show decreased splanchnic blood flow. Ischemic damage to the mucosa may therefore play a role. Unlike chronic benign gastric ulcers, which are generally found along the lesser curvature and in the antrum, acute erosive lesions usually involve the body and fundus and spare the antrum.
Hence, the correct option is (D).

81. Metropathia hemorrhagica should be regarded as a specialized form of dysfunctional uterine hemorrhage. The disease is most prevalent in women over the age of 40 years, the maximum incidence being between the ages of 40 and 45 years.

Occasionally, it develops in young girls under the age of 20 years. Parity is not related to its incidence. The symptoms are very typical. The most common complaint is continuous vaginal bleeding, which may last for many weeks. In half the cases, the continuous bleeding is preceded by a short period of amenorrhea, an interval of about 8 weeks elapsing between the last period and the onset of the continuous hemorrhage. The bleeding is always painless, since it is anovulatory.

Irregular ripening and shredding are examples of ovulatory DUB in which period of amenorrhea is not seen.
Hence, the correct option is (C).

82. The image shows that the child has bow legs. His chest radiograph shows expansion of the anterior rib ends (arrows), marked reduction in bone density, cortical tunnelling and fraying, and splaying of the proximal humeral growth plate (arrowheads). Cupping s observed in the x-ray of hands. These multiple bony abnormalities are characteristic of Rickets.

. Rickets is caused by failure of action of calcitriol (1,25-dihydroxycholecalciferol), the active form of vitamin D. The bony abnormalities in rickets are caused by failure of osteoid matrix to calcify, leading to excess accumulation of osteoid, increased thickness of the epiphyseal growth plates, and other skeletal deformities.

Many of the effects of calcitriol deficiency are mediated by increased release of parathyroid hormone (PTH). PTH stimulates bony osteoblastic activity, which is represented by an increase in serum alkaline phosphatase.
Hence, the correct option is (B).

83. Mittelschmerz is the pain associated with the rupture of ovarian follicle at the time of ovulation (Ovular pain). **Its characteristics are :**

a) It appears in mid-menstrual period

b) Pain is usually situated in the hypogastrium or iliac fossa

c) Pain changes side according to which ovary is ovulating

d) It rarely lasts for more than 12 hours

e) It may be associated with slight vaginal bleeding or mucoid discharge

f) The probable factors are: include increased tension of graffian follicle just prior to rupture;

Paritoneal irritation by follicular fluid following ovulation; contraction of tubes and uterus
Hence, the correct option is (C).

84. Reflux esophagitis is an esophageal mucosal injury that occurs secondary to retrograde flux of gastric contents into the esophagus. Clinically, this is referred to as gastroesophageal reflux disease (GERD).

Heartburn is a characteristic symptom of reflux esophagitis and may be associated with regurgitation.
The clinical symptoms of GERD can be divided into 2 groups: esophageal and extra-esophageal. The typical presentation of GERD includes esophageal symptoms such as heartburn, acid dyspepsia, regurgitation, and chest pain. The extra-esophageal symptoms are also referred to as "atypical" symptoms of reflux disease and include, but are not limited to, cough, asthma, throat pain, aspiration pneumonia, globus sensation, and hoarseness due to pharyngitis, laryngitis, or sinus problems.
Hence, the correct option is (D).

85. The epiglottis is a flap that is made of elastic cartilage tissue covered with a mucous membrane, attached to the entrance of the larynx. It projects obliquely upwards behind the tongue and the hyoid bone, pointing dorsally. The term, like tonsils, is often incorrectly used to refer to the uvula. There are taste buds on the epiglottis.
Hence, the correct option is (A).

86. Axillary sheath is fibrous neurovascular sheath formed as an extension of the prevertebral layer of deep cervical fascia through the cervicoaxillary canal that encloses the first part of the axillary artery, the axillary vein, and the brachial plexus.
Hence, the correct option is (A).

87. Prolonged rupture of the membranes increases the risk of ascending infection via the genital tract, as does a prolonged second stage. Operative delivery (whether vaginal or abdominal) carries a higher risk than spontaneous delivery. If the membranes are not ruptured then there is no increased risk associated with prolonged pregnancy.
Hence, the correct option is (B).

88. During starvation, less than half the energy used by the brain comes from metabolized glucose. Because the human brain can use ketone bodies as major fuel sources, the body is not forced to break down skeletal muscles at a high rate, thereby maintaining both cognitive function and mobility for up to several weeks.

The body's glycogen stores are consumed in about 24 hours. The body also engages in gluconeogenesis to convert glycerol and glucogenic amino acids into glucose for metabolism. Another adaptation is the Cori cycle, which involves shuttling lipid-derived energy in glucose to peripheral glycolytic tissues, which in turn send the lactate back to the liver for resynthesis to glucose. Because of these processes, blood glucose levels remain relatively stable during prolonged starvation.

However, the main source of energy during prolonged starvation is derived from triglycerides. These are broken down to fatty acids via lipolysis. Epinephrine precipitates lipolysis by activating protein kinase A, which phosphorylates hormone sensitive lipase (HSL) and perilipin. These enzymes, along with CGI-58 and adipose triglyceride lipase (ATGL), forms complex at the surface of lipid droplets. The concerted action of ATGL and HSL liberates the first two fatty acids. Cellular monoacylglycerol lipase (MGL) liberates the final fatty acid. The remaining glycerol enters gluconeogenesis.

Fatty acids by themselves cannot be used as a direct fuel source. They must first undergo beta oxidation in the mitochondria (mostly of skeletal muscle, cardiac muscle, and liver cells). Fatty acids are transported into the mitochondria as an acyl-carnitine via the action of the enzyme CAT-1. This step controls the metabolic flux of beta oxidation. The resulting acetyl-CoA enters the TCA cycle and undergoes oxidative phosphorylation to produce ATP. The body invests some of this ATP in gluconeogenesis to produce more glucose.

Triglycerides and long-chain fatty acids are too hydrophobic to cross into brain cells, so the liver must convert them into short-chain fatty acids and ketone bodies through ketogenesis. The resulting ketone bodies, acetoacetate and ß-hydroxybutyrate, are amphipathic and can be transported into the brain (and muscles) and broken down into acetyl-CoA for use in the TCA cycle. Acetoacetate breaks down spontaneously into acetone, and the acetone is released through the urine and lungs to produce the "acetone breath" that accompanies prolonged fasting. The brain also uses glucose during starvation, but most of the body's glucose is allocated to the skeletal muscles and red blood cells.

ß-Hydroxybutyric acid is able to cross the blood-brain-barrier into the central nervous system. Levels of ß-hydroxybutyric acid increase in the liver, heart, muscle, brain, and other tissues with exercise, calorie restriction, fasting, and ketogenic diets. The compound has been found to act as a histone deacetylase (HDAC) inhibitor.
Hence, the correct option is (A).

89. Arachidonate 5-lipoxygenase inhibitors are compounds that slow or stop the action of the arachidonate 5-lipoxygenase (5-lipoxygenase or 5-LOX) enzyme, which is responsible for the production of inflammatory leukotrienes. The overproduction of leukotrienes is a major cause of inflammation in asthma and allergic rhinitis and Osteoarthritis. Examples of 5-LOX inhibitors include drugs, such as meclofenamate sodium and zileuton.

Montelukast is a leukotriene receptor antagonist (LTRA) used for the maintenance treatment of asthma and to relieve symptoms of seasonal allergies.

Terbutaline is a β2 adrenergic receptor agonist, used as a reliever inhaler in the management of asthma symptoms.

Sodium cromoglycate belongs to the class of medications called mast cell stabilizers. It is used to prevent symptoms associated with asthma that are caused by exposure to certain substances or conditions.
Hence, the correct option is (A).

90. 1) Ca^{2+}, Cl^-, Fe^{2+}, $(SO_4)^{2-}$, long chain fatty acids & vitamins (except B12) are mainly absorbed in upper small intestine (i.e. jejunum & duodenum).

2) Sugar & amino acids are mainly absorbed in mid small intestine whereas bile salts & Vit. B12 in lower small intestine (ileum).

3) Na^+ mainly absorbed in upper & lower SI (jejunum & ileum) & colon.
Hence, the correct option is (C).

91. It is useful to divide the body into the areas such as: face/arms/legs, left/ right, proximal/distal. This allows a rapid diagnosis of where the lesion might be.

In this case, the left side of the face is affected but so is the right side of his body. This is an example of crossed signs and can only be produced by a brainstem lesion. A left brainstem lesion would affect cranial nerves exiting on that side (LMN left-sided droop) and the cortical spinal tracts as they descend which then go on to cross at the medulla (UMN right arm and leg weakness).

A right brainstem lesion would cause the opposite.

Our patient does not have any signs, such as aphasia, or apraxia to suggest a cortical lesion.
Hence, the correct option is (C).

92. MacConkey agar is a selective and differential culture medium for bacteria designed to selectively isolate Gram-negative and enteric (normally found in the intestinal tract) bacilli and differentiate them based on lactose fermentation.It contains bile salts (to inhibit most Gram-positive bacteria), crystal violet dye (which also inhibits certain Gram-positive bacteria), neutral red dye (which turns pink if the microbes are fermenting lactose).By utilizing the lactose available in the medium, Lac+ bacteria such as Escherichia coli, Enterobacter and Klebsiella will produce acid, which lowers the pH of the agar below 6.8 and results in the appearance of pink colonies. The bile salts precipitate in the immediate neighbourhood of the colony, causing the medium surrounding the colony to become hazy.
Hence, the correct option is (D).

93.

Classification of disorders of sexual development (DSD)		
Old name	New name	Possible diagnosis
True hermaphrodite	Oyotesticular DSD	46XX/46XY 45X/46XY (mixed gonadal dysgenesis)
Male pseudohermaphrodite Undervirilisation of an XY male Undermasculinisation of an XY male	46XY DSD*	Androgen insensitivity syndrome (partial or complete) 5-a-reductase deficiency
Female pseudo-hermaphrodite Over virilisation of an XX female Masculinisation of an XX female	46XX DSD	Congenital adrenal hyperplasia
XX male or XX sex reversal	46XX testicular DSD	Males with external ambiguities or males have both internal and external genital ambiguities
XY sex reversal	46XY complete Gonadal dysgenesis	Completely undeveloped ('streak') gonads
Gonadal dysgenesis	Sex chromosome	45XO Turner 47XXY Klinefelter

	DSD
Although Y chromosome is the principal decisive factor in human sexual differentiation, prominent exception is 46XY females with complete androgen insensitivity syndrome (cAls).	

Hence, the correct option is (D).

94. 1. Heart Disease is a relative common postmortem finding in HIV infected patients.

2. Cardiovascular disease may be seen as a direct consequence of

a. HIV infection or

b. As a consequence of ARV therapy

c. As a part of lipodystrophy syndrome

3. The most common clinically significant finding as a result of primary consequence of HIV infection is

a. HIV associated cardiomyopathy (dilated cardiomyopathy associated with congestive cardiac failure). This generally occurs as a late complication of HIV infection and histologically displays elements of myocarditis.

4. Patients with HIV infection also presents with cardiomyopathy as a side effect of IFN - a or nucleoside analogue theraphy.

5. A variety of other cardiovascular problems are found in HIV infection, which are

a. Pericardial effusion (due to T.B., CHF, Mycobacterial infection, Cryptococcal infects)

b. Pericarditis (K.S.)

c. Tamponade and death

d. Nonbacterial thromnoticendocarditis

Hence, the correct option is (C).

95. Iceberg of disease

A concept closely related to the spectrum of disease is the concept of the iceberg phenomenon of disease. According to this concept, disease in a community may be compared with an iceberg. The floating tip of the iceberg represents what the physician sees in the community, i.e., clinical cases. The vast submerged portion of the iceberg represents the hidden mass of disease, i.e., latent, in apparent, presymptomatic and undiagnosed cases and carriers in the community. The "waterline" represents the demarcation between apparent and in apparent disease.

In some diseases (e.g., hypertension, diabetes, anemia, malnutrition, mental illness) the unknown morbidity (i.e., the submerged portion of the iceberg) far exceeds the known morbidity. The hidden part of the iceberg thus constitutes an important, undiagnosed reservoir of infection or disease in the community, and its detection and control is a challenge to modern techniques in preventive medicine. One of the major deterrents in the study of chronic diseases of unknown etiology is the absence of methods to detect the subclinical state - the bottom of the iceberg.

Hence, the correct option is (D).

96. Barium swallow shows an esophageal dilation with tapering at the esophageal junction, known as "bird beak." It is suggestive of diagnosis of Achalasia cardia. It is characterized by absence of ganglion cells from the myenteric plexus leading to impaired relaxation of the lower esophageal sphincter (LES) and absence of esophageal peristalsis.

The gold standard for diagnosing achalasia is esophageal manometry; radiographic and endoscopic evaluation provides supplementary information. A chest X-ray may show a widened mediastinum and an air-fluid level in the esophagus. A barium esophagram shows esophageal dilation with tapering at the esophageal junction, known as a "bird beak". If the esophagus is severely dilated, it can occupy the entire mediastinum, assuming an S curve, known as a sigmoid esophagus. Endoscopy is performed to evaluate for secondary causes of achalasia; it cannot be used for diagnosis as it is often normal.

The hallmark findings of achalasia on manometry are absence of esophageal peristalsis and incomplete or partial LES relaxation with wet swallows. Basal LES pressure and intraesophageal pressure may be elevated, but not uniformly. High-resolution esophageal manometry has led to the description of 3 subtypes of achalasia: type I or classic achalasia with low intraesophageal pressure, type II with panesophageal pressurization, and type III with highamplitude spastic contractions. Classification is beneficial as different types have variable responses to similar therapies, with type II having the most favorable response.

Achalasia cardia predisposes to esophageal malignancy due to chronic stasis and mucosal irritation.

Hence, the correct option is (A).

97. Beta-adrenergic antagonist, particularly propranolol, decreases plasma renin activity, tremors, heart rate and cardiac output. They should not be used in patients with diabetes taking oral hypoglycemic drugs, as they decrease the hypoglycemic control. They inhibit glycogenolysis and delay recovery from hypoglycemia. They also mask the warning symptoms of hypoglycemia.

Hence, the correct option is (D).

98. Enzymes involved in free radical detoxification :

1. SOD
2. Glutathione peroxidase
3. Catalase

Vitamin C and E are also implicated in detoxification of free radicals.

Food with increased lutein content will reduce cataract formation

Vitamin C also helps to modulate HMP pathway of lens

Chromophores present in lens act as sensitizers of photo oxidation of lens proteins. These chromophores contribute to protein cross linking and aggregation which leads to cataract development.

Hence, the correct option is (A).

99. Huntington disease is a hereditary degenerative brain disease that is characterized by a loss of neurons from the cerebral cortex and striatum, the latter causing severe involuntary movements. It is believed that loss of Y-aminobutyric acid (GABA)-mediated inhibition of dopaminergic neurons produces the motor disturbance. The neurochemical imbalance is opposite that in Parkinson disease and patients may benefit from dopaminergic antagonists, whereas levodopa and other dopaminergic drugs make the condition worse.

Hence, the correct option is (C).

100. Shown in the diagram is granulocyte. Granulocyte-colony stimulating factor (G-CSF or GCSF), also known as colony-

stimulating factor 3 (CSF 3), is a glycoprotein that stimulates the bone marrow to produce granulocytes and stem cells and release them into the bloodstream.
Hence, the correct option is (B).

101. While all organisms listed are associated with GI symptoms, this case is descriptive of peptic ulcer disease, which is associated with H. pylori infection. The other organisms cause diarrheal diseases.
Hence, the correct option is (C).

102. The indicated structure is a gray ramus communicans. Gray rami communicantes are located along the entire length of the sympathetic chain, connecting sympathetic chain ganglia with individual spinal nerves. They convey postsynaptic sympathetic fibers from the sympathetic chain to spinal nerves, for distribution to the body wall and limbs. White rami communicantes convey presynaptic sympathetic axons from spinal nerves into the sympathetic chain ganglia.

Nuclei housing presynaptic parasympathetic neurons are associated with four cranial nerve outflow tracts in the brainstem (Oculomotor nerve or CN III; Facial nerve or CN VII; Glossopharyngeal nerve or CN IX; Vagus nerve or CN X) and sacral levels S2-4. Because parasympathetic fibers emerge from both cranial and sacral levels of the central nervous

system, this division of the autonomic nervous system is described as having a craniosacral outflow. Though presynaptic parasympathetic neurons reach the thorax via the vagus nerve (CN X), these fibers do not enter or leave the sympathetic chain, so cutting a gray ramus communicans would not damage these nerve fibers.

Parasympathetic fibers below the head travel through the vagus nerve or sacral spinal nerves, but these nerves carry presynaptic parasympathetic axons, which have no attachments to the sympathetic chain. The postsynaptic parasympathetic axons have their cell bodies in intrinsic ganglia, which lie within the organ that is being innervated.
Hence, the correct option is (C).

103. Pruriceptive itch mostly originates when specific sensory nerve terminals, generally located in the skin, are activated. The excitation of sensory nerve fibers in the skin leading to pruriceptive itch occurs upon exposure of certain sensory nerve terminals to a pruritic substance and frequently follows skin damage or inflammation. Sensory nerve fibers in the skin originate from the distal processes of primary afferent dorsal root ganglion neurons.

Sensory nerve fibers in the skin are broadly classified according their condition of velocity and the sensory modalities that excite them. Fast conducting myelinated nerve fibers (Aβ) respond to non-noxious mechanical stimulation of the skin, while slow conducting myelinated (Aδ) and unmyelinated (C) nerves fibers respond to noxious stimulation and temperature changes of the skin. Studies in humans and non-human primates have demonstrated that slowly conducting unmyelinated nerve fibers (i.e. C-fibers) detect and signal pruriceptive information to the central nervous system. C-fibers are classified according to the stimuli that excite them.
Hence, the correct option is (A).

104. Premenstrual syndrome (PMS) and its more severe variant, that is, premenstrual dysphoric disorder (PMDD) are characterized by a constellation of physical and/or behavioral changes that occur in the second half of the menstrual cycle. These changes might include headache, weight gain, bloating, breast tenderness, mood fl uctuation, restlessness, irritability, anxiety, depression, fatigue, and a feeling of being out of control. These symptoms must occur in the 2 weeks prior to menstruation and there must be at least a 7-day symptom-free interval in the first half of the menstrual cycle. Symptoms must occur in at least two consecutive cycles for the diagnosis to be made.

The exact etiology of PMS and PMDD is unknown but is likely multifactorial and includes both physiologic and psychological causes. Studies have suggested that although women with PMS and PMDD have normal levels of estrogen and progesterone, they may have an abnormal response to normal hormonal changes.

Effective treatments for PMS and PMDD have been identified after systematic reviews. The selective serotonin reuptake inhibitors (SSRIs) have demonstrated clear efficacy in treating both the physical and mood symptoms of these disorders.

The serotonin and norepinephrine reuptake inhibitor (SNRI) Effexor (venlafaxine) and the benzodiazepine Xanax (alprazolam) have also shown efficacy in treating these disorders. In small trials, both Lupron (leuprolide acetate) and Danocrine (danazol) have shown efficacy in treating PMS and PMDD. Their side effects, however, prevent widespread use of these options.

Several older studies showed oral contraceptives to have no greater efficacy than placebo in managing PMS and PMDD.

Several studies have looked at vitamin supplementation as a treatment for PMS and PMDD. There appears to be some role for the use of calcium (600 mg BID), vitamin D (800 IU/day), vitamin B6 (=100 mg/day), magnesium (200 to 360 mg/day), and chasteberry extract (one tablet/day) in the treatment of these disorders.

There is some suggestion that exercise and relaxation techniques may improve the symptoms.

Other supplements such as evening primrose oil, essential fatty acids, and ginkgo biloba extract have not been found to be effective nor has the use of progesterone and progestins.
Hence, the correct option is (D).

105. Rheumatic fever is associated with five major criteria that include carditis or pancarditis, which involves the pericardium, myocardium, and endocardium. Patients typically present with sinus tachycardia, murmur of mitral regurgitation, evidence of heart failure, and presence of a pericardial friction rub or cardiomegaly on examination. Healing of the rheumatic valvulitis causes the classic fibrous thickening of the mitral valves. This leads to valvular stenosis and/or regurgitation. A migratory polyarthritis is present in as many as 75% of cases and most often affects the ankles, wrists, knees, and elbows over a period of days. Sydenham's chorea is a rare complication occurring in less than 10% of patients and is typically a late finding and may occur as long as several months after the presentation of acute rheumatic fever. Erythema marginatum is a rare manifestation occurring in less than 5% of cases. It presents as an evanescent macular eruption with rounded borders, usually concentrated on the trunk. Group A Streptococci can be recovered only in less than 25-40% of patients at the time of diagnosis. After initiation of standard conventional antibiotic treatment, secondary prophylaxis should be initiated to prevent subsequent colonization. In high-risk patients, benzathine penicillin-G given every 3 weeks is

effective in reducing the risk of recurrent rheumatic fever.
Hence, the correct option is (C).

106. Huntington disease is an autosomal dominant, fatal, progressive degeneration and atrophy of the striatum (caudate nucleus and putamen). The disorder is characterized by an increased number of trinucleotide (CAG) repeats in the HD (huntingtin) gene on the short arm of chromosome 4.

Degeneration of the upper and lower motor neurons is characteristic of ALS.

Dopamine depletion and depigmentation of the substantia nigra is characteristic of Parkinson disease.

Neurofibrillary tangles and amyloid plaques are found in Alzheimer disease.
Hence, the correct option is (C).

107. The baroreflex or baroreceptor reflex is one of the body's homeostatic mechanisms that helps to maintain blood pressure at nearly constant levels. The baroreflex provides a rapid negative feedback loop in which an elevated blood pressure reflexively causes the heart rate to decrease and also causes blood pressure to decrease. Decreased blood pressure decreases baroreflex activation and causes heart rate to increase and to restore blood pressure levels. The baroreflex can begin to act in less than the duration of a cardiac cycle (fractions of a second) and thus baroreflex adjustments are key factors in dealing with postural hypotension, the tendency for blood pressure to decrease on standing due to gravity.
Hence, the correct option is (A).

108. A pupillary diameter of less than 3 mm can cause general depression of the field. It is best to test the field with a pupil larger than or at least 3 mm diameter. If it is not possible to dilate the pupil to 3mm, the test should be performed with a pupil that is no smaller than that which existed during previous tests. Patients taking pilocarpine may need to refrain from taking the medication for 24 hours before the test or be dilated at the time of their examination.
Hence, the correct option is (B).

109. The signs and symptoms of Cushing syndrome can vary depending on the levels of excess cortisol.

Common signs and symptoms involve progressive obesity and skin changes, such as:

Weight gain and fatty tissue deposits, particularly around the midsection and upper back, in the face (moon face), and between the shoulders (buffalo hump)

Pink or purple stretch marks (striae) on the skin of the abdomen, thighs, breasts and arms

Thinning, fragile skin that bruises easily

Slow healing of cuts, insect bites and infections

Acne

Women with Cushing syndrome may experience:

Thicker or more visible body and facial hair (hirsutism)

Irregular or absent menstrual periods

Men with Cushing syndrome may experience:

Decreased libido

Decreased fertility

Erectile dysfunction

Other signs and symptoms include:

Severe fatigue

Muscle weakness

Depression, anxiety and irritability

Loss of emotional control

Cognitive difficulties

New or worsened high blood pressure

Headache

Bone loss, leading to fractures over time

In children, impaired growth

Cushing's disease is a form of Cushing's syndrome

Cushing's disease is the most common form of endogenous Cushing's syndrome. It is caused by a tumor in the pituitary gland that secretes excessive amounts of a hormone called Adrenocorticotropic hormone, or ACTH. Fortunately, this type of tumor is typically benign. Unlike a cancerous (malignant) tumor, a benign tumor stays in its original location and will not spread.

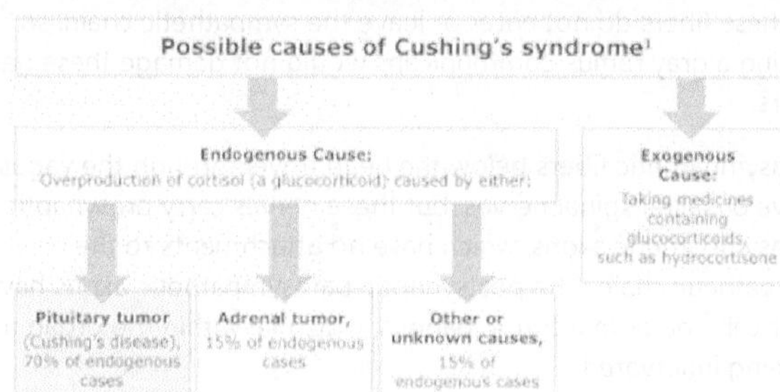

Hence, the correct option is (D).

110. Imbert Fick law states that pressure inside a sphere (P) is equal to the force (W) required to flatten its surface, divided by the area of flattening (A), i.e. P=W/A

The concept of applanation tonometry is based on this law.
Hence, the correct option is (D).

111. Tropomyosin is identifies in the diagram.

Myofibrils consist of two types of protein filaments, called thin filaments and thick filaments. Tropomyosin molecules, together with troponin and actin molecules, form the thin filaments which have a helix structure.

The key function of tropomyosin is to inhibit muscle contraction by blocking the interaction of actin and myosin (which is part of the thick filaments), except when influenced by troponin.

The binding of the myosin heads to the muscle actin is a highly regulated process. The thin filament is made of actin, tropomyosin, and troponin. The contraction of skeletal muscle is triggered by nerve impulses that in turn stimulate the release of Ca^{2+}. The release of Ca^{2+} from the sarcoplasmic reticulum causes an increase in the concentration of Ca^{2+} in the cytosol. Ca^{2+} initiates contraction by

binding to troponin C. In resting muscle, troponin I is tightly bound to actin and tropomyosin covers the sites where myosin heads bind to actin. Thus, the troponin-tropomyosin complex constitutes a "relaxing protein" that inhibits the interaction between actin and myosin. When the Ca^{2+} released by the action potential binds to troponin C, the binding of troponin I to actin is presumably weakened, and this permits the tropomyosin to move laterally. This movement uncovers binding sites for the myosin heads. ATP is then split and contraction occurs. Seven myosin-binding sites are uncovered for each molecule of troponin that binds a calcium ion.
Hence, the correct option is (D).

112. The Bender Visual Motor Gestalt Test (Bender-Gestalt) is the most frequently administered and thoroughly researched of all of the drawing (copying) tests. It consists of nine geometric designs (numbered A and 1-8) originally developed by Wertheimer to demonstrate the perceptual tendencies to organize visual stimuli into configural wholes (Gestalten). Each design is presented sequentially to the subject whose task is to reproduce them on a blank sheet of paper. It is used in wide variety of clinical groups, including mentally retarded, organically brain-damaged, and psychotic patients.

Bender Gestalt test detects errors like rotations, omissions, preservation on drawing the standard pictures shown to patient. Preservation is main diagnostic of organic pathology. Rest all other tests are projective tests for psychiatric diagnosis.
Hence, the correct option is (B).

113. Cholera toxin is a protein complex secreted by the bacterium Vibrio cholerae. The toxin is an oligomeric protein composed of one A subunit and five B subunits (AB_5). After entrance into intestinal epithelial cells (enterocytes) via receptor-mediated endocytosis, the A subunit detaches and becomes activated by proteolytic cleavage, allowing it to catalyze the ADP-ribosylation of the $G\alpha_s$ subunit of the heterotrimeric G protein resulting in constitutive cAMP production.
Hence, the correct option is (A).

114. Class $I_B$anti-arrhythmic drugs (Lignocaine, Mexiletine, Phenytoin) shorten the action potential duration and selectively act on diseased or ischemic tissue. Lignocaine suppresses the electrical activity of the arrhythmogenic tissues. Lignocaine is used in the treatment of ventricular arrhythmias associated with AMI and with cardiac surgery. Lignocaine is not useful in atrial arrhythmias. Phenytoin is useful in digitalis induced cardiac arrhythmia and ventricular arrhythmias in children
Hence, the correct option is (A).

115. Isopropyl thiogalactoside (IPTG) are galactosides; they are strong inducers of β-galactosidase in E.coli but do not act as substrate for enzyme, such compounds are known as non metabolisable inducers or gratuitous inducers. Allolactose is a natural inducer of β-galactosidase. Lactose on transglycodylation form allolactose. It is an intermediate in the hydrolysis of lactose by β-galactosidase. Allolactose and lactose are substrates for β-galactosidase. Glucose is the end product of lactose metabolism by β-galactosidase.
Hence, the correct option is (B).

116. The Shine-Dalgarno (SD) sequence is a ribosomal binding site in bacterial and archaeal messenger RNA, generally located around 8 bases upstream of the start codon AUG. The RNA sequence helps recruit the ribosome to the messenger RNA (mRNA) to initiate protein synthesis by aligning the ribosome with the start codon.

Initiation of translation in prokaryotes involves the assembly of the components of the translation system, which are: the two ribosomal subunits (50S and 30S subunits); the mature mRNA to be translated; the tRNA charged with N-formylmethionine (the first amino acid in the nascent peptide); guanosine triphosphate (GTP) as a source of energy, and the three prokaryotic initiation factors IF1, IF2, and IF3, which help the assembly of the initiation complex. The selection of an initiation site (usually an AUG codon) depends on the interaction between the 30S subunit and the mRNA template. The 30S subunit binds to the mRNA template at a purine-rich region (the Shine-Dalgarno sequence) upstream of the AUG initiation codon. The Shine-Dalgarno sequence is complementary to a pyrimidine rich region on the 16S rRNA component of the 30S subunit.

Mutations in the Shine-Dalgarno sequence can reduce or increase translation in prokaryotes. This change is due to a reduced or increased mRNA-ribosome pairing efficiency, as evidenced by the fact that compensatory mutations in the 3'-terminal 16S rRNA sequence can restore translation.
Hence, the correct option is (B).

117. Thiazides and thiazides like diuretics (e.g., chlorthalidonemetolazone) may elevate blood glucose levels due to decreased release of insulin from the pancreas, increased glycogenolysis and decreased glucogenosis and a reduction in the conversion of proinsulin to insulin
Hence, the correct option is (C).

118. The vascular cast sign is the radiographic appearance of cyanoacrylate and hyperdense lipiodol polymerizing within the pulmonary vasculature (giving the appearance as if a cast of the vessels have been made). A deep sulcus sign and a white line at the lung apex may indicate a pneumothorax, but are not related to cyanoacrylate embolization. Choice D and E are signs of left heart failure and would not be expected in the case of cyanoacrylate embolization.
Hence, the correct option is (A).

119. Aripiprazole diverges from traditional atypical profile, in that it has higher affinity for D2 receptors than for 5-HT2A receptors and more importantly, it is a partial agonist, rather than an antagonist at D2 receptors.

As a partial agonist it may diminish subcortical DA hyperfunction by competing with Dopamine for receptor binding, while simultaneously enhancing dopaminergic neurotransmission in prefrontal cortex by acting as agonist. The dual mechanism afforded by partial agonist may thus treat both positive and negative symptoms associated with schizophrenia.
Hence, the correct option is (B).

120. Rebound phenomenon results from the inability to brake the movement, which results in exaggerated opposite movement. This is because of the stretch on the particular muscle stimulate the stretch receptors, which than causes the contraction of that muscle. In the absence of cerebellum when the stretch is removed the simultaneous correction cannot occur rapidly in the body resulting rebound phenomenon.
Hence, the correct option is (B).

121. Alpha-fetoprotein (AFP):

It is a protein that in humans is encoded by the AFP GENE

This gene encodes alpha-fetoprotein, a major plasma protein produced by the yolk sac and the liver during fetal life.

The protein is thought to be the fetal counterpart of serum albumin and the alpha-fetoprotein and albumin genes are present in tandem on chromosome 4.

Alpha-fetoprotein is found in monomeric as well as dimeric and trimeric forms, and binds copper, nickel, fatty acids and bilirubin.

In humans, AFP levels decrease gradually after birth, reaching adult levels by 8 to 12 months. Normal adult AFP levels are low, but detectable; however, AFP has no known function in healthy adults.

In normal fetuses, AFP binds the hormone estradiol. AFP is measured in pregnant women, using maternal blood or amniotic fluid as a screening test for a subset developmental abnormalities: it is principally increased in open neural tube defects and omphalocoele & decreased in Down syndrome.

It is also measured in pregnant women, other adults, and children, serving as a biomarker to detect a subset of tumors, principally hepatocellular carcinoma, hepatoblastoma and endodermal sinus tumors.
Hence, the correct option is (B).

122. Given the history of excessive intake of milk, a food known to be low in iron, and the presentation of pallor, initial testing should focus on the hemoglobin and iron status. The reticulocyte count and the mean corpuscular volume (MCV) generally are low in iron deficiency. Chest radiography and stool smears for ova and parasites are not indicated. Serum haptoglobin is low in state of hemolysis, but that is not the most likely cause of anemia in this case.
Hence, the correct option is (C).

123. Medullary carcinoma of the thyroid is a calcitonin-producing tumor of C cells of the thyroid. Calcitonin contributes to amyloid deposition within the tumor.

Tumor cells with "Orphan Annie" nuclei and the presence of psammoma bodies are seen in papillary carcinoma of the thyroid.

Infiltrates of lymphocytes with germinal center formation are seen in Hashimoto thyroiditis.
Hence, the correct option is (A).

124. Gallstone ileus results in "tumbling" intestinal obstruction due to the intermittent nature of the condition. Previous choledochoduodenostomy could give air in the biliary tree but not obstruction
Hence, the correct option is (B).

125. The figure depicts Onycholysis.

Onycholysis - the nail becomes detached from the underlying nail bed and a gap develops under the nail. When it starts there is a white or yellowish patch at the tip of the nail, and this then extends down to the cuticle. The gap between the nail and the nail bed can become colonised by particular bacteria, such as pseudomonas, which can then produce a dark green pigment. The nail can become infected and discoloured and can easily be mistaken for melanoma under the nail.

It is the most common manifestation of psoriasis.
Hence, the correct option is (B).

126. Dobutamine activates mainly ß1 adrenoceptors. The subsequent actiivation of cyclic adenosine monophosphate (cAMP)-dependent protein kinase A increases the opening of membrane voltage-gated calcium channels (causing an increased speed and strength of myocyte contract ion), as well as the opening of sarcoplasmic calcium channels (causing an increased reuptake of Ca^{2+} by the sarcoplasmic reticulum). Therefore, both the speed of contraction and the speed of relaxation of myocytes are increased.

Inhibition of phosphodiesterase is the mechanism of action of milrinone.

Inhibition of the Ca^{2+}/Na^{+} exchanger in cardiac cell membrane is triggered by digoxin, not dobutamine.
Activation of phospholipase A2 is triggered by activation of a receptors, not ß receptors.
Hence, the correct option is (B).

127. Risk factors for stroke in a patient with atrial fibrillation include :

1. History of stroke, TIA
2. Hyperytension
3. Diabetes Mellitus
4. Mitral stenosis
5. Age more than 75 years
6. Congestive heart failure
7. LEFT ventricular dysfunction
8. Marked left atrial enlargement
9. Spontaneous echo contrast

Hence, the correct option is (D).

128. This patient has a popliteal artery aneurysm which accounts for 70% of all peripheral aneurysms. The history is typical of thrombosis in the aneurysm (Fig.), a recognized complication. An angiogram is done to see the 'run off' followed by femoro-distal bypass using the patient's reversed long saphenous vein. Surgery can be unsuccessful because the distal vessels are thrombosed; 50% of such limbs are not salvageable. An asymptomatic aneurysm should be repaired if the diameter is 2.5 cm or more to prevent complications such as distal emboli or thrombosis.

Popliteal artery aneurysm accounts for 70 per cent of all peripheral aneurysms; two-thirds are bilateral. Examination of the abdominal aorta is indicated if a popliteal aneurysm is found because one-third are accompanied by aortic dilatation. Popliteal aneurysms present as a swelling behind the knee or with symptoms caused by complications, such as severe ischaemia following thrombosis or distal ischaemia as a result of emboli. The diagnosis is usually confirmed with duplex scanning, but assessment of the distal vessels (with CT, MR or DSA) is important prior to repair if the foot pulses are diminished or absent. An asymptomatic aneurysm should be considered for elective repair to prevent future complications, especially if it exceeds 25 mm in diameter. Some surgeons would also offer elective repair if the sac contained thrombus because this may predispose to distal emboli. Surgery usually involves a medial approach to the above and below knee popliteal arteries, ligation of the aneurysm and restoration of flow to the foot with a bypass graft using saphenous vein. An alternative is a posterior approach and an inlay graft. In the acute situation, the presentation is usually with a thrombosed aneurysm and an ischaemic foot. Surgery is often unsuccessful because the distal vessels are thrombosed and difficult to clear. Attempts should be made with a Fogarty catheter and intra-arterial thrombolysis. The limb loss rate is high (50 per cent).

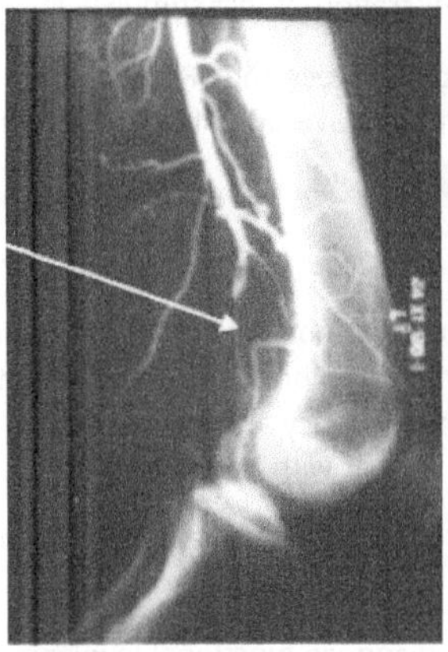

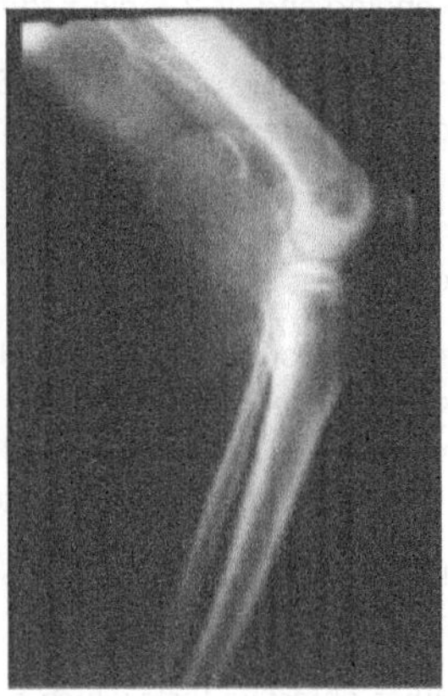

Hence, the correct option is (C).

129. It has significantly longer half-life than does isosorbide dinitrate

For isosorbide dinitrate, sublingual adm produces peak conc by 6 min and fall in conc is rapid (half life- 45 min). The primary initial metabolites, Isosorbide-2-mononitrate and Isosorbide-5-mononitrate have longer half lives that are presumed to contribute to therapeutic efficacy of the drug.
Hence, the correct option is (C).

130. In patients older than 40 years, 75% of neck masses are neoplastic. The most common cause of a unilateral neck mass is squamous cell carcinoma.

Masses can be initially mobile and then fixed as the cancer invades surrounding tissue.

They can become superinfected and present as abscesses.
Hence, the correct option is (C).

131. Intravascular hemolysis from blood transfusion is usually due to ABO incompatibility, often resulting from a human error. Symptoms of intravascular hemolysis include flushing, pain at the infusion site, chest or back pain, restlessness, anxiety, nausea, and diarrhea. Signs include fever and chills, shock, and renal failure. In this process, the donor's red blood cells are destroyed by recipient's preformed antibodies through the activation of complement system. Thus, the donor's red blood cells break open and releases haemoglobin into the blood. The haemoglobin is then excreted into urine, causes haemoglobinuria. Meanwhile, haemoglobin can also pass through the liver system and process into bilirubin, which accumulates under the skin, causing jaundice. The release of red blood cell debris and the activation of complement system causes uncontrolled clotting (disseminated intravascular coagulation) and circulatory shock. In comatose patients, hemoglobulinuria or bleeding from disseminated intravascular coagulation can be the first sign. Management is supportive.

Acute hemolysis can also result from antibodies directed against other RBC antigens such as Rh, Kell, or Duffy.
Hence, the correct option is (C).

132. It occurs in middle-aged women. It is a gradual painless goiter with local symptoms due to compression of esophagus, trachea, neck veins or recurrent laryngeal nerves. There is dense fibrosis disrupting thyroid gland. Thyroid dysfunction is uncommon. It needs open biopsy. Surgery to relive fibrosis is done. Tamoxifen may be beneficial. Ridel's thyroiditis is associated with idiopathic fibrosis of retroperitoneum, mediastinum, biliary tree, lung and orbit.
Hence, the correct option is (D).

133. Meningitis is the most common neurological event that occurs in the setting of early Lyme disease dissemination.

In this clinical setting CSF is always abnormal and shows

- Pleocytosis with predominantly lymphocytosis

- Increased protein

- Low to normal glucose

- Specific IgM, IgG, IgA appear in CSF and indicates intrathecal antibody synthesis.

Hence, the correct option is (C).

134. Puberty is said to be delayed when secondary sex characters do not appear by 13-14 years or menarche by 16 years.

Causes of delayed puberty are :-

Hypergonadotrophic hypogonadism

Gonodal dysgenesis 46 XO

Pure gonadal dysgenesis 46XX, 46XY

Ovarian failure 46 XX

Hypogonadotropic hypogonadism

Constitutional delay

Chronic illness

Primary hypothyroidism

Kallmann's syndrome

Intracranial lesions

Anatomical -

Mullerian agenesis

Imperforate hymen

Transverse vaginal septum

Constitutional is the most commonest.
Hence, the correct option is (D).

135. To walk down stairs, one has to have the ability to move the eyes down when they are in the medial position. This involves the use of cranial nerve IV (trochlear nerve), which innervates the superior oblique muscle (whose action is to pull the eye downward when in the medial position). If there is damage to this nerve on one side, the eyes will not be able to focus on the same visual field, thus producing double vision. Cranial nerve IV is classified as a general somatic efferent fiber because it innervates skeletal muscle and it is derived from somites.
Hence, the correct option is (C).

136. Postterm pregnancy is not associated with transient tachypnea of the newborn, which is seen more commonly in cesarean deliveries and in early term births at 37 and 38 weeks of gestation.

Oligohydramnios, macrosomia, meconium aspiration, and intrauterine fetal demise are all risks associated with postterm pregnancy.
Hence, the correct option is (A).

137. A reduction in carotid sinus pressure due to a decrease in mean blood pressure would elicit a baroreceptor reflex tending to restore blood pressure to normal. The reflex response includes an increase in sympathetic nervous system activity, which would cause an increase in heart rate and myocardial contractility, both of which would tend to increase cardiac output. Sympathetic stimulation would also cause constriction of both the arterioles and venous vessels. Arteriolar constriction would cause an increase in total peripheral resistance. Sympathetic stimulation of the venous vessels would cause a decrease in venous compliance
Hence, the correct option is (D).

138. Women who have invasive vulvar carcinoma usually are treated surgically. If the lesion is unilateral, is not associated with fixed or ulcerated inguinal lymph nodes, and does not involve the urethra, vagina, anus, or rectum, then treatment usually consists of radical vulvectomy and bilateral inguinal lymphadenectomy. If inguinal lymph nodes show evidence of metastatic disease, bilateral pelvic lymphadenectomy is usually performed. Radiation therapy, though not a routine part of the management of women who have early vulvar carcinoma, is employed (as an alternative to pelvic exenteration with radical vulvectomy) in the treatment of women who have local, advanced carcinoma.
Hence, the correct option is (D).

139. In uncal herniation, which is a common subtype of transtentorial herniation, the innermost part of the temporal lobe, the uncus, can be squeezed so much that it moves towards the tentorium and puts pressure on the brainstem, most notably the midbrain.

A) Sub falcine herniation - shift of cingulate gyrus of one hemisphere under falx cerebri and across to contralateral side.

B) Tentorial herniation - downward shift of midbrain structures through tentorial hiatus.
Hence, the correct option is (B).

140. Lanugo hair (Latin lanugo: down, like the fine small hairs of plants): Fine, soft, downy, usually un-pigmented hair on the body of the fetus and newborn. It is the first hair to be produced by the fetal hair follicles, and it usually appears around sixteen weeks of gestation and is abundant by week twenty. It is normally shed before birth, around seven or eight months of gestation, but is sometimes present at birth. It disappears on its own within a few weeks.

It is replaced by hair covering the same surfaces, which is called vellus hair. This hair is thinner and more difficult to see. The more visible hair that persists into adulthood is called terminal hair. It forms in specific areas and is hormone-dependent.
Hence, the correct option is (B).

141. Malingering/Nonorganic hearing loss (also called pseudohypacusis)

• Occasionally patients willfully or subconsciously exaggerate their hearing loss.

• This is functional hearing loss or pseudohypacusis or malingering

- The signs in the test behavior that suggest functional component include:

a. Inconsistent responses

b. Significant differences between the threshold obtained using ascending and descending administration of test stimuli

c. A discrepancy of more than 8 dB between the SRT (speech reception threshold) and the pure tone average of 500-2000 Hz

d. Positive Stenger test

Stenger Test

• It is used to identify unilateral or asymmetrical functional hearing loss. It is based on the concept that when both ears are stimulated simultaneously by a tone equal in frequency and phase, the auditory percept is lateralized to the ear with better hearing.

• If speech stimulus is used in Strenger test it is k/a Speech Stenger test or modified Stenger test.

• Other objective tests which can diagnose functional involvement are:

- Acoustic reflexes: It saying hearing loss but normal acoustic reflex indicates NOHL

- Auditory brainstem response

- otoacoustic emission
Hence, the correct option is (A).

142. The internal carotid arteries are two major arteries, one on each side of the head and neck. They arise from the common carotid arteries where these bifurcate into the internal and external carotid artery, and they supply the brain.

The following are the branches of the internal carotid artery, listed by segment :

C1: Branches from the cervical portion - none.

C2: Branches from the petrous portion

o Caroticotympanic arteries

o vidian artery

C3: Branches from the lacerum portion - none

C4: Branches from the cavernous portion

o Branches of the meningohypophyseal trunk:

+ Tentorial basal branch

+ Tentorial marginal branch

+ Meningeal branch - helps supply blood to the meninges of the anterior cranial fossa

+ Clivus branches - tiny branches that supply the clivus

+ Inferior hypophyseal artery

o Capsular branches - supplies wall of cavernous sinus

o Branches of the inferolateral trunk:

+ Branches to trigeminal ganglion - provide blood to trigeminal ganglion

+ Artery of the foramen rotundum

+ Branches to nerves

C5: Branches from the clinoid portion - none

C6: Branches from the ophthalmic portion

o Ophthalmic artery

o Superior hypophyseal artery

C7: Branches from the communicating portion

o Posterior communicating artery

o Anterior choroidal artery

o Anterior cerebral artery (a terminal branch)

o Middle cerebral artery (a terminal branch)

Posterior Choroidal is not a branch of interior carotid artery
Hence, the correct option is (B).

143. Antimuscarinic drugs relax the detrusor muscle, so voiding of the bladder becomes more diffcult. This can be especially dangerous in patients with prostatic hyperplasia who already have diffulty in micturition, due to prostate-induced narrowing of the urethra. In these pat ients, antimuscarinic drugs can precipitate acute urinary retention.

Alpha-1 antagonists such as prazosin are actually indicated in prostatic hyperplasia, as they relax the internal sphincter of the bladder.

Beta-blockers tend to contract the smooth muscle, as they block β_2 receptor-mediated relaxation. However, these drugs have little influence on nonvascular smooth muscles, which are mainly under parasympathetic control.

Alpha-2 agonists activate α_2 receptors, which are mainly presynaptic. This activation in turn can decrease the release of norepinephrine, thereby decreasing the contractility of the internal sphincter of the bladder.
Hence, the correct option is (B).

144. The placenta is a unique vascular organ that receives blood supplies from both the maternal and the fetal systems and thus has two separate circulatory systems for blood: (1) the maternal-placental (uteroplacental) blood circulation, and (2) the fetal-placental (fetoplacental) blood circulation. The uteroplacental circulation starts with the maternal blood flow into the intervillous space through decidual spiral arteries. Exchange of oxygen and nutrients take place as the maternal blood flows around terminal villi in the intervillous space. The in-flowing maternal arterial blood pushes deoxygenated blood into the endometrial and then uterine veins back to the maternal circulation. The fetal-placental circulation allows the umbilical arteries to carry deoxygenated and nutrient-depleted fetal blood from the fetus to the villous core fetal vessels. After the exchange of oxygen and nutrients, the umbilical vein carries fresh oxygenated and nutrient-rich blood circulating back to the fetal systemic circulation. At term, maternal blood flow to the placenta is approximately 600-700 ml/minute.
Hence, the correct option is (D).

145. Arterial ulcers are usually caused by atherosclerosis in the elderly. Men are more commonly affected. Pain is common, as is claudication. Distinguishing features of arterial ulcers are their sharply defined borders and round, punched-out appearance. They tend to be smaller than venous ulcers and are usually deep enough to expose muscle or tendons. Commonly affected sites include the toes, pretibial areas, and dorsum of the feet. Patients may have signs of livedo reticularis, pallor, and cyanosis. The legs may feel cold and clammy. Decreased peripheral pulses are commonly noted. Treatment consists of alleviating underlying risk factors. Pentoxifylline can be used in some cases. Surgical evaluation should be considered.
Hence, the correct option is (B).

146. A first-degree tear involves the vaginal mucosa or perineal skin, but not the underlying tissue. In a second-degree episiotomy, the underlying subcutaneous tissue is also involved, but not the rectal sphincter or rectal mucosa. In a third-degree tear, the rectal sphincter is affected. A fourth-degree episiotomy involves a tear that extends into the rectal mucosa.
Hence, the correct option is (C).

147. The auricular branch of the vagus nerve is often termed the Alderman's nerve or Arnold's nerve. It arises from the jugular ganglion, and is joined soon after its origin by a filament from the petrous ganglion of the glossopharyngeal; it passes behind the internal jugular vein, and enters the mastoid canaliculus on the lateral wall of the jugular fossa.
Hence, the correct option is (D).

148. The clinical presentation of laryngeal disorder is often ambiguous because breathing difficulties frequently masquerate as swallowing or voice disorders. Conversely, swallowing difficulties that result in failure to clear food particles from the throat may interfere with breathing. Laryngeal obstruction may be noted by the complaint of shortened phrasing and excessively effortful speaking, singing, or both. Conversely, laryngeal complaints often reflect disorders of the pharynx or esophagus such as gastroesophageal reflux disease. Aside from patients being obviously dyspneic, the sign and symptoms of laryngeal obstruction vary according to the cause of the obstruction.

Acute obstruction due to foreign bodies, trauma, or anaphylactic reactions is associated with abrupt onset of throat constriction, panic, and inability to phonate. Cough may be muted or not possible if a foreign body is firmly lodged in the upper trachea such that passage of air is virtually impossible. Salivation may occur. Patients may grab at their throat to identify the point of blockage. Vital signs may show tachycardia and elevated blood pressure or the conserve, depending on the degree of hypoxia and/or hypercarbia. Their level of consciousness is affected by the same factor. If the obstruction is almost complete, there may be virtually no audible breath sounds; whereas if the obstruction is partial, laryngeal wheezes (that transmit to the chest and may be mistaken as lower airway wheezing) are best heard directly over the trachea.
Hence, the correct option is (C).

149. Acrodermatitis enteropathica is a rare inherited form of zinc deficiency, characterized by periorificial and acral dermatitis, alopecia, and diarrhea.

Zinc is an essential trace nutrient required for the proper function of more than 100 enzymes and plays a crucial role in nucleic acid metabolism.

Acrodermatitis enteropathica is an autosomal recessive disorder postulated to occur as a result of mutations in the SLC39A4 gene located on band 8q24.3. The SLC39A4 gene encodes a transmembrane protein that is part of the zinc/iron-regulated transporter-like protein (ZIP) family required for zinc uptake. This

protein is highly expressed in the enterocytes in the duodenum and jejunum; therefore, affected individuals have a decreased ability to absorb zinc from dietary sources. Absence of a binding ligand needed to transport zinc may further contribute to zinc malabsorption.
Hence, the correct option is (B).

150. FIFTH DISEASE or Erythema infectiosum is a mild, moderately contagious disease seen most commonly in children 3 to 12 years old. It is caused by human parvovirus B19. The rash develops after fever has resolved, as a bright blanchable erythema on the cheeks (slapped cheek appearance) with perioral pallor.
Hence, the correct option is (A).

151. In RISING SUN SIGN there is red vascular hue seen behind the intact tympanic membrane. it is seen in glomus jugulare tumour, high jugular bulb and aberant carotid artery in the floor of middle ear.

Glomus jugulare tumour arises from the floor of the middle ear cavity. As the tumour increases in size, it fills in the middle ear cavity. It can be seen through the tympanic membrane as a red mass arising from the floor (thus called a RISING SUN SIGN). At times, a high jugular bulb can also mimic rising sun.
Hence, the correct option is (A).

152. Interpretation of hepatitis B Serologic Test Results

Tests	Results	Interpretation
HBsAg anti-HBc anti-HBs	negative negative negative	Susceptible
HBsAg anti-HBc anti-HBs	negative positive positive	Immune due to natural infection
HBsAg anti-HBc anti-HBs	negative negative positive	Immune due to hepatitis B vaccination
HBsAg anti-HBc IgM anti-HBC anti-HBS	positive positive positive negative	Acutely infected
HBsAg anti-HBc IgM anti-HBc anti-HBs	positive positive negative negative	Chronically infected
HBsAg anti-HBc anti-HBs	negative positive negative	Interpretation unclear; four possibilities: 1. Resolved infection (most common) 2. False-positive anti-HBc, thus susceptible 3. "Low level"chronic infection 4. Resolving acute infection

hepatitis B surface antigen (HBsAg): A protein on the surface of HBV; it can be detected in high levels in serum during acute or chronic HBV infection. The presence of HBsAg indicates that the person is infectious. The body normally produces antibodies to HBsAg as part of the normal immune response to infection. HBsAg is the antigen used to make hepatitis B vaccine.

hepatitis B surface antibody (anti-HBs): The presence of anti-HBs is generally interpreted as indicating recovery and immunity from HBV infection. Anti-HBs also develops in a person who has been successfully vaccinated against hepatitis B.

Total hepatitis B core antibody (anti-HBc): Appears at the onset of symptoms in acute hepatitis B and persists for life. The presence of anti-HBc indicates previous or ongoing infection with HBV in an undefined time frame.

IgM antibody to hepatitis B core antigen (IgM anti-HBc): Positivity indicates recent infection with HBV ($\leq$6) months). Its presence indicates acute infection.

Adapted from: A Comprehensive Immunization Strategy to Eliminate Transmission of hepatitis B Virus Infection in the United States: Recommendations of the Advisory Committee on Immunization Practices. Part I: Immunization of Infants, Children, and Adolescents.

Hence, the correct option is (B).

153. C. botulinum organisms are noninvasive. They cause disease primarily by production of an exotoxin, the botulinum toxin, which is the major virulence factor of the bacteria.

All toxins except C2 are neurotoxins; the neurotoxin acts specifically on cholinergic nerves; it acts by preventing the release of acetyl choline at the synapses and at the neuromuscular junctions.

Inhibition of glycine and GABA (choice B) describes the action of Tetanus toxin which causes a rigid paralysis.

The toxin of Clostridium perfringens is a lecithinase (choice C) which directly disrupts cell membranes.

Toxic shock syndrome toxin- 1 and the pyrogenic exotoxins of Streptococcus pyogenes act as superantigens (choice D) which cause systemic inflammatory response syndrome.
Hence, the correct option is (A).

154. Figure shows Malignant Acanthosis Nigricans on the dorsum of the foot and the lower one-third of the leg.

Acanthosis nigricans is associated with hyperpigmented areas that typically affect flexural folds (axilla). The two basic types of acanthosis nigricans are benign and malignant. The benign form is associated with obesity, diabetes, Stein-Leventhal syndrome, Cushing's disease, Addison's disease, pituitary disorders, and hyperandrogenic syndromes. Drugs, including glucocorticoids, nicotinic acid, diethylstilbestrol, and growth hormone therapy, have also caused acanthosis nigricans. Many cases are idiopathic. Malignant acanthosis nigricans is associated with an intestinal cancer such as gastric carcinoma.
Hence, the correct option is (B).

155. One significant and dangerous complication of placenta previa is placenta accreta, increta, and percreta. This is usually seen when a placenta previa gets implanted over previously injured sites such as scar of cesarean section, myomectomy, dilatation and curettage.

Placenta accreta refers to the placenta being attached to the myometrium but does not invade the muscle; increta is seen with the villi invades the myometrium; and percreta is seen when the villi penetrates through the entire uterine wall and into the bladder or rectum. Nitabuch's fibrinoid layer is absent.

The presence of placenta previa in a patient with a prior cesarean section is associated with accreta in 10-35% of cases. With multiple cesarean sections, the risk may be as high as 60-65%. USG and color Doppler assessment are very helpful in demonstrating marked or turbulent blood flow within the placenta and extending into the surrounding tissues, which is also described as lacunar flow. MRI can demonstrate placental tissue extension through the uterus.

Careful attention should be paid to the lower uterine segment after delivery of the placenta. If bleeding persists despite the usual postpartum uterotonic agents and uterine or hypogastric artery ligation, hysterectomy must be considered. It is considered a definitive and the safest treatment in these cases. Other methods to control the bleeding should be considered before hysterectomy such as oversewing the lower uterine segment, uterine artery ligation, ligation of internal iliac and uterine packing.
Hence, the correct option is (D).

156. Respiratory syncytial virus (RSV) is the most important cause of bronchiolitis in infants and young children and causes acute respiratory tract illness in patients of all ages. Typical roentgenographic findings include hyperinflation, peribronchial thickening, and atelectasis especially involving the right upper lobe. Infiltrates are typically associated with bacterial pneumonia. Pleural effusions and hilar adenopathy are findings not typically associated with bronchiolitis.
Hence, the correct option is (A).

157. Urobilinogen is normally present in urine in low concentrations. It is formed in the intestine from bilirubin, and a portion of it is absorbed back into the bloodstream. When urine urobilinogen is low or absent in a person with urine bilirubin and/or signs of liver dysfunction, it can indicate the presence of hepatic or biliary obstruction.

Positive test results help detect liver diseases such as hepatitis and cirrhosis and conditions associated with increased RBC destruction. Hemolytic anemia involves increased fecal and urinary urobilinogen. Increased amounts of bilirubin are formed in hemolysis, which generates increased urobilinogen in the gut. In liver disease (such as hepatitis), the intrahepatic urobilinogen cycle is inhibited also increasing urobilinogen levels. Urobilinogen is converted to the yellow pigmented urobilin apparent in urine.
Hence, the correct option is (B).

158. Penetrating injuries of the anterior neck that violate the platysma are considered significant because of the density of the critical structures in this region.
Hence, the correct option is (C).

159. Subacute hematoma appears isodense on nonenhanced CT. It shows hyperintense signal on T1-weighted and hypointense signal on T2- weighted images because of intracellular methemoglobin. Progression occurs from periphery to center.
Hence, the correct option is (B).

160. Mucopolysaccharidoses (MPSs) are inheritable storage diseases caused by a deficiency of lysosomal enzymes that degrade glycosaminoglycans (GAGs, previously called mucopolysaccharides). The MPSs are a heterogeneous group characterized by the intralysosomal accumulation of GAGs, excessive urinary excretion of GAGs, and variable degrees of progressive mental and physical deterioration and, in severe forms, premature death. Each type has a specific lysosomal enzyme deficiency, and many have variable phenotypic expression with characteristic degrees of organ involvement and rates of deterioration. Depending on the enzyme deficiency, the metabolism of dermatan sulfate, heparan sulfate, or keratan sulfate may be blocked alone or in combination. Lysosomal accumulation of the GAGs eventually results in cell, vascular, tissue, and organ dysfunction. The MPS disorders share many clinical features, although in variable degrees. These include a chronic and progressive course, multisystem involvement, organomegaly, dysostosis multiplex, and abnormal facial features. Vision, hearing, airway and cardiovascular function, and joint mobility may be affected. Mental retardation is a common feature of the severe forms. There is clinical similarity among different enzyme deficiencies and, conversely, a wide spectrum of clinical severity within any enzyme deficiency. MPSs are characterized by autosomal recessive traits, except for MPS II, which is an X-linked recessive condition.

MUCOPOLYSACCHARIDOSIS I: Deficiency of iduronidase results in a wide range of clinical involvement from the most severe, Hurler syndrome, to the mild Scheie syndrome, which are ends of a broad clinical spectrum. Hurler syndrome is the prototype for describing MPSs, but this is misleading because it is only representative of the most severe end of a spectrum.

Hurler Syndrome. This form of MPS I is a severe progressive disorder with multiple organ and tissue involvement that results in premature death, usually by 10 yr of age. An infant with Hurler syndrome appears normal at birth. Diagnosis is made between 6-24 mo with evidence of hepatosplenomegaly, skeletal deformity, coarse facial features, corneal clouding, large tongue, prominent forehead, joint stiffness, and short stature. Acute cardiomyopathy may be a feature in some infants younger than 1 yr of age. Most children with Hurler syndrome acquire only limited language skills because of developmental delay, chronic hearing loss, and an enlarged tongue. Hearing loss is common and is caused by a combination of conductive and neurosensory problems. Most patients have recurrent upper respiratory tract and ear infections, noisy breathing, and persistent copious nasal discharge. Progressive ventricular enlargement with increased intracranial pressure caused by communicating hydrocephalus also occurs. Corneal clouding, glaucoma, and retinal degeneration are common. Obstructive airway disease develops in many patients, necessitating tracheostomy. Obstructive airway disease, respiratory infection, and cardiac complications are the common causes of death.

Radiographic changes represent the many skeletal abnormalities in the MPSs and are known as dysostosis multiplex. The skull is large, with thickened calvarium, premature closure of lambdoid and sagittal sutures, shallow orbits, enlarged J-shaped sella, and abnormal spacing of teeth with dentigerous cysts. Anterior hypoplasia of the lumbar vertebrae with kyphosis is seen early. The diaphyses of the long bones are enlarged with an irregular appearance of the metaphyses; the epiphyseal centers are not well developed. The pelvis is usually poorly formed with small femoral heads and coxavalga. The clavicles are short, thickened, and irregular. The ribs have been described as oar-shaped-narrowed at the vertebral ends and flat and broad at their sternal ends. The phalanges are short and trapezoid with widening of the diaphyses.
Hence, the correct option is (A).

161. Examples of viral inclusion bodies:

Intracytoplasmic eosinophilic (acidophilic)-

Negri bodies in Rabies

Guarnieri bodies in vaccinia, variola

Paschen bodies in variola or small pox

Bollinger bodies in fowlpox

Henderson-Patterson bodies in Molluscum contagiosum

Intranuclear eosinophilic (acidophilic)-

Cowdry type A in Herpes simplex virus and Varicella zoster virus

Torres bodies in Yellow fever

Cowdry type B in Polio

Intranuclear basophilic-

Cowdry type B in Adenovirus

"Owl's eye appearance" in cytomegalovirus

Both intranuclear and intracytoplasmic-

Warthin–Finkeldey bodies in Measles

Hence, the correct option is (D).

162. Viral and immune markers are detectable in blood, and characteristic antigen-antibody patterns evolve over time. The first detectable viral marker is HBsAg, followed by hepatitis B e antigen (HBeAg) and HBV DNA. Titers may be high during the incubation period, but HBV DNA and HBeAg levels begin to fall at the onset of illness and may be undetectable at the time of peak clinical illness.7 Core antigen does not appear in blood, but antibody to this antigen (anti-HBc) is detectable with the onset of clinical symptoms.

HBeAg is another viral marker detectable in blood. It correlates with active viral replication and therefore high viral load and infectivity. HBeAg in serum reflects active viral replication, and the clinical outcome of infection is correlated with HBeAg status. Conversion to HBeAg-negative and HBeAb-positive status in patients with chronic hepatitis B typically leads to decreased inflammation, with normalizing transaminase levels and decreased levels of HBV DNA in serum: the inactive carrier state. The e antigen marker is also absent in patients with core or precore mutants.

Hence, the correct option is (B).

163. Acute glomerulonephritis is defined as inflammation and subsequent damage of the glomeruli leading to hematuria, proteinuria, and azotemia; it may be caused by primary renal disease or systemic conditions. The glomerular filtration rate is decreased, leading to activation of the renin-aldosterone system and subsequent salt and water retention, resulting in edema and hypertension. Most intrinsic causes of acute glomerulonephritis fall under the classification of nephritic syndromes. Nephritic syndromes are classified by hematuria, proteinuria, and red blood cell casts with hypertension and decreased urine production.

Nephrotic syndromes are due to impaired filtration of the glomeruli secondary to loss of function of the electrical barrier in the basement membrane, leading to loss of protein (primarily albumin) in large amounts (more than 3.5 g/day). The loss of albumin results in generalized edema from the loss of oncotic pressure that typically holds the fluid within the intravascular space.

Nephrolithiasis specifically refers to calculi in the kidneys. Acute onset of severe flank pain radiating to the groin, gross or microscopic hematuria, nausea, and vomiting not associated with an acute abdomen are symptoms that most likely indicate renal colic caused by an acute ureteral or renal pelvic obstruction from a calculus.

Diabetic nephropathy is a clinical syndrome characterized by persistent albuminuria (greater than 300 mg/d or 200 μg/min) that is confirmed on at least 2 occasions 3-6 months apart, progressive decline in the glomerular filtration rate (GFR) and elevated arterial blood pressure.

Hence, the correct option is (D).

164. The lienorenal (splenorenal) ligament is the portion of the greater omentum that connects the hilum of the spleen with the left kidney. It conveys the splenic vessels and also contains the tail of the pancreas. The mesenteries are double layers of peritoneum that support the abdominopelvic viscera and transmit associated neurovascular structures. The splenic artery is the largest branch of the celiac trunk. It weaves along the superior border of the pancreas and enters the splenorenal ligament to reach the spleen. In its course, it gives branches to the pancreas, fundus and greater curvature of the stomach, and greater omentum.

The hepatoduodenal ligament is the portion of the lesser omentum that attaches the porta hepatis of the liver to the first part of the duodenum. Its free margin forms the anterior wall of the epiploic foramen and conveys three significant structures: proper hepatic artery, bile duct, and portal vein. The coronary ligament connects the diaphragmatic surface of the liver to the diaphragm. It defines the bare area of the liver but does not transmit any major neurovascular structures.

The gastrolienal (gastrosplenic) ligament is the portion of the greater omentum that runs from the left part of the greater curvature of the stomach to the hilum of the spleen. It carries the short gastric and the left gastroomental (gastroepiploic) vessels.

Hence, the correct option is (C).

165. Mammography also is used to guide interventional procedures, including needle localization and needle biopsy. Specific mammographic features that suggest a diagnosis of breast cancer include a solid mass with or without stellate features, asymmetric thickening of breast tissues, and clustered microcalcifications. The presence of fine, stippled calcium in and around a suspicious lesion is suggestive of breast cancer and occurs in as many as 50% of nonpalpable cancers. These microcalcifications are an especially important sign of cancer in younger women, in whom it may be the only mammographic abnormality.

The combination of diagnostic mammography, ultrasound or stereotactic localization, and fine-needle aspiration (FNA) biopsy achieves almost 100% accuracy in the preoperative diagnosis of breast cancer. However, although FNA biopsy permits cytologic evaluation, core-needle permits the analysis of breast tissue architecture and allows the pathologist to determine whether invasive cancer is present. Core-needle biopsy is preferred over open biopsy for nonpalpable breast lesions because a single surgical procedure can be planned based on the results of the core biopsy. The advantages of core-needle biopsy include a low complication rate, minimal scarring, and a lower cost compared with excisional breast biopsy.

Hence, the correct option is (A).

166. Nitrous oxide is an anesthetic gas that has good analgesic and sedative properties without the skeletal muscle-relaxing effects. It can be used along with other inhaled agents decreasing their concentrations and thus their side effects.

Enflurane produces anesthesia, hypnosis, and muscle relaxation, as do the others, and is very pungent. Thiopental is a barbiturate that is too short acting for this application. Halothane has a pleasant odor and produces a smooth and relatively rapid induction but decreases cardiac output and can result in an unpredictable hepatotoxicity.
Hence, the correct option is (B).

167. Patients with chronic granulomatous disease have defective functioning of phagocytic neutrophils and monocytes due to an inability to produce hydrogen peroxide. That is, their phagocytic cells have a decreased oxidative or respiratory burst. The most common cause of chronic granulomatous disease is defective NADPH oxidase, which is an enzyme on the membrane of lysosomes that converts O_2 to superoxide and stimulates oxygen burst. This deficiency results in recurrent infections with catalase-positive organisms, such as S. aureus.

The classic form of chronic granulomatous disease usually affects boys and causes death before the age of 10.

Key findings in chronic granulomatous disease include lymphadenitis, hepatosplenomegaly, eczematoid dermatitis, pulmonary infiltrates that are associated with hypergammaglobulinemia, and defective ability of neutrophils to kill bacteria.
Hence, the correct option is (A).

168. Venlafaxine is a potent inhibitor of serotonin and norepinephrine reuptake and a weak inhibitor of dopamine reuptake. It has a better percentage response and completeness of response than fluoxetine in patients with severe depression. Venlafaxine must be tapered over 2 to 4 weeks. Clinical trials have shown that blood pressure increases with the 375-mg/day dose but not with 75 to 225 mg/day. Venlafaxine has been successful in reducing the insomnia, irritability, and excessive tension related to generalized anxiety disorder.
Hence, the correct option is (D).

169. CT has long been considered the gold standard in detecting calcification. When the Hounsfield units (Hu) exceed an established threshold (100 Hu), the source is believed to be calcification. In MRI, calcification appears with various signal intensities on conventional spin echo (SE) T1 or T2 weighted images, which makes it difficult to identify definitively as calcium. In gradient-echo acquisitions, calcifications usually appear as hypointense and cannot be differentiated from hemorrhage.
Hence, the correct option is (C).

170. Calcium metabolism is regulated in large part by the parathyroid hormone (PTH)-vitamin D endocrine system, which is characterized by a series of homeostatic feedback loops. The rapid release of mineral from the bone is essential to maintain adequate levels of ionized calcium in serum.

In general, mean calcium absorption and calcium intake are directly related. However, fractional calcium absorption varies inversely with calcium intake when the intake is very low. This type of adaptation occurs within 1 to 2 weeks and is accompanied by a decline in serum calcium concentration and a rise in serum PTH and calcitriol concentrations. The fraction of calcium absorbed rises adaptively as intake is lowered. However, this rise is not sufficient to offset the loss in absorbed calcium that occurs as a result of the lower intake of calcium-however modest that decrease may be-and thus net calcium absorption is reduced.

Reduced active calcium absorption leads to increased PTH secretion as the calcium sensing receptor in the parathyroid gland senses changes in circulating ionic calcium.
Hence, the correct option is (C).

171. Fanconi syndrome is a proximal tubule transport disorder which leads to hypophosphatemia, hypokalemia, and a hyperchloremic metabolicacidosis. The most common inherited cause in children is cystinosis, a disorder in which cystine accumulates in the lysosomes eventually leading to cell dysfunction. Children with this disorder typically are healthy for the first few months of life, and then develop the symptoms described. Two other choices, tyrosinemia and glycogen storage disease also are associated with Fanconi syndrome.
Hence, the correct option is (A).

172. There are many procedures that will provide successful correction of stress urinary incontinence. One of the abdominal procedures that successfully cures stress incontinence is the Marshall-Marchetti-Krantz (MMK) procedure, which involves the attachment of the periurethral tissue to the symphysis pubis.

The long-term cure rate for an MMK procedure is around 80%.

In approximately 1% to 2% of patients undergoing the procedure, the painfully debilitating condition of osteitis pubis will develop. Treatment of this aseptic inflammation of the symphysis is suboptimal, and the course is usually chronic.

Urinary retention after an MMK procedure occasionally occurs, but the problem usually resolves within 1 week. Short-term intermittent or indwelling catheterization is the treatment for urinary retention.

Enteroceles may occur in approximately 5% of women who have undergone the MMK procedure.
Hence, the correct option is (B).

173. Enterococci are Gram-positive cocci that often occur in pairs (iplococcic) or short chains. nterococci are facultative anaerobic organisms, i.e., they are capable of cellular respiration in both oxygen-rich and oxygen-poor environments. Though they are not capable of forming spores, enterococci are tolerant of a wide range of environmental conditions: extreme temperature (10-45°C), pH (4.5-10.0), and high sodium chloride concentrations. Enterococci typically exhibit gamma-hemolysis on sheep's blood agar.

The enterococci are commensal microorganisms that act as opportunistic agents of infections, particularly in elderly patients with serious underlying diseases and other immunocompromised patients who have been hospitalized for prolonged periods, have been treated with invasive devices and / or have received broad-spectrum antimicrobial therapy.

An important feature of this genus is the high level of intrinsic antibiotic resistance. Some enterococci are intrinsically resistant to β-lactam-based antibiotics (penicillins, cephalosporins, carbapenems), as well as many aminoglycosides. In the last two decades, particularly virulent strains of Enterococcus that are resistant to vancomycin (vancomycin-resistant Enterococcus, or

VRE) have emerged in nosocomial infections of hospitalized patients, especially in the US.

As Enterococci are increasingly becoming resistant to Vancomycin so should be screened.Urinary tract infections can be treated specifically with nitrofurantoin, even in cases of vancomycin resistance.
Hence, the correct option is (B).

174. The case describes a patient with mild persistent asthma. Asthma severity is classified by frequency of symptoms during the day and symptoms at night. The treatment of mild persistent asthma is the initiation of a controller medication plus the use of albuterol as needed-the most effective controller is a low dose inhaled corticosteroid twice daily. Albuterol alone will not control the persistent nature of this patient's symptoms. Over the counter cough medication does not address the root of the problems and symptoms will persist. Albuterol twice daily may help with symptoms, but albuterol should be given on an as needed basis and a controller medication given twice daily. Systemic steroids daily are used for acute exacerbations of asthma for a short course and for severe persistent asthma as a long term therapy.
Hence, the correct option is (C).

175. Neuroleptic malignant syndrome (NMS) is a rare, but life-threatening, idiosyncratic reaction to neuroleptic medications that is characterized by fever, muscular rigidity, altered mental status, and autonomic dysfunction. NMS often occurs shortly after the initiation of neuroleptic treatment, or after dose increases.

Signs and symptoms

The key to diagnosis is that NMS occurs only after exposure to an neuroleptic drug. On average, onset is 4-14 days after the start of therapy; 90% of cases occur within 10 days. However, NMS can occur years into therapy. Once the syndrome starts, it usually evolves over 24-72 hours.

Cardinal features are as follows:

Severe muscular rigidity

Hyperthermia (temperature more than 38°C)

Autonomic instability

Changes in the level of consciousness

A summary of the clinical features of neuroleptic malignant syndrome includes the following:

Muscular rigidity (typically, "lead pipe" rigidity)

Hyperthermia (temperature more than 38°C)

Diaphoresis

Pallor

Dysphagia

Dyspnea

Tremor

Incontinence

Shuffling gait

Psychomotor agitation

Delirium progressing to lethargy, stupor, coma

Other general examination findings indicative of autonomic dysregulation include the following:

Diaphoresis

Sialorrhea

Tachycardia

Tachypnea, respiratory distress (31% of cases)

Increased or labile blood pressure

Hypoxemia (low pulse oximeter reading)

See Clinical Presentation for more detail.

Diagnosis

No laboratory test result is diagnostic for NMS. Laboratory studies are used to assess severity and complications or rule out other diagnostic possibilities. A summary of the laboratory abnormalities that may be found in neuroleptic malignant syndrome includes the following:

Increased LDH

Increased creatine kinase (50-100% of cases)

Increased AST and ALT

Increased alkaline phosphatase

Hyperuricemia

Hyperphosphatemia

Hyperkalemia

Myoglobinemia

Leukocytosis (70-98% of cases)

Thrombocytosis

Proteinuria

Decreased serum iron

Increased CSF protein

Hypocalcemia

Myoglobinuria

Metabolic acidosis
Hence, the correct option is (C).

176. Secondary prevention

Secondary prevention can be defined as "action which halts the progress of a disease at its incipient stage and prevents complications". The specific interventions are early diagnosis (e.g., screening tests, case finding programmes) and adequate treatment. By early diagnosis and adequate treatment, secondary prevention attempts to arrest the disease process; restore health by seeking out unrecognized disease and treating it before irreversible pathological changes have taken place; and reverse communicability of infectious diseases. It may also protect others in the community from acquiring the infection and thus provide, at once, secondary prevention for the infected individuals and primary prevention for their potential contacts.

Secondary prevention is largely the domain of clinical medicine. The health programmes initiated by governments are usually at the level of secondary prevention. The drawback of secondary prevention is that the patient has already been subject to mental anguish, physical pain; and the community to loss of productivity. These situations are not encountered in primary prevention.

Secondary prevention is an imperfect tool in the control of transmission of disease. It is often more expensive and less effective than primary prevention. In the long run, human health, happiness and useful longevity will be achieved at far less expense with less suffering through primary prevention than through secondary prevention.
Hence, the correct option is (C).

177. Rules of Consent

i. Consent should be free, voluntary, clear, intelligent, informed, direct and personal. There should be no undue influence, fraud, misrepresentation of facts, compulsion, coercion or other consequences.

ii. Informed consent is legally not required to be in writing, but provides evidence that consent was in fact obtained, if necessity arises.

• It should be in a proper form and suitably drafted for the circumstances. The more specific the consent, the less likely it will be construed against the doctor or hospital in the court.

• The written consent should be witnessed by another person, present at the signing to prevent any allegation that the consent was forged or obtained under pressure. Hence, it has to be signed by the patient (unless minor, unconscious or insane wherein a legal guardian should sign), doctor and an independent witness.

iii. Any procedure beyond routine physical examination, such as operation, blood transfusion or collection of blood requires expressed consent.

iv. The doctor should explain the object of examination to the patient, and patient should be informed that the findings would be included in the report.

v. Patient should be informed that he has right to refuse to submit to examination. If he refuses, he cannot be examined.

vi. A person greater than 18 years of age can give valid consent to suffer any harm, which may result from an act not intended or not known to cause death or grievous hurt (Sec. 87 IPC).

vii. A person can give valid consent to suffer any harm which may result from an act not intended or not known to cause death, done in good faith and for his benefit (Sec. 88 IPC).

viii. A child less than 12 years of age and an insane person cannot give valid consent to suffer any harm which may result from an act done in good faith and for his benefit. The consent of the parent or guardian should be taken (Sec. 89 IPC).

Loco parentis (Latin, 'in place of a parent'): In an emergency involving children, when their parents or guardians are not available, consent is taken from the person-in-charge of the child, e.g. a school teacher can give consent for treating a child who becomes sick during a picnic away from home, or the consent of the principal of a residential school.

ix. The consent given by an insane or intoxicated person, who is unable to understand the nature and consequences of that to which he gives his consent is invalid (Sec. 90 IPC).

x. Sec. 92 IPC deals with cases of emergency, e.g. head injury requiring urgent decompression.34 It states that any harm caused to a person in good faith, even without the person's consent, is not an offence, if the circumstances are such that it is impossible for that person to signify consent and has no guardian or other person in lawful charge of him from whom it is possible to obtain consent in time for the thing to be done in benefit.

In an emergency, the law implies consent.

xi. Even in emergency, unless patient is unconscious, the consent offered by the parents of major (more than 18 years) is void and amount to negligence.

xii. Nothing is said to done in good faith which is done without due care and attention (Sec. 52 IPC).

xiii. Consent of the in-mates of the hostel is necessary, if they are greater than 12 years of age. Within 12 years, the principal or warden can give consent.

xiv. In civil cases, examination should not be done without the consent of the person.

xv. In criminal cases, the victim cannot be examined without his/her consent. The court cannot force a person to get medically examined.

• In rape cases, victim should not be examined without her written consent.

• In medico-legal cases of pregnancy, delivery and abortion, the woman should not be examined without her consent.

xvi. Under Sec. 53 (1) CrPC, an accused can be examined by a doctor by using reasonable force, if requested by a police officer (not below S.I.), if examination* may provide evidence to the commission of the offence.

Whenever an accused female is to be examined, the examination shall be made only by, or under the supervision of a female medical practitioner. Such an examination by a male doctor must not be carried out even in the presence of a female nurse [Sec. 53 (2) CrPC].

xvii. Under Sec. 54 CrPC, an arrested person may be examined by a doctor at his request to detect evidence in his favor, a copy of the report is to be furnished by the doctor to the arrested person.

xviii. Consent of one's spouse is not necessary for the treatment of other. Husband or wife has no right to refuse consent to any operation, which is required to safeguard the health of the partner.

xix. For contraceptive sterilization and artificial insemination, consent of both husband and wife should be obtained.

xx. Consent given for a diagnostic procedure cannot be considered as consent for therapeutic treatment. Consent given for a specific treatment/ procedure is not valid for conducting some other treatment/procedure. The fact that the unauthorized additional surgery is beneficial to the patient, or that it would save considerable time and expense to the patient, or would relieve the patient from pain and suffering in future, are not grounds of defense in an action for negligence. The only exception to this rule is if the unauthorized procedure was done to save the life or preserve the health of the patient.

xxi. There can be a common consent for:

• Diagnostic and operative procedures where they are contemplated

• Particular surgical procedure and an additional/ further procedure that may become necessary during the course of surgery.

xxii. The law provides the consent in any procedure made compulsory by state, e.g. mass immunization.

xxiii. In case of consent for donation of organ after death, the will of the deceased is enough.

xxiv. In prenatal diagnostic procedures, informed written consent of pregnant woman is obtained and a copy of the consent is given to the woman.

xxv. Pathological autopsy should not be carried out without the consent of next of kin of the deceased.

xxvi. Medico-legal autopsy does not require any consent from the relatives of the deceased.
Hence, the correct option is (C).

178. Clostridium is a diverse genus of bacteria, many of which are abundant and normal inhabitants of the human gastrointestinal tract (GIT). Many of the Clostridium species can have beneficial effects on the metabolism and health of the GIT in part by breakdown of polysaccharides, saccharolytic fermentation of carbohydrates to short chain fatty acids, and regulation of immune function.

While non-pathogenic Clostridium species are predominantly saccharolytic, toxin-producing species tend to be strongly proteolytic.

Proteolytic fermentation produces toxic metabolites such as ammonia, amines, volatile phenols and indoles which are pharmacologically active and affect a variety of physiological functions; including adverse effects in the central nervous system.
C. sporogenes is proteolytic; others given in the option are saccharolytic.
Hence, the correct option is (C).

179. Unregulated production of ADH results in increased water retention by the kidney, increased total body water, and moderate expansion of plasma volume. Plasma hypotonicity fails to supress the secretion of ADH. Hyponatremia, plasma hypo-osmolality, and inability to excrete maximally diluted urine are the consequences of SIADH.
Hence, the correct option is (C).

180.

Additional viscera and materials reguired in certain cases		
S.No	Material	Poisoning/circumstances suspected
1	Heart	Strychnine, digitalis
2	Brain	Alkaloids, organophosphorus, opiates, strychnine, carbon monoxide, cyanide, barbiturates and volatile organic poisons; hydrophobia/rabies (for negri bodies)
3	Spinal cord	Strychnine
4	CSF	Alcohol
5	Vitreous humor	Alcohol, chloroform
6	Lung	Gaseous poisons, hydrocyanic acid, alcohol, chloroform
7	Skin	Injected poisons (insulin, morphine, heroin, cocaine and other illicit drugs), firearm injuries
8	Bone, hair, and nails	Heavy metals (arsenic, antimony, thallium)
9	Fatty tissue	Pesticides and insecticides
10	Uterus and its appendages	Criminal abortion
11	Muscle	Decomposition

Hence, the correct option is (D).

181. The common carotid artery bifurcates at or just beyond the fourth cervical vertebral level, at the upper border of the thyroid cartilage.

The pharyngo-esophageal junction is typically at the level of the lower border of the cricoids cartilage, corresponding to the level of lower border of the 6th cervical vertebra. In front of pharynx and esophagus respectively, larynx and trachea are situated. The laryngotracheal junction is at the same horizontal level as the pharyngo-esophageal junction.
Hence, the correct option is (C).

182. In Tourette disorder, multiple motor tics and one or more vocal tics must be present at sometime during the illness. The motor and vocal tics do not need to occur concurrently.

Onset is before the age of 18. The average age of onset is 7. Tics must be present nearly every day or intermittently for at least 1 year, with no tic-free period longer than 3 consecutive months.
Hence, the correct option is (D).

183. The man is naturally angry, anxious, and sensitive at being reprimanded by his employer. He has found it difficult to express his feelings toward the disturbing person, the employer. Instead of suppressing or repressing the anger, or sublimating his tension in more forceful work, he displaces his anger onto a safer target, his wife. This is an example of displacement.
Hence, the correct option is (A).

184. The eyeball is an ablate spheroid, consisting of two modified spheres fused together. The cornea is a part of the anterior smaller sphere with radius of 7.8 mm and the sclera is a part of the posterior larger sphere with radius of about 12 mm.

The dimensions of the adult eyeball are :

Antero posterior diameter: 24 mm

Lateral (Horizontal) diameter: 23.5 mm

Vertical diameter: 23 mm

Circumference : 75 mm

Volume: 6.5 ml

Weight: 7 gms
Hence, the correct option is (D).

185.

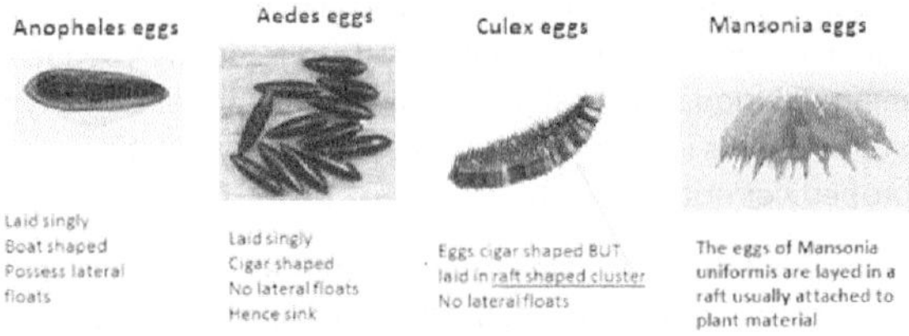

Hence, the correct option is (A).

186. Xanthogranulomatous pyelonephritis is a chronic infective condition of the kidney which is bilateral. It is important because it may be mistaken for cancer of the kidney. It occurs more commonly in females and may occur at any age. Symptoms include fever, weight loss, lassitude, nausea and vomiting. Urine culture shows Proteus (implicated in 60%), E. coli, Klebsiella, Pseudomonas and Enterobacter. The kidney is enlarged with a dilated pelvis lined by a yellowish zone which is friable. Often abscesses with surrounding yellowish zones are seen. Theses yellow zones are composed of an admixture of foam cells, plasma are composed of an admixture of foam cells, plasma cells, fibroblasts, polymorphs and foreign body giant cells. Focal calcification is a frequent finding.
Hence, the correct option is (C).

187. Coeliac disease is a common disorder that can arise at any age and typically presents with a broad spectrum of symptoms. The disease is thought to be underdiagnosed, in part owing to the fact that coeliac disease is often characterized by associated conditions and extraintestinal manifestations that can misdirect and impede diagnosis. Some of these manifestations are direct consequences of autoimmunity, such as dermatitis herpetiformis or gluten ataxia, whereas others are indirectly related to inflammation and/or malabsorption including anaemia, osteoporosis, short stature and delayed puberty.

A diagnosis of Dermatitis herpetiformis is made in this case.

A course of dapsone, a sulphone antibiotic, will reduce the symptoms of itching. In addition, avoiding gluten-based food may also clear the lesions slowly. Dermatitis herpetiformis does not respond well to systemic steroids, although topical steroid-antibiotic preparations have shown benefit. NSAIDs may help with pain but are not considered first-line therapy. Aciclovir is not recommended in the treatment of dermatitis herpetiformis.
Hence, the correct option is (B).

188. Burns involving less than 20% tsa in otherwise healthy individuals are rarely associated with life threatening infections.
Hence, the correct option is (B).

189. Keratitis, an inflammation of the cornea that frequently arises due to infection, is a threat to corneal transparency. Species of Aspergillus may cause keratitis. Aspergillus keratitis is an important ophthalmological problem worldwide, especially in outdoor workers in agricultural communities, where it frequently occurs following traumatic inoculation of Aspergillus conidia into the cornea through injury.

A presumptive diagnosis ofAspergillus keratitis can be established by a careful clinical examination and by direct microscopic examination of stained smears of corneal scrape material; Aspergillus hyphae in corneal material need to be distinguished from hyphae of other hyaline filamentous fungi such as species of Fusarium and Acremonium (Aspergillus hyphae may exhibit dichotomous branching whereas the other hyaline filamentous fungi usually do not) and hyphae of phaeohyphomycetes such as Curvularia (the hyphae of phaeohyphomycetes exhibit brown coloration). The diagnosis can be confirmed by culture of corneal scrape or corneal biopsy material.
Hence, the correct option is (B).

190. Older adults with radiographic evidence of calcified arteries often have Mönckeberg arteriosclerosis, beginning in the internal elastic lamina. This is a benign process that is a form of arteriosclerosis, often with no serious sequelae. The distal extremities, pelvis, thyroid, and breast regions are the most common locations.

Such focal peripheral arterial calcification is far less likely to be a consequence of atherosclerosis, with diabetes mellitus or with hypercalcemia.

Hypertension is most likely to affect small renal arteries, with hyaline or hyperplastic arteriolosclerosis, and calcification is not a major feature, although hypertension also is a risk factor for atherosclerosis.
Hence, the correct option is (A).

191. The Clostridia are a highly polyphyletic class of Firmicutes. They are obligate anaerobes and oxygen is toxic to them. Species of the class Clostridia are often but not always Gram-positive and have the ability to form spores.

The toxins produced by certain members of the genus Clostridium are among the most dangerous known. Examples are tetanus toxin (known as tetanospasmin) produced by C. tetani and botulinum toxin produced by C. botulinum. Some species have been isolated from women with bacterial vaginosis.

Clostridial necrotizing enteritis is necrosis of the jejunum and ileum caused by Clostridium perfringens. C. perfringens type C occasionally causes severe necrosis in the small bowel (primarily the jejunum). Disease is caused by clostridial beta-toxin, which is very sensitive to proteolytic enzymes and is inactivated by normal cooking. Necrosis is segmental, involving small or large patches with varying degrees of hemorrhage and intramural gas; necrosis ranges from mucosal injury to full-thickness necrosis and perforation.

Pathogenic C. difficile strains produce multiple toxins. The best-characterized are enterotoxin (Clostridium difficile toxin A) and cytotoxin (Clostridium difficile toxin B), both of which may produce diarrhea and inflammation in infected patients. The diarrhea may range from a few days of intestinal fluid loss to life-threatening pseudomembranous colitis. Pseudomembranous colitis is associated with intense inflammation of the colon and formation of pseudomembranes on the intestinal mucosal surface.

Bacillary dysentery is a type of dysentery, and is a severe form of shigellosis. It is associated with species of bacteria from the Enterobacteriaceae family. The term is usually restricted to Shigella infections.
Hence, the correct option is (C).

192. The MRI shows abnormal signal in the area of the dorsal midbrain (Fig. arrow). Skew deviation, lid retraction (Collier sign), and pupillary light-near dissociation are all signs of Parinaud dorsal midbrain syndrome. The sixth nerve arises in the pons (Fig. curved arrow) and should not be affected by this lesion.

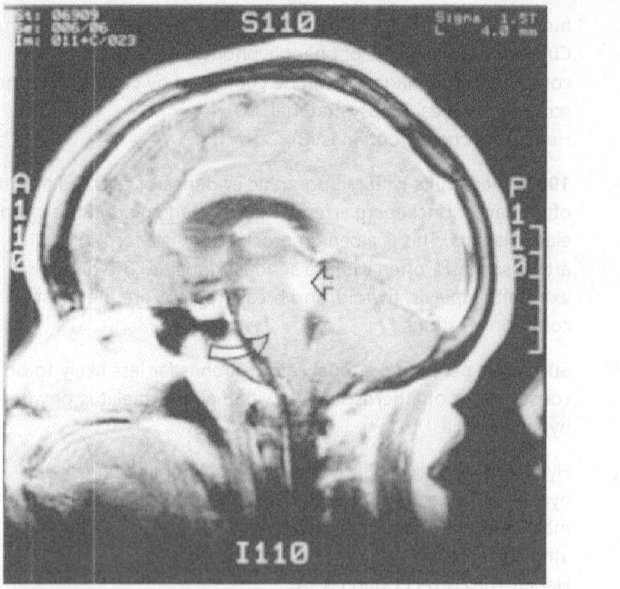

Hence, the correct option is (A).

193. In the years leading up to menopause, women begin having variations in the length of their menstrual cycle. This is a mormal physiologic change and on average a woman begins menopause at 51 years old. Premature ovarian failure is the cessation of menstrual periods prior to age 40 years old.
Hence, the correct option is (C).

194. Penoscrotal and perineal hypospadias often have bifid scrotum and should be considered to have intersex problems.
Hence, the correct option is (D).

195. Burkitt lymphoma (BL) (or small noncleaved cell lymphoma) is one of the highly aggressive B-cellnon-Hodgkin lymphomas (NHL) that is characterized by the translocation and deregulation of the c-MYC gene on chromosome 8.

Major signs of Burkitt lymphoma include a soft-tissue mass associated with the involvement of the jaw or other facial bones, rapidly enlarged cervical lymph nodes, abdominal masses, and ascites. The physical examination findings depend on the sites of extranodal involvement and may include the following:

- Abdominal tenderness
- Ascites
- Abdominal mass
- Hepatosplenomegaly
- Palpable tumor of the mandibulomaxillary region
- Ecchymosis and/or petechiae (as a result of thrombocytopenia)
- Meningeal signs (from CNS disease)
- Painless lymphadenopathy

The tumor consists of sheets of a monotonous population of medium-sized lymphoid cells with high proliferative activity and apoptotic activity. The "starry sky" appearance is seen under low power due to scattered body-laden macrophages (macrophages containing dead apoptotic tumor cells).
Hence, the correct option is (D).

196. Shown in the image is nonsense mutation. A nonsense mutation is a change in one DNA base pair. Instead of substituting one amino acid for another, however, the altered DNA sequence prematurely signals the cell to stop building a protein. This type of mutation results in a shortened protein that may function improperly or not at all.

Missense mutation: This type of mutation is a change in one DNA base pair that results in the substitution of one amino acid for another in the protein made by a gene.

Frameshift mutation: This type of mutation occurs when the addition or loss of DNA bases changes a gene's reading frame. A reading frame consists of groups of 3 bases that each code for one amino acid. A frameshift mutation shifts the grouping of these bases and changes the code for amino acids. The resulting protein is usually nonfunctional. Insertions, deletions, and duplications can all be frameshift mutations.

Insertion: An insertion changes the number of DNA bases in a gene by adding a piece of DNA. As a result, the protein made by the gene may not function properly.
Hence, the correct option is (A).

197. Findings: T1 and T2 weighted images show a fluid (CSF)-filled cleft extending from the surface of the right hemisphere to the left lateral ventricle. The margins of the cleft are lined by dysplastic/polymicrogyric gray matter (arrows).

- Schizencephaly is a disorder in which there is a cleft between the surface of the brain and the ventricle. The cleft is lined by dysplastic or polymicrogyric brain.
- The etiology of schizencephaly is controversial. Most cases are thought to be due to an early destructive insult occurring before neuronal migration. Later, when neuronal migration occurs from the germinal matrix, the cleft becomes lined with gray matter, in rare cases, a genetic mutation may be responsible.
- Patients may have seizures, motor deficit, spasticity, or developmental delay. Clinical severity is related to the extent and location of the cleft(s) and the associated malformations.
- The cleft may be wide open and filled with CSF (open-lip schizencephaly) or narrow/closed (closed-lip schizencephaly). The clefts may be unilateral or bilateral.
- In closed-lip schizencephaly, a "dimple" along the wall of the lateral ventricle may point to the abnormality.
- Schizencephaly is associated with other malformations, such as septo-optic dysplasia and corpus callosum anomalies.
- Some porencephalic or postoperative cavities may also represent a CSF-filled connection between the brain surface and the ventricle, but these will not be lined by gray matter.

Management:

Treatment is supportive and may include anticonvulsant for seizures.
Hence, the correct option is (C).

198. Von-Willebrand disease is a congenital disorder of hemostasis characterized by defective or deficient Von-Willebrand factor (vWF). There are several subtypes of Von-Willebrand disease. The most common type (80% of cases) is type I, which is caused by a quantitative decrease in vWF; type IIA and type IIB are results of qualitative protein abnormalities; and type III is a rare, autosomal recessive disorder characterized by a near-complete quantitative deficiency of vWF.

The laboratory diagnosis of von-Willebrand disease includes normal or abnormal Partial thromboplastin time (APTT) and normal prothrombin time (PT); prolonged bleeding time; decrease in factor VIII, vWF antigen (vWF:Ag), and vWF activity (ristocetin cofactor activity); normal platelet aggregation except in the presence of ristocerin; and mildly prolonged PTT. A normal APTT does not exclude the diagnosis of von-Willebrand disease.
Hence, the correct option is (B).

199. Morphological changes such as mediastinal shift, elevation of the hemidiaphragm and crowding of the ribs occur after pneumonectomy to contract the pneumonectomy space, which fills with tissue fluid. Dehiscence of the bronchial stump occurs in bronchopleural fistula to establish communication between colonised bronchial tree and sterile pneumonectomy space. Invariably, the pneumonectomy space and contained fluid get infected due to the bronchopleural fistula. Signs of systemic infection (pyrexia) with clinical (expectorating purulent sputum) and radiological (high fluid level) evidences of infected collection in the chest warrant immediate chest drain insertion, to control the source of sepsis. Further management of bronchopleural fistula is undertaken in specialised centres.
Hence, the correct option is (B).

200. Clinging behavior and inordinate pining may be early signs of prolonged grief as described by Parks. More recently, childhood experiences of early parental death or divorce, sudden or violent death of a loved one, and high levels of dependency on the deceased for a sense of personal well-being are thought to be associated with prolonged grief. Several of these factors suggest the role of attachment insecurity in increasing a person's vulnerability to complicated bereavement.
Hence, the correct option is (A).

201. CVP catheterization is done through Seldinger technique in which the catheter is threaded over J wire. The point of insertion is at cricoid level and the guide to direction is ipsilateral nipple. The tip should lie at the junction of superior vena cava with right atrium.
Hence, the correct option is (B).

202. Shown in the image is Elek's test, also known as the immuno diffusion technique. It is an in vitro virulence test performed upon Corynebacterium diphtheriae. It is used to test for toxigenicity of C. diphtheriae.

A filter paper strip impregnated with diphtheria antitoxin is buried just beneath the surface of a special agar plate before the agar hardens. Strains to be tested, known positive and negative toxigenic strains are streaked on the agar's surface in a line across the plate, and at a right angle to the antitoxin paper strip. After 24 hours of incubation at 37 degrees Celsius, plates are examined with transmitted light for the presence of fine precipitin lines at a 45-degree angle to the streaks. The presence of precipitin lines indicates that the strain produced toxin that reacted with the antitoxin.
Hence, the correct option is (B).

203. In contrast to a normal, mature neutrophil, which has from two to five nuclear lobes, the neutrophil shown has at least six lobes and is an illustration of neutrophilic hypersegmentation. Granulocytic hypersegmentation is significant and among the first hematologic findings in the peripheral blood of patients who have megaloblastic anemia in its developmental stages. Neutrophilic hypersegmentation is generally considered a sensitive indicator of megaloblastic anemia, which can be caused by a deficiency in vitamin B12, in folate, or in both.

This deficiency impairs DNA synthesis and delays mitotic division, which in turn causes the nuclei to be enlarged. The synthesis of RNA and cytoplasmic elements is not affected, however, so there is nuclearcytoplasmic asynchrony. These cellular changes affect all rapidly proliferating cells in the body, but in the bone marrow they result in enlarged erythroid precursors, which are referred to as megaloblasts. These abnormal cells produce abnormally enlarged red cells, which are called macroovalocytes. These megaloblasts also undergo autohemolysis within the bone marrow, resulting in ineffective erythropoiesis. Granulocyte precursors are also enlarged and are called giant metamyelocytes. These abnormal cells produce enlarged hypersegmented neutrophils. The megakaryocytes are large and have nuclear abnormalities, but, although the platelet count is decreased, the platelets are not enlarged.
Hence, the correct option is (B).

204. Regular arrangements of groups of amino acids located near each other in the linear sequence of a polypeptide are the secondary structure of a protein. The α helix, β sheet, and β bend are the secondary structures usually observed in proteins. In both the α helix and the β sheet, all the peptide bond components participate in hydrogen bonding. That is, the oxygen components of the peptide bond form hydrogen bonds with the amide hydrogens. In the case of the α helix, all hydrogen bonding is intrachain and stabilizes the helix.

In the case of β sheets, the bonds are interchain when formed between the polypeptide backbones of separate polypeptide chains and intrachain when the β sheet is formed by a single polypeptide chain folding back on itself.

While the spiral of the α helix prevents the chain from being fully extended, the chains of β sheets are almost fully extended and relatively flat.

The chains of β sheets can be either parallel or antiparallel. When the N-terminals of chains run together, the chain or segment is considered parallel. In contrast, when N- and C-terminal ends of the chains alternate, the β strand is considered antiparallel.
Hence, the correct option is (A).

205. Mutations in the gene for barttin, also known as BSND, have been associated with Bartter syndrome with sensorineural deafness. Bartter syndrome is due to defective transport in the thick ascending limb. It is characterized by chronic Na+ loss in the urine, with resultant hypovolemia causing stimulation of renin and aldosterone secretion without hypertension, plus hyperkalemia and alkalosis. BSND encodes an essential beta subunit for CLC chloride channels. These heteromeric channels localize to basolateral membranes of renal tubules and of potassium-secreting epithelia of the inner ear.
Hence, the correct option is (A).

206. Keratoacanthoma

Classically, this is a symmetrical, cutaneous growth with a central crater filled with a keratin plug (Fig.). It is twice as common in men and is usually found on the face of 50-70 year olds. The aetiology of keratoacanthoma is unclear but may be caused by a papilloma virus in a hair follicle during the growth phase. It has also been associated with smoking and chemical carcinogen exposure.

Keratoacanthoma, is usually a rapidly growing solitary tumour with a predilection for sun-exposed areas. It can grow to between 1 and 3 cm in a 6-week period and then typically resolve spontaneously over the subsequent six months. Removal of the central keratin plug may speed resolution. Excision is recommended as the differential diagnosis includes anaplastic SCC and the excision scar is often better than that which remains after resolution. Patients with multiple keratoacanthomas or with sebaceous differentiation should be evaluated for Muir-Torre syndrome, which is associated with visceral malignant tumours.
Hence, the correct option is (C).

207. Ceramide is an important signaling molecule for apoptosis and is a precursor for glycosphingolipids and gangliosides. Sphingolipids and phospholipids are structural lipids in membranes. Multiple sclerosis is a demyelinating disease in which both phospholipid and sphingolipid levels are decreased, unlike lipid storage diseases, which affect sphingolipid levels.
Hence, the correct option is (D).

208. Ventilatory function can be easily measured with lung volume measurement and the FEV1/FVC ratio.

A decreased FEV1/FVC ratio is characteristic of obstructive lung diseases. Alternatively, low lung volumes, specifically decreased total lung capacity (TLC), and occasionally decreased residual volume (RV) are characteristic of restrictive lung diseases.

In patients with idiopathic pulmonary fibrosis, a restrictive ventilatory defect is typically present. Vital capacity, functional residual capacity, total lung capacity, and forced vital capacity (FVC) all are reduced.

With extensive air trapping in obstructive lung disease, TLC is often increased, and RV may also be increased. Vital capacity (VC) is proportionally decreased.

Maximal inspiratory pressure (MIP) measures respiratory muscle strength and is decreased in patients with neuromuscular disease.

Ppatients with idiopathic pulmonary fibrosis will have normal muscle strength and subsequently a normal MIP but decreased TLC and RV. In some cases of pulmonary parenchymal restrictive lung disease, the increase in elastic recoil results in an increased FEV1/FVC ratio.

The hallmark of obstructive lung disease, such as chronic obstructive pulmonary disease (COPD), is a decreased FEV1/FVC ratio.
Hence, the correct option is (B).

209. Ethylene glycol by itself it is a harmless substance but it is broken down in the body into oxalic acid (a deadly poison) by the enzyme, alcohol dehydrogenase. Eethanol acts as a competitive inhibitor for alcohol dehydrogenase.

Ethylene glycol is metabolised via alcohol dehydrogenase to glycolaldehyde which is rapidly metabolised to glycolate, the metabolite mainly responsible for the metabolic acidosis in ethylene glycol poisoning. Glycolate is metabolised by various pathways, including one to oxalate which rapidly precipitates with calcium in various tissues and in the urine. Toxicity is mainly due to the severe metabolic acidosis caused by glycolate and to the calcium oxalate precipitation.

Ethanol is also metabolised by alcohol dehydrogenase, but has a much higher affinity for this enzyme than ethylene glycol. Presence of ethanol will therefore inhibit formation of toxic metabolites ethylene glycol. Because ethanol has a much higher affinity for alcohol dehydrogenase, about a 100-times greater affinity, it successfully blocks the breakdown of ethylene glycol into glycolaldehyde, which prevents the further degradation. Without oxalic acid formation, the nephrotoxic effects can be avoided, but the ethylene glycol is still present in the body. It is eventually excreted in the urine, but supportive therapy for the CNS depression and metabolic acidosis will be required until the ethylene glycol concentrations fall below toxic limits.
Hence, the correct option is (D).

210. Tricuspid valve endocarditis would produce emboli that would not be able to reach intestine due to pulmonary filtration.
Hence, the correct option is (A).

211. Metabolism of Atracurium is by Hoffmann's elimination and nonspecific ester hydrolysis, the kidneys not having to play a major role in it, making it the drug of choice in renal patients.

Pancuronium is eliminated majorly (80%) by the kidneys. Vecuronium undergoes about 25% of renal excretion, rapacuronium gets metabolized its 3 desacetyl derivative which has an accumulative property. About 20% is by renal excretion.
Hence, the correct option is (B).

212. Respiratory burst is a type of cellular defence mechanism. Phagocytic cells like monocytes, nutrophils, eosinophils and macrophages remove foreign cell (e.g. bacteria) by phagocytosis. At this time the phagocytic cells are activated and there is rapid increase in consumption of oxygen which is known as respiratory burst. During this phenomenon there is production of reactive derivatives such as O^{2-}, H_2O_2, OH^-, OCl^-. Some of these products are potent microbicidal agents. NADPH Oxidase present in plasma membrane of phagocytic cells is responsible for this respiratory burst.
Hence, the correct option is (C).

213. So far only one disease, smallpox, has been eradicated by vaccines, saving approximately 5 million lives annually. Polio could be next. Over 80% of the world's children are now being immunized against the polio virus, and the annual number of cases has been cut from 400,000 in 1980 to 90,000 in the mid-1990s.

Eradication literally means to "tear out by roots".

Eradication of disease implies termination of all transmission of infection by extermination of the infectious agent (31). As the name implies, eradication is an absolute process, and not a relative goal. It is "all or none phenomenon". The word eradication is reserved to cessation of infection and disease from the whole world.

Today, smallpox is the only disease that has been eradicated globally. Every disease like every human being is unique with its own epidemiological characteristics and specific strategies for control.

During recent years, three diseases have been seriously advanced as candidates for global eradication within the foreseeable future: polio, measles and dracunculiasis. The feasibility of eradicating polio appears to be greater than that of others and the goal is in sight.

Experience gained from eradication programmes (e.g., malaria, yaws) has shown that once the morbidity of a disease reaches a very

low level, a "residual" infection usually persists in the population leading to a state of equilibrium between the agent, host and environmental components of the disease process. In this situation, there are always hidden foci of infection, unrecognized methods of transmission, resistance of the vector or organism, all of which may again flare up when the agent-host-environment equilibrium is disturbed. Failure to understand this led to disappointment in the eradication programmes mounted against malaria, yaws, plague, kala-azar and yellow fever.
Hence, the correct option is (A).

214. Sestamibi does not redistribute as well as thallium does in hibernating myocardium. Positron emission tomography is the "gold standard" for detecting myocardial viability but is not routinely available. Thallium, which is dependent on the Na_, K_-ATPase pump for uptake, can be used to assess the viability of myocardial tissue. Dipyrimadole is an inhibitor of adenosine metabolism and can result in bronchospasm. Therefore, caution must be used in patients with severe (FEV _40% of predicted) obstructive 1 pulmonary disease. The side effects of dipyridamole can be reversed by the administration of intravenous theophylline, an adenosine receptor antagonist.
Hence, the correct option is (D).

215. One should consider pyoderma gangrenosum in the differential of a patient who presents with rapid skin ulcerations, undermined borders, and a history of autoimmune disorders including rheumatoid arthritis. Pyoderma granulosum is a diagnosis of exclusion, and biopsy is used to rule out other causes.

Squamous cell carcinoma rarely propagated this quickly. This tumor's borders are often raised and irregular.

Rheumatoid vasculitis can produce ulcerative lesions in patients suffering from rheumatoid arthritis, especially in those with titers of rheumatoid factor. However, the ulcers produced in this condition lack undermined borders, cribiform scarring, and pathergy.

Keratoacanthoma (KA) is a rapidly growing skin cancer usually appearing as a volcano-like bump on the sun-exposed skin of middle-aged and elderly individuals.

Pyoderma gangrenosum is an ulcerative process associated with other autoimmune diseases, such as rheumatoid arthritis and inflammatory bowel disease.

Pyoderma gangrenosum is in the rapidly progressive skin ulcerations, undermined borders, and a history of autoimmune disorders.
Hence, the correct option is (B).

216. R-factor (resistance) plasmids contain genes for proteins that degrade antibiotics or alter antibiotic transport, thus conferring antibiotic resistance. They also carry transfer genes, which facilitate their intercellular transfer to other genomes.

The R factor may carry one antibiotic resistance gene or may carry two or more of these genes. The R factor carrying more than two genes has many clinical implications:

- First and foremost, a bacterium carrying such genes will show resistance to more than one type of antibiotics, such as penicillins and aminoglycosides.

- The second importance is that the use of an antibiotic that selects an organism for a bacterium resistant to one antibiotic (such as penicillin) will select for a bacterium resistant to other antibiotics (such as tetracyclines, aminoglycosides, chloramphenicol, erythromycin, etc.).

Hence, the correct option is (B).

217. Endophthalmitis as a complication of IV drug abuse has been widely reported. The most common organisms in these cases are fungal in origin and often occur in the absence of fungemia. Bacterial causes are predominantly a result of Staphylococcus species; however, recently B. cereus has been reported as an important pathogen. Although H. influenzae can cause infection, it would be unusual in this setting.
Hence, the correct option is (D).

218. An ostium secundum atrial septal defect is an abnormally large opening in the atrial septum at the site of the foramen ovale and the ostium secundum.

An ECG demonstrates sinus rhythm, often with evidence of right atrial enlargement manifested by tall, peaked P waves (usually best seen in leads II and V2) and prolongation of the PR interval. The QRS axis is slightly directed to the right (+100 degree), and the precordial leads reveal right ventricular enlargement of the so-called volume overload type that is characterized by an rSR' pattern in leads V3 R and V1 with normal T waves.

The QRS duration may be mildly prolonged because of right ventricular dilation. This mimics the finding in right ventricular conduction delay.

In ostium primum defect RV conduction defect is associated with Left axis Deviation.

Varying degrees of right atrial and right ventricular hypertrophy may occur with each type of defect.
Hence, the correct option is (A).

219. A true neoplasm is a monoclonal proliferation of cells, whereas a reactive proliferation of cells is not monoclonal. Molecular genetic analysis, such as allelotype analysis with microsatellite markers, shows clonality. Reactive and neoplastic cellular proliferations may have similar histochemical and immunohistochemical staining patterns based on the type of cells and proteins that are present. Flow cytometry is effective at indicating the DNA content, aneuploidy, and growth fraction, but does not indicate clonality.
Hence, the correct option is (D).

220. In epidemiology, a case fatality rate (CFR) is the proportion of deaths within a designated population of "cases", over the course of the disease. A CFR is conventionally expressed as a percentage and represents a measure of risk. CFRs are most often used for diseases with discrete, limited time courses, such as outbreaks of acute infections.

In the given question, in an outbreak of cholera in a village of 2000 population, 20 cases have occurred and 5 have died.

Thus, CFR = (5/20) x 100 = 25 %
Hence, the correct option is (D).

221. Sleep apnea syndrome is the most common cause of daytime sleepiness in the elderly. The prevalence (at east in sleep disorder centers) increases with advancing age. Narcolepsy and periodic limb movement disorder (restless legs) are other common causes of excessive daytime sleepiness.
Hence, the correct option is (A).

222. Montenegro skin test (or Leishman skin test) is to test Leishmaniasis (Kala Azar). An intradermal injection of a suspension of killed promastigotes (leishmania flagellate) measures delayed type hypersensitivity reactions ranging from few days to months. A positive wheal formation indicates an infection.
Hence, the correct option is (C).

223. Most ovarian neoplasms are epithelially derived. Typically, ovarian carcinoma presents in an indolent fashion with abdominal fullness at an advanced stage with extensive inter peritoneal metastasis. However, a small subset of ovarian neoplasms are germ cell tumors, which are capable of producing sex hormones such as androgens, leading to virilization, as noted in this patient. Such ovarian germ cell tumors should be treated in an analogous fashion to testicular cancer in the male, since they are highly responsive to cisplatin and etoposide.
Hence, the correct option is (D).

224. Sensitivity

The term sensitivity was introduced by Yerushalmy in 1940s as a statistical index of diagnostic accuracy. It has been defined as the ability of a test to identify correctly all those who have the disease, that is "true-positive". A 90 per cent sensitivity means that 90 per cent of the diseased people screened by the test will give a "true-positive" result and the remaining 10 per cent a "false-negative" result.
Hence, the correct option is (A).

225. Because surgical wound infect ions are major nosocomial in fections, antimicrobial prophylaxis is advisable in open heart surgery, surgery for placement of prosthetic materials, any surgeries performed on an immunocompromised host, high-risk patients in preparation for contaminated and cleancontaminated surgical procedures, and orthopedic surgery, as in this case. The goal of antimicrobial prophylaxis is to decrease bacterial counts below the critical level necessary to cause infection. Cefazolin is the drug most frequently used for surgical prophylaxis when skin flora is the source of contaminat ion because of its excellent activity against staphylococci.

Metronidazole is not used for surgical prophylaxis, as it is active only against anaerobic microorganisms.

Tetracycline: Bacteriostatic agents are not used for microbial prophylaxis because bacteremia can reoccur when the drug is no longer present.

Aztreonam is active only against gram-negative bacteria and therefore is not suitable to prevent infection due to staphylococci.
Hence, the correct option is (D).

226. Conduct Money

• It is the money given or paid to a witness in civil cases to meet the expenses towards attending the court.

• In civil cases, conduct money is paid to the doctor at the time of serving the summons. If the money is not paid or the doctor feels that the sum paid is inadequate, he can inform the court accordingly. Then the judge will decide regarding the amount to be paid.

• In criminal cases, no such money is paid to the witness at the time of serving the summons. The witness must attend the court because every citizen is duty bound to attend the court whenever summoned. However, conveyance charges and daily allowance is paid to the doctor according to the prevailing government rules.
Hence, the correct option is (C).

227. Leishmania recidivans is caused by L. tropica.

1. Donovani visceral LEISHMANIASIS

2. Tropicacutaneous leishmaniasis oriental sore, Delhi boil

3. Braziliensismucocutaneous leishmaniasis, espundia (severe lower extremity involved)

4. Braziliensis peruvianauta or dumdum fever or Asian fever or infantile splenomegaly
Hence, the correct option is (A).

228. Encephalocele is a neural tube defect characterized by sac like protrusions of the brain and the membranes that cover it through openings in the skull. These defects are caused by failure of the neural tube to close completely during fetal development.
Hence, the correct option is (C).

229. Pelvic splanchnic nerves or nervi erigentes are splanchnic nerves that arise from sacral spinal nerves S2, S3, S4 to provide parasympathetic innervation to the hindgut. It provides the sacral parasympathetic outflow that supplies the gut tube below the left colic flexure, the pelvic viscera, and the perineum. Part of the distribution route for the parasympathetic nerves to the descending colon, sigmoid colon, and upper rectum is to ride along the arterial branches that supply those organs. Because the left colic artery is the parent vessel to those structures, damage to the pelvic splanchnic nerves would affect the organs supplied by the left colic artery.

The right colic artery carries parasympathetic fibers derived from the vagus nerve to the ascending colon. This vessel/organ pairing is outside the pelvic splanchnic territory.

Renal arteries supply the kidneys and suprarenal glands. Again, any parasympathetic supply to these organs is derived from vagal branches that travel with the renal arteries.

The lumbar arteries supply structures in the posterior abdominal wall (e.g., psoas muscles, vertebral column). Parasympathetic nerves do not supply the body walls and limbs. Thus, the lumbar arteries do not convey parasympathetic fibers.
Hence, the correct option is (B).

230.

Uncojugated hyperbilirubinermia	Conjugated hyperbillirubinemia
Criggler Najjarsy syndrome-I	Dubin Johnson syndrome
Criggler Najjar syndrome-=II	Rotor syndrome
Gilbert syndrome	

Hence, the correct option is (D).

231. The most common complication of mumps virus infection in postpubertal males is orchitis, occurring in about 33% to 50% of cases. Other complications occur at lower frequencies including myocarditis, meningoencephalitis, Guillain-Barré syndrome, mastitis, pneumonia, thyroiditis, pancreatitis, hearing loss, and immune thrombocytopenia purpura, which may be associated with hemorrhage. Oophoritis occurs in approximately 7% of postpubertal females.
Hence, the correct option is (B).

232. All the listed techniques have been suggested for dealing with residual common duct stones. Duct flushing techniques have not proved effective for impacted distal common duct stone although removal: via the T-tube tract is feasible, transduodenal papillotomy with endoscopic stone extraction is more effective with a stone impacted in the distal part of the common bile duct. Operative removal is reserved for situations where other techniques have failed.
Hence, the correct option is (D).

233. The most common clinical presentation of hypoplastic left heart syndrome is respiratory distress on the second or third day of life. Prostaglandin E1 maintains patency of the ductus arteriosus and thereby preserves blood flow to the systemic circulation.Although this is deoxygenated blood due to total mixing, there is adequate oxygen delivery to maintain life. Milrinone is a phosphodiesterase inhibitor whose cardiovascular effects include increased inotropy and peripheral vasodilatation. These effects are similar to dobutamine which acts through beta 1, 2 - adrenergic receptors.
Hence, the correct option is (B).

234. 1. Renal sinus and perinephric simple cysts seen. (On sonography, characteristics of simple cysts are seen).

2. Kidneys may show loss of cortico-medullary differentiation. (Kidneys may appear enlarged, and cortico-medullary differentiation may be lost).

3. Kidneys are usually large. (Kidneys may appear enlarged, and cortico-medullary differentiation may be lost).

4. Cysts are fluid density on CT scan. (The attenuation within the cysts lies in the range of fluid).

5. Surrounding structures are not invaded but displaced. (Surrounding structures are not seen to be invaded, but only abutted or displaced. Ascites may be found, and is a known complication).
Hence, the correct option is (D).

235. Hamartomatous polyp in intussusception in Peutz-Jeghers syndrome.

A - Gross specimen of resected small bowl demonstrating intussception.

B - Opened small-bowel resection revealing gross appearance of polyps, indicated by circles

C and D - A hamartomatous polyp from the small-bowel resection with both gross (C) and histologic (D) cross-sections demonstrating extension of the smooth muscle layer from the muscularis propria into the core of the polyp, characteristic of a hamartomatous polyp.

Peutz-Jeghers syndrome is characterized by the development of noncancerous growths called hamartomatous polyps in the gastrointestinal tract (particularly the stomach and intestines) and a greatly increased risk of developing certain types of cancer.

Children with Peutz-Jeghers syndrome often develop small, dark-colored spots on the lips, around and inside the mouth, near the eyes and nostrils, and around the anus. These spots may also occur on the hands and feet. They appear during childhood and often fade as the person gets older. In addition, most people with Peutz-Jeghers syndrome develop multiple polyps in the stomach and intestines during childhood or adolescence. Polyps can cause health problems such as recurrent bowel obstructions, chronic bleeding, and abdominal pain.

People with Peutz-Jeghers syndrome have a high risk of developing cancer during their lifetimes. Cancers of the gastrointestinal tract, pancreas, cervix, ovary, and breast are among the most commonly reported tumors.
Hence, the correct option is (C).

236. The history of the patient suggests a bronchial adenoma. Up to 60% of patients have no symptoms. When present, symptoms are related to the presence and degree of endobronchial occlusion and the vascularity of the tumor. Hemoptysis occurs in 18%, recurrent infection or cough in 17%, dyspnea or wheezing in 2%, and carcinoid syndrome in 1%.

Chest radiography films may demonstrate a nodule, mass, infiltrate or atelectasis, mediastinal or hilar lymphadenopathy, or pleural effusion. Findings may be due to bronchial obstruction. Radiological findings are frequently nondiagnostic. The most appropriate next test would be a lung CT to demonstrate a lesion.

The other tests are not appropriate for identifying the source of bleeding.
Hence, the correct option is (B).

237. A straight blade is generally more suitable for use in infants than a curved blade because it better elevates the base of the tongue to expose the glottic opening and the tube used should be uncuffed to prevent trauma to subglottic area as subglottis is the narrowest part.
Hence, the correct option is (C).

238. The goal of therapeutic radiation is selective destruction of neoplastic cells, in which formation of free radicals within the tumor and tissues has the greatest effect.

Gamma irradiation is not converted to heat.

K cell lysis is a feature of innate immunity and may play a role in tumor surveillance. Radiation therapy, however, tends to reduce immune function if the irradiated field includes tissues of the immune system, such as bone marrow and lymph nodes.

There are long-term vascular changes in radiated tissues, but the doses are divided and spread over time to avoid significant immediate tissue damage.
Hence, the correct option is (C).

239. IgM is basically a pentamer, composed of five immunoglobulin subunits (monomeric subunits, IgMs) and one molecule of J chain. Each monomeric IgM is composed of two light chains (κ or γ light chains) and two heavy chains (μ).

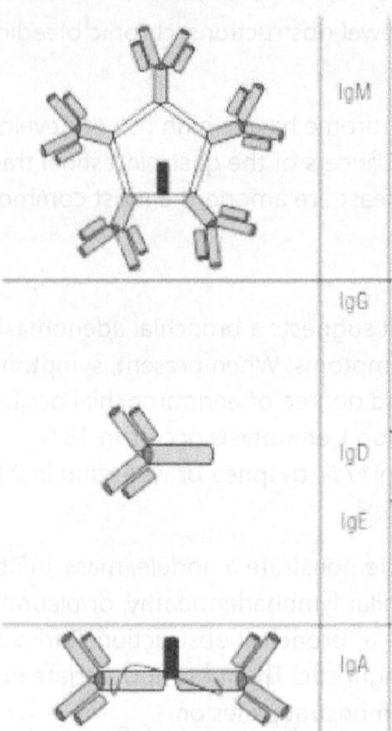

Hence, the correct option is (C).

240. Main early complication of TIPSS is perforation of liver capsule.

- Shunt stenosis is the main long term complicationof TIPSS- 50% at 1 year.
- Main indications for shunt currently- childs grade a cirrhosis in whom initial bleed has been controlled by sclerotherapy.

Hence, the correct option is (A).

241. Vasomotor rhinitis is a non-infective, non-allergic condition characterised by profuse rhinorrhoea and sneezing, with or without nasal obstruction, occurring in attacks which may be either paroxysmal or parennial. The running of the nose and sneezing may be so severe as to even disable the patient.

Malcomson showed conclusively that stimulation of the parasympathetic or interruption of the sympathetic nerve supply to the nasal mucous membrane caused vasodilatation, hypersecretion and sneezing, and hence it is reasonable to assume that under normal conditions there exists a balance between the two systems. The symptoms of vasomotor rhinitis seem to be due to an imbalance between these two systems.

While the causes of vasomotor rhinitis could be psychogenic or due to drugs like methyldopa or rauwolfia, or endocrine, the logical step in the treatment of idiopathic nasal vasomotor imbalance is vidian neurectomy, when it is found that all other available methods of treatment have failed and the symptoms are severe enough to justify surgery.

The principle underlying vidian neurectomy is to sever the preganglionic fibres that reach the sphenopalatine ganglion through the vidian nerve. Several routes have been described to approach the deep seated vidian nerve: (1) Transantral (a) Classic, (b) Subperiosteal, (2) Transeptal, (3) Transpalatal, (4) Transethmoidal, and (5) Transnasal.
Hence, the correct option is (A).

242. AIDS-defining illnesses are classified as being directly associated with advanced HIV infection. Many of these diseases are seen outside the realm of HIV but are considered AIDS-defining either because they are more prevalent in HIV-positive people or are rarely seen outside of immune suppressive disorder.

The current case definition of AIDS in a patient with HIV infection is done by symptoms and CD4+ T-lymphocyte cell count. Any category C symptoms (e.g., cervical cancer, mycobacterium avium infection, CMV, retinitis, Kaposi sarcoma, etc.) indicates frank AIDS as does a CD4+ T-cell count less than 200/μL regardless of symptoms.

<u>The current list of AIDS-defining illnesses</u>

- Candidiasis of bronchi, trachea, or lungs
- Candidiasis esophageal
- Coccidioidomycosis, disseminated or extrapulmonary
- Cryptococcosis, extrapulmonary
- Cryptosporidiosis, chronic intestinal for longer than 1 month
- Cytomegalovirus disease (other than liver, spleen or lymph nodes)
- Cytomegalovirus retinitis (with loss of vision)
- Encephalopathy (HIV-related)
- Herpes simplex: chronic ulcer(s) (for more than 1 month); or bronchitis, pneumonitis, or esophagitis
- Histoplasmosis, disseminated or extrapulmonary
- Isosporiasis, chronic intestinal (for more than 1 month)
- Kaposi's sarcoma
- Lymphoma, Burkitt's
- Lymphoma, immunoblastic (or equivalent term)
- Lymphoma, primary, of brain
- Mycobacterium avium complex or Mycobacterium kansasii, disseminated or extrapulmonary
- Mycobacterium, other species, disseminated or extrapulmonary
- Mycobacterium tuberculosis, any site (extrapulmonary)
- Pneumocystis jirovecii pneumonia (formerly Pneumocystis carinii)
- Progressive multifocal leukoencephalopathy
- Salmonella septicemia (recurrent)
- Toxoplasmosis of the brain
- Tuberculosis, disseminated
- Wasting syndrome due to HIV
- Cervical cancer (invasive)
- Mycobacterium tuberculosis, any site (pulmonary)
- Pneumonia (recurrent)

<u>Additional conditions are included for children younger than 13:</u>

- Bacterial infections, multiple or recurrent
- Lymphoid interstitial pneumonia or pulmonary lymphoid hyperplasia complex

Shingles and thrush are category B symptoms.
Hence, the correct option is (B).

243. Hemarthrosis (or haemarthrosis) is a bleeding into joint spaces. It is a common feature of Hemophilia. The most common presentation is with pain in a weight bearing joint such as the hip, knee or ankle. Hematuria is also common. Bleeding can occur at almost any site without prior trauma.
Hence, the correct option is (D).

244. Stratified sampling is used when the population is heterogeneous with regards to characteristic under study. When subpopulations within an overall population vary, it is advantageous to sample each subpopulation (stratum) independently. Stratification is the process of dividing members of the population into homogeneous subgroups before sampling. The strata should be mutually exclusive: every element in the population must be assigned to only one stratum. The strata should also be collectively exhaustive: no population element can be excluded. Then simple random sampling or systematic sampling is applied within each stratum. This often improves the representativeness of the sample by reducing sampling error. It can produce a weighted mean that has less variability than the arithmetic mean of a simple random sample of the population.

Snowball sampling technique is often used in hidden populations which are difficult for researchers to access It is a non-probability sampling technique where existing study subjects recruit future subjects from among their acquaintances. Thus the sample group is said to grow like a rolling snowball.

Cluster sampling is used when units of population are natural groups or clusters. In this sampling plan, the total population is divided into these groups (known as clusters) and a simple random sample of the groups is selected. The elements in each cluster are then sampled.

Multistage sampling refers to sampling plans where the sampling is carried out in several stages using smaller and smaller sampling units at each stage.
Hence, the correct option is (B).

245. Cryoprecipitate is formed by thawing fresh frozen plasma from a recent donation and is rich in fibrinogen and factor VIII. It is not however free of the risk of non-A non-B hepatitis, and it contains the same degree of risk of infection with hepatitis Band HIV as other blood products, i.e. it depends on effective donor screening. It does appear to be useful in reversing the platelet defect in uraemia although the mechanism is unclear, but it is relatively deficient in factor IX and is of no therapeutic value in haemophilia B.
Hence, the correct option is (D).

246. MRI with gadolinium is the most sensitive test for the detection of microadenomas, revealing them in 10%-20% of normal women. Oversecretion of prolactin is present in only 30%-50% of patients with pituitary adenomas. Impaired GH response to insulin-induced hypoglycemia or visual field changes would occur only in those tumors that are large enough to interfere with normal pituitary function or to compress the optic chiasm. CT scans reveal very small adenomas, but MRI with gadolinium is even more sensitive.
Hence, the correct option is (D).

247. The causative agent is Rickettsia conorii, a member of the spotted fever group of rickettsiae, the best known member of which is R. rickettsii the causative agent of Rocky Mountain spotted fever.

Hence, the correct option is (B).

248. Penicillinase resistant penicillins are antibiotics, which are not inactivated by the penicillinase enzyme. Some bacteria produce the enzyme penicillinase that destroys the beta-lactam ring of the antibiotic, making the penicillin ineffective. Penicillinase resistant penicillins are used to treat resistant strains of staphylococci and other infections.

Three major penicillinase-resistant penicillins are dicloxacillin, oxacillin and nafcillin. Dicloxacillin is orally available; oxacillin and nafcillin have both oral and parenteral formulations, the latter being given by the intramuscular or intravenous route. Other formulations available include methicillin, cloxacillin and flucloxacillin, which have been associated with a higher frequency of side effects including hepatic injury. The major indications for dicloxacillin, oxacillin and nafcillin are moderate-to-serious infections with susceptible penicillinase-producing staphylococci; these agents are also active against organisms susceptible to natural penicillins, but are less active than the natural penicillins.
Hence, the correct option is (D).

249. Portal bridging fibrosis and nodular hepatocyte regeneration are features of cirrhosis. If liver stem cells support hepatocyte regeneration, and ductular reactions are minimal, then cirrhosis may be less progressive, and thin septae suggest some degree of regression. If the patient is currently not drinking alcohol, no fatty change (steatosis) would be present. The architectural changes of cirrhosis persist for decades after cirrhosis develops.

Concentric bile duct fibrosis is seen in primary sclerosing cholangitis, which may be idiopathic or may appear in association with inflammatory bowel disease.

Interface hepatitis is a characteristic of chronic active HBV or HCV infection.

Massive hepatocellular necrosis may occur rarely as a complication of HAV infection or ingestion of massive amounts of acetaminophen.

α1-Antitrypsin deficiency with the PAS-positive periportal globules is associated with development of cirrhosis, but this is far less common than alcoholic cirrhosis.
Hence, the correct option is (D).

250. The prevalence of phaeochromocytoma in patients with hypertension is 0.1-0.6 per cent with an overall prevalence of 0.05 per cent in autopsy series. In total, 4 per cent of incidentalomas are phaeochromocytomas. Sporadic phaeochromocytomas occur around the fourth decade whereas patients with hereditary forms are diagnosed earlier. Phaeochromocytoma is known as the '10 per cent tumour' as 10 per cent of tumours are inherited, 10 per cent are extra-adrenal, 10 per cent are malignant, 10 per cent are bilateral and 10 per cent occur in children. With the recent advent of detailed genetic tests, however, the incidence of hereditary phaeochromocytomas has been shown to be higher.

Clinical features

Symptoms and signs are caused by catecholamine excess and are typically intermittent. In total, 90 per cent of patients with the combination of headache, palpitations and sweating have a phaeochromocytoma. Hypertension may occur continuously, be intermittent or absent.

Diagnosis

The first step in the diagnosis of a phaeochromocytoma is the determination of adrenaline and noradrenaline breakdown products, metanephrine and normetanephrine level, in a 12- or 24-hour urine collection. Levels that exceed the normal range by 2-40 times will be found in affected patients. Determination of plasma-free metanephrine and normetanephrine levels also has a high sensitivity. Biochemical tests should be performed at least twice. The biochemical diagnosis is followed by the localisation of the phaeochromocytoma. MRI is preferred because contrast media used for CT scans can provoke paroxysms. Classically, phaeochromocytomas show a 'Swiss cheese' configuration (Fig. a). 123I-MIBG (metaiodobenzylguanidine) single-photon emission computed tomography (SPECT) will identify about 90 per cent of primary tumours and is essential for the detection of multiple extra-adrenal tumours and metastases (Fig. b). PET scanning using FDG PET or DOPA PET is yet more sensitive in detecting metastatic foci.

Treatment

Laparoscopic resection is now routine in the treatment of phaeochromocytoma. If the tumour is larger than 8-10 cm or radiological signs of malignancy are detected, an open approach should be considered.

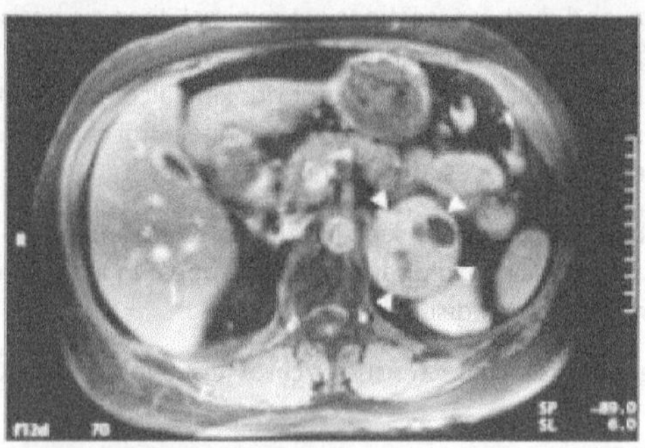

Fig: a

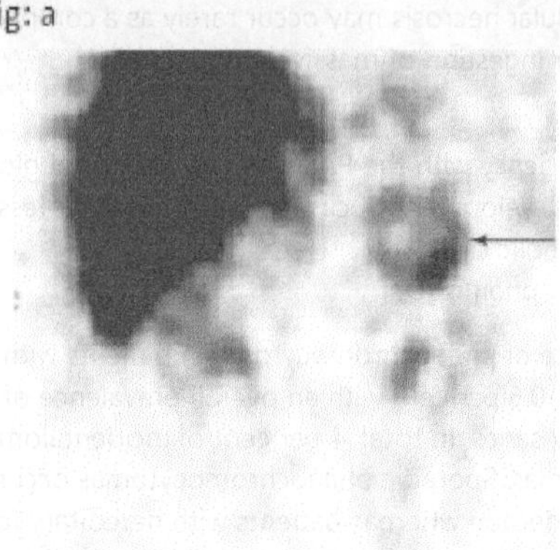

Fig: b

Hence, the correct option is (C).

251. Ebstein anomaly is an uncommon congenital cardiac anomaly, characterized by a variable developmental anomaly of the tricuspid valve. Findings on chest radiographs largely depend on the severity of the abnormality and the degree to which the tricuspid valve is displaced downwards.

There is often severe right-sided cardiomegaly due to an elongated and enlarged right atrium which may result in an elevated apex. Classically, the heart is described as having a "box shape" on a frontal chest radiograph.

Characteristic heart shapes in other CHDs:

Truncus arteriosus: Sitting duck shape

TOF: Boot shaped heart

D-TGA: Egg on end shape

Hence, the correct option is (A).

252. Case fatality rate: Case fatality rate measures the risk of persons dying from a certain disease within a given time period. Case fatality rate is calculated as number of deaths from a specific disease during a specific time period divided by number of cases of the disease during the same time period, usually expressed as per 100. The case fatality rate is used to link mortality to morbidity. One function of the case fatality rate is to measure various aspects or properties of a disease such as its pathogenicity, severity, or virulence.

It can also be used in poisonings, chemical exposures, or other short-term non-disease cause of death.

Hence, the correct option is (D).

253. There are many methods for tubal ligation including laparoscopic methods to burn (cautery), clip (Hulka or Filshie clip), cut and remove a section of fallopian tube, band (Falope Ring - small thick rubber band that strangulates the tissue), removal of the distal end of the tube (Krohner fimbriectomy), or complete removal of the fallopian tube (salpingectomy).

Shown in the image is the Hulka clip method. The Hulka clip is made from a soft pliable plastic known as Silastic. The Silastic clip is "spring-loaded" and clips to the fallopian tube. Clips cannot be simply "unclipped" to open the tubes as they damage the tubal tissue. Surgical reversal with tubal reconnection is necessary. The Hulka clip has the advantage of causing the least damage to the fallopian tube (if only 1 clip is placed) and may therefore be the easiest to reverse.
Hence, the correct option is (A).

254. Osteomalacia

The deficiency of vitamin D in adults is osteomalacia which is rare. It can occur:

- In pregnancy and lactation: Where there is an additional requirement of this vitamin and drainage of it in milk.
- In women who observe purdah or in climates where sunshine is scanty, calcium and phosphorus absorption is decreased. Consequently, the mineralization of osteoid to form bone is impaired. Such bones become soft. This particularly affects pelvic bones.

Hence, the correct option is (D).

255. Influenza is an acute respiratory tract infection caused by the influenza virus, of which there are 3 types - A, B, and C. All known pandemics were caused by influenza A strains. The disease is characterized by sudden onset of chills, malaise, fever, muscular pains, and cough.

- Hepatitis B is endemic throughout the world.
- Influenza B and C does not cause Pandemics.

Hence, the correct option is (B).

256. Chlamydia trachomatis is a gram-negative bacterium that infects the columnar epithelium of the cervix, urethra, and rectum, as well as nongenital sites. Nucleic acid amplification tests are the most sensitive tests for detecting chlamydia infection and may be performed on endocervical, urethral, vaginal, pharyngeal, rectal, or urine samples. This test is more sensitive and rapid than cell culture.

Neither cytology nor serology is used to diagnose infections with this organism.
Hence, the correct option is (A).

257. This refers to a blue discoloration of the skin and mucous membranes; it is due to the presence of deoxygenated hemoglobin in superficial blood vessels. The hemoglobin molecule changes color from blue to red when oxygen is added to it in the lungs. If more than about 50 g/L of deoxygenated hemoglobin is present in the capillary blood, the skin will have a bluish tinge. Cyanosis does not occur in anemic hypoxia because the total hemoglobin content is low. Cyanosis is more easily detected in fluorescent light than in daylight.

Central cyanosis means that there is an abnormal amount of deoxygenated hemoglobin in the arteries and that a blue discoloration is present in parts of the body with good circulation, such as the tongue. This must be distinguished from peripheral cyanosis, which occurs when the blood supply to a certain part of the body is reduced and the tissues extract more oxygen than normal from the circulating blood: for example, the lips in cold weather are often blue, but the tongue is spared. The presence of central cyanosis should lead one to a careful examination of the cardiovascular and respiratory systems.

All the clinical conditions in the options can cause central cyanosis, except for any condition with severe anemia.
Hence, the correct option is (A).

258. A rheumatoid nodule is a local swelling or tissue lump, usually rather firm to touch, like an unripe fruit, which occurs almost exclusively in association with rheumatoid arthritis. Very rarely rheumatoid nodules occur as 'rheumatoid nodulosis' in the absence of arthritis.

They are usually subcutaneous especially over bony prominences such as the tip of the elbow or olecranon or over the finger knuckles. Less commonly they occur in the lining of the lung and other internal organs. The commonest site for rheumatoid nodules is over Olecranon process.
Hence, the correct option is (A).

259. The Ayre spatula was developed in 1947 and it has been widely used. It is especially designed with a bifid end, one end of the scraper slightly longer than the other, so that the spatula fits the external os. The scraper is rotated 360°, the longer end used as a pivot within the external os. Smears obtained with Ayre's spatula results in adequate yield and are easy to screen.

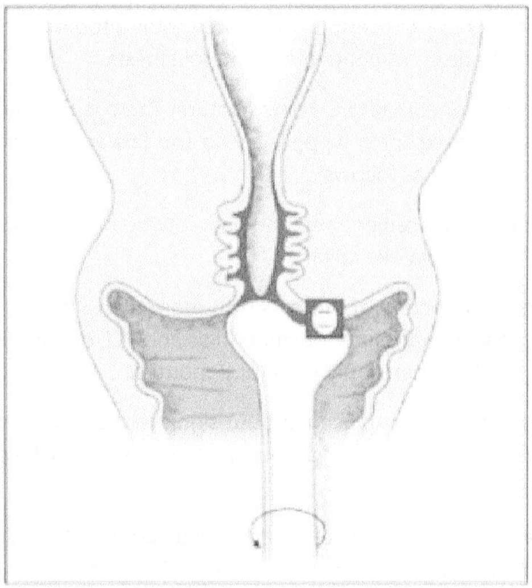

Collection of cervical smear by Ayre spatula
Hence, the correct option is (D).

260. The angular gyrus is the most inferior portion of the posterior parietal lobe, lying immediately behind Wernicke's area and fusing posteriorly into the visual areas of the occipital lobe as well. If this region is destroyed the stream of visual experiences passing into Wernicke's area from the visual cortex is mainly blocked. Therefore, the person may be able to see words and even know that they are words but not be able to interpret their meanings. This is a condition called dyslexia, or word blindness.

Damage to the mammillary bodies due to thiamine deficiency is implied in the pathogenesis of Wernicke-Korsakoff syndrome. Symptoms include impaired memory, also called anterograde amnesia, suggesting that the mammillary bodies may be important for memory. Lesions of the medial dorsal and anterior nuclei of the thalami and lesions of the mammillary bodies are commonly involved in amnesic syndromes in humans.

Lesions in the categorical hemisphere produce language disorders. Broca's Area Provides the Neural Circuitry for Word Formation. Hence lesions in this area may result in slow speech.

Lesions in the representational hemisphere produce astereognosis - the inability to identify objects by feeling them- and other agnosias. Lesions producing these defects are generally in the parietal lobe. Especially when lesions of the parietal lobe are in the representational hemisphere, it causes unilateral inattention and neglect.
Hence, the correct option is (C).

261. PO_2 of the atmospheric air is 159 mm Hg. But when this air reaches it is humidified that is it is diluted by the addition of water vapour pressure (PO_2 becomes 149 mmHg). At normal tidal breathing, about 2300 ml of air is present in the lung at the end of normal expiration. The inspired air (350 ml) with the PO_2 of 149 mm Hg gets mixed with the 2300 ml of air (with PO_2 of 40 mm of Hg in the alveoli. This changes the PO_2 to 104 mm Hg) circulation but later with the admixture from bronchial blood (deoxygenated) the PO_2 changes to 95 mm Hg.
Hence, the correct option is (D).

262. A hangman's fracture is a traumatic spondylolisthesis of C2 on C3 as a result of the bilateral fracture of C2 pars or pedicles. The mechanism of injury is an extension injury (causes pars fracture) with a secondary flexion (disrupts the posterior longitudinal ligament and the disc) resulting in the anterolisthesis.

In 30% there is a concomitant C-spine fracture. There is usually no neurological deficit except in type III. Levine and Edwards have classified this fracture as follows:

Type I - minimal displacement and angulation with an intact disc. Treatment: Philadelphia-like collar.

Type II - displaced fracture of the pars with more than 3mm displacement and significant angulation (disc and PLL disrupted). Reduce with traction then apply halo for 2 months.

Type IIA - no horizontal displacement but significant angulation. Reduction with hyperextension without traction then apply halo for 2 months.

Type III - is associated with bilateral facet dislocation and requires an open reduction of the dislocation with C2/C3 fusion.
Hence, the correct option is (B).

263. Tachypnea, retractions, cyanosis, and grunting are common findings in neonatal respiratory distress syndrome (RDS). Pallor and poor perfusion may also be present but is not the most common initial manifestation. Wheezing is not a feature of RDS. The clinical findings related to the pathogenesis of the disease, which primarily is atelectasis due to the collapse of the terminal airways caused by surfactant deficiency.
Hence, the correct option is (C).

264. Morbilliform drug eruptions are the most common drug reactions. They typically begin on the trunk and consist of symmetric macules and papules that may become confluent. Moderate to severe pruritus is common. In contrast to Stevens-Johnson syndrome and toxic shock syndrome, the involvement of mucus membranes is uncommon. The principal differential diagnosis is viral exanthem, particularly in children. The rash usually develops within 1 week of initiation of therapy and resolves with discontinuation. The most common drugs that cause morbilliform eruptions include penicillin derivatives, allopurinol, sulfonamides, and nonsteroidal anti-inflammatories. Urticaria consists of superficial well-defined weals that are pruritic. Penicillins may cause IgE-mediated urticaria.
Hence, the correct option is (A).

265. It is inherited as an autosomal dominant disorder and noted in nearly 1/5000 births. The NF-1 gene encodes a protein neurofibromin that plays a role in neuroectodermal differentiation and cardiac development.
Hence, the correct option is (C).

266. Transient neonatal pustular melanosis, a benign idiopathic skin condition is mainly seen in newborns with the skin of dark color. It has distinctive features characterized by vesicles, superficial pustules, and pigmented macules. The lesions of transient neonatal pustular melanosis are present at birth. They occur on the chin, neck, forehead, chest, buttocks, back, and, less often, on the palms and soles. The vesicles and pustules rupture easily and resolve within 48 hours. The brown macules may persist for several months.

Erythema toxicum neonatorum is the most common transient rash in a healthy neonate, which is a benign, self-limiting, physiological rash affecting about 50% of term newborn. They usually begin at 1 to 2 days of age, but may occur at any time until about the fourth day. Blotchy erythematous macules 1 to 3 cm in diameter with a 1 to 4 mm central vesicle or pustule are seen. The number of lesions can vary from one or two to several hundred.

Transient neonatal cephalic pustulosis presents in the first 3 weeks of life, characterized by erythematous papulopustules, surrounded by an erythematous halo, on the cheeks, chin, eyelids, neck, and upper chest in an otherwise healthy neonate. It has been postulated that Malassezia furfur is the causal agent of neonatal cephalic pustulosis. The absence of comedones and the presence of pustules surrounded by erythematous halo help to differentiate this entity from neonatal acne.

The onset of Sclerema Neonatorum is usually within the first week of life. It is a form of panniculitis in severely ill, premature infants and often fatal. It presents with diffuse woody hardening of the skin, spares genitalia, palms and soles.
Hence, the correct option is (B).

267. Erythema, pruritus, and dark pigmentation are not associated with malignancy. Although most cancers have slow, progressive growth, rapid growth does not rule out a malignancy.
Hence, the correct option is (C).

268. A most common type of precocious puberty in girls is idiopathic, it is essential to ensure close long-term follow-up of these patients to ascertain that there is no serious underlying pathology, such as tumors of the central nervous system or ovary. Only 1% to 2% of patients with precocious puberty have an estrogen-producing ovarian tumor as the causative factor. McCune-Albright syndrome (polyostotic fibrous dysplasia) is also relatively rare and consists of fibrous dysplasia and cystic degeneration of the long bones, sexual precocity, and café au lait spots on the skin. Hypothyroidism is a cause of precocious puberty in some children, making thyroid function tests mandatory in these cases. Tumors of the central nervous system as a cause of precocious puberty occur more commonly in boys than in girls; they are seen in about 11% of girls with precocious puberty.
Hence, the correct option is (A).

269. In certain cases of poisoning, the following articles are preserved.

(1) Heart: strychnine, digitalis.

(2) Brain: 100 gm. of cerebrum or cerebellum: alkaloids, organophosphorus compounds, opiates, CO, cyanide, strychnine, barbiturates anesthetics, and volatile organic poisons.

(3) Spinal cord entire length: strychnine and gelsemium.

(4) C.S.F: alcohol.

(5) Bile: It is best removed by puncturing the gall bladder in situ. Narcotic drugs, cocaine, methadone, glutathione, barbiturates, and some tranquilizers

(6) Vitreous humour: alcohol, chloroform, etc.

(7) Lung: one lung in gaseous poisons, hydrocyanic acid, alcohol, chloroform, etc. Use a nylon bag which should be heat-sealed.

(8) Skin: in deaths where hypodermic injection marks, or areas where absorption of it through the skin may have occurred and in corrosive poisons, an area of 10 cm. radius about the site, with as much underlying fat and muscle as possible, and the whole needle track is removed. Control specimens should be taken from the opposite side of the body. The usual substances injected are insulin, morphine, heroin, cocaine, and other illicit drugs.

(9) Bone: 10 cm. of the shaft of the femur is taken in cases of subacute or chronic poisoning by arsenic, antimony, thallium, or radium.

(10) Hair: In case of heavy metal poisoning (arsenic, antimony, thallium), an adequate sample (20 to 30) of head hair should be removed with a tweezer to remove the roots, and tied in locks.

(11) Nails: In case of heavy metal poisoning (arsenic, antimony, thallium), all the nails should be removed entirely by inserting the blade of a Spencer- Wells forceps under the nail-plate, grasping it and twisting.

(12) Uterus: Uterus and appendages and upper part of vagina are preserved in cases of criminal abortion. Sticks and foreign bodies found in the genital tract are preserved separately.

(13) Muscle: If the internal organs are badly putrefied, muscle tissue (3x3cm) especially of thigh is well preserved and can be analyzed.

(14) Fat: 10 g from abdominal wall or perinephric region in cases of poisoning by pesticides and insecticides.
Hence, the correct option is (C).

270. **INFECTIVITY**: The period of communicability of patients with varicella is estimated to range from 1 to 2 days before the appearance of the rash, and 4 to 5 days thereafter. The virus tends to die out before the pustular stage. The patient ceases to be infectious once the lesions have crusted.
Hence, the correct option is (B).

271. Cock's peculiar tumor is one of the complications of the sebaceous cyst. When the sebaceous cyst of the scalp ulcerates, excessive granulation tissue forms resembling fungating epithelioma, this is called Cock's peculiar tumor.
Hence, the correct option is (B).

272. Diphenhydramine has significant antimuscarinic (atropine-like) activity, and may cause dry mouth, blurred vision, urinary retention, and tachycardia. Sedation is commonly observed in most patients, but children may paradoxically experience excitement.
Hence, the correct option is (C).

273. A cholesteatoma may be congenital or acquired. It is a small sac lined with epithelium-containing debris. Acquired cholesteatoma can present in children with recurrent otitis media, or in the face of a chronically draining ear. The mass can grow aggressively, leading to CNS complications like facial nerve damage, hearing loss, and intracranial extension. Referral to an otolaryngologist is required; a CT scan of the temporal bones can define the extent of disease.

Tympanosclerosis would present with scarring on the surface of the tympanic membrane. Acute otitis media with perforation and drainage would present with a hole in the tympanic membrane and with (often) purulent drainage. Dislocation of the malleus from its insertion in the tympanic membrane can occur, but would not produce a mass extending through the tympanic membrane.
Hence, the correct option is (A).

274. This is saw-scaled viper. It can be identified by carefully checking very dry looking body covered with rough scales, light color rounded patches on top which are surrounded by two wavy lines from head to posterior body. Its venom is hemotoxic. It is known to prevent blood from clotting, which is useful for anticoagulant drugs.
Hence, the correct option is (B).

275. No change in seizure frequency is observed in 60-85% of patients on getting pregnant.

Women with epilepsy have an increased risk of congenital anomalies in the fetus over and above the risk that is due to the anticonvulsant medications (epilepsy itself increases the risk even if the patient is not on any anticonvulsant medications).

There is a two-fold increased risk of malformed fetus in an epileptic patient on anticonvulsant medication. The risk in decreasing order is observed with various medications such as primidone, valproate, phenytoin, carbamazepine, phenobarbitone.

The embryotoxicity of these medications is due to their intermediate metabolites and is genetically mediated. There is a defect in detoxification. All these drugs commonly alter the CNS of the fetus leading to NTDS, and folic acid is known to be protective.

The drug concentration in breast milk is minimal, and hence breastfeeding is quite safe.
Hence, the correct option is (B).

276. Muscle function is best tested by working individuals or groups of muscles against resistance while in their optimal mechanical alignment. This patient is being asked to flex his leg against resistance to test the hamstring muscles in the posterior compartment of the thigh. While some other muscles (e.g., gracilis, gastrocnemius) do contribute to flexion of the leg, the hamstrings are by far the major flexors at the knee.

The four quadriceps femoris muscles are parts of the anterior compartment of the thigh. Their major action is extension of the knee. Thus, testing of this group is best accomplished by asking the patient to extend the knee against resistance from the flexed position.

The adductors are the muscles of the medial compartment of the thigh. Their major action is the adduction of the thigh. The basic test for integrity here is the adduction of the thigh against resistance.

The triceps surae ("three heads of the calf") group is composed of the gastrocnemius (with two heads) and soleus (with one head) muscles in the posterior superficial compartment of the leg. The primary action of this group is plantar flexion of the foot. Testing can be accomplished by plantar flexion against resistance from the prone position, or, by asking the patient to stand on their tiptoes.
Hence, the correct option is (B).

277. The case diagnosis is post-streptococcal glomerulonephritis caused by group A strep. The Lancefield group is determined by the C carbohydrate and the serotype is determined via the M proteins. This is particularly important in post-streptococcal glomerulonephritis, as certain strains, such as the M l 2 serotype, are more commonly associated with this type of nonsuppurative sequela.
Hence, the correct option is (B).

278. Glucose and galactose are examples of epimeric pairs which differ only with respect of C4 (Fig.). Similarly, mannose and glucose are epimers in respect of C2.

Epimerization: The process by which one epimer is converted to another is called epimerization and it requires the enzyme epimerase, e.g. conversion of galactose to glucose in the liver.

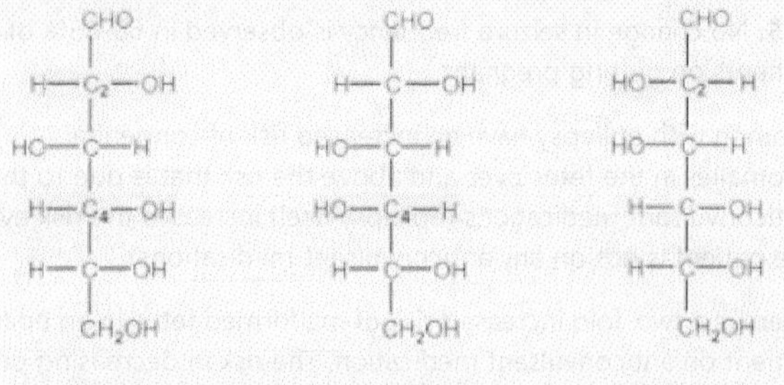

D-Glucose D-Galactose D-Mannose

Hence, the correct option is (B).

279. The condition shown in the image is 'Wrist drop'. It is a condition in which a person cannot extend his wrist and it hangs flaccidly. Radial nerve dysfunction is a problem with the radial nerve. Damage to the radial nerve leads to problems with movement in the arm and wrist and with sensation in the back of the arm or hand.

The radial nerve travels down the arm and controls movement of the triceps muscle at the back of the upper arm. It also controls the ability to bend the wrist and fingers backward and helps with the movement and sensation of the wrist and hand.
Hence, the correct option is (B).

280. The child has JXG (nevoxanthoendothelioma) of the iris. This is a benign cutaneous disorder of infants with typical raised orange skin lesions occurring singly or in crops and regressing spontaneously. Ocular involvement is rather rare and occurs mostly under 6 months of age.

Children may present with spontaneous anterior chamber hemorrhage and secondary glaucoma.

Histologically, the lesion is characterized by a diffuse granulomatous inflammatory reaction with many histiocytes and Touton giant cells, as seen in the figure. The histiocytes are positive for antibodies binding to macrophages (e.g., CD 68).
Hence, the correct option is (B).

281. Amiodarone is categorized as a class III antiarrhythmic agent and interferes with outward potassium current. It prolongs phase 3 of the cardiac action potential, the repolarization phase where there is normally decreased calcium permeability and increased potassium permeability.

Amiodarone slows conduction rate and prolongs the refractory period of the SA and AV nodes. It also prolongs the refractory periods of the ventricles, bundles of His, and the Purkinje fibres without exhibiting any effects on the conduction rate. Amiodarone has been shown to prolong the myocardial cell action potential duration and refractory period and is a non-competitive β-adrenergic inhibitor.

It also shows beta blocker-like and calcium channel blocker-like actions on the SA and AV nodes increases the refractory period via sodium- and potassium-channel effects, and slows intra-cardiac conduction of the cardiac action potential, via sodium-channel effects.

β-Receptor antagonists are considered class II antiarrhythmics.

Class I antiarrhythmics block fast sodium channels.

Amiodarone has a rather long half-life, up to 100 days.
Hence, the correct option is (C).

282. TOOLS OF MEASUREMENT IN EPIDEMIOLOGY:

- Rate: Numerator (a) is a part of the denominator (b) and the multiplier is 1000 or 10,000 or 100,000 or so on.
- Ratio: Numerator (a) is not a part of the denominator (b) and BOTH numerator and denominator are unrelated.
- Proportion: Numerator (a) is a part of the denominator (b) and the multiplier is 100.
- Proportion is always expressed in percentage (%).
- Incidence is a rate, Prevalence is a proportion.

Hence, the correct option is (C).

283. PAIR =

P = Percutaneous

A = Aspiration

I = Infusion (of scolicidal agents)

R = Reinfusion

Contraindications for pair technique:

1. Early pregnancy.
2. Cyst in lung, spine, brain, and heart.
3. Inaccessible cyst or cysts in risky locations.
4. Superficially located cysts (risk of spillage).
5. Inactive or calcified lesions.
6. Cysts communicating with the biliary tree.

Hence, the correct option is (A).

284. VACCINATION: Highly effective live attenuated vaccine is now available for the prevention of mumps. Widely-used live attenuated mumps vaccine strains include the Jeryl- Lynn, RIT 4385, Leningrad-3, L-Zagreb, and Urabe strains.

Live attenuated mumps vaccine strains used only on a limited scale include the Hoshino, Torii, and NKM-46 strains. The WHO recommends that the Rubini mumps vaccine strain should not be used in national immunization programs because of its demonstrated low effectiveness.

A single dose (0.5 ml) intramuscularly produces detectable antibodies in 95 percent of vaccines. The duration of long-term immunity is not known. It is recommended for routine immunization for children over 1 year of age, either alone or in combination with other virus vaccines, eg. in MMR vaccine or as a quadrivalent vaccine with varicella. A second dose is recommended for children at 4 - 6 years of age i.e., before starting school. The current mumps strain (Jeryl Lynn) has the lowest associated incidence of post-vaccine aseptic meningitis (from 1 in 150,000 to 1 in 1.8 million). There are no known cases of long-term sequelae associated with mumps vaccination.

Countries including mumps vaccines in their national immunization program are advised by WHO to set disease control targets (control or elimination) and to design their mumps immunization strategy accordingly. Strategies to achieve mumps elimination include very high coverage with the first dose of mumps vaccine, ensuring a second opportunity for vaccination and conducting catch-up immunization of susceptible cohorts.

As with most other live virus vaccines, the mumps vaccine should not be administered to pregnant women, patients receiving immunosuppressive therapy, or those who are severely ill.
Hence, the correct option is (A).

285. Scrotal hydroceles resolve spontaneously unless associated with a patent processus vaginalis and an inguinal hernia. Most newborn infants, male & female, have some breast enlargement. Towards the end of the first week of life, this may become engorged and secrete milk. The swollen tender tissue may appear inflamed and the milk resembles pus, but only very rarely does true mastitis occur. The majority of sacral dimples are shallow and innocent.

Femoral pulses are not always easy to palpate but genuine absence suggests coarctation of the aorta. Newborn children with coarctation of the aorta are usually asymptomatic at birth. The onset of symptoms is related to closure of the ductusarteriosus within the first 7-10 days of life. The degree of severity of symptoms following ductal closure depends on the severity of the coarctation. With ductal closure, newborn children with severe coarctation may initially have periods of poor color, appearing ashen or dusky, or present with poor feeding and irritability. Children with severe coarctation present with circulatory collapse and shock, with poor or no palpable pulses and usually no audible murmurs.
Hence, the correct option is (D).

286.

- N-acetyl derivative of D-Glucosamine occur as a constituent of certain mucopolysaccharides (MPS).
- Glucosamine is the chief organic constituent of the cell wall of fungi, and a constituent of shells of crustacea (crabs, Lobsters, etc), where it occurs as Chitin, which is made of repeating units of N-acetylated glucosamine. Hence Glucosamine is often called Chitosamine.
- Galactosamine occurs as N-acetyl-Galactosamine in chondroitin sulphates which are present in cartilages, bones, tendons, and heart valves. Hence Galactosamine is also known as Chondrosamine.

Hence, the correct option is (C).

287. Tolazoline is a non-selective competitive α-adrenergic receptor antagonist. It is a vasodilator that is used to treat spasms of peripheral blood vessels. It is an imidazoline compound with a structure similar to that of clonidine and has both central and peripheral nonspecific α-adrenergic inhibitory effects.

Tolazoline is similar to phentolamine. It is somewhat less potent than phentolamine but is better absorbed from the gastrointestinal tract.

It is a vasodilator that apparently has direct actions on blood vessels and also increases cardiac output. Tolazoline can interact to some degree with histamine, adrenergic, and cholinergic receptors, but the mechanisms of its therapeutic effects are not clear. It is used in the treatment of persistent pulmonary hypertension of the newborn.
Hence, the correct option is (B).

288. Myeloproliferative disorders and myelofibrosis in particular, are known to cause massive splenomegaly. As hematopoiesis is reduced in the marrow, it moves elsewhere (extramedullary hematopoiesis) such as the spleen.

Myelofibrosis is a clonal neoplastic disorder of hematopoiesis, the formation of blood cellular components. It is one of the myeloproliferative disorders, diseases of the bone marrow in which excess cells are produced. Production of cytokines such as fibroblast growth factor by the abnormal hematopoietic cell clone (particularly by megakaryocytes) leads to the replacement of the hematopoietic tissue of the bone marrow by connective tissue via collagen fibrosis. The decrease in hematopoietic tissue impairs the patient's ability to generate new blood cells, resulting in progressive pancytopenia, a shortage of all blood cell types. However, the proliferation of fibroblasts and deposition of collagen is a secondary phenomenon, and the fibroblasts themselves are not part of the abnormal cell clone.

The principal site of extramedullary hematopoiesis in myelofibrosis is the spleen, which is usually markedly enlarged, sometimes weighing as much as 4000 g. As a result of massive enlargement of the spleen, multiple subcapsular infarcts often occur in the spleen, meaning that oxygen supply to the spleen is interrupted, leading to partial or complete tissue death. On the cellular level, the spleen contains red blood cell precursors, granulocyte precursors, and megakaryocytes, with the megakaryocytes prominent in their number and in their bizarre shapes. Megakaryocytes are believed to be involved in causing the secondary fibrosis seen in this condition. Sometimes the unusual activity of the red blood cells, white blood cells, or platelets is seen.

A spleen will rarely be larger than 1000 gm in a patient (such as a chronic alcoholic with micronodular cirrhosis of liver) who has portal hypertension. The spleen may be slightly enlarged and tender but is not massively enlarged with Epstein-Barr virus infection, which lasts a few weeks. There may be increased iron stores and the spleen may be some-what enlarged with hemochromatosis, but massive enlargement does not occur.
Hence, the correct option is (A).

289. Human leukocyte antigen B27 (HLA-B27) is a protein that contributes to immune system dysfunction. It is a class I surface antigen encoded by the B locus in the major histocompatibility complex (MHC) on chromosome 6 and presents antigenic peptides (derived from self and non-self antigens) to T cells. It is associated with a wide range of pathology, particularly seronegative spondyloarthropathy, but it does not appear to be the sole mediator in development of disease. The presence of HLA-B27 is associated with certain autoimmune and immune-mediated diseases, including:

• ankylosing spondylitis, which causes inflammation of the bones in spine

• reactive arthritis (Reiter's Syndrome), which causes inflammation of joints, urethra, and eyes, and sometimes lesions on skin

• psoriatic arthritis

• juvenile rheumatoid arthritis

• anterior uveitis, which causes swelling and irritation in the middle layer of eye

• ulcerative colitis

Susceptibility to SLE is associated with HLA class II, in particular with haplotypes bearing the DRB1 alleles.
Hence, the correct option is (B).

290. Phase-4 depolarization is caused by activation of a Na channel. This channel is called as funny channel because it is activated when the membrane hyperpolarizes. Potassium conductance decreases during phase-4 depolarization & thus the flow of potassium out of the cell is diminished. However, this change in potassium current is not responsible for phase -4 depolarization. Chloride conductance does not change during phase-4. The Na/Ca exchanger maintains low intracellular ca2+ at rest but may reverse its direction and pump ca2+ into the cell during phase 2 of the cardiac action. However, neither the Na/Ca exchanger nor the Na-K pump is involved in phase-4 depolarization.
Hence, the correct option is (A).

291. With antiepileptic drugs, there is increased liver metabolism so to counterbalance this, standard dose oral contraceptive pillsare used which contain 50 µg of ethinyl estradiol.

Ultra low dose, low dose or sequential pills will not be effective.
Hence, the correct option is (C).

292. Penicillin G is metabolized mainly in kidney. Its pharmacokinetics is dominated by very rapid renal excretion (10%), by glomerular filtration and rest by tubular secretion (90%).

Rest of the drugs i.e. erythromycin, rifampicin and phenytoin are metabolized in the liver.
Hence, the correct option is (A).

293. A major cause of spontaneous abortions in the first trimester is chromosomal abnormalities; however, the causes of losses in the second trimester are more likely to be uterine or environmental in origin. Patients should be screened for thyroid function, diabetes mellitus, and collagen vascular disorders. There is also a correlation between patients with a positive lupus anticoagulant and recurrent miscarriages. A hysterosalpingogram should be performed to rule out uterine structural abnormalities, such as bicornuate uterus, septate uterus, unicornuate uterus, submucous fibroids, or intrauterine adhesions. Endometrial biopsy is performed to rule out an insufficiency of the endometrium. If no abnormalities are found, both the husband and wife should be karyotyped to see if a balanced translocation or 45,X mosaicism exists.

A postcoital test is useful for couples who can not conceive, but does not address postconception losses.
Hence, the correct option is (D).

294. The spinal muscular atrophies (SMAs), are characterized by degeneration of nerve cells (motor nuclei) within the lowest region of the brain (lower brainstem) and certain motor neurons in the spinal cord (anterior horn cells) leading to muscle weakness of the truncal, and extremity muscles initially, followed by chewing, swallowing and breathing difficulties.
Hence, the correct option is (C).

295. A number of staining techniques have been employed for demonstration of oocysts of c. parvum in the stool specimen. Modified acid fast staining is the method of choice and by this method oocysts appear as red acidfast spheres, against a blue background (Fig.). Yeast closely resembles oocysts of c. parvum in shape and size but can be diff erentiated by using acidfast stain, as they are not acidfast and appear blue in color. The staining can also be used for demonstration of oocysts in other specimens like sputum, bronchial washing, etc.

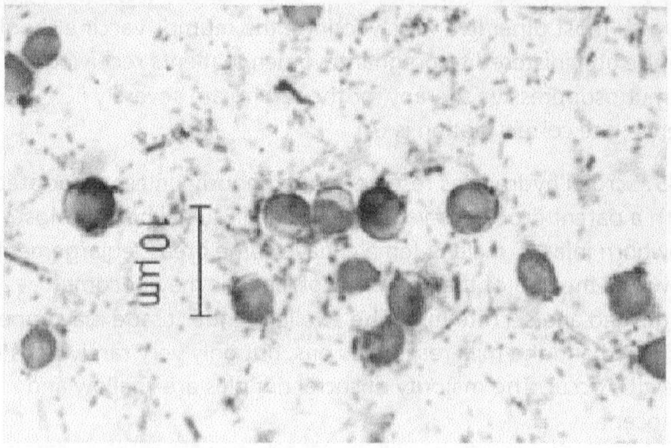

Hence, the correct option is (C).

296. The thyroid does not form a part of the neuroendocrine pathway to the stress response. Following any form of injury, the afferent nociceptive pathways consist of the spinal cord, thalamus, hypothalamus and the pituitary. The hypothalamus secretes corticotrophin releasing factor (CRF), which acts on the anterior pituitary to secrete adrenocorticotrophic hormone (ACTH), which, in turn, acts on the adrenal glands to release cortisol. Classically it has been described as the 'fight or flight' response. This occurs as a result of a concerted interplay between neural, endocrine and inflammatory factors.

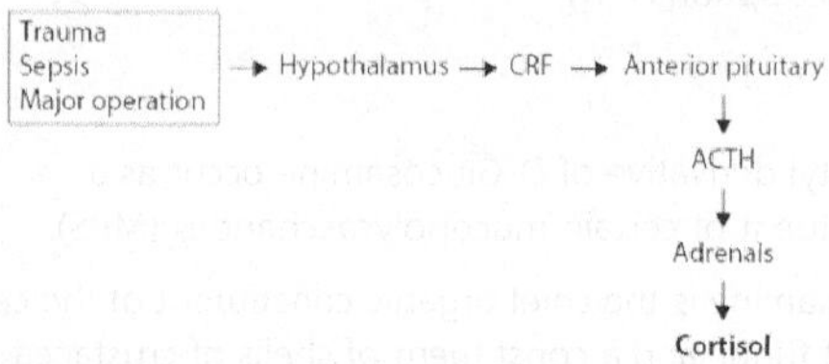

The release of cortisol.

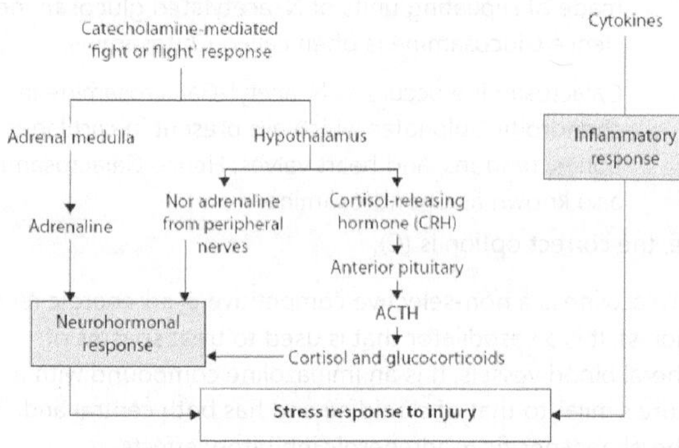

Interplay of neural, endocrine and inflammatory factors.
Hence, the correct option is (B).

297. Shown in the image is a stratified squamous epithelium, which consists of squamous (flattened) epithelial cells arranged in layers upon a basal membrane. Only one layer is in contact with the basement membrane; the other layers adhere to one another to maintain structural integrity. Although this epithelium is referred to as squamous, many cells within the layers may not be flattened; this is due to the convention of naming epithelia according to the cell type at the surface. In the deeper layers, the cells may be columnar or cuboidal. There are no intercellular spaces. This type of epithelium is well suited to areas in the body subject to constant abrasion, as the thickest layers can be sequentially sloughed off and replaced before the basement membrane is exposed. It forms the outermost layer of the skin and the inner lining of the mouth,

esophagus and vagina.
Hence, the correct option is (C).

298. Chondrosarcomas are malignant cartilaginous tumours that account for about 25% of all primary malignant bone tumours. They are most commonly found in older patients within the long bones and can arise de novo or secondary from an existing benign cartilaginous neoplasm. On imaging, these tumours have ring-and-arc chondroid matrix mineralisation with aggressive features such as lytic pattern, deep endosteal scalloping and soft-tissue extension.

The typical presentation is in the 4th and 5th decades and there is a slight male predominance. Patients usually present with pain, pathological fracture, a palpable lump or local mass effect.

It may arise in any bone but is common in flat bones such as scapula, pelvis, ribs and also spine. Nearly 45% occur in long bones as the cartilage is more abundant in the long, tubular bones.

Plain radiograph characteristics:

• lytic (50%)

• intralesional calcifications: ~70% (rings and arcs calcification or popcorn calcification)

• endosteal scalloping: affecting more than two-thirds of the cortical thickness (c.f. less than two-thirds in enchondromas)

• moth-eaten appearance or permeative appearance in higher grade tumours (see chondrosarcoma grading), e.g. myxoid, dedifferentiated and mesenchymal chondrosarcomas

• cortical remodelling, thickening and periosteal reaction are also useful in distinguishing between an enchondroma and low-grade chondrosarcoma (see enchondroma vs. low-grade chondrosarcoma)
Hence, the correct option is (B).

299. Benign positional vertigo (BPV) is a condition in which a person develops a sudden sensation of spinning, usually with specific head movement such as turning over onto one side in bed; or reaching for an object above head level with head rotated cause vertigo of short duration.

It is due to a disturbance within the inner ear. Otoliths (calcium carbonate particles) are normally attached to a membrane inside the utricle and saccule. The utricle is connected to the semicircular ducts.

These otoliths may become displaced from the utricle to enter the posterior semicircular duct since this is the most dependent of the 3 ducts and has favourable anatomical position. The most widely accepted theory of the pathophysiology of BPV is that changing head position relative to gravity causes the free otoliths to gravitate longitudinally through the canal and the concurrent flow of endolymph stimulates the hair cells of the affected semicircular canal, causing vertigo.

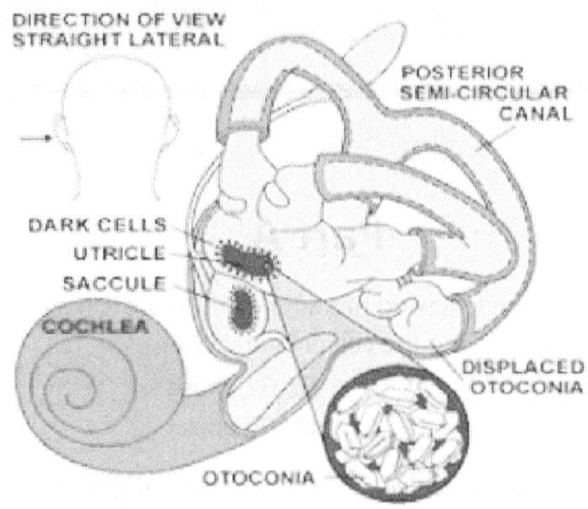

Hence, the correct option is (C).

300. The Barium enema finding shows **"lead pipe appearance"** which is the classical finding in chronic ulcerative colitis.

Ulcerative colitis is an inflammatory bowel disease that not only predominantly affects the colon, but also has extraintestinal manifestations.

Clinically patients have chronic diarrhoea (sometimes bloody) associated with tenesmus, pain and fever.

Double contrast barium enema allows for exquisite detail of the colonic mucosa and also allows the bowel proximal to strictures to be assessed. It is however contraindicated if acute severe colitis is present due to the risk of perforation.

Mucosal inflammation leads a granular appearance to the surface of the bowel. As inflammation increases, the bowel wall and haustra thicken.

Mucosal ulcers are undermined (button-shaped ulcers). When most of the mucosa has been lost, islands of mucosa remain giving it a pseudopolyp appearance.

In chronic cases, the bowel becomes featureless with the loss of normal haustral markings, luminal narrowing and bowel shortening (lead pipe sign).

Small islands of residual mucosa can grow into thin worm-like structures (so-called filiform polyps)

Colorectal carcinoma in the setting of ulcerative colitis is more frequently sessile and may appear to be a simple stricture.
Hence, the correct option is (C).

Mock Test 08

Part A

Q.1 Which of the following has a function of protein synthesis and cell growth during the cell division cycle?

A. S phase **B.** G1 phase
C. G2 phase **D.** G0 phase

Q.2 Which nerve is involved in a patient suffering from defective adduction of the hip joint and pains in the hip and knee joint.

A. Saphenous nerve **B.** Femoral nerve
C. Obturator nerve **D.** Sciatic nerve

Q.3 Muscle(s) causing dorsiflexion of foot is/are -

a) Extensor digitorum longus
b) Extensor hallucis longus
c) Flexor digitorum longus
d) Flexor hallucis longus
e) Tibialis anterior

A. a,b,c **B.** a,e,d **C.** a,b,e **D.** b,c,d

Q.4 Artery/arteries supplying occipital cortex is -

A. PCA **B.** MCA
C. MCA + PCA **D.** ACA

Q.5 Which artery is the main source of blood for the arm?

A. Ulnar artery **B.** Radial artery
C. Brachial artery **D.** Profunda branchii

Q.6 The diagram below shows the relationship between the esophagus, stomach, and duodenum. The area labeled A is the region that contains which of the following types of cells?

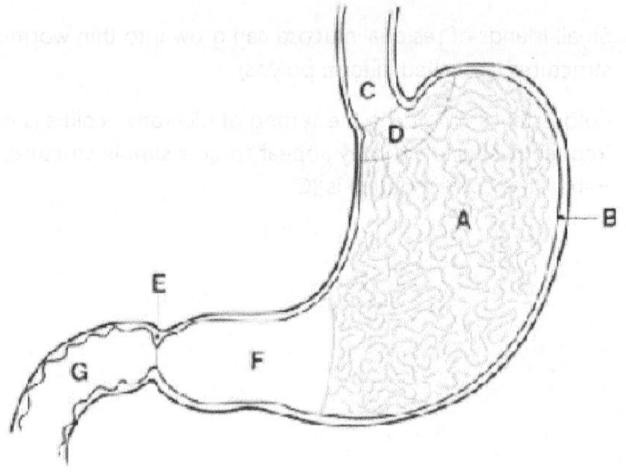

A. Cells that secrete gastric intrinsic factor
B. Most of the Paneth cells
C. Cells that secrete mucus and gastrin
D. Cells that secrete mucus and bicarbonate

Q.7 The arrow represents the dark structure in the midbrain, in this midsagittal MRI represents a passage for which of the following?

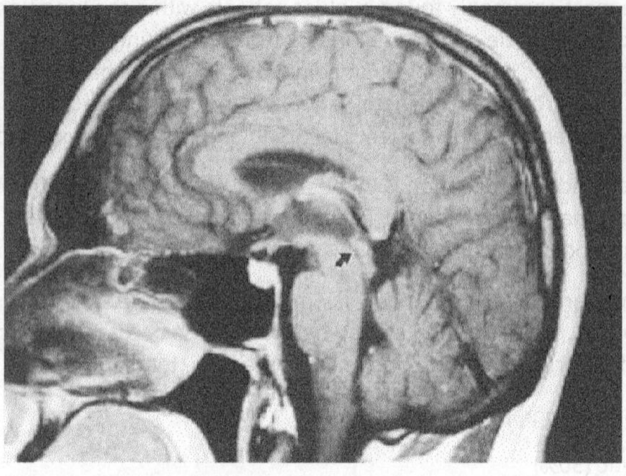

A. Venous blood
B. Cerebrospinal fluid
C. Neurons of the corticospinal tract
D. Arterial blood (in the basilar artery)

Q.8 The spinal nerve is related to

A. Glossopharyngeal **B.** Vagus
C. Hypoglossal **D.** Facial

Q.9 Name the muscle attached at point 'X' ?

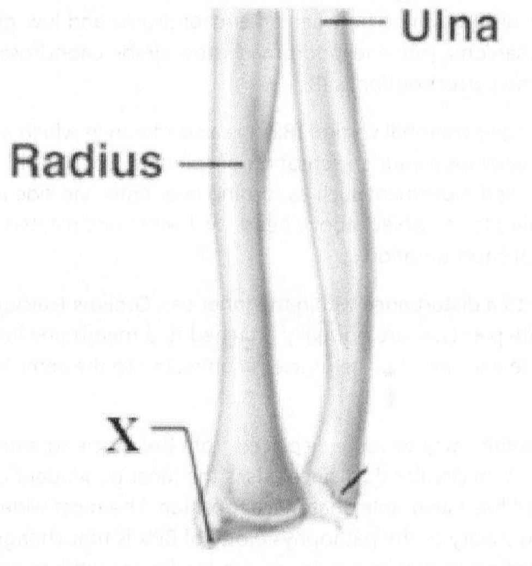

A. Brachioradialis
B. Pronator quadratus
C. Pronator teres
D. Lateral collateral ligament

Q.10 Rasmussen's aneurysm involves

A. Bronchial artery **B.** Pulmonary artery
C. Intercostal artery **D.** Aorta

Q.11 Hortega cells are:

A. Microglia
B. Modified macrophages
C. Astrocytes

D. Neutrophils

Q.12 End arteries occur in all of the following except :

A. Brain
B. Kidneys
C. Liver
D. The regions of the joints

Q.13 Most lateral deep cerebellar nucleus is:

A. Fastigial nucleus
B. Emboliform nucleus
C. Dentate nucleus
D. Globose nucleus

Q.14 Bed of tonsil is formed by -

A. Superior constrictor **B.** Middle constrictor
C. Inferior constrictor **D.** Platysma

Q.15 Depressor of Temporomandibular joint is

A. Temporal is muscle
B. Masseter muscle
C. Lateral pterygoid muscle
D. Medial pterygoid muscle

Q.16 A branch of Supraclinoid segment of Internal Carotid Artery is :

A. Ophthalmic artery
B. Medullary branches
C. Branches to pituitary
D. Anterior cerebral artery

Q.17 Which of the following structures does the fetal allantoic duct become in the adult ?

A. Cloaca
B. Medial umbilical ligament
C. Urachus
D. Ureter

Q.18 Collagen of which type is found in hyaline cartilage:

A. Type III **B.** Type IV **C.** Type II **D.** Type I

Q.19 Sorensess and pain in muscels after vigrous exercise is due to -

A. Hyperkalemia **B.** Hyperthermia
C. Lactic acidosis **D.** Hyponatremia

Q.20 Pulmonary vasoconstriction is caused by

A. Prostacyclin **B.** Alpha-2 stimulation
C. Hypoxia **D.** Histamine

Q.21 Hypopnea is a condition where:

A. The airway becomes partially obstructed.
B. The blood does not clot properly.
C. The lungs cannot eliminate the excess carbon dioxide from the body.
D. The blood oxygen levels are abnormally low.

Q.22 Find faulty statement regarding muscle spindle.

A. Central zone has no actin & myosin
B. Peripheral zone has no actin & myosin
C. Type 1 nuclear bag fibers has low myosin ATPase activity
D. Type 2 nuclear bag fiber has high level of myosin ATPase activity

Q.23 Which of the following is not the thermoreceptor.

A. Cold receptor & warm receptor
B. Pain receptor
C. Stretch receptor & pressure receptor
D. None of the above.

Q.24 Marey's Law states:

A. Relationship of HR with CO.
B. Relationship of HR with Stroke volume.
C. Relationship of HR with Presystolic pressure.
D. Relationship of HR with BP.

Q.25 Normal alveolar ventilation pressure on inspiration is

A. –1 cm water **B.** -1 cm Hg
C. +1 cm water **D.** +1 cm Hg

Q.26 Hormone that increases "Post Menopausal" is:

A. Progesterone **B.** Estrogen
C. FSH **D.** Androgens

Q.27 "Major Basic Protein" is secreted by:

A. Basophil **B.** Macrophage
C. Eosinophil **D.** Monocyte

Q.28 Which of the following is freely filtered by kidney across glomerular capillaries

A. Creatinine
B. Albumin (across glomerular capillaries)
C. Globulin
D. All of the above

Q.29 The mechanism involved in the absorption of glucose from the small intestine is

A. Passive diffusion
B. Facilitated diffusion
C. Secondary active co-transport with sodium
D. Actively by insulin dependent uptake

Q.30 The radiograph below was taken in a 36-year old man who presented to the ED with severe left flank pain and one episode of hematuria. Which of the following measures could cause another episode of this pathology?

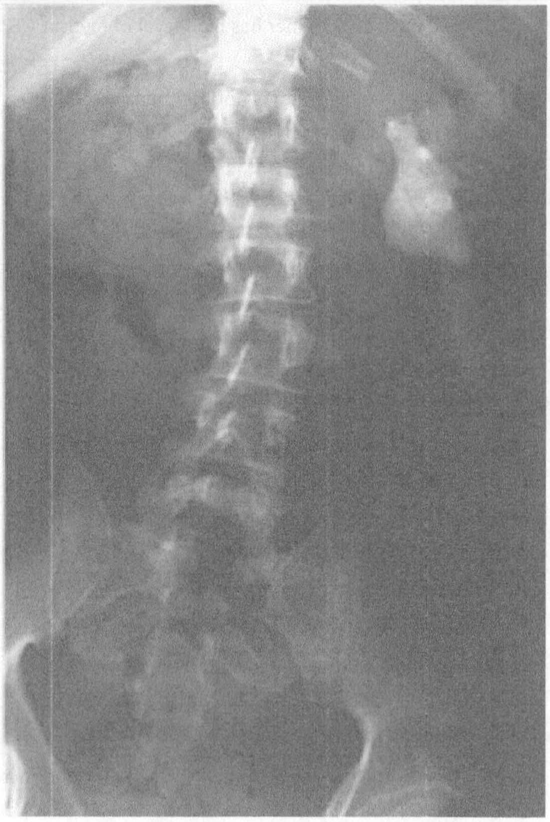

A. Calcium restriction
B. Increased fluid intake (> 2 L/d)
C. Protein restriction
D. Sodium restriction

Q.31 The action potentials shown in below figure represent which kind of cells?

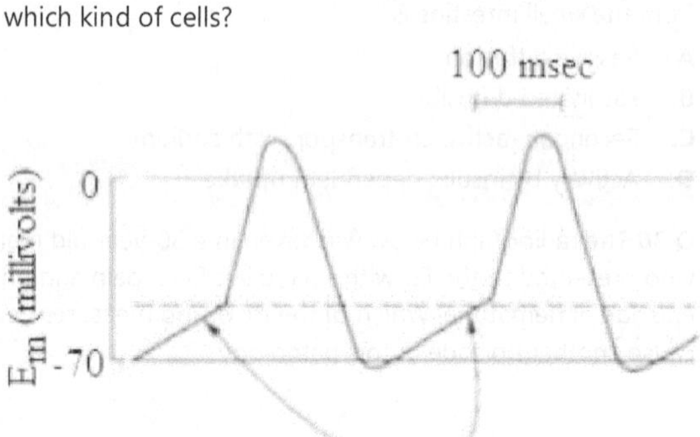

A. Cardiac nodal cells
B. Myelinated motor axons
C. Sensory neurons
D. Skeletal muscle cells

Q.32 What is an individual contractile unit known as?
A. Sarcomere **B.** Sarcolemma
C. Myofibril **D.** Sarcotubular system

Q.33 Transport of two substances in the same direction is called as?
A. Symport **B.** Antiport
C. Exocytosis **D.** Pinocytosis

Q.34 What is/are the effect(s) on membrane when extracellular concentration of K^+ is decreased
a) ↓magnitude of RMP
b) ↑negativity of the membrane
c) ↑magnitude of RMP
d) ↓negativity of membrane
A. b and c **B.** a and b **C.** b and d **D.** a and c

Q.35 Selenium is co-factor for
A. Glutathione peroxidase
B. Glutathione reductase
C. Glutathione synthetase
D. Glutathione dehydrogenase

Q.36 Which of the following is a functional enzyme:
A. Creatine kinase (CK)
B. Alkaline phosphatase
C. Lipoprotein lipase
D. Lactate dehydrogenase (LDH)

Q.37 In which of the following conditions a low/controlled glycemic index diet is preferred?
A. Diabetes **B.** Hypertension
C. Children **D.** Normal adults

Q.38 In beta-oxidation of fatty acids, carnitine is required for
A. Conversion of short chain fatty acids to long chain fatty acids
B. Transport of long chain fatty acid to mitochondrial inner layer
C. Transport of long chain fatty acid to cytoplasm
D. Conversion of long chain fatty acids to short chain fatty acids

Q.39 Find the amino acid which is justifiable to be found in the transmembrane region of a protein
A. Lysine **B.** Arginine
C. Leucine **D.** Aspartate

Q.40 Regarding glutathione which of the following is not true?
A. It helps in absorption of certain amino acids
B. It inactivates some enzymes
C. It helps in mebrane transport
D. It helps in conjugation reactions

Q.41 Absorption of iron is increased by?
A. Tea **B.** Coffee
C. EDTA **D.** Vitamin C

Q.42 All of the following abbreviations are true except
a) AMP-Adenosine monophosphate
b) CMP-Cytidine monophosphate
c) GMP-Guanosine monophosphate
d) TMP-Thymine monophosphate
e) UMP-Uracil monophosphate
A. a and b **B.** d and e **C.** c and d **D.** b and d

Q.43 True about DNA supercoiling is all except
A. Underwinding results in negative superhelical density & supercoiling

B. Underwinding strain is normally accommodated by strand separation

C. Topoisomerase II change linking number in increments of 2

D. Most cellular DNA is underwound

Q.44 True about polymorphism is

A. Single locus → multiple normal alleles

B. Single locus → multiple abnormal alleles

C. Single phenotype : Single locus → multiple normal alleles

D. Single phenotype : Single locus → multiple abnormal alleles

Q.45 Coenzyme associated with glycogen phosphorylase is -

A. Pyridoxal Phosphate

B. Tetrahydrofolate

C. Thiamine

D. FMN

Q.46 A 30-year-old man is diagnosed with type I familial dyslipidemia. He has had recent laboratory studies showing elevated triglycerides and normal cholesterol levels. Which of the following explains the pathophysiology of this disease?

A. Apolipoprotein E deficiency

B. LDL cholesterol receptor deficiency

C. Lipoprotein lipase deficiency

D. VLDL cholesterol clearance deficiency

Q.47 Heme synthesis occurs in the bone marrow and liver. Deficiency of δ-aminolevulinic acid hydrase would lead to the accumulation of which of the following

A. δ-Aminolevulinic acid

B. Coproporphyrinogen

C. Glycine

D. Porphobilinogen

Q.48 Rate limiting enzyme in heme synthesis

A. ALA dehydratase

B. Hmg coa reductase

C. ALA synthase

D. Uroporphyrinogen 1 synthase

Q.49 Hormone Synthesized from Tyrosine is:

A. Cortisol **B.** Calcitonin

C. Calcitrol **D.** Thyroxine

Q.50 Enzyme catalyzing reversible step in glycolysis is/are

A. Glucokinase / Hexokinase

B. Phosphofructokinase-I

C. Pyruvate kinase

D. Enolase

Part B

Q.51 Fat necrosis is seen in?

A. Breast **B.** Brain **C.** Kidney **D.** Spleen

Q.52 Central to apoptosis is the utilization of -

A. Nitrous oxide **B.** Adenyl cyclase

C. Caspases **D.** c-AMP

Q.53 Increased permeability in acute inflammation is due to

A. IL-2 **B.** Histamine

C. TGF-p **D.** FGF

Q.54 Mallory bodies are composed of -

A. Fat droplets

B. Microfilaments

C. Lysosomal enzymes

D. Intermediate filaments

Q.55 Identity the disease shown in photograph by its Granuloma

A. Brucellosis **B.** Syphilis

C. Leprosy **D.** TB

Q.56 Provisional matrix is made up of -

A. Fibrin **B.** Hemoglobin

C. Insulin **D.** Albumin

Q.57 HLA is present on –

A. Short arm of chromosomes 6

B. Short arm of chromosomes 3

C. Long arm of chromosomes 3

D. Long arm of chromosomes 6

Q.58 Function of CD4 is all except

A. Memory

B. Immunoglobulin production

C. Activation of macrophages

D. Cytotoxicity

Q.59 Comment on the diagnosis?

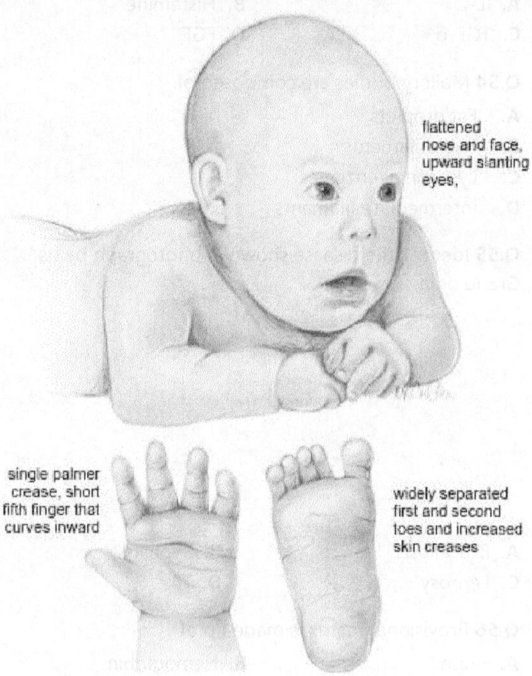

A. Turner Syndrome
B. Down syndrome
C. Prader-Willi syndrome
D. Patau syndrome

Q.60 Increased risk of cancer is seen in
A. Fibroadenoma of breast
B. Chronic ulcerative colitis
C. Bronchial asthma
D. Leiomyoma of the uterus

Q.61 Lynch syndrome is associated with cancers of the
A. Colon, endometrium, ovary
B. Breast, endometrium, ovary
C. Breast, colon, endometrium
D. Breast, colon, ovary

Q.62 In atherosclerosis, increased LDL in monocyte/macrophage is due to -
A. LDL receptors on macrophage
B. LDL receptors on endothelium
C. Lipids in LDL get oxidized
D. All of the above

Q.63 A 3-month-old infant is brought to the physician because of difficulty feeding, failure to thrive, and episodes of bluish pale skin during crying or feeding, Physical examination reveals a harsh systolic ejection murmur that is heard over the pulmonic area and left sternal border, A chest radiograph at shows a boot-shaped heart,
Which of the following events will most likely explain the embryologic mechanism responsible for the development of this condition?
A. Anterosuperior displacement of the infundibular septum
B. Failure of aorticopulmonary septum to divide
C. Failure of aorticopulmonary septum to spiral
D. Incomplete absorption of the sinus venosus into the right atrium

Q.64 Bite cells are seen in -
A. G6PD deficiency
B. SCA
C. Hereditary spherocytosis
D. Trauma

Q.65 A 9-year-old boy with elevation in both PT and APTT. What is the diagnosis?
A. Defect in extrinsic pathway
B. Defect in intrinsic pathway
C. Platelet function defect
D. Defect in common pathway

Q.66 If PTT is high in bleeding disorders then what will happen ?

a) Hemophilia A
b) Hemophilia B
c) Henoch-schonlein purpura
d) Bernard-soulier syndrome
e) Von-Willebrand disease

A. a,b,e **B.** b,c,d **C.** c,d,e **D.** a,c,d

Q.67 Classical markers for Hodgkin's disease -
A. CD_{15} and CD_{30} **B.** CD_{15} and CD_{22}
C. CD_{15} and CD_{20} **D.** CD_{20} and CD_{30}

Q.68 Characteristic histopathological finding in shock lung-
A. Diffuse alveolar necrosis
B. Interstitial pulmonary edema
C. Diffuse interstitial inflammation
D. Intra-cellular debris

Q.69 Commonest histological type of carcinoma testis is -
A. Teratoma **B.** Yolk sac tumor
C. Seminoma **D.** Choriocarcinoma

Q.70 Chronic gastritis is caused by all except
A. H. Pylori
B. Pernicious anemia
C. Alcohol
D. Overuse of salicylates

Q.71 Which of the following is not true regarding viral hepatitis -
A. Raised transaminase level correlates well with hepatic injury
B. Variable elevation of transaminase in prodromal phase.
C. The first sign of liver damage is inflammation.
D. Liver failure.

Q.72 A 20 year old female is diagnosed with granulosa cell tumor of the ovary. Which of the following biomarkers would be most useful for follow-up of patient?
A. CA 19-9
B. CA 50
C. Inhibin
D. Neuron-specific -enolase

Q.73 Tophi in gout found in all regions except -

a) Joint capsule
b) Skin
c) Muscle
d) Articular cartilage
e) Synovial membrane

A. a,e **B.** b **C.** a,b **D.** a,d

Q.74 Most common cause of Heridetary Spherocytosis is:

A. Glycophyrin **B.** Spectrin
C. Band 4 **D.** Ankyrin

Q.75 Asteroid bodies are seen in :

A. Sarcoidosis
B. Both of them (Sarcoidosis and Sporotrichosis)
C. Sporotrichosis
D. Anaphylaxis

Q.76 This antihistaminic drug can cause cardiac arrhythmia at a high dose by blocking cardiac K+ channels. It is most likely to be :

A. Levocetirizine **B.** Fexofenadine
C. Astemizole **D.** Loratadine

Q.77 What did Pavlov conclude from his experiments with the dog?

A. Conditional response
B. Unconditioned response
C. Procedural memory
D. Familiarity

Q.78 Selective 5–$HT_{1B/1D}$ receptor agonist useful in acute migraine is :

A. Buspirone **B.** Ondansetron
C. Frovatriptan **D.** Ketanserin

Q.79 Mycobacterium lepree was discovered by:

A. Robert Koch **B.** Hansen
C. Edward Jenner **D.** Louis Pasteur

Q.80 Dr. Sunil used edrophonium for differentiating a myasthenic crisis from the cholinergic crisis. He preferred it over other anticholinesterase agents because of its :

A. Shorter duration of action
B. Longer duration of action
C. Direct action on muscle end plate
D. Selective inhibition of true cholinesterase

Q.81 All are true about starting of beta-blocker therapy in a patient with congestive heart failure except :

A. They should be started with optimum doses
B. They should be gradually increased over weeks
C. Special precautions should be taken in cases of NYHA class III and IV
D. Carvedilol and metoprolol are the preferred drugs.

Q.82 Drugs that have been found to be useful in compensated heart failure include all of the following except :

A. Na^+ K^+ ATPase inhibitors
B. Alpha blockers
C. Beta receptor agonists
D. Beta receptor antagonists

Q.83 A pregnant female Salma with thyrotoxicosis is planned for surgery. Before surgery can be done, her gland should be reduced in size and vascularity by administering :

A. Iodide ion **B.** Propranolol
C. Propylthiouracil **D.** Radioactive iodine

Q.84 Which of the following is not true :

A. If a drug is administered rectally it follow 1st order kinetics
B. If a drug is administered I.M. it follows zero order kinetics
C. If a drug is administered I.V. it follows 1st order kinetics
D. All of these

Q.85 A drug X is secreted through renal tubules, tubular secretion of this drug can be confirmed if renal clearance of drug X is :

A. More than the GFR
B. Equal to the GFR
C. Less than the GFR
D. More than volume of distribution

Q.86 In a patient of head injuries with rapidly increasing intracranial tension without hematoma, the drug of choice for initial management would be :

A. Furosemide **B.** Steroids
C. 20% Mannitol **D.** Glycine

Q.87 Amiloride can cause hyperkalemia due to its action on :

A. Electrogenic K^+ channels
B. Electrogenic Na^+ channels
C. Non electrogenic Na^+-$C1^-$ symporter
D. H^+-K^+ ATPase

Q.88 Busulfan

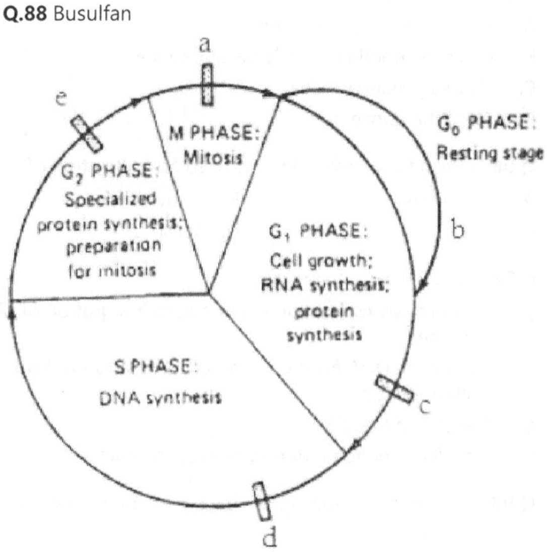

A. a **B.** b **C.** c **D.** d

Q.89 The plasma concentration of drug Y is 50 mg/L, and it is eliminated at a rate of 2 mg/ min. Which of the following is the clearance rate of drug Y ?

A. 0.01 L/min **B.** 0.04 L/min
C. 4 L/min **D.** 10 L/min

Q.90 A 40-year-old man has been diagnosed with glioblastoma multiforme. The patient's neurologist must choose an appropriate cancer drug to treat this tumor. Which of the following can cross the blood–brain barrier for effective treatment of brain tumors ?

A. Cytarabine
B. Etoposide
C. Nitrosoureas
D. Selective estrogen receptor modulators

Q.91 If a drug is repeatedly administered at dosing intervals that are equal to its elimination half-life, the number of doses required for the plasma concentration of the drug to reach the steady state is

A. 2 to 3 **B.** 4 to 5 **C.** 6 to 7 **D.** 8 to 9

Q.92 Postoperative vomiting is uncommon with this intravenous anaesthetic agent and patients are able to ambulate sooner than those who receive other anaesthetic agents :

A. Ketamine **B.** Enflurane
C. Propofol **D.** Remifentanil

Q.93 Dissociative anaesthesia is seen on administration of :

A. Ether **B.** Halothane
C. Enflurane **D.** Ketamine

Q.94 All are true about cephalosporins, EXCEPT :

A. Ceftazidime is a 3rd generation cephalosporin.
B. Cefoperazone has got antipseudomonal effect.
C. Cefoxitin has got no activity against anaerobes.
D. Cephalosporins act by inhibiting cell wall synthesis.

Q.95 Biclutamide is a drug. True about it is:

A. Binds to androgen receptors
B. Given as montherapy in prostatic cancer
C. Causes gynaecomastia
D. All of the above

Q.96 Human fibroblast cell line is used for cultivation of -

A. Adenovirus **B.** Poliovirus
C. HIV **D.** Measles

Q.97 Lysogenic conversion is -

A. New properties in a bacterium due to integration of phage genome
B. Transfer of DNA from one bacterium to another by a bacteriophage
C. Transfer of free DNA
D. Transfer of genome during physical contact

Q.98 Which of the following is a bacteria taxonomically -

a) Chlamydia
b) Rickettsia
c) Mycoplasma
d) Prion
e) Bacteriophage

A. a,b **B.** a,b,c **C.** a,c,d **D.** b,c,d

Q.99 Apart from T & B lymphocytes, the other class of lymphocytes is -

A. Macrophages **B.** Astrocytes
C. NK cells **D.** Langerhans cells

Q.100 A possible source of "second signal" to a B-cell bound by specific antigen include -

A. EB virus
B. Endotoxin
C. Antigen-specific T-cells
D. Plasma cells

Q.101 Which of the following is not a mechanism for resistance to MRSA -

A. Resistance is chromosomally mediated
B. Produced mainly by alteration in PBP's
C. MRSA resistance is absolutely beta lactamase dependent
D. Intrinsic resistance is known

Q.102 Reverse transcriptase polymerase chain reactions can aid in the diagnosis of all of the following viral infections except -

A. Adenovirus **B.** Astrovirus
C. Rotavirus **D.** Poliovirus

Q.103 All are true about Entamoeba Histolytica except -

A. Cyst are 4 nucleated
B. Trophozoites colonise in the colon
C. The chromatid bodies are stained by Iodides
D. None of the above.

Q.104 Which amongst the following biological agents carries the least potential for use as a biological weapon for microbial terrorism?

A. Plague (Yersinia pestis)
B. Small pox (Variola major)
C. Botulism (Clostridium botulinum)
D. Brucellosis (Brucella sp)

Q.105 A person gets infected in a hospital and clinical manifestation appear after he is discharged this is called -

A. Nosocomial infection
B. Opportunistic infection
C. Epizootic infection
D. Physician induced

Q.106 There is an outbreak of MRSA infection in a ward. What is the best way to control the infection-

A. Vancomycin given emperically to all the patients
B. Fumigation of ward frequently
C. Washing hand before & after attending patient
D. Wearing mask before any invasive procedure in ICU

Q.107 Correctly matched stain -

A. Mucicarmine - Cryptococcus
B. Giemsa - Candida
C. Gram's - Pneumocystis carinii
D. Fontana- Histoplasma

Q.108 The following figure represents :-

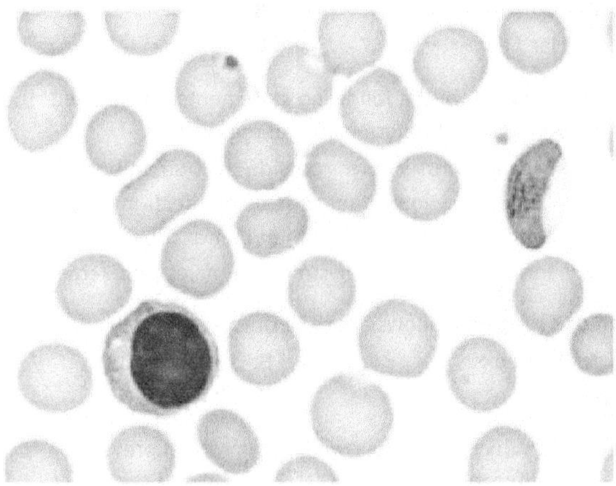

A. Gametocyte – Plasmodium malariae
B. Gametocyte – Plasmodium falciparum
C. Trophozoites – Plasmodium falciparum
D. Trophozoites – Plasmodium vivax

Q.109 The organism shown here is most likely :-

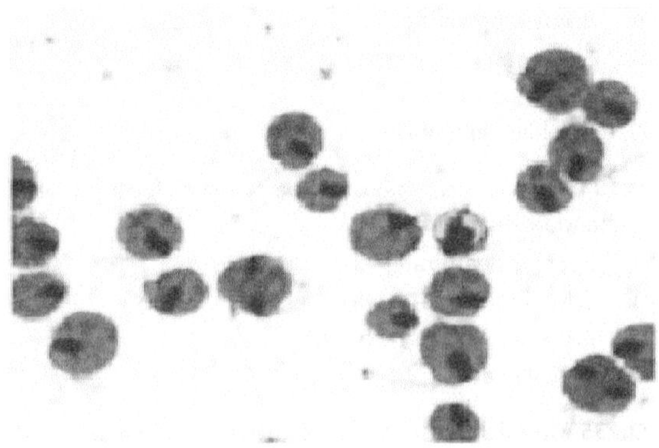

A. Giardia lambia
B. Trichomonas vaginalis
C. Leishmania donovani
D. None

Q.110 This image describes multiple, erythematous papules that develop at a site and progress to severely pruritic, serpinginous, dark skin lesions which elongate daily. This condition could be most likely due to :-

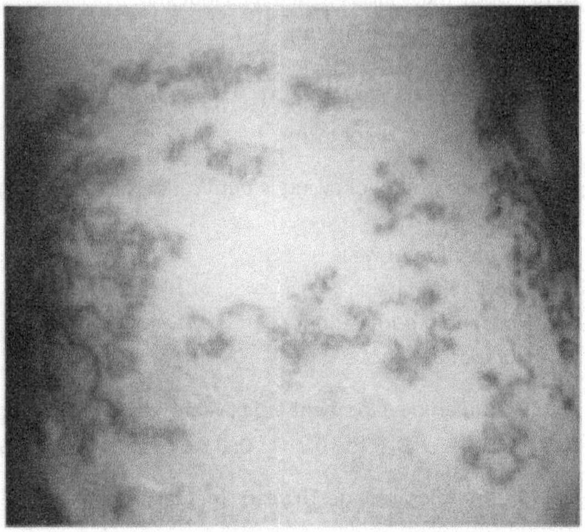

A. Ancylostoma caninum
B. Ancylostoma braziliense
C. Ancylostoma duodenale
D. Uncinaria stenocephala

Q.111 The following section describes a fungal organism obtained from nasal sinus of a neutropenic patient. The most likely organism is :-

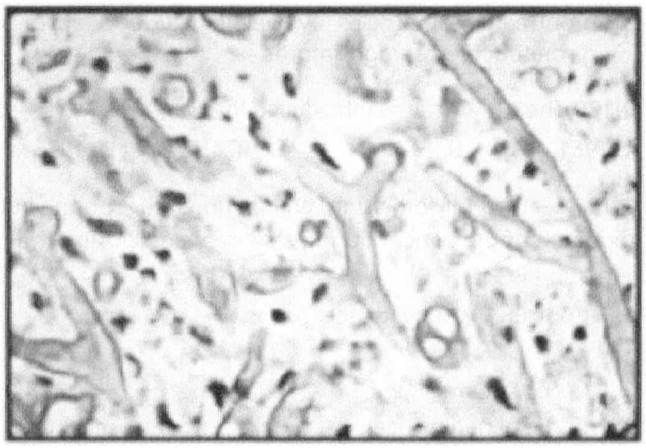

A. Aspergillus **B.** Rhizopus
C. Candida **D.** Histoplasma

Q.112 What is the correct order of reagents in the Gram stain?
A. Gentian violet → Iodine → Carbol fuchsin
B. Iodine → Gentian violet → Carbol fuchsin
C. Carbol fuchsin → Iodine → Gentian violet
D. Carbol fuchsin → Gentian violet → Iodine

Q.113 Stain is not taken by capsule in gram negative organisms because the capsule consist of -
a) Polysaccharides
b) Lipopolysaccharides
c) Lipids
d) Protein
A. b **B.** c **C.** ac **D.** ad

Q.114 Electron microscopy is used for the following except -
A. To differentiate T & B lymphocytes
B. IgG deposits in kidney
C. TPI
D. Flagella

Q.115 Peptide binding site on class I MHC molecules for presenting processed antigens to CD_8 T cells is formed by -
A. Proximal domain of α subunits
B. Distal domain of α subunit
C. Proximal domains of α and β subunit
D. Distal domains of α and β subunit

Q.116 IPC 197 is related to –
A. Causing disappearance of evidence
B. Giving false evidence
C. Issuing false certificate by doctor
D. Examination of accused

Q.117 Punishment for issuing false certificate –
A. 7 years **B.** 5 years **C.** 3 years **D.** 20 years

Q.118 Injury by Lathi

A. Laceration B. Stab wound
C. Abrasion D. Contusion

Q.119 Cadaveric spasm is -

A. Shows primary relaxation
B. Occurs immediately after death
C. It does not indicates the nature of death
D. Contraction of muscles involved in cadaveric sapsm is less pronounced than rigor mortis

Q.120 The MTP Act was introduced in -

A. 1961 B. 1971 C. 1974 D. 1975

Q.121 Leaving (or forgetting) an instrument or sponge in the abdomen of the patient during a surgery and closing the operation is -

A. Contributory negligence
B. Civil
C. Corporate negligence
D. Criminal negligence

Q.122 Thanatology deals with the study of:

A. Snakes B. Poison
C. Finger prints D. Death

Q.123 All of the following are true about death by strangulation except -

A. Dribbling of saliva down the chin
B. Bleeding from nose is common
C. Hyoid fracture is common
D. Fracture dislocation of cervical ventebrae is rare

Q.124 Cephalic index is most useful in the identification of -

A. Age B. Sex C. Religion D. Race

Q.125 Post mortem staining in case of "CO" poisoning is:

A. Brown B. Bright red
C. Cherry red D. Blue

Q.126 Due to an effective prevention program, the prevalence of an infectious disease in a community has been reduced by 90%. A physician continues to use the same diagnostic test for the disease that she has always used. How have the test's characteristics changed ?

A. Its sensitivity has increased
B. Its positive predictive value has increased
C. Its negative predictive value has increased
D. The test's characteristics have not changed

Q.127 The term 'Hidden Hunger' refers to:

A. Hunger amongst tribal communities
B. Hunger amongst war-torn area residents
C. Micronutrient deficiency
D. Severe malnutrition in young children

Q.128 Under the National Programme, NCD clinic is established at:

A. Anganwadi B. Sub-centre
C. PHC D. CHC

Q.129 Kyasanur forest disease is transmitted by:

A. House fly B. Sand fly
C. Hard tick D. Soft tick

Q.130 Which of the following statements is true about the epidemiological determinants of measles -

A. Measles virus survives outside the human body for 5 days
B. Carriers are important sources of infection
C. Secondary attack is less than that of rubella
D. Incidence of measles is more in males than females

Q.131 MTP act allows abortion upto:

A. 10 weeks B. 12 weeks
C. 16 weeks D. 20 weeks

Q.132 Which of the following is primordial prevention for non communicable Disease [NCD]

A. Salt restriction in high NCD area
B. Smoking cessation in high NCD area
C. Preservation of traditional diet in low NCD area
D. Early diagnosis & Treatment

Q.133 Immunization is-

A. Primary prevention
B. Secondary prevention
C. Tertiary prevention
D. Disability limitation

Q.134 Following can be used as a yardstick for the assessment of standards of therapy -

A. Specific death rate
B. Case fatality rate
C. Proportional mortality rate
D. Survival rate

Q.135 Modifiable risk factors for hypertension is ?

A. Ethinicity B. Age
C. Sex D. Obesity

Q.136 Which is most economical and best screening-

A. Mass screening
B. High risk screening
C. Multiphasic screening
D. Any of the above

Q.137 Body mass index (Quetelet's index) is:

A. Weight (Kg)/Height^2 (m)
B. Weight (Kg)/Height (m)
C. Weight^2 (Kg)/Height (m)
D. Weight^2 (Kg)/Height^2 (m)

Q.138 Which of the following is purification of water at large scale -

A. Disinfection of well
B. Rapid sand filter
C. Household purification
D. None of the above

Q.139 Human development index value ranges between:

A. 0 to 100 B. 0 to 10 C. 0 to 1 D. 0 to 0.5

Q.140 Chronological age 10 years, mental age 4 years. What that person called as?

A. Imbecile B. Idiot C. Normal D. Genius

Q.141 Diagnostic power of the test is reflected by-

A. Sensitivity
B. Specificity
C. Predictive value
D. Population attributable risk

Q.142 Ergonomics –

A. Adjusting the Worker to his job
B. Study of human behavior
C. Study of social mobility
D. None

Q.143 Mercury is disposed by

A. Controlled combustion
B. Deep burial
C. Chemical treatment
D. Safely collect and re-use

Q.144 PERT type of system is used for –

A. Cost effective analysis
B. Cost benefit analysis
C. Network analysis
D. Input-Output analysis

Q.145 Under the National Programme for Control of Blindness in India, medical colleges are classified as eye care centers of –

A. Primary level B. Secondary level
C. Tertiary level D. None of the above

Q.146 A group of experts discussing and interacting about a particular topic in presence of audience is :

A. Panel discussion B. Chalk and talk
C. Group discussion D. Workshop

Q.147 Disease which does not come under Integrated Disease Surveillance Project is:

A. Tuberculosis
B. Meningoencephalitis
C. Herpes Zoster
D. Cholera

Q.148 National AIDS control Programme was started on –

A. 1977 B. 1985 C. 1986 D. 1990

Q.149 Occurrence in the community of a number of cases of disease that is unusually large or unexpected

A. Endemic B. Epidemic
C. Pandemic D. Infection

Q.150 The proportion of disease incidence that can be attributed to a specific exposure

A. Relative risk B. Odds ratio
C. Attributable risk D. Potential risk

Part C

Q.151 Which of the following is/are not the cause of hypopigmentation –

A. Leprosy B. Pinta
C. Syphilis D. Pytriasis alba

Q.152 Most common association with Acanthosis nigricans -

A. Hypertension B. DM
C. Obesity D. Hypothyroidism

Q.153 Glial cells are the most abundant cells in:

A. Lungs B. Kidney
C. Gallbladder D. Nervous system

Q.154 Caterpillar bodies are seen in

A. Dyskeratosis congenita
B. Amyloidosis
C. Porphyria cutanea tarda
D. Lipoid proteinosis

Q.155 Most common organism causing T. capitis is –

A. Trichoderma B. Microsporum
C. Epidermophyton D. Candida albicans

Q.156 Drug not causing exatithematous skin eruption –

A. Phenytoin B. Hydrocortisone
C. Ampicillin D. Phenylbutazone

Q.157 Which is not a connective tissue

A. Blood B. Bone C. Cartilage D. Muscle

Q.158 A child is presenting with erythmatous follicular papules on trunk. There are areas of normal skin within the lesions. There is thickening of palms & soles. This child is suffering from –

A. Pityriasis rosea
B. Pityriasis rubra pilaris
C. Psoriasis
D. Seborrheic dermatitis

Q.159 A 50 years old man has a 2 year history of facial bullae & oral ulcers. Microscopic smear from skin lesions is most likely to disclose –

a) Tzanck cells
b) Acantholytic cells
c) Necrosis
d) Koilocytosis

A. c B. d C. ab D. ac

Q.160 Thalidomide is drug of choice for .... , if two courses of glucocorticoids fail.

A. Lepra I reaction
B. Lepra II reaction
C. Both Lepra I & II reactions
D. Nerve abscess

Q.161 Incubation period of scabies is –

A. 7 days B. 2 weeks C. 4 weeks D. 2–3 days

Q.162 In which of the following Palpable pupura is not seen –

A. Cryoglobulinuria
B. H.S. pupura
C. Gaint cell arteritis
D. Drug induced vasculitis

Q.163 In which of the following flaky paint dermatosis is observed

A. Dermatitis B. Pellagra
C. Marasmus D. Kwashiorkor

Q.164 Isolated 3rd nerve palsy is seen in-

A. Frontal lobe tumour
B. Diabetes
C. Webers syndrome
D. Lateral medullary syndrome

Q.165 Locus heterogeneity is a feature of which of the following?

A. Familial adenomatous polyposis
B. Turcot syndrome
C. Osteogenesis imperfecta
D. All of the above

Q.166 Which one of the following veins does not drain into coronary sinus?

A. Middle cardiac vein
B. Anterior cardiac vein
C. Oblique cardiac vein
D. Small cardiac vein

Q.167 Mayer–Rokitansky–Kuster–Hauser syndrome (MRKH) syndrome is associated with -

A. Ovarian agenesis
B. Absent fallopian tube
C. Vaginal atresia
D. Bicornuate uterus

Q.168 Duroziez's sign is seen in?

A. Aortic regurgitation B. Aortic stenosis
C. Mitral stenosis D. Mitral regurgitation

Q.169 The most common cause of Pulmonary thromboembolism

A. DIC
B. DVT
C. Coagulopathy
D. Venous hypertension

Q.170 In hyperkalemia with bradycardia treatment is -

A. Calcium gluconate B. Steroid
C. Salbutamol D. K+resin

Q.171 All are true regarding anaemia of chronic diseases, except

A. Decreased serum Fe
B. Decreased ferritin
C. Decreased total Fe binding capacity
D. Increased bone marrow Fe

Q.172 In which leukemia, autoimmune hemolytic anemia is most common in

A. Acute lymphoblastic leukemia (ALL)
B. Acute myeloid leukemia (AML)
C. Clinical manifestations of immediate hypersensitivity (CMIL)
D. Chronic lymphocytic leukemia (CLL)

Q.173 All of the following feature of hallucination EXCEPT-

a) Depends on will of observer and is under voluntary control
b) Occur in inner subjective space
c) It is vivid as sensory perception
d) It occurs in absence of perceptual stimulus

A. ac B. a C. ad D. ab

Q.174 All are examples of cortical dementia except -

A. Alzheimer's disease
B. Multiple sclerosis
C. Creutzfeldt–Jakob disease (CJD)
D. Pick's disease

Q.175 A boy is having diarrhoea, rhinorrhoea, sweating & lacrimation, What is the most probable diagnosis -

A. Cocaine withdrawal B. Heroin withdrawal
C. Alcohol withdrawal D. LSD withdrawal

Q.176 Naltrexone is used in opioid dependence to -

A. Prevent respiratory depression
B. Treat withdrawal symptoms
C. Prevent relapse
D. Treatment of opioid overdose

Q.177 Secretion of growth hormone is stimulated by which of the following?

A. Increased plasma glucose levels
B. Deep sleep
C. Free fatty acids
D. Somatostatin

Q.178 The term "Dementia praecox" was coined by -

A. Freud B. Bleuler
C. Kraepelin D. Schneider

Q.179 Nihilistic delusions are seen in -

a) Endogenous depression
b) Double depression
c) Depression in involutional stage
d) Cyclothymia
e) Dysthymia

A. ab B. abc C. acd D. bce

Q.180 Delusion of Nihilism and Early morning insomnia are characteristic features of -

A. Mania B. Major depression
C. Personality disorder D. Schizophrenia

Q.181 Treatment of choice for the phobic disorder is -

A. Psychotherapy B. Behaviour therapy
C. SSRI D. Benzodiazepam

Q.182 Which of the following is false about somatization disorder -

A. Involves 2 sexual disturbance Symptoms
B. Two GI symptoms
C. Four pain symptoms
D. Multiple recurrent symptoms

Q.183 Hallucinations which arises when a patient is falling asleep -

A. Hypnagogic hallucination
B. Hypnopompic hallucination
C. Non specific hallucinations
D. Jactatio nocturna capitis

Q.184 How to differentiate between psychological and organic erectile dysfunction -
A. Nocturnal penile tumescence
B. PIPE therapy
C. Sildenafil induced erection
D. Stop-squeeze technique

Q.185 A young lady is present with repeated episode of overeating followed by purging using laxatives, she probably suffering from -
A. Bulimia nervosa
B. Schizophrenia
C. Anorexia nervosa
D. Binge eating disorders

Q.186 Following drugs are used in the treatment of ADHD ?
A. Amphetamine **B.** Modafinil
C. Methylphenidate **D.** All of the above

Q.187 Treatment of hyperkinetic syndrome include -
a) Imipramine
b) Methylphenidate
c) Haloperidol
d) Clozapine
e) Amphetamine
A. ab **B.** ad **C.** be **D.** ce

Q.188 Memory disturbance of ECT recovers in -
A. Few days to few weeks
B. Few weeks to few months
C. Few months to few year
D. Permanent

Q.189 All are true about RVF Except :
A. Hepatomegaly **B.** Nocturia
C. Normal JVP **D.** Ascites

Q.190 Schrimer's Test is used for evaluation of function of :
A. Optic nerve **B.** Abducent nerve
C. Occulomotor nerve **D.** Facial nerve

Q.191 Urinary VMA levels are increased in :
A. Carcinoid syndrome
B. Conn's syndrome
C. Phaeochromocytoma
D. Hepatocellular carcinoma

Q.192 Non-oliguric renal failure is seen with :
A. NSAID **B.** PSGN
C. Hypovolemia **D.** Gentamycin

Q.193 Not a cause of Diarrhea:
A. Hypercalcemia **B.** Diabetes mellitus
C. Carcinoid **D.** Hyperythyroidism

Q.194 N-myc gene is seen in:
A. Retinoblastoma **B.** Neuroblastoma
C. Williams tumor **D.** Nephroblastoma

Q.195 Hepatitis B is not transmitted through :
A. Semen **B.** Milk **C.** Blood **D.** Stool

Q.196 Barret's esophagus can lead to -
a) Stricture
b) Reflux esophagitis
c) Peptic ulcer
d) Achalasia
A. a and c **B.** b and c **C.** a and d **D.** b

Q.197 True about achalasia cardio, all except :
A. elevated resting LES tone
B. increased primary peristaltic waves in the esophagus
C. increased baseline intraesophageal pressure
D. pre malignant

Q.198 Artery to bleed in duodenal ulcer haemorrhage -
A. Splenic artery
B. Gastroduodenal artery
C. Left gastric artery
D. Superior mesenteric artery

Q.199 Anomaly associated with duodenal atresia is
A. Down syndrome
B. Duodenal adenomas
C. Limb defects
D. Autoimmune disorders

Q.200 Portal hypertension following portal vein thrombosis are guided by -
a) ↑ in splenic pulp pressure
b) ↑ in portal vein pressure
c) ↑ in hepatic vein pressure
d) Portal vein doppler study
A. abd **B.** bcd **C.** abc **D.** ab

Q.201 Indication of aspiration in liver abscess is all, except:
A. Left lobe abscess
B. Deep & less than $5\ mm$ size
C. Multiple
D. Recurrent

Q.202 Which of the following is not an indication for cholecystectomy
A. 70-year-old male with symptomatic gallstones
B. 20-year-old male with sickle cell anaemia and symptomatic gallstones
C. 65-year-old female with a large gallbladder polyp
D. 55-year-old with an asymptomatic gallstone

Q.203 CBD stone may present with
A. decreased bilirubin
B. ↓WBC count
C. ↓serum alkaline phosphatase
D. cholangitis

Q.204 Which of the following parameters will fall the earliest in iron deficiency

A. MCV
B. MCH
C. MCHC
D. Red cell distribution width

Q.205 Raised MCV in pregnancy can be due to all except
A. Megaloblastic Anaemia
B. Iron Deficiency
C. Hypothyroidism
D. Alcohol use

Q.206 Meckels diverticulum represents which structure of the embryonic life ?
A. Vitellointestinal duct
B. Wolfian duct
C. Mullerian duct
D. Paramesonophric duct

Q.207 All of the following are significant risk factors for colonic carcinoma in an adenomatous polyp except
A. Pedunculated polyp B. Villous histology
C. Size > 2 cm D. Atypia

Q.208 Non-union is a complication of
A. Inter-trochanteric of hip
B. Colles' fracture
C. Supracondylar humerus
D. Scaphoid

Q.209 In anterior cruciate ligament tear, which of these tests are positive -
A. Lachman's test
B. McMuny's test
C. Posterior drawer test
D. Apley's test

Q.210 Increased alkaline phosphate in seen in -
A. Multiple myeloma
B. Chronic renal failure
C. Osteoporosis
D. All of the above

Q.211 The most visually disabling type of cataract is:
A. Cortical cataract
B. Nuclear cataract
C. Posterior subcapsular cataract
D. Anterior capsular cataract

Q.212 Housemaids knee is bursitis of -
A. Prepatellar bursa B. Infrapatellar bursa
C. Olecranon D. Ischial bursa

Q.213 The correct order of priorities in the initial management of head injury is -
A. Airway, Breathing, Circulation, treatment of extra cranial injuries
B. Treatment of extracranial injuries, Airway, Breathing, Circulation
C. Circulation, airway, Breathing, treatment of extra cranial injuries
D. Airway, circulation, breathing, treatment of extra cranial injuries

Q.214 Maximum weight for skin traction -
A. 1-2 kg B. 4-5 kg C. 10-15 kg D. 15-20 kg

Q.215 Bone resorption markers are -
A. Serum propeptide of type I procollagen
B. Osteocalcin
C. Urine total free deoxypyridinoline
D. Free glutamic acid cross linkage

Q.216 A 20-years old male presents with anterior shoulder dislocation. This injury is usually caused as a combination of which of the following -
A. Abduction & external rotation
B. Adduction & external rotation
C. Abduction & internal rotation
D. Adduction & internal rotation

Q.217 Cubitus valgus is seen in
A. Intercondylar of humerus
B. Of the olecranon
C. Head of the radius
D. Lateral condyle of humerus

Q.218 Late complication of acetabular fracture
A. vascular necrosis of head of the femur
B. Avascular necrosis of lilac crest
C. Fixed deformity of the hip joint
D. None of the above

Q.219 Ratio of $O_2 : N_2O$ in Entonox is –
A. 50 : 50 B. 60 : 40 C. 40 : 60 D. 25 : 75

Q.220 Circuit of choice for controlled ventilation
A. Magill circuit B. Type B
C. Type C D. Type D

Q.221 Identify the type of waves shown in the photograph.

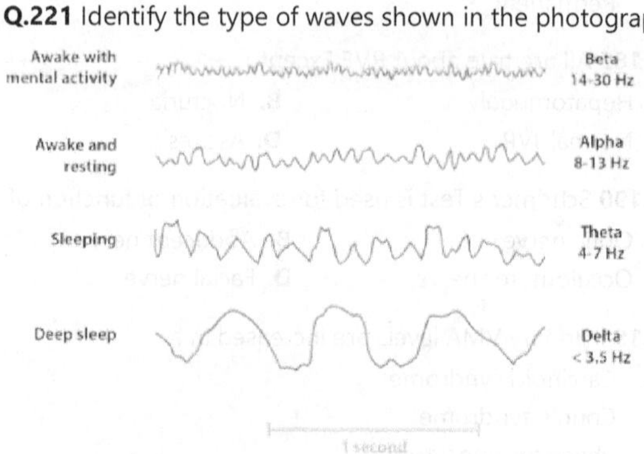

A. ECG B. EEG C. JVP D. PCWP

Q.222 Capnography is useful for –
A. Determining vaporizer malfunction or contamination.
B. Determining circuit hypoxia.
C. Determining the appropriate placement of endotracheal tube.
D. Detecting concentration of oxygen in the anesthetic circuit.

Q.223 All are the complication of CVP line, except:
A. Airway injury B. Haemothroax

C. Air embolism **D.** Septicemia

Q.224 Pentothiol sodium should preferablay be injected into –

A. Femoral vein
B. Antecubital vein
C. Neck vein
D. Veins on outer aspect of fore arm

Q.225 Cerebral metabolism and O_2 consumption are increased by –

A. Propofol **B.** Ketamine
C. Atracurium **D.** Fentanyl

Q.226 Addition of epinephrine to lignocaine –

A. Increaseses distribution of LA
B. Decreases absorption of LA
C. Decreases duration of LA
D. Increases metabolism of LA

Q.227 Local anaesthetic with maximum ionized form at physiological pH –

A. Lidocaine **B.** Etidocaine
C. Bupivacaine **D.** Chloroprocaine

Q.228 Cocaine was first used as local anaesthetic by –

A. Carl Kollar **B.** Horace Wells
C. Morton **D.** None

Q.229 Upper respiratory tract infection is a common problem in children. All the following anaesthetic complications can occur in children with respiratory infections, except –

A. Bacteremia
B. Halothane granuloma
C. Increased mucosal bleeding
D. Larygospasm

Q.230 Right anterior oblique view of chest X-ray true is/are

A. Cassette near right shoulder
B. Cassette near the left shoulder
C. Arch of Aorta best seen
D. Mitral & tricuspid valves better seen

Q.231 Figure of 8 in chest X-ray is seen in –

A. Ebstein anomaly
B. Total anomalous pulmonary venous connection (TAPVC)
C. Tetrology of fallot
D. Transposition of great vessels

Q.232 Soap bubble appearance in X-ray is seen in –

A. Multiple cystic kidney
B. Neuroblastoma
C. Cystic lymphangiectasis
D. Meconium ileus

Q.233 Which of following is not a feature of renovascular hypertension on intravenous urography -

A. Delayed 'wash - out' of contrast
B. Filling defect in calyces
C. Ureteral kinking
D. Normal or small sized kidney

Q.234 76 year old man presents with a lytic lesion in the vertebrae. X-ray skull showed multiple punched out lesions. The diagnosis is –

A. Metastasis
B. Multiple myeloma
C. Osteomalacia
D. Hyperparathyroidism

Q.235 A 20 year female patient with 6th cranial nerve palsy on T_2 weighted MRI shows a hyperintense lesion in cavernous sinus which shows homogenous contrast enhancement. Most probable diagnosis is?

A. Schwannoma
B. Meningioma
C. Cavernous sinus hemangioma
D. Cavernous hemangioma

Q.236 In Radionuclide imaging the most useful radiopharmaceutical for skeletal imaging is –

A. Gallium 67 (^{67}Ga)
B. Technetium–sulphur-colloid (^{99m}Tc–Sc)
C. Technetium–99m linked to Methylene diphosphonate (^{99m}Tc–MDP)
D. None of the above

Q.237 Which of the following liver metastasis appear hypoechoic on Ultrasonography –

A. Breast cancer
B. Colon cancer
C. Renal cancer
D. Mucinous adenocarcinoma

Q.238 Tracheal bifurcation on X-ray corresponds to –

A. Thoracic inlet **B.** T_4T_5
C. T_5T_6 **D.** None of the above

Q.239 A newborn presenting with intestinal obstruction showed on abdominal X-ray, multiple air-fluid levels. The diagnosis is not likely to be –

A. Pyloric obstruction **B.** Duodenal atresia
C. Heal atresia **D.** Ladd's bands

Q.240 Looser's zone is seen in –

A. Osteoporosis
B. Hyperparathyrodism
C. Osteomalacia
D. Both (B) and (C)

Q.241 All are used for contraception in sickle cell anaemia except

A. IUCD
B. Oral Pill
C. Progestin only pill
D. Progesterone Impants

Q.242 Rupture of membrane is said to be premature when it occurs at :

A. 38 weeks of pregnancy
B. 32 weeks of pregnancy
C. Prior to 1st stage of labour
D. II stage of labour

Q.243 Birth weight of a baby can be increased by :

A. Cessation of smoking
B. Aspirin
C. Ca^{++} and vitamin D supplement
D. Bed rest

Q.244 Cephalhematoma :

A. Is caused by oedema of the subcutaneous layers of the scalp
B. Should be treated by aspiration
C. Most commonly lies over the occipital bone
D. Does not vary in tension with crying

Q.245 The number of fontanelles present in a newborn child is:

A. 1 **B.** 2 **C.** 4 **D.** 6

Q.246 Which of the following method is the best predictor for ovulation in a female infertility patient during a menstrual cycle

A. Basal body temperature
B. Hormonal Study
C. Endometrial biopsy
D. Fern study

Q.247 Not an indication for blood transfusion

A. Moderate anemia at 24-30 weeks
B. Severe anemia at 36 weeks
C. Blood loss anemia
D. Refractory anemia

Q.248 Postcoital test (PCT) is done for :

A. Cervical receptivity
B. Sperm motility
C. Absolute sperm count
D. Viable sperm count

Q.249 Type of maternal anaemia based on Photograph of the peripheral smear

A. Iron deficiency anemia
B. Thalassemia
C. Sickle cell anemia
D. Sideroblastic anemia

Q.250 The following statements are related to the therapy of iron deficiency anaemia except :

A. Oral iron can be given only if anemia is detected before 20 weeks of pregnancy
B. Parenteral iron therapy markedly increases the reticulocytic count within 7-14 days
C. Parenteral therapy is ideal during 30-36 weeks
D. Blood transfusion may be useful in severe anaemia beyond 36 weeks

Q.251 Drug given to reduce uterine contractions during preterm labour with least side effects :

A. Ritodrine
B. Nifidipine
C. Magnessium sulphate
D. Progesterone

Q.252 Blood will interfere with the nitrazine test for detecting ruptured membranes because :

A. It is acid
B. It is alkaline
C. It contains increased amounts of sodium chloride
D. It contains decreased amounts of sodium chloride

Q.253 Early date for detection of fetal heart :

A. 6.0-6.5 week **B.** 6.5-7 week
C. 7.1-7.5 week **D.** 8 week

Q.254 Diagnostic factor for choriocarcinoma is :

A. Hypoplastic trophoblasts
B. Lung Metastasis
C. HCG Level less than 35,000Miu/ml
D. None of them

Q.255 Late deceleration is due to :

A. Cord compression
B. Abdominal compression
C. Placental insufficiency
D. Head compression

Q.256 The triangular area bounded by clitoris, fourchette and labia minora is

A. Fossa navicularis **B.** Fouchette
C. Vestibule **D.** Vulva

Q.257 True about clomiphene citrate is :

A. Enclomiphene has antiestrogenic affect
B. Chance of pregnancy is three fold as compared to placebo
C. Risk of multiple pregnancy is 2-4%
D. It can also be used for male infertility with oligozoospermia

Q.258 Most common site of ectopic pregnancy is

A. Ovary **B.** Peritoneum
C. Fallopian tube **D.** Cervix

Q.259 Best prenatal treatment CAH is

A. Betamethasone **B.** Prednisolone
C. Hydrocortisone **D.** Dexamethasone

Q.260 Acute PID is treated by:

a) IV antibiotics (broad spectrum)
b) Drainage of TO mass
c) Abdominal hysterectomy
d) Laparoscopic exploration

A. acd **B.** bcd **C.** abd **D.** ab

Q.261 Among the surgeries of stress incontinence, the long-term success rate is maximum with

A. Stamey's repair
B. Burch's colposuspension
C. Kelly's stitch
D. Aldridge surgery

Q.262 The fallopian tube
A. Is lined entirely by ciliated columnar epithelium
B. Has a submucous layer
C. Undergoes shedding during menstrual cycle
D. Surrounded by peritoneum on all sides except along the line of attachment of mesosalpinx

Q.263 Granulosa cells produces estrogen with the help of the enzyme:
A. Alkaline phosphatase
B. Aromatase
C. Acid phosphatase
D. Glucuronidase

Q.264 Which of the following infection affects fetal growth?
A. CMV B. Rubella
C. Herpes simplex D. All

Q.265 OCP gives protection against following cancers:
a) Endometrial
b) Ovary
c) Cervix
d) Breast
e) Liver
A. ac B. a C. ad D. ab

Q.266 The drug which reduces the size of myoma include
A. Danazol B. Progesterone
C. GnRH agonist D. Mifepristone

Q.267 Submucosal fibroid is detected by
A. Hysteroscopy
B. Hysterosalpingography
C. USG(Transabdominal)
D. Laparoscopy

Q.268 Endometriosis is commonly associated with:
A. B/L chocolate cyst of ovary
B. Adenomyosis
C. Fibroid
D. Luteal cyst

Q.269 Causes of dysfunctional uterine bleeding can be:
a) Uterine polyp
b) Fibroid
c) Granulosa cell tumour
d) Irregular ripening of endometrium
e) Irregular shedding of endometrium
A. ab B. bc C. cd D. be

Q.270 Long-term tamoxifen therapy may cause:
A. Endometrium Ca B. Ovary Ca
C. Cervix Ca D. Vagina Ca

Q.271 Child draws triangle at what age ?
A. 3 years B. 5 years C. 6 years D. 7 years

Q.272 Newborn babies are able to breathe and suck at the same time due to –
A. Wide short tongue B. Short soft palate
C. High larynx D. Short pharynx

Q.273 Persistence of Moro's reflex is abnormal beyond the age of –
A. 3rd month B. 4th month
C. 5th month D. 6th month

Q.274 A child with central cyanosis and enlarged left ventricle the probable diagnosis is –
A. Tricuspid atresia
B. Eisenmenger's syndrome
C. tetralogy of fallot
D. Anomolous pulmonary artery

Q.275 The following is false about Atrial septal defect –
A. Ostium secundum most common
B. Right to Left Shunt
C. May be associated with TAPVC
D. CCF is very rare

Q.276 A most common cause of Bronchiolitis is?
A. RSV B. Adenovirus
C. Parainfluenza D. Mycoplasma

Q.277 Glioma of the optic nerve is usually –
A. Gemistocytic B. Pilocytic
C. Fibrillary D. Lamellar

Q.278 Most important cause of abdominal distension in intestinal obstruction –
A. Cases produced by bacterial activity
B. Cases diffused from blood
C. Swallowed air
D. Products of digestion

Q.279 What is the probable diagnosis for a cyst in a child which is located at and associated with vertebral defects –
A. Myelocele B. Bronchogenic cyst
C. Neuroenteric cyst D. Neuroblastoma

Q.280 Potter's syndrome is associated with –
A. Renal anomalies
B. Severe oligohydramnios
C. Flattened nose
D. All the above

Q.281 Paranasal sinus opening in middle meatus includes all except-
A. Maxillaly B. Anterior ethmoid
C. Frontal D. Sphenoid

Q.282 Percentage of newborn with deviation of nasal septum -
A. 2% B. 10% C. 20% D. 50%

Q.283 The highest frequency of palpable metastasis in neck on presentation is -
A. Carcinoma tongue B. Buccal mucosa

C. Alveolus **D.** Lip

Q.284 Surgery on eardrum is done using

A. Operative microscope
B. Laser
C. Direct vision
D. Blindly

Q.285 Tympanic membrane develops from:

A. Ectoderm
B. Mesoderm
C. Endoderm
D. All the three germinal layers

Q.286 Stapes superstructure develops from:

A. Meckel's cartilage
B. Reichert's cartilage
C. Both (A) and (B)
D. Both (A) and (B) plus bony otic capsule

Q.287 Intratemporal lesion of chorda tympani nerve result in -

A. Loss of taste sensations from papilla of tongue
B. Loss of taste sensations from anterior 2/3rd of tongue
C. Loss of secretomotor fibres to the submandibular salivery gland
D. Loss of taste sensations from posterior 1/3rd of tongue

Q.288 Which one of the following statements is correct in facial paralysis -

A. The nasolabial fold is obliterated on same side
B. The nasolabial fold is obliterated on opposite side
C. The face deviates to the opposite side
D. Both (A) and (C)

Q.289 Maxillary sinus epithelium is

A. Squamous
B. Non ciliated columnar
C. Non-Keratinized squamous
D. Ciliated columnar

Q.290 All of the following are true about retropharyngeal abscess except -

A. Confined to one side of the midline
B. Can be palpable per orally by pressing the finger on posterior pharyngeal wall
C. Lies behind the prevertebral fascia
D. Presents with dysphagia & difficulty in breathing

Q.291 Treatment of Phylenticular conjunctivitis is:

A. Miotics **B.** Mydriatics
C. Antibiotics **D.** Steroid

Q.292 A soft contact lens wearer developed pain and itching of the eye and showed a reticular pattern on the corneal epithelium. The cause could be –

A. Corneal dystrophy **B.** Acanthamoeba
C. Pseudomonas **D.** Virus

Q.293 All of the following may lead to corneal opacity in newborn except –

A. Endothelial dystrophy
B. Sclerocornea
C. Mucopolysaccharidosis
D. Droplet keratopathy

Q.294 Vogt Koyanagi–Harada (VKH) syndrome is –

A. Chronic granulomatous uveitis
B. Chronic non-granulomatous uveitis
C. Acute purulent uveitis
D. None

Q.295 Cataract in diabetic patients is because of the accumulation of sorbitol in the lens. The enzyme responsible for this is

A. Hexokinase
B. NADPH$^+$ dependant aldolase reductase
C. Glucokinase
D. Phosphofructo isomerase

Q.296 Treatment of acute congestive glaucoma includes all except –

a) Sclerectomy
b) Trabeculectomy
c) Trabeculoplasty
d) Vitrectomy
e) Iridotomy

A. ab **B.** bc **C.** ed **D.** cd

Q.297 Diabetes mellitus can lead to –

A. Vitreous haemorrhage
B. Rubeosis iridis
C. Retinal detachment
D. All of the above

Q.298 A child presents with sudden loss of vision with painful ocular movements. The eye is white and there are no obvious signs on ophthalmoscopy. The most likely diagnosis is -

A. Optic nerve glioma **B.** Retrobulbar neuritis
C. Craniopharyngioma **D.** Papillitis

Q.299 Which is the commonest cause of occular morbidity in the community -

A. Cataract
B. Refractive error
C. Occular injury
D. Vitamin A deficiency

Q.300 The condition shown in Figure may be associated with which one of the following choices?

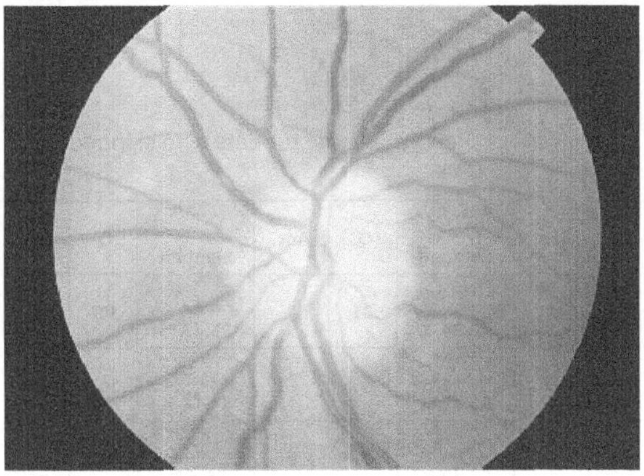

A. Visual loss
B. Papilledema
C. Autosomal recessive inheritance
D. Bilaterality in 25%

// Smart Answer Sheet //

Correct — Percentage of students who answered correctly. Skipped — Percentage of students who skipped.

Q.	Ans.	Correct	Skipped	Q.	Ans.	Correct	Skipped	Q.	Ans.	Correct	Skipped	Q.	Ans.	Correct	Skipped	Q.	Ans.	Correct	Skipped	Q.	Ans.	Correct	Skipped
1	C	44.53 %	3.92 %	22	B	17.54 %	38.74 %	43	B	9.72 %	44.8 %	64	A	20.11 %	50.88 %	85	A	15.25 %	55.47 %	106	C	18.35 %	57.63 %
2	C	30.5 %	15.92 %	23	C	26.45 %	38.06 %	44	C	18.08 %	43.59 %	65	D	20.24 %	51.42 %	86	C	34.41 %	54.12 %	107	A	10.53 %	59.24 %
3	C	38.06 %	21.45 %	24	D	14.04 %	38.86 %	45	A	21.59 %	43.05 %	66	A	20.11 %	52.49 %	87	B	10.53 %	55.6 %	108	B	16.19 %	59.38 %
4	A	21.05 %	24.7 %	25	A	18.22 %	38.6 %	46	C	16.46 %	43.46 %	67	A	19.57 %	51.42 %	88	B	12.42 %	57.35 %	109	B	15.52 %	58.7 %
5	C	39.68 %	28.07 %	26	C	23.21 %	37.25 %	47	A	23.21 %	42.51 %	68	A	13.09 %	51.55 %	89	B	17.14 %	56.95 %	110	B	15.65 %	58.98 %
6	A	25.51 %	26.04 %	27	C	15.92 %	38.33 %	48	C	20.24 %	42.65 %	69	C	31.98 %	51.42 %	90	C	8.5 %	57.36 %	111	B	14.84 %	58.17 %
7	B	39.27 %	27.94 %	28	A	24.97 %	37.24 %	49	D	28.34 %	42.38 %	70	D	9.58 %	51.28 %	91	B	15.65 %	56.95 %	112	A	16.73 %	58.03 %
8	C	19.57 %	28.74 %	29	C	31.58 %	37.92 %	50	D	11.07 %	42.37 %	71	A	9.45 %	53.44 %	92	C	17.54 %	55.2 %	113	D	4.45 %	58.84 %
9	A	17.81 %	30.64 %	30	A	16.6 %	39.81 %	51	A	41.7 %	36.44 %	72	C	14.04 %	52.49 %	93	D	24.02 %	54.93 %	114	C	11.34 %	59.38 %
10	B	19.97 %	31.99 %	31	A	20.65 %	40.62 %	52	C	28.34 %	42.38 %	73	A	8.91 %	53.17 %	94	C	19.03 %	56.68 %	115	B	5.13 %	61.27 %
11	A	11.74 %	33.06 %	32	A	33.47 %	39.13 %	53	B	26.86 %	44.66 %	74	D	13.5 %	52.09 %	95	D	20.78 %	56.68 %	116	C	19.57 %	59.78 %
12	D	22.13 %	31.99 %	33	A	47.91 %	39.0 %	54	D	11.61 %	45.88 %	75	B	21.73 %	52.9 %	96	B	11.74 %	56.41 %	117	A	12.15 %	58.57 %
13	C	22.27 %	33.2 %	34	A	13.9 %	40.49 %	55	D	22.0 %	47.23 %	76	C	13.9 %	53.71 %	97	A	10.53 %	56.81 %	118	D	25.51 %	57.76 %
14	A	20.92 %	33.06 %	35	A	21.59 %	40.89 %	56	A	26.86 %	48.58 %	77	A	21.59 %	52.63 %	98	B	21.46 %	56.14 %	119	B	15.79 %	58.03 %
15	C	31.17 %	33.61 %	36	C	17.41 %	41.16 %	57	A	25.24 %	48.17 %	78	C	22.0 %	52.63 %	99	C	24.7 %	55.19 %	120	B	22.94 %	58.57 %
16	A	16.06 %	36.17 %	37	A	44.26 %	40.36 %	58	B	16.19 %	47.91 %	79	B	4.86 %	54.38 %	100	C	19.57 %	57.22 %	121	D	17.54 %	58.3 %
17	C	24.16 %	34.95 %	38	B	22.4 %	42.38 %	59	B	36.98 %	48.04 %	80	A	15.38 %	53.99 %	101	C	15.38 %	57.63 %	122	D	24.97 %	57.76 %
18	C	27.67 %	34.54 %	39	C	14.04 %	41.83 %	60	B	29.55 %	48.18 %	81	A	10.12 %	54.12 %	102	A	8.37 %	58.03 %	123	A	9.18 %	58.16 %
19	C	43.99 %	34.82 %	40	B	15.25 %	42.91 %	61	A	15.11 %	49.13 %	82	C	20.38 %	55.33 %	103	C	10.66 %	58.71 %	124	D	21.19 %	57.89 %
20	C	23.62 %	35.22 %	41	D	41.16 %	40.89 %	62	C	7.42 %	50.88 %	83	C	22.13 %	53.31 %	104	D	12.28 %	57.76 %	125	C	28.74 %	58.03 %
21	A	15.65 %	37.52 %	42	B	19.57 %	42.64 %	63	A	11.61 %	50.87 %	84	D	17.81 %	55.74 %	105	A	29.96 %	56.95 %	126	C	9.58 %	60.06 %

Q.	Ans.	Correct	Skipped	Q.	Ans.	Correct	Skipped	Q.	Ans.	Correct	Skipped	Q.	Ans.	Correct	Skipped	Q.	Ans.	Correct	Skipped	Q.	Ans.	Correct	Skipped
127	C	21.32 %	59.92 %	148	C	15.25 %	60.05 %	169	B	26.32 %	56.81 %	190	D	12.96 %	59.37 %	211	C	13.77 %	59.91 %	232	D	9.72 %	60.32 %
128	D	11.88 %	60.86 %	149	B	20.24 %	59.25 %	170	C	10.26 %	57.22 %	191	C	27.26 %	59.11 %	212	A	18.22 %	60.05 %	233	B	5.26 %	62.22 %
129	C	16.87 %	59.78 %	150	C	20.11 %	59.51 %	171	B	9.72 %	57.49 %	192	D	8.5 %	60.06 %	213	A	22.4 %	59.11 %	234	B	25.78 %	59.92 %
130	C	9.45 %	61.0 %	151	C	21.32 %	48.32 %	172	D	5.67 %	58.16 %	193	A	11.61 %	59.51 %	214	B	13.9 %	60.73 %	235	B	4.32 %	61.27 %
131	D	16.06 %	59.78 %	152	C	17.54 %	51.69 %	173	D	7.02 %	58.57 %	194	B	14.98 %	59.11 %	215	C	7.96 %	60.73 %	236	C	18.62 %	60.73 %
132	C	13.23 %	58.56 %	153	D	19.57 %	54.11 %	174	B	11.34 %	58.43 %	195	D	21.86 %	58.3 %	216	A	14.84 %	59.79 %	237	A	6.61 %	61.27 %
133	A	29.55 %	58.57 %	154	C	12.42 %	54.38 %	175	B	10.8 %	57.89 %	196	A	4.99 %	58.98 %	217	D	15.79 %	59.78 %	238	B	20.78 %	60.33 %
134	D	8.64 %	60.19 %	155	B	10.66 %	55.2 %	176	C	8.5 %	57.22 %	197	B	11.47 %	59.65 %	218	A	9.85 %	60.06 %	239	A	10.39 %	60.33 %
135	D	32.66 %	58.57 %	156	B	14.57 %	56.69 %	177	B	15.79 %	57.35 %	198	B	20.38 %	59.24 %	219	A	9.72 %	61.13 %	240	D	14.17 %	60.46 %
136	B	17.81 %	59.92 %	157	D	13.9 %	54.79 %	178	C	12.28 %	59.38 %	199	A	18.35 %	58.98 %	220	D	5.53 %	61.41 %	241	B	9.45 %	60.86 %
137	A	23.89 %	58.57 %	158	B	13.77 %	56.41 %	179	B	10.93 %	60.86 %	200	A	8.64 %	60.19 %	221	B	17.68 %	63.02 %	242	C	13.63 %	59.78 %
138	B	17.81 %	58.84 %	159	C	20.65 %	56.41 %	180	B	17.68 %	59.51 %	201	B	14.3 %	60.06 %	222	C	16.87 %	60.19 %	243	A	11.07 %	59.92 %
139	C	11.88 %	59.64 %	160	B	18.35 %	55.6 %	181	B	19.03 %	58.03 %	202	D	19.97 %	59.92 %	223	A	13.77 %	60.18 %	244	D	5.26 %	59.65 %
140	A	21.73 %	59.24 %	161	C	11.47 %	56.28 %	182	A	11.61 %	60.72 %	203	D	20.24 %	59.38 %	224	D	6.21 %	61.94 %	245	D	12.55 %	59.92 %
141	C	10.53 %	59.24 %	162	C	12.28 %	57.22 %	183	A	15.38 %	59.52 %	204	A	11.47 %	59.65 %	225	B	11.74 %	61.67 %	246	B	16.06 %	59.65 %
142	A	17.27 %	59.79 %	163	D	12.82 %	56.28 %	184	A	12.55 %	58.84 %	205	B	14.44 %	59.38 %	226	B	12.96 %	60.99 %	247	A	19.7 %	60.46 %
143	D	10.8 %	60.46 %	164	B	8.1 %	56.68 %	185	A	23.62 %	57.62 %	206	A	25.91 %	58.71 %	227	D	2.7 %	61.54 %	248	A	14.04 %	60.45 %
144	C	14.04 %	60.99 %	165	C	4.99 %	57.9 %	186	D	21.19 %	58.7 %	207	A	12.82 %	60.59 %	228	A	9.45 %	60.86 %	249	C	31.04 %	59.78 %
145	C	24.43 %	59.92 %	166	B	9.31 %	58.98 %	187	C	7.83 %	59.92 %	208	D	9.18 %	59.92 %	229	B	9.99 %	60.73 %	250	A	13.9 %	61.54 %
146	A	22.0 %	59.51 %	167	C	11.61 %	57.76 %	188	B	9.31 %	60.33 %	209	A	13.23 %	61.13 %	230	A	5.8 %	61.95 %	251	B	11.61 %	60.86 %
147	C	17.27 %	59.92 %	168	A	17.14 %	58.43 %	189	C	22.81 %	59.51 %	210	B	3.24 %	59.11 %	231	B	20.24 %	59.65 %	252	B	9.85 %	62.21 %

Q.	Ans.	Correct / Skipped	Q.	Ans.	Correct / Skipped	Q.	Ans.	Correct / Skipped	Q.	Ans.	Correct / Skipped	Q.	Ans.	Correct / Skipped	Q.	Ans.	Correct / Skipped
253	A	17.81 % / 60.46 %	261	B	11.34 % / 61.8 %	269	D	9.04 % / 61.54 %	277	B	10.66 % / 62.35 %	285	D	22.13 % / 61.14 %	293	D	5.26 % / 62.62 %
254	D	4.72 % / 61.14 %	262	D	11.34 % / 60.72 %	270	A	19.03 % / 60.73 %	278	C	13.36 % / 61.27 %	286	B	8.37 % / 61.81 %	294	A	9.58 % / 62.08 %
255	C	13.63 % / 61.13 %	263	B	19.03 % / 60.86 %	271	B	15.92 % / 60.19 %	279	C	8.77 % / 61.68 %	287	C	6.75 % / 62.75 %	295	B	18.35 % / 61.27 %
256	C	14.57 % / 60.19 %	264	D	26.05 % / 60.18 %	272	C	16.87 % / 60.32 %	280	D	22.94 % / 61.41 %	288	D	21.19 % / 61.4 %	296	D	5.67 % / 62.62 %
257	A	5.94 % / 61.67 %	265	D	10.12 % / 60.73 %	273	D	12.55 % / 60.46 %	281	D	14.71 % / 61.13 %	289	D	12.82 % / 61.13 %	297	D	26.45 % / 60.32 %
258	C	33.47 % / 59.51 %	266	C	12.01 % / 61.4 %	274	A	4.45 % / 60.6 %	282	B	8.91 % / 61.94 %	290	C	10.39 % / 62.75 %	298	B	14.98 % / 62.08 %
259	D	9.72 % / 61.27 %	267	A	9.04 % / 60.46 %	275	B	10.93 % / 61.27 %	283	A	11.34 % / 61.8 %	291	D	15.11 % / 61.68 %	299	B	15.92 % / 60.33 %
260	C	13.63 % / 60.73 %	268	A	19.43 % / 60.19 %	276	A	20.65 % / 60.19 %	284	A	23.08 % / 61.54 %	292	B	17.0 % / 61.27 %	300	A	5.13 % / 59.92 %

//Hints and Solutions//

1. The G2 phase of cell division has a function of protein synthesis and cell growth.

- In this phase, the cell grows and prepares itself for cell division.
- G1, S phase, and G2 phase are part of the interphase.
- In the G1 phase, the cell grows but DNA replication is absent in this phase is the synthesis phase-in which DNA synthesis and replication lead to double the number of DNA.
- The G0 phase is the resting or inactive phase of the cell cycle.
- It is also known as the quiescent stage.

Hence, the correct option is (C).

2. Option (C) is correct because the adductor compartment is supplied by the obturator nerve. The obturator nerve is responsible for the sensory innervation of the skin of the medial aspect of the thigh. The nerve is also responsible for the motor innervation of the adductor muscles of the lower limb. Thus, obturator nerve block is used in the management of pain after lower limb surgery or for chronic hip pain.

Option (A) is incorrect as the saphenous nerve (long or internal saphenous nerve) is the largest cutaneous branch of the femoral nerve. It is a strictly sensory nerve and has no motor function.

Option (B) is incorrect as the femoral nerve is one of the largest nerves in your leg. It's located near the groin and controls the muscles that help straighten your leg and move your hips. It also provides feeling in the lower part of your leg and the front of your thigh.

Option (D) is incorrect because the sciatic nerve also called the ischiadic or ischiadic nerve, is a large nerve in humans and other vertebrate animals which begins in the lower part of the sacral plexus and runs through the hip joint and down the lower limb. It is the longest and widest single nerve in the human body, going from the top of the leg to the foot on the posterior aspect.

Hence, the correct option is (C).

3. Option (C) is correct because dorsiflexion of ankle joint is mainly by tibialis anterior. It is also supported for the movement by extensor digitorum longus, extensor hallucis longus and peroneus tertius.

Option (A) is incorrect because the flexor digitorum longus is situated on the tibial side of the leg. At its origin, it is thin and pointed, but it gradually increases in size as it descends. This muscle serves to curl the second, third, fourth, and fifth toes (flexion of phalanges II-V).

Option (B) is incorrect as flexor hallucis longus is a powerful muscle located on the posterior aspect of the fibular below the deep fascia of the calf. In its own synovial sheath, the tendon passes downwards, deep to the flexor retinaculum, crossing the posterior ankle joint, lateral to flexor digitorum longus.

Option (D) is incorrect because plantar flexion is mainly by soleus and gastrocnemius. It is supported for the movement by plantaris, flexor hallucis longus, flexor digitorum longus and tibialis posterior.

Hence, the correct option is (C).

4. Option (A) is correct because of the arterial circle and arteries of the brain. The posterior cerebral arteries (bottom forks) arise from the basilar artery (center). The posterior cerebral artery (PCA) is one of a pair of arteries that supply oxygenated blood to the occipital lobe, part of the back of the human brain.

Option (B) is incorrect as the middle cerebral artery (MCA) is one of the three major paired arteries that supply blood to the cerebrum. The MCA arises from the internal carotid and continues into the lateral sulcus where it then branches and projects to many parts of the lateral cerebral cortex. It also supplies blood to the anterior temporal lobes and the insular cortices.

Option (C) is incorrect as it is only related to PCA and not with MCA.

Option (D) is incorrect as the anterior cerebral artery (ACA) is one of a pair of arteries on the brain that supplies oxygenated blood to most midline portions of the frontal lobes and superior medial parietal lobes.

Hence, the correct option is (A).

5. Brachial artery is the main source of blood for arm. When axillary artery reaches the lower border of teres major it becomes brachial arteries. It continues down the ventral surface of the arm until it reaches the cubital fossa at the elbow.

Hence, the correct option is (C).

6. Option (A) is correct as the cells in the region labeled A synthesize pepsinogen, acid, and gastric intrinsic factor. Region A is the fundus of the stomach. Its mucosa is comprised of gastric glands containing mucous cells, chief cells that synthesize pepsinogen, and parietal cells that synthesize hydrochloric acid and gastric intrinsic factor. Gastric intrinsic factor is required for the absorption of vitamin B12 from the small intestine.

Option (B) is incorrect as paneth cells synthesize and secrete substantial quantities of antimicrobial peptides and proteins. Perhaps more intriguing, Paneth cells secrete factors that help sustain and modulate the epithelial stem and progenitor cells that cohabitate in the crypts and rejuvenate the small intestinal epithelium.

Option (C) is incorrect as, in anatomy, the G cell or gastrin cell is a type of cell in the stomach and duodenum that secretes gastrin. It works in conjunction with gastric chief cells and parietal cells. G cells are found deep within the pyloric glands of the stomach antrum, and occasionally in the pancreas and duodenum.

Option (D) is incorrect because to prevent disastrous effects, mucus and bicarbonate ions (HCO_3^-) are secreted by the foveolar cells. The mucus allows the acid at pH above 4 to penetrate lining, but below pH 4 (i.e. when acid is more concentrated) the acid cannot penetrate the mucus.

Hence, the correct option is (A).

7. Option (B) is correct as the arrow indicates the cerebral aqueduct, which is the narrow canal connecting the third and fourth ventricles. The cerebrospinal fluid produced in the lateral and third ventricles must reach the fourth ventricle to escape into the subarachnoid space through the foramina of Luschka and Magendie.

Option (A) is incorrect as venous blood is deoxygenated blood that flows from tiny capillary blood vessels within the tissues into progressively larger veins to the right side of the heart. Venous blood is the specimen of choice for most routine laboratory tests.

Option (C) is incorrect the corticospinal tract is a white matter motor pathway starting at the cerebral cortex that terminates on lower motor neurons and interneurons in the spinal cord, controlling movements of the limbs and trunk. The corticospinal tract is one of the pyramidal tracts, the other being the corticobulbar tract.

Option (D) is incorrect as the basilar artery is part of the blood supply system for the brain and central nervous system. It is formed where the two vertebral arteries join at the base of the skull. The basilar artery carries oxygenated blood to the cerebellum, brainstem, and occipital lobes.

Hence, the correct option is (B).

8. Option (C) is correct as the anterior primary ramus of C1 joins with hypoglossal nerve, which distributes the motor fibres to the geniohyoid and thyroid muscles. C1 is the first spinal nerve which is unique in that it contains only motor fibres.

Option (A) is incorrect as the glossopharyngeal nerve, known as the ninth cranial nerve (CN IX), is a mixed nerve that carries afferent sensory and efferent motor information. It exits the brainstem out from the sides of the upper medulla, just anterior (closer to the nose) to the vagus nerve.

Option (B) is incorrect as the vagus nerve, historically cited as the pneumogastric nerve, is the tenth cranial nerve or CN X, and interfaces with the parasympathetic control of the heart, lungs, and digestive tract. The vagus nerves are normally referred to in the singular.

Option (D) is incorrect as the facial nerve is the seventh cranial nerve, or simply CN VII. It emerges from the pons of the brainstem, controls the muscles of facial expression, and functions in the conveyance of taste sensations from the anterior two-thirds of the tongue.

Hence, the correct option is (C).

9. Option (A) is correct as Brachioradialis is one of the muscles that comprise the posterior compartment of the forearm. It is the most superficial muscle of the radial side of the forearm, forming the lateral wall of the cubital fossa.

Option (B) is incorrect as the pronator quadratus is a square-shaped muscle on the distal forearm that acts to pronate (turn so the palm faces downwards) the hand. As it is on the anterior side of the arm, it is innervated by a branch of the median nerve, the anterior interosseous nerve.

Option (C) is incorrect as the pronator teres is a muscle (located mainly in the forearm) that, along with the pronator quadratus, serves to pronate the forearm.

Option (D) is incorrect as the lateral collateral ligament (LCL) is the ligament located in the knee joint. Ligaments are thick, strong bands of tissue that connect bone to bone. The LCL runs along the outside of the knee joint, from the outside of the bottom of the thighbone (femur) to the top of the lower-leg bone.

Hence, the correct option is (A).

10. Option (B) is correct as Rasmussen's aneurysm refers to an aneurysm of the small to medium pulmonary artery branches that develop in the vicinity of a tuberculous cavity.

Option (A) is incorrect as, in human anatomy, the bronchial arteries supply the lungs with nutrition and oxygenated blood. Although there is much variation, there are usually two bronchial arteries that run to the left lung, and one to the right lung.

Option (C) is incorrect as the intercostal artery refers to the set of blood vessels that direct blood flow to an area within the ribs known as the intercostal space. The intercostal artery is divided into three groups of smaller blood vessels. Two of the groups originate from the front, and the other group is found near the back.

Option (D) is incorrect as the aorta is the main artery that carries blood away from your heart to the rest of your body. After the blood leaves the heart through the aortic valve, it travels through the aorta, making a cane-shaped curve that connects with other major arteries to deliver oxygen-rich blood to the brain, muscles, and other cells.

Hence, the correct option is (B).

11. Option (A) is correct because Hortega or Gitter cells are microglial phagocytic cells of the Central Nervous System which are laden with degenerating myelin. The cells are spherical with a bubbly margin and with a reduced nucleus. They are also known as compound granular corpuscles, scavenger cells, and fat granule cells.

Option (B) is incorrect as macrophages are a type of white blood cell of the immune system, that engulfs and digests cellular debris, foreign substances, microbes, cancer cells, and anything else that does not have the type of proteins specific to healthy body cells on its surface in a process called phagocytosis.

Option (C) is incorrect as astrocytes also known collectively as astroglia, are characteristic star-shaped glial cells in the brain and spinal cord. The proportion of astrocytes in the brain is not well defined.

Option (D) is incorrect as neutrophils are a type of white blood cell that helps heal damaged tissues and resolve infections. Neutrophil blood levels increase naturally in response to infections, injuries, and other types of stress. They may decrease in response to severe or chronic infections, drug treatments, and genetic conditions.

Hence, the correct option is (A).

12. An end artery (or terminal artery) is an artery that is the only supply of oxygenated blood to a portion of tissue. Arteries which do not anastomose with their neighbors are called end arteries. Their blockage results in infarct or necrosis of the area of supply. Functional end arteries are those which have limited communication with adjacent arteries and are not adequate to establish a viable collateral circulation if one of them is blocked. Joints are surrounded by freely communicating arterial anastomoses.

Thus, end arteries do not occur in regions of the joints.

Hence, the correct option is (D).

13.

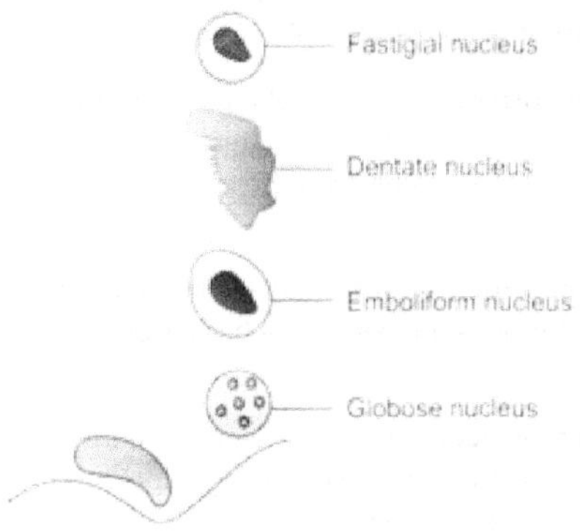

Option (C) is correct as the dentate is the most lateral and largest and is an irregularly folded sheet of neurones, which encloses a mass of fibres mainly derived from dentate neurones. It resembles a leather purse, the opening of which is directed medially.

Option (A) is incorrect because fastigial nucleus is smaller than the nucleus dentatus but somewhat larger than the nucleus emboliformis and nucleus globosus.

Option (B) is incorrect as the emboliform nucleus (or anterior interposed nucleus) is a deep cerebellar nucleus that lies immediately to the medial side of the nucleus dentatus, and partly covering its hilum.

Option (D) is incorrect as globose nucleus is located medial to the emboliform nucleus and lateral to the fastigial nucleus. This nucleus contains primarily large and small multipolar neurons.

Hence, the correct option is (C).

14. Option (A) is correct as tonsilar bed is formed from within to outwards by:-

- Pharyngobasilar fascia
- Superior constrictor and palatopharyngeus muscle
- Styloglossus
- Buccopharyngeal fascia

Option (B) is incorrect as the contraction of the middle pharyngeal muscle, in coordination with the superior and inferior pharyngeal constrictors, constricts and closes the pharynx during deglutition to propel the food bolus from the oropharynx downward to the esophagus. The middle pharyngeal constrictor works specifically on the mid-portion of the pharynx.

Option (C) is incorrect as Zenker's diverticulum develops between the two bellies of the inferior constrictor (Thyropharyngeal and Cricopharyngeal) in a small gap called Killian's dehiscence. A diverticulum can form where a balloon of mucosa becomes trapped outside the pharyngeal boundaries.

Option (D) is incorrect as platysma draws the corners of the mouth inferiorly and widens it (as in expressions of sadness and fright). Also draws the skin of the neck superiorly when teeth are clenched.

Hence, the correct option is (A).

15. Option (C) is correct because depression is brought about mainly by lateral pterygoid. The lateral pterygoid depresses and protrudes the mandible.

Option (A) is incorrect because temporalis muscle performs elevation and retraction of the mandible.

Option (B) is incorrect as the action of masseter muscle is elevation (as in the closing of the mouth) and protrusion of the mandible.

Option (D) is incorrect as it elevates mandible, closes jaw, helps lateral pterygoids in moving the jaw from side to side.

Hence, the correct option is (C).

16. Option (A) is correct as Supraclinoid segment of Internal Carotid Artery (ICA) has 3 branches ophthalmic artery, posterior communicating artery, and anterior choroidal artery. The Supraclinoid segment runs above the clinoid process through the dura into the subarachnoid space.

Option (B) is incorrect as the segmental medullar artery is a branch of the cervical part (V2 segment) of the vertebral artery that follows the spinal branches and supplies the meninges of the spinal cord and vertebral bodies, and is involved in the formation of the arterial plexus in the vertebral canal.

Option (C) is incorrect as most of the anterior pituitary blood is brought in from the superior hypophysial arteries, which branch from the internal carotids, and the posterior communicating branch from the circle of Willis.

Option (D) is incorrect as the anterior cerebral artery (ACA) is one of a pair of arteries on the brain that supplies oxygenated blood to most midline portions of the frontal lobes and superior medial parietal lobes.

Hence, the correct option is (A).

17. Option (C) is correct because urachus is an embryonic remnant resulting from involution of the allantoic duct and the ventral cloaca. Attaching the bladder dome to the umbilicus, the urachus should close during gestation. It is a canal that drains the urinary bladder of the fetus that joins and runs within the umbilical cord.

Option (A) is incorrect as cloaca, in vertebrates, common chamber and outlet into which the intestinal, urinary, and genital tracts open. It is present in amphibians, reptiles, birds, elasmobranch fishes (such as sharks), and monotremes. A cloaca is not present in placental mammals or in most bony fishes.

Option (B) is incorrect because the medial umbilical ligament is a paired structure found in human anatomy. It is on the deep surface of the anterior abdominal wall and is covered by the medial umbilical folds.

Option (D) is incorrect as the ureter is a tube that carries urine from the kidney to the urinary bladder. There are two ureters, one attached to each kidney.

Hence, the correct option is (C).

18. Option (C) is correct as Type II is found predominantly in cartilage (hyaline). The principal collagen of cartilage matrix is type II as a homotrimer of three alpha I (type II) chains. The chondrocyte is the dominant cell of cartilage; it releases to the extracellular matrix type II collagen and vesicles that are rich in alkaline phosphatase and that may be a central organelle for accumulating calcium in preparation for mineralizing cartilage. Keratan sulfate has been assayed as a marker of cartilage metabolism, and collagen type II as a marker of cartilage destruction.

Option (A) is incorrect because Type III is found in association with Type I, although the ratio varies in different tissues.

Option (B) is incorrect because Type IV collagen is found in basement membranes in association with mucopolysaccharides and laminin.

Option (D) is incorrect as Type I collagen is the major structural component of bones, skin, and tendons.

Hence, the correct option is (C).

19. Option (C) is correct as immediate-onset soreness is characterized by pain during and immediately after exercise. This type of soreness is thought to be caused by stimulation of pain receptors by metabolic byproducts of cellular respiration, especially H+ associated with increased lactic acid levels.

Option (A) is incorrect as hyperkalemia is the medical term that describes a potassium level in your blood that's higher than normal. Potassium is a chemical that is critical to the function of nerve and muscle cells, including those in your heart. Your blood potassium level is normally 3.6 to 5.2 millimoles per litre (mmol/L).

Option (B) is incorrect as hyperthermia, also known simply as overheating, is a condition where an individual's body temperature is elevated beyond normal due to failed thermoregulation. The person's body produces or absorbs more heat than it dissipates.

Option (D) is incorrect as hyponatremia is an important and common clinical problem. The etiology is multifactorial. Hyponatremia may be euvolemic, hypovolemic or hypervolemic.

Hence, the correct option is (C).

20. Option (C) is correct because pulmonary vasoconstriction is caused by hypoxia. Hypoxia is a condition in which the body or a region of the body is deprived of adequate oxygen supply at the tissue level. Hypoxia may be classified as either generalized, affecting the whole body, or local, affecting a region of the body.

Option (A) is incorrect as prostacyclin inhibits platelet activation and is also an effective vasodilator.

Option (B) is incorrect as Alpha 2 receptor agonists such as clonidine or guanabenz reduce central and peripheral sympathetic overflow and via peripheral presynaptic receptors may reduce peripheral neurotransmitter release.

Option (D) is incorrect as histamine is involved in the inflammatory response and has a central role as a mediator of itching.

Hence, the correct option is (C).

21. Hypopnea is related to sleep apnea and is a part of the same family of sleep disorders. In hypopnea, there is a decrease of airflow for at least 10 seconds in respirations, a 30-percent reduction in ventilation, and a decrease in oxygen saturation. It is overly shallow breathing or an abnormally low respiratory rate.

Thus, in hypopnea, the airway becomes partially obstructed.

Hence, the correct option is (A).

22. Option (B) is correct as in a muscle spindle, the central part is non-contractile while the peripheral part is contractile. So actin and myosin are present in the peripheral part, not in the central part.

Option (A) is incorrect as the central part of muscle spindles is extended to the side due to sensory (afferent) and motor (efferent) endings of nerve fibres located predominantly in this fragment. And it has no actin and myosin.

Option (C) is incorrect as Type 1 nuclear bag fibres has low myosin ATPase activity because the bag1 fibre has a slow weak contraction followed by creep.

Option (D) is incorrect as Type 2 nuclear bag fibre has a high level of myosin ATPase activity because the bag2 fibre has more elastic tissue and a larger contraction.

Hence, the correct option is (B).

23. Option (C) is correct because these receptors transmit information along the vagus nerve (10th cranial nerve) to the central nervous system. And these are not counted as thermoreceptors.

Option (A) is incorrect as cold receptor & warm receptor are thermoreceptor. A thermoreceptor is a non-specialised sense receptor, or more accurately the receptive portion of a sensory neuron, that codes absolute and relative changes in temperature, primarily within the innocuous range. Warm receptors will turn up their signal rate when they feel warmth or heat transfer into the body. Cooling or heat transfer out of the body results in a decreased signal rate. Cold receptors, on the other hand, increase their firing rate during cooling and decrease it during warming.

Option (B) is incorrect because pain receptors, also called thermal nociceptors, are a group of sensory neurons with specialized nerve endings widely distributed in the skin, deep tissues (including the muscles and joints), and most of the visceral organs.

Option (D) is incorrect as option C is correct and pain receptor is not the thermoreceptor.

Hence, the correct option is (C).

24. Marey's law states that there is an inverse relationship between the rate of heart rate (HR) and blood pressure (BP). Marey's reflex is a cardioinhibitory reflex that decreases heart rate when blood pressure increases. Increased Blood pressure $\rightarrow$ Stimulation of baroreceptors $\rightarrow$ Stimulation of vasodilator area $\rightarrow$ Increase in vagal tone $\rightarrow$ Bradycardia. It is the basis for the baroreceptor reflex.

Hence, the correct option is (D).

25. Option (A) is correct because during inspiration, alveolar pressure is -1 to -2 cm of water and at the end of inspiration or beginning of expiration, it is zero.

Option (B) is incorrect as 1 cm Hg = 5.3524 in H_2O, where negative sign indicates inspiration.

Option (C) is incorrect because the alveolar pressure is +1 to +2 cm of water during expiration.

Option (D) is incorrect because 1 cm Hg = 5.3524 in H_2O, where positive sign indicates expiration.

Hence, the correct option is (A).

26. Option (C) is correct because in menopause estrogen levels decrease and FSH (Follicle Stimulating Hormone) plus LH (Luteinizing Hormone) levels increase. These vary markedly during the perimenopause and single measures are unreliable. Elevated FSH levels may be helpful in confirming the menopause in later stages. FSH levels of greater than 30 IU/L are generally considered to be in the post menopausal range and should be repeated in 4-8 weeks to confirm this.

Option (A) is incorrect because elevated levels of progesterone potently reduce the sodium-retaining activity of aldosterone, resulting in natriuresis and a reduction in extracellular fluid volume.

Option (B) is incorrect as estrogen enters passively into the cell where it binds to and activates the estrogen receptor. In menopause estrogen levels decrease. Estradiol is the main form of estrogen found in premenopausal women. A normal level is 30-400 picograms per milliliter (pg/mL), but after menopause, it falls below 30 pg/mL.

Option (D) is incorrect as the androgens function as paracrine hormones required by the Sertoli cells to support sperm production. They are also required for masculinization of the developing male fetus (including penis and scrotum formation).

Hence, the correct option is (C).

27. Option (C) is correct as MBP (Major Basic Protein) is a toxic cationic protein that is the principal protein found in the granules of eosinophils and that is capable of damaging tissue if released into extracellular spaces. Eosinophils secrete:

- Eosinophil peroxidase
- Major Basic Protein
- Eosinophil cationic protein
- Eosinophil derived neurotoxin
- Interleukin 4 and 5

Option (A) is incorrect as when activated, basophils degranulate to release histamine, proteoglycans (e.g. heparin and chondroitin), and proteolytic enzymes (e.g. elastase and lysophospholipase). They also secrete lipid mediators like leukotrienes (LTD-4), and several cytokines.

Option (B) is incorrect as when macrophages are exposed to inflammatory stimuli, they secrete cytokines such as tumour necrosis factor (TNF), IL-1, IL-6, IL-8, and IL-12.

Option (D) is incorrect because monocytes secrete chemokines, and proliferate in response to infection and injury.

Hence, the correct option is (C).

28. Option (A) is correct as creatinine is freely filtered by kidney across glomerular capillaries. Creatinine is a waste product produced by muscles from the breakdown of creatine phosphate from muscle and protein metabolism. It is released at a constant rate by the body.

Option (B) is incorrect as albumin is a protein made by your liver. Albumin helps keep fluid in your bloodstream so it doesn't leak into other tissues. It also carries various substances throughout your body, including hormones, vitamins, and enzymes. Low albumin levels can indicate a problem with your liver or kidneys.

Option (C) is incorrect because the globulins are a family of globular proteins that have higher molecular weights than albumins and are insoluble in pure water but dissolve in dilute salt solutions. Some globulins are produced in the liver, while others are made by the immune system.

Option (D) is incorrect as freely filterable substances by the glomerulus are:

- Water
- Na^+
- Cl^-
- HCO_3^-
- Inulin
- Glucose
- Creatinine
- Free calcium or phosphate

Hence, the correct option is (A).

29. Option (C) is correct because, in the intestine, glucose and galactose are transported along with Na^+ by secondary active transport through SGLT1.

Option (A) is incorrect as diffusion is a passive process of transport. A single substance tends to move from an area of high concentration to an area of low concentration until the concentration is equal across space.

Option (B) is incorrect as facilitated diffusion (also known as facilitated transport or passive-mediated transport) is the process of spontaneous passive transport (as opposed to active transport) of molecules or ions across a biological membrane via specific transmembrane integral proteins.

Option (D) is incorrect as insulin mediates glucose uptake into adipose tissue and skeletal muscle through GLUT4 glucose transporters. Vesicles containing GLUT4 glucose transporters are mobilized to the plasma membrane by insulin stimulation, thereby affecting glucose transport into the cell.

Hence, the correct option is (C).

30. Option (A) is correct because this patient has a left ureteral stone. Eighty percent of patients with renal calculi form calcium stones, most often calcium oxalate. Various forms of diet modification can help prevent calculus formation. Even though hypercalciuria is commonly found in patients who form stones, decreased calcium intake actually increases absorption and excretion of oxalate, thereby enhancing stone formation. Calcium restriction is therefore not recommended for prevention of stones.

Option (B) is incorrect as increasing fluid intake to above 2 L/d will increase the urine flow rate and lower the urine solute concentration, both of which protect against stone formation.

Option (C) is incorrect as the restriction of protein intake is recommended as a means of decreasing the dietary phosphorus intake and the risk for hyperphosphatemia because of its frequent association with cardiovascular disease (CVD) in patients with chronic kidney disease (CKD).

Option (D) is incorrect as reducing sodium intake can lower blood pressure in both normotensive and hypertensive patients.

Hence, the correct option is (A).

31. Option (A) is correct as the action potentials illustrated must be those of cardiac nodal cells (SA node or AV node). The cardiac action potential is a brief change in the voltage (membrane potential) across the cell membrane of heart cells.

Option (B) is incorrect as the duration of these action potentials is too long for motor axons.

Option (C) is incorrect the duration of these action potentials is too long for sensory neurons also. Also, the configuration is different and a pacemaker potential is clearly present.

Option (D) is incorrect because a skeletal muscle action potential is generated when the motor endplate potential is sufficient to raise the surrounding sarcolemmal potential above the threshold for activation of the voltage-gated Na^+ channels that are abundant throughout the sarcolemma.

Hence, the correct option is (A).

32. Option (A) is correct as the basic structural and functional unit of a muscle cell is the sarcomere, which consists of thin filaments of the protein actin and thicker filaments of the protein myosin.

Option (B) is incorrect as the sarcolemma is the cell membrane of a striated muscle fibre cell. It consists of a lipid bilayer and a thin outer coat of polysaccharide material (glycocalyx) that contacts the basement membrane.

Option (C) is incorrect as a myofibril (also known as a muscle fibril) is a basic rod-like unit of a muscle cell. Muscles are composed of tubular cells called myocytes, known as muscle fibres in striated muscle, and these cells, in turn, contain many chains of myofibrils.

Option (D) is incorrect as sarcotubular system is a network of membranes that are found in striated muscle fibers, and includes two components consisting of transverse tubules and cisternal formations.

Hence, the correct option is (A).

33. Option (A) is correct because when the transported molecule and cotransported ion move in the same direction, the process is called symport.

Option (B) is incorrect as when the transported molecule and cotransported ion move in opposite directions, the process is called antiport.

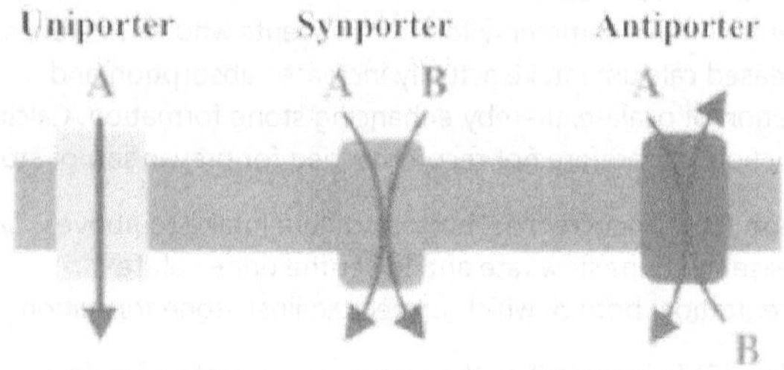

Option (C) is incorrect because exocytosis is an important process of plant and animal cells as it performs the opposite function of endocytosis. In endocytosis, substances that are external to a cell are brought into the cell. In exocytosis, membrane-bound vesicles containing cellular molecules are transported to the cell membrane.

Option (D) is incorrect as pinocytosis is a process by which liquid droplets are ingested by living cells.

Hence, the correct option is (A).

34. Option (A) is correct as if the concentration of K^+ in ECF (extracellular fluid) is decreased The concentration gradient of K^+ is increased. More leaking of K^+ from ICF (intracellular fluid) to ECF. Thus there is more negativity of the membrane or less positivity of the membrane or increased magnitude of RMP.

Option (B) is incorrect because the magnitude of RMP decreases when the concentration gradient of K^+ is increased.

Option (C) is incorrect because it is not possible as both the points are contradictory,i.e. in option (B) negativity of the membrane is increasing and in option (D) it is mentioned as decreasing.

Option (D) is incorrect because it is not possible as both the points are contradictory,i.e. in option (A) magnitude of RMP is decreasing and in option (C) it is mentioned as increasing.

Hence, the correct option is (A).

35. Option (A) is correct because Glutathione peroxidases, also known as selenoproteins, are a family of antioxidant enzymes that speed up the reaction between glutathione and free radicals, particularly toxic hydrogen peroxide, which selenium-containing glutathione peroxidases help transform to harmless water. These enzymes act both inside and outside the cells maximizing antioxidant protection.

In cases of selenium deficiency and with the resulting impaired function of glutathione peroxidases destructive hydrogen peroxide breaks down into even more dangerous hydroxyl radical which damages cell membranes and cell DNA eventually leading to serious disease. Selenium is directly involved in the preservation of cell membrane integrity and DNA integrity.

Option (B) is incorrect as Glutathione reductase (GR) is a homodimer containing one FAD per monomer that catalyzes the reduction of glutathione disulfide (GSSG) to glutathione (GSH).

Option (C) is incorrect as Glutathione synthetase (GSS) is the second enzyme in the glutathione (GSH) biosynthesis pathway. It catalyses the condensation of gamma-glutamylcysteine and glycine, to form glutathione. Glutathione synthetase is also a potent antioxidant.

Option (D) is incorrect as in enzymology, a Glutathione dehydrogenase (ascorbate) is an enzyme that catalyzes the chemical reaction.

Hence, the correct option is (A).

36. Option (C) is correct as Lipoprotein lipase is functional enzyme that degrades circulating triglycerides in the bloodstream. These triglycerides are embedded in very low-density lipoproteins (VLDL) and in chylomicrons that travel through the bloodstream.

Option (A) is incorrect as Creatine kinase (CK) is a non-functional enzyme that increases in heart, brain, and skeletal muscle diseases.

Option (B) is incorrect as Alkaline phosphatase is a non-functional enzyme that increases in obstructive liver diseases, bone diseases and hyperparathyroidism.

Option (D) is incorrect as Lactate dehydrogenase (LDH) is also a non-functional enzyme that increases in heart, liver, and blood diseases.

Hence, the correct option is (C).

37. Option (A) is correct as the glycemic index is a measure of the ability of a food type to raise blood glucose in comparison to reference food (glucose). Obviously, the low glycemic index diet should be given to diabetic patients.

The effect of low glycaemic index (GI) diet was compared with higher glycaemic index diet or control in adult patients with type 2 diabetes. The higher-GI or control diets were classified as having a higher glycaemic index based on the lower GI values of the intervention diets (low-GI diet).

Option (B) is incorrect as diet preferred for hypertension includes eating foods that are low insaturated fat, total fat, and cholesterol, and high in fruits, vegetables, and low-fat dairyfoods.

Option (C) is incorrect as diet preferred for must be high in carbohydrate-rich foods as well as nutritious high carbohydrate snacks between meals.

Option (D) is incorrect as diet preferred for normal adults is low in saturated fats, trans fats, cholesterol, salt (sodium), and added sugars.

Hence, the correct option is (A).

38. Option (B) is correct because carnitine is essential for the transfer of long-chain fatty acids across the inner mitochondrial membrane for subsequent beta-oxidation. It can be synthesized by the body or assumed with the diet from meat and dairy products. Defects in carnitine biosynthesis do not routinely result in low plasma carnitine levels.

Option (A) is incorrect as short-chain fatty acids are carnitine-independent.

Option (C) is incorrect as free fatty acids are formed in the cytoplasm by the action of lipase on stored triglycerides, but the fatty acids themselves are degraded and oxidized only in the mitochondria and peroxisomes.

Option (D) is incorrect as fatty acids (long-chain) are activated, and monoacylglycerols are converted to triacylglycerols at the smooth endoplasmic reticulum.

Hence, the correct option is (B).

39. Option (C) is correct as hydrophobic or nonpolar amino acids are present in the transmembrane region. Hydrophilic or polar amino acids are present on the outer surface of the membrane. Leucine is hydrophobic so it lies in the transmembrane region.

Option (A) is incorrect as lysine is an amino acid (the building block of protein). People use it to make medicine. Lysine is used for preventing and treating cold sores (caused by the virus called herpes simplex labialis). It is taken by mouth or applied directly to the skin for this use.

Option (B) is incorrect as L-arginine is a chemical building block called an amino acid. It is obtained from the diet and is necessary for the body to make proteins. L-arginine is found in red meat, poultry, fish, and dairy products. It can also be made in a laboratory and used as medicine.

Option (D) is incorrect because aspartic acid (or aspartate) is a non-essential amino acid, meaning that it is readily and naturally synthesized by mammals. It is one of the 20 building-block amino acids of proteins, 3-letter code is ASP, one letter code is D. The DNA codons encoding aspartic acid are GAC and GAU.

Hence, the correct option is (C).

40. Option (B) is correct because glutathione helps in keeping some enzymes in an active state by preventing the oxidation of their sulfhydryl (-SH) group. Therefore, glutathione is required for the catalytic activity of many enzymes. Glutathione is involved in the transport of amino acids across the cell membrane of the kidney and intestine. Glutathione is used to conjugate xenobiotics.

Option (A) is incorrect as amino acids are absorbed by a co-transport mechanism with sodium ions. Both sodium ion and amino acid combine with a cell surface protein receptor.

Option (C) is incorrect as cell membranes have to allow the passage of various polar molecules, such as ions, sugars, amino acids, nucleotides, and many cell metabolites that cross synthetic lipid bilayers only very slowly. Special membrane transport proteins are responsible for transferring such solutes across cell membranes.

Option (D) is incorrect as conjugation reactions are catalyzed by enzymes known as transferases. They involve a cofactor that binds to the enzyme in close proximity to the substrate and carries the endogenous molecule or moiety to be transferred.

Hence, the correct option is (B).

41. Option (D) is correct because inorganic iron is absorbed in $Fe2^{+}$ state (reduced state). Thus, reducing agents promote the absorption of Iron. Most important among these are vitamin C, alcohol, and fructose.

Option (A) is incorrect as absorption of iron is impaired by calcium (in milk and milk products). And tea is a product of milk. Thus, it will impair the absorption of iron.

Option (B) is incorrect because coffee is also a product of milk. Thus, it will impair the absorption of iron.

Option (C) is incorrect as EDTA is a chemical that binds and holds on to (chelates) minerals and metals such as chromium, iron, lead, mercury, copper, aluminum, nickel, zinc, calcium, cobalt, manganese, and magnesium. When they are bound, they can't have any effects on the body and they are removed from the body.

Hence, the correct option is (D).

42. Option (B) is correct because of TMP is the abbreviation of Thymidine monophosphate, also known as thymidylic acid, deoxythymidine monophosphate, or deoxythymidylic acid and not of Thymine monophosphate, and UMP is the abbreviation of Uridine monophosphate, also known as 5'-uridylic acid and not of Uracil monophosphate. Hence, this is the required answer.

Option (A) is incorrect because AMP is the abbreviation of Adenosine monophosphate, also known as 5'-adenylic acid and CMP is the abbreviation of Cytidine monophosphate, also known as 5'-cytidylic acid or simply cytidylate. So, this is not the required answer.

Option (C) is incorrect as GMP is the abbreviation of Guanosine monophosphate whereas TMP is not correctly expanded. So, this is not the required answer.

Option (D) is incorrect because here CMP-Cytidine monophosphate is right whereas TMP is not correctly expanded. So, this is not the required answer.

Hence, the correct option is (B).

43. Option (B) is correct because this strain introduced by underwinding is generally accommodated by supercoiling rather than strand separation because coiling the axis of DNA usually requires less energy than breaking the hydrogen bonds. So, supercoiling is a result of underwinding. However, underwinding represent a form of stored energy and makes separation of DNA strands easier.

Option (A) is incorrect as superhelical density or specific linking difference (σ) is a measure of a number of turns removed relative to the number present in relaxed DNA. It is independent of the length of the DNA molecule. The negative sign indicates that the change in linking number is due to the underwinding of DNA. So, the supercoiling induced by underwinding is called negative supercoiling. Overwinding results in positive supercoiling.

Option (C) is incorrect as linking number can be defined as number of times the 2nd strand pierces the surface of the 1st strand which is visualized as a circle. It is defined as positive (+ve) if strands are interwound in right-handed helix and (-ve) in the left-handed helix. So linking number is the number of turns. Topoisomerase II breaks both DNA strands and changes the linking number in increments of 2.

Option (D) is incorrect as closed circular (B form) DNA with one turn of double helix per 10.5 bp (base pair) is relaxed. An 84 bp segment of a circular DNA in the relaxed state would contain 8 double-helical turns or 1 for every 10.5 bp. If one of these turns were removed, there would be 84 bp/7 = 12 bp/turn rather than 10.5 bp/turn in B-DNA. This would result in a thermodynamically strained DNA. Most cellular DNA is underwound.

Hence, the correct option is (B).

44. Option (C) is correct as a clinically harmless variation of DNA sequences that don't affect the phenotype.

They constitute single base pair substitution, deletions & insertions in the noncoding region.

They don't alter the protein-coding sequence because of degeneracy of genetic code.

So, polymorphism is a single phenotype, single-locus & multiple normal alleles.

Option (A) is incorrect as single phenotype is also one of the properties of polymorphism along with single locus and multiple normal alleles.

Option (B) is incorrect multiple alleles combine in different ways in a population, and produce different phenotypes. These phenotypes are caused by the proteins encoded for by the various alleles. And the point doesn't tell about phenotypes.

Option (D) is incorrect as a null allele is a gene variant that lacks the gene's normal function because it either is not expressed, or the expressed protein is inactive. And polymorphism contains multiple normal alleles.

Hence, the correct option is (C).

45. Option (A) is correct as vitamin B6 includes pyridoxal, pyridoxine, and pyridoxamine. These are converted to "pyridoxal-5-phosphate" which acts as a "coenzyme" in "decarboxylation and transamination" of amino acids, such as in the decarboxylation of 5-hydroxytryptophan in the formation of serotonin and in the metabolism of glycogen and fatty acids.

Pyridoxal phosphate is the coenzyme for both glutamic decarboxylase and gamma-aminobutyric acid transaminase; each is necessary for normal brain metabolism. It participates in the active transport of amino acids across cell membranes, chelates metals, and participates in the synthesis of arachidonic acid from linoleic acid.

Option (B) is incorrect as tetrahydrofolate or tetrahydrofolic acid is a folic acid derivative that serves as a coenzyme for metabolic reactions involving amino acids and nucleic acids. The term "folate" denoted a water-soluble B-complex vitamin that functions in the transfer process of single-carbon groups at different stages of oxidation and essential for the biosynthesis of certain amino acid, purine bases and thymine which is a type of pyrimidine base.

Option (C) is incorrect as the active form of thiamine is thiamine pyrophosphate (TPP), which functions as a coenzyme in the metabolism of carbohydrates, lipids, and branched-chain amino acids. It is involved in the decarboxylation of α-keto acids during adenosine triphosphate (ATP) synthesis and maintenance of reduced glutathione in erythrocytes.

Option (D) is incorrect as FMN is a flavin mononucleotide that is riboflavin (vitamin B2) in which the primary hydroxy group has been converted to its dihydrogen phosphate ester. It has a role as a coenzyme, a bacterial metabolite, a human metabolite, a mouse metabolite and a cofactor.

Hence, the correct option is (A).

46. Option (C) is correct because Type I dyslipidemia is caused by a deficiency of lipoprotein lipase. This enzyme exists in capillary walls of adipose and muscle tissue and cleaves triglycerides into free fatty acids and glycerol. The enzyme is activated by apolipoprotein C-II, which is found on VLDL cholesterol and chylomicrons. Type I dyslipidemia is characterized by an accumulation of triglyceride-rich lipoproteins in the plasma. It can also occur with an alteration in apolipoprotein C-II.

Option (A) is incorrect because Apolipoprotein E deficiency (or its abnormalities in humans) is associated with a series of pathological conditions including dyslipidemia, atherosclerosis, Alzheimer's disease, and shorter life span.

Option (B) is incorrect because familial hypercholesterolemia (FH) is a genetic disorder characterized by high cholesterol levels, specifically very high levels of low-density lipoprotein (LDL, "bad cholesterol"), in the blood and early cardiovascular disease. For example, high LDL (often due to LDL receptor defect) is type 2.

Option (D) is incorrect as hyperlipidemia is a common feature of diabetes and is related to cardiovascular disease. The very low-density lipoprotein receptor (VLDL-R) is a member of the low-density lipoprotein receptor (LDL-R) family. It binds and internalizes triglyceride-rich lipoproteins with high specificity.

Hence, the correct option is (C).

47. Option (A) is correct as δ-Aminolevulinic acid (δ-ALA) synthase irreversibly catalyzes the first reaction, glycine + succinyl-CoA → δ-ALA. This is the rate-limiting and committed step in heme synthesis. δ-ALA dehydratase catalyzes the second step in heme synthesis, 2δ-ALA → porphobilinogen. Since δ-aminolevulinic synthetases action is irreversible, only δ-ALA would accumulate.

Option (B) is incorrect because coproporphyrinogen III is a metabolic intermediate in the biosynthesis of many compounds that are critical for living organisms, such as haemoglobin and chlorophyll. It is a colorless solid. The compound is a porphyrinogen, a class of compounds characterized by a hexahydroporphine core with various side chains.

Option (C) is incorrect as glycine (symbol Gly or G) is an amino acid that has a single hydrogen atom as its side chain. It is the simplest amino acid (since carbamic acid is unstable), with the chemical formula NH_2-CH_2-COOH. Glycine is one of the proteinogenic amino acids.

Option (D) is incorrect because porphobilinogen is an organic compound that occurs in living organisms as an intermediate in the biosynthesis of porphyrins, which include critical substances like hemoglobin and chlorophyll. The name is often abbreviated PBG.

Hence, the correct option is (A).

48. Option (C) is correct as ALA Synthase is the committed step of the heme synthesis pathway, & is usually rate-limiting for the overall pathway. Heme functions as a feedback inhibitor, repressing transcription of the ALA Synthase gene in most cells.

Option (A) is incorrect because the ALA dehydratase reaction occurs in the cytoplasm; the product is porphobilinogen (pronounce). The substrates are two molecules of ALA.

Option (B) is incorrect as HMG-CoA Reductase (or 3-hydroxy-3-methyl-glutaryl-CoA reductase or HMGR) is the rate-controlling enzyme of the mevalonate pathway, responsible for cholesterol and another isoprenoid biosynthesis. HMGR is a transmembrane protein, containing 8 domains, that is anchored in the membrane of the endoplasmic reticulum.

Option (D) is incorrect as in living organisms, uroporphyrinogen I occurs as a side branch of the main porphyrin synthesis pathway. In the normal pathway, the linear tetrapyrrole precursor preuroporphyrinogen (a substituted hydroxymethylbilane) is converted by the enzyme uroporphyrinogen-III cosynthase into the cyclic uroporphyrinogen III; which is then converted to coproporphyrinogen III on the way to porphyrins like heme.

Hence, the correct option is (C).

49. Option (D) is correct because Tyrosine, obtained from ingested protein and synthesized endogenously from phenylalanine, is used for protein synthesis and is a precursor of

- Dopamine,
- Norepinephrine,
- Epinephrine,
- Melanin, and
- Thyroxine.

The thyroid hormones are iodinated amino acids, Thyroxine (T 4) and Triiodothyronine (T 3). In the thyroid they are an integral part of thyroglobulin, in which they are synthesized and stored In the plasma, they circulate as free amino acids in reversible equilibrium with the thyroid hormone-binding proteins.

Option (A) is incorrect as Cortisol is one of the steroid hormones and is made in the adrenal glands. Most cells within the body have cortisol receptors. Secretion of the hormone is controlled by the hypothalamus, the pituitary gland, and the adrenal gland, a combination glands often referred to as the HPA axis.

Option (B) is incorrect because Calcitonin is a hormone that is produced in humans by the parafollicular cells (commonly known as C-cells) of the thyroid gland. Calcitonin is involved in helping to regulate levels of calcium and phosphate in the blood, opposing the action of parathyroid hormone.

Option (C) is incorrect as Calcitriol is produced in the proximal tubular cells in the kidney. The synthesis of 1α,25(OH)2D3 by renal 1α-hydroxylase (CYP27B1) is tightly regulated by the levels of plasma 1α,25(OH)2D3, calcium and parathyroid hormone (PTH).

Hence, the correct option is (D).

50. Option (D) is correct as reversible steps are catalyzed by :

- Phosphohexose isomerase,
- Aldolase,
- Phosphotriose isomerase,
- Glyceraldehyde 3-phosphate dehydrogenase,
- Phosphoglycerate kinase,
- Phosphoglycerate mutase,
- Enolase.

Option (A) is incorrect as a hexokinase is an enzyme that phosphorylates hexoses (six-carbon sugars), forming hexose phosphate. And it is used as an enzyme catalyzing irreversible step in glycolysis.

Option (B) is incorrect as phosphofructokinase is a kinase enzyme that phosphorylates fructose 6-phosphate in glycolysis.

Option (C) is incorrect because pyruvate kinase is the enzyme involved in the last step of glycolysis. It catalyzes the transfer of a phosphate group from phosphoenolpyruvate to adenosine diphosphate, yielding one molecule of pyruvate and one molecule of ATP.

Hence, the correct option is (D).

51. Option (A) is correct because fat necrosis is seen in breast. It does not denote a specific pattern of necrosis; rather it is a focal area of fat destruction, due to the release of pancreatic lipase. It is a lump of dead or damaged breast tissue that sometimes appears after breast surgery, radiation, or another trauma. Fat necrosis is harmless and doesn't increase your cancer risk. It usually isn't painful, but it can cause anxiety.

Option (B) is incorrect because liquefactive necrosis is a type of necrosis in which the dead tissue turns into a liquid substance. This condition usually occurs in the central nervous system, especially in the brain.

61. Option (A) is correct because Lynch syndrome (LS) is an autosomal dominant familial cancer risk syndrome that occurs due to a germline mutation in one of several mismatch repair genes and is associated with an increased risk of colorectal (colon), endometrial, and ovarian cancer.

Option (B) is incorrect because polycystic ovary syndrome (PCOS) is a common endocrine disorder among women of reproductive age. In a nationwide population-based retrospective cohort study to analyze the association between PCOS and the subsequent development of gynecological cancers, namely endometrial, breast, and ovarian cancer.

Option (C) is incorrect because the aggregation of colon, endometrial, ovarian, and possibly breast cancers in families has been described as a cancer family syndrome (now called Lynch syndrome II).

Option (D) is incorrect because Lynch syndrome is not associated with breast.

Hence, the correct option is (A).

62. Option (C) is correct because atherosclerosis is a chronic, progressive disease that eventually leads to coronary heart disease (CHD), ischemic stroke, and another atherosclerotic cardiovascular disease (ASCVD). Numerous studies have demonstrated an atherogenic role of oxidized low-density lipoprotein (ox-LDL) in the progression of ASCVD.

Option (A) is incorrect because macrophages and endothelial cells generate oxygen free radicals that induce a chemical change in LDL to yield oxidized (modified) LDL.

Option (B) is incorrect because LDL infiltrates in the arterial wall and interacts with the proteoglycan matrix promoting the retention and modification of LDL to a toxic form, which results in endothelial cell (EC) activation and vascular inflammation.

Option (D) is incorrect because, in atherosclerosis, increased LDL in monocyte/macrophage is due to lipids in LDL get oxidized. So, there is no relation of the question to macrophage and endothelium.

Hence, the correct option is (C).

63. Option (A) is correct because the anterosuperior displacement of the infundibular septum will most likely explain the embryologic mechanism responsible for the development of this condition. Anterior displacement of the infundibular septum was associated with coarctation or interruption of the aortic arch in 88% of the cases, whereas posterior displacement resulted in subpulmonary narrowing in 100% of the cases.

Option (B) is incorrect because persistent truncus arteriosus describes the failure of septum formation that divides the truncus arteriosus into the aorta and pulmonary artery, leaving only one combined outflow tract for the blood that is ejected by each ventricle.

Option (C) is incorrect because TGA (Transposition of the Great Arteries) occurs when the conotruncal septum fails to spiral and instead descends straight downward. The aorta originates from the right ventricle and the pulmonary artery from the left.

Option (D) is incorrect because the absorption of the sinus venosus into the atrium is incomplete there will be a persistent communication with the vestibule adjacent to the mouths of the superior vena cava and pulmonary veins.

Hence, the correct option is (A).

64. Option (A) is correct because bite cells are primarily caused by G6PD deficiency and unstable hemoglobins probably from red-cell enzymopathies involving the pentose phosphate shunt. People receiving large quantities of aromatic drugs or metabolites are more prone to have degmacytes.

Option (B) is incorrect because the cause of SCD is a defective gene, called a sickle cell gene. People with the disease are born with two sickle cell genes, one from each parent. If you are born with one sickle cell gene, it's called sickle cell trait.

Option (C) is incorrect because spherocytosis most often refers to hereditary spherocytosis. This is caused by a molecular defect in one or more of the proteins of the red blood cell cytoskeleton, including spectrin, ankyrin, Band 3, or Protein 4.2.

Option (D) is incorrect because resident cutaneous interfollicular stem cells are derivatives of mesenchymal stem cells and collectively they contribute to immunomodulation, angiogenesis, chemotaxis, anti-fibrosis, and preservation of stem cell homeostasis [90,91]. Skin trauma causes the local and systemic release of IL-6, TNF-α, and IL-1β.

Hence, the correct option is (A).

65. Option (D) is correct because defect in the common pathway, both the intrinsic and extrinsic pathways lead to activation of the common pathway. Factor X is activated to Xa, which then stimulates the conversion of prothrombin to thrombin, facilitated by the presence of phospholipid.

Option (A) is incorrect because the extrinsic pathway is initiated by the release of microsomal lipoproteins from damaged tissue. This tissue factor (TF) combines with the normal small amounts of circulating activated factor VII (VIIa) to activate factors X and IX.

Option (B) is incorrect because defects in the intrinsic pathway coagulation factors (factors VIII, IX, and XI) are associated with a significant bleeding tendency. The X-linked recessive disorders, hemophilia A (factor VIII) and B (factor IX) are the principal examples of this type of abnormality.

Option (C) is incorrect because congenital platelet function defects are bleeding disorders that cause reduced platelet function. Glanzmann thrombasthenia is a condition caused by the lack of a protein needed for platelets to clump together. Platelets are typical of normal size and number. This disorder may also cause severe bleeding.

Hence, the correct option is (D).

66. Hemophilia A and Hemophilia B are suspected in patients with recurrent bleeding, unexplained hemarthroses, or a prolongation of the PTT.

The aPTT is mildly prolonged in approximately 50% of patients with Von-Willebrand disease. The prolongation is secondary to low levels of FVIII because one of the normal functions of vWF is to protect FVIII from degradation.

Henoch–Schonlein purpura (HSP), also known as IgA vasculitis, is a disease of the skin, mucous membranes, and sometimes other organs that most commonly affects children.

Bernard–Soulier syndrome (BSS), is a rare autosomal recessive bleeding disorder that is caused by a deficiency of glycoprotein Ib (GpIb), the receptor for von Willebrand factor. The incidence of BSS is estimated to be less than 1 case per million persons, based on cases reported from Europe, North America, and Japan.

According to the above explanation statements a, b, and e are correct.

Hence, the correct option is (A).

67. Option (A) is correct because CD_{30} and CD_{15} are expressed on Reed-Sternberg cells typical for Hodgkin's lymphoma. CD_{30} is associated with anaplastic large cell lymphoma. It is expressed in embryonal carcinoma but not in seminoma and is thus a useful marker in distinguishing between these germ cell tumors.

Option (B) is incorrect because CD_{22}, which is expressed by the vast majority of B-cell cancers but not by lymphocyte precursors of memory B cells, also represents an attractive target for non-Hodgkin lymphoma therapy. CD_{15} is expressed on Reed-Sternberg cells typical for Hodgkin's lymphoma. But both cannot be expressed for Hodgkin's, so it cannot be the correct answer.

Option (C) is incorrect because CD_{20} is an antigen that is found on the surface of B cells but not T cells. CD_{20} can be used to tell the difference between these two cancers in that test results for CD_{20} would usually be positive in the case of DLBCL but negative for ALCL. CD_{15} is expressed on Reed-Sternberg cells typical for Hodgkin's lymphoma. But both cannot be expressed for Hodgkin's, so it cannot be the correct answer.

Option (D) is incorrect because diagnosis of peripheral T-cell lymphoma (PTCL) with aberrant expression of CD_{30}, CD_{15}, and CD_{20} was rendered.

Hence, the correct option is (A).

68.

Option (A) is correct because shock lung is a clinical syndrome caused by diffuse alveolar capillary damage. It is characterized by the rapid onset of severe life-threatening respiratory insufficiency, cyanosis, and severe arterial hypoxemia that is refractory to oxygen therapy.

Option (B) is incorrect because pulmonary edema, especially acute, can lead to fatal respiratory distress or cardiac arrest due to hypoxia. It is a cardinal feature of congestive heart failure.

Option (C) is incorrect because Sjogren's syndrome is caused due to diffuse interstitial inflammation.

Option (D) is incorrect because histiocytic necrotizing lymphadenitis (Kikuchi's disease) is a benign, self-limited disorder that is characterized by collections of histiocytes and lymphocytes surrounding areas of necrosis containing fragments of karyorrhectic nuclear debris (intra-cellular debris).

Hence, the correct option is (A).

69. Option (C) is correct because seminoma is the most common pure germ cell tumor (GCT) of the testis, accounting for up to 50% of cases. Among mixed GCTs, seminoma is also commonly present, in which the combination of teratoma, seminoma, yolk sac tumor, and embryonal carcinoma represent about one-third of mixed cases.

Option (A) is incorrect because a teratoma is a tumor made up of several different types of tissue, such as hair, muscle, teeth, or bone. They typically form in the ovary, testicle, or tailbone and less commonly in other areas. Symptoms may be minimal if the tumor is small. A testicular teratoma may present as a painless lump.

Option (B) is incorrect because a yolk sac tumor is a rare, malignant tumor of cells that line the yolk sac of the embryo. These cells normally become ovaries or testes; however, the cause of a yolk sac tumor is unknown. It is most often found in children before the ages of 1 to 2 but can occur throughout life.

Option (D) is incorrect because choriocarcinoma is a very rare and fast-growing type of testicular cancer in adults. Pure choriocarcinoma is likely to spread rapidly to other parts of the body, including the lungs, bones, and brain. More often, choriocarcinoma cells are seen with other types of non-seminoma cells in a mixed germ cell tumor.

Hence, the correct option is (C).

70. Option (D) is correct because the overuse of salicylates cause acute gastritis. It is acute mucosal injury, usually transient in injury and is associated with neutrophilic infiltration.

Option (A) is incorrect because H pylori is associated with chronic gastritis. Helicobacter pylori is the leading cause of chronic gastritis, peptic ulcer disease, gastric adenocarcinoma, and primary gastric lymphoma. The bacteria survive within the mucous layer that covers the gastric surface epithelium and the upper portions of the gastric foveolae.

Option (B) is incorrect because Pernicious anemia (PA) is often called autoimmune gastritis or type gastritis, which is defined as a type of chronic atrophic gastritis restricted to the body mucosa, characterized by severe, diffuse atrophy of the oxyntic glands and hypochlorhydria, and normal antral mucosa.

Option (C) is incorrect because gastritis can be caused by irritation due to excessive alcohol use, chronic vomiting, stress, or the use of certain medications such as aspirin or other anti-inflammatory drugs.

Hence, the correct option is (D).

71. Option(A) is correct because serum aspartate aminotransferase (AST) and the alanine aminotransferase (ALT) activities increase to variable levels during the prodromal phase of acute hepatitis and precede elevations in bilirubin.

Option(B) is incorrect because very high elevations of the transaminases suggest severe liver damage, such as viral hepatitis, liver injury from lack of blood flow, or injury from drugs or toxins.

Option(C) is incorrect because Hepatitis C causes damage to the liver mainly in the form of inflammation, which then leads to scarring or fibrosis. Hepatitis C results in the death of liver cells.

Option(D) is incorrect because viral hepatitis is still one of the key causes of acute liver failure (ALF) in the world.

Hence, the correct option is (A).

72. Option (C) is correct because peptide hormones inhibin and antimullerian hormone (AMH), both produced by the granulosa cells, are potential candidates for diagnosis and follow-up of granulosa cell tumors (GCTs). Thus, inhibin is a biomarker for assessment GCT.

Option (A) is incorrect because CA 19-9 is a type of antigen released by pancreatic cancer cells. It can also be referred to as a tumor marker. The CA 19-9 Radioimmunoassay (RIA) is a blood test that measures the CA 19-9 level in the blood.

Option (B) is incorrect because CA 50 is a new tumor marker based on a monoclonal antibody (MAb) against a human colorectal carcinoma cell line. The CA 50 antigen is similar, but not identical, to the tumor marker CA 19-9.

Option (D) is incorrect because in neuronal injury biomarkers for assessment of the individual cognitive reserve in clinically suspected Alzheimer's disease.

Hence, the correct option is (C).

73. A tophus (plural: tophi) happens when crystals of the compound known as sodium urate monohydrate, or uric acid, builds up around your joints. Tophi often look like swollen, bulbous growths on your joints just under your skin. They commonly develop in the fingers, hands, feet, the tough band extending from the calf muscles to the heel (Achilles tendon), or around the elbows. Tophi form in the joints, cartilage, bones, and other places throughout the body. Sometimes, tophi break through the skin and appear as white or yellowish-white, chalky nodules.

According to the above explanation statements, a and e are correct.

Hence, the correct option is (A).

74. Option (D) is correct because Hereditary spherocytosis is Inherited hemolytic anemia characterized by dense, osmotically fragile, partially spherical red cells that are selectively trapped by the spleen "Ankyrin defects are the most frequent" (>> 30 to 60% of cases). These occur in-both dominant and recessive HS and are characterized by a combined deficiency of ankyrin and spectrin (which binds to ankyrin) in roughly equivalent proportions.

Option (A) is incorrect because Glycophorin A (also known as membrane inhibitor of reactive lysis type II, MIRL II) may function as a complement regulator and is a receptor for bacteria, viruses, and Plasmodium falciparum malaria parasites.

Option (B) is incorrect because Mutations of spectrin lead to various human diseases such as hereditary hemolytic anemia, type 5 spinocerebellar ataxia, cancer, as well as others.

Option (C) is incorrect because White band disease is a coral disease that affects acroporid corals and is distinguishable by the white band of dead coral tissue that it forms. The disease completely destroys the coral tissue of Caribbean acroporid corals, specifically elkhorn coral (Acropora palmata) and staghorn coral

Hence, the correct option is (D).

75. Option (B) is correct because asteroid bodies are seen in an irregularly star-shaped inclusion body found in the giant cells in sarcoidosis and other diseases. The finding of large asteroid bodies (radiate eosinophilic material surrounding fungal yeast cells) provides presumptive evidence of sporotrichosis. Thus, asteroid bodies are seen in both Sarcoidosis and Sporotrichosis.

Option (A) is incorrect because an asteroid body is a microscopic finding seen within the giant cells of granulomas in diseases such as sarcoidosis and foreign-body giant cell reactions. But asteroid body is seen in Sporotrichosis also so, only one option i.e., individually cannot be true.

Option (C) is incorrect because, in sporotrichosis, the asteroid bodies are seen in is extracellular eosinophilic structures, 15-35 microm in diameter, and located within abscesses. In this, only we have talked about Sporotrichosis, but asteroid bodies are seen in both Sarcoidosis and Sporotrichosis as explained above. so, it can't be the correct option.

Option (D) is incorrect because anaphylaxis is a severe allergic reaction to venom, food, or medication. Anaphylaxis causes a series of symptoms, including a rash, low pulse, and shock, which is known as anaphylactic shock.

Hence, the correct option is (B).

76. Option (C) is correct because the use of terfenadine and astemizole, two long-acting nonsedating histamine H1 receptor antagonists, has been associated with prolongation of the QT interval, development of ventricular arrhythmias, particularly torsade de points, and sudden cardiac death.

Option (A) is incorrect because levocetirizine is an antihistamine used to relieve allergy symptoms such as watery eyes, runny nose, itching eyes/nose, and sneezing. It is also used to relieve itching and hives. It works by blocking a certain natural substance (histamine) that your body makes during an allergic reaction.

Option (B) is incorrect because fexofenadine lacks the cardiac effects of its parent drug, and so the risk of QT prolongation and subsequent ventricular arrhythmias at therapeutic doses is mostly apparent when metabolic pathway is inhibited.

Option (D) is incorrect because loratadine is an antihistamine that reduces the effects of the natural chemical histamine in the body. Histamine can produce symptoms of sneezing, itching, watery eyes, and runny nose. Loratadine is used to treat sneezing, runny nose, watery eyes, hives, skin rash, itching, and other cold or allergy symptoms.

Hence, the correct option is (C).

77. Option (A) is correct because in classical conditioning, the conditioned stimulus (which usually does not produce the response), when paired with the unconditioned stimulus (stimulus which usually produces a response), directly produces a response. The typical example of classical conditioning is Pavlov's experiment.

Option (B) is incorrect because, in behaviorist terms, food is an unconditioned stimulus and salivation is an unconditioned response. In his experiment, Pavlov used a metronome as his neutral stimulus.

Option (C) is incorrect because procedural memory refers to sensorimotor habits or automatic skills, which are largely unconscious. The structures implicated in these habits are the basal ganglia.

Option (D) is incorrect because the mere-exposure effect is a psychological phenomenon by which people tend to develop a preference for things merely because they are familiar with them. In social psychology, this effect is sometimes called the familiarity principle.

Hence, the correct option is (A).

78. Option (C) is correct because Frovatriptan is a selective 5-HT1B/1D receptor agonist with a long half-life (26-30 h) and a low headache recurrence rate within 24 hours of taking the drug. It constricts cranial vessels, inhibits neuropeptide release, and reduces pain transmission in trigeminal pathways.

Option (A) is incorrect because Buspirone, sold under the brand name Buspar among others, is a medication primarily used to treat anxiety disorders, a particularly generalized anxiety disorder.

Option (B) is incorrect because Ondansetron, marketed under the brand name Zofran, is a medication used to prevent nausea and vomiting caused by cancer chemotherapy, radiation therapy, or surgery.

Option (D) is incorrect because Ketanserin is a drug used clinically as an antihypertensive agent and in scientific research to study the serotonin system; specifically, the 5-HT_2 receptor family. It was discovered at Janssen Pharmaceutica in 1980.

Hence, the correct option is (C).

79. The discovery of Mycobacterium leprae by G. H. Armauer Hansen (1841-1912) in 1873 represents a link in a chain of development in international medicine that was influenced by two main concepts, namely, that germs may be causes of disease and that social conditions may be related to disease, either as causes or consequences or both.

Hence, the correct option is (B).

80. Option (A) is correct because simple quaternary compounds, such as edrophonium, form electrostatic bonds with the anionic site of the enzyme and hydrogen bonds with the imidazole nitrogen atom of the esteratic site. In all such cases, inhibition is rapidly reversible, and such drugs have a very short duration of inhibitory action.

Option (B) is incorrect because edrophonium (by the so-called Tensilon test) is used to differentiate myasthenia gravis from cholinergic crisis and Lambert-Eaton. In myasthenia gravis, the body produces autoantibodies which block, inhibit or destroy nicotinic acetylcholine receptors in the neuromuscular junction.

Option (C) is incorrect because edrophonium is an effective acetylcholinesterase inhibitor that will reduce the muscle weakness by blocking the enzymatic effect of acetylcholinesterase (AChE) enzymes, prolonging the presence of acetylcholine in the synaptic cleft. It binds to a Serine-103 allosteric site, while pyridostigmine and neostigmine bind to the AchE active site for their inhibitory effects.

Option (D) is incorrect because cholinergic crisis is a clinical condition that develops as a result of overstimulation of nicotinic and muscarinic receptors at the neuromuscular junctions and synapses. This is usually secondary to the inactivation or inhibition of acetylcholinesterase (AChE), the enzyme responsible for the degradation of acetylcholine (ACh). Excessive accumulation of acetylcholine (ACh) at the neuromuscular junctions and synapses causes symptoms of both muscarinic and nicotinic toxicity. These include cramps, increased salivation, lacrimation, muscular weakness, paralysis, muscular fasciculation, diarrhea, and blurry vision

Hence, the correct option is (A).

81. Option (A) is correct because of Clinical use of β_2 adrenergic receptor antagonists in heart failure. These are now recommended for routine use in patients with an ejection fraction < 35% and NYHA class II or III symptoms in conjunction with an ACE inhibitor or angiotensin-receptor antagonist, and diuretics. These should be initiated at very low doses, generally less than one-tenth of the final target dose.

Option (B) is incorrect because of Beta-blockers can slow the progression of systolic forms of heart failure. Beta-blockers may be used to treat left ventricular systolic dysfunction in people who are stable and have no symptoms or only mild to moderate heart failure symptoms. Beta-blockers may be used together with other medicines that are usually used to treat heart failures, such as angiotensin-converting enzyme (ACE) inhibitors or diuretics. So, they cannot be gradually increased over the weeks.

Option (C) is incorrect because of NYHA Class IIIB and IV patients should be approached with a high level of caution; and in recently decompensated heart failure, beta-blockers should not be used until the patients are stabilized for several days to weeks.

Option (D) is incorrect because of Carvedilol is considered a non-selective beta-blocker that has activity on alpha and beta receptors. Alpha receptors are partly responsible for vasoconstriction and high blood pressure while beta receptors play a major role in the heart. Metoprolol is classified as a beta-1 selective blocker. Metoprolol is approved to treat high blood pressure, angina, and acute heart attacks.

Hence, the correct option is (A).

82. Option (C) is correct because β2 (beta2) adrenergic receptor agonists, also known as adrenergic β2 receptor agonists, are a class of drugs that act on the β2 adrenergic receptor. Like other β adrenergic agonists, they cause smooth muscle relaxation. β2 adrenergic agonists' effects on smooth muscle cause dilation of bronchial passages, vasodilation in muscle and liver, relaxation of the uterine muscle, and release of insulin. They are primarily used to treat asthma and other pulmonary disorders, such as COPD.

Option (A) is incorrect because Na^+ K^+ ATPase inhibitors are indicated for the treatment of acute decompensated Congestive heart failure (CHF). Digitalis (Na^+ - K^+ ATPase inhibitor) is indicated both for acute treatment as well as maintenance in CHF as digoxin is the only orally effective inotropic drug available.

Option (B) is incorrect because Alpha-blockers typically isn't the first treatment option for high blood pressure. Instead, they're used in combination with other drugs, such as diuretics, when your high blood pressure is difficult to control.

Option (D) is incorrect because of stimulation of β1 receptors by epinephrine and norepinephrine induces a positive chronotropic and inotropic effect on the heart and increases cardiac conduction velocity and automaticity. Stimulation of β1 receptors on the kidney causes renin release. Stimulation of β2 receptors induces smooth muscle relaxation, induces tremor in skeletal muscle, and increases glycogenolysis in the liver and skeletal muscle.

Hence, the correct option is (C).

83. Option (C) is correct because of Propylthiouracil (PTU) is an oral medication that is used to manage hyperthyroidism which is due to an overactive thyroid gland. It is an anti-thyroid drug that has a mechanism of action that is similar to methimazole (Tapazole). Graves' disease is the most common cause of hyperthyroidism. It is an autoimmune disease where an individual makes antibodies to thyroid stimulating hormone receptors on cells of the thyroid gland and then trigger overproduction of thyroid hormone by the cells.

Option (A) is incorrect because of

- Iodides are commonly used to decrease the size and vascularity of thyroid gland before surgery.
- As this patient is pregnant, iodides and radioactive iodine are contra-indicated.
- Propylthiouracil is safe in pregnancy and is used for this purpose.

Iodide ion: An iodide ion is the ion I^-. Compounds with iodine in formal oxidation state −1 are called iodides.

Option (B) is incorrect because Propranolol, sold under the brand name Inderal among others, is a medication of the beta-blocker class.

Option (D) is incorrect because Radioiodine therapy is a nuclear medicine treatment for an overactive thyroid, a condition called hyperthyroidism, and also may be used to treat thyroid cancer.
Hence, the correct option is (C).

84. Option (D) is correct because of

Definition Zero-order elimination kinetics : "Elimination of a constant quantity per time unit of the drug quantity present in the organism."

Definition First order elimination kinetics : "Elimination of a constant fraction per time unit of the drug quantity present in the organism. The elimination is proportional to the drug concentration."

Option (A) is incorrect because of When drug elimination proceeds by first-order kinetics, a constant proportion or fraction of drug is eliminated per unit time (e.g., 25%/hr). As a result, plasma drug concentrations decline exponentially.

Option (B) is incorrect because of if the substance follows a zero-order elimination, the amount eliminated will be dependent of time and not the amount ingested, which can be contrasted to first-order kinetics, which the amount eliminated will be dependent on the maximum blood/plasma concentration and not of time.

Option (C) is incorrect because of In clinical pharmacology, first-order kinetics are considered as a linear process because the rate of elimination is proportional to the drug concentration. This means that the higher the drug concentration, the higher its elimination rate. But I.V. does not follow this.

Hence, the correct option is (D).

85. Option (A) is correct because of Passively cleared compounds are generally well predicted from animal data because of CLr = GFR × fu (where CLr is renal clearance, GFR glomerular filtration rate, fu the fraction unbound). Hence, simple, related, allometric relationships can be readily established.

Option (B) is incorrect because of the renal clearance of a drug is the volume of plasma that the kidneys completely clear of that drug per unit of time. Although empirical, the renal clearance of a drug can be used to describe renal drug excretion quantitatively and study the physiological processes that affect it and so, the value can not be equal to the GFR.

Option (C) is incorrect because when renal clearance is less than the product of glomerular filtration rate by the unbound fraction, then renal reabsorption is assumed.

Option (D) is incorrect because when renal clearance is greater than the product of glomerular filtration rate by the unbound fraction, then secretion is thought to be present.
Hence, the correct option is (A).

86. Option (C) is correct because mannitol is an osmotic diuretic indicated for cerebral edema and glaucoma. It is contra-indicated inactive bleeding in the brain.

Option (A) is incorrect because furosemide is used to reduce extra fluid in the body (edema) caused by conditions such as heart failure, liver disease, and kidney disease.

Option (B) is incorrect because anabolic steroids are often used illegally to build muscle. But corticosteroids are used to treat a variety of health problems.

Option (D) is incorrect because glycine is an amino acid that has a single hydrogen atom as its side chain. It is the simplest amino acid (since carbamic acid is unstable), with the chemical formula NH_2 - CH_2 - COOH. Glycine is one of the proteinogenic amino acids.

Hence, the correct option is (C).

87.

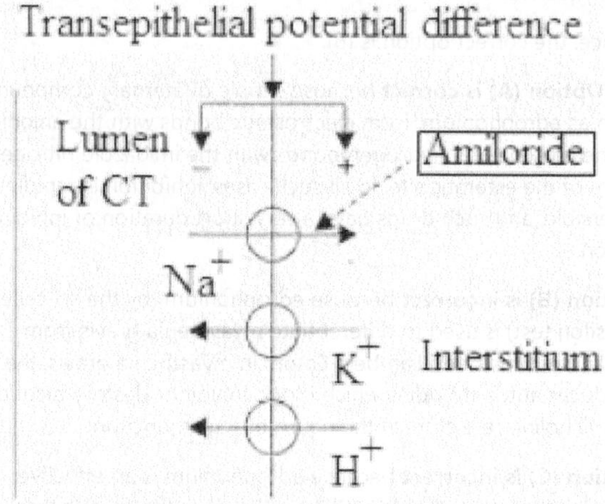

Option (B) is correct because of amiloride and triamterene are K+ sparing diuretics that act by inhibiting epithelial Na+ channels.

Option (A) is incorrect because of Amiloride can not cause hyperkalemia due to its action on Electrogenic K^+ channels.

Option (C) is incorrect because of In the distal tubules and collecting ducts, three separate channels are present (one for Na^+, K^+ and H^+ each). Aldosterone acts on DCT and CD to cause reabsorption of Na^+. This generates a lumen negative potential difference across the membrane of this part of the nephron. To maintain the electric neutrality, K^+ and H^+ are secreted in the lumen.

Option (D) is incorrect because ofwhen amiloride and triamterene inhibit epithelial Na^+ channels, the transepithelial potential difference is not generated and therefore K^+ and H^+ are not secreted in the lumen. Thus due to more retention of K^+, amiloride may result in hyperkalemia.
Hence, the correct option is (B).

88. -The G_0 phase or resting phase is a period in the cell cycle in which cells exist in a quiescent state. G_0 phase is viewed as either an extended G_1 phase, where the cell is neither dividing nor preparing to divide or a distinct quiescent stage that occurs outside of the cell cycle.

-The G_1 phase, or Gap 1 phase, is the first of four phases of the cell cycle that takes place in eukaryotic cell division. In this part of interphase, the cell synthesizes mRNA and proteins in preparation for subsequent steps leading to mitosis.

-S phase is the phase of the cell cycle in which DNA is replicated, occurring between the G_1 phase and G_2 phase. Since accurate duplication of the genome is critical to successful cell division, the processes that occur during S-phase are tightly regulated and widely conserved.

-G_2 phase, or Gap 2 phase, is the third subphase of interphase in the cell cycle directly preceding mitosis. It follows the successful completion of S phase, during which the cell's DNA is replicated.

-In cell biology, mitosis is a part of the cell cycle when replicated chromosomes are separated into two new nuclei. Cell division gives rise to genetically identical cells in which the number of chromosomes is maintained.

Option (B) is correct -According to the above explanation .

Option (A) is incorrect-According to the above explanation.

Option (C) is incorrect-According to the above explanation.

Option (D) is incorrect -According to the above explanation.

Hence, the correct option is (B).

89. Clearance is calculated as $\frac{rate\ of\ drug\ elimination}{plasma\ drug\ concentration} = \frac{2}{50}$

= 0.04 L/min.

Option (B) is correct - According to the above solution .

Option (A) is incorrect - According to the above solution .

Option (C) is incorrect - According to the above solution .

Option (D) is incorrect - According to the above solution .

Hence, the correct option is (B).

90. Option (C) is correct because of the lipophilic nitrosoureas, such as carmustine and lomustine, are alkylating agents that can penetrate the blood-brain barrier, making them excellent drugs for the treatment of brain tumours. The nitrosoureas are metabolized to active products and excreted in the urine.

Option (A) is incorrect because of Cytarabine, also known as cytosine arabinoside, is a chemotherapy medication used to treat acute myeloid leukaemia, acute lymphocytic leukaemia, chronic myelogenous leukaemia, and non-Hodgkin's lymphoma.

Option (B) is incorrect because of Etoposide, sold under the brand name Etopophos among others, is a chemotherapy medication used for the treatments of a number of types of cancer including testicular cancer, lung cancer, lymphoma, leukaemia, neuroblastoma, and ovarian cancer.

Option (D) is incorrect because of Selective estrogen receptor modulators (SERMs) are a class of drugs that act on the estrogen receptor (ER). A characteristic that distinguishes these substances from pure ER agonists and antagonists (that is, full agonists and silent antagonists) is that their action is different in various tissues, thereby granting the possibility to selectively inhibit or stimulate estrogen-like action in various tissues.

Hence, the correct option is (C).

91. When a drug is administered in multiple doses and each dose is given prior to the complete elimination of the previous dose, the mean plasma concentration (C) of the drug during each dose interval rises as shown in the following figure:

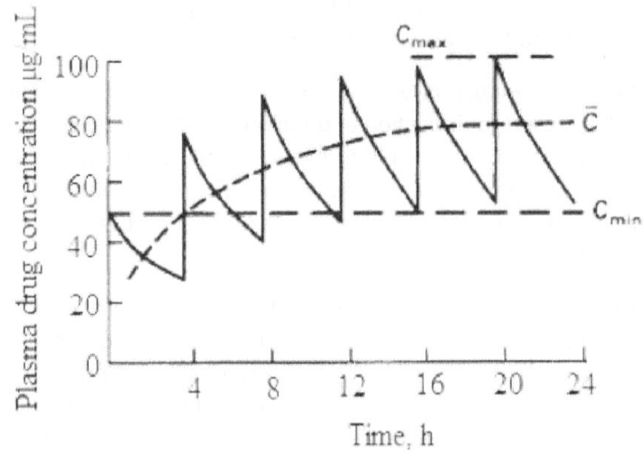

The plasma concentration will continue to rise until it reaches a plateau or steady-state. At this time, the plasma concentration will fluctuate between a maximum (Cmax) and a minimum (Cmin) level, but, more importantly, the amount of drug eliminated per dose interval will equal the amount of drug absorbed per dose. When a drug is given at a dosing interval that is equal to its elimination half-life, it will reach 50% of its steady-state plasma concentration after one half-life, 75% after two half-lives, 87.5% after three, 93.75% after four, and 96.87% after five. Thus, from a practical viewpoint, regardless of the magnitude of the dose or the half-life, the steady-state will be achieved in 4 to 5 half-lives.

Option (A) is incorrect-According to the above explanation.

Option (B) is correct-According to the above explanation.

Option (C) is incorrect-According to the above explanation.

Option (D) is incorrect-According to the above explanation.

Hence, the correct option is (B).

92. Option (A) is incorrect because of Ketamine is a medication mainly used for starting and maintaining anaesthesia. It induces a trance-like state while providing pain relief, sedation, and memory loss.

Option (B) is incorrect because of Enflurane is a halogenated ether. Developed by Ross Terrell in 1963, it was first used clinically in 1966. It was increasingly used for inhalational anaesthesia during the 1970s and 1980s but is no longer in common use.

Option (C) is correct because of Propofol is the most commonly used anaesthetic agent for daycare surgery. Propofol is a short-acting medication that results in a decreased level of consciousness and a lack of memory for events. Its uses include the starting and maintenance of general anaesthesia, sedation for mechanically ventilated adults, and procedural sedation.

Option (D) is incorrect because of Remifentanil (marketed by Abbott as Ultiva) is a potent ultra short-acting synthetic opioid analgesic drug. It is given to patients during surgery to relieve pain and as an adjunct to an anaesthetic. Remifentanil is a specific mu-type-opioid receptor agonist.

Hence, the correct option is (C).

93. Option (A) is incorrect because ether was safely and effectively used as an inhalation anesthetic for over one hundred years. Dissociative anesthesia is a form of anesthesia characterized by catalepsy, catatonia, analgesia, and amnesia. It does not necessarily involve loss of consciousness and thus does not always imply a state of general anesthesia. A pleasant-smelling, colorless and highly flammable liquid, ether can be vaporized into a gas that numbs pain but leaves patients conscious.

Option (B) is incorrect because of halothane is a general inhalation anesthetic used for induction and maintenance of general anesthesia. It reduces the blood pressure and frequently decreases the pulse rate and depresses respiration. It induces muscle relaxation and reduces pains sensitivity by altering tissue excitability.

Option (C) is incorrect because of enflurane (2-chloro-1,1,2,-trifluoroethyl-difluoromethyl ether) is a halogenated ether. Developed by Ross Terrell in 1963, it was first used clinically in 1966. It was increasingly used for inhalational anesthesia during the 1970s and 1980s but is no longer in common use. Enflurane is a structural isomer of isoflurane.

Option (D) is correct because of dissociative anaesthesia is seen in the administration of Ketamine. Ketamine produces the so-called dissociative anaesthetic state that has been described as functional and electrophysiological dissociation between the thalamo-neocortical and limbic systems.

Hence, the correct option is (D).

94. Option (A) is incorrect because ceftazidime is in the third-generation cephalosporin family of medications and works by interfering with the bacteria's cell wall. It is sold under the brand name Fortaz among others and is an antibiotic useful for the treatment of a number of bacterial infections.

Option (B) is incorrect because cefoperazone has an antipseudomonal effect. Cefoperazone is highly active against Enterobacteriaceae. Its activity against Staphylococcus aureus is comparable to that of the other newer cephem antibiotics. Cefoperazone is also active against all beta-hemolytic streptococci and Streptococcus pneumonia and is relatively inactive against methicillin-resistant S.

Option (C) is correct because when the in vitro susceptibility of 155 strains of anaerobic bacteria to five cephalosporin antibiotics was tested, cefoxitin was the most active against 33 isolates of Bacteroides fragilis; 82% of the strains were sensitive at 16 μg/ml. At 64 μg/ml cefazolin and cephaloridine were also generally effective. Cefoxitin, cephaloridine, cefazolin, and cephalothin showed comparable activity against 122 strains of anaerobes other than B. fragilis. Thus, Cefoxitin has activity against anaerobes.

Option (D) is incorrect because penicillins and cephalosporins are the major antibiotics that inhibit bacterial cell wall synthesis. They are called beta-lactams because of the unusual 4-member ring that is common to all their members.

Hence, the correct option is (C).

95. Bicalutamide has been assessed at the membrane androgen receptors (mARs) and found to act as a potent antagonist of ZIP9 (IC50 = 66.3 nM), whereas it does not appear to interact with GPRC6A.

Bicalutamide is approved for and mainly used in locally advanced prostate cancer (LAPC) in men as monotherapy in high doses.

The side effect profile of bicalutamide is highly dependent on sex; that is, on whether the person is male or female. In men, due to androgen deprivation, a variety of side effects of varying severity may occur during bicalutamide treatment, with breast pain/tenderness and gynecomastia (breast development/enlargement) being the most common.

Option (A) is incorrect-According to the above explanation.

Option (B) is incorrect-According to the above explanation.

Option (C) is incorrect-According to the above explanation.

Option (D) is correct-According to the above explanation, option (D) consist all part.

Hence, the correct option is (D).

96. Option (A) is incorrect because adenoviruses are common viruses that cause a range of illness. They can cause cold-like symptoms, fever, sore throat, bronchitis, pneumonia, diarrhoea, and pink eye (conjunctivitis). You can get an adenovirus infection at any age.

Option (B) is correct because the Human diploid fibroblasts (HDF) cell line is used for cultivation of coxsackie A7, 9, 16; CMV; echovirus; enteroviruses; HSV-1, 2; poliovirus; parainfluenza virus, rhinovirus and VZV. Thus, human fibroblast cell line is used for cultivation of poliovirus.

Option (C) is incorrect because the human immunodeficiency viruses (HIV) are two species of Lentivirus (a subgroup of retrovirus) that infect humans. Over time they cause acquired immunodeficiency syndrome (AIDS), a condition in which progressive failure of the immune system allows life-threatening opportunistic infections and cancers to thrive.

Option (D) is incorrect because measles is a childhood infection caused by a virus. Once quite common, measles can now almost always be prevented with a vaccine. Also called rubeola, measles can be serious and even fatal for small children.

Hence, the correct option is (B).

97. Option (A) is correct because lysogenic conversion is when a temperate phage induces a change in the phenotype of the infected bacteria that is not part of a usual phage cycle. An example is a lysogenic conversion in diphtheria bacilli, which acquire toxigenicity (virulence) by lysogenisation with the beta phage.

Option (B) is incorrect because the transfer of DNA from one bacterium to another by a bacteriophage is known as transduction.

Option (C) is incorrect because the transfer of free DNA is transformation.

Option (D) is incorrect because the transfer of genome by physical contact is conjugation.

Hence, the correct option is (A).

98. (a) Chlamydia is a common sexually transmitted disease. It is caused by bacteria called Chlamydia trachomatis. It can infect both men and women. Women can get chlamydia in the cervix, rectum, or throat. Men can get chlamydia in the urethra (inside the penis), rectum, or throat.

(b) Rickettsia is a genus of nonmotile, gram-negative, non-spore forming, highly pleomorphic bacteria that may occur in the forms of cocci, bacilli, or threads.

(c) Mycoplasma is a genus of bacteria that lack a cell wall around their cell membranes. This characteristic makes them naturally resistant to antibiotics that target cell wall synthesis. They can be parasitic or saprotrophic.

(d) Prions are misfolded proteins with the ability to transmit their misfolded shape onto normal variants of the same protein. They characterize several fatal and transmissible neurodegenerative diseases in humans and many other animals.

(e) Bacterial viruses are called phages or bacteriophages. They only attack bacteria; phages are harmless to people, animals, and plants. Bacteriophages are the natural enemies of bacteria.

Thus, chlamydia, rickettsia, and mycoplasma are taxonomically bacteria.

According to the above explanation **option (A) is incorrect.**

According to the above explanation **option (B) is correct.**

According to the above explanation **option (C) is incorrect.**

According to the above explanation **option (D) is incorrect.**

Hence, the correct option is (B).

99. Option (C) is correct because the cells of the lymphoid system are lymphocytes.

On the basis of function and surface markers, there are two major types of lymphocytes-

1- T- cells

2- B- cells

When circulating lymphocytes are classified by their surface markers into T and B cells, about 5-10 per cent of cells are found to lack features of either type they are called null cells/Large granular lymphocytes.

Large granular lymphocytes include:

- Natural killer cells (N.K Cells)
- Antibody-dependent cytotoxic cells/killer cells (ADCC).
- Lymphokine-activated killer cells (LAK cells).

Option (A) is incorrect because of Macrophages are specialised cells involved in the detection, phagocytosis and destruction of bacteria and other harmful organisms. In addition, they can also present antigens to T cells and initiate inflammation by releasing molecules (known as cytokines) that activate other cells.

Option (B) is incorrect because of Astrocytes (Astro from Greek astron = star and cyte from Greek "kytos" = cavity but also means cell), also known collectively as astroglia, are characteristic star-shaped glial cells in the brain and spinal cord. The proportion of astrocytes in the brain is not well defined.

Option (D) is incorrect because of Langerhans cells (LC) are members of the family of the dendritic cells, residing in the basal and suprabasal layers of the epidermis and in the epithelia of the respiratory, digestive and urogenital tracts. They specialize in antigen presentation and belong to the skin immune system (SIS).

Hence, the correct option is (C).

100. Option (C) is correct because of

Role of T cell in antibody formation:

- Antigen with class II MHC on antigen-presenting cells activates the CD4 helper T cells. CD4 helper T cells produce cytokines that stimulate B cells which have already exposed to similar antigen.
- Though antibody is produced by B cells (after differentiating into plasma cells), coordination of helper (CD 4) T cells is also necessary.
- In antibody formation, T cells are involved earlier than B cells.
- After antigen exposure, antigen-presenting cells present antigen to CD 4 helper T cells, which then secrete cytokines that induce differentiation of B cells (which have already been exposed to the same antigen) to plasma cells.
- Plasma cells form an antibody against that specific antigen.

Antigen + Antigen presenting cell with MHC class II
↓
CD4 T cell activation
↓
Release of cytokines
↓
Stimulation of B cells bound by specific antigen
↓
Plasma cells
↓
Antibody production

Option (A) is incorrect because Epstein-Barr (EB) is the virus that causes mononucleosis. It spreads primarily through saliva. It is one of the most common human viruses. EB virus is found all over the world. Most people get infected with EBV at some point in their lives.

Option (B) is incorrect because endotoxin is a type of pyrogen and is a component of the exterior cell wall of gram-negative bacteria, like E. coli. Endotoxin is a lipopolysaccharide or LPS. LPS consists of the lipid A portion containing fatty acids and disaccharide phosphates, core polysaccharides, and the O-antigen.

Option (D) is incorrect because plasma cells, also called plasma B cells, are white blood cells that originate in the bone marrow and secrete large quantities of proteins called antibodies in response to being presented specific substances called antigens.

Hence, the correct option is (C).

101. Option (C) is correct because MRSA resistance is not absolutely beta-lactamase dependent. Though altered penicillin-binding protein is involved in most strains, rarely beta-lactamase production is also involved.

Option (A) is incorrect as resistance to MRSA is chromosomally mediated.

Option (B) is incorrect as it involves the production of an altered penicillin-binding protein (PBP2a).

Option (D) is incorrect as intrinsic resistance is known, that means an alteration in intrinsic PBPs is also one of the mechanisms for resistance in MRSA.

Hence, the correct option is (C).

102. Option (A) is correct as normally in transcription, there is the formation of RNA from DNA. Reverse transcriptase will cause transcription in reverse fashion i.e synthesis of DNA from RNA. Then fresh RNA is formed from DNA. Amongst the given options, the only adenovirus is a DNA virus. All others are RNA viruses. Reverse transcriptase induces the formation of DNA from RNA. So it can be used in the diagnosis of RNA viruses only.

Option (B) is incorrect because astroviruses (AstV) are single-stranded, positive-sense, nonenveloped RNA viruses of icosahedral particle symmetry that cause a variety of clinical diseases ranging from diarrhea to encephalitis, or asymptomatic infection in a wide range of mammals and birds.

Option (C) is incorrect because rotavirus is a genus of double-stranded RNA viruses in the family Reoviridae. Rotaviruses are the most common cause of diarrhoeal disease among infants and young children.

Option (D) is incorrect as poliovirus, the causative agent of polio (also known as poliomyelitis), is a serotype of the species Enterovirus C, in the family of Picornaviridae. Poliovirus is composed of an RNA genome and a protein capsid.

Hence, the correct option is (A).

103. Option (C) is correct as chromatid bodies do not stain with iodine but are seen as refractile oblong bars with rounded ends in preparations with normal saline and as black when stained with iron-haematoxylin., i. e. this is not true about Entamoeba Histolytica. Thus, this is the required answer.

Option (A) is incorrect as cyst of E. histolytica is quadrinucleate (4 nuclei). Thus, it is true about Entamoeba Histolytica. Hence this is not the required answered.

Option (B) is incorrect as trophozoites colonize cecum and ascending colon, sigmoid colon, rectum and appendix in order of frequency. Thus, it is true about Entamoeba Histolytica. And hence this is not the required answered.

Option (D) is incorrect as option (C) is not true about Entamoeba Histolytica.

Hence, the correct option is (C).

104. Option (D) is correct because Brucellosis (Brucella sp.) is classified as 'Category B' agent with second highest priority/potential for use as a biological weapon for microbial terrorism. Whereas plague, smallpox and Botulism belong to 'Category A' as defined by CDC (Centers for Disease Control and Prevention) with the highest potential for use as biological weapons.

Option (A) is incorrect as Yersinia pestis is a gram-negative, non-motile, rod-shaped, coccobacillus bacterium, with no spores. It is a facultative anaerobic organism that can infect humans via the oriental rat flea. It causes the disease plague, which takes three main forms: pneumonic, septicemic, and bubonic.

Option (B) is incorrect because variola major was the severe and most common form, with a more extensive rash and higher fever, resulting in confluent smallpox, which had a high death rate. Variola minor was a less common presentation, causing less severe disease, discrete smallpox, with historical death rates of one percent or less.

Option (C) is incorrect as clostridium botulinum is a gram-positive, rod-shaped, anaerobic, spore-forming, motile bacterium with the ability to produce the neurotoxin botulinum.

Hence, the correct option is (D).

105. Option (A) is correct because the term hospital infection, hospital-acquired infection, or nosocomial infection are applied to infections developing in hospitalized patients, not present or in incubation at the time of their admission. Such infections may become evident during their stay in hospital or, sometimes, only after their discharge.

Option (B) is incorrect because an opportunistic infection is an infection caused by pathogens (bacteria, viruses, fungi, or protozoa) that take advantage of an opportunity not normally available, such as a host with a weakened immune system, an altered microbiota (such as a disrupted gut microbiota), or breached integumentary barriers.

Option (C) is incorrect because, in epizoology, an epizootic is a disease event in a nonhuman animal population, analogous to an epidemic in humans. An epizootic may be: restricted to a specific locale, general, or widespread.

Option (D) is incorrect as physician-induced demand exists when the physician influences a patient's demand for care against the physician's interpretation of the best interests of the patient.

Hence, the correct option is (A).

106. Option (C) is correct as the best way to control the MRSA infection is by washing hands before & after attending to the patient. MRSA is usually spread by direct contact with an infected wound or from contaminated hands, usually those of healthcare providers. Also, people who carry MRSA but do not have signs of infection can spread the bacteria to others.

Option (A) is incorrect because vancomycin is only active against gram-positive bacteria.

Option (B) is incorrect as fumigation is done only in the high-risk areas like ICU, PICU, NICU, Labour room. OTwards are excluded for fumigation (done only if required).

Option (D) is incorrect as masks are worn to decrease the risk ofpatient exposure to contamination or infection from thesurgical team.

Hence, the correct option is (C).

107. Option (A) is correct because, in Cryptococcus, stains used are:

- For Capsule: India ink/Nigrosin stain, and Alcian blue.
- For melanin: Masson Fontana.
- For cell wall: Mayer's mucicarmine.
- For biopsy: H and E, Methenamine silver, PAS, Calcofluor white.

Option (B) is incorrect because, in Candida, stains used are: Gram stain, Calcofluor white H and E (tissue biopsy specimens).

Option (C) is incorrect because, in Pneumocystis carinii, stains used is: Methenamine silver.

Option (D) is incorrect because, in Histoplasma, stains used are: Giemsa, PAS, and Methenamine silver.

Hence, the correct option is (A).

108. Option (B) is correct as the gametocytes of Plasmodium falciparum have a crescent or banana shape as evident in the picture.

Option (A) is incorrect as the gametocytes of Plasmodium malariae have a round shape about the size of red blood cells. They have a fine granular appearance.

Option (C) is incorrect as trophozoites of Plasmodium falciparum have the characteristic signet ring shape. Also, unique to Plasmodium falciparum is the presence of multiple trophozoites in one cell ie multiple ring forms are present in one RBC.

Option (D) is incorrect as Plasmodium vivax trophozoites show amoeboid cytoplasm, large chromatin dots, and have fine, yellowish-brown pigment.

Hence, the correct option is (B).

109. Option (B) is correct as Trichomoniasis, is a common sexually transmitted disease (STD) that affects both men and women. Trichomoniasis is caused by a protozoan parasite called Trichomonas vaginalis and is a cause of vaginal infections in women and urethral infections in men.

Option (A) is incorrect as Giardia duodenalis, also known as Giardia intestinalis and Giardia lamblia, is a flagellated parasitic microorganism, that colonizes and reproduces in the small intestine, causing giardiasis. The parasite attaches to the epithelium by a ventral adhesive disc or sucker and reproduces via binary fission.

Option (C) is incorrect as Leishmania donovani is a species of intracellular parasites belonging to the genus Leishmania, a group of haemoflagellate kinetoplastids that cause the disease leishmaniasis. It is a human blood parasite responsible for visceral leishmaniasis or kala-azar, the most severe form of leishmaniasis.

Option (D) is incorrect as the organism shown in the figure is Trichomonas vaginalis.

Hence, the correct option is (B).

110. Option (B) is correct as the image describes cutaneous larva migrans which is caused by the penetration of the skin by zoonotic (eg cat, dog. or other mammals) nematode larvae.

It is an intestinal parasite of domestic cats and dogs. Severe infection is often fatal to these pets, especially in puppies and kittens. The infection is particularly endemic in the southern United States.

Option (A) is incorrect because Ancylostoma caninum, the dog hookworm, can also inhabit humans, causing diarrhoea, abdominal pain, and severe eosinophilic gastroenteritis.

Option (C) is incorrect as Ancylostoma duodenale is a species of the roundworm genus Ancylostoma. It is a parasitic nematode worm and commonly known as the old world hookworm. It lives in the small intestine of hosts such as humans, cats and dogs, where it is able to mate and mature.

Option (D) is incorrect as Uncinaria stenocephala is a nematode that parasitizes dogs, cats, and foxes as well as humans.
Hence, the correct option is (B).

111. Option (B) is correct as the images describe (irregular hyphae broad, ribbon-like, ranging from 6-50 microns in width and is aseptate) broad aseptate fungi - Zygomycetes. Members of the class Zygomycetes - namely, Rhizopus, Mucor Rhizomucor, and Absidia - produce severe, necrotizing, invasive, opportunistic infections that begin in the nasal sinuses or lungs. The infections they produce are usually called mucormycosis or zygomycoses.

Option (A) is incorrect because Aspergillus is a fungus whose spores are present in the air we breathe but does not normally cause illness. In those people with a weakened immune system, damaged lungs or with allergies, Aspergillus can cause disease. Common Aspergillus infections include invasive aspergillosis, ABPA CPA and aspergilloma.

Option (C) is incorrect as Candidiasis is a fungal infection caused by a yeast (a type of fungus) called Candida. Some species of Candida can cause infection in people; the most common is Candida albicans. Candida normally lives on the skin and inside the body, in places such as the mouth, throat, gut, and vagina, without causing any problems.

Option (D) is incorrect as Histoplasmosis is a disease caused by a fungus (or mold) called Histoplasma. The fungus is common in the eastern and central United States. It grows in soil and material contaminated with bat or bird droppings. You get infected by breathing the fungal spores.

Hence, the correct option is (B).

112. Option (A) is correct as the order is as follows :

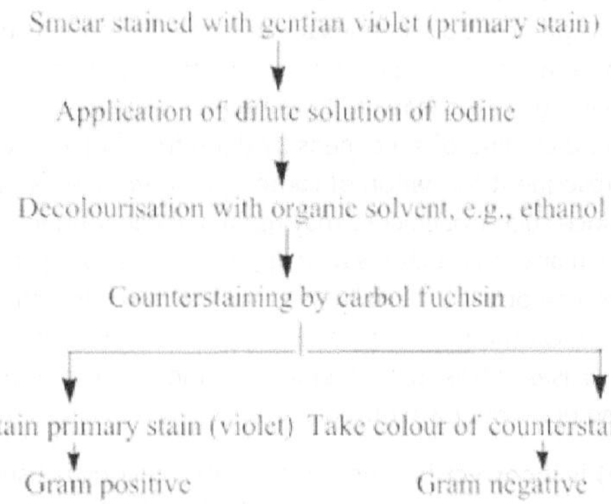

Option (B) is incorrect because this is not the correct order as :

Gram-positive → Resist decolourization and retain primary stain, appear violet.

Option (C) is incorrect because it is also not following the correct order as counterstaining by carbol fuchsin is the last step.

Option (D) is incorrect as the correct order is:

Gentian violet → Iodine → Carbol fuchsin

Hence, the correct option is (A).

113. Option (D) is correct as:

- For single option go-ahead for option 'a', i.e. polysaccharide because, except for Bacillus anthracis, the

- capsule of almost all the important bacteria is composed of sugar (polysaccharide).
- Don't get confused with word gram-negative in question because the capsule, whether it is of grain positive or gram-negative bacteria, is not visible on gram staining.

Option (A) is incorrect as lipopolysaccharides (LPS), also known as lipoglycans and endotoxins, are large molecules consisting of a lipid and a polysaccharide composed of O-antigen, outer core and inner core joined by a covalent bond; they are found in the outer membrane of Gram-negative bacteria.

Option (B) is incorrect because a lipid is chemically defined as a substance that is insoluble in water and soluble in alcohol, ether, and chloroform. Lipids are an important component of living cells. Together with carbohydrates and proteins, lipids are the main constituents of plant and animal cells. Cholesterol and triglycerides are lipids.

Option (C) is incorrect as :

- Capsules are protective walls that surround the cell membranes of gram-positive and gram-negative bacteria.
- They are usually composed of simple sugar (polysaccharide) except in Bacillus anthracis it is made up of polypeptide (protein).
- The capsule is not visible in gram stained smear as it has little affinity for basic dyes.

Hence, the correct option is (D).

114. Option (C) is correct because the scanning Electron microscopy is a recent development which provides a higher resolution and 3-dimensional image of the object. Although the substantial increases in a resolution power of Electron microscopy have led to significant discoveries a major disadvantage is the inability to examine living cells. a method introduced to overcome this disadvantage is the inability to examine living cells. a method involves rapid cooling of specimens by deep freezing in liquid gas and the subsequent formation of carbon platinum replicas of the material. since such frozen cells may remain viable it enables the study of cellular ultrastructures as it appears in the living state. Electron microscopy is especially used for the rapid detection of viruses in clinical samples. it is particularly useful for detecting non-cultivable viruses. ultrastructural study of various microorganisms may also be done by this method.

Option (A) is incorrect because electron microscopy is used To differentiate T and B lymphocytes. T and B lymphocytes are difficult to distinguish morphologically even with electron microscopy, and antibodies are generally used to make the distinction. Observations of electron microscopy revealed that B lymphocytes are more likely to lose surface antigens and intracellular organelles than T lymphocytes, which allows the visual distinction between T and B lymphocytes.

Option (B) is incorrect as electron microscopy used in IgG deposits in kidney. Electron microscopy has been used for the morphological diagnosis of glomerular diseases. Proliferative glomerulonephritis with monoclonal immunoglobulin G deposit (PGNMID), a recently described pathologic entity in native kidneys, has been recognized in kidney transplant patients, where it can present as either recurrent or de novo disease.

Option (D) is incorrect because a flagellum (plural: flagella) is a long, whip-like structure that helps some single-celled organisms move. It is composed of microtubules. They help propel cells and organisms in a whip-like motion. The flagellum of eukaryotes usually moves with an "S" motion and is surrounded by a cell membrane.

Hence, the correct option is (C).

115. Option (B) is correct as the distal domain (alpha 1 and alpha 2) have highly variable amino-acid sequences and are folded to form a groove between them (between alpha 1 and alpha 2). Protein antigen processed by macrophages or dendritic cells are bound to this groove for presentation to CD_8-T cells.

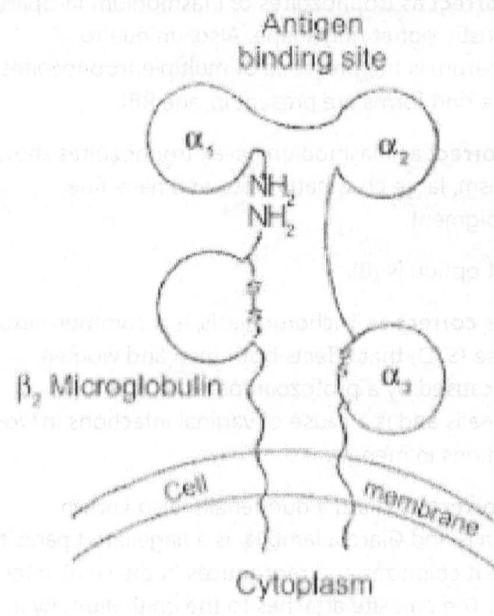

HLA Class I Molecule

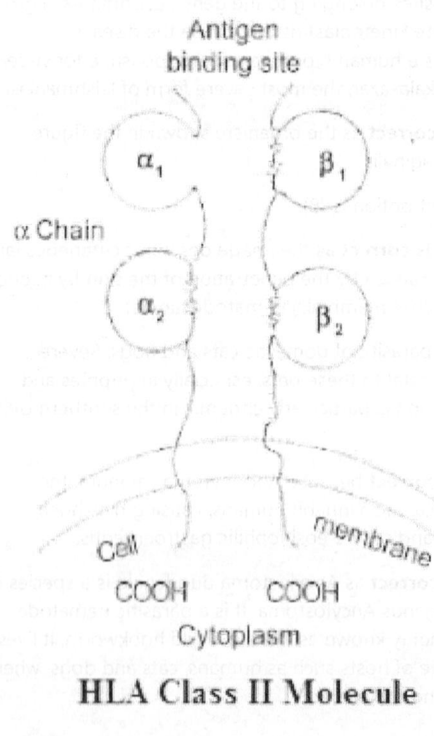

HLA Class II Molecule

Option (A) is incorrect as long & heavy α - chain, consists of three globoid domains α1, α2 and α3.

Option (C) is incorrect because each chain has two domains, the proximal domains being constant and the distal being variable.

Option (D) is incorrect because the two distal domains (α_1 and β_1) constitute the antigen-binding site for recognition by CD_4-T cells.

Hence, the correct option is (B).

116. Option (C) is correct because it is Sec 197 IPC which states that whoever issues or signs any certificate required by law to be given or signed, or relating to any fact of which such certificate is by law admissible in evidence, knowing or believing that such certificate is false in any material point, shall be punished in the same manner as if he gave false evidence.

Option (A) is incorrect because it is section IPC 201 which states that if someone is knowing or having a reason to believe that an offence was committed causes the disappearance of the evidence shall be punished under this section.

Option (B) is incorrect as it is Section 194 that states about false evidence, fabricated evidence, forged evidence or tainted evidence is information created or obtained illegally, to sway the verdict in a court case. Falsified evidence could be created by either side in a case (including the police/prosecution in a criminal case), or by someone sympathetic to either side.

Option (D) is incorrect as the accused is examined in every enquiry or trial by enabling him to explain personally to circumstances appearing in the evidence against him. Section 313 of Criminal Procedure Code, 1973 envisages power of the trial court to examine the accused to explain evidence adduced against him.

Hence, the correct option is (C).

117. Option (A) is correct as IPC Section 197 states that whoever issues or signs any certificate required by law to be given or signed, or relating to any fact of which such certificate is by law admissible in evidence, knowing or believing that such certificate is false in any material point, shall be punished in the same manner as if he gave false evidence. The person who presents false evidence in court can be liable to imprisonment for a term of 7 years and a fine.

Option (B) is incorrect as Section 326 B in the Indian Penal Code lays down the punishment for attempted acid attacks. The minimum punishment is 5 years imprisonment.

Option (C) is incorrect as the punishment for theft is up to three years imprisonment, a fine, or both.

Option (D) is incorrect as stringent punishment for rape of a girl under 12 years has been provided with the minimum jail term being 20 years which may go up to life in prison or death sentence.

Hence, the correct option is (A).

118. Option (D) is correct as:

- Contusion (Bruises) is the effusion of blood into tissues, due to rupture of blood vessels and due to blunt violence. Lathi injury is an injury caused by blunt force.
- In contusion, there is a painful swelling and crushing or tearing of the subcutaneous tissue, usually without destruction of the skin.

Option (A) is incorrect because a laceration is a wound that is produced by the tearing of soft body tissue. This type of wound is often irregular and jagged.

Option (B) is incorrect because a stab wound is a specific form of penetrating trauma to the skin that results from a knife or a similar pointed object. While stab wounds are typically known to be caused by knives, they can also occur from a variety of implements, including broken bottles and ice picks.

Option (C) is incorrect because an abrasion is a partial thickness wound caused by damage to the skin and can be superficial involving only the epidermis to deep, involving the deep dermis.

Hence, the correct option is (D).

119. Option (B) is correct as cadaveric spasm occurs immediately after death.

Option (A) is incorrect as cadaveric spasm occurs without going into a phase of primary relaxation.

Option (C) is incorrect because cadaveric spasm tells the mode of death, suicide/homicide.

Option (D) is incorrect because the contraction of muscles is more pronounced and requires more (great) force to overcome than rigor mortis.

Hence, the correct option is (B).

120. Option (B) is correct as the MTP act was introduced in 1971. The Medical Termination of Pregnancy (MTP) Act 1971, as amended in 2002 to facilitate better implementation and increase access for women, especially in the private health sector.

Option (A) is incorrect as the Maternity benefit act was passed in 1961 by the Parliament house with the object of providing maternity leave and benefits to protect the dignity of motherhood.

Option (C) is incorrect as it is the Privacy Act, Public Law 93-579 that was created in 1974 in response to concerns about how the creation and use of computerized databases might impact individuals' privacy rights.

Option (D) is incorrect as MICRA, or the Medical Injury Compensation Reform Act, was signed into law by California Governor Jerry Brown during his first governorship in 1975 with the intent to reduce medical malpractice insurance premiums.

Hence, the correct option is (B).

121. Option (D) is correct as leaving (or forgetting) an instrument or sponge in the abdomen of the patient during surgery and closing the abdomen at operation amounts to criminal negligence. It refers to conduct in which a person ignores a known or obvious risk, or disregards the life and safety of others.

Option (A) is incorrect because contributory negligence states that if a person was injured in part due to his/her own negligence (his/her negligence "contributed" to the accident), the injured party would not be entitled to collect any damages (money) from another party who supposedly caused the accident.

Option (B) is incorrect as civil negligence is the failure of one person to act with reasonable care in his dealings with others so as not to cause injury or damage. Negligence is not intentional, it is an accident, and we all know that accidents will happen.

Option (C) is incorrect as corporate negligence is the legal doctrine that holds healthcare facilities and hospitals liable for any patient injury. Prior to the enactment of the corporate negligence doctrine, hospitals were often immune to lawsuit for the malpractice or negligence of its doctors and medical staff.

Hence, the correct option is (D).

122. Option (D) is correct as thanatology or deathlore is the scientific study of death and the losses brought about as a result. It investigates the mechanisms and forensic aspects of death, such as bodily changes that accompany death and the post-mortem period, as well as wider psychological and social aspects related to death.

Option (A) is incorrect because it is herpetology is the branch of zoology which deals with the study of reptiles and amphibians such as snakes, turtles, and iguanas.

Option (B) is incorrect because toxicology is a scientific discipline, overlapping with biology, chemistry, pharmacology, and medicine, that involves the study of the adverse effects of chemical substances on living organisms and the practice of diagnosing and treating exposures to toxins and toxicants.

Option (C) is incorrect because the scientific study of fingerprints is called dermatoglyphics.

Hence, the correct option is (D).

123. Option (A) is correct as dribbling of saliva is a feature of hanging (not strangulation). Hence, this is the required answer.

Option (B) is incorrect because bleeding from the nose and transverse ligature mark are common features of strangulation.

Option (C) is incorrect as hyoid bone fracture is commonly associated with strangulation and rarely occurs in isolation. The hyoid bone fracture is a very rare fracture of the hyoid bone, accounting for 0.002% of all fractures in humans.

Option (D) is incorrect as fracture and dislocation of the cervical vertebra in accidental ligature strangulation by chunni (a cloth worn around the neck by Indian women) are very rare and have not been reported previously.

Hence, the correct option is (A).

124. Option (D) is correct because the cephalic index is used for the determination of race. Race determination of skeleton.

Option (A) is incorrect as index fossils are of organisms that lived over a wide area. They lived for a fairly short period of time. An index fossil allows a scientist to determine the age of the rock.

Option (B) is incorrect because the demarking point of the ischiopubic index was more useful in sex determination assigning sex to 69% males and 81% females.

Option (C) is incorrect as the Duke University Religion Index (DUREL) is a five-item measure of religious involvement, and was developed for use in large cross-sectional and longitudinal observational studies.

Hence, the correct option is (D).

125. Option (C) is correct as in case of CO poisoning, post mortem staining is cherry red colour.

Option (A) is incorrect as in the case nitrate or nitrobenzene poisoning, post mortem staining is reddish brown.

Option (B) is incorrect as in case of HCN poisoning, post mortem staining is bright red colour.

Option (D) is incorrect as in case of copper sulfate poisoning, post mortem staining is blue colour.

Hence, the correct option is (C).

126. The positive and negative predictive values (PPV and NPV respectively) of a screening test depend on:

– Sensitivity

– Specificity

– Prevalence of disease in the population

Option (C) is correct as NPV is inversely proportional to the Prevalence of disease in a population. As the prevalence of disease increases in a population, NPV decreases for the screening test. Therefore, since the prevalence of an infectious disease in a community has been reduced by 90%, its PPV will reduce and its NPV will increase.

Option (A) is incorrect since a physician continues to use the same diagnostic test for the disease that she has always used, sensitivity and specificity of the test will remain the same.

Option (B) is incorrect as the predictive value of a test (PPV and NPV) depends on the prevalence of a disease in a population. PPV is directly proportional to the prevalence of the disease in the population. As the prevalence of disease increases in a population, PPV increases for the screening test. But the prevalence of the disease has been reduced, so PPV will also reduce.

Option (D) is incorrect as NPV is increasing and PPV is decreasing depending on the prevalence of a disease.

Hence, the correct option is (C).

127. Hidden hunger is a lack of vitamins and minerals. Hidden hunger occurs when the quality of food people eat does not meet their nutrient requirements, so the food is deficient in micronutrients such as the vitamins and minerals that they need for their growth and development. Thus, hidden hunger is micronutrient deficiency.

Hence, the correct option is (C).

128. Under NPCDCS (National Programme for Prevention and Control of Cancer, Diabetes, Cardiovascular diseases and Stroke), NCD Cells are being established at National, State and District levels for programme management, and NCD Clinics are being set up at District and CHC levels, to provide services for early diagnosis, treatment and follow-up for common NCDs.

Hence, the correct option is (D).

129. Kyasanur Forest disease virus is transmitted by the bite of the tick Haemaphysalis spinigera, a tick often found at the forest margins. Rodents, bats and shrews as well as monkeys are also susceptible to the virus. It is a tick-borne viral haemorrhagic fever endemic to South-western part of India. Thus, Kyasanur forest disease is transmitted by hard tick.

Hence, the correct option is (C).

130. Option (C) is correct as:

SAR of some important infectious diseases

- Measles → 80%
- Rubella → 90 - 95%
- Chickenpox → 90%
- Pertussis → 90%
- Mumps → 86%

Individuals at risk for measles include children too young to be vaccinated, those who have not been vaccinated for medical or other reasons, those who have not received a second dose of measles vaccine, and those for whom the vaccine failed to elicit a protective immune response (a very small fraction of those immunized with two doses of vaccine).

Option (A) is incorrect because measles virus can live for up to two hours on a surface or in an airspace where the infected person coughed or sneezed. The CDC states, If other people breathe the contaminated air or touch the infected surface, then touch their eyes, noses, or mouths, they can become infected.

Option (B) is incorrect because measles transmission is airborne by respiratory droplet nuclei spread or by direct contact with infected nasal or throat secretions. The transmission has been reported to people whose only apparent source of infection was a room previously occupied by a patient with measles.

Option (D) is incorrect as unvaccinated males and females are equally susceptible to infection by the measles virus.

Hence, the correct option is (C).

131. Medical termination of pregnancy (MTP) or medical abortion is the use of abortion pills for terminating a pregnancy. The MTP Act allows for termination of pregnancy up to 20 weeks of pregnancy. In case termination of pregnancy is immediately necessary to save the life of the woman, this limit does not apply.

Hence, the correct option is (D).

132. Option (C) is correct as primordial prevention aims at preventing the emergence of risk factors. This is primary prevention in its purest sense, that is, prevention of emergence or developments of risk factors in countries or population groups in which they have not yet appeared.

Option (A) is incorrect because food for patients with high blood pressure and CVDs are salt-free or salt-reduced. Patients with NCDs are advised to reduce their salt intake to the WHO recommended level of <5 g/day.

Option (B) is incorrect as premature mortality due to NCDs in young age is high in the region with 34% of the deaths due to NCDs occurring below the age of 60 years, and 48% below the age of 70 years.

Option (D) is incorrect if a diagnosis is made early on in the course of the disease, the patient and supportive others are given the opportunity to educate themselves about the condition. In turn, they are able to make informed choices and plan effectively for the future.

Hence, the correct option is (C).

133. Option (A) is correct because primary prevention includes:

- Immunization (vaccination)
- Chemoprophylaxis
- Nutritional supplementation programmes
- Chlorination of water
- Using a mosquito net
- Health education

Option (B) is incorrect as secondary prevention includes:

- Screening test
- Case finding programmes
- Early diagnosis and treatment

Option (C) is incorrect as tertiary prevention including rehabilitation uses:

- Establishing schools for blinds
- Provision of aids for crippled
- Reconstructive surgery in leprosy
- Muscle re-education and graded exercise in a neurological disorder like polio
- Changing profession for a more suitable one

Option (D) is incorrect as disability limitation includes resting the affected limb in a neutral position in PRPP to prevent deformity.

Hence, the correct option is (A).

134. Option (D) is correct as:

- Survival rate is the proportion of survivors in a group (e.g. of patients) studied and followed over a period of time.
- It is a method of describing prognosis in certain disease conditions.
- Survival experience can used as a yardstick for the assessment of standard of therapy.
- Survival rates have received special attention in cancer studies.

5 years of survival rate = Total no. of patients alive after 5 years/Total no. of patients diagnosed or treated x 100

Option (A) is incorrect because specific death rate is the number of deaths from a specified cause per 100,000 person-years at risk. The numerator is typically restricted to resident deaths in a specific geographic area (country, state, county, etc).

Option (B) is incorrect because case fatality rate is calculated by dividing the number of deaths from a specified disease over a defined period of time by the number of individuals diagnosed with the disease during that time; the resulting ratio is then multiplied by 100 to yield a percentage.

Option (C) is incorrect as proportionate mortality describes the proportion of deaths in a specified population over a period of time attributable to different causes. Each cause is expressed as a percentage of all deaths, and the sum of the causes must add to 100%.

Hence, the correct option is (D).

135. Option (D) is correct as obesity is a modifiable risk factor. Excess dietary salt, low dietary potassium, overweight and obesity, physical inactivity, excess alcohol, smoking, socioeconomic status, psychosocial stressors, and diabetes are considered modifiable risk factors for hypertension.

Option (A) is incorrect as ethnic background family history of heart disease is a non-modifiable risk factor.

Option (B) is incorrect because the older you are, the more likely you are to develop coronary heart disease or to have a cardiac event (angina, heart attack or stroke).

Option (C) is incorrect as sex is considered an untreatable and non-modifiable risk factor.

Hence, the correct option is (D).

136. Option (B) is correct as high risk screening is most economical and best screening. High risk screening is applied selectively to the high-risk group, i.e., the group which has increased risk of developing certain disease/cancer. For example screening of lung cancer in heavy smokers. It is the most productive screening because the screening is done on the concerned group (high risk), so there is the proper utilization of resources.

Option (A) is incorrect as mass screening means the screening of a whole population or subgroup. It is offered to all, irrespective of the particular risk individual may run of contracting the disease in question. So, it is not a very useful preventive measure and is not the most economical and best screening.

Option (C) is incorrect as multiphasic screening has defined the application of two or more screening test in combination to a large number of people at one time than to carry out separate screening tests for a single disease. It increases the cost of health services without any observable benefit.

Option (D) is incorrect as the most economical and best screening is high-risk screening.

Hence, the correct option is (B).

137. Body mass index (BMI) is a measure of body fat based on height and weight that applies to adult men and women. It is a person's weight in kilograms divided by the square of his/her height in meters.

Hence, the correct option is (A).

138. Option (B) is correct as rapid sand filter is process of water purification on large scale. The rapid sand filter or rapid gravity filter is a type of filter used in water purification and is commonly used in municipal drinking water facilities as part of a multiple-stage treatment system.

Option (A) is incorrect as disinfection of well is a process of water purification on a small scale.

Option (C) is incorrect as household purification is process of water purification on small scale. The most promising and accessible of technologies for household water treatment are filtration with ceramic filters, chlorination with storage in an improvised vessel, solar disinfection in clear bottles by the combined action of UV radiation and heat, etc.

Option (D) is incorrect as a rapid sand filter is the filtration method of water purification on a large scale.

Hence, the correct option is (B).

139. The UNDP classifies each country into one of three development groups: Low human development for HDI scores between 0.0 and 0.5, Medium human development for HDI scores between 0.5 and 0.8. High human development for HDI scores between 0.8 and 1.0. Thus, human development index value ranges between 0 to 1.

Hence, the correct option is (C).

140. Option (A) is correct as an imbecile person whose mental age is less than chronological age. The term imbecile denotes a category of people with moderate to severe intellectual disability.

- IQ of this child = 4/10 x 100 = 40.
- An imbecile child has an IQ between 25-49.

Option (B) is incorrect because an idiot child has an IQ between 0 to 25.

Option (C) is incorrect because the average or normal, range of IQ is 90 to 110.

Option (D) is incorrect because a genius child has an IQ between 140 to 160.

Hence, the correct option is (A).

141. Option (C) is correct as predictive value reflects the diagnostic power of the test. The predictive value refers to the likelihood for determining an outbreak or non-outbreak of an infectious disease based on early warning results. Predictive values can be classified into the predictive value for a positive test (PVP) and the predictive value for a negative test (PVN).

Option (A) is incorrect as sensitivity defines how good a test is at correctly identifying subjects who have the disease.

Option (B) is incorrect as specificity defines how good the test is at correctly identifying subjects without the disease.

Option (D) is incorrect as population attributable risk (PAR) is the proportion of the incidence of disease in the population (exposed and unexposed) that is due to exposure.

Hence, the correct option is (C).

142. Option (A) is correct as ergonomics simply means fitting the job to the worker. The object of ergonomics is to achieve the best mutual adjustment of man and his work, for the improvement of human efficiency and well being.

Option (B) is incorrect because human behaviour is studied by the social sciences, which include psychology, sociology, economics, and anthropology. Behaviour changes throughout an individual's life, as they move through different stages of life. For example, adolescence, parenthood and retirement. Human behaviour is shaped by psychological traits.

Option (C) is incorrect as social mobility is the movement of individuals, families, households, or other categories of people within or between social strata in a society. It is a change in social status relative to one's current social location within a given society.

Option (D) is incorrect as ergonomics is related to adjusting the worker to his job.

Hence, the correct option is (A).

143. Option (D) is correct because when products containing mercury are placed in the trash, the mercury doesn't disappear, it finds its way into the environment. That's why mercury-containing products cannot be disposed of with regular trash or poured down the drain. Mercury products and compounds must be recycled or managed as hazardous waste.

Option (A) is incorrect as controlled combustion is not used for disposal of mercury. Controlled combustion, which occurs at conditions of high preheat and low O_2 concentration, is the result of chemical processes which are fundamentally different from conventional combustion processes.

Option (B) is incorrect as all private healthcare facilities are treating their biomedical waste by deep burial method.

Option (C) is incorrect as chemical treatment (of hazardous waste) refers to the treatment methods that are used to effect the complete breakdown of hazardous waste into non-toxic gases or, more frequently, to modify the chemical properties of the waste, for example, through reduction of water solubility or neutralisation of acidity or alkalinity.

Hence, the correct option is (D).

144. Option (C) is correct as:

- A network analysis is a graphic of all events and activities to be completed in order to reach an end objective.
- It brings greater discipline in planning.
- The two common types of network technique are :

1. Programme Evaluation and Review technique (PERT)
2. Critical Path Method (CPM)

Option (A) is incorrect because Cost-effectiveness analysis (CEA) is a form of economic analysis that compares the relative costs and outcomes (effects) of different courses of action.

Option (B) is incorrect because Cost-benefit analysis (CBA), sometimes also called benefit-cost analysis or benefit costs analysis, is a systematic approach to estimating the strengths and weaknesses of alternatives used to determine options which provide the best approach to achieving benefits while preserving savings (for example, in transactions, activities, and functional business requirements).

Option (D) is incorrect as Input-output analysis ("I-O") is a form of macroeconomic analysis based on the interdependencies between economic sectors or industries. This method is commonly used for estimating the impacts of positive or negative economic shocks and analyzing the ripple effects throughout an economy.

Hence, the correct option is (C).

145. Option (C) is correct as tertiary level is provided by -

- These services are usually established in the national or regional capitals and often associated with
- Medical Colleges and
- Institutes of medicine

It involves sophisticated eye care such as -

- Retinal detachment surgery
- Corneal grafting and
- Other complex forms of management

Option (A) is incorrect as primary level is provided by -

- Locally trained primary health care workers e.g.
- Village-health guides
- Multipurpose workers
- The workers are also trained to refer difficult cases to the nearest PIFIC or district hospital.

Primary care involves treatment and prevention of following eye conditions-

- Acute conjunctivitis
- Ophthalmia neonatorum
- Trachoma
- Superficial foreign bodies
- Xerophthalmia

Option (B) is incorrect as secondary level is provided by -

- Primary Health Care Centers and
- District hospitals.

Secondary care involves definitive management of common blinding conditions such as -

- Cataract
- Trichiasis
- Entropion
- Ocular trauma
- Glaucoma
- The secondary care may also involve the use of mobile eye clinics for instance cataract eye camps.

Option (D) is incorrect as Under the National Programme for Control of Blindness in India, medical colleges are classified as eye care centres of tertiary level.

Hence, the correct option is (C).

146. Option (A) is correct as in panel discussion 4-8 qualified people talk about a topic and discuss a given problem in the presence of an audience.

Option (B) is incorrect because a chalk talk is an illustrated performance in which the speaker draws pictures to emphasize lecture points and create a memorable and entertaining experience for listeners. Chalk talks differ from other types of illustrated talks in their use of real-time illustration rather than static images.

Option (C) is incorrect as group discussion refers to a communicative situation that allows its participants to share their views and opinions with other participants. It is a systematic exchange of information, views and opinions about a topic, problem, issue or situation among the members of a group who share some common objectives.

Option (D) is incorrect as workshop is a series of meetings usually four or more with emphasis on individual work, within a group with the help of consultants and resource personnel.

Hence, the correct option is (A).

147. Option (C) is correct as Herpes zoster does not come under Integrated Disease Surveillance Project. Herpes zoster is a viral infection that occurs with reactivation of the varicella-zoster virus. It is usually a painful but self-limited dermatomal rash. Symptoms typically start with pain along the affected dermatome, which is followed in 2-3 days by a vesicular eruption.

Option (A) is incorrect as tuberculosis come under the Integrated Disease Surveillance Project.

Option (B) is incorrect as meningoencephalitis is one of the diseases that come under the Integrated Disease Surveillance Project.

Option (D) is incorrect as cholera also comes under the Integrated Disease Surveillance Project.

Hence, the correct option is (C).

148. Option (C) is correct as the National AIDS Control Programme is a government health organization of Tanzania. It was founded in 1986 and it operates under the purview of the country's Ministry of Health. The NACP is a policy-making board, on the issue of HIV and AIDS in Tanzania.

Option (A) is incorrect as the Revised National Tuberculosis Control Programme was launched from April 1977.

Option (B) is incorrect as the Narcotic Drugs and Psychotropic Substances Act, 1985, commonly referred to as the NDPS Act, is an Act of the Parliament of India that prohibits a person the production/manufacturing/cultivation, possession, sale, purchasing, transport, storage, and/or consumption of any narcotic drug or psychotropic substance. It was published on 23 August 1985 and commenced on 14 November 1985.

Option (D) is incorrect as the ARI Control Programme was started in India in 1990. It sought to introduce scientific protocols for case management of pneumonia with co-trimoxazole. Initially, 14 pilot districts were selected and later on, new districts were included.

Hence, the correct option is (C).

149. Option (B) is correct because an epidemic is defined as the occurrence of an illness or health-related event that is unusually large or unexpected. Epidemics are commonly caused by a disease of infectious or parasitic origin.

Option (A) is incorrect as in epidemiology, an infection is said to be endemic in a population when that infection is constantly maintained at a baseline level in a geographic area without external inputs. For example, chickenpox is endemic in the United Kingdom, but malaria is not.

Option (C) is incorrect because a pandemic is a disease outbreak that spreads across countries or continents. It affects more people and takes more lives than an epidemic.

Option (D) is incorrect as an infection is the invasion of an organism's body tissues by disease-causing agents, their multiplication, and the reaction of host tissues to the infectious agents and the toxins they produce.

Hence, the correct option is (B).

150. Option (C) is correct as attributable risk is a measure of the proportion of the disease occurrence that can be attributed to a certain exposure. It is a measure of the prevalence of a condition or disease.

Option (A) is incorrect as the relative risk (RR) or risk ratio is the ratio of the probability of an outcome in an exposed group to the probability of an outcome in an unexposed group.

Option (B) is incorrect as an odds ratio (OR) is a measure of association between an exposure and an outcome. The OR represents the odds that an outcome will occur given a particular exposure, compared to the odds of the outcome occurring in the absence of that exposure.

Option (D) is incorrect as potential risk means the potential for harm to public health and welfare and the environment posed by a vessel as calculated through vessel screening.

Hence, the correct option is (C).

151. Option (C) is correct as syphilis is a bacterial infection usually spread by sexual contact. The disease starts as a painless sore — typically on your genitals, rectum or mouth. Syphilis spreads from person to person via skin or mucous membrane contact with these sores.

Hypopigmentation is caused by a lack of melanin, the pigment-producing protein that gives our hair, skin and eyes color. Often, hypopigmentation is the result of skin inflammation or trauma caused by pimples, cuts, lesions, and scrapes.

Option (A) is incorrect because leprosy is a cause of hypopigmentation and it occurs due to defective transfer of melanin into keratinocytes.

Option (B) is incorrect because pinta is a rare infectious tropical disease affecting the skin that is caused by the bacterium Treponema carateum, which is transmitted by direct, nonsexual contact. Treponemas caused several infectious diseases including pinta, hypopigmentation, yaws, and syphilis.

Option (D) is incorrect because hypopigmentation in extensive pityriasis alba may be primarily caused by the reduced numbers of active melanocytes and the decrease in the number and size of melanosomes in the affected skin.

Hence, the correct option is (C).

152. Option (C) is correct as Acanthosis nigricans has the most common association is with obesity. Obesity associated acanthosis nigricans may be a marker for higher insulin needs in obese women with gestational diabetes. Acanthosis nigricans has been shown to be a reliable early marker for metabolic syndrome in pediatric patients.

Option (A)is incorrect as hypertension (HTN or HT), also known as high blood pressure (HBP), is a long-term medical condition in which the blood pressure in the arteries is persistently elevated. High blood pressure typically does not cause symptoms.

Option (B)is incorrect as in obese patients, the presence of acanthosis nigricans is an indicator of insulin resistance or diabetes mellitus (DM).

Option (D) is incorrect as hypothyroidism, also called underactive thyroid or low thyroid, is a disorder of the endocrine system in which the thyroid gland does not produce enough thyroid hormone. It can cause a number of symptoms, such as poor ability to tolerate cold, a feeling of tiredness, constipation, depression, and weight gain.

Hence, the correct option is (C).

153. Glial cells are the most abundant cells in the nervous system, as the nervous system is primarily made up of two types of cells, Neurons & Glial cells.

1. Neurons: These are the structural and functional units of the nervous system. Neurons are microscopic structures

that perform the function of conduction of electrical impulses carrying information.

2. Glial cells: These are also called neuroglia cells. They are majorly found in the brain and the spinal cord. They do not conduct electrical impulses.

Their primary function is to provide support to the neurons. About 50% of the total brain cells are neuroglial cells. There are different types of neuroglial cells present in the CNS & PNS respectively.

Hence, the correct option is (D).

154. Caterpillar bodies are eosinophilic, elongated, segmented bodies located within the roofs of blisters and are considered to represent a specific histopathologic feature of porphyric bullous eruptions, including porphyria cutanea tarda and erythropoietic protoporphyria.

Hence, the correct option is (C).

155. Option (B) is correct as Tinea capitis is caused by fungi of species of genera Trichophyton and Microsporum. Tinea capitis is the most common pediatric dermatophyte infection worldwide. Microsporum is a genus of fungi that causes tinea capitis, tinea corporis, ringworm, and other dermatophytoses (fungal infections of the skin).

Option (A) is incorrect as Trichoderma is a genus of fungi in the family Hypocreaceae, that is present in all soils, where they are the most prevalent culturable fungi. Many species in this genus can be characterized as opportunistic avirulent plant symbionts.

Option (C) is incorrect as Epidermophyton is a genus of fungus causing superficial and cutaneous mycoses, including E. floccosum, and causes tinea corporis (ringworm), tinea cruris (jock itch), tinea pedis (athlete's foot), and tinea unguium (fungal infection of the nail bed).

Option (D) is incorrect as Candida albicans is the most prevalent cause of fungal infections in people. Its species name, albicans, comes from the Latin word for "white." The yeast appears white when cultured on a plate. And in the case of certain infections, like thrush, it can create white patches.

Hence, the correct option is (B).

156. Option (B) is correct because Drugs causing exanthematic reactions

Most common: - Ampicillin and penicillin, Phenylbutazone and other pyrazolones, Sulphonamides, Phenytoin,

Carbamazepine, Gold, Gentamicin, Meprobamate, Atropine

Less common: - Cephalosporins, Barbiturates, Thiazides, Naproxen, Isoniazid, Phenothiazines, Quinidine.And it takes place in Hydrocortisone

Option (A) is incorrect as Phenytoin, sold under the brand name Dilantin among others, is an anti-seizure medication. It is useful for the prevention of tonic-clonic seizures and focal seizures, but not absence seizures. The intravenous form is used for status epilepticus that does not improve with benzodiazepines.

Option (C) is incorrect as Ampicillin is a penicillin antibiotic that is used to treat or prevent many different types of infections such as bladder infections, pneumonia, gonorrhoea, meningitis, or infections of the stomach or intestines. Ampicillin may also be used for purposes not listed in this medication guide.

Option (D) is incorrect as Phenylbutazone is a nonsteroidal anti-inflammatory drug (NSAID) effective in treating fever, pain, and inflammation in the body. As a group, NSAIDs are non-narcotic relievers of mild to moderate pain of many causes, including injury, menstrual cramps, arthritis and other musculoskeletal conditions.

Hence, the correct option is (B).

157. Option (D) is correct because muscular tissue consists of muscle fibres, it is not a connective tissue. The human body possesses four types of tissues, namely muscle, epithelial, connective and nervous. Connective tissue is further divided into six types, blood, lymph, bone, cartilage, adipose tissue, tendons and ligaments.

Option (A) is incorrect because blood is considered a connective tissue because it has a matrix. The living cell types are red blood cells, also called erythrocytes, and white blood cells also called leukocytes. Blood Tissue is a connective tissue that has a fluid matrix, called plasma, and no fibres.

Option (B) is incorrect because bone is a connective tissue that has a large amount of two different types of matrix material. The organic matrix is materially similar to other connective tissues, including some amount of collagen and elastic fibres. This gives strength and flexibility to the tissue.

Option (C) is incorrect because cartilage is a form of connective tissue in which the ground substance is abundant and of a firmly gelated consistency that endows this tissue with unusual rigidity and resistance to compression. The cells of cartilage, called chondrocytes, are isolated in small lacunae within the matrix.

Hence, the correct option is (D).

158. Option (B) is correct because the diagnosis of Pityriasis rubra pilaris includes:

Erythematous follicular papules

Involvement of trunk

Thickening of Palm and soles (Palmo-Planter keratoderma)

The most important one is presence of normal skin within the lesions.

Option (A) is incorrect as Pityriasis rosea is a rash that usually begins as a large circular or oval spot on your chest, abdomen or back. Called a herald patch, this spot can be up to 4 inches (10 centimetres) across.

Option (C) is incorrect as Psoriasis is a long-lasting autoimmune disease characterized by patches of abnormal skin. These skin patches are typically red, or purple on some people with darker skin, dry, itchy, and scaly. Psoriasis varies in severity from small, localized patches to complete body coverage.

Option (D) is incorrect as Seborrheic dermatitis is a common skin disease that causes an itchy rash with flaky scales. It causes redness on light skin and light patches on darker skin. It's also called dandruff, cradle cap, seborrhea, seborrheic eczema, and seborrheic psoriasis.

Hence, the correct option is (B).

159. Option (C) is correct As Facial bulla and oral ulcers (mucosal involvement) in a 50 years man suggest the diagnosis of pemphigus vulgaris. The smear from the lesions will show Acantholytic cells also referred to as Tzanck cells, which are separated keratinocytes.

Option (A) is incorrect As Necrosis is the death of body tissue. It occurs when too little blood flows to the tissue. This can be from injury, radiation, or chemicals. Necrosis cannot be reversed. When large areas of tissue die due to a lack of blood supply, the condition is called gangrene.

Option (B) is incorrect As Koilocytes, also known as halo cells, are a type of epithelial cell that develops following a human papillomavirus (HPV) infection. Koilocytes are structurally different from other epithelial cells. For instance, their nuclei, which contain the cell's DNA, are an irregular size, shape, or color.

Option (D) is incorrect because According to the option A which explain the reason for Necrosis but this is not related to the question hence this option is incorrect.

Hence, the correct option is (C).

160. Option (B) is correct as Thalidomide is the drug of choice for treating Erythema nodosum leprosum (ENL), also known as lepra type 2 reaction (Lepra II reaction). Prednisone is added to the treatment when the reactions are difficult to control, or when there are complications, especially neuritis.

Option (A) is incorrect as reversal reaction, or lepra type 1 reaction, is a delayed-type hypersensitivity reaction that arises when borderline leprosy shifts toward borderline lepromatous leprosy with treatment.

Option (C) is incorrect because Lepra I reaction is not correct for this question. Thalidomide is drug of choice for Lepra II reaction, if two courses of glucocorticoids fail.

Option (D) is incorrect Nerve abscesses are infrequently observed complications of tuberculoid and borderline leprosy.

Hence, the correct option is (B).

161. Scabies is a skin infestation caused by a mite known as the Sarcoptes scabiei. Untreated, these microscopic mites can live on your skin for months. They reproduce on the surface of your skin and then burrow into it and lay eggs. This causes an itchy, red rash to form on the skin. Itching occurs due to hypersensitivity to saliva of mite, and it takes 4-6 weeks are required for the hypersensitivity to develop. So, incubation period of scabies is 4-6 weeks.

Hence, the correct option is (C).

162. Option (C) is correct As Giant cell arteritis (GCA) is the most common form of vasculitis that occurs in adults. Almost all patients who develop giant cell arteritis are over the age of 50. GCA commonly causes headaches, joint pain, facial pain, fever, and difficulties with vision, and sometimes a permanent visual loss in one or both eyes.

Option (A) is incorrect because Cryoglobulinemia is a medical condition in which the blood contains large amounts of pathological cold sensitive antibodies called cryoglobulins – proteins (mostly immunoglobulins themselves) that become insoluble at reduced temperatures.

Option (B) is incorrect because H.S. pupura (HSP) is a disease involving inflammation of small blood vessels. It most commonly occurs in children. The inflammation causes blood vessels in the skin, intestines, kidneys, and joints to start leaking. Adults with HSP are more likely to have the more severe disease compared to children.

Option (D) is incorrect As Drug-induced vasculitis is an inflammation of blood vessels caused by the use of various pharmaceutical agents. Vasculitis causes changes in the walls of blood vessels, including thickening, weakening, narrowing and scarring.

Hence, the correct option is (C).

163. Option (D) is correct as flaky paint dermatosis is observed in Kwashiorkor.

(1) Hair changes in Kwashiorkor

- Hair is thin, dry and brittle, easily pluckable.
- Straight and hypopigmented.
- Flag sign (Alternate bands of Hypo and hyperpigmented hair corresponding to the period of under and proper nutrition).

(2) Skin changes in Kwashiorkor

- Large areas of skin show erythema followed by hyperpigmentation.
- Flaky paint dermatosis → Hyperpigmentation patches desquamate to expose raw hypopigmented areas. It gives the appearance of paint flaking off the surface of the wood.

Option (A) is incorrect because Dermatitis is a common condition that has many causes and occurs in many forms. It usually involves itchy, dry skin or a rash on swollen, reddened skin. Or it may cause the skin to blister, ooze, crust or flake off. Examples of this condition are atopic dermatitis (eczema), dandruff and contact dermatitis.

Option (B) is incorrect as Pellagra is a disease caused by low levels of niacin, also known as vitamin B-3. It's marked by dementia, diarrhea, and dermatitis, also known as "the three Ds". If left untreated, pellagra can be fatal.

Option (C) is incorrect as Marasmus is a form of severe malnutrition characterized by energy deficiency. It can occur in anyone with severe malnutrition but usually occurs in children. Body weight is reduced to less than 62% of the normal (expected) body weight for the age.

Hence, the correct option is (D).

164. Option (B) is correct because diabetes, hypertension and vascular disease are major risk factors where isolated nuclear oculomotor palsy is rare. In this region, isolated third-nerve palsy is very common. The primary causes of isolated palsy include aneurysms, diabetes mellitus, and extradural hematoma

Option (A) is incorrect as frontal lobe tumours may cause: behavioural and emotional changes; impaired judgment, motivation or inhibition; an impaired sense of smell or vision loss; paralysis on one side of the body; reduced mental abilities and memory loss.

Option (C) is incorrect as Weber's syndrome, also known as superior alternating hemiplegia, is a form of stroke characterized by the presence of an ipsilateral oculomotor nerve palsy and contralateral hemiparesis or hemiplegia.

Option (D) is incorrect because lateral medullary syndrome is a neurological disorder causing a range of symptoms due to ischemia in the lateral part of the medulla oblongata in the brainstem. The lateral medullary syndrome is also called Wallenberg's syndrome, posterior inferior cerebellar artery (PICA) syndrome and vertebral artery syndrome.

Hence, the correct option is (B).

165. Option (C) is correct because Locus heterogeneity refers to the situation in which a similar disease phenotype results from mutations at different genetic loci. For example: Osteogenesis imperfecta, Albinism, Muscular dystrophy syndromes (dystrophin, most common cause of mus dystrophy and has large gene size).

Option (A) is incorrect as Familial adenomatous polyposis (FAP) is an autosomal dominant inherited condition in which numerous adenomatous polyps form mainly in the epithelium of the large intestine. While these polyps start out benign, malignant transformation into colon cancer occurs when they are left untreated.

Option (B) is incorrect as Turcot syndrome is characterized by the formation of multiple benign growths (polyps) in the colon that occur in association with a primary brain tumor. These growths are associated with bleeding from the rectum, diarrhea, constipation, abdominal pain, and/or weight loss.

Option (D) is incorrect as option C is correct, so not all options are correct.

Hence, the correct option is (C).

166. Option (B) is correct as anterior cardiac veins drain directly into the right atrium, through its anterior wall. Thus, anterior cardiac vein does not drain into coronary sinus.

Option (A) is incorrect because the middle cardiac vein or posterior interventricular vein is a vein of the heart which accompanies the posterior interventricular artery. It courses in the posterior interventricular groove and drains directly into the coronary sinus close to its termination.

Option (C) is incorrect because the oblique vein of the left atrium (oblique vein of Marshall) is a small vessel which descends obliquely on the back of the left atrium and ends in the coronary sinus near its left extremity; it is continuous above with the ligament of the left vena cava.

Option (D) is incorrect because the small cardiac vein is a vein of the heart which accompanies the acute marginal artery from the RCA. It courses in the right posterior atrioventricular groove and drains into the coronary sinus close to its termination but may drain directly into the right atrium. It drains the right ventricle.

Hence, the correct option is (B).

167. Vaginal atresia in combination with an abnormal absent uterus is called Mayer–Rokitansky–Kuster–Hauser syndrome. Vaginal agenesis is a rare disorder that occurs when the vagina doesn't develop, and the womb (uterus) may only develop partially or not at all. This condition is present before birth, and may also be associated with kidney, heart or skeletal abnormalities.

Hence, the correct option is (C).

168. Option (A) is correct because Duroziez's sign is a sign of aortic regurgitation. It consists of an audible diastolic murmur which can be heard over the femoral artery when it is compressed with the bell of a stethoscope. It is named for Paul Louis Duroziez.

Option (B) is incorrect as aortic stenosis is one of the most common and most serious valve disease problems. Aortic stenosis is a narrowing of the aortic valve opening. Aortic stenosis restricts the blood flow from the left ventricle to the aorta and may also affect the pressure in the left atrium.

Option (C) is incorrect as mitral stenosis is a narrowing of the mitral valve opening that blocks (obstructs) blood flow from the left atrium to the left ventricle. Mitral stenosis usually results from rheumatic fever, but infants can be born with the condition. Mitral stenosis does not cause symptoms unless it is severe.

Option (D) is incorrect as mitral regurgitation (MR) is defined as an abnormal reversal of blood flow from the left ventricle (LV) to the left atrium (LA). It is caused by a disruption in any part of the mitral valve (MV) apparatus.

Hence, the correct option is (A).

169. Option (B) is correct because the most common cause of pulmonary thromboembolism is deep vein thrombosis (DVT). Deep vein thrombosis (DVT) is a serious condition that occurs when a blood clot forms in a vein located deep inside your body. In most cases, pulmonary thrombosis is caused by blood clots that travel to the lungs from deep veins in the legs or, rarely, from veins in other parts of the body (deep vein thrombosis).

Option (A) is incorrect as disseminated intravascular coagulation (DIC) is a serious disorder in which the proteins that control blood clotting become overactive.

Option (C) is incorrect as coagulopathy (also called a bleeding disorder) is a condition in which the blood's ability to coagulate (form clots) is impaired. This condition can cause a tendency toward prolonged or excessive bleeding (bleeding diathesis), which may occur spontaneously or following an injury or medical and dental procedures.

Option (D) is incorrect as high pressure in the veins of the legs is called chronic venous hypertension. Chronic venous hypertension may be due to venous insufficiency, a condition where the blood leaks downward due to the effect of gravity through leaky one-way valves.
Hence, the correct option is (B).

170. Option (C) is correct as the change in serum potassium affects the repolarisation part of the action potential. Hyperkalemia leads to a flattening of the angle of this part of the action potential which can lead to a slower heart rate.

Option (A) is incorrect As Calcium gluconate is the calcium salt of gluconic acid, an intravenous medication used to treat conditions arising from calcium deficiencies such as hypocalcemic tetany, hypocalcemia related to hypoparathyrodism, and hypocalcemia due to rapid growth or pregnancy.

Option (B) is incorrect because Steroids are a man-made version of chemicals, known as hormones, that are made naturally in the human body. Steroids are designed to act like these hormones to reduce inflammation. They're also known as corticosteroids, and are different to anabolic steroids used by bodybuilders and athletes.

Option (D) is incorrect As Two important characteristics of K-Resin SBC are its crystal clarity and exceptional shatter resistance. In addition to this excellent clarity and impact strength, K-Resin SBC is easy to process, provides for design versatility, has the thermal stability required to permit recycling of scrap, and has the necessary physical properties for a broad spectrum of applications. Hence, the correct option is (C).

171. Option (B) is correct because a lower-than-normal ferritin level can indicate that you have an iron deficiency, which can happen when you don't consume enough iron in your daily diet. Another condition that affects iron levels is anemia, which is when you don't have enough red blood cells for iron to attach to.

Option (A) is incorrect as abnormally low iron levels may mean you haven't consumed enough iron or your body isn't absorbing the iron properly. Regularly having heavy menstrual periods can also lead to low iron levels. Low iron levels may indicate anemia.

Option (C) is incorrect as a total iron binding capacity value above 450 mcg/dL usually means that there's a low level of iron in your blood. This may be caused by a lack of iron in the diet, increased blood loss during menstruation, pregnancy, or a chronic infection.

Option (D) is incorrect because Iron is needed to form hemoglobin, part of red blood cells that carry oxygen and remove carbon dioxide (a waste product) from the body. Iron is mostly stored in the body in the hemoglobin. About one-third of iron is also stored as ferritin and hemosiderin in the bone marrow, spleen, and liver.

Hence, the correct option is (B).

172. Option (D) is correct because Chronic lymphocytic leukemia (CLL) is the most common of the known causes of autoimmune hemolytic anemia (AIHA). The clinical course of patients with B-cell chronic lymphocytic leukemia (CLL) is often made complicated by autoimmune phenomena which mainly target the blood cells. Among them, autoimmune hemolytic anemia (AIHA) is the most common form.

Option (A) is incorrect as Acute lymphoblastic leukemia (ALL) is a fast-growing cancer of a type of white blood cell called a lymphoblast. All occurs when the bone marrow produces a large number of immature lymphoblasts. All prevents healthy blood cells from being made.

Option (B) is incorrect as Acute myeloid leukemia (AML) is cancer that starts inside bone marrow. This is the soft tissue in the center of bones that helps form all blood cells. The cancer grows from cells that would normally turn into white blood cells. Acute means the disease grows quickly and usually has an aggressive course.

Option (C) is incorrect as clinical manifestations of immediate hypersensitivity (CMIL) diseases are caused by the release of proinflammatory mediators (histamine, leukotrienes, and prostaglandins) from immunoglobulin E (IgE) sensitized effector cells (mast cells and basophils) when cell-bound IgE antibodies interact with allergen.

Hence, the correct option is (D).

173. Option (D) is correct because Statements 'a''b' explains

- Hallucinations are not under voluntary control of observer .
- Hallucinations are perceived as being in external objective space (not in inner subjective space).
- Hence this is not true about Hallucinations ,so this option is correct .

Option (A) is incorrect because Hallucinations are not under voluntary control of observer. hence statement 'a' is not correct in the case of Hallucinations.

Option (B) is incorrect because Hallucinations are not under voluntary control of observer. hence this option is also not correct.

Option (C) is incorrect for the statement 'd'Hallucinations occurs in absence of perceptual stimulus it is true hence according to the question this option will not be correct.

Hence, the correct option is (D).

174. Option (B) is correct because Multiple sclerosis (MS) is a potentially disabling disease of the brain and spinal cord (central nervous system). In MS, the immune system attacks the protective sheath (myelin) that covers nerve fibers and causes communication problems between your brain and the rest of your body.

Option (A) is incorrect as Alzheimer's disease is a progressive disorder that causes brain cells to waste away (degenerate) and die. Alzheimer's disease is the most common cause of dementia — a continuous decline in thinking, behavioral, and social skills that disrupts a person's ability to function independently.

Option (C) is incorrect because Creutzfeldt–Jakob disease (CJD), also known as classic Creutzfeldt–Jakob disease, is a fatal degenerative brain disorder. Early symptoms include memory problems, behavioral changes, poor coordination, and visual disturbances.

Option (D) is incorrect as Pick's disease is a kind of dementia similar to Alzheimer's but far less common. It affects parts of the brain that control emotions, behavior, personality, and language. It's also a type of disorder known as frontotemporal dementia (FTD) or frontotemporal lobar degeneration (FTLD).

Hence, the correct option is (B).

175. Option (B) is correct as diarrhoea, rhinorrhea, sweating, and lacrimation are symptoms of opioid withdrawal (Heroin/morphine withdrawal).

Option (A) is incorrect as cocaine withdrawal occurs when someone who has used a lot of cocaine cuts down or quits taking the drug. Symptoms of withdrawal can occur even if the user is not completely off cocaine and still has some of the drugs in their blood.

Option (C) is incorrect as if you drink alcohol heavily for weeks, months, or years, you may have both mental and physical problems when you stop or seriously cut back on how much you drink. This is called alcohol withdrawal.

Option (D) is incorrect as LSD is not an addictive drug and therefore does not negate physical withdrawal symptoms. It is a mental detox that requires counseling and careful observance. LSD withdrawal symptoms are uncommon, though psychological side effects have been reported following long-term use.

Hence, the correct option is (B).

176. Option (C) is correct as Naltrexone is a pure opioid antagonist. It is a competitive antagonist at all opioid receptors. It can be used orally, to assist in the rehabilitation of ex-opioid abusers who are fully withdrawn (otherwise it will induce an acute withdrawal syndrome). A patient who then takes an opioid fails to experience the kick or euphoria because of the opioid antagonistic actions of the Naltrexone.

Option (A) is incorrect as Opioid-induced respiratory depression occurs both in the acute and chronic treatment settings. Opioid-induced respiratory depression is caused by the activation of μ-opioid receptors expressed on the surface of neurons in brainstem respiratory centres. hence respiratory depression can not be prevented.

Option (B) is incorrect as Naltrexone has been used to treat opioid dependence for many years with naltrexone not begin until signs and symptoms of acute alcohol withdrawal.

Option (D) is incorrect as Naltrexone is an opioid-receptor antagonist that blocks the euphoric effects of opioids. Unlike other treatments for opioid use disorder, including buprenorphine/naloxone and methadone, naltrexone is not associated with the development of tolerance and dependence, and lacks the potential for misuse and diversion.

Hence, the correct option is (C).

177. Deep sleep induces the greatest daily peak in the secretion of growth hormone. Synthesis and secretion of growth hormone by the anterior pituitary are regulated by a variety of metabolic factors, many of which act to alter the balance between release of growth hormone—releasing hormone (GHRH) and somatostatin (SS) from the hypothalamus. Insulin-induced hypoglycemia is a major stimulus for release of growth hormone. Amino acids are also potent stimuli for release of growth hormone, whereas fatty acids are inhibitory.

Hence, the correct option is (B).

178. Option (C) is correct because one of the first to classify mental disorders into different categories was the German physician, Emile Kraepelin. Dr. Kraepelin used the term "dementia praecox" for individuals who had symptoms that we now associate with schizophrenia.

Option (A) is incorrect as the psychoanalytic movement originated in the clinical observations and formulations of Austrian psychiatrist Sigmund Freud, who coined the term psychoanalysis. During the 1890s, Freud worked with Austrian physician and physiologist Josef Breuer in studies of neurotic patients under hypnosis. Freud and Breuer observed that when the sources of patients' ideas and impulses.

Option (B) is incorrect because, in 1908, Bleuler coined the term schizophrenia to describe a group of diseases that cause changes in thought processes and behaviour in humans as well as difficulties relating to the world.

Option (C) is correct because one of the first to classify mental disorders into different categories was the German physician, Emile Kraepelin. Dr. Kraepelin used the term "dementia praecox" for individuals who had symptoms that we now associate with schizophrenia.

Option (D) is incorrect because Schneider coined the term endogenous depression, derived from Emil Kraepelin's use of the adjective to mean biological in origin, and reactive depression, more usually seen in outpatients, in 1920.

Hence, the correct option is (C).

179. Option (B) is correct as Psychotic features (delusions, hallucination) can occur in endogenous depression (not in reactive/neurotic depression) and occurs later in life (involutional depression).

Major endogenous depression on top of dysthymia is called double depression → Psychotic features may occur.

Option (A) is incorrect as Nihilistic delusions are seen in the process a, b both like Psychotic features (delusions, hallucination) can occur in endogenous depression. Major endogenous depression on top of dysthymia is called double depression → Psychotic features may occur.

Option (C) is incorrect as Cyclothymia, also known as a cyclothymic disorder, is a mental disorder that involves numerous periods of symptoms of depression and periods of symptoms of hypomania. These symptoms, however, are not sufficient to be a major depressive episode or a hypomanic episode. Hence here in this option from the explanation of statement d it is clear that it will not be the correct option.

Option (D) is incorrect as Persistent depressive disorder also called dysthymia (dis-THIE-me-uh), is a continuous long-term (chronic) form of depression. Though the persistent depressive disorder is not as severe as major depression, your current depressed mood may be mild, moderate or severe.

Hence, the correct option is (B).

180. Option (B) is correct because Nihilistic delusion, insomnia and early morning awakening are seen in major depression.

Option (A) is incorrect because an abnormally elevated mood state characterized by such symptoms as inappropriate elation, increased irritability, severe insomnia, grandiose notions, increased speed and/or volume of speech, disconnected and racing thoughts, increased sexual desire, markedly increased energy and activity level, poor judgment, and inappropriate social behavior.

Option (C) is incorrect as a personality disorder is a type of mental disorder in which you have a rigid and unhealthy pattern of thinking, functioning, and behaving. A person with a personality disorder has trouble perceiving and relating to situations and people

Option (D) is incorrect as schizophrenia is a chronic and severe mental disorder that affects how a person thinks, feels, and behaves. People with schizophrenia may seem like they have lost touch with reality. Although schizophrenia is not as common as other mental disorders, the symptoms can be very disabling.

Hence, the correct option is (B).

181. Option (B) is correct because the most studied and most effective treatment for phobias is behavior therapy.

Option (A) is incorrect because psychotherapy (psychological therapy or talking therapy) is the use of psychological methods, particularly when based on regular personal interaction with adults, to help a person change behavior and overcome problems in desired ways.

Option (C) is incorrect because SSRI stands for Selective Serotonin Reuptake Inhibitor. SSRI antidepressants are a type of antidepressant that works by increasing levels of serotonin within the brain. Serotonin is a neurotransmitter that is often referred to as the "feel-good hormone".

Option (D) is incorrect as benzodiazepines possess psycholeptic, sedative, hypnotic, anxiolytic, anticonvulsant, muscle relaxant, and amnesic actions, which are useful in a variety of indications such as alcohol dependence, seizures, anxiety disorders, panic, agitation, and insomnia.

Hence, the correct option is (B).

182. Option (A) is correct Somatic symptom disorder (SSD is formerly known as "somatization disorder" or "somatoform disorder") is a form of mental illness that causes one or more bodily symptoms, including pain. The symptoms can involve one or more different organs and body systems, such as pain, neurologic problems, and gastrointestinal complaints. For diagnostic criteria at least 1 sexual symptom should be there (not two).

Option (B) is incorrect because for diagnostic criteria two gastrointestinal symptoms are required other than pain (eg, nausea, bloating, vomiting, or intolerance of several different foods).

Option (C) is incorrect because for diagnostic criteria four different pain are required (eg, head, abdomen, back, joints, extremities, chest, rectum) or painful functions (eg, menstruation, sexual intercourse, urination)

Option (D) is incorrect because, in the latest version of the International Statistical Classification of Diseases and Related Health Problems, somatization syndrome is described as: The main features are multiple, recurrent and frequently changing physical symptoms of at least two years duration.

Hence, the correct option is (A).

183. Option (A) is correct because hallucinations just before falling asleep are called hypnagogic hallucinations.

Option (B) is incorrect because hallucinations just before awakening are called hypnopompic hallucinations.

Option (C) is incorrect because there is not any kind of non-specific hallucinations, only hypnagogic hallucinations and hypnopompic hallucinations are considered normal phenomena. Hypnagogic hallucinations can occur as one is falling asleep and hypnopompic hallucinations occur when one is waking up.

Option (D) is incorrect because jactatio capitis nocturna is an infancy and childhood sleep-related disorder characterized by repetitive movements occurring immediately prior to sleep onset and sustained into light sleep.

Hence, the correct option is (A).

184. Option (A) is correct as one of the important methods to distinguish psychogenic impotence from organic impotence is nocturnal penile tumescence & early morning erection which are preserved in psychogenic impotence but not in the organic cause of impotence.

Option (B) is incorrect as pharmacologically induced penile erection (PIPE) is used as a maintenance treatment for erectile impotence.

Option (C) is incorrect as sildenafil treats erectile dysfunction by increasing blood flow to the penis during sexual stimulation. This increased blood flow can cause an erection. Sildenafil treats pulmonary arterial hypertension (PAH) by relaxing the blood vessels in the lungs to allow blood to flow easily.

Option (D) is incorrect as the stop-squeeze technique is a form of ejaculatory control. It allows you to near the point of climax and then back off suddenly by holding the tip of the penis until the sensation subsides. You can repeat the stop-squeeze several times, or you can do it once.

Hence, the correct option is (A).

185. Option (A) is correct as Bulimia nervosa is characterized by episodes of uncontrollable excessive eating (binge) followed by vigorous weight-reducing measures like self-induced vomiting, purgative abuse, etc.

Option (B) is incorrect as schizophrenia is a chronic and severe mental disorder that affects how a person thinks, feels, and behaves. People with schizophrenia may seem like they have lost touch with reality. Although schizophrenia is not as common as other mental disorders, the symptoms can be very disabling.

Option (C) is incorrect as anorexia nervosa is a serious psychological and eating disorder. The complications can be fatal, but treatment and recovery are possible.

Option (D) is incorrect as binge eating followed by self-induced vomiting or purgative abuse can also be seen in anorexia nervous, but it is not the characteristic feature of anorexia nervosa. The characteristic presenting feature of anorexia nervosa is self-imposed dietary restrictions.

Hence, the correct option is (A).

186. Option (D) is correct because this option includes all other options which all are drugs used in the treatment of ADHD so it will be the correct option.

Option (A) is incorrect because Amphetamines are used to treat adults with ADHD. Amphetamines are drugs, structurally related to catecholamines, it is the most commonly prescribed medications for ADHD. They are often the first course of drugs used for ADHD treatment.

Option (B) is incorrect as Modafinil is a wakefulness-promoting prescription drug that reduces the extreme sleepiness that accompanies sleep disorders including narcolepsy, obstructive sleep apnea, and shift work disorder (SWD). It is sometimes used off-label to treat symptoms of ADHD in adults 18 years of age and older.

Option (C) is incorrect as Methylphenidate is used to treat attention deficit hyperactivity disorder (ADHD). Methylphenidate belongs to a class of drugs known as stimulants. It can help increase your ability to pay attention, stay focused on an activity, and control behavior problems.

Hence, the correct option is (D).

187. Option (C) is correct As Amphetamine activates receptors in the brain and increases the activity of a number of neurotransmitters, especially norepinephrine and dopamine.

Option (A) is incorrect because Imipramine is used in the treatment of depression and certain anxiety disorders. It is similar in efficacy to the antidepressant drug moclobemide. It has also been used to treat nocturnal enuresis because of its ability to shorten the time of delta wave stage sleep, where wetting occurs.

Methylphenidate is a central nervous system stimulant. It affects chemicals in the brain and nerves that contribute to hyperactivity and impulse control. Methylphenidate is used to treat attention deficit disorder (ADD), attention deficit hyperactivity disorder (ADHD), and narcolepsy.

Option (B) is incorrect because Clozapine is an antipsychotic medication. It works by changing the actions of chemicals in the brain. Clozapine is used to treat severe schizophrenia, or to reduce the risk of suicidal behavior in people with schizophrenia or similar disorders.

Option (D) is incorrect because Haldol (haloperidol) is an antipsychotic drug that decreases excitement in the brain. Haldol is used to treat psychotic disorders like schizophrenia, to control motor (movement) and verbal (for example, Tourette's syndrome) tics and is used to treat severe behavior problems in children.

Hence, the correct option is (C).

188. "However, some people may be advised not to return to work, make important decisions, or drive until few weeks to few months after the last ECT in a series, or for at least 24 hours after a single treatment during maintenance therapy. "

Option (B) is correct According to above explanation this option is correct.

Option (A) is incorrect According to above explanation this option is not correct.

Option (C) is incorrect According to above explanation this option is not correct.

Option (D) is incorrect According to above explanation this option is not correct.

Hence, the correct option is (B).

189. Option (C) is correct As the liver is typically enlarged and tender in right heart failure. If the onset is acute, right upper quadrant pain may result from constraint of the swollen liver by its tight capsule. Splenomegaly is uncommon except in prolonged passive congestion of the liver, and pain or tenderness of the spleen should raise the question of superimposed systemic embolization and splenic infarction.

Option (A) is incorrect As Pressure in the jugular venous system, a useful index of right atrial pressure, may be estimated from the height of the column of blood distending the cervical veins. It is increased in RVF.

Option (B) is incorrect because Kidney. Oliguria occurs with decompensation in isolated right or left heart failure but is more prominent in the latter or in biventricular failure. The urine is sodium poor but has a relatively high specific gravity. Prerenal azotemia is common, particularly in the presence of intrinsic renal disease or after vigorous diuresis.. Blood urea nitrogen (BUN) is typically elevated out of proportion to serum creatinine. Proteinuria is common but does not usually exceed 1 gram per day. Nocturia is also seen.

Option (D) is incorrect because the presence of free fluid in the abdominal cavity is a late manifestation of right heart failure, usually associated with systemic venous hypertension, peripheral edema, and hydrothorax.

Hence, the correct option is (C).

190. Option (D) is correct because the Schirmer's test is used to assess the function of facial nerve by testing lacrimation, It determines the ability of eyes to produce enough tears to keep it moist.

Option (A) is incorrect because the optic nerve is the nerve that transmits visual information from the retina to the brain. The optic nerve is composed of retinal ganglion cell axons and support cells.

Option (B) is incorrect because the abducens nerve (or abducens nerve) is the sixth cranial nerve (CNVI), in humans, that controls the movement of the lateral rectus muscle, responsible for outward gaze. It is a somatic efferent nerve.

Option (C) is incorrect because the oculomotor nerve is the third cranial nerve (CN III). It enters the orbit via the superior orbital fissure and innervates extrinsic eye muscles that enable most movements of the eye and that raise the eyelid.

Hence, the correct option is (D).

191. Option (C) is correct as increased urinary metanephrines have the highest diagnostic sensitivity and specificity for pheochromocytoma.

Option (A) is incorrect as carcinoid syndrome is a paraneoplastic syndrome comprising the signs and symptoms that occur secondary to carcinoid tumors. The syndrome includes flushing and diarrhea, and less frequently, heart failure, vomiting and bronchoconstriction. It is caused by endogenous secretion of mainly serotonin and kallikrein.

Option (B) is incorrect as Conn's syndrome is a rare health problem that occurs when the adrenal glands make too much aldosterone. This problem is also known as primary hyperaldosteronism. Aldosterone is a hormone that controls salt and potassium levels in the blood. Too much leads to high blood pressure.

Option (D) is incorrect because hepatocellular carcinoma (HCC) is the most common type of primary liver cancer. Hepatocellular carcinoma occurs most often in people with chronic liver diseases, such as cirrhosis caused by hepatitis B or hepatitis C infection.

Hence, the correct option is (C).

192. Option (D) is correct because Gentamicin, sold under brand name Garamycin among others, is an antibiotic used to treat several types of bacterial infections. This may include bone infections, endocarditis, pelvic inflammatory disease, meningitis, pneumonia, urinary tract infections, and sepsis among others.

Causes of Non Oliguria Renal Failure :

- Ischemic ATN
- Radiocontrast induced RF
- Polymyxin B
- Lithium
- Cisplatin
- Tubulointerstitial disease
- Aminoglycosides

Option (A) is incorrect because Nonsteroidal anti-inflammatory drugs (NSAIDs) are members of a drug class that reduces pain, decreases fever, prevents blood clots, and in higher doses, decreases inflammation.

Option (B) is incorrect because Poststreptococcal glomerulonephritis (PSGN) is a kidney disease that develops 10 to 14 days after a skin or throat infection. The main symptoms are blood in your child's wee and swollen ankles or puffy eyes.

Option (C) is incorrect because Hypovolemia, also known as volume depletion or volume contraction, is a state of decreased intravascular volume. This may be due to either a loss of both salt and water or a decrease in blood volume. Hypovolemia refers to the loss of extracellular fluid and should not be confused with dehydration.

Hence, the correct option is (D).

193. Option (A) is correct because Hypercalcemia is caused by: Overactive parathyroid glands. The most common cause of hypercalcemia, overactive parathyroid glands (hyperparathyroidism) can stem from a small, noncancerous (benign) tumor or enlargement of one or more of the four parathyroid glands, cancer.

Option (B) is incorrect A person with diabetes has high blood sugar levels due to a problem with insulin. Neuropathy that affects the digestive system is diabetic enteropathy. Nerve damage in the gastrointestinal tract can impact the consistency and frequency of bowel movements and lead to diarrhea, constipation, and other problems.

Option (C) is incorrect because Carcinoid Syndrome Diarrhea. Diarrhea occurs in 80% of patients with carcinoid syndrome. The pathophysiology of carcinoid syndrome diarrhea involves the presence of excess serotonin, which stimulates secretion of colonic mucus, increases peristalsis, and inhibits absorption in the GI tract—all of which lead to diarrhea.

Option (D) is incorrect because hyperthyroidism leads to an overactivity of the sympathetic system. It also goes on to mention that this sympathetic hyperstimulation in the gut leads to increased motility leading to diarrhea and malabsorption.

Hence, the correct option is (A).

194. Option (B) is correct As

Oncogenes :

RAS: (signal transducing proteins)

- K RAS: colon , lung, pancreatic tumors
- N RAS: melanoma, AML
- H RAS: Bladder, kidney tumors

ABL

MYC

- C - MYC: Burkitts lymphoma
- N-MYC: Neuroblastoma
- L-MYC: Small cell lung cancer
- WNT 1
- ERB -B2
- FOS
- JUN
- AKTI, AKT2
- BRAF

Option (A) is incorrect Retinoblastoma is an eye cancer that begins in the retina and the sensitive lining on the inside of your eye. Retinoblastoma most commonly affects young children, but can rarely occur in adults.

Option (C) is incorrect because Williams tumor is a rare kidney cancer that is highly treatable. Most kids with Wilms tumor survive and go on to live normal, healthy lives. Also known as nephroblastoma, Wilms tumor can affect both kidneys, but usually develops in just one.

Option (D) is incorrect As Wilms' tumor is a rare kidney cancer that primarily affects children. Also known as nephroblastoma, it's the most common cancer of the kidneys in children. Wilms' tumor most often affects children ages 3 to 4 and becomes much less common after age 5.

Hence, the correct option is (B).

195. Option (D) is correct because Hepatitis B is not transmitted through stool. Unlike Hepatitis A, the transmission of Hepatitis B by the fecal-oral route is relatively unimportant. The Hepatitis B virus is spread when blood, semen, or other body fluid infected with the Hepatitis B virus enters the body of a person who is not infected. People can become infected with the virus from sex with an infected partner, sharing needles, syringes, or drug preparation equipment.

Option (A) is incorrect because semen, vaginal fluids, and blood all contain the Hepatitis B virus (HBV), and the higher the viral load, the more infectious one's blood, and body fluids are. Even if a man has an undetectable viral load, studies show his semen still contains some HBV and can spread infection, though the risk is lower.

Option (B) is incorrect as Hepatitis B virus (HBV) is passed from person to person through infected blood, most commonly by sharing contaminated needles or having sex with an infected person. HBV transmission, however, does not occur through breast milk, making it perfectly safe for infants unless there is a risk of contact HBV-infected blood.

Option (C) is incorrect as the Hepatitis B virus is spread when blood infected with the Hepatitis B virus enters the body of a person who is not infected. People can become infected with the virus from birth (spread from an infected mother to her baby during birth).

Hence, the correct option is (D).

196. The typical complications of Barrett's esophagus include :

- Peptic ulcers in the columnar lined segment of esophagus
- High and long strictures and
- Dysplasia - cancer sequence.

Barrett's esophagus is a condition in which the cells that make up your esophagus begin to look like the cells that make up your intestines. This often happens when cells are damaged by exposure to acid from the stomach. This condition often develops after years of experiencing gastroesophageal reflux (GERD).

Hence, the correct option is (A).

197. Option (B) is correct because Loss of primary peristaltic waves in the esophageal body, but disorganized muscular activity may be present.

Increased intraesophageal baseline pressure relative to gastric baseline.

Option (A) is incorrect because There are two main defects in achalasia:

(1) obstruction at the esophagogastric junction, and

(2) abnormal esophageal peristalsis.

Obstruction was initially attributed to spasm of the cardia or lower esophageal sphincter (LES), and the condition was called "cardiospasm." Subsequently, uninfused manometric techniques revealed that the LES was not hypertensive, but showed absence of relaxation with swallowing, resulting in the term "achalasia," which literally means "failure of relaxation."

Option (C) is incorrect As explained above in option B ,it is related to the achalasia cardio.

Option (D) is incorrect As achalasia of the esophagus is presumed by many to be a premalignant lesion leading to an increased risk of squamous cell carcinoma. A review of the available literature on the subject has disclosed a wide range of reported cancer risks in achalasia patients, from zero to 33 times that of the normal population.

Hence, the correct option is (B).

198. Option (B) is correct because gastroduodenal artery is the most common artery involved in duodenal ulcer hemorrhage. The gastroduodenal artery can be the source of a significant gastrointestinal bleed, which may arise as a complication of peptic ulcer disease.

Option (A) is incorrect as the splenic artery or lienal artery is the blood vessel that supplies oxygenated blood to the spleen. It branches from the celiac artery, and follows a course superior to the pancreas.

Option (C) is incorrect as in human anatomy, the left gastric artery arises from the celiac artery and runs along the superior portion of the lesser curvature of the stomach. Branches also supply the lower esophagus. The left gastric artery anastomoses with the right gastric artery, which runs right to left.

Option (D) is incorrect in human anatomy, the superior mesenteric artery (SMA) arises from the anterior surface of the abdominal aorta, just inferior to the origin of the celiac trunk, and supplies the intestine from the lower part of the duodenum through two-thirds of the transverse colon, as well as the pancreas primary peristaltic waves in the esophagus.

Hence, the correct option is (B).

199. Duodenal atresia has been reported in association with various malformations and syndromes common being Down syndrome, malrotation, and annular pancreas. Duodenal atresia is a condition that occurs when a portion of the duodenum doesn't form. This condition results in a blockage (atresia) that stops food or fluid from leaving the baby's stomach. Down syndrome (sometimes called Down's syndrome) is a condition in which a child is born with an extra copy of their 21st chromosome — hence its other name, trisomy 21. This causes physical and mental developmental delays and disabilities.

Hence, the correct option is (A).

200. Option (A) is correct because Splenic pulp pressure gives a measure of the portal vein pressure. It can be measured by inserting a needle percutaneously.

Option (B) is incorrect as portal vein pressure measured by Splenic pulp pressure explained above.

Option (C) is incorrect because Portal venous pressure is the blood pressure in the hepatic portal vein, and is normally between 5-10 mmHg. Raised portal venous pressure is termed portal hypertension, and has numerous sequelae such as ascites and hepatic encephalopathy. hence it is not related to the question part.

Option (D) is incorrect because Portal vein Doppler study is the most useful noninvasive investigation for assessing thrombosis of the main portal vein branches.

Hence, the correct option is (A).

201. Option (B) is correct as indication of aspiration in liver abscess is large abscess (>10%), infected abscess, failure of drug therapy, large left lobe abscess, seronegative abscess, abscess in pregnancy where drug therapy cannot be used.

Option (A) is incorrect because the indications for drainage of an amebic liver abscess include the following: Presence of a left-lobe abscess more than 10 cm in diameter. Impending rupture and abscess that does not respond to medical therapy within 3-5 days.

Option (C) is incorrect as a liver abscess can be solitary or multiple and commonly affects the right lobe. Biliary tract infection is the main cause of pyogenic abscess and accounts for 21-30%. Biliary obstruction encourages bacterial proliferation and can cause multiple liver abscesses.

Option (D) is incorrect as the pyogenic liver abscess is more commonly recurrent in patients with underlying biliary tract disease. Irrespective of diabetic status or cryptogenic aetiology, the recurrence of K. pneumonia-infected liver abscess is low in the long-term.

Hence, the correct option is (B).

202. Option (D) is correct because in asymptomatic gallstones, "Prophylactic cholecystectomy is not warranted." Hence, this is the required answer.

Option (A) is incorrect because patients with symptomatic gallstones are always candidates for cholecystectomy.

Option (B) is incorrect as Cholecystectomy is done in all patients with symptomatic polyps.

Option (C) is incorrect as Risk factors associated with malignancy in gall bladder polyps include Old age (>60 years).

Hence, the correct option is (D).

203. Option (D) is correct because Clinical presentation of a CBD stone includes cholangitis - may present with fever, pain or jaundice or pancreatitis.

Option (A) is incorrect as due to biliary obstruction

↑ serum bilirubin

Option (B) is incorrect as if cholangitis is associated

↑ WBC count

Option (C) is incorrect as due to biliary obstruction

↑ serum alkaline phosphatase

Hence, the correct option is (D).

204. Option (A) is correct as MCV is reduced in iron deficiency while a high value indicates macrocytic anaemia. The first red cell index to become abnormal is MCV.

A typical iron deficiency anaemia shows the following blood values for

MCV — less than 75 μ3

Option (B) is incorrect as A typical iron deficiency anaemia shows the following blood values for

MCH—less than 25 pg

Option (C) is incorrect as A typical iron deficiency anaemia shows the following blood values for

MCHC — less than 30%

Option (D) is incorrect as A typical iron deficiency anaemia shows the following blood values for

Red blood cells —less than 4 million/mm^3

Hence, the correct option is (A).

205. Option (B) is correct because when iron levels are low, the red blood cells are unable to carry oxygen to the body's tissues. Although it is normal to experience mild anaemia during pregnancy due to increased blood volume, severe anaemia may put you and your baby at risk of premature delivery and low birth weight. So, this is the required answer.

Option (A) is incorrect as megaloblastic: folate deficiency, vitamin B12 deficiency, and orotic aciduria can raise MCV during pregnancy. Hence, this is not the required answer.

Option (C) is incorrect as non-megaloblastic: liver disease, alcoholism, reticulocytosis, hypothyroidism can raise MCV during pregnancy. Hence, this is not the required answer.

Option (D) is incorrect as alcohol use can raise MCV during pregnancy. Hence, this is not the required answer.

Hence, the correct option is (B).

206. Option (A) is correct because Meckel's diverticulum is present in 2% of the population; it is situated on the anti-mesenteric border of the small intestine, commonly 60cm from the ileocaecal valve, and is usually 3-5 cm long. Many variations occur (2% - 2 feet - 2 inches is a useful aide-memoire). It represents the patent intestinal end of the vitellointestinal duct.

Option (B) is incorrect because the duct of the mesonephros that persists in the female chiefly as part of the epoophoron and in the male as the duct system leaving the testis and including the epididymis, vas deferens, seminal vesicle, and ejaculatory duct. —called also Leydig's duct, mesonephric duct.

Option (C) is incorrect because the müllerian ducts are the primordial anlage of the female reproductive tract. They differentiate to form the fallopian tubes, uterus, the uterine cervix, and the superior aspect of the vagina. A wide variety of malformations can occur when this system is disrupted.

Option (D) is incorrect because paramesonephric ducts (or Müllerian ducts) are paired ducts of the embryo that run down the lateral sides of the urogenital ridge and terminate at the sinus tubercle in the primitive urogenital sinus. In the female, they will develop to form the fallopian tubes, uterus, cervix, and the upper one-third of the vagina.

Hence, the correct option is (A).

207. Option (A) is correct as in anatomy, a polyp is an abnormal growth of tissue projecting from a mucous membrane. If it is attached to the surface by a narrow elongated stalk, it is said to be pedunculated; if it is attached without a stalk, it is said to be sessile. Hence, this is the required answer.

Option (B) is incorrect because approximately 15 percent of polyps detected in colon cancer screening are villous or tubulovillous adenomas. This type of polyp carries a high risk of turning cancerous.

Option (C) is incorrect as the size of a colonic polyp is a biomarker that correlates with its risk of malignancy and guides its clinical management. The risk of malignancy increases with increasing polyp size.

Option (D) is incorrect because Atypia, on histology, seen anywhere, is a risk factor for cancer.

Hence, the correct option is (A).

208. Missed scaphoid fractures have a high risk of non-union or malunion. Non-union occurs in up to 12% of patients if an occult fracture is not detected and treated. Scaphoid non-unions are especially challenging to treat successfully, and if untreated, they can progress to carpal collapse and degenerative arthritis.

Hence, the correct option is (D).

209. Option (A) is correct as the following tests are used for ACL injury :

1. Lachman's test
2. Anterior drawer test
3. Pivot shift test
4. Flexion-rotation drawer test
5. Jerk test
6. Loose's test

Option (B) is incorrect because the McMurray test, also known as the McMurray circumduction test is used to evaluate individuals for tears in the meniscus of the knee. A tear in the meniscus may cause a pedunculated tag of the meniscus which may become jammed between the joint surfaces.

Option (C) is incorrect as Doctors often perform a posterior drawer test to assess the function of the posterior cruciate ligament (PCL)—one of the four ligaments of the knee. If your doctor suspects a PCL tear, the posterior drawer test is the best test to diagnose it.

Option (D) is incorrect because the Apley's grind test (Apley Compression test) is used to evaluate individuals for problems of the meniscus in the knee.

Hence, the correct option is (A).

210. Option (B) is correct because the conditions in which osteoblastic activity is increased and hence the alkaline phosphatase in increased are: -

Rickets/osteomalacia

Primary hyperparathyroidism

Renal osteodystrophy (secondary hyperparathyroidism)

Chronic renal failure and secondary hyperparathyroidism

Paget's disease (osteitis deformans)

Osteoblastic secondaries

Option (A) is incorrect because multiple myeloma is cancer that starts in the bone marrow's plasma cells. Symptoms and signs include anaemia, skin lesions, weakness, and bone fractures.

Option (C) is incorrect as osteoporosis occurs when bone density decreases. This affects the structure and strength of bones and makes fractures more likely.

Option (D) is incorrect because all cannot be the answer as out of all options only in chronic renal failure increased alkaline phosphate is seen.

Hence, the correct option is (B).

211. A posterior subcapsular cataract is the most visually disabling type of cataract since the clouding is close to the nodal point. It often interferes with the near reading vision especially in bright light and causes glare and halos around light at night. Anything that constricts the pupil makes it very difficult for people with this type of cataract. PSCC is associated with aging, steroids, trauma, ionizing radiation, intraocular inflammation, high myopia, atopic dermatitis and retinitis pigmentosa.

Hence, the correct option is (C).

212. Prepatellar bursitis is called housemaid's knee. It is caused by inflammation of a small fluid-filled sac (the bursa) in front of the kneecap. It more commonly occurs in people who spend long periods of time kneeling. Treatment is usually supportive only and the outlook is generally very good.

Hence, the correct option is (A).

213. Option (A) is correct because any trauma patient should be managed in following sequent of events (ABCDEF) : -

- Airway management
- Breathing (ventilation)
- Circulation
- Disability (neurological status) assessment
- Exposure and environmental central
- Fracture splintage: - Adequate immobilization of the cervical spine or other fracture splintage.

Option (B) is incorrect as the firsts step in the initial management of the head injury is airway. So, this option cannot be true.

Option (C) is incorrect as the order is ABCDEF and the option has the order as FEDABC. So, this option is incorrect.

Option (D) is incorrect for the same reasons as (B) and (C).

Hence, the correct option is (A).

214. Option (B) is correct as skin traction → 4-5 kg.

Option (A) is incorrect because in the application of skin traction or Buck traction, usually, 10% of the patient's body weight (up to a maximum of 10 lb) is recommended.

Option (C) is incorrect because at weights greater than 10 lb, superficial skin layers are disrupted and irritated.

Option (D) is incorrect as skeletal traction → 20 kg.

Hence, the correct option is (B).

215. Option (C) is correct as:

Markers of bone resorption

Urine & serum cross-linked N telopeptide

Urine & serum cross-linked C telopeptide

Urine total free deoxypyridinoline

Urine hydroxyproline

Urine hydroxylysine glycosides

Serum tartrate-resistant acid phosphatase

Serum bone sialoprotein

Option (A) is incorrect as serum propeptide of type I procollagen: The aminoterminal propeptide of type I procollagen (PINP) in serum is a sensitive indicator of the synthesis of type I collagen.

Option (B) is incorrect because Osteocalcin, also known as bone gamma-carboxy glutamic acid-containing protein (BGLAP), is a small (49-amino-acid) noncollagenous protein hormone found in bone and dentin, first identified as a calcium-binding protein in chick bone. Because osteocalcin has gla domains, its synthesis is vitamin K dependent.

Option (D) is incorrect because the pyridinoline cross-linking amino acids of collagen have received much attention as bone resorption markers in urine (4,5). Two forms exist, the more abundant hydroxylysyl pyridinoline (HP or pyridino- line) and lysyl pyridinoline (LP or deoxypyridinoline).

Hence, the correct option is (C).

216. Option (A) is correct as Anterior shoulder dislocation

Indirect force (most common) → Abduction, external rotation, extension.

Direct force (less common) → Blow from the posterior aspect of the shoulder.

Option (B) is incorrect as most common mechanism of injury for anterior dislocation of the shoulder is fall on outstretched hand or throwing, with abduction, external rotation, and extension at the shoulder.

Option (C) is incorrect because, during internal rotation, the insertion of the supraspinatus muscle, the main initiator of abduction,14, 15 is displaced anteriorly. In this position, the moment arm for the supraspinatus to abduct the shoulder is unfavourable. The same is applicable to the pectoralis major, biceps long head, and coracobrachialis.

Option (D) is incorrect because the subscapularis muscle internally rotates the humerus; the upper portion of the muscle influences abduction, while the lower area influences adduction. It is considered a multipennate muscle.

Hence, the correct option is (A).

217. Option (D) is correct because :

- Fractures commonly showing cubitus valgus deformity due to malunion :
- Fracture lateral condyle humerus
- Monteggia Fracture Dislocation
- Complications of lateral condylar humerus fractures
- Cubitus valgus
- Cubitus Pseudovirus (lateral spur)
- Tardy ulnar nerve palsy
- Osteonecrosis of the trochlea

Option (A) is incorrect as an intercondylar fracture of the humerus is one of the commonest fractures of young adult and counts for about 30% of all elbow fractures. The treatment of these fractures continues to present challenges despite advances in internal fixation.

Option (B) is incorrect as Olecranon fracture is a fracture of the bony portion of the elbow. The injury is fairly common and often occurs following a fall or direct trauma to the elbow.

Option (C) is incorrect because of the radius and ulna of the left forearm, posterior surface. The top is proximal (elbow) and the bottom is distal (wrist). The head of the radius has a cylindrical form, and on its upper surface is a shallow cup or fovea for articulation with the capitulum of the humerus.

Hence, the correct option is (D).

218. The potential late complication with an acetabular fracture is avascular necrosis, in which the blood supply to the femoral head is sufficiently damaged or stretched from dislocation that the bone subsequently dies and collapses, resulting in hip pain.

An acetabular fracture is a break in the socket portion of the "ball-and-socket" hip joint. Avascular necrosis is the death of bone tissue due to a lack of blood supply. Also called osteonecrosis, it can lead to tiny breaks in the bone and the bone's eventual collapse. A broken bone or dislocated joint can interrupt the blood flow to a section of bone.

Hence, the correct option is (A).

219. Option (A) is correct as Entonox contain equal amount (50/50) of N_2O and O_2.

Option (B) is incorrect as ENTONOX is a ready-to-use medical gas mixture consisting of 50% nitrous oxide and 50% oxygen for use in all situations where analgesia and sedation with rapid onset and offset is sought.

Option (C) is incorrect because the amount must be equal.

Option (D) is incorrect for the same reason as point (B) and point (C).

Hence, the correct option is (A).

220. Option (D) is correct as Mapleson D, E, F require higher fresh gas flow to prevent rebreathing. But they are better than Mapleson A for controlled ventilation.

Option (A) is incorrect because A three-way T-tube is connected to the fresh gas outlet (F), a breathing bag (B) and a reservoir tube (R). The other end of the reservoir tube is connected to the patient (P) and a spring-loaded expiratory valve (V).

Option (B) is incorrect because the C circuit is compact and was used for short transports before self-inflating bags became available. Acceptable CO2 levels could be achieved with a FGF of 2 x MV and mild hyperventilation. If the cylinder became empty ventilation was impossible.

Option (C) is incorrect for the same reason as point (B).

Hence, the correct option is (D).

221. Option (B) is correct because of the latter analyses the type of neural oscillations (popularly called "brain waves") that can be observed in EEG signals in the frequency domain. EEG is most often used to diagnose epilepsy, which causes abnormalities in EEG readings.

Option (A) is incorrect as the electrocardiogram (ECG) is one of the most common, enduring, and important tests in all of the medicine.

Option (C) is incorrect because the wave corresponds to right atrial contraction and ends synchronously with the carotid artery pulse. The peak of the 'a' wave demarcates the end of atrial systole. The x descent follows the 'a' wave and corresponds to atrial relaxation and rapid atrial filling due to low pressure.

Option (D) is incorrect because the V wave in the left atrial pressure (LAP) or pulmonary capillary wedge pressure (PCWP) tracing represents left atrial filling against a closed mitral valve. If severe mitral valve regurgitation is present, the V wave will be significantly accentuated.

Hence, the correct option is (B).

222. Capnography can be used to detect displaced tracheal tubes and tracheostomy tubes and to diagnose inadvertent oesophageal intubation. In addition, capnography has other uses in ICU relating to airway management and monitoring of respiratory and cardiovascular function.

Thus, it can be used for determining the appropriate placement of endotracheal tube.

Hence, the correct option is (C).

223. Complications of CVP are air embolism, thromboembolism, cardiac arrhythmias, pneumothorax, hemothorax, chylothorax, cardiac tamponade, sepsis, trauma to the phrenic nerve, carotid artery (can cause pseudoaneurysm) and brachial plexus.

Thus, airway injury is not a complication of CVP line.

Hence, the correct option is (A).

224. Option (D) is correct because inadvertent intra-arterial injection occurs when thiopentone is injected in antecubital vein because in 10% of the cases brachial artery divides above elbow giving a very superficial abnormal artery which lies deep to an antecubital vein. Therefore thiopentone injection should be given in the veins over the outer aspect of the forearm (not in antecubital vein).

Option (A) is incorrect because the femoral vein (Latin: vena femoralis) is a large blood vessel of the thigh formed by the popliteal vein. The femoral vein arises at the adductor canal as the continuation of the popliteal vein. The femoral vein ends at the inferior margin of the inguinal ligament, becoming the external iliac vein.

Option (B) is incorrect because the antecubital fossa is the shallow depression located in front of the median cubital vein of your arm. The median cubital vein joins the two longest vessels that run up the length of your arm, called the cephalic vein and the basilic vein.

Option (C) is incorrect as a Jugular vein, any of several veins of the neck that drain blood from the brain, face, and neck, returning it to the heart via the superior vena cava. The main vessels are the external jugular vein and the interior jugular vein.

Hence, the correct option is (D).

225. Option (B) is correct as Cerebral blood flow, metabolism, oxygen consumption and ICT all are increased by ketamine → ketamine is contraindicated in raised ICT.

Option (A) is incorrect because Propofol, marketed as Diprivan among other names, is a short-acting medication that results in a decreased level of consciousness and lack of memory for events. Its uses include the starting and maintenance of general anaesthesia, sedation for mechanically ventilated adults, and procedural sedation.

Option (C) is incorrect as Atracurium besylate, is a medication used in addition to other medications to provide skeletal muscle relaxation during surgery or mechanical ventilation.

Option (D) is incorrect as Fentanyl, also spelt fentanil, is an opioid used as a pain medication and together with other medications for anesthesia. Fentanyl is also used as a recreational drug, often mixed with heroin or cocaine. It has a rapid onset and its effects generally last less than two hours.

Hence, the correct option is (B).

226. Option (B) is correct as Vasoconstrictors are used along with LA which prolongs the duration of action as the rate of absorption is decreased due to vasoconstriction.

Option (A) is incorrect as the half-life of local anaesthetics is also prolonged, secondary to a greater volume of distribution and decreased hepatic metabolism.

Option (C) is incorrect as it is mentioned in point (B) that the duration of LA increases instead of decreasing.

Option (D) is incorrect as for the same reason, metabolism of LA is reduced and toxicity is decreased as there is lesser absorption of LA.

Hence, the correct option is (B).

227. Option (D) is correct as Chloroprocaine has the highest pKa value, hence maximum ionized form at physiological pH , i.e.

Local anaesthetics with pKa value in increasing order

Mepivacaine (7.6) < Etidocaine (7.7) < Lidocaine (7.8) = Prilocaine (7.8) < Bupivacaine (8.1)

= Ropivacaine (8.1) < Tetracaine (8.2) < Cocaine (8.7) < Procaine (8.9) < Chloroprocaine (9.0)

Option (A) is incorrect as

Lidocaine (7.8)<Chloroprocaine (9.0)

Option (B) is incorrect as

Etidocaine (7.7)<Chloroprocaine (9.0)

Option (C) is incorrect as

Bupivacaine (8.1)<Chloroprocaine (9.0)

Hence, the correct option is (D).

228. Option (A) is correct as cocaine was first used as local anaesthetic by Carl Koller. It was used for the anaesthetizing cornea.

Option (B) is incorrect as Horace Wells was an American dentist who pioneered the use of anaesthesia in dentistry, specifically nitrous oxide.

Option (C) is incorrect because William Thomas Green Morton was an American dentist who first publicly demonstrated the use of inhaled ether as a surgical anaesthetic in 1846.

Option (D) is incorrect as Carl Kollar used first cocaine as a local anaesthetic.

Hence, the correct option is (A).

229. Option (B) is correct as :

Due to local infection, there is hyperemia of the local area & trauma can result in mucosal bleeding.

Due to local oedema & inflammation laryngospasm can be a complication. Halothane toxicity usually occurs in elderly women & obese; rare in children.

Option (A) is incorrect as Systemic infection can lead to Bacteremia.

Option (C) is incorrect as Mucosal bleeding symptoms are most commonly associated with vWD and can be accentuated in the presence of inherited platelet dysfunction, plasminogen activator deficiency 1 (PAI-1) or a vascular disorder such as Ehlers Danlos syndrome.

Option (D) is incorrect as Laryngospasm refers to a sudden spasm of the vocal cords. Laryngospasms are often a symptom of an underlying condition. Sometimes they can happen as a result of anxiety or stress. They can also occur as a symptom of asthma, gastroesophageal reflux disease (GERD), or vocal cord dysfunction.

Hence, the correct option is (B).

230. Option (A) is correct because, in RAO view of chest, the patient is rotated 45° to the left (right side is more forward) and the cassette is close to the right front (right shoulder) of the patient.

Option (B) is incorrect as it is explained in point (A) that its right side is more forward.

Option (C) is incorrect because the RAO view is generally used for the assessment of the pulmonary artery, right ventricle, and size of the left atrium.

Option (D) is incorrect for the same reason as point (C).

Hence, the correct option is (A).

231. Option (B) is correct as Snowman's sign or figure of 8 sign is seen in supracardiac TAPVC. Snowman sign, also sometimes referred to as a dumbell sign, is a radiologic sign related to conditions that have a shape which resembles a snowman. This includes snowman sign (total anomalous pulmonary venous return).

Option (A) is incorrect as Ebstein anomaly is a congenital malformation of the heart that is characterized by apical displacement of the septal and posterior tricuspid valve leaflets, leading to the materialization of the right ventricle with a variable degree of malformation and displacement of the anterior leaflet.

Option (C) is incorrect because the Tetralogy of Fallot is a combination of four congenital abnormalities. The four defects include a ventricular septal defect (VSD), pulmonary valve stenosis, a misplaced aorta and a thickened right ventricular wall (right ventricular hypertrophy).

Option (D) is incorrect as Transposition of the great vessels (TGV) is a group of congenital heart defects involving an abnormal spatial arrangement of any of the great vessels: superior and/or inferior venae cavae, pulmonary artery, pulmonary veins, and aorta.

Hence, the correct option is (B).

232. Option (D) is correct because soap bubble appearance is seen in meconium ileus due to admixture of gas with meconium.

Option (A) is incorrect typically, only one cyst occurs on the surface of a kidney, but multiple cysts can affect one or both kidneys. However, simple kidney cysts aren't the same as the cysts that form with polycystic kidney disease. Simple kidney cysts that don't cause signs or symptoms usually don't require treatment.

Option (B) is incorrect as Neuroblastoma is cancer that develops from immature nerve cells found in several areas of the body. Neuroblastoma most commonly arises in and around the adrenal glands, which have similar origins to nerve cells and sit atop the kidneys.

Option (C) is incorrect as Lymphangiectasia is a pathologic dilation of lymph vessels. When it occurs in the intestines of dogs, and more rarely humans, it causes a disease known as "intestinal lymphangiectasia". This disease is characterized by lymphatic vessel dilation, chronic diarrhoea and loss of proteins such as serum albumin and globulin. It is considered to be a chronic form of protein-losing enteropathy.

It is also known as "lymphangiectasis".

Hence, the correct option is (D).

233. Option (B) is correct as filling defect in calyces is not counted as a feature of intravenous urography. Hence, this is the required answer.

Option (A) is incorrect as delayed or absent nephrogram is intravenous urography (IVU) findings of renovascular hypertension.

Option (C) is incorrect as ureteral kinking (in retroperitoneal fibrosis) is a feature of intravenous urography.

Option (D) is incorrect as normal or atrophic kidney without calyceal deformity or abnormality is also one of the IVU findings of renovascular hypertension.

Hence, the correct option is (B).

234. Option (B) is correct as Punched out lesions of the skull are seen both in Eosinophilic granuloma and multiple myeloma. However, bevelled edges (double contour) is characteristic of eosinophilic granuloma due to uneven destruction of the inner and outer table of the skull.

Punched out lesions of skull → Multiple myelomas

Punched out lesions with bevelled edges → Eosinophilic granuloma

Option (A) is incorrect as Metastasis is a pathogenic agent's spread from an initial or primary site to a different or secondary site within the host's body; the term is typically used when referring to metastasis by a cancerous tumour. The newly pathological sites, then, are metastases.

Option (C) is incorrect as Osteomalacia is a disease characterized by the softening of the bones caused by impaired bone metabolism primarily due to inadequate levels of available phosphate, calcium, and vitamin D, or because of resorption of calcium. The impairment of bone metabolism causes inadequate bone mineralization.

Option (D) is incorrect as Hyperparathyroidism is a condition in which one or more of the parathyroid glands become overactive and secrete too much parathyroid hormone (PTH). This causes the levels of calcium in the blood to rise, a condition known as hypercalcemia.

Hence, the correct option is (B).

235. Option (B) is correct as "Meningioma usually have similar characteristics to schwannomas, being isointense on T1 image and hyperintense on T2 weighted image. However; Homogeneous and significant contrast enhancement is a characteristic appearance of meningioma".

Option (A) is incorrect as Schwannomas show Heterogeneous (non-homogenous) and moderate contrast enhancement.

Option (C) is incorrect as "Cavernous sinus (paracellular) meningiomas present with retro-orbital pain and sixth cranial nerve palsy".

Option (D) is incorrect as Cavernous hemangioma also shows homogenous contrast enhancement but it is a moderate enhancement (not intense). Further cavernous hemangioma does not cause 6th nerve palsy.

Hence, the correct option is (B).

236. Option (C) is correct as Tc 99 is the most common radiopharmaceutical used for imaging in nuclear medicine. For skeletal imaging Diphosphonate Ligands are used as these agents are deposited on sites of actively growing bone. The diphosphonate ligand has a high affinity for actively growing bone. ^{99}Tc-MDP is the most widely used of the diphosphonate ligands- Bone Scintigraphy.

Option (A) is incorrect as A gallium scan is a type of nuclear medicine test that uses either a gallium-67 (67Ga) radiopharmaceutical to obtain images of a specific type of tissue or disease state of the tissue.

Option (B) is incorrect because it contains a radioactive substance called technetium linked to a substance called sulfur colloid. Sulfer colloid is taken up by special cells in lymph tissue, and in the liver, spleen, and bone marrow after it is injected. Also called Tc 99m sulfur colloid and Tc-99m SC.

Option (D) is incorrect as Technetium–99m linked to Methylene diphosphonate (^{99m}Tc-MDP) is the most useful radiopharmaceutical for skeletal imaging in Radionuclide imaging.

Hence, the correct option is (C).

237. Option (A) is correct because metastases from breast cancer are typically hypoechoic (Echopoor) on ultrasonography. Metastases from carcinoma colon and renal cell carcinoma are typically hyper-echoic (or echogenic) while metastasis from mucinous adenocarcinoma typically appears 'calcified'.

Option (B) is incorrect because colon cancer is a type of cancer that begins in the large intestine (colon). The colon is the final part of the digestive tract. Colon cancer typically affects older adults, though it can happen at any age. It usually begins as small, noncancerous (benign) clumps of cells called polyps that form on the inside of the colon. Over time some of these polyps can become colon cancers.

Option (C) is incorrect as renal cell cancer (also called kidney cancer or renal cell adenocarcinoma) is a disease in which malignant (cancer) cells are found in the lining of tubules (very small tubes) in the kidney. There are two kidneys, one on each side of the backbone, above the waist. Tiny tubules in the kidneys filter and clean the blood

Option (D) is incorrect as Mucinous adenocarcinoma is one of the histological subtypes of colorectal cancer. Mucinous colorectal adenocarcinomas comprise approximately 1 to 6 percent of all colorectal epithelial cancers. Frequently are more advanced at diagnosis and have a poorer prognosis than nonmucinous colorectal adenocarcinomas.

Hence, the correct option is (A).

238. Option (B) is correct as tracheal bifurcation (carina) is located at about 4th thoracic vertebral body or T_4T_5 disc space posteriorly and sternal angle of Louis anteriorly.

Option (A) is incorrect as the thoracic inlet is a narrow opening defined by the anterior edge of the body of the first thoracic vertebra, the inner curvature of the first rib on each side and the posterior border of the manubrium sterni.

Option (C) is incorrect as it is explained in point (B) that carina is located at about 4th vertebral body.

Option (D) is incorrect as point (B) is the required answer.

Hence, the correct option is (B).

239. Option (A) is correct because this newborn is presenting with intestinal obstruction and pylorus is a part of the stomach (not the intestine). Pyloric obstruction shows a single bubble (single air-fluid) appearance (not multiple air-fluid levels).

Option (B) is incorrect as Duodenal atresia show double bubble.

Option (C) is incorrect because Heal atresia shows multiple bubbles (multiple air-fluid levels).

Option (D) is incorrect for the same reason as point (B) as it also shows a double bubble.

Hence, the correct option is (A).

240. Option (D) is correct as Looser's zone or pseudofracture is pathognomonic for osteomalacia, However, it may occur rarely also in Paget's disease, Fibrous dysplasia, Hyperparathyroidism, Renal osteodystrophy, Hyperphosphatasia, and osteogenesis imperfecta.

Option (A) is incorrect because Osteoporosis is a bone disease that occurs when the body loses too much bone, makes too little bone, or both. As a result, bones become weak and may break from a fall or, in serious cases, from sneezing or minor bumps. Osteoporosis means "porous bone." Viewed under a microscope, healthy bone looks like a honeycomb.

Option (B) is incorrect even when the looser's zone is seen in Hyperparathyroidism because when you have the option that contains all the true options, go for that option instead of selecting an individual option.

Option (C) is incorrect for the same reason as point (B).

Hence, the correct option is (D).

241. Option (B) is correct as:

- Combined oestrogen progesterone should be avoided for contraception
- Intrauterine devices are not preferred due to the risk of infection

Progesterone only contraception is ideal. Progesterone is known to prevent sickle cell crisis

Option (A) is incorrect as an Intrauterine Contraceptive Device (IUCD) is a device which is inserted into the uterus (womb) to prevent pregnancy. There are many types of IUCDs and they come in different shapes and sizes. Commonly used types are IUCDs containing copper.

Option (C) is incorrect as the progestin-only pill (POP), also called the "Mini-pill," is a type of birth control pill (oral contraceptive) that comes in a pack of 28 pills. Instead of containing the hormones progestin and estrogen, it only contains progestin. It's often called the "Mini-Pill" because it doesn't contain estrogen.

Option (D) is incorrect as progestin implants for contraception are highly effective, safe, and the most convenient choice for many women.

Hence, the correct option is (B).

242. Option (C) is correct as premature rupture of membranes (PROM) is defined as spontaneous rupture of membranes before the onset of labour. Preterm premature rupture of membranes (PPROM) is defined as premature rupture of membranes before 37 completed weeks.

Option (A) is incorrect as it occurs before completion of 37 weeks not 38 weeks.

Option (B) is incorrect for the same reason as point (A).

Option (D) is incorrect as it occurs before first stage and not at the second stage of labour.

Hence, the correct option is (C).

243. Option (A) is correct as "Smoking is the single most preventable cause of IUGR in infants born in the united states—women who quit smoking at 7 months gestation have newborns with higher mean birthweights than do women who smoke throughout the pregnancy. Women who quit smoking before 16 weeks of gestation are not at any increased risk for an IUGR infant."

"In the prevention of fetal growth restriction – smoking cessation is critical".

Option (B) is incorrect because Aspirin, also known as acetylsalicylic acid, is a medication used to reduce pain, fever, or inflammation. Specific inflammatory conditions which aspirin is used to treat include Kawasaki disease, pericarditis, and rheumatic fever. Aspirin given shortly after a heart attack decreases the risk of death.

Option (C) is incorrect as Vitamin D helps the body absorb calcium, which is why the two nutrients are often paired up in supplements. According to the Institute of Medicine (IOM), women over age 50 need 1,200 milligrams (mg) of calcium a day, and 600 to 800 international units (IU) of vitamin D a day.

Option (D) is incorrect as some doctors suggest bed rest for conditions like growth problems in the baby, high blood pressure or preeclampsia, vaginal bleeding from placenta previa or abruption, preterm labor, cervical insufficiency, threatened miscarriage, and other problems.

Hence, the correct option is (A).

244. Option (D) is correct as Cephalhematoma does not vary in tension with crying.

Option (A) is incorrect as it is caused generally by forceps delivery but may also be met with following normal labour.

Option (B) is incorrect as no active treatment is necessary.

Option (C) is incorrect as it lies over a parietal bone.

Hence, the correct option is (D).

245. Option (D) is correct as 6 fontanelles are present in fetal skull:

- Anterior fontanelle (bregma) – 1
- Posterior fontanelle (lambda) – 1
- Anterolateral fontanelle – 1
- Posteriolateral fontanelle – 1

Option (A) is incorrect as the number of fontanelles present in a newborn child is 6, not 1.

Option (B) is incorrect for the same reason as point (A).

Option (C) is incorrect for the same reason as point (A) and point (B).

Hence, the correct option is (D).

246. Option (B) is correct as Hormonal Study is the best predictor for ovulation in a female infertility patient during a menstrual cycle.

Option (A) is incorrect as Basal body temperature (BBT) falls at the time of ovulation by about 1/2degree. During the progestational half of the cycle, the temperature is slightly raised above the preovulatory level. But it is now obsolete because:

1. Tedious daily recording
2. Not very accurate
3. Better modalities are available

Option (C) is incorrect as in endometrial biopsy endometrium from the uterus is curetted preferably 1 or 2days prior to the onset of menstruation. A histological examination done for secretory changes. Nowadays endometrial biopsy is omitted as a routine investigation of infertility. Only used in suspected tubercular endometritis.

Option (D) is incorrect because Fern test: cervical mucus is examined under a low power microscope. During the estrogenic phase, it shows a characteristic fern pattern which disappears after ovulation.

Hence, the correct option is (B).

247. Option (A) is correct as :

1. To correct anaemia due to blood loss and to combat postpartum haemorrhage
2. Patient with severe anaemia seen in later months of pregnancy (beyond 36 weeks)
3. Refractory anaemia: Anemia not responding to either oral or parenteral therapy in spite of correct treatment
4. Associated infection

Option (B) is incorrect because Low B12 or folate can also make you anaemic, even without iron deficiency. If your ferritin level is low, this confirms that you don't have enough iron. If you are more than 36 weeks pregnant, there may not be enough time for iron tablets to work before your baby is born.

Option (C) is incorrect as Anemia due to excessive bleeding results when loss of red blood cells exceeds the production of new red blood cells. When blood loss is rapid, blood pressure falls, and people may be dizzy. When blood loss occurs gradually, people may be tired, short of breath, and pale.

Option (D) is incorrect as refractory anaemia (RA) is a low-risk MDS with mono-lineage dysplasia characterized by anaemia, dyserythropoietic, and the low percentage of blasts in the bone marrow and peripheral blood.

Hence, the correct option is (A).

248. Option (A) is correct as Postcoital test (Sim's/Huhner's test) Advantage of this test is that cervical mucus can be simultaneously studied for oestrogenic effect and ovulation, it's the capability to allow sperm penetration and the presence of any anti-sperm antibodies.

Option (B) is incorrect because the definition of motility is the ability of an organism or fluid to move. Sperm motility refers to the movement and swimming of sperm. 1 Poor sperm motility means that the sperm do not swim properly, which can lead to male infertility.

Option (C) is incorrect as a normal sperm count ranges from 15 million sperm to more than 200 million sperm per millilitre (mL) of semen. Anything less than 15 million sperm per millilitre, or 39 million sperm per ejaculate, is considered low. A high, or above average, sperm count is over 200 million sperm per millimetre.

Option (D) is incorrect as sperm viability refers to the percentage of live sperm in the semen sample. This is especially important to measure if sperm motility is low, so differentiate between live non-motile sperm and dead sperm.

Hence, the correct option is (A).

249. Option (C) is correct as Sickle cell anaemia (Description: Peripheral smear shows Sickle-shaped RBCs).

Option (A) is incorrect as With more severe iron-deficiency anaemia, the peripheral blood smear may show hypochromic, pencil-shaped cells and, occasionally, small numbers of nucleated red blood cells.

Option (B) is incorrect because Abnormally shaped red blood cells are a sign of thalassemia.

Option (D) is incorrect as Sideroblastic anaemia is defined as microcytic anaemia in which the bone marrow produces sideroblasts, i.e., ring-shaped blood cells.

Hence, the correct option is (C).

250. Overview of Management of Iron Deficiency Anemia in Pregnancy:

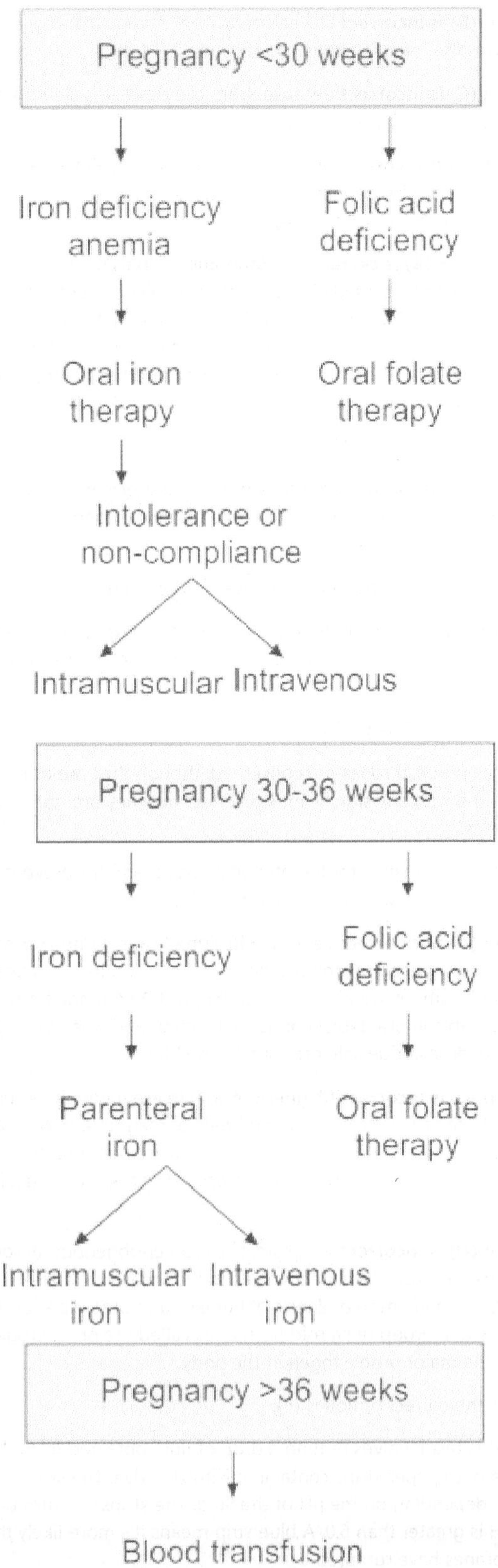

Option (A) is correct as Oral iron is useful in anaemias before 30 weeks of pregnancy and not 20 weeks. So, this is the required answer.

Option (B) is incorrect as Parenteral iron therapy markedly increases the reticulocytotic count within 7-14 days.

Option (C) is incorrect because, from the chart, it is clear that parenteral iron is ideal during 30–36 weeks.

Option (D) is incorrect as blood transfusion is useful in severe anaemia beyond 36 weeks.
Hence, the correct option is (A).

251. Option (B) is correct As "Randomized trials have demonstrated that nifedipine is a better tocolytic agent than ritodrine and terbutaline. Nifedipine is the best first line tocolytic agent available at this time. Headaches are the main maternal side effect but overall the drug is well tolerated and has no apparent fetal effects."

Fernando Arias 3/e, p 224

"When tocolysis is indicated for women in preterm labor, calcium channel blockers are preferred to other tocolytic agents compared mainly with betamimetics."

Mgt of High Risk Pregnancy, SS Trivedi , Manju Puri

So undoubtedly nifedipine is the answer of choice as well as the tocolytic of choice. IInd choice tocolytics are - Beta adrenergic drugs.

Fernando Arias 3/e, p 224

As far as progesterones are concerned, though they are not associated with any significant side effect but they are not used as tocolytics.

They are used mainly for threatened abortion and for preventing preterm labor in patients who have risk factors for preterm labor.

Option (A) is incorrect because Ritodrine (trade name Yutopar) is a tocolytic drug used to stop premature labor. This drug has been removed from the US market, according to FDA Orange Book. It was available in oral tablets or as an injection and was typically used as the hydrochloride salt, ritodrine hydrochloride.

Option (C) is incorrect Magnesium sulfate is a naturally occurring mineral used to control low blood levels of magnesium. Magnesium sulfate injection is also used for pediatric acute nephritis and to prevent seizures in severe pre-eclampsia, eclampsia, or toxemia of pregnancy.

Option (D) is incorrect Progesterone is an endogenous steroid and progesterone sex hormone involved in the menstrual cycle, pregnancy, and embryogenesis of humans and other species. It belongs to a group of steroid hormones called the progestogens, and is the major progestogen in the body.

Hence, the correct option is (B).

252. This test involves putting a drop of fluid obtained from the vagina onto paper strips containing Nitrazine dye. The strips change colour depending on the pH of the fluid. The strips will turn blue if the pH is greater than 6.0. A blue strip means it's more likely the membranes have ruptured.

This test, however, can produce false positives. If blood gets in the sample or if there is an infection present, the pH of the vaginal fluid may be higher than normal. Semen also has a higher pH, so recent vaginal intercourse can produce a false reading.

According to the above explanation **Option (B) is correct.**

According to the above explanation **Option (A) is incorrect.**

According to the above explanation **Option (C) is incorrect.**

According to the above explanation **Option (D) is incorrect.**

Hence, the correct option is (B).

253. "A fetal heartbeat may first be detected by a vaginal ultrasound as early as **6.0-6.5 week** after gestation. That's when a fetal pole, the first visible sign of a developing embryo, can sometimes be seen. But between 6.5 to 7 weeks after gestation, a heartbeat can be better assessed"

Option (A) is correct because according to above explanation the time duration of Early date for detection of fetal heart is given 6.0-6.5 week, hence this option is correct.

Option (B) is incorrect because according to above explanation this option is not correct.

Option (C) is incorrect because according to above explanation this option is not correct.

Option (D) is incorrect because according to above explanation this option is not correct.
Hence, the correct option is (A).

254. Option (D) is correct According to all explanation given above it is shows that none of them are factors and the real factors are Persistence of detectable hCG after mole evacuation is a feature.

Diagnosis of choriocarcinoma is by Histology of uterine wall showing penetration with marked hyperplastic trophoblastic cells

Persistent high HCG levels

X ray chest showing cannon ball shadows.

On lapratomy:

a. Perforation of uterus through which purple fungating growth is visible

b. By haemoperitoneum

Option (A) is incorrect as Hypoplasia is underdevelopment or incomplete development of a tissue or organ. Although the term is not always used precisely, it properly refers to an inadequate or below-normal number of cells. where as Trophoblasts are cells forming the outer layer of a blastocyst, which provide nutrients to the embryo and develop into a large part of the placenta. it explains that it is not the Diagnostic factor for choriocarcinoma.

Option (B) is incorrect Lung metastasis is cancer that started in another part of the body and spread to the lungs. It's sometimes called secondary lung cancer or metastatic lung tumours. Lung metastasis is not the same as cancer that starts in the lung (called primary lung cancer).

Option (C) is incorrect because HCG appears in the blood and urine of pregnant women as early as 10 days after conception. Quantitative HCG measurement helps determine the exact age of the fetus. It can also assist in the diagnosis of abnormal pregnancies, such as ectopic pregnancies, molar pregnancies, and possible miscarriages. hence it is not Diagnostic factor of choriocarcinoma.

Hence, the correct option is (D).

255. Option (C) is correct As The fetal heart rate response to uterine contraction can be an index of either uterine perfusion or placental function. A late deceleration is a smooth, gradual symmetrical decrease in fetal heart rate beginning at or after the peak of the contraction and returning to baseline only after the contraction is over.

Murata and Co workers showed that the late deceleration was a consequence of uteroplacental induced hypoxia,

Generally any condition that causes maternal hypotension, excessive uterine activity or placental dysfunction can cause late deceleration's.

- Early deceleration: head compression
- Late deceleration: placental insufficiency
- Variable deceleration: cord compression

Option (A) is incorrect As Spinal cord compression is caused by any condition that puts pressure on your spinal cord. Spinal cord compression can occur anywhere from your neck (cervical spine) down to your lower back (lumbar spine). Symptoms include numbness, pain, weakness, and loss of bowel and bladder control.

Option (B) is incorrect because An abdominal binder is a wide compression belt that encircles your abdomen. An abdominal binder may be used to speed-up the recovery process after abdominal surgery. Hence it is not a cause of Late deceleration.

Option (D) is incorrect because A compression headache is a type of headache that starts when you wear something tight across your forehead or scalp. Hats, goggles, and headbands are common culprits. These headaches are sometimes referred to as external compression headaches since they involve pressure from something outside your body.

Hence, the correct option is (C).

256. Option (C) is correct because It is a triangular area bounded

- Anteriorly by clitoris
- Posteriorly by fourchette
- Either side by labia minus

Option (A) is incorrect as the fossa navicularis refers to a normal mild dilatation of the urethra. It occurs at the most distal/downstream portion of the urethra. It is more evident in males, where it occurs in the penile/pendulous urethra, near the urethral meatus.

Option (B) is incorrect because Fourchette A fork-shaped structure, specifically the fold of skin where the labia minora meet above the perineum

Option (D) is incorrect because the vulva is the external part of the female genitalia. It protects a woman's sexual organs, urinary opening, vestibule and vagina and is the center of much of a woman's sexual response. The outer and inner 'lips' of the vulva are called the labia majora and labia minora.

Hence, the correct option is (C).

257. Option (A) is correct As Enclomiphene is the trans-isomer of clomiphene citrate, it is slight estrogenic activity and moderate antiestrogenic activity, but the most striking effect was the inhibition of the pituitary's gonadotropic function.

Option (B) is incorrect because Chance of pregnancy is three fold as compared to placebo is not related to clomiphene citrate. so this is not correct option.

Option (C) is incorrect because Women carrying multiples have a high risk of gestational diabetes. This condition can increase the risk of preeclampsia and of developing diabetes mellitus later in life. Newborns may have breathing problems or low blood sugar levels. Diet, exercise, and sometimes medication can reduce the risk of these complications. hence this is also not topic regarding question.

Option (D) is incorrect As Some men with oligospermia can still conceive despite lower sperm counts. ... Other men with oligospermia may have no problem with conception, despite the low sperm numbers. Some of the most common causes of oligospermia also increase a man's risk for other fertility issues. This includes sperm motility problems. hence this is also not related to the question.

Hence, the correct option is (A).

258. Option (C) is correct As a most common site for ectopic pregnancy is fallopian tubes

- In fallopian tubes most common site in descending order is - Ampulla> isthmus> infundibulum>intersum.
- Thus ampulla is the most common site for ectopic and intersum is the least common site in the fallopian tubes.
- The ampulla is the most common site of tubal abortion.
- Isthmus is the most common site of tubal rupture.
- Time of termination is earliest at the isthmus as it is the narrowest part.
- Time of termination is the latest at the intersumas myometrium is distensible and supports the growing sac.

Option (A) is incorrect because The ovary is an organ found in the female reproductive system that produces an ovum. When released, this travels down the fallopian tube into the uterus, where it may become fertilized by a sperm.

Option (B) is incorrect because the peritoneum is the serous membrane forming the lining of the abdominal cavity or coelom in amniotes and some invertebrates, such as annelids. It covers most of the intra-abdominal (or coelomic) organs, and is composed of a layer of mesothelium supported by a thin layer of connective tissue.

Option (D) is incorrect because The cervix is a cylinder-shaped neck of tissue that connects the vagina and uterus. Located at the lowermost portion of the uterus, the cervix is composed primarily of fibromuscular tissue.

Hence, the correct option is (C).

259. Option (D) is correct As Dexamethasone is a steroid that prevents the release of substances in the body that cause inflammation. Dexamethasone is used to treat many different conditions such as allergic disorders, skin conditions, ulcerative colitis, arthritis, lupus, psoriasis, or breathing disorders

Option (A) is incorrect As Betamethasone is a highly potent steroid that prevents the release of substances in the body that cause inflammation. Betamethasone topical (for the skin) is used to treat the inflammation and itching caused by a number of skin conditions such as eczema or psoriasis

Option (B) is incorrect As It is used to treat conditions such as arthritis, blood problems, immune system disorders, skin and eye conditions, breathing problems, cancer, and severe allergies. It decreases your immune system's response to various diseases to reduce symptoms such as pain, swelling and allergic-type reactions.

Option (C) is incorrect As This medication is used to treat a variety of skin conditions (e.g., insect bites, poison oak/ivy, eczema, dermatitis, allergies, rash, itching of the outer female genitals, anal itching). Hydrocortisone reduces the swelling, itching, and redness that can occur in these types of conditions.

Hence, the correct option is (D).

260. -The main intervention for acute PID is the use of broad-spectrum antibiotics which cover Chlamydia trachomatis, Neisseria gonorrhoeae, and anaerobic bacteria, administered intravenously, intramuscularly, or orally.

-A tubo-ovarian abscess (TOA) is a complex infectious mass of the adnexa that forms as a sequela of pelvic inflammatory disease. Classically, a TOA manifests with an adnexal mass, fever, elevated white blood cell count, lower abdominal-pelvic pain, and/or vaginal discharge; however, presentations of this disease can be highly variable.

-An abdominal hysterectomy is a surgical procedure that removes your uterus through an incision in your lower abdomen. Your uterus - or womb - is where a baby grows if you're pregnant. A partial hysterectomy removes just the uterus, leaving the cervix intact

-Laparoscopic treatment of severe PID resulting in TOA is generally successful, but some patients will develop chronic pelvic pain secondary to adhesion formation. It is doubtful that the chronic pain is directly related to the laparoscopic approach. antibiotics.

According to the above explanation **Option (C) is correct.**

According to the above explanation **Option (A) is incorrect.**

According to the above explanation **Option (B) is incorrect.**

According to the above explanation **Option (D) is incorrect.**

Hence, the correct option is (C).

261. Option (B) is correct As Burch colposuspension is used to treat stress urinary incontinence (SUI). Stress urinary incontinence is the involuntary leakage of urine during periods of increased intra-abdominal pressure, including exertion such as laughing, coughing, sneezing, coughing, and jumping. hence in this case the long-term success rate is maximum for the surgeries of stress incontinence.

Option (A) is incorrect The Stamey procedure has gained a favourable reputation as a highly effective operation for the treatment of genuine stress incontinence in the female. Technical ease, short operating time, brief hospitalization and minimal postoperative morbidity have all been claimed as particular advantages of this procedure.

Option (C) is incorrect because It is a minimally invasive operation that is done through an incision in the anterior vaginal wall but only has a cure rate of 20-30 % for stress urinary incontinence.

Option (D) is incorrect because The Aldridge procedure, first described in 1942, overcame this difficulty by utilising the rectus abdominis fascia as the sling material. This is harvested through an abdominal incision, with two lateral strips of fascia passed through the retropubic space and secured beneath the urethra.

Hence, the correct option is (B).

262. Option (D) is correct Structure of fallopian Tube—It consists of 3 layers:

1. Serous: Consists of peritoneum on all sides except along the line of attachment of mesosalpinx (i.e. option d is correct).

2. Muscular: Arranged in two layers — outer longitudinal and inner circular.

3. The mucous membrane is thrown into longitudinal folds. It is lined by columnar epithelium, partly ciliated, others secretory nonciliated and 'Peg cells'. There is no submucosal layer nor any glands. Changes occur in the tubal epithelium during menstrual cycle but are less pronounced and there is no shedding during the menstrual cycle (option c is incorrect).

Option (A) is incorrect because the fallopian tube is lined with ciliated columnar epithelium. Blockage of the fallopian tube may cause infertility and predispose to the development of ectopic pregnancy. Ectopic pregnancy most often occurs in the fallopian tube but can occur in the peritoneal cavity as a result of an abnormal implantation event.

Option (B) is incorrect because there is only these are layers name As in this explanation-A cross-section of a fallopian tube shows four distinct layers, from outer to inner: serosa, subserosa, lamina propria and innermost mucosal. Subserosa is composed of loose adventitious tissue, blood vessels, lymphatics, an outer longitudinal and inner circular smooth muscle coats.

Option (C) is incorrect As If the egg is fertilized by a sperm as it travels down the fallopian tube, then pregnancy occurs. The fertilized egg attaches to the lining of the uterus. If the egg does not become fertilized, the lining of the uterus (endometrium) is shed during menstruation. The average menstrual cycle lasts 28 days.

Hence, the correct option is (D).

263. Option (B) is correct because Aromatase, An enzyme involved in the production of estrogen that acts by catalyzing the conversion of testosterone (an androgen) to estradiol (an estrogen). Aromatase is located in estrogen-producing cells in the adrenal glands, ovaries, placenta, testicles, adipose (fat) tissue, and brain.

Option (A) is incorrect because Alkaline phosphatase (ALP) is an enzyme found in several tissues throughout the body. The highest concentrations of ALP are present in the cells that comprise bone and the liver. Elevated levels of ALP in the blood are most commonly caused by liver disease or bone disorders. it does not used in Granulosa cells to produce estrogen.

Option (C) is incorrect because Acid phosphatase is a ubiquitous lysosomal enzyme that hydrolyses organic phosphates at an acid pH. Although the post pubescent prostatic epithelial cell contains a uniquely high concentration of acid phosphatase, cellular components of bone, spleen, kidney, liver, intestine, and blood also contain this enzyme.

Option (D) is incorrect Human β-glucuronidase is a type of glucuronidase (a member of glycosidase Family 2) that catalyzes hydrolysis of β-D-glucuronic acid residues from the non-reducing end of mucopolysaccharides (also referred to as glycosaminoglycans) such as heparan sulfate. Human β-glucuronidase is located in the lysosome.

Hence, the correct option is (B).

264. Option (D) is correct As all other options are included in this option so this option will be correct.

Option (A) is incorrect because CMV can cause mononucleosis or hepatitis (liver problem). People with weakened immune systems who get CMV can have more serious symptoms affecting the eyes, lungs, liver, esophagus, stomach, and intestines. Babies born with CMV can have brain, liver, spleen, lung, and growth problems.

Option (B) is incorrect because Rubella - commonly known as German measles or 3-day measles — is an infection that mostly affects the skin and lymph nodes. It is caused by the rubella virus (not the same virus that causes measles).

Option (C) is incorrect because Herpes simplex virus infection causes recurring episodes of small, painful, fluid-filled blisters on the skin, mouth, lips (cold sores), eyes, or genitals. This very contagious viral infection is spread by direct contact with sores or sometimes contact with an affected area when no sores are present.

Hence, the correct option is (D).

265. Taking the pill may help cut your risk of ovarian cancer and endometrial (uterine) cancer. That's probably because women who take the pill ovulate, or release eggs from the ovaries, fewer times than women who don't take the pill. The more times you ovulate over your lifetime, the more hormones you're exposed to.

Option (D) is correct because according to above explanation this option will be correct.

Option (A) is incorrect According to above explanation only ovarian cancer and endometrial (uterine) cancer are protected by OCP not the cervix cancer. hence this option will not be correct.

Option (B) is incorrect because according to above explanation this option will not be correct.

Option (C) is incorrect because according to above explanation this option will not be correct.

Hence, the correct option is (D).

266. Option (C) is correct because These drugs include leuprolide acetate (Lupron); the first GnRH agonist to be approved in the United States, nafarelin acetate (Synarel); and goserelin acetate (Zoladex). Approved indications for these drugs, depending on the specific agent, include advanced prostate cancer, endometriosis, and precocious puberty.

Option (A) is incorrect As Danazol affects the ovaries and pituitary gland and prevents the release of certain hormones in the body. Danazol is used to treat endometriosis and fibrocystic breast disease. Danazol is also used to prevent attacks of angioedema in people with an inherited form of this disorder (hereditary angioedema)

Option (B) is incorrect because Oral micronized progesterone (OMP), which allowed progesterone to be taken by mouth, was introduced in 1980. A large number of synthetic progestogens, or progestins, have been derived from progesterone and are used as medications as well. Examples include medroxyprogesterone acetate and norethisterone.

Option (D) is incorrect because Mifepristone is used in combination with misoprostol (Cytotec) to end an early pregnancy. Early pregnancy means it has been 70 days or less since your last menstrual period began. Mifepristone is in a class of medications called anti progestational steroids

Hence, the correct option is (C).

267. Option (A) is correct because of These methods are useful to detect submucous fibroid in unexplained infertility and repeated pregnancy wastage. The presence and site of submucous fibroid can be diagnosed by direct visualization during hysteroscopy or indirectly as a filling defect on HSG. Hysteroscopy also allows its excision under direct vision.

Option (B) is incorrect because of Hysterosalpingography, also known as uterosalpingography, is a radiologic procedure to investigate the shape of the uterine cavity and the shape and patency of the fallopian tubes. This means it is a special x-ray using dye to look at the womb and Fallopian tubes.

Option (C) is incorrect because of Ultrasound is the most readily available, least costly imaging technique to diagnose fibroid. It checks the number, location, and size of fibroids and helps to reduce overlooking small fibroids during surgery (which might lead to persistence or recurrence of symptoms).

Option (D) is incorrect because of is helpful if the uterine size is less than 12 weeks, for detection of subserous fibroid and not submucous. It can also differentiate a pedunculated fibroid from an ovarian tumour not revealed by clinical examination and ultrasound. Hence, the correct option is (A).

268. Option (A) is correct because Chocolate cysts are noncancerous, fluid-filled cysts that typically form deep within the ovaries. They get their name from their brown, tar-like appearance, looking something like melted chocolate. They're also called ovarian endometriomas.

Option (B) is incorrect because Adenomyosis is a condition in which the inner lining of the uterus (the endometrium) breaks through the muscle wall of the uterus (the myometrium). Adenomyosis can cause menstrual cramps, lower abdominal pressure, and bloating before menstrual periods and can result in heavy periods

Option (C) is incorrect because Fibroids are abnormal growths that develop in or on a woman's uterus. Sometimes these tumors become quite large and cause severe abdominal pain and heavy periods. In other cases, they cause no signs or symptoms at all. The growths are typically benign, or noncancerous.

Option (D) is incorrect because a corpus luteum cyst is a type of ovarian cyst which may rupture about the time of menstruation, and take up to three months to disappear entirely. A corpus luteum cyst rarely occurs in women over the age of 50, because eggs are no longer being released after menopause.

Hence, the correct option is (A).

269. DUB is defined as a state of abnormal uterine bleeding without any clinically detectable organic pelvic pathology.

-Fibroids are small growths that occur within the uterus, uterine lining, or uterine muscle. Like polyps, the causes of uterine fibroids are unknown. But estrogen seems to play a role in their growth. A variety of things can cause Dysfunctional uterine bleeding. Fibroids (small and large growths) in the uterus can also cause bleeding.

-Regular monthly menstrual cycles flush out the endometrial lining, which is the blood-enriched layer of tissue that grows inside the uterus. Lighter periods, or spotting between periods, may represent an endometrial lining that is unstable and leaking, either because hormonal levels don't adequately support it or because the lining may be too thick.

From the given reasons only b and e is satisfying. Hence,

According to the above explanation **option (D) is correct.**

According to the above explanation **option (A) is incorrect.**

According to the above explanation **option (B) is incorrect.**

According to the above explanation **option (C) is incorrect.**

Hence, the correct option is (D).

270. Option (A) is correct As Long-term tamoxifen therapy is a predisposing factor for endometrial hyperplasia and cancers.

Malignancies caused by Long-term tamoxifen therapy:

- Carcinoma endometrium-it is the most common carcinoma associated with it.
- Uterine sarcoma.
- Rarely liver cancer with a long-term high dose.

Non-malignant effects of tamoxifen on uterus:

- Endometrial hyperplasia
- Endometriosis
- Fibroid uterus
- Ovarian cysts
- Menstrual irregularities or amenorrhea.

Option (B) is incorrect because In general, cancer begins when a cell develops errors (mutations) in its DNA. The mutations tell the cell to grow and multiply quickly, creating a mass (tumor) of abnormal cells. The abnormal cells continue living when healthy cells would die. They can invade nearby tissues and break off from an initial tumor to spread elsewhere in the body

Option (C) is incorrect As Cervical cancer is a type of cancer that occurs in the cells of the cervix — the lower part of the uterus that connects to the vagina. Various strains of the human papillomavirus (HPV), a sexually transmitted infection, play a role in causing most cervical cancer.

Option (D) is incorrect because in general, cancer begins when healthy cells acquire a genetic mutation that turns normal cells into abnormal cells.

Healthy cells grow and multiply at a set rate, eventually dying at a set time. Cancer cells grow and multiply out of control, and they don't die. The accumulating abnormal cells form a mass (tumor). Hence, the correct option is (A).

271.

Age	Milestone
12-24 months	Tries to scribble spontaneously
2 years	Draws a vertical or horizontal line.
3 years	Draws a circle
4 years	Draws a cross (plus sign) and draws a rectangle
5 years	Draws a triangle

According to the above explanation **option (B) is correct.**

According to the above explanation **option (A) is incorrect.**

According to the above explanation **option (C) is incorrect.**

According to the above explanation **option (D) is incorrect.**

Hence, the correct option is (B).

272.

- The infant larynx differs markedly from its adult counterpart. Although it is about one - third adult size, it is proportionately larger.
- Its lumen is short and funnel-shaped and disproportionately narrower than that of an adult. It lies higher in the neck than the adult larynx. At rest, the upper border of the infant epiglottis is at the level of the second or third cervical vertebra; when the larynx is elevated, it reaches the level of the first cervical vertebra.
- This high position enables an infant to use its nasal airway to breath while sucking.

According to the above explanation **option (C) is correct.**

According to the above explanation **option (A) is incorrect.**

According to the above explanation **option (B) is incorrect.**

According to the above explanation **option (D) is incorrect.**

Hence, the correct option is (C).

273.

- "In a normal infant, the Moro's reflex begins to fade at three months of age and gradually disappears at 4-6 months.
- When it persists beyond 6 months it indicates a delay in CNS development." Tachdjian
- "Moro's reflex disappears by six months in a normal infant." Ghai

According to the above explanation **option (D) is correct.**

According to the above explanation **option (A) is incorrect.**

According to the above explanation **option (B) is incorrect.**

According to the above explanation **option (C) is incorrect.**

Hence, the correct option is (D).

274. Option (A) is correct because of Tricuspid atresia is a type of heart disease that is present at birth (congenital heart disease), in which the tricuspid heart valve is missing or abnormally developed. The defect blocks blood flow from the right atrium to the right ventricle.

Option (B) is incorrect because of Eisenmenger's syndrome is defined as the process in which a long-standing left-to-right cardiac shunt caused by a congenital heart defect (typically by a ventricular septal defect, atrial septal defect, or less commonly, patent ductus arteriosus) causes pulmonary hypertension.

Option (C) is incorrect because of Tetralogy of Fallot. Tetralogy of Fallot is a combination of four congenital abnormalities. The four defects include a ventricular septal defect (VSD), pulmonary valve stenosis, a misplaced aorta and a thickened right ventricular wall (right ventricular hypertrophy).

Option (D) is incorrect because of Anomalous right or left pulmonary artery arising from the aorta are relatively rare congenital heart disease entities. This rare disease is thought to come about because of failure of migration of the embryonic branch pulmonary artery to reach the pulmonary trunk end of the truncoaortic sac before septation occurs.

Hence, the correct option is (A).

275. Option (B) is correct because of An atrial septal defect (ASD) is an opening in the interatrial septum, causing a left-to-right shunt and volume overload of the right atrium and right ventricle.

Option (A) is incorrect because the ostium Secundum atrial septal defect is the most common type of atrial septal defect and comprises 6–10% of all congenital heart diseases. The Secundum atrial septal defect usually arises from an enlarged foramen ovale, inadequate growth of the septum Secundum, or excessive absorption of the septum primum.

Option (C) is incorrect because of the pulmonary veins are the four blood vessels (two on each side) that return oxygen-rich blood from the lungs to the left atrium (left upper chamber) of the heart. Total anomalous pulmonary venous return (TAPVR) is a rare congenital malformation in which all four pulmonary veins do not connect normally to the left atrium. Instead, the four pulmonary veins drain abnormally to the right atrium (right upper chamber) by way of an abnormal (anomalous) connection.

Option (D) is incorrect because of carotid cavernous fistulas are a rare but treatable cause of orbital injury and vision loss. Endovascular embolization of CCFs with coiling or liquid agents is the treatment modality of choice. With appropriate treatment, progressive resolution of symptoms is expected in most patients.

Hence, the correct option is (B).

276. Option (A) is correct as Bronchiolitis is one of the common serious acute lower respiratory tract infection in infants. Affected infants are between the ages of 1 and 6 months but the disease can affect children up to 2 years old. The disease usually occurs in winter and spring.

The respiratory syncytial virus is implicated in most cases.

Option (B) is incorrect as Adenoviruses most commonly cause respiratory illness. The illnesses can range from the common cold to pneumonia, croup, and bronchitis. Depending on the type, adenoviruses can cause other illnesses such as gastroenteritis, conjunctivitis, cystitis, and, less commonly, neurological disease.

Option (C) is incorrect because Parainfluenza viruses are responsible for disease throughout the year, but winter outbreaks of respiratory tract infections, especially croup, in children throughout the temperate zones of the northern and southern hemispheres represent peak periods of prevalence.

Option (D) is incorrect as several Mycoplasma species can cause disease, including M. pneumoniae, which is an important cause of atypical pneumonia (formerly known as "walking pneumonia"), and M. genitalium, which has been associated with pelvic inflammatory diseases.

Hence, the correct option is (A).

277. Option (B) is correct as Optic nerve glioma, also referred to as juvenile pilocytic astrocytoma, is the most frequent tumour of the optic nerve in childhood.

Option (A) is incorrect because these cells usually appear during acute injury; after that, they gradually shrink in size. Astrocytes participating in gliosis are referred to as reactive astrocytes.

Option (C) is incorrect as Fibrillary GN is a disease which affects the millions of filtering units that make up the kidney. These filtering units are called glomeruli. Each individual glomerulus is composed of multiple layers of straining material. In this condition, the body produces a large volume of unusual proteins.

Option (D) is incorrect as a sheet like membrane found within a chloroplast of an autotrophic cell. They act as a type of wall at which chloroplasts can be fixed within, achieving the maximum light possible.

Hence, the correct option is (B).

278. Option (C) is correct because

- In intestinal obstruction distension of the intestine is caused by the accumulation of gas and fluid proximal to and within the obstructed segmented.
- 70-80% of this intestinal gas consists of swallowed air.

Option (A) is incorrect as pathogenic bacteria contribute to other globally important diseases, such as pneumonia, which can be caused by bacteria such as Streptococcus and Pseudomonas, and foodborne illnesses, which can be caused by bacteria such as Shigella, Campylobacter, and Salmonella.

Option (B) is incorrect as breathing in and out is a mechanical action, not diffusion, but the oxygen actually enters your bloodstream through diffusion.

Option (D) is incorrect as your digestive system breaks nutrients into parts small enough for your body to absorb and use for energy, growth, and cell repair.

- Proteins break into amino acids.
- Fats break into fatty acids and glycerol.
- Carbohydrates break into simple sugars.

Hence, the correct option is (C).

279. Option (C) is correct as Vertebral defect in association with intraspinal cyst suggest the diagnosis of the neurenteric cyst.

Option (A) is incorrect as Spina bifida is a birth defect in which there is incomplete closing of the spine and membranes around the spinal cord during early development in pregnancy. There are three main types: spina bifida occulta, meningocele and myelomeningocele. Myelomeningocele, also known as open spina bifida, is the most severe form.

Option (B) is incorrect as A bronchogenic cyst is a rare congenital cystic lesion in the mediastinum or lung parenchyma and can be asymptomatic. In conclusion, the congenital pericardial defect may be associated with the bronchogenic cyst and in most cases, it is asymptomatic.

Option (D) is incorrect as Neuroblastoma may spread (metastasize) to other parts of the body, such as the lymph nodes, bone marrow, liver, skin and bones. Spinal cord compression. Tumors may grow and press on the spinal cord, causing spinal cord compression. Spinal cord compression may cause pain and paralysis.

Hence, the correct option is (C).

280. Option (D) is correct as it covers all the above options those after combining defines Potter's syndrome, i.e.

Potter syndrome

Potter syndrome is characterized by -

1. Bilateral renal agenesis
2. Pulmonary hypoplasia
3. Potter facies → widely separated eyes with epicanthic folds, low set ears, broad compressed flat nose, receding chin.

- This condition is incompatible with life, death occurs shortly after birth from pulmonary hypoplasia.
- Maternal USG demonstrates -
  a. Oligohydramnios
  b. Nonvisulization of bladder
  c. Absent kidney

Option (A) is incorrect even when Potter's syndrome is characterized by Bilateral renal agenesis. As other options are also associated with the syndrome, choosing individual option can not be considered as correct.

Option (B) is incorrect for the same reason as point (A) as Maternal USG demonstrates -

1. Oligohydramnios
2. Nonvisulization of bladder
3. Absent kidney

Option (C) is incorrect for the same reason as point (A) and point (B) that all the options are a feature of Potter's syndrome. Potter facies → widely separated eyes with epicanthic folds, low set ears, broad compressed flat nose, receding chin.

Hence, the correct option is (D).

281. Option (D) is correct as the sphenoid sinus is the opening of Sphenoethmoidal recess.

Option (A) is incorrect as the middle part of the lateral nasal wall includes opening of maxillaly sinus. So, this is not the required answer.

Option (B) is incorrect as the middle part of the lateral nasal wall includes the opening of Anterior ethmoid sinus. So, this is not the required answer.

Option (C) is incorrect because Frontal sinus is also one of the opening of the middle meatus. So, this is not the required answer.

Hence, the correct option is (D).

282. Option (B) is correct as

- Birth trauma may result in nasal septal deviation. Nasal deformities are estimated to occur in 1.25 - 23 % of newborns. Forceps - assisted or breech delivery is often mentioned as the aetiology of injury.
- Three options are coming in the range, i.e., 1.25 - 23 % : - Option 'a' (2 %), 'b' (10 %) and 'c' (20 %).
- So, the answer is given, which is the average of the range.

Option (A) is incorrect even it comes under the defined range but the other options also follow the range. So the answer will be estimated on an average basis.

Option (C) is incorrect for the same reason as point (A).

Option (D) is incorrect as it is out of the defined range.

Hence, the correct option is (B).

283. Option (A) is correct as "Among oral cavity cancers, cancers of the mobile tongue have a high incidence of occult and clinical cervical lymph node metastasis".

Option (B) is incorrect as the buccal mucosa is the lining of the cheeks and the back of the lips, inside where they touch the teeth. Development of cancer cells or tumour in this area leads to carcinoma buccal mucosa, which is a type of oral cancer. It generally starts in the squamous cells that are thin and flat, and line the lips and the mouth.

Option (C) is incorrect as Alveoli are tiny sacs within our lungs that allow oxygen and carbon dioxide to move between the lungs and bloodstream.

Option (D) is incorrect because the lips surround the entrance to the oral cavity. They function to provide competence to the oral cavity during mastication and at rest.

Hence, the correct option is (A).

284. Option (A) is correct as Myringotomy is ideally performed under an operating microscope using a sharp myringotomy and good suction apparatus.

Option (B) is incorrect because in stapedectomy surgery for otosclerosis, the laser is used to remove the fixed stapes bone with minimal trauma to surrounding structures.

Option (C) is incorrect as Otoendoscopy offers a large field of vision using direct vision and lateral vision endoscopes, particularly in the supratubal recess and sinus tympani, for which visualization is excellent with reduced surgical approaches.

Option (D) is incorrect as Blind sac closure is a very effective way of managing the chronically discharging ear in the presence of a profound hearing loss, or large conductive losses not amenable to surgical correction. It is associated with a low rate of complications and recurrent disease.

Hence, the correct option is (A).

285. Option (D) is correct as the Tympanic membrane develops from all the three germinal layers.

Outer epithelial layer develops from the epithelium lining the first branchial cleft.

Inner mucosal layer develops from the lining of tubotympanic recess which is a derivative of the first pharyngeal pouch and partly of the second pouch.

Intermediate fibrous layer is derived from mesoderm.

Option (A) is incorrect as it is one of the parts of the Tympanic membrane and the other options are also the part of it. So, selecting an individual option will not be considered as the correct answer.

Option (B) is incorrect for the same reason as defined in point (B). Mesoderm is one of the layer in the Tympanic membrane.

Option (C) is incorrect for the same reason as defined in option (A) and (B) as Endoderm is also a part of the Tympanic membrane.

Hence, the correct option is (D).

286. Option (B) is correct as Stapes superstructure, i.e. its head, neck and both crura develop from Reichert's cartilage (second arch).

Option (A) is incorrect as the Meckelian Cartilage, also known as "Meckel's Cartilage", is a piece of cartilage from which the mandibles (lower jaws) of vertebrates evolved.

Option (C) is incorrect as both are transitorily important to the formation of the skull—the one serving as part of the anterior wall of the primordial facial canal, the other becoming partially enveloped by bone of the medial alveolar wall of the mandible.

Option (D) is incorrect as Stapes footplate has a dual origin both from the otic capsule and second arch.

Hence, the correct option is (B).

287. Option (C) is correct as from the explanation of point (B).

- Any lesion of chorda tympani thus leads to dryness of the mouth.

Option (A) is incorrect because a deficiency in the function of taste may be caused by age, drugs, disease, or trauma. For example as humans age, there is a decrease in the number of papillae containing taste buds and a reduction in the sensitivity to many taste solutes; however, older people still enjoy sweet, tasting foods.

Option (B) is incorrect as Chorda tympani carries fibres of : -

1. Taste for the anterior two-thirds of the tongue.
2. Secretomotor fibres to the submandibular and sublingual salivary gland.

- So, Ideally, a lesion of chorda tympani should impair both these functions but-sensations from anterior 2/3rd of the tongue are not impaired as an alternate pathway passing through the nerve of the pterygoid canal to the otic ganglion exists (which does not pass through middle ear) which is preserved in lesions of chorda tympani.

Option (D) is incorrect as damage to the glossopharyngeal nerve can result in loss of taste sensation to the posterior one third of the tongue, and impaired swallowing.
Hence, the correct option is (C).

288. Option (D) is correct as it covers both the point (A) and point (C), i.e.

- LMN causes ipsilateral paralysis : -
- Nasolabial fold of same side is obliterated.
- Face sags and is drawn across to the opposite side on smiling.

Option (A) is incorrect as Lower motor neuron lesion is more common and until unless specified, All facial palsy are taken as LMN type. LMN causes ipsilateral paralysis : -

A nasolabial fold of the same side is obliterated.

In case of more than one options being correct, going for an individual option will not be considered as the right answer.

Option (B) is incorrect as it produces contradiction from the explanation in point (A).

Option (C) is incorrect for the same reason as point (A).

Hence, the correct option is (D).

289. Option (D) is correct because the sinus is lined with mucoperiosteum, with cilia that beat down the Ostia.

This membrane is referred to as the Schneiderian membrane, which is histologically a bilaminar membrane with ciliated columnar epithelium cells on the internal side and periosteum.

Option (A) is incorrect as Squamous epithelial cells can become squamous cell carcinomas. This is the most common type of cancer in the nasal cavity and paranasal sinuses. These cancers usually are found on sun-exposed areas of the skin but can form on the lining of the nasal cavity and sinuses or other areas inside the body.

Option (B) is incorrect as Single-layered non-ciliated columnar epithelium tends to indicate an absorptive function.

Option (C) is incorrect as Non-keratinizing squamous cell carcinoma is one of the most common types of skin cancer that involves abnormal growth of cells within the epidermis.

Hence, the correct option is (D).

290. Option (C) is correct because Retropharyngeal space, and therefore retropharyngeal abscess, lies anterior to prevertebral fascia. So, this is not true about a retropharyngeal abscess. Hence, this is the required answer.

Option (A) is incorrect as a retropharyngeal abscess is confined to one side of the midline. So, this is not the required answer.

Option (B) is incorrect as a retropharyngeal abscess can be palpable per orally by pressing the finger on the posterior pharyngeal wall.

Option (D) is incorrect as it is true for retropharyngeal abscess. Thus, it is not the required answer.
Hence, the correct option is (C).

291. Option (D) is correct as phylenticular conjunctivitis is a nodular affection occurring as an allergic response of conjunctival and corneal epithelium to some endogenous allergens to which they have become sensitized

- Type IV hypersensitivity reaction.
- Due to staph aureus(MC) and tuberculous protein.
- Koeppes nodule,
- Busaca nodules are manifestations.
- MC allergic manifestation is Koppes nodule
- Phylecten is hence due to endogeneous causes, (papules at limbus)
- Doc: topical steroids.

Option (A) is incorrect as a muscarinic cholinergic agonist used on the eye to treat elevated intraocular pressure, various types of glaucoma, and to induce miosis. Also available orally to treat symptoms of dry mouth associated with Sjogren's syndrome and radiotherapy.

Option (B) is incorrect because topical mydriatics are used during an eye examination to allow visualization of the retina and other structures deep within the eye. Mydriatics may also be used to treat inflammatory eye conditions such as iritis and cyclitis and to reduce cycloplegia (a painful paralysis of the ciliary muscle of the eye).

Option (C) is incorrect because Antibiotics are used to treat or prevent some types of bacterial infection. They work by killing bacteria or preventing them from reproducing and spreading. Antibiotics aren't effective against viral infections, such as the common cold, flu, most coughs and sore throats.

Hence, the correct option is (D).

292. Option (B) is correct as:

- The reticular pattern of keratitis in a contact lens wearer is seen in Acanthamoeba.
- Initially, the Acanthamoeba keratitis shows typical reticular pattern due to radial keratoiritis (Radial perineuritis), i.e. infiltrates along corneal nerves.
- Due to this, the pain is very severe (neurological due to perineuritis) which is out of proportion to the degree of inflammation.
- Later, reticular superficial keratitis advanced to the ring-shaped lesion in the central or paracentral region.

Option (A) is incorrect as it appears as greyish white lines, circles, or clouding of the cornea. Corneal dystrophy can also have a crystalline appearance. There are over 20 corneal dystrophies that affect all parts of the cornea.

Option (C) is incorrect as A Pseudomonas infection that reaches the bloodstream tends to be more severe. The areas of the body that the infections are most likely to affect are the ears, skin, lungs, soft tissue, and blood. Common symptoms of the infections Pain and redness in the eye.

Option (D) is incorrect as often, a person will experience symptoms that may include a runny nose, coughing, nausea, fatigue, and body aches. While not every person experiences a fever when they have a virus, a fever can be a sign that the body is trying to fight off the infection.

Hence, the correct option is (B).

293. Option (D) is correct as climatic droplet keratopathy (CDK) is a degenerative condition characterized by the accumulation of translucent material in the superficial corneal stroma within the interpalpebral strip, beginning peripherally and spreading centrally. It doesn't lead to corneal opacity, this is the required answer.

Option (A) is incorrect as Endothelial dystrophy is one of the causes of congenital opacities of cornea and is classified in congenital hereditary, posterior polymorphous, stromal. Hence, this is not the required answer.

Option (B) is incorrect as Sclerocornea can be defined as a tear in Descemet's membrane that can cause corneal opacity and has classification as Congenital glaucoma, birth trauma. Hence, this is not the required answer.

Option (C) is incorrect as Mucopolysaccharidosis is metabolic and can cause corneal opacity. So, this is also not the required answer.

Hence, the correct option is (D).

294. Option (A) is correct as VKH syndrome is a multisystem disorder characterized by chronic granulomatous uveitis with an exudative retinal detachment that is often associated with neurological and cutaneous manifestations.

Option (B) is incorrect as non-granulomatous uveitis typically has an acute onset and shows fine KP. It is more likely to be idiopathic.

Option (C) is incorrect because the exact cause of uveitis is often unclear, but some factors increase the chance of it happening. These include Juvenile arthritis, psoriasis and other autoimmune disorders, such as rheumatoid arthritis. Inflammatory disorders, such as Crohn's disease, ulcerative colitis.

Option (D) is incorrect as Vogt Koyanagi–Harada (VKH) syndrome is associated with chronic granulomatous uveitis i.e. option (A). Hence, the correct option is (A).

295. Option (B) is correct as NADPH+ dependent aldolase reductase reduces excessive glucose to sorbitol and intracellular accumulation of sorbitol causes osmotic changes resulting in cataract development.

Option (A) is incorrect because a hexokinase is an enzyme that phosphorylates a six-carbon sugar, a hexose, to a hexose phosphate. In most tissues and organisms, glucose is the most important substrate of hexokinases, and glucose 6-phosphate the most important product.

Option (C) is incorrect as Glucokinase is an enzyme responsible for the conversion of glucose into glucose-6 phosphate and plays a central role as a glucose sensor in the regulation of glucose homeostasis.

Option (D) is incorrect as Phosphoglucose isomerase, as its name suggests, is the enzyme crucial for the interconversion of D-glucose 6-phosphate and D-fructose 6-phosphate. PGI is the enzyme responsible for the second step of glycolysis and is involved in glucogenesis. Thus, it is highly conserved in bacteria and eukaryotes.

Hence, the correct option is (B).

296. Option (D) is correct as both the Trabeculoplasty and Vitrectomy is not the treatment part of acute congestive glaucoma. So, this is the required answer.

Option (A) is incorrect it is a non-penetrating filtration surgery (deep sclerectomy, viscoanulostomy) for treatment of acute congestive glaucoma. Hence, this is not the required answer.

Option (B) is incorrect as Trabeculectomy is Partial-thickness fistula filtration surgery used for the treatment of acute congestive glaucoma while Trabeculoplasty is not the part of the treatment of the same. So, this is not the right answer.

Option (C) is incorrect as treatment of choice:- Peripheral laser iridotomy (1st choice), surgical peripheral iridectomy (when laser not available) while Vitrectomy is not the part of the treatment of the same. So, this is not the right answer.

Hence, the correct option is (D).

297. Option (D) is correct as it is covering all the above points, i.e.

- Complications of diabetic retinopathy:- Vitreous haemorrhage, neovascular glaucoma (rubeosis iridis), traction retinal detachment.
- Other ocular manifestations of DM → Secondary cataract (snowflake/snowstorm cataract); Cranial nerve palsies: 3rd (most common) 4th, 6th & 7th; Myopia because of fluid imbibition and swelling of lens. In rare cases, hypermetropia may also be caused by diabetes.

Option (A) is incorrect as Vitreous haemorrhage is one of the complication of diabetic retinopathy. In case of other options being true, choosing an individual option will not be considered as the correct answer.

Option (B) is incorrect as Rubeosis iridis is one of the complications of diabetic retinopathy. In case of other options being true, choosing an individual option will not be considered as the correct answer.

Option (C) is incorrect for the same reason as of point (A) and point (B) as Retinal detachment can be caused by Diabetes mellitus.

Hence, the correct option is (D).

298. Option (B) is correct as information in this question is:-

1. Sudden loss of vision
2. Painful ocular movement
3. Normal fundus on ophthalmoscopy

- All are seen in retrobulbar neuritis and last two features are more characteristics of retrobulbar neuritis and differentiate it from papillitis.

Option (A) is incorrect because an optic nerve glioma is a type of brain tumour that forms in or around the optic nerve, which connects the eye to the brain.

Option (C) is incorrect as it has the following symptoms :

- Headaches, including morning headache or headache that goes away after vomiting.
- Vision changes.
- Nausea and vomiting.
- Loss of balance or trouble walking.
- Increase in thirst or urination.
- Unusual sleepiness or change in energy level.
- Changes in personality or behavior.
- Short stature or slow growth.
- Hearing loss.
- Weight gain.

Option (D) is incorrect as papillitis and retrobulbar neuritis have almost the same clinical features except Painful ocular movement is more common in retrobulbar neuritis than papillitis

The fundus is normal in retrobulbar neuritis while papillitis has characteristic fundus abnormalities.

Hence, the correct option is (B).

299. Option (B) is correct the most common cause of low vision is refractive errors. And, refractive errors cause low vision in 100% of cases. So, refractive errors should be the most common cause of ocular morbidity in India.

Option (A) is incorrect as the most common cause of blindness in India is the cataract.

Option (C) is incorrect as Ocular trauma is one of the most under-recognized causes of vision loss in the developed world. Blunt or penetrating ocular trauma can lead to vision loss through cataract or glaucoma.

Option (D) is incorrect as Vitamin A deficiency is the leading cause of preventable childhood blindness, and is critical to achieving Millennium Development Goal 4 to reduce child mortality. The prevalence of night blindness due to VAD is also high among pregnant women in many developing countries.
Hence, the correct option is (B).

300. Option (A) is correct as Visual loss can occur and is thought to result from axonal compression, subretinal haemorrhage, or choroidal neovascular membrane formation.

Option (B) is incorrect as the nerve head may be elevated, but no axonal swelling or edema exists.

Option (C) is incorrect as optic nerve drusen may be inherited in an autosomal dominant fashion and occur more frequently in whites.

Option (D) is incorrect because optic nerve drusen occur in 2% of optic nerve specimens on histopathology and are bilateral in 50%.
Hence, the correct option is (A).

// Notes //